TWO PHASE FLOW, PHASE CHANGE AND NUMERICAL MODELING

Edited by **Amimul Ahsan**

Two Phase Flow, Phase Change and Numerical Modeling
Edited by Amimul Ahsan

Published by InTech
Janeza Trdine 9, 51000 Rijeka, Croatia

Publishing Process Manager Ivana Lorković

Technical Editor Teodora Smiljanic

Cover Designer InTech Design Team

Additional hard copies can be obtained from orders@intechopen.com

Two Phase Flow, Phase Change and Numerical Modeling, Edited by Amimul Ahsan
p. cm.
ISBN 978-953-307-584-6

For EU product safety concerns:
IN TECH d.o.o., Prolaz Marije Krucifikse Kozulić 3, 51000 Rijeka, Croatia,
info@intechopen.com or visit our website at intechopen.com.

Meet the editor

Dr. Amimul Ahsan was born in Netrokona, Bangladesh, 1982. He is a Senior Lecturer, Department of Civil Engineering, Faculty of Engineering, University Putra Malaysia, Malaysia. He received a Ph.D in Civil Engineering from the University of Fukui, Japan. He has been involved in collaboration research with many researchers and scientists in the world since 2004 and published in diverse areas of Civil and Environmental Engineering. He has published 3 books, 6 book chapters, over 19 technical papers, and is a member of the editorial board of numerous international technical journals. He has been serving on the scientific and editorial board of InTech Open Access Publisher since 2010.

Contents

Preface

The heat transfer and analysis on laser beam, evaporator coils, shell-and-tube condenser, two phase flow, nanofluids, and on phase change are significant issues in a design of wide range of industrial processes and devices. This book introduces advanced processes and modeling of heat transfer, flat miniature heat pipe, gas-solid fluidization bed, solidification phenomena, thermal approaches to laser damage, and temperature and velocity distribution to the international community. It includes 25 advanced and revised contributions, and it covers mainly (1) numerical modeling of heat transfer, (2) two phase flow, (3) nanofluids, and (4) phase change.

The first section introduces numerical modeling of heat transfer on laser beam, evaporator coils, shell-and-tube condenser, rarefied gas, flat miniature heat pipe, particles in binary gas-solid fluidization bed, solidification phenomena, profile evolution, heated solid wall, axisymmetric swirl, thermal approaches to laser damage, ultrafast heating characteristics, and temperature and velocity distribution. The second section covers density wave instability phenomena, gas and spray-water quenching, spray cooling, wettability effect, liquid film thickness, and thermosyphon loop.

The third section includes nanofluids for heat transfer, nanofluids in minichannels, potential and engineering strategies on nanofluids, nanostructures using the fractal approximation, micro DMFC, and heat transfer at nanoscale and in complex fluids. The forth section presents time-dependent melting and deformation processes of phase change material (PCM), thermal energy storage tanks using PCM, capillary rise in a capillary loop, phase change in deep CO_2 injector, and phase change thermal storage device of solar hot water system.

The readers of this book will appreciate the current issues of modeling on laser beam, evaporator coils, rarefied gas, flat miniature heat pipe, two phase flow, nanofluids, complex fluids, and on phase change in different aspects. The approaches would be applicable in various industrial purposes as well. The advanced idea and information described here will be fruitful for the readers to find a sustainable solution in an industrialized society.

The editor of this book would like to express sincere thanks to all authors for their high quality contributions and in particular to the reviewers for reviewing the chapters.

ACKNOWLEDGEMENTS

All praise be to Almighty Allah, the Creator and the Sustainer of the world, the Most Beneficent, Most Benevolent, Most Merciful, and Master of the Day of Judgment. He is Omnipresent and Omnipotent. He is the King of all kings of the world. In His hand is all good. Certainly, over all things Allah has power.

The editor would like to express appreciation to all who have helped to prepare this book. The editor expresses the gratefulness to Ms. Ivana Lorkovic, Publishing Process Manager InTech Open Access Publisher, for her continued cooperation. In addition, the editor appreciatively remembers the assistance of all authors and reviewers of this book.

Gratitude is expressed to Mrs. Ahsan, Ibrahim Bin Ahsan, Mother, Father, Mother-in-Law, Father-in-Law, and Brothers and Sisters for their endless inspirations, mental supports and also necessary help whenever any difficulty.

Amimul Ahsan
Department of Civil Engineering,
Faculty of Engineering,
University Putra Malaysia
Malaysia

Part 1

Numerical Modeling of Heat Transfer

1

Modeling the Physical Phenomena Involved by Laser Beam – Substance Interaction

Marian Pearsica, Stefan Nedelcu, Cristian-George Constantinescu, Constantin Strimbu, Marius Benta and Catalin Mihai
"Henri Coanda" Air Force Academy
Romania

1. Introduction

The mathematical model is based on the heat transfer equation, into a homogeneous material, laser beam heated. Because transient phenomena are discussed, it is necessary to consider simultaneously the three phases in material (solid, liquid and vapor), these implying boundary conditions for unknown boundaries, resulting in this way analytical and numerical approach with high complexity.

Because the technical literature (Belic, 1989; Hacia & Domke, 2007; Riyad & Abdelkader, 2006) does not provide a general applicable mathematical model of material-power laser beam assisted by an active gas interaction, it is considered that elaborating such model, taking into account the significant parameters of laser, assisting gas, processed material, which may be particularized to interest cases, may be an important technical progress in this branch. The mathematical methods used (as well the algorithms developed in this purpose) may be applied to study phenomena in other scientific/technical branches too. The majority of works analyzing the numerical and analytical solutions of heat equation, the limits of applicability and validity of approximations in practical interest cases, is based on results achieved by Carslaw and Jaeger using several particular cases (Draganescu & Velculescu, 1986; Dowden, 2009, 2001; Mazumder, 1991; Mazumder & Steen, 1980).

The main hypothesis basing the mathematical model elaboration, derived from previous research team achievements (Pearsica et al., 2010, 2009; Pearsica & Nedelcu, 2005), are: laser processing is a consequence of photon energy transferred in the material and active gas jet, increasing the metal destruction process by favoring exothermic reactions; the processed material is approximated as a semi-infinite region, which is the space limited by the plane $z = 0$, the irradiated domain being much smaller than substance volume; the power laser beam has a "Gaussian" type radial distribution of beam intensity (valid for TEM_{00} regime); laser beam absorption at z depth respects the Beer law; oxidations occurs only in laser irradiated zone, oxidant energy being "Gaussian" distributed; the attenuation of metal vapors flow respects an exponential law. One of the mathematical hypothesis needing a deeper analysis is the shape of the boundaries between liquid and vaporization, respectively liquid and solid states, supposed as previously known, the parameters characterizing them being computed in the thermic regime prior to the calculus moment.

The laser defocusing effect, while penetrating the processed metal is taken into consideration too, as well as energy losses by electromagnetic radiation and convection. The proposed method solves simultaneously the heat equation for the three phases (solid, liquid and vapor), computing the temperature distribution in material and the depth of penetration of the material for a given processing time, the vaporization speed of the material being measurable in this way.

2. Analytical model equations

The invariant form of the heat equation for an isotropic medium is given by (1).

$$\frac{c_v \cdot \rho}{k}\frac{\partial T}{\partial t} = \Delta T \tag{1}$$

where: $\rho\,[kg/m^3]$ is the mass density; $c_v\,[J \cdot kg^{-1} \cdot K^{-1}]$ - volumetric specific heat; $T[K]$ - temperature; $k[W \cdot m^{-1} \cdot K^{-1}]$ - heat conductivity of the material; $t[s]$ - time; Δ - Laplace operator.
Because the print of the laser beam on the material surface is a circular one, thermic phenomena produced within the substantial, have a cylindrical symmetry. Oz is considered as symmetry axis of the laser beam, the object surface equation is $z = 0$ and the positive sense of Oz axis is from the surface to the inside of the object. The heat equation within cylindrical coordinates (θ, r, z) will be:

$$\frac{1}{K}\frac{\partial T}{\partial t} = \frac{1}{r^2}\frac{\partial^2 T}{\partial \theta^2} + \frac{1}{r}\frac{\partial}{\partial r}\left(r\frac{\partial T}{\partial r}\right) + \frac{\partial^2 T}{\partial z^2} \tag{2}$$

where: $K[m^2/s]$ is the diffusivity of the material.
Limit and initial conditions are attached to heat equation according to the particularly cases which are the discussed subject. These conditions are time and space dependent. In time, the medium submitted to the actions of the laser presents the solid, liquid and vapor state separated by previously unknown boundaries. A simplifying model taking into consideration these boundaries, by considering them as having a cylindrical symmetry, was proposed. By specifying the pattern D, the temperature initial conditions and the conditions on D pattern boundaries, one can have the solution of heat equation, T(x,y,z,t) for a certain substantial.

2.1 Temperature source modeling

The destruction of the crystalline network of the material and its vaporization, along the pre-established curve, is completed by the energy of photons created inside the material, and by the jet of the assisting gas (O_2). This gas intensifies the material destroying action due to the exothermic reactions provided. Dealing with a semi-infinite solid heated by a laser beam uniform absorbed in its volume, it is assumed that Beer law governs its absorption at z depth. It is considered a radial "Gaussian" distribution of the laser beam intensity, which corresponds to the central part of the laser beam. It is assumed that photons energy is totally transformed in heat. So, the heat increasing rate, owing the photons energy, at z depth (under surface) is given by:

$$\frac{dQ}{dt \cdot dV} = h\nu \cdot \sigma \cdot \rho \cdot I(r,z) = \frac{P_L}{\pi d^2 \cdot l} e^{-\left[\left(\frac{r}{d}\right)^2 + \frac{z}{l}\right]} \tag{3}$$

where: $dV[m^3]$ and $dt[s]$ are the infinitesimal volume and time respectively, $\sigma[m^2/kg]$ - the absorption cross section, $\sigma = 1/\rho \cdot l$, $I(rt)[W/m^2]$ - photons distribution in material volume, $l[m]$ - the attenuation length of laser radiation, $P_L[W]$ - the laser power; $\pi d^2[m^2]$ - irradiated surface, $r[m]$ - radial coordinate, and $h\nu[J]$ - the energy of one photon.
The vaporized material diffuses in oxygen atmosphere and oxidizes exothermic, resulting in this way an oxidizing energy, which appears as an additional kinetic energy of the surface gas constituents, leading to an additional heating of the laser processed zone. It is assumed an exponential attenuation of the metal vapors flow and oxidizing is only inner laser irradiated zone, the oxidizing energy being "Gaussian" distributed. The rate of oxidizing energy release on the material is given by (4):

$$\frac{dQ_{ox}}{dt \cdot dV} = \eta_o \cdot \sigma_{ox} \cdot \rho \cdot n_{o_2} \cdot v_s \cdot \frac{\varepsilon}{M} e^{\left[\frac{z}{l_{ox}} - \left(\frac{r}{d}\right)^2\right]} \tag{4}$$

where: η_o is the oxidizing efficiency, $\varepsilon[J]$ - oxidizing energy on completely oxidized metal atom, $\sigma_{ox}[m^2/kg]$ - effective oxidizing section, $n_{o_2}[m^{-3}]$ - oxygen atomic concentration, $v_s[m/s]$ - vaporization boundary speed, $M[kg]$ - atomic mass of metal, and $l_{ox}[m]$ - oxidizing length, $l_{ox} = 1/(n_{o_2} \cdot \sigma_{ox})$. In (4), z is negative outside the material, so the attenuation is obvious. The full temperature source results as a sum of (3) and (4), and assuming a constant vaporization boundary speed, the instantaneous expression of temperature source is given by (Pearsica et al., 2010):

$$S(r,z) = e^{-\left(\frac{r}{d}\right)^2} \cdot \left[\frac{P_L}{\pi d^2 \cdot l} e^{-\frac{z - v_s \cdot t}{l}} \cdot h(z - v_s \cdot t) + \eta_o \frac{\varepsilon \cdot \rho \cdot v_s}{M \cdot l_{ox}} e^{-\frac{v_s \cdot t - z}{l_{ox}}} \cdot h(v_s \cdot t - z)\right] \tag{5}$$

where h(x) is Heaviside function. In temperature source expression, z origin is the same with the vaporization boundary, which advance in profoundness as the material is drawn. The spatial and temporal temperature distribution in material is governed by the full temperature source and results by solving the heat equation.

2.2 Boundary and initial conditions for heat equation

a. Dirichlet conditions

Let $S_1 \subset S$. For S_1 surface points it is assumes that the temperature T is known as a function f(M,t), and the remaining surface, S, the temperature is constant, T_a:

$$T(M,t) = \begin{cases} f(M,t), & M \in S_1 \\ T_a, & M \in S \setminus S_1 \end{cases} \tag{6}$$

b. Neumann conditions

Let $S_2 \subset S$. It is known the derivate in the perpendicular n direction to the surface S_2:

$$\frac{\partial T(M,t)}{\partial n} = g(M,t), \quad M \in S_2 \tag{7}$$

c. Initial conditions

It is assumed that at $t = t_o$ time is known the thermic state of the material in D pattern:

$$T(M,t_o)=T_o(M), \quad M\in D \tag{8}$$

In time, successions the phases the object suffers while irradiate by the power laser beam are the following:

- phase 1, for $0\le t<t_{top}$;
- phase 2, for $t_{top}\le t<t_{vap}$;
- phase 3, for $t\ge t_{vap}$, where t_{top} and t_{vap} are the starting time moments of the melting, respectively vaporization of the material.

The surfaces separating solid, liquid and vapor state are previously unknown and will be determined using the conditions of continuity of thermic flow on separation surfaces of two different substantial, knowing the temperature and the speed of separation surface (Mazumder & Steen, 1980; Shuja et al., 2008; Steen & Mazumder, 2010).

The isotropic domain D is assumed to be the semi-space $z\ge 0$, so its border, S, is characterized by the equation $z=0$. The laser beam acts on the normal direction, developing thermic effects described by (1). In the initial moment, $t=0$, the domain temperature is the ambient one, T_a. If the laser beam radius is d and axis origin is chosen on its symmetry axis, then the condition of type (7) (thermic flow imposed on the surface of the processed material) yields:

$$\left.\frac{\partial T}{\partial x}\right|_{z=0}=\begin{cases}-\dfrac{1}{k}\varphi_S(M,t), & x^2+y^2\le d^2,\ z=0\\ 0, & x^2+y^2>d^2,\ z=0\end{cases} \tag{9}$$

where $\varphi_S(M,t)[W/m^2]$ is the power flow on the processed surface, corresponding to the solid state:

$$\varphi_S(M,t)=\frac{A_S\cdot P_L}{\pi d^2}e^{-\left(\frac{r}{d}\right)^2},\quad r^2=x^2+y^2,\ z=0 \tag{10}$$

where: A_S is the absorbability of solid surface, and $P_L[W]$ – the power of laser beam.

Regarding the working regime, two kinds of lasers were taken into consideration: continuous regime lasers (P_L = constant) and pulsated regime lasers (P_L has periodical time dependence, governed by a "Gaussian" type law). If the laser pulse period is $t_p=t_{on}+t_{off}$, then the expression used for the laser power is the following:

$$P_L=\begin{cases}C\left[e^{-\frac{1}{4}}-e^{-\left(\frac{t-\frac{t_{on}}{2}-k\,t_p}{t_{on}}\right)^2}\right], & t\in\left[k t_p,\ k t_p+t_{on}\right]\\ 0, & t\in\left((k+1)t_p-t_{off},\ (k+1)t_p\right)\end{cases};\ k\in N \tag{11}$$

where: $C=P_{L\max}\cdot e^{1/4}$. Due to the cylindrical symmetry, $\dfrac{\partial^2 T}{\partial\theta^2}=0$, so (2) changes to:

$$\frac{1}{K}\frac{\partial T}{\partial t}=\frac{1}{r}\frac{\partial T}{\partial r}+\frac{\partial^2 T}{\partial r^2}+\frac{\partial^2 T}{\partial z^2} \tag{12}$$

Equations (6) and (7) will be:

$$T(r,z,0)=T_a,\quad (r,z)\in[0,\ r_\infty]\times[0,\ r_\infty] \tag{13}$$

$$\frac{\partial T(r,0,t)}{\partial z}=\begin{cases}-\dfrac{1}{k}\varphi(r,0,t), & r\le d\\ 0, & r>d\end{cases} \tag{14}$$

Because it was assumed that the area of thermic influence neighboring the processing is comparable to the processing width it may consider that $r_\infty \approx 6d$, and is valid the relation (Dirichlet condition):

$$T(r_\infty,z,t)=T_a,\quad z>0 \tag{15}$$

In order to avoid the singularity in $r=0$ it is considered that:

$$\frac{\partial T(0,z,t)}{\partial r}=0 \tag{16}$$

The power flow on the processed surface corresponding to the solid state is given by the relation (10).

As a result of laser beam action, the processed material surface heats, the temperature reaching the melting value, T_{top} at a certain moment of time. The heating goes on, so in another moment of time, the melted material temperature reaches the vaporization value, T_{vap}. That moment onward the vapor state appears in material. The equations (12), (13), (14), and (15) still govern the heating process in all of three states (solid, liquid and vapor), changing the material constants k and K, which will be denoted according to the state of the point M(r,z), as it follows: k_1, K_1 - for the solid state, k_2, K_2 - for the liquid state, respectively k_3, K_3 - for the vapor state.

The three states are separated by time varying boundaries. To know these boundaries is essential to determine the thermic regime at a certain time moment. If the temperature is known, then the following relations describe the boundaries separating the processed material states:

- solid and liquid states boundary:

$$T(r,z,t)=T_{top},\quad (r,z)\in C_l(t) \tag{17}$$

- liquid and vapor states boundary:

$$T(r,z,t)=T_{vap},\quad (r,z)\in C_v(t) \tag{18}$$

The material temperature rises from T_{top} to T_{vap} between the boundaries $C_l(t)$ and $C_v(t)$. The power flow on the processed surface corresponding to the liquid state is given by:

$$\varphi_L(M,t)=\frac{A_L\cdot P_L}{\pi d^2}e^{-\left(\frac{r}{d}\right)^2},\quad r^2=x^2+y^2,\ z=0 \tag{19}$$

where A_L is the absorbability on liquid surface.
The power flow on the processed surface corresponding to vapor state is given by:

$$\varphi_V(M,t)=C_G\cdot e^{-\left(\frac{r}{d_V}\right)^2},\quad r^2=x^2+y^2,\ z=z_f \tag{20}$$

where: $C_G=C_{G_1}+C_{G_2}=\frac{P_L}{\pi d_V^2}+\frac{\eta_o\cdot\varepsilon\cdot\rho_v\cdot v_S}{M}$ ($d_V[m]$ - radius of the laser beam on the separation boundary between vapor state and liquid state and it is calculated with the relation (21), z_f - z coordinate corresponding to the boundary between vapor state and liquid state; C_{G_2} is considered only in the vapor state, because the vaporized metal diffusing in atmosphere suffers an exothermic air oxidation, thus resulting an oxidizing energy which provides supplemental heating of the laser beam processed zone).

$$d_V=d+\frac{D-d}{f}\cdot z_f \tag{21}$$

where: $D[m]$ is the diameter of the generated laser beam and $f[m]$ is the focusing distance of the focusing system.
In (14), the power losses through electromagnetic radiation, $\varphi_r[W/m^2]$ and convection, $\varphi_c[W/m^2]$ were taken into account (Pearsica et al., 2008a, 2008b):

$$\varphi_r=\sigma_b\left(T_{vap}^4-T_a^4\right),\ \varphi_c=H\left(T_{vap}-T_a\right) \tag{22}$$

where: σ_b is Stefan-Boltzmann constant, H - substantial heat transfer constant. The emittance of irradiated area was considered as equal to 1.

2.3 Separating boundaries equations

To solve analytical the presented problem is a difficult task. The method described bellow is a numerical one. An iterative process will be used to find the surfaces $C_l(t)$ and $C_v(t)$. An inverse method was applied, choosing the boundaries as surfaces with rotational symmetry, ellipsoid type (Pearsica et al., 2008a, 2008b). Because the rotational ellipsoid is characterized by a double parametrical equation:

$$\frac{r^2}{\alpha^2}+\frac{z^2}{\beta^2}=1 \tag{23}$$

it's enough to know the points (r_1,z_1) and (r_2,z_2) on the considered surface in order to determine the parameters α and β. The points $(r(t),0)$ and $(0,z(t))$, with $r(t_{top})=r^*$ and $z(t_{top})=z^*$ were chosen, where t_{top} is the time moment when the temperature is T_{top}.
On the surface $C_l(t)$ is known the equation relating temperature gradient and the surface movement speed in this (normal) direction:

$$\frac{\partial T}{\partial n} = -\frac{\rho_2 L_2}{k_2} v_n \tag{24}$$

where: $k_2 [W \cdot m^{-1} \cdot K^{-1}]$ is the heat conductivity that belongs to liquid state, $L_2 [J / kg]$ - the latent melting heat, $\rho_2 [kg / m^3]$ - the mass density that belongs to liquid state, and $v_n [m / s]$ is the movement speed of the boundary surface, $C_1(t)$, in the direction of its external normal vector $\overline{n}$.

The boundary at the t moment is supposed as known, respectively the points $(r(t), 0)$ and $(0, z(t))$ on it. It is enough to determine the points $(r(t+\Delta t), 0)$ and $(0, z(t+\Delta t))$ in order to find $C_1(t+\Delta t)$. In the point $(r(t), 0)$, (24) yields:

$$\frac{\partial T}{\partial r} = -\frac{\rho_2 L_2}{k_2} v_r \;\Rightarrow\; v_r = -\frac{k_2}{\rho_2 L_2}\frac{\partial T}{\partial r} \tag{25}$$

where: $\frac{\partial T}{\partial r} = \frac{T(r+\Delta r) - T_{top}}{\Delta r}$

It obtains:

$$r(t+\Delta t) = r(t) + v_r \cdot \Delta t \tag{26}$$

In $(0, z(t))$ point, (24) yields:

$$\frac{\partial T}{\partial z} = -\frac{\rho_2 L_2}{k_2} v_z \;\Rightarrow\; v_z = -\frac{k_2}{\rho_2 L_2}\frac{\partial T}{\partial z} \tag{27}$$

where: $\frac{\partial T}{\partial z} = \frac{T(z+\Delta z) - T_{top}}{\Delta z}$. It results:

$$z(t+\Delta t) = z(t) + v_z \cdot \Delta t \tag{28}$$

The new boundary parameters, $\alpha(t+\Delta t)$ and $\beta(t+\Delta t)$, are returned by (26) and (28):

$$\alpha(t+\Delta t) = r(t+\Delta t),\; \beta(t+\Delta t) = z(t+\Delta t) \tag{29}$$

The moment t_{top} is the first time when the above procedure is applied. $z(t_{top}) = 0$ and $r(t_{top}) = 0$ at this moment of time. Because the temperature gradient (having the z direction,) is known in $z = 0$ and $r = 0$:

$$\left.\frac{\partial T}{\partial z}\right|_{z=0} = -\frac{1}{k_1}\varphi_L(0,0,t) \tag{30}$$

in (28) results:

$$z(t_{top} + \Delta t) = \frac{\varphi_L(0,0,t)}{\rho_2 L_2}\Delta t \tag{31}$$

where φ_L is the power flow on the processed surface corresponding to the liquid state. In these conditions, (26) becomes:

$$r\left(t_{top}+\Delta t\right)=\frac{T_{top}-T\left(\Delta r\right)}{\Delta r\cdot\rho_2\cdot L_2}k_2\cdot\Delta t \tag{32}$$

The same procedure is applied to find the $C_v(t)$ boundary, taking into account the latent heat of vaporization $L_3[J/kg]$, the mass density corresponding to vapor state $\rho_3[kg/m^3]$ and respectively the heat conductivity corresponding to vapor state $k_3[W\cdot m^{-1}\cdot K^{-1}]$.

2.4 Digitization of heat equation, boundary and initial conditions

The first step of the mathematical approach is to make the equations dimensionless (Mazumder, 1991; Pearsica et al., 2008a, 2008c). In heat equation case it will be achieved by considering the following (r_∞ and z_∞ are the studied domain boundaries, where the material temperature is always equal to the ambient one):

$$r=xr_\infty,\quad z=yr_\infty,\quad T=T_a u,\quad t=\frac{r_\infty^2}{K_1}\tau \tag{33}$$

The heat equation (12) in the new variables x, y, τ, and u yields:

$$\frac{1}{x}\frac{\partial u}{\partial x}+\frac{\partial^2 u}{\partial x^2}+\frac{\partial^2 u}{\partial y^2}=\frac{K_1}{K_i}\frac{\partial u}{\partial \tau},\quad (x,y)\in[0,1]\times[0,1],\ \ \tau\geq 0,\text{ and } i=1,2,3 \tag{34}$$

The initial and limit conditions for the unknown function, u yield:

- phase 1, for $0\leq t<t_{top}$

$$u(x,y,0)=1,\quad (x,y)\in[0,1]\times[0,1] \tag{35}$$

$$u(1,y,\tau)=1,\quad y\in[0,1],\ \ \tau\in[0,\tau_{top}],\ \ \tau_{top}=\frac{K_1}{r_\infty^2}t_{top} \tag{36}$$

$$u(x,1,\tau)=1,\quad x\in[0,1],\ \ \tau\in[0,\tau_{top}] \tag{37}$$

- phase 2, for $t_{top}\leq t<t_{vap}$

$$u(0,0,\tau_{top})=u_{top} \tag{38}$$

$$u(x,y,\tau_{top})=u_1(x,y,\tau_{top}),\quad (x,y)\in(0,1]\times(0,1] \tag{39}$$

where: τ_{top} is the τ value when $u=u_{top}$, $u_{top}=T_{top}/T_a$, and $u_1(x,y,\tau_{top})$ is the heat equation solution in according to phase 1.

If $\tau\in[\tau_{top},\tau_{vap})$ both solid and liquid phases coexist in material, occupying $D_s(\tau)$ and $D_l(\tau)$ domains respectively, which are separated by a time varying boundary, $C_l(\tau)$, so $u(x,y,\tau)=u_{top}$ on it. The projection of the domain $D_l(\tau)$ on $y=0$ plane is the set $\{x/x\leq x_1\}$. For $x=1$ and $y=1$ respectively, the conditions are:

$$u(1,y,\tau)=u(x,1,\tau)=1 \tag{40}$$

Phase 2 is going on while $\tau\in[\tau_{top},\tau_{vap})$, where: $\tau_{vap}=\frac{t_{vap}\cdot K_1}{r_\infty^2}$.

- phase 3, for $t\geq t_{vap}$

$$u(0,0,\tau_{vap})=u_{vap} \tag{41}$$

$$u(x,y,\tau_{vap})=u_2(x,y,\tau_{vap}),\ \ (x,y)\in D_l(\tau_{vap})\setminus(0,0) \tag{42}$$

$$u(x,y,\tau_{vap})=u_1(x,y,\tau_{vap}),\ \ (x,y)\in D_s(\tau_{vap}) \tag{43}$$

where $u_2(x,y,\tau_{vap})$ is the heating equation solution from phase 2. In this temporal phase all the three (solid, liquid and vapor) states coexist in material, occupying the domains: $D_s(\tau)$, $D_l(\tau)$ and $D_v(\tau)$, separated by mobile boundaries $C_l(\tau)$ and $C_v(\tau)$, on which $u(x,y,\tau)=u_{vap}$. The projection of the domains $D_l(\tau)$ and $D_v(\tau)$ on plane $y=0$ are the sets: $\{x/x\in[x_2,x_1]\}$ and $\{x/x\in[0,x_2]\}$. According to phase 3, the conditions on $y=0$ surface (Neumann type conditions) are:

a. $x_2\leq x_1\leq\frac{d}{r_\infty}$:

$$\frac{\partial u}{\partial y}=\begin{cases}-\frac{r_\infty}{T_a\cdot k_3}\left[\varphi_V(x,y_f,\tau)-\varphi_r-\varphi_c\right], & x\in[0,x_2]\\ -\frac{r_\infty}{T_a\cdot k_2}\varphi_L(x,0,\tau), & x\in(x_2,x_1]\\ -\frac{r_\infty}{T_a\cdot k_1}\varphi_S(x,0,\tau), & x\in\left(x_1,\frac{d}{r_\infty}\right]\\ 0, & x\in\left(\frac{d}{r_\infty},1\right]\end{cases} \tag{44}$$

b. $x_2\leq\frac{d}{r_\infty}\leq x_1$:

$$\frac{\partial u}{\partial y}=\begin{cases}-\frac{r_\infty}{T_a\cdot k_3}\left[\varphi_V(x,y_f,\tau)-\varphi_r-\varphi_c\right], & x\in[0,x_2]\\ -\frac{r_\infty}{T_a\cdot k_2}\varphi_L(x,0,\tau), & x\in\left(x_2,\frac{d}{r_\infty}\right]\\ 0, & x\in\left(\frac{d}{r_\infty},1\right]\end{cases} \tag{45}$$

c. $x_2 > \frac{d}{r_\infty}$:

$$\frac{\partial u}{\partial y} = \begin{cases} -\frac{r_\infty}{T_a \cdot k_3}\left[\varphi_V(x, y_f, \tau) - \varphi_r - \varphi_c\right], & x \in \left[0, \frac{d}{r_\infty}\right] \\ 0, \quad x \in \left(\frac{d}{r_\infty}, 1\right] \end{cases} \tag{46}$$

Similar Neumann type conditions are settled for temporal phases 1 and 2, accordingly to their specific parameters.
For $x = 1$, and $y = 1$ respectively, the conditions are given by (40).

2.5 Digitization of equations on separation boundaries

The speed of time variation of separation boundaries, v_n, is given by (47), where n is the external normal vector of the boundary.

$$v_n = -\frac{k_e}{\rho_e \cdot L_e}\frac{\partial T}{\partial n}, \quad e = 2,3 \tag{47}$$

For $y = 0$ and $x = x_f$, it results:

$$v_r(x_f, 0) = -\frac{k_e}{\rho_e \cdot L_e}\frac{\partial T}{\partial r} = -\frac{k_e \cdot T_a}{\rho_e \cdot L_e \cdot r_\infty}\frac{\partial u}{\partial x}, \quad e = 2,3 \tag{48}$$

respectively,

$$v_r(x_f, 0) = \frac{dr}{dt} = \frac{K_1}{r_\infty}\frac{dx}{d\tau} \tag{49}$$

It results:

$$\frac{dx}{d\tau} = -\frac{k_e \cdot T_a}{\rho_e \cdot L_e \cdot K_1}\frac{\partial u}{\partial x}, \quad e = 2,3 \tag{50}$$

The α parameter of separation boundary at $\tau + \Delta\tau$ moment is:

$$\alpha = x_f(\tau + \Delta\tau) = x_f(\tau) + \frac{dx}{d\tau}\Delta\tau = x_f(\tau) - \frac{k_e \cdot T_a}{\rho_e \cdot L_e \cdot K_1}\frac{\partial u}{\partial x}\Delta\tau, \quad e = 2,3 \tag{51}$$

where:

$$\frac{\partial u}{\partial x} \approx \frac{u(x_k, 0) - u(x_f, 0)}{x_k - x_f} \tag{52}$$

where $x_k \in$ digitization network. For $\tau = \tau_{top}$ and $\tau = \tau_{vap}$ respectively, (52) yields:

$$\frac{\partial u}{\partial x} = \frac{u_1(x_1, 0) - u_{top}}{x_1}, \quad x_f(\tau_{top}) = 0 \tag{53}$$

$$\frac{\partial u}{\partial x}=\frac{u_2(x_1,0)-u_{vap}}{x_1}, \quad x_f(\tau_{vap})=0 \tag{54}$$

For $x=0$ and $y=y_f$, it results:

$$v_z(0,y_f)=-\frac{k_e}{\rho_e\cdot L_e}\frac{\partial T}{\partial z}=-\frac{k_e\cdot T_a}{\rho_e\cdot L_e\cdot r_\infty}\frac{\partial u}{\partial y}, \quad e=2,3 \tag{55}$$

respectively,

$$v_z(0,y_f)=\frac{dz}{dt}=\frac{K_1}{r_\infty}\frac{dy}{d\tau} \tag{56}$$

It results:

$$\frac{dy}{d\tau}=-\frac{k_e\cdot T_a}{\rho_e\cdot L_e\cdot K_1}\frac{\partial u}{\partial y}, \quad e=2,3 \tag{57}$$

The β parameter of separation boundary at $\tau+\Delta\tau$ moment is:

$$\beta=y_f(\tau+\Delta\tau)=y_f(\tau)+\frac{dy}{d\tau}\Delta\tau=y_f(\tau)-\frac{k_e\cdot T_a}{\rho_e\cdot L_e\cdot K_1}\frac{\partial u}{\partial y}\Delta\tau, \quad e=2,3 \tag{58}$$

where:

$$\frac{\partial u}{\partial y}\approx\frac{u(0,y_k)-u(0,y_f)}{y_k-y_f} \tag{59}$$

For $\tau=\tau_{top}$ it results:

$$\frac{\partial u}{\partial y}=-\frac{r_\infty}{T_a\cdot k_2}\varphi_L(0,0,\tau_{top}), \quad y_f(\tau_{top})=0 \tag{60}$$

For $\tau=\tau_{vap}$ it results:

$$\frac{\partial u}{\partial y}=-\frac{r_\infty}{T_a\cdot k_3}\left[\varphi_V(0,0,\tau_{top})-\varphi_r-\varphi_c\right], \quad y_f(\tau_{vap})=0 \tag{61}$$

3. Determination of temperature distribution in material

Using the finite differences method, the domain $[0,1]\times[0,1]$ is digitized by sets of equidistant points on Ox and Oy directions (Pearsica et al., 2008a, 2008b).

3.1 Digitization of mathematical model equations

In the network points, the partial derivatives will be approximated by:

$$\left.\frac{\partial u}{\partial x}\right|_{(i,j)}\approx\frac{u_{i+1,j}-u_{i-1,j}}{2\Delta x}, \quad \left.\frac{\partial^2 u}{\partial x^2}\right|_{(i,j)}\approx\frac{u_{i+1,j}-2u_{i,j}+u_{i-1,j}}{(\Delta x)^2} \tag{62}$$

$$\left.\frac{\partial u}{\partial y}\right|_{(i,j)} \approx \frac{u_{i,j+1}-u_{i,j-1}}{2\Delta y}, \quad \left.\frac{\partial^2 u}{\partial y^2}\right|_{(i,j)} \approx \frac{u_{i,j+1}-2u_{i,j}+u_{i,j-1}}{(\Delta y)^2} \tag{63}$$

$$\left.\frac{\partial u}{\partial \tau}\right|_{(i,j)} \approx \frac{u_{i,j}(\tau+\Delta\tau)-u_{i,j}(\tau)}{\Delta\tau} \tag{64}$$

With these approximations, in each inner point of the network the partial derivatives equations become an algebraic system such:

$$a^j_{i,i-1}u_{i-1,j}+a^j_{i,i}u_{i,j}+a^j_{i,i+1}u_{i+1,j}+b^j_{i,i}u_{i,j-1}+c^j_{i,i}u_{i,j+1}=f_{i,j} \tag{65}$$

The system coefficients are linear expressions of the partial derivatives equation, computed in the network points. If there are M and N points on Ox and Oy axis respectively, the system will include $M\times N$ equations with $(M+1)\times(N+1)$ unknowns. Adding the conditions for the domain boundaries, the system is determinate.

The implicit method, involving evaluations of the equation terms containing spatial derivatives at $\tau+\Delta\tau$ moment, is used to obtain the unknown function $u(x,y,\tau)$ distribution in network points. The option is on this method because there are no restrictions on choosing the time and spatial steps $(\Delta\tau,\Delta x,\Delta y)$. According to this method, an additional index is introduced, representing the time moment. With these explanations, the heat equation with finite differences yields:

$$\left[\frac{1}{x}\frac{\partial u}{\partial x}+\frac{\partial^2 u}{\partial x^2}+\frac{\partial^2 u}{\partial y^2}\right]_{i,j,n+1}=\frac{K_1}{K_e}\left(\frac{\partial u}{\partial \tau}\right)_{i,j,n+1}, \quad e=1,2,3 \tag{66}$$

Finally, the algebraic system yields:

$$\lambda_1\left(1-\frac{\Delta x}{2x_i}\right)u_{i-1,j,n+1}-\left[\frac{K_1}{K_e}+2\lambda_1(1+\lambda_2)\right]u_{i,j,n+1}+\lambda_1\left(1+\frac{\Delta x}{2x_i}\right)u_{i+1,j,n+1}+$$
$$+\lambda_1\lambda_2 u_{i,j-1,n+1}+\lambda_1\lambda_2 u_{i,j+1,n+1}=-u_{i,j,n}\cdot\frac{K_1}{K_e}, \quad e=1,2,3 \tag{67}$$

where: $\lambda_1=\frac{\partial\tau}{(\Delta x)^2}$, $\lambda_2=\left(\frac{\Delta x}{\Delta y}\right)^2$, and $x_i=x_o+(i-1)\cdot\Delta x$. The value x_o is very close to zero and it was chosen to avoid the singularity appearing in heating equation at $x=0$. Formally, this singularity appears because if $x=0$, then $\frac{\partial u}{\partial x}=0$ too. If $\Delta x=1/M$ and $\Delta y=1/N$ will result $i=\overline{1,M+1}$ and $j=\overline{1,N+1}$.

Equation (67) will be written for $i=\overline{2,M}$ and $j=\overline{2,N}$. In case $j=N+1$ and $i=M+1$, the constraints imposed to u are:

$$u_{i,N+1,n+1}=1, \quad u_{M+1,j,n+1}=1 \tag{68}$$

The initial condition is for $n=0$:

$$u_{i,j,1}=1,\ \forall(i,j) \tag{69}$$

For $i=1,\ j\neq 1$, (67) is still valid, observing that $u_{0,j,n+1}=u_{2,j,n+1}$, because the solution is symmetrical related to $x=0$. In this case, (67) yields:

$$-\left[\frac{K_1}{K_e}+2\lambda_1(1+\lambda_2)\right]u_{1,j,n+1}+2\lambda_1 u_{2,j,n+1}+\lambda_1\lambda_2 u_{1,j-1,n+1}+\lambda_1\lambda_2 u_{1,j+1,n+1}=$$

$$=-u_{1,j,n}\cdot\frac{K_1}{K_e},\ e=1,2,3 \tag{70}$$

For $j=1$, when writing the initial conditions for the boundary $y=0$, the temporal phase of the material must be taken into account. Only the equations corresponding to the third phase ($t\geq t_{vap}$) will be presented, because it is the most complex one, all the three states (solid, liquid and vapor) being taken into account. Similar results were obtained for the other two phases, in a similar way, accordingly to their influencing parameters. The initial conditions are:

$$u_{1,1,n_0}=u_{vap},\quad \tau_{vap}=\Delta\tau\cdot n_0 \tag{71}$$

$$u_{i,j,n_0}=u^{(2)}_{i,j,n_0},\quad (x_i,y_j)\in D_l\setminus(0,0) \tag{72}$$

$$u_{i,j,n_0}=u^{(1)}_{i,j,n_0},\quad (x_i,y_j)\in D_s \tag{73}$$

where $u^{(2)}$ is the solution of the problem corresponding to the second temporal phase ($t_{top}\leq t<t_{vap}$).
The boundary corresponding to the n_0+1 time moment will be determined hereinafter. The parameters of the boundary separating the vapor and liquid will be:

$$\alpha_{n_0+1}=\frac{T_a\cdot k_3\cdot\Delta\tau}{K_1\cdot\rho_v\cdot L_3\cdot\Delta x}\left(u_{1,1,n_0}-u_{2,1,n_0}\right),\quad \beta_{n_0+1}=\frac{r_\infty\cdot\Delta\tau}{\rho_v\cdot L_3\cdot K_1}\varphi_V(0,0,\tau) \tag{74}$$

The boundary equation will be:

$$x=\frac{\alpha_{n_0+1}}{\beta_{n_0+1}}\sqrt{\beta^2_{n_0+1}-y^2} \tag{75}$$

The boundary separating liquid and solid phases exists at the moment n_0, as well at a certain moment n, its parameters being given by (51) and (58). The situation corresponding to the third phase is illustrated in figure 1.
In the marked points, the heating equation must be changed, because its related partial derivatives approximation by using finite differences is not possible anymore (the associated Taylor series in A and B will be used, where $AC=a\Delta x$ and $BC=b\Delta y$). In order

to know if a point is nearby the boundary previously determined, the points $(x_i^{'}, y_i^{'})$ and $(x_j^{''}, y_j^{''})$ respectively will be obtain by intersecting the network lines $(x_i = x_o + (i-1)\Delta x$, $y_j = (j-1)\Delta y)$ and the boundary $x = \frac{\alpha}{\beta}\sqrt{\beta^2 - y^2}$. It results $h = \left[\frac{y_i^{'}}{\Delta y}\right] + 1$ (floor() + 1) as solution of the equation $(h-1)\Delta y = y_i^{'}$, and:

$$b_p(i,h) = \frac{y_i^{'}}{\Delta y} - \left[\frac{y_i^{'}}{\Delta y}\right],\quad b_m(i,h) = 1,\quad b_m(i,h+1) = 1 - b_p(i,h),\quad b_p(i,h+1) = 1 \tag{76}$$

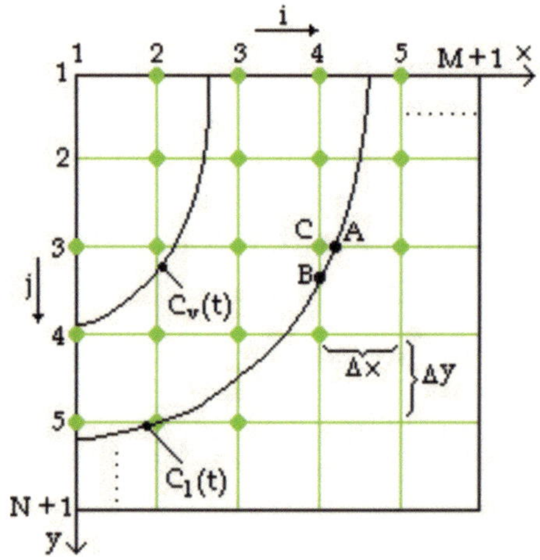

Fig. 1. The boundaries separating the phases

It results (similar) $k = \left[\frac{x_j^{''}}{\Delta x}\right] + 1$ as solution of the equation $(k-1)\Delta x = x_j^{''}$, and:

$$a_p(k,j) = \frac{x_j^{''}}{\Delta x} - \left[\frac{x_j^{''}}{\Delta x}\right],\quad a_m(k,j) = 1,\quad a_m(k+1,j) = 1 - a_p(k,j),\quad a_p(k+1,j) = 1 \tag{77}$$

For the regular points (the ones which are not nearby the boundary), the above mentioned parameters will be:

$$b_p(i,j) = b_m(i,j) = a_p(i,j) = a_m(i,j) = 1 \tag{78}$$

The unified heating equation in a network point (i, j) will be:

$$\begin{gathered}\frac{2\lambda_1}{a_m(a_m + a_p)}\left(\frac{a_p \Delta x}{2x_i} - 1\right) u_{i-1,j,n+1} + \left(\frac{K_1}{K_3} + \frac{a_m - a_p}{a_m a_p}\frac{\lambda_1 \Delta x}{x_i} + \frac{2\lambda_1}{a_m a_p} + \frac{2\lambda_1\lambda_2}{b_m b_p}\right) u_{i,j,n+1} - \\ - \frac{\lambda_1(2x_i + a_m \Delta x)}{a_p(a_m + a_p)x_i} u_{fx,n+1} - \frac{2\lambda_1\lambda_2}{b_m(b_p + b_m)} u_{i,j-1} - \frac{2\lambda_1\lambda_2}{b_p(b_m + b_p)} u_{fy,n+1} = u_{i,j,n} \cdot \frac{K_1}{K_3}\end{gathered} \tag{79}$$

where the coefficients a_m, a_p, b_m, and b_p depends on point (i, j), and $u_{fx} = u_{i+1,j}$ and $u_{fy} = u_{i,j+1}$, if the point where derivatives are approximated is not nearby the boundary. For $i = 1$, (79) becomes:

$$\left(\frac{K_1}{K_e} + \frac{2\lambda_1}{a_p a_m} + \frac{2\lambda_1\lambda_2}{b_p b_m} - \frac{a_p - a_m}{a_p a_m}\frac{\lambda_1 \cdot \Delta x}{x_i}\right)u_{1,j,n+1} + \frac{2\lambda_1}{a_p + a_m}\left(\frac{a_p \Delta x}{2a_m x_i} - \frac{1}{a_m} - \frac{a_m \Delta x}{2a_p x_i} - \frac{1}{a_p}\right)u_{2,j,n+1} - \frac{2\lambda_1\lambda_2}{b_m(b_m + b_p)}u_{1,j-1,n+1} - \frac{2\lambda_1\lambda_2}{b_p(b_m + b_p)}u_{1,j+1,n+1} = u_{1,j,n} \cdot \frac{K_1}{K_e} \tag{80}$$

There are as well vapor, liquid and solid zones on the boundary $y = 0$. Depending on the position of the intersecting points between boundary and $y = 0$, the following situations may occur:

a. $x_1 \le \frac{d}{r_\infty}$:

$$u_{i,1,n+1} - u_{fr} = \frac{\Delta y \cdot a_m \cdot r_\infty}{T_a \cdot k_3}\varphi_V(x_i, y_f, \tau), \quad x_i \in [0, x_2] \tag{81}$$

$$u_{i,1,n+1} - u_{i,2,n+1} = \frac{\Delta y \cdot r_\infty}{T_a \cdot k_2}\varphi_L(x_i, 0, \tau), \quad x_i \in (x_2, x_1] \tag{82}$$

$$u_{i,1,n+1} - u_{i,2,n+1} = \frac{\Delta y \cdot r_\infty}{T_a \cdot k_1}\varphi_S(x_i, 0, \tau), \quad x_i \in \left(x_1, \frac{d}{r_\infty}\right] \tag{83}$$

b. $x_2 \le \frac{d}{r_\infty} < x_1$:

$$u_{i,1,n+1} - u_{fr} = \frac{\Delta y \cdot a_m \cdot r_\infty}{T_a \cdot k_3}\varphi_V(x_i, y_f, \tau), \quad x_i \in [0, x_2] \tag{84}$$

$$u_{i,1,n+1} - u_{i,2,n+1} = \frac{\Delta y \cdot r_\infty}{T_a \cdot k_2}\varphi_L(x_i, 0, \tau), \quad x_i \in \left(x_2, \frac{d}{r_\infty}\right] \tag{85}$$

c. $x_2 > \frac{d}{r_\infty}$:

$$u_{i,1,n+1} - u_{fr} = \frac{\Delta y \cdot a_m \cdot r_\infty}{T_a \cdot k_3}\varphi_V(x_i, y_f, \tau), \quad x_i \in \left[0, \frac{d}{r_\infty}\right] \tag{86}$$

If $x_i > \frac{d}{r_\infty}$, in all of the three mentioned cases:

$$u_{i,1,n+1} = u_{i,2,n+1} \tag{87}$$

Because the discrete network parameters do not influence the initial moment of laser interaction with the material, the temperature gradient on z direction was replaced by the temporal temperature gradient in the initial condition on $z = 0$ boundary (Draganescu & Velculescu, 1986). So, the digitized initial condition on $z = 0$ boundary yields:

$$u_{i,1,n+1} = u_{i,1,n} + \frac{r_\infty}{k}\sqrt{\frac{K \cdot d\tau}{K_1 \cdot n}} \cdot \varphi(x_i, 0, \tau) \tag{88}$$

The equations system obtained after digitization and boundary determination will be solved by using an optimized method regarding the solving run time, namely the column wise method. It is an exact type method, preferable to the direct matrix inversing method.

3.2 The column wise solving method

From the algebraic system of $(M+1)\times(N+1)$ equations, the minimum dimension will be chosen as unknowns' column dimension. It is assumed to be $M+1$. It is to notice that writing the system in the point (i,j) involves as well the points $(i-1,j)$, $(i+1,j)$, $(i,j-1)$, and $(i,j+1)$ (Pearsica et al., 2008a, 2008b). The system and transformed conditions may be organized, writing in sequence all the equations for each fixed j and variable i, as a vector system. So, by keeping j constant, it results a relationship between columns j, $j-1$, and $j+1$. By denoting $[A_j]$, $[B_j]$, and $[C_j]$ the unknowns coefficients matrixes of the columns j, $j-1$, and $j+1$ respectively, the system for j constant will be:

$$[A_j]\cdot\{U_j\} + [B_j]\cdot\{U_{j-1}\} + [C_j]\cdot\{U_{j+1}\} = \{F_j\} \tag{89}$$

where: $[X]$ is a quadratic matrix, $\{X\}$ is a column vector, $\{F_j\}$ is the free terms vector, $[A_j]$ is a tri-diagonal matrix whose non-null components are $a_{i,i-1}$, $a_{i,i}$ and $a_{i,i+1}$, and $[B_j]$ and $[C_j]$ are diagonal matrixes. The components of matrixes $[A_j]$, $[B_j]$ and $[C_j]$, are the coefficients of the unified caloric equation written in a point (i,j) of the network, equation (79). The components of $\{F_j\}$ are:

$$f_{i,j} = u_{i,j,n} \cdot \frac{K_1}{K_e}, \quad j \neq 1, \quad e = 1,2,3 \tag{90}$$

For $j = 1$, (90) yields ($[A_1] = [I]$ - unity matrix, and $[B_1] = [C_1] = [0]$):

$$[A_1]\cdot\{U_1\} = \{F_1\} \tag{91}$$

The components of $\{F_1\}$ are computed using the relation:

$$f_{i,1} = \begin{cases} u_{i,1,n} + \dfrac{r_\infty}{k}\sqrt{\dfrac{K \cdot d\tau}{K_1 \cdot n}} \cdot \varphi(x_i, 0, \tau), & i \le i_d \\ u_{i,1,n}, & i > i_d \end{cases} \tag{92}$$

where i_d is the laser beam limit. Taking into account the relation linking two successive columns, U_{j-1} and U_j:

$$\{U_{j-1}\} = [E_j] \cdot \{U_j\} + \{R_j\} \tag{93}$$

and by denoting:

$$[T_j] = ([A_j] + [B_j] \cdot [E_j])^{-1} \tag{94}$$

The following relation results:

$$\{U_j\} = -[T_j] \cdot [C_j] \cdot \{U_{j+1}\} + [T_j](\{F_j\} - [B_j] \cdot \{R_j\}) \tag{95}$$

By comparing (93) and (95) the recurrence relations to find matrixes $[E_j]$ and $\{R_j\}$ yield:

$$[E_{j+1}] = -[T_j] \cdot [C_j], \quad \{R_{j+1}\} = [T_j](\{F_j\} - [B_j] \cdot \{R_j\}) \tag{96}$$

The initial matrixes $[E_1]$ and $\{R_1\}$ are chosen so that (92) is respected:

$$[E_1] = [0], \quad \{R_j\} = \{0\} \tag{97}$$

A sequence determination of the matrixes $[E_j]$ and $\{R_j\}$ till $j = N + 1$ and then, using (93) of $\{U_N\}$, $\{U_{N-1}\}$,…,$\{U_2\}$, bases the computing process. The simplified logical diagram of the function computing the temperature distribution in material is shown in figure 2.

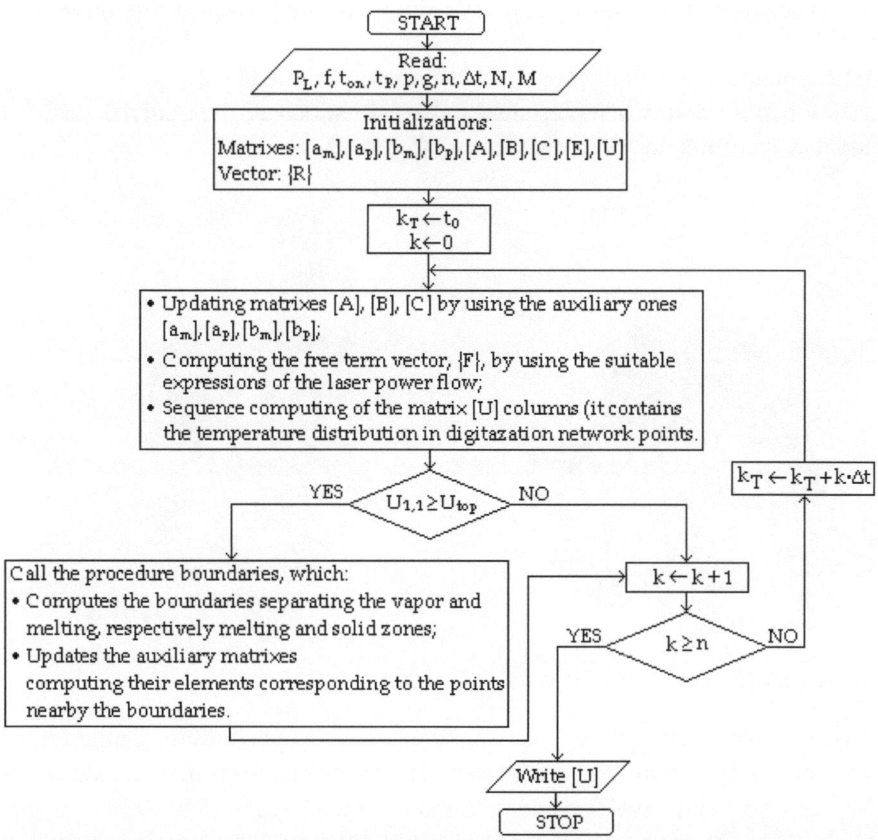

Fig. 2. Logical diagram of the function computing the temperature distribution in material

Input data: P_L - laser power, f - focal distance of the focusing system, t_{on} - laser pulse duration, t_p - laser pulse period, p - additional gas pressure, g - material thickness, n - number of time steps that program are running for, Δt - time step, M, N - number of digitization network in Ox and Oy directions, respectivelly.
Both procedures (the main function and the procedure computing the boundaries) were implemented as MathCAD functions.

4. Numeric results

The model equations were solved for a cutting process of metals with a high concentration of iron (steel case). In table 1 is presented the temperature distribution in material, computed in continuous regime lasers, with the following input data: $P_L = 1kW$ (laser power), $\eta_o = 0.74$ (oxidizing efficiency), $p = 0.8bar$ (additional gas pressure), $d = 0.16mm$ (focalized laser beam radius), $D = 10mm$ (diameter of the generated laser beam), $f = 145mm$ (focal distance of the focusing system), $g = 6mm$ (material thickness) $A_S = 0.49$ (absorbability on solid surface), $A_L = 0.68$ (absorbability on liquid surface), $\Delta t = 10^{-5}s$ (time step), $t = 10ms$ (operation time), $M = 8$ (number of intervals on x direction), $N = 32$ (number of intervals on y direction), $k_T = 1000$ (number of iterations). The iron material constants were taken into consideration, accordingly to the present (solid, liquid or vapor) state.
The real temperatures in material are the below ones multiplied by 25.
Temperature distribution was represented in two situations: at the material surface and at the material evaporating depth $(z = 4.192mm)$ (figure 3).

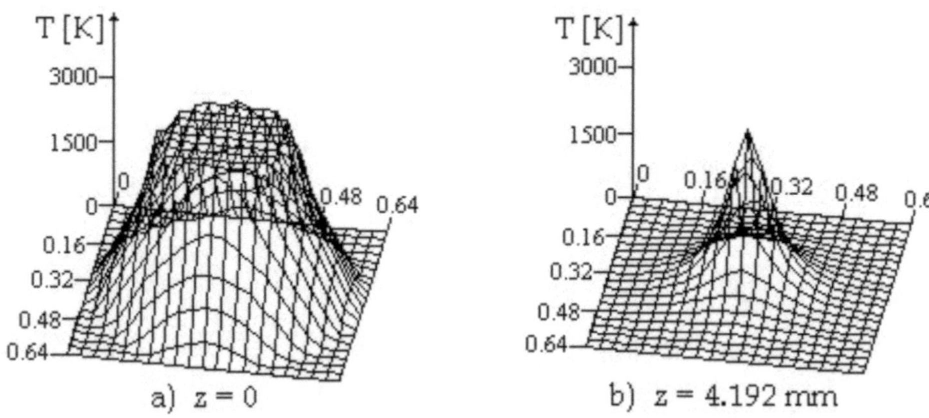

Fig. 3. Temperature distribution, $P_L = 1kW, t = 10ms$

The depths corresponding to the melting and vaporization temperatures are: $z_{top} = 4.288mm$, respectively $z_{vap} = 4.192mm$. The moments when material surface reaches the vaporization and melting temperatures are: $t_{vap} = 0.181 \cdot 10^{-5}s$, respectively $t_{top} = 0.132 \cdot 10^{-5}s$. The temperature distributions at different depths within the material, for laser power $P_L = 400W$, and processing time $t = 1ms$, are presented in figure 4.

N \ M	1	2	3	4	5	6	7	8	9
1	120.3	120.3	120.3	120.3	120.3	71.6	45.0	21.4	1.0
2	120.3	120.3	120.3	120.3	71.6	71.6	45.0	21.4	1.0
3	120.3	120.3	120.3	120.3	71.6	71.7	44.8	21.3	1.0
4	120.3	120.3	120.3	120.3	71.6	71.6	44.7	21.3	1.0
5	120.3	120.3	120.3	120.3	71.6	71.6	44.3	21.1	1.0
6	120.3	120.3	120.3	120.3	71.6	68.4	42.1	20.1	1.0
7	120.3	120.3	120.3	120.3	71.6	64.9	40.0	19.1	1.0
8	120.3	120.3	120.3	120.3	71.6	61.7	38.0	18.2	1.0
9	120.3	120.3	120.3	120.3	71.6	59.0	35.4	17.4	1.0
10	120.3	120.3	120.3	120.3	71.6	56.8	35.0	16.8	1.0
11	120.3	120.3	120.3	120.3	71.6	54.9	33.9	16.3	1.0
12	120.3	120.3	120.3	120.3	71.6	53.4	33.0	15.8	1.0
13	120.3	120.3	120.3	120.3	71.6	52.2	32.3	15.5	1.0
14	120.3	120.3	120.3	120.3	71.6	51.3	31.7	15.2	1.0
15	120.3	120.3	120.3	120.3	71.6	50.3	31.0	14.9	1.0
16	120.3	120.3	120.3	94.9	64.4	47.2	29.5	14.2	1.0
17	120.3	120.3	120.3	71.6	64.0	42.5	26.0	12.5	1.0
18	120.3	120.3	120.3	71.6	57.3	38.3	23.5	11.4	1.0
19	120.3	120.3	120.3	71.6	53.1	35.2	21.4	10.3	1.0
20	120.3	120.3	120.3	71.6	47.4	29.6	17.4	8.4	1.0
21	120.3	120.3	71.6	61.2	37.5	23.2	13.5	6.5	1.0
22	120.3	120.3	71.6	45.0	25.8	14.7	8.0	3.9	1.0
23	120.3	86.0	39.3	18.7	9.2	5.0	2.9	1.7	1.0
24	25.6	7.6	4.2	2.7	1.9	1.5	1.2	1.1	1.0
25	1.5	1.3	1.2	1.1	1.1	1.0	1.0	1.0	1.0
26	1.0	1.0	1.0	1.0	1.0	1.0	1.0	1.0	1.0
...	...	...	...	...	...	...	...	...	...
33	1.0	1.0	1.0	1.0	1.0	1.0	1.0	1.0	1.0

Table 1. Temperature distribution in material

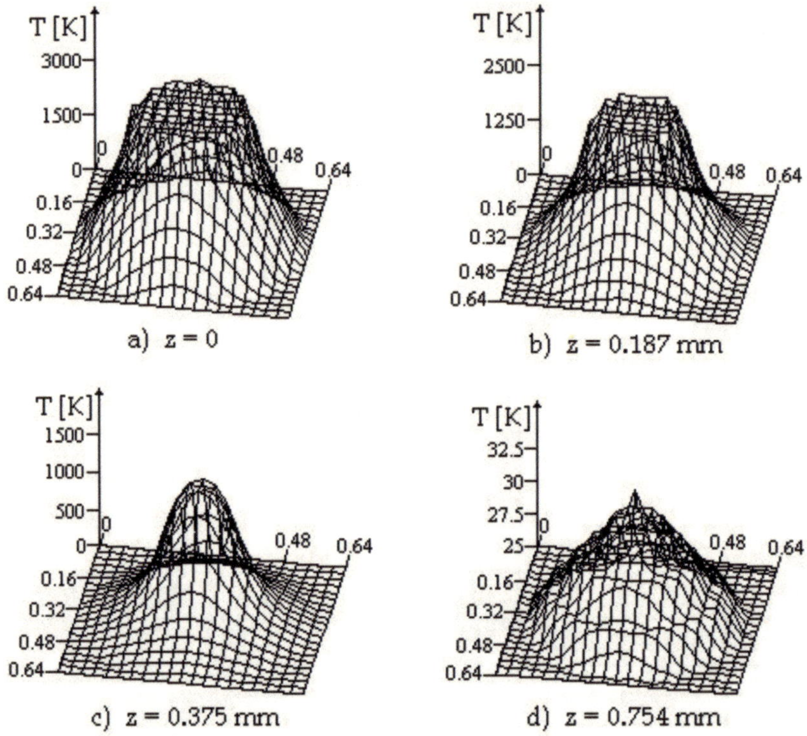

Fig. 4. Temperature distribution, $P_L = 400W, t = 1ms$

The temperature distributions on the material surface $(z = 0)$ are quite identical in both mentioned cases (figures 3 and 4). The material vaporization depth is depending on the processing time, and the considered input parameters as well. So, for a 10 times greater processing time and a 2.5 times greater laser power, one may observe a 10.94 times greater vaporization depth, compared with the previous case $(z = 0.383\,\text{mm})$. If comparing the obtained results, it results a quite small dimension of the liquid phase (difference between z_{top} and z_{vap}), within $0.006 \div 0.085$ mm.

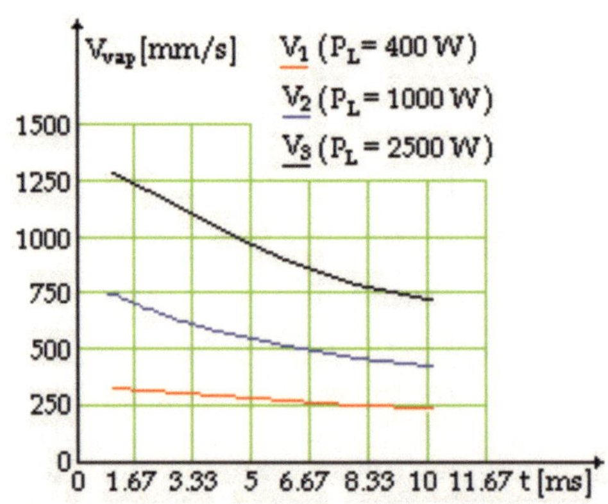

Fig. 5. The vaporization speed variation vs. processing time

Knowing the vaporization depth at a certain processing time allows evaluating the vaporization speed and limited processing speed. The vaporization speed variation as a function of processing time is presented in figure 5. It may be observed that vaporization speed is decreasing function (it decreases as the laser beam advances in material).

The decreasing of the vaporization speed as the vaporization depth increases is owed to the laser beam defocusing effect, which augments once the laser beam advances in material.

The processing speed is computed for a certain material thickness, as a function of vaporization speed corresponding to processing moment when vaporization depth is equal to material thickness. So, for a certain processing time, results the thickness of the material that may be processed, which is equal to vaporization depth.

As a consequence of the mass-flow conserving law, in order to cut a material with a certain thickness, the time requested by moving the irradiated zone must be equal to the time requested by material breakdown. The following relation derives in this way, allowing evaluating the processing speed as a function of vaporization speed:

$$v_T = v_{vap} \cdot \frac{2d}{g} \tag{98}$$

In figure 6 are compared the processing speeds: analytically determined, experimentally determined and returned by the above presented method (Pearsica et al., 2010, 2008c).

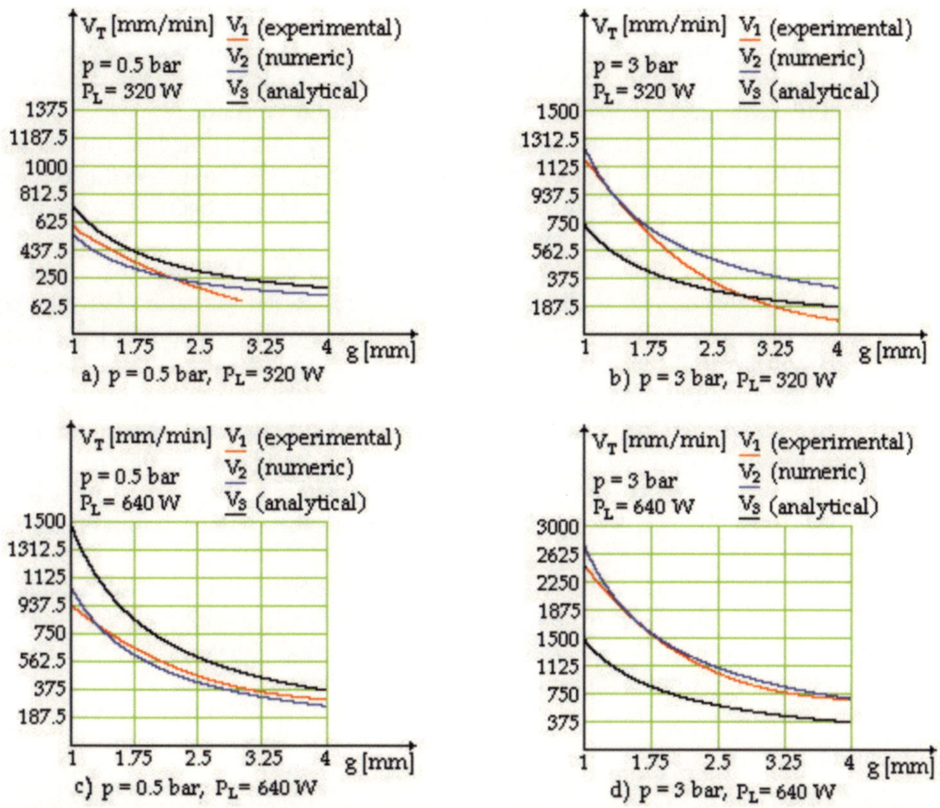

Fig. 6. Processing speed variation

The experimental processing speeds were determined for a general use steel (OL 37), and iron material parameters were considered for the theoretical speeds. It may be observed in the presented figures that processing speed numerical results are a quite good approximation for the experimental ones, for the laser power $P_L = 640\,W$, the maximum error being 11.3% for $p = 3\,bar$ and, 17.28%, for $p = 0.5\,bar$. In case of $P_L = 320\,W$, the numerical determined processing speed matches better the experimental one for small thickness of processed material (for $g = 1\,mm$, the error is 10.2%, for $p = 0.5\,bar$, and 6.89%, for $p = 3\,bar$), the error being greater at bigger thickness (for $g = 3\,mm$ and $p = 0.5\,bar$ the error is 89.4%, and for $g = 4\,mm$ and $p = 3\,bar$ the error is 230.52%).
According to the presented situation, it may be considered that, in comparison with the analytical processing speed, the numerical determined one match better the experiments.

5. Conclusion

The computing function allowed determination of: temperature distribution in material, melting depth, vaporization depth, vaporization speed, working speed, returned data allowing evaluation of working and thermic affected zones widths too.
The equations of the mathematical proposed model to describe the way the material submitted to laser action reacts were solved numerically by finite differences method. The algebraic system returned by digitization was solved by using an exact type method, known in literature as column solving method.
The variables and the unknown functions were non-dimensional and it was chosen a net of equidistant points in the pattern presented by the substantial. Because the points neighboring the boundary have distances up to boundary different from the net parameters, some digitization formulas with variable steps have been used for them.
An algebraic system of equation solved at each time-step by column method was obtained after digitization and application of the limit conditions. The procedure is specific to implicit method of solving numerically the heat equation and it was chosen because there were no restrictions on the steps in time and space of the net.
Among the hypothesis on which the mathematics model is based on and hypothesis that need a more thorough analysis is the hypothesis on boundaries formation between solid state and liquid state, respectively, the liquid state and vapor state, supposed to be known previously, parameters that characterize the boundaries being determined from the thermic regime prior to the calculus moment.
The analytical model obtained is experiment dependent, because there are certain difficulties in oxidizing efficiency η_o determination, which implies to model the gas-metal thermic transfer mechanism. As well, some material parameters $(c, k, \rho, A_S, ...)$ (which were assumed as constants) are temperature dependent. Their average values in interest domains were considered.
The indirect results obtained as such (the thickness of penetrating the substantial, the vaporization speed) certify the correctness of the hypothesis made with boundary formula. The results thus obtained are placed within the limits of normal physics, which constitutes a verifying of the mathematics model equation.

6. Acknowledgment

This work was supported by The National Authority for Scientific Research, Romania – CNCSIS-UEFISCDI: Grant CNCSIS, PN-II-ID-PCE-2008, no. 703/15.01.2009, code 2291:

"Laser Radiation-Substance Interaction: Physical Phenomena Modeling and Techniques of Electromagnetic Pollution Rejection".

7. References

Belic, I. (1989). A Method to Determine the Parameters of Laser Cutting. *Optics and Laser Technology*, Vol.21, No.4, (August 1989), pp. 277-278, ISSN 0030-3992

Draganescu, V. & Velculescu, V.G. (1986). *Thermal Processing by Lasers*, Academy Publishing House, Bucharest, Romania

Dowden, J.M. (2009). *The Theory of Laser Materials Processing: Heat and Mass Transfer in Modern Technology*, Springer, ISBN 140209339X, New York, USA

Dowden, J.M. (2001). *The Mathematics of Thermal Modeling*, Chapman & Hall, ISBN 1-58488-230-1, Boca Raton, Florida, SUA

Hacia, L. & Domke, K. (2007). Integral Modeling and Simulating in Some Thermal Problems, *Proceedings of 5th IASME/WSEAS International Conference on Heat and Mass Transfer (THE'07)*, pp. 42-47, ISBN 978-960-6766-00-8, Athens, Greece, August 25-27, 2007

Mazumder, J. (1991). Overview of Melt Dynamics in Laser Processing. *Optical Engineering*, Vol.30, No.8, (August 1991), pp. 1208-1219, ISSN 0091-3286

Mazumder, J. & Steen, W.M. (1980). Heat Transfer Model for C.W. Laser Materials Processing. *Journal of Applied Physics*, Vol.51, No.2, (February 1980), pp. 941-947, ISSN 0021-8979

Pearsica, M.; Baluta, S.; Constantinescu, C.; Nedelcu, S.; Strimbu, C. & Bentea, M. (2010). A Mathematical Model to Compute the Thermic Affected Zone at Laser Beam Processing. *Optoelectronics and Advanced Materials*, Vol.4, No.1, (January 2010), pp. 4-10, ISSN 1842-6573

Pearsica, M.; Constantinescu, C.; Strimbu, C. & Mihai, C. (2009). Experimental Researches to Determine the Thermic Affected Zone at Laser Beam Processing of Metals. *Metalurgia International*, Vol.14, Special issue no.12, (August 2009), pp. 224-228, ISSN 1582-2214

Pearsica, M.; Ratiu, G.; Carstea, C.G.; Constantinescu, C.; Strimbu, C. & Gherman, L. (2008). Heat Transfer Modeling and Simulating for Laser Beam Irradiation with Phase Transformations. *WSEAS Transactions on Mathematics*, Vol.7, No.11, (November 2008), pp. 2174-2180, ISSN 676-685

Pearsica, M.; Ratiu, I.G.; Carstea, C.G.; Constantinescu, C. & Strimbu, C. (2008). Electromagnetic Processes at Laser Beam Processing Assisted by an Active Gas Jet, *Proceedings of 10th WSEAS International Conference on Mathematical Methods, Computational Technique and Intelligent Systems*, pp. 187-193, ISBN 978-960-474-012-3, Corfu, Greece, October 26-28, 2008

Pearsica, M.; Baluta, S.; Constantinescu, C. & Strimbu, C. (2008), A Numerical Method to Analyse the Thermal Phenomena Involved in Phase Transformations at Laser Beam Irradiation, *Journal of Optoelectronics and Advanced Materials*, Vol.10, No.5, (August 2008), pp. 2174-2181, ISSN 1454-4164

Pearsica, M. & Nedelcu, S. (2005). A Simulation Method of Thermal Phenomena at Laser Beam Irradiation, *Proceedings of 10th International Conference „Applied Electronics"*, pp. 269-272, ISBN 80-7043-369-8, Pilsen, Czech Republic, September 7-8, 2005

Riyad, M. & Abdelkader, H. (2006). Investigation of Numerical Techniques with Comparison Between Anlytical and Explicit and Implicit Methods of Solving One-

Dimensional Transient Heat Conduction Problems. *WSEAS Transactions on Heat and Mass Transfer*, Vol.1, No.4, (April 2006), pp. 567-571, ISSN 1790-5044

Shuja, S.Z.; Yilbas, B.S. & Khan, S.M. (2008). Laser Heating of Semi-Infinite Solid with Consecutive Pulses: Influence of Material Properties on Temperature Field. *Optics and Laser Technology*, Vol.40, No.3, (April 2008), pp. 472-480, ISSN 0030-3992

Steen, W.M. & Mazumder, J. (2010). *Laser Material Processing*, Springer-Verlag, ISBN 978-1-84996-061-8, London, Great Britain

2

Numerical Modeling and Experimentation on Evaporator Coils for Refrigeration in Dry and Frosting Operational Conditions

Zine Aidoun, Mohamed Ouzzane and Adlane Bendaoud
CanmetENERGY-Varennes Natural Resources Canada
Canada

1. Introduction

The drive to improve energy efficiency in refrigeration and heat pump systems necessarily leads to a continuous reassessment of the current heat transfer surface design and analysis techniques. The process of heat exchange between two fluids at different temperatures, separated by a solid wall occurs in many engineering applications and heat exchangers are the devices used to implement this operation. If improved heat exchanger designs are used as evaporators and condensers in refrigerators and heat pumps, these can considerably benefit from improved cycle efficiency. Air coolers or coils are heat exchangers applied extensively in cold stores, the food industry and air conditioning as evaporators. In these devices, heat transfer enhancement is used to achieve high heat transfer coefficients in small volumes, and extended surfaces or fins, classified as a passive method, are the most frequently encountered. Almost all forced convection air coolers use finned tubes. Coils have in this way become established as the heat transfer workhorse of the refrigeration industry, because of their high area density, their relatively low cost, and the excellent thermo physical properties of copper and aluminum, which are their principal construction materials. Compact coils are needed to facilitate the repackaging of a number of types of air conditioning and refrigeration equipment: a reduced volume effectively enables a new approach to be made to the modular design and a route towards improving performance and size is through appropriate selection of refrigerants, heat transfer enhancement of primary and secondary surfaces through advanced fin design and circuit configurations. Circuiting, although practically used on an empirical basis, has not yet received sufficient attention despite its potential for performance improvement, flow and heat transfer distribution, cost and operational efficiency. In the specific case of refrigeration and air conditioning, a confined phase changing refrigerant exchanges heat in evaporators with the cold room, giving up its heat. The design and operation of refrigeration coils is adapted to these particular conditions. Geometrically they generally consist of copper tubing to which aluminum fins are attached to increase their external surface area over which air is flowing, in order to compensate for this latter poor convection heat transfer. Coils generally achieve relatively high heat transfer area per unit volume by having dense arrays of finned tubes and the fins are generally corrugated or occasionally louvered plates with variable spacing and number of passes. Internal heat transfer of phase changing refrigerant is high and varies with flow regimes occurring along the tube passes. Flow on the secondary surfaces (outside of tubes and fins) in cooling, refrigeration or deep freezing, becomes rapidly complicated by the mass transfer during the commonly occurring processes of condensation and frost deposition, depending on the air prevailing conditions. Overall, geometric and operational considerations make these components very complex to design and analyse theoretically.

2. Previous research highlights

An inherent characteristic of plate fin-and-tube heat exchangers being that air-side heat transfer coefficients are generally much lower than those on the refrigerant side, an effective route towards their performance improvement is through heat transfer enhancement. Substantial gains in terms of size and cost are then made, on heat exchangers and related units, during air dehumidification and frost formation. In the specific case of evaporators and condensers treated here, it is the primary and secondary surfaces arrangements or designs that are of importance i.e. fins and circuit designs. These arrangements are generally known as passive enhancement, implying no external energy input for their activation. Fins improve heat exchange with the airside stream and come in a variety of shapes. In evaporators and condensers, round tubes are most commonly encountered and fins attached on their outer side are either individually assembled, in a variety of geometries or in continuous sheets, flat, corrugated or louvered. For refrigeration, fins significantly alleviate the effect of airside resistance to heat transfer. Heat exchangers of this type are in the class of compact heat exchangers, characterized by area densities as high as 700 m^2/m^3. Heat transfer enhancement based on the use of extended surfaces and circuiting has received particular attention in our studies. By discussing some of the related current research in the context of work performed elsewhere, it is our hope that researchers and engineers active in the field will be able to identify new opportunities, likely to emerge in their own research. Our efforts are successfully articulated around experimentation with CO_2 as refrigerant for low temperature applications and novel modeling treatment of circuit design and frost deposition control.

2.1 Modeling

Modeling of refrigeration heat exchangers for design and performance prediction has been progressing during the last two decades or so in view of the reduced design and development costs it provides, as opposed to physical prototyping. Most models handle steady state, dry, wet or frosting operating conditions. They fall into two main approaches: zone-by-zone and incremental. Zone-by-zone models divide the heat exchanger into subcooled, two-phase and superheated regions which are considered as independent heat exchangers hooked in series. Incremental methods divide the heat exchanger in an arbitrary number of small elements. They can be adapted to perform calculations along the refrigerant flow path and conveniently handle circuiting effects, as well as fluid distributions. Several models of both types are available in the literature for design and simulation, with different degrees of sophistication. Only a representative sample of existing research on heat exchanger coils is reported here and the main features highlighted. (Domanski, 1991) proposed a tube-by-tube computation approach which he applied to study the effect of non-uniform air distribution on the performance of a plate-and-tube heat exchanger. Based on the same approach, (Bensafi et al., 1997) developed a general tool for design and simulation of finned-tube heat exchangers for a limited number of pure and mixed refrigerants in evaporation or condensation. This model can handle circuiting but requires user intervention to fix mass flows in each circuit. Since hydrodynamic and thermal aspects are treated independently, this manual intervention may affect the final thermal results, thus limiting the application to only simple cases. (Corberan et al., 1998) developed a model of plate- finned tube evaporators and condensers, for refrigerant R134a. They then compared the predicting efficiency of a number of available correlations in the literature for heat transfer and friction factor coefficients. This model is limited to computing the refrigerant side conditions. (Liang et al., 1999) developed a distributed simulation model for coils which accounts for the refrigerant pressure drop along the coil and the partially or totally wet fin conditions on the air side. (Byun et al., 2007) conducted their study, based on the tube-by-tube method and EVSIM model due to (Domanski, 1989) in which they updated the correlations in order to suit their conditions. Performance analysis included different refrigerants, fin geometry and inner tube configuration. Other detailed models such as those of (Singh et al., 2008) and (Singh et al., 2009) respectively account for fin heat conduction and arbitrary fin sheet, encompassing variable tube location and size, variable pitches and several other interesting features. (Ouzzane&Aidoun, 2008), simulated the thermal behaviour of the wavy fins and coil heat exchangers, using refrigerant CO_2. The authors used a forward marching technique to solve their conservation equations by discretizing the quality of the refrigerant. The iterative process fixes the outlet refrigerant conditions and computes the inlet conditions which are then compared with the real conditions until convergence is achieved. This method requires manual adjustments during the iterative process and is therefore not well adapted to handle complex circuiting. Moreover, on the air side, mean inlet temperatures are used before each tube, resulting in up to 3.5 % capacity variation, depending on the coil depth. In an effort to address the weaknesses of the above mentioned procedure and extend its computational capabilities (Bendaoud et al., 2011) further developed a new distributed model simultaneously accounting for the thermal and hydrodynamic behaviour and handling complex geometries, dry, humid and frosting conditions. The equations describing these aspects are strongly coupled, and their decoupling is reached by using an original method of resolution. The heat exchanger may be subdivided into several elementary control volumes, allowing for detailed information in X, Y and Z directions. Among the features which are being recognized by the research community as having an important impact on plate fin-and-tube heat exchangers in the refrigeration context, are the following:

2.1.1 Circuiting

In many cases the heat exchanger performance enhancement process focuses on identifying refrigerant circuitry that provides maximum heat transfer rates for given environmental constraints. In fact, refrigerant circuitry may have a significant effect on capacity and operation. However, the numerous possible circuitry arrangements for a finned tube heat exchanger are a contributing factor to the complexity of its modeling and analysis. Designing maximized performance refrigerant circuitry may prove to be even more challenging for new refrigerants with no previous experience or design data available. It is perhaps one reason that only a limited amount of work has been devoted to advance research and development on theses yet important aspects. (Domanski's, 1991) tube-by-tube model was designed to handle simple circuits in counter-current configurations and (Elison et al., 1981), also using the tube-by-tube method built a model for a specified circuitry on fin and tube condensers. The same approach was adopted by (Vardhan et al., 1998) to study simple circuited plate-fin-tube coils for cooling and dehumidification. The effectiveness-NTU method was used but information was provided neither on refrigerant heat transfer and pressure drop conditions, nor on the airside pressure losses. Later (Liang et al., 2000) and (Liang et al., 2001) performed two studies on refrigerant circuitry for finned tube condensers and dry evaporators respectively. The condenser model combined the flexibility of a distributed model to an exergy destruction analysis to evaluate performance. The same modeling approach was applied to cooling evaporators. Six coil configurations with different circuiting were compared. In both condensers and evaporators the authors reported that adequate circuiting could reduce the heat transfer area by approximately 5%. It is to be noted however that only simple circuiting could be conveniently handled and no account was taken of the airside pressure drop. In common to the reported approaches, the hydrodynamics of the problem was not detailed. Circuiting arrangements with several refrigerant inlets and junctions were not fully taken care of, so that the user must fix a mass flux of the refrigerant in each inlet and in the process, the thermal-hydrodynamic coupling is lost, affecting the results. (Liu et al., 2004) developed a steady state model based on the pass-by-pass approach, accounting for heat conduction between adjacent tubes and circuitry by means of a matrix that fixes the configuration. (Jiang et al., 2006) proposed CoilDesigner, in the form of easy-to-use software. It handles circuitry in a similar manner to Liu's model but uses a segment by segment computational approach in order to capture potential parameter variations occurring locally. Mean values of heat transfer coefficients on both air and refrigerant sides are then calculated. This approximation generally leads to important differences between numerical and experimental results. CoilDesigner does not provide air-side pressure losses which may be important in large refrigeration installations. Another interesting indexing technique for complex circuitry was proposed by (Kuo et al., 2006). It is based on a connectivity matrix similar to those used in (Liu et al., 2004) and (Jiang et al., 2006) but introduces additional indices to indicate the number of main flows, first and second level circuitry. The related model is of distributed type for cooling with dry and wet conditions. The details of the modeling procedure for the coupled thermal hydraulic system represented by the air and refrigerant sides are not provided.

2.1.2 Frosting

Frost forms on evaporator coil surfaces on which it grows when operating temperatures are below 0 °C and the air dew point temperature is above the coil surface temperature. It affects considerably the performance by reducing the refrigeration capacity and the system efficiency. This performance degradation occurs because frost is a porous medium composed of air and ice with poor thermal conductivity. The frost layer increases the air-refrigerant thermal resistance. Moreover, frost accumulation eventually narrows the flow channels formed by tubes and adjoining fins, imposing an increasingly higher resistance to air flow. This effect is marked at the leading edge, causing a rapid decline in heat transfer and early blockage of the channels at this location. Consequently, the rows of finned tubes located at the rear of multi-row coils may become severely underused. It is the authors' belief that circuiting can play a role to alleviate this effect by more uniformly distributing capacity and temperature among rows. Available theoretical literature on coil frosting is limited due to complex equipment geometries. Selected work is reported herein:

(Kondepudi et al., 1993a) developed an analytical model for finned-tube heat exchangers under frosting conditions by assuming a uniform distribution of frost to develop over the entire external surface. They used the ideal gas theory to calculate the mass of water diffused in the frost layer on a single circuit through which was circulated a 50% ethylene-glycol/water mixture as the refrigerating fluid. (Seker et al., 2004a, 2004b) carried out numerical and experimental investigations on frost formation. The authors used a custom-made heat exchanger on the geometry of which little information is available. The experiments were performed with a large temperature difference (17°C) between air and refrigerant. The authors used a correlation for airside heat transfer, based on their own heat exchanger data which cannot be extrapolated to other coil conditions. (Yang et al., 2006a, 2006b) optimized fin spacing of a frost fin-and-tube evaporator to increase coil performance and operational time between defrost cycles.

In common to most of the theoretical and modeling work reported herein, validations generally relied on the data available in the open literature or on private collaborative exchanges. A limited number however did have their proper validation set-ups, ((Liang et al., 1999), (Bendaoud et al., 2011), (Liang et al., 2000), (Liang et al., 2001), (Seker et al., 2004a, 2004b)).

2.2 Experiments

Relatively, experimental work on finned tube heat exchangers has been more prolific because the complexity of air flow patterns across finned tubes is quite problematic for theoretical treatments. (Rich, 1973) and (Rich, 1975) conducted a systematic study on air side heat transfer and pressure drop on several coils with variable fin spacing and tube rows. (Wang et al., 1996) and (Wang et al., 1997) investigated the effect of fin spacing, fin thickness, number of tube rows on heat transfer and pressure drop with commonly used tube diameters in HVAC coils, under dry and humid conditions respectively. (Chuah et al., 1998) investigated dehumidifying performance of plain fin-and-tube coils. They measured the effects of air and water velocities which they compared to predictions based on existing methods. Regarding frost formation on coils, (Stoecker, 1957) and (Stoecker, 1960) was among the pioneers who recommended using wide fin spacing and over sizing the coils operating under these conditions in order to limit the defrosting frequency. (Ogawa et al., 1993) showed that combining front staging and side staging respectively reduced air flow blockage and promoted more heat transfer at the rear, globally reducing pressure losses and improving performance. (Guo et al., 2008) conducted their study on the relation between frost growth and the dynamic performance of a heat pump system. They distinguished three stages in frost build up, which they related to the capacity and COP of the heat pump. They found that performance declined rapidly in the third stage during which a fluffy frost layer was formed, particularly when the outdoor temperature was near 0°C. Last but not least is the work reported by (Aljuwayhel et al., 2008) about frost build up on a real size evaporator in an industrial refrigeration ammonia system operating below -34 °C. In-situ measurements of temperatures, flow rates and humidity were gathered to assess capacity degradation as a result of frost. Capacity losses as high as 26%, were recorded after 42 hours of operation. A detailed review of plate fin-and-tube refrigeration heat exchangers is beyond the scope of this paper, because some new material on circuit and frost modeling, as well as analysis results will be introduced. For a detailed review of operational details and data under different conditions, the reader is referred to (Seker et al., 2004a, 2004b), (Wang et al., 1996) and (Wang et al., 1997).

3. Research at CanmetENERGY

3.1 Theoretical approach

Two essential and most uncertain coil design parameters are the heat transfer coefficients and the pressure losses on both air and refrigerant sides. Their theoretical assessment requires rather involved mathematics due to the coupling of heat, mass and momentum transfer as well as geometry, thermo physical and material aspects. As a result of this complexity, the various geometric configurations, the different fin types and arrangements, the design has been generally empirical, relying on experimental data, graphical information and or correlations. (Kays&London, 1984) expressed this information in terms of the Colburn j and f friction factors, which now form the basis for all the subsequent empirical and semi-empirical work currently available. As a consequence, heat exchanger analysis treats traditionally the design and the rating as two separate problems. However, due to the new developments in modeling and simulation techniques, supported by the modern computational power, it is possible to effectively tackle the two aspects simultaneously, to yield both a satisfactory design and knowledge of its sensitivity to geometric and specification changes. Working along the lines of lifting to as large extent as possible the limitations imposed by empirical techniques, an extensive research and development program was set at the laboratories of Natural Resources Canada with the objectives of developing detailed models for coil design and simulation in the context of dry or frosting conditions. Complementary to the theoretical work, a fully instrumented test bench was built to generate data in a large interval of operating conditions. However, a comprehensive experimental study of coil performance under various conditions remains expensive because of the high costs related the large number of possible test configurations and operator time. Numerical modeling, on the other hand has the potential of offering flexible and cost-effective means for the investigation. A typical refrigeration coil sample is represented in (Fig. 1). Refrigeration coils are generally arranged in the form of several circuits. This study focused on CO_2 coils employed in low temperature secondary loops. Air flows on the outside, across the finned coil and carbon dioxide flows inside the tube. Aluminum fins of wavy, rectangular shape are assembled on the copper tubes.

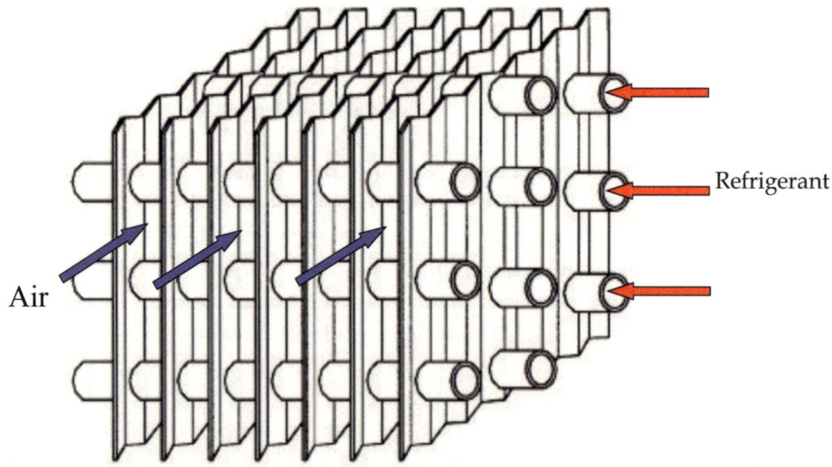

Fig. 1. Schematic of a typical refrigeration evaporator coil

Model development to design coils with different geometric configurations and simulate their thermal hydraulic behaviour revolved around similar geometries. They were performed in two steps: the first development by (Ouzzane &Aidoun, 2008) handled dry cases and the second one by (Bendaoud et al., 2011) was for coils with frost formation. The approach consisted in dividing the heat exchanger into incremental elements over which fundamental conservation equations of mass, momentum and energy were applied (Fig.2).

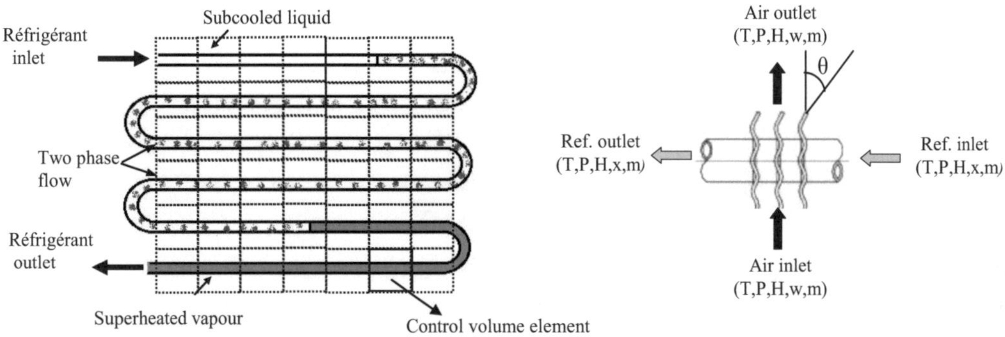

a) Evaporation process and mesh grid b) Control volume element

Fig. 2. Evaporator coil and discretization

3.1.1 Main assumptions

- One dimensional flow of refrigerant inside the tube coil.
- Gravity forces for both air and refrigerant neglected.
- Negligible heat losses to the surroundings.
- Uniform air velocity across each tube row.
- System in steady and quasi-steady state conditions for dry and frosting conditions respectively.
- Uniform frost distribution on the entire control volume and the frost layer, characterised by average properties.

3.1.2 Conservation equations and correlations

Conservation equations of mass, momentum and energy are successively applied to a control volume element (Fig. 2). The resulting relations are summarized as:

Equation of mass

$$\left(\sum \dot{m}_r\right)_{ou} = \left(\sum \dot{m}_r\right)_{in} \text{ and } \left(\dot{m}_a\right)_{ou} = \left(\dot{m}_a\right)_{in} \tag{1}$$

Equation of momentum

Pressure losses are calculated in tubes and return bends as follows:
For tubes:

$$\left(P_r\right)_{ou} = (P_r)_{in} - (\Delta P_r)_1 \tag{2a}$$

For return bends:

$$\left(P_r\right)_{ou} = \left(P_r\right)_{in} - \left(\Delta P_r\right)_b \tag{2b}$$

For single phase, subcooled liquid and superheated vapour, the Darcy-Weisbach equation is used to calculate the linear pressure drop as:

$$\left(\Delta P_r\right)_l = f.\Delta L.\frac{8.(\dot{m}_r)^2}{\rho_r.\pi^2.D_{in}^5} \tag{3}$$

The friction factor f is calculated by using the correlation given by (Drew et al., 1932) Pressure losses in bends are calculated by:

$$\left(\Delta P_r\right)_b = f_b.\frac{8.(\dot{m}_r)^2}{\rho_r.\pi^2.D_{in}^4} \tag{4}$$

Where, the friction coefficient f_b is given by (Kays &London, 1984).
For two phase flow the linear pressure drop is calculated by the equation:

$$\left(\Delta P_r\right)_l = \left[\frac{f}{2.D_{in}}\Delta L.v_{tp(ou)} + \left(v_{tp(ou)} - v_{tp(in)}\right)\right]G^2 \tag{5}$$

With G being the mass flow rate per unit area, and f being the friction factor coefficient determined on the basis of the homogeneous model reported by (Rohsenow et al., 1998). Two-phase pressure drop in bends is based on the correlations due to (Geary, 1975).

$$\left(\Delta P_r\right)_b = \left(f_b\right)_{tp}.\frac{L_b.x^2.G^2}{2.\left(\rho_r\right)_g.D_{in}} \tag{6}$$

L_b is the length of the bend, and $(f_b)_{tp}$ is the friction factor for a return bend calculated by:

$$\left(f_b\right)_{tp} = \frac{80352.10^{-8}.Re_g^{0.5}}{\exp(0.215.C_d / D_{in}).x^{1.25}} \tag{7}$$

Where C_d is the bend's centre-to-centre distance and Re_g is the Reynolds number based on the refrigerant vapour phase.

Equation of energy

The equations resulting from the energy balance are summarized as:

$$\dot{Q} = \dot{m}_r.\left[\left(H_r\right)_{ou} - \left(H_r\right)_{in}\right] \tag{8a}$$

$$\dot{Q} = \dot{m}_a.\left[\left(H_a\right)_{in} - \left(H_a\right)_{ou}\right] \tag{8b}$$

and

$$\dot{Q} = h_r.A_{in}(\overline{T_w} - \overline{T_r}) \tag{9a}$$

$$\dot{Q} = h_a.A_{ou}\left(\overline{T_a} - \overline{T_w}\right) \tag{9b}$$

$\dot{Q}$ is the heat transfer rate, h_r and h_a the heat transfer coefficients for the refrigerant and air, respectively.

Heat transfer coefficient for CO_2

For single phase, the heat transfer coefficient h_r is calculated using the correlation proposed by Petukhov and Kirillov reported by (Kakaç et al., 1998). For two phase flow, the correlations developed by Bennet-Chen and modified by (Hwang et al., 1997) were used to calculate h_r. This is based on the superposition principle, which consists of assuming that h_r is the sum of nucleate boiling coefficient h_{nb} and convection heat transfer coefficient h_{bc} as:

$$h_r = h_{nb} + h_{bc} \tag{10}$$

Where h_{nb} and h_{bc} are given respectively by:

$$h_{nb} = \Omega.\left(T_w - T_{sat}(P_l)\right)^{0.4}.\left(P_{sat}(T_w) - P_l\right)^{0.75}.S \tag{11}$$

And

$$h_{bc} = h_l.Pr^{0.6}.F.(1-x)^{0.8} \tag{12}$$

h_l is the convective heat transfer coefficient for the liquid phase, calculated by Dittus-Boelter correlation (Incropera et al., 2002). The expressions of Ω, S and Fin equations (11) and (12) can be found in (Hwang et al., 1997).

Air side heat transfer coefficient

For air flowing over wavy plate-finned tubes, the (Wang et al., 2002) correlations for heat transfer and pressure drop are used. Heat transfer is expressed by the Colburn coefficient as:

$$J = 0.0646.Re_{Dc}^{J_1}.\left(\frac{D_c}{D_h}\right)^{J_2}.\left(\frac{F_s}{S_t}\right)^{-1.03}\left(\frac{S_1}{D_c}\right)^{0.432}.J_3 \tag{13a}$$

And

$$J = \frac{h_a.D_c}{k_a.Re_{Dc}.Pr_a^{1/3}} \tag{13b}$$

D_c and D_h are the fin collar outside and the hydraulic diameters respectively.
The pressure drop across the coil can be computed by the expression proposed by (Kays &London, 1984)

$$\Delta P_a = \frac{G_{max}^2}{2\rho_{a,in}}\left[f_a\left(\frac{A_c}{A_{min}}.\frac{\rho_{a,in}}{\rho_m}\right) + \left(\left(1+\beta^2\right)\left(\frac{\rho_{a,in}}{\rho_{a,ou}} - 1\right)\right)\right] \tag{14}$$

ρ_m is calculated at the mean temperature between air inlet and outlet.
A_c : total air side heat transfer area.

A_{min}: minimum free flow area through which air passes across the coil.
β: ratio of free-flow to frontal area.
The air friction factor f_a is calculated by the correlation proposed by (Wang et al., 2002)

$$f_a = 0.228 Re_{Dc}^{f1}.(\tan\theta)^{f2}\left(\frac{F_s}{S_1}\right)^{f3}\left(\frac{S_1}{D_c}\right)^{f4}.f_5 \quad (14a)$$

Air properties are calculated using the standard psychometric relations (ASHRAE, 1993). Expressions for J_1, J_2, f_1, f_2, f_3, f_4 and f_5 are given in (Wang et al., 2002).
The rate of frost formation is expressed as a loss of humidity as water vapour condenses on the cold coil surface.

$$m_f = m_{da}.(\omega_{in} - \omega_{ou}).\Delta t \quad (15)$$

The mass of the dry air is expressed as:

$$m_{da} = \frac{\dot{m}_t.\Delta t}{1+\omega_{in}} \quad (16)$$

Frost properties

The frost distribution on the entire control volume is assumed to be uniform, and the frost layer is characterised by average properties. When the saturated air passes over the coil surface at a temperature below the dew point, the first frost layer appears. The initial conditions for frost height and density are important as the results are sensitive to their selection (Shokouhmand et al., 2009). (Jones & Parker, 1975) tested the initial conditions by changing the values of the initial frost thickness and density, they found that the prediction results of the frost growth rate would not be affected significantly if the initial frost thickness approaches a low value (~ 2 x 10^{-2} mm). They also found that as long as the initial value of the frost density is significantly smaller than the frost density during growth, it will not affect the solution for the frost growth rate of densification, the recommended value being (~ 30 kg.m^{-3}). Hence, in this work, the initial conditions for the frost temperature, thickness and density are fixed as:

$$T_f^0 = T_w \quad , \quad \delta_f^0 = 2.10^{-5}\,m \quad , \quad \rho_f^0 = 30\ kg/m^3$$

The water vapour transferred, from moist air to the frost surface, increases both the frost density and thickness. This phenomenon can be expressed as:

$$m_f = m_\delta + m_\rho \quad (17)$$

The mass flux from the frost density absorbed into the frost layer is given by (Lee et al., 1997):

$$m_\rho = \int_{\delta_f=0}^{\delta_f=Y_f} \alpha_f \rho_w.\Delta t.d\delta_f \quad (18)$$

Were α_f represents an absorption coefficient calculated by:

$$\alpha_f = D_v.\left[\frac{\cosh^{-1}}{\delta_f}\left\{\frac{\rho_{w,sat}(T_{f,s})}{\rho_{w,sat}(T_w)}\right\}\right]^2 \quad (19)$$

The thermal conductivity, valid for $30 \le \rho_f \le 400 \quad kg.m^{-3}$, is given by:

$$k_f = 0.132 + 3.13.10^{-4}.\rho_f + 1.6.10^{-7}.\rho_f^2 \quad (20)$$

The diffusion coefficient D_v is valid for $-50 \le \overline{T}_a \le +20\,^\circ C$ and is given by:

$$D_v = \left(a + b\overline{T}_a + c\overline{T}_a^2 + d\overline{T}_a^3\right).10^{-5} \quad (21)$$

With:

$$a = 2.219928,\ b = 0.0137779,\ c = -0.0000065,\ d = -5.32937434.10^{-7}$$

The frost density and thickness for each time interval are calculated as follows, (Kondepudi et al., 1993a):

$$\Delta\rho_f = \frac{\dot{m}_\rho \Delta t}{A_{c,d}\delta_f} \quad (22)$$

$$\Delta\delta_f = \frac{\dot{m}_\delta \Delta t}{A_{c,d}\rho_f} \quad (23)$$

$A_{c,d}$: convective heat transfer area in dry condition.

3.1.3 Solution procedure

Two different solution procedures were developed in the modeling process: Forward Marching Technique (FMT) (Ouzzane & Aidoun, 2004) and Iterative Solution for Whole System (ISWS) (Bendaoud et al., 2010). The Forward Marching Technique allowed local tracking of relevant operational parameters. Differential lengths of tubing were used where single phase flow prevailed and differential variations of quality were employed in zones of two-phase flow. Taking advantage of the relative flexibility offered by this technique, it was upgraded by (Aidoun & Ouzzane, 2009) to handle simple circuitry. In this case the method calls for iterations where a guess on the refrigerant conditions at exit is made and the inlet conditions are calculated. These are compared to the fixed inlet conditions. Iterations are repeated until convergence between fixed and computed inlet conditions are met. The ISWS procedure is intended to cover a large range of operating conditions and handle complex circuiting configurations. In order to achieve this objective, the solution procedure is based on the adoption of an original strategy for the convention of numbering and localizing the tubes, identifying refrigerant entries, exits, tube connections, as well as control volume variables. Rows are counted according to the air flow direction.

J(I,K) is a matrix indicating the presence or absence of a junction between two tubes; the coordinates I and K indicate the direction of flow: incoming and destination, respectively. The values of J(I,K) are:

$$J(I,K) = \begin{cases} 0 & \text{no connection between I and K tubes} \\ 1 & \text{connection between I and K tubes} \end{cases}$$

Index 1 for I or K is allowed only for the exit or entry to the system. (Fig. 3) shows an example of a heat exchanger with 9 tubes arranged in three rows and three lines with one entrance in tube 5 and two exits in tubes 2 and 10. J(1,5) means that the refrigerant enters in tube 5. J(2,1) and J(10,1)) indicate exits from tubes 2 and 10 respectively. J(4,3) is the junction between tubes 4 and 3 and the flow is from tube 4 through to tube 3.

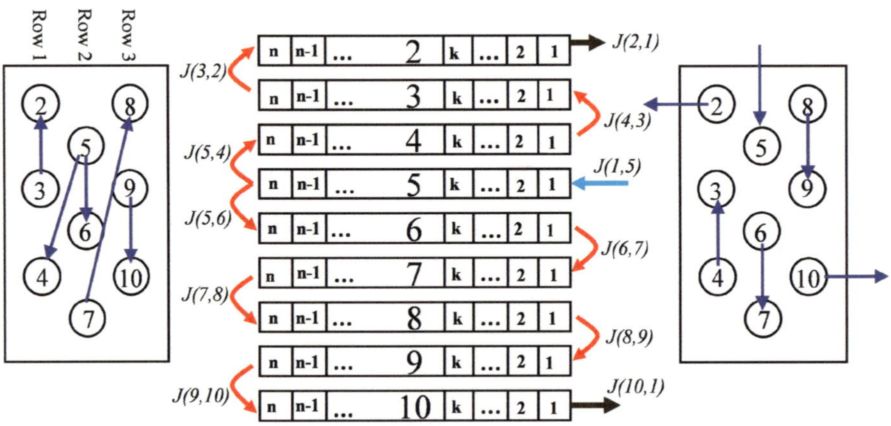

Fig. 3. An example of circuiting configuration with volume control elements and conventions

Each tube I is divided into n control volume elements, starting either from the left or from the right, depending on the refrigerant flow direction entrance. For this purpose, a parameter DIR(I) having a value of 1 or -1 is allocated to each tube. In (Fig. 3), the direction of the upper entrance tube is chosen as a positive reference (DIR(I)=1). In this way, DIR(5)=DIR(3)=DIR(7)=DIR(9)= +1 and DIR(2)=DIR(4)=DIR(6)=DIR(8)=DIR(10)= -1. As for FMT, the resolution still relies on an iterative method but it is applied on matrix system.The main steps of theses two computing procedures are indicated in the flow charts of (Fig. 4) and (Fig.5). Geometric and operation data are first introduced, then the thermodynamic state of the refrigerant is defined (at the outlet for FMT and at the inlet for ISWS), using subroutine REFPROP (NIST, 1998). Three cases are possible:

- Two-phase: calculations are made according to the steps on the right branch of the flowchart.
- Superheat for FMT or subcooling for ISWS: the case is treated according to the steps on the left branch.
- Subcooling for FMT or superheat for: no calculations are performed since there is no evaporation.

If operating under frost condition with ISWS (Fig. 5) and when hydrodynamic and thermal convergence is obtained, the subroutine HUMI is called to compute the air relative humidity at inlet and outlet of each volume element. Data are stored in matrices $[\Phi_{in}]$ and $[\Phi_{ou}]$ respectively. The program then checks, for each volume element if the conditions of frost formation are verified, i.e. saturated air and T_s below the freezing point. For the elements under the dew point temperature, the subroutine computes the mass of the frost formed, distributed into diffused (m_ρ) and solidified (m_δ) mass parts. Next, the program calls the subroutine UPCOILGEO to update the geometric configuration of the heat exchanger (outer tube diameter, fin thickness, convective heat transfer area, free flow area) and stores the information in respective matrices. By considering the most recent geometry resulting from frost deposition over a time step, the hydrodynamic, thermal and psychometric calculations are repeated for each time step Δt until the total working period of the heat exchanger is covered.

3.2 Experimental validation

In the first instance, results from the FMT and ISWS procedures were compared as part of the model validation process. For dry and frosting conditions further comparison was respectively performed with the available information from the literature (Kondepudi et al., 1993b) and with data from the CanmetENERGY's experimental stand (Ouzzane & Aidoun, 2008). This installation, shown in (Fig.6), complies with ASHRAE standards for forced air cooling and heating coils (ASHRAE, 2000). Evaporating carbon dioxide is the working fluid in the loop of interest (L1), which includes a CO_2 pump, a mass flow meter, a CO_2-air coil with aluminum wavy fins and copper tubes, a brazed plate condenser and a reservoir for CO_2 condensate. The loop is well instrumented for the purpose of heat and mass transfer balances and fluid flow. For a flexible control of temperature and capacity, a brine loop (L2) was used to cool down the CO_2 condenser. The temperature control of this loop is achieved by a mechanical refrigeration system (L3). Loop (L1) is located in a closed room with two compartments corresponding to inlet and outlet of the coil: air flows from one compartment to the other through a duct enclosing the coil. Air circulation is maintained by a blower. The compartments are well insulated in order to reduce infiltration of outside air and moisture.

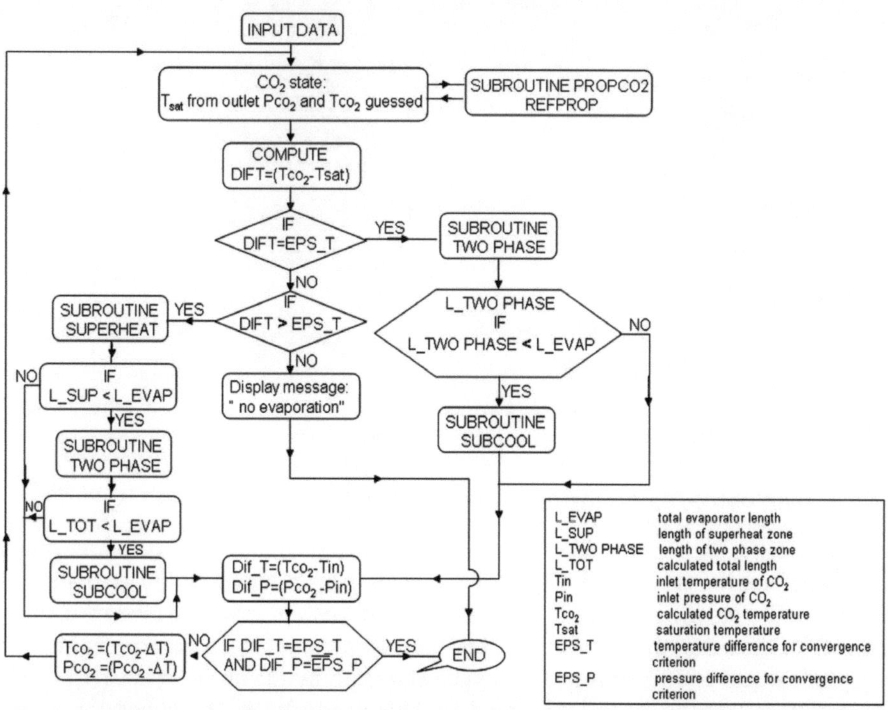

Fig. 4. Flow chart of the computing procedure for FMT

Means of adjusting air temperature and humidity conditions at the duct inlet are provided by a brine cooler, electric heating and a steam generator. Both compartments are equipped with temperature, pressure, flow and dew point sensors set in accordance with ASHRAE standards (ASHRAE, 1987). The coil is 0.22 m deep with a face area of 0.61m x 0.32 m. The configuration employed is similar to that represented on Figure1 and has eight rows of ten tubes, 8.7 mm internal diameter, 4 fins per inch, arranged in one circuit.

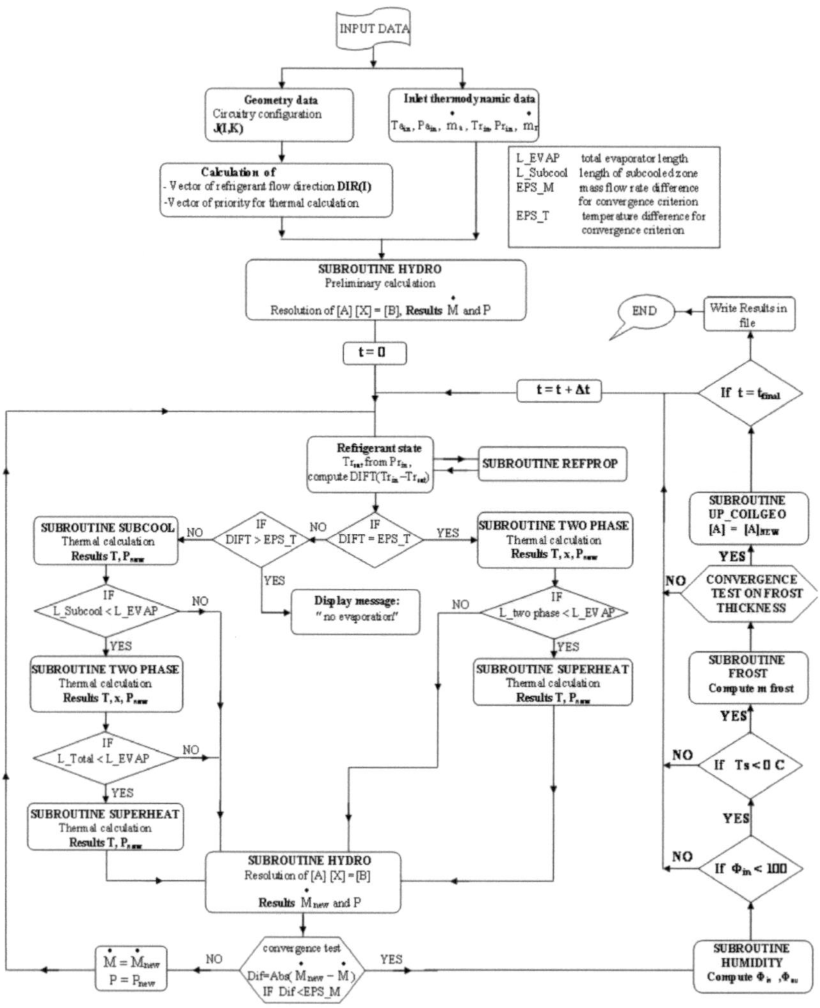

Fig. 5. Flow chart of the computing procedure for ISWS

At temperatures of -10 °C and -15 °C as used here, air absorbs only a very low quantity of vapour. Therefore, it is very difficult to vary and to control air humidity at the evaporator coil entrance. The steam injected in the test chamber instantaneously freezes on the walls and injector orifice. For this reason the injection system is designed to ensure sufficient steam superheat and residence time for it to be absorbed by the ambient air. (Fig. 7) shows a schematic of the steam injection. Saturated vapour produced in the generator flows in an insulated pipe to an electrical superheater. The desired level of superheat and the required steam quantities result from a combined adjustment of the heaters and the solenoid valves for the steam injection and water drainage. Operation of the heaters is controlled to ensure the required temperature for the injected steam. Presented below are some comparison examples and validations performed. For dry surfaces, four different experimental cases are selected, with their operating conditions summarized in Table 1.

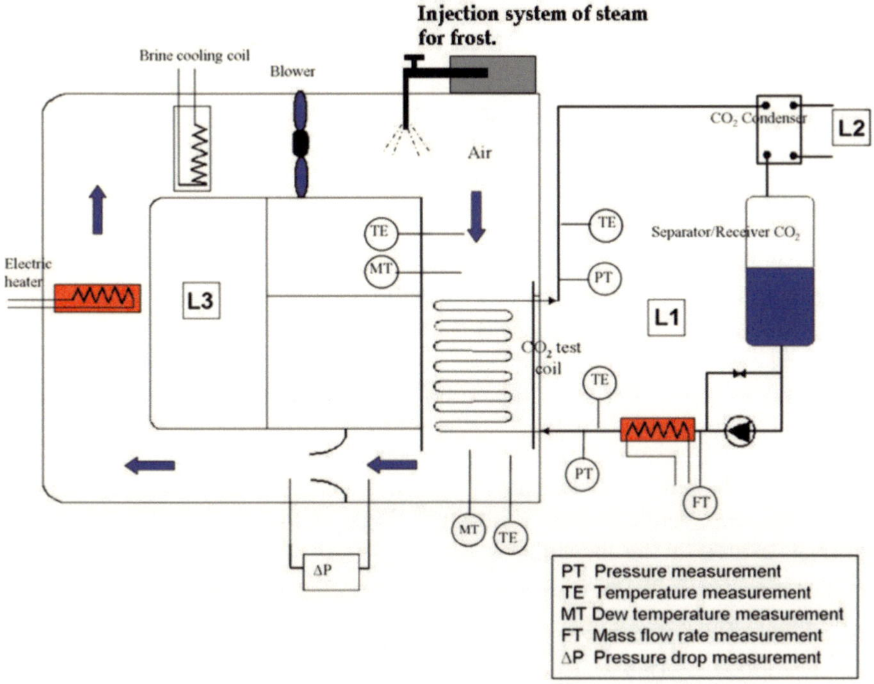

Fig. 6. Schematic diagram of CanmetENERGY test set-up

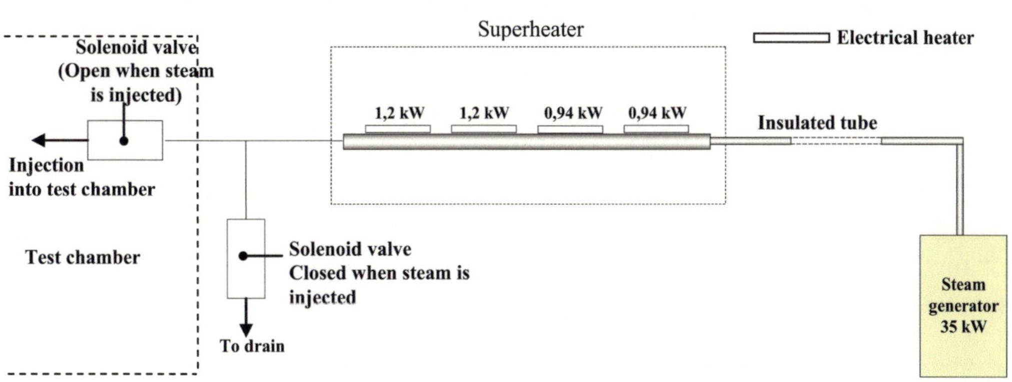

Fig. 7. Schematic of injection system of steam

In all these cases, the refrigerant is entering the coil in a saturated state with an assumed quality of 0 %. The results in Table 2 show that the coil capacity predicted by the ISWS procedure is in good agreement with the experimental data, the maximum discrepancy being less than 6.5 %. Comparison with FMT procedure of (Ouzzane & Aidoun, 2008) shows differences of less than 14 %.

	Mass flow rate (kG/s)		Inlet temperature (°C)		Inlet pressure (kPa)	
	Air	CO_2	Air	CO_2	Air	CO_2
CASE 1	0.5865	0.02700	-15.5	-26.07	101.325	1624.7
CASE 2	0.6070	0.01864	-15.6	-26.93	101.325	1580.5
CASE 3	0.5865	0.01619	-16.0	-27.29	101.325	1560.3
CASE 4	0.6090	0.01472	-20.3	-24.03	101.325	1732.8

Table 1. Input conditions for validation

The results show also that the refrigerant pressure drop predicted by ISWS procedure is in good agreement with the experimental data. The cumulative errors resulting from the iterative process applied with correlations for pressure drop whose overall uncertainty is ± 50% (Rohsenow et al., 1998) and for the heat transfer coefficient whose uncertainty on the predictions is ± 40 % (Hwang et al., 1997) are well within the acceptable range. In the analysis performed by (Ouzzane & Aidoun, 2008), the pressure drop for the saturated refrigerant flow is strongly affected by the quality of the refrigerant. Since the iterative process in the present approach is based on tube length increments, and because quality results from computations, it is possible that surges in quality occur towards the end of the evaporation process and result in correspondingly high departures of the pressure drop outside the range covered by the correlations used.

		Capacity (W)		Outlet quality	ΔP (kPa)	Outlet temperature (°C)		Outlet relative humidity (%)
		Air	CO_2	CO_2	CO_2	Air	CO_2	Air
CASE 1	ISWS	4091.0	4112.9	52.8 %	170.2	-22.4	-29.4	-
	FMT	4438.3	4530.6	58.0 %	195.2	-23.0	-29.9	-
	Experiments	4083.3	-	51.4 %	171.6	-22.4	-29.6	66.0
CASE 2	ISWS	4444.6	4435.2	80.7 %	152.5	-22.9	-30.0	-
	FMT	4811.5	4914.1	89.0 %	149.6	-23.5	-29.9	-
	Experiments	4471.0	-	75.0 %	132.2	-22.9	-29.6	65.6
CASE 3	ISWS	1402.4	1379.1	32.5 %	29.3	-22.6	-24.5	-
	FMT	1557.2	1550.0	36.5 %	38.6	-22.8	-24.8	-
	Experiments	1495.9	-	35.5 %	44.4	-22.7	-24.9	76.0
CASE 4	ISWS	5588.8	5590.6	45.3%	195.0	-19.4	-26.6	-
	FMT	5869.4	5683.8	47.5%	398.9	-19.8	-30.8	-
	Experiments	5458.0	-	43.5 %	303.4	-19.1	-28.8	54.7

Table 2. Comparison of numerical results from two resolution procedures and experiments

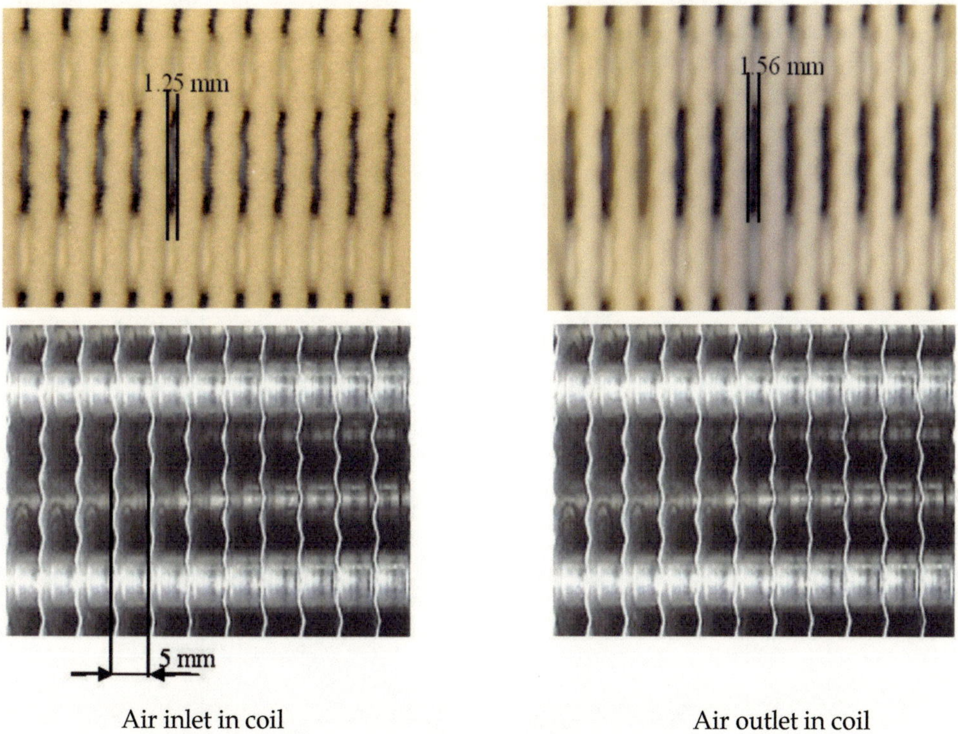

Fig. 8. Pictures showing the frost formed on tubes and fins

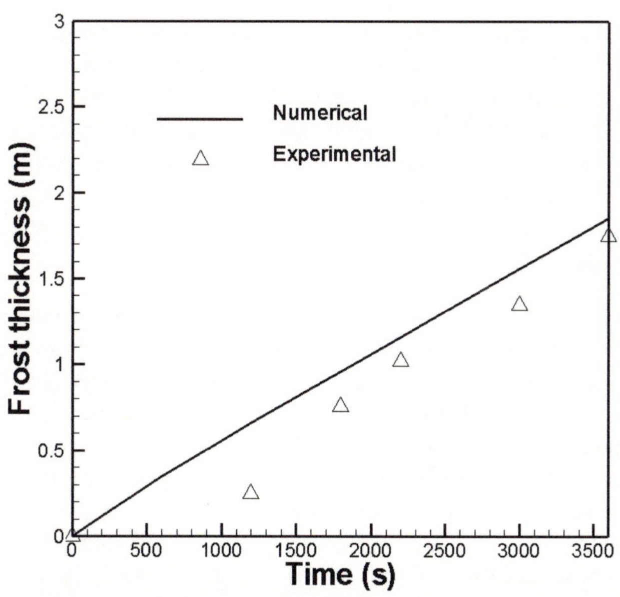

Fig. 9. Variation of the frost thickness with time

Under frosting conditions, several tests were performed on the test bench at CanmetENERGY, some of which were selected to validate the theoretical model. From the pictures taken by digital cameras located at the inlet and outlet of the coil (Fig. 8), the frost thickness is estimated. The coil with no frost is used as a reference for the scale and the frost thickness variation with time is shown in (Fig. 8).

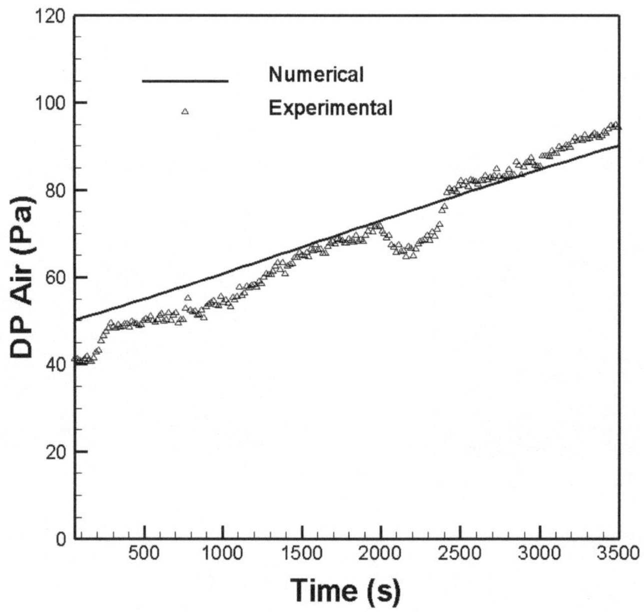

Fig. 10. Variation of the air pressure drop with time

Variations of the frost thickness and air pressure drop with time are presented in Fig. 9 and Fig. 10. As frost accumulates air flow passage cross-sections reduce, thereby increasing the pressure drop. Agreement between experimental and numerical calculations is quite satisfactory. The first measurable frost layer thickness is only observed after 20 minutes from the start. This is due to difficulties in accurately estimating slowly developing frost layer thicknesses.

4. Simulation results

The developed theoretical tool using FMT and ISWS procedures was used to perform several studies. An interesting feature is that all relevant operation parameters can be determined locally along the coil and mapped. In the example represented in (Fig. 11), typical results are shown for the air temperature from inlet to outlet, row after row. The general tendency towards temperature decrease with the row number can be expected but the distribution along tube lines is less obvious and will depend on the configuration and the operating conditions. In the first and the last rows (A-A and D-D sections), we can clearly see zones where single phase refrigerant prevails. Subcooled liquid and superheated vapour, are represented in blue and red respectively. The same kind of results can be presented for relative humidity (Ouzzane & Aidoun, 2004), in which case the locations where frost formation may first develop are indicated.

4.1 Effect of recirculation

Experience from large ammonia refrigeration installations reveals that circulation makes better use of the evaporators' surfaces, with enhanced heat transfer and improved overall system performance. This technique is now being proposed in more modest sizes as well, by inserting an accumulator in the system. In these systems a separator supplies liquid refrigerant to the evaporator while saturated vapour is fed to the compressor. At the evaporator exit saturated refrigerant in the state of liquid-vapour mixture is sent back to the separator (x<1). The overall impact is a performance improvement through a refrigerant flow rate increase (with a corresponding internal heat exchange improvement) and a reduction or elimination of superheat at the compressor suction.

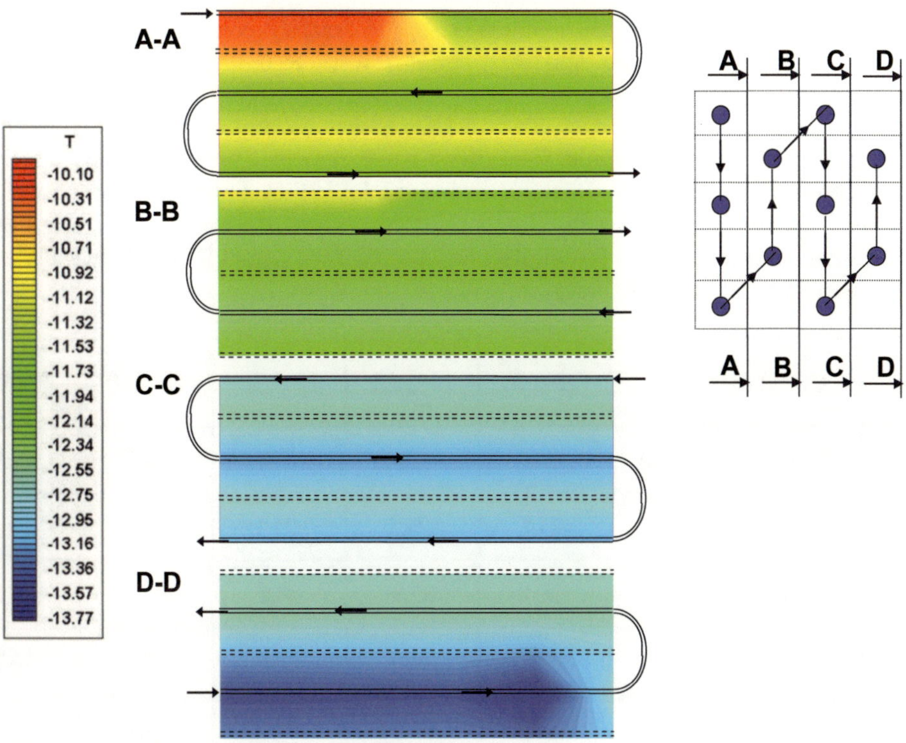

Fig. 11. Typical temperature field inside the coil

However this improvement comes with saturation pressure and related temperature variations, resulting in property values reductions. These opposing effects are expected to lead to an optimum circulation ratio with traditional refrigerants and ammonia. Using an actual installation to obtain data however, imposes limitations on their range and on the extent of the corresponding parametric analysis that will be derived. In (Ouzzane & Aidoun, 2007), circulation of CO_2 was studied as part of secondary loops with phase change, as found in supermarkets. The purpose was to investigate the impact of the circulation practice on heat transfer and heat exchangers performance, through modeling and test bench data for CO_2. In the first instance this will be limited to the evaporator. The circulation ratio, N was varied in the range 1 to 4 and corresponding heat transfer coefficients, internal pressure drop and saturation temperature variations were obtained. Despite a substantial improvement in heat transfer due to circulation (in the order of 180% for N=4), the coil capacity remained almost unchanged while pressure drop considerably increased and the corresponding saturation temperature dropped from 1.7 °C for N=1 to 6.4 °C for N=4. In the following analysis and discussion, two sets of results will be considered. The first set comes from experiments performed on a test bench with coil characteristics specified in the previous section. The second set of results comes from simulations. Since the purpose of this investigation is to study the evaporator coil under the conditions of circulation, operating conditions are adjusted so that only two-phase flow exists ($0 < x < 1$). The range of circulation ratios covered experimentally was from 1 to 5.5 approximately. The coil geometric specifications are those reported in the above section and operating conditions as well as resulting performance parameters are recapitulated in Table 3. On the airside temperature and flow rate were maintained approximately constant. On the CO_2 side saturation conditions (pressure and temperature) were also maintained approximately constant while the flow rate was progressively increased. Assuming negligible heat losses to the surrounding, a heat balance on air and CO_2 allows estimating coil capacity and exit quality, while pressure drop results from direct measurement. The coil capacity appears to be quasi-constant despite some fluctuations around 1.5 kW at these conditions. Bearing in mind that the amplitude of these fluctuations is within the uncertainty range of the measurements and because of the limited number of data points it is not possible at this stage to identify a variation tendency.

	Circulation ratio	N=1.0	N=1.23	N=1.50	N=2.90	N=5.42
CO_2	Mass flow rate (g/s)	5.1	6.23	7.6	14.7	27.5
	Tin (C)	-24.1	-24.3	-24.1	-24.1	-24.1
	x (%) (exit)	100.0	82.8	68.8	36.2	19.7
	ΔP (kPa)	10.0	19.5	27.8	45.3	78.1
Air	$Tair_{in}$ (C)	-20.0	-19.95	-20.0	-20.2	-20.3
	Mass flow rate (g/s)	605.1	589	605.7	606.4	603.1
	Capacity (kW)	1.48	1.501	1.521	1.534	1.514

Table 3. Results from measurement for different circulation ratios

The pressure drop on the other hand increases very rapidly with circulation ratio. Further investigation of this effect was performed by simulation of a typical refrigeration case for supermarket conditions. The coil operating conditions and the corresponding results are summarized in Table 4 for circulation ratios ranging from 1 to 4.

Circulation affects positively the refrigerant side heat transfer coefficient, as is shown by (Fig. 12). This is due to the combination of good thermo physical properties of CO_2 and increasing flow rates. The increase is at least 85% when going from N=1 to N=4. However, the maximum local increase of the overall heat transfer coefficient is no more than 10% (Ouzzane & Aidoun, 2007).

Geometry and conditions		Circulation ratio	1	2	3	4
Inner diameter = 8.7mm Ext. diameter = 9.5mm Fins (27.8×31.8×0.19) 118 fins/m, L = 90 m T_{co2}=-30C, $Tair_{in}$=-24C $\dot{m}_{air} = 1.105$ (kG / s)	CO_2	$\dot{m}_{CO2}$(g / s)	11.6	23.2	34.8	46.4
		x (%) (exit)	99.66	55.48	37.99	29.89
		ΔP (kPa)	82.66	164.02	220.74	288.26
		Q (kW)	3.551	3.774	3.749	3.672
		ΔT_{CO2}	1.744	3.533	4.81	6.3944

Table 4. Calculation results for different circulation ratios

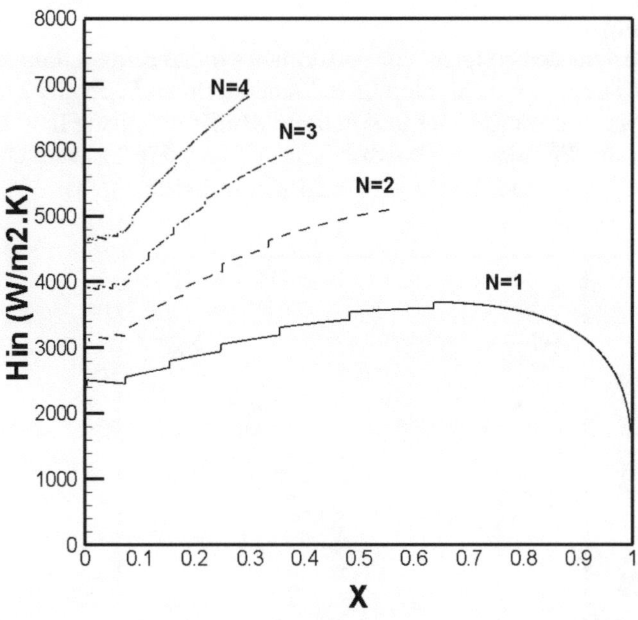

Fig. 12. Internal heat transfer coefficient distribution for different circulation ratios

This is not surprising since the controlling factor is the air side heat transfer, which is known to be limiting. As pointed out earlier, pressure drop increases very rapidly with coil length, (Fig. 13). Up to 90% of this pressure drop occurs in the first half of the coil, particularly for lower circulation ratios, where refrigerant qualities are lower. This study was limited to the coil; however it should be extended to all the system to assess the overall impact.

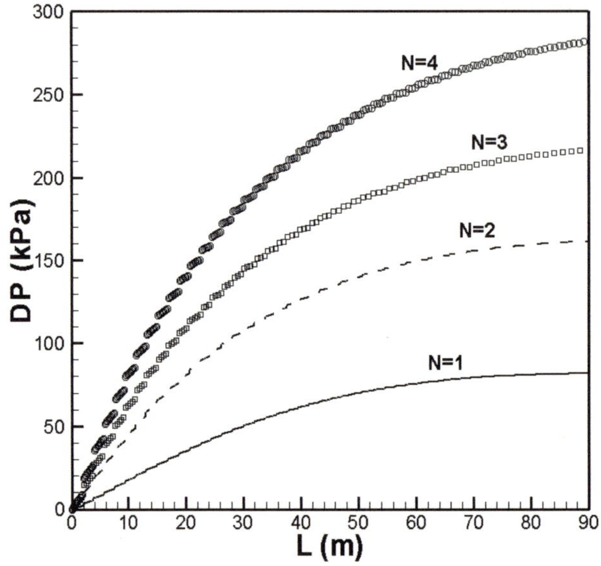

Fig. 13. Internal cumulative pressure drop distribution for different circulation ratios

4.2 Effect of circuiting

Circuiting is an important design factor for performance enhancement, improved flow and air temperature distribution. By combining tube diameter, fin and circuitry arrangements, it is possible to maximise heat transfer per unit volume while minimising flow resistance both internally and externally. Simulations shown in (Fig. 19) and (Fig.20) were obtained for the following conditions: 16 pass coil, T_r=-30 °C, T_a=-25 °C and ϕ=50%.

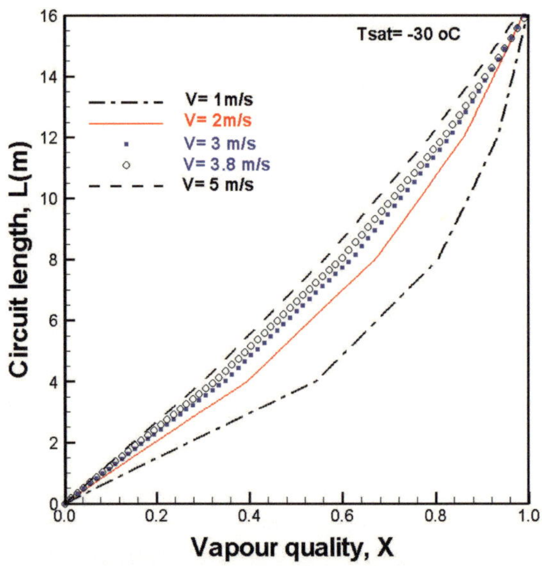

Fig. 14. Distribution of refrigerant quality in the circuit

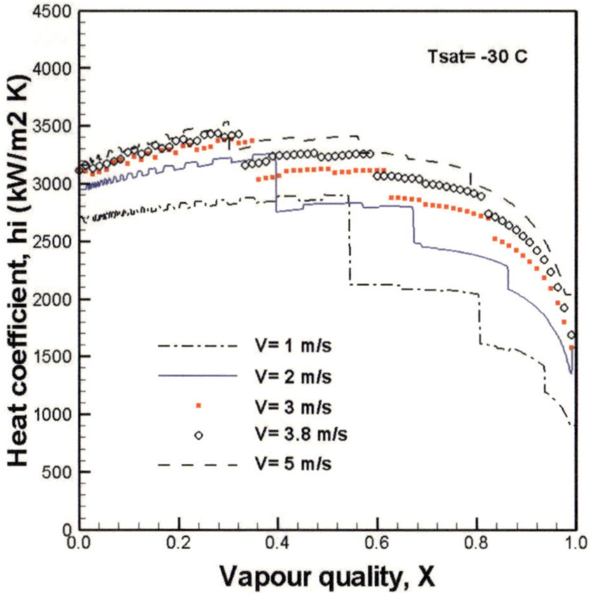

Fig. 15. Heat transfer distribution with quality

(Figure 14) indicates that for x ≥ 0.75 approximately the required tube length for evaporation increases. For the case considered, 35% of the total length is used in the quality range 0.75 - 1, while only 17.5% is used in the quality range of 0. - 0.25. This is a consequence of more efficient heat transfer in the range of moderate qualities. This condition is expressed in terms of the heat transfer coefficient in figure 15 for different air velocities. The internal heat transfer coefficient h_i on this figure is highest at low qualities and it maintains a stable value up to 50%. From 50% to 75%, its value decreases gradually up to 75%, beyond which the heat transfer declines rapidly, particularly towards 90% quality. On the other hand, it was shown by (Ouzzane & Aidoun, 2005) that internal pressure drop, expressed in terms of the pressure gradient for similar conditions steadily increased in the quality range of 0. ≤ x ≤ 0.8 before decreasing again. In the range of qualities x ≤ 0.5 and x ≥ 0.8, pressure losses are moderate. Under such conditions it is possible to use high flow rates in the low and high quality ranges for better heat transfer and less pressure loss penalty. The flow may be reduced in the medium range qualities where high heat transfer and high-pressure losses prevail. These important observations are put into practice in the example that follows, where circuiting is expected to play a major role in the design of large capacity coils. Optimized circuits may reduce the coil overall size, better distribute the flow and reduce frost formation. Most hydro fluorocarbons can accommodate only limited tube lengths due to excessive pressure drop in refrigeration coils as is shown for R507A in (Fig. 17), corresponding to the coil geometry of (Fig. 16). Due to the thermo physical properties of R507A, it was found that internal pressure losses were very high, rapidly resulting in a significant drop of saturation temperature over relatively short tube lengths. In order to maintain a reasonably constant temperature across an evaporator this temperature drop must be small (ideally less than 2°C) and in order to fulfill this condition, several short length circuits were needed with synthetic refrigerants, while only one circuit was required with carbon dioxide under similar working conditions (Aidoun & Ouzzane, 2009).

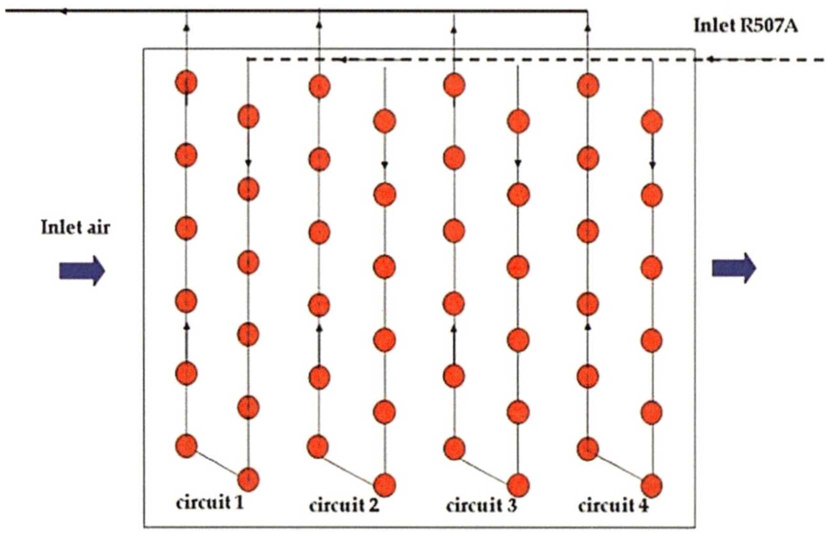

Fig. 16. Case of application for circuiting

In the event of frost formation it is expected to be more uniform and to occur over a longer period of time in comparison to ordinary synthetic refrigerants. With refrigerant R507A, several iterative attempts were performed before obtaining a reasonable temperature drop. At least four circuits were found to be necessary to satisfy this condition. The four circuits selected were 2 rows each, arranged in parallel. In such a case, the circuits are well balanced and the temperature drop in the saturation temperature is of the order of 2.6 °C in each circuit (22.5 metres) while it's only of the order of 1.8 °C for CO_2 in all the coil length (90 metres).

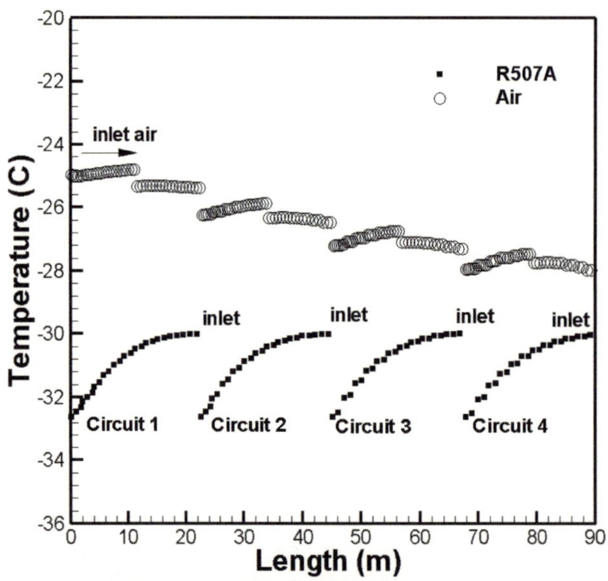

Fig. 17. Temperature distribution for air and R507A with coil length

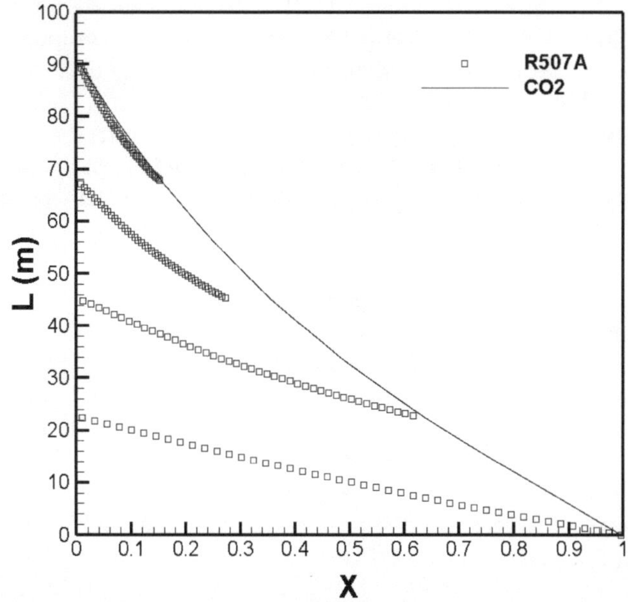

Fig. 18. Evaporation level in different circuits

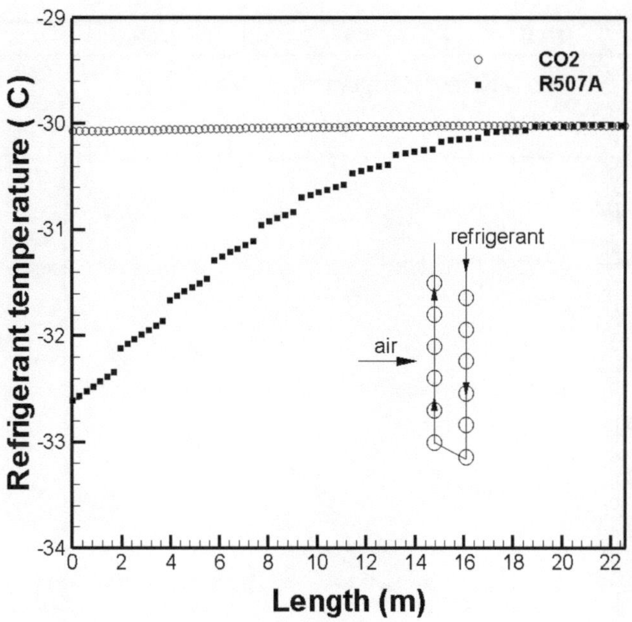

Fig. 19. Effect of refrigerant on temperature glide

(Fig. 18) shows the amount of evaporation taking place in each circuit. CO_2 uses only one circuit and evaporates 100% of the available refrigerant. R505A needs four circuits to deliver the same capacity. In this case only the frontal circuit works at full capacity. The other three are increasingly underused from the coil front to rear because of their exposure to an increasingly cold air flowing across the coil. In (Fig.19) and considering a representative circuit, the temperature distribution for CO_2 and R507A are compared in the same conditions. Because of its properties, particularly the low viscosity and the high saturation pressure, CO_2 temperature glide with pressure loss is negligible. This in turn insures uniform air cooling and small temperature gradients between refrigerant and air. R507A does not provide the same advantages. The temperature slide is high and as a consequence it is more difficult to obtain uniform air temperature otherwise than by multiplying the number of circuits.

4.3 Effect of refrigerant and geometrical parameters

4.3.1 Effect of refrigerant

Carbon dioxide is considered to be a potential environmentally innocuous replacement in many applications where HCFC'S and HFC'S are currently used. In this context, a comparative study of CO_2, R22 and R134A was performed on a 15 pass, 15 m length staggered counter-current flow tube coil (Aidoun & Ouzzane, 2005). The refrigerant mass flow was adjusted for complete evaporation for R22 which was taken as the reference case. CO_2 was shown to present a very low pressure drop in comparison with R22 and R134a, especially for low saturation temperatures.

Refrigerant	Psat [kPa]	Exit state	Dptotal [Pa]	Q [W]
R22	296.2	x=100 %	4966.2	779.4
CO_2	2288.0	x= 74.5 %	1210.9	726.5
R134A	163.9	x = 91.7%	6486.3	691.6

Table 5. Comparison between different refrigerants

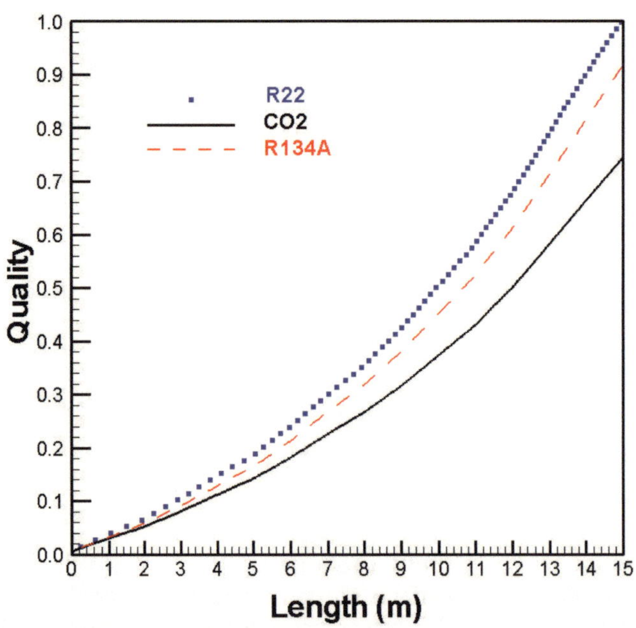

Fig. 20. Quality distribution for different refrigerants

At -20°C, R22 has a pressure drop six times higher than that of CO_2, resulting in higher compression power. (Fig. 20) presents the quality distribution through the tubes for R22, CO_2 and R134A, at -15°C. Air and refrigerant inlet conditions were kept constant. For these conditions, only R22 was completely evaporated (x=1 at exit). The evaporator size is however not sufficient to complete the evaporation of CO_2 and R134A. Due to better internal heat transfer, R22 gives the highest capacity (Table 5). At -15 °C, R134A latent heat of evaporation is comparable to that of R22 (209.5 kJ /kg and 216.5 kJ/kg), respectively. However, because of its other properties, R134A performs less than R22. CO_2 has a comparatively higher latent heat of evaporation (ΔH_L=270.9 kJ/kg]), resulting in the lowest exit quality (x=74.5%). Its lowest pressure drop however allows increasing the mass flow rate with a corresponding increase in heat transfer or decreasing tube diameter.

4.3.2 Effect of fin spacing

Fin spacing was shown to generally enhance heat transfer in dry coils and condensers. Increasing the fin number reduces fin spacing, increases the Reynolds number and the overall heat transfer coefficient. The heat transfer area also increases thereby increasing the heat exchanger capacity and efficiency. When operating at low temperatures the fin number needs to be reduced because of frost formation. Frost build up reduces air flow channels cross section, eventually obstructing them and affects considerably the performance. Overall operation time is reduced because of frequent defrosting, which also means increased energy consumption and decreased production. Simulated results for the conditions of 90% relative humidity and -25 °C evaporation temperature are represented.

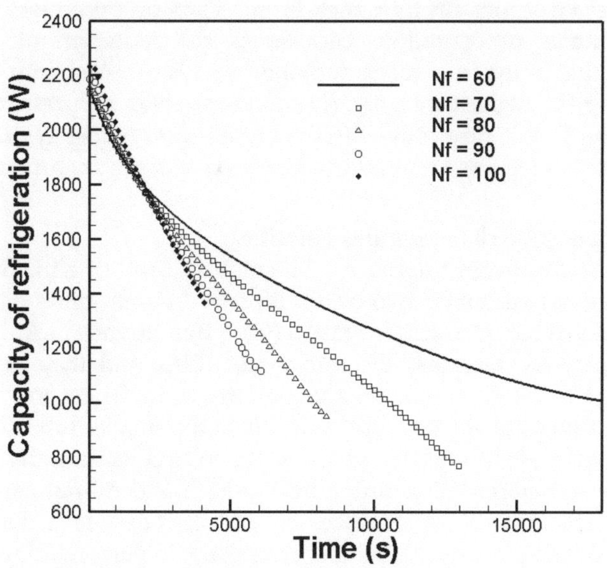

Fig. 21. Cooling capacity for different fin spacing

In this case study, calculations are stopped after five hours of operation or when the first control volume is totally blocked by frost. The effect of fin density on air pressure drop and coil capacity is respectively represented in (Fig. 21) and (Fig. 22). The fin density was varied from 60 to 100, which initially increases capacity but this advantage is lost after approximately 30 minutes due frost growth.

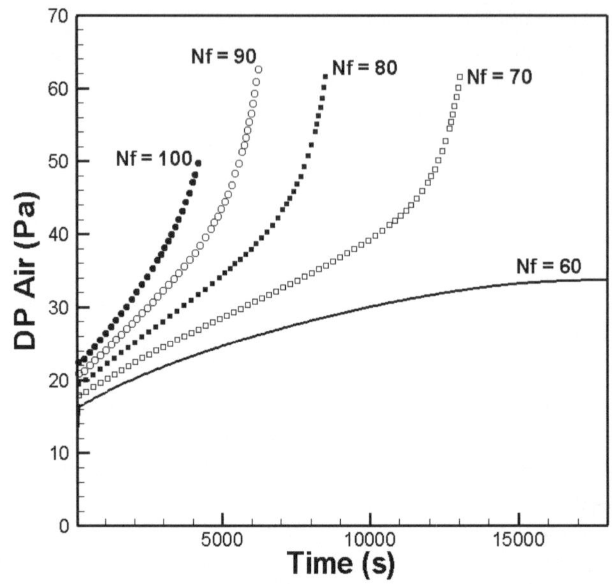

Fig. 22. Air pressure drop for different fin spacing

(Fig. 21) shows heat exchangers with 100 fins per meter get blocked after 66 minutes from the start while those with 60 fins per meter continue to work after 5 hours. (Fig. 21) indicates that as long as the frost layer remains thin, high fin numbers produce more capacity. After approximately 30 minutes of operation, because of the reduction of the exchanger effectiveness which is due to the frost formation, the trend is reversed with the coil having the least fins producing the highest capacity. (Fig. 22) represents air pressure drop in coils with frost development. In this case coils with the highest fin number systematically incur higher losses than those having less fin numbers, irrespective of the amount of frost formed.

4.3.3 Combined effect of tube diameter and circuiting

In order to outline the advantages offered by the combined use of circuiting and CO_2, a comparative study was carried out on two coils with two different tubes diameters: a base configuration (Case A) and circuited configuration (Case B) (Ouzzane & Aidoun, 2008). For Case B and for comparison purposes, the number of tubes and their arrangement are selected in such a way that the frontal section, perpendicular to the air flow is equal to that of Case A. In contrast with Case A (base case) and due to the smaller tube diameter used in Case B, it is not possible to use a single circuit or even two circuits since the pressure losses and the glide of the evaporation temperature are too high and do not correspond to the conditions normally encountered in practice. Several iterative tests have had to be performed in order to obtain a reasonable temperature drop. In particular it was found to be impossible to use less than three circuits for this case (case B). Therefore the configuration selected was that of three circuits, respectively 3, 4 and 4 rows deep (in the direction of air flow). The geometry, core dimensions and relevant operating conditions for both configurations are summarized in Table 6.

Two types of results deserve attention: global results summarized in Table 7 and detailed results presented in (Fig. 23) and (Fig. 24). Table 7 shows that when reducing the tube diameter in Case B, internal pressure losses (refrigerant side) increase significantly, a fact that results in an important evaporation temperature glide. It can be observed that for the given conditions, while the base configuration of Case A results in a pressure loss of 58 kPa over a single circuit in excess of 90 m, the Case B configuration uses three circuits with the respective lengths of 45.12 m, 60.16 m, 60.16 m. The internal pressure loss in each of them is 66 kPa, corresponding to a temperature glide of 1.4 °C. These results have direct repercussions on the total capacity produced by each coil: the configuration of Case B gives a 19% increase in capacity over the base configuration (Case A), mainly due to better heat transfer across the coil. The first and second circuits perform well while the third circuit produces less than half the capacity of the first circuit, evaporating only 20% of the available CO_2. This is due to the more important temperature gradients between air and CO_2, available for the first rows, corresponding to air inlet.

		Case A (Base Case)	Case B
Internal/external diameter		d_i/d_o=9.525/12.7 mm	d_i/d_o=6.35/9.52 mm
Longitudinal and transversal tube pitch		P_l/P_t=28.03/31.75 mm	P_l/P_t=20.39/23.81 mm
Tubes number/total length (m)		48/90.24 m	88/165.44 m
		118 fins/m, fin thickness= 0.19 mm, Pass length =1.88 m	
Inlet conditions	Air	$Tair_{in}$=-24.0 °C, $Pair_{in}$=101.3 kPa, HR_{in}=0.5, $\dot{m}_{air} = 1.105 kg/s$	
	CO_2	Tco_{2in}=-30.0 °C, quality=X=0%	

Table 6. Geometrical data and operational conditions

		Case A (Base case)	Case B
CO_2	Total pressure drop per circuit (kPa)	58.0	66.3
	ΔT of refrigerant per circuit (C)	1.19	1.4
	CO_2 mass flow rate per circuit (g/s)	12.2	6.7 circuit n°1 6.7 circuit n°2 15.0 circuit n°3
	Outlet CO_2 quality (%)	100	100.0 circuit n°1 73.5 circuit n°2 20.0 circuit n°3
	Power (W)	3699.8	2032.4 circuit n°1 1488.6 circuit n°2 874.8 circuit n°3 4395.8 (total)
Air	Total pressure drop (Pa)	48.87	49.35
Mass (kG)	Tubes	44.67	58.50
	Fins	1.60	1.56
	Total Coil Mass (kG)	46.27	60.06

Table 7. Results of comparison

The effect of tube diameter can also be presented in colors by the distribution of air temperature in (Fig. 23) and (Fig. 24). It is important to point out that the -28 °C of air temperature at the exit of the coil in case A can be reached at the end of the eighth row in case B. This means that the coil volume as well as the mass of material can be reduced by 27 % without affecting the evaporation capacity. It was previously shown that under the same operating conditions, using CO_2 as a refrigerant in coils having tube diameters of 3/8 inches incur a smaller internal pressure drop in comparison with other commonly used synthetic refrigerants such as R507A for the case of supermarkets. Taking these results into account allows the use of longer circuits (as in Case A), therefore reducing their number and simplifying the overall configuration for a given capacity. The tube diameter has a great impact on the capacity and pressure drop of CO_2. Advantage can be taken of CO_2 thermo physical properties by using more tubes with small diameter, arranged in an appropriate number of circuits such that it becomes possible to reduce both the size and the mass of the coil while maintaining or even improving the capacity.

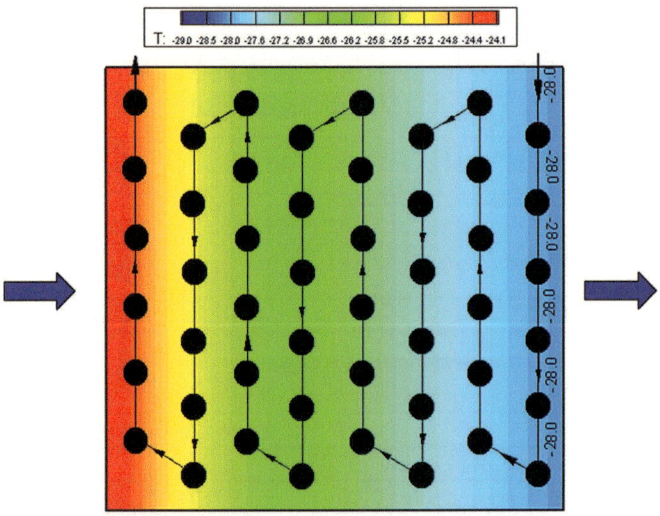

Fig. 23. Isotherms Case A (Base case)

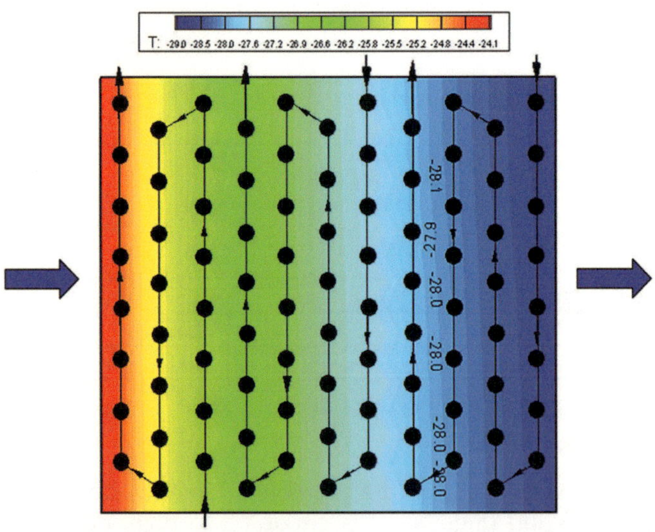

Fig. 24. Isotherms Case B

5. Conclusion

Finned tube heat exchangers are almost exclusively used as gas-to-liquid heat exchangers in a number of generic operations such as HVAC, dehumidification, refrigeration, freezing etc…, because they can achieve high heat transfer in reduced volume at a moderate cost. An improved coil design can considerably benefit the cycle efficiency, which is reflected in the coefficient of performance (COP). To this end, two different solution procedures were introduced in the modeling: the Forward Marching Technique (FMT) and the Iterative Solution for Whole System (ISWS). FMT solves the conservation equations one elementary control volume at a time before moving to the next while ISWS resolves simultaneously the conservation equations arranged in a matrix form for all the elements. Both procedures offer good flexibility for local simulations. The first was limited to dry operation and simple circuitry as a trade-off against relative simplicity while the second with its original indexing and parameterization method of flow directions, circuits and other relevant information offers extended capabilities for complex configurations and frosting conditions. The proposed models were validated against sets of data obtained on a dedicated refrigeration facility, and from the literature. Comparison of numerical predictions and experimental results were shown to be in very good agreement.

The tool was then successfully applied to predict coil performance under different practical conditions and simulation results were analysed. More particularly, it was shown that with this procedure, parameters of a three-dimensional coil could be represented by using a 1-dimensional approach, within reasonable limits of calculation accuracy, by tracking refrigerant and air flows inside tubes and across passes. The influence of non uniformities in air flow and the refrigerant local behavior could in this way be tackled. CO_2, a natural refrigerant was selected as the main fluid of study with which some other current refrigerants were compared. Its pressure drop in typical refrigeration conditions was shown to be very low in comparison to traditional refrigerants and resulting in very small temperature glides.

The effect of frost growth was studied in conjunction with the fin effect. This has shown that in general, frost initially enhanced heat transfer as long as the frost layer was sufficiently thin. Beyond this, the trend was changed with the least fins being more efficient. Large fin spacing delayed channel blockage and extended operation time.

The tool was also applied to study circuiting and its effects on coil operation and performance for different configurations of evaporation paths with CO_2 as the working fluid. The basic unit had only one circuit forming the whole coil and served as a reference. The other configurations had two circuits with different refrigerant paths but with the same total area and tube length. Comparison between these units has shown that circuiting affected performance and general coil operation. Internal pressure drop and corresponding temperature glides were greatly reduced, making it possible to use longer and fewer circuits with CO_2 as opposed to other refrigerants for similar refrigeration capacities. Combined effects of circuiting and tube diameters were then used to take advantage of the favourable thermo-physical characteristics of CO_2 in order to highlight the benefits in terms of size reductions. This exercise has demonstrated that by reducing the tube diameter and by increasing the number of circuits, it was possible to reduce both the size and the mass of the coil by at least 20% without affecting its capacity.

6. Acknowledgments

Funding for this work was mainly provided by the Canadian Government's Program on Energy Research and Development (PERD). The authors thank the Natural Sciences and

Engineering Research Council of Canada (NSERC) for the scholarship granted to the third author.

7. References

Aidoun Z. & Ouzzane M., 2005, Evaporation of Carbon Dioxide: A Comparative Study With Refrigerants R22 and R134A, *20th Canadian Congress of Applied Mechanics (CANCAM2005),* May 30-June 2, Mc Gill, Montreal, Quebec, Canada.

Aidoun Z. & Ouzzane M., 2009, A Model Application to Study Circuiting and Operation in CO_2 Refrigeration Coils, *Applied Thermal Engineering,* Vol. 29, 2544-2553.

Aljuwayhel N.F., Reindl D.T., Klein S.A. & Nellis G.F., 2008, Comparison of parallel and counter-flow circuiting in an industrial evaporator under frosting conditions, *International Journal of Refrigeration,* 31: 98-106.

ASHRAE, 1993, *ASHRAE Handbook of Fundamentals,* SI Edition, chapter 6, pp.1-17, U.S.A.

ASHRAE, 2000, Methods of testing forced circulation air cooling and heating coils, *ASHRAE Standard* 33-2000, Atlanta, Georgia, U.S.A.

ASHRAE, 1987, Standard Methods for Laboratory Airflow Measurement, *ANSI/ASHRAE Standard* 41.2 (RA92), Atlanta, Georgia, U.S.A.

Bendaoud A., Ouzzane M., Aidoun Z. & Galanis N., Oct. 2010, A New Modeling Procedure for Circuit Design and Performance Prediction of Evaporator Coil Using CO_2 as Refrigerant, *Applied Energy,* Vol. 87, Issues 10, 2974-2983.

Bendaoud A., Ouzzane M., Aidoun Z. & Galanis N., July 2011, A Novel Approach to Study the Performance of Finned-Tube Heat Exchangers Under Frosting Conditions, *Journal of Applied Fluid Mechanics,* will be published in Vol. 4, Number 2, Issue 8 in July 2011.

Bensafi A., Borg S. & Parent D., 1997, CYRANO: A computational model for the detailed design of plate-fin-and-tube heat exchangers using pure and mixed refrigerants, *International Journal of Refrigeration,* 20(3): 218–28.

Byun J. S., Lee J. & Choi J. Y., 2007,Numerical analysis of evaporation performance in a finned-tube heat exchanger, *International Journal of Refrigeration,* 30: 812-820.

Chuah Y.K., Hung C.C.& Tseng P.C., 1998, Experiments on the dehumidification performance of a finned tube heat exchanger, *HVAC&R Research,* 4(2): 167-178.

Corberan J.M. & Melon M.G., 1998, A modeling of plate finned tube evaporators and condensers working with R134A, *International Journal of Refrigeration,* 21(4): 273–83.

Domanski P.A., 1989, EVSIM- An evaporator simulation model accounting for refrigerant with and one-dimensional air distribution, NIST report, *NISTIR,* 89-4133.

Domanski, P.A., 1991, Simulation of an evaporator with non-uniform one-dimensional air distribution, *ASHRAE Transaction,* 97 (1), 793-802.

Drew T.B., Koo E.C. & Mc Adams W.H., 1932, The friction factors for clean round pipes, *Trans. AIChE,* Vol. 28-56.

Ellison, P.R., F.A. Crewick, S.K. Ficher & W.L. Jackson, 1981, A computer model for air-cooled refrigerant condenser with specified refrigerant circuiting, *ASHRAE Transaction,* 1106-1124.

Geary D.F., 1975, Return bend pressure drop in refrigeration systems, *ASHRAE Transactions,* Vol. 81, No. 1, pp. 250-264.

Guo X.M., Chen Y.G., Wang W.H. & Chen C.Z., 2008, Experimental study on frost growth and dynamic performance of air source heat pump system, *Applied Thermal Engineering*, 28: 2267-2278.

Hwang Y., Kim B.H. & Radermacher R., Nov. 1997, Boiling heat transfer correlation for carbon dioxide, *IIR international conference*, Heat Transfer Issues in Natural Refrigeration.

Incropera F.P. & DeWitt D.P., 2002, *Fundamentals of heat and mass transfer*, John Wiley and Sons, 5th edition, NY.

Jones & Parker J.D., 1975, Frost formation with varying environmental parameters, *Journal of Heat Transfer*,Vol.97, pp. 255–259.

Jiang H., Aute V. & Radermacher R., 2006, Coil Designer: A general-purpose simulation and design tool for air-to-refrigerant heat exchangers, *International Journal of Refrigeration*, 601–610.

Kakaç S. & Liu H., 1998, *Heat exchangers, Selection, Rating and Thermal Design*, CRC Press LLC.

Kays W. M. & London A. L., 1984, *Compact Heat Exchangers,* 3rd edition, New York, McGraw-Hill.

Kondepudi S.N. & O'Neal D.L., 1993a, Performance of finned-tube heat exchangers under frosting conditions: I. Simulation model, *International Journal of Refrigeration*, Vol. 16, No. 3, pp. 175-180.

Kondepudi S. N. & O'Neal D. L., 1993b, Performance of Finned-Tube Heat Exchangers Under Frosting Conditions II : Comparison of Experimental Data with Model, *International Journal of Refrigeration,* Vol.16,No 3, 181-184.

Kuo M.C., Ma H. K., Chen S. L. & Wang C.C., 2006, An algorithm for simulation of the performance of air-cooled heat exchanger applications subject to the influence of complex circuitry, *Applied Thermal Engineering*, 26: 1- 9.

Lee K.S., Kim W.S. & Lee T.H., 1997, A one-dimensional model for frost formation on a cold flat surface, *International Journal of Heat Mass Transfer,* Vol. 40 No.18, pp. 4359-4365.

Liang S.Y., Liu M., Wong T. N. & Nathan G. K., 1999, Analytical study of evaporator coil in humid environment, *Applied Thermal Engineering,* 19: 1129-1145.

Liang, S.Y., Wong, T.N. & Nathan, G.K., 2001, Numerical and experimental studies of refrigerant circuitry of evaporator coils, *International Journal of Refrigeration,* 24, pp.823-833.

Liang S. Y., Wong T. N. & Nathan G. K., 2000, Study on refrigerant circuitry of condenser coils with exergy destruction analysis, *Applied Thermal Engineering,* 20: 559-577.

Liu J., Wei W., Ding G., Zhang C., Fukaya M., Wang K. & Inagaki T., 2004, A general steady state mathematical model for fin-and-tube heat exchanger based on graph theory, *International Journal of Refrigeration,* 27: 965- 973.

NIST, July 1998, *Thermodynamic and Transport Properties of Refrigerant Mixtures-REFPROP*, Version 6.01, U.S. Department of Commerce, Technology Administration.

Ogawa K., Tanaka N. & Takeshita M., 1993, Performance improvement of plate-fin-and-tube heat exchangers under frosting conditions, *ASHRAE Transactions,* CH-93-2-4: 762-771.

Ouzzane M. & Aidoun Z., 2008, A Numerical Study of a Wavy Fin and Tube CO_2 Evaporator Coil, *Heat Transfer Engineering,* Vol. 29, 12, 1008-1017.

Ouzzane M. & Aidoun Z., 2004, A numerical procedure for the design and the analysis of plate finned evaporator coils using CO_2 as refrigerant, *CSME Forum (The Canadian Society for the Mechanical Engineering),* June1-4, 2004, London, Ontario, Canada.

Ouzzane M. & Aidoun Z., 2007, A Study of The Effect of Recirculation On An Air-CO_2 Evaporator Coil in A Secondary Loop of A Refrigeration System; *Heat SET 2007 Conference,* Chambery, 18-20 April, pp. 877-884, France.

Ouzzane M. & Aidoun Z., 2008, A Study of a Wavy Fin and Tube CO_2 Evaporator Coil for a Secondary Loop in a Low Temperature Refrigeration System, *International Conference, Design and Operation of Environmentally Friendly Refrigeration and AC Systems,* October 15-17, Poznan, Poland.

Rich D.G., 1973, The effect of fin spacing on the heat transfer and friction performance of multi-row, plate fin-and-tube heat exchangers, *ASHRAE Transactions,* 79 (2): 137-145.

Rich D.G., 1975, The effect of number of tube row on heat transfer performance of smooth plate fin-and-tube heat exchangers, ASHRAE Transactions, 81 (1): 307-317.

Rohsenow, W.M., Hartnett, J.P. and Cho and Y.I., 1998, *Handbook of Heat Transfer,* Third Edition, Mc Graw Hill, New York, pp. 17.89-17.97.

Seker D., Karatas H. & Egrican N., 2004a, Frost formation on fin-and-tube heat exchangers. Part I-Modeling of frost formation on fin-and-tube heat exchangers, *International Journal of Refrigeration,* 27(4): 367-374.

Seker D., Karatas H. & Egrican N., 2004b, Frost formation on fin-and-tube heat exchangers. Part II-Experimental investigation of frost formation on fin- and tube heat exchangers, *International Journal of Refrigeration,* 27(4): 375-377.

Singh V., Aute V. & Radermacher R., 2008, Numerical approach for modeling air-to-refrigerant fin-and-tube heat exchanger with tube-to-tube heat transfer, *International Journal of Refrigeration,* 31: 1414-1425.

Singh V., Aute V. & Radermacher R., 2009, A heat exchanger model for air-to- refrigerant fin-and-tube heat exchanger with arbitrary fin sheet, *International Journal of Refrigeration,* 32: 1724-1735.

Shokouhmand H., Esmaili E., Veshkini A. & Sarabi Y., Jan. 2009, Modeling for predicting frost behaviour of a fin-tube heat exchanger with thermal contact resistance, *ASHRAE Transactions,* pp. 538-551.

Stoecker W.F., 1957, How frost formation on coils effects refrigeration systems, Refrigeration Engineering, 42.

Stoecker W.F., 1960, Frost formation on refrigeration coils, *ASHRAE Trans.,* 66:91.

Vardhan A., Dhar P.L., 1998, A new procedure for performance prediction of air conditioning coils, *International Journal of Refrigeration,* 21(1): 77–83.

Wang C. C., Chang Y. J., Hsieh Y. C. & Lin Y. T., 1996, Sensible heat and friction characteristics of plate-fin-and-tube heat exchangers having plain fins, *International Journal of Refrigeration,* 19(4): 223-230.

Wang C.C., Hsieh Y. C. & Lin Y. T., 1997, Performance of plate finned tube heat exchangers under dehumidifying conditions, *Journal of Heat Transfer,* 11(9): 109-117.

Wang, C.C., Hwang, Y.M. & Lin, Y.T., 2002, Empirical correlations for heat transfer and flow friction characteristics of herringbone wavy fin-and-tube heat exchangers, *International Journal of Refrigeration,* Vol. 25, pp.673- 680.

Yang D., Lee K. & Song S., 2006a, Modeling for predicting frosting behaviour of a fin-tube heat exchanger, International *Journal of Heat and Mass Transfer,* 49 (7-8): 1472-1479.

Yang D., Lee K. & Song S., 2006b, Fin spacing optimization of a fin-tube heat exchanger under frosting conditions, *International Journal of Heat and Mass Transfer,* 49 (15-16): 2619-2625.

3

Modeling and Simulation of the Heat Transfer Behaviour of a Shell-and-Tube Condenser for a Moderately High-Temperature Heat Pump

Tzong-Shing Lee and Jhen-Wei Mai
Department of Energy and Refrigerating Air-Conditioning Engineering
National Taipei University of Technology, Taipei
Taiwan

1. Introduction

For many countries, increasing energy efficiency and reducing greenhouse gas emissions are key countermeasures to cope with the energy crisis and climate change. Of the various heating equipment such as heat pumps, gas-fired boilers, oil-fired boilers, or electric boilers, heat pumps are widely adopted for space heating, water heating, and process heating by households, business, and industry due to high energy efficiency and effective reduction of greenhouse gases. The main components in a heat pump include the compressor, the expansion valve and two heat exchangers referred to as evaporator and condenser. Condenser is the essential component for heat pump transferring heat from refrigerant-side to water-side. Among many types of heat exchangers, shell-and-tube condensers are probably the most common type for using in heat pump as a heat exchanger for heating water, because of their relatively simple manufacturing and adaptability to various operating conditions.

When heat pumps are used for residential and commercial hot water supply, the outlet water temperature of condenser is generally kept below 60°C. However, when heat pumps are used for process heating, the hot water outlet water temperature of condenser can range anywhere from 60 to 95°C. Such heat pumps are referred to as a moderately high-temperature heat pump. Under such operating conditions, the shell-and-tube condensers may face several issues: (1) the temperature difference between hot water inlet and outlet temperatures is high; generally above 40K and even up to 60K; (2) the condensing temperature increases as the outlet temperature increases contributing to the increase in the sensible heat ratio of refrigerants during the condensing process by as much as 25%; (3) as condensing temperature increases, the discharge temperature of compressor also increases, resulting in a decrease in energy efficiency of heat pump units. Therefore, under conditions of large temperature difference, high sensible heat ratio, and high outlet water temperature, how to effectively recover sensible heat, reduce condensing temperature, and thus improve the performance of heat pump units have become key challenges for this type of shell-and-tube condenser design. Because the factors that can influence heat transfer performance of heat exchangers are many, including flow arrangement, tube size, geometric configuration, and inlet/outlet conditions on the water and refrigerant sides, in order to effectively shorten or reduce the time and cost in the development and design of this type of heat exchanger, computer-aided design of moderately high-temperature heat pump condensers, as well as relevant simulation studies, is worth further investigation.

Lately, several studies dealt with shell-and-tube heat exchangers. Kara & Güraras (2004) made a computer-based design model for preliminary design of shell-and-tube heat exchangers with single-phase fluid flow both on shell and tube side. The program determined the overall dimensions of the shell, the tube bundle, and optimum heat transfer surface area required to meet the specified heat transfer duty by calculating minimum or allowable shell side pressure drop, and selected an optimum exchanger among total number of 240 exchangers. Moita et al. (2004) summarized the current existing criteria in a general design algorithm to show a path for the calculations of the main design variables of shell-and-tube heat exchangers. They also introduced an economic strategy design algorithm to allow a feasible design which minimizes the cost of heat exchanger. Karlsson & Vamling (2005) carried out a 2-D CFD calculations to investigate the behaviour of vapor flow and the rate of condensation for a geometry similar to a real shell-and-tube conenser with 100 tubes.

It is shown that: (1) The vapour flow behaviour for a zeotropic mixed refrigerant in a shell-and-tube condenser is complex and can be significantly different from that for a pure refrigerant. (2) The clearance size between the tube bundle and the shell has no greater influence on the flow field for the mixed refrigerant, but it has an influence on the flow field for pure refrigerant. (3) Small adjustments of the inlet design can influence the average heat flux by up to 24% for a low temperature driving force, and up to 8% for a high temperature driving. force. Karno & Ajib (2006) developed a new model for calculation, simulation and optimization of shell-and-tube heat exchangers, and investigated the effects of transverse and longitudinal tube pitch in the in-line and staggered tube arrangements on Nusselt numbers, heat transfer coefficients, and thermal performance of the heat exchangers. It is shown that a good agreement is observed between the calculated values and the lierature values. Selbas et al. (2006) presented a method using genetic algorithms (GA) to find the optimal design parameters of a shell-and-tube heat exchanger and using LMTD method to determine the heat transfer area for a given design configuration. Allen & Gosselin (2008) presented a model for estimating the total cost of shell-and-tube heat exchangers with condensation in tubes or in the shell, as well as a designing strategy for minimizing this cost. The optimization process is based on a genetic algorithm, and two case studies are presented. Patel & Rao (2010) presented particle swarm optimization (PSO) for design optimization of shell-and-tube heat exchangers from economic view point. Three design variables such as shell internal diameter, outer tube diameter and baffle spacing are considered for optimization. Triangle and square tube layout were also considered for optimization. Four different case studies were presented to demonstrate the effectiveness and accuracy of the proposed algorithm. And the results were compared with those obtained by using genetic algorithm (GA). Wang et al. (2010) experimentally studied flow and heat transfer characteristics of the shell-and-tube heat exchanger with continuous helical baffles (CH-STHX) and segmental baffles (SG-STHX). Experimental results that the CH-STHX can increase the heat transfer rate by 7–12% than the SG-STHX for the same mass flow rate although its effective heat transfer area had 4% decrease. The heat transfer coefficient and pressure drop of the CH-STHX also had 43–53% and 64–72% increase than

those of the SG-STHX. Li et al. (2010) investigated the flow field and the heat transfer characteristics of a shell-and-tube heat exchanger for the cooling of syngas. The results show that higher operation pressure can improve the heat transfer, however brings bigger pressure drop. The components of the syngas significantly affect the pressure drop and the heat transfer. The arrangement of the baffles influences the fluid flow. Ghorbani et al. (2010) studied an experimental investigation of the mixed convection heat transfer in a coil-in-shell heat exchanger for various Reynolds and Rayleigh numbers, various tube-to-coil diameter ratios and dimensionless coil pitch. They purposed to assess the influence of the tube diameter, coil pitch, shell-side and tube-side mass flow rate over the performance coefficient and modified effectiveness of vertical helical coiled tube heat exchangers. It was found that the mass flow rate of tube-side to shell-side ratio was effective on the axial temperature profiles of heat exchanger. Vera-Garcia et al. (2010) proposed a simplified model of shell-and-tubes heat exchangers, and it is implemented and tested in the modelization of a general refrigeration cycle by using R22, the results are compared with data obtained from a specific test bench for the analysis of shell-and-tubes heat exchangers.
Throughout the literature review, the study on the modeling and simulation of a shell-and-tube condenser utilizing in moderately high-temperature heat pumps is still lacking. This chapter will present a study experimentally and theoretically investigating the heat transfer modeling of a new shell-and-tube condenser with longitude baffels, designed for an air-source moderately high-temperature heat pump water heater. Experimental data and theoretical methods were applied in order to develop a theoretical model that can simulate the heat transfer behavior of this type of heat exchanger. Cases study for sizing and rating of the heat exchanger was then demonstrated. Some topics will be covered in this chapter:

i. Experimental measurements of the shell-and-tube condenser,
ii. Modeling, and validation of the heat transfer behavior of the shell-and-tube condenser
iii. Cases study for sizing and rating by using modified model.

The results of this study can be used as a reference in development of computer-aided design and simulation of heat transfer performance of shell-and-tube condensers for moderately high-temperature heat pumps.

2. Experimental setup and test conditions

2.1 Experimental apparatus

An air-source moderately high-temperature heat pump system with its condenser for heating water has been built and tested in this study. The aims of this study were focused mainly on the heat transfer performance of the new condenser designed for operating under large temperature difference, high sensible heat ratio, and high outlet water temperature. Figure 1 shows the schematic diagram of the experimental setup and the location of the sensors. The testing system consists of a compressor, a condenser, a throttling device, and an evaporator. R134a was selected as the working refrigerant in the testing system. The compressor is a type of semi-hermetic scroll with a displacement volume of 46.5 m^3/hr. The condenser, shown in Figure 2 and 3, is a type of shell-and-tube heat exchanger with longitude baffles, twelve tube passes, and 48 copper tubes. The evaporator is a cross flow air-to-refrigerant heat exchanger of finned-tube type. The throttling device is a thermostatic expansion valve with an external equalizer. Heat released from the condenser is transferred to water while the evaporator takes heat from air in a controlled environment room as heat source. The temperature and humidity of ambient air entering to the finned-tube evaporator was controlled by a testing facility used to conduct the heat pump experiment. The inlet water temperature is adjusted by circulating the generated hot water and mixing with colder water from both cooling tower and water main supply. The temperatures of water, refrigerant, and air at various points in the heat pump system were measured by T-type thermocouples with an accuracy of ±0.1K. The measurement of refrigerant pressures is made by calibrated pressure transducers with an accuracy of ±0.15%. The water flow rate of condenser is measured by an electromagnetic flowmeter with accuracy of ±0.5%, while the power consumed by compressor and fan are measured by power meter with an accuracy of ±0.5%.

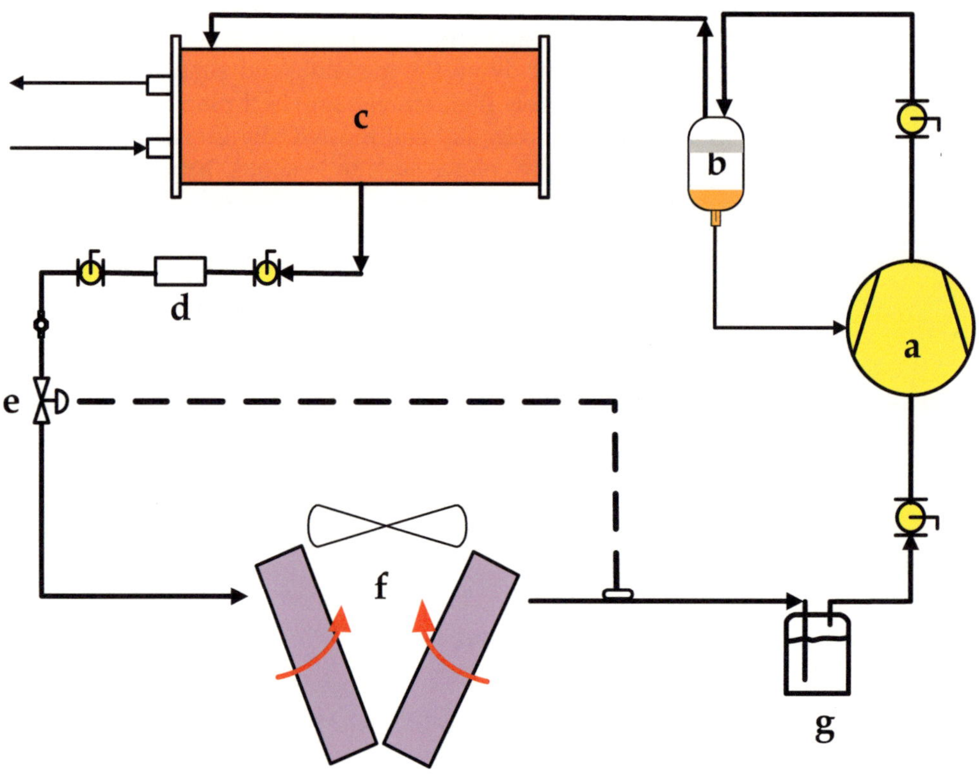

a. compressor
b. oil separator
c. condenser
d. dryer
e. expansion valve
f. evaporator
g. liquid-gas separator

Fig. 1. Schematic diagram of an air-source moderately high-temperature heat pump system

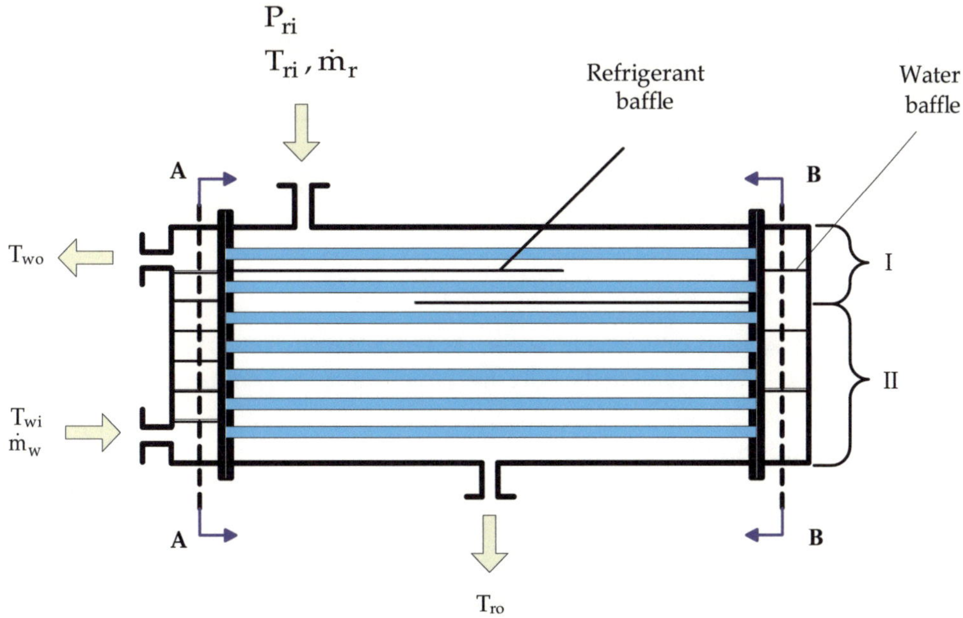

Fig. 2. Schematic diagram of the shell-and-tube condenser with longitude baffles

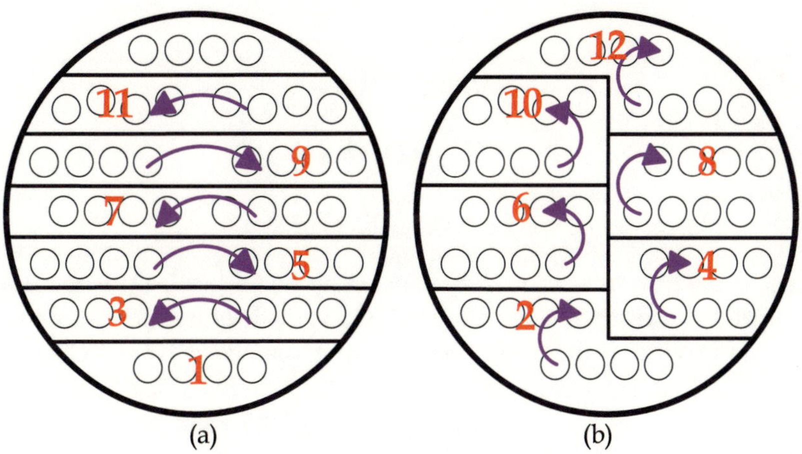

Fig. 3. Passes layout for the shell-and-tube condenser (a) A-A section view, (b) B-B section view

2.2 Test condition and procedures

The experimental parameters of this work are inlet and outlet states of refrigerant, inlet and outlet water temperatures, and water flow rate passing through condenser. In order to investigate the effect of those parameters on the heating capacity and performance of moderately high-temperature air-source heat pump, this work conducted 27 experiments. The detail of testing conditions of this work is listed in Table 1. The test data sets were acquired and recorded every five minutes intervals through the data logger system connected to a notebook computer after the testing system operation had reached steady state. The reliability of experimental data recorded was confirmed by energy balance method with less than 5% between the measured and calculated values.

2.3 Data reduction

The heating capacity of shell-and-tube condenser for heat pump can be determined as follows.

$$\dot{Q}_H = \dot{F}_c \rho_w c_{pw} (T_{wo} - T_{wi}) \ [\text{kW}] \tag{1}$$

where $\dot{F}_c$ is the volumetri flow rate of water, ρ_w is the density of water c_{pw} is the specific heat of water, T_{wi} and T_{wo} represent the inlet and outlet water temperatures, respectively.

3. Mathematical models

3.1 Heat transfer rate

In the shell-and-tube condenser as shown in Fig. 2, water flows inside the tubes and refrigerant flows outside the tubes through the shell. The heat transfer rate between refrigerant and water can be determined in three ways:

$$\dot{Q}_{Model} = \dot{Q}_r = \dot{Q}_w \tag{2}$$

and

$$\dot{Q}_{Model} = UAF\Delta T_m \tag{3}$$

$$\dot{Q}_r = \dot{m}_r (h_{ri} - h_{ro}) \tag{4}$$

$$\dot{Q}_w = \dot{m}_w c_{pw} (T_{wo} - T_{wi}) \tag{5}$$

where $\dot{Q}_{Model}$ is the heat transfer rate determined by Eq.(3) [kW], $\dot{Q}_r$ is the heat transfer rate determined by refrigerant-side data [kW], $\dot{Q}_w$ is the heat transfer rate determined by water-side data [kW], U is the overall heat transfer coefficient [W/m^2°C], A is the heat transfer area [m^2], F is a correction factor, ΔT_m represents log mean temperature difference, $\dot{m}_r$ is the mass flow rate of refrigerant [kg/s], h_{ri} and h_{ro} are, respectively, the inlet and outlet enthalpy of refrigerant [kJ/kg], $\dot{m}_w$ is the mass flow rate of water[kg/s], c_{pw} is the specific heat of water [kJ/kgK], T_{wi} and T_{wo} are the inlet and outlet temperature of water [°C], respectively.

3.2 Heat transfer area

The heat transfer area (A) of the shell-and-tube condenser is computed by:

$$A = L\pi d_o N_t \tag{6}$$

where L is the tube length [m], d_o is the tube outside diameter [m], and N_t is the number of tubes.

3.3 Correction factor

In design the heat exchangers, a correction factor is applied to the log mean temperature difference (LMTD) to allow for the departure from true countercurrent flow to determine the true temperature difference. The correction factor *F* for a multi-pass and crossflow heat exchanger and given for a two-pass shell-and-tube heat exchangers is calculated by (Kara & Güraras, 2004):

$$F = \frac{\sqrt{R^2+1}\ln(\frac{1-P}{1-PR})}{(R-1)\ln\{[\frac{2-P(R+1-\sqrt{R^2+1}}{2-P(R+1+\sqrt{R^2+1})}]\}} \tag{7a}$$

and

$$P = \frac{(T_{co}-T_{ci})}{(T_{hi}-T_{ci})} \tag{7b}$$

$$R = \frac{(T_{hi}-T_{ho})}{(T_{co}-T_{ci})} \tag{7c}$$

where P is the thermal effectiveness, and R is the heat capacity flow-rate ratio. The value of correction factor for a condenser is 1, regardless of the configuration of the heat exchanger (Hewitt, 1998).

3.4 Log-mean temperature difference

The log mean temperature difference ΔT_m for countercurrent flow is determined by:

$$\Delta T_m = \frac{(T_{hi}-T_{co})-(T_{ho}-T_{ci})}{\ln\frac{T_{hi}-T_{co}}{T_{ho}-T_{ci}}} \tag{8}$$

where T_{hi} and T_{ho} are, respectively, the inlet and outlet temperature for hot fluid, T_{ci} and T_{co} are the inlet and outlet temperature for cool fluid, respectively.

3.5 Overall heat transfer coefficient

Overall heat transfer coefficient *U* depends on the tube inside diameter, tube outside diameter, tube side convective coefficient, shell side convective coefficient, tube side fouling resistance, shell side fouling resistance, and tube material, which is given by (Kara & Güraras, 2004):

$$U = \frac{1}{\frac{1}{h_s}+\frac{d_o\ln(\frac{d_o}{d_i})}{2k_m}+R_{fo}+\frac{d_o}{d_i}(R_{fi}+\frac{1}{h_t})} \tag{9}$$

where h_s is the shell-side heat transfer coefficient [W/m²K], h_t is the tube-side heat transfer coefficient [W/m²K], d_i and d_o are, respectively, the inside and outside diameters of tubes

[m], k_m is the thermal conductivity [W/mK], R_{fi} and R_{fo} are the tube-side and shell-side fouling resistances [m^{2}K/W], respectively.

3.6 Shell-side heat transfer coefficient in single phase flow

In this work, the shell-side heat transfer coefficient h_s in single phase flow is given by (Kern, 1950):

$$Nu_s = \frac{h_s D_e}{k_s} = 0.36 \mathrm{Re}_s^{0.55} \mathrm{Pr}_s^{1/3} (\frac{\mu_s}{\mu_{wts}})^{0.14} \quad (10)$$

and

$$\mathrm{Re}_s = \frac{\dot{m}_s D_e}{A_s \mu_s} \quad (11)$$

$$D_e = \frac{4[0.86 P_T^2 - (\frac{\pi d_o^2}{4})]}{\pi d_o} \quad \text{for triangular pitch} \quad (12)$$

$$A_s = D_i B(1 - \frac{d_o}{P_T}) \quad (13)$$

$$\mathrm{Pr}_s = \frac{\mu_s c_{ps}}{k_s} \quad (14)$$

where D_e is the hydraulic diameter [m], $\dot{m}_s$ is the mass flow rate of refrigerant [kg/s], μ_s is dynamic viscosity [Pa-s], μ_{wts} is wall dynamic viscosity [Pa-s], d_o is the tube outside diameter[m], P_T is the tube pitch[m], As is the shell-side pass area [m^2], Di is inside diameter [m], B is the baffles spacing [m], cps is the specific heat [kJ/kgK], and k_s is the thermal conductivity [W/mK].

3.7 Shell-side heat transfer coefficient in condensation flow

The average heat transfer coefficient h_s for horizontal condensation outside a single tube is given by the equation (Edwards, 2008):

$$h_s = C[\frac{k_f^3 \rho_f^2 g h_{fg}}{\mu_f d_o \Delta T_f}]^{0.25} \quad (15a)$$

where C=0.943, k_f is the film thermal conductivity [W/mK], ρ_f is the film density [kg/m^3], μ_f is the film dynamic viscosity[Pa s], h_{fg} is the latent heat of vaporization [J/kg], g is gravitational acceleration [m/s^2], d_o is the tube outside diameter[m], ΔT_f is the film temperature difference[°C].

For a bundle of N_t tubes, the heat transfer coefficient can be modified by the Eissenberg expression as following (Kakac & Liu, 2002):

$$\frac{h_N}{h_1} = 0.60 + 0.42 N^{-1/4} \quad (15b)$$

where hN is the average heat transfer coefficient for a vertical column of N tubes, and h_1 is the heat transfer coefficient of the top tube in the row.

3.8 Tube-side heat transfer coefficient

According to flow regime, the tube-side heat transfer coefficient h_t can be computed by following relations (Patel & Rao, 2010):

$$Nu_t = \frac{h_t d_i}{k_t} = [3.657 + \frac{0.0677(\mathrm{Re}_t \mathrm{Pr}_t \frac{d_i}{L})^{1.33}}{1 + 0.1\mathrm{Pr}_t (\mathrm{Re}_t \frac{d_i}{L})^{0.3}}] \quad \text{for } Re_t < 2300 \tag{16}$$

$$Nu_t = \frac{h_t d_i}{k_t} = \{\frac{\frac{f_t}{8}(\mathrm{Re}_t - 1000)\mathrm{Pr}_t}{1 + 12.7\sqrt{\frac{f_t}{8}}(\mathrm{Pr}_t^{0.67} - 1)}[1 + (\frac{d_i}{L})^{0.67}]\} \quad \text{for } 2300 < Re_t < 10000 \tag{17}$$

$$Nu_t = \frac{h_t d_o}{k_t} = 0.027\mathrm{Re}_t^{0.8}\mathrm{Pr}_t^{1/3}(\frac{\mu_t}{\mu_{wt}})^{0.14} \quad \text{for } Re_t > 10000 \tag{18}$$

and

$$\mathrm{Re}_t = \frac{\rho_t v_t d_i}{\mu_t} \tag{19}$$

$$v_t = \frac{\dot{m}_t}{\frac{\pi d_o^2}{4}\rho_t}\frac{n_p}{N_t} \tag{20}$$

$$\mathrm{Pr}_t = \frac{\mu_t c_{pt}}{k_t} \tag{21}$$

$$f_t = (1.82\log_{10}\mathrm{Re}_t - 1.64)^{-2} \tag{22}$$

where Nu_t is tube-side Nusselt number, Re_t is tube-side Reynolds number, Pr_t is tube-side Prandtl number, k_t is the thermal conductivity [W/mK], d_i is the tube inside diameter[m], L is tube length[m], v_t is tube-side fluid velocity [m/s], $\dot{m}_t$ is tube-side mass flow rate[kg/s], d_o is tube outside length [m], ρ_t is tube-side density [kg/m³], n_p is number of tube passes, N_t is number of tubes, μ_t is viscosity at tube wall temperature [Pa-s], μ_{wt} is viscosity at core flow temperature [Pa-s], f_t is Darcy friction factor (Hewitt, 1998).

3.9 Coefficient of variation of root-mean-square error

This study uses the coefficient of variation of root-mean-square error (CV) to indicate how well the model predicting value fits the experimental data, defined as follows:

$$CV = \frac{\sqrt{\frac{\sum_{i=1}^{n}(y_i - x_i)^2}{n}}}{\left|\frac{\sum_{i=1}^{n} y_i}{n}\right|} \times 100\% \tag{23}$$

where x_i is the predicting value by present model, y_i is experimental data, and n is the number of experimental data set.

3.10 Solution procedures

According to the configuration of the horizontal baffles in the heat exchanger, the condenser can be separate into two regions, Section-I and II, as indicated in Figure 2-4. Section-I has three tube passes and two horizontal baffles, while Section-II has nine tube passes without any horizontal baffle. In Section-I, both water and refrigerant are in single phase. The temperature variations of the refrigerant and water streams are shown in Figure 4. In the interface between Section-I and II, the entering water temperature T_w and the leaving refrigerant temperature Tr should be determined by iteration method.

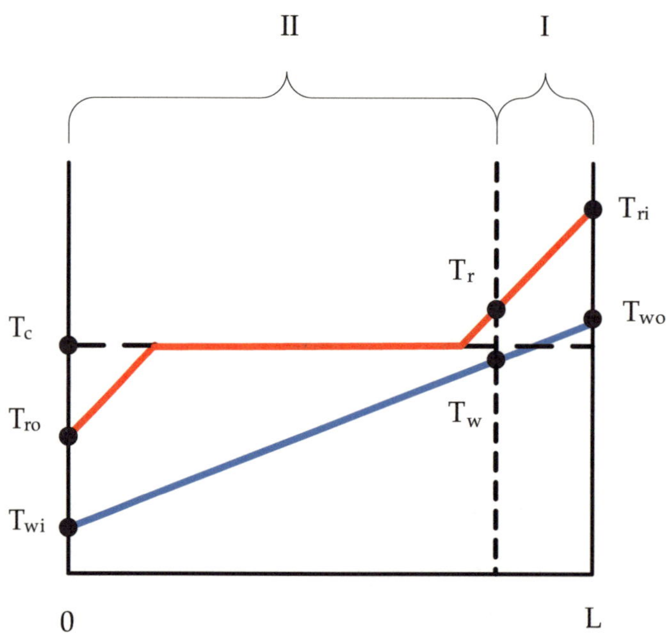

Fig. 4. Temperature variations of two steams in the condenser

The total heat transfer rate of the condenser is the sum of individual heat transfer rate of the two sections.

$$\dot{Q}_{Model} = \dot{Q}_{Model,I} + \dot{Q}_{Model,II} \tag{24}$$

where $\dot{Q}_{Model,I}$ and $\dot{Q}_{Model,II}$ represent the heat transfer rate in Section-I and II, respectively, and can be determined as following equations.

$$\dot{Q}_{Model,I} = (U_{Model} AF\Delta T_m)_I \tag{25}$$

$$\dot{Q}_{Model,II} = (U_{Model} AF\Delta T_m)_{II} \tag{26}$$

The overall heat transfer coefficient for the two sections can be calculated by

$$U_{Model,I} = \frac{1}{\frac{1}{h_{s,I}} + \frac{d_o \ln(\frac{d_o}{d_i})}{2k_m} + R_{fo} + \frac{d_o}{d_i}(R_{fi} + \frac{1}{h_t})} \tag{27}$$

$$U_{Model,II} = \frac{1}{\frac{1}{h_{s,II}} + \frac{d_o \ln(\frac{d_o}{d_i})}{2k_m} + R_{fo} + \frac{d_o}{d_i}(R_{fi} + \frac{1}{h_t})} \tag{28}$$

The heat transfer areas for the two sections can be calculated as

$$A_I = L\pi d_o N_{t,I} \tag{29}$$

$$A_{II} = L\pi d_o N_{t,II} \tag{30}$$

The tube-side heat transfer rates for Section-I and II are:

$$\dot{Q}_w = \dot{Q}_{w,I} + \dot{Q}_{w,II} \tag{31}$$

$$\dot{Q}_{w,I} = \dot{Q}_{r,I} = \dot{m}_r (h_{ri} - h_r) = (U_{Exp} A\Delta T_m)_I \tag{32}$$

$$T_w = T_{wo} - \frac{\dot{Q}_{w,I}}{\dot{m}_w c_{pw}} \tag{33}$$

$$\dot{Q}_{w,II} = \dot{m}_w c_{pw} (T_w - T_{wi}) = (U_{Exp} A\Delta T_m)_{II} \tag{34}$$

where the log mean temperature difference for Section-I and II can be determined by:

$$\Delta T_{m,I} = \frac{(T_{ri} - T_{wo}) - (T_r - T_w)}{\ln(\frac{T_{ri} - T_{wo}}{T_r - T_w})} \tag{35}$$

$$\Delta T_{m,II} = \frac{(T_r - T_w) - (T_{ro} - T_{wi})}{\ln(\frac{T_r - T_w}{T_{ro} - T_{wi}})} \tag{36}$$

The present modeling procedures for determining the total heat transfer rate are shown as Fig. 5 and detailed as following steps:

1. Input design parameters and geometry factors:
   Design parameters include the refrigerant inlet and outlet temperatures (T_{ri}, T_{ro}), the refrigerant inlet pressure P_{ri}, the water inlet and outlet temperatures (T_{wi}, T_{wo}), the water and refrigerant mass flow rate ($\dot{m}_w$, $\dot{m}_r$), the condensing temperature T_c, and the number of tubes N_t. Geometry factors include the tube inside and outside diameters (d_i, d_o), the shell inside diameter D_i, the baffles distance B, the tube pitch P_T, and the tube length L.
2. Initial guess a shell-side outlet temperature (T_r) for Section-I.
3. Determine relative physical quantities for Section-I:
   The physical quantities include the heat transfer areas, the shell-side hydraulic diameter, the tube-side fluid velocity, the Reynolds numbers, the tube- and shell-side heat transfer coefficients, overall heat transfer coefficient, log mean temperature difference, the heat transfer rate ($\dot{Q}_{w,I}$) computed from water-side data and the heat transfer rate ($\dot{Q}_{Model,I}$) predicting by present model.
4. If the percent error $\left|\frac{Q_{w,I} - Q_{Model,I}}{Q_{w,I}}\right|$ <0.01%, then output T_r, T_w, $\dot{Q}_{Model,I}$ and $\dot{Q}_{w,I}$ and go to step 5. If not, gives a new shell-side outlet temperature and goes back to step 2. Iteration of the previous steps until the relative error is within the value of 0.01%.
5. Determine relative physical quantities for Section-II:
   The relative physical quantities needing to determine in the section include the heat transfer area (A_{II}), the shell-side heat transfer coefficient ($h_{s,II}$), the overall heat transfer coefficient ($U_{Model,II}$), the log mean temperature difference ($\Delta T_{m,II}$), the heat transfer rate ($\dot{Q}_{w,II}$) computing from water-side data, and the heat transfer rate ($\dot{Q}_{Model,II}$) predicting by present model.
6. Compute total heat transfer rate by water-side data ($\dot{Q}_w$) and present model ($\dot{Q}_{Model}$)
7. Output calculation results.

4. Results and discussions

A shell-and-tube condenser designed for moderately high-temperature heat pump system were built and tested in this study. Twenty-seven sets of experiment results are shown in Table 1.

By observing the data listed in Table 1, we found that, except for the data set 2-5, the water outlet temperature is higher than the condensing temperature for most data sets. These results were in line with our expectations. This is because that at the beginning of design stage, in order to effectively recover the sensible heat from superheating vapour at refrigerant-side inlet of the condenser, two horizontal baffles were placed on the refrigerant-side to extend the contact time between the refrigerant and the water.

The new shell-and-tube condenser has divided into two sections, according to whether or not the refrigerant-side has placed horizontal baffles, as shown in Figure 2. By using the theoretical model and solution procedure introduced previously, numerical simulation of heat transfer behaviour was carried out for Section-I first and then for Section-II. After substituting the same conditions similar to the 27 sets of experiments, the preliminary comparison of the simulated and the experimental results are shown in Figure 6a and Figure 6b.

Examining Figure 6a showed that the simulation results for the Section-I of condenser are very close to the deduced results from the experiment. This is because in the Section-I iteration process solving the heat transfer rates for refrigerant- and the water-side, the convergence constrain was set within 0.01% in order to meet energy conservation requirements.

The output results from Section-I calculation were set as the input data for the following Section-II calculation. The computation results for the Section-II calculation were compared to the deduced results from Eq. (34), and the difference between the two results is shown in Figure 6b, the CV value of Section-II is 23.01%.

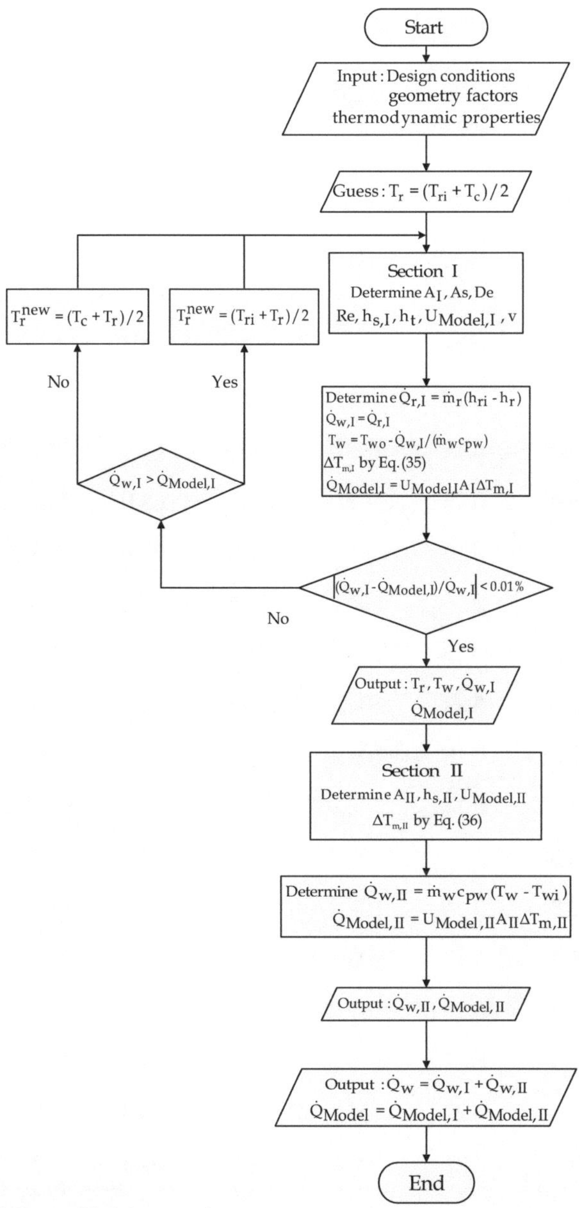

Fig. 5. Algorithm of the model

Case	T_{wi} (°C)	T_{wo} (°C)	$\dot{m}_w$ (kg/s)	T_{ri} (°C)	P_{ri} (MPa)	T_{ro} (°C)	T_c (°C)	$\dot{m}_r$ (kg/s)	$\dot{Q}_H$ (kW)
1	24.9	74.9	0.16	100.4	2.20	64.3	71.8	0.19	33.4
2	25.0	45.1	0.41	70.5	1.20	39.1	46.2	0.18	35.0
3	25.1	45.4	0.48	71.9	1.22	39.7	47.0	0.21	40.8
4	24.9	55.1	0.27	80.2	1.50	46.6	55.2	0.18	34.6
5	25.1	55.1	0.33	79.4	1.53	47.6	55.9	0.22	41.3
6	25.0	64.9	0.20	91.0	1.84	53.6	63.7	0.18	34.1
7	25.1	65.1	0.24	89.0	1.88	57.0	64.7	0.23	40.4
8	24.9	70.7	0.16	97.1	2.09	59.1	69.4	0.17	30.5
9	25.0	73.7	0.16	97.3	2.23	64.4	72.2	0.19	32.4
10	25.0	74.0	0.16	98.0	2.22	63.7	72.1	0.19	32.7
11	25.1	75.0	0.18	99.3	2.26	67.1	72.9	0.23	38.8
12	25.1	75.1	0.18	99.2	2.24	71.1	72.5	0.24	38.1
13	24.9	75.2	0.16	100.5	2.22	64.5	72.1	0.19	33.6
14	24.9	75.4	0.16	102.9	2.23	61.0	72.2	0.19	33.9
15	25.1	75.4	0.18	99.3	2.25	71.0	72.8	0.24	38.3
16	25.2	78.3	0.16	104.0	2.34	68.4	74.5	0.21	35.5
17	25.1	78.8	0.18	103.7	2.43	73.1	76.2	0.25	40.4
18	25.0	80.0	0.19	104.1	2.47	73.8	76.9	0.28	44.7
19	25.1	80.6	0.18	103.4	2.49	74.8	77.3	0.27	41.4
20	25.1	84.8	0.14	106.9	2.65	78.0	80.2	0.24	35.6
21	24.9	85.0	0.12	108.2	2.63	73.9	79.8	0.20	31.8
22	34.9	84.3	0.16	107.4	2.62	77.8	79.8	0.22	32.9
23	35.0	85.5	0.18	108.5	2.71	78.7	81.4	0.25	38.3
24	35.1	85.1	0.19	109.5	2.70	78.5	81.0	0.27	40.7
25	35.1	85.1	0.17	109.0	2.69	79.0	81.0	0.25	37.0
26	39.9	75.2	0.22	104.3	2.26	63.5	72.9	0.19	33.1
27	40.1	75.3	0.25	100.9	2.31	69.3	73.9	0.23	38.0

Table 1. Experimental results

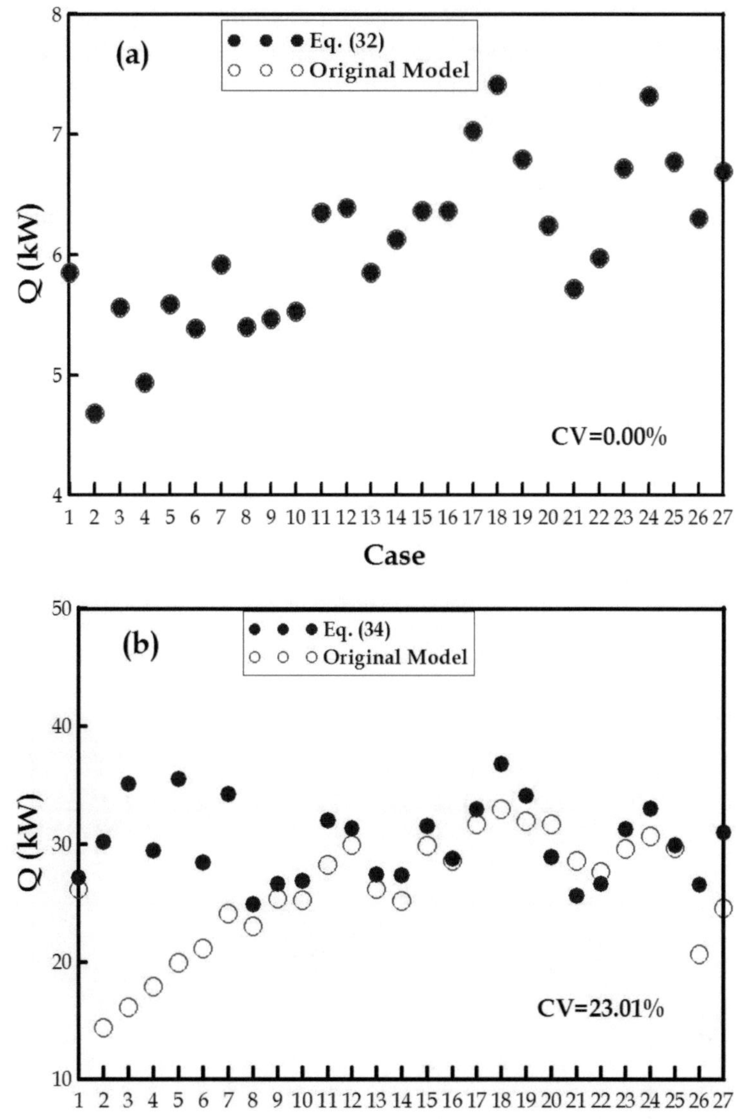

Fig. 6. The computation results of heat transfer rate for (a) Section-I and (b) Section-II

From Figure 7a and Figure 7b, the difference from data sets numbered 2-7 and 26-27 are greater than 10%, the percent error for the rest data sets are all within 10%. Table 1 also showed that, as compared with the other data sets, these eight cases with larger difference occurred when changing water outlet temperature and mass flow rate. We know from the theoretical model that the major variables of heat transfer rate of condenser include water inlet/outlet temperatures, water mass flow rate, and overall heat transfer coefficient U. Among them, the overall heat transfer coefficient is influenced by the tube-side as well as the shell-side heat transfer coefficients. The change in tube-side heat transfer coefficient is mainly due to the effect of water flow rate, while the shell-side heat transfer coefficient is influenced by the flow characteristic of refrigerant and tube arrangement in the condenser, which make the actual heat transfer behaviour much complex and difficult to accurately predict. Thus, observation of the effect of operating parameters on the overall heat transfer coefficient, establishment of a rule governing the overall heat transfer coefficient of the changing parameters, and the establishment of a modified correlation of heat transfer coefficient can all help increase the prediction accuracy of the model for heat transfer rate. Since in this study the hot water inlet temperature was almost constant, thus the operating parameters to be discussed include water outlet temperature (T_{wo}), and water mass flow-rate ($\dot{m}_w$).

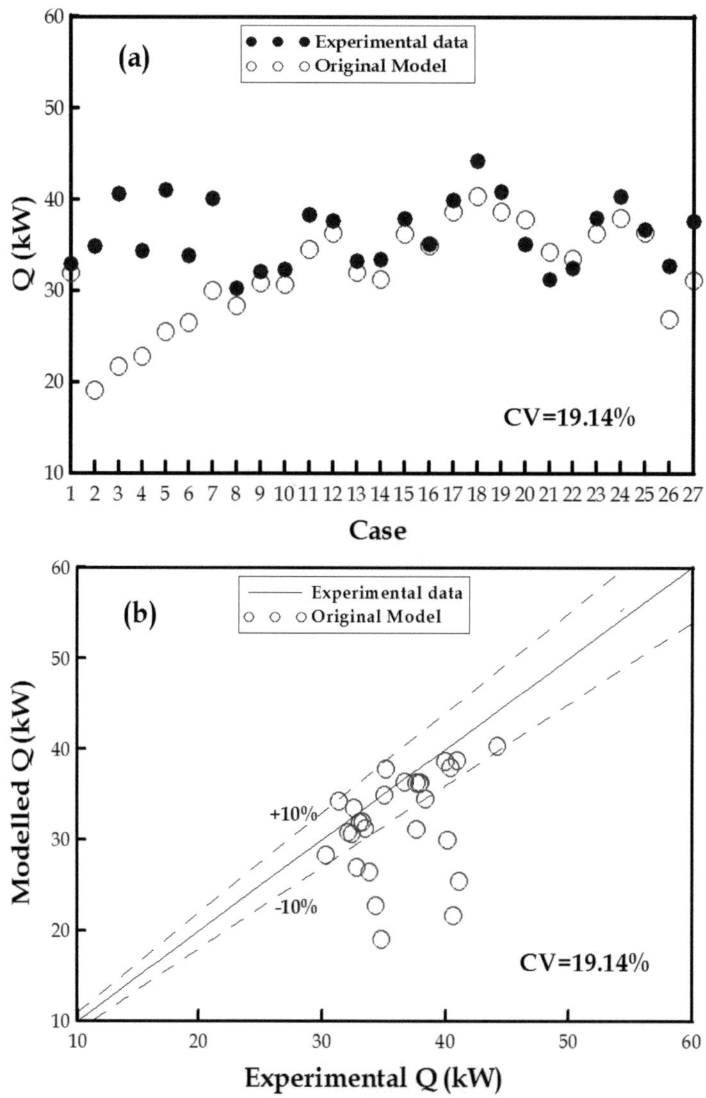

Fig. 7. (a) Comparison between the simulation results and the experimental data, (b) relative error analysis for overall heat transfer rate

As the water outlet temperature changes due to various physical parameters such as water mass flow rate, the ratio of the model predicted to experimental data for the overall heat transfer coefficient at Section-II, $U_{model,II}/U_{exp,II}$, is depicted in Figure 8.

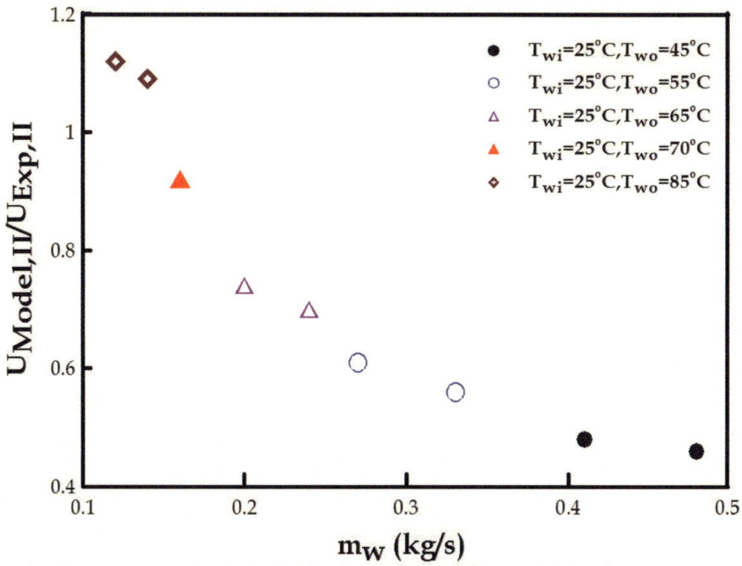

Fig. 8. Variation of the ratio of overall heat transfer coefficient with water mass flow rate under various water outlet temperatures

Figure 8 clearly shows that when the hot water outlet temperature is higher, or when the hot water mass flow rate is lower, the ratio of $U_{Model,II}/U_{exp,II}$ becomes larger. This means that as the hot water outlet temperature becomes higher, or when the hot water mass flow rate becomes lower, the simulated value of the overall heat transfer coefficient will change as a result. From this, we can learn that any change in the overall heat transfer coefficient at Section-II has to be related to these two physical parameters. Therefore, modification of the relationship between the overall heat transfer coefficients before and after the change in hot water outlet temperature can be expressed as a function of hot water outlet water temperature and mass flow rate, as Eq. (37) shows:

$$U'_{Model,II} = (c_0 + c_1 T_{wo} + c_2 \dot{m}_w + c_3 T_{wo} \dot{m}_w + c_4 T_{wo}^2 + c_5 \dot{m}_w^2) U_{Model,II} \tag{37}$$

The fitting coefficients in the equation were respectively calculated, using least square regression method, as c_o= 3.47931, c_1= -0.06503, c_2= 2.39712, c_3= 0.018492, c_4= 0.000340667, and c_5= -2.68725.

The modified overall heat transfer coefficient was used to simulate heat transfer rate for condenser. The comparison of model predicting results versus experimental results, and the relative errors are shown in Figure 9a and 9b, respectively.

Using experimental data as a benchmark, the pre-revision calculation error derived from the heat transfer rate prediction model was 19.14 %, but post-revision calculation error dropped significantly to 2.03 %, indicating that the revision function in Eq. (37) is indeed feasible. Therefore, our study will use the current revision model with modified overall heat transfer coefficient for follow-up research with regard to sizing and performance ratings.

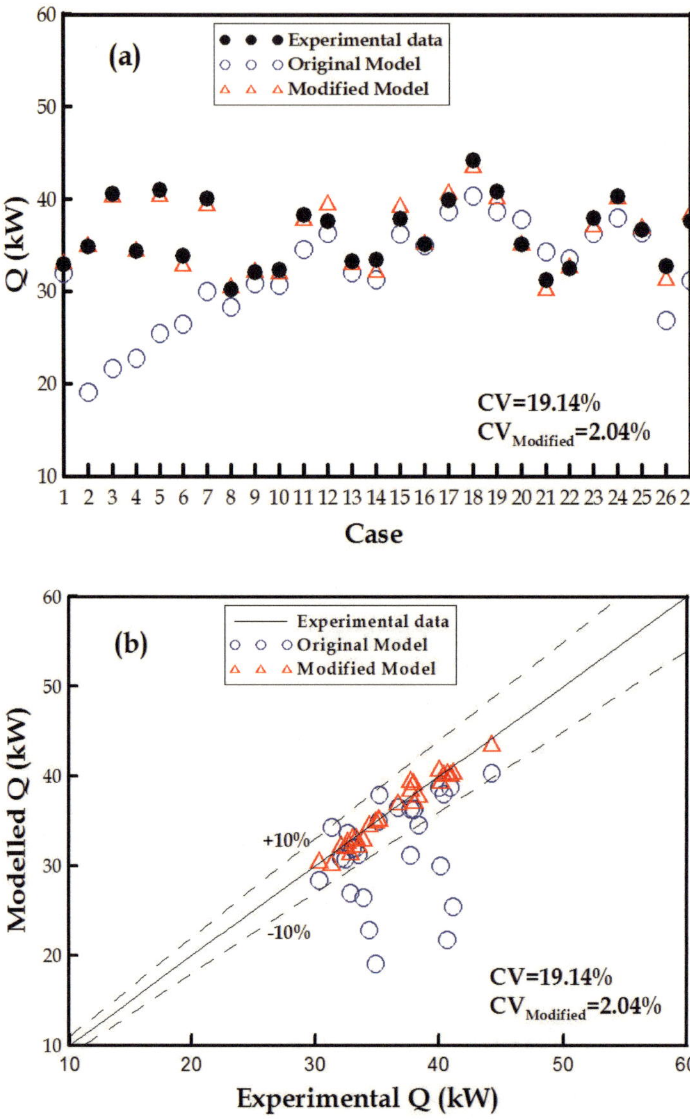

Fig. 9. (a) Comparison between the experimental data and the simulation results by either modified or original models, (b) relative error analysis for overall heat transfer rate

5. Cases study

5.1 Sizing problem (Estimation of unit size)

Sizing is to estimate the tube length for a heat exchanger by present model when the inlet/outlet conditions on the refrigerant side, the inlet/outlet conditions on the hot water side, and the diameter of the heat exchanger are known.

The estimation procedures for sizing a shell-and-tube condenser is shown as follows:

- Input design parameters:
- Input design parameters include: refrigerant inlet/outlet temperatures, refrigerant inlet pressure, water inlet/outlet temperatures, water and refrigerant mass flow rates, condensing temperature, number of copper tubes, tube inner/outer diameters, shell inner diameter, baffle spacing, and copper tube spacing.
- Give a tube length and shell-side outlet temperature to be initial guess values for Section-I calculation.
- Calculate the physical properties for Section-I and Section-II.
- Calculate the overall heat transfer rates by present model.
- Check the percent error between model predicting and experimental data for overall heat transfer rates. If the percent error is less than the value of 0.01%, then output the tube length and end the estimation process; if it is larger than the percent error, then set a new value for *L* and return to the second step.

In accordance with the above estimation procedures, the resulting length is 0.694 m when input the experimental data set, Case 1, as the design parameters for sizing. The same estimation procedures are utilizing to another 26 cases, and the results are shown in Figure 10.

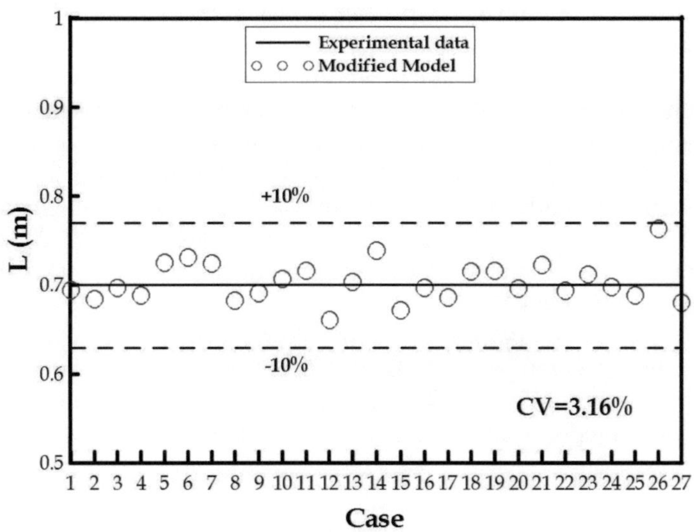

Fig. 10. Estimation results for sizing condensers

Comparisons between the estimating values length for all the cases and the experimental data (0.7 m) indicats that the relative error were within ± 10 % with an average CV value of 3.16 %. In summary, the results from the application of present model on heat exchanger sizing calculation are satisfactory.

5.2 Rating problem (Estimation of thermal performance)

For performance rating procedure, all the geometrical parameters must be determined as the input into the heat transfer correlations. When the condenser is available, then all the geometrical parameters are also known. In the rating process, the basic calculation is the

calculations of heat transfer coefficient for both shell- and refrigerant-side stream. If the condenser's refrigerant inlet temperature and pressure, water inlet temperature, hot water and refrigerant mass flow rates, and tube size are specified, then the condenser's water outlet temperature, refrigerant outlet temperature, and heat transfer rate can be estimated.
The estimation process for rating a condenser:

- Input design parameters:
  The input design parameters include: refrigerant inlet/outlet temperatures, refrigerant inlet pressure, water inlet temperature, mass flow rate of hot water/refrigerant, and geometric conditions.
- Give a refrigerant outlet temperature as an initial guess for computing the hot water outlet temperature: $T_{wo} = T_{wi} + \dfrac{\dot{Q}_w}{\dot{m}_w C_{pw}}$.
- Give an outlet temperature (T_r) as an initial guess for Section-I.
- Calculate the properties for Section-I and Section-II.
- Calculate the overall heat transfer rates by present model.
- Check the percent error between model predicting and experimental data for overall heat transfer rates. If the percent error is less than the value of 0.01%, then output the refrigerant outlet temperature, water outlet temperature, and heat transfer rate; if it is larger than the percent error, then reset a new refrigerant outlet temperature, and return to the second step.

In accordance with the above calculation process, the experimental data of Case 1 can be used as input into the present model for rating calculations. The calculation results give the water outlet temperature is 74.84°C, refrigerant outlet temperature is 64.35°C, and heat transfer rate was is 33.01 kW. Experimental data of Case 2 were used as input into the rating calculation process, and another set of result tell: water outlet water temperature is 45.16 °C, refrigerant outlet temperature is 39.04 °C, and heat transfer rate is 35.03 kW. Repeat the same procedures for the remaining 26 sets of experimental data, the calculation results for rating are displayed in Figures 11.
As depicted in Figure 11, comparison of the model predicting and the experimental data for water outlet temperature, refrigerant outlet temperature and heat transfer rates show that the average CV values are 0.63%, 0.36%, and 1.02% respectively. In summary, the predicting accuracies of present model on shell-and-tube condenser have satisfactory results.

6. Conclusion

This study investigated the modelling and simulation of thermal performance for a shell-and-tube condenser with longitude baffles, designed for a moderately high-temperature heat pump. Through the validation of experimental data, a heat transfer model for predicting heat transfer rate of condenser was developed, and then used to carry out size estimation and performance rating of the shell-and-tube condenser for cases study. In summary, the following conclusions were obtained:

- A model for calculation, size estimation, and performance rating of the shell-and-tube condenser has been developed, varified, and modified. A good agreement is observed between the computed values and the experimental data.
- In applying the present model, the average deviations (CV) is within 3.16% for size estimation, and is within 1.02% for performance rating.

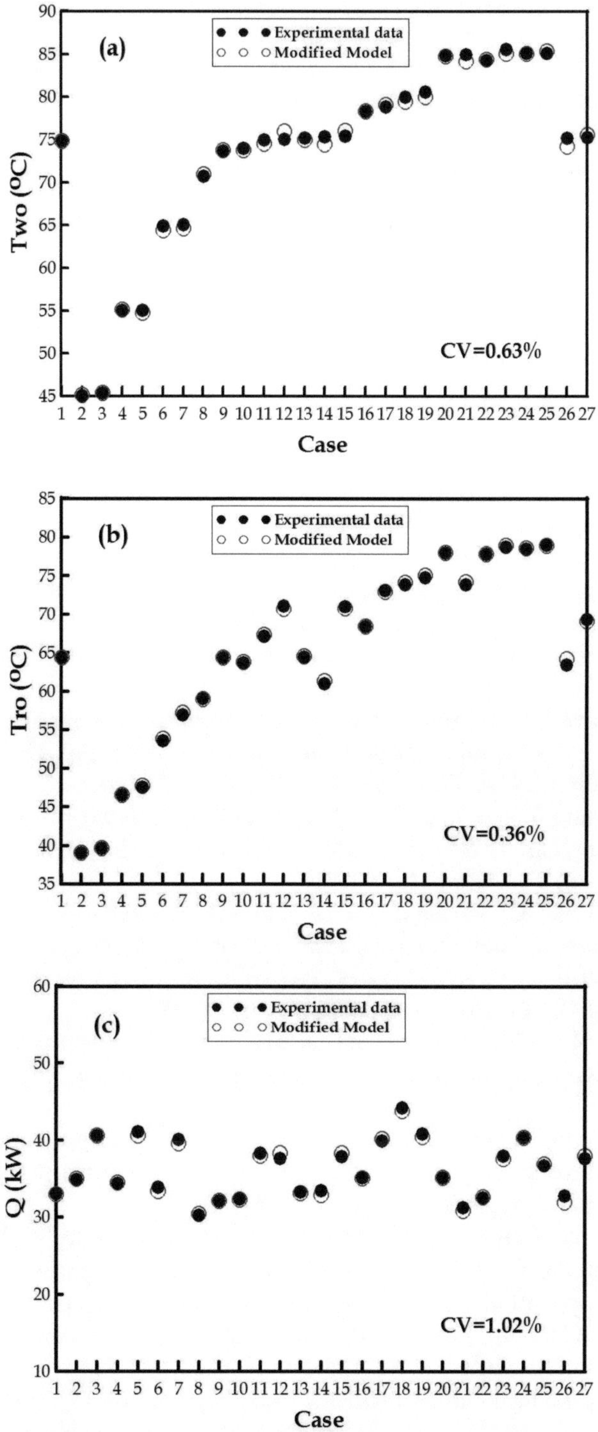

Fig. 11. Simulation results of rating condensers for (a) water outlet temperature, (b) refrigerant outlet temperature, and (c) heat transfer rate

7. References

Allen, B., & Gosselin, L. (2008). Optimal geometry and flow arrangement for minimizing the cost of shell-and-tube condensers. *International Journal of Energy Research,* Vol. 32, pp. 958-969.

Caputo, A.C., Pelagagge, P.M., & Salini, P. (2008). Heat exchanger design based on economic optimisation. *Applied Thermal Engineering,*Vol. 28, pp. 1151–1159.

Edwards, J.E. (2008). *Design and Rating Shell and Tube Heat Exchangers,* P & I Design Ltd, Retrieved from <www.pidesign.co.uk>.

Ghorbani, N., Taherian, H., Gorji, M., & Mirgolbabaei, H. (2010). An experimental study of thermal performance of shell-and-coil heat exchangers. *International communications in Heat and Mass Transfer,* Vol. 37, pp. 775-781.

Hewitt, G.F. (1998). *Heat Exchanger Design Handbook,* ISBN 1-56700-097-5, Begell House, New York.

Holman, J.P. (2000). *Heat Transfer,* ISBN 957-493-199-4, McGraw-Hill, New York.

Kakac, S., & Liu, H. (2002). Design correlations for condensers and Evaporators, In:Heat Exchangers, pp. 229-236, CRC press, ISBN 0-8493-0902-6, United Ststes of America.

Kara, Y.A., & Güraras, Ö. (2004). A computer program for designing of shell-and-tube heat exchangers. *Applied Thermal Engineering,* Vol. 24, pp. 1797-1805.

Karlsson, T., & Vamling, L. (2005). Flow fields in shell-and-tube condensers: comparison of a pure refrigerant and a binary mixture. *International Journal of Refrigeration* , Vol. 28, pp. 706-713.

Karno, A., & Ajib, S. (2006). Effect of tube pitch on heat transfer in shell-and-tube heat exchangers—new simulation software. *Springer-Verlag,* Vol. 42, pp. 263-270.

Kern, D.Q. (1950). *Process Heat Transfer,* ISBN 0070341907, McGraw-Hill, New York.

Li, Y., Jiang, X., Huang, X., Jia, J., & Tong, J. (2010). Optimization of high-pressure shell-and-tube heat exchanger for syngas cooling in an IGCC. *International Journal of Heat and Mass Transfer,* Vol. 53, pp. 4543-4551.

Moita, R.D., Fernandes, C., Matos, H.A., & Nunes, C.P. (2004). A Cost-Based Strategy to Design Multiple Shell and Tube Heat Exchangers. *Journal of Heat Transfer,* Vol. 126, pp. 119-130.

NIST. (2007). REFPROP, In: *The United States of America,* 2007.

Patel, V.K., & Rao, R.V. (2010). Design optimization of shell-and-tube heat exchanger using particle swarm optimization technique. *Applied Thermal Engineering,* Vol. 30, pp. 1417-1425.

Selbas, R., Kızılkan, Ö., & Reppich, M. (2006). A new design approach for shell-and-tube heat exchangers using genetic algorithms from economic point of view. *Chemical Engineering and Processing,* Vol. 45, pp. 268-275.

Vera-García, F., García-Cascales, J.R., Gonzálvez-Maciá, J., Cabello, R., Llopis, R., Sanchez, D., & Torrella, E. (2010). A simplified model for shell-and-tubes heat exchangers: Practical application. *Applied Thermal Engineering,* Vol. 30, pp. 1231-1241.

Wang, Q.W., Chen, G.D., Xu, J., & Ji, Y.P. (2010). Second-Law Thermodynamic Comparison and Maximal Velocity Ratio Design of Shell-and-Tube Heat Exchangers with Continuous Helical Baffles. *Journal of Heat Transfer,* Vol. 132, pp. 1-9.

4

Simulation of Rarefied Gas Between Coaxial Circular Cylinders by DSMC Method

H. Ghezel Sofloo
Department of Aerospace Engineering, K.N.Toosi University of Technology, Tehran Iran

1. Introduction

In every system, if Knudsen number is larger than 0.1, the Navier-Stokes equation will not be satisfied for investigation of flow patterns. In this condition, the Boltzmann equation, presented by Ludwig Boltzmann in 1872, can be useful. The conditions that this equation can be used were investigted by Cercignani in 1969. The most successful method for solving Boltzmann equation for a rarefied gas system is Direct Simulation Monte Carlo (DSMC) method. This method was suggested by Bird in 1974. The cylindrical Couette flow and occurrence of secondry flow (Taylor vortex flow) in a annular domin of two coaxial rotating cylinders is a classical problem in fluid mechanics. Because this type of gas flow can occur in many industrial types of equipment used in chemical industries, Chemical engineers are interested in this problem. In 2000, De and Marino studied the effect of Knudsen number on flow patterns and in 2006 the effect of temperature gradient between two cylinders was investigated by Yoshio and his co-workers. The aim of the present paper is investigation of understanding of the effect of different conditions of rotation of the cylinders on the vortex flow and flow patterns.

2. Mathematical model

In the Boltzmann equation, the independent variable is the proption of molecules that are in a specific situation and dependent variables are time, velocity components and molecules positions. We consider the Boltzmann equation as follow:

$$\frac{\delta f}{\delta t}+\bar{v}.\frac{\delta f}{\delta \bar{x}}+\bar{F}.\frac{\delta f}{\delta \bar{v}}=\frac{1}{Kn}Q(f,f) \tag{1}$$

The bilinear collision operator, Q(f,f), describes the binary collosion of the particles and is given by:

$$Q(f,f)=\iint_{R^3 S^2}\sigma(\left|\bar{v}-\bar{v}_*\right|,\omega)(f'\,f'_*-ff_*)d\omega dv_* \tag{2}$$

Where, w is a unit vector of the shere S^2, so w is an element of the area of the surface of the unit sphere S^2 in R^3. With using this assumption that $\vec{f}$ is zero, we can rewrite equation 2 as:

$$Q(f,f)=\int_{R^3}\int_{S^2}\sigma(|\vec{v}-\vec{v}_*|,\omega)f'\,f'_*d\omega d\vec{v}_*-\int_{R^3}\int_{S^2}\sigma(|\vec{v}-\vec{v}_*|,\omega)ff_*d\omega d\vec{v}_* \quad (3)$$

The sign $'$ is refered to values of distribution function after collision. The value of above integral is not related on $\vec{V}$, then we have

$$Q(f,f)=\int_{R^3}\int_{S^2}\sigma(|\vec{v}-\vec{v}_*|,\omega)f'\,f'_*d\omega d\vec{v}_*-f\int_{R^3}\int_{S^2}\sigma(|\vec{v}-\vec{v}_*|,\omega)f_*d\omega d\vec{v}_* \quad (4)$$

Inasmuch as the values of distribution function depend on its value before collision, we have:

$$Q(f,f)=P(f,f)-f\mu(\vec{v}) \quad (5)$$

Where $\mu(\vec{v})$ is the mean value of the collision of the particles that move with $\vec{v}$ velocity. Then we can estimate $\mu(\vec{v})$ as

$$\mu(\vec{v})=\mu=\frac{\kappa p}{m} \quad (6)$$

Then the Boltzmann equation can be written as

$$\frac{\delta f}{\delta t}+\vec{v}.\frac{\delta f}{\delta \vec{x}}=\frac{1}{Kn}\left[P(f,f)-f\mu(\vec{v})\right] \quad (7)$$

For solving this equation, we use fractional step method, so we have

$$\frac{\delta f}{\delta t}=-\vec{v}.\frac{\delta f}{\delta \vec{x}} \quad (8)$$

$$\frac{\delta f}{\delta t}=\frac{1}{Kn}Q(f,f)=\frac{1}{Kn}\left[P(f,f)-f\mu(\vec{v})\right] \quad (9)$$

Equation 8 describes the movement of the particles and equation 9 explains the collision of the particles. For estimation of new position of a mobile particle, we use following realationship

$$\vec{x}^{new}=\vec{x}^{old}+\vec{v}.\Delta t \quad (10)$$

For solving equation 9 by a numerical method, we can write it as

$$\frac{f^{n+1}-f^n}{\Delta t}=\frac{1}{Kn}\left[P(f^n,f^n)-\mu f^n\right] \quad (11)$$

If we rearrange it, we will have

$$f^{n+1}=\frac{\mu\Delta t}{Kn}.\frac{P(f^n,f^n)}{\mu}+(1-\frac{\mu\Delta t}{Kn})f^n \quad (12)$$

The first term on the right side of Eq. (12) is refered to probability of collision and the second term is refred to situation that no collision occurs.

Equation (12) is solved using the DSMC method. DSMC is a molecule-based statistical simulation method for rarefied gas introduced by Bird (2). It is a numerical solution method to solve the dynamic equation for gas flow by at least thousands of simulated molecules. Under the assumption of molecular chaos and gas rarefaction, the binary collisions are only considered. Therefore, the molecules' motion and their collisions are uncoupling if the computational time step is smaller than the physical collision time. After some steps, the macroscopic flow characteristics should be obtained statistically by sampling molecular properties in each cell and mean value of each property should be recorded. For estimation of macroscopic characteristics we used following realationship

$$\rho = \int_{\Re^3} f d\vec{v} \tag{13}$$

$$\rho \vec{u} = \int_{\Re^3} \vec{v} f d\vec{v} \tag{14}$$

$$T = \frac{1}{3\rho} \int_{\Re^3} (\vec{v} - \vec{u}) f d\vec{v} \tag{15}$$

$$p = \frac{\rho}{m} kT \tag{16}$$

3. Results and discussion

We consider a rarefied gas inside an annular domin of coaxial rotating cylinders. The radius of the inlet and the outlet cylinder are R1 and R2 (R1<R2). The bottom and top end of cylinders are covered with plates located at z=0 and z=L, repectively. Thus we consider a cylindrical domin R1<R2 ، $0 \le \Theta \le 2\pi$ and $0 \le z \le L$. Two cylinders are rotating around z-axes at surfac velocities $V_{\Theta 1}$ and $V_{\Theta 2}$ in the Θ direction. We will investigate the behavior of the gas numerically on the basis of Kinetic theory. The flow field is symmetric and the gas molecules are Hard-Sphere undergo diffuse reflection on the surface of the cylinders and specular reflection on the bottom and top boundaries. Here $Kn_0 = \lambda_0 / \Delta R$ is the Knudsen number with λ_0 being the mean free path of the gas molecules in the equilibrium state at rest with temerature T_0 and density ρ_0. The distance between two cylinders is $\Delta R = R2 - R1$. In this work, R2/R1=2 and L/R1=1 and the number of cells are 100×100. The working gas was Argon, characterized by a specific haet ratio $\gamma = 5/3$. Considering as a Hard-Sphere gas the molecular diamete equal to $d = 4.17 \times 10^{-10} m$ and a molecular mass is $m = 6.63 \times 10^{-26} kgm^{-3}$ respectively.

Fig. 2 shows temperature contour when teperature of the inlet cylinder and the teperature of oulet cylinder are 300 and 350 K. Figs. 3 and 4 show flow field with a vortex flow. In Fig. 3, teperature of the inlet cylinder and the teperature of oulet cylinder are 300 and 350 K. In Fig. 4 teperature of the inlet cylinder and the teperature of oulet cylinder are 350 and 300 K. It can be seen that the direction of vortex in Fig. 3 is inverted in Fig. 4. Fig. 5 shows the temperature plot at pressure 4, 40 and 400 Pa. It can be seen when the outlet cylinder is stagnant, the maximum amount of the temperature gradient occurs at the middle section and near the walls of the inlet cylinder. Fig. 6 shows density contour at pressure 4 Pa then maximum amount of density is near the walls of the outlet cylinder. Fig. 7 shows density contour at $V_{\Theta 1} / (2R\,T_0)^{1/2} = 0.26$ and $V_{\Theta 2} / (2R\,T_0)^{1/2} = 0.52$. Fig. 8 shows the flow field of single vortex flow at $V_{\Theta 1} / (2R\,T_0)^{1/2} = 0.81$ and $V_{\Theta 2} / (2R\,T_0)^{1/2} = -0.237$.

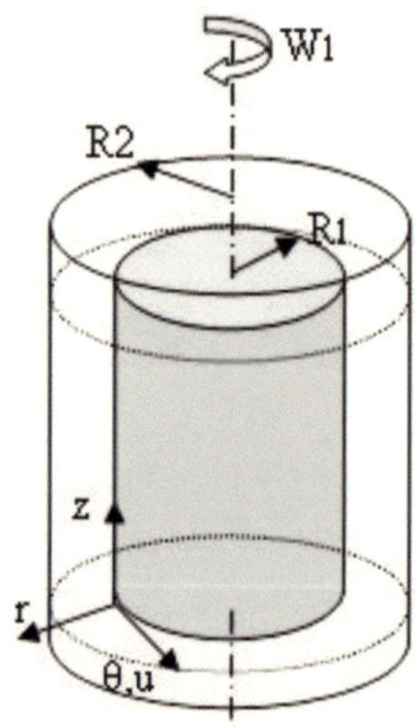

Fig. 1. Definition of the problem

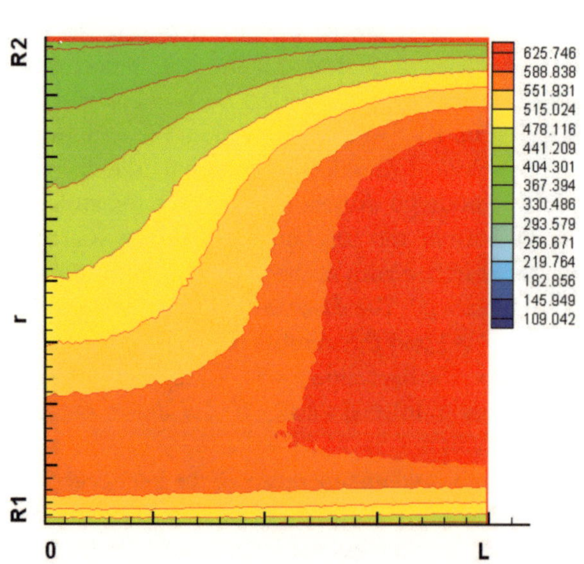

Fig. 2. Temperature contour when when teperature of the inlet cylinder and the teperature of oulet cylinder are 300 and 350 K

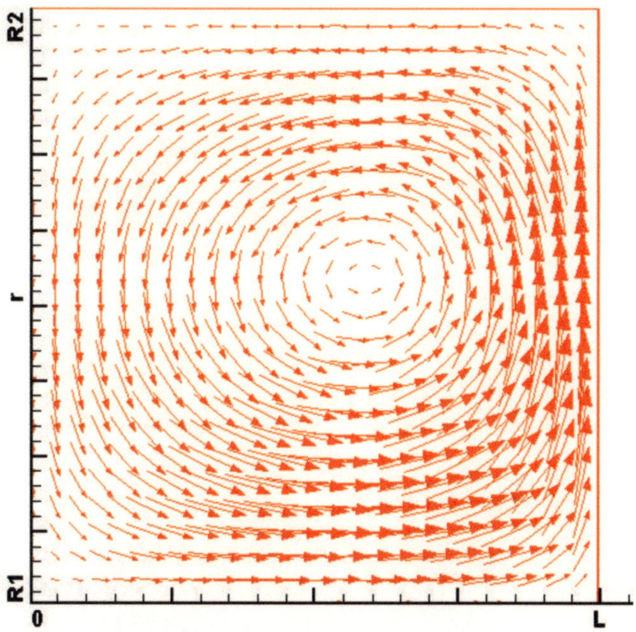

Fig. 3. Flow filed of single-vortex Flow when teperature of the inlet cylinder and the teperature of oulet cylinder are 300 and 350 K

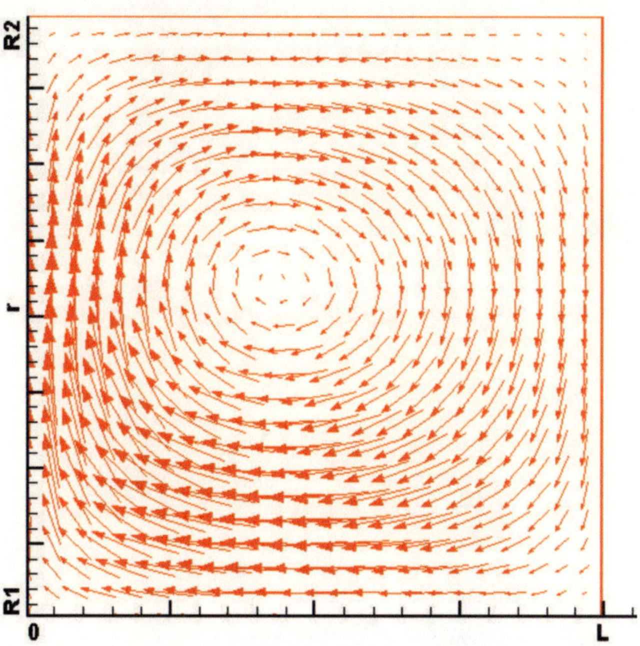

Fig. 4. Flow filed of single-vortex Flow when teperature of the inlet cylinder and the teperature of oulet cylinder are 350 and 300 K

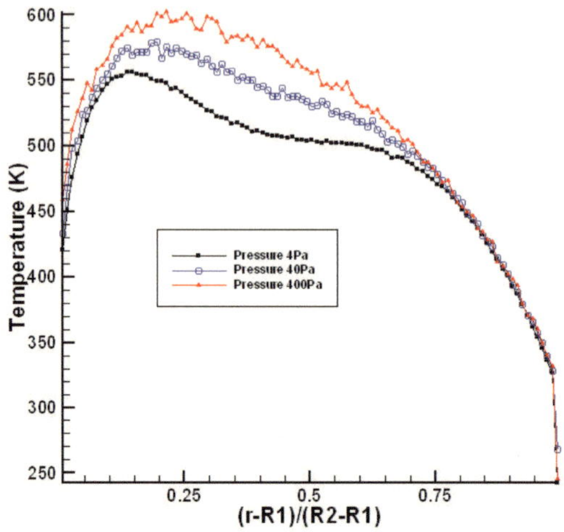

Fig. 5. Temperature at 4, 40 and 400 Pa

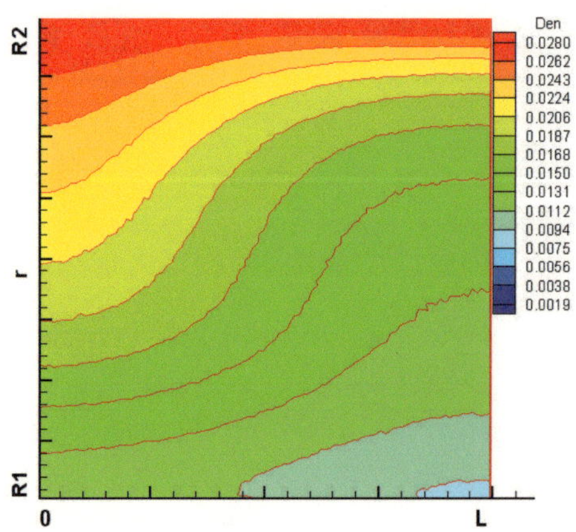

Fig. 6. Density contour at 4 Pa

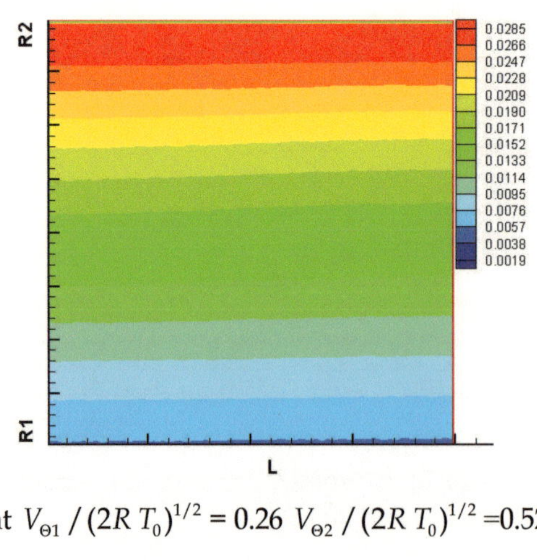

Fig. 7. Density contour at $V_{\Theta 1} / (2R\,T_0)^{1/2} = 0.26$ $V_{\Theta 2} / (2R\,T_0)^{1/2} = 0.52$

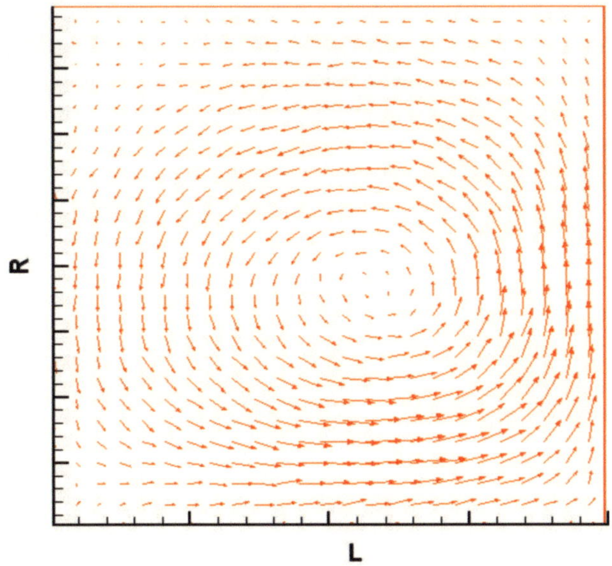

Fig. 8. Flow filed of single-vortex Flow $V_{\Theta 1} / (2R\,T_0)^{1/2} = 0.81$ $V_{\Theta 2} / (2R\,T_0)^{1/2} =-0.237$

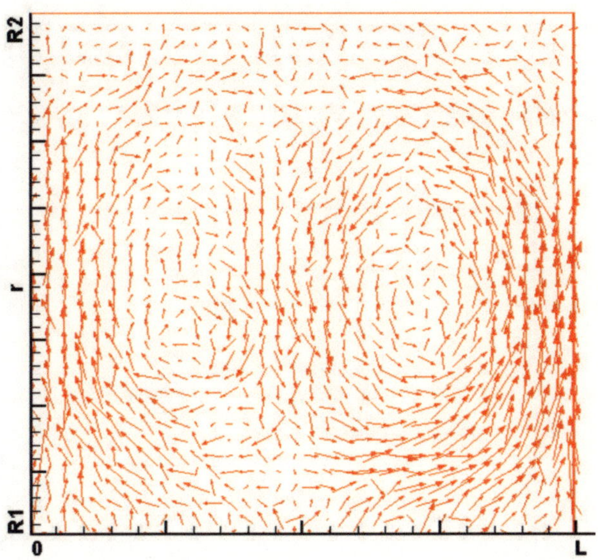

Fig. 9. Flow filed of double-vortex Flow $V_{\Theta 1} / (2R\,T_0)^{1/2} = 0.81$ $V_{\Theta 2} / (2R\,T_0)^{1/2} =-0.27$

Figure 8 shows the flow field of double-vortex flow at $V_{\Theta 1} / (2R\,T_0)^{1/2} = 0.81$ and $V_{\Theta 2} / (2R\,T_0)^{1/2} = -0.27$. Figure 10 Fig. 8 shows the flow field of single vortex flow at $V_{\Theta 1} / (2R\,T_0)^{1/2} = 0.81$ and $V_{\Theta 2} / (2R\,T_0)^{1/2} = -0.311$. It can be seen from these figures when pressure increases, we have weaker vortex flow. Figure 11 shows density when $V_{\Theta 1} = 1000$ m/s is constant and $V_{\Theta 2}$ is 200, 500 and 1000 m/s. According to this figure, if the velocity of the outlet cylinder increases, density changes rapidly. Figure 12 shows temperature changes when $V_{\Theta 1} = 1000$ m/s is constant and $V_{\Theta 2}$ is 200, 500 and 1000 m/s. It can be seen that maximum temperature occurs when the velocity of the outlet cylinder is 200 m/s. Figure 13 shows radial velocity at 4, 40 and 400 Pa. The results show different flow patterns at different temperature and pressure.

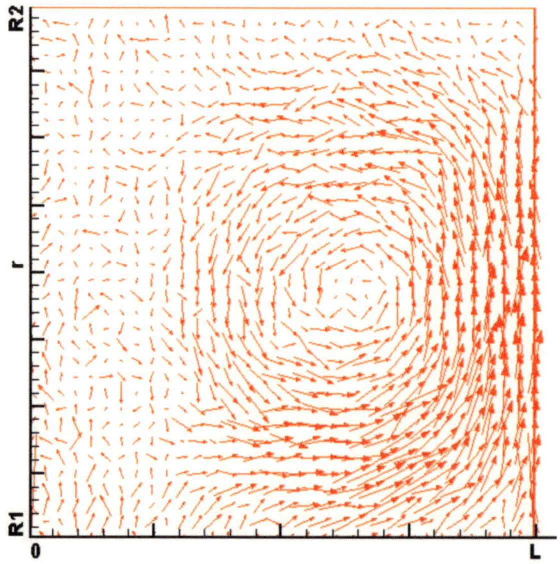

Fig. 10. Flow filed of single-vortex Flow $V_{\Theta 1} / (2R\,T_0)^{1/2} = 0.81$ $V_{\Theta 2} / (2R\,T_0)^{1/2} = -0.311$

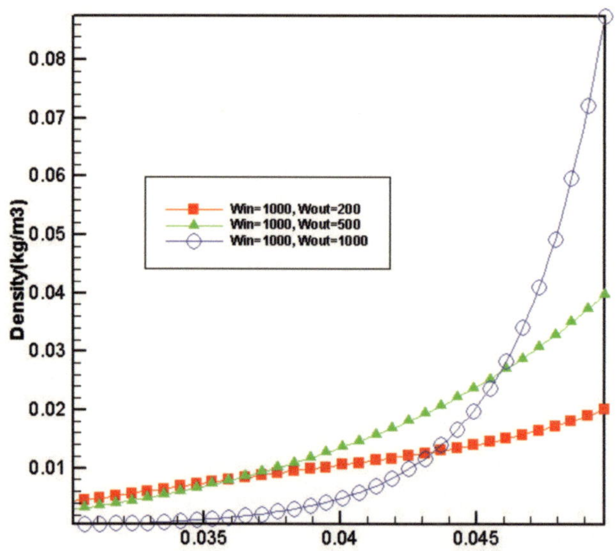

Fig. 11. Density at $V_{\Theta 1} = 1000$ m/s is constant and $V_{\Theta 2}$ is 200, 500 and 1000 m/s

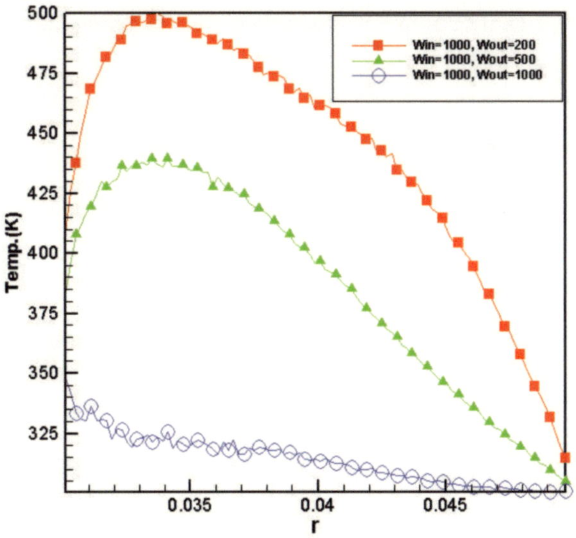

Fig. 12. Temperature changes at $V_{\Theta 1} = 1000$ m/s is constant and $V_{\Theta 2}$ is 200, 500 and 1000 m/s.

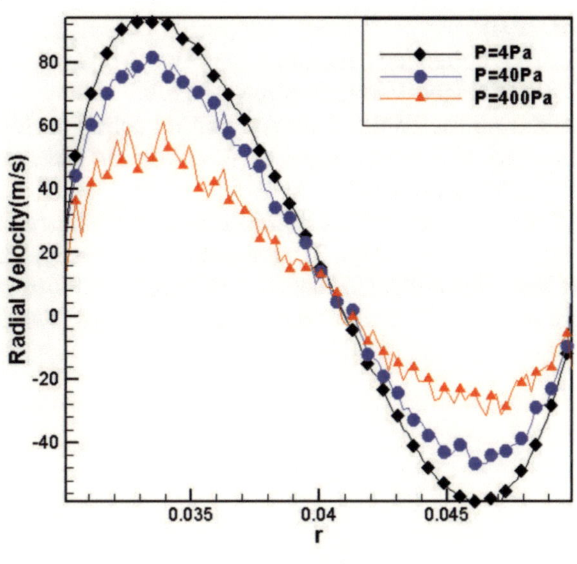

Fig. 13. Radial velocity at 4, 40 and 400 Pa

4. Conclusions

In this work, The Couette-Taylor flow for a rarefied gas is supposed to be contained in an annular domain, bounded by two coaxial rotating circular cylinders. The Boltzmann equation was solved with DSMC method. The results showed different type of flow patterns, as Couette-Taylor flow or single and double vortex flow, can be created in a wide range of speed of rotation of inner and outer cylinders. This work shows if size or number of cells is not proper, we cannot obtain reasonable results by using DSMC method.

5. Nomenclature

f = density distribution function
F = external forces filed
K = Boltzmann constant
K_n =Knudsen number
m = molecular wieght
p = pressure
Q = collision integral
T = temperature
$R1$ =radius of the inlet cylinder
$R2$ =radius of the outlet cylinder
T_{tr} =translational temperature
u = free stream velocity
v = molecular velocity
κ = molecular constant
μ = collision rate per unit of time and volume
ρ = density of gas
σ = hard sphere diameter
Subscripts
* = other investigated features
Superscripts
2 = two dimentional phase
3 = three dimentional phase
′ = value of feature after collision Abbreviations
DSMC = Direct Simulation Monte Carlo

6. References

Bird, G.A., Molecular Gas Dynamics and the Direct Simulation of Gas Flows (Clarendon Press, Oxford, 1994).

Cercignani, C. 1988, The Boltzmann Equation and Its Applications, *Lectures Series in Mathematics*, 68, Springer- Verlag,Berlin,New York.

DE, L.M., Cio, S. and Marino, L., 2000, Simulation and modeling of flows between rotating cylinders: Influence of knudsen number, *Mathematical models and method in applied seiences,* Vol. 10, No.10, pp. 73-83.

Ghezel Sofloo H., R. Ebrahimi, Analysis of MEMS gas flows with pressure boundaries, *17th Symposium, NSU-XVII,* Dec. 2008, Banaras Hindu University, Varanasi, India.

Yoshio, S., Masato, H. and Toshiyuki, D., 2006, Ghost Effect and Bifurcation in Gas between Coaxial Circular Cylinder with Different Temperatures, *Physical of fluid*, Vol. 15, No. 10.

5

Theoretical and Experimental Analysis of Flows and Heat Transfer Within Flat Mini Heat Pipe Including Grooved Capillary Structures

Zaghdoudi Mohamed Chaker, Maalej Samah and Mansouri Jed
University of Carthage – Institute of Applied Sciences and technology
Research Unit Materials, Measurements, and Applications
Tunisia

1. Introduction

Thermal management of electronic components must solve problems connected with the limitations on the maximum chip temperature and the requirements of the level of temperature uniformity. To cool electronic components, one can use air and liquid coolers as well as coolers constructed on the principle of the phase change heat transfer in closed space, i.e. immersion, thermosyphon and heat pipe coolers. Each of these methods has its merits and draw-backs, because in the choice of appropriate cooling one must take into consideration not only the thermal parameters of the cooler, but also design and stability of the system, durability, technology, price, application, etc.

Heat pipes represent promising solutions for electronic equipment cooling (Groll et al., 1998). Heat pipes are sealed systems whose transfer capacity depends mainly on the fluid and the capillary structure. Several capillary structures are developed in order to meet specific thermal needs. They are constituted either by an integrated structure of microchannels or microgrooves machined in the internal wall of the heat spreader, or by porous structures made of wire screens or sintered powders. According to specific conditions, composed capillary structures can be integrated into heat pipes.

Flat Miniature Heat Pipes (FMHPs) are small efficient devices to meet the requirement of cooling electronic components. They are developed in different ways and layouts, according to its materials, capillary structure design and manufacturing technology. The present study deals with the development of a FMHP concept to be used for cooling high power dissipation electronic components. Experiments are carried out in order to determine the thermal performance of such devices as a function of various parameters. A mathematical model of a FMHP with axial rectangular microchannels is developed in which the fluid flow is considered along with the heat and mass transfer processes during evaporation and condensation. The numerical simulations results are presented regarding the thickness distribution of the liquid film in a microchannel, the liquid and vapor pressures and velocities as well as the wall temperatures along the FMHP. By comparing the experimental results with numerical simulation results, the reliability of the numerical model can be verified.

2. Nomenclature

A	Constant in Eq. (8), Section, m^2
C_p	Specific heat, J/kg.K
d	Side of the square microchannel, m
D_g	Groove height, m
D_h	Hydraulic diameter, m
f	Friction factor
g	Gravity acceleration, m/s^2
h	Heat transfer coefficient, $W/m^2.K$
I	Current, A
Ja*	Modified Jacob number
k	Poiseuille number
l	Width, m
L	FMHP overall length, m
La	Laplace constant, m
l_c	Condenser width, m
L_c	Condenser length, m
l_e	Evaporator width, m
L_e	Evaporator length, m
$\dot{m}$	Mass flow rate, kg/s
m_1	Constant in Eq. (8)
m_2	Constant in Eq. (8)
m_3	Constant in Eq. (8)
N_g	Number of grooves
Nu	Nüsselt number
P	Pressure, N/m^2
Pr	Prandtl number
q	Heat flux, W/m^2
Q	Heat transfer rate, W
Q_a	Axial heat flux rate, W
r_c	Radius of curvature, m
Re	Reynolds number
R_{th}	Thermal resistance, K/W
S_g	Groove spacing, m
S	Heat transfer area, m^2
S_g	Groove spacing, m
t	Thickness, m
T	Temperature, °C
T_c	Wall condenser temperature, °C
T_{ev}	Wall evaporator temperature, °C
T_f	Film temperature, °C
T_{sf}	Heat sink temperature, °C
T_w	Wall temperature, °C
V	Voltage, V
V_e	Velocity, m/s
w	Axial velocity, m/s
W	FMHP width, m
W_g	Groove width, m
z	Coordinate, m

Greek Symbols

α	Contact angle, °
β	Tilt angle, °
ΔT	Temperature difference = $T_{ev} - T_c$, K
Δh_v	Latent heat of vaporization, J/kg
ΔP	Pressure drop, N/m^2
λ	Thermal conductivity, W/m.K
μ	Dynamic viscosity, kg/m.s
θ	Angle, °
ρ	Density, kg/m^3
σ	Surface tension, N/m
τ	Shear stress, N/m^2

Subscripts and superscripts

a	Adiabatic
b	Blocked
c	Condenser, Curvature
d	Dry
Cu	Copper
ev	Evaporator
eff	Effective
exp	Experimental
f	Film
il	Interfacial (liquid side)
iv	Interfacial (vapor side)
l	Liquid
lw	Liquid-Wall
max	Maximum
sat	Saturation
sf	Heat sink
t	Total
v	Vapor
vw	Vapor-Wall
w	Wall

3. Literature survey on mini heat pipes prototyping and testing

This survey concerns mainly the FMHPs made in metallic materials such as copper, aluminum, brass, etc. For the metallic FMHPs, the fabrication of microgrooves on the heat pipe housing for the wick structure has been widely adopted as means of minimizing the size of the cooling device. Hence, FMHPs include axial microgrooves with triangular, rectangular, and trapezoidal shapes. Investigations into FMHPs with newer groove designs have also been carried out, and recent researches include triangular grooves coupled with arteries, star and rhombus grooves, microgrooves mixed with screen mesh or sintered metal. The fabrication of narrow grooves with sharp corner angle is a challenging task for conventional micromachining techniques such as precision mechanical machining. Accordingly, a number of different techniques including high speed dicing and rolling method (Hopkins et al., 1999), Electric-Discharge-Machining (EDM) (Cao et al., 1997; Cao and Gao, 2002; Lin et al., 2002), CNC milling process (Cao and Gao, 2002; Gao and Cao, 2003; Lin et al., 2004; Zaghdoudi and Sarno, 2001, Zaghdoudi et al., 2004; Lefèvre et al., 2008), drawing and extrusion processes (Moon et al., 2003, 2004; Romestant et al., 2004; Xiaowu, 2009), metal forming process (Schneider et al., 1999a, 1999b, 2000; Chien et al., 2003), and flattening (Tao et al., 2008) have been applied to the fabrication of microgrooves. More recently, laser-assisted wet etching technique was used in order to machine fan-shaped microgrooves (Lim et al., 2008). A literature survey of the micromachining techniques and capillary structures that have been used in metallic materials are reported in table 1.

It can be seen from this overview that three types of grooved metallic FMHP are developed:

i. Type I: FMHPs with only axial rectangular, triangular or trapezoidal grooves (Murakami et al., 1987; Plesh et al., 1991; Sun and Wang, 1994; Ogushi and Yamanaka., 1994; Cao et al., 1997; Hopkins et al., 1999; Schneider et al., 1999a, 1999b, 2000; Avenas et al., 2001, Cao and Gao, 2002, Lin et al., 2002; Chien et al., 2003; Moon et al., 2003, 2004; Soo Yong and Joon Hong, 2003; Lin et al., 2004; Romestant et al., 2004; Zhang et al., 2004; Popova et al., 2006; Lefevre et al., 2008; Lim et al., 2008; Tao et al., 2008, Zhang et al., 2009; Xiaowu et al., 2009). These FMHPs allow for high heat fluxes for horizontal or thermosyphon positions (up to 150 W/cm^2). However, in the majority of the cases, the thermal performances of such FMHP don't meet the electronic cooling requirements when the anti-gravity position is requested since the FMHP thermal performances are greatly altered for these conditions because the standard capillary grooves are not able to allow for the necessary capillary pumping able to overcome the pressure losses.

ii. Type II: FMHPs with mixed capillary structures such as grooves and sintered metal powder or grooves and screen meshes (Schneider et al.,1999a, 1999b, 2000; Zaghdoudi et al., 2004; Popova et al., 2005, 2006). Depending on the characteristics of the capillary structures such as the pore diameter, the wire diameter, the wire spacing and the number for screen wick layers, these FMHPs could meet the electronic cooling requirements especially for those applications where the electronic devices are submitted to forces such as gravity, acceleration and vibration forces (Zaghdoudi and Sarno, 2001). However, for standard applications, these FMHPs allow for low thermal performances (lower heat fluxes and higher thermal resistance) when compared to those delivered by the FMHPs of Type I.

iii. Type III: wickless FMHPs (Cao and Gao, 2002; Gao and Cao, 2003). These FMHPs utilize the concept of the boiling heat transfer mechanism in narrow space. These FMHPs can remove high heat flux rates with great temperature gradient between the hot source and the cold one.

Author	Micromachining Technique	Material	Capillary structure
Murakami et al. (1987)	—[a]	Brass	Triangular and rectangular grooves
Plesh et al. (1991)	—[a]	Copper	Axial and transverse rectangular grooves
Sun and Wang (1994)	—[a]	Aluminum	V-shaped axial grooves
Ogushi and Yamanaka (1994)	—[a]	Brass	Triangular and trapezoidal axial grooves
Cao et al. (1997)	Electric-discharge-machining (EDM)	Copper	Rectangular axial grooves
Hopkins et al. (1999)	Rolling method High-speed dicing saw	Copper	Trapezoidal diagonal grooves Rectangular axial grooves
Schneider et al. (1999a, 1999b, 2000)	Metal forming process	AlSiC	Triangular axial grooves
Avenas et al. (2001)	—[a]	Brass	Rectangular axial grooves
Zaghdoudi and Sarno (2001)	Milling process and sintering	Copper	Rectangular axial grooves and sintered powder wick
Cao and Gao (2002)	Milling process Electric Discharge Machining (EDM)	Aluminum Copper	Perpendicular network of crossed grooves Triangular axial grooves
Lin et al. (2002)	Electric-discharge-machining (EDM)	Copper	Rectangular axial grooves
Chien et al. (2003)	Metal forming process	Aluminum	Radial rectangular grooves
Gao and Cao (2003)	Milling process	Aluminum	Waffle-like cubes (protrusions)
Moon et al. (2003)	Drawing and extrusion process	Copper	Triangular and rectangular axial grooves with curved walls
Soo Yong and Joon Hong (2003)	—[a]	—[a]	Rectangular axial grooves with half circle shape at the bottom
Lin et al. (2004)	Etching, CNC milling, and sintering	Copper	Radial diverging grooves and sintered powder wick
Moon et al. (2004)	Drawing process	Copper	Triangular and rectangular grooves with incurved walls

Romestant et al. (2004)	Extrusion	Aluminum	Triangular axial grooves
Zaghdoudi et al. (2004)	Milling process	Copper	Triangular axial grooves and meshes
Zhang et al. (2004)	—[a]	Copper Stainless steel Copper	Rectangular axial grooves Trapezoidal axial grooves
Iavona et al. (2005)	Direct Bounded Copper technology	Copper/Alumina	Fiber mixed material of Al_2O_3 and SiO_2
Popova et al. (2005)	—[a]	Copper	Rectangular grooves machined in sintered copper structure
Popova et al. (2006)	—[a]	Copper	Rectangular grooves machined in sintered copper structure
Lefèvre et al. (2008)	Milling process	Copper	Rectangular axial grooves
Lim et al (2008)	Laser micromachining	Copper	Triangular axial grooves with curved walls
Tao et al. (2008)	Flattening of cylindrical finned tubes	Copper	Rectangular axial grooves with half circle shape at the bottom
Zhang et al. (2009)	—[a]	Copper	Radial diverging grooves
Xiaowu et al. (2009)	Extrusion-ploughing process	—[a]	V-shaped grooves

[a] Not specified in the reference

Table 1. Overview of the micromachining techniques of microgrooves for metallic FMHPs

From the studies published in open literature, the following points can be outlined:

i. The importance of the choice of the microchannel geometry. Indeed, according to the shape of a corner, the capillary pressure generated by the variation of the liquid-vapor interface curvature between the evaporator and the condenser, can be improved. An optimal shape of a corner permits to supply efficiently the evaporation zone in liquid, so that more heat power can be dissipated, and dry-out, which causes heat transfer degradation, can be avoided.
ii. The choice and the quantity of the introduced fluid in the microchannel play a primordial role for the good operation of the FMHP.
iii. Although the heat flux rates transferred by FMHPs with integrated capillary structure are low, these devices permit to transfer very important heat fluxes avoiding the formation of hot spots. Their major advantage resides in their small dimensions that permit to integrate them near the heat sources.

4. Literature survey on micro/mini heat pipe modeling

For FMHPs constituted of an integrated capillary structure including microchannels of different shapes, the theoretical approach consists of studying the flow and the heat transfer in isolated microchannels. The effect of the main parameters, of which depends the FMHP operation, can be determined by a theoretical study. Hence, the influence of the liquid and vapor flow interaction, the fill charge, the contact angle, the geometry, and the hydraulic diameter of the microchannel can be predicted by models that analyze hydrodynamic aspect coupled to the thermal phenomena.

Khrustalev and Faghri (1995) developed a detailed mathematical model of low-temperature axially grooved heat pipes in which the fluid circulation is considered along with the heat and mass transfer processes during evaporation and condensation. The results obtained are compared to existing experimental data. Both capillary and boiling limitations are found to be important for the flat miniature copper-water heat pipes, which is capable of withstanding heat fluxes on the order of 40 W/cm^2 applied to the evaporator wall in the vertical position. The influence of the geometry of the grooved surface on the maximum heat transfer capacity of the miniature heat pipe is demonstrated.

Faghri and Khrustalev (1997) studied an enhanced flat miniature heat pipes with capillary grooves for electronics cooling systems, They survey advances in modeling of important steady-state performance characteristics of enhanced and conventional flat miniature axially-grooved heat pipes such as the maximum heat flow rate, thermal resistance of the evaporator, incipience of the nucleate boiling, and the maximum heat flux on the evaporator wall.

Khrustalev and Faghri (1999) analyze Friction factor coefficients for liquid flow in a rectangular microgroove coupled with the vapor flow in a vapor channel of a miniature two-phase device. The results show that the effect of the vapor-liquid frictional interaction on the liquid flow decreases with curvature of the liquid-vapor interface. Shear stresses at the liquid-vapor interface are significantly non-uniform, decreasing towards the center of the liquid-vapor meniscus.

Lefevre et al. (2003) developed a capillary two-phase flow model of flat mini heat pipes with micro grooves of different cross-sections. The model permits to calculate the maximum heat transfer capabilities and the optimal liquid charge of the FMHP. The results are obtained for trapezoidal and rectangular micro grooves cross-sections.

Launay et al. (2004) developed a detailed mathematical model for predicting the heat transport capability and the temperature distribution along the axial direction of a flat miniature heat pipe, filled with water. This steady-state model combines hydrodynamic flow equations with heat transfer equations in both the condensing and evaporating thin films. The velocity, pressure, and temperature distributions in the vapor and liquid phases are calculated. Various boundary conditions fixed to the FMHP evaporator and condenser have been simulated to study the thermal performance of the micro-heat-pipe array below and above the capillary limit. The effect of the dry-out or flooding phenomena on the FMHP performance, according to boundary conditions and fluid fill charge, can also be predicted.

Tzanova et al. (2004) presented a detailed analysis on maximum heat transfer capabilities of silicon-water FMHPs. The predictive hydraulic and thermal models were developed to define the heat spreader thermal performances and capillary limitations. Theoretical results of the maximal heat flux that could be transferred agree reasonably well with the experimental data and the developed model provides a better understanding of the heat transfer capability of FMHPs.

Angelov et al. (2005) proposed theoretical and modeling issues of FMHPs with parallelepipedal shape with regard to the capillary limit and the evaporator boiling limit. An improved model is suggested and it is compared with the simulation and experimental results. The improved model implements a different analytically derived form of the friction factor-Reynolds number product (Poiseuille number). The simulated results with the proposed model demonstrate better coherence to the experiment showing the importance of accurate physical modeling to heat conduction behavior of the FMHP.

Shi et al. (2006) carried out a performance evaluation of miniature heat pipes in LTCC by numerical analysis, and the optimum miniature heat pipe design was defined. The effect of the groove depth, width and vapor space on the heat transfer capacity of miniature heat pipes was analyzed.

Do et al. (2008) developed a mathematical model for predicting the thermal performance of a FMHP with a rectangular grooved wick structure. The effects of the liquid-vapor interfacial shear stress, the contact angle, and the amount of liquid charge are accounted for in the present model. In particular, the axial variations of the wall temperature and the evaporation and condensation rates are considered by solving the one-dimensional conduction equation for the wall and the augmented Young-Laplace equation, respectively. The results obtained from the proposed model are in close agreement with several existing experimental data in terms of the wall temperatures and the maximum heat transport rate. From the validated model, it is found that the assumptions employed in previous studies may lead to significant errors for predicting the thermal performance of the heat pipe. Finally, the maximum heat transport rate of a FMHP with a grooved wick structure is optimized with respect to the width and the height of the groove by using the proposed model. The maximum heat transport rate for the optimum conditions is enhanced by approximately 20%, compared to existing experimental results.

Do and Jang (2010) investigated the effect of water-based Al2O3 nanofluids as working fluid on the thermal performance of a FMHP with a rectangular grooved wick. For the purpose, the axial variations of the wall temperature, the evaporation and condensation rates are considered by solving the one-dimensional conduction equation for the wall and the augmented Young-Laplace equation for the phase change process. In particular, the thermophysical properties of nanofluids as well as the surface characteristics formed by nanoparticles such as a thin porous coating are considered. From the comparison of the thermal performance using both water and nanofluids, it is found that the thin porous coating layer formed by nanoparticles suspended in nanofluids is a key effect of the heat transfer enhancement for the heat pipe using nanofluids. Also, the effects of the volume fraction and the size of nanoparticles on the thermal performance are studied. The results show the feasibility of enhancing the thermal performance up to 100% although water-based Al2O3 nanofluids with the concentration less than 10% is used as working fluid. Finally, it is shown that the thermal resistance of the nanofluid heat pipe tends to decrease with increasing the nanoparticle size, which corresponds to the previous experimental results.

5. Experimental study

5.1 FMHP fabrication and filling procedure

A FMHP has been designed, manufactured, and tested. The design parameters are based on some electronic components that require high power dissipation rate. The design is subjected to some restrictions such as the requirements for size, weight, thermal resistance, working temperature, and flow resistance. For comparison purposes, a solid heat sink that has the same size but more weight than the FMHP is also tested. The test sample is made of the same copper and their dimensions are 100 mm length, 50 mm width, and 3 mm

thickness. The FMHP body is manufactured in two halves. Manufacturing of the FMHP begins with the capillary grooves being mechanically machined by a high speed dicing process in the first half (2 mm thick) and the second half, which consists of a copper cover slip 1 mm thick, is bonded to the first half by an electron beam welding process. The heat pipe charging tube (2 mm diameter), from which the fluid working is introduced, is bounded to the heat pipe end by a classic welding technique. The geometrical dimensions of the FMHP are indicated in table 2 and in Fig. 1. A view of the microchannels is shown in Fig. 2.
Filling the FMHP presents one of the greatest challenges. In this study, a boiling method is used for the filling purpose. The filling assembly includes a vacuum system, a boiler filled with distilled water, vacuum tight electrovalves, a burette for a precise filling of the FMHP and a tubular adapter. The degassing and charging procedure consists of the following steps: (i) degassing water by boiling process, (ii) realizing a vacuum in the complete set-up, (iii) charging of the burette, and (iv) charging of the FMHP. An automatic process controls the whole steps. After charging the FMHP, the open end (a 2 mm diameter charging tube) is sealed. The amount of liquid is controlled by accurate balance. Indeed, the FMHP is weighed before and after the fill charging process and it is found that the optimum fill charge for the FMHP developed in this study is 1.2 ml.

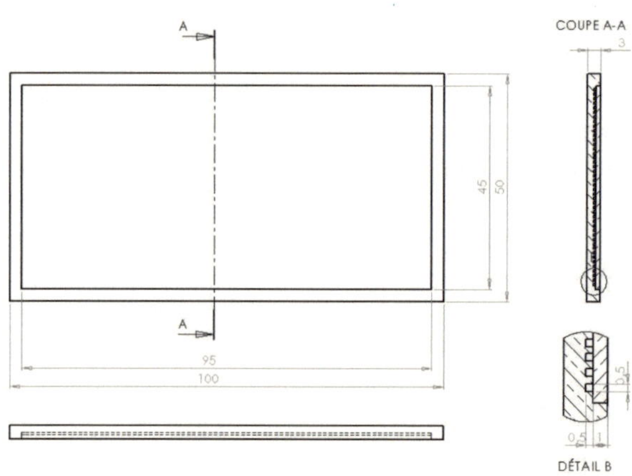

Fig. 1. Sketch of the FMHPs

Fig. 2. View of the microchannels

FMHP width, W	50
FMHP overall length, L_t	100
FMHP thickness, t	3
Microchannel height, D_g	0.5
Microchannel width W_g (mm)	0.5
Microchannel spacing S_g (mm)	1
Overall width of the microchannels	45
Overall length of the microchannels (mm)	95
Number of the microchannels, N_g	47

Dimensions are in mm.

Table 2. Main geometrical parameters of the FMHP

5.2 Experimental set-up and procedures

Heat input is delivered by an electric resistance cartridge attached at one end of the FMHP and it is provided on the grooved side of the FMHP. The power input to the heater is controlled through a variable transformer so that a constant power is supplied to the heated section, and the voltage and current are measured using digital voltmeter and ammeter. Both the evaporator and the adiabatic sections are thermally insulated. The heat loss from the insulation surface to the ambient is determined by evaluating the temperature difference and the heat transfer coefficient of natural convection between the insulated outer surface and ambient. Heat is removed from the FMHP by a water cooling system. A thermally conductive paste is used to enhance the heat transfer between the copper FMHP and the aluminum blocks. The lengths of the evaporator, adiabatic, and condenser zones are L_e = 19 mm, L_a = 35 mm, and L_c = 45 mm, respectively. The temperature distribution across the surface of the FMHP and the copper plate is obtained using 6 type-J surface mounted thermocouples. The thermocouples are located, respectively at 5, 15, 27, 42, 60, and 90 mm from the end cap of the evaporator section. In order to measure the evaporator and condenser temperatures, grooves are practiced on the FMHP wall and thermocouples are inserted along the grooves. The thermocouples locations and the experimental set-up are shown in Figs. 3 and 4.

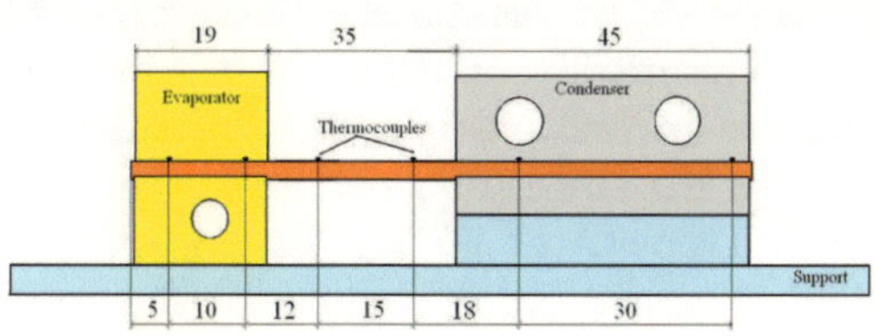

Fig. 3. Thermocouple locations

The experimental investigation focuses on the heat transfer characteristics of the FMHP at various heat flux rates, Q, and operating temperatures, T_{sf}. Input power is varied in increments from a low value to the power at which the evaporator temperature starts to increase rapidly. In the process, the temperature distribution of the heat pipe along the longitudinal axis is observed and recorded. All experimental data are obtained with a systematic and consistent methodology that is as follows. First, the flat miniature heat pipe is positioned in the proper orientation and a small heat load is applied to the evaporator section. Secondly, the heat sink operating temperature is obtained and maintained by adjusting the cooling water flow to the aluminum heat sink. Once the heat sink temperature is obtained, the system is allowed to reach steady-state over 10-15 minutes. After steady-state is reached, temperature readings at all thermocouples are recorded and power to the evaporator is increased by a small increment. This cycle is repeated until the maximum capillary limit is reached which is characterized by a sudden and steady rise of the evaporator temperature.

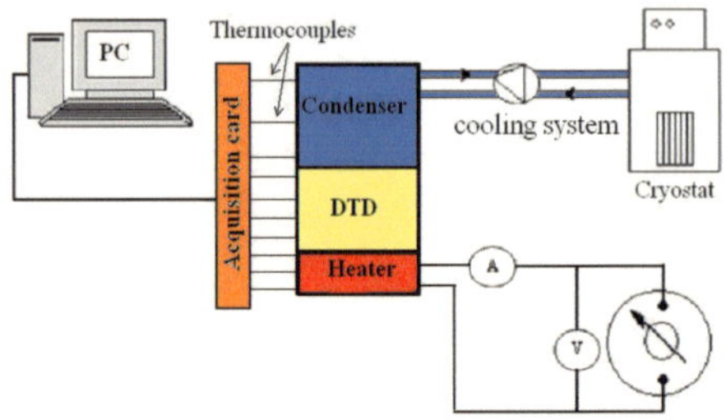

Fig. 4. Experimental set-up

The data logger TC-08 acquisition system is used to make all temperature measurements. The type J thermocouples are calibrated against a precision digital RTD and their accuracy over the range of interest is found to be within 0.5 °C. In the steady-state, the wall thermocouples fluctuate within 0.2 °C. The uncertainty of the thermocouples is 0.3°C + 0.03 $\times 10^{-2}$ T, where T is the measured temperature. The uncertainty of the thermocouples locations is within 0.5 mm in the heat pipe axial direction. A pair of multimeters is used to determine and record the power supplied to the resistors. The first multimeter is used to measure voltage across the film resistor and has an accuracy of 2 % of true voltage while the second measures the AC current and has accuracy 2 % of true AC current. The power input to the electric heater is calculated using the measured current and voltage ($Q = V \times I$). The thermal resistance, R_{th}, of the heat pipe is defined as the ratio of the temperature drop, $\Delta T = T_{ev} - T_c$, across the heat pipe to the input heat power Q.

5.3 Experimental results and analysis

5.3.1 Combined effects of the heat input power and the heat sink temperature

Figs 5a to 5c illustrate typical steady temperature profiles for the FMHP prototypes for 10 W to 60 W at a heat sink temperature, T_{sf}, of 10 °C, 20 °C, and 40 °C, when it is oriented horizontally. The maximum evaporator temperature and temperature gradients for the FMHP are considerably smaller than those obtained for copper plate (Fig. 5d). For instance, for T_{sf} = 40 °C, at an input power of 60 W, the maximum steady-state evaporator temperature for the FMHP is nearly 100 °C, while for the copper plate the maximum evaporator temperature is 160°C. This results in a decrease in temperature gradients of approximately 60 °C. The heat source-heat sink temperature difference, $\Delta T = T_{ev} - T_c$, for T_{sf} = 40 °C when the FMHP is oriented horizontally, are plotted as a function of the applied heat flux rate in Fig. 6. Also shown for comparison is the heat source-heat sink temperature difference for a copper plate. The maximum evaporator temperature and temperature gradients for the FMHP are considerably smaller than those obtained for the copper plate. As shown in Fig. 6, the heat pipe operation reduces the slope of the temperature profile for the FMHP. This gives some indication of the ability of such FMHP to reduce the thermal gradients or localized hot spots. The size of the source-sink temperature difference for the FMHP increases in direct proportion of the input heat flux rate and varies from almost 10 °C at low power levels to approximately 50 °C at input power levels of approximately 60 W.

This plot again shows the effectiveness of the enhanced FMHP and clearly indicates the temperature reduction level that can be expected at higher heat flux rates prior to dry-out. The effective end cap to end cap thermal resistance of the FMHP is given in Fig. 7. Effective end cap to end cap thermal resistance, R_{tht}, defined here as the overall en cap to end cap temperature drop divided by the total applied heat load, Q. A common characteristic of the thermal resistance presented here is that the thermal resistance of the FMHP is high at low heat loads as a relatively thick liquid film resides in the evaporator. However, this thermal resistance decreases rapidly to its minimum value as the applied heat load is increased. This minimum value corresponds to the capillary limit. When the applied heat flux rate becomes higher than the capillary limit, the FMHP thermal resistance increases since the evaporator becomes starved of liquid. This is due to the fact that the capillary pumping cannot overcome the pressure losses within the FMHP. The decrease of the FMHP thermal resistance is attributed mainly to the decrease of the evaporator thermal resistance when the heat flux increases. Indeed, increasing the heat flux leads to the enhancement evaporation process in the grooves. The decrease of R_{tht} is observed when the evaporation process is dominated by the capillary limit. However, for heat flux rates higher than the maximum capillary limit, intensified boiling process may occur in the capillary structure, and consequently the evaporator thermal resistance increases. This results in an increase of the overall FMHP thermal resistance.

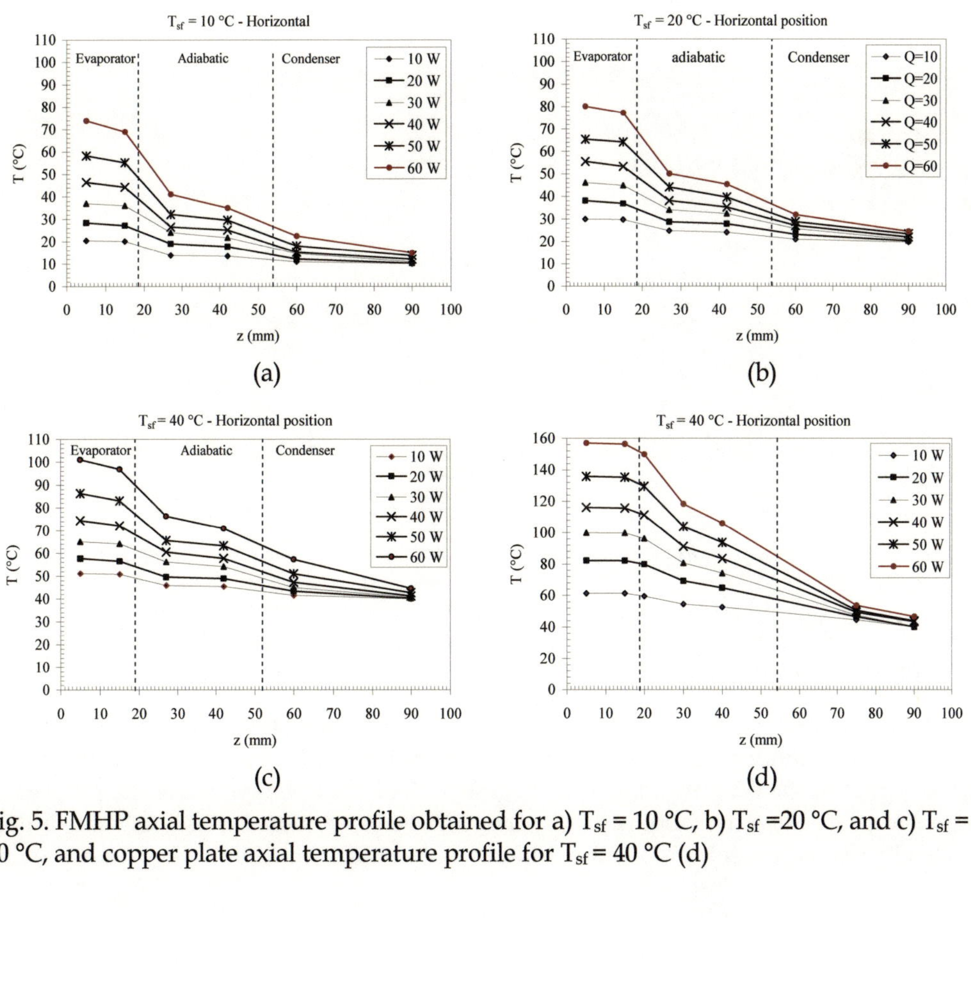

Fig. 5. FMHP axial temperature profile obtained for a) T_{sf} = 10 °C, b) T_{sf} =20 °C, and c) T_{sf} = 40 °C, and copper plate axial temperature profile for T_{sf} = 40 °C (d)

It is also noticed that for a given heat flux rate the thermal resistance decreases as the heat sink temperature increases and the capillary limit, Q_{max}, increases. The increase in Q_{max} with T_{sf} is due to the decrease of the overall pressure drop ($\Delta P_l + \Delta P_v$). Indeed, when T_{sf} increases, the vapor temperature, T_{sat}, increases too. This results in a dramatic decrease of the vapor friction factor and consequently the vapor pressure drop ΔP_v decreases. However, the liquid pressure drop, ΔP_l increases with T_{sf} because an augmentation of the liquid mass flow rate is allowed by a decrease of the liquid friction factor with T_{sf}. Since the increase in ΔP_l is lower than the decrease in ΔP_v, the overall pressure drop ($\Delta P_l + \Delta P_v$) decrease. As shown in Fig. 7, the effect the heat sink temperature on the FMHP thermal resistance is effective when the heat input power is greater than the capillary limit.

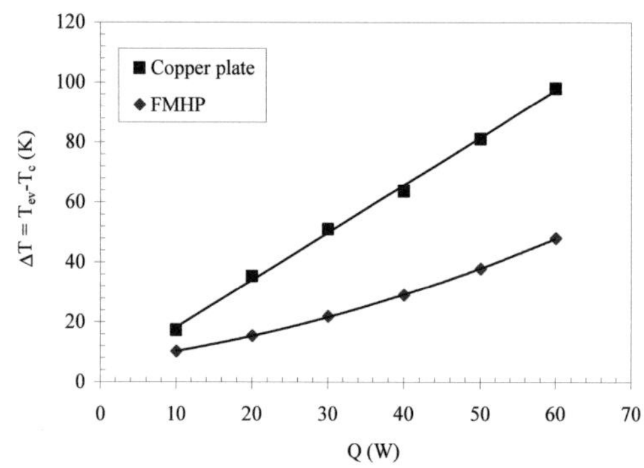

Fig. 6. T_{ev} - T_c variations Vs. Q

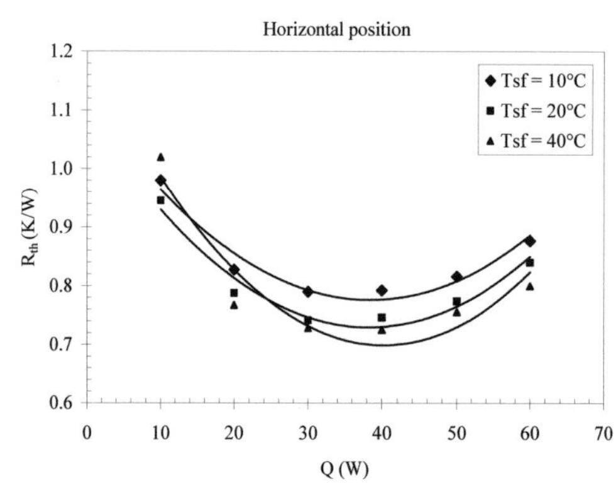

Fig. 7. FMHP thermal resistance Vs. Q, for

In order to quantify the experimental results better, additional data are taken from which an effective FMHP conductivity, λ_{eff}, could be calculated using Fourier's law. The axial heat flux rate, that is, the heat transported through the FMHP in the direction of the grooves, is computed by dividing the input power by the FMHP cross-sectional area. This value is then divided by the source-sink temperature difference. The obtained result is then multiplied by the linear distance between the points at which the source and sink temperatures are measured. As depicted in Fig. 8, the increasing trend observed in the effective thermal conductivity of the FMHP results from the decreasing temperature gradient occurring at high heat flux rates which makes the heat pipes perform more effectively.

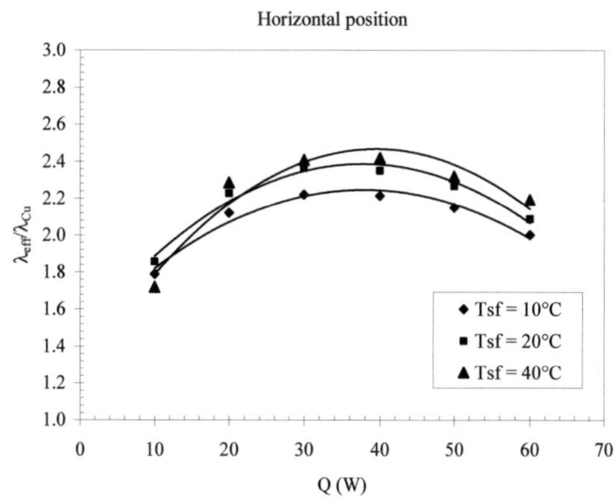

Fig. 8. Effective thermal conductivity enhancement variations Vs. Q, for different heat sink temperatures

The heat transfer coefficients in the evaporator and condenser zones are calculated according to the following expressions

$$h_{ev} = \frac{1}{\frac{(T_{ev} - T_{sat})}{q_{ev}} - \frac{t_w}{\lambda_w}} \qquad (1)$$

$$h_c = \frac{1}{\frac{(T_{sat} - T_c)}{q_c} - \frac{t_w}{\lambda_w}} \qquad (2)$$

q_{ev} and q_c are the heat fluxes calculated on the basis the evaporator and condenser heat transfer areas. t_w and λ_w are the thickness and the thermal conductivity of the wall, respectively.

The variations of the evaporation and condensation heat transfer as a function of the heat input power are depicted in Fig. 9, for different heat sink temperatures. The evaporation heat transfer coefficients are larger than the condensation ones. For a given heat sink temperature, the evaporation heat transfer coefficient exhibits a maximum which corresponds to the capillary limit, Q_{max}. The degradation of the evaporation process is caused by the fact that, for heat input powers which are higher than the capillary limit, the evaporator becomes starved of liquid and dry-out occurs since the capillary pumping is not sufficient for these conditions to overcome the liquid and vapor pressure losses. The condensation heat transfer coefficient increases with the heat input power, Q. This is due to the fact that the FMHP is correctly filled, and the blocking zone at the end of the condenser section is not large. For a given heat input power, the evaporation heat transfer coefficient increases with the heat sink temperature, however, the condensation heat transfer coefficient seems to decrease when the heat sink temperature increases. Hence, the evaporation process in the grooves is enhanced when the heat sink temperature increases; meanwhile the condensation process is altered.

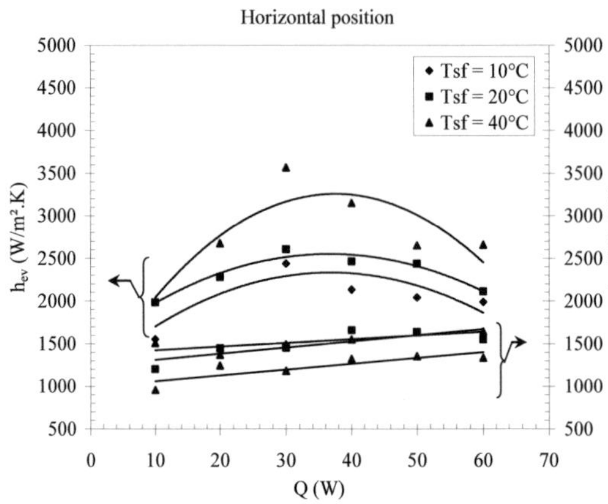

Fig. 9. Evaporation and condensation heat transfer coefficients Vs. Q, for different heat sink temperatures

5.3.2 Combined effects of the heat input power and the tilt angle

To determine the significance of the gravitational forces, experiments are carried out with different FMHP orientations: horizontal, thermosyphon, and anti-gravity positions. The heat sink temperature is fixed at T_{sf} = 40°C. The FMHP thermal resistances variations as a function of the heat input power are depicted in Fig. 10, for different FMHP orientations. For heat flux rates Q > 40 W, the FMHP thermal resistances are nearly the same for the different positions (if we consider the uncertainties on thermal resistance). However, for heat flux rates Q < 40 W, the FMHP becomes sensitive to the orientation. The Anti-gravity position exhibits the highest thermal resistances, while the thermosyphon and the horizontal positions exhibit similar thermal resistances which are lower than those obtained for the anti-gravity position.

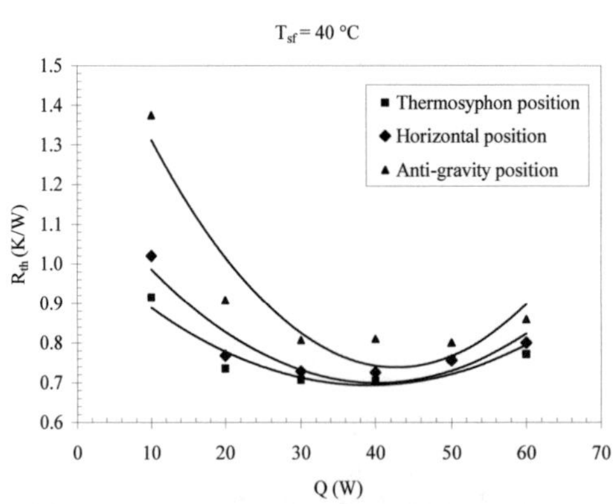

Fig. 10. FMHP thermal resistance Vs. Q, for different orientations

In Fig. 11 are depicted the variations of the ratio of the effective thermal conductivity, λ_{eff}, to the copper thermal conductivity, λ_{Cu}, as a function of the heat power input. The enhancement of the effective thermal conductivity of the FMHP amounts to an increase of nearly 240 percent for an input heat flux rate of about 40 W, for the horizontal and thermosyphon positions, however, for the anti-gravity position, the enhancement is lower and varies from nearly 30% for a heat input power of 10 W to 220% for a heat input power of 40 W, and decreases to 200% for Q = 60 W.

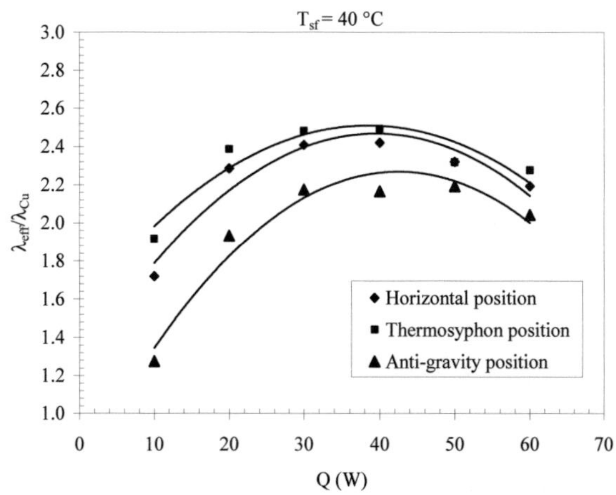

Fig. 11. Effective thermal conductivity enhancement variations as a function of Q, for different orientations (T_{sf} = 40 °C)

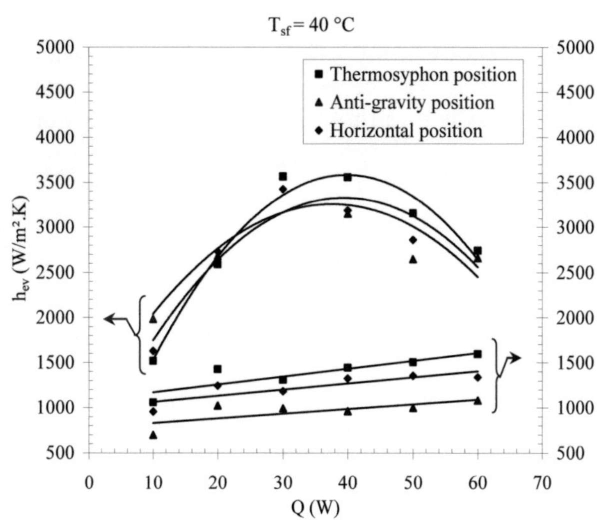

Fig. 12. Evaporation and condensation heat transfer coefficient Vs. Q, for different orientations (T_{sf} = 40 °C)

Fig. 12 shows the variations of the evaporator and condensation heat transfer coefficients as a function of the heat input power, Q. As it can be noticed, the evaporator heat transfer coefficients are not very sensitive to the FMHP orientation (if we consider the uncertainties). We can also notice that for heat input powers, which are higher than the capillary limit, the evaporator heat transfer coefficients are higher than those obtained for the horizontal and anti-gravity positions. However, the condensation heat transfer coefficient is sensitive to the orientation. These results can be explained by the liquid distribution inside the FMHP which is dependent on its orientation since the thermosyphon position is favorable to the return of the liquid to the evaporator.

5.3.3 Heat transfer law

In order to quantify the heat transfer mechanisms in the evaporator and condenser zones, we have processed the experimental data in dimensionless numbers in order to obtain heat transfer laws. The dimensionless analysis is carried out on the basis of Vaschy-Backingham theorem (or π theorem). The heat transfer coefficients in the evaporator and condenser zones are calculated according to equations (1) and (2).The following dimensionless numbers are evidenced from the π analysis:

i. the Laplace constant (obtained for Bond number equal to unity), La

$$La = \sqrt{\frac{\sigma}{(\rho_l - \rho_v)g}} \tag{3}$$

where σ is the liquid surface tension. ρ_l and ρ_v are the liquid and vapor densities, respectively. g is the gravity acceleration.

ii. the Reynolds number, Re

$$Re = \frac{\rho_l V_e La}{\mu_l} = \frac{\dot{m}}{\mu_l S} = \frac{Q}{\mu_l S \Delta h_v} = \frac{q}{\mu_l \Delta h_v} \tag{4}$$

where V_e is the liquid or the vapor velocity. μ_l is the liquid dynamic viscosity, and Δh_v is the latent heat. S is the heat transfer area in the evaporator ($L_e \times l_e$) or condenser section ($L_c \times l_c$), Q is the heat flux rate, and q is the heat flux transferred in the evaporator or the condenser zone.

iii. the Prandtl number, Pr

$$Pr = \frac{\mu_l C_{pl}}{\lambda_l} \tag{5}$$

where C_{pl} is the liquid specific heat, and λ_l is the liquid thermal conductivity.

iv. the Nüsselt number, Nu

$$Nu = \frac{h La}{\lambda_l} \tag{6}$$

where h is the heat transfer coefficient in the evaporator or condenser section.

v. the modified Jakob number, Ja*

$$Ja^* = \frac{\rho_l}{\rho_v} \frac{C_{pl} T_{sat}}{\Delta h_v} \tag{7}$$

Hence, the heat transfer coefficients can be calculated by

$$Nu = A\,Re^{m_1}\,Pr^{m_2}\,Ja^{*m_3} \tag{8}$$

A, m_1, m_2, and m_3 are constant, which are determined from the experimental results. For the evaporation heat transfer, relation (8) is calculated by taking the liquid physical properties at the saturation temperature and the vapor physical properties at the film temperature ($T_f = (T_{sat}+T_w)/2$). For condensation heat transfer, the liquid and vapor physical properties are determined by considering the film and saturation temperatures, respectively.
The constants of equation (8) are determined from the experimental data by a linear regression analysis, for the evaporation and the condensation phenomena. It is found that the heat transfer law proposed by equation (8), the experimental results are well correlated when considering $A = 902$, $m_1 = 0.825$, $m_2 = 0.333$, $m_3 = -0.999$, and $m_4 = -0.020$, for the evaporation phenomena, and $A = 2.165 \times 10^{-12}$, $m_1 = 1.001$, $m_2 = -0.032$, $m_3 = 2.644$, and $m_4 = 1.907$, for the condensation phenomena. The variations of the calculated Nüsselt number as a function of the Nüsselt number obtained experimentally are depicted in Fig. 13. As it can be seen from Fig. 13, the experimental Nüsselt number for the heat transfer by evaporation is well represented by equation (8). For the evaporation heat transfer, the coefficient of correlation is 0.751 and the deviation from the experimental results is ± 20%. For the condensation heat transfer law, the experimental results are very well represented by equation (8) with a coefficient of correlation of 0.978, and the deviation from the experimental results is ± 10%.

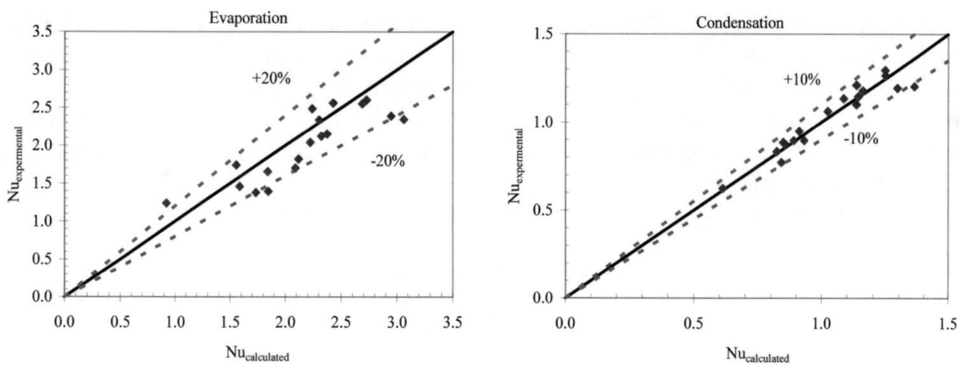

Fig. 13. Comparison between the Nusselt number obtained from the experimental results and that obtained from equation (8) for (a) the evaporation heat transfer, (b) the condensation heat transfer

6. FMHP modeling

6.1 Equations of the model

The section of the FMHP is illustrated by Fig. 1 (square microchannels with $D_g = W_g = d$). The liquid accumulates in the corners and forms four meniscuses (Fig. 14). Their curvature radius, r_c, is related to the difference of pressure, between vapor and liquid phase, by the Laplace-Young equation.

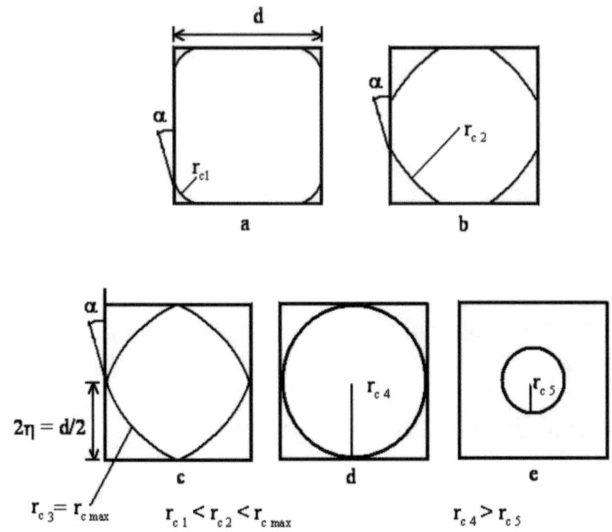

Fig. 14. Evolution of the curvature radius along a microchannel

In the evaporator and adiabatic zones, the curvature radius, in the parallel direction of the microchannel axis, is lower than the one perpendicular to this axis. Therefore, the meniscus is described by only one curvature radius. In a given section, r_c is supposed constant. The axial evolution of r_c is obtained by the differential of the Laplace-Young equation. The part of wall that is not in contact with the liquid is supposed dry and adiabatic.

In the condenser, the liquid flows toward the microchannel corners. There is a transverse pressure gradient, and a transverse curvature radius variation of the meniscus. The distribution of the liquid along a microchannel is presented in Fig. 14.

The microchannel is divided into several elementary volumes of length, dz, for which, we consider the Laplace-Young equation, and the conservation equations written for the liquid and vapor phases as it follows

Laplace-Young equation

$$\frac{dP_v}{dz} - \frac{dP_l}{dz} = -\frac{\sigma}{r_c^2}\frac{dr_c}{dz} \tag{9}$$

Liquid and vapor mass conservation

$$\frac{d\,(\rho_l\, w_l\, A_l)}{dz} = \frac{1}{\Delta h_v}\frac{dQ}{dz} \tag{10}$$

$$\frac{d\,(\rho_v\, w_v\, A_v)}{dz} = -\frac{1}{\Delta h_v}\frac{dQ}{dz} \tag{11}$$

Liquid and vapor momentum conservation

$$\rho_l \frac{d(A_l w_l^2)}{dz} dz = \frac{d(A_l P_l)}{dz} dz + A_{il}\left|\tau_{il}\right| + A_{lw}\left|\tau_{lw}\right| - \rho_l\, g\, A_l \sin\beta\, dz \tag{12}$$

$$\rho_v \frac{d(A_v w_v^2)}{dz} dz = -\frac{d(A_v P_v)}{dz} dz - |\tau_{il}| A_{il} - |\tau_{vw}| A_{vw} - \rho_v g A_v \sin\beta \, dz \tag{13}$$

Energy conservation

$$\lambda_w \frac{\partial^2 T_w}{\partial z^2} - \frac{h}{t_w}(T_w - T_{sat}) = -\frac{1}{1 \times t_w} \frac{dQ}{dz} \tag{14}$$

The quantity dQ/dz in equations (10), (11), and (14) represents the heat flux rate variations along the elementary volume in the evaporator and condenser zones, which affect the variations of the liquid and vapor mass flow rates as it is indicated by equations (10) and (11). So, if the axial heat flux rate distribution along the microchannel is given by

$$Q = \begin{cases} Q_a z/L_e & 0 \le z \le L_e \\ Q_a & L_e < z < L_e + L_a \\ Q_a \left(1 + \dfrac{L_e + L_a - z}{L_c - L_b}\right) & L_e + L_a \le z \le L_t - L_b \end{cases} \tag{15}$$

we get a linear flow mass rate variations along the microchannel.

In equation (15), h represents the heat transfer coefficient in the evaporator, adiabatic and condenser sections. For these zones, the heat transfer coefficients are determined from the experimental results (section 5.3.3). Since the heat transfer in the adiabatic section is equal to zero and the temperature distribution must be represented by a mathematical continuous function between the different zones, the adiabatic heat transfer coefficient value is chosen to be infinity.

The liquid and vapor passage sections, A_l, and A_v, the interfacial area, A_{il}, the contact areas of the phases with the wall, A_{lp} and A_{vp}, are expressed using the contact angle and the interface curvature radius by

$$A_l = 4 * r_c^2 \left(\sin^2\theta - \theta + \frac{\sin 2\theta}{2}\right) \tag{16}$$

$$A_v = d^2 - A_l \tag{17}$$

$$A_{il} = 8 \times \theta \times r_c \times dz \tag{18}$$

$$A_{lw} = \frac{16}{\sqrt{2}} r_c \sin\theta \, dz \tag{19}$$

$$A_{vw} = \left(4 \times d - \frac{16}{\sqrt{2}} r_c \sin\theta\right) dz \tag{20}$$

$$\theta = \frac{\pi}{4} - \alpha \tag{21}$$

The liquid-wall and the vapor-wall shear stresses are expressed as

$$\tau_{lw} = \frac{1}{2}\rho_l w_l^2 f_l \,,\ f_l = \frac{k_l}{R_{e_l}} \,,\ R_{el} = \frac{\rho_l w_l D_{hlw}}{\mu_l} \tag{22}$$

$$\tau_{vw} = \frac{1}{2}\rho_v w_v^2 f_v \,,\ f_v = \frac{k_v}{R_{ev}} \,,\ R_{ev} = \frac{\rho_v w_v D_{hvw}}{\mu_v} \tag{23}$$

Where k_l and k_v are the Poiseuille numbers, and D_{hlw} and D_{hvw} are the liquid-wall and the vapor-wall hydraulic diameters, respectively.
The hydraulic diameters and the shear stresses in equations (22) and (23) are expressed as follows

$$D_{hlw} = \frac{\sqrt{2} \times r_c \left(\sin^2\theta - \theta + \frac{\sin 2\theta}{2}\right)}{\sin\theta} \tag{24}$$

$$D_{hvw} = \frac{d^2 - 4r_c^2\left(\sin^2\theta - \theta + \frac{\sin 2\theta}{2}\right)}{d - \frac{4}{\sqrt{2}}\sin\theta \times r_c} \tag{25}$$

$$\tau_{lw} = \frac{1}{2}\frac{k_l w_l \mu_l \sin\theta}{2\sqrt{2}\left(\sin^2\theta - \theta + \frac{\sin\theta}{2}\right) r_c} \tag{26}$$

$$\tau_{vw} = \frac{k_v w_v \mu_v \left(d - \left(\frac{4}{\sqrt{2}}\sin\theta\right) r_c\right)}{2\left(d^2 - 4r_c^2\left(\sin^2\theta - \theta + \frac{\sin\theta}{2}\right)\right)} \tag{27}$$

The liquid-vapor shear stress is calculated by assuming that the liquid is immobile since its velocity is considered to be negligible when compared to the vapor velocity ($w_l << w_v$). Hence, we have

$$\tau_{il} = \frac{1}{2}\frac{\rho_v w_v^2 k_v}{R_{eiv}} \,,\ R_{eiv} = \frac{\rho_v |w_v| D_{hiv}}{\mu_v} \tag{28}$$

where D_{hiv} is the hydraulic diameter of the liquid-vapor interface. The expressions of D_{hiv} and τ_{iv} are

$$D_{hi} = \frac{d^2 - 4r_c^2\left(\sin^2\theta - \theta + \frac{\sin 2\theta}{2}\right)}{2\ \theta\ r_c} \tag{29}$$

$$\tau_{il} = \frac{k_v \theta\ r_c w_v \mu_v}{d^2 - 4r_c^2\left(\sin^2\theta - \theta + \frac{\sin 2\theta}{2}\right)} \tag{30}$$

The equations (9-14) constitute a system of six first order differential, nonlinear, and coupled equations. The six unknown parameters are: r_c, w_l, w_v, P_l, P_v, and T_w. The integration starts in the beginning of the evaporator (z = 0) and ends in the condenser extremity ($z = L_t - L_b$), where L_b is the length of the condenser flooding zone. The boundary conditions for the adiabatic zone are the calculated solutions for the evaporator end. In z = 0, we use the following boundary conditions:

$$\begin{cases} r_c|^0 = r_{cmin} & \text{(a)} \\ w_l|^0 = w_v|^0 = 0 & \text{(b)} \\ P_v|^0 = P_{sat}(T_v) & \text{(c)} \\ P_l|^0 = P_v - \dfrac{\sigma}{r_{cmin}} & \text{(d)} \end{cases} \quad (31)$$

The solution is performed along the microchannel if r_c is higher than r_{cmin}. The coordinate for which this condition is verified, is noted L_{as} and corresponds to the microchannel dry zone length. Beyond this zone, the liquid doesn't flow anymore. Solution is stopped when $r_c = r_{cmax}$, which is determined using the following reasoning: the liquid film meets the wall with a constant contact angle. Thus, the curvature radius increases as we progress toward the condenser (Figs. 14a and 14b). When the liquid film contact points meet, the wall is not anymore in direct contact with vapor. In this case, the liquid configuration should correspond to Fig. 14c, but actually, the continuity in the liquid-vapor interface shape imposes the profile represented on Figure 14d. In this case, the curvature radius is maximum. Then, in the condenser, the meniscus curvature radius decreases as the liquid thickness increases (Fig. 14e). The transferred maximum power, so called capillary limit, is determined if the junction of the four meniscuses starts precisely in the beginning of the condenser.

6.2 Numerical results and analysis

In this analysis, we study a FMHP with the dimensions which are indicated in Table 1. The capillary structure is composed of microchannels as it is represented by the sketch of Fig. 1. The working fluid is water and the heat sink temperature is equal to 40 °C. The conditions of simulation are such as the dissipated power is varied, and the introduced mass of water is equal to the optimal fill charge.

The variations of the curvature radius r_c are represented in Fig. 15. In the evaporator, because of the recession of the meniscus in the channel corners and the great difference of pressure between the two phases, the interfacial curvature radius is very small on the evaporator extremity. It is also noticed that the interfacial curvature radius decreases in the evaporator section when the heat flux rate increases. However, it increases in the condenser section. Indeed, when the heat input power increases, the liquid and vapor pressure losses increase, and the capillary pressure becomes insufficient to overcome the pressure losses. Hence, the evaporator becomes starved of liquid, and the condenser is blocked with the liquid in excess.

The evolution of the liquid and vapor pressures along the microchannel is given in Figs. 16 and 17. We note that the vapor pressure gradient along the microchannel is weak. It is due to the size and the shape of the microchannel that don't generate a very important vapor

pressure drop. For the liquid, the velocity increase is important near of the evaporator extremity, which generates an important liquid pressure drop.
Fig. 18 presents the evolution of the liquid phase velocity along a microchannel. In the evaporator section, as the liquid passage section decreases, the liquid velocity increases considerably. On other hand, since the liquid passage section increases along the microchannel (adiabatic and condenser sections), the liquid velocity decreases to reach zero at the final extremity of the condenser. In the evaporator, the vapor phase velocity increases since the vapor passage section decreases. In the adiabatic zone, it continues to grow with the reduction of the section of vapor passage. Then, when the condensation appears, it decreases, and it is equal to zero on the extremity of the condenser (Fig. 19).

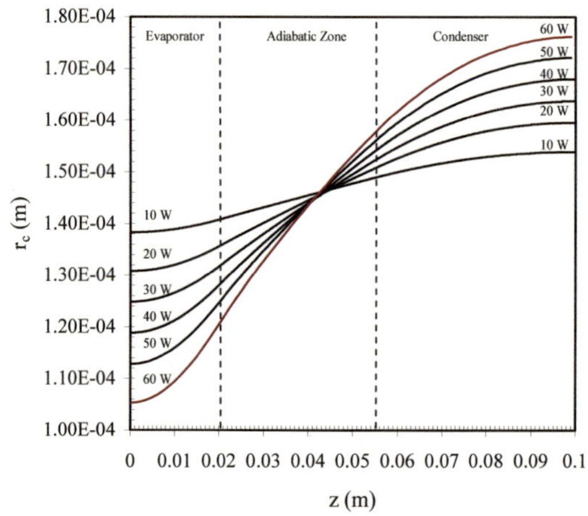

Fig. 15. Variations of the curvature radius r_c of the meniscus

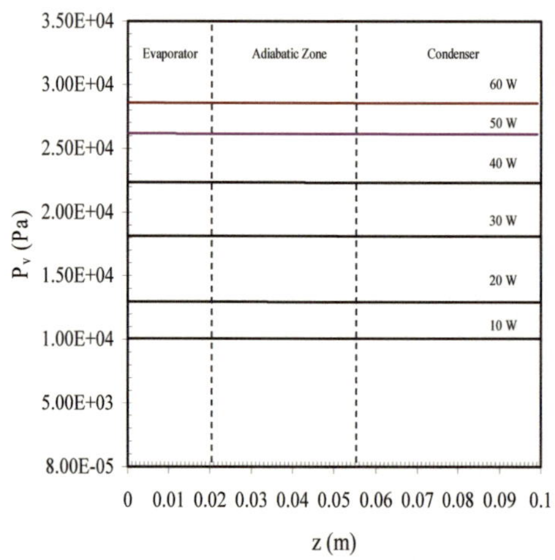

Fig. 16. Variations of the vapor pressure P_v

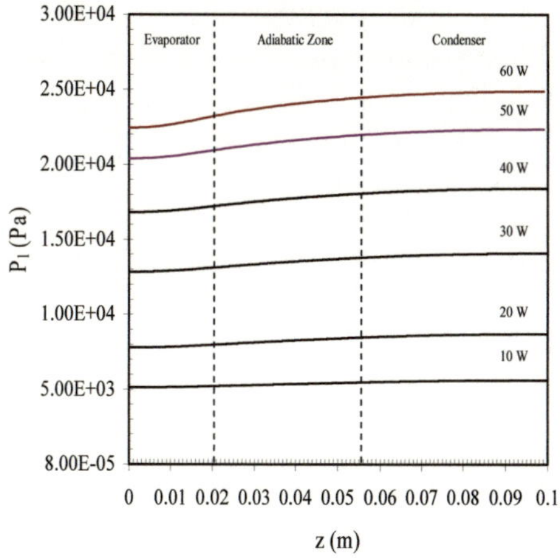

Fig. 17. Variations of the liquid pressure P_l

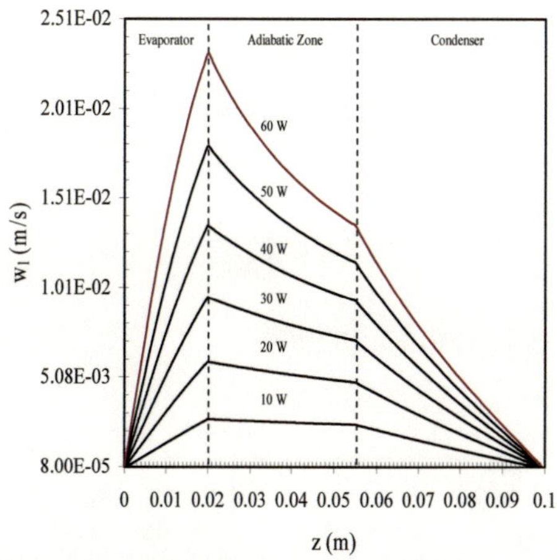

Fig. 18. The liquid phase velocity distribution

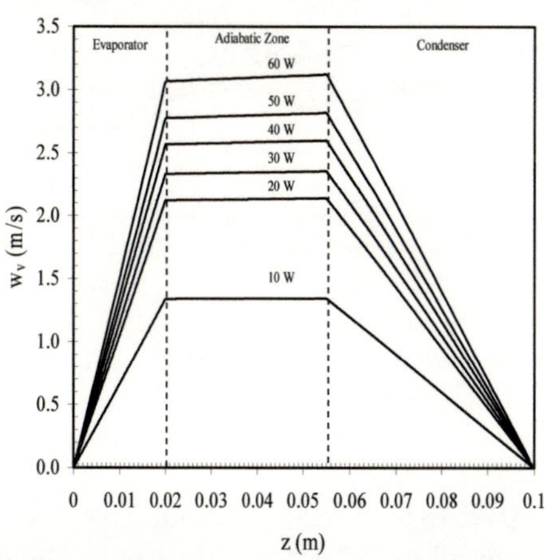

Fig. 19. The vapor phase velocity distribution

The variations of the wall temperature along the microchannel are reported in Fig. 20. In the evaporator section, the wall temperature decreases since an intensive evaporation appears due the presence of a thin liquid film in the corners. In the adiabatic section, the wall temperature is equal to the saturation temperature corresponding to the vapor pressure. In the condenser section, the wall temperature decreases. In this plot, are shown a comparison between the numerical results and the experimental ones, and a good agreement is found between the temperature distribution along the FMHP computed from the model and the temperature profile which is measured experimentally. An agreement is also noticed between the temperature distribution which is obtained from a pure conduction model and that obtained experimentally (Fig. 21).

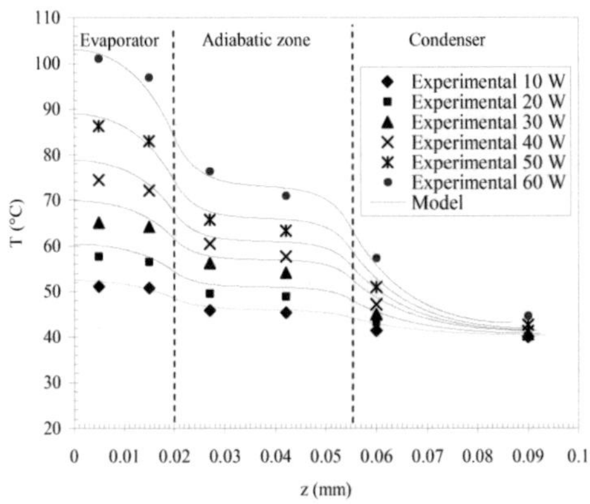

Fig. 20. Variations of the FMHP wall temperature

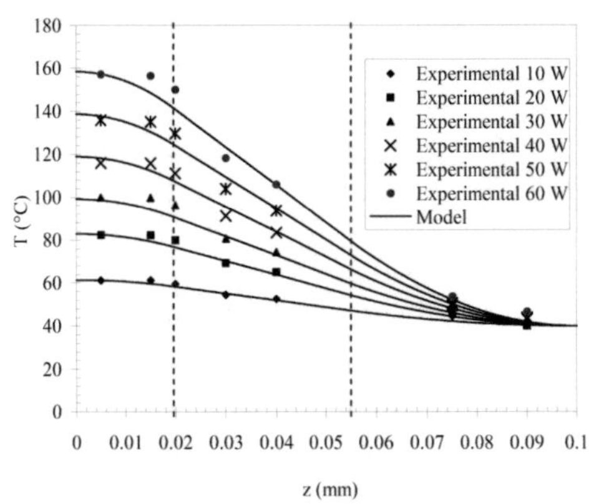

Fig. 21. Variations of the copper plate wall temperature

7. Conclusion

In this study, a copper FMHP is machined, sealed and filled with water as working fluid. The temperature measurements allow for a determination of the temperature gradients and maximum localized temperatures for the FMHPs. The thermal FMHP are compared to those of a copper plate having the same dimensions. In this way, the magnitude of the thermal enhancement resulting from the FMHP could be determined. The thermal measurements show significantly reduced temperature gradients and maximum temperature decrease when compared to those of a copper plate having the same dimensions. Reductions in the source-sink temperature difference are significant and increases in the effective thermal conductivity of approximately 250 percent are measured when the flat mini heat pipes operate horizontally.

The main feature of this study is the establishment of heat transfer laws for both condensation and evaporation phenomena. Appropriate dimensionless numbers are introduced and allow for the determination of relations, which represent well the experimental results. This kind of relations will be useful for the establishment of theoretical models for such capillary structures.

Based on the mass conservation, momentum conservation, energy conservation, and Laplace-Young equations, a one dimensional numerical model is developed to simulate the liquid-vapor flow as well as the heat transfer in a FMHP constituted by microchannels. It allows to predict the maximum power and the optimal mass of the fluid. The model takes into account interfacial effects, the interfacial radius of curvature, and the heat transfer in both the evaporator and condenser zones. The resulting coupled ordinary differential equations are solved numerically to yield interfacial radius of curvature, pressure, velocity, temperature information as a function of axial distance along the FMHP, for different heat inputs. The model results predict an almost linear profile in the interfacial radius of curvature. The pressure drop in the liquid is also found to be about an order of magnitude larger than that of the vapor. The model predicts very well the temperature distribution along the FMHP.

Although not addressing several issues such as the effect of the fill charge, FMHP orientation, heat sink temperature, and the geometrical parameters (groove width, groove height or groove spacing), it is clear from these results that incorporating such FMHP as part of high integrated electronic packages can significantly improve the performance and reliability of electronic devices, by increasing the effective thermal conductivity, decreasing the temperature gradients and reducing the intensity and the number of localized hot spots.

8. References

Angelov, G., Tzanova, S., Avenas, Y., Ivanova, M., Takov, T., Schaeffer, C. & Kamenova, L. (2005). Modeling of Heat Spreaders for Cooling Power and Mobile Electronic Devices, *36th Power Electronics Specialists Conference (PESC 2005)*, pp. 1080-1086, Recife, Brazil, June 12-15, 2005

Avenas, Y., Mallet, B., Gillot, C., Bricard, A., Schaeffer, C., Poupon, G. & Fournier, E. (2001). Thermal Spreaders for High Heat Flux Power Devices, *7th THERMINIC Workshop*, pp. 59-63, Paris, France, September 24-27, 2001

Cao, Y., Gao, M., Beam, J.E. & Donovan, B. (1997). Experiments and Analyses of Flat Miniature Heat Pipes, *Journal of Thermophysics and Heat Transfer*, Vol.11, No.2, pp. 158-164

Cao, Y. & Gao, M. (2002). Wickless Network Heat Pipes for High Heat Flux Spreading Applications, *International Journal of Heat and Mass Transfer*, Vol.45, pp. 2539-2547

Chien, H.T., Lee, D.S., Ding, P.P., Chiu, S.L. & Chen, P.H. (2003). Disk-shaped Miniature Heat Pipe (DMHP) with Radiating Micro Grooves for a TO Can Laser Diode Package, *IEEE Transactions on Components and Packaging Technologies*, Vol.26, No.3, pp. 569-574

Do, K.H., Kim, S.J. & Garimella, S.V. (2008). A Mathematical Model for Analyzing the Thermal Characteristics of a Flat Micro Heat Pipe with a Grooved Wick, *International Journal Heat and Mass Transfer,* Vol.51, No.19-20, pp. 4637-4650

Do, K.H. & Jang, S.P. (2010). Effect of Nanofluids on the Thermal Performance of a Flat Micro Heat Pipe with a Rectangular Grooved Wick, *International Journal of Heat and Mass Transfer*, Vol.53, pp. 2183-2192

Gao, M. & Cao, Y. (2003). Flat and U-shaped Heat Spreaders for High-Power Electronics, *Heat Transfer Engineering,* Vol.24, pp. 57-65

Groll, M., Schneider, M., Sartre, V., Zaghdoudi, M.C. & Lallemand, M. (1998). Thermal Control of electronic equipment by heat pipes, *Revue Générale de Thermique*, Vol.37, No.5, pp. 323-352

Hopkins, R., Faghri, A. & Khrustalev, D. (1999). Flat Miniature Heat Pipes with Micro Capillary Grooves, *Journal of Heat Transfer*, Vol.121, pp. 102-109

Khrustlev, D. & Faghri, A. (1995). Thermal Characteristics of Conventional and Flat Miniature Axially Grooved Heat Pipes, *Journal of Heat Transfer,* Vol.117, pp. 1048-1054

Faghri, A. & Khrustalev, D. (1997). Advances in modeling of enhanced flat miniature heat pipes with capillary grooves, Journal of Enhanced Heat Transfer, Vol.4, No.2, pp. 99-109

Khrustlev, D. & Faghri, A. (1999). Coupled Liquid and Vapor Flow in Miniature Passages with Micro Grooves, *Journal of Heat Transfer*, Vol.121, pp. 729-733

Launay, S., Sartre, V. & Lallemand, M. (2004). Hydrodynamic and Thermal Study of a Water-Filled Micro Heat Pipe Array, *Journal of Thermophysics and Heat Transfer*, Vol.18, No.3, pp. 358-363

Lefèvre, F., Revellin, R. & Lallemand, M. (2003). Theoretical Analysis of Two-Phase Heat Spreaders with Different Cross-section Micro Grooves, *7th International Heat Pipe Symposium*, pp. 97-102, Jeju Island, South Korea, October 12-16, 2003

Lefèvre, F., Rullière, R., Pandraud, G. & Lallemand, M. (2008). Prediction of the Maximum Heat Transfer Capability of Two-Phase Heat Spreaders-Experimental Validation, *International Journal of Heat and Mass Transfer*, Vol.51, No.15-16, pp. 4083-4094

Lim, H.T., Kim, S.H., Im, H.D., Oh, K.H. & Jeong, S.H. (2008). Fabrication and Evaluation of a Copper Flat Micro Heat Pipe Working under Adverse-Gravity Orientation, *Journal of Micromechanical Microengineering,* Vol.18, 8p.

Lin, L., Ponnappan, R. & Leland, J. (2002). High Performance Miniature Heat Pipe, *International Journal of Heat and Mass Transfer*, Vol.45, pp. 3131-3142

Lin, J.C., Wu, J.C., Yeh, C.T. & Yang, C.Y. (2004). Fabrication and Performance Analysis of Metallic Micro Heat Spreader for CPU, *13th International Heat Pipe Conference*, pp. 151-155, Shangai, China, September 21-25, 2004

Moon, S.H., Hwang, G., Ko, S.C. & Kim, Y.T. (2003). Operating Performance of Micro Heat Pipe for Thin Electronic Packaging, *7th International Heat Pipe Symposium*, pp. 109-114, Jeju Island, South Korea, October 12-16, 2003

Moon, S.H., Hwang, G., Ko, S.C. & Kim, Y.T. (2004). Experimental Study on the Thermal Performance of Micro-Heat Pipe with Cross-section of Polygon, *Microelectronics Reliability*, Vol.44, pp. 315-321

Murakami, M., Ogushi, T., Sakurai, Y., Masumuto, H., Furukawa, M. & Imai, R. (1987). Heat Pipe Heat Sink, *6th International Heat Pipe Conference*, pp. 257-261, Grenoble, France, May 25-29, 1987

Ogushi, T. & Yamanaka, G. (1994). Heat Transport Capability of Grooves Heat Pipes, *5th International Heat Pipe Conference*, pp. 74-79, Tsukuba, Japan, May 14-18, 1994

Plesh, D., Bier, W. & Seidel, D. (1991). Miniature Heat Pipes for Heat Removal from Microelectronic Circuits, *Micromechanical Sensors, Actuators and Systems*, Vol.32, pp. 303-313

Popova, N., Schaeffer, C., Sarno, C., Parbaud, S. & Kapelski, G. (2005). Thermal management for stacked 3D microelectronic packages, *36th Annual IEEE Power Electronic Specialits Conference (PESC 2005)*, pp. 1761-1766, recife, Brazil, June 12-16, 2005

Popova, N., Schaeffer, C., Avenas, Y. & Kapelski, G. (2006). Fabrication and Experimental Investigation of Innovative Sintered Very Thin Copper Heat Pipes for Electronics Applications, *37th IEEE Power Electronics Specialist Conference (PESC 2006)*, pp. 1652-1656, Vol. 1-7, Cheju Island, South Korea, June 18-22, 2006

Romestant, C., Burban, G. & Alexandre, A. (2004). Heat Pipe Application in Thermal-Engine Car Air Conditioning, *13th International Heat Pipe Conference*, pp. 196-201, Shanghai, China, September 21-25, 2004

Schneider, M., Yoshida, M. & Groll, M. (1999a). Investigation of Interconnected Mini Heat Pipe Arrays For Micro Electronics Cooling, *11th International Heat Pipe conference*, 6p., Musachinoshi-Tokyo, Japan, September 12-16, 1999

Schneider, M. Yoshida, M. & Groll, M. (1999b). Optical Investigation of Mini Heat Pipe Arrays With Sharp Angled Triangular Grooves, *Advances in Electronic Packaging*, EEP-Vol. 26-1 and 26-2, 1999, pp. 1965-1969.

Schneider, M. Yoshida, M. & Groll, M. (2000). Cooling of Electronic Components By Mini Heat Pipe Arrays, *15th National Heat and Mass transfer Conference and 4th ISHMT/ASME Heat and Mass Transfer Conference, 8p.*, Pune, India, January 12-14, 2000

Soo Yong, P. & Joon Hong, B. (2003). Thermal Performance of a Grooved Flat-Strip Heat Pipe with Multiple Source Locations, *7th International Heat Pipe Symposium*, pp. 157-162, Jeju Island, South Korea, October 12-16, 2003

Shi, P.Z., Chua, K.M., Wong, S.C.K. & Tan, Y.M. (2006). Design and Performance Optimization of Miniature Heat Pipe in LTCC, *Journal of Physics: Conference Series*, Vol.34, pp. 142-147

Sun, J.Y. & Wang, C.Y. (1994). The Development of Flat Heat Pipes for Electronic Cooling, *4th International Heat Pipe Symposium*, pp. 99-105, Tsukuba, Japan, May 16-18, 1994

Tao, H.Z., Zhang, H., Zhuang, J. & Bowmans, J.W. (2008). Experimental Study of Partially Flattened Axial Grooved Heat Pipes, *Applied Thermal Engineering*, Vol.28, pp. 1699-1710

Tzanova, S., Ivanova, M., Avenas, Y. & Schaeffer, C. (2004). Analytical Investigation of Flat Silicon Micro Heat Spreaders, *Industry Applications Conference, 39th IAS Annual Meeting Conference Record of the 2004 IEEE*, pp. 2296-2302, Vol.4, October 3-7, 2004

Xiaowu, W., Yong, T. & Ping, C. (2009). Investigation into Performance of a Heat Pipe with Micro Grooves Fabricated by Extrusion-Ploughing Process, *Energy Conversion and Management*, Vol.50, pp.1384-1388

Zaghdoudi, M.C. & Sarno, C. (2001). Investigation on the Effects of Body Force Environment on Flat Heat Pipes, *Journal of Thermophysics and Heat Transfer*, Vol.15, No.4, pp. 384-394

Zaghdoudi, M.C., Tantolin, C. & Godet, C. (2004). Experimental and Theoretical Analysis of Enhanced Flat Miniature Heat Pipes, *Journal of Thermophysics and Heat Transfer*, Vol.18, No.4, pp. 430-447

Zhang, L., Ma, T., Zhang, Z.F. & Ge, X. (2004). Experimental Investigation on Thermal Performance of Flat Miniature Heat Pipes with Axial Grooves, *13th International Heat Pipe Conference*, pp. 206-210, Shangai, China, September 21-25, 2004

Zhang, M., Liu, Z. & Ma, G. (2009). The Experimental and Numerical Investigation of a Grooved Vapor Chamber, *Applied Thermal Engineering*, Vol.29, pp. 422-430

6

Modeling Solidification Phenomena in the Continuous Casting of Carbon Steels

Panagiotis Sismanis
SIDENOR SA
Greece

1. Introduction

In recent years the quest for advanced steel quality satisfying more stringent specifications by time has forced research in the development of advanced equipment for the improvement of the internal structure of the continuously cast steels. A relatively important role has played the better understanding of the solidification phenomena that occur during the final stages of the solidification. Dynamic soft-reduction machines have been placed in industrial practice with top-level performance. Nevertheless, the numerical solution of the governing heat-transfer differential equation under the proper initial and boundary conditions continues to play the paramount role for the fundamental approach of the whole solidification process. Steel properties are critical upon the solidification behaviour. Different chemical analyses of carbon steels alter the solidus and liquidus temperatures and therefore influence the calculated results. Shell growth, local cooling rates and solidification times, solid fraction, and secondary dendrite arm-spacing are some important metallurgical parameters that need to be ultimately computed for specific steel grades once the heat transfer problem is solved.

2. Previous work and current status

Solidification heat-transfer has been extensively studied throughout the years and there are numerous works on the subject in the academic and industrial fields. Towards the development of continuous casting machines adapted to the needs of the various steel grades a great deal of research work has been published in this metallurgical domain. In one of the early works (Mizikar, 1967), the fundamental relationships and the means of solution were described, but in a series of articles (Brimacombe, 1976) and (Brimacombe et al, 1977, 1978, 1979, 1980) some important answers to the heat transfer problem as well as to associated product internal structures and continuous-casting problems were presented in detail. The crucial knowledge-creation practice of combining experiments and models together was the main method applied to most of these works. In this way, the shell thickness at mold exit, the metallurgical length of the caster, the location down the caster where cracks initiate, and the cooling practice below the mold to avoid reheating cracks were some of the points addressed. At that time, the first finite-element thermal-stress models of solidification were applied in order to understand the internal stress distribution in the solidifying steel strand below the mold. The need for data with respect to the mechanical properties of steels and specifically creep at high temperatures as a means for controlling the continuous casting events was realized from the early years of analysis (Palmaers, 1978). In a similar study, the bulging produced by creep in the continuously cast slabs was analyzed (Grill & Schwerdtfeger, 1979) with a finite-element model. In order to simulate the unbending process in a continuous casting machine a multi-beam model was proposed (Tacke, 1985) for strand straightening in the caster. With the advent of the computer revolution more advanced topics relevant to the fluid flow in the mold were addressed. Unsteady-state turbulent phenomena in the mold were tackled using the large eddy simulation method of analysis (Sivaramakrishnan et al, 2000); in extreme cases, it was reported that the computer program could take up to a month to converge and come up with a solution. Nevertheless, computational heat-transfer programs have helped in the development of better internal structure continuously-cast steels mostly for two main reasons: [1] the online control of the casting process and, [2] the offline analysis of factors which are more intrinsic to the specific nature of a steel grade under investigation, i.e., chemical analysis and internal structure. Continuing the literature survey more focus will be given to selected published works relevant to the second [2] influential reason.

The formation of internal cracks that influence the internal structure of slabs was investigated from the early years (Fuji et al, 1976) of continuous casting. It was proven that internal cracks are formed adjacent to the solid-liquid interface and greatly influenced by bulging. As creep was critical upon bulging in continuously cast slabs a model was proposed (Fujii et al, 1981) with adequate agreement between theory and practice for low and medium carbon aluminum-killed steels. In another study (Matsumiya et al, 1984) a mathematical analysis model was established in order to investigate the interdendritic micro-segregation using a finite difference scheme and taking into consideration the diffusion of a solute in the solid and liquid phases. As mechanical behavior of plain carbon steel in the austenite temperature region was proven of paramount importance in the continuous casting process a set of simple constitutive equations was developed (Kozlowski et al, 1992) for the elastoplastic analysis used in finite element models. Chemical composition of steel and specifically equivalent carbon content as well as the Mn/S ratio were found to define a critical strain value above which internal structure problems could appear (Hiebler et al, 1994). As analysis deepened into the internal structure and specifically into micro- and macro-segregation, relationships between primary and secondary dendrite arm spacing (Imagumbai, 1994) started to appear. In fact, first order analysis revealed that secondary dendrite arm-spacing is about one-half of the primary one. The effect of cooling rate on zero-strength-temperature (ZST) and zero-ductility-temperature (ZDT) was found to be significant (Won et al, 1998) due to segregation of solute elements at the final stage of solidification. The calculated temperatures at the solid fractions of 0.75 and 0.99 corresponded to the experimentally measured ZST and ZDT, respectively. Furthermore, a set of relationships that take under consideration steel composition, cooling rate, and solid fraction was proposed; the suggested prediction equation on ZST and ZDT was found in relative agreement with experimental results. In a monumental work (Cabrera-Marrero et al, 1998), the dendritic microstructure of continuously-cast steel billets was analyzed and found in agreement with experimental results. In fact, the differential equation of heat transfer was numerically solved along the sections of the caster and local solidification times related to microstructure for various steel compositions were computed. Based on the Clyne-Kurz model a simple model of micro-segregation during solidification of steels was developed

(Won & Thomas, 2001). In this way, the secondary dendrite arm spacing can be sufficiently computed with respect to carbon content and local cooling rates. In another study (Han et al, 2001), the formation of internal cracks in continuously cast slabs was mathematically analyzed with the implementation of a strain analysis model together with a micro-segregation model. The equation of heat transfer was also numerically solved along the caster. Total strain based on bulging, unbending, and roll-misalignment attributed strains, was computed and checked against the critical strain. Consequently, internal structure problems could be identified and verified in practice. The unsteady bulging was found to be (Yoon et al, 2002) the main reason of mold level hunching during thin slab casting. A finite difference scheme for the numerical solution of the heat transfer equation together with a continuous beam model and a primary creep equation were developed in order to match experimental data. A 2D unsteady heat-transfer model (Zhu et al, 2003) was applied to obtain the surface temperature and shell thickness of continuous casting slabs during the process of solidification. Roll misalignment was proven to provoke internal cracks once total strain at the solid/liquid interface exceeded the critical strain for the examined chemical composition of steel slabs. As creep was proven to be important in the continuous casting of steels, an evaluation of common constitutive equations was performed (Pierer at al, 2005) and tested against experimental data. The proposed results could help in the development of more sophisticated 2D finite element models. Once offline computer models are proven correct they can be applied online in real-time applications and minimize internal defects (Ma et al, 2008).

Consequently, very advanced types of continuous casting machines have appeared in the international market as a result of these investigations. Different steel grades are classified into groups which are processed in the continuous casters as heats cast with similar design and operating parameters. Automation plays an important role supervising the whole continuous casting process by running in two levels, i.e., controlling the process, and computing the final solidification front as a real-time solution to the heat-transfer problem case. The numerous steel products of excellent quality manifest the success of these sophisticated casting machines.

3. Present work

In this work the modelling of the solidification phenomena for two slab casters installed in different plants, one in Stomana, Pernik, Bulgaria, and the other in Sovel, Almyros, Greece, is presented. Both plants belong to the SIDENOR group of companies. Simple design and operating parameters together with the chemical analyses of the steel grades cast are the basic data to approximate the heat transfer solution, compute the temperature distributions inside the continuously cast slabs in every section of the caster, and investigate the solidification phenomena from the metallurgical point of view. A 3D numerical solution of the differential equation of heat transfer was developed and tested in a previous publication (Sismanis, 2010) and is not to be presented in detail here. Some routines were also implemented in the main core of that developed software in order to cover the extra computational work required for the metallurgical analysis of the solidification phenomena. Furthermore, strain analysis for any slab bulging and for the straightening positions was implemented as well. The methodology applied for tackling the continuous casting problem for different carbon steel grades from the metallurgical point of view is maybe what makes this purely computational study more intriguing and specific in nature. Critical formulas that bind the heat transfer problem with the various solidification parameters and strains in the slab are presented and discussed.

3.1 The heat transfer model applied

The general 3D heat transfer equation that describes the temperature distribution inside the solidifying body is given by the following equation (Carslaw & Jaeger, 1986) and (Incropera & DeWitt, 1981):

$$\rho C_P \frac{\partial T}{\partial t} = \nabla \cdot k \nabla T + S \tag{1}$$

The source term S, in units $W \cdot m^{-3}$, may be considered (Patankar, 1980) to be of the form:

$$S = S_C + S_P \cdot T \tag{2}$$

that is, by a constant term and a temperature dependent term and can be related to correspond to the latent heat of phase change. Furthermore, T is the temperature, and ρ, C_p, and k are the density, heat capacity, and thermal conductivity of steel, respectively. The heat transfer equation in Cartesian coordinates may be written as:

$$\rho C_p \frac{\partial T}{\partial t} = \frac{\partial}{\partial x}\left(k \frac{\partial T}{\partial x}\right) + \frac{\partial}{\partial y}\left(k \frac{\partial T}{\partial y}\right) + \frac{\partial}{\partial z}\left(k \frac{\partial T}{\partial z}\right) + S \tag{3}$$

The solidification problem in the continuous casting may be considered as such of studying the advance of the solidification front by means of mathematical solution of the global heat transfer involved in the specific geometry, and the local heat transfer in the mushy zone. In the present study, the heat conduction along the casting direction is considered to be negligible. So, (3) can be written as:

$$\rho C_P \frac{\partial T}{\partial t} = \frac{\partial}{\partial x}\left(k \frac{\partial T}{\partial x}\right) + \frac{\partial}{\partial y}\left(k \frac{\partial T}{\partial y}\right) + S \tag{4}$$

The boundary conditions applied in order to solve (4) are as follows:
Heat flux in the mold is equalized to the empirical equation used by other researchers (Lait et al, 1974),

$$q_m = 2.67 \times 10^6 - 2.21 \times 10^5 \sqrt{t_d} \tag{5}$$

The mold heat-flux (q_m) is given in W/m^2, and t_d (in seconds) is the dwell time of the strand inside the mold. Involving an expression for the local heat-transfer coefficient inside the mold (Yoon et al, 2002) a more realistic formula was derived that exhibited good results in the present study:

$$h_m = 1.35 \cdot 10^{-3} \cdot (1 - 0.8z) \cdot q_m \tag{6}$$

The heat fluxes due to water spraying and radiation of the strand in the secondary cooling zones were calculated using the following expressions:

$$q_s = h_s \cdot (T - T_{w0}) \tag{7}$$

$$q_r = h_r \cdot (T - T_{env}) \quad with \quad h_r = \sigma\varepsilon \cdot \frac{T^4 - T_{env}{}^4}{T - T_{env}} \tag{8}$$

$$q_c = h_c \cdot (T - T_{env}) \tag{9}$$

where h_s, h_r, and h_c are the heat transfer coefficients for spray cooling, radiation, and convection, respectively, T_{w0} is the water temperature, T_{env} is the ambient temperature, σ is the Stefan-Boltzmann constant, and ε is the steel emissivity (equal to 0.8 in the present study). Natural convection was assumed to prevail at the convection heat transfer as stagnant air-flow conditions were considered due to the low casting speeds of the strand applied in practice. The strand was assumed to be a long horizontal cylinder with an equivalent diameter of a circle having the same area with that of the strand cross-sectional area, and a correlation valid for a wide Rayleigh number range proposed by (Churchill & Chu, 1975) was applied, written in the form proposed by (Burmeister, 1983):

$$\sqrt{Nu_D} = 0.60 + 0.387B^{1/6} \qquad B = Ra_D\left[1 + \left(\frac{0.559}{\mathrm{Pr}}\right)^{9/16}\right]^{16/9} \qquad (10^{-5} < B < 10^{13}) \tag{10}$$

where Nu, Ra, and Pr are the dimensionless Nusselt, Rayleigh, and Prandtl numbers, respectively. In this way, h_c is calculated by means of the Nu_D number. It is worth mentioning, however, that the radiation effects are more pronounced than the convection ones in the continuous casting of steels. From various expressions proposed in the literature for the heat transfer coefficient in water-spray cooling systems the following formula was applied as approaching the present casting conditions:

$$h_s = 1570 \cdot W^{0.55} \cdot \frac{1 - 0.0075T_{w0}}{4} \tag{11}$$

where W is the water flux for any secondary spray zone in liters/m²/sec, and h_s is in W/m²/K. At any point along the secondary zones (starting just below the mold) of the caster the total flux q_{tot} is computed according to the following formula, taking into account that q_s may be zero at areas where no sprays are applied:

$$q_{tot} = q_s + q_r + q \tag{12}$$

In mathematical terms, considering a one-fourth of the cross-section of a slab assuming perfect symmetry, the aforementioned boundary conditions can be written as:

$$-k\frac{\partial T}{\partial x} = \begin{cases} q_m \;\; at\; x = W_x,\; 0 \le y \le W_y,\; 0 \le z \le L_m \\ q_{tot} \;\; at\; x = W_x,\; 0 \le y \le W_y,\; z > L_m \end{cases} \tag{13}$$

$$-k\frac{\partial T}{\partial y} = \begin{cases} q_m \;\; at\; y = W_y,\; 0 \le x \le W_x,\; 0 \le z \le L_m \\ q_{tot} \;\; at\; y = W_y,\; 0 \le x \le W_x,\; z > L_m \end{cases} \tag{14}$$

where z follows the casting direction starting from the meniscus level inside the mold; consequently, the mold has an active length of L_m. W_x and W_y are the half-width and the half-thickness of the cast product, respectively. Due to symmetry, the heat fluxes at the central planes are considered to be zero:

$$-k\frac{\partial T}{\partial x}=0 \ at\ x=0,\ 0\leq y\leq W_y,\ z\geq 0 \tag{15}$$

$$-k\frac{\partial T}{\partial y}=0 \ at\ y=0,\ 0\leq x\leq W_x,\ z\geq 0 \tag{16}$$

Finally, the initial temperature of the pouring liquid steel is supposed to be the temperature of liquid steel in the tundish:

$$T=T_0 \text{ at } t=0 \text{ (and } z=0\text{)},\ 0<x<W_x,\ 0<y<W_y \tag{17}$$

The thermo-physical properties of carbon steels were obtained from the published work of (Cabrera-Marrero et al, 1998); the properties were given as functions of carbon content for the liquid, mushy, solid, and transformation temperature domain values. The liquidus and solidus temperatures were obtained from the work of (Thomas et al, 1987):

$$\begin{aligned}T_L &= 1537-88(\%C)-8(\%Si)-5(\%Mn)-30(\%P)-25(\%S)\\ &\quad -4(\%Ni)-1.5(\%Cr)-5(\%Cu)-2(\%Mo)-2(\%V)-18(\%Ti)\end{aligned} \tag{18}$$

$$\begin{aligned}T_S &= 1535-200(\%C)-12.3(\%Si)-6.8(\%Mn)-124.5(\%P)-183.9(\%S)\\ &\quad -4.3(\%Ni)-1.4(\%Cr)-4.1(\%Al)\end{aligned} \tag{19}$$

At any time step the simulating program computes whether a given nodal point is at a lower or higher temperature than the liquidus or solidus temperatures for a given steel composition. Consequently, the instantaneous position of the solidification front is derived, and therefore, in the solidification direction the last solidified nodal point at the solidus temperature.

3.1.1 Strain analysis computations

Bulging strain ε_B was computed based on the analysis by (Fujii et al, 1976) in which primary creep was taken under consideration. Equations (20) through (27) contain the necessary formulas used in these computations:

$$\varepsilon_B = 1600\cdot\delta_B\cdot S/\ell_P^{\,2} \tag{20}$$

$$\delta_B=\beta\sqrt{t_P}\ /S^3 \quad and \quad t_P=\ell_P/u_C \tag{21}$$

$$\beta = 12(1-\nu^2)\cdot\sigma_P\cdot\alpha_5\cdot A_0\cdot\ell_P^{\,4} \tag{22}$$

$$\alpha_5=\frac{2}{\pi^5\cosh(\psi)}\{2\cosh(\psi)-\psi\tanh(\psi)-2\} \quad and \quad \psi=\frac{\pi W_x}{\ell_P} \tag{23}$$

Some important parameters are included in the expressions: ℓ_P is the roll pitch in the part of the caster under consideration, u_C is the casting speed, t_P is time in seconds, S is the thickness of the solidified shell at the point of analysis along the caster, and ν is the Poisson ratio for steel which is related to steel according to the following relationship (Uehara et al, 1986):

$$\nu = 0.278 + 8.23 \times 10^{-5} \cdot T_P \quad and \quad T_P = \frac{1}{2}\left(T_S + T_{Surf}\right) \tag{24}$$

The T_P value (in °C) is taken as the average value between the solidus and the surface temperature of the slab. Primary creep data were taken from the work of (Palmaers, 1978) and applied with good results mostly for low and medium carbon steel slabs produced at Sovel. Table 1 presents the data used. Equation (25) illustrates the expression used for the calculation of the primary creep strain and σ_P (in MPa) resembles the ferro-static pressure (26) at a point along the caster which has a distance H_5 measured along the vertical axis from the meniscus level; it is clarified that the maximum value of H_5 can be around the caster radius (27).

$$\varepsilon_C = A_0 \cdot \sigma_P{}^n \cdot t_P{}^m \cdot \exp(-\frac{Q_C}{RT}) \tag{25}$$

$$\sigma_P = \rho g H_5 \tag{26}$$

$$H_{5,\max} = R_C \tag{27}$$

For the steel slabs produced at Stomana, the constitutive equations for model II (Kozlowski et al, 1992) were applied after integration (T in Kelvin=T_P+273.16):

$$\dot{\varepsilon}_P = C \cdot \exp(-Q_{C,K} / T) \cdot \sigma_P{}^n \cdot t_P{}^m \tag{28}$$

where, $Q_{C,K}$ = 17160 and:

$$C = 0.3091 + 0.2090 \cdot (\%C) + 0.1773 \cdot (\%C)^2 \tag{29}$$

$$n = 6.365 - 4.521 \cdot 10^{-3} \cdot T + 1.439 \cdot 10^{-6} \cdot T^2 \tag{30}$$

$$m = -1.362 + 5.761 \cdot 10^{-4} \cdot T + 1.982 \cdot 10^{-8} \cdot T^2 \tag{31}$$

So, after appropriate integration of the strain rate (28), the following expression was applied for the primary creep that exhibited better results than the correlations of (Palmaers, 1978) specifically for the Stomana slabs, probably due to their much larger size compared to the size of the slabs produced at Sovel:

$$\varepsilon_P = (C / (m+1)) \cdot \exp(-Q_{C,K} / T) \cdot \sigma_P{}^n \cdot t^{m+1} \tag{32}$$

The unbending strain was computed according to equation (33) where R_{n-1}, R_n are the unbending radii of the caster, (Uehara et al, 1986) and (Zhu et al, 2003).

$$\varepsilon_S = 100 \cdot (W_y - S) \cdot \left| \frac{1}{R_{n-1}} - \frac{1}{R_n} \right| \tag{33}$$

Any caster misalignment of value δ_M can be computed according to (34), as described in the works of (Han et al, 2001) and (Zhu et al, 2003):

$$\varepsilon_M = 300 \cdot S \cdot \delta_M / \ell_P^{\,2} \qquad (34)$$

The total strain ε_{tot} that a slab may undergo at a specific point along the caster is the sum of all the aforementioned strains:

$$\varepsilon_{tot} = \varepsilon_B + \varepsilon_S + \varepsilon_M \qquad (35)$$

The total strain should never exceed the value for the critical strain ε_{Cr} which is a function of the carbon equivalent value (36) and the Mn/S ratio, as this could cause internal cracks during casting (Hiebler et al, 1994). It should be pointed out that low carbon steels with high Mn/S (>25) ratios are the least prone for cracking during casting.

$$C_{eq,C} = (\%C) + 0.02(\%Mn) + 0.04(\%Ni) - 0.1(\%Si) - 0.04(\%Cr) - 0.1(\%Mo) \qquad (36)$$

%Carbon	Temperature range, °C	A_0	m	n	Q_C (kJ/mol)
0.090 (low carbon)	< 1000	0.349	0.35	3.1	150.6
0.090 (low carbon)	1000-1250	2.422	0.33	2.5	146.4
0.090 (low carbon)	> 1250	6.240	0.21	1.6	123.4
0.185 (medium carbon)	< 1000	141.1	0.36	3.1	211.3
0.185 (medium carbon)	1000-1250	1.825	0.37	2.5	144.3
0.185 (medium carbon)	> 1250	1.342	0.25	1.5	102.5

Table 1. Data used for primary creep

3.1.2 Solid fraction analysis

The solid fraction values f_S are very important especially at the final stages of solidification in which soft reduction is applied in many slab casters in an attempt to reduce or minimize any internal segregation problems. The following expressions extracted from the work of (Won et al, 1998) were used:

$$f_S = (1 - 2\Omega\kappa)^{-1} \left\{ 1 - \left(\frac{1536 - T}{\sum_j f'(C_j)} \right)^{\Lambda} \right\} \quad \text{and} \quad \Lambda = \frac{1 - 2\Omega\kappa}{\kappa - 1} \qquad (37)$$

$$\sum_j f'(C_j) = 67.51(\%C) + 9.741(\%Si) + 3.292(\%Mn) + 82.18(\%P) + 155.8(\%S) \qquad (38)$$

$$\Omega = \alpha(1 - \exp(-1/\alpha)) - \frac{1}{2}\exp(-1/(2\alpha)) \qquad (39)$$

$$\alpha = 33.7 \cdot C_R^{-0.244} \tag{40}$$

$$\kappa = 0.265 \quad \text{and} \quad \kappa = (\kappa^{\delta/L} + \kappa^{\gamma/L}) / 2 \tag{41}$$

As described by equations (37) through (41), considering an average equilibrium partition coefficient κ=0.265 for carbon at the delta/liquid and gamma/liquid phase transformations, respectively, and a local cooling rate C_R, solid fraction values can be computed as a function of mushy-zone temperatures and specific chemical analysis of steel. Dendrites are characterized by means of the primary λ_{PRIM} and secondary λ_{SDAS} dendritic arm spacing. The dependence of both λ_{PRIM} and λ_{SDAS} spacing on the chemical composition and solidification conditions is needed for a correct microstructure prediction whose results can be employed for micro- and macro-segregation appraisal. Primary dendrite arm spacing is related to the solidification rate r and thermal gradient G in the mushy zone according to the following formula (Cabrera-Marrero et al, 1998):

$$\lambda_{PRIM} = n_{rg} \cdot r^{-\frac{1}{4}} \cdot G^{-\frac{1}{2}} \tag{42}$$

Solidification rate r is actually the rate of shell growth:

$$r = \frac{dS}{dt} \tag{43}$$

and the thermal gradient G is defined as:

$$G = \frac{(T_L - T_S)}{w} \tag{44}$$

where w is the width of the mushy zone. It is interesting to note that local solidification times T_F are related to the local cooling rates with the expressions:

$$T_F = \frac{T_L - T_S}{C_R} = \frac{T_L - T_S}{rG} = \frac{T_L - T_S}{G\left(\frac{dS}{dt}\right)} \tag{45}$$

Furthermore, λ_{SDAS} is an important parameter as it plays a great role in the development of micro-segregation towards the final stage of solidification. For this reason it has received more attention than λ_{PRIM}. Consequently, recalling the work of (Won & Thomas, 2001) secondary dendrite arm spacing λ_{SDAS} (in μm) was computed using the following equation:

$$\lambda_{SDAS} = \begin{cases} (169.1 - 720.9 \cdot (\%C)) \cdot C_R^{-0.4935} & \text{for } 0 < (\%C) \leq 0.15 \\ 143.9 \cdot C_R^{-0.3616} \cdot (\%C)^{(0.5501 - 1.996 \cdot (\%C))} & \text{for } (\%C) > 0.15 \end{cases} \tag{46}$$

4. Results and discussion

For the Stomana slab caster that normally casts slab sizes of 220x1500 mm x mm two chemical analyses for steel were examined depending on the selected carbon concentrations, as presented on Table 2.

%C	%Si	%Mn	%P	%S	%Cu	%Ni	%Cr	%Al	T_{liq}(°C)	T_{sol}(°C)
0.100	0.30	1.20	0.025	0.015	0.35	0.30	0.10	0.03	1515	1495
0.185	0.30	1.20	0.025	0.015	0.35	0.30	0.10	0.03	1508	1479

Table 2. Steel chemical analyses examined for Stomana

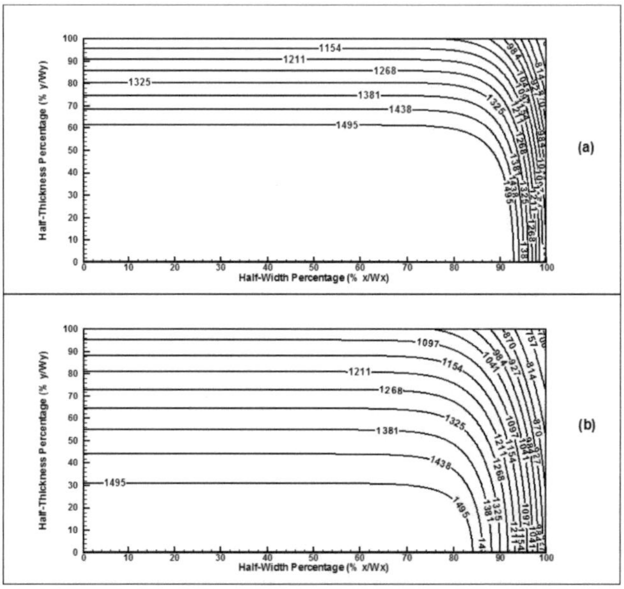

Fig. 1. Temperature distribution in sections of a 220 x 1500 mm x mm Stomana slab, at 5.1 m for part (a) and 10 m for part (b) from the meniscus, respectively. %C = 0.10; casting speed: 0.80 m/min; SPH: 20 K; solidus temperature = 1495°C; *(all temperatures in the graph are in °C)*

In addition to this, two levels for superheat *SPH* ($=T_{cast}-T_L$) were selected at the values of 20K and 40K. Two levels for the casting speed u_c were also examined at the 0.6 and 0.8 m/min. Fig. 1 presents the temperature distribution till solidus temperature inside a slab at two different positions in the caster; parts (a) and (b) show results at about 5.1 m and 10.0 m from the meniscus level in the mold, respectively. The dramatic progress of the solidification front is illustrated. The following casting parameters were selected in this case: %C=0.10, *SPH*= 20K, and u_c = 0.8 m/min. It is interesting to note that the shell grows faster along the direction of the smaller size, i.e., the thickness than the width of the slab. Fig. 2 presents some more typical results for the same case. The temperature in the centre is presented by line 1, and the temperature at the surface of the slab is presented by line 2. The shell thickness S and the distance between liquidus and solidus w are presented by dotted lines 3 and 4, respectively. In part (b) of Fig. 2 the rate of shell growth (dS/dt), the cooling rate (C_R), and the solid fraction (f_S) in the final stages of solidification are presented. Finally, in part (c) the local solidification time T_F, and secondary dendrite arm spacing λ_{SDAS} are also presented. It is interesting to note that the rate of shell growth is almost constant for the major part of solidification. Computation results show that solid fraction seems to significantly increase towards solidification completion. Apart from unclear fluid-flow phenomena that may adversely affect the uniform development of dendrites in the final stages of solidification and influence the local solid-fraction values, the shape of the f_S curve at the values of f_S above 0.8 seem to be influenced by the selected set of equations (37)-(41). Fig. 3 depicts computed strain results along the caster.

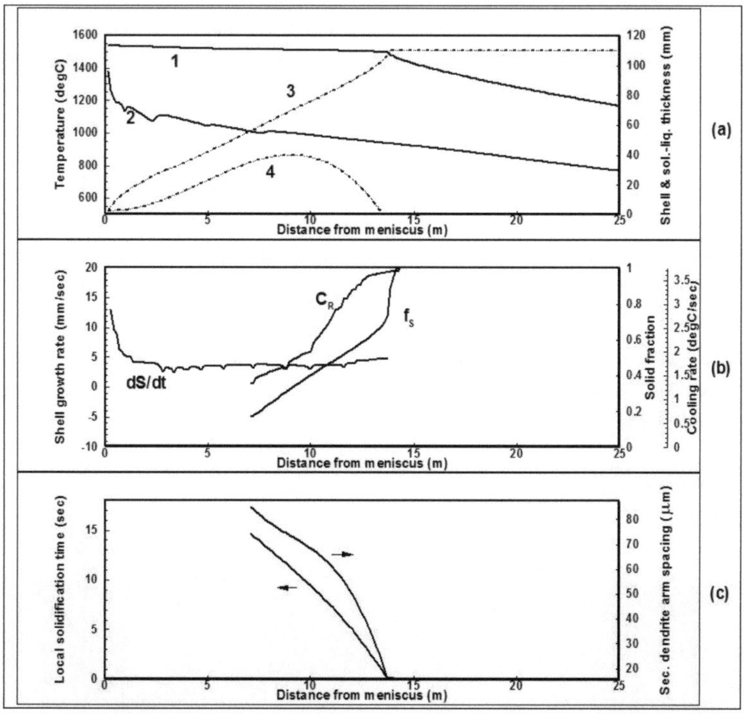

Fig. 2. Results with respect to distance from the meniscus: In part (a), lines (1) and (2) illustrate the centreline and surface temperatures of a 220 x 1500 mm x mm Stomana slab; lines (3) and (4) depict the shell thickness and the distance between the solidus and liquidus temperatures; in part (b), the solid fraction f_S, the local cooling-rate C_R, and the rate of shell growth dS/dt are presented; in part (c), the local solidification time and secondary dendrite arm spacing are depicted, as well. Casting conditions: %C = 0.10; casting speed: 0.80 m/min; SPH: 20 K; solidus temperature = 1495°C; *(all temperatures in the graph are in °C)*

In part (a) of Fig. 3 line 1 depicts the bulging strain along the caster with the aforementioned formulation. Left-hand-side (LHS) axis is used to present the bulging strain which is also presented by dashed line 2 with the means of another formulation (Han et al, 2001) which is presented by the following equations:

$$\delta_{B,2} = \frac{\sigma_P \ell_P^{\;4}}{32 E_e S^3} \sqrt{t_P} \tag{47}$$

where most parameters were defined in the appropriate section and E_e is an equivalent elastic modulus that was calculated using the following equation:

$$E_e = \frac{T_S - T_P}{T_S - 100} \times 10^4 \quad \text{in MPa} \tag{48}$$

Consequently, the bulging strain is computed by equation (20) in which δ_B is substituted by $\delta_{B,2}$. It seems that the computed results in the latter case are much higher than the ones computed with the generally applied method as described in 3.1.1. Furthermore, the recently presented formulation (47)-(48) was proven to be of limited applicability in most cases for the Sovel slab caster and in some cases in the Stomana caster as it gave rise to extremely high values for the bulging strain. Coming back to Fig. 3, the right-hand-side (RHS) axis in part (a) presents the misalignment and unbending strains in a smaller scale. In order to emphasize the misalignment effect upon the strain two different values, 0.5 mm and 1.0 mm of rolls misalignment were chosen at two positions, about 8.9 m and 13.4 m, respectively, along the caster. In this way, these values are depicted by lines 3 and 4 in part (a) of Fig. 3. The caster radius is 10.0 m while two unbending points with radii 18.0 m and 30.0 m at the 13.5 m and 18.0 m positions along the caster were selected in order to simulate the straightening process. Line 8 in part (a) of Fig. 3 actually presents the strain from the first unbending point. The LHS axis in part (b) of Fig. 3 represents the total strains as computed by the two methods for bulging strain and illustrated by lines 5 and 6. In this case, the total strain is less than the critical strain (as measured on the RHS axis and illustrated by straight line 7) throughout the caster.

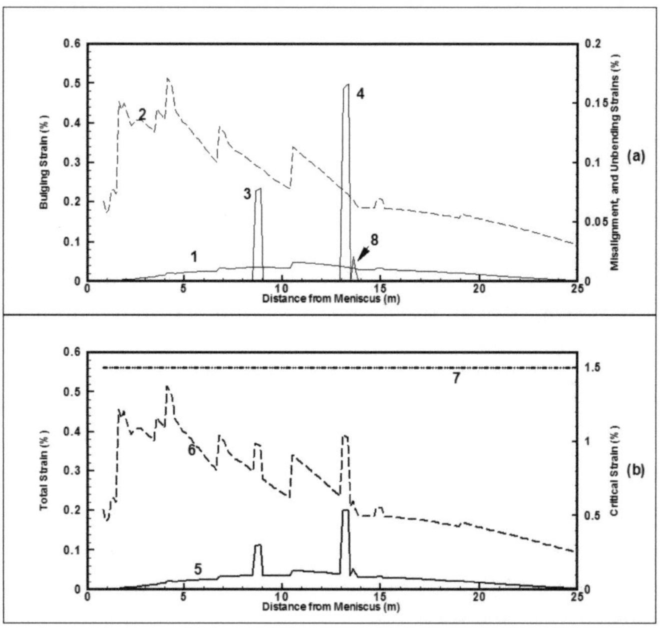

Fig. 3. In part (a), bulging strain (LHS axis), and misalignment and unbending strains (RHS axis) are illustrated. Bulging strain is depicted by two lines (1) and (2) depending on the applied formulation: line (1) is based on the formulation presented in section 3.1.1, and line (2) is based on the formulation described by equations (47) & (48). Lines (3) and (4) depict the strains resulting from 0.5 mm and 1.0 mm rolls-misalignment, respectively. Line (8) shows the strain from unbending at this position of the caster. In a similar manner, the total strains (LHS axis) are presented in part (b); the critical strain (RHS axis) is also, included. Casting conditions: 220 x 1500 mm x mm Stomana slab;%C = 0.10; casting speed: 0.80 m/min; SPH: 20 K; solidus temperature = 1495°C

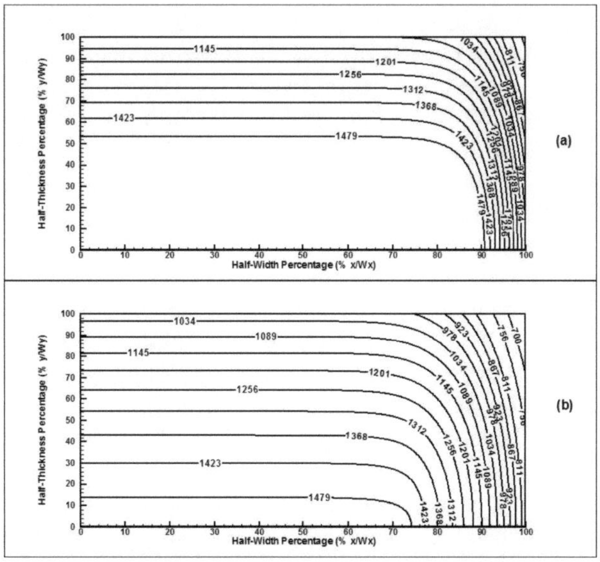

Fig. 4. Temperature distribution in sections of a 220 x 1500 mm x mm Stomana slab, at 8.0 m for part (a) and 16 m for part (b) from the meniscus, respectively. %C = 0.185; casting speed: 0.80 m/min; SPH: 20 K; solidus temperature = 1479°C; *(all temperatures in the graph are in °C)*

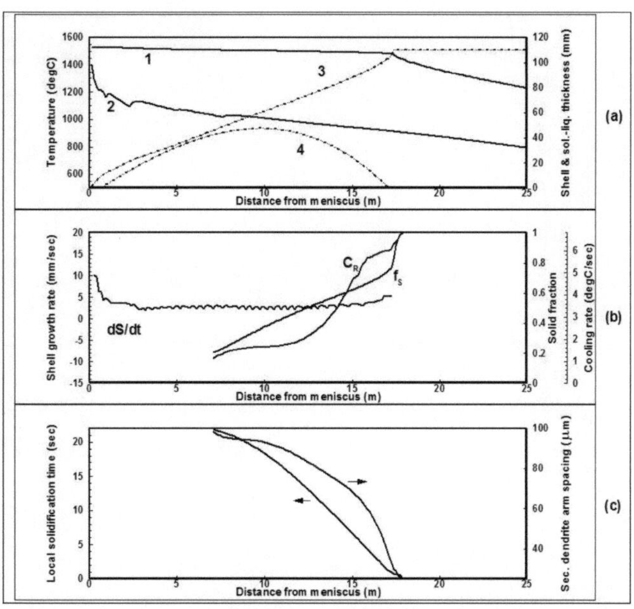

Fig. 5. Results with respect to distance from the meniscus: In part (a), lines (1) and (2) illustrate the centreline and surface temperatures of a 220 x 1500 mm x mm Stomana slab; lines (3) and (4) depict the shell thickness and the distance between the solidus and liquidus temperatures; in part (b), the solid fraction f_S, the local cooling-rate C_R, and the rate of shell growth dS/dt are presented; in part (c), the local solidification time and secondary dendrite arm spacing are depicted, as well. Casting conditions: %C = 0.185; casting speed: 0.80 m/min; SPH: 20 K; solidus temperature = 1479°C; *(all temperatures in the graph are in °C)*

Fig. 4 presents the temperature distribution till solidus temperature inside a slab at two different positions in the caster; parts (a) and (b) show results at about 8.0 m and 16.0 m from the meniscus level in the mold, respectively. The following casting parameters were selected in this case: %C=0.185, *SPH*= 20K, and u_c = 0.8 m/min. It is interesting to note that the shell grows faster along the direction of the smaller size, i.e., the thickness than the width of the slab. Fig. 5 presents some more typical results for the same case. The temperature in the centre is presented by line 1, and the temperature at the surface of the slab is presented by line 2. The shell thickness *S* and the distance between liquidus and solidus *w* are presented by dotted lines 3 and 4, respectively. In part (b) of Fig. 2 the rate of shell growth (d*S*/dt), the cooling rate (C_R), and the solid fraction (f_S) in the final stages of solidification are presented. Finally, in part (c) the local solidification time T_F, and secondary dendrite arm spacing λ_{SDAS} are also presented. It is interesting to note that the rate of shell growth is almost constant for the major part of solidification.

In part (a) of Fig. 6 line 1 depicts the bulging strain along the caster with the aforementioned formulation. LHS axis is used to present the bulging strain, while the RHS axis in part (a) presents the misalignment and unbending strains in a smaller scale. The strains due to the applied misalignment values are depicted by lines 2 and 3 in part (a) of Fig. 6. Line 4 presents the strain from the first unbending point. The LHS axis in part (b) of Fig. 6 represents the total strain and is illustrated by line 5. In this case, the total strain is less than the critical strain (as measured on the RHS axis and illustrated by straight line 6) throughout the caster.

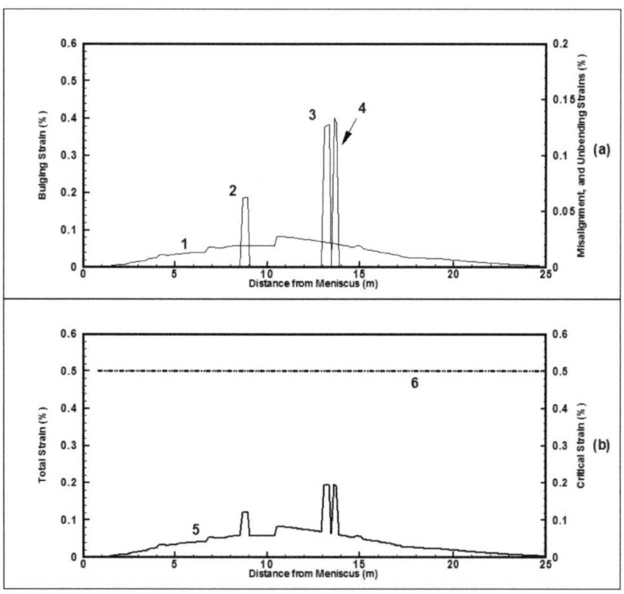

Fig. 6. In part (a), bulging strain (LHS axis), and misalignment and unbending strains (RHS axis) are illustrated. Bulging strain is depicted by line (1); lines (2) and (3) depict the strains resulting from 0.5 mm and 1.0 mm rolls-misalignment, respectively; line (4) shows the strain from unbending at this position of the caster. In a similar manner, the total strain (LHS axis) is presented in part (b); the critical strain (RHS axis) is also, included. Casting conditions: 220 x 1500 mm x mm Stomana slab; %C = 0.185; casting speed: 0.80 m/min; SPH: 20 K; solidus temperature = 1479°C

Fig. 7 presents the temperature distribution till solidus temperature inside a slab at two different positions in the caster; parts (a) and (b) show results at about 9.3 m and 20.0 m from the meniscus level in the mold, respectively. The following casting parameters were selected in this case: %C=0.185, *SPH*=40K, and u_c = 0.8 m/min. It is interesting to note that the shell grows faster along the direction of the smaller size, i.e., the thickness than the width of the slab. Fig. 8 presents some more typical results for the same case. The temperature in the centre is presented by line 1, and the temperature at the surface of the slab is presented by line 2. The shell thickness *S* and the distance between liquidus and solidus *w* are presented by dotted lines 3 and 4, respectively. In part (b) of Fig. 2 the rate of shell growth (d*S*/dt), the cooling rate (C_R), and the solid fraction (f_S) in the final stages of solidification are presented. Finally, in part (c) the local solidification time T_F, and secondary dendrite arm spacing λ_{SDAS} are also presented. It is interesting to note that the rate of shell growth is almost constant for the major part of solidification.

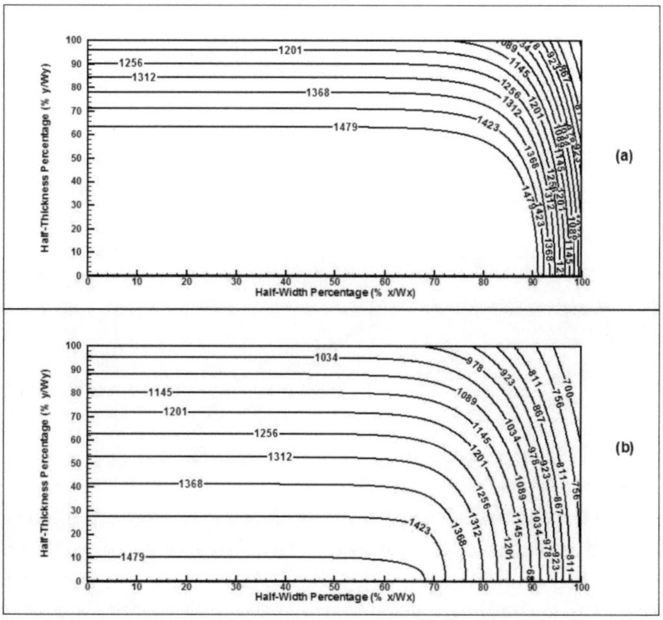

Fig. 7. Temperature distribution in sections of a 220 x 1500 mm x mm Stomana slab, at 9.3 m for part (a) and 20 m for part (b) from the meniscus, respectively. %C = 0.185; casting speed: 0.80 m/min; SPH: 40 K; solidus temperature = 1479°C; *(all temperatures in the graph are in °C)*

In part (a) of Fig. 9 line 1 depicts the bulging strain along the caster with the aforementioned formulation. LHS axis is used to present the bulging strain, while the RHS axis in part (a) presents the misalignment and unbending strains in a smaller scale. The strains due to the applied misalignment values are depicted by lines 2 and 3 in part (a) of Fig. 9. Line 4 presents the strain from the first unbending point, while line 5 presents the strain from the second unbending point. The LHS axis in part (b) of Fig. 9 represents the total strain and is illustrated by line 6. In this case, the total strain is less than the critical strain (as measured on the RHS axis and illustrated by straight line 7) throughout the caster.
For the Sovel slab caster that normally casts slab sizes of 130x390 and 130x360 (mm x mm) two chemical analyses for steel were examined depending on the selected carbon

concentrations, as presented on Table 3. For the cases presented in this study only the slab size of 130x390 was examined.

%C	%Si	%Mn	%P	%S	%Cu	%Ni	%Cr	%V	%Al	T_{liq}(°C)	T_{sol}(°C)
0.100	0.25	1.20	0.025	0.010	0.28	0.30	0.10	0.05	0.04	1516	1497
0.165	0.25	1.20	0.025	0.010	0.28	0.30	0.10	0.05	0.04	1511	1484

Table 3. Steel chemical analyses examined for Sovel

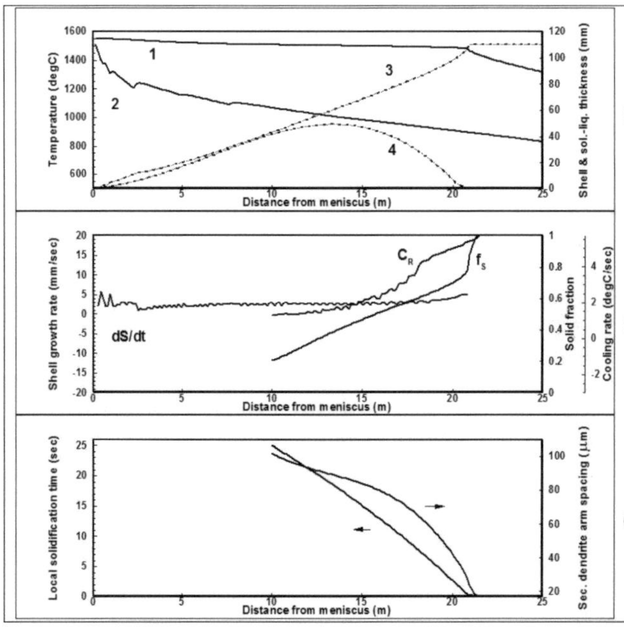

Fig. 8. Results with respect to distance from the meniscus: In part (a), lines (1) and (2) illustrate the centreline and surface temperatures of a 220 x 1500 mm x mm Stomana slab; lines (3) and (4) depict the shell thickness and the distance between the solidus and liquidus temperatures; in part (b), the solid fraction f_S, the local cooling-rate C_R, and the rate of shell growth d*S*/dt are presented; in part (c), the local solidification time and secondary dendrite arm spacing are depicted, as well. Casting conditions: %C = 0.185; casting speed: 0.80 m/min; SPH: 40 K; solidus temperature = 1479°C; *(all temperatures in the graph are in °C)*

Fig. 10 presents the temperature distribution till solidus temperature inside a slab at two different positions in the caster; parts (a) and (b) show results at about 3.3 m and 6.0 m from the meniscus level in the mold, respectively. The following casting parameters were selected in this case: %C=0.10, *SPH*= 20K, and u_c = 1.1 m/min. It is interesting to note that the shell grows faster along the direction of the smaller size, i.e., the thickness than the width of the slab. Fig. 11 presents some more typical results for the same case. The temperature in the centre is presented by line 1, and the temperature at the surface of the slab is presented by line 2. The shell thickness *S* and the distance between liquidus and solidus *w* are presented by dotted lines 3 and 4, respectively. In part (b) of Fig. 11 the rate of shell growth (d*S*/dt), the cooling rate (C_R), and the solid fraction (f_S) in the final stages of solidification are presented. Finally, in part (c) the local solidification time T_F, and secondary dendrite arm spacing λ_{SDAS} are also presented. It is interesting to note that the rate of shell growth is almost constant for the major part of solidification.

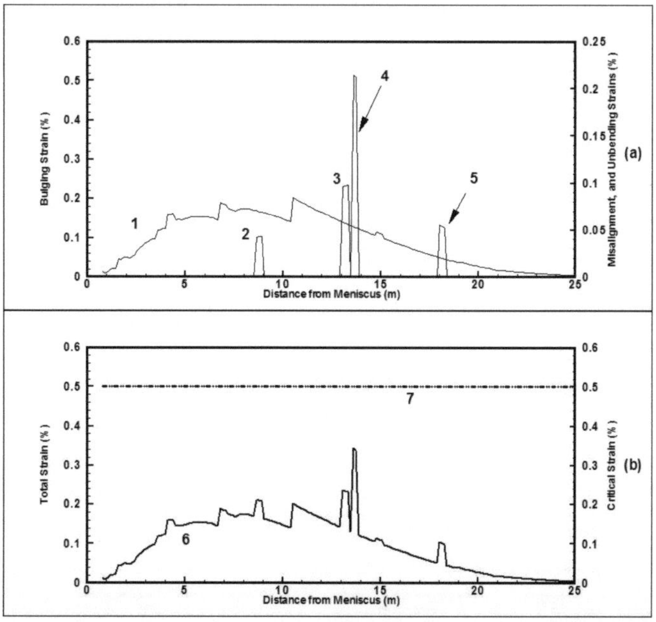

Fig. 9. In part (a), bulging strain (LHS axis), and misalignment and unbending strains (RHS axis) are illustrated. Bulging strain is depicted by line (1); lines (2) and (3) depict the strains resulting from 0.5 mm and 1.0 mm rolls-misalignment, respectively; lines (4) and (5) show the strain from unbending at these positions. In a similar manner, the total strain (LHS axis) is presented in part (b) as line (6); the critical strain (RHS axis) is also included as line (7). Casting conditions: 220 x 1500 mm x mm Stomana slab; %C = 0.185; casting speed: 0.80 m/min; SPH: 40 K; solidus temperature = 1479°C

In part (a) of Fig. 12 line 1 depicts the bulging strain along the caster with the aforementioned formulation. LHS axis is used to present the bulging strain, while the RHS axis in part (a) presents the misalignment and unbending strains in a larger scale. The caster radius is 9.0 m and unbending takes place at a point about 13.5 m apart from meniscus level with a straightening radius of about 16.0 m. It seems that the computed unbending strains are relatively low. Due to the small size of the produced slabs the design of the caster has a relatively small number of rolls at large distances from each other. Roll pitches have values from 2.5 m up to 3.0 m. In this way the caster is somewhat "forgiving" in the cases that misalignment gets a bit out of hand. Actually, in this study relatively large misalignment values from 20 mm up to 50 mm were examined. The strains due to the applied misalignment values are depicted by line 2 in part (a) of Fig. 12, and seem to be low indeed. For the Sovel caster, bulging strains were computed by the formulation presented in section 3.1.1; too high values for bulging strains were computed with the formulation presented by equations (47) and (48). The LHS axis in part (b) of Fig. 12 represents the total strain and is illustrated by line 3. In this case, the total strain is less than the critical strain (as measured on the RHS axis and illustrated by straight line 4) throughout the caster.

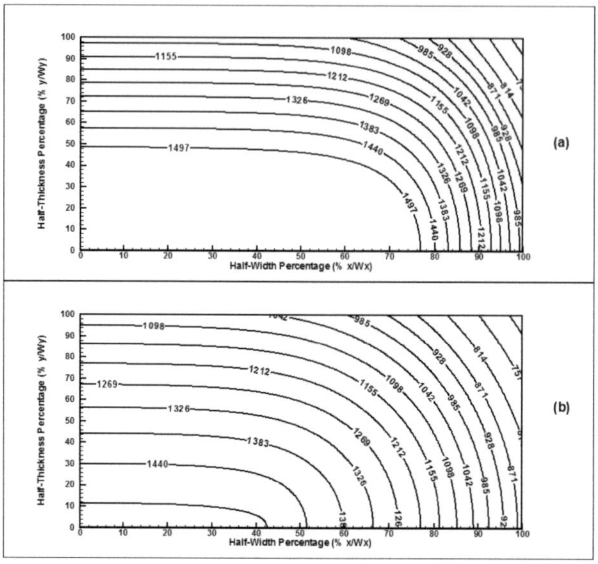

Fig. 10. Temperature distribution in sections of a 130 x 390 mm x mm Sovel slab, at 3.3 m for part (a) and 6.0 m for part (b) from the meniscus, respectively. %C = 0.10; casting speed: 1.1 m/min; *SPH*: 20 K; solidus temperature = 1497°C; *(all temperatures in the graph are in °C)*

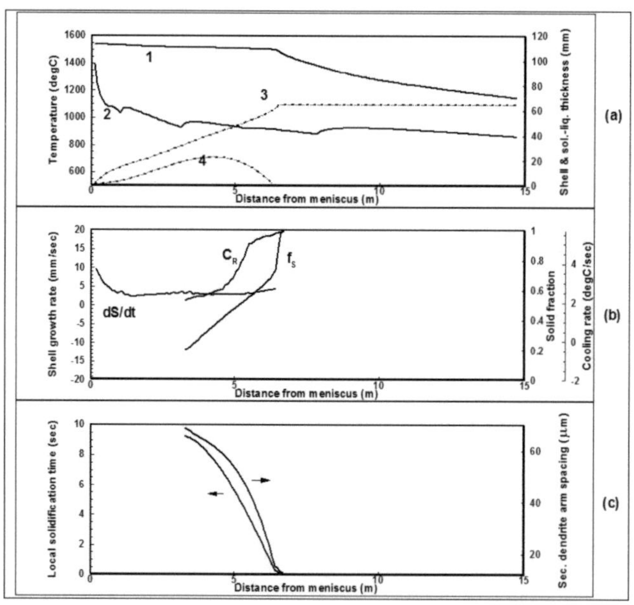

Fig. 11. Results with respect to distance from the meniscus: In part (a), lines (1) and (2) illustrate the centreline and surface temperatures of a 130 x 390 mm x mm Sovel slab; lines (3) and (4) depict the shell thickness and the distance between the solidus and liquidus temperatures; in part (b), the solid fraction f_S, the local cooling-rate C_R, and the rate of shell growth dS/dt are presented; in part (c), the local solidification time and secondary dendrite arm spacing are depicted, as well. Casting conditions: %C = 0.10; casting speed: 1.1 m/min; SPH: 20 K; solidus temperature = 1497°C; *(all temperatures in the graph are in °C)*

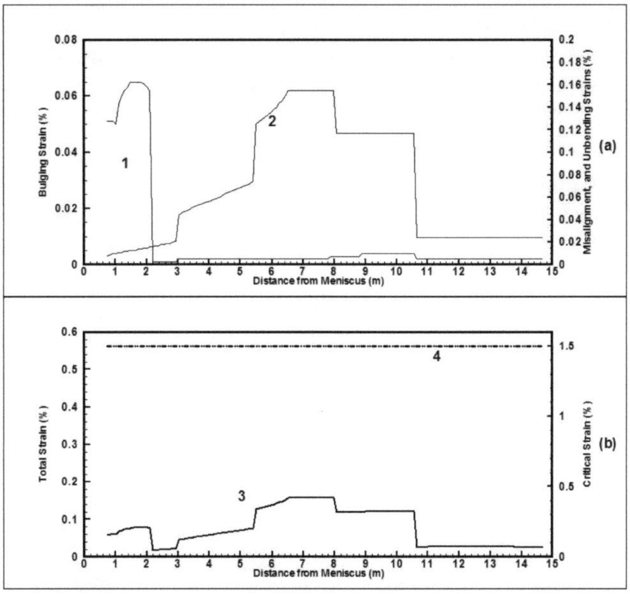

Fig. 12. In part (a), bulging strain (LHS axis), and misalignment and unbending strains (RHS axis) are illustrated by lines (1) and (2), respectively. In a similar manner, the total strain (LHS axis) is presented in part (b) as line (3); the critical strain (RHS axis) is also included as line (4). Casting conditions: 130 x 390 mm x mm Sovel slab; %C = 0.10; casting speed: 1.1 m/min; SPH: 20 K; solidus temperature = 1497ºC

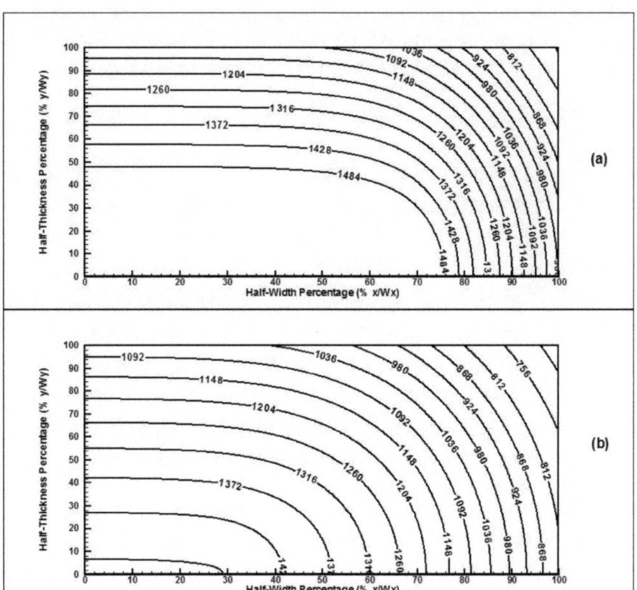

Fig. 13. Temperature distribution in sections of a 130 x 390 mm x mm Sovel slab, at 4.0 m for part (a) and 7.7 m for part (b) from the meniscus, respectively. %C = 0.165; casting speed: 1.1 m/min; *SPH*: 20 K; solidus temperature = 1484ºC; *(all temperatures in the graph are in ºC)*

Fig. 13 presents the temperature distribution till solidus temperature inside a slab at two different positions in the caster; parts (a) and (b) show results at about 4.0 m and 7.7 m from the meniscus level in the mold, respectively. The following casting parameters were selected in this case: %C=0.165, *SPH*= 20K, and u_c = 1.1 m/min. It is interesting to note that the shell grows faster along the direction of the smaller size, i.e., the thickness than the width of the slab. Fig. 14 presents some more typical results for the same case. The temperature in the centre is presented by line 1, and the temperature at the surface of the slab is presented by line 2. The shell thickness *S* and the distance between liquidus and solidus *w* are presented by dotted lines 3 and 4, respectively. In part (b) of Fig. 14 the rate of shell growth (d*S*/dt), the cooling rate (C_R), and the solid fraction (f_S) in the final stages of solidification are presented. Finally, in part (c) the local solidification time T_F, and secondary dendrite arm spacing λ_{SDAS} are also presented. It is interesting to note that the rate of shell growth is almost constant for the major part of solidification.

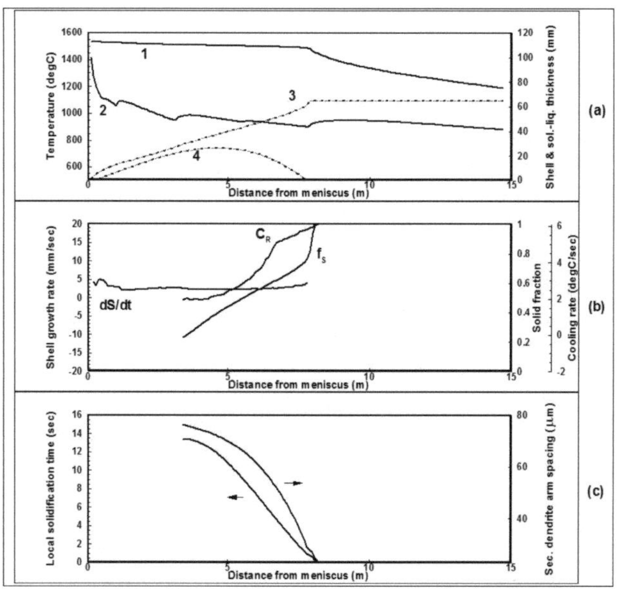

Fig. 14. Results with respect to distance from the meniscus: In part (a), lines (1) and (2) illustrate the centreline and surface temperatures of a 130 x 390 mm x mm Sovel slab; lines (3) and (4) depict the shell thickness and the distance between the solidus and liquidus temperatures; in part (b), the solid fraction f_S, the local cooling-rate C_R, and the rate of shell growth d*S*/dt are presented; in part (c), the local solidification time and secondary dendrite arm spacing are depicted, as well. Casting conditions: %C = 0.165; casting speed: 1.1 m/min; SPH: 20 K; solidus temperature = 1484°C; *(all temperatures in the graph are in °C)*

In part (a) of Fig. 15, line 1 depicts the bulging strain along the caster with the aforementioned formulation. LHS axis is used to present the bulging strain, while the RHS axis in part (a) presents the misalignment and unbending strains in the same scale. The strains due to the applied misalignment values are depicted by line 2 in part (a) of Fig. 15, and seem to be low indeed. The LHS axis in part (b) of Fig. 15 represents the total strain and is illustrated by line 3. In this case, the total strain is less than the critical strain (as measured on the RHS axis and illustrated by straight line 4) throughout the caster.

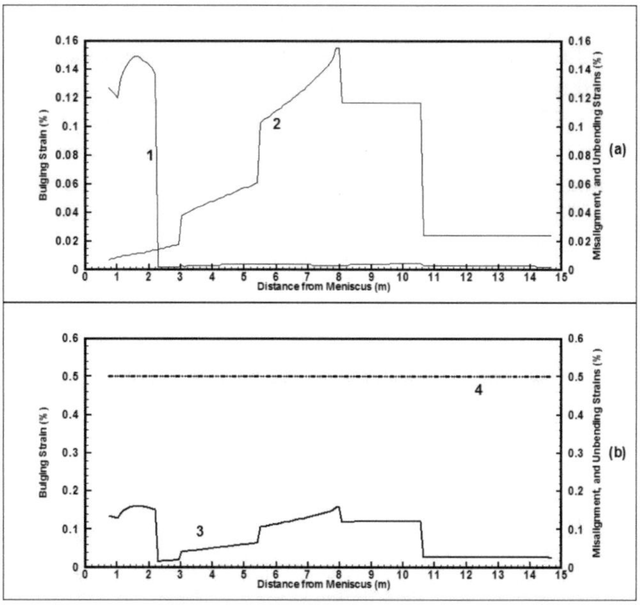

Fig. 15. In part (a), bulging strain (LHS axis), and misalignment and unbending strains (RHS axis) are illustrated by lines (1) and (2), respectively. In a similar manner, the total strain (LHS axis) is presented in part (b) as line (3); the critical strain (RHS axis) is also included as line (4). Casting conditions: 130 x 390 mm x mm Sovel slab; %C = 0.165; casting speed: 1.1 m/min; SPH: 20 K; solidus temperature = 1484°C

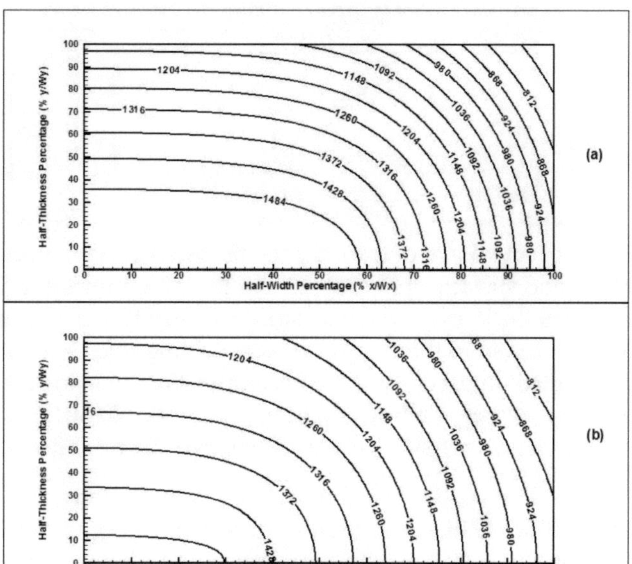

Fig. 16. Temperature distribution in sections of a 130 x 390 mm x mm Sovel slab, at 7.3 m for part (a) and 9.5 m for part (b) from the meniscus, respectively. %C = 0.165; casting speed: 1.1 m/min; *SPH*: 40 K; solidus temperature = 1484°C; *(all temperatures in the graph are in °C)*

Fig. 16 presents the temperature distribution till solidus temperature inside a slab at two different positions in the caster; parts (a) and (b) show results at about 7.3 m and 9.5 m from the meniscus level in the mold, respectively. The following casting parameters were selected in this case: %C=0.165, *SPH*= 40K, and u_c = 1.1 m/min. It is interesting to note that the shell grows faster along the direction of the smaller size, i.e., the thickness than the width of the slab. Fig. 17 presents some more typical results for the same case. The temperature in the centre is presented by line 1, and the temperature at the surface of the slab is presented by line 2. The shell thickness *S* and the distance between liquidus and solidus *w* are presented by dotted lines 3 and 4, respectively. In part (b) of Fig. 17 the rate of shell growth (d*S*/dt), the cooling rate (C_R), and the solid fraction (f_S) in the final stages of solidification are presented. Finally, in part (c) the local solidification time T_F, and secondary dendrite arm spacing λ_{SDAS} are also presented. It is interesting to note that the rate of shell growth is almost constant for the major part of solidification.

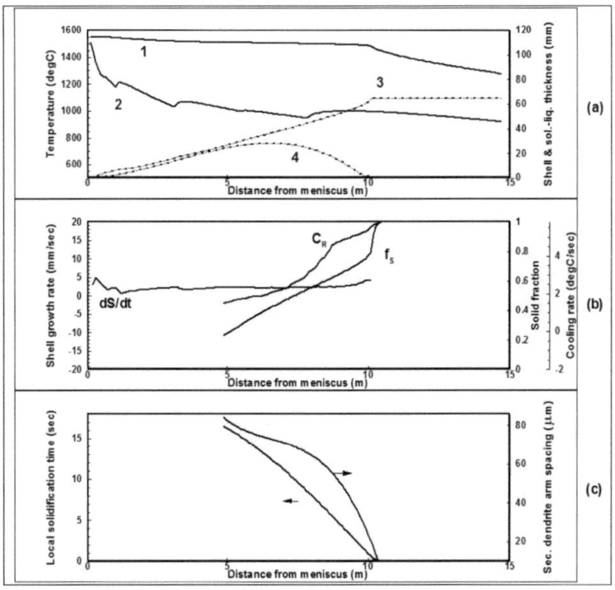

Fig. 17. Results with respect to distance from the meniscus: In part (a), lines (1) and (2) illustrate the centreline and surface temperatures of a 130 x 390 mm x mm Sovel slab; lines (3) and (4) depict the shell thickness and the distance between the solidus and liquidus temperatures; in part (b), the solid fraction f_S, the local cooling-rate C_R, and the rate of shell growth d*S*/dt are presented; in part (c), the local solidification time and secondary dendrite arm spacing are depicted, as well. Casting conditions: %C = 0.165; casting speed: 1.1 m/min; SPH: 40 K; solidus temperature = 1484°C; *(all temperatures in the graph are in °C)*

In part (a) of Fig. 18 line 1 depicts the bulging strain along the caster with the aforementioned formulation. LHS axis is used to present the bulging strain, while the RHS axis in part (a) presents the misalignment and unbending strains in the same scale. The strains due to the applied misalignment values are depicted by line 2 in part (a) of Fig. 18, and seem to be low indeed. The LHS axis in part (b) of Fig. 18 represents the total strain and is illustrated by line 3. However in this case, the total strain is larger than the critical strain (as measured on the RHS axis and illustrated by straight line 4) in as far as the first 4 m of the caster are concerned. The effect of high SPH is affecting the internal slab soundness in a negative way.

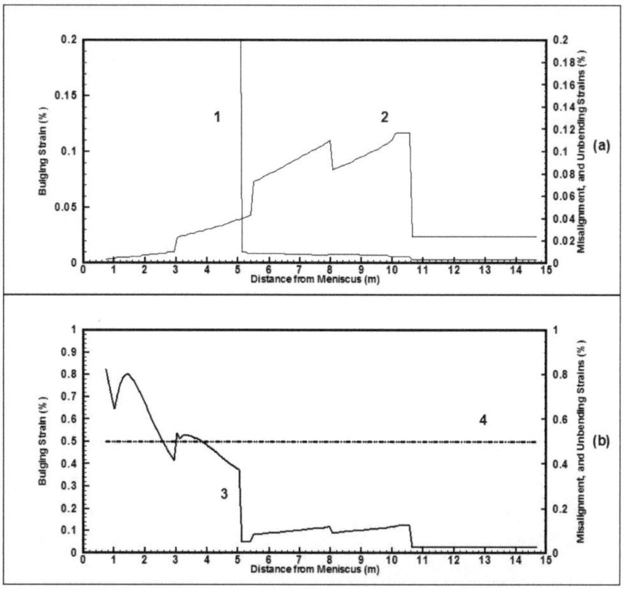

Fig. 18. In part (a), bulging strain (LHS axis), and misalignment and unbending strains (RHS axis) are illustrated by lines (1) and (2), respectively. In a similar manner, the total strain (LHS axis) is presented in part (b) as line (3); the critical strain (RHS axis) is also included as line (4). Casting conditions: 130 x 390 mm x mm Sovel slab; %C = 0.165; casting speed: 1.1 m/min; SPH: 40 K; solidus temperature = 1484°C

As of figures 1, 4, 7, 10, 13, and 16 it is obvious that the temperature distribution is presented only for the one-quarter of the slab cross-section, the rest one is omitted as redundant due to symmetry. It is interesting to note that due to the values of the shape factors, i.e., 1500/220 = 6.818, and 390/130 = 3.0 for the Stomana and Sovel casters, respectively, the shell proceeds faster across the largest size (width) than across the smallest one (thickness). This is well depicted with respect to the plot of the temperature distributions in the sections till the solidus temperatures for the specific chemical analyses under study. It should be pointed out that due to this, macro-segregation phenomena occasionally appear at both ends and across the central region of slabs. These defects appear normally as edge defects later on at the plate mill once they are rolled.

Comparing figures 2 and 5, it becomes evident that the higher the carbon content the more it takes to solidify downstream the Stomana caster. For the Sovel caster similar results can be obtained by comparing the graphs presented by figures 11 and 14.

Comparing figures 5 and 8, it is interesting to note that the higher the superheat the more time it takes for a slab to completely solidify in the caster at Stomana. Similar results have been obtained for the Sovel caster, just by comparing the results presented in figures 14 and 17.

Furthermore, the higher the casting speed the more it takes to complete solidification in both casters, although computed results are not presented at different casting speeds. For productivity reasons, the maximum attainable casting speeds are selected in normal

practice, so to avoid redundancy only results at real practice casting speeds were selected for presentation in this study.
The ratio of the shape factors for the two casters, i.e., 6.818/3.0 = 2.27 seems to play some role for the failure of the application of the second formulation presented by equations (47) and (48) for the Sovel caster compared with the formulation for the bulging calculations presented in 3.1.1. In addition to this, even for the Stomana caster the computed bulging results were too high and not presented at higher carbon and superheat values. Low carbon steel grades seem to withstand better any bulging, misalignment, and unbending strains for both casters as illustrated by figures 3 and 6 for Stomana, and figures 12 and 15 for Sovel, respectively. The higher critical strain values associated with low carbon steels give more "room" for higher superheats and any caster design or maintenance problems.
Another critical aspect that is worth mentioning is the effect of SPH upon strains for the same steel grade and casting speed. For the Stomana caster, comparing the results presented in figures 6 and 9 it seems that by increasing the superheat from 20K to 40K the bulging and misalignment strains increase by an almost double value; furthermore, the unbending strain at the second straightening point becomes appreciable and apparent in figure 9. In the case of the Sovel caster, higher superheat gives rise to such high values for bulging strains that may create significant amount of internal defects in the first stages of solidification, as presented in Fig. 18 compared with Fig. 15. Consequently, although Sovel's caster is more "forgiving" than Stomana's one with respect to unbending and misalignment strains it gets more prone to create defects due to bulging strains at higher superheats.
In Fig. 19, an attempt to model static soft reduction is presented for the Stomana caster. In fact, statistical analysis was performed based upon the overall computed results and the following equation was developed from regression analysis giving the solidification point (*SP*) in meters, that is, the distance from meniscus at which the slab is completely solidified:

$$SP = 0.16 \times SPH + 37.5 \times \%C + 19.7 \times u_C - 8.5 \tag{49}$$

Equation (49) is statistically sound with a correlation coefficient R^2=0.993, an F-test for the regression above 99.5%, and t-test for every coefficient above 99.5%, as well. In general, industrial practice has revealed that in the range of solid fraction from 0.3 up to 0.7 is the most fruitful time to start applying soft reduction. In the final stages of solidification, internal segregation problems may appear. In the Stomana caster, the final and most critical segments are presented in Fig. 19 with the numbers 5, 6, and 7. A scheme for static soft reduction (*SR*) is proposed with the idea of closing the gaps of the rolls according to a specific profile. In this way, the reduction of the thickness of the final product per caster length in which static soft reduction is to be applied will be of the order of 0.7 mm/m, which is similar to generally applied practices of the order of 1.0 mm/m. At the same time, for the conditions presented in Fig. 19, the solid fraction will be around 0.5 at the time soft reduction starts. Consequently, the point within the caster at which static soft reduction can be applied (starting $f_S \approx 0.5$) is given by:

$$SR_{start} \simeq SP - 5.5 \tag{50}$$

where, SR_{start} designates the caster point in meters at which static soft reduction may prove very promising.

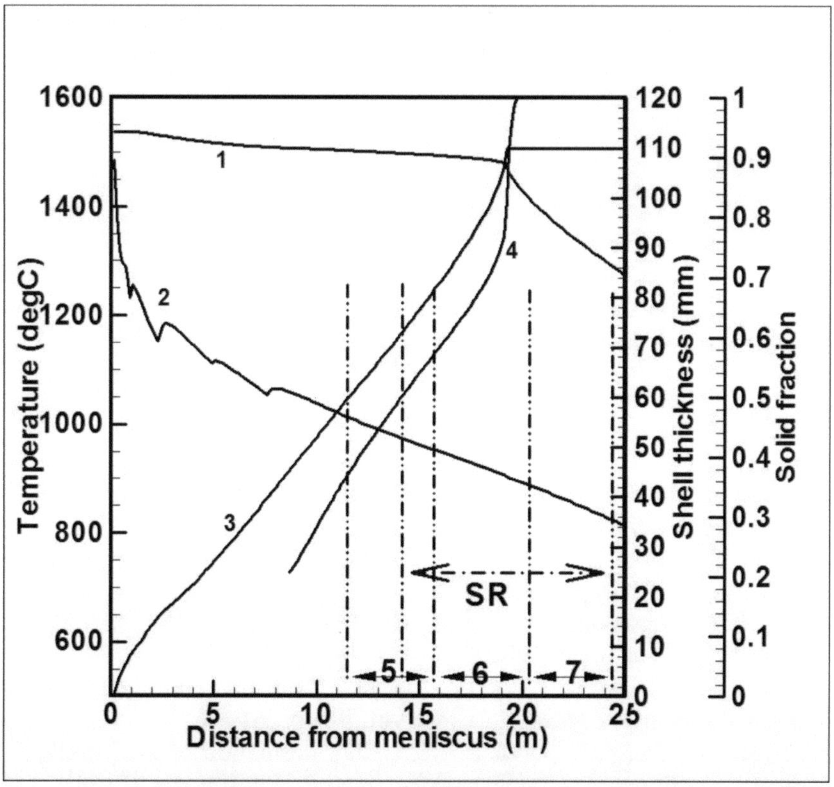

Fig. 19. Suggested area for static soft reduction (SR) in the Stomana caster: Casting conditions: 220x1500 mm x mm slab; %C = 0.185; *SPH* = 30 K; u_C = 0.8 m/min. Lines 1 and 2 depict the centreline and surface temperature, respectively. Lines 3 and 4 illustrate the shell growth and solid fraction, respectively. The borders of the final casting segments 5, 6, and 7 are also presented

Closing the discussion it should be added that the proper combination of low superheat and high casting speed values satisfies a proper slab unbending in the caster. The straightening process is successfully carried out at slab temperatures above 900°C without any surface defects for the products.

5. Conclusion

In this computational study the differential equation of heat transfer was numerically solved along a continuous caster, and results that are interesting from both the heat-transfer and the metallurgical points of view were presented and discussed. The effects of superheat, casting speed, and carbon levels upon slab casting were examined and computed for Stomana and Sovel casters. Generally, the higher the superheat the more difficult to solidify and produce a slab product that will be free of internal defects. Carbon levels are related to the selected steel grades, and casting speeds to the required maximum productivities so both are more difficult to alter under normal conditions. In order to tackle any internal defects coming from variable superheats from one heat to another, dynamic soft reduction has been put into practice by some slab casting manufacturers worldwide. In this study, some ideas for applying static soft reduction in practice at the Stomana caster have been proposed; in this case, more stringent demands for superheat levels from one heat to another are inevitable.

6. Acknowledgment

The continuous support from the top management of the SIDENOR group of companies is greatly appreciated. Professor Rabi Baliga from McGill University, Montreal, is also acknowledged for his guidelines in the analysis of many practical computational heat-transfer problems. The help of colleague and friend, mechanical engineer Nicolas Evangeliou for the construction of the graphs is also greatly appreciated.

7. References

Brimacombe J.K. (1976). Design of Continuous Casting Machines based on a Heat-Flow Analysis : State-of-the-Art Review. *Canadian Metallurgical Quarterly, CIM,* Vol. 15, No. 2, pp. 163-175

Brimacombe J.K., Sorimachi K. (1977). Crack Formation in the Continuous Casting of Steel. *Met. Trans.B,* Vol. 8B, pp. 489-505

Brimacombe J.K., Samarasekera I.V. (1978). The Continuous-Casting Mould. *Intl. Metals Review,* Vol. 23,No. 6, pp. 286-300

Brimacombe J.K., Samarasekera (1979). The Thermal Field in Continuous Casting Moulds. *CanadianMetallurgical Quarterly, CIM,* Vol. 18, pp. 251-266

Brimacombe J.K., Weinberg F., Hawbolt E.B. (1979). Formation of Longitudinal, Midface Cracks inContinuously Cast Slabs. *Met. Trans. B,* Vol. 10B, pp. 279-292

Brimacombe J.K., Hawbolt E.B., Weinberg F. (1980). Formation of Off-Corner Internal Cracks inContinuously-Cast Billets, *Canadian Metallurgical Quarterly, CIM,* Vol. 19, pp. 215-227

Burmeister L.C. (1983). Convective Heat Transfer. *John Wiley & Sons,* p. 551

Cabrera-Marrero, J.M., Carreno-Galindo V., Morales R.D., Chavez-Alcala F. (1998). Macro-Micro Modeling of the Dendritic Microstructure of Steel Billets by Continuous Casting. *ISIJ International,* Vol. 38, No. 8, pp. 812-821

Carslaw, H.S, & Jaeger, J.C. (1986). Conduction of Heat in Solids. *Oxford University Press.* New York

Churchill, S.W., & Chu, H.H.S. (1975). Correlating Equations for Laminar and Turbulent Free Convection from a Horizontal Cylinder. *Int. J. Heat Mass Transfer,* 18, pp. 1049-1053

Fujii, H., Ohashi, T., & Hiromoto, T. (1976). On the Formation of Internal Cracks in Continuously Cast Slabs. *Tetsu To Hagane-Journal of the Iron and Steel Institute of Japan,* Vol. 62, pp. 1813-1822

Fujii, H., Ohashi, T., Oda, M., Arima, R., & Hiromoto, T. (1981). Analysis of Bulging in Continuously Cast Slabs by the Creep Model. *Tetsu To Hagane-Journal of the Iron and Steel Institute of Japan,* Vol. 67, pp. 1172-1179

Grill A., Schwerdtfeger K. (1979). Finite-element analysis of bulging produced by creep in continuously cast steel slabs. *Ironmaking and Steelmaking,* Vol. 6, No. 3, pp. 131-135

Han, Z., Cai, K., & Liu, B. (2001). Prediction and Analysis on Formation of Internal Cracks in Continuously Cast Slabs by Mathematical Models. *ISIJ International,* Vol. 41, No. 12, pp. 1473-1480

Hiebler, H., Zirngast, J., Bernhard, C., & Wolf, M. (1994). Inner Crack Formation in Continuous Casting: Stress or Strain Criterion? *Steelmaking Conference Proceedings,* ISS, Vol. 77, pp. 405-416

Imagumbai, M. (1994). Relationship between Primary- and Secondary-dendrite Arm Spacing of C-Mn Steel Uni-directionally Solidified in Steady State. *ISIJ International,* Vol. 34, No. 12, pp. 986-991

Incropera, F.P., & DeWitt, D.P. (1981). Fundamentals of Heat Transfer. *John Wiley & Sons,* p. 49

Kozlowski, P.F., Thomas, B.G., Azzi, J.A., & Wang, H. (1992). Simple Constitutive Equations for Steel at High Temperature. *Metallurgical Transactions A,* Vol. 23A, (March 1992), pp. 903-918

Lait, J.E., Brimacombe, J.K., Weinberg, F. (1974). Mathematical Modelling of Heat Flow in the Continuous Casting of Steel. *Ironmaking and Steelmaking,* Vol. 1, No.2, pp. 90-97

Ma, J., Xie, Z., & Jia G. (2008). Applying of Real-time Heat Transfer and Solidification Model on the Dynamic Control System of Billet Continuous Casting. *ISIJ International,* Vol. 48, No. 12, pp. 1722-1727

Matsumiya, T., Kajioka, H., Mizoguchi, S., Ueshima, Y., & Esaka, H. (1984). Mathematical Analysis of Segregations in Continuously-cast Slabs. *Transactions ISIJ,* Vol. 24, pp. 873-882

Mizikar, E.A. (1967). Mathematical Heat Transfer Model for Solidification of Continuously Cast Steel

Slabs. *Trans. TMS-AIME,* Vol. 239, pp. 1747-1753

Palmaers, A. (1978). High Temperature Mechanical Properties of Steel as a Means for Controlling Casting. *Metall. Report C.R.M.,* No. 53, pp. 23-31

Patankar, S.V. (1980). Numerical Heat Transfer and Fluid Flow. *Hemisphere Publishing Corporation,* Washington

Pierer, R., Bernhard, C., & Chimani, C. (2005). Evaluation of Common Constitutive Equations for Solidifying Steel. *BHM,* Vol. 150, No. 5, pp. 1-13

Sismanis P.G. (2010). Heat transfer analysis of special reinforced NSC-columns under severe fire conditions. *International Journal of Materials Research (formerly: Zeitschrift fuer Metallkunde),* Vol. 101, (March 2010), pp. 417-430, DOI 10.3139/146.110290

Sivaramakrishnan S., Bai H., Thomas B.G., Vanka P., Dauby P., & Assar M. (2000). *Ironmaking Conference Proceedings,* Pittsburgh, PA, ISS, Vol. 59, pp. 541-557

Tacke K.-H. (1985). Multi-beam model for strand straightening in continuous caster. *Ironmaking and Steelmaking,* Vol. 12, No. 2, pp. 87-94

Thomas, B.G., Samarasekera, I.V., Brimacombe, J.K. (1987). Mathematical Model of the Thermal Processing of Steel Ingots: Part I. Heat Flow Model. *Metallurgical Transactions B,* Vol. 18B, (March 1987), pp. 119-130

Uehara, M., Samarasekera, I.V., Brimacombe, J.K. (1986). Mathematical modeling of unbending of continuously cast steel slabs. *Ironmaking and Steelmaking.* Vol. 13, No. 3, pp. 138-153

Won, Y-M, Kim, K-H, Yeo, T-J, & Oh, K. (1998). Effect of Cooling Rate on ZST, LIT and ZDT of Carbon Steels Near Melting Point. *ISIJ International,* Vol. 38, No. 10, pp. 1093-1099

Won, Y-M, & Thomas, B. (2001). Simple Model of Microsegregation during Solidification of Steels. *Metallurgical and Materials Transactions A,* Vol. 32A, (July 2001), pp. 1755-1767

Yoon, U-S., Bang, I.-W., Rhee, J.H., Kim, S.-Y., Lee, J.-D., & Oh, K.-H. (2002). Analysis of Mold Level Hunching by Unsteady Bulging during Thin Slab Casting. *ISIJ International,* Vol. 42, No. 10, pp. 1103-1111

Zhu, G., Wang, X., Yu, H., & Wang, W. (2003). Strain in solidifying shell of continuous casting slabs. *Journal of University of Science and Technology Beijing,* Vol. 10, No. 6, pp. 26-29

7

Modelling of Profile Evolution by Transport Transitions in Fusion Plasmas

Mikhail Tokar
Institute for Energy and Climate Research – Plasma Physics, Research Centre Jülich
Germany

1. Introduction

In tokamaks, the most advanced types of fusion devices, electric currents, flowing both in external coils and inside the plasma itself, produce nested closed magnetic surfaces, see Fig. 1. This allows confining charged plasma components, electrons and deuterium-tritium fuel ions, throughout times exceeding by orders of magnitudes those which particles require to pass through the device if they would freely run away with their thermal velocities. Under conditions of ideal confinement charged particles would infinitely move along and rotate around magnetic field lines forming the surfaces. In reality, diverse transport processes lead to losses of particles and energy from the plasma. On the one hand, this hinders the attainment and maintenance of the plasma density and temperature on a required level and forces to develop sophisticated and expansive methods to feed and heat up the plasma components. On the other hand, if the fusion conditions are achieved the generated α-particles have to be transported out to avoid suffocation of the thermonuclear burning in a reactor. Therefore it is very important to investigate, understand, predict and control transport processes in fusion plasmas.

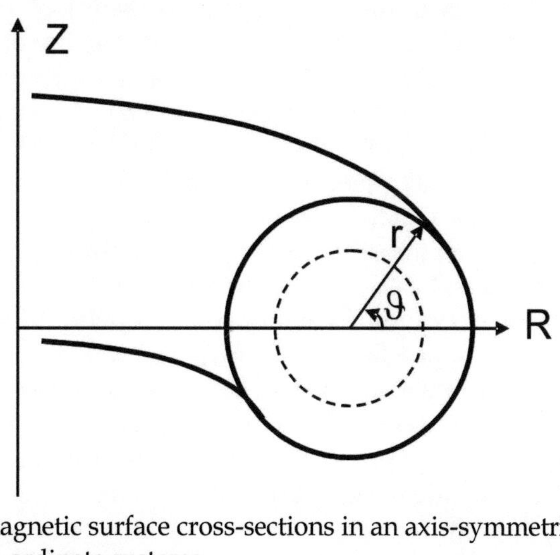

Fig. 1. Geometry of magnetic surface cross-sections in an axis-symmetrical tokamak device and normally used co-ordinate systems

1.1 Classical and neoclassical transport

Plasmas in magnetic fusion devices of the tokamak type are media with complex non-trivial characteristics of heat and mass transfer across magnetic surfaces. The most basic mechanism for transport phenomena is due to coulomb collisions of plasma components, electrons and ions. By such collisions the centres of Larmor circles, traced by particles, are displaced across the magnetic field B. In the case of light electrons this displacement is of their Larmor circle radiusρ_{Le}. Due to the momentum conservation the Larmor centres of ions are shifted at the same distance. Therefore the transport is automatically ambipolar and is determined by the electron characteristics only. The level of this so called classical diffusion can be estimated in a random step approximation, see, e.g., Ref. (Wesson, 2004):

$$D_{cl} \approx \rho_{Le}^2 \nu_e \tag{1}$$

with ν_e being the frequency of electron-ion collisions. Normally D_{cl} is very low, 10^{-3} m^{2}s^{-1}, and practically no experimental conditions have been found up to now in real fusion plasmas where the measured particle diffusivity would not significantly exceed this level. Mutual electron-electron and ion-ion collisions do not lead to net displacements and transfer of particles. But in the presence of temperature gradients they cause heat losses because particles of different temperatures are transferred across the magnetic surfaces in opposite directions. This heat transfer is by a factor of $(m_i/m_e)^{1/2}$ larger for ions than for electrons, where m_i and m_e are the corresponding particle masses, (Braginskii, 1963).

In a tokamak magnetic field lines are curved and, by moving along them, the charged particles are subjected to centrifugal forces. The plasma current produces the so called poloidal component of the magnetic field and therefore field lines have a spiral structure, displacing periodically from the outer to the inner side of the torus. Thus, when moving along them, charged particles go through regions of different field magnitude since the latter varies inversely proportional to the distance R from the torus axis analogously to the field from a current flowing along the axis. Because of their Larmor rotation the particles possess magnetic momentums and those fill a force in the direction of the field variation, i.e. in the same direction R as that of the centrifugal force. Both forces cause a particle drift motion perpendicular to the magnetic field and R, i.e. in the vertical direction Z, see Fig.1. In the upper half of the torus, $Z > 0$, this drift is directed outwards the magnetic surface and in the lower one, $Z < 0$, - towards the surface. Thus, after one turn in the poloidal direction ϑ the particle would not have a net radial displacement. This is not however the case if the particle motion is chaotically interrupted by coulomb collisions. As a result, the particle starts a new Larmor circle at a radial distance from the original surface exceeding the Larmor radius by q times where the safety factor q characterizes the pitch-angle of the field lines. This noticeably enhances, by an order of magnitude, the classical particle and energy transfer. Even more dramatic is the situation for particles moving too slowly along magnetic field: these are completely trapped in the local magnetic well at the outer low field side. They spent much longer time in the same half of the magnetic surface and deviate from it by a factor of $(R/r)^{1/2}$ stronger than passing particles freely flying along the torus. The poloidal projections of trajectories of such trapped particle look like "bananas". For the existence of "banana" trapped particles should not collide too often, i.e. the collision length λ_c has not to exceed $qR(R/r)^{3/2}$. In spite of the rareness of collisions, these lead to a transport contribution from trapped particles exceeding significantly, by a factor of $q^2(R/r)^{3/2}$, the classical one, see

Ref. (Galeev & Sagdeev, 1973). In an opposite case of very often collisions, where $\lambda_c << qR$, there are not at all particles passing a full poloidal circumference without collisions. In this, the so called Pfirsch-Schlüter, collision dominated regime the transport is enhanced with respect to the classical one by a factor of q^2. In the intermediate "plateau" range the transport coefficients are formally independent of the collision frequency. The transport contribution due to toroidal geometry described above is referred to as a "neoclassical" transport and is universally present in toroidal fusion devices. Fortunately, under high thermonuclear temperatures it causes only a small enough and, therefore, quite acceptable level of losses.

1.2 Anomalous transport

The sources of charged particles and energy inside the plasma result in sharp gradients of the temperature T and density n in the radial direction r across the magnetic surfaces. Thus, a vast reservoir of free energy is stored in the plasma core. This may be released by triggering of drift waves, perturbations of the plasma density and electric potential travelling on magnetic surfaces in the direction y perpendicular to the field lines. Through the development of diverse types of micro-instabilities the wave amplitudes can grow in time. This growth introduces such a phase shift between density and potential perturbations so that the associated y-component of the electric field induces drift flows of particles and heat in the radial direction. These Anomalous flows tremendously enhance the level of losses due to classical and neoclassical transport contributions.

Different kinds of instabilities are of the most importance in the hot core and at the relatively cold edge of the plasma (Weiland, 2000). In the former case the so called toroidal ion temperature gradient (ITG) instability (Horton et all 1981) is considered as the most dangerous one. Spontaneous fluctuations of the ion temperature generate perturbations of the plasma pressure in the y-direction. These induce a diamagnetic drift in the radial direction bringing hotter particles from the plasma core and, therefore, enhancing the initial temperature perturbations. This mechanism is augmented by the presence of trapped electrons those can not move freely in the toroidal direction and therefore are in this respect similar to massive ions. On the one hand, the fraction of trapped particles is of $\sqrt{2r/(r+R)}$ and increases by approaching towards the plasma boundary. On the other hand, the plasma collisionality has to be low enough for the presence of "banana" trajectories. Therefore the corresponding instability branch, TE-modes (Kadomtsev & Pogutse, 1971), is normally at work in the transitional region between the plasma core and edge.

At the very edge the plasma temperature is low and coulomb collisions between electrons and ions are very often. They lead to a friction force on electrons when they move along the magnetic field in order to maintain the Boltzmann distribution in the perturbation of the electrostatic potential caused by a drift wave. As a result a phase shift between the density and potential fluctuations arises and the radial drift associated with the perturbed electric field brings particles from the denser plasma core. Thus, the initial density perturbation is enhanced and this gives rise to new branches of drift wave instabilities, drift Alfvén waves (DA) (Scott, 1997) and drift resistive ballooning (DRB) modes, see (Guzdar et al, 1993). The reduction of DA activity with heating up of the plasma edge is discussed as an important perquisite for the transition from the low (L) to high (H) confinement modes (Kerner et al, 1998). The development of DRB instability is considered as the most probable reason for the

density limit phenomena (Greenwald, 2002) in the L-mode, leading to a very fast termination of the discharge (Xu et al, 2003; Tokar, 2003).
Roughly the contribution from drift wave instabilities to the radial transport of charged particles can be estimated on the basis of the so called "improved mixing length" approximation (Connor & Pogutse, 2000):

$$D_{an} \approx \frac{\gamma_{\max}}{k_{y,\max}^2} \frac{\gamma_{\max}^2}{\gamma_{\max}^2 + \omega_{r,\max}^2} \tag{2}$$

Here γ and ω_r are the imaginary and real parts of the perturbation complex frequency, correspondingly; the former is normally refer to as the growth rate. Both γ and ω_r are functions of the y-component of the wave vector, k_y; the subscript "max" means that these values are computed at $k_y = k_{y,\max}$ at which γ approaches its maximum value. Such a maximum arises normally due to finite Larmor radius effects. For ITG-TE modes $k_{y,\max} \approx 0.3/\rho_{Li}$ and for DA-DRB drift instabilities $k_{y,\max} \approx 0.1/\rho_{Li}$, with ρ_{Li} being the ion Larmor radius.

1.3 Transitions between different transport regimes

Both the growth rate and real frequency of unstable drift modes and, therefore, the characteristics of induced anomalous transport depend in a complex non-linear way on the radial gradients of the plasma parameters. For ITG-TE modes triggered by the temperature gradients of ions and electrons, respectively, the plasma density gradient brings a phase shift between the temperature fluctuations and induced heat flows. As a result the fluctuations can not be fed enough any more and die out. For pure ITG-modes this impact is mimicked in the following simple estimate for the corresponding transport coefficient:

$$D_{an,ITG} \approx \frac{cT}{eBRk_{y,\max}} \sqrt{4\varepsilon_T - \varepsilon_n^2} \tag{3}$$

where $\varepsilon_{n,T} = R/(2L_{n,T})$ are the dimensionless gradients of the density and temperature, with $L_T = -T/\partial_r T$ and $L_n = -n/\partial_r n$ being the e-folding lengths of these parameters, correspondingly. Since the density profile is normally very peaked and ε_n is large at the plasma edge, ITG instability is suppressed in the plasma boundary region. Several sophisticated models have been developed to calculate firmly anomalous fluxes of charged particles and energy in tokamak plasmas (Waltz et al, 1997; Bateman et al, 1998). The solid curve in Fig. 2 shows a typical dependence on the dimensionless density gradient of the radial anomalous particle flux density computed by taking into account the contributions from ITG-TE modes calculated with the model from Ref. (Weiland, 2000), DA waves estimated according to Ref. (Kerner et al, 1998) and neoclassical diffusion from Ref. (Wesson, 2004), for parameters characteristic at the plasma edge in the tokamak JET (Wesson 2004): $R = 3\ m$, $r = 1\ m$, $B = 3\ T$, $n = 5 \cdot 10^{19}\ m^{-3}$, $T = 0.5\ keV$ and $L_T = 0.1\ m$. The dash-dotted curve provides the diffusivity formally determined according to the relation $D = -\Gamma/(dn/dr)$.
One can see that the total flux density Γ has an N-like shape. In stationary states the particle balance is described by the continuity equation $\nabla \cdot \Gamma = S$. Here S is the density of charged particle sources due to ionization of neutrals, entering the plasma volume through the separatrix, and injected with frozen pellets and energetic neutral beams. Since these sources

are, to some extent, in our hands, the stationary radial profile of the flux of charged particles can be also considered as prescribed. If at a certain radial position it is in the range $\Gamma_{\min} \leq \Gamma \leq \Gamma_{\max}$, see the thick dashed line in Fig.2, three steady states given by the black intersection points can be realized. They are characterised by very different values of the density gradient. The smallest gradient value corresponds to a very high particle transport and the largest one - to very low losses. In two neighbouring spatial points with close values of Γ the plasma can be in states belonging to different branches of the $\Gamma(\varepsilon_n)$ curve. Thus, a sudden change in the transport nature should happen between these points and this manifests itself in the formation of a transport barrier (TB).

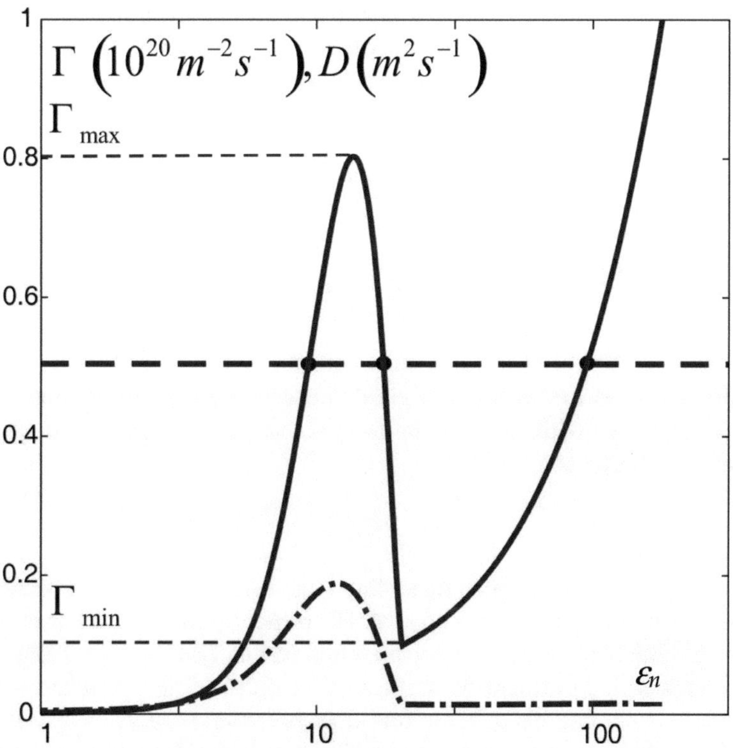

Fig. 2. The flux density (solid line) and diffusivity (dash-dotted line) of charged particles induced by unstable ITG, TE and DA modes and with neoclassical contribution

A stationary transport equation does not allow, nonetheless, defining uniquely the positions of the TB interfaces. This can be done only by solving non-stationary transport equations. Henceforth we consider this equation, applied to a variable Z, in a cylindrical geometry. After averaging over the magnetic surface it looks like:

$$\partial_t Z + \partial_r (r\Gamma)/r = S \tag{4}$$

In the present chapter it is demonstrated that this is not a straightforward procedure to integrate Eq.(4) with the flux density Γ being a non-monotonous function of the gradient $\partial_r Z$. Numerical approaches elaborated to overcome problems arising on this way are presented and highlighted below on several examples.

2. Numerical approach

2.1 Stability problems

For a positive dependence of the flux on the gradient, e.g. $\Gamma \sim (|\partial_r Z|)^p$ with $p > 0$, a numerical solution of Eq.(4) with a fully implicit scheme is absolutely stable for arbitrary time steps, see Ref. (Shestakov et al, 2003) . However for a non-monotonic dependence like that shown in Fig.1 there is a range with $p < 0$ and we have to analyze the numerical stability in this case. Let $\Psi(t,r)$ is the genuine solution of Eq.(4) with given initial and boundary conditions. Consider a deviation $\zeta(t,r)$ from $\Psi(t,r)$ that arises by a numerical integration of Eq.(4). By substituting $Z(t,r) = \Psi(t,r) + \zeta(t,r)$ into Eq.(4), we discretize linearly the time derivative, $\partial_t \zeta \approx [\zeta(t,r) - \zeta(t-\tau,r)]/\tau$. As a result one gets an ordinary differential equation (ODE) of the second order for the radial dependence of the variable ζ at the time moment $t = m\tau$, $\zeta_m(r)$. Not very close to the plasma axis, $r = 0$, we look for the solution of this equation in the form of plane waves (Shestakov et al, 2003):

$$\zeta_m = \lambda^m \exp(i\xi r) \tag{5}$$

with small enough wave lengths, $\xi >> |\Psi/\partial_r \Psi|, |\partial_r \Psi/\partial_r(\partial_r \Psi)|$. This results in:

$$\lambda \approx 1/\left(1 + \tau D p \xi^2\right) \tag{6}$$

where the diffusivity has been introduced according to the definition $D \equiv -\Gamma/\partial_r \Psi$. For a numerical stability $|\lambda| < 1$ is required. If $p > 0$, the absolute stability for any τ is recovered from Eq.(6), in agreement with Ref. (Shestakov et al, 2003). For negative p in question, $|\lambda| > 1$ and a numerical solution is unstable if

$$\tau < 2/\left(D|p|\xi^2\right) \tag{7}$$

i.e. for small enough time steps. Such instability was, most probably, the cause of problems arisen with small time steps by modelling of TB formation in Ref. (Tokar et al, 2006). It is also necessary to note that the approach elaborated in Ref. (Jardin et al, 2008) for solving of diffusion problems with a gradient-dependent diffusion coefficient and based on solving of a system of non-linear equations by iterations, does not work reliably as well in the situation in question: the convergence condition for a Newton-Raphson method used there is very easy to violate under the inequality (7). The limitation (7) on the time step does not allow following transport transitions in necessary details. Moreover, as it has been demonstrated in Ref. (Tokar, 2010), calculations with too large time steps can even lead to principally wrong solutions, with improper characteristics of final stationary states.

Thus, even in a normally undemanding one-dimensional cylindrical geometry normally used by modelling of the confined plasma region in fusion devices with numerical transport codes like JETTO (Cennachi& Troni, 1988), ASTRA (Pereverzev & Yushmanov, 1988), CRONOS (Basiuk et al, 2003), RITM (Tokar, 1994), it is not a trivial task to simulate firmly the time evolution of radial profiles if fluxes are non-monotonous functions of parameter gradients and transport bifurcations can take place. The development of reliable numerical schemes for such a kind of problems is an issue of permanent importance and has been tackled, in particular, in the framework of activities of the European Task Force on Integrated Tokamak Modelling (ITM, 2010).

2.2 Change of dependent variable

Analysis shows that problems with numerical stability considered above arise due to the contribution from the dependent variable at the previous time step, $Z(t-\tau,r)$, in the discretized representation of the time derivative in Eq.(4). Therefore one may presume that they can be avoided by the change to the variation of this variable after one time step, $\xi(r) = Z(t,r) - Z(t-\tau,r)$, proposed in Ref. (Tokar, 2010). However, it should be seen that such a change introduces into the source term on the right hand side (r.h.s.) a contribution from the flux divergence at the previous time moment. By calculating with large time steps, this contribution may be too disturbing and also lead to numerical instabilities. Therefore in the present study we suggest the change of variables in the following form:

$$\xi(r) = Z(t,r) - Z(t-\tau,r)\cdot e^{-\tau/\tau_0} \tag{8}$$

where τ_0 is some memory time. In the limits of large, $\tau >> \tau_0$, and small, $\tau << \tau_0$, time steps, $\xi(t,r)$ reproduces the representations of the dependent variable considered above, the original variable $Z(t,r)$ and its variation after the time step $Z(t,r) - Z(t-\tau,r)$, respectively. As a result, with linearly discretized time derivative Eq.(4) takes the form:

$$\frac{\xi(r)}{\tau} + \frac{1}{r}\partial_r(r\Gamma) = S + Z(t-\tau,r)\frac{1-e^{-\tau/\tau_0}}{\tau} \tag{9}$$

Due to nonlinear dependence of the flux density Γ on the density gradient the latter ODE have to be solved by iterations at any given time moment t. For a certain iteration level we represent Γ as a sum of diffusive and convective parts:

$$\Gamma = -D\cdot\partial_r Z + V\cdot Z \tag{10}$$

The diffusivity $D(r)$ can be chosen in a form convenient for us. Then the convection velocity $V(r)$ is determined from the requirement that the flux density Γ_-, found according to the transport model with the dependent variable Z_- at the previous iteration level, is reproduced by Eq.(10). This leads to:

$$V = (\Gamma_- + D\cdot\partial_r Z_-)/Z_- \tag{11}$$

An appropriate solver has to provide, of course, the same solution $Z(t,r)$ independently of a choice for the diffusivity $D(r)$.

For transport models, reproducing the formation of TB, we expect, at least in stationary states, a step-like change of the solution gradient at the position of the TB boundaries. Therefore such a discontinuity is also duplicated in the convection velocity V computed according to Eq. (11). As an alternative option, the situation with $V = 0$ but discontinuous D will be considered below. Such discontinuities in transport coefficients lead to difficulties by integrating Eq.(9): with the flux density represented by Eq.(10) it contains the radial derivatives of the transport coefficients D and V approaching to infinity at the position of the TB boundary. To avoid this we integrate Eq.(9), multiplied by r and obtain:

$$\frac{1}{\tau r}\int_0^r \xi\rho d\rho - D\cdot\partial_r\xi + V\cdot\xi = J \tag{12}$$

where

$$J = \frac{1}{r}\int_0^r \left[S + Z(t-\tau,r)\frac{1-e^{-\tau/\tau_0}}{\tau} \right]\rho d\rho + \left[D\cdot\partial_r Z(t-\tau,r) - V\cdot Z(t-\tau,r) \right] e^{-\tau/\tau_0} \tag{13}$$

Finally, an integral counterpart of the variable $\xi(r)$ is introduced:

$$y(r) = \frac{1}{r^2}\int_0^r \xi(\rho)\rho d\rho \tag{14}$$

and Eq. (12) is reduced to the second order ODE to y:

$$d^2y/dr^2 + a\cdot dy/dr = by - f \tag{15}$$

with the coefficients $a = 3/r - V/D$, $b = 1/(\tau D) + 2V/(rD)$ and $f = J/(rD)$.
Equation (15) has to be supplemented by boundary conditions. Due to axial symmetry the original variable Z has a zero derivative at the plasma axis, $r = 0$. From the relations above it follows that dy/dr also reduces to zero here. However, there is a singularity in Eq.(15) at $r = 0$ because the coefficient a becomes infinite here. Therefore, by a numerical realization the boundary condition has to be transferred to the point $r_1 > 0$. The error introduced by this procedure can be arbitrarily small by decreasing r_1. In the range $0 \le r \le r_1$ one can use the Taylor's expansion:

$$y(0\le r\le r_1) = y(r_1) + (r-r_1)\frac{dy}{dr}(r_1) + \frac{(r-r_1)^2}{2}\frac{d^2y}{dr^2}(r_1)$$

and the requirement dy/dr $(r = 0) = 0$ reduces to:

$$r_1 b(r_1) y(r_1) - \left[1 + r_1 a(r_1)\right]\frac{dy}{dr}(r_1) = r_1 f(r_1) \tag{16}$$

The condition at the boundary of the confined plasma region, r_n, corresponds normally to a prescribed value of the variable Z or its e – folding length, $-dr/d\,(\ln Z) = \delta$. In the latter case we get for the variable y:

$$\left[r_n/\tau + 2(D/\delta + V)\right]y + r_n(D/\delta + V)\cdot dy/dr = J \tag{17}$$

2.3 Numerical solution

The coefficients in Eq.(15) are finite everywhere but discontinuous at the boundaries of a TB. Therefore, by integrating it, one can run to difficulties with applying established approaches, e.g., finite difference, finite volume and finite element methods, see Refs. (Versteeg & Malalasekera, 1995; Tajima, 2004; Jardin, 2010). In these approaches the derivatives of the dependent variable are discretized on a spatial grid with knots $r_{1,\ldots,n}$. This procedure implies a priory a smooth behaviour of the solution in the vicinity of grid knots. Usually it is supposed that this can be described by a quadratic or higher order spline. However, in the situation in question we expect a discontinuity of the derivative of y due to discontinuous transport coefficients. Thus, by following Ref. (Tokar, 2010), Eq.(15) is approximated in the vicinity $r_i^- \le r \le r_i^+$ of the grid knots i =2,...n-1, with $r_i^\pm = (r_{i\pm1} + r_i)/2$, by the second order ODEs with constant coefficients $a = a_i \equiv a(r_i)$, $b = b_i \equiv b(r_i)$, and $f = f_i \equiv f(r_i)$. Exact analytical solutions of such equations are given as follows:

$$y^i(r) = y(r_i^- \le r \le r_i^+) = C_{i,1}y_{i,1}(r) + C_{i,2}y_{i,2}(r) + y_{i,0} \quad (18)$$

The discriminant of Eq.(15) is positive. Indeed,

$$\Delta = \frac{a^2}{4} + b = \frac{1}{4}\left(\frac{3}{r} - \frac{V}{D}\right)^2 + \frac{1}{\tau D} + \frac{2V}{rD} = \frac{2}{r^2} + \frac{1}{4}\left(\frac{1}{r} + \frac{V}{D}\right)^2 + \frac{1}{\tau D} > 0$$

Thus the general solutions in Eq.(18) are exponential functions, $y_{i,k=1,2} = \exp\left[\lambda_{i,k}(r - r_i)\right]$, with $\lambda_{i,k} = -a_i/2 - (-1)^k \sqrt{\Delta(r_i)}$; the partial solution we chose in the form $y_{i,0} = f_i/b_i$. The continuity of the solution and its first derivative at the interfaces $r_i^\pm$ of the grid knot vicinities allow to exclude the coefficients $C_{i,k}$ and to get a three-diagonal system of linear equations for the values y_i of the solution in the grid knots:

$$y_i = y_{i-1}g_{i,1} + y_{i+1}g_{i,2} + \chi_i$$

where $g_{i,k}$ and χ_i are expressed through $y_{i,k}(r_i^\pm)$, $y_{i,0}$ and $\lambda_{i,k}$, see Ref. (Tokar, 2010) for details. These equations have to be supplemented by the relations following from the boundary conditions (16) and (17) where the approximations $dy/dr\ (r_1) \approx (y_2 - y_1)/(r_2 - r_1)$ and $dy/dr\ (r_n) \approx (y_n - y_{n-1})/(r_n - r_{n-1})$ are applied.
With $y_{1,\dots,n}$ known, the original dependent variable $Z(t,r)$ is determined by using the relations (8) and (14):

$$Z(t,r) = Z(t-\tau,r) \cdot e^{-\tau/\tau_0} + 2y + r\,dy/dr \quad (19)$$

One can see, $Z(t,r)$ is defined through both y and its derivative. Since the latter changes abruptly at the TB border, it is essential to calculate dy/dr as exact as possible, i.e. by using the expression (18) directly:

$$dy/dr(r_i) = C_{i,1}\lambda_{i,1} + C_{i,2}\lambda_{i,2}$$

Finally a new estimation for the transport coefficients is calculated with the new approximation to the solution $Z(t,r)$. Normally it is, however, necessary to use a stronger relaxation by applying some mixture of the old approximation, with the subscript (-), and the new one marked by the subscript (+). For example, for the convection velocity we have:

$$V = V_- \cdot (1 - A_{mix}) + V_+ \cdot A_{mix}$$

For the given time moment iterations continue till the convergence criterion:

$$\text{Error} = \sqrt{\sum_i \left[V_-(r_i) - V_+(r_i)\right]^2 \Big/ \sum_i \left[V_-(r_i) + V_+(r_i)\right]^2} \le 10^{-5} A_{mix}$$

is fulfilled.

3. Examples of applications

3.1 Temperature profile with the edge transport barrier

The most prominent example of TB in fusion tokamak plasmas is the edge transport barrier (ETB) in the H-mode with improved confinement (Wagner et al, 1982). The ETB may be triggered by changing some controlling parameters, normally by increasing the heating power (ASDEX Team, 1989). It is, however, unknown *a priory* when and where such a transport transition, inducing a fast modification of the parameter profiles, can happen. Regardless of the long history of experimental and theoretical studies, it is still not clear what physical mechanisms lead to suppression of anomalous transport in the ETB. The main line of thinking is the mitigation of drift instabilities and non-linear structures, arising on a non-linear stage of instabilities, through the shear of drift motion induced by the radial electric field (Diamond 1994, Terry 2000). Other approaches speculate on the role of the density gradient at the edge in the suppression of ITG-TE modes (Kalupin et al, 2005) and reduction of DA instabilities with decreasing plasma collisionality (Kerner, 1998; Rogers et al, 1998; Guzdar, 2001), the sharpness of the safety factor profile in the vicinity of the magnetic separatrix in a divertor configuration, etc. To prove the importance of a particular physical mechanism, the ability to solve numerically heat transport equations, allowing the formation of ETB, and to calculate the time evolution of the plasma parameter profiles is of principle importance.

Henceforth we do not rely on any particular mechanism for the turbulence and anomalous transport suppression but take into account the fact that in the final state the plasma core with a relatively low temperature gradient, $\partial_r T$, co-exists with the ETB where the temperature gradient is much larger. Since there are no any strong heat sources at the interface between two regions, the strong discontinuity in $\partial_r T$ is a consequence of an instantaneous reduction in the plasma heat conduction κ. Most roughly such a situation is described as a step-like drop of κ if $|\partial_r T|$ exceeds a critical value $|\partial_r T|_{cr}$. For convenience, however, we adopt that this happens if the *e*-folding length L_T drops below a certain L_{cr} ; κ is equal to constant values κ_0 for $L_T > L_{cr}$ and $\kappa_1 << \kappa_0$ for $L_T < L_{cr}$, see Fig.3.

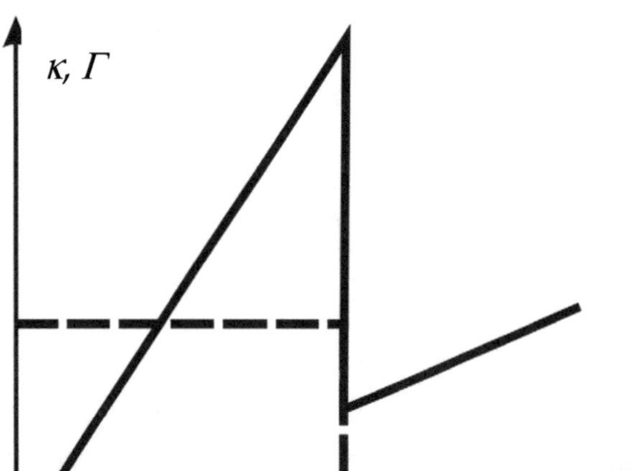

Fig. 3. Step-model for heat conduction (dashed line) and flux density (solid line) dependence on the dimensionless temperature gradient

The temperature profile $T(r)$ is described by Eq. (4) and it is assumed that the source density S is independent of the time and radial position. First consider stationary states with $\partial T/\partial t = 0$. In this case the heat flux density increases linearly with the radius, $\Gamma = Sr/2$. The corresponding radial profiles can be found analytically if one accepts that the transition from the strong transport in the plasma core, $\kappa = \kappa_0$, to the low transport at the edge, $\kappa = \kappa_1$, occurs at a position r_*. The existence of a central region with intense transport is ensured by the fact that L_T is infinite at the plasma axis, $r = 0$, where $\partial T/\partial r = 0$. At the boundary r_n we fix the temperature $T(r_n) = T_1$. The latter is governed by transport processes outside the last closed flux surface, in the scrape-off layer (SOL), where magnetic field lines hit a material surface. Stationary temperature profiles are given as follows:

$$T(0 \le r \le r_*) = \frac{S}{4}\left(\frac{r_*^2 - r^2}{\kappa_0} + \frac{r_n^2 - r_*^2}{\kappa_1}\right) + T_1$$
$$T(r_* \le r \le r_n) = \frac{S}{4}\frac{r_n^2 - r^2}{\kappa_1} + T_1 \tag{20}$$

At the position of the interface between the region of strong transport and the ETB the heat flux density $\Gamma(r_*)$ should be in the range where its dependence on the temperature *e*-folding length is ambiguous, i.e. the following inequalities have to be satisfied:

$$\frac{\kappa_1 T(r_*)}{L_{cr}} \le \frac{Sr_*}{2} \le \frac{\kappa_0 T(r_*)}{L_{cr}}$$

These give quadratic equations for the upper and lower boundaries of the interface position r_*. From these equations one gets the range of possible positions of the ETB interface:

$$r_*^{\min} \equiv \sqrt{L_{cr}^2 + r_n^2 + 4\kappa_1 T_1/S} - L_{cr} \le r_* \le \sqrt{\left(L_{cr}\,\kappa_1/\kappa_0\right)^2 + r_n^2 + 4\kappa_1 T_1/S} - L_{cr}\,\kappa_1/\kappa_0 \equiv r_*^{\max} \tag{21}$$

For the existence of ETB the lower limit has to be smaller than r_n. In agreement with observations this results in the requirement that the heating power has to exceed a minimum value:

$$S \ge S_{\min} \equiv 2\kappa_1 T_1/(r_n L_{cr}) \tag{22}$$

The stationary analysis above does not allow fixing the position of the interface between regions with different transport levels and for this purpose the non-stationary equation (4) has to be solved. This is done for different initial conditions in the form:

$$T(0,r) = T_1 + \alpha\frac{S}{4}\frac{r_n^2 - r^2}{\kappa_1}$$

By increasing the factor α one can reproduce different situations from a flat initial profile $T(r) = T_1$ for $\alpha = 0$ with very small thermal capacity, to a very peaked temperature for $\alpha > 1$ with a total thermal energy exceeding that in any stationary state. Calculations were done with the parameters $\kappa_1/\kappa_0 = 0.1$ and $L_{cr}/r_n = 1$. Only these combinations are of importance by calculating the dimensionless temperature $\Theta = \kappa_0 T/(Sr_n^2)$ as a function of the dimensionless radius $\rho = r/r_n$ and time $t/(r_n\kappa_0)$. The boundary condition Θ (ρ = 1) =0.01 ensures the existence of an ETB. The stationary profiles obtained by a numerical solution of the time-dependent equation with the time step $\tau = 10^{-3}/(r_n\kappa_0)$, the memory time $\tau_0 = 10^3\tau$ and an equidistant spatial grid with the total number of points n = 500 are shown in Fig.4 for different magnitudes of the parameter α. The analytical profiles (20) with r_* obtained from the numerical solutions are presented by thick bars. One can see a perfect agreement between analytical and numerical solutions and that the total interval $r_*^{min} \leq r_* \leq r_*^{max}$ can be realized by changing the steepness α of the initial temperature profile. It is also important to notice that only for sufficiently small τ and large τ_0 calculations provide the same final profiles. Thus, it is of principal significance to make the change of variable according to the relation (8) and operate with the temperature variation after a time step but not with the temperature itself. Finally we compare the results above with those obtained by the method described in Ref. (Tokar, 2006b), which has been also applied to non-linear transport models allowing bifurcations resulting in the ETB formation. Independently of initial conditions and time step this method provides final stationary states with the TB interface at $r_* = r_*^{max}$. In Ref. (Tokar, 2006b) the solution was found by going from the outmost boundary, $r = r_n$, where the plasma state is definitely belongs to those with the low transport level. If in the point r_{i-1} solutions with three values of the gradient are possible, see Fig.2, the one with the gradient magnitude closest to that in the point r_i has been selected. This constraint is, probably, too restrictive since it allows transitions between different transport regimes only in points where the optimum flux values Γ_{min} and Γ_{max} are approached.

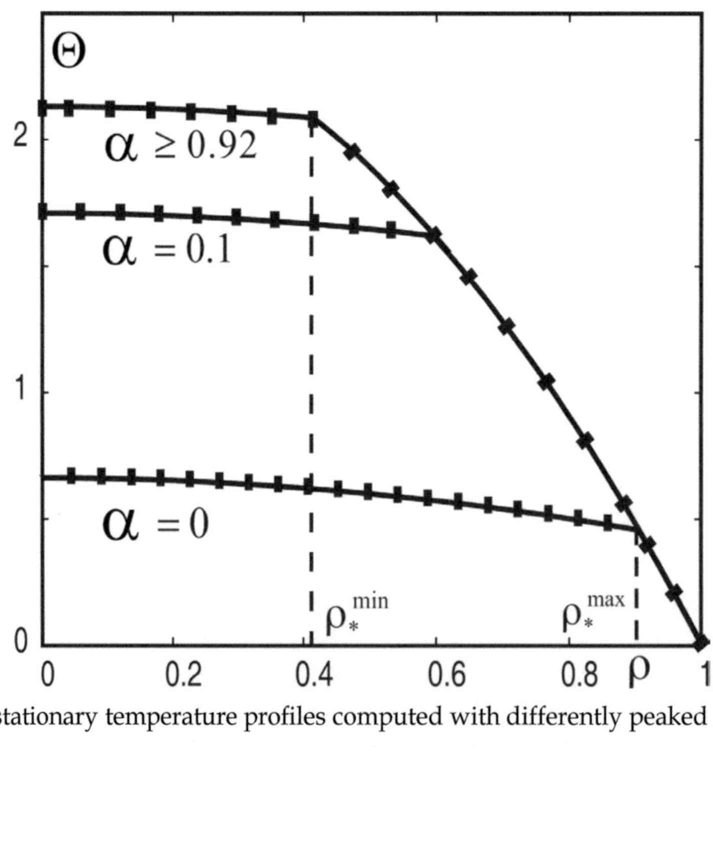

Fig. 4. Final stationary temperature profiles computed with differently peaked initial profiles

As another example we consider a plasma with a heating under the critical level where the formation of ETB is paradoxically provoked by enhanced radiation losses from the plasma edge. In fusion devices such losses are generated due to excitation by electrons of impurity particles eroded from the walls and seeded deliberately for diverse purposes. Normally radiation losses lead to plasma cooling and reduction of the temperature (Wesson, 2004). However, under certain conditions an increasing temperature has been observed under impurity seeding (Lazarus et al, 1984; Litaudon et al, 2007). Usually effects of impurities on the anomalous transport processes, in particular through a higher charge of impurity ions compared with that of the main particles, is discussed as a possible course of such a confinement improvement (Tokar, 2000a). Particularly it has been demonstrated that ITG-instability can be effectively suppressed by increasing the ion charge. Here, however, we do not consider such effects but take into account radiation energy losses in Eq.(4) by replacing the heat source S with the difference S-R, where R is the radiation power density. The latter is a non-linear function of the electron temperature and for numerical calculations in the present study we take it in the form (Tokar, 2000b):

$$R = R_0(t)\cdot\exp\left[-\left(\sqrt{\frac{T_{\min}}{T}}-\sqrt{\frac{T}{T_{\max}}}\right)^2\right] \tag{23}$$

The factor R_0 is proportional to the product of the densities of radiating impurity particles and exciting electrons. The exponent function takes into account two facts: (i) for temperatures significantly lower than the level $T_{\min}$ electrons can not excite impurities and (ii) for temperatures significantly exceeding $T_{\max}$ impurities are ionized into states with very large excitation energies. For neon, often used in impurity seeding experiments (Ongena, 2001), $T_{\min}$ is of several electron-volts and $T_{\max} \approx 100\ eV$, see Ref.(Tokar, 1994). Thus the radiation losses are concentrated at the plasma edge where the temperature is essentially smaller than several keV typical for the plasma core.

Why additional energy losses with radiation can provoke the formation of ETB? Consider stationary temperature profile in the edge region where the heating can be neglected compared with the radiation, i.e. $T_{\min} < T < T_{\max}$. By approximating R with R_0, the heat transport equation is reduced to the following one:

$$\kappa d^2T/dx^2 \approx R_0 \tag{24}$$

where $x = r_n - r$ is the distance from the LCMS. This equation can be straightforwardly integrated leading to:

$$\frac{dT}{dx} \approx \frac{R_0}{\kappa}x + \frac{T(0)}{\delta},\ T \approx \frac{R_0}{\kappa}\frac{x^2}{2} + T(0)\cdot\left(\frac{x}{\delta}+1\right) \tag{25}$$

The temperature value at the LCMS, $T(0)$, has to be found from the conditions at the inner boundary of the radiation layer, $x = x_{rad}$, where $T \approx T_{\max}$ and the heat flux density from the core, $\kappa\ dT/dx$, is equal to the value q_{heat} prescribed by the central heating. The plane geometry adopted in this consideration implies $x_{rad} << r_n$. From Eqs.(25) one finds:

$$L_T = \frac{\chi^2\gamma_{rad}/2 + (\chi + \delta/x_{rad})(1-\gamma_{rad})}{\chi\gamma_{rad} + 1 - \gamma_{rad}} \tag{26}$$

where the dimensionless co-ordinate $0 \le \chi \equiv x / x_{rad} \le 1$ and radiation level $\gamma_{rad} \equiv R_0 x_{rad} / q_{heat}$ are introduced. For δ / x_{rad} and γ_{rad} large enough the χ-dependence of the r.h.s. in Eq.(26) is non-monotonous: with χ increasing from zero it first goes down and then up. Qualitatively the decrease of L_T means that if the heat contact with the SOL-region out of the confined plasma is weak, i.e. δ is large, the radiation losses lead to a stronger decrease of the temperature than of the conductive heat flux in the radiation layer. At the plasma boundary, $x = 0$, we assume $L_T = \delta > L_{cr}$, i.e. there is no ETB without radiation. With radiation the condition for the transport reduction, $L_T < L_{cr}$, can be, however, fulfilled somewhere inside the radiation layer, $0 < x < x_{rad}$.

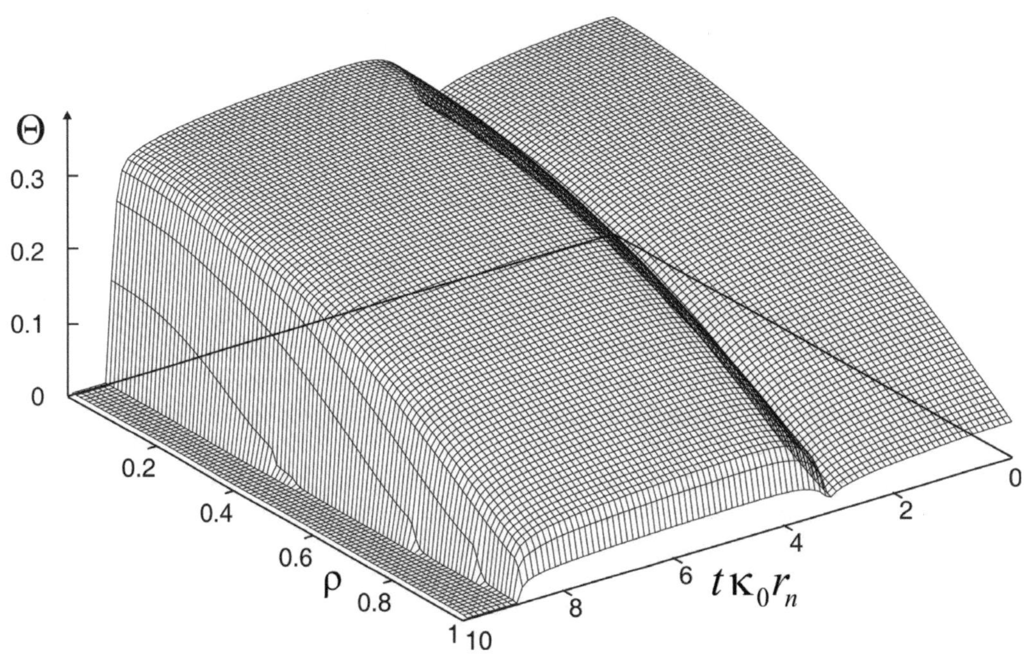

Fig. 5. The time evolution of the temperature profile under conditions of sub-critical heating with the ETB formation induced by the radiation energy losses increasing linearly in time. Finally the radiation triggers plasma collapse

If the radiation intensity is too high the state with the radiation layer at the plasma edge does not exist at all. This can be seen if, by using Eqs.(25) and the conditions at the inner interface of the radiation zone with the plasma core, one calculates $T(0)$:

$$T(0) = \left(R_0 \delta \pm \sqrt{R_0^2 \delta^2 + q_{heat}^2 - 2\kappa R_0 T_{\max}} \right) \delta / \kappa \qquad (27)$$

If the discriminant in Eq.(27) is positive, as it is the case for R_0 small enough, there are two values for $T(0)$ but only the state with the edge temperature given by Eq.(27) with the sign (+), i.e., with larger $T(0)$, is stable. Indeed, in the state with (-) in Eq.(27) and smaller $T(0)$ the total energy loss increases with decreasing $T(0)$. If the temperature spontaneously drops, the radiation layer widens and the radiation losses grow up leading to a further drop of $T(0)$. With increasing R_0 the discriminant approaches to its minimum level $q_{heat}^2 - \left(\kappa T_{\max} / \delta \right)^2$

at $R_0 = \kappa T_{\max}/\delta^2$. If the flux from the plasma core is smaller than the critical value $\kappa T_{\max}/\delta$, there are no stationary states at all with the radiation layer located at the plasma edge if R_0 exceeds the level:

$$R_0^{\max} = \left(1 - \sqrt{1 - q_{heat}^2 \delta^2 / \kappa^2 T_{\max}^2}\right) \kappa T_{\max} / \delta^2 \tag{28}$$

In such a case the radiation zone spreads towards the plasma core and a radiation collapse takes place. Figure 5 demonstrates the corresponding time evolution of the radial profile for the dimensionless temperature Θ found from Eq.(4) with the radiation losses computed according to Eq.(3) where the amplitude grows up linearly in time, $R_0(t) \sim t$. As the initial condition a stationary profile in the state without any radiation and ETB ($\delta > L_{cr}$), has been used. One can see that at a low radiation the total temperature profile is first settled down with increasing R_0. However, at a certain moment a spontaneous formation of the ETB takes place. The ETB spreads out with the further increase of the radiation amplitude. When the latter becomes too large radiation collapse develops.

3.2 Time evolution of the plasma density profile

As the next example the evolution of the plasma density profile by an instantaneous formation of the ETB will be considered. This evolution results from the interplay between transport of charged particles and their production due to diverse sources in fusion plasmas. Normally the most intensive contribution is due to ionization of neutral particles which are produced by the recombination on material surfaces of electrons and ions lost from the plasma. If the surfaces are saturated with neutral particles they return into the plasma in the process of "recycling" (Nedospasov & Tokar, 2003). Thus the densities of neutral atoms, n_a, and charged particles, n, are interrelated and the source term in Eq.(4) for charged particles, $S = k_{ion} n n_a$, where k_{ion} is the ionization rate coefficient, depends non-linearly on n. This non-linearity may be an additional cause for numerical complications. The transport of recycling neutrals is treated self-consistently with that of charged particles and n_a is determined by the continuity equation:

$$\partial_t n_a + 1/r \cdot \partial_r (r j_a) = -S \tag{29}$$

with the flux density j_a computed in a diffusive approximation, see, e.g., (Tokar, 1993) :

$$j_a = -\frac{T_a}{m_a (k_{ion} + k_{cx}) n} \partial_r n_a \tag{30}$$

This approximation takes into account that the rate coefficient for the charge-exchange of neutrals with ions, k_{cx}, is noticeably larger than k_{ion}. Thus, before the ionization happens neutrals charge-exchange with ions many times and change their velocities chaotically, i.e., a Brownian like motion takes place. At the entrance to the confined plasma, $r = r_n$, the temperature T_a of recycling neutrals is normally lower than that of the plasma, $T_a(t, r = a) < T(t, r = a)$. However after charge-exchange interactions the newly produced atoms acquire the ion kinetic energy and T_a approaches to T. This evolution is governed by the heat balance equation:

$$n_a \partial_t T_a + j_a \partial_r T_a = k_{cx} n n_a (T - T_a) \tag{31}$$

By discretizing this in time and in space, one gets the following recurrent relation:

$$T_{a,i} = \frac{n_{a,i} T_{a,i}^{-}/\tau - j_{a,i} T_{a,i+1}/(r_{i+1} - r_i) + (k_{cx} n n_a T)_i}{n_{a,i}/\tau - j_{a,i}/(r_{i+1} - r_i) + (k_{cx} n n_a)_i}$$

allowing to calculate the atom temperature profile at the time moment t, $T_{a,i<n} \equiv T_a(t, r_{i<n})$, from that at the previous time $t - \tau$, $T_{a,i<n}^{-} \equiv T_a(t-\tau, r_{i<n})$, and boundary condition $T_{a,n} \equiv T_a(t, r_n)$. In this consideration we assume that the radial profile of the plasma temperature T, assumed the same for electrons and ions, is prescribed as follows:

$$T(r) = T(0) - [T(0) - T(r_n)](r/r_n)^2 \tag{32}$$

Figure 6 shows the time evolution of the central plasma density, $n(t,r = 0)$, computed for the conditions of the tokamak TEXTOR (Dippel et al, 1987) with the minor radius of the LCLS r_n = 0.46 m, the central plasma temperature $T(0)$ =1.5 keV and the following parameters at the LCMS: the plasma temperature, $T(r_n)$ =50 eV , the neutral density $n_a(r_n)$ =$2{\cdot}10^{16} m^{-3}$ and temperature $T(r_n)$ = 25 eV. The initial profile of the plasma density was assumed parabolic and given by a formula similar to Eq.(32) with the values at the axis $n(0)$ =$5{\cdot}10^{19} m^{-3}$ and at the LCMS $n(r_n)$ =$10^{19} m^{-3}$, respectively. To investigate the impact of nonlinearities introduced by the coupling of the densities of neutral and charged particles only, these computations have been done for a smooth radial variation of the plasma particle diffusivity D also given by a formula similar to Eq.(32) with D(0)=0.2m^2s^{-1} and $D(r_n)$ =0.8 m^2s^{-1} and zero convection velocity V.

Different panels and curves in Fig.6 show the results obtained for different time steps τ and memory times τ_0. One can see in Fig.6a that for $\tau_0 << \tau$ problems arise by computing with small τ. This happens in spite of the fact that the calculations were done with particle transport characteristics independent of the density gradient, i.e. p = 1 in the flux dependence on $\partial_r n$, see page 3. The reason for such behaviour can be the non-linearity in the source S due to the ionization of neutrals and the involvement of the solution at the previous time moment $t - \tau$ into the inhomogeneous term f in Eq.(15) for the variable y. Indeed, for $\tau_0 << \tau$ this contribution is given by the integral from $n(t-\tau,r)/\tau$ that becomes unboundedly large with decreasing time step. As a result a large error can accumulate after many time steps and no stationary state is achieved for $\tau = 10^{-4}$s and $\tau_0 = 10^{-6}$s.

The behaviour described above contradicts both physical expectations and the existence of stationary analytical solution found for a plane geometry approximation applicable for the neutral penetration depth significantly less than the plasma radius r_n, and with the plasma diffusivity D and particle temperatures T, T_a constant along the radius, see, e.g., Ref. (Tokar 1993). Under these conditions one can introduce the dimensionless co-ordinate

$$u = \int_r^{r_n} \sigma_* n d\rho$$

where $\sigma_* = \sqrt{m_a k_{ion} (k_{ion} + k_{cx})/T_a}$ is the effective cross-section for the attenuation of neutrals in the plasma,. With this variable change Eqs. (29), (30) are reduced to a very simple one:

$$d^2 n_a / du^2 = n_a$$

and the physically meaning solution, decaying towards the plasma core, is:

$$n_a \approx n_a(r_n)\cdot\exp(-u)$$

Then the stationary continuity equation for charged particles is as follows:

$$d^2u/dr^2 = \exp(-u)\cdot n_a(r_n)k_{ion}/D$$

By multiplying both sides of the latter with $2du/dr$, we get after a straightforward integration:

$$n(u) \equiv \frac{`1}{\sigma_*}\frac{du}{dr} = \frac{`1}{\sigma_*}\sqrt{\left[\delta\frac{n_a(r_n)k_{ion}}{D}\right]^2 + 2\frac{n_a(r_n)k_{ion}}{D}\left[1-\exp(-u)\right]}$$

where to determine the integration constant we have used the boundary condition at the LCMS, dn/dr = - n/δ. The explicit dependences $u(r)$ and $n(r)$ can be obtained from this relation, see, e.g., Ref. (Tokar, 1993), by using table of integrals (Gradshteyn & Ryzhik, 1965). Interesting that the latter one reproduces hyperbolic tangent law often used to approximate experimentally found density profiles.

The solution is stable if τ is increased, however, the larger the time step the more details of the time dynamics are lost. Figure 6b demonstrates the results found for $\tau << \tau_0 = 10s$. In this case calculations with all $\tau < 1s$ are numerically stable and result in the same final stationary value of the central density of $5.4{\cdot}10^{19}m^{-3}$. Nonetheless, a numerical instability reappears again for τ exceeding some critical value of 1s. A probable reason for this behaviour is again the involvement of the solution at the previous time moment into the term J in Eq.(13). Now the problem arises because of two last two terms in J which do not become smaller with increasing τ as this is the case for the integral contribution. For large time steps these terms are dubious. Improper impacts of the solution at the previous time in Eq.(15) can be avoided if the memory time τ_0 is suitably chosen. In Fig.6c we show the time behaviour of $n(t,r{=}0)$ found with τ_0 = 1s. The solutions have similar time evolution for any τ, as one may expect for a given time step, and approach to the same stationary value of $5.4{\cdot}10^{19}m^{-3}$.

It is not obviously how to choose a proper τ_0 in a particular situation. The consideration above indicates that for small time steps the second term under the integral in J, Eq.(13), has not to exceed the last two contributions and for large τ the ordering has to be opposite. As a rough condition satisfying both constraints one can adopt the equality of these terms averaged over the whole computation domain. This results in:

$$\tau_0 = \frac{\tau}{\ln(1+\tau/\tau_c)} \tag{33}$$

where the "confinement" time is defined as follows:

$$\tau_c = \frac{1}{r_n\Gamma(r_n)}\int_0^{r_n} n(t-\tau,r)rdr$$

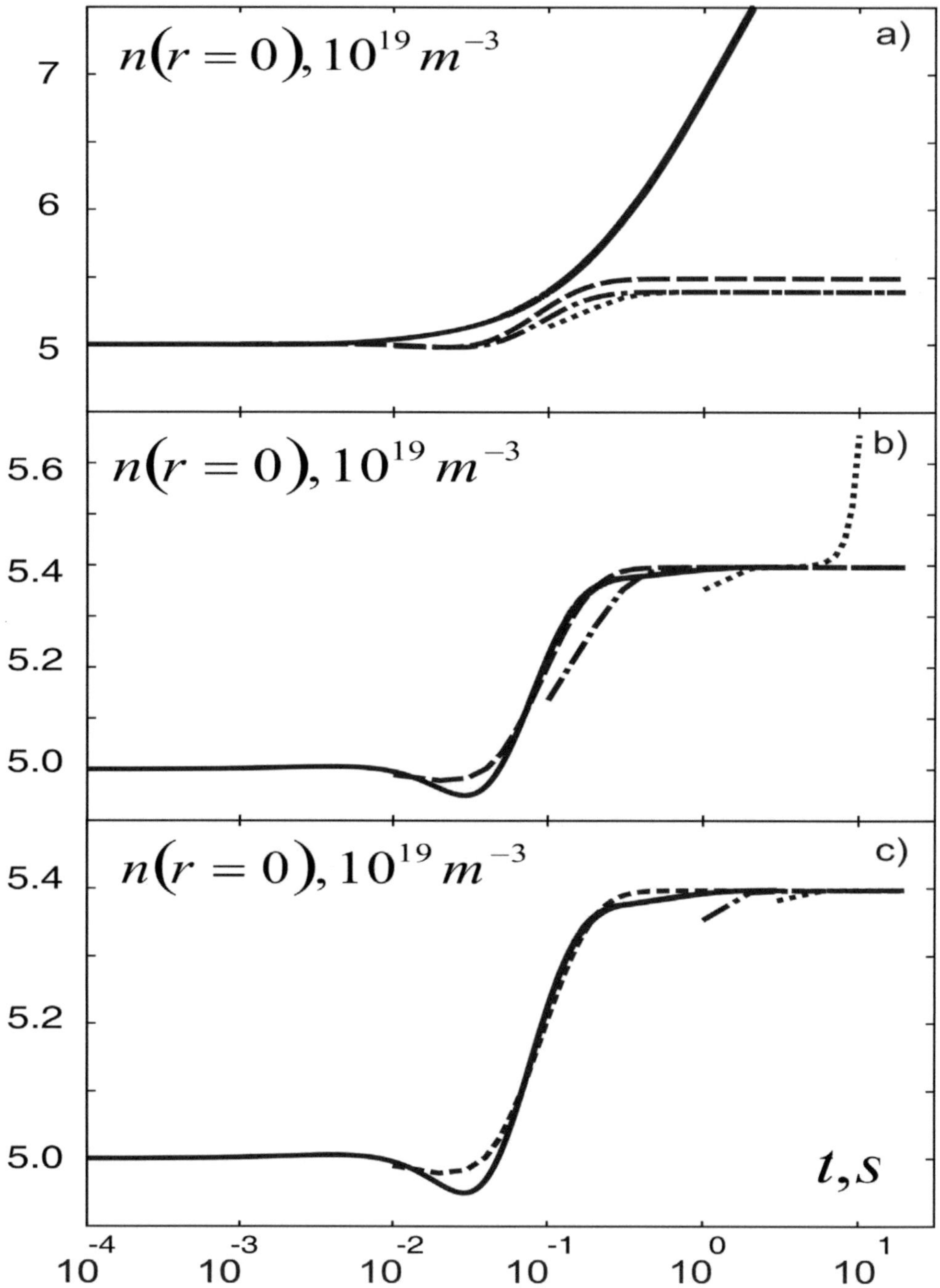

Fig. 6. The time evolution of the central plasma density computed with different memory times and time steps: $\tau_0 = 10^{-6}$ s , $\tau = 10^{-4}$ s (solid line), 10^{-3} s (dashed line), 10^{-2} s (dash-dotted line) and 10^{-1} s (dotted line) (a) ; $\tau_0 = 10$ s , $\tau = 10^{-4}$ s (solid line), 10^{-2} s (dashed line), 10^{-1} s (dash-dotted line) and 1s (dotted line) (b); $\tau_0 = 1$ s , $\tau = 10^{-4}$ s (solid line), 10^{-2} s (dashed line), 1s (dash-dotted line) and 3 s (dotted line) (c). All curves begin after the first time step, at $t = \tau$

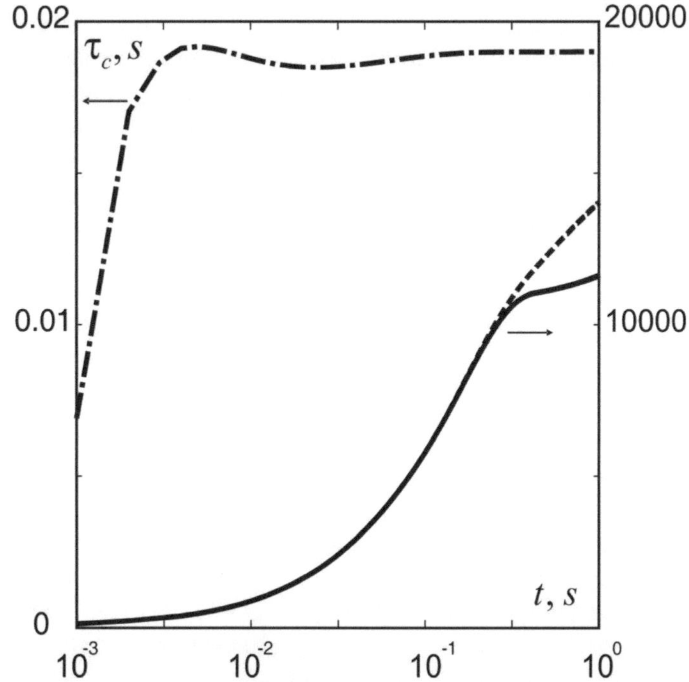

Fig. 7. The number of iterations done to the time t by calculating with the fixed memory time τ_0 (dashed curve), with the optimized one calculated according to Eq.(33) (solid line) and the time variation of the confinement time τ_c (dash-dotted line)

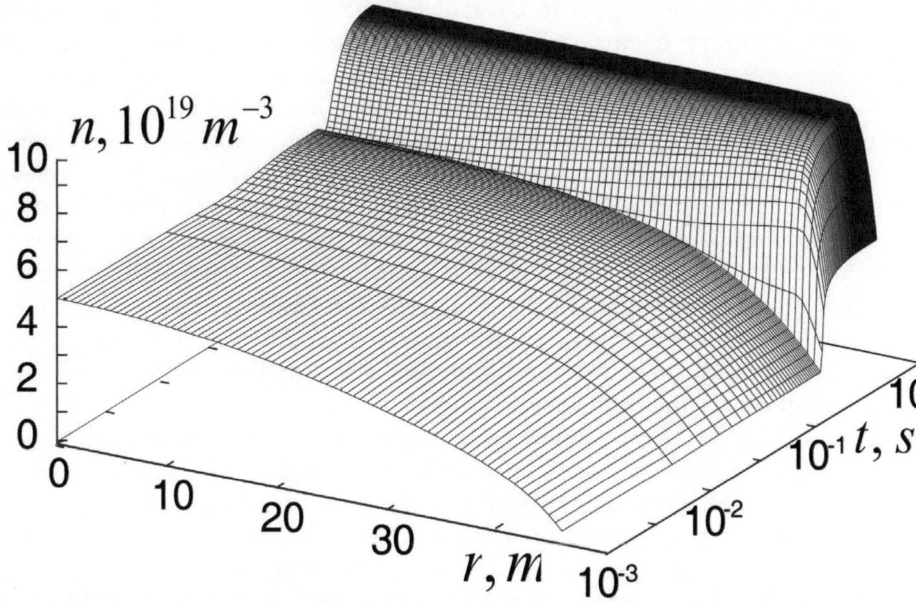

Fig. 8. The time evolution of the plasma density profile with formation of the ETB computed with $\tau = 10^{-3}$ s and τ_0 defined according to Eq.(33)

In the limit cases, $\tau << \tau_c$ and $\tau_c << \tau$ we have $\tau_0 \approx \tau_c$ and $\tau_0 \approx \tau/\ln(\tau/\tau_c)$, respectively. Figure 7 shows the time variation of τ_c for the density evolution calculated with $\tau = 10^{-3}$s and τ_0 = 1s. Also the number of iterations done to the time t by computations with τ_0 = 1s and with τ_0 determined according to Eq.(33) are demonstrated. One can see that in the latter case the number of iterations decreases significantly by approaching to the steady state at large t.

The estimate (33) gives a good hint for a proper memory time also in calculations with the formation of transport barriers. The results of this calculation are demonstrated in Fig.8 showing the time evolution of the density profile obtained by assuming that at time t = 0.3 s there is an instantaneous reduction by a factor of 10 of the charged particle diffusivity D in the edge region $r_n - \Delta \le r \le r_n$ with $\Delta = 0.02$ m. In this case computations with $\tau_0 >> 0.5$ s, i.e. significantly exceeding τ_c, are unstable.

4. Conclusion

Transport processes in fusion plasmas can be caused by diverse physical mechanisms. The most straightforward one is due to Coulomb collisions between charged particles. Due to conservation of momentum collisions provoke a net particle displacement only by interactions of particles of opposite charges, i.e. electrons and ions. For such a classical diffusion the characteristic mean free path is of the electron Larmor radius and the level of induced particle losses is very low. In a tokamak with curved magnetic field lines these losses are enhanced significantly by the drift motion originated from the field inhomogeneity and curvature of field lines. Nonetheless, the corresponding so called neo-classical transport does not provide obstacles to confine and heat plasmas to thermonuclear temperatures. Much more dangerous are innumerable drift instabilities triggered by sharp gradients of the plasma parameters in the radial direction across the magnetic surfaces. These instabilities enhance anomalously, by orders of magnitude, the particle and energy losses over the neoclassical level. Different types of such instabilities are of importance in the hot core and at the relatively cold edge of the plasma. In the core instabilities triggered by the radial temperature gradients, namely, ion temperature gradient and collisionless trapped electron modes are of the most importance. At the edge where coulomb collisions are often enough drift Alfvén waves and drift resistive ballooning modes may be dominant. Important characteristics of unstable modes, e.g., growth rates are essentially dependent on the plasma parameter gradients. Therefore some instability can be completely suppressed if certain critical gradients are approached. As a result the induced fluxes of particles and energy are non-linear non-monotonous functions of the gradients. Such behaviour results in an ambiguity of local gradient values in stationary states and provides possibilities for bifurcations like the formation of transport barriers.

It is demonstrated that in the case of fluxes decaying with increasing gradient the numerical solution of a diffusion-like equation is unstable for time steps smaller than a critical one. This does not allow describing time dynamics of transport transitions in necessary details and leads even to principally wrong plasma final states resulting from this calculation. An approach based on a proper change of dependent variable proposed in the present chapter allows avoiding difficulties outlined above. It includes several principal elements: (i) change over to a new dependent variable ξ relating the values of the original one Z at the present and previous time moments through the time step and a memory time τ_0, (ii) transition to an

integral form of the primary equation and change to an integral counterpart y of the variable ξ and (iii) approximation of the second order ODE for y in the vicinities of grid knots by ODEs with constant coefficients whose exact analytical solutions are conjugated by requiring the continuity of the solution and its first spatial derivative.
The approach elaborated is demonstrated by modelling of the development of the edge transport barrier in a tokamak. The plasma heat conduction dependence on the temperature gradient is assumed as a dropping abruptly at a critical value of the temperature *e*-folding length. First a situation with a heating exceeding a critical level is considered that corresponds to a L_T magnitude at the LCMS smaller than L_{cr}. Calculations have shown that, depending on the initial temperature profile, the whole range of the radial position of the interface between ETB and the core region with strong transport, predicted by an analytical model, can be realized in the final stationary state. Computations also demonstrate that an ETB can be triggered even with a subcritical heating if impurity radiation localized at the very plasma edge is enhanced to a certain critical level. This may improve the understanding of the radiation improved mode observed in several tokamaks.
Modelling of the plasma density profile involves additional non-linearity through the coupling between the densities of charged and neutral particles. This can lead to numerical instabilities in calculations with both too small and too large memory times. With a proper chosen τ_0 such difficulties can be avoided. An approach is proposed to choose the memory time. Itis based on the equilibration of different contributions to the free term in the equation for y and relates τ_0 to the confinement time. The optimization of the τ_0 selection procedure allows reducing noticeably the total number of iterations required to achieve the stationary solution. It allows also modelling reliably the plasma density evolution by a spontaneous formation of the ETB. The methods developed can be applied by simulations of other physical phenomena in fusion plasmas having a bifurcation-like character, e.g., density limits, and phase transitions in other media.

5. References

ASDEX Team (1989) The H-mode in ASDEX , *Nucl. Fusion* Vol. 29, No. 11 (November 1989), pp. 1959–2040, ISSN 0029-5515

Basiuk, V. et al (2003) Simulations of steady-state scenarios for Tore Supra using the CRONOS code, *Nuclear Fusion* Vol. 43, No. 9 (September 2003), pp. 822–830, ISSN 0029-5515

Bateman, G. et al (1998) Predicting temperature and density profiles in tokamaks, *Phys. of Plasmas*, Vol.5, No.5 (May 1998), pp. 1793-1799, ISSN 1070-664X

Braginskii, S.I. (1963) Transport processes in a plasma, in *Reviews of Plasma Physics*, edited by Leontovich M., Vol.1, pp.205-310, Library of Congress Catalog Card Number 64-23244, Consultants Bureau, New York, US

Cennachi, G. & Taroni, A. (1988) JETTO: A Free-Boundary Plasma Transport Code (Basic Version), *Rep. JET-IR(88)03*, JET Joint Undertaking, Abingdon, UK

Connor, J.W. & Pogutse, O.P. (2001) On the relationship between mixing length and strong turbulence estimates for transport due to drift turbulence, *Plasma Physics and Controlled Fusion*, Vol.43, No.2, (February 2001), pp. 155-176, ISSN 0741-3335

Diamond, P.H. et al (1994) Self-regulating shear flow turbulence: a paradigm for the L to H transition, *Physical Review Letters,* Vol.72, No.16, (April 1994), pp. 2565-2568, ISSN 0031-9007

Dippel, K.H. et al (1987) Plasma-wall interaction and plasma performance in TEXTOR – A review, *J. Nuclear Mater.* Vol. 145-147, No.2 (February 1987), pp. 3-14, ISSN 0022-3115

Galeev, A.A., and Sagdeev, R.Z., (1973) Theory of neoclassical diffusion, in *Reviews of Plasma Physics,* edited by Leontovich M., Vol.7, pp.257-343, ISBN 0-306-17067-1, Consultants Bureau, New York, US

Gradshteyn, I.S. & Ryzhik, I.M. (1965) Table of integrals, series and products, Academic Press, Library of congress catalog card number 65-29097, New York, US

Greenwald, M. (2002) Density limits in toroidal plasmas. *Plasma Physics and Controlled Fusion,* Vol.44, No.8, (August 2002), pp. R27-R80, ISSN 0741-3335

Guzdar, P.N. et al (2001) Zonal flow and zonal magnetic field generation by finite ß drift waves: a theory for low to high transitions in tokamaks, *Physical Review Letters,* Vol.87, No.1, (July 2001), pp. 015001-1-4, ISSN 0031-9007

Guzdar, P.N. et al. (1993) Three-dimensional fluid simulations of the nonlinear drift-resistive ballooning modes in tokamak edge plasmas, *Phys. Fluids B,* Vol.5, No. 10, (October 1997), pp. 3712-3727, ISSN 0899-8221

Horton Jr., W. et al (1981) Toroidal drift modes driven by ion pressure gradient, *Phys. Fluids,* Vol. 24, No. 6, (June 1981), pp. 1077-1085, ISSN 0031-9171

ITM (2010) http://www.efda-itm.eu/

Jardin, S. (2010) Computational Methods in Plasma Physics, Chapman and Hall/CRC, ISBN 978-1-4398-1021-7, Boca Raton, US

Jardin, S.C. et al (2008) On 1D diffusion problems with a gradient-dependent diffusion coefficient, *J. Comp. Phys.* Vol. 227, No.20, (October 2008), pp. 8769-8775, ISSN 0021-9991

Kadomtsev, B.B. and Pogutse, O.P. (1971) Trapped particles in toroidal magnetic systems, *Nuclear Fusion,* Vol. 11, No. 1, (January 1971), pp. 67-92, ISSN 0029-5515

Kalupin, D. et al, Predictive modelling of L and H confinement modes and edge pedestal characteristics, *Nuclear Fusion* Vol. 45, No. 6 (June 2005), pp. 468–476, ISSN 0029-5515

Kerner, W. (1998) The scaling of the edge temperature in tokamaks based on the Alfven drift-wave turbulence, *Contributions to Plasma Physics,* Vol.38, No.1-2, (January 1998), pp.118-123, ISSN 0863-1042

Lazarus, E.A. et al (1984) Confinement improvement in beam heated ISX-B discharges with low-*z* impurity injection, *J. Nuclear Mater.* Vol. 121, No.1 (May 1984), pp. 61-68, ISSN 0022-3115

Litaudon, X. et al (2007) Development of steady-state scenarios compatible with ITER-like wall conditions, *Plasma Physics and Controlled Fusion,* Vol.49, No.12B, (December 2007), pp. B529-B550, ISSN 0741-3335

Nedospasov, A.V. & Tokar, M.Z. (1993) Plasma edge in tokamaks, in *Reviews of Plasma Physics,* edited by Kadomtsev, B.B., Vol.18, pp.68-20, ISBN 0-306-11007-5, Consultants Bureau, New York, US

Ongena, J. et al (2001) Recent progress toward high performance above the Greenwald density limit in impurity seeded discharges in limiter and divertor tokamaks, *Phys. Plasmas* Vol. 8, No.5 (May 2001), pp. 1364513-1-13, ISSN 1070-664X

Pereverzev, G.V. & Yushmanov, P.N. (1988) Automated System for Transport Analysis in a Tokamak, *IPP Report 5/98*, Max-Planck-Institut für Plasmaphysik, Garching, Germany

Rogers, B.N. et al (1998) Phase space of tokamak edge turbulence, the L-H- transition, and formation of the edge pedestal, *Physical Review Letters*, Vol.81, No.20, (November 1998), pp. 4396-4399, ISSN 0031-9007

Scott, B. (1997) Three-dimensional computation of collisional drift wave turbulence and transport in tokamak geometry, *Plasma Physics and Controlled Fusion*, Vol.39, No.3, (March 1993), pp. 471-504, ISSN 0741-3335

Shestakov, A.I. et al (2003) Self-consistent modelling of turbulence and transport, *J. Comp. Phys.*, Vol.185, No. 2 (March 2003), pp. 399-426, ISSN 0021-9991

Tajima, T. (2004) Computational plasma physics, Westview Press, Boulder, US

Terry, P.W. (2000) Suppression of turbulence and transport by sheared flow, *Rev. Mod. Phys.*, Vol.72, No.1, (January 2000), pp. 109-165, ISSN 0034-6861

Tokar, M.Z. (1993) The possible nature of the localized recycling effect on the plasma edge in tokamaks, *Plasma Physics and Controlled Fusion*, Vol.35, No.9, (September 2007), 1119-1135, ISSN 0741-3335

Tokar, M.Z. (1994) Effect of radial particle transport on radiation from light impurities, *Nuclear Fusion* Vol. 34, No. 6 (June 1994), pp. 853–861, ISSN 0029-5515

Tokar, M.Z. (1994) Modelling of detachment in a limiter tokamak as a nonlinear phenomenon caused by impurity radiation, *Plasma Phys. and Contr. Fusion* Vol. 36, No 11 (November 1994), pp. 1819-1844, ISSN 0741-3335

Tokar, M.Z. (2000a) Model for the transition to the radiation improved mode in a tokamak, *Physical Review Letters*, Vol.84, No.5, (January 2000), pp. 895-898, ISSN 0031-9007

Tokar, M.Z. (2000b) On threshold of radial detachment in tokamaks, *Phys. Plasmas* Vol. 7, No.6 (June 2000), pp. 2432-2438, ISSN 1070-664X

Tokar, M.Z. (2003) Synergy of anomalous transport and radiation in the density limit, *Physical Review Letters*, Vol.91, No.9, (August 2001), pp. 095001-1-4, ISSN 0031-9007

Tokar, M.Z. (2006) Numerical solution of continuity equation with a flux non-linearly depending on the density gradient, *J. Comp. Phys.* Vol. 220, No.1, (December 2006), pp. 2625-2633, ISSN 0021-9991

Tokar, M.Z. (2010) Numerical modeling of transport barrier formation, *J. Comp. Phys.* Vol. 229, No.7, (April 2010), pp. 2625-2633, ISSN 0021-9991

Tokar, M.Z. et al. (2006) Numerical solution of transport equations for plasmas with transport barrier, *Comp. Phys. Comm.* Vol. 175, No.1, (January 2006), pp. 30-35, ISSN 0010-4655

Versteeg, H.K. & Malalasekera, W. (1995) An introduction to computational fluid dynamics: The finite volume method, Harlow: Longman Scientific \& Technical, US

Wagner, F. et al. (1982) Regime of Improved Confinement and High Beta in Neutral-Beam-Heated Divertor Discharges of the ASDEX Tokamak, *Physical Review Letters*, Vol.49, No.19, (November 1982), pp. 1408-1412, ISSN 0031-9007

Waltz, R.E. et al (1197) A gyro-Landau-fluid transport model, *Phys. of Plasmas*, Vol.4, No.7 (July 1997), pp. 2482-2496, ISSN 1070-664X

Weiland, J. (2000) Collective Modes in Inhomogeneous Plasma, Institute of Physics Publishing, ISBN 0-7503-0589-4-hbk, Bristol, Great Britain

Wesson, J. (2004) *Tokamaks, 3rd edition*, Oxford Science Publications, ISBN 0-19-8509227, Oxford, GB

Xu, X.Q et al (2003) , Transitions of turbulence in plasma density limits, *Phys. Plasmas* Vol. 10, No.5 (May 2003), pp. 1773-1781, ISSN 1070-664X

8

Numerical Simulation of the Heat Transfer from a Heated Solid Wall to an Impinging Swirling Jet

Joaquín Ortega-Casanova
Área de Mecánica de Fluidos, ETS de Ingeniería Industrial, C/ Dr. Ortiz Ramos s/n, Universidad de Málaga, 29071 Málaga Spain

1. Introduction

Swirling jets are frequently used in many industrial applications such as those related with propulsion, cleaning, combustion, excavation and, of course, with heat transfer (e.g. cooling/heating), among others. The azimuthal motion is usually given to the jet by different mechanisms, being the most used by means of nozzles with guided-blades (e.g. Harvey, 1962); by entering the fluid radially to the device (e.g. Gallaire et al., 2004); by the rotation of some solid parts of the device (e.g. Escudier et al., 1980); or by inserting helical pieces inside a cylindrical tube (e.g. Lee et al., 2002), among other configurations. The way the swirl is given to the flow will finally depend on the particular application it will be used for.

Impinging swirling (or not swirling) jets against heated solid walls have been extensively used as a tool to transfer heat from the wall to the jet. In the literature, one can find many works that study this kind of heat transfer related problem from a theoretical, experimental or numerical point of view, being the last two techniques presented in many papers during the last decade. In that sense, Sagot et al. (2008) study the non-swirling jet impingement heat transfer problem from a flat plate, when its temperature is constant, both numerically and experimentally to obtain an average Nusselt number correlation as a function of 4 non-dimensional parameters. And, what is most important from a numerical point of view, their numerical results, obtained with the commercial code Fluent© and the Shear Stress Transport (SST) $k-\omega$ turbulence model for values of Reynolds number (*Re*) ranging from 10E3 to 30E3, agree very well with previous experimental results obtained by Fenot et al. (2005), Lee et al. (2002) and Baughn et al. (1991).

More experimental results are given by O'Donovan & Murray (2007), who studied the impinging of non-swirling jets, and by Bakirci et al. (2007), about the impinging of a swirling jet, against a solid wall. The last ones visualize the temperature distribution on the wall and evaluate the heat transfer rate. In Bakirci et al. (2007), the swirl is given to the jet by means of a helical solid insert with four narrow slots machined on its surface and located inside a tube. The swirl angle of the slots can be varied in order to have jets with different swirl intensity levels. This is a commonly extended way of giving swirl to impinging jets in heat transfer applications, as can be seen in Huang & El-Genk (1998), Lee et al. (2002), Wen & Jang (2003) or Ianiro et al. (2010). On the other hand, Angioletti et al. (2005), and for Reynolds numbers ranging between 1E3 and 4E3, present turbulent numerical simulations of the impingement of a non-swirling jet against a solid wall. Their results are later validated by Particle Image

Velocimetry (PIV) experimental data: when the Reynolds number is small, their numerical results, obtained with the SST $k-\omega$ turbulence model, fit very well the experimental data, while for high Reynolds number values, either the Re-Normalization Group (RNG) $k-\epsilon$ model or the Reynolds Stress Model (RSM) works better. Others previous numerical studies, as the ones by Akansu (2006) and by Olson et al. (2004), show that the SST $k-\omega$ turbulence model is able to predict very well the turbulence in the near-wall region in comparison with other turbulence models. This fact is essential to obtain accurately the turbulent heat transfer from the wall.

Another different turbulent model, presented by Durbin (1991), is used by Behnia et al. (1998; 1999) to predict numerically the heat transfer from a flat solid plate by means of turbulent impinging jets, showing their results good agreement with experimental data. The inconvenient of this last turbulent model is that it does not come originally with Fluent package, so it is ruled out as an available turbulent model.

The work presented here in this chapter deals with the numerical study about the heat transfer from a flat uniform solid surface at a constant temperature to a turbulent swirling jet that impinges against it. To that end, the commercial code Fluent© is used with the corresponding turbulent model and boundary conditions. As any turbulent numerical study where jets are involved, it needs as boundary condition the velocity and turbulence intensity profiles of the jet, and the ones measured experimentally, by means of a Laser Doppler Anemometry (LDA) technique, at the exit of a swirl generator nozzle will be used. The nozzle, experimental measurements and some fitting of the experimental data will be shown in Section 2. Different information, about the computational tasks and decisions taken, will be presented in Section 3, such as those related with the computational domain, its discretization, the numerical methods and boundary conditions used and the grid convergence study. After that, in Section 4 the different results obtained from the numerical simulations will be presented and discussed. They will be divided into two subsections: one to see the effect of varying the Reynolds number; and another to see the effect of increasing or decreasing the nozzle-to-plate distance. Finally, the document will conclude with Section 5, where a summary of the main conclusions will be presented together with some recommendations one should take into account to enhance the heat transfer from a flat plate when a turbulent swirling jet impinges against it.

2. Experimental considerations

Regarding the experimental swirling jet generation, it is created by a nozzle where the swirl is given to the flow by means of swirl blades with adjustable angles located at the bottom of the nozzle (see Fig. 1). After the fluid moves through the blades, it finally exits the nozzle as a swirling jet. Due to the fact that blades can be mounted with five different angles, swirling jets with different swirl intensities can be generated. Thus, for a given flow rate, or Reynolds number (defined below), through the nozzle, five different swirling jets with five different swirl intensities, or swirl numbers (defined below), can be obtained. When the blades are mounted radially, no swirl is imparted to the jet and the swirl number will be practically zero. This blade configuration will be referred in what follows as R. However, with the blades rotated the maximum possible angle, the jet will have the highest swirl levels (and then the highest swirl numbers). This configuration will be referred as $S2$. Between R and $S2$ configurations there are other 3 possible blade orientations, but only the one with the most tangential orientation, $S2$, will be considered in this work. Fig. 2 shows a 2-D view of the

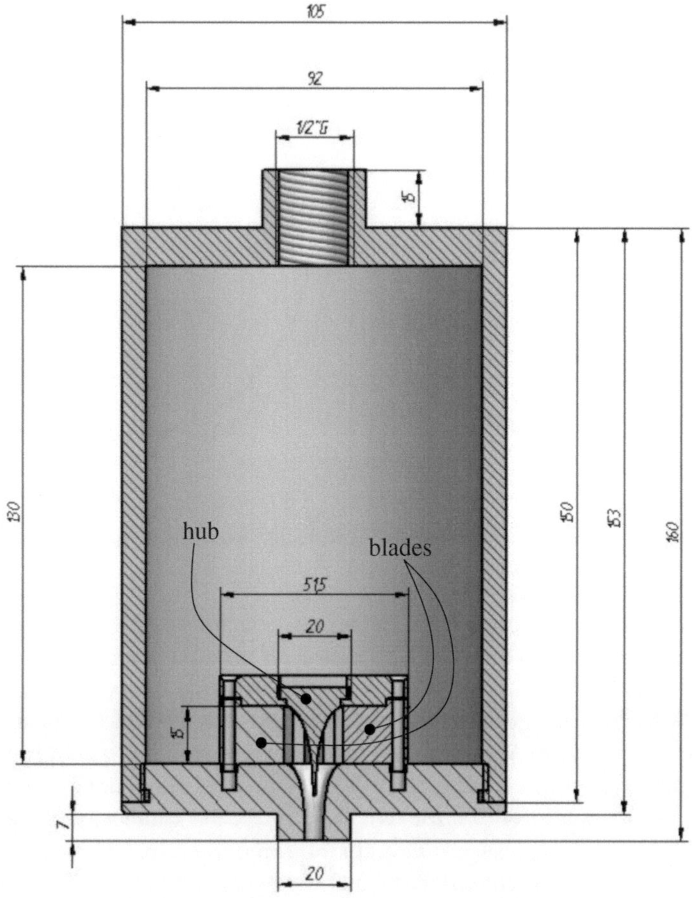

Fig. 1. 2D view of the nozzle. The dimensions are in mm.

swirl blades mounted radially and with the most tangential angle, *R* and *S*2 configuration, respectively.

Similar devices to the one used here to generate the swirling jet are commonly used in several industrial applications, but its use in this work is motivated by two reasons: firstly, by seabed excavation devices that usually use a swirl component to enhance their excavation performance (see Redding, 2002), instead of using a totally axial jet; and secondly, to compare the heat transfer performance of the impinging swirling jet with that obtained experimentally by the same kind of impinging swirling jets but under seabed excavation tasks and reported in Ortega-Casanova et al. (2011). They show that better results (in terms of the size of the scour created) are obtained when the swirl blades are rotated the maximum possible angle, *S*2 configuration, and for the highest nozzle-to-plate distance studied. Thus, the objective of this numerical study is to be able to answer the question about whether or not the *S*2 configuration and the largest nozzle-to-plate distance, also give the highest heat transfer from the plate to the jet.

To model the swirling turbulent jet created by the nozzle is necessary to know both the average velocity field and its turbulent structure at the exit nozzle. In a cylindrical coordinate system

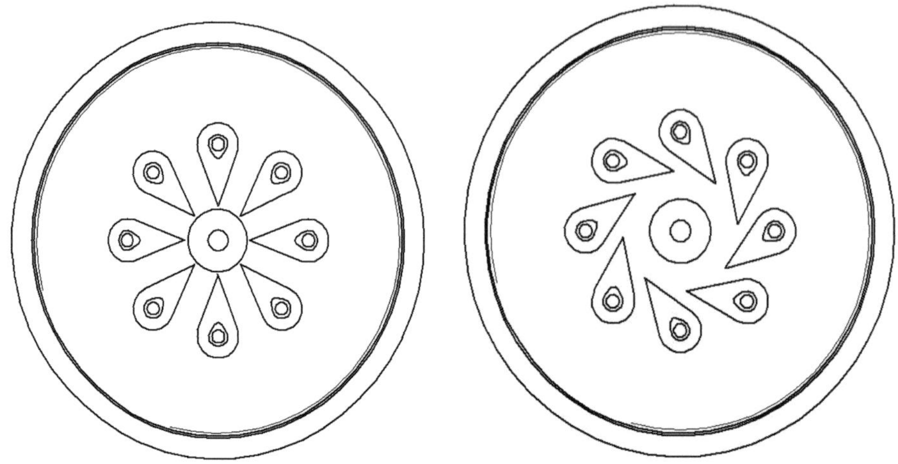

(a) (b)

Fig. 2. 2D view of the guided blades: mounted radially, R configuration, (a); and rotated the maximum angle, $S2$ configuration, (b).

(r,θ,z), the mean velocity components of the velocity vector will be indicated by $\vec{V}(r,\theta,z) = (U,V,W)$, while the jet turbulence will be take into account by the velocity fluctuations, $\vec{v}'(r,\theta,z) = (u',v',w')$. Both vectors have been previously measured experimentally by means of a LDA system and, due to the shape of the exit tube of the nozzle (see Fig. 1), the radial component of both $\vec{V}$ and $\vec{v}'$ has been considered small enough to be neglected: $U = 0 = u'$. Typical non-dimensional mean velocity profiles at the nozzle exit, together with its fluctuations, are shown in Fig. 3 for two flow rates, the smallest and the highest used, $Q \approx 100$ l/h and $Q \approx 270$ l/h, respectively. In the same figure is also included, with a solid line, the fitting of the experimental data (see Ortega-Casanova et al., 2011, for more details about the fitting models used). In Fig. 3, the velocity has been made dimensionless using the mean velocity W_c based on the flow rate through the nozzle, $W_c = 4Q/(\pi D^2)$, and the radial coordinate with the radius of the nozzle exit $D/2$.
In addition, Fig. 3 shows that, for a given blade orientation, $S2$ in our case, the swirl intensity of the jet will depend on the flow rate Q through the nozzle, since the azimuthal velocity profile is different depending on Q, too. Due to this, the one and only non-dimensional parameter governing the kind of jet at the nozzle exit is the Reynolds number:

$$Re = \frac{\rho W_c D}{\mu} = \frac{4\rho Q}{\mu \pi D}, \tag{1}$$

where ρ and μ are the density and viscosity of the fluid, respectively: in Ortega-Casanova et al. (2011) the flow rate ranges from 100 l/h to 270 l/h, so the Reynolds number ranges from 7E3 to 18.3E3, approximately. On the other hand, once the blade orientation is given, $S2$ [shown Fig. 2(b)], the swirl intensity of the jet will depend only on the Reynolds number, and following Chigier et al. (1967), an integral swirl number S_i can be defined to quantify the swirl intensity of the jet as

$$S_i = \frac{\int_0^\infty r^2 WV\, dr}{(D/2)\int_0^\infty r\left(W^2 - \frac{1}{2}V^2\right) dr}. \tag{2}$$

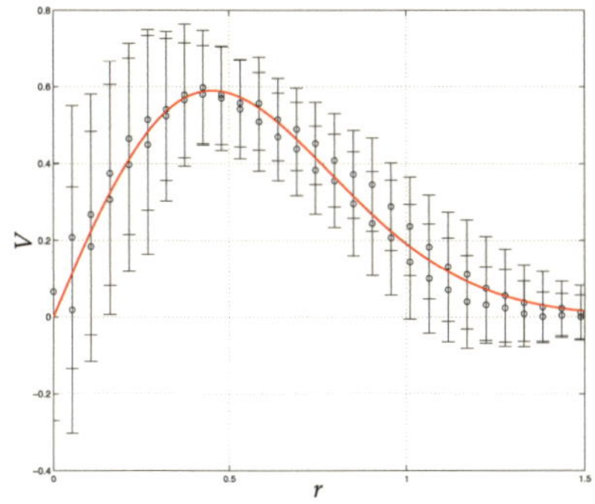

(a)

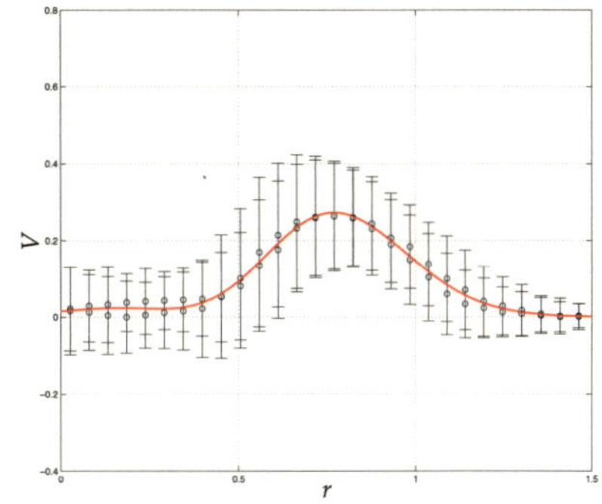

(b)

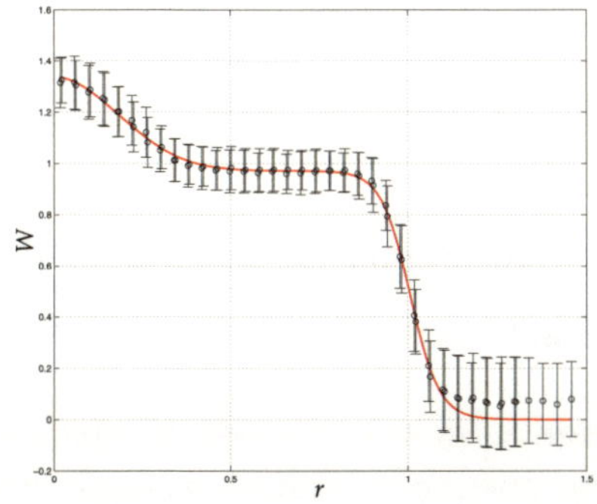

(c)

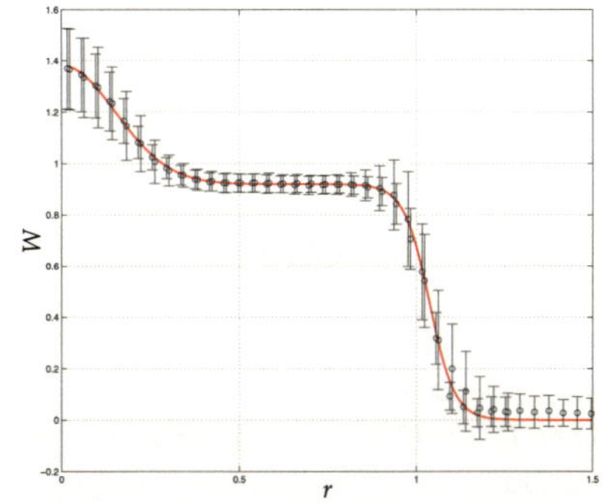

(d)

Fig. 3. Dimensionless azimuthal, (a) and (b), and axial, (c) and (d), velocity profiles for $S2$ configuration. $Q \approx 100$ l/h for (a) and (c); and $Q \approx 270$ l/h for (b) and (d). The circles indicate mean velocity values and the error bars its fluctuations.

The evolution of S_i versus the Reynolds number for the blade orientation under study is shown in Fig. 4.

As it has been pointed out previously, the swirl intensity of the jet S_i will depend on the blade orientation and the flow rate. As can be seen in Fig. 4, $S2$ configuration produces jets with variable levels of swirl, with its maximum around $Re \approx$ 9E3. This Reynolds number divides the curve in two parts: the left one, $Re \lesssim$ 9E3, in which S_i increases with Re; and the right one, $Re \gtrsim$ 9E3, in which S_i decreases with Re. S_i has been calculated using (2) and the non-dimensional mean axial and azimuthal velocity profiles measured just downstream of the nozzle exit. Both components of the velocity are depicted in Fig. 5 for all Reynolds numbers experimentally studied. From this figure can easily be understood the behavior of S_i for $S2$ configuration. These profiles are also shown in Ortega-Casanova et al. (2011), but are reproduced here again in order to have a complete and general idea of the swirling jets generated by the nozzle configuration under study. When the swirl increases with the rotation of the blades, not only the dimensional azimuthal velocity increases, as it was expected, but also the maximum axial velocity at the axis, appearing a well defined overshoot around it (see the axial and azimuthal velocity profiles for other blade orientations in Ortega-Casanova et al., 2011). In addition to this, another effect associated with the increasing of the blade rotation

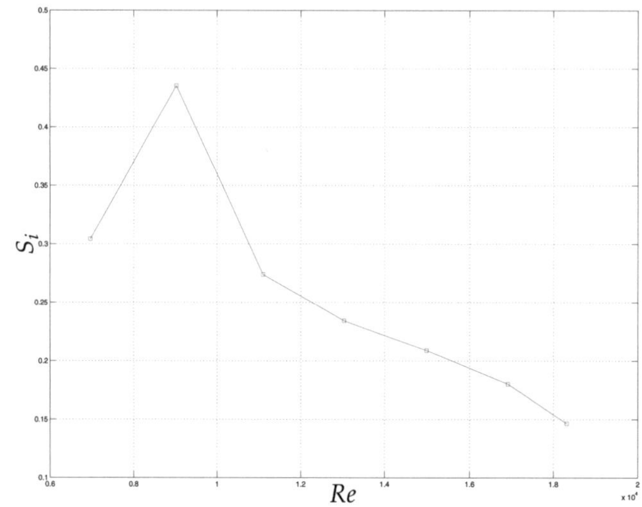

Fig. 4. Integral swirl number S_i as a function of the Reynolds number. $S2$ configuration.

is the appearance of a swirless region near the axis and a shift of all the azimuthal motion to a region off the axis when the Reynolds number is above a certain value, as can be seen in Fig. 5(a) for $Re > 11E3$. This swirless region has nothing to do with vortex breakdown since the axial velocity [Fig. 5(b)] does not have any characteristic of this phenomena, like a reverse flow at the axis with a stagnation point at a certain radius of the profile. This phenomena has been recently observed experimentally by Alekseenko et al. (2007), where vortex breakdown occurs for jet swirl intensities above a critical value (see, e.g., Lucca-Negro & O'Doherty, 2001, for a recent review about that phenomena).

Also, in Ortega-Casanova et al. (2011) is shown that the best combination for excavation purposes in order to produce deeper and wider scours on sand beach is the axial overshoot together with the shift of the azimuthal motion to an annular region. They also discuss and give the mathematical models that better fit the experimental data, shown also in Fig. 3 with solid lines. Obviously, when $S2$ configuration is used, as it is here, the azimuthal velocity models depend on the Reynolds number considered, being different the one used for low Reynolds numbers ($Re \leq 11E3$) than for high ones ($Re \geq 13E3$).

Those models will be used now as a boundary condition to specify the velocity components of the swirling jet in the numerical simulations. However, not only the model of the velocity profiles are needed to model the turbulent jet, but also is necessary to model its turbulence. Once the velocity fluctuations $\vec{v}'$ have been measured, the turbulent intensity I of the jet can be estimated as

$$I = \frac{\sqrt{u'^2 + v'^2 + w'^2}}{W_c} \simeq \frac{\sqrt{v'^2 + w'^2}}{W_c}. \tag{3}$$

In order to have an analytical function of the turbulent intensity profile to be used as boundary condition, all turbulent intensity I profiles must be fitted and it is found that the best fitting is achieved with the Gaussian model

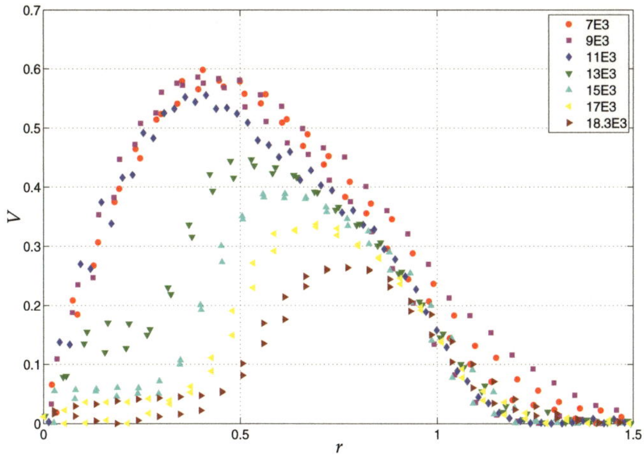

(a)

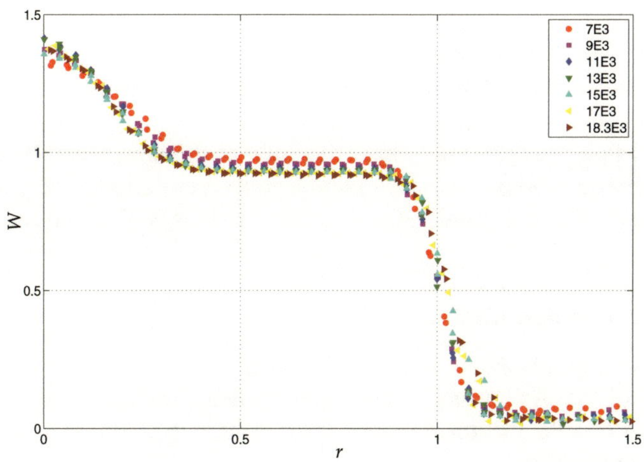

(b)

Fig. 5. Mean dimensionless azimuthal (a) and axial (b) velocities measured just downstream the nozzle exit.

$$I = \sum_{i=1}^{n} a_i \mathrm{e}^{\left[-\left(\frac{r-b_i}{c_i}\right)^2\right]}, \tag{4}$$

where r is the dimensionless radial coordinate and a_i, b_i and c_i are fitting parameters depending on the Reynolds number. It has been checked that $n = 3$ is enough to fit quite well, and with the simplest model, the radial I profile for any value of Re. Fig. 6 shows the profile of I for two values of the Reynolds number. For low Re and almost all radial positions, the swirling jet is more turbulent than for high Re, with the highest levels of turbulence around the axis, while for high Re, the turbulence is more uniform. The profiles shown in Fig. 6

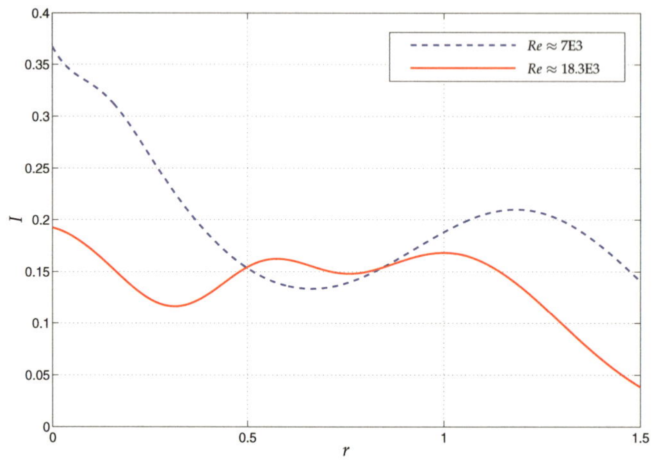

Fig. 6. Turbulent intensity radial distribution when the Reynolds numbers are the indicated in the legend.

has been obtained with (3) and the velocity fluctuations shown in Fig. 3. Once this turbulent magnitude has been fitted, it will be used later to specify the appropriate boundary conditions in the turbulent model used (see next section).
The turbulent swirling jets measured experimentally at the nozzle exit by means of a LDA system are ready to be used as boundary condition in the numerical simulations thank the models of both azimuthal and axial velocity components as well as the one of the turbulent intensity.

3. Computational considerations

The numerical simulations have been carried out by means of the commercial code Fluent© (version 6.2.16). As for any numerical turbulent simulations, some previous things must be chosen, such as the turbulent model, the optimum grid, the computational geometry and boundary conditions, etc.
Firstly, the computational geometry together with the corresponding boundary conditions used will be presented. The problem is considered to be axisymmetric, so only a 2D $r-z$ section of the three-dimensional geometry will be solved. Fig. 7 shows a sketch of the heat transfer problem solved in this work together with the different boundary conditions used: the swirl generator nozzle is located at a distance H above the solid hot plate (whose radius is $\mathcal{R}$) where the swirling jet will impinge once it leaves the nozzle as a swirling jet (the non-dimensional nozzle-to-plate distance will be indicated by the ratio H/D); once the impinging takes place, the fluid leaves the computational domain through either the side or top surface. The velocity and turbulent intensity profiles shown in the previous section will be introduced into the simulations by a "velocity inlet" boundary condition at the left-top of the domain by means of a User Defined Function (abbreviated as UDF in what follows) in order to model the nozzle above the plate. As can be seen in Fig. 7, the nozzle exit is surrounded by an annular solid part of the nozzle. It will be modeled giving to the velocity components in that region an almost zero value through the velocity profile at the "velocity inlet" boundary

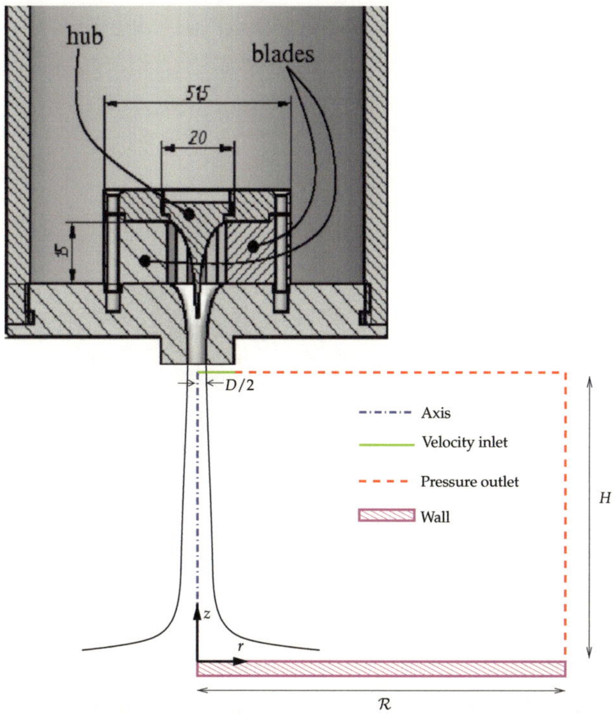

Fig. 7. Sketch of the computation domain. The nozzle and type of boundary condition used are also included.

condition. However, Fluent does not allow to specify a turbulent intensity distribution or profile but a constant value. Due to this, in order to indicate the turbulent structure of the swirling jet when it leaves the swirl generator nozzle by the measurements taken experimentally, the turbulent intensity I must be turned into other turbulent magnitudes that will depend on the turbulent model used, as it will be shown later. The surfaces where the fluid is allowed to leave the computational domain (the right and top side) will be indicated as "pressure-outlet" boundary conditions. The bottom of the geometry represents the solid hot plate where the fluid will impinge and is considered as a no-slip surface with a prescribed temperature and modeled as a "wall" boundary condition (Sagot et al., 2008, showed that almost similar results can be obtained when the boundary condition on the solid plate is either a prescribed temperature or heat flux). Finally, the left line from the nozzle exit to the plate at the bottom will be indicated as an "axis" boundary condition, since it represents the axis of symmetry of the problem.

Regarding the turbulent model, the $k - \omega$ one will be used, in particular, its version SST. This decision is based on the previous works review presented in the Introduction because is the one used by Sagot et al. (2008) (where good agreement between numerical and experimental solutions are shown) and because the Reynolds number used here, in this work, ranges between 7E3 and 18.3E3, close to those employed in Sagot et al. (2008).

The flow we are interested in solving with this problem is considered turbulent, steady and axisymmetric with the fluid (water) having its density constant (incompressible fluid) as in Ortega-Casanova et al. (2011). Thus, the steady Reynolds Averaged Navier-Stokes (RANS)

equations are solved numerically to obtain any fluid magnitude. They can be written in Cartesian tensor notation as:
the continuity equation:

$$\frac{\partial V_i}{\partial x_i} = 0; \tag{5}$$

the momentum equations:

$$\frac{\partial (V_i V_j)}{\partial x_j} = -\frac{1}{\rho}\frac{\partial p}{\partial x_i} + \nu \frac{\partial}{\partial x_j}\left[\frac{\partial V_i}{\partial x_j} + \frac{\partial V_j}{\partial x_i} - \frac{2}{3}\delta_{ij}\frac{\partial V_l}{\partial x_l}\right] + \frac{\partial\left(-\overline{v_i' v_j'}\right)}{\partial x_j}; \tag{6}$$

and the energy equation:

$$\frac{\partial}{\partial x_i}\left[V_i(\rho e + p)\right] = \frac{\partial}{\partial x_j}\left[K_{eff}\frac{\partial T}{\partial x_j}\right] \tag{7}$$

with

$$e = h - \frac{p}{\rho} + \frac{\vec{V}\cdot\vec{V}}{2}, \tag{8}$$

where ν is the kinematic viscosity, h is the enthalpy, K is the thermal conductivity and $K_{eff} = K + K_t$ is the effective thermal conductivity that takes into account the turbulent thermal conductivity K_t: $K_t = c_p\mu_t/Pr_t$. c_p is the specific heat, μ_t is the turbulent dynamic viscosity and Pr_t is the turbulent Prandtl number. Also, two closure equations are needed: one to know the turbulent kinetic energy k and another one for the specific turbulent dissipation rate ω:

$$\rho\frac{\partial}{\partial x_i}(kV_i) = \frac{\partial}{\partial x_j}\left(\Gamma_k\frac{\partial k}{\partial x_j}\right) + G_k - Y_k, \tag{9}$$

$$\rho\frac{\partial}{\partial x_i}(\omega V_i) = \frac{\partial}{\partial x_j}\left(\Gamma_\omega\frac{\partial \omega}{\partial x_j}\right) + G_\omega - Y_\omega, \tag{10}$$

where: Γ_k and Γ_ω are the effective diffusivity of k and ω, respectively; G_k and G_ω are the generation of k and ω, respectively, due to mean velocity gradients; and Y_k and Y_ω are the dissipation of k and ω, respectively. To know more about their definition and implementation in Fluent, the reader is remitted to Fluent 6.2 User's Guide (2005).
Regarding the boundary conditions shown in Fig. 7, their implementation in Fluent was as follows:

Axis: since this line is an axis of symmetry, the boundary conditions "axis" was chosen;

Pressure outlet: both the side and top surfaces were supposed to be at the same constant pressure, so the boundary condition "pressure-outlet" was chosen;

Wall: this surface is considered as a smooth no-slip stationary solid surface at constant temperature T_W, so the boundary condition "wall" was chosen, imposing its temperature at the known constant value.

Velocity inlet: in this surface, the corresponding radial dependence axial and azimuthal velocity profile associated with the corresponding Reynolds number under study was imposed trough an UDF file through a "velocity-inlet" boundary condition. The models used to fit the velocity profiles shown in Fig. 3 are given in Ortega-Casanova et al. (2011), and the reader is remitted there to know more about them. On the other hand, regarding the specification of the swirling jet turbulence levels, the turbulence intensity can be estimated from the LDA measurements, eq. (3), and fitting to a radial profile, eq. (4), but Fluent does not allow to specify as boundary condition a radial dependence profile for the turbulence intensity but a constant value. For that reason, and in order to specify the radial turbulence distribution of the jet, the turbulence intensity is turned into the variables k and ω for which are possible to indicate a radial profile as boundary condition. Once the mean axial and azimuthal velocities are measured, W and V, respectively, together with its fluctuations, w' and v', respectively, and with the turbulent intensity I given by (3), k and ω can be obtained as

$$k = \frac{3}{2}\left(\overline{U}\, I\right)^2, \tag{11}$$

$$\omega = \frac{800}{25}\frac{\overline{U}\, I}{D_H}, \tag{12}$$

where I is in %, $\overline{U} = \sqrt{W^2 + V^2}$, and D_H is the hydraulic diameter of the nozzle exit. While (11) is given by Fluent 6.2 User's Guide (2005), (12) has been obtained numerically giving different values to $\overline{U}$, I and D_H on a velocity inlet boundary condition, and relating the ω value giving by Fluent on that boundary with them [(11) has been also confirmed by the same methodology]. On the other hand, the jet leaves the nozzle at a constant temperature T_j.

The presence of solid surfaces when turbulent flows are solving numerically, needs special attention in order to solve efficiently the boundary layer along the solid surface. This fact is crucial in our problem since there is a solid surface where the swirling jet impinges and the heat transfer from the surface must be solved precisely. This requires that the nearest grid point to the solid hot plate must be as close to the surface as possible to have an $y+$ of unity order. To achieve this, rectangular stretched meshes with different node densities have been generated with the total nodes ranging from 13 000 to 60 000. All meshes have in common that the mesh nodes density is higher near the solid hot plate, the axis, the mixing layer and the nozzle exit. The grid independence study were done with five grids in order to choose from them the optimum one. The number of nodes, with the maximum value of $y+$ along the solid hot plate indicated in parenthesis, used were: 13 041 (8.0); 22 321 (4.0); 30 000 (0.4); 37 901 (0.4) and 60 551 (0.4). The $y+$ values previously indicated were obtained from the numerical simulation of the most unfavorable case studied (see next section): the one with the highest Reynolds number ($Re \approx$ 18.3E3), and the shortest nozzle-to-plate distance, i.e. $H/D = 5$. The grid density near the solid hot plate selected as the optimum for this H/D will be reproduced, in that zone, for other nozzle-to-plate distances, or H/D values, that is, the radial node distribution and the one next to the plate along axial direction: meshes for different values of H/D will differ only on the axial node distribution and the number of nodes along that direction.

The minimum $y+$ obtained in the grid independence process was 0.4, but in 3 different grids, so the optimum will be selected in terms of the area-weighted average Nusselt number along the solid hot plate. On the one hand, the Nusselt number will be defined as

$$Nu(r, Re) = \frac{q(r)\,D}{K\,\Delta T}, \tag{13}$$

where q is the total heat flux from the solid hot wall to the fluid and ΔT is the temperature difference between the wall (T_w) and the swirling jet emerging from the nozzle (T_j). And, on the other hand, the area-weighted average Nusselt number along a surface S is defined as

$$\overline{Nu}(Re) = \frac{1}{S}\int_S Nu(r, Re)\,\mathrm{d}S, \tag{14}$$

which is a measurement of the dimensionless mean heat transferred from the solid hot plate to the jet.

Using the finest grid (60 551 nodes), $\overline{Nu}$ on the solid hot plate only changes $\approx 1\%$ and the computational time increases by 78% with respect to the grid with $\simeq 38\,000$ nodes. For these reasons, the grid chosen as the optimum was the one with $nr \times nz = 37\,901$ nodes (nr and nz are the number of nodes along r and z directions, respectively). Regarding the radial direction, the optimum mesh has $nr = 251$ non uniform nodes compressed around the axis ($r = 0$) and the mixing layer ($r \simeq D/2$). On the other hand, the number of nodes along the axial direction depends on the nozzle-to-plate distance. Thus, for $H/D = 5$, $nz = 151$; for $H/D = 10$, $nz = 201$ and for $H/D = 30$, $nz = 301$. The first node from both the solid hot plate, along the axial direction, and the axis, along the radial direction, is at a distance equal to 0.0025 mm.

To conclude this section, new computational information is added below. A typical simulation requires about 70E3 iterations to converge, detected by the convergence with the iterations of: the equation residuals; a monitor, defined as the area-weighted average Nusselt number on the solid hot plate; and the mass conservation between the inlet and outlets of the computational domain. About one fifth of the total iterations were done using first order methods to discretize the convective terms of the transport equations, while the remaining iterations were done with the second order schemes PRESTO (PREssure STaggering Option) and QUICK (Quadratic Upwind Interpolation for Convective Kinematics). The Pressure-Velocity Coupling were carried out with the SIMPLE (Semi-Implicit Method for Pressure-Linked Equations) scheme. On the other hand, the gravity effects have been not taken into account since the inertial forces are much bigger than the gravitational ones, so that the Froude number is much bigger than one.

4. Results

In this section, the results obtained will be presented, once the heat transfer from the solid hot wall to the impinging swirling jet has been solved numerically. This section will be divided in two subsections dedicated to present the effect of increasing both the nozzle-to-plate distance and the Reynolds number. The results will be discussed in terms of both the Nusselt number $Nu(r, Re)$ and the area-weighted average Nusselt number $\overline{Nu}(Re)$, both calculated on the solid hot plate. Three distances, $H/D = 5, 10$ and 30, and seven Reynolds numbers, $Re \approx$ 7E3, 9E3, 11E3, 13E3, 15E3, 17E3 and 18.3E3, have been studied, as in Ortega-Casanova et al. (2011). Previous works related with both heat transfer and impinging jets have focused their attention in distances H/D smaller than 10 (see Brown et al., 2010, for recent results

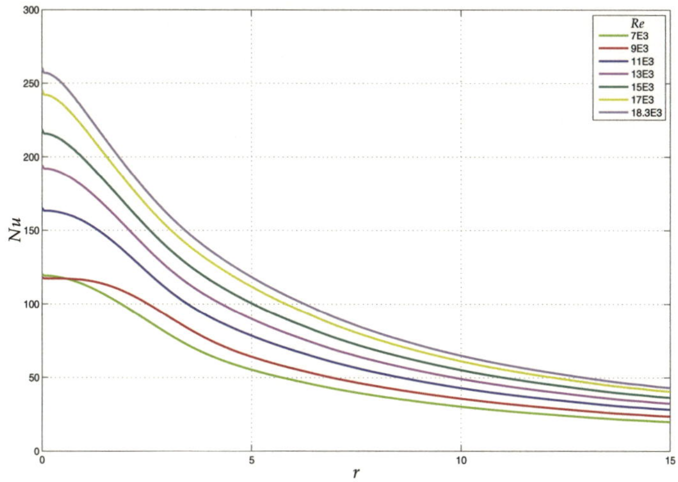

Fig. 8. Nu evolution for $H/D = 5$ and the Re indicated in the legend.

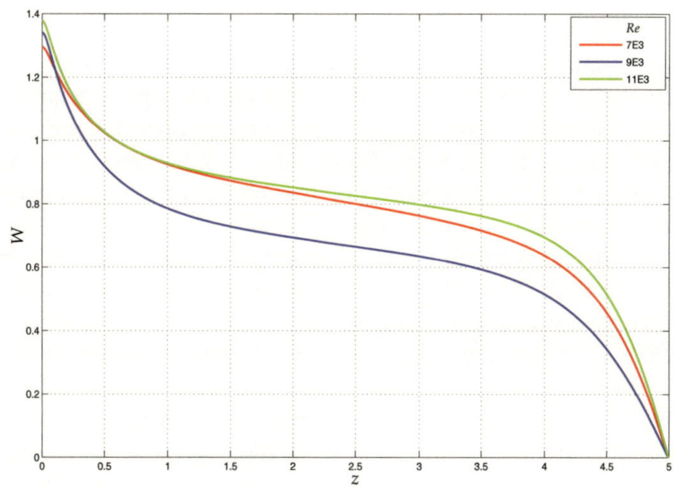

Fig. 9. Evolution of W along the axis: $H/D = 5$ and the Reynolds numbers are indicated in the legend. z has been made dimensionless with D.

when H/D ranges between 0.5 and 10), so that, the behavior for larger distances will be also discussed in this work.

4.1 Effect of Reynolds number.

First of all, it must be remembered that the swirl intensity of each jet is different according with Fig. 4, and that its value will be important in order to explain how Nusselt number on the solid hot plate changes with Reynolds number.

In Fig. 8 is plotted the evolution of Nu along the solid hot plate for the different Reynolds numbers studied and the smaller nozzle-to-plate distance, $H/D = 5$. For this smallest distance, when Re increases, Nu increases for any radial position, except for $Re \approx$ 9E3, the one with the highest S_i (see Fig. 4), for which there exists a small region around the axis where Nu is smaller than the one for $Re \approx$ 7E3. Therefore, the jet with the highest S_i, the one corresponding to $Re \approx$ 9E3, produces a more uniform region around the axis where Nu is almost constant, being at the stagnation point $r = 0$ slightly smaller than that of the previous and smaller Reynolds number.

The above mentioned uniform Nu region near the axis when $Re \approx$ 9E3 is due to the high swirl intensity of the jet for which a deceleration of the vortex along the axis occurs, without appearing its breakdown, that would require higher swirl intensity levels to appear, as it does in Alekseenko et al. (2007), where the vortex breakdown of a turbulent impinging swirling jet is observed experimentally above a critical jet swirl intensity. In order to explain the previously commented deceleration of the swirling jet, in Fig. 9 is depicted the axial evolution of the dimensionless axial velocity along the axis for three Reynolds numbers. One can observe how the jet with the highest S_i produces a slower jet along the axis than the other two. Probably, swirling jets with $S_i \gtrsim 0.45$ could finally undergo breakdown downstream the swirl generator nozzle but they have not been obtained experimentally with the $S2$ configuration. For this small nozzle-to-plate distance, it must be noted an imperceptible decreasing of the Nusselt number in the region near to the axis, close to the stagnation point, thing that happens for all Reynolds numbers.

When the nozzle-to-plate distance is doubled, i.e. $H/D = 10$, things are quite similar. Fig. 10 shows the radial evolution of Nu along the solid hot plate when the different jets impinged against it. The main difference with respect to the previous and smaller separation is that the swirl intensity of the jet when $Re \approx$ 9E3 is not big enough to decelerate the jet along the axis in order to produce a more uniform Nu number region than for $Re \approx$ 7E3: the higher the nozzle-to-plate distance, the higher the S_i needed to decelerate the flow around the axis in order to reach the vortex breakdown conditions. This was also shown in Ortega-Casanova et al. (2008), where the impingement of a family of swirling jets against a solid wall were studied numerically: higher swirl intensity levels were needed to observe vortex breakdown when the separation of the impinged plate increased. Therefore, since there is not enough deceleration of the jet, always that Re increases, Nu increases, too, for any radial coordinate (see Fig. 10). On the other hand, comparing Fig. 8 and 10, one can also observe that the Nusselt number at the stagnation point decreases when the separation increases.

When the nozzle-to-plate distance is the highest studied, the behavior is the same than for $H/D = 10$: increasing Re, the corresponding swirling jet produces a higher Nu distribution at any radial position than lower Reynolds number jets, but Nu levels are lower in comparison with smaller nozzle-to-plate distances. Therefore, the increasing of the separation between the nozzle and the solid hot plate will produce lower heat transfer from the plate to the jet at any radial location on the plate, assuming a constant Re. This comment can be seen clearly at the stagnation point $r = 0$ if the Nusselt number there is plotted against the Reynolds number for the different distances studied, as it is shown in Fig. 12(a). On the other hand, if one takes into account the area-weighted average Nusselt number, given in (13), on the solid hot plate and is plotted versus the Reynolds number, as it is done in Fig. 12(b), one can see that $\overline{Nu}$ increases almost linearly with Re for small nozzle-to-plate distances, $H/D = 5, 10$, while for the highest distance studied, $H/D = 30$, the tend is nonlinear for the highest Reynolds numbers. From

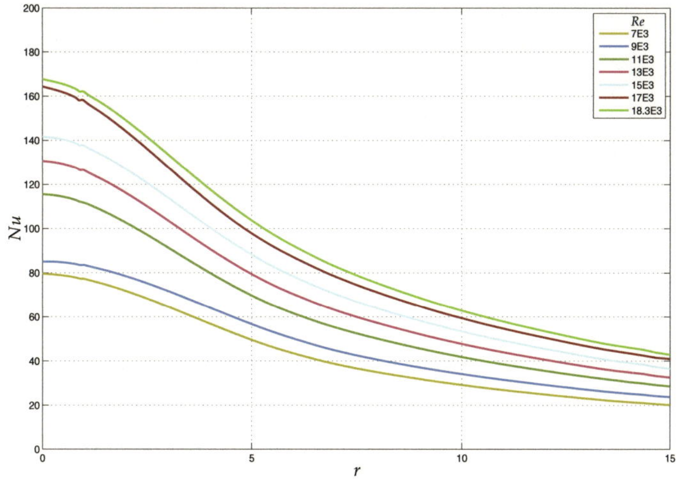

Fig. 10. As in Fig. 8, but for $H/D = 10$.

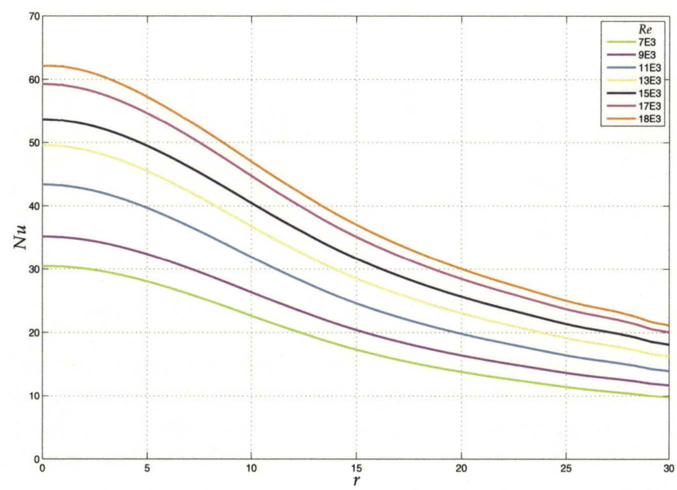

Fig. 11. As in Fig. 8, but for $H/D = 30$.

this last figure, it could be interesting to know how $\overline{Nu}$ changes with Re in comparison with $\overline{Nu}(7E3)$, that is, the ratio given by

$$\frac{\overline{Nu}(Re)}{\overline{Nu}(7E3)} \equiv \overline{Nu}^{Re}_{7E3}. \tag{15}$$

This function is depicted in Fig. 13: for $H/D = 5, 10$, $\overline{Nu}^{Re}_{7E3}$ is almost the same and linearly varying with Re; however, when $H/D = 30$ the evolution is nonlinear, being remarkable what happens for high Reynolds numbers, in comparison with the other smaller values of H/D.

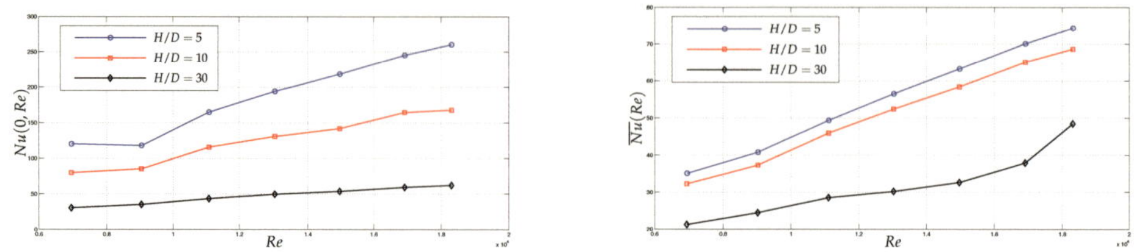

(a) (b)

Fig. 12. Evolution of: (a) $Nu(0, Re)$; and (b) $\overline{Nu}(Re)$. The corresponding value of H/D is indicated in the legend.

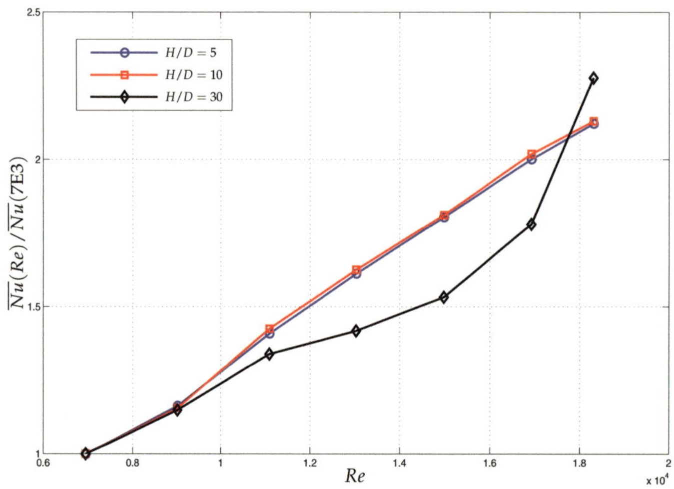

Fig. 13. Evolution of $\overline{Nu}^{Re}_{7E3}$ for the values of H/D given in the legend.

From these curves, very different predictions are obtained if they are extrapolated to higher Reynolds numbers than the ones studied. Consequently, the benefits of using the highest Reynolds number swirling jet, generated by the $S2$ configuration, to transfer heat from an impinged solid hot plate to the jet, are higher than using the low/medium Reynolds number ones when the distance between the nozzle and the plate is the highest possible: from Fig. 13 can easily be seen that for $H/D = 5, 10$, $\overline{Nu}(18.3\text{E}3) \simeq 2.1 \times \overline{Nu}(7\text{E}3)$, while for $H/D = 30$ this ratio is a little bit higher, that is, $\overline{Nu}(18.3\text{E}3) \simeq 2.3 \times \overline{Nu}(7\text{E}3)$. If one takes a look at Fig. 5(a), the previously commented facts could be explained in a different way: the effect of the displacement of the azimuthal velocity to an annular region off the axis, appearing at high Reynolds numbers, has more influence in the heat transfer at high distances between the nozzle and the solid hot plate.

4.2 Effect of the nozzle-to-plate distance.

When Reynolds number is considered constant, the effect of increasing the nozzle-to-plate distance gives as result a quick decreasing of the heat transfer from the solid hot plate to the impinging jet. The decreasing rate is higher at high Reynolds numbers than at low ones, as

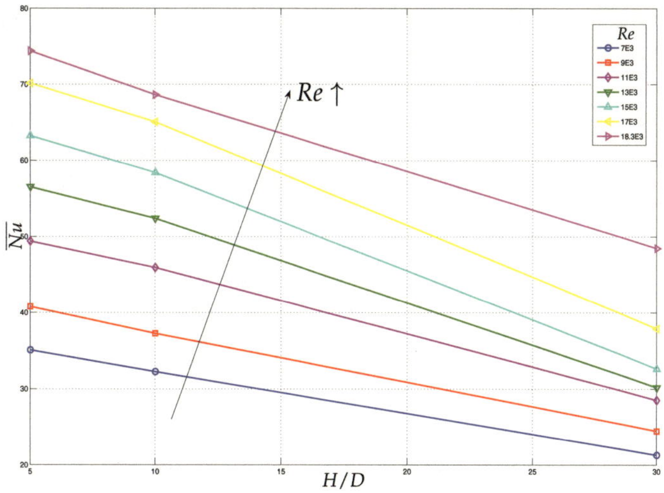

Fig. 14. Evolution of $\overline{Nu}$ for the constant values of *Re* indicated in the legend.

can be seen in Fig. 14, where the evolution of $\overline{Nu}$ for each *Re* studied is shown versus the nozzle-to-plate distance: for a given Reynolds number, the heat transfer always decreases when the separation increases; the decreasing will be higher or lower depending on the corresponding value of *Re*.

5. Conclusion

In this work, numerical simulations of the impingement of a turbulent swirling jet against a solid hot plate at constant temperature have been presented. The jet has been modeled by experimental measurements taken by means of a LDA equipment at the exit of a nozzle that imparts the swirl to the jet by guided blades, and with the jet swirl intensity depending only on the Reynolds number. Seven Reynolds numbers and three nozzle-to-plate distances have been simulated, which gives a total of 21 numerical simulations. The analysis of the results gives the following conclusions:

Firstly, taken into account that the main objective of this work was to see if the performance of the heat transfer was higher for the highest nozzle-to-plate distance than for lower ones, as in Ortega-Casanova et al. (2011) under seabed excavation tasks, it must be said that the question is answered negatively: the heat transfer from the solid hot plate to the impinging swirling jet always decreases when the separation increases, at least for the type of jets used here. Therefore, the sand, that is, the granular media used in Ortega-Casanova et al. (2011) on which the swirling jet impinged, plays an important role in reaching the scour its final shape, especially when $H/D = 30$ and the highest Reynolds number jets are used. For that combination, the impinging swirling jet creates the deepest and widest scours. When the same swirling jet impinges against undeformable solid surfaces, the qualitative results, in term of the heat transferred from the surface, are totally different from those obtained when the impingement takes place against granular media and cannot be extrapolated from excavation related problems to heat transfer ones, and vice versa.

Secondly, the area-weighted average Nusselt number on the solid hot plate, always increases with Reynolds number and for any value of the nozzle-to-plate distance, i.e. for any H/D. Almost the same happens with the Nusselt evaluated at the stagnation point $r = 0$: only for $Re \approx$ 9E3 and $H/D = 5$, this is not true due to the combination of the highest jet swirl intensity and the smallest nozzle-to-plate distance, for which a deceleration of the swirling jet takes place but without being high enough for the vortex breakdown to be observed. The effect of the deceleration was not to increase the Nusselt number at the stagnation point but to create a more uniform Nu region around the axis. Despite that decreasing in the stagnation point Nusselt number, the mean heat transfer, i.e. $\overline{Nu}$, on the surface always increases with Re. On the other hand, for high nozzle-to-plate distances, the benefits of using high Reynolds number jets instead of low ones, are higher than at small nozzle-to-plate distances. This fact has much to do with the displacement of the azimuthal motion of the swirling jet to an annular region off the axis that has more influence on the heat transferred from the solid hot plate when the nozzle-to-plate is the highest studied. The above mentioned displacement of the azimuthal motion takes place for Reynolds numbers greater than 13E3, approximately. It could have been interesting to study the heat transfer when the solid hot wall is impinged with swirling jets that have undergone breakdown and to compare the Nusselt distributions on the solid hot wall due to the impingement of swirling jets with and without breakdown. Unfortunately, vortex breakdown has not been observed experimentally with the nozzle configuration and flow rates used in this work.

And finally, the area-weighted average Nusselt number always decreases with the increasing of the nozzle-to-plate distance: for a given Reynolds number, the smaller the nozzle-to-plate distance, the higher the heat transferred from the plate to the jet.

6. Acknowledgement

The author wants to thank Nicolás Campos Alonso, who was the responsible for taking the LDA measurements at the laboratory of the Fluid Mechanics Group at the University of Málaga.

All the numerical simulations were performed in the computer facility "Taylor" at the Computational Fluid Dynamic Laboratory of the Fluid Mechanic Group at the University of Málaga.

7. References

Akansu, S. O. (2006). Heat transfers and pressure drops for porous-ring turbulators in a circular pipe. *Applied Energy*, 83, 280-298.

Alekseenko, S. V.; Bilsky, A. V.; Dulin V. M. & Markovich, D. M. (2007). Experimental study of a impinging jet with different swirl rates. *International Journal of Heat and Fluid Flow*, 28, 1340-1359.

Angioletti, M.; Nino, E. & Ruocco, G. (2005). CFD turbulent modeling of jet impingement and its validation by particle image velocimetry and mass transfer measurements. *International Journal of Thermal Sciences*, 44, 349-356.

Bakirci, K. & Bilen, K. (2007). Visualization of heat transfer for impinging swirl flow. *Experimental Thermal and Fluid Science*, 32, 182-191.

Baughn, J. W.; Hechanova, A. E. & Yan, X. (1991). An experimental study of entrainment effect on the heat transfer from a flat surface to a heated circular impinging jet. *Journal of Heat Transfer*, 113, 1023-1025.

Behnia, M.; Parneix, S. & Durbin, P. A. (1998). Prediction of heat transfer in an axisymmetric turbulent jet impinging on a flat plate. *International Journal of Heat and Mass Transfer*, 41, 1845-1855.

Behnia, M.; Parneix, S.; Shabany, Y. & Durbin, P. A. (1999). Numerical study of turbulent heat transfer in confined and unconfined impinging jets. *International Journal of Heat and Fluid Flow*, 20, 1-9.

Brown, K. J.; Persoons, T. & Murray, D. B. (2010). Heat transfer characteristics of swirling impinging jets. *In Proceedings of the 14th International Heat Transfer Conference, IHTC14*. pp 14. Washington, DC, USA. August 8-13, 2010. Edited by ASME, New York.

Chigier, N. A. & Chervinsky, A. (1967). Experimental investigation of swirling vortex motion in jets. *Journal of Applied Mechanics*, 34, 443-451.

Durbin, P. 1991. Near-wall turbulence closure without damping functions. *Theoretical and Computational Fluid Dynamics*, 3, 1-13.

Escudier, M. P.; Bornstein, J. & Zehnder, N. 1980. Observations and LDA measurements of confined turbulent vortex flow. *Journal of Fluid Mechanics*, 98, 49-63.

Fenot, M.; Vullierme, J.-J.; & Dorignac, E. (2005). Local heat transfer due to several configurations of circular air jets impinging on a flat plate with and without semi-confinement. *International Journal of Thermal Sciences*, 44, 665-675.

Fluent 6.2 user's guide (2005). Fluent Incorporated, Centerra Resource Park, 10, Cavendish Court, Lebanon (NH) 03766 USA.

Gallaire, F.; Rott, S. & Chomaz, J. M. (2004). Experimental study of a free and forced swirling jet. *Physics of Fluids*, 16, 2907-2917.

Harvey, J. K. (1962). Some observations of the vortex breakdown phenomenon. *Journal of Fluid Mechanics*, 14, 585-592.

Huang, L. & El-Genk, M. S. (1998). Heat transfer and flow visualization experiments of swirling, multi-channel, and conventional impinging jets. *International Journal of Heat and Mass Transfer*, 41, 583-600.

Ianiro, A.; Cardone, G. & Carlomagno, G. M. (2010). Convective Heat-Transfer in swirling Impinging jets. Book of Papers of the 5th International Conference on Vortex Flow and Vortex Methods. ISBN: 978-88-905218-6-7. 8-10 November, Caserta (Italy).

Lee, D. H.; Won, S. Y.; Kim, Y. T. & Chung, Y.S. (2002). Turbulent heat transfer from a flat surface to a swirling round impinging jet. *International Journal of Heat and Mass Transfer*, 45, 223-227.

Lucca-Negro, O. & O'Doherty, T. (2001). Vortex breakdown: a review. Progress in Energy and Combustion Science, 27, 431-481.

O'Donovan, T. S. & Murray, D. B. (2007). Jet impingement heat transfer - Part I: Mean and root-mean-square heat transfer and velocity distributions. *International Journal of Heat and Mass Transfer*, 50, 3291-3301.

Olsson, E. E. M.; Ahrné, L. M. & Trägardh, A. C. (2004). Heat transfer from a slot air jet impinging on a circular cylinder. *Journal of Food Engineering*, 63, 393-401.

Ortega-Casanova, J.; Martín-Rivas, S. & del Pino, C. (2008). Estudio numérico del impacto de un chorro con giro, turbulento y axilsimétrico contra una superficie sólida (in Spanish). In *Nolineal 2008, edited by F. Marqués and A. Delshams*. pp. 101. ISBN: 978-84-96739-48-1. CIMNE. Barcelona.

Ortega-Casanova, J.; Campos, N. & Fernandez-Feria, R. (2011). Experimental study on sand bed excavation by impinging swirling jet. Submitted to the *Journal of Hydraulic Research* (accepted for publication).

Redding, J. H. (2002). The SILT X-Cavator: technical aspects and modes of operation. In: Dredging' 02: Key Technology for Global Prosperity. Orlando.

Sagot, B.; Antonini, G.; Christgen, A. & Buron, F. (2008). Jet impingement heat transfer on a flat plate at a constant wall temperature. *International Journal of Thermal Sciences*, 47, 1610-1619.

Wen, M. Y. & Jang, K. J. (2003). An impingement cooling on a flat surface by using circular jet with longitudinal swirling strips. *International Journal of Heat and Mass Transfer*, 46, 4657-4667.

9

Recent Advances in Modeling Axisymmetric Swirl and Applications for Enhanced Heat Transfer and Flow Mixing

Sal B. Rodriguez[1] and Mohamed S. El-Genk[2]
[1]*Sandia National Laboratories,*
[2]*University of New Mexico*
USA

1. Introduction

The concept of enhanced heat transfer and flow mixing using swirling jets has been investigated for nearly seven decades (Burgers, 1948; Watson and Clarke, 1947). Many practical applications of swirling jets include combustion, pharmaceuticals, tempering of metals, electrochemical mass transfer, metallurgy, propulsion, cooling of high-power electronics and computer chips, atomization, and the food industry, such as improved pizza ovens. Recently, swirling jet models have been applied to investigate heat transfer and flow mixing in nuclear reactors, including the usage of swirling jets in the lower plenum (LP) of generation-IV very high temperature gas-cooled reactors (VHTRs) to enhance mixing of the helium coolant and eliminate the formation of hot spots in the lower support plate, a safety concern (Johnson, 2008; Kim, Lim, and Lee, 2007; Laurien, Lavante, and Wang, 2010; Lavante and Laurien, 2007; Nematollahi and Nazifi, 2007; Rodriguez and El-Genk, 2008a, b, c, and d; Rodriguez, Domino, and El-Genk, 2010; Rodriguez and El-Genk, 2010a and b; Rodriguez and El-Genk, 2011).

There are many devices and processes for generating vortex fields to enhance flow mixing and convective heat transfer. Figure 1 shows a static helicoid device that can be used to generate vortex fields based on the swirling angle, θ. Recent advances in swirling jet technology exploit common characteristics found in axisymmetric vortex flows, and these traits can be employed to design the vortex flow field according to the desired applications; among these are the degree of swirl (based on the swirl number, S) and the spatial distributions of the radial, azimuthal, and axial velocities.

For a 3D helicoid, the vortex velocity in Cartesian coordinates can be approximated as:

$$\vec{V}_o(x,y,z) = u_o \sin(2\pi y)\vec{i} - u_o \sin(2\pi x)\vec{j} + w_o\vec{k} \quad (1)$$

For a jet with small radius r, the above velocity distribution can be represented in cylindrical coordinates as

$$v_\theta(r) = u_o \sin(\pi r) \quad (2)$$

and

$$w_z(r) = w_o \,. \tag{3}$$

Whereas there are about a dozen or so definitions of the swirling number S, we define it as a pure geometric entity, consistent with various investigators in the literature (Arzutug and Yapici, 2009; Bilen *et al*. 2002; Kerr and Fraser, 1965; Mathur and MacCallum, 1967):

$$S = \frac{2}{3}\tan(\theta) \tag{4}$$

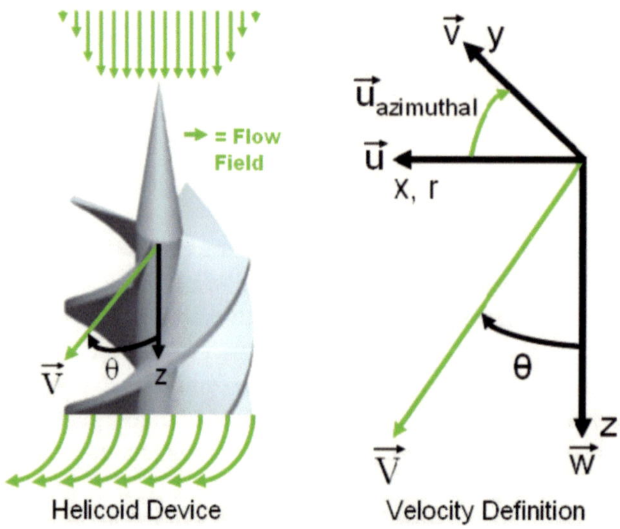

Fig. 1. Helicoid swirl device and associated velocity distribution

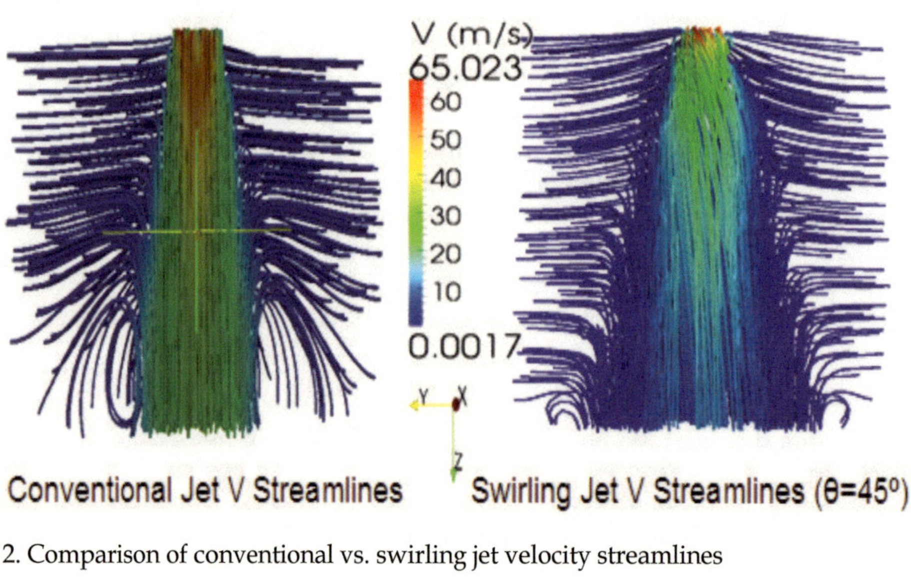

Fig. 2. Comparison of conventional vs. swirling jet velocity streamlines

Increasing S has been shown to increase the entrainment of the surrounding fluid (K_e) linearly (Kerr and Fraser, 1965) as:

$$K_e = 0.35 + 1.4S\,. \tag{5}$$

As a result of the increased entrainment, mixing, and turbulence, a swirling jet has a wider core diameter than a conventional impinging jet, as shown in Figure 2. Further, the azimuthal velocity of the helicoid vortex increases as S increases,

$$\frac{v_{\theta,0}}{V_0} = \frac{1}{\left(1+\dfrac{4}{9S^2}\right)^{\frac{1}{2}}} \tag{6}$$

while the axial velocity decreases (Rodriguez and El-Genk, 2010b),

$$\frac{w_{z,0}}{V_0} = \frac{2}{3S}\frac{1}{\left(1+\dfrac{4}{9S^2}\right)^{\frac{1}{2}}}. \tag{7}$$

V_0 is the velocity at the jet exit when no swirling occurs (conventional jet).

2. Vortex modeling

For this discussion, the broad field of turbulent vortex flows is narrowed down to swirling Newtonian fluid jets that are axisymmetric and incompressible. These vortices have been studied in many coordinates. A rather "unnatural" selection is Cartesian coordinates, as the flow field rotates about the axisymmetric axis, which is generally selected as the z coordinate. Therefore, the axisymmetric vortex flow is symmetric about the z axis as the flow rotates in the azimuthal direction, and continues to expand in the z direction.

As noted in Figure 2, both impinging and swirling jets have the same source diameter and expand into an open domain. While the conventional jet experiences no azimuthal rotation, the swirling jet with $\theta = 45^{o}$ has a strong rotational flow component. Note that the swirling jet has a wider jet core diameter, a higher degree of entrainment of surrounding fluid, and its azimuthal rotation causes more fluid mixing than the conventional impinging jet. Because part of the axial momentum in the swirling jet is converted to azimuthal momentum, the axial velocity component decays much faster than for the conventional jet.

Vortex research in Cartesian coordinates includes the Green-Taylor vortex (Taylor and Green, 1937) and the helicoid vortex discussed herein (Rodriguez and El-Genk, 2008a, 2010b and d). Various researchers selected spherical coordinates (Gol'Dshtik and Yavorskii, 1986; Hwang and Chwang, 1992; Tsukker, 1955), but the vast majority of the research found in the literature is in cylindrical coordinates (Aboelkassem, Vatistas, and Esmail, 2005; Batchelor, 1964; Burgers, 1948; Chepura, 1969; Gortler, 1954; Lamb, 1932; Loitsyanskiy, 1953; Martynenko, 1989; Newman, 1959; Rankine, 1858; Rodriguez and El-Genk, 2008a, 2010b and d; Sullivan, 1959; Squire, 1965). Cylindrical coordinates are chosen primarily due to its geometric simplicity and excellent mapping of the vortex behavior onto a coordinate system—in particular, as a 3D vortex spins azimuthally, stretching about the z axis, the vortex velocity field engulfs a cylindrical geometry. Certainly, conical coordinates could be used, but they are not as convenient to manipulate mathematically. Indeed, as the vortex expands, forming a 3D cone, care needs to be taken such that the swirl field is not so large that it generates a field with an angle that is larger than the conical coordinate system.

Consider a cylindrical coordinate system with r, θ, and z as the radial, azimuthal, and axial components, as defined in Figure 1. For 3D, steady state, negligible gravitational effect, incompressible, Newtonian fluids with symmetry about the z axis (axisymmetry), the momentum and conservation of mass equations are given as:

$$u\frac{\partial u_r}{\partial r}-\frac{v^2}{r}+w\frac{\partial u}{\partial z}=-\frac{1}{\rho}\frac{\partial p}{\partial r}+\nu\left(\frac{\partial^2 u}{\partial r^2}+\frac{1}{r}\frac{\partial u}{\partial r}-\frac{u}{r^2}+\frac{\partial^2 u}{\partial z^2}\right) \tag{8}$$

$$u\frac{\partial v}{\partial r}+\frac{vu}{r}+w\frac{\partial v}{\partial z}=\nu\left(\frac{\partial^2 v}{\partial r^2}+\frac{1}{r}\frac{\partial v}{\partial r}-\frac{v}{r^2}+\frac{\partial^2 v}{\partial z^2}\right) \tag{9}$$

$$u\frac{\partial w}{\partial r}+w\frac{\partial w}{\partial z}=-\frac{1}{\rho}\frac{\partial p}{\partial z}+\nu\left(\frac{\partial^2 w}{\partial r^2}+\frac{1}{r}\frac{\partial w}{\partial r}+\frac{\partial^2 w}{\partial z^2}\right) \tag{10}$$

$$\frac{\partial u}{\partial r}+\frac{u}{r}+\frac{\partial w}{\partial z}=0 \tag{11}$$

An inspection of the literature over the past 150 years shows that the above equations are generally the departure point for generating analytic solutions for axisymmetric swirling flows (vortices) (Aboelkassem, Vatistas, and Esmail, 2005; Batchelor, 1964; Burgers, 1948; Chepura, 1969; Gortler, 1954; Lamb, 1932; Loitsyanskiy, 1953; Martynenko, 1989; Newman, 1959; Rankine, 1858; Rodriguez and El-Genk, 2010b; Sullivan, 1959; Squire, 1965).

3. Helicoid swirl modeling

Helicoids for the generation of swirling-flow fields may be produced by various methods. One method is via a geometrical specification of a static, swirl device that consists of helicoidal surfaces, and another is a mathematical description of a swirl boundary condition (BC) that reproduces the flow field. It has been reported in the literature and confirmed herein that if a computational fluid mechanics (CFD) code does not have a swirl boundary option, it would be customary to develop the geometry for a swirl device and then mesh it (Duwig *et al.* 2005; Fujimoto, Inokuchi, and Yamasaki, 2005; Garcia-Villalba, Frohlich, and Rodi, 2005; Rodriguez and El-Genk, 2008a, b, c, and d; Rodriguez, Domino, and El-Genk, 2010; Rodriguez and El-Genk, 2010a and b; Rodriguez and El-Genk, 2011). Several static swirl devices are shown in Figure 3 (Huang, 1996; Huang and El-Genk, 1998; Larocque, 2004; Rodriguez and El-Genk, 2010a and b; Rodriguez and El-Genk, 2011). The swirl device considered in this chapter consists of a sharp cone that surrounds four helical surfaces off-set by 90° and spiral symmetrically around the cylinder (Figure 4, LHS). Because the swirling device is static, the fluid flows around the helicoid surfaces, producing a swirling motion as it travels around the surfaces.

Deciding on a particular swirl angle *a priori* for the swirling device, and then meshing its geometry, is computationally-intensive and time consuming, not to mention that it is a tedious, error-prone, and expensive process. Instead, as will be shown *a posteriori*, having a closed form, mathematical formulation for the swirling field not only simplifies the computation requirements but also yields significant insights concerning the behavior of the velocity fields and their impact on heat transfer.

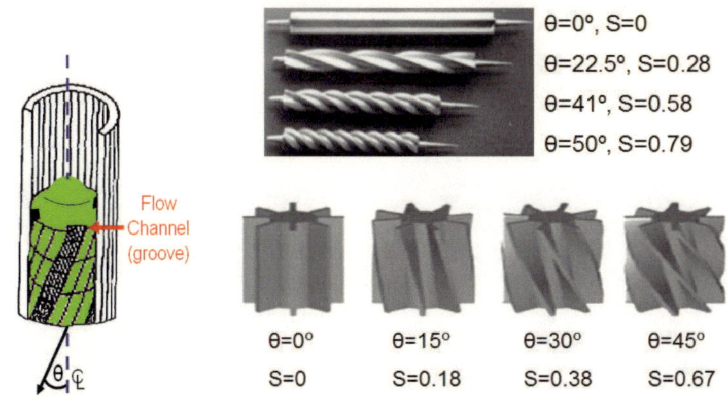

Fig. 3. Various Swirl Devices Found in the Literature (Huang, 1996; Huang and El-Genk, 1998; Larocque, 2004; Rodriguez and El-Genk, 2010a and b; Rodriguez and El-Genk, 2011)

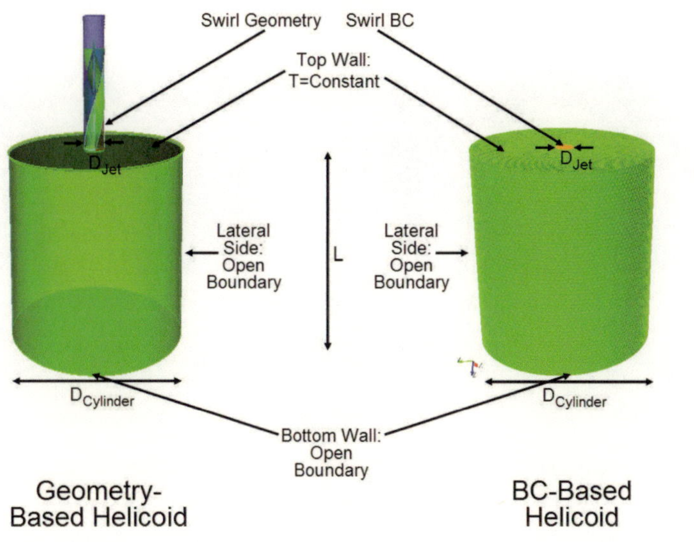

Fig. 4. Comparison of Geometric and BC Swirl Models

Now, once a mathematical swirl formulation is derived, it is a straightforward matter to apportion the jet velocity fields such that a given swirl angle is uniquely specified (Equations 4, 6, and 7). As a result, a mathematically-generated velocity field with no helicoid surfaces (i.e. just swirl BCs) can very closely approximate the swirl fields of the geometric helicoid devices shown in Figure 1. To demonstrate this, two meshes are shown: one with a geometric swirl device and the other with swirl BCs (see Figure 4). The CFD computation for both meshes has the same S.

A comparison of both models shows that the total velocity vector streamlines are essentially indistinguishable, as shown in Figure 5. The azimuthal velocity compared in Figure 6, again shows that the velocity streamlines are fairly identical. This methodology results in significant savings in the meshing and computational effort, especially because the helicoid geometry requires finite elements that are about four times smaller than the rest of the model, and further, the time step is dominated by the smallest finite element.

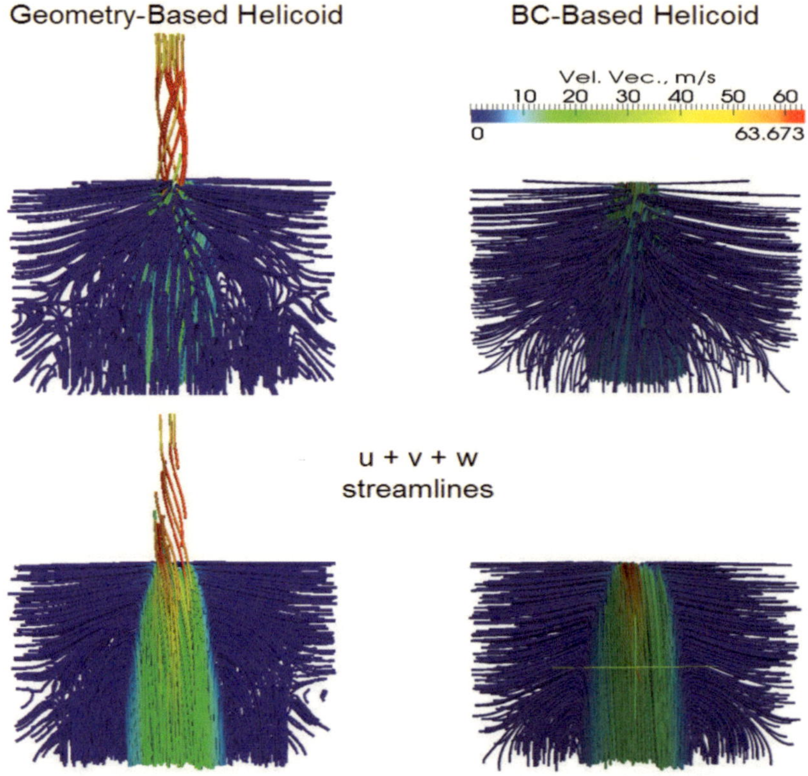

Fig. 5. Comparison of the Geometric and BC Swirl Models: U + V + W Streamlines

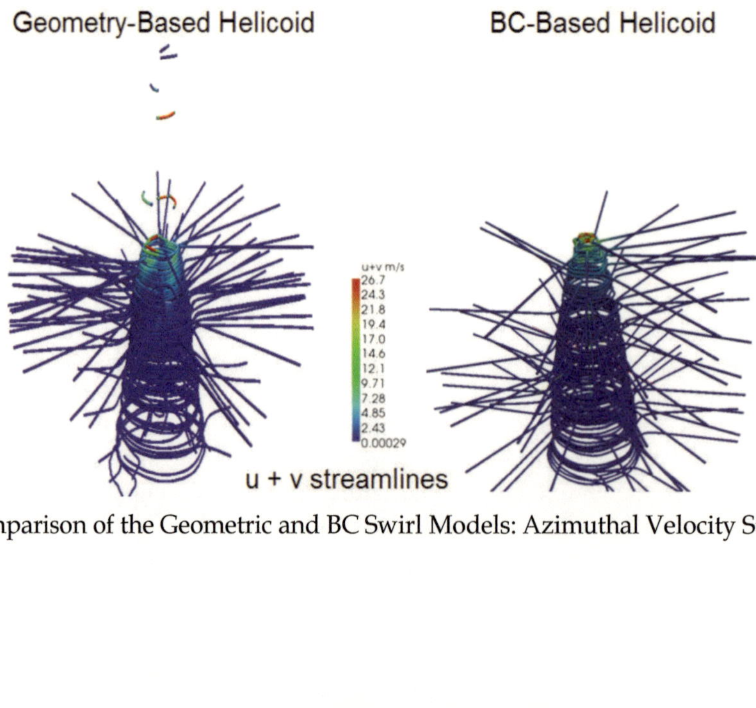

Fig. 6. Comparison of the Geometric and BC Swirl Models: Azimuthal Velocity Streamlines

4. Swirling jet strongest domain

The results of CFD calculations with swirl BCs agree with both theory and experimental data for weak to intermediate S, showing that the peak azimuthal velocity v_θ decays as $1/z^2$, while the peak axial velocity w decays as 1/z (Blevins, 1992; Billant *et al.* 1998; Chigier and Chervinsky, 1967; Gortler, 1954; Loitsyanskiy, 1953; Mathur and MacCallum, 1967). This issue, defined as "swirl decay", was first reported by Loitsyanskiy. In particular, as z becomes large, the peak azimuthal velocity decays much faster. That is,

$$w = \frac{C_1}{z} \tag{12}$$

and

$$v_\theta = \frac{C_2}{z^2}\,. \tag{13}$$

Based on a curve-fit of the reported data in the literature (Blevins, 1992), it is possible to obtain $C_1 = -2.6S^3+12S^2+19S+12$, while the reported value in the literature for $C_2 \sim 4$ to 11, and may be a function of S (Blevins, 1992).
Because the azimuthal velocity for a swirling jet decays faster than the axial velocity, there is a point, z*, where for $z \le z^*$, $w \le v_\theta$. Setting z = z* and solving for $v_\theta(z^*)=w(z^*)$, yields:

$$z^* = \frac{C_2}{C_1} = \frac{C_2}{-2.6S^3+12S^2+19S+12} \tag{14}$$

Clearly, the magnitude of z* that maximizes the azimuthal momentum vs. the axial momentum depends strongly on the value of S. For example, for S = 0.2 and 0.6, z* = 1.3 and 2.6, respectively. Therefore, if the purpose is to optimize the flow mixing and convective heat transfer caused by swirl, a guideline is to have $w \le v_\theta$, such that Equation 14 is satisfied.

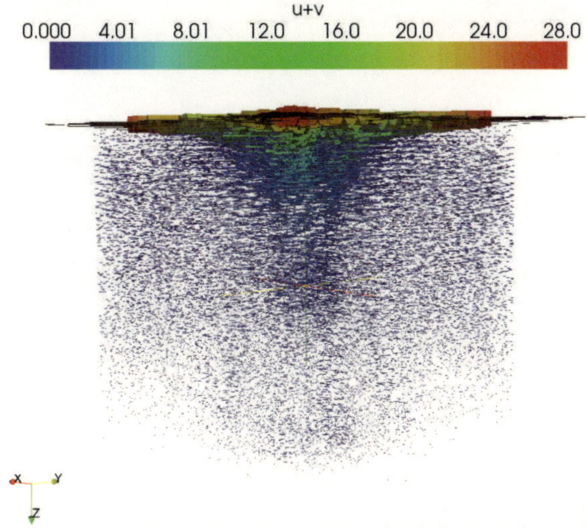

Fig. 7. Fast Decay of the Azimuthal Velocity

A consequence of the azimuthal rotation is that swirling jets experience swirl decay (see Figure 7). Therefore, there is a point beyond which the azimuthal velocity will decay to a degree whereby it no longer significantly impacts the flow field. This factor is crucial in the design of swirling jets, and in any applications that employ swirling jets for enhancing heat and mass transfer, combustion, and flow mixing.

5. Impact of S on the Central Recirculation Zone

As the azimuthal velocity increases and exceeds the axial velocity, a low pressure region prevails near the jet exit where the azimuthal velocity is the highest. The low pressure causes a reversal in the axial velocity, thus producing a region of backflow. Because the azimuthal velocity forms circular planes, and the reverse axial velocity superimposes onto it, the net result is a pear-shaped central recirculation zone (CRZ). From a different point of view, for an incompressible swirling jet, as S increases, the azimuthal momentum increases at the expense of the axial momentum (see Equations 6 and 7). This is consistent with the data in the literature (Chigier and Chervinsky, 1967).
The CRZ formation results in a region where vortices oscillate, similar to vortex shedding for flow around a cylinder. The enhanced mixing associated with the CRZ is attributable to the back flow in the axial direction; in particular, the back flow acts as a pump that brings back fluid for further mixing. The CRZ vortices tend to recirculate and entrain fluid into the central region of the swirling jet, thus enhancing mixing and heat transfer within the CRZ.

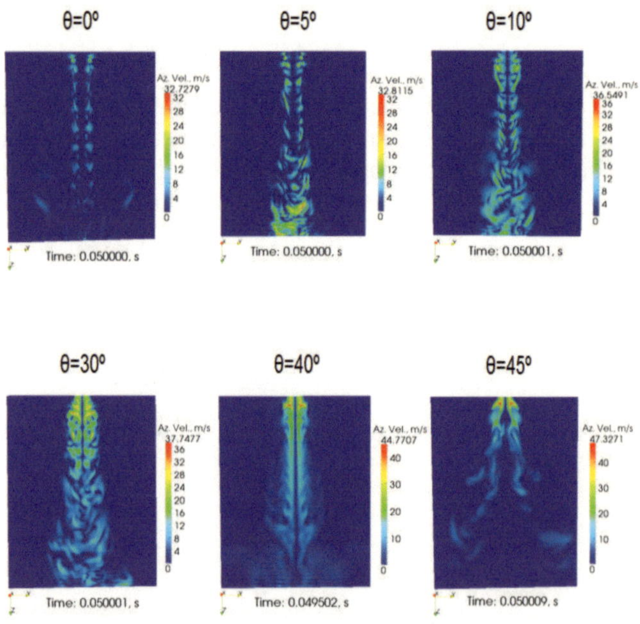

Fig. 8. Effect of Swirl Angle on the Azimuthal Velocity

The Fuego CFD code was used to compute the flow fields shown in Figures 8 through 10 (Fuego, 2009). Figure 8 shows the effect of the swirl angle on the azimuthal flow for an unconfined swirling jet. Figure 9 shows the velocity vector, azimuthal velocity, and the axial velocity for a weak swirl, while Figure 10 shows the same, but for moderate to strong swirl.

Note the dramatic changes that occur in the axial and azimuthal velocity distributions as the CRZ forms – the most significant change occurs in the z-direction, which is the axis normal to the jet flow. For example, for θ = 40° (no CRZ), the maximum azimuthal velocity at the bottom of the domain along the z axis is 15 m/s. But, when the CRZ forms at θ = 45°, the maximum azimuthal velocity is essentially 0. The same effect can be observed for the axial velocity for pre- and post-CRZ velocity distributions. Note that the region near the bottom of the z-axis for θ = 45° forms a stagnant cone that is surrounded by azimuthal flow moving around the cone at ~15 m/s, and likewise for the axial velocity.

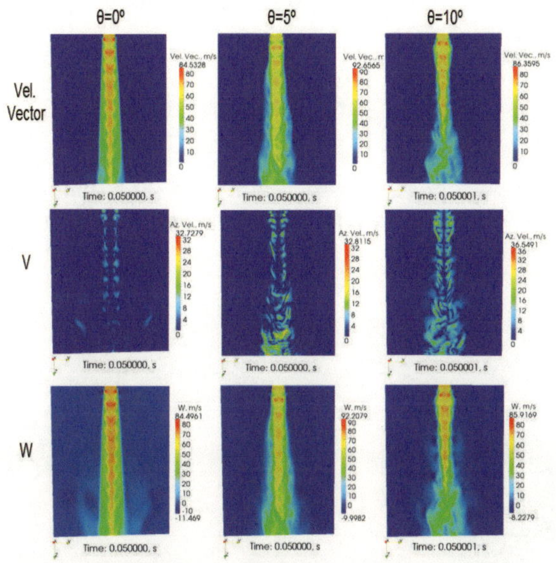

Fig. 9. Various Velocities for a Small Swirl Angle

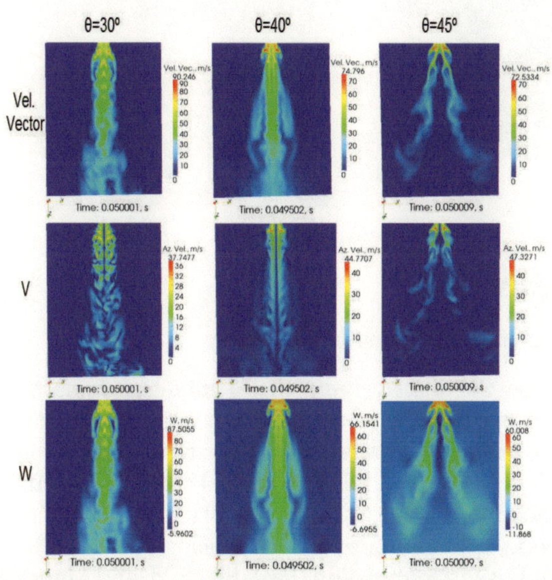

Fig. 10. Various Velocities for Moderate to Strong Swirl Angle

From Figure 10, it is quite evident that the CRZ acts as a "solid" body around which the strong swirling jet flows. This is important, as the CRZ basically has two key impacts on the flow domain: 1) it diminishes the momentum along the flow axis and 2) both the axial and azimuthal velocities drop much faster than $1/z$ and $1/z^2$, respectively. *Therefore, whether a CRZ is useful in the design problem or not depends on what issue is being addressed. In particular, if it is desirable that a hot fluid be dispersed as rapidly as possible, then the CRZ is useful because it more rapidly decreases the axial and azimuthal velocities of a swirling jet. However, if having a large conical region with nearly zero axial and azimuthal velocity is undesirable, then it is recommended that $S < 0.67$.* In the case of the VHTR, the support plate temperatures decrease as S increases; an $S = 2.49$ results in the lowest temperatures.

6. Impact of Re and S on mixing and heat transfer

In this section, two models are discussed in order to address this issue: (1) a cylindrical domain with a centrally-positioned swirling air jet and (2) a quadrilateral domain with six swirling jets. The single-jet model and its results are presented first, followed by the six-jet model discussion and results.

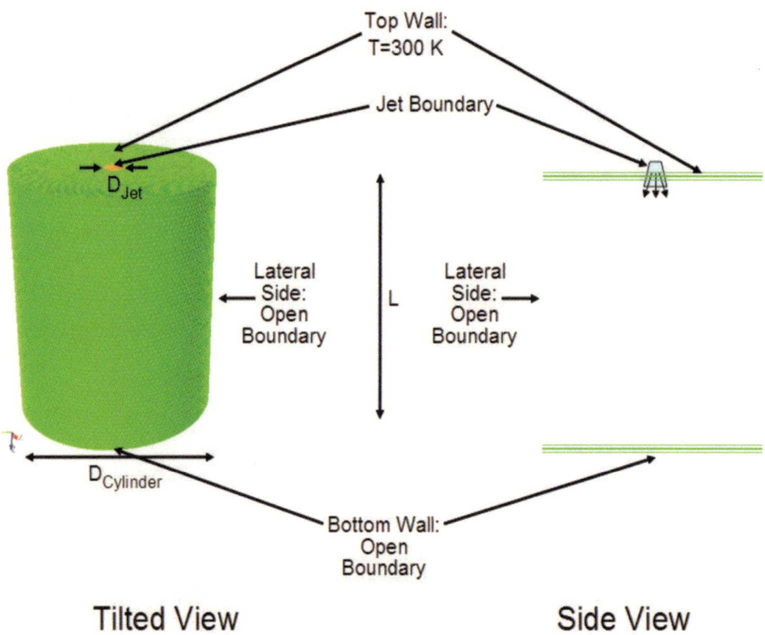

Fig. 11. Cylinder with a Single Swirling-Jet Boundary

Both models are run on the massively-parallel Thunderbird machine at Sandia National Laboratories (SNL). The initial time step used is 0.1 μs, and the maximum Courant-Friedrichs-Lewy (CFL) condition of 1.0, which resulted in a time step on the order of 1 μs. The simulations are typically run for about 0.05 to several seconds of transient time. Both models are meshed using hexahedral elements with the CUBIT code (CUBIT, 2009). The temperature-dependent thermal properties for air are calculated using a CANTERA XML input file that is based on the Chapman-Enskog formulation (Bird, Steward, and Lightfoot, 2007). Finally, both models used the dynamic Smagorinsky turbulence scheme (Fuego, 2009; Smagorinsky, 1963).

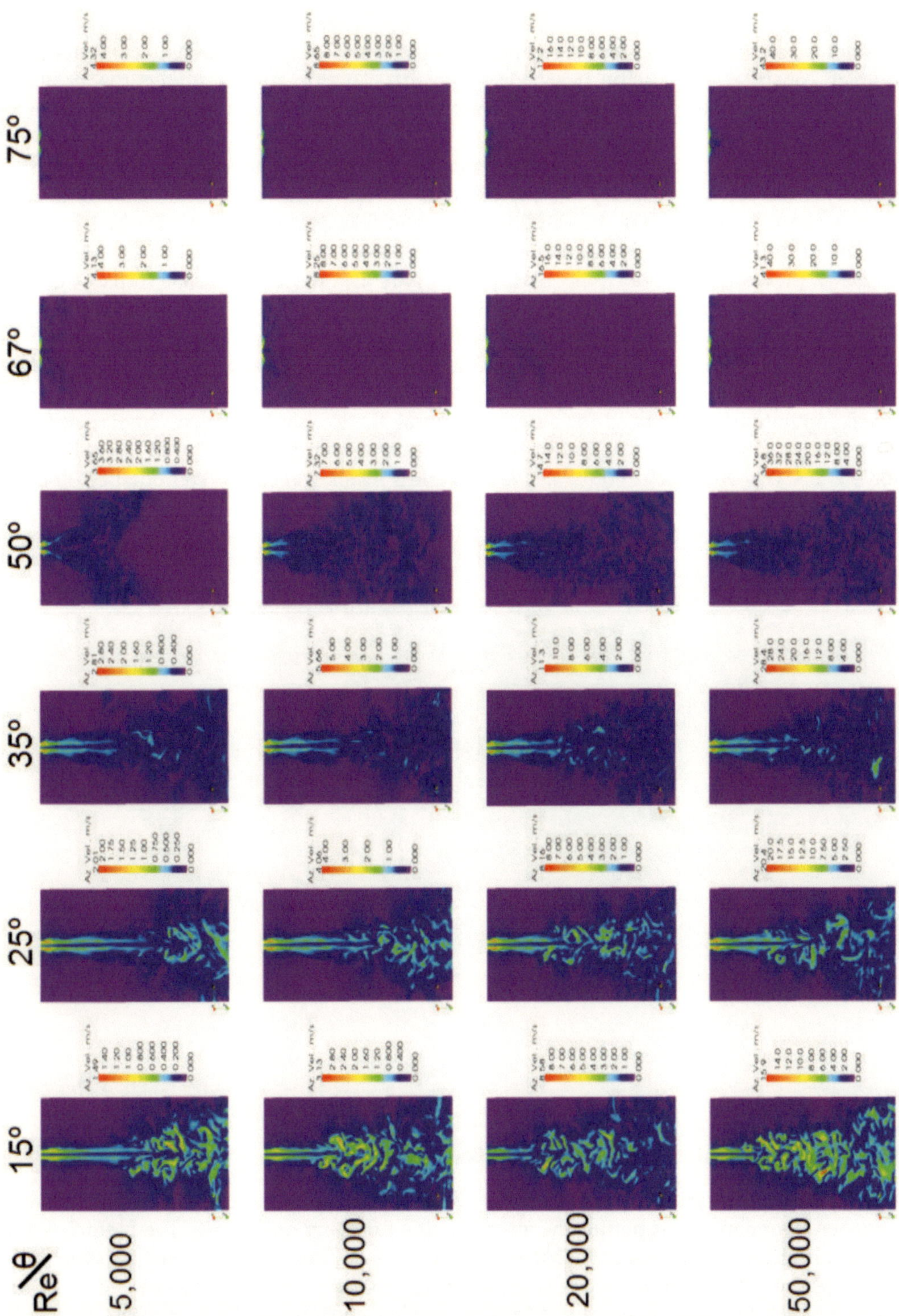

Fig. 12. Impact of Re and θ on Azimuthal Velocity Field

The single-jet computation domain consisted of a right cylinder that enclosed a centrally-positioned single, unbounded, swirling air jet (Figure 11). The meshed computational domain consisted of 1 million hexahedral elements. The top surface (minus the jet BC) is modeled as a wall, while the lateral and bottom surfaces of the cylindrical domain are open boundaries.

Figure 12 shows the effect of the swirl angle and Reynolds number (Re) on the azimuthal velocity field for θ = 15, 25, 35, 50, 67, and 75° (S =0.18, 0.31, 0.79, 1.57, and 2.49, respectively). Re was 5,000, 10,000, 20,000, and 50,000. For fixed S, as Re increases the azimuthal velocity turbulence increases, and the jet core becomes wider. For a fixed Re, as S increases the azimuthal velocity increases. The figure also shows the strong impact the CRZ formation has on how far the swirling jet travels before it disperses. *Thus, as soon as the CRZ appears, the azimuthal velocity field does not travel as far, even as Re is increased substantially. In other words, although Re increased 10-fold as shown in the figure, its impact was not as great on the flow field as that of S once the CRZ developed.*

The computational mesh used for the quadrilateral 3D domain for the six circular, swirling air jets is shown in Figure 13. The air temperature and approach velocity in the z direction for the jets was 300 K and 60 m/s. The numerical mesh grid in the computation domain consisted of 2.5×10^5 to 5×10^6 hexahedral elements.

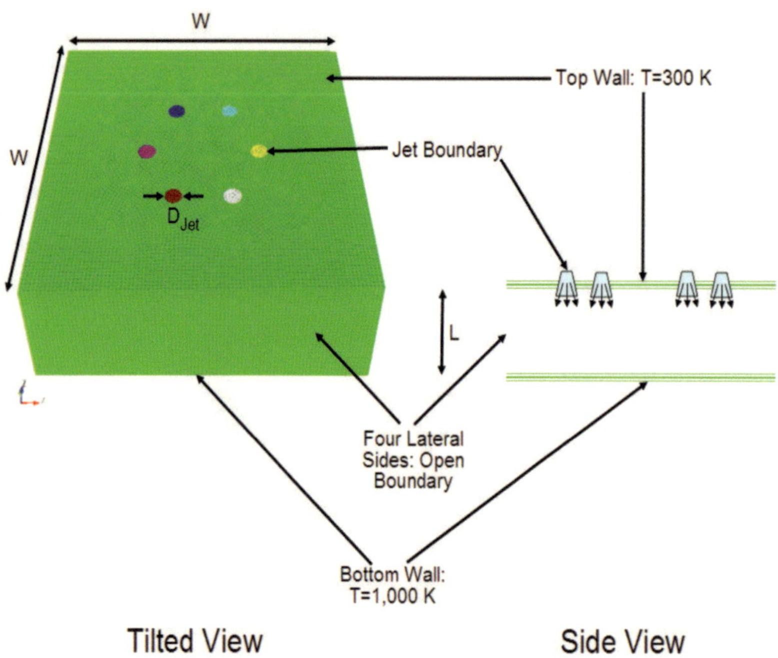

Fig. 13. Quadrilateral with Six Swirling-Jet Boundaries

The top surface of the domain (minus the jet BCs) is adiabatic. The lateral quadrilateral sides are open boundaries that permit the air to continue flowing outwardly. The bottom of the domain is an isothermal wall at 1,000 K. The swirling air flowing out the six jets eventually impinges the bottom surface, thereby transferring heat from the plate. The heated air at the surface of the hot plate is entrained by the swirling and mixing air above the plate. The calculations are conducted for θ = 0 (conventional jet), 5, 10, 15, 20, 25, 50, and 75° (S = 0,

0.058, 0.12, 0.18, 0.24, 0.31, 0.79, and 2.49, respectively). With the exception of varying the swirl angle, the calculations used the same mesh (L/D=3), Fuego CFD version (Fuego, 2009), and input. A similar set of calculations used L/D=12.

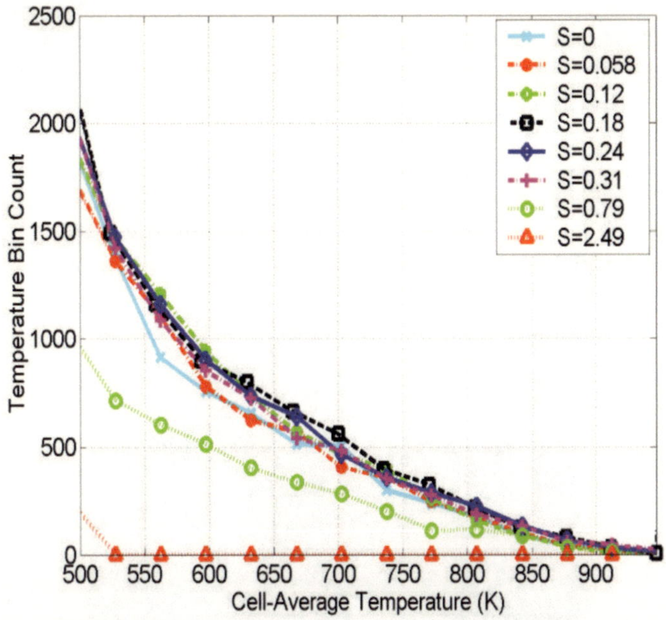

Fig. 14. Temperature Bin Count for All Elements with L/D = 12 Mesh

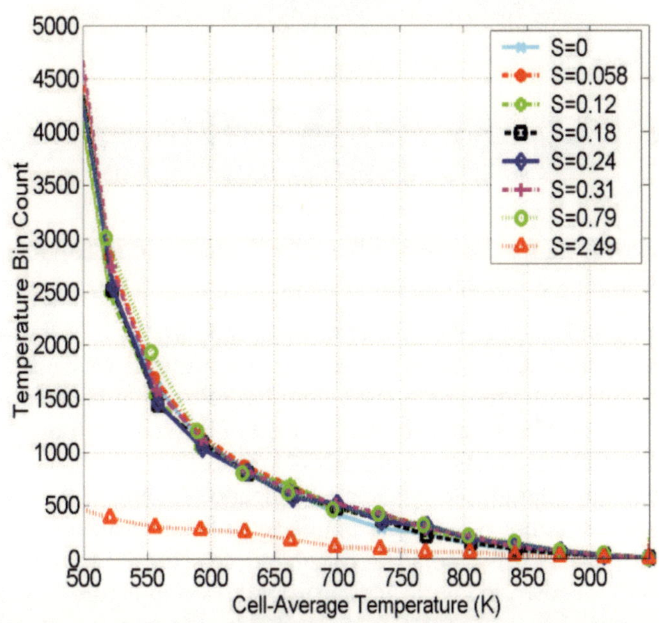

Fig. 15. Temperature Bin Count for All Elements with L/D = 3 Mesh

As a way to quantify S vs. cooling potential, all the hexahedral elements cell-averaged temperatures are grouped according to a linear temperature distribution ("bins"). The calculated temperature bins presented in Figures 14 and 15 show that at a given L/D and for S in a certain range, there are a higher number of hotter finite elements in the flow field. This is indicative of the swirling jet enhanced heat transfer ability over a conventional impinging jet to remove heat from the isothermal plate. For example, Figure 14 shows that for L/D = 12, and S ranging from 0.12 to 0.31, the swirling jets removed more heat from the plate, and thus are hotter than the impinging jet with S = 0. Additionally, the best cooling is achievable when S = 0.18. However, Figure 15 shows that for L/D = 3, and S ranging from 0.12 to 0.79, the swirling jets removed more heat from the plate, and are thus hotter than the impinging jet with S = 0. The best swirling jet cooling under these conditions is when S = 0.79. The results confirmed that for $S \leq 0.058$, the flow field closely approximates the flow field for an impinging jet, S = 0, with insignificant enhancement to the heat transfer.

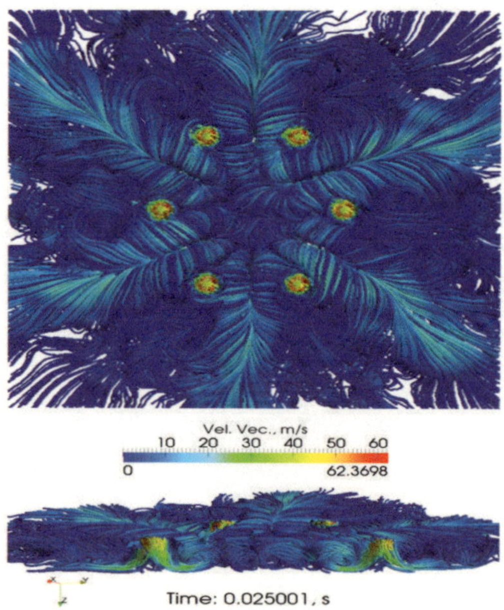

Fig. 16. Velocity Flow Field for the Mesh with L/D = 3 and S = 0.79. Top Image: Domain View of Top; Bottom Image: Domain Cross-Section

The back flow zone manifested as the CRZ appears to enhance the heat transfer compared to the swirling flow with no CRZ, as evidenced by the multiple-jet calculations shown in Figures 14 and 15. As noted previously, the azimuthal velocity of the swirling jet decays as $1/z^2$. Therefore, the largest heat transfer enhancement of the swirling occurs within a few jet diameters as evidenced by the results in Figures 14 and 15.

It is not surprising that the multiple swirling jets enhance cooling of the bottom isothermal plate only when the azimuthal velocity has not decayed before reaching the intended target (i.e. the isothermal plate in this case). The calculated velocity field for the swirling jet for L/D = 3 and S = 0.79 is shown in Figure 16. The upper insert in Figure 16 shows the velocity distribution at the top of the computation domain near the nozzle exit, while the bottom insert shows a cross-section view of the domain. The circulation roles appear as a result of the interaction of the flow field by the multiple jets, rather than the value of S (the roles for S = 0.0 are very similar to those for S = 0.79). Note that the flow field shows that the jets impinge on the isothermal plate at velocities ranging from 25 to 35 m/s, which is a significant fraction of the initial velocity of 60 m/s. Thus, the azimuthal momentum is significant, inducing significant swirl that results in more mixing and therefore more cooling of the plate.

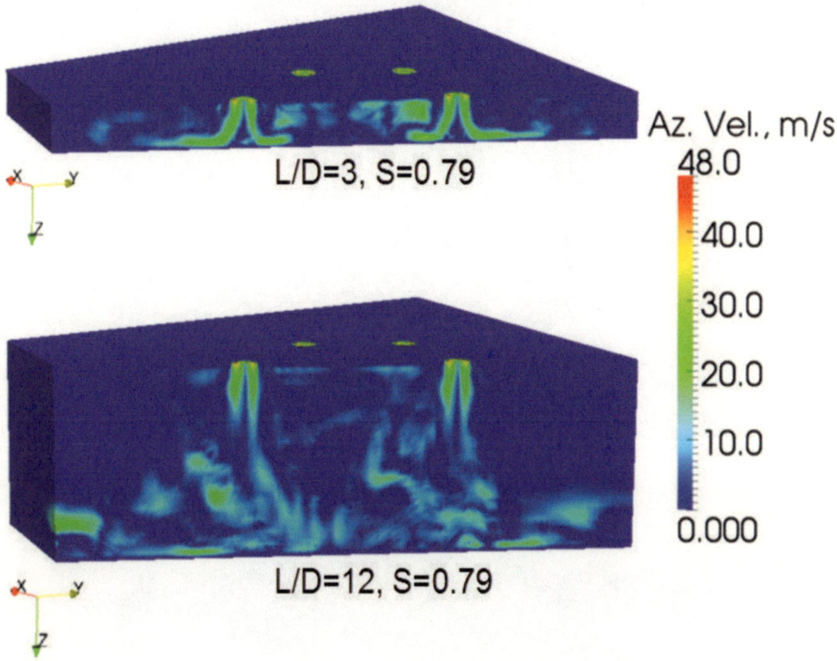

Fig. 17. Azimuthal Flow Field for S = 0.79. Top Image: L/D = 3; Bottom Image: L/D = 12

The high degree of enhanced cooling and induced mixing by swirling jets can be better understood by comparing the azimuthal flow fields shown in Figure 17 for S = 0.79 (the top has L/D = 3 and the bottom has L/D = 12). Note that for L/D = 3, the azimuthal velocity is approximately 25 to 35 m/s by the time it reaches the isothermal plate, but for the case with L/D = 12, the azimuthal velocity at the isothermal plate is 15 to 25 m/s. The calculated temperature field for S = 0.79 and L/D = 3 is shown in Figure 18. Thus, because the azimuthal velocity decays rapidly with distance from the nozzle exit, the value of L/D determines if there will be a significant azimuthal flow field by the time the jet reaches the isothermal bottom plate. Therefore, smaller L/D results in more heat transfer enhancement as S increases.

Results also show that the swirling jet flow field transitions to that of a conventional jet beyond a few jet diameters. For example, according to weak swirl theory, at L/D = 10, the swirling jet's azimuthal velocity decays to ~1% of its initial value, so the azimuthal momentum becomes negligible at this point; instead, the flow field exhibits radial and axial momentum, just like a conventional jet. Therefore, a free (unconstrained) swirling jet that becomes fully developed will eventually transition to a conventional jet, which is consistent with the recent similarity theory of Ewing (Semaan, Naughton, and Ewing, 2009). Clearly, then, the advantages offered by the swirl are only available within a few jet diameters from the nozzle exit, depending on the value of S and Re.

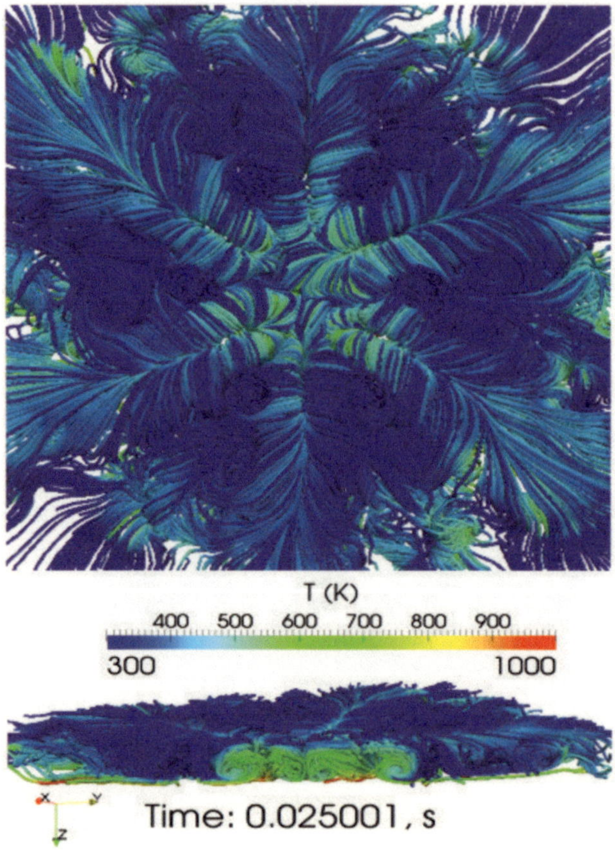

Fig. 18. Temperature Field for the Mesh with L/D = 3 and S = 0.79. Top Image: Domain View of Top; Bottom Image: Domain Cross-Section

7. Multiphysics, advanced swirling-jet LP modeling

For another application of swirling jets, calculations are performed for the LP of a prismatic core VHTR. The helium gas flowing in vertical channels cools the reactor core and exits as jets into the LP. The graphite blocks of the reactor core and those of the axial and radial reflectors are raised using large diameter graphite posts in the LP. These posts are structurally supported by a thick steel plate that is thermally insulated at the bottom. The issue is that the exiting conventional hot helium jets could induce hot spots in the lower support region, and together with the presence of the graphite posts, hinder the helium gas mixing in the LP chamber (Johnson and Schultz, 2009; McEligot and McCreery, 2004).
The performed calculation pertinent to these critical issues of operation safety of the VHTR included the following:

- Fuego-Calore coupled code,
- Helicoid vortex swirl model,

- Dynamic Smagorinsky large eddy simulation (LES) turbulence model,
- Participating media radiation (PMR),
- 1D conjugate heat transfer (CHT), and
- Insulation plate at the bottom of the LP.

The PMR model calculates the impact of radiation heat transfer for the high temperature helium gas behavior as a participating media. For the CHT, it is assumed that the LP wall conducts heat, which is subsequently removed by convection to the ambient fluid.

The full-scale, half-symmetry mesh used in the LP simulation had unstructured hexahedral elements and accounted for the graphite posts, the helium jets, the exterior walls, and the bottom plate with an insulating outer surface (Allen, 2004; Rodriguez and El-Genk, 2011). The impact of using various swirl angles on the flow mixing and heat transfer in the LP is investigated. For these calculations, the exit velocity for the conventional helium jets in the +z direction is V_0 = 67 m/s. The emerging gas flow from the coolant channels in the Cartesian x, y, and z directions has v_x, v_y, and v_z velocity components, respectively, whose magnitude depends on the swirl angle of the insert, θ, placed at the exit of the helium coolant channels into the LP. The initial time step used is 0.01 µs, and the simulation transient time is five to 25 s, with the CFL condition set to 1.0. In three helium jets (used as tracers), the temperature of the exiting helium gas is set to 1,473 K in order to investigate their tendency to form hot spots in the lower support plate and thermally-stratified regions in the LP; the exiting helium gas from the rest of the jets is at 1,273 K (Rodriguez and El-Genk, 2011). For these calculations S = 0.67.

Figure 19 shows key output from the coupled calculation, including the velocity streamlines (A), plate temperature distribution (B), fluid temperature as seen from the top (C), and fluid temperature shown from the bottom side (D). At steady state, Re in the LP ranges from 500 to 35,000. The lower RHS region in the LP experiences the lowest crossflow (Re ~ 500), as shown in Figure 19A. As a consequence of the low crossflow, the hot helium jet that exists strategically in that vicinity is able to reach the bottom plate with higher temperature (Figure 19B, RHS) than the other two tracer hot channels (LHS) that inject helium onto regions with much higher crossflow (Rodriguez and El-Genk, 2011). Consequently, Figure 19C shows that these two jets are unable to reach the lower plate. This is a basic effect of conventional jets in crossflow (Blevins, 1992; Chassaing *et al.*, 1974; Goldstein and Behbahani, 1982; Kamotani and Greber, 1974; Kavsaoglu and Schetz, 1989; Kawai and Lele, 2007; Kiel *et al.*, 2003; Patankar, Basu, and Alpay, 1977; Rivero, Ferre, and Giralt, 2001; Sucec and Bowley, 1976; Nirmolo, 1970; Pratte and Baines, 1967), and swirling jets in crossflow (Denev, Frohlich, and Bockhorn, 2009; Kamal, 2009; Kavsaoglu and Schetz, 1989): *the higher the ratio of crossflow velocity to the jet velocity, the faster the jet will bend in a parabolic profile.* Figure 19D shows the fluid temperature as seen from the bottom.

Figure 20 shows the velocity threshold for the three hot tracer helium flow channels. The results confirm that despite the fact that there are a total of 138 jets in the half-symmetry model of the VHTR LP, each jet follows a rather narrowly-defined path that widens two to seven times the initial jet diameter, and follows the classic parabolic trajectory of a jet in crossflow. Figure 21 shows the fluid temperature (based on thresholds) for the hot helium tracer channels. Due to the induced mixing, the helium gas temperature drops ~ 100 K within a few jet diameters from the channel exit. These figures allow the systematic tracing of velocity and temperature profiles of the three selected jets, without obstruction from other adjacent, cooler jets.

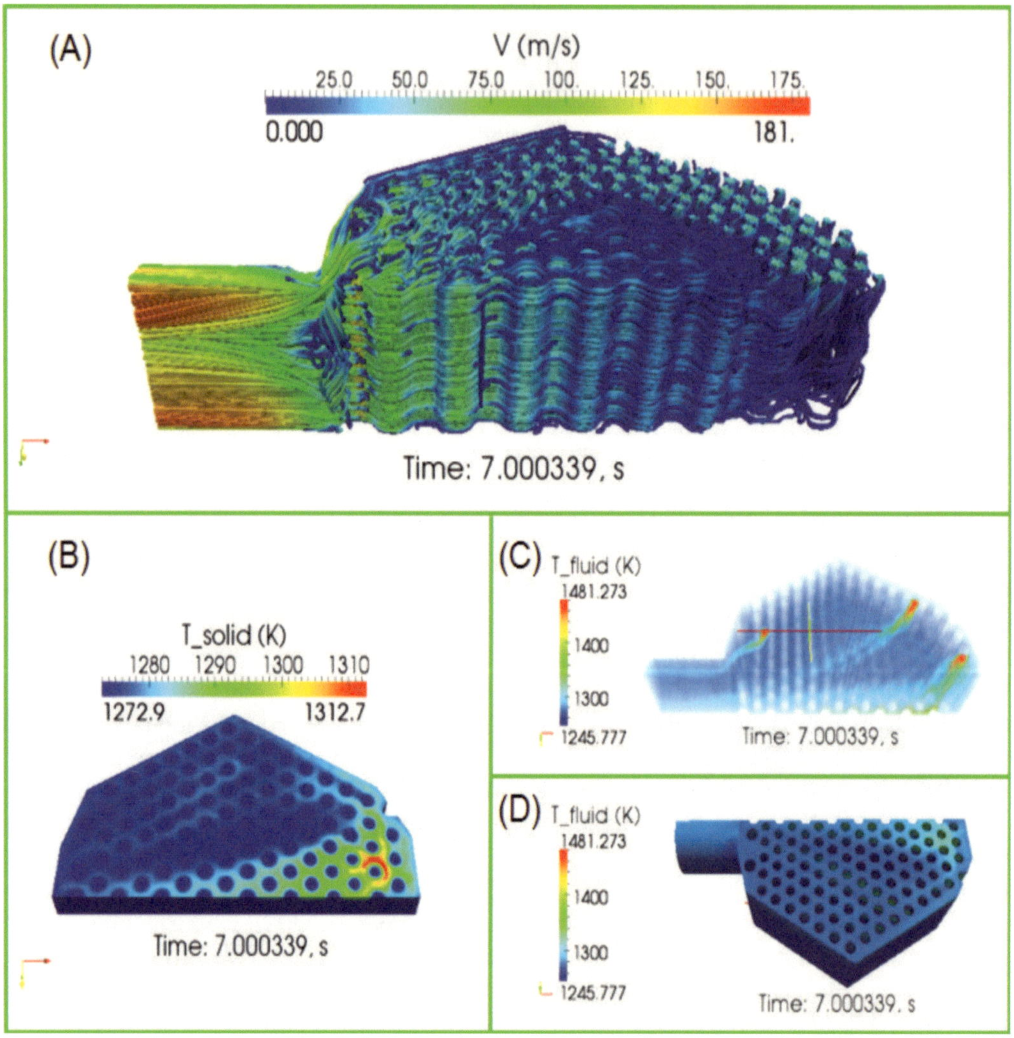

Fig. 19. Fuego-Calore Output Showing: (A) Velocity Streamlines. (B) Plate Temperature Distribution, (C) Volume Rendering of Fluid Temperature, and (D) Fluid Temperature at the Bottom Side

Calculations with S ranging from 0 to 2.49 were also conducted (Rodriguez and El-Genk, 2011). Note that for low S, there is less mixing in the region adjacent to the jet exit, but the jet is able to reach the bottom plate. Conversely, for higher S, there is more mixing near the jet exit, but significantly less of the jet's azimuthal momentum reaches the bottom plate. For a sufficiently large S and tall LP, the azimuthal momentum decays before reaching the bottom plate. The optimal height for swirling jets (with no crossflow) can be calculated via z, as discussed in Section 4.*

Figures 20 and 21 indicate that the jet penetration in the axial direction is a strong function of the crossflow. So, the lower the crossflow (RHS of said figures), the deeper the jets are able to penetrate, and vice-versa (LHS of said figures). Therefore, due to swirl decay and crossflow issues, S needs to be adjusted according to the local flow field conditions and desired LP height.

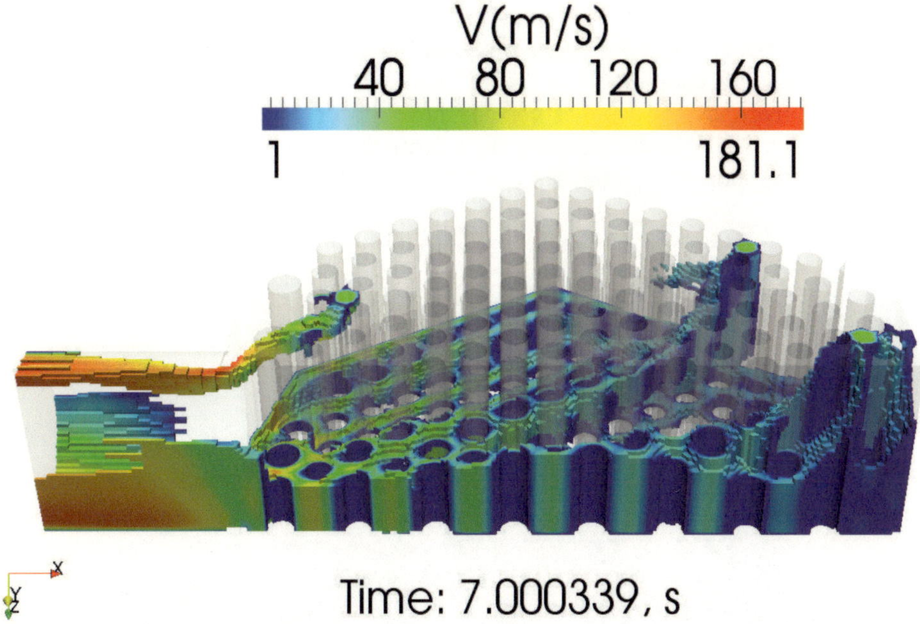

Fig. 20. Velocity Threshold for the Three Hot Channels

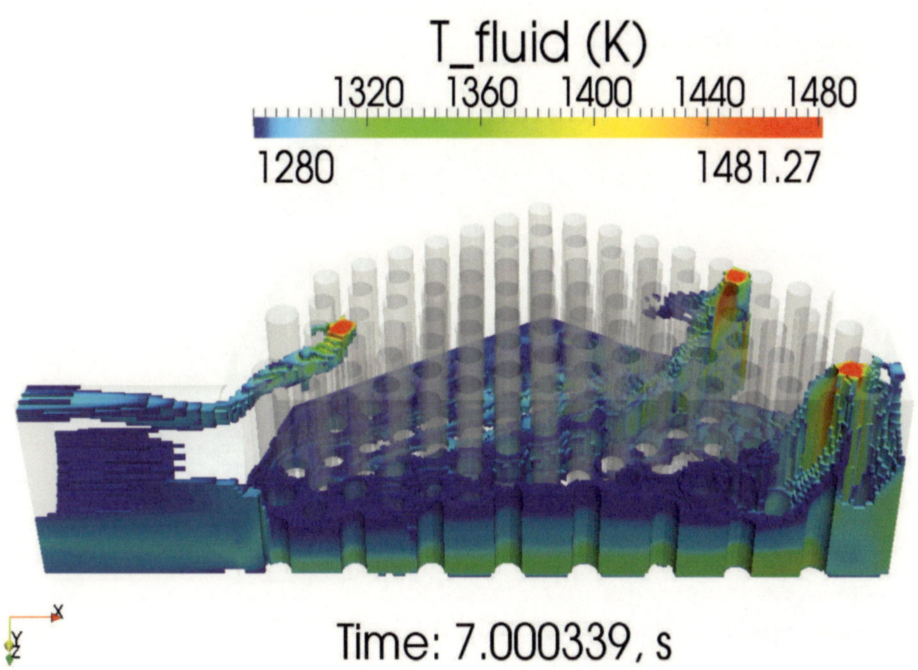

Fig. 21. Temperature Threshold for the Three Hot Channels

Figure 22 shows the bottom plate temperature. Note that the higher temperatures occur in areas of the LP where the helium gas jets are able to reach the bottom. Thus, the peak temperature corresponds to the jet that impinges onto the region with the lowest Re (opposite end of the LP outlet). Figure 23 shows the convective heat transfer coefficient, h. Its magnitude is small, comparable to that of forced airflow at 2 m/s over a plate (Holman, 1990). Because the relatively low jet velocity near the LP bottom plate (0 - 20 m/s), the values for h ~ 2 to 12 W/m^2K are reasonable. Note that h is zero (of course) in the region occupied by the support posts (shown as the large, dark blue circles).

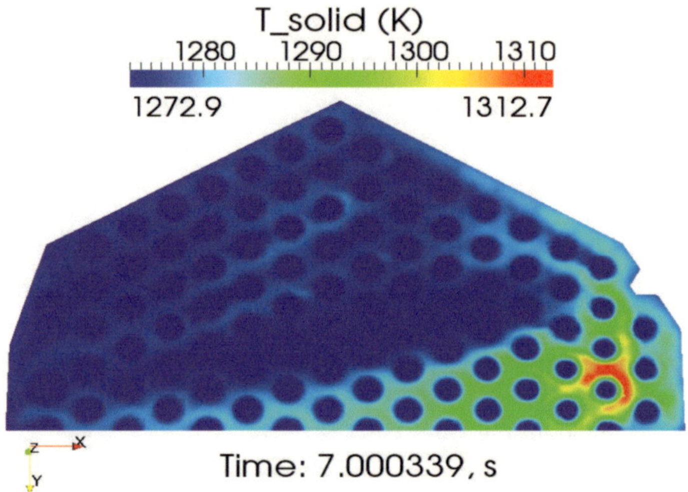

Fig. 22. Bottom Plate Temperature

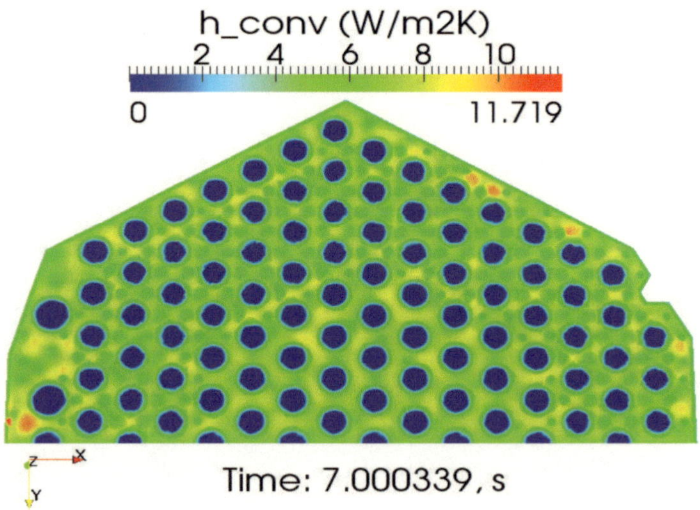

Fig. 23. Bottom Plate Heat Transfer Coefficient

The above figures confirm that swirling jets can mitigate thermal stratification and the formation of hot spots in the lower support plate in the VHTR LP. The mitigation of those two issues is achievable by adding swirl inserts at the exit of the helium coolant channels in the VHTR core, slightly increasing the pressure drop in the channels and across the LP. *An inspection of the pressure drop caused by the static helicoid device on a single, standalone helicoid shows that there was a relatively small drop of approximately 1,000 Pa (0.15 psi), as shown in Figure 24. This result is consistent with those found in the literature for hubless swirlers (Mathur and MacCallum, 1967). Given the benefits related to enhanced mixing and turbulence gained as a result of the swirling device, such small pressure drop is clearly justified.*

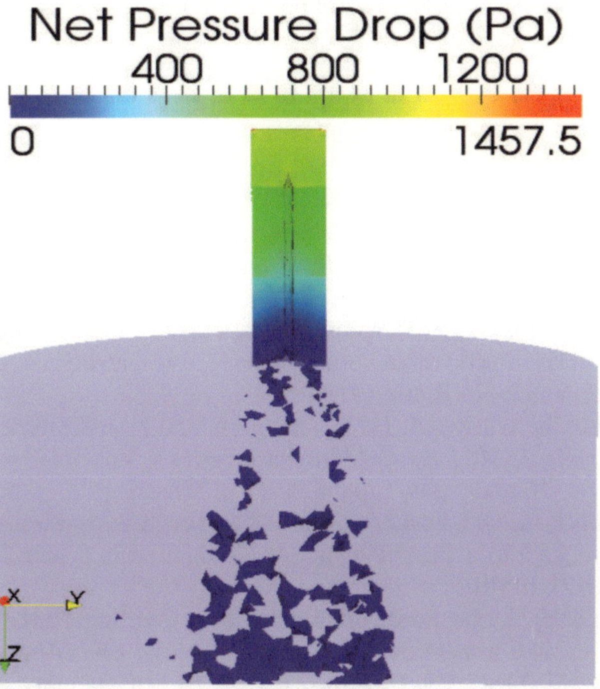

Fig. 24. Net Pressure Drop Across Helicoid Geometry

8. Conclusion

A helicoid vortex swirl model, along with the Fuego CFD and Calore heat transfer codes are used to investigate mixing and heat transfer enhancements for a number of swirling jet applications. Critical parameters are S, CRZ, swirl decay, jet separation distance, and Re. As soon as the CRZ forms, the azimuthal velocity field for the swirling jets does not travel as far, even when Re increases substantially. For example, once the CRZ develops, a 10-fold increase in Re has a smaller impact on the flow field than S.

Knowing at a more fundamental level how vortices behave and what traits they have in common allows for insights that lead to vortex engineering for the purpose of maximizing heat transfer and flow mixing. Because the CRZ is a strong function of the azimuthal and axial velocities, shaping those velocity profiles substantially affect the flow field.

As applications for the material discussed herein, simulations are performed for: (1) unconfined jet, (2) jets impinging on a flat plate, and (3) a VHTR LP. The calculations show the effects of S, CRZ, L/D, swirl decay, and Re. For the VHTR LP calculations, results demonstrated that hot spots and thermal stratification in the LP can be mitigated using swirling jets, while producing a relatively small pressure drop.

9. References

Aboelkassem, Y., Vatistas, G. H., and Esmail, N. (2005). Viscous Dissipation of Rankine Vortex Profile in Zero Meridional Flow, *Acta Mech. Sinica*, Vol. 21, 550 - 556

Allen, T. (2004). Generation IV Systems and Materials, Advanced Computational Materials Science: Application to Fusion and Generation-IV Fission Reactors, U. of Wisconsin

Batchelor, G. K. (1964). Axial Flow in Trailing Line Vortices, *J. Fluid Mech.*, Vol. 20, Part 4, 645 - 658

Billant, P., Chomaz, J.-M., and Huerre, P. (1998). Experimental Study of Vortex Breakdown in Swirling Jets, *J. Fluid Mech.*, Vol. 376, 183 - 219

Bird, R., Stewart, W., and Lightfoot, E. (2007). *Transport Phenomena*, John Wiley & Sons, 2nd Edition

Blevins, R. (1992). *Applied Fluid Dynamics Handbook*, Krieger Publishing Co., Florida

Burgers, J. M. (1948) *Advances in Applied Mechanics*, Vol. 1, Academic Press, New York, 171

Chassaing, P. *et al.* (1974). Physical Characteristics of Subsonic Jets in a Cross-Stream, *J. Fluid Mech.*, Vol. 62, Part 1, 41 - 64

Chepura, I. B. *et al.* (1969). On the Tangential Component of the Velocity Field in a Smooth-Wall Vessel Equipped with a Radial-Blade Mixer, *Teoreticheskie Osnovy Khimichesko i Tekhnologii*, Vol. 3, No. 3, 404 - 411

Chigier, N. A. and Chervinsky, A. (1967). Experimental Investigation of Swirling Vortex Motion in Jets, *ASME J. Applied Mechanics*, Series E, Vol. 3, 443 - 451

CUBIT, (2009). www/cs.sandia.gov/capabilities/CubitMeshingProgram/index.html

Denev, J. A., Frohlich, J., and Bockhorn, H. (2009). Large Eddy Simulation of a Swirling Transverse Jet into a Crossflow with Investigation of Scalar Transport, *Physics of Fluids*, Vol. 21, 015101

Duwig, C. *et al.* (2005). Large Eddy Simulation of a Swirling Flame Response to Swirl Modulation with Impact on Combustion Stability, 43rd AIAA Aerospace Sciences Meeting and Exhibit, AIAA 2005-1275, Reno, Nevada, January 10-13

Fuego (2009). SIERRA/Fuego Theory Manual - 4.11, Sandia National Laboratories

Fujimoto, Y., Inokuchi, Y., and Yamasaki, N. (2005). Large Eddy Simulation of Swirling Jet in Bluff-Body Burner, *J. Thermal Science*, Vol. 14, No. 1, 28 - 33

Garcia-Villalba, M., Frohlich, J., and Rodi, W. (2005). Large Eddy Simulation of Turbulent Confined Coaxial Swirling Jets, *Proc. Appl. Math. Mech.*, Vol. 5, 463 - 464

Gol'Dshtik, M. A. and Yavorskii, N. I. (1986). On Submerged Jets, *Prikl. Matem. Mekhan.* USSR, Vol. 50, No. 4, 438 - 445

Goldstein, R. J. and Behbahani, A. I. (1982). Impingement of a Circular Jet with and without Cross Flow, *Int. J. Heat Mass Transfer*, Vol. 25, No. 9, 1377 - 1382

Gortler, H. (1954). Decay of Swirl in an Axially Symmetrical Jet, Far from the Orifice, *Revista Matematica Hispano-Americana*, Vol. 14, 143 - 178

Huang, L. (1996). Heat Transfer and Flow Visualization of Conventional and Swirling Impinging Jets, Ph.D. Diss., University of New Mexico

Huang, L. and El-Genk, M. (1998). Heat Transfer and Flow Visualization Experiments of Swirling, Multi-Channel, and Conventional Impinging Jets, *Int. J. Heat Mass Transfer*, Vol. 41, No. 3, 583 - 600

Hwang, W.-S. and Chwang, A. T. (1992). The Swirling Round Laminar Jet, *J. of Engineering Mathematics*, Vol. 26, 339 - 348

Johnson, G. A. (2008). Power Conversion System Evaluation for the Next Generation Nuclear Plant (NGNP), Proc. International Congress on Advances in Nuclear Power Plants (ICAPP 08), American Nuclear Society, Paper 8253, Anaheim, CA

Johnson, R. W. and Schultz, R. R. (2009). Computational Fluid Dynamic Analysis of the VHTR Lower Plenum Standard Problem, INL/EXT-09-16325, Idaho Nat. Lab.

Kamal, M. M. (2009). Combustion in a Cross Flow with Air Jet Nozzles, *Combust. Sci. and Tech.*, Vol. 181, 78 - 96

Kamotani, Y. and Greber, I. (1974). Experiments on Confined Turbulent Jets in Cross Flow, NASA CR-2392

Kavsaoglu, M. S. and Schetz, J. A. (1989). Effects of Swirl and High Turbulence on a Jet in a Crossflow, *J. Aircraft*, Vol. 26, No. 6, 539 - 546

Kawai, S. and Lele, S. K. (2007). Mechanisms of Jet Mixing in a Supersonic Crossflow: A Study Using Large-Eddy Simulation, Center for Turbulence Research, Annual Research Briefs, 353 - 365

Kiel, B. *et al.* (2003). Experimental Investigation of Vortex Shedding of a Jet in Crossflow, 41st Aerospace Sciences Meeting and Exhibit, AIAA 2003-182, Reno, Nevada

Kim, M.-H., Lim, H.-S, and Lee, W.-J. (2007). A CFD Analysis of a Preliminary Cooled-Vessel Concept for a VHTR, Korea Atomic Energy Research Institute

Lamb, H. (1932). *Hydrodynamics*, 6th Ed., Cambridge Univ. Press

Larocque, J. (2004). Heat Transfer Simulation in Swirling Impinging Jet, Institut National Polytechnique de Grenoble, Division of Heat Transfer

Laurien, E., Lavante, D. v., and Wang, H. (2010). Hot-Gas Mixing in the Annular Channel Below the Core of High-Power HTR's, Proceedings of the 5th Int. Topical Meeting on High Temperature Reactor Technology, HTR 2010-138, Prague, Czech Republic

Lavante, D. v. and Laurien, E. (2007). 3-D Simulation of Hot Gas Mixing in the Lower Plenum of High-Temperature Reactors, *Int. J. for Nuclear Power*, Vol. 52, 648 - 649

Loitsyanskiy, L. G. (1953). The Propagation of a Twisted Jet in an Unbounded Space Filled with the Same Fluid, *Prikladnaya Matematika i Mekhanika*, Vol. 17, No. 1, 3 - 16

Martynenko, O. G., Korovkin, V. N., and Sokovishin, Yu. A. (1989). A Swirled Jet Problem, *Int. J. Heat Mass Transfer*, Vol. 32, No. 12, 2309 - 2317

Mathur, M. L. and MacCallum, N. R. L. (1967). Swirling Air Jets Issuing from Vane Swirlers. Part 1: Free Jets, *Journal of the Institute of Fuel*, Vol. 40, 214 - 225

McEligot, D. M. and McCreery, G. E. (2004). Scaling Studies and Conceptual Experiment Designs for NGNP CFD Assessment, Idaho National Engineering and Environment Laboratory, INEEL/EXT-04-02502

Nematollahi, M. R. and Nazifi, M. (2007). Enhancement of Heat Transfer in a Typical Pressurized Water Reactor by New Mixing Vanes on Spacer Grids, ICENES

Newman, B. G. (1959). Flow in a Viscous Trailing Vortex, *The Aero. Quarterly*, 149 - 162

Nirmolo, A. (2007). Optimization of Radial Jets Mixing in Cross-Flow of Combustion Chambers Using Computational Fluid Dynamics, Ph.D. Diss., Otto-von-Guericke U. of Magdeburg, Germany

Patankar, S. V., Basu, D. K., and Alpay, S. A. (1977). Prediction of the Three-Dimensional Velocity Field of a Deflected Turbulent Jet, *J. of Fluids Engineering*, 758 - 762

Pratte, B. D. and Baines, W. D. (1967). Profiles of Round Turbulent Jets in a Cross Flow, Procs. of the American Society of Civil Engineers, *J. Hydraulics Div.*, Vol. 92, 53 - 64

Rankine, W. J. (1858). *A Manual of Applied Mechanics*, 9th Ed., C. Griffin and Co., London, UK

Rivero, A., Ferre, J. A., and Giralt, F. (2001). Organized Motions in a Jet in Crossflow, *J. Fluid Mech.*, Vol. 444, 117 - 149

Rodriguez, S. B. and El-Genk, M. S. (2008a). Using Helicoids to Eliminate 'Hot Streaking' and Stratification in the Very High Temperature Reactor Lower Plenum, *Proceedings of ICAPP '08*, American Nuclear Society, Paper 8079, Anaheim, CA

Rodriguez, S. B. and El-Genk, M. S. (2008b). On Eliminating 'Hot Streaking' and Stratification in the VHTR Lower Plenum Using Helicoid Inserts, *HTR-08*, American Society of Mechanical Engineers, Paper 58292, Washington, DC

Rodriguez, S. B., Domino, S., and El-Genk, M. S. (2010). Safety Analysis of the NGNP Lower Plenum Using the Fuego CFD Code, CFD4NRS-3 Workshop, Experimental Validation and Application of CFD and CMFD Codes to Nuclear Reactor Safety Issues, Washington, DC

Rodriguez, S. B. and El-Genk, M. S. (2010a). Numerical Investigation of Potential Elimination of 'Hot Streaking' and Stratification in the VHTR Lower Plenum using Helicoid Inserts, *Nuclear Engineering and Design Journal*, Vol. 240, 995 - 1004

Rodriguez, S. B. and El-Genk, M. S. (2010b). Cooling of an Isothermal Plate Using a Triangular Array of Swirling Air Jets, *14th Int. Heat Transfer Conference*, Wash. DC

Rodriguez, S. B. and El-Genk, M. S. (2010c). On Enhancing VHTR Lower Plenum Heat Transfer and Mixing via Swirling Jet, *Procs. of ICAPP 10*, Paper 10160, S. Diego, CA

Rodriguez, S. B. and El-Genk, M. S. (2010d). Heat Transfer and Flow Field Characterization of a Triangular Array of Swirling Jets Impinging on an Adiabatic Plate, *Proc. 14th Int. Heat Transfer Conference*, Washington DC

Rodriguez, S. B. and El-Genk, M. S. (2011). Coupled Computational Fluid Dynamics and Heat Transfer Analysis of the VHTR Lower Plenum, Proceedings of ICAPP-11, Paper 11247, Nice, France

Semaan, R., Naughton, J., and Ewing, F. D. (2009). Approach Toward Similar Behavior of a Swirling Jet Flow, 47th AIAA Aero. Sc. Mtg., Orlando, Florida, Paper 2009-1114

Smagorinsky, J. (1963). General Circulation Experiments with the Primitive Equations I. The Basic Experiment, Dept. of Com., *Monthly Weather Rep.*, Vol. 91, No. 3, 99 - 164

Squire, H. B. (1965). The Growth of a Vortex in a Turbulent Flow, *The Aeronautical Quarterly*, Vol. 16, Part 1, 302 - 306

Sucec, J. and Bowley, W. W. (1976). Prediction of the Trajectory of a Turbulent Jet Injected into a Crossflowing Stream, *J. of Fluids Engineering*, 667 - 673

Sullivan, R. D. (1959). A Two-Cell Vortex Solution of the Navier-Stokes Equations, *J. of the Aerospace Sciences*, Vol. 26, No. 11, 767 - 768

Taylor, G. I. and Green, A. E. (1937). Mechanism of the Production of Small Eddies from Large Ones, *Proceedings of the Royal Society of London, Series A, Mathematical and Physical Sciences*, Vol. 158, No. 895, 499 - 521

Tsukker, M. S. (1955). A Swirled Jet Propagating in the Space Filled with the Same Fluid, *Prikladnaja Matematika i Mehanika*, Vol. 19, No. 4, 500 - 503

Watson, E. A. and Clarke, J. S. (1947). Combustion and Combustion Equipment for Aero Gas Engines, *J. Inst. Fuel*, Vol. 21, 572 - 579

10

Thermal Approaches to Interpret Laser Damage Experiments

S. Reyné[1], L. Lamaignère[2], J-Y. Natoli[3] and G. Duchateau[4]
[1,2]*Commissariat à l'Energie Atomique, Centre du Cesta Avenue des Sablières, Le Barp*
[3]*Institut Fresnel, UMR-CNRS D.U. St Jérôme, Marseille*
[4]*Commissariat à l'Energie Atomique, Centre du Ripault, Monts France*

1. Introduction

Laser-Induced Damage (LID) resistance of optical components is under considerations for Inertial Confinement Fusion-class facilities such as NIF (National Ignition Facility, in US) or LMJ (Laser MegaJoule, in France). These uncommon facilities require large components (typically 40 × 40 cm^2) with high optical quality to supply the energy necessary to ensure the fusion of a Deuterium-Tritium mixture encapsulated into a micro-balloon. At the end of the laser chain, the final optic assembly is in charge for the frequency conversion of the laser beam from the 1053 nm (1ω) to 351 nm (3ω) before its focusing on the target. In this assembly, frequency converters in KH_2PO_4 (or KDP) and DKDP (which is the deuterated analog), are illuminated either by one wavelength or several wavelengths in the frequency conversion regime. These converters have to resist to fluence levels high enough in order to avoid laser-induced damage. This is actually the topic of this study which interests in KDP crystals laser damage experiments specifically. Indeed, pinpoints can appear at the exit surface or most often in the bulk of the components. This is a real issue to be addressed in order to improve their resistance and ensure their nominal performances on a laser chain.

KDP crystals LID in the nanosecond regime, as localized, is now admitted to occur due to the existence of precursors defects (Demos et al., 2003; Feit & Rubenchik, 2004) present in the material initially or induced during the laser illumination. Because these precursors can not be identified by classical optical techniques, their size is supposed to be few nanometers. Despite the several attempts to identify their physical and chemical properties (Demos et al., 2003; Pommiès et al., 2006), their exact nature remains unknown or their role in the LID mechanisms is not clearly established yet. From the best of our knowledge, the main candidates to be proposed are linked to hydrogen bonds (Liu et al., 2003;?; Wang et al., 2005) which may induce point defects. Indeed, atomic scale defects such as interstitials or oxygen vacancies may be responsible for LID in KDP crystals. Also, point defects can migrate into structural defects (such as cracks, dislocations...) to create bigger defects (Duchateau, 2009). In the literature, many experimental and theoretical studies have been performed to explain the LID in KDP crystal (Demos et al., 2010; Duchateau, 2009; Duchateau & Dyan, 2007; Dyan et al., 2008; Feit & Rubenchik, 2004; Reyné et al., 2009; 2010). These studies highlight the great improvements obtained in the KDP laser-induced damage field but also the difficulties to refine its understanding.

This chapter presents an overview of the LID in KDP when illuminated by a nanosecond laser beam. A review of the thermal approaches which have been developed over the last ten years is proposed. In Section 2, a description of two models including the heat transfer in defects of sub-micrometric size is carried out. We first propose a description of the DMT (Drude - Mie - Thermal) model (Dyan et al., 2008) which considers the incident laser energy absorption by a plasma ball (i.e. an absorbing zone), that may lead to a damage. Then, we describe a model coupling statistics and heat transfer (Duchateau, 2009; Duchateau & Dyan, 2007) which indicates that LID may be induced by the thermal cooperation of point defects. These two models are based on the resolution of the standard Fourier's equation where the features of the model under considerations are included. Also, the damage occurrence is determined according to a criterion defined by a critical temperature, which corresponds to the temperature reached by the defect to induce a damage site.

The previous models account for most of the classical results and trends on KDP LID published in the literature. In Section 3, some applications of these models are presented to interpret several sets of new experimental results. To interpret these new results, these thermal models have been adapted. First in the mono-wavelength case, it is shown that the DMT model accounts for the influence of the crystal orientation on the LID by considering defects with an ellipsoid geometry (Reyné et al., 2009). Then, when a KDP crystal is illuminated by two different wavelengths at the same time, it exists a coupling effect between the wavelength that induces a drastic drop in the laser damage resistance of the component. The model then addresses the resolution of the Fourier's equation by taking into account the presence of two wavelength at the same time (Reyné et al., 2010).

2. Review of thermal approaches to model LID

Section 2 presents different thermal approaches to explain the main results of laser-induced damage in KDP crystals. This section aims at giving a review of the last attempts to model laser-induced damage in KDP crystals (Duchateau & Dyan, 2007; Dyan et al., 2008). Modeling is mainly based on the resolution of the Fourier's equation on a precursor defect whose optical properties have to be characterized. Heat transfer in the KDP lattice may be considered either as the result of individual defects or as the cooperation of several point defects. These models can thus help to obtain more information on precursor defects and identify them.

2.1 DMT model

Since this study deals with conditions where the temperature evolution is strongly driven by thermal diffusion mechanisms, LID modeling attempts have to be based on the resolution of the Fourier equation. This has been first studied by Hopper and Uhlmann (Hopper & Uhlmann, 1970). Walker *et al.* improved the latter model by introducing an absorption efficiency that depends on the sphere radius (Walker et al., 1981). In this work, they considered only particular cases of the general Mie theory (Van de Hulst, 1981). Always on the basis of a heat transfer driven temperature evolution, Sparks and Duthler refined the characterization of the absorbing properties of the plasma through a Drude model but did not take into account the influence of the plasma ball radius (Sparks et al., 1981). In all these works, no importance has been given to the scaling law exponent x linking the laser pulse density energy F_c to the pulse duration τ as $F_c = \alpha\tau^x$ where α is a constant. Indeed, this temporal scaling law has motivated many research groups in order to obtain information on the mechanisms responsible for laser-induced damage in dielectrics. Unlike the standard 0.5 value of x that has been demonstrated in a lot of materials by both experimental (Stuart et al., 1996) and simple physical considerations (Bliss, 1971; Feit & Rubenchik, 2004; Wood, 2003), LID in KDP exhibits a lower value of x that is close to 0.35 at 3ω (Adams et al., 2005; Burnham et al., 2003). A first attempt has been made by Feit and co-workers to explain this deviation from 0.5 (Feit & Rubenchik, 2004; Trenholme et al., 2006). Hereafter, in the tradition of the state-of-the-art above-mentioned thermal modeling, an introduction to the general model is done. This model that takes into account all relevant physical mechanisms involved in LID in order to predict x values that depart from the standard 0.5. Under a few assumptions, this is achieved by coupling a Drude model, the Mie theory and Thermal diffusion. The resulting model hereafter referred to as DMT is presented in Sec. 2.1.1. It allows to predict the values of F_c and x with respect to the optical constants of the plasma (see Sec. 2.1.3). The inverse problem (Gallais et al., 2004) is considered in order to determine the modeling physical parameters from experimental data. It permits to draw up conclusions about the electronic plasma density. Further, the evolution of the scaling law exponent is studied with respect to the laser pulse duration interval that is used to evaluate it.

2.1.1 Thermal modeling and absorption efficiency

Since LID consists of a set of pinpoints distributed randomly within the bulk (Adams et al., 2005), the model considers the heating of a set of plasma balls whose radius varies from a few nanometers to hundreds of nanometers (Feit & Rubenchik, 2004). The main assumptions of the model are the following :

- continuity of the size distribution, i.e. it exists at least one sphere for each size,
- since it deals with a plasma, a high thermal conductivity of the absorbing sphere is assumed. It follows that the temperature is constant inside the plasma,
- the absorption efficiency is independent of time, i.e. it is assumed that the plasma reaches its stationary state in a time much shorter than the laser pulse duration,
- when the critical temperature T_c is reached at the end of the pulse, an irreversible damage occurs,
- the physical parameters do not depend on the temperature.

The heating model for one sphere is based on the standard diffusion equation (Feit & Rubenchik, 2004; Hopper & Uhlmann, 1970) that can be written in spherical symmetry as :

$$\frac{1}{D}\frac{\partial T}{\partial t} = \frac{1}{r^2}\frac{\partial}{\partial r}(r^2\frac{\partial T}{\partial r}) \tag{1}$$

where T is the temperature, r is the radial coordinate and D is the bulk thermal diffusivity defined as $D = \frac{\lambda_t}{\rho C}$ with λ_t, ρ, C being the thermal conductivity, the density and the specific heat capacity of the KDP bulk respectively. Eq. (1) is solved under the following initial and boundary conditions :

i. at $t = 0$, $T = T_0 = \text{constant} \; \forall \; r$, where T_0 is the initial ambient temperature set to 300 K,

ii. T tends to T_0 when r tends to infinity,

iii. the following enthalpy conservation at the interface between the bulk and the absorber is considered:

$$\frac{4\pi}{3}a^3\rho_p C_p \frac{\partial T}{\partial t}\bigg]_{r=a} = I_0 Q_{abs}(m,y)\pi a^2 + 4\pi a^2 \lambda_t \frac{\partial T}{\partial r}\bigg]_{r=a} \tag{2}$$

where a, ρ_p and C_p are the radius, the density and the specific heat capacity of the absorber respectively. $Q_{abs}(m, y)$ is defined as the absorption efficiency that can be evaluated through the Mie theory (Van de Hulst, 1981). m is the complex optical index of the absorber related to the one of the bulk and y is the size parameter. Finally, I_0 is the laser intensity that is assumed to be constant with respect to time in order to correspond to an experimental top hat temporal profile.

Eq. (1) can be solved in the Laplace space (Carslaw & Jaeger, 1959) and the use of the initial and boundary conditions leads to the following solution for $r = a$:

$$T(a,\tau) = T_0 + \frac{Q_{abs} I_0 \sqrt{4D\tau}}{4\lambda_t} \xi(U, A) \tag{3}$$

with

$$\xi(U, A) = \frac{UA}{1 - X^2} \left(\phi(\frac{X}{A}) - X^2 \phi(\frac{1}{XA}) \right) \tag{4}$$

where $U = \sqrt{\frac{\kappa}{D}}$, $X = U + \sqrt{U^2 - 1}$ and $A = \frac{a}{\sqrt{4\kappa\tau}}$ are dimensionless. Note that $\xi(U, A)$ is a function that gives acoount for the material properties. The notation $\kappa = \frac{3\lambda_t}{4\rho_p C_p}$ is also introduced and has units of a thermal diffusivity, but mixes the properties of the bulk and the absorber. The function ϕ is defined as $\phi(z) = 1 - \exp(z^2)\ \mathrm{erfc}(z)$ where erfc is the complementary error function. Also, the fluence can be written as $F = I_0\tau$ which allows Eq. 3 to be re-formulated. The plot of F as a function of a exhibits a minimum (Hopper & Uhlmann, 1970) (see Fig. 1) and since the existence of at least one absorber of size a is assumed, the critical fluence necessary to reach the critical temperature T_c (set to 10000 K in all the calculations (Carr et al., 2004)) can thus be written as :

$$F_c = \frac{2\lambda_t (T_c - T_0)}{Q_{abs}(a_c)\sqrt{D}} \frac{\sqrt{\tau}}{\xi(U, A_c)} \tag{5}$$

where a_c is the radius that corresponds to the minimum fluence to reach T_c.
Moreover, for the case where Q_{abs} does not depend on a, one can show from Eq. (5) and Fig. 1 that the critical fluence reaches a minimum for the critical radius a_c :

$$a_c(\tau) = 2\sqrt{\kappa\tau}\, B(U) \tag{6}$$

where B is a function of U. It can be shown that $B(\infty) = 1$ and $B(0) \simeq 0.89$. Elsewhere, the function $B(U)$ has to be evaluated numerically. If Q_{abs} does not depends on a, then $x = 1/2$. It is worth noting that the value of x can be refound from considerations about the enthalpy conservation at the interface.

The second step consists in showing by simple considerations how the introduction of the Mie theory permits to deviate from the standard $x = 1/2$ value. From that theory, Q_{abs} depends on the sphere radius. More precisely, one can reasonably write $Q_{abs} \propto a_c^\delta$ where $\delta \in [-1; 1]$. $\delta = -1$ corresponds to the case $a_c > \lambda$ and large values of the imaginary part k of the optical index (typically a few unities as for metals) whereas $\delta = 1$ corresponds to the Rayleigh regime ($a_c \ll \lambda$). As above mentioned, a_c is a function of the pulse duration that can be written as $a_c \propto \tau^\gamma$ where γ is close to $1/2$. It follows that $F_c \propto \tau^{1/2-\delta\gamma}$ with $-1/2 \leq \delta\gamma \leq 1/2$ and therefore x lies in the range $[0; 1]$.

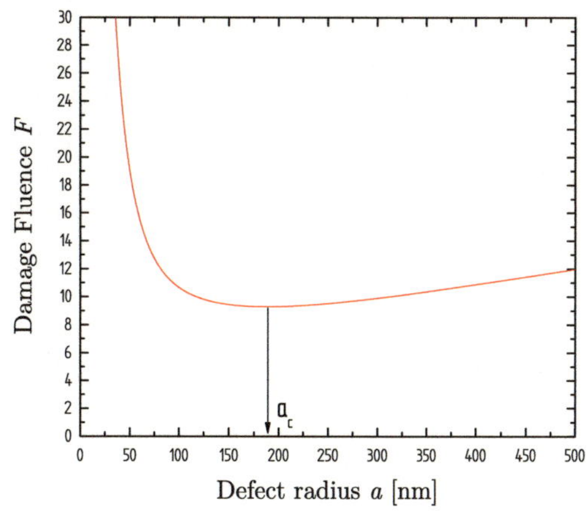

Fig. 1. Evolution of the damage fluence F_c as a function of the defect size a. A minimum is obtained for $a = a_c$ which is associated to the critical fluence F_c.

2.1.2 Determination of the plasma optical indices within the Drude model framework

Since the laser absorption is due to a plasma state, for which free electrons oscillate in the laser electric field and undergo collisions with ions, the optical indices of the plasma can be derived from the standard Drude model with damping (see for example Hummel (2001)). In that framework, the response of the electron gas to the external laser electric field is given by the following complex dielectric function :

$$\varepsilon = 1 - \frac{\omega_p^2}{\omega(\omega - i/\tau_{coll})} = \varepsilon_1 - i\varepsilon_2 \tag{7}$$

In this expression, ω_p is the electron plasma frequency given by $\omega_p = (n_e e^2/\varepsilon_0 m_*)^{1/2}$ where n_e is the free electrons density and m_* is the effective mass of the electron. τ_{coll} stands for the collisional time, i.e. the time elapsed between two collisions with ions. The dielectric function is linked to the complex optical index $m = n - ik$ by the relation $m^2 = \varepsilon$. It follows that $\varepsilon_1 = n^2 - k^2$ and $\varepsilon_2 = 2nk$. In the case where m and hence ε are known, the characteristic parameters of the plasma n_e and τ_{coll} can be determined by inversing Eq. (7). The laser-induced electron density cannot exceed a critical value n_c above which the plasma becomes opaque. This critical density is determined setting ω_p to ω, which leads to $n_c = m_* \epsilon_0 \omega^2/e^2$. In the next section, we will see that it is of interest to know the values of the optical index satisfying the physical requirement $n_e \leq n_c$ (or equivalently $\omega_p \leq \omega$) appearing in laser-induced experiments. By setting n_e to n_c, the couples $(\varepsilon_1, \varepsilon_2)$ have to satisfy $(\varepsilon_1 - 1/2)^2 + \varepsilon_2^2 = (1/2)^2$ that is nothing but the equation of a circle centered at $(1/2, 0)$ and of radius $1/2$. Each point inside the circle satisfies the required condition $n_e \leq n_c$.

2.1.3 Results

A description of the procedure that is used to compute all physical parameters of interest for the present paper is done first. For given pulse duration and (n, k) values, the plot of the fluence required to reach the critical temperature T_c as a function of the absorber radius – the plot that exhibits a minimum a_c (Feit & Rubenchik, 2004) – allows to determine the critical fluence F_c, i.e. the fluence for which the first damage appears. It is also possible to associate the critical Mie absorption efficiency $Q_{abs}(a_c)$ evaluated for $a = a_c$. In order to determine the scaling law exponent x corresponding to a couple (n,k), one only has to apply the last procedure for different pulse durations. It is then assumed that one can write $F_c = A\tau^x$ and the values of the parameters A and x are determined with a fitting procedure based on a Levenberg-Marquardt algorithm (*Numerical Recipies*, n.d.).

Now, within this modeling framework, the optical constants of the plasma can be determined by using experimental data that provide F_c and x. To do so, by applying the above-described procedure, the theoretical evolution of F_c and x have been evaluated as a function of (n,k) on Figs. 2 (a) and 2 (b) respectively. Fig. 2 (a) has been obtained with $\tau = 3\ ns$ whereas, for Fig. 2 (b), τ varies in the interval $[1.\ ns\ ;10.\ ns]$ which is used experimentally (Burnham et al., 2003). The particular behavior of F_c can be explained in a simple way. From Eq. (5), F_c is proportional to $1/Q_{abs}$, Q_{abs} being itself proportional to $\varepsilon_2 = 2nk$ since it deals with conditions close to the Rayleigh regime (Van de Hulst, 1981) ($a_c \simeq 100\ nm$ and thus $a/\lambda < 1$) and $\varepsilon_2 \ll 1$. Iso-fluence curves as shown on Fig. 2 (a) correspond to $F_c =$ const, that is to say $1/Q_{abs} =$ const and subsequently $k \propto 1/n$. This hyperbolic behavior is all the more pronounced that τ is short. As regards the scaling law exponent, the main feature appearing on Fig. 2 (b) is that x depends essentially on k, this trend becoming more pronounced as k goes up. Indeed, for large enough values of k whatever the value of n, the shape of Q_{abs} with respect to a remains almost the same that imposes the value of x. Now, the optical constants can be determined from experimental data $F_c = 10 \pm 1\ J/cm^2$ (Carr et al., 2004) and $x = 0.35 \pm 0.05$ (Burnham et al., 2003). The theoretical index range providing these two values is obtained by performing a superposition of Figs. 2 (a) and 2 (b) as shown on Fig. 2 (c). In addition, the intersection region is restricted by the above-mentioned condition $\omega_p \leq \omega$. Since the uncertainty on F_c is relatively small, the shape of the intersection region is elongated. The extremal points in the (n,k) plane are roughly $(0.16, 0.16)$ ($n_e = n_c$ and $\tau_{coll} = 3.50$ fs) and $(0.40, 0.06)$ ($n_e = 0.84 n_c$ and $\tau_{coll} = 3.27$ fs). The optical index satisfying $F_c = 10\ J.cm^{-2}$ and $x = 0.35$ is $(0.22, 0.12)$ ($n_e = 0.97 n_c$ and $\tau_{coll} = 3.40$ fs). Also, we find values of n_e and τ_{coll} that are close to the plasma critical density and the standard femtosecond range respectively. It is worth noting that the associated Mie absorption efficiency with the latter optical indices is $Q_{abs}(a_c) = 6.5\ \%$ where $a_c \simeq 100\ nm$. In order to compare to experiments where the ionized region size is estimated to 30 μm (Carr et al., 2004) in conditions where the fluence is twice the critical fluence (for such a high energy, the plasma spreads over the whole focal laser spot), we have evaluated Q_{abs} with the above found index and $a = 30\ \mu m$. In that case, $Q_{abs} \simeq 10\ \%$ which is close to the 12 % experimental value (Carr et al., 2004). It is noteworthy that Q_{abs} saturates with respect to a for such values of the optical index and absorber size.

2.2 Coupling statistics and heat tranfer

In order to characterize experimentally the resistance of KDP crystals to optical damaging, a standard measurement consists in plotting the bulk damage probability as a function of the laser fluence F (Adams et al., 2005) that gives rise to the so-called S-curves. In order to explain this behavior, thermal models based on an inclusion heating have been proposed (Dyan et al., 2008; Feit & Rubenchik, 2004; Hopper & Uhlmann, 1970). In these approaches, statistics (Poisson law) and inclusion size distributions are assumed. On the other hand, pure statistical approaches mainly devoted to the onset determination and that do not take into account thermal processes have been considered (Gallais et al., 2002; Natoli et al., 2002; O'Connell, 1992; Picard et al., 1977; Porteus & Seitel, 1984). On the basis of the above-

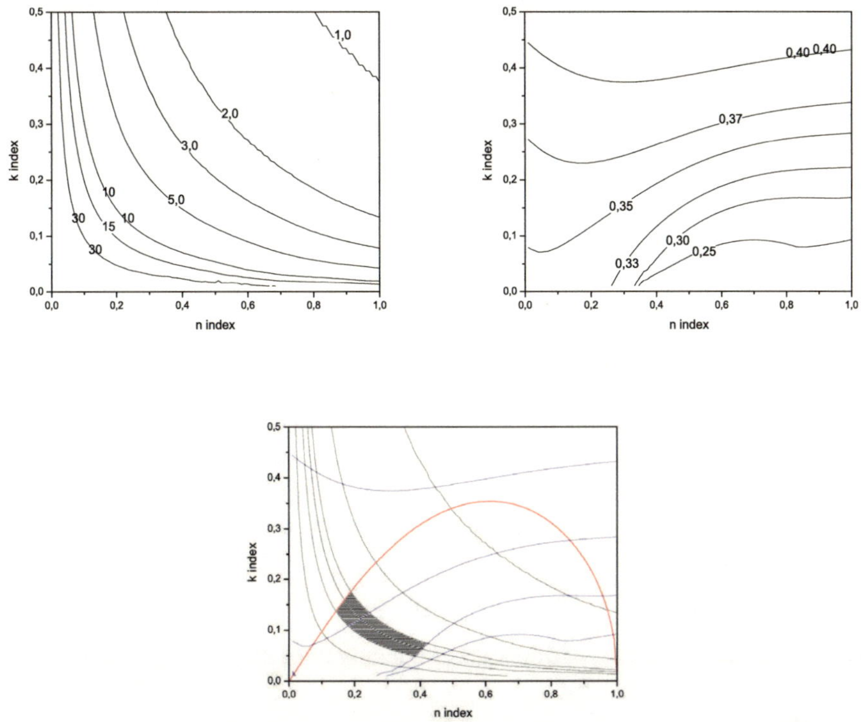

Fig. 2. (top left) Critical fluence F_c in $J.cm^{-2}$ as a function of n and k for $\tau = 3\ ns$. (top right) Scaling law exponent x as a function of n and k for $\tau \in [1.\ ns;\ 10.\ ns]$. (bottom) Intersection of (a) and (b), the highlighted area delimits the region satisfying experimental data.

mentioned assumption of defects aggregation, this section proposes a model where Absorbing Defects of Nanometric Size, hereafter referred to as ADNS, are distributed randomly and may cooperate to the temperature rise ΔT through heat transfer within a given micrometric region of the bulk that corresponds to an heterogeneity. Since this approach combines statistics and heat transfer, it allows to provide the cluster size distribution, damage probability as a function of fluence, and scaling laws without any supplementary hypothesis. The present section aims at introducing the general principle of this model and giving first main results that are compared with experimental facts. A particular attention has been payed to scaling laws since they are very instructive in terms of physical mechanisms. More precisely, a deviation from the standard $\tau^{1/2}$ law has recently been observed within KDP crystals (Adams et al., 2005) and this model (as the DMT one previously presented) also proposes a plausible explanation of this fact based on thermal cooperation effects and statistics. Despite the 2D and 3D representation was tackled (Duchateau, 2009; Duchateau & Dyan, 2007), this section focuses on a one dimensional modeling that gives a good insight about physics and seems to provide a nice counterpart to experimental tendencies.

This section is organized as follows: Sec. 2.2.1 deals with the model coupling statistics and heat transfer. In a first part, the principle of the approach is exposed. Secondly, numerical predictions of the model are provided in terms of damage probability S-curves and temporal scaling laws. Results are discussed and compared with experimental facts in Sec. 2.2.2.

2.2.1 Random distribution of absorbing defects

This model considers a set of ADNS that are distributed on a spatial domain. When a crystal cell contains a defect, it is called an alterate cell which may absorb laser energy much more efficiently than a pure cell crystal. Therefore, from heat transfer point of view, the alterate cell may be seen as a very tiny source inducing temperature rising. This source of size a is assumed to be close to the characteristic crystal cell dimension, i.e. one nanometer. Within a 1D framework, the domain of size Na, that is assumed to correspond to an heterogeneity, then is composed of two kinds of cells. The temperature evolution is governed by the Fourier's equation:

$$\frac{\partial T}{\partial t} = D\frac{\partial^2 T}{\partial x^2} + \frac{A}{\rho C}\sum_{i=1}^{n_{ADNS}} \Pi(x - x_i) \tag{8}$$

where $x_i \in [0, Na]$ stands for the position of ADNS or alterate cells whose number is n_{ADNS} and A is the absorbed power per unit of volume. Material physical parameters such as thermal diffusivity D and conductivity λ, density ρ or specific heat capacity C, linked by the relation $D = \lambda/\rho C$, are assumed to remain constant in the course of interaction. The function Π is defined as follows:

$$\begin{cases} \Pi(x) = 1 \text{ if } x \in [x - a/2; x + a/2] \\ \Pi(x) = 0 \text{ elsewhere} \end{cases} \tag{9}$$

The way to distribute defects is addressed in the next paragraph. A general solution of (8) is given by (Carslaw & Jaeger, 1959):

$$T(x,t) = T_0 + \sum_{i=1}^{n_{ADNS}} \Delta T^{(i)}(x,t) \tag{10}$$

where $T_0 = 300K$ is the initial temperature of the crystal and where the temperature rise $\Delta T^{(i)}(x,t)$ induced by one ADNS is solution of the following equation:

$$\frac{\partial \Delta T^{(i)}}{\partial t} = D\frac{\partial^2 \Delta T^{(i)}}{\partial x^2} + \frac{A}{\rho C}\Pi(x - x_i) \tag{11}$$

Now, since conditions are $a \ll \sqrt{Dt}$ (for $D_{KDP} = 6.5 \times 10^{-7} m^2.s^{-1}$ and $\tau = 1ns$, it leads to $\sqrt{Dt} \simeq 25nm$), in order to deal with simple formula allowing fast numerical calculations, the function $\Pi(x)$ is replaced by the Dirac delta function $\delta(x)$, i.e.it is imposed that the energy absorbed by a finite-size defect is in fact absorbed by a point source. The ADNS then may be seen as a heating point source. Within this framework, a good approximated solution of Eq. (11) is given by:

$$\theta_{1D}(x,t) = \frac{Aa}{2\lambda}\left\{2\left(\frac{Dt}{\pi}\right)^{1/2} \exp\left(-\frac{x^2}{4Dt}\right) - x \operatorname{erfc}\left(\frac{x}{2\sqrt{Dt}}\right)\right\} \tag{12}$$

The reliability of this approximation has been checked by performing a full numerical resolution of Eq. (8) based on a finite differences scheme. In order to illustrate the main principle of the model, Fig. 3 plots the evolution of the temperature (10) as a function of the 1D spatial coordinate in a case for which $n_{ADNS} = 15$, $A/\rho C = 10^{13} K.s^{-1}$ and $\tau = 1\ ns$. This

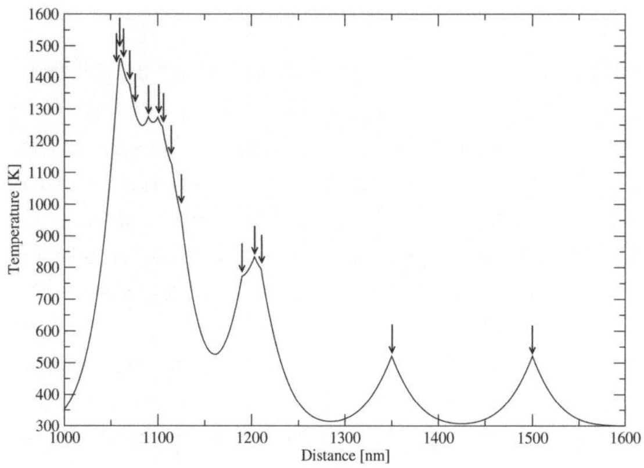

Fig. 3. Spatial temperature evolution resulting from a particular random throwing. 15 ADNS are present, $A/\rho C = 10^{13} K.s^{-1}$ and $\tau = 1\ ns$ are used. The temperature rise is enhanced when several ADNS aggregate. Defects positions are shown by vertical arrows.

graph shows a characteristic spatial behavior where it clearly appears that cooperative effect leads to a locally higher temperature.

From these calculations, it is then possible to construct a damage probability law. For a given fluence F, a number n_{draw} of ADNS distribution are generated, and it is checked whether or not each ADNS distribution induces a temperature higher than the critical temperature T_c. Let n_{dam} be the number of ADNS configurations leading to $T \geq T_c$. Then, the damage probability is simply given by $P(F) = n_{dam}(F)/n_{draw}$. In order to plot the damage probability as a function of fluence, the source term of Eq. (11) has to be evaluated. Since the defect nature is unknown, the absorbed power per unit of volume A cannot be evaluated theoretically thus leading to an empirical evaluation from experimental data. From dimensional analysis, it can be written that $A = \xi F/l\tau$ where ξ and l may be identified to a dimensionless absorption efficiency and an effective cluster size respectively. In conditions where thermal diffusion is not taken into account, the temperature rise induced by the laser pulse reads $\Delta T = \Delta\rho_E/\rho C$ where $\Delta\rho_E = \xi F/l$ and $C = 0.023 \times 900 \simeq 2\ J.K^{-1}.cm^{-3}$ are the absorbed energy per unit of volume and the heat capacity per unit volume of KDP respectively. From black body measurements (Carr et al., 2004), it turns out that the temperature rise associated with damage induced by a $3ns$ laser pulse with $F \simeq 10J.cm^{-2}$ is roughly $10000K$. That allows to estimate the unknown ratio ξ/l to about $2 \times 10^3 cm^{-1}$. In fact, thermal diffusion processes take place, and ξ/l must be higher. Therefore, we choose $\xi/l = 10^4 cm^{-1}$ and we will check in Sec. 2.2.2 that it is consistent with experimental data. Since we are working within the Rayleigh regime for which $\xi \propto l$ (defects clusters are assumed to be well smaller than $\lambda = 351nm$), it is assumed that ξ/l to remain almost unchanged when l varies. Also, the use of $A = 10^4 \times F/\tau$ as the source term empirical expression of Eq. (11) in numerical calculations is done.

In following calculations, critical temperature is fixed to $T_c = 5000\ K$ (Carr et al., 2004). The Laser-Induced Damage Threshold (LIDT) is then defined as the value of the fluence F_c such that the damage probability equals 10%. As usually in Physics, this choice indicates actually the departure from perturbative conditions. It is worth noting that taking 5% or 20% will not affect the main conclusions of this model.

2.2.2 Results

Let us begin with the 1D case. The damage probability as a function of the laser fluence is shown on Fig. 4 for $\tau = 250ps$, $1ns$, $4ns$ and $16ns$. In all cases, we choose $n_{ADNS} = 100$, $N = 10000$ and statistics is supported by 200 drawings. The general shape of curves exhibits a standard behavior for which damage probabilities increase monotonically with the fluence. Further, calculations for $\tau = 3\ ns$ show that the LIDT is close to $9\ J.cm^{-2}$ that is in a good agreement with Carr *et al.*'s experiment (Carr et al., 2004). Also, *a posteriori*, this result confirms the reliability of the evaluation of the coefficient ξ/l that has been set to $10^4 cm^{-1}$. For a given pulse duration, probability becomes non-zero when, within at least one drawing, a group of ADNS is sufficiently aggregated to form a cluster whose size and density are enough to reach locally the critical temperature.

When the fluence goes up, the critical temperature may be reached by smaller or less dense cluster. Since they are in a larger number, the probability increases itself. A probability close to one corresponds to the lowest cooperative effect, i.e. involving the smallest number of ADNS around the place where $T \geq T_c$. This number is determined counting ADNS that contribute significantly to the place x_c where $T \geq T_c$. To do so, the counting is made in the range $[x_c - 4\sqrt{D\tau}, x_c + 4\sqrt{D\tau}]$. It appears that, for a given pulse duration, the larger the fluence, the lesser the number of ADNS involved in the damage.

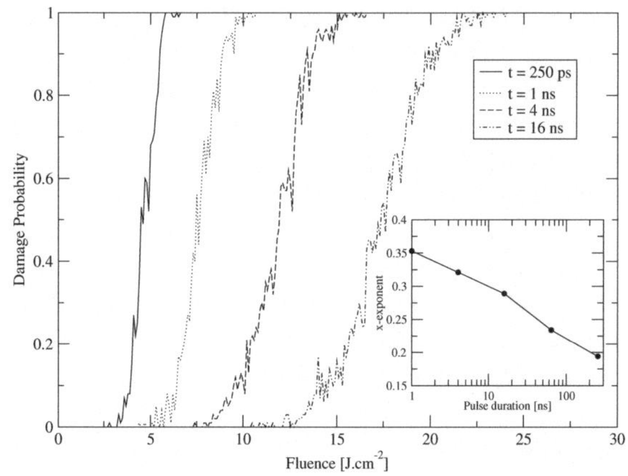

Fig. 4. Evolution of the damage probability as a function of fluence within the 1D model. Four pulse durations are considered : $\tau = 250ps, 1ns, 4ns$ and $16ns$. Parameters are $n_{ADNS} = 100$ and $N = 10000$. 200 drawings have been performed for each fluence. Sub-figure displays the scaling law exponent as a function of the pulse duration (see text).

Now, les us focus on the influence of the pulse duration on the damage probability curves and, more precisely, the scaling law linking the fluence to the pulse duration. Fig. 4 shows clearly that the LIDT is shifted towards higher fluence when τ increases. Actually, for long pulse, the thermal diffusion process is more efficient and more energy is needed to reach the critical temperature for a given ADNS configuration. For instance, the temperature rises as $\sqrt{\tau}$ (Carslaw & Jaeger, 1959) thus implying the scaling law $F_{c1}/F_{c2} = \sqrt{\tau_1/\tau_2}$. In order to establish the scaling law in our model, it is assumed that $F_{c1}/F_{c2} = (\tau_1/\tau_2)^x$ may be written. The exponent x is determined from the knowledge of F_{c1}, F_{c2}, τ_1 and τ_2. In fact, $\tau_2 = 4\tau_1$ is stated and the x exponent is evaluated as a function of τ_2 ranging from 1 ns to 16 ns. The values of F_c and x are displayed for the above-mentioned values of τ in Table 1. Note that more drawings than in Fig. 4 have been performed in order to determine F_c with a correct numerical precision. It appears that x differs from the expected $1/2$ value and takes values

	F_c $[J.cm^{-2}]$	x
$\tau = 250ps$	3.85	
$\tau = 1ns$	6.28	0.353
$\tau = 4ns$	9.80	0.321
$\tau = 16ns$	14.60	0.288

Table 1. Critical fluence and x-exponent as a function of the pulse duration

that depends on the pulse duration. For the sake of completeness, the values of x for a large range of pulses ratios is plotted on sub-figure of Fig. 4. The evolution of x can be fitted by the empirical following expression:

$$x = -\alpha \ln \tau + \beta \tag{13}$$

with $\alpha = 2.92 \times 10^{-2}$ and $\beta = 0.3592$. The fit error is close to 2% and may be due to statistical uncertainties. We have checked that a different ratio τ_2/τ_1 leads to the same general expression of x but where the coefficients α and β differ slightly. For a given ADNS spatial configuration, this behavior of x can be understood by the following consideration: for a single ADNS, since $\Delta T \propto \tau^{1/2}$, the according scaling law reads $F_c \propto \tau^{1/2}$. For a given pulse duration, since several ADNS are involved, whose effective cluster size is non negligible in comparison with the diffusion length, the temperature goes up faster than $\tau^{1/2}$ and the scaling law exponent is accordingly lower than $1/2$. Now, when τ increases, since the contribution length is proportional to $\sqrt{D\tau}$, more and more defects take part in the temperature rise. It is like if the laser pulses *sees* different target sizes with respect to its duration. It then turns out that less energy is needed than in a situation where all target components always contribute for any interaction time. Consequently, the scaling law deviates from the standard $x = 1/2$ value as the pulse duration goes up.

3. Evolutions of the thermal models and interpretation of the experiments

Sec. 2 has presented different thermal approaches capable to explain the most of usual results of laser-induced damage in KDP crystals in the nanosecond range. Despite some approximations, these models allow a good interpretation of the complex scenario of KDP laser damage but do not include any polarization influence nor the presence of two laser pulses with different wavelengths. In this section, the latter influences are thus addressed. First, we focus on the effect of polarization on the laser damage resistance of KDP. Then we will highlight the effect of multiple wavelength interacting with the crystal simultaneously and the consequences on its resistance.

3.1 The effect of laser polarization on KDP crystal resistance: influence of the precursor defects geometry

3.1.1 Experimental results at 1ω: laser damage density versus fluence and Ω

Test protocol

Generally, laser damage tests yield to the Standard (*ISO Standard No 11254-1:2000; ISO Standard No 11254-2:2001*, 2001). The so-called 1-on-1 procedure has been used here to test the KDP crystal. Specific data treatments described in (Lamaignère et al., 2009) allow to extract the bulk damage densities as a function of fluence. This part interests more particularly in the effect of the polarization on KDP crystals resistance. Then the Ω notation is introduced as the angle between the polarization of the incident laser beam and the propagation axis. In substance, $\Omega = 0°$corresponds to the case where the laser polarization $\vec{E}$ is collinear to the ordinary axis of the crystal. When $\Omega = +90°$, $\vec{E}$ is collinear to the extraordinary axis of the crystal.

Evolution of the laser damage density versus fluence

Fig. 5 presents the evolution of the laser damage density as a function of 1ω fluence. Tests have been performed for two orthogonal positions of the crystal, i.e. (a) the laser polarization along the ordinary axis (blue triangles), (b) the laser polarization along the extraordinary axis (red squares).

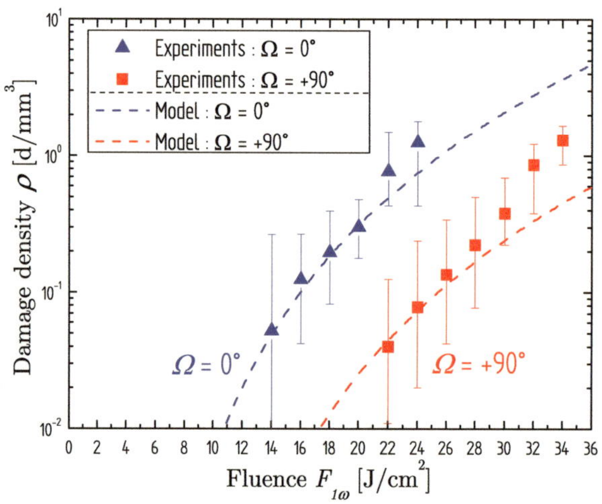

Fig. 5. Evolution of the laser damage density as a function of the 1ω fluence. Blue triangles correspond experimental results for the ordinary position ($\Omega = 0°$) and red squares to extraordinary position ($\Omega = 90°$). Modeling results are represented in dash lines, respectively for each test positions. Modeling results are discussed in Sec. 3.1.3. Damage densities evolve as a power law of the fluence.

According to Fig. 5, results clearly appear different between the two positions as we can estimate a shift of about 10 J/cm^2. This implies a factor 1.4 - 1.5 on the fluence at constant damage density.

Laser damage density versus Ω at 1ω

Studying the laser damage density as a function of the rotation angle Ω has been carried out to investigate a potential effect due to fluence. It is worth noting that rotating the crystal is equivalent to turning the beam polarization. This test has been performed for two different fluences $F_{1\omega}$ (i.e. at 19 J/cm^2 and 24.5 J/cm^2). Note that the choice of these $F_{1\omega}$ test fluences allows scanning damage probabilities in the whole range [0 ; 1]. Fig. 6 illustrates the damage density as a function of Ω. Red squares and blue triangles respectively correspond to tests carried out at $F_{1\omega} = 24.5$ J/cm^2 and at $F_{1\omega} = 19$ J/cm^2.

Fig. 6 highlights the influence of crystal orientation on LID. To address this point, one may interest in the variations of the damage density as a function of Ω. In the range [0°, 90°], apart from the points referenced by the black arrows (see explanations after), it can be observed that the laser damage density globally decreases in the range [0°, 90°]. If considering now the black arrows, these points correspond to local generation of SHG. It has been noticed that for these particular points (i.e. Ω = 40°and Ω = 60°) the laser damage density is punctually altered as an indication that SHG tends to cooperate to damage initiation.

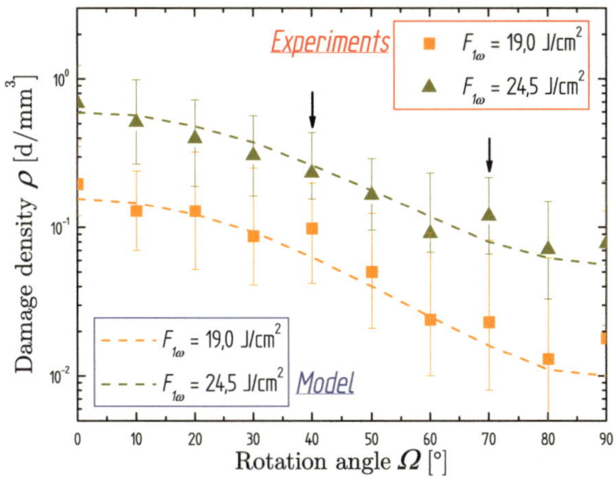

Fig. 6. Evolution of laser damage density as a function of Ω, for two different 1ω fluences. Green triangles and orange squares respectively correspond to $F_{1\omega}$ = 19 J/cm^2 and $F_{1\omega}$ = 24.5 J/cm^2. Modeling results are represented in dash lines, respectively for each fluence. Modeling results are discussed in Sec. 3.1.3.

Many assumptions may be done to explain these observations. Crystal inhomogeneity, tests repeatability, self-focusing, walk-off and SHG (Demos et al., 2003; Lamaignère et al., 2009; Zaitseva et al., 1999;?) were suspected to be possible causes for these results due to their orientation dependence they may induce. But it has been ensured that these mechanisms were not the main contributors (even existing, participating or not) to explain the influence of polarization on KDP laser damage resistance. This assessment has to be nuanced in the case of SHG. These conclusions are also in agreement with literature relative to (non)-linear effects in crystals, qualitatively considering the same range of operating conditions (ns pulses, beams of few hundreds of microns in size, intensity level below a hundred GW/cm^2, etc).
To conclude on the experimental part, it is thus necessary to find another explanation (than SHG). This is addressed in the next section which introduces defects geometry dependence and proposes a modeling of the damage density versus fluence and Ω.

3.1.2 Modeling: coupling DMT and DDscat models

DMT model

The DMT code presented in Sec. 2.1 is capable to extract damage probabilities or damage densities as a function of fluence, i.e. directly comparable to most of experimental results. To do so, DMT model considers a distribution of independent defects whose size is supposed to be few tens of nanometers that may initiate laser damage. Considering that any defect leads to a damage site, damage density is obtained from Eq. (14):

$$\rho(F) = \int_{a_-(F)}^{a_+(F)} D_{def}(a).da \tag{14}$$

Where $[a_-(F), a_+(F)]$ is the range of defects size activated at a given damage fluence level, $D_{def}(a)$ is the density size distribution of absorbers assumed to be (as expressed in (Feit & Rubenchik, 2004)):

$$D_{def}(a) = \frac{C_{def}}{a^{p+1}} \tag{15}$$

Where C_{def} and p are adjusting parameters. This distribution is consistent with the fact that the more numerous the precursors (even small and thus less absorbing), the higher the damage density. In Sec. 2.1.1, Eq. (5) has defined the critical fluence F_c necessary to reach the critical temperature T_c for which a first damage site occurs, which can be written again as (Dyan et al., 2008):

$$F_c \propto \gamma \frac{T_c - T_0}{Q_{abs}(a_c)} \tau^x \tag{16}$$

Where γ is a factor dependent of material properties, T_0 is the room temperature, τ is the pulse duration and Q_{abs} is the absorption efficiency. What is interesting in Eq. (16) is the dependence in Q_{abs}. Eq. (16) shows that to deviate F_c from a factor $\sim$1.5 (this value is observed on Fig. 5 between the two positions of the crystal), it is necessary to modify Q_{abs} by the same factor. It follows that an orientation dependence can be introduced through Q_{abs}. It is then supposed that the geometry of the precursor defect can explain the previous experimental results.

Geometries of defects

As regards KDP crystals, lattice parameters a, b and c are such as $a = b \neq c$ conditions. The defects are assumed to keep the symmetry of the crystal so that the defects are isotropic in the (ab) plane due to the multi-layered structure of KDP crystal. The principal axes of the defects match with the crystallographic axes. Assuming this, it is possible to encounter two geometries (either $b/c < 1$ or $b/c > 1$), the prolate (elongated) spheroid and the oblate (flattened) spheroid, represented on Fig. 7.

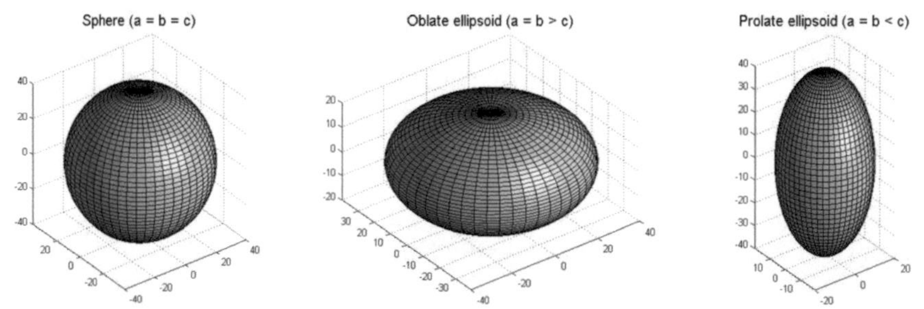

(a) (b) (c)

Fig. 7. Geometries proposed for modeling: (a) a sphere, which is the standard geometry used, (b) the oblate ellipsoid (flattened shape) and (c) the prolate ellipsoid (elongated shape). The value of the aspect ratio (between major and minor axis) is set to 2.

DDScat model

Defining an anisotropic geometry instead of a sphere implies to reconsider the set of equations (i.e. Fourier's and Maxwell's equations) to be solved. Concerning Fourier's equation, to our knowledge, it does not exist a simple analytic solution. So temperature determination remains solved for a sphere. This approximation remains valid as long as the aspect ratio does not deviate too far from unity. This approximation will be checked in the next paragraph. As regards the Maxwell's equation, it does not exist an analytic solution in the general case. It is then solved numerically by using the discrete dipole approximation. We addressed this issue by the mean of DDScat 7.0 code developed by Draine and co-workers (Draine & Flatau, 1994; 2008; n.d.). This code enables the calculations of electromagnetic scattering and absorption from targets with various geometries. Practically, orientation, indexes from the dielectric constant and shape aspect of the ellipsoid have to be determined. One would note that SHG is not taken into account in this model since it has been shown experimentally in Sec. 3.1.1 that SHG does not contribute to LID regarding the influence of orientation.

Parameters of the models
The main parameters for running the DMT code are set as follow. Parameters can be divided into two categories: those that are fixed to describe the geometry of the defects (e.g. the aspect ratio) and those we adapt to fit to the experimental damage density curve for $\Omega = 0°(T_c, n_1, n_2, C_{def}$ and $p)$. The value of each parameter is reported in Table 2 and their choice is explained below. We assume a critical damage density level at 10^{-2} d/mm^3 (it is consistent with experimental results in Fig. 5 that it would be possible to reach with a larger test area). This criterion corresponds to a critical fluence F_c = 11 J/cm^2 and a critical temperature T_c = 6,000 K. This latter value agrees qualitatively with experimental results obtained by Carr *et al.* (Carr et al., 2004), other value (e.g. around 10,000 K) would not have significantly modified the results. Complex indices have been fixed to n_1 = 0.30 and n_2 = 0.11. C_{def} and p necessary to define the defects size distribution are chosen to ensure that damage density must fit with experimentally observed probabilities (i.e. P = 0.05 to P = 1).

Critical damage density	T_c	n_1	n_2	C_{def}	p	Aspect ratio	Rotation angle Ω
10^{-2} d/mm^3	6,000 K	0.30	0.11	5.5 10^{-47}	7.5	2	0 to 90°

Table 2. Definition of the set of parameters for the DMT code at 1064 nm.

It is worth noting that these parameters have been fixed for $F_{1\omega}$ = 19 J/cm^2, and remained unchanged for the calculations at $F_{1\omega}$ = 24.5 J/cm^2 (other experimental fluence used in this study). Consequently, the dependence is given by Ω only, through the determination of Q_{abs} for each position. In other words, this model is expected to reproduce the experimental results for any fluence $F_{1\omega}$ tested on this crystal.

3.1.3 Comparison model versus experiments: $\rho_{|F=cst} = f(\Omega)$ and $\rho = f(F_{1\omega})$

Through DDScat, the curve $Q_{abs} = f(\Omega)$ can be finally extracted which is then re-injected in DMT code to reproduce the curve $\rho_{|F=cst} = f(\Omega)$, i.e. the evolution of the laser damage density as a function of Ω. Calculations have been performed turn by turn with the two geometric configurations previously presented. For each configuration, defects are considered as all oriented in the same direction comparatively to the laser beam. For the prolate geometry, Q_{abs} variations are correlated to the variations of $\rho(\Omega)$. As regards the oblate one which has also been proposed, it has been immediately leaved out since variations introduced by the Q_{abs} coefficient were anti-correlated to those obtained experimentally. Note that other geometries (not satisfying the condition $a = b$) have also been studied. Results (not presented here) show that either the variations of Q_{abs} are anti-correlated or its variations are not large enough to reproduce experimental results whatever the 1ω fluence.

On Fig. 5, green and orange dash lines respectively correspond to fluence $F_{1\omega}$ = 19 J/cm^2 and fluence $F_{1\omega}$ = 24.5 J/cm^2. As said in Sec. 3.1.1, one would note that it is important to dissociate the impact of the SHG on the damage density from the geometry effect due to the rotation angle Ω. For a modeling concern, it is thus not mandatory to include SHG as a contributor to laser damage. So, in the range [0°, 90°], one can clearly see that modeling is in good agreement with experimental results for both fluences. Moreover, given the error margins, only the points linked to SHG peaks are out of the model validity. Now considering the positions $\Omega = 0°$and $\Omega = 90°$, this modeling reproduces the experimental damage density as function of the fluence on the whole range of the scanned fluences. This approach, with the introduction of an ellipsoidal geometry, enables to reproduce the main experimental trends whereas modeling based on spherical geometry can not.

3.2 Multi-wavelength study: coupling of LID mechanisms

In the previous section, we have highlighted the effect of polarization on the laser damage resistance of KDP crystals. It has been demonstrated that precursor defects and more precisely their geometries could impact the physical mechanisms responsible for laser damage in such material. In Sec. 3.2, we are going to focus on the identification of these physical process. To do so, it is assumed that the use of multi-wavelengths damage test is an original way to discriminate the mechanisms due to their strong dependence as a function of the wavelength.

3.2.1 Experimental results in the multi-wavelengths case

In the case of mono-wavelength tests, damage density evolves as a function of the fluence following a power law. As an example, this can be represented on Fig. 8 (a) for two tests carried out at 1ω and 3ω. Mono-wavelength tests can be considered as the identity chart of the crystal. Note that the damage resistance of KDP is different as a function of the wavelength: the longer the wavelength, the better the crystal can resist to photon flux.
In the case of multi-wavelength tests, the damage density ρ is thus extracted as a function of each couple of fluences ($F_{3\omega}$,$F_{1\omega}$). Fig. 8 (b) exhibits the evolution of $\rho(F_{3\omega},F_{1\omega})$, symbolized by color contour lines.

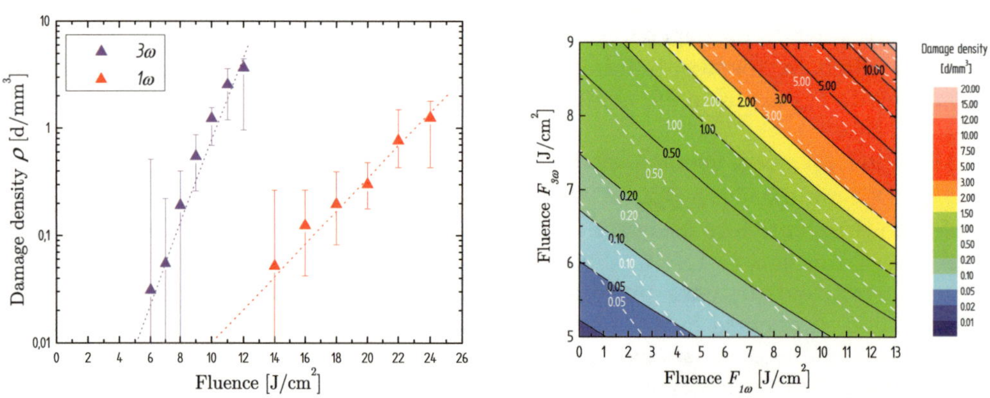

Fig. 8. (a) Damage density versus fluence in the mono-wavelength case: for 1ω and 3ω. (b) Evolution of the LID densities (expressed in dam./mm^3) as a function of $F_{3\omega}$ and $F_{1\omega}$. The color levels stand for the experimental damage densities. Modeling results are represented in white dash contour lines for $\delta = 3$. Modeling results are discussed in Sec. 3.2.3.

A particular pattern for the damage densities stands out. Indeed, each damage iso-density is associated to a combination between $F_{3\omega}$ and $F_{1\omega}$ fluences. If now we compare results obtained in the mono- and multi-wavelengths cases, it is possible to observe a coupling between the 3ω and 1ω wavelengths (Reyné et al., 2009). Indeed, we can observe that:

$$\rho = f(F_{3\omega}, F_{1\omega}) \neq \rho(F_{1\omega}) + \rho(F_{3\omega}) \quad (17)$$

On Fig. 8 (a), for $F_{3\omega}$ = 5 J/cm^2 and $F_{1\omega}$ = 10 J/cm^2, the resulting damage density (if we do the sum) would be $\rho = 2.10^{-2}$ d/mm^3. Whereas on Fig. 8 (b) for the same couple of fluences $F_{3\omega}$ and $F_{1\omega}$, the resulting damage density is $\rho = 2.10^{-1}$ d/mm^3, i.e. one order of magnitude higher. Other experimental results (DeMange et al., 2006) indicates that it is possible to predict the damage evolution of a KDP crystal when exposed to several different wavelengths from the damage tests results. It can be said that mono-wavelength results are necessary but not sufficient due to the existence of a coupling effect.
Besides, it is possible to define a 3ω-equivalent fluence F_{eq}, depending both on $F_{3\omega}$ and $F_{1\omega}$, which leads to the same damage density that would be obtained with a $F_{3\omega}$ fluence only. F_{eq} can be determined using approximately a linear relation between $F_{3\omega}$ and $F_{1\omega}$, linked by a slope s resulting in

$$F_{eq} = f(F_{3\omega}, F_{1\omega}) = sF_{1\omega} + F_{3\omega} \quad (18)$$

By evidence, s contains the main physical information about the coupling process. Thus, in the following we focus our attention on this physical quantity. For $\rho \geq 3$ dam./mm^3, a constant value for s_{exp} close to -0.3 is obtained from Fig. 8 (b).

3.2.2 Model: introducing two wavelengths

To interpret these data, the DMT$_{2\lambda}$ code has been developed on the basis of the mono-wavelength DMT model. To address the multiple wavelengths case, the DMT$_{2\lambda}$ model takes into account the presence of two wavelengths at the same time: here the 3ω and 1ω. For this configuration, a particular attention has been paid to the influence of the wavelength on the defects energy absorption.
First, a single population of defects is considered: the one that is used to fit the experimental densities at 3ω only. Secondly, it is assumed that the temperature elevation results from a combination of each wavelength absorption efficiency such as

$$Q_{abs}^{(\omega)} I_{(\omega)} = Q_{abs}^{(3\omega)}(3\omega, 1\omega) I_{3\omega} + Q_{abs}^{(1\omega)}(3\omega, 1\omega) I_{1\omega} \quad (19)$$

Where $Q_{abs}^{(3\omega)}(3\omega, 1\omega)$ and $Q_{abs}^{(1\omega)}(3\omega, 1\omega)$ are the absorption efficiencies at 3ω and 1ω. It is noteworthy that *a priori* each absorption efficiency depends on the two wavelengths since both participate into the plasma production. Thirdly, calculations are performed under conditions where the Rayleigh criterion ($a \leq 100$ nm) is satisfied: under this condition, an error less than 20 % is observed when the approximate expression of $Q_{abs}^{(\omega)}$ is used. So, $Q_{abs}^{(3\omega)}(3\omega, 1\omega)$ and $Q_{abs}^{(1\omega)}(3\omega, 1\omega)$ contain the main information about the physical mechanisms implied in LID.
According to a Drude model, $Q_{abs}^{(\omega)} \propto \epsilon_2 \propto n_e$ where n_e is mainly produced by multiphoton ionization (MPI), ϵ_2 representing the imaginary part of the dielectric function (Dyan et al., 2008). Indeed, electronic avalanche is assumed to be negligible (Dyan et al., 2008) at first glance. It follows that $n_e \propto F_{(\omega)}^{\delta}$ where δ is the multiphotonic order (Agostini & Petite, 88). For KDP crystals, at 3ω three photons at 3.54 eV are necessary for valence electrons to break through the 7.8 eV band gap (Carr et al., 2003) whereas at 1ω seven photons at 1.18 eV would

be required, lowering drastically the absorption cross-section. Then, it is assumed that $n_e = n_e^{(3\omega)} + n_e^{(1\omega)}$, where $n_e^{(3\omega)}$ and $n_e^{(1\omega)}$ are the electron densities produced by the 3ω and 1ω pulses. Here the interference between both wavelengths are neglected. This assumption is reliable since the conditions permit to consider that the promotion of valence electrons to the Conduction Band (CB) is mainly driven by the 3ω pulse ($F_{3\omega} \geq 5\,\mathrm{J/cm^2}$). As a consequence, we consider that the 3ω is the predominant wavelength to promote electrons in the CB.
So for the 3ω it results that $Q_{abs}^{(3\omega)}(3\omega, 1\omega) = Q_{abs}^{(3\omega)}(3\omega)$ while for the 1ω, since $Q_{abs}^{(1\omega)} \propto n_e$ in the Rayleigh regime, the 1ω-energy absorption coefficient can be written as

$$Q_{abs}^{(1\omega)}(3\omega, 1\omega) = \beta F_{3\omega}^{\delta} + Q_{abs}^{(1\omega)} \tag{20}$$

β is a parameter which is adjusted to obtain the best agreement with the experimental data. It is noteworthy that β has no influence on the slopes s predicted by the model. Finally, the $DMT_{2\lambda}$ model is able to predict the damage densities $\rho(F_{3\omega}, F_{1\omega})$ from which the slope s is extracted.

3.2.3 Modeling results

Fig. 9 represents the evolution of the modeling slopes s as a function of δ for the damage density $\rho = 5\,\mathrm{d/mm^3}$. One can see that the intersection between s_{exp} and the modeling slopes is obtained for $\delta \simeq 3$. These calculations have also been performed for various iso-densities ranging from 2 to 15 d./mm^3.

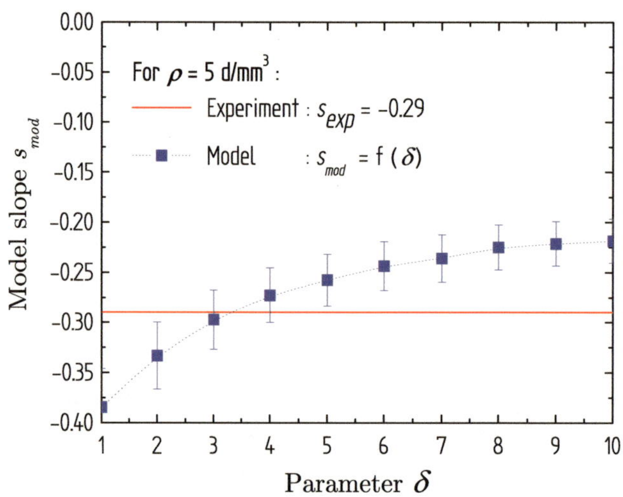

Fig. 9. Evolution of the modeling slopes s as a function of δ for the damage iso-density $\rho = 5$ d/mm^3. For this density level, the experimental slope is $s_{exp} \simeq -0.3$.

As a consequence, observations result in Fig. 10 which shows that $\delta \simeq 3$ for $\rho \geq 3\,\mathrm{d/mm^3}$. Actually, it is most likely that $\delta = 3$ considering errors on the experimental fluences, uncertainties on the linear fit to obtain s_{exp}, and owing to the band gap value. Therefore, the comparison between this experiment and the model indicates that the free electron density leading to damage is produced by a three-photon absorption mechanism. It is noteworthy

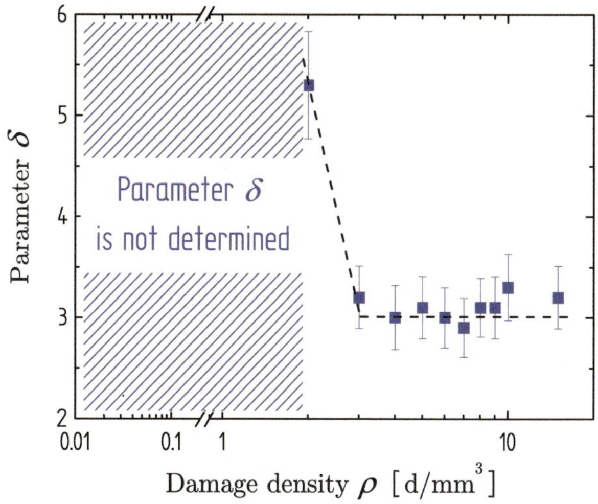

Fig. 10. Evolution of the best parameter δ which fits the experimental slope s_{exp}, as a function of ρ. Given a damage density, the error bars are obtained from the standard deviation observed between the minimum and maximum slopes.

that this absorption is assisted by defects that induce intermediate states in the band gap (Carr et al., 2003).
Finally, as reported in Fig. 8 (b) the trends given by this model (plotted in white dashes) are in good agreement with the experimental results for $\rho \geq 3$ d/mm^3.
However, this model cannot reproduce the experimental trends on the whole range of fluences and particularly fails for the lowest damage densities. To explain the observed discrepancy, two explanations based on the defects size are proposed. First, it has been suggested that the defects size may impact on the laser damage mechanisms. For the lowest densities, the size distribution (Feit & Rubenchik, 2004) used to calculate the damage densities implies larger defects (i.e. $a \geq 100$ nm). Thus, it oversteps the limits of the Rayleigh criterion: indeed, an error on Q_{abs} larger than several tens of percents is observed when $a \geq 100$ nm.
Secondly, the contribution of larger size defects which is responsible for the lowest densities may also be consistent with an electronic avalanche competing with the MPI dominant regime. Indeed, for a given density n_e produced by MPI, since avalanche occurs provided that it exists at least one free electron in the defect volume (Noack & Vogel, 1999), the largest defects are favorable to impact ionization. Once engaged, avalanche enables an exponential growth of n_e (which is assumed to be produced by the $F_{3\omega}$ fluence essentially). Mathematically, the development of this exponential leads to high exponents of the fluence which is then consistent with $\delta > 5$ or more. In Fig. 10, it corresponds to the hashed region where the modeling slopes do not intercept the experimental ones.
In other respects, the nature of the precursor defects has partially been addressed in the mono-wavelength configuration (DeMange et al., 2008; Feit & Rubenchik, 2004; Reyné et al., 2009). In the DMT$_{2\lambda}$ model, we consider a single distribution of defects, corresponding to a population of defects both sensitive at 3ω and 1ω. Calculations with two distinct distributions have also been performed. It comes out that no significant modification is observed between the results obtained with only one distribution: e.g. the damage densities pattern nearly

remains unchanged and the slopes s as well. Also these observations do not dismiss that two populations of defects may exist in KDP (DeMange et al., 2008).

4. Conclusion

The laser-induced damage of optical components used in megajoule-class lasers is still under investigation. Progress in the laser damage resistance of optical components has been achieved thanks to a better understanding of damage mechanisms. The models proposed in this study mainly deal with thermal approaches to describe the occurrence of damage sites in the bulk of KDP crystals. Despite the difficulty to model the whole scenario leading to damage initiation, these models account for the main trends of KDP laser damage in the nanosecond regime.

Based on these thermal approaches, direct comparisons between models and experiments have been proposed and allow: *(i)* to obtain some main information on precursor defects and their link to the physical mechanisms involved in laser damage and *(ii)* to improve our knowledge in LID mechanisms on powerful laser facilities.

5. References

Adams, J., Weiland, T., Stanley, J., Sell, W., Luthi, R., Vickers, J., Carr, C., Feit, M., Rubenchik, A., Spaeth, M. & Hackel, R. (2005). Pulse length dependence of laser conditioning and bulk damage in KD_2PO_4, *Proc. SPIE 5647*, p. 265.

Agostini, P. & Petite, G. (1988). Photoelectric effect under strong irradiation, *Contemporary Physics* 29: 55–77.

Bliss, E. (1971). Pulse duration dependence of laser damage mechanism, *Opto-electronics* 3: 99.

Burnham, A., Runkel, M., Feit, M., Rubenchik, A., Floyd, R., Land, T., Siekhaus, W. & Hawley-Fedder, R. (2003). Laser-induced damage in deuterated potassium dihydrogen phosphate, *Appl. Opt.* 42, 27: 5483–5495.

Carr, C., Radousky, H. & Demos, S. (2003). Wavelength dependence of laser-induced damage: determining the damage initiation mechanisms, *Phys. Rev. Lett.* 91, 12: 127402.

Carr, C., Radousky, H., Rubenchik, A., Feit, M. & Demos, S. (2004). Localized dynamics during laser-induced damage in optical materials, *Phys. Rev. Lett.* 92, 8: 087401.

Carslaw, H. & Jaeger, J. (1959). *Conduction of heat in solids*, Oxford Science Publications (2nd ed.).

Van de Hulst, H. C. (1981). *Light scattering by small particles*, Dover publications Inc., New York.

DeMange, P., Negres, R. & Rubenchick, A. (2006). Understanding and predicting the damage performance of $K_2H_{(2-x)}D_xPO_4$ crystal under simultaneous exposure to 532- and 355-nm pulses, *Appl. Phys. Lett.* 89: 181922.

DeMange, P., Negres, R., Rubenchik, A., Radousky, H., Feit, M. & Demos, S. (2008). The energy coupling efficiency of multiwavelenght laser pulses to damage initiating defects in deuterated KH_2PO_4 nonlinear crystals, *J. Appl. Phys.* 103: 083122.

Demos, S., DeMange, P., Negres, R. & Feit, M. (2010). Investigation of the electronic and physical properties of defect structures responsible for laser-induced damage in DKDP crystal, *Opt. Express* 18, 12: 13788–13804.

Demos, S., Staggs, M. & Radousky, H. (2003). Bulk defect formations in KH_2PO_4 crystals investigated using fluorescence microscopy, *Phys. Rev. B* 67: 224102.

Draine, B. & Flatau, P. (1994). Discrete-dipole approximation for scattering calculations, *J. Opt. Soc. Am. B* 11: 1491–1499.

Draine, B. & Flatau, P. (2008). The discrete dipole approximation for periodic targets: theory and tests, *J. Opt. Soc. Am. A* 25: 2693–2703.

Draine, B. & Flatau, P. (n.d.). *User guide for the discrete dipole approximation code DDScat 7.0.*

Duchateau, G. (2009). Simple models for laser-induced damage and conditioning of potassium dihydrogen phosphate crystals by nanosecond pulses, *Opt. Express* 17, 13: 10434–10456.

Duchateau, G. & Dyan, A. (2007). Coupling statistics and heat transfer to study laser-induced crystal damage by nanosecond pulses, *Opt. Express* 18, 8: 4557–4576.

Dyan, A., Enguehard, F., Lallich, S., Piombini, H. & Duchateau, G. (2008). Scaling laws in laser-induced KDP crystal damage by nanosecond pulses at 3ω, *J. Opt. Soc. Am. B* 25, 6: 1087–1095.

Feit, M. & Rubenchik, A. (2004). Implications of nanoabsorber initiators for damage probability curves and pulselength scaling and laser conditioning, *Proc. SPIE 5273*, pp. 527374–82.

Gallais, L., Natoli, J. & Amra, C. (2002). Statistical study of single and multiple pulse laser-induced damage in glasses, *Opt. Express* 10: 1465–1474.

Gallais, L., Voarino, P. & Amra, C. (2004). Optical measurement of size and complex index of laser-damage precursors: the inverse problem, *J. Opt. Soc. Am. B* 21: 1073–1080.

Hopper, R. & Uhlmann, D. (1970). Mechanism of inclusion damage in laser glass, *J. Appl. Phys.* 41, 10: 4023–4037.

Hummel, R. (2001). *Electronic properties of materials*, Springer and Third Edition.

ISO Standard No 11254-1:2000; ISO Standard No 11254-2:2001 (2001).

Lamaignère, L., Donval, T., Loiseau, M., Poncetta, J., Razé, G., Meslin, C., Bertussi, B. & Bercegol, H. (2009). Accurate measurements of laser-induced bulk damage density, *Meas. Sci. Technol.* 20: 095701.

Liu, C., Kioussis, N., Demos, S. & Radousky, H. (2003). Electron- or hole-assisted reactions of H defects in hydrogen-bonded KDP, *Phys. Rev. Lett.* 91, 1: 015505.

Liu, C., Zhang, Q., Kioussis, N., Demos, S. & Radousky, H. (2003). Electronic structure calculations of intrinsic and extrinsic hydrogen point defects in KH_2PO_4, *Phys. Rev. B* 68, 22: 224107.

Natoli, J., Gallais, L., Akhouayri, H. & Amra, C. (2002). Laser-induced damage of materials in bulk and thin film and and liquid forms, *App Opt.* 41, 16: 3156–3166.

Noack, J. & Vogel, A. (1999). Laser-induced plasma formation in water at nanosecond to femtosecond time scales: calculation of thresholds, absorption coefficients, and energy density, *IEEE J. Quant. Electron.* 35: 1156–1167.

Numerical Recipies (n.d.).

O'Connell, R. (1992). Onset threshold analysis of defect-driven surface and bulk laser damage, *Appl. Optics* 31, 21: 4143.

Picard, R., Milam, D. & Bradbury, R. (1977). Statistical analysis of defect-caused laser damage in thin films, *Appl. Opt.* 16: 1563–1571.

Pommiès, M., Damiani, D., Bertussi, B., Piombini, H., Mathis, H., Capoulade, J. & Natoli, J. (2006). Detection and characterization of absorption heterogeneities in KH_2PO_4 crystals, *Opt. Comm.* 267: 154–161.

Porteus, J. & Seitel, S. (1984). Absolute onset of optical surface damage using distributed defect ensembles, *Appl. Optics* 23, 21: 3796–3805.

Reyné, S., Duchateau, G., Natoli, J.-Y. & Lamaignère, L. (2009). Laser-induced damage of KDP crystals by 1ω nanosecond pulses: influence of crystal orientation, *Opt. Express* 17, 24: 21652–21665.

Reyné, S., Duchateau, G., Natoli, J.-Y. & Lamaignère, L. (2010). Pump-pump experiment in KH_2PO_4 crystals: Coupling two different wavelengths to identify the laser-induced damage mechanisms in the nanosecond regime, *Appl. Phys. Lett.* 96: 121102–121104.

Reyné, S., Loiseau, M., Duchateau, G., Natoli, J.-Y. & Lamaignère, L. (2009). Towards a better understanding of multi-wavelength effects on KDP crystals, *Proc. SPIE 7361*, p. 73610Z.

Sparks, M., Mills, D., Warren, R., Holstein, T., Maradudin, A., Sham, L., Loh, E., Jr. & King, D. (1981). Theory of electron-avalanche breakdown in solids, *Phys. Rev. B* 24, 6: 3519–3536.

Stuart, B., Feit, M., Herman, S., Rubenchik, A., Shore, B. & Perry, M. (1996). Nanosecond-to-femtosecond laser-induced breakdown in dielectrics, *Phys. Rev. B* 53, 4: 1749.

Trenholme, J., Feit, M. & Rubenchik, A. (2006). Size-selection initiation model extended to include shape and random factors, *Proc. SPIE 5991*, p. 59910X.

Walker, T., Guenther, A. & Nielsen, P. (1981). Pulsed laser-induced damage to thin film optical coatings - part 2: Theory, *IEEE J. Quantum Electron.* QE-17, 10: 2053.

Wang, K., Fang, C., Zhang, J., Liu, C., Boughton, R., Wang, S. & Zhao, X. (2005). First-principles study of interstitial oxygen in potassium dihydrogen phosphate crystals, *Phys. Rev. B* 72: 134110.

Wood, R. (2003). *Laser-induced damage of optical materials*, Institute Of Physics publishing series in optics ans optoelectronics, Bristol and Philadelphia.

Zaitseva, N., Atherton, J., Rozsa, R., Carman, L., Smolsky, I., Runkel, M., Ryon, R. & James, L. (1999). Design and benefits of continuous filtration in rapid growth of large KDP and DKDP crystals, *J. Crystal Growth* 97, 4: 911–920.

Zaitseva, N., Carman, L., Smolsky, I., Torres, R. & Yan, M. (1999). The effect of impurities and supersaturation on the rapid growth of KDP crystals, *J. Crystal Growth* 204, 4: 512.

11

Ultrafast Heating Characteristics in Multi-Layer Metal Film Assembly Under Femtosecond Laser Pulses Irradiation

Feng Chen, Guangqing Du, Qing Yang, Jinhai Si and Hun Hou
Xi'an Jiaotong University, School of Electronics and Information Engineering
China

1. Introduction

In recent years, ultrashort pulsed laser micromachining of multi-layer metal film assembly had attracted great attention because the multi-layer configuration can be well applied for satisfaction of thermal, optical and electronic requirements in development of MEMs, photoelectric equipments and biochips (Liu, 2007). Generally, the thermal properties for metals are physically originated from the collision mechanisms for electron-electron and electron-phonon in the metal targets. For the multi-layer metal film assembly, the thermal properties, such as the electron-phonon coupling strength can actually vary significantly for different layers of the assembly, so the heating of muti-layer film assembly would take on various characteristics for different padding layer configurations. In this article, the ultrafast heating characteristics in multi-layer metal film assemblies irradiated by femtosecond laser pulse were investigated by numerical simulations. The effect of different padding layer configurations on the ultrafast thermalization characteristics for the multi-layer metal film assemblies are well discussed. The ultrafast heat transfer processes in the layered metal film systems after the femtosecond pulse excitation are described based on the two temperature model (TTM), in which the electron and phonon is considered at two different temperatures, and heat transfer is mainly due to the hot electron diffusion among the sub-electron system and the electron energy transfer to the local lattice characterized by the electron-phonon coupling strength. The thermal properties for the respective metal film layers and the optical surface reflectivity are all defined as temperature dependent parameters in order to well explore the ultrafast heating characrastics of the multi-layer metal assemblies. The coupling two temperature equations are calculated by the Finite Element Method (FEM) with respect to temperature dependent thermal and optical properties. The ultrafast two-dimension (2-D) temperature field evolutions for electron and phonon subsystems in the multi-layer metal film assemblies are obtained, which show that the electron and phonon temperature field distributions can be largely effected by adjusting padding layer configurations. The physical origins for the discrepant temperature field distributions in multi-layer film assemblies are analyzed in details. It indicates that electron-phonon coupling strength and phonon thermal capacity play key roles in determining the temperature field distributions of the multi-layer film assembly.

2. Modelling and methods

2.1 Mathematical model

For pulsed laser ablation of metals, the ultrafast heating mechanisms perform great disparity for femtosecond and nanosecond pulse duration. In fact, the electron and phonon thermally relax in harmony for the nanosecond laser ablation, however, which are out of equilibrium severely for femtosecond laser ablation due to the femtosecond pulse duration is quite shorter compared to the electron–phonon relaxation time. So, it is expected that the basic theory for describing the femtosecond laser pulses interactions with metal is quite different from that of nanosecond laser pulses. In general, for femtosecond laser pulses, the heating involves high-rate heat flow from electrons to lattices in the picosecond domains. The ultrafast heating processes for femtosecond pulse interaction with metals are mainly consist two steps: the first stage is the absorption of laser energy through photon–electron coupling within the femtosecond pulse duration, which takes a few femtoseconds for electrons to reestablish the Fermi distribution meanwhile the metal lattice keep undisturbed. The second stage is the energy distribution to the lattice through electron–phonon coupling, typically on the order of tens of picoseconds until the electron and phonon reaches the thermal equilibrium. The different heating processes for electron and phonon were first evaluated theoretically in 1957 (Kaganov et al.,1957). Later, Anisimov et al. proposed a Parabolic Two Temperature Model (PTTM), in which the electron and phonon temperatures can be well characterized (Anisimov et al.,1974). By removing the assumptions that regard instantaneous laser energy deposition and diffusion, a Hyperbolic Two Temperature Model (HTTM) based on the Boltzmann transport equation was rigorously derived by Qiu (Qiu et al.,1993). Further, Chen and Beraun extended the conventional hyperbolic two temperature model and educed a more general version of the Dual-Hyperbolic Two Temperature Model (DHTTM), in which the electron and phonon thermal flux are all taken into account (Chen et al., 2001). The DHTTM has been well applied in the investigation of ultrashort laser pulse interaction with materials. The mathematical models for describing the DHTTM can be represented in the following coupling partial differential equations:

$$C_e \frac{\partial T_e}{\partial t} = -\nabla q_e - G(T_e - T_p) + Q \tag{1}$$

$$C_p \frac{\partial T_p}{\partial t} = -\nabla q_p + G(T_e - T_p) \tag{2}$$

where subscripts e and p stands for electron and phonon, respectively. T denotes temperature, C the heat capacity, q the heat flux, G the electron-phonon coupling strength, and Q is the laser heat source. The first equation describes the laser energy absorption by electron sub-system, electrons thermal diffusion and electrons heat coupling into localized phonons. The second equation is for the phonon heating due to coupling with electron sub-system. For metal targets, the heat conductivity in phonon subsystem is small compared to that for the electrons so that the phonon heat flux q_p in Eq.(2) can be usually neglected. The heat flux terms in Eq.(1) with respect to the hyperbolic effect can be written as

$$q_e = -(k_e \nabla T_e + \tau_e \, \partial q_e / \partial t) \tag{3}$$

here k_e and τ_e denotes the electron heat conductivity and the electron thermal relaxation time. Further, letting the electron thermal relaxation time τ_e be zero. Consequently the DHTTM can be reduced to the Parabolic Two Temperature Model (PTTM), which had been widely used for investigation of the ultrashort laser pulse interaction with metal films.
For the multi-layered metal film assembly, the PTTM can be modified from Eqs.(1)-(3) and written as the following form for the respective layers:

$$C_e^{(i)}\frac{\partial T_e^{(i)}}{\partial t}=-\nabla q_e^{(i)}-G(T_e^{(i)}-T_p^{(i)})+Q^{(1)} \tag{4}$$

$$C_p^{(i)}\frac{\partial T_p^{(i)}}{\partial t}=G^{(i)}\left(T_e^{(i)}-T_p^{(i)}\right) \tag{5}$$

where $q_e^{(i)}$ is the heat flux vector, described as $-k_e^{(i)}\nabla T_e^{(i)}$. The superscript i relates to the layer number in the multi-layer assembly. The laser heat source term is usually considered as Gaussian shapes in time and space, which can be written as

$$Q^{(1)}=S(x,y)\cdot T(t) \tag{6}$$

where

$$S(x,y)=\sqrt{\frac{4\ln 2}{\pi}}\frac{1-R}{t_p(\delta+\delta_b)}F\times\exp\left[-\frac{x}{\delta+\delta_b}-\left(\frac{y-y_0}{y_s}\right)^2\right] \tag{7}$$

$$T(t)=\exp\left(-4\ln 2\left(\frac{t-2t_p}{t_p}\right)^2\right) \tag{8}$$

here, R is the film surface reflectivity, t_p is the FWHM (full width at half maximum) pulse duration, $\delta+\delta_b$ is defined as the effective laser penetration depth with δ and δ_b denoting the optical penetration depth and electron ballistic range, respectively. F is the laser fluence. y_0 is the coordinate of central spot of light front at the plane of incidence and y_s is the profile parameter. When a laser pulse is incident on metal surface, the laser energy is first absorbed by the free electrons within optical skin depth. Then, the excited electrons is further heated by two different processes, which includes the thermal diffusion due to electron collisions and the ballistic motion of excited electrons. So, we use the effective laser penetration depth in order to account for the effect of ballistic motion of the excited electrons that make laser energy penetrating into deeper bulk of a material.

2.2 Initial and boundary conditions

The calculation starts at time t=0. The electrons and phonons for the respective layers in the multi-layer film systems are assumed to be room temperature at 300 K before laser pulse irradiation. Thus, the initial conditions for the multi-layer metal film assembly are:

$$T_e^{(1)}(t=0)=T_e^{(2)}(t=0)=\cdots=T_e^{(i)}(t=0)=300\text{K} \tag{9}$$

$$T_p^{(1)}(t=0)=T_p^{(2)}(t=0)=\cdots=T_p^{(i)}(t=0)=300\text{K} \tag{10}$$

For the exterior boundaries of the multi-layer assembly, it is reasonable to assume that heat losses from the metal film to the surrounding as well as to the front surface are neglected during the femtosecond-to-picosecond time period. The perfect thermal insulation condition between bottom layer of assembly with the substrate can also be established at rear surface of the multi-layer film assembly. Therefore, the exterior boundary conditions can be written as:

$$\frac{\partial T_e}{\partial n}\Big|_\Omega=\frac{\partial T_p}{\partial n}\Big|_\Omega=0 \tag{11}$$

here, Ω represents the four borderlines of the 2-D metal film assembly.

For the interior interfaces of the multi-layer systems, we assume the perfect thermal contacts for electron subsystem between the respective layers herein, leading to

$$T_e^{(1)}\Big|_\Gamma=T_e^{(2)}\Big|_\Gamma=\cdots=T_e^{(i)}\Big|_\Gamma \tag{12}$$

$$q_e^{(1)}\Big|_\Gamma=q_e^{(2)}\Big|_\Gamma=\cdots q_e^{(i)}\Big|_\Gamma \tag{13}$$

where, Γ represents the interior interfaces of the multi-layer assembly. Additionally, the phonon thermal transfer at layer interface is considered to be impracticable due to the small phonon heat conductivity during the picosecond timescale. So, the phonon temperature and thermal flux are all treated as discontinuous physical quantities at the layer interfaces of the multi-layer film assemblies in current simulations.

2.3 Temperature dependent thermal properties

Most of the previous researches considered the thermal parameters for gold film as constant values for simplification of the calculations and saving the computer time. Herein we treat all the thermal properties including thermal capacity, thermal conductivity and the electron-phonon coupling strength as temperature dependent parameters in order to well explore the heating characteristics in the metal films assembly under ultrashort laser pulse irradiation. According to the Sommerfeld theory, electron thermal conductivity at low temperature is given in paper (Christensen et al., 2007)

$$k_e=\frac{1}{3}v_F^2C_e^{'}T_e\left(\frac{1}{\tau_{ee}}+\frac{1}{\tau_{ep}}\right) \tag{14}$$

where $1/\tau_{ee}=AT_e^2$ and $1/\tau_{ep}=BT_p$ is temperature dependent electron-electron and the electron-phonon scattering rates, with which the temperature dependent thermal conductivity can be educed. We assume that the electrons and phonons are isotropic across the target so that the isotropic thermal properties for the targets can be applied in the current simulations. In the regime of high electron temperature, the electron-electron interactions must be taken into account, leading to

$$k_{e1}=B_ek_{e,0}\frac{T_e}{A_eT_e^2+B_pT_p} \tag{15}$$

However, when the electron temperature is low enough that electron-electron interactions compared to electron-phonon collisions can be neglected, the electron thermal conductivity is written as

$$k_{e2} = k_{e,0} T_e / T_p \tag{16}$$

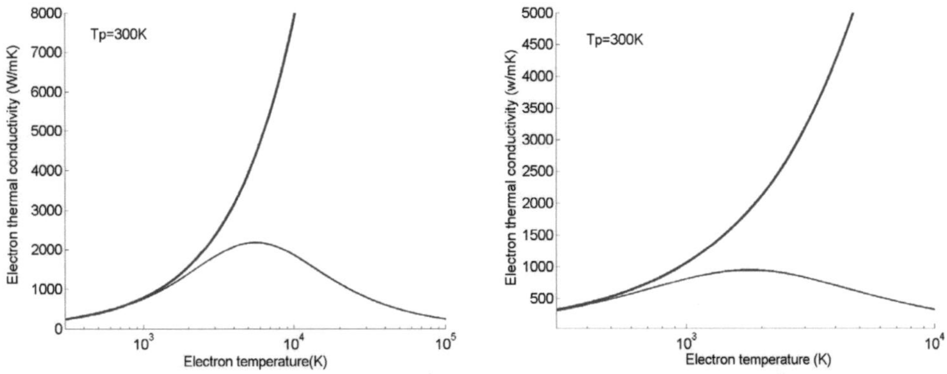

(a) (b)

Fig. 1. The electron thermal conductivity as a function of electron temperature for the targets of Au (a) and Al (b), the thick line stands for k_{e2}, the thin line stands for k_{e1}

The electron thermal conductivity as a function of electron temperature for the targets of Au and Al are shown in Fig.1. We can see that the electron thermal conductivity when ignoring the term of electron-electron collisions increases dramatically with increasing the electron temperature. However, as the electron-electron collisions term is taken into account, the thermal conductivity curve appears a peak approximately at the temperature of 5500 K for Au, and 1900 K for Al, and the peak thermal conductivity for Au is twice larger than for Al. It indicates that the effect of electron-electron collisions on the electron thermal conductivity is significant in the range of high electron temperature, but not exhibits large difference in low electron temperature regime.

The temperature dependent electron heat capacity is taken to be proportional to the electron temperature with a coefficient B_e (Kanavin et al.,1998):

$$C_e(T_e) = B_e T_e \tag{17}$$

An analytical expression for the electron-phonon coupling strength was proposed by Chen et. al., which can be represented as follows (Chen et al., 2006):

$$G(T_e, T_p) = G_0 \left[\frac{A_e}{B_p}(T_e + T_p) + 1 \right] \tag{18}$$

Fig.2 shows the electron-phonon coupling strength as a function of electron temperature for the targets of Au and Al. We fix the phonon temperature at room temperature of 300K. It is shown that the electron-phonon coupling strength increases obviously with increasing the electron temperature. It indicates that more electron energy can be transferred to localized phonon due to the increase of electron-phonon coupling strength as a result of the rise of electron temperature. Meanwhile, the excited phonons sub-system also help strengthen the electron-phonon coupling process, leading to the further promotion of phonon temperature. It can be seen that the electron-phonon coupling strength is one order of magnitude larger for Al than Au in the temperature range of 300 K to 100000 K, which would result in the distinct phonon heating processes in the multi-layer metal film assembly for different layers.

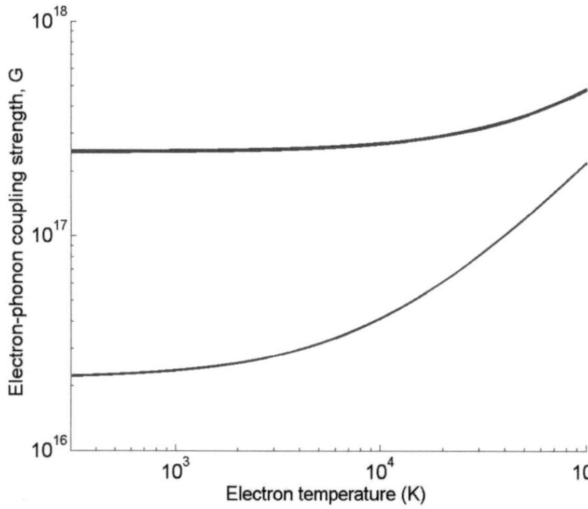

Fig. 2. The electron-phonon coupling strength as functions of electron temperature for Au and Al. The thick line stands for Al, the thin line stands for Au. The unit of G is J m^{-3} s^{-1} K^{-1}

2.4 Temperature dependent optical parameters

For femtosecond pulse heating of the metal film assembly, the electron sub-system for the surface layer can be initially heated to several thousand Kelvin during the pulse duration. So the effect of electron temperature on the optical properties such as the surface reflectivity should be carefully taken into account for accurately predicting the ultrafast electron and phonon heating processes in multi-layer metal film assemblies. The laser energy reflection from metal surface is physically originated to the particles collisions mechanisms including electron-electron and electron-phonon collisions in the target materials. For ultra-high non-equilibrium heating of the electron and phonon sub-systems under the femtosecond pulse excitation, the total scattering rates can be written as $v_m = A_e T^2 + B_b T_p$, in which the electron and phonon temperatures can jointly contribute to the total scattering rates. The connection between the metal surface reflectivity and the total scattering rate usually relates to the well-known Drude absorption model. After some derivations from Drude model, the reflective index n and absorptive coefficient k can be immediately written as:

$$n^2 = \frac{1}{2}\left[\left(1-\frac{\omega_p^2}{\omega^2+v_m^2}\right)^2 + \left(\frac{v_m}{\omega}\frac{\omega_p^2}{\omega^2+v_m^2}\right)^2\right]^{\frac{1}{2}} + \frac{1}{2}\left(1-\frac{\omega_p^2}{\omega^2+v_m^2}\right) \tag{19}$$

$$k^2 = \frac{1}{2}\left[\left(1-\frac{\omega_p^2}{\omega^2+v_m^2}\right)^2+\left(\frac{v_m}{\omega}\frac{\omega_p^2}{\omega^2+v_m^2}\right)^2\right]^{\frac{1}{2}}-\frac{1}{2}\left(1-\frac{\omega_p^2}{\omega^2+v_m^2}\right) \tag{20}$$

where ω_p denotes the plasma frequency of the free electron sub-system, expressed as $\sqrt{e^2 n/(\varepsilon_0 m_e^*)}$, ω is the angular frequency of the laser field. Applying the Fresnel law at the surface, we can get the surface reflectivity coefficient:

$$R(T_e,T_p,\omega) = \frac{(n-1)^2+k^2}{(n+1)^2+k^2} \tag{21}$$

3. Results and discussion

Fig.3 shows the temporal evolution of electron and phonon temperature fields in the two layer Au/Ag film assembly. The laser is incident from left, the parameters for the laser pulse and the assembly are listed as follows: laser fluence F=0.1 J/cm^2, pulse duration t_p=65 fs, laser wavelength 800 nm, the thickness of padding layers $T_{Au} = T_{Ag} = 100\text{nm}$. Herein, the electron ballistic effect is included in the simulations. At time of 500 fs, the electron subsystem for the film assembly is dramatically heated, the maximal electron temperature at the front and rear surfaces of the two layer Au/Ag film assembly get 2955K and 1150K, respectively. However, the phonon subsystem for the bottom Ag film layer of the assembly is slightly heated at 500 fs, the phonon temperature field is mostly centralized at the first layer, approximately 20 nm under the Au film surface, the maximal phonon temperatures at front surface and the layer interface gets to 317K and 305K, respectively. At time of 1 ps, the electron temperature field penetrates into deeper region of the assembly, indicating that the electron heat conduction amongst electron subsystem is playing an important role during this period. The maximal electron temperature at the front surface drops down to 2100K and rises to 1500K at the rear surface. Simultaneously, the phonon temperature at the respective Au and Ag layers begins to rise, the maximal phonon temperatures at the front and the rear surfaces of the assembly climbs to 328 K and 313 K at 1ps. The bottom Ag layer phonon thermalization can actually be attributed to the electron thermal transfer from the first layer Au film to the Ag electron subsystem, and the following process in which the overheated electron coupling its energy to localized Ag film phonon subsystem through electron-phonon coupling. At time of 4ps, the electron temperature field is significantly weakened across the Au/Ag assembly and the phonon temperature fields are mostly distributed near the front surfaces of the respective Au and Ag layers at this time, the maximal phonon temperature at the front surface of the Au film and the Ag layer is 353.3 K and 345 K, respectively. With time, the electron and phonon subsystems ultimately would get the thermal equilibrium state and bears the united temperature distribution across the assembly. It should be emphasized that the temperature field distributions for electrons and phonons are quite different at the middle interface layer which is actually originated from the physical fact that phonon thermal flux can be ignored and electron presents excellent thermal conduction at the middle interface of the assembly during the picosecond time period.

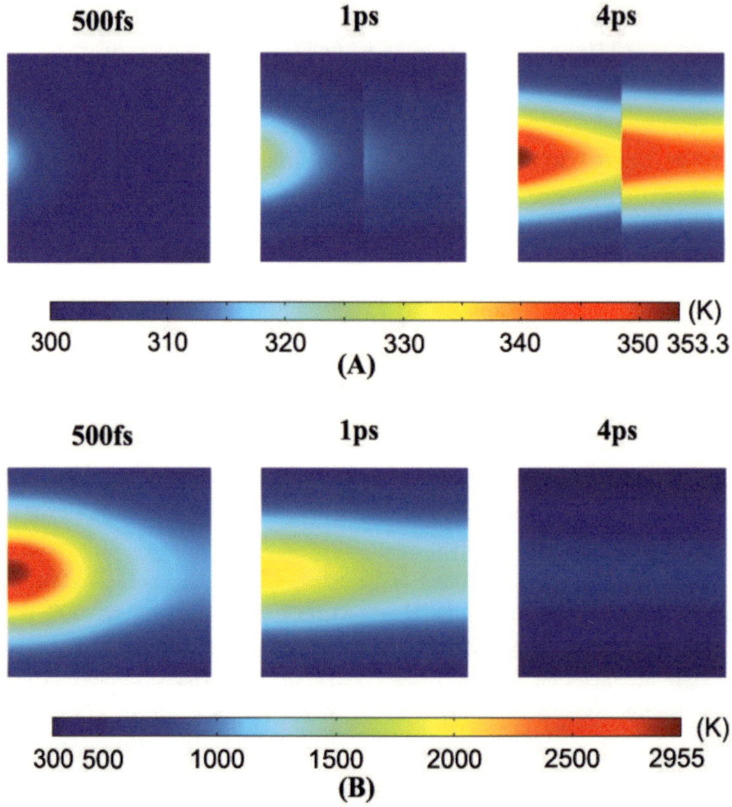

Fig. 3. The temporal evolution of electron and phonon temperature fields in two layer Au/Ag film assembly. (A) Phonon temperature fields at 500fs, 1ps and 4ps; (B) Electron temperature fields at 500 fs, 1ps and 4ps

Fig.4 shows the temporal evolution of electron and phonon temperature fields in the two layer Au/Al film assembly. The laser is incident from left, the laser pulse and the assembly parameters are listed as follows: laser fluence F=0.1 J/cm^2, pulse duration t_p= 65 fs, laser wavelength 800 nm, the thickness of padding layers T_{Au}=T_{Al}= 100 nm. It can be clearly seen from Fig.4(A) that the phonon temperature fields evolution for the Au/Al assembly exhibits different tendency as for the Au/Ag film assembly. At time of 500 fs, the surface Au layer phonon in the Au/Al film assembly is less heated, the deposited thermal energy is mainly concentrated at substrate Al layer. The maximal phonon temperature at front surface and middle interface of the assembly is 310 K and 330K, respectively. At time of 1ps, the phonon subsystem for the bottom Al layer is dominantly heated, while the surface Au layer phonon temperature keeps close to room temperature, the maximal phonon temperature at front surface and middle interface comes to 320K and 371 K at this time. Generally, the rapid rise of the bottom Al layer phonon temperature is primarily attributed to larger electron-phonon coupling strength for the Al layer compared to that of Au layer. The laser energy is firstly coupled into the electron of the surface Au layer, then the excited electron conducts it's energy to electron subsystem of bottom Al layer through electron thermal conduction. Immediately after that the Al layer electron couples it's energy to the local phonon, leading to preferential heating of the bottom Al film. At time of 4ps, the phonon subsystem of the Al film is further heated and the phonon temperature at Au layer continues to rise very slowly, the maximal phonon temperature at front surface and the middle interface is 351K and 443K at this time. In Fig.4(B), the electron temperature field evolution for Au/Al film assembly dose not show significant difference from that of the Au/Ag film assembly. The electron subsystem of the two layer Au/Al film assembly is dramatically overheated at 500 fs, the maximal electron temperature at the front surface of the assembly reaches 2922 K. At time of 1ps, the electron subsystem continues diffusing it's thermal energy to the Al substrate, and the electron temperature for the surface Au film bears a severe drop. The maximal electron temperature comes down to 1900K at the front surface, and rises to 750K at the rear surface at 1ps. At time of 4ps, the electron temperature across the assembly goes down to 400K and 350K at front surface and rear surface, respectively. With time, the electron and phonon subsystems also would get the thermal equilibrium state, and if the united electron and phonon temperature in assembly is higher than padding layers melting point, the two layer film assembly will be damaged.

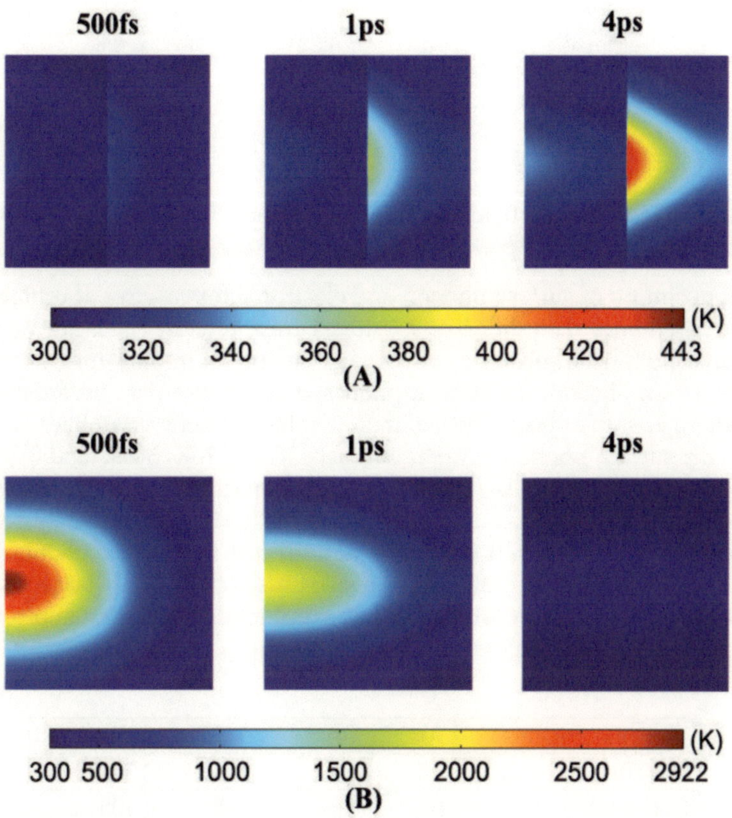

Fig. 4. The temporal evolution of electron and phonon temperature fields in two layer Au/Al film assembly. (A) Phonon temperature fields at 500fs, 1ps and 4ps; (B) Electron temperature fields at 500fs, 1ps and 4ps

Fig.5 presents the phonon temperature field distributions for the three layer film assemblies with different layer configurations at 5 ps. The laser and film parameters for the simulations are listed as follows: laser fluence is F=0.1 J/cm^2, pulse duration t_p=65 fs, laser wavelength

800 nm, the thicknesses of the respective padding layers are T_{Au}=T_{Ag}=T_{Al} =50 nm. The laser pulse is incident from left. It is shown in Fig.5 (A) that the phonon energy is concentrated at bottom of the assembly for Au/Ag/Al configuration, however, which is mostly distributed at the surface layer for Al/Ag/Au configuration as can be seen from Fig.5(B). The results can be partly interpreted as large electron-phonon coupling strength for Al compared to Au, which is beneficial for transferring the overheating surface electron thermal energy into the bottom layer phonon.

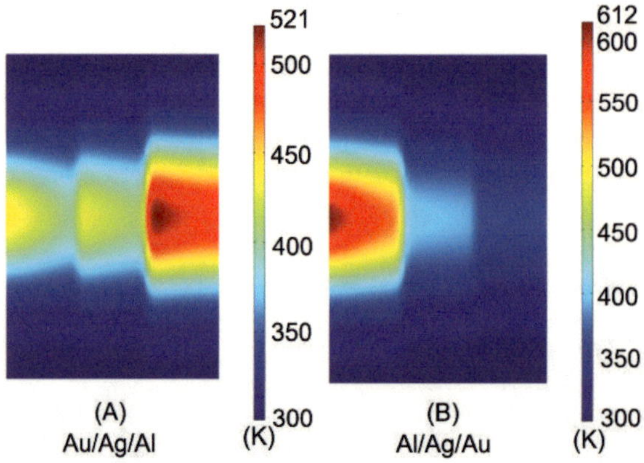

Fig. 5. The phonon temperature fields for three layer metal film assemblies with different layer configurations at time of 5 ps

The temporal evolution of surface phonon and electron temperatures at center of laser spot for Au coated assemblies with different substrates are shown in Fig.6. The applied thermal physical parameters for the substrates of Au, Ag, Cu and Al in the simulations are listed in table 1. As shown in Fig.6(a), the surface phonon temperature rises accordantly for the all assemblies before 1ps, then begins to separate for the different assemblies with increasing time. Finally, the surface phonon temperature gets 380K, 370K, 349K, and 386K at 15ps for assemblies of Au/Au, Au/Ag, Au/Cu and Au/Al, respectively. Fig.6(b) shows the surface electron temperature of the Au coated metals also evolutes synchronously before 1ps, but becomes discrepantly after 1 ps. It should be noticed that the surface phonon and electron temperatures at 15ps for the Au coated Al film substrate are obviously larger than that of the assemblies with other metal film substrates. It is expected that the thermal properties for the substrate layers can play an important role in enhancing surface temperature evolution on the Au coated metal assemblies.

Parameters	Au	Ag	Cu	Al
$G_0(10^{16}\,J\,m^{-3}\,s^{-1}\,K^{-1})$	2.1	3.1	10	24.5
$C_{e0}(J\,m^{-3}\,K^{-2})$	68	63	97	135
$k_{e0}(J\,m^{-1}\,s^{-1}\,K^{-1})$	318	428	401	235
$C_l(10^6\,J\,m^{-3}\,K^{-1})$	2.5	2.5	3.5	0.244
$A(10^7\,s^{-1}\,K^{-2})$	1.18	0.932	1.28	0.376
$B(10^{11}\,s^{-1}\,K^{-1})$	1.25	1.02	1.23	3.9

Table 1. Thermal physical parameters for Au, Ag, Cu and Al, the datum are cited from references (Chen et al., 2010 ; Wang et al., 2006)

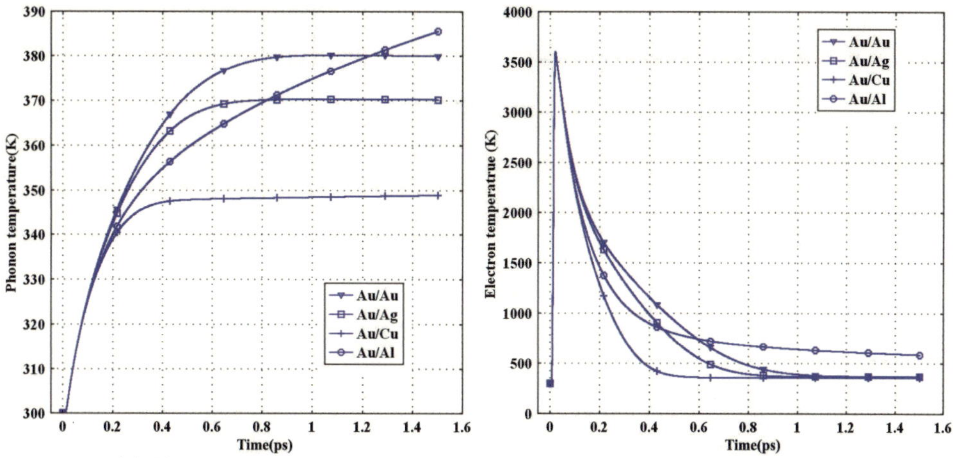

(a) Phonon temperature (b) Electron temperature

Fig. 6. Temporal evolution of phonon and electron temperatures at center of laser spot on surface of Au surfaced two layer metal film assemblies

In general, the physical mechanism in dominating the temperature field distributions has no difference for the two layer and the three layer metal film assemblies because of the similar physical boundary and the mathematical processing for them. So, the two layer Au coated metal assembly is here taken as example in order to explore what causes can definitely give rise to the distinct temperature field distributions in the metal film assembly with different substrate configurations? Fig.7 shows effect of the substrates thermal parameters on surface phonon temperature of the two layers Au coated assembly. The thermal parameters such as electron thermal capacity, electron thermal conductivity, electron-phonon coupling strength and phonon thermal capacity are all selected falling into the ranges for the actual materials as listed in table 1. As shown in Fig.7(a) and (b), the surface Au layer phonon temperature decreases slightly with increasing electron thermal capacity and electron thermal conductivity of the substrates. However, increasing of electron-phonon coupling strength or phonon thermal capacity for the substrate layers can both result in the dramatic drops of surface phonon temperature as shown in Fig.7(c) and (d), indicating the substrate layer electron-phonon coupling strength and phonon thermal capacity both play key roles in determining the surface heating process in the Au coated metal assembly. From table 1, it can be found out that the electron-phonon coupling strengths for the substrates is in the order of $G_{Au}<G_{Ag}<G_{Cu}$, so the surface Au phonon would be preferentially heated for Au/Au, Au/Ag, Au/Cu orderly as had be observed in Fig.6. However, the obvious rise of the Au surface phonon temperature for Au/Al assembly is actually attributed to the quite smaller phonon thermal capacity for the Al substrate compared to other metal substrates.

Fig.8 shows temporal evolution of electron and phonon temperature in the two layer Au/Al assembly at different depths. The laser parameters are t_p=65 fs, F=0.1 J/cm^2, wavelength is 800 nm. It can be seen from Fig.8(a) that when the depth exceeds 100 nm, the pulse-like distribution of electron temperature profile fades away, which can be related to the role of the electron ballistic effect. Beyond the ballistic range, taken as 100 nm here, the temporal information of laser pulse can less be delivered to the electron temperature for the Au/Al assembly. We can see from Fig.8(b) that the phonon temperature evolutions for the surface layer at depths of 0 nm and 50 nm is severely inhibited, however, which rises dramatically at depths of 150 nm and 200 nm for the substrate layer. It indicates the phonon subsystem is heated in priority from substrate to the surface layer for the Au/Al assembly.

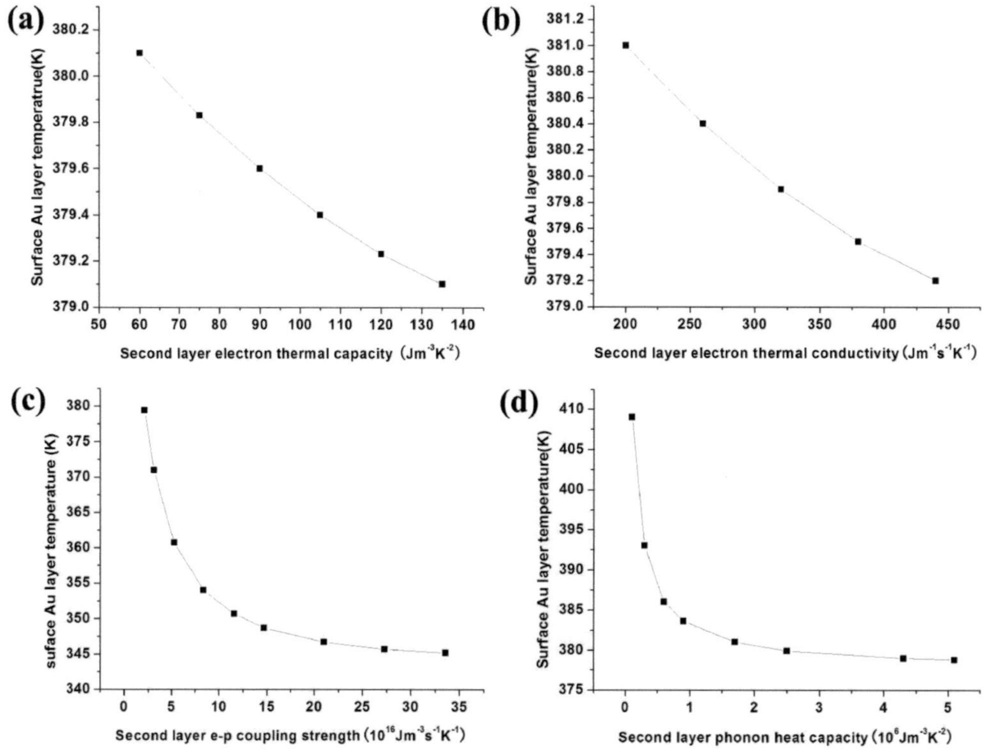

Fig. 7. Effect of thermal parameters of the substrate layer on surface phonon temperature of the two layer Au/substrate assembly

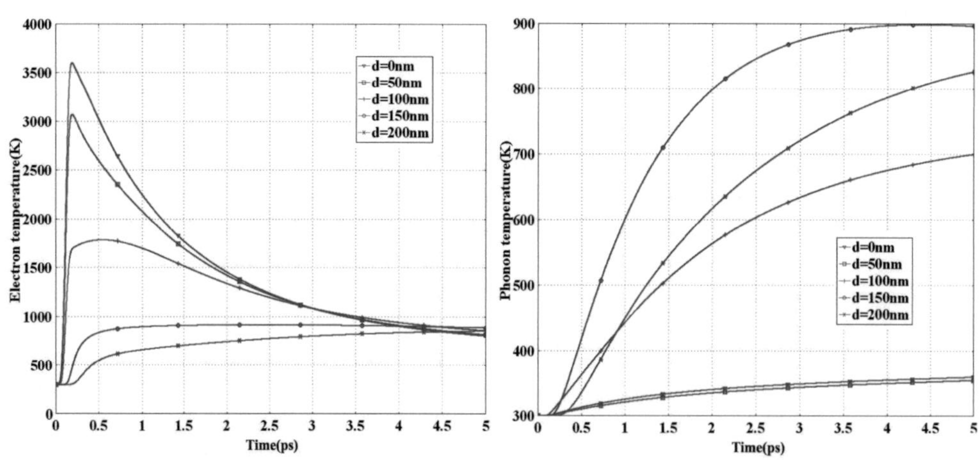

(a) Electron temperature (b) Phonon temperature

Fig. 8. Temporal evolutions of electron and phonon temperature for the Au/Al film assembly at different depths of the target

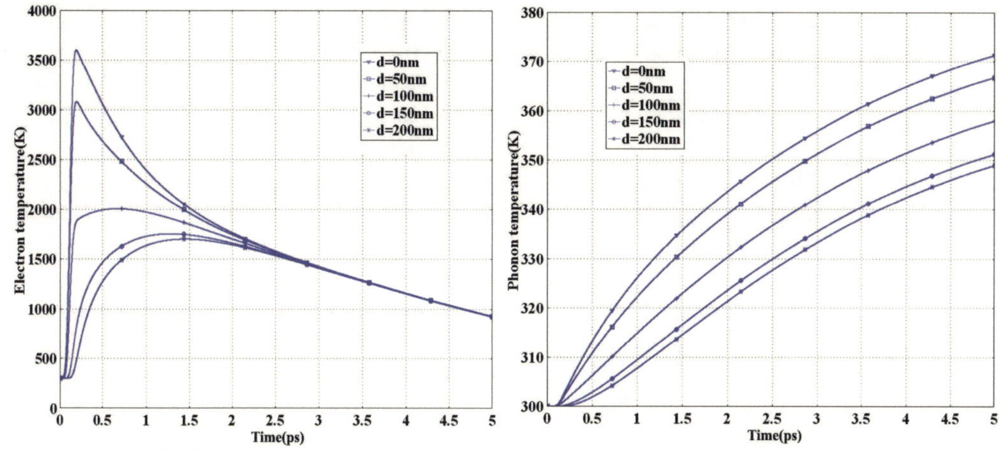

(a) Electron temperature (b) Phonon temperature

Fig. 9. Temporal evolution of electron and phonon temperature for the Au/Ag film assembly at different depths of the target

The temporal evolution of electron and phonon temperature for the Au/Ag film assembly at different depths of the target are given in Fig.9. The laser parameters are t_p=65 fs, F=0.1 J/cm^2, wavelength is 800 nm. As show in Fig.9(a), the electron temperature peak decreases orderly with increasing the depth. As the depth exceeds 100 nm, the electron temperature profile still maintains the pulse-like distribution, although the sharp pulse structure is weakened for the Au/Ag film assembly, which is different from that of the Au/Al film assembly. From Fig.9(b), it can be seen that the phonon temperature rises more rapidly from depths of d=0 nm to d=200 nm. In fact, the thermal parameters between Au and Ag is very close to each other so that the electron and phonon temperature evolutions in the Au/Ag assembly perform the normal tendency as usually found in single layer metal film heating, namely, the film is preferentially heated from surface to the bottom.

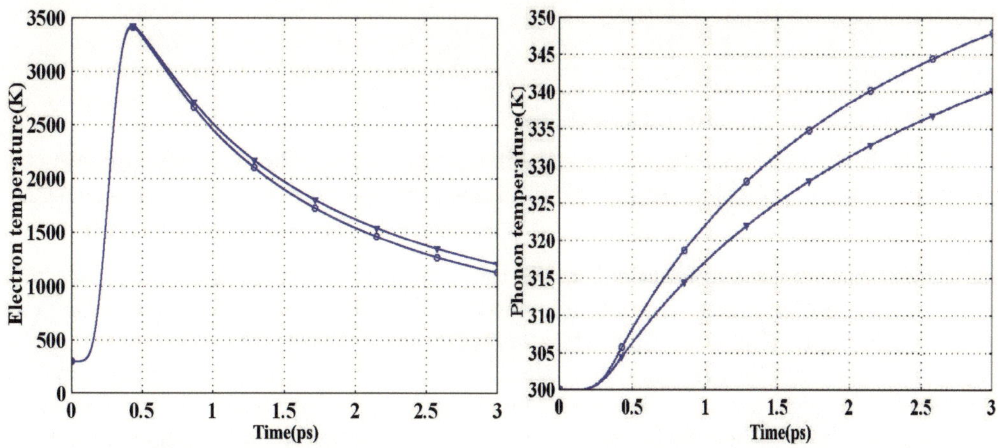

(a) Electron temperature (b) Phonon temperature

Fig. 10. The surface electron temperature of the two layer Au/Al film assembly at center of laser spot as a function of delay time. (The circle represents the temperature dependent electron-phonon coupling strength, and the triangle represents constant coupling strength)

Fig.10 shows surface electron and phonon temperatures of the two layer Au/Al assembly at center of laser spot as a function of delay time with respect to the temperature dependent and constant electron-phonon coupling strengths. The laser parameters are t_p=150 fs, F=0.1 J/cm^2, laser wavelength is 800 nm. The temporal evolutions of electron and phonon temperatures are almost identical during the femtosecond laser pulse duration and becomes discrepantly after 300 fs. The simulated electron temperature using temperature dependent electron-phonon coupling strength is slightly lower compared to that applying the constant electron-phonon coupling strength. However, as seen in Fig.10 (b), the phonon temperature evaluated by the temperature dependent electron-phonon coupling strength is rather higher than using the constant electron-phonon strength mainly after 300 fs. For femtosecond laser ablation, material damage usually occurs after the electron-phonon relaxation termination on timescale of picoseconds. So, it is important to use the temperature dependent electron-phonon coupling strength to predict ultrafast heating characteristics in multi-layer metal film assembly for target material ablation.

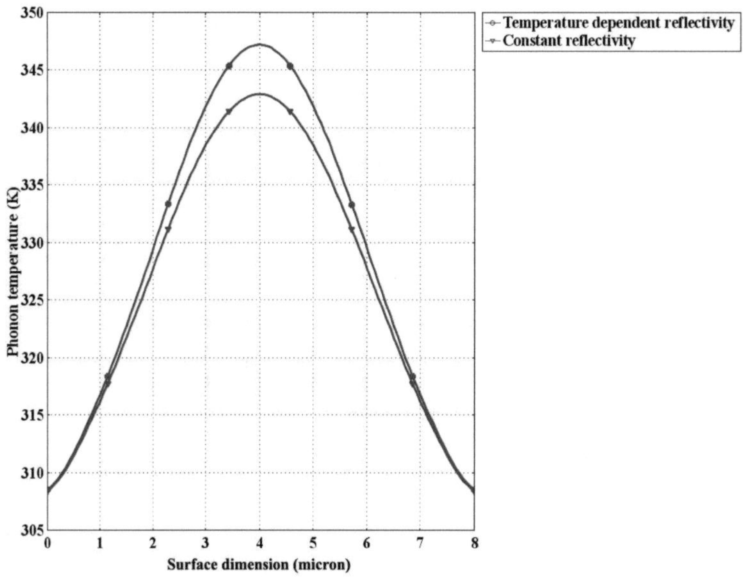

Fig. 11. The surface phonon temperature of the two layer Au/Al film assembly under the irradiation of laser spot at time of 15ps with respect to temperature dependent and constant reflectivity

The surface phonon temperature fields in the two layer Au/Al film assembly at 15 ps under range of laser spot with respect to the temperature dependent and the constant reflectivity are shown in Fig.11. The laser parameters are t_p=150 fs, F=0.05 J/cm^2, laser wavelength is 800 nm. It can be seen that the constant surface reflectivity definitely makes a low estimation of the surface phonon temperature, especially at center of the laser spot. The results can be explained as follows: When the femtosecond laser pulse irradiation on the target surface, the electron subsystem can be rapidly heated and the electron temperature is immediately evaluated to higher level during femtosecond laser pulse heating, causing dramatic increase of the total scattering rates. The large particle scattering rate is beneficial for reducing surface reflectivity as predicted by the Drude model with respect to temperature dependent particle scattering processes. So the surface phonon temperature for the target with consideration of the temperature dependent reflectivity can be thus promoted as a result of reduction of the surface reflectivity for laser energy absorption by electron subsystem and the following energy coupling to phonon after the femtosecond laser pulse duration.

4. Conclusions

The ultrafast heating characteristics in the two layers and three layers metal film assemblies irradiated by femtosecond laser pulses are investigated by numerical simulations, in which the metals such as Au, Ag, Cu and Al are taken as the targets. The ultrafast 2-D temperature field evolutions on picosecond timescale with regard to the temperature dependent material properties for different film layer configurations of the multi-layer assemblies are obtained by Finite Element Method (FEM). The comparations for phonon temperature field evaluated by constant and temperature dependent electron-phonon coupling strength and reflectivity are given, which show the temperature dependent material properties must be taken into account for well exploring the ultrafast heating processes in multi-layer film assemblies. It is shown that the temperature field evolutions exhibit distinct characteristics for different layer configurations in the multi-layer assemblies. For the two layer Au/Ag assembly, the phonon temperature field is mainly distributed at the surface Au layer, while which can dominantly diffuse into the substrate layer for the Au/Al configuration after several picoseconds. Some similar results can also be observed in three layer metal film assemblies. It is demonstrated that electron-phonon coupling strength and phonon thermal capacity for the substrate layer play important roles in determining the temperature field distributions at the surface of Au coated assemblies. The increasing of second layer electron-phonon coupling strength and phonon thermal capacity both can result in severe drop of the surface Au layer phonon temperature. But, the electron thermal parameters including electron thermal conductivity and electron thermal capacity have less effect on the Au surface layer phonon temperature.

5. Acknowledgment

The work was supported by National High Technology R&D Program of China under the Grant No.2009AA04Z305 and National Science Foundation of China under the Grant No. 60678011.

6. References

Anisimov S., Kapeliovich B., and Perel'man T. (1974). Electron Emission from Metal Surfaces Exposed to Ultrashort Laser Pulses, *Sov. Phys. JETP,* Vol. 39, No. (August 1974),pp. 375-377.

Chen A.; Xu H.; Jiang Y.; Sui L.; Ding D.;Liu H. & Jin M. (2010). Modeling of Femtosecond Laser Damage Threshold on the Two-layer Metal Films. *Applied Surface Science,* Vol. 257, No.5, (December 2010),pp.1678-1683. ISSN 0169-4332

Chen J. & Beraun J. (2001).Numerical Study of Ultrashort Laser Pulse Interactions with Metal Films. *Numer. Heat Transfer A,* Vol. 40, No.1 (July 2001),pp. 1-20, ISSN 1040-7782

Chen J.; Tzou D.& Beraun J. (2006). A Semiclassical Two-temperature Model for Ultrafast Laser Heating. *International Journal of Heat and Mass Transfer*, Vol.49, No.1-2, (January 2006), pp.307-316.ISSN 0017-9310

Christensen B.; Vestentoft K. & Balling P. (2007). Short-pulse Ablation Rates and the Two Temperature Model. *Applied Surface Science*,Vol. 235, No.15, (May 2007),pp.6347-6352,ISSN 0169-4332

Kaganov M.; Lifshitz I.; & Tanatarov L.(1957). Relaxation Between Electrons and Crystalline Lattices. *Sov. Phys. JETP*, Vol. 4, No. 173, (1957),pp. 173-178

Kanavin A.; Smetanin I.; Isakov V.; Afanasiev Yu.; Chichkov B.; Wellegehausen B.; Nolte S.; Momma C. & Tünnermann A. (1998). Heat Transport in Metals Irradiated by Ultrashort Laser Pulses. *Physics. Review. B*, Vol.57, No.23, (June 1998),pp.14698-14703, ISSN 0163-1829

Liu K. (2007). Analysis of Thermal Behavior in Multi-layer Metal Thin Films Based on Hyperbolic Two-Step Model. *International Journal of Heat and Mass Transfer*,Vol.50,No.7-8, (April 2007), pp.1397-1407, ISSN 0017-9310

Qiu T.& Tien C. (1993). Heat Transfer Mechanisms During Short-Pulse Laser Heating of Metals, *ASME J. Heat Transfer*, Vol. 115, No.4,(November 1993), pp. 835-841, ISSN 0022-1481

Wang H.; Dai W.; Nassar R.& Melnik R. (2006).A Finite Difference Method for Studying Thermal Deformation in a Thin Film Exposed to Ultrashort-Pulsed Lasers. *International Journal of Heat and Mass Transfer*, Vol.49, No. 15-16, (July 2006),pp.2712-2723, ISSN 0017-9310

Part 2

Two Phase Flow

12

On Density Wave Instability Phenomena – Modelling and Experimental Investigation

Davide Papini, Antonio Cammi, Marco Colombo and Marco E. Ricotti
Department of Energy, CeSNEF – Nuclear Engineering Division, Politecnico di Milano
Italy

1. Introduction

Density Wave Oscillations (DWOs) are dealt with in this work as the most representative instabilities frequently encountered in the boiling systems. This *dynamic type* instability mode - resulting from multiple feedback effects between the flow rate, the vapour generation rate and the pressure drops in the boiling channel - constitutes an issue of special interest for the design of industrial systems and equipments involving vapour generation (Yadigaroglu, 1981). In the nuclear area, instability phenomena can be triggered both in Boiling Water Reactor (BWR) fuel channels (where they are moreover coupled through neutronic feedbacks with the neutron field), and in steam generators, which experience boiling phenomena inside parallel tubes. The latter is typical configuration of all the *once-through* steam generators, considered in this work with respect to integral Small-medium Modular Reactors (SMRs)[1] applications.

Extensive attention is required because parallel channel instability is very difficult to be immediately detected when occurs in steam power systems, being the total mass flow of the system stable while the instability is locally triggered among some of the parallel channels. Thermally induced oscillations of the flow rate and system pressure are undesirable, as they can cause mechanical vibrations, problems of system control, and in extreme cases induce heat transfer surface burn-out. Large amplitude fluctuations in the heater wall temperature (so named *thermal oscillations*) usually occur under DWO conditions. Continual cycling of the wall temperature can lead to thermal fatigue problems which may cause tube failure.

It is clear from these examples that the flow instabilities must be avoided in the design and operation of the various industrial systems. The safe operating regime of a two-phase heat exchanger can be determined by instability threshold values of system parameters such as flow rate, pressure, inlet temperature and exit quality. To the aim, both basic experiments and numerical analyses are necessary.

This work is dedicated to the study (from theoretical, numerical and experimental point of view) of density wave phenomena, aimed at instability threshold prediction, DWO characterization and linear stability analysis as well.

---

[1] The *integral layout* - shared by the SMR designs - provides that all the primary system components are hosted inside the reactor vessel. This permits to reduce by design risks and effects of several postulated accidents, as well as to introduce improved technological solutions for the single plant components (e.g., the helically coiled steam generators fitting with the increased compactness of the system).

First, modelling effort based on the development of an analytical dynamic model - via integration of the 1D governing equations - is described. The simplest Homogeneous Equilibrium Model (HEM), in which phasic slip and subcooled boiling are neglected, has been considered. Non-linear features of the modelling equations have permitted to represent the complex interactions between the variables triggering the instability. Several sensitivity studies have been carried out, on the operating conditions, on system geometrical features, and on the empirical coefficients used to better model two-phase flow structure. Theoretical predictions from analytical model are then verified via qualified numerical simulation tools. Both the thermal-hydraulic dedicated code RELAP5 and the multi-physics code COMSOL have been applied.
Final objective of the developed modelling on density wave instabilities has been to prepare (pre-test analyses) and interpret (post-test analyses) an experimental campaign carried out at SIET labs (Piacenza, Italy), where parallel channel instability phenomena have been directly investigated with a test section reproducing in full scale two helical tubes of the IRIS (International Reactor Innovative and Secure) steam generator (Papini et al., 2011). Due to the complexity of the helical geometry, the basic experimental investigation provided is of utmost importance for the diffusion of such helically coiled steam generators.
The chapter is structured as follows. Physical insight into the distinctive features leading to DWO mechanism is provided in Section 2. Modelling and experimental investigations on instability phenomena available from the open literature are described in Section 3. Section 4 and 5 present the analytical modelling developed in this work for DWO theoretical predictions, whereas numerical modelling (using RELAP5 and COMSOL codes) is briefly discussed in Section 6. Modelling efforts start necessarily from the simplifying and sound case of straight vertical tube geometry, which is referenced for validating the whole modelling tools. Description of the experimental campaign for DWO characterization in helical coil tubes is shortly presented in Section 7. The peculiar influence of the helical shape on the instability occurrence is examined in Section 8. Suited modifications of the models are introduced in order to simulate the experimental results.

2. Density Wave Oscillations (DWOs)

The classical interpretation of density wave oscillations, proposed e.g. by Yadigaroglu & Bergles (1972) and recently confirmed by the noteworthy review of Kakaç & Bon (2008), ascribes the origin of the instability to waves of *heavier* and *lighter* fluids, and respective delays through the channel.
The difference in density between the fluid entering the heated channel (subcooled liquid) and the fluid exiting (low density two-phase mixture) triggers delays in the transient distribution of pressure drops along the tube, which may induce self-sustained oscillations. A constant pressure drop (or better, the same, not necessarily constant with time, pressure drop for the multiple parallel channels) is the proper boundary condition that can excite those dynamic feedbacks which are at the source of the instability mechanism. A remark is now mandatory. The mentioned boundary condition can be provided by connecting two or more parallel channels with common upper and lower headers (for this reason, *density wave instabilities* are commonly referred to as *parallel channel instabilities*). When dealing with DWO investigation in a single boiling channel, the experimental apparatus must be designed such to effectively maintain a constant pressure variation along the tube. In case of

modelling, it is enough to impose the boundary condition $\Delta P = P_{in} - P_{out} = const$; in case of experimental investigation, a system configuration with a large bypass tube parallel-connected to the heated channel must be used to properly reproduce the phenomenon. The suited boundary condition is preserved only for a sufficiently large ratio between bypass area and heated channel area (Collins & Gacesa, 1969).

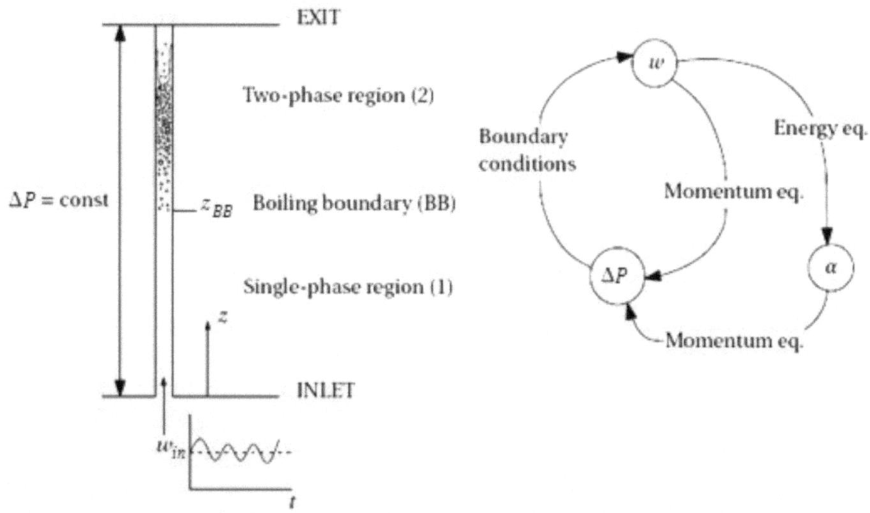

Fig. 1. Density wave instability mechanism in a single boiling channel, and respective feedbacks between main physical quantities. (Reproduced from (Yadigaroglu, 1981))

Going more into details, the physical mechanism leading to the appearance of DWOs is now briefly described (Yadigaroglu & Bergles, 1972). A single heated channel, as depicted in Fig. 1, is considered for simplicity. The instantaneous position of the boiling boundary, that is the point where the bulk of the fluid reaches saturation, divides the channel into a single-phase region and a two-phase region. A sudden outlet pressure drop perturbation, e.g. resulting from a local microscopic increase in void fraction, can be assumed to trigger the instability by propagating a corresponding low pressure pulse to the channel inlet, which in turn causes an increase in inlet flow. Considered as a consequence an oscillatory inlet flow entering the channel (Lahey Jr. & Moody, 1977), a propagating enthalpy perturbation is created in the single-phase region. The boiling boundary will respond by oscillating according to the amplitude and the phase of the enthalpy perturbation. Changes in the flow and in the length of the single-phase region will combine to create an oscillatory single-phase pressure drop perturbation (say $\Delta P_{1\phi}$). The enthalpy perturbation will appear in the two-phase region as quality and void fraction perturbations and will travel with the flow along the channel. The combined effects of flow and void fraction perturbations and the variation of the two-phase length will create a two-phase pressure drop perturbation (say $\Delta P_{2\phi}$). Since the total pressure drop across the boiling channel is imposed:

$$\delta\Delta P_{tot} = \delta\Delta P_{1\phi} + \delta\Delta P_{2\phi} = 0 \tag{1}$$

the two-phase pressure drop perturbation will create a feedback perturbation of the opposite sign in the single-phase region. That is (Rizwan-Uddin, 1994), in order to keep the *constant-pressure-drop boundary condition*, the increase of exit pressure drop (following the positive perturbation in inlet velocity that transforms into a wave of *higher density)* will result indeed into an instantaneous drop in the inlet flow. The process is now reversed as the density wave, resulting from the lower inlet velocity, travels to the channel exit: the pressure drop at channel exit decreases as the wave of *lower density* reaches the top, resulting in an increase in the inlet flow rate, which starts the cycle over again. With correct timing, the flow oscillation can become self-sustained, matched by an oscillation of pressure and by the single-phase and two-phase pressure drop terms oscillating in counter-phase.

In accordance with this description, as a complete oscillating cycle consists in the passage of two perturbations through the channel (*higher density* wave and *lower density* wave), the period of oscillations T should be of the order of twice the mixture transit time τ in the heated section:

$$T = 2\tau \tag{2}$$

In recent years, Rizwan-Uddin (1994) proposed indeed different descriptions based on more complex relations between the system parameters. His explanation is based on the different speeds of propagation of velocity perturbations between the single-phase region (speed of sound) and the two-phase region (so named *kinematic velocity*). This behaviour is dominant at high inlet subcooling, such that the phenomenon seems to be more likely related to mixture velocity variations rather than to mixture density variations. In this case, the period of oscillations is larger than twice the mixture transit time.

2.1 Stability maps

The operating point of a boiling channel is determined by several parameters, which also affect the channel stability. Once the fluid properties, channel geometry and system operating pressure have been defined, major role is played by the mass flow rate Γ, the total thermal power supplied Q and the inlet subcooling Δh_{in} (in enthalpy units). Stable and unstable operating regions can be defined in the three dimensional space (Γ, Q, Δh_{in}), whereas mapping of these regions in two dimensions is referred to as the stability map of the system. No universal map exists. Moreover, the usage of dimensionless stability maps is strongly recommended to cluster the information on the dynamic characteristics of the system.

The most used dimensionless stability map is due to Ishii & Zuber (1970), who introduced the *phase change number* N_{pch} and the *subcooling number* N_{sub}. The phase change number scales the characteristic frequency of phase change Ω to the inverse of a single-phase transit time in the system, instead the subcooling number measures the inlet subcooling:

$$N_{pch} = \frac{\Omega}{\frac{w_{in}}{H}} = \frac{\frac{Q}{AH\,h_{fg}}\frac{v_{fg}}{}}{\frac{w_{in}}{H}} = \frac{Q}{\Gamma h_{fg}}\frac{v_{fg}}{v_f} \tag{3}$$

$$N_{sub} = \frac{\Delta h_{in}}{h_{fg}}\frac{v_{fg}}{v_f} \tag{4}$$

Fig. 2 depicts a typical stability map for a boiling channel system on the stability plane N_{pch}–N_{sub}. The usual stability boundary shape shows the classical *L shape* inclination, valid in general as the system pressure is reasonably low and the inlet loss coefficient is not too large (Zhang et al., 2009). The stability boundary at high inlet subcooling is a line of constant equilibrium quality. It is easy to demonstrate (by suitably rearranging Eqs.(3), (4)) that the constant exit quality lines are obtained as:

$$N_{sub} = N_{pch} - x_{ex} \frac{v_{fg}}{v_f} \tag{5}$$

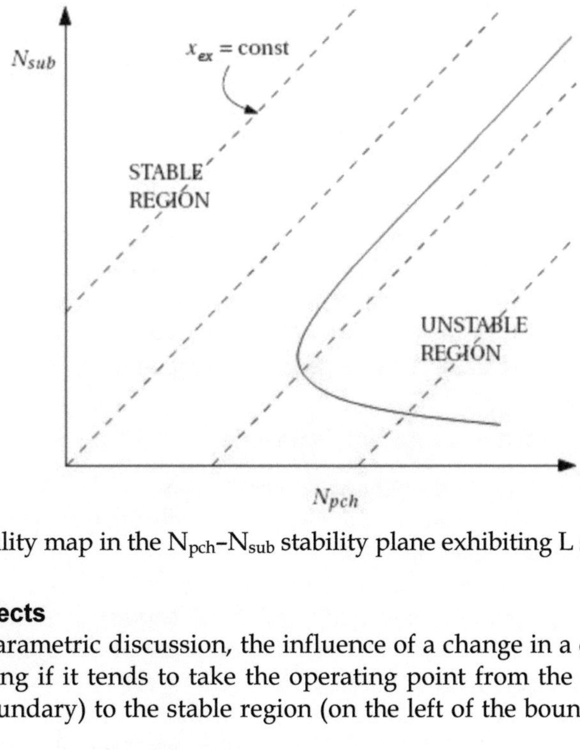

Fig. 2. Typical stability map in the N_{pch}-N_{sub} stability plane exhibiting L shape

2.2 Parametric effects

In the following parametric discussion, the influence of a change in a certain parameter is said to be stabilizing if it tends to take the operating point from the unstable region (on the right of the boundary) to the stable region (on the left of the boundary) (Yadigaroglu, 1981).

2.2.1 Effects of thermal power, flow rate and exit quality

A stable system can be brought into the unstable operating region by increases in the supplied thermal power or decreases in the flow rate. Both effects increase the exit quality, which turns out to be a key parameter for system stability.

The destabilizing effect of increasing the ratio Q/Γ is universally accepted.

2.2.2 Effects of inlet subcooling

The influence of inlet subcooling on the system stability is multi-valued. In the high inlet subcooling region the stability is strengthened by increasing the subcooling, whereas in the low inlet subcooling region the stability is strengthened by decreasing the subcooling. That is, the inlet subcooling is stabilizing at high subcoolings and destabilizing at low

subcoolings, resulting therefore in the so named *L shape* of the stability boundary (see Fig. 2).
Intuitively this effect may be explained by the fact that, as the inlet subcooling is increased or decreased, the two-phase channel tends towards stable single-phase liquid and vapour operation respectively, hence out of the unstable two-phase operating mode (Yadigaroglu, 1981).

2.2.3 Effects of pressure level

An increase in the operating pressure is found to be stabilizing, although one must be careful in stating which system parameters are kept constant while the pressure level is increased. At constant values of the dimensionless subcooling and exit quality, the pressure effect is made apparent by the specific volume ratio v_{fg}/v_f (approximately equal to the density ratio ρ_f/ρ_g). This corrective term, accounting for pressure variations within the Ishii's dimensionless parameters, is such that the stability boundaries calculated at slightly different pressure levels are almost overlapped in the N_{pch}–N_{sub} plane.

2.2.4 Effects of inlet and exit throttling

The effect of inlet throttling (single-phase region pressure drops) is always strongly stabilizing and is used to assure the stability of otherwise unstable channels.
On the contrary, the effect of flow resistances near the exit of the channel (two-phase region pressure drops) is strongly destabilizing. For example, stable channels can become unstable if an orifice is added at the exit, or if a riser section is provided.

3. Review of density wave instability studies

3.1 Theoretical researches on density wave oscillations

Two general approaches are possible for theoretical stability analyses on a boiling channel:

i. frequency domain, linearized models;
ii. time domain, linear and non-linear models.

In *frequency domain* (Lahey Jr. & Moody, 1977), governing equations and necessary constitutive laws are linearized about an operating point and then Laplace-transformed. The transfer functions obtained in this manner are used to evaluate the system stability by means of classic control-theory techniques. This method is inexpensive with respect to computer time, relatively straightforward to implement, and is free of the numerical stability problems of finite-difference methods.
The models built in *time domain* permit either 0D analyses (Muñoz-Cobo et al., 2002; Schlichting et al., 2010), based on the analytical integration of conservation equations in the competing regions, or more complex but accurate 1D analyses (Ambrosini et al., 2000; Guo Yun et al., 2008; Zhang et al., 2009), by applying numerical solution techniques (finite differences, finite volumes or finite elements). In these models the steady-state is perturbed with small stepwise changes of some operating parameter simulating an actual transient, such as power increase in a real system. The stability threshold is reached when undamped or diverging oscillations are induced. Non-linear features of the governing equations permit to grasp the feedbacks and the mutual interactions between variables triggering a self-sustained density wave oscillation. Time-domain techniques are indeed rather time consuming when used for stability analyses, since a large number of cases must be run to

produce a stability map, and each run is itself time consuming because of the limits on the allowable time step.

Lots of lumped-parameter and distributed-parameter stability models, both linear and non-linear, have been published since the '60-'70s. Most important literature reviews on the subject - among which are worthy of mention the works of Bouré et al. (1973), Yadigaroglu (1981) and Kakaç & Bon (2008) - collect the large amount of theoretical researches. It is just noticed that the study on density wave instabilities in parallel twin or multi-channel systems represents still nowadays a topical research area. For instance, Muñoz-Cobo et al. (2002) applied a non-linear 0D model to the study of out-of-phase oscillations between parallel subchannels of BWR cores. In the framework of the future development of nuclear power plants in China, Guo Yun et al. (2008) and Zhang et al. (2009) investigated DWO instability in parallel multi-channel systems by using control volume integrating method. Schlichting et al. (2010) analysed the interaction of PDOs (*Pressure Drop Oscillations*) and DWOs for a typical NASA type phase change system for space exploration applications.

3.2 Numerical code simulations on density wave oscillations

On the other hands, qualified numerical simulation tools can be successfully applied to the study of boiling channel instabilities, as accurate quantitative predictions can be provided by using simple and straightforward nodalizations.

In this frame, the best-estimate system code RELAP5 - based on a *six-equations* non-homogeneous non-equilibrium model for the two-phase system[2] - was designed for the analysis of all transients and postulated accidents in LWR nuclear reactors, including Loss Of Coolant Accidents (LOCAs) as well as all different types of operational transients (US NRC, 2001). In the recent years, several numerical studies published on DWOs featured the RELAP5 code as the main analysis tool. Amongst them, Ambrosini & Ferreri (2006) performed a detailed analysis about thermal-hydraulic instabilities in a boiling channel using the RELAP5/MOD3.2 code. In order to respect the imposed *constant-pressure-drop boundary condition*, which is the proper boundary condition to excite the dynamic feedbacks that are at the source of the instability mechanism, a single channel layout with impressed pressures, kept constant by two inlet and outlet plena, was investigated. The Authors demonstrated the capability of the RELAP5 system code to detect the onset of DWO instability.

The multi-purpose COMSOL Multiphysics® numerical code (COMSOL, Inc., 2008) can be applied to study the stability characteristics of boiling systems too. Widespread utilization of COMSOL code relies on the possibility to solve different numerical problems by implementing directly the systems of equations in PDE (*Partial Differential Equation*) form. PDEs are then solved numerically by means of finite element techniques. It is just mentioned that this approach is globally different from previous one discussed (i.e., the RELAP5 code), which indeed considers finite volume discretizations of the governing equations, and of course from the simple analytical treatments described in Section 3.1. In this respect, linear and non-linear stability analyses by means of the COMSOL code have been provided by

[2] The RELAP5 hydrodynamic model is a one-dimensional, transient, *two-fluid model* for flow of two-phase steam-water mixture. Simplification of assuming the same interfacial pressure for the two phases, with equal phasic pressures as well, is considered.

Schlichting et al. (2007), who developed a 1D drift-flux model applied to instability studies on a boiling loop for space applications.

3.3 Experimental investigations on density wave oscillations

The majority of the experimental works on the subject - collected in several literature reviews (Kakaç & Bon, 2008; Yadigaroglu, 1981) - deals with straight tubes and few meters long test sections. Moreover, all the aspects associated with DWO instability have been systematically analysed in a limited number of works. Systematic study of density wave instability means to produce well-controlled experimental data on the onset and the frequency of this type of oscillation, at various system conditions (and with various operating fluids).

Amongst them, are worthy of mention the pioneering experimental works of Saha et al. (1976) - using a uniformly heated single boiling channel with bypass - and of Masini et al. (1968), working with two vertical parallel tubes. To the best of our knowledge, scarce number of experiments was conducted studying full-scale long test sections (with steam generator tubes application), and no data are available on the helically coiled tube geometry (final objective of the present work). Indeed, numerous experimental campaigns were conducted in the past using refrigerant fluids (such as R-11, R-113 ...), due to the low critical pressure, low boiling point, and low latent heat of vaporization. That is, for instance, the case of the utmost work of Saha et al. (1976), where R-113 was used as operating fluid.

In the recent years, some Chinese researches (Guo Yun et al., 2010) experimentally studied the flow instability behaviour of a twin-channel system, using water as working fluid. Indeed, a small test section with limited pressure level (maximum pressure investigated is 30 bar) was considered; systematic execution of a precise test matrix, as well as discussions about the oscillation period, are lacking.

4. Analytical lumped parameter model: fundamentals and development

The analytical model provided to theoretically study DWO instabilities is based on the work of Muñoz-Cobo et al. (2002). Proper modifications have been considered to fit the modelling approach with steam generator tubes with imposed thermal power (representative of typical experimental facility conditions).

The developed model is based on a *lumped parameter approach* (0D) for the two zones characterizing a single boiling channel, which are single-phase region and two-phase region, divided by the boiling boundary. Modelling approach is schematically illustrated in Fig. 3.

Differential conservation equations of mass and energy are considered for each region, whereas momentum equation is integrated along the whole channel. Wall dynamics is accounted for in the two distinct regions, following lumped wall temperature dynamics by means of the respective heat transfer balances. The model can apply to *single boiling channel* and *two parallel channels* configuration, suited both for instability investigation according to the specification of the respective boundary conditions:

i. constant ΔP across the tube for *single channel;*
ii. same $\Delta P(t)$ across the two channels (with constant total mass flow) for *parallel channels* (Muñoz-Cobo et al., 2002).

The main assumptions considered in the provided modelling are: *(a)* one-dimensional flow (straight tube geometry); *(b)* homogeneous two-phase flow model; *(c)* thermodynamic equilibrium between the two phases; *(d)* uniform heating along the channel (linear increase of quality with tube abscissa *z*); *(e)* system of constant pressure (pressure term is neglected within the energy equation); *(f)* constant fluid properties at given system inlet pressure; *(g)* subcooled boiling is neglected.

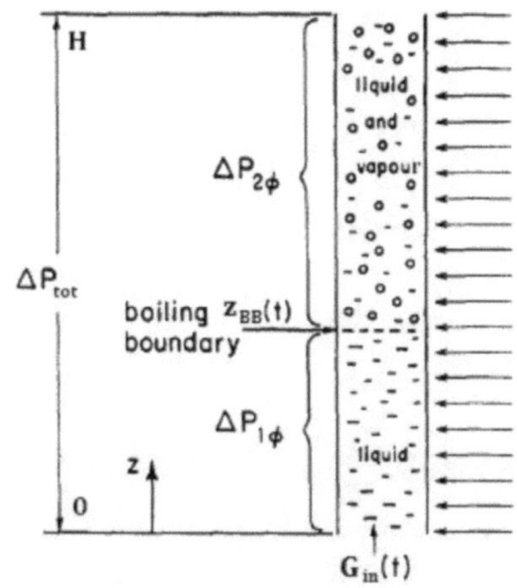

Fig. 3. Schematic diagram of a heated channel with single-phase ($0 < z < z_{BB}$) and two-phase ($z_{BB} < z < H$) regions. Externally impressed pressure drop is ΔP_{tot}. (Adapted from (Rizwan-Uddin, 1994))

4.1 Mathematical modelling

Modelling equations are derived by the continuity of mass and energy for a single-phase fluid and a two-phase fluid, respectively.
Single-phase flow equations read:

$$\frac{\partial \rho}{\partial t}+\frac{\partial G}{\partial z}=0 \tag{6}$$

$$\frac{\partial (\rho h)}{\partial t}+\frac{\partial (Gh)}{\partial z}=Q''' \tag{7}$$

Two-phase mixture is dealt with according to homogeneous flow model. By defining the homogeneous density ρ_H and the reaction frequency Ω (Lahey Jr. & Moody, 1977) as follows:

$$\rho_H=\rho_f\left(1-\bar{\alpha}\right)+\rho_g\bar{\alpha}=\frac{1}{v_f+\bar{x}v_{fg}} \tag{8}$$

$$\Omega(t)=\frac{Q(t)v_{fg}}{AHh_{fg}} \tag{9}$$

one gets:

$$\frac{\partial \rho_H}{\partial t} + \frac{\partial G}{\partial z} = 0 \tag{10}$$

$$\frac{\partial j}{\partial z} = \Omega(t) \tag{11}$$

Momentum equation is accounted for by integrating the pressure balance along the channel:

$$\int_0^H \frac{\partial G(z,t)}{\partial t} dz = \Delta P(t) - \Delta P_{acc} - \Delta P_{grav} - \Delta P_{frict} \tag{12}$$

As concerns the wall dynamics modelling, a lumped two-region approach is adopted. Heated wall dynamics is evaluated separately for single-phase and two-phase regions, following the dynamics of the respective wall temperatures according to a heat transfer balance:

$$\frac{dQ^{1\phi}}{dt} = M_h^{1\phi} c_h \frac{dT_h^{1\phi}}{dt} = Q^{1\phi} - (hS)^{1\phi} \left(T_h^{1\phi} - T_{fl}^{1\phi}\right) \tag{13}$$

$$\frac{dQ^{2\phi}}{dt} = M_h^{2\phi} c_h \frac{dT_h^{2\phi}}{dt} = Q^{2\phi} - (hS)^{2\phi} \left(T_h^{2\phi} - T_{fl}^{2\phi}\right) \tag{14}$$

4.2 Model development

Modelling equations are dealt with according to the usual principles of lumped parameter models (Papini, 2011), i.e. via integration of the governing PDEs (*Partial Differential Equations*) into ODEs (*Ordinary Differential Equations*) by applying the Leibniz rule. The hydraulic and thermal behaviour of a single heated channel is fully described by a set of 5 non-linear differential equations, in the form of:

$$\frac{d\eta_i}{dt} = f_i(\eta) \qquad i = 1, 2, ..., 5 \tag{15}$$

where the state variables are:

$$\begin{array}{lll} \eta_1 = z_{BB} & \eta_2 = x_{ex} & \eta_3 = G_{in} \\ \eta_4 = T_h^{1\phi} & \eta_5 = T_h^{2\phi} & \end{array} \tag{16}$$

In case of *single boiling channel modelling*, boundary condition of constant pressure drop between channel inlet and outlet must be simply introduced by specifying the imposed ΔP of interest within the momentum balance equation (derived following Eq. (12), consult (Papini, 2011)).

In case of *two parallel channels modelling*, mass and energy conservation equations are solved for each of the two channels, while parallel channel boundary condition is dealt imposing within the momentum conservation equation: *(i)* the same pressure drop dependence with time – $\Delta P(t)$ – across the two channels; *(ii)* a constant total flow rate.

First, steady-state conditions of the analysed system are calculated by solving the whole set of equations with time derivative terms set to zero. Steady-state solutions are then used as initial conditions for the integrations of the equations, obtaining the time evolution of each computed state variable. Input variable perturbations (considered thermal power and channel inlet and exit loss coefficients according to the model purposes) can be introduced both in terms of step variations and ramp variations.

The described dynamic model has been solved through the use of the MATLAB software SIMULINK® (The Math Works, Inc., 2005).

4.3 Linear stability analysis

Modelling equations can be linearized to investigate the neutral stability boundary of the nodal model.

The linearization about an unperturbed steady-state initial condition is carried out by assuming for each state variable:

$$\eta(t) = \eta^0 + \delta\eta \cdot e^{\lambda t} \tag{17}$$

To simplify the calculations, modelling equations are linearized with respect to the three state variables representing the hydraulic behaviour of a boiling channel, i.e. the boiling boundary $z_{BB}(t)$, the exit quality $x_{ex}(t)$, and the inlet mass flux $G_{in}(t)$. That is, linear stability analysis is presented by neglecting the dynamics of the heated wall ($Q(t) = const$).

The initial ODEs - obtained after integration of the original governing PDEs - are (Papini, 2011):

Mass-Energy conservation equation in the single-phase region:

$$\frac{dz_{BB}}{dt} = b_1 \tag{18}$$

Mass-Energy conservation equation in the two-phase region:

$$\frac{dx_{ex}}{dt} = b_4 = b_2 + b_3 \frac{dz_{BB}}{dt} \tag{19}$$

Momentum conservation equation (along the whole channel):

$$\frac{dG_{in}}{dt} = b_5 \tag{20}$$

By applying Eq. (17) to the selected three state variables, as:

$$z_{BB}(t) = z_{BB}^0 + \delta z_{BB} \cdot e^{\lambda t} \tag{21}$$

$$x_{ex}(t) = x_{ex}^0 + \delta x_{ex} \cdot e^{\lambda t} \tag{22}$$

$$G_{in}(t) = G_{in}^0 + \delta G_{in} \cdot e^{\lambda t} \tag{23}$$

the resulting linear system can be written in the form of:

$$\delta z_{BB} E_{11} + \delta x_{ex} E_{12} + \delta G_{in} E_{13} = 0 \tag{24}$$

$$\delta z_{BB}E_{21} + \delta x_{ex}E_{22} + \delta G_{in}E_{23} = 0 \quad (25)$$

$$\delta z_{BB}E_{31} + \delta x_{ex}E_{32} + \delta G_{in}E_{33} = 0 \quad (26)$$

The calculation of the system eigenvalues is based on solving:

$$\begin{vmatrix} E_{11} & E_{12} & E_{13} \\ E_{21} & E_{22} & E_{23} \\ E_{31} & E_{32} & E_{33} \end{vmatrix} = 0 \quad (27)$$

which yields a cubic characteristic equation, where λ are the eigenvalues of the system:

$$\lambda^3 + a\lambda^2 + b\lambda + c = 0 \quad (28)$$

5. Analytical lumped parameter model: results and discussion

Single boiling channel configuration is referenced for the discussion of the results obtained by the developed model on DWOs. For the sake of simplicity, and availability of similar works in the open literature for validation purposes (Ambrosini et al., 2000; Ambrosini & Ferreri, 2006; Muñoz-Cobo et al., 2002), typical dimensions and operating conditions of classical BWR core subchannels are considered.
Table 1 lists the geometrical and operational values taken into account in the following analyses.

Heated channel	
Diameter [m]	0.0124
Length [m]	3.658
Operating parameters	
Pressure [bar]	70
Inlet temperature [°C]	151.3 - 282.3
k_{in}	23
k_{ex}	5

Table 1. Dimensions and operating conditions selected for the analyses

5.1 System transient response

To excite the unstable modes of density wave oscillations, input thermal power is increased starting from stable stationary conditions, step-by-step, up to the instability occurrence. Instability threshold crossing is characterized by passing through damping out oscillations (Fig. 4-(a)), limit cycle oscillations (Fig. 4-(b)), and divergent oscillations (Fig. 4-(c))). This process is rather universal across the boundary. From stable state to divergent oscillation state, a narrow transition zone of some kW has been found in this study.
The analysed system is non-linear and pretty complex. Trajectories on the phase space defined by boiling boundary z_{BB} vs. inlet mass flux G_{in} are reported in Fig. 4 too. The operating point on the stability boundary (Fig. 4-(b)) is the cut-off point between stable (Fig. 4-(a)) and unstable (Fig. 4-(c)) states. This point can be looked as a bifurcation point. The

limit oscillation is a quasi-periodic motion; the period of the depicted oscillation is rather small (less than 1 s), due to the low subcooling conditions considered at inlet.

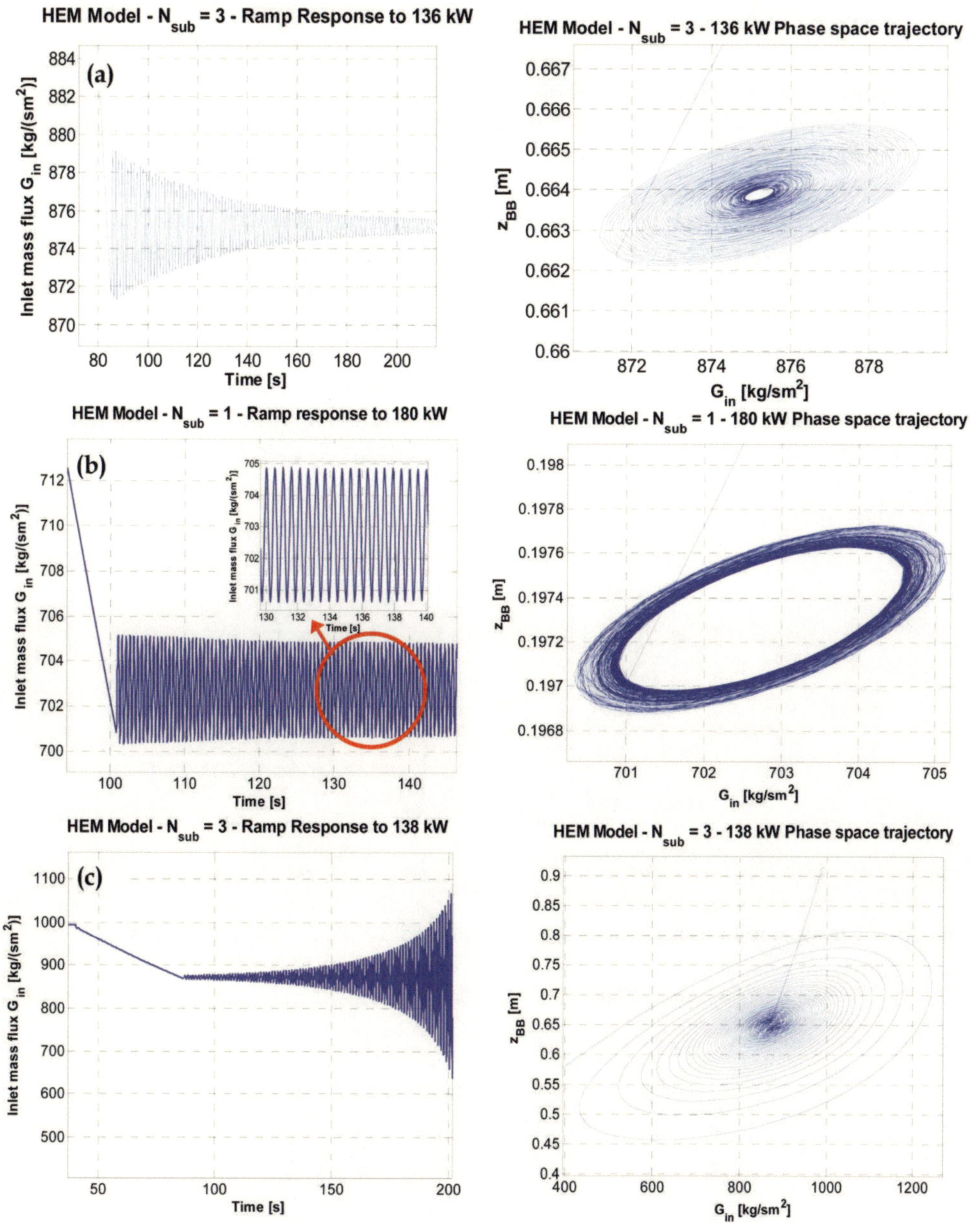

Fig. 4. Inlet mass flux oscillation curves and corresponding trajectories in the phase space
(a) Stable state - (b) Neutral stability boundary - (c) Unstable state

With reference to the eigenvalue computation, by solving Eq. (28), at least one of the eigenvalues is real, and the other two can be either real or complex conjugate. For the complex conjugate eigenvalues, the operating conditions that generate the stability boundary are those in which the complex conjugate eigenvalues are purely imaginary (i.e., the real part is zero). Crossing the instability threshold is characterized by passing to positive real part of the complex conjugate eigenvalues, which is at the basis of the diverging response of the model under unstable conditions.

5.2 Description of a self-sustained DWO

The simple two-node lumped parameter model developed in this work is capable to catch the basic phenomena of density wave oscillations. Numerical simulations have been used to gain insight into the physical mechanisms behind DWOs, as discussed in this section.
The analysis has shown good agreement with some findings due to Rizwan-Uddin (1994). Fully developed DWO conditions are considered. By analysing an inlet velocity variation and its propagation throughout the channel, particular features of the transient pressure drop distributions are depicted.
The starting point is taken as a variation (increase) in the inlet velocity. The boiling boundary responds to this perturbation with a certain delay (Fig. 5), due to the propagation of an enthalpy wave in the single-phase region. The propagation of this perturbation in the two-phase zone (via quality and void fraction perturbations) causes further lags in terms of two-phase average velocity and exit velocity (Fig. 6).

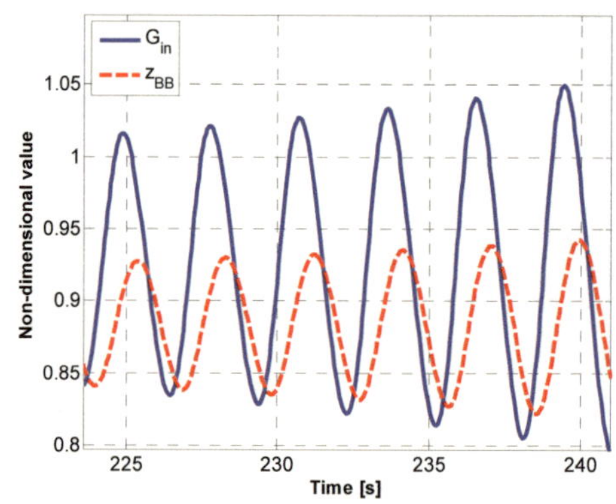

Fig. 5. Dimensionless inlet mass flux and boiling boundary. $N_{sub} = 8$; $Q = 133$ kW

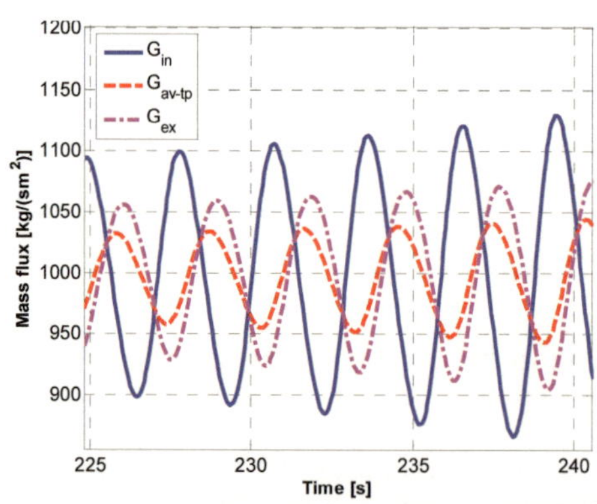

Fig. 6. Mass flux delayed variations along the channel. $N_{sub} = 8$; $Q = 133$ kW

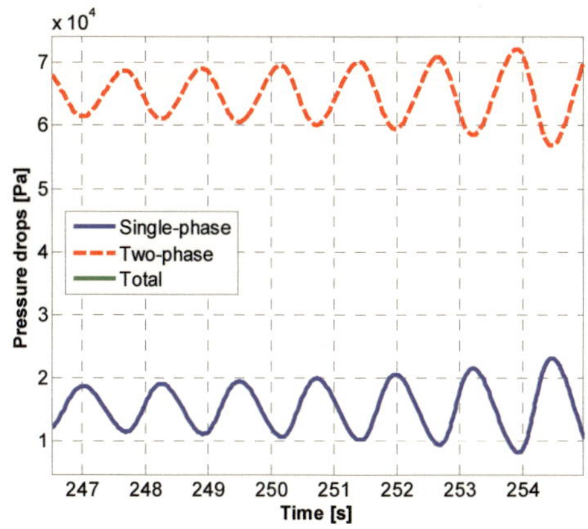

Fig. 7. Oscillating pressure drop distribution. N_{sub} = 2; Q = 103 kW

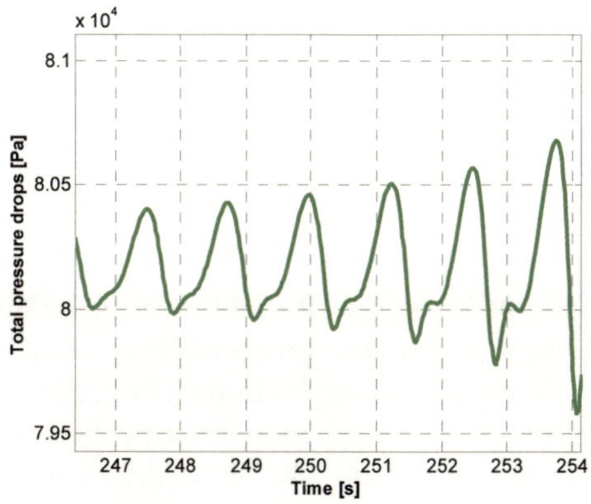

Fig. 8. "Shark-fin" oscillation of total pressure drops. N_{sub} = 2; Q = 103 kW

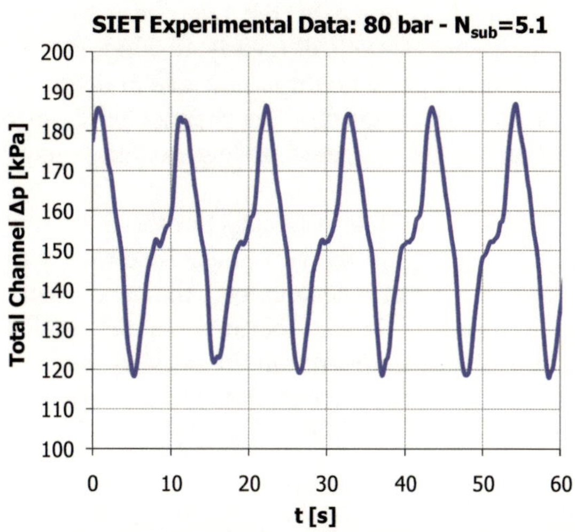

Fig. 9. Experimental recording of total pressure drop oscillation showing "shark-fin" shape (SIET labs)

All these delayed effects combine in single-phase pressure drop term and two-phase pressure drop term acquiring 180° out-of-phase fluctuations (Fig. 7). What is interesting to notice, indeed, is that the 180° phase shift between single-phase and two-phase pressure drops is not perfect (Rizwan-Uddin, 1994). Due to the delayed propagation of initial inlet velocity variation, single-phase term increase is faster than two-phase term rising. The superimposition of the two oscillations - in some operating conditions - is such to create a total pressure drop along the channel oscillating as a non-sinusoidal wave. The peculiar trend obtained is shown in Fig. 8; relating oscillation shape has been named "shark-fin" shape. Such behaviour has found corroboration in the experimental evidence collected with the facility at SIET labs (Papini et al., 2011). In Fig. 9 an experimental recording of channel total pressure drops is depicted. The experimental pressure drop oscillation shows a fair qualitative agreement with the phenomenon of "shark-fin" shape described theoretically.

5.3 Sensitivity analyses and stability maps

In order to provide accurate quantitative predictions of the instability thresholds, and of their dependence with the inlet subcooling to draw a stability map (as the one commonly drawn in the N_{pch}–N_{sub} stability plane (Ishii & Zuber, 1970), see e.g. Fig. 2), it is first necessary to identify most critical modelling parameters that have deeper effects on the results.

Several sensitivity studies have been carried out on the empirical coefficients used to model two-phase flow structure. In particular, specific empirical correlations have been accounted for within momentum balance equation to represent two-phase frictional pressure drops (by testing several correlations for the two-phase friction factor multiplier Φ_{lo}^2 [3]).

In this respect, a comparison of the considered friction models is provided in Table 2: Homogeneous Equilibrium pressure drop Model (HEM), Lockhart-Martinelli multiplier, Jones expression of Martinelli-Nelson method and Friedel correlation are selected (Todreas & Kazimi, 1993), respectively, for the analysis. It is worth noticing that the main contribution to channel total pressure drops is given by the two-phase terms, both frictional and in particular concentrated losses at channel exit (nearly 40-50%). Fractional distribution of the pressure drops along the channel plays an important role in determining the stability of the system. Concentration of pressure drops near the channel exit is such to render the system prone to instability: hence, DWOs triggered at low qualities may be expected with the analysed system.

The effects of two-phase frictions on the instability threshold are evident from the stability maps shown in Fig. 10. The higher are the two-phase friction characteristics of the system (that is, with Lockhart-Martinelli and Jones models), the most unstable results the channel (being the instability induced at lower thermodynamic quality values). Moreover, RELAP5 calculations about DWO occurrence in the same system are reported as well (see Section 6). In these conditions, Friedel correlation for two-phase multiplier is the preferred one.

---

[3] When *"lo"* subscript is added to the friction multiplier, *liquid-only* approach is considered. That is, the liquid phase is assumed to flow alone with total flow rate.

Conversely, when *"l"* subscript is applied, *only-liquid* approach is considered. That is, the liquid phase is assumed to flow alone at its actual flow rate.

	HEM		Lockhart-Martinelli		Jones		Friedel	
Term	*ΔP [kPa]*	*% of total*	*ΔP [kPa]*	*% of total*	*ΔP [kPa]*	*% of total*	*ΔP [kPa]*	*% of total*
ΔP_{grav}	12.82	17.31%	12.82	7.96%	12.82	10.96%	12.82	14.62%
ΔP_{acc}	10.24	13.84%	10.24	6.36%	10.24	8.76%	10.24	11.68%
ΔP_{in}	15.35	20.74%	15.35	9.54%	15.35	13.12%	15.35	17.51%
$\Delta P_{frict,1\phi}$	0.96	1.29%	0.96	0.59%	0.96	0.82%	0.96	1.09%
$\Delta P_{frict,2\phi}$	10.61	14.33%	39.84	24.75%	23.54	20.12%	14.97	17.07%
ΔP_{ex}	24.06	32.50%	81.73	50.79%	54.07	46.22%	33.36	38.04%
ΔP_{tot}	74.03	100%	160.94	100%	116.97	100%	87.69	100%

Table 2. Fractional contributions to total channel pressure drop (at steady-state conditions). Test case: $\Gamma = 0.12$ kg/s; $T_{in} = 239.2$ °C; $Q = 100$ kW ($x_{ex} = 0.40$)

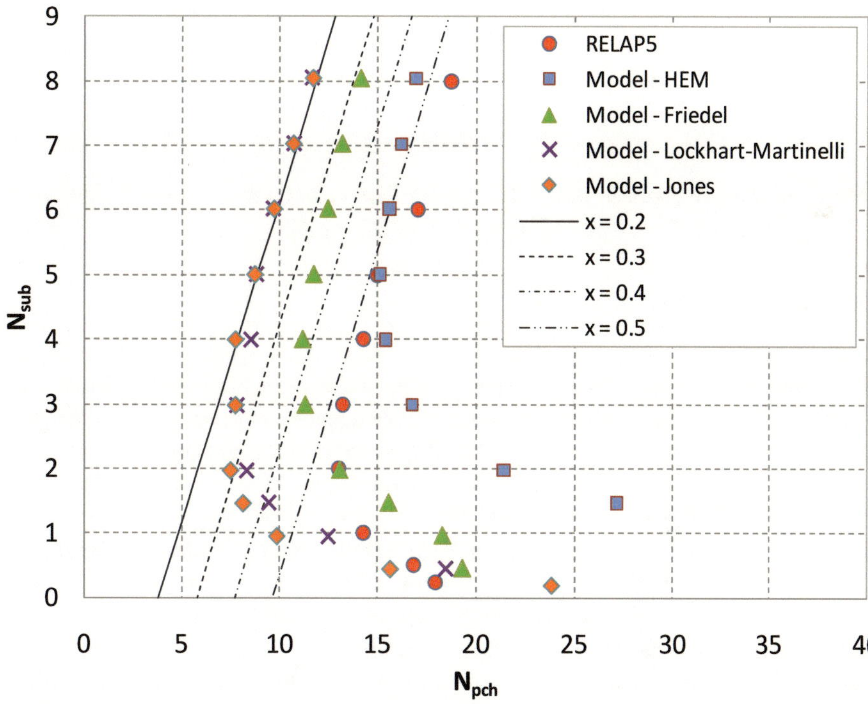

Fig. 10. Stability maps in the N_{pch}–N_{sub} stability plane, drawn with different models for two-phase friction factor multiplier

The influence of the two-phase friction multiplier on the system stability (via the channel pressure drop distribution) is made apparent also in terms of eigenvalues computation. Fig. 11 reports the results of the linear stability analysis corresponding to the four cases depicted in Table 2.

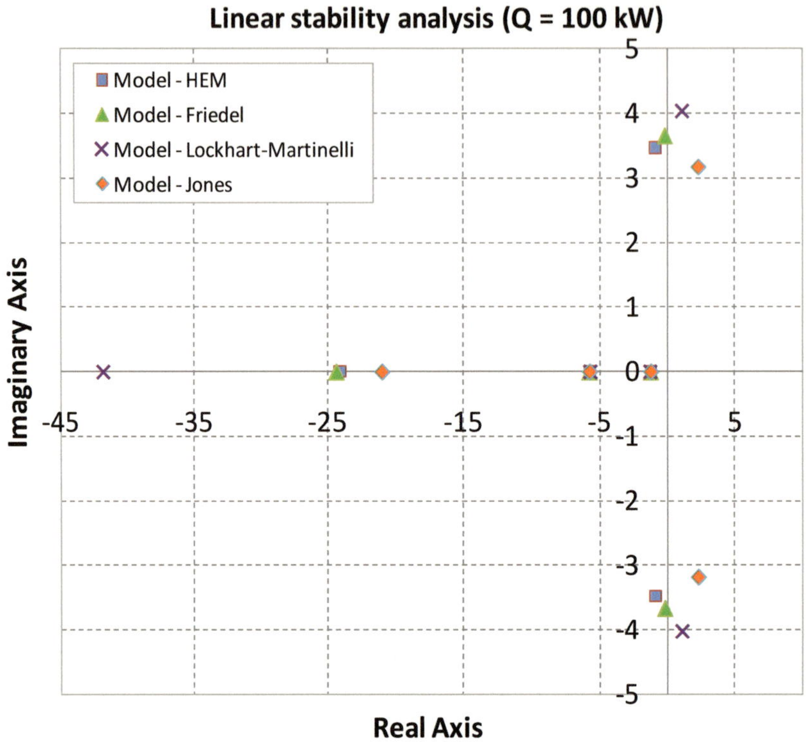

Fig. 11. Sensitivity on two-phase friction factor multiplier in terms of system eigenvalues. Test case: Γ = 0.12 kg/s; T_{in} = 239.2 °C; Q = 100 kW (x_{ex} = 0.40)

6. Numerical modelling

Theoretical predictions from analytical model have been then verified via qualified numerical simulation tools. Both, the thermal-hydraulic dedicated code RELAP5 and the multi-physics code COMSOL have been successfully applied to predict DWO inception and calculate the stability map of the single boiling channel system (vertical tube geometry) referenced in Section 4 and 5. The final benchmark - considering also the noteworthy work of Ambrosini et al. (2000) - is shown in Fig. 12.

As concerns the RELAP5 modelling, rather than simulating a fictitious configuration with single channel working with imposed ΔP, kept constant throughout the simulation (as provided by Ambrosini & Ferreri (2006)), the attempt to reproduce realistic experimental apparatus for DWO investigation has been pursued. For instance, the analyses on a single boiling channel have been carried out by considering a large bypass tube connected in parallel to the heated channel. As discussed in Section 2, the bypass solution is in fact the typical layout experimentally adopted to impose the constant-pressure-drop condition on a single boiling channel[4]. Instability inception is established from transient analysis, by increasing the power generation till fully developed flow oscillations occur.

[4] As a matter of fact, in the experimental apparatus the mass flow rate is forced by an external feedwater pump, instead of being freely driven according to the supplied power level.

As concerns the COMSOL modelling, a thermal-hydraulic 1D simulator valid for water-steam mixtures has been first developed, via implementation in the code of the governing PDEs for single-phase and two-phase regions, respectively. Linear stability analysis has been then computed to obtain the results reported in Fig. 12, where both, homogeneous model for two-phase flow structure (as assumed by the analytical model) and appropriate drift-flux model accounting for slip effects as well are considered. As the proper prediction of the instability threshold depends highly on the effective frictional characteristics of the reproduced channel (see Section 5.3), the possibility of implementing most various kinds of two-phase flow models (drift-flux kind, with different correlations for the void fraction) renders the developed COMSOL model suitable to apply for most different heated channel systems.

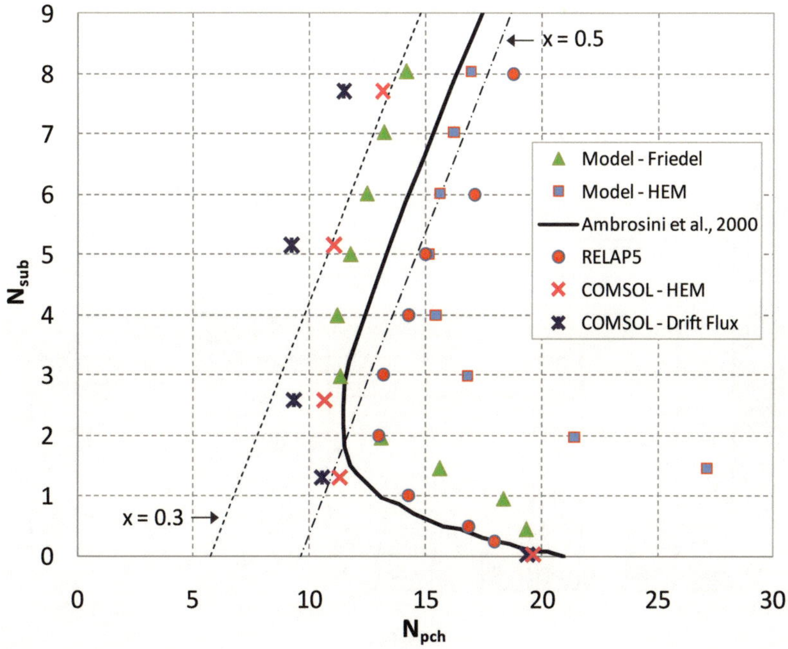

Fig. 12. Validation benchmark between analytical model and numerical models with RELAP5 and COMSOL codes

7. Experimental campaign with helical coil tube geometry

In order to experimentally study DWOs in helically coiled tubes, a full-scale open-loop test facility simulating the thermal-hydraulic behaviour of a helically coiled steam generator for applications within SMRs was built and operated at SIET labs (Piacenza, Italy) (Papini et al., 2011). Provided with steam generator full elevation and suited for prototypical thermal-hydraulic conditions, the facility comprises two helical tubes (1 m coil diameter, 32 m length, 8 m height), connected via lower and upper headers. Conceptual sketch is depicted in Fig. 13, whereas global and detailed views are shown in Fig. 14.

The test section is fed by a three-cylindrical pump with a maximum head of about 200 bar; the flow rate is controlled by a throttling valve positioned downwards the feed water pump and after a bypass line. System pressure control is accomplished by acting on a throttling valve placed at the end of the steam generator. An electrically heated helically coiled pre-heater is located before the test section, and allows creating the desired inlet temperature. To excite flow unstable conditions starting from stable operating conditions, supplied electrical power was gradually increased (by small steps, 2-5 kW) up to the appearance of permanent and regular flow oscillations.

Nearly 100 flow instability threshold conditions have been identified, in a test matrix of pressures (80 bar, 40 bar, 20 bar), mass fluxes (600 kg/m²s, 400 kg/m²s, 200 kg/m²s) and inlet subcooling (from -30% up to saturation). Effects of the operating pressure, flow rate and inlet subcooling on the instability threshold power have been investigated, pointing out the differences with respect to classical DWO theory, valid for straight tubes.

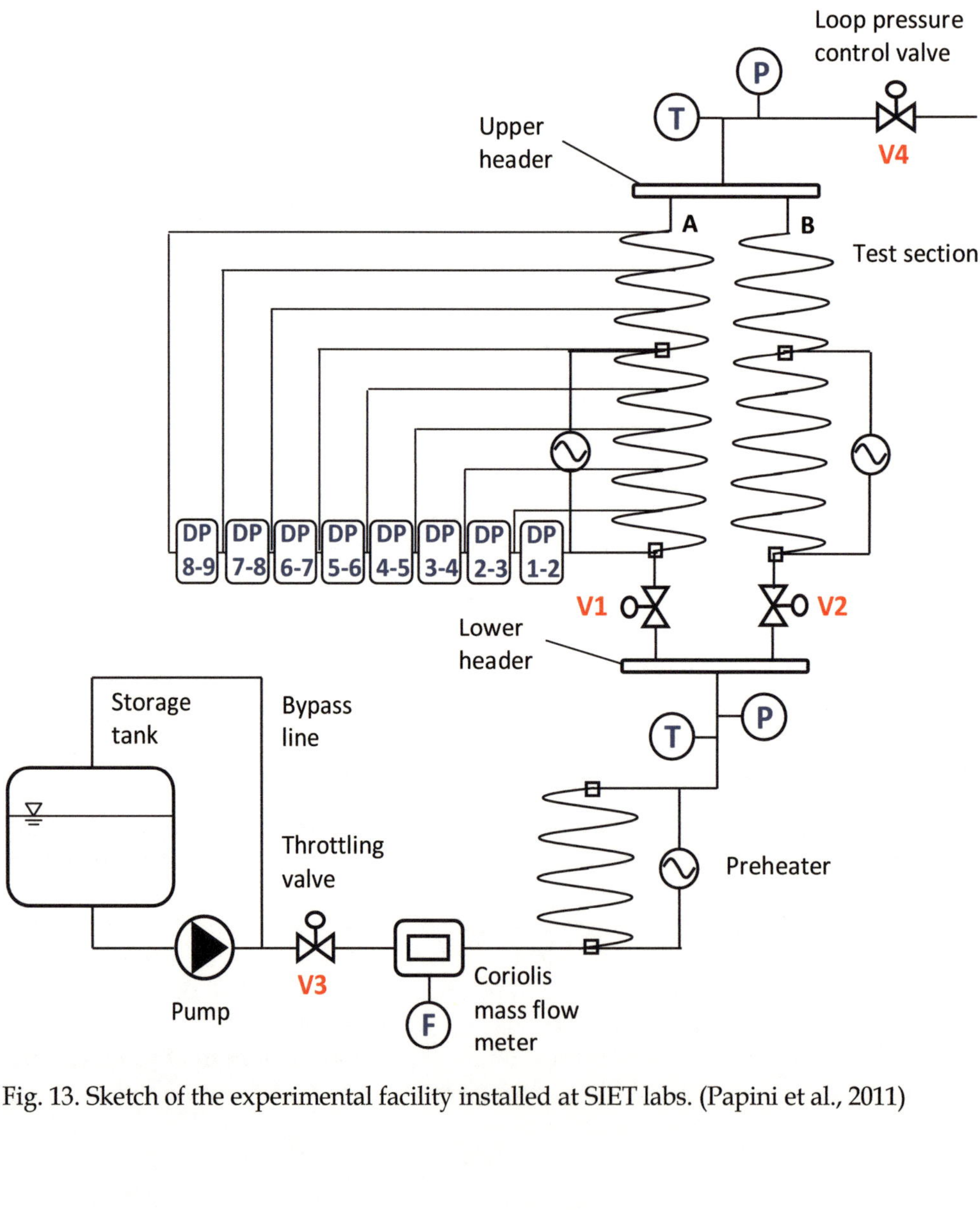

Fig. 13. Sketch of the experimental facility installed at SIET labs. (Papini et al., 2011)

Fig. 14. Global view (a) and detailed picture (b) of the helical coil test facility (SIET labs)

7.1 Experimental characterization of a self-sustained DWO

DWO onset can be detected by monitoring the flow rate, which starts to oscillate when power threshold is reached. Calibrated orifices installed at the inlet of both parallel tubes permitted to measure the flow rate through the recording of the pressure drops established across them. Oscillation amplitude grows progressively as the instability is incepted. Throughout our analyses the system was considered completely unstable (corresponding to instability threshold crossing) when flow rate oscillation amplitude reached the 100% of its steady-state value. Obviously, the flow rate in the two channels oscillates in counter-phase, as shown in Fig. 15-(a). The "square wave" shape of the curves is due to the reaching of instruments full scale.

The distinctive features of DWOs within two parallel channels can be described as follows.

System pressure oscillates with a frequency that is double if compared with the frequency of flow rate oscillations (Fig. 15-(b)).

Counter-phase oscillation of single-phase and two-phase pressure drops can be noticed within each channel. Pressure drops between pressure taps placed on different regions of Channel A, in case of self-sustained instability, are compared in Fig. 15-(c). Pressure drops in the single-phase region (DP 2-3) oscillate in counter-phase with respect to two-phase pressure drops (DP 6-7 and DP 8-9). The phase shift is not abrupt, but it appears gradually along the channel. As a matter of fact, the pressure term DP 4-5 (low-quality two-phase region) shows only a limited phase shift with respect to single-phase zone (DP 2-3).

Moreover, large amplitude fluctuations in channel wall temperatures, so named *thermal oscillations* (Kakaç & Bon, 2008), always occur (Fig. 15-(d)), associated with fully developed density wave oscillations that trigger intermittent film boiling conditions.

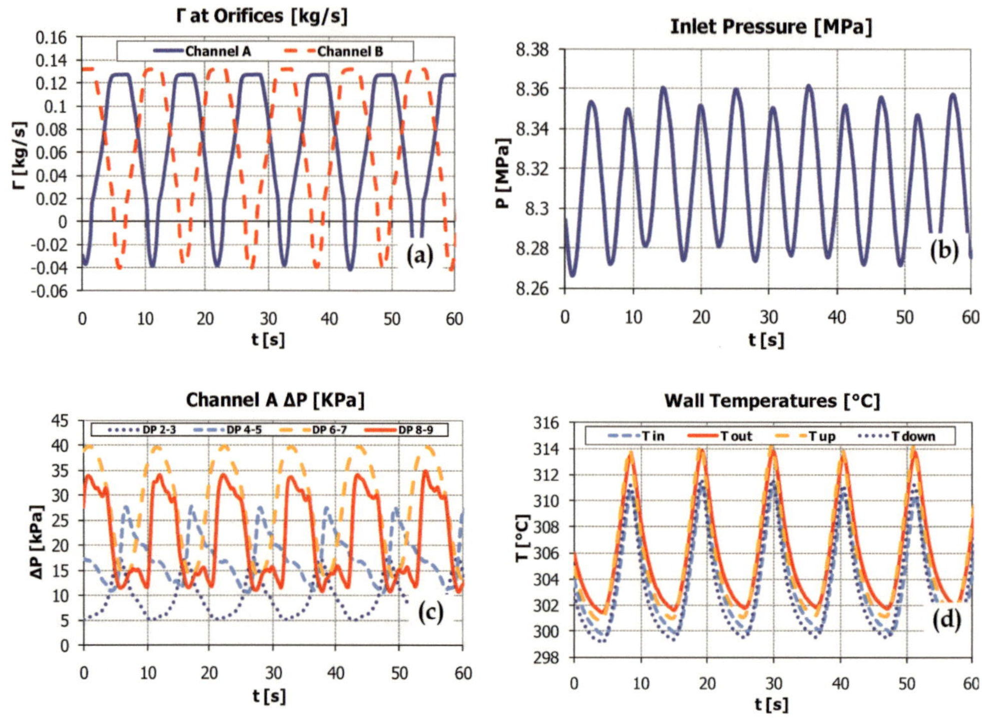

Fig. 15. Flow rate oscillations (a), system pressure oscillations (b), pressure drops oscillations (c) and wall temperature oscillations (d) during fully developed instabilities.
Data collected with: P = 83 bar; T_{in} = 199 °C; G = 597 kg/m^{2}s; Q = 99.3 kW

7.2 Experimental results

The experimental campaign provided a thorough threshold database useful for model validation. Collected threshold data have been clustered in the N_{pch}–N_{sub} stability plane.

Peculiar influence of the helical coil geometry (ascribable to the centrifugal field induced by tube bending) has been main object of investigation. For the sake of brevity, just the experimental results at P = 40 bar are hereby presented. Instability threshold data for the three values of mass flux (G = 600 kg/m^{2}s, 400 kg/m^{2}s and 200 kg/m^{2}s) are depicted in Fig. 16, whereas limit power dependence with the inlet subcooling is shown in Fig. 17.

The effects on instability of the thermal power and mass flow rate do not show differences in the helical geometry when compared to the straight tube case (refer to the parametric discussion of Section 2.2). In short, an increase in thermal power or a decrease in channel mass flow rate are found to trigger the onset of DWOs; both effects increase the exit quality, which turns out to be a key parameter for boiling channel instability.

Instead, it is interesting to focus the attention on the effects of the inlet subcooling. With respect to the *L shape* of the stability boundary, generally exhibited by vertical straight tubes, the present datasets with helical geometry show indeed two different behaviours: *(a)* "conventional" at medium-high subcoolings, with iso-quality stability boundary and slight stabilization in the range N_{sub} = 3 ÷ 6 (close to *L shape*); *(b)* "non-conventional" at low subcoolings, with marked destabilizing effects as the inlet temperature increases and approaches the saturation value.

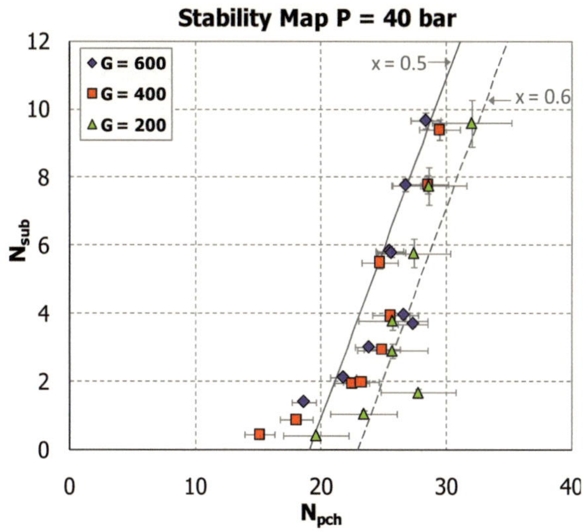

Fig. 16. Stability map obtained at P = 40 bar and different mass fluxes (G = 600 kg/m²s, 400 kg/m²s, 200 kg/m²s)

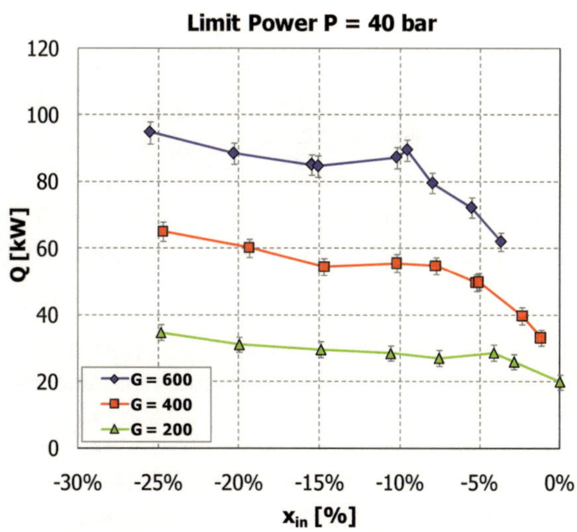

Fig. 17. Limit power for instability inception at P = 40 bar as function of inlet subcooling and for different mass fluxes

8. Comparison between models and experimental results

To reproduce and interpret the highlighted phenomena related to the investigated helical coil geometry, both the analytical lumped parameter model and the RELAP5 code have been applied. Proper modifications to simulate the experimental facility configuration (Table 3) include introduction of a riser section downstream the heated section and approximation of the helical shape by assuming a straight channel long as the helical tube and with the same inclination of the helix.

Heated channel	
Diameter [m]	0.01253
Heated length [m]	24
Riser length [m]	8
Helix inclination angle [deg]	14.48°
Operating parameters	
Pressure [bar]	20 - 40 - 80
Mass flux (per channel) [kg/m²s]	200 - 400 - 600
Inlet subcooling [%]	-30 ÷ 0
k_{in}	45
k_{ex}	0

Table 3. Dimensions and operating conditions of the experimental facility

8.1 Analytical modelling of the experimental facility

Best results have been obtained via the analytical model, on the basis of a modified form of the widespread and sound Lockhart-Martinelli two-phase friction multiplier, previously tuned on the frictional characteristics of the system (Colorado et al., 2011). The modified Lockhart-Martinelli multiplier (*only-liquid* kind) used for the calculations reads:

$$\Phi_l^2 = 1 + \frac{3.2789}{X_{tt}} + \frac{0.3700}{X_{tt}^{2.0822}} \tag{29}$$

To comply with the form of the modelling equations, passing from *"only-liquid"* to *"liquid-only"* mode is required. The following relation (Todreas & Kazimi, 1993) is considered:

$$\Phi_{lo}^2 = \Phi_l^2 (1-x)^{1.75} \tag{30}$$

Though the developed analytical model seems to underestimate the instability threshold conditions (that is, the predicted instabilities occur at lower qualities), rather satisfactory results turn out at low flow rate values (G = 200 kg/m²s). In these conditions, fair agreement is found with the peculiar instability behaviour of helical coil geometry, characterized by a marked destabilization near the saturation when inlet temperature is increased (i.e., inlet subcooling is reduced). Fig. 18-(a) shows how the peculiar stability boundary shape, experimentally obtained for the present helical-coiled system, is well predicted. Finally, the comparison between model and experimental findings is considerably better at high pressure (P = 80 bar; Fig. 18-(b)), where the homogenous two-phase flow model - at the basis of the modelling equations - is more accurate.

8.2 RELAP5 modelling of the experimental facility

Marked overestimations of the instability onset come out when applying the RELAP5 code to the helical coil tube facility simulation (see Fig. 18), mainly due to the lack in the code of specific thermo-fluid-dynamics models (two-phase pressure drops above all) suited for the complex geometry investigated.

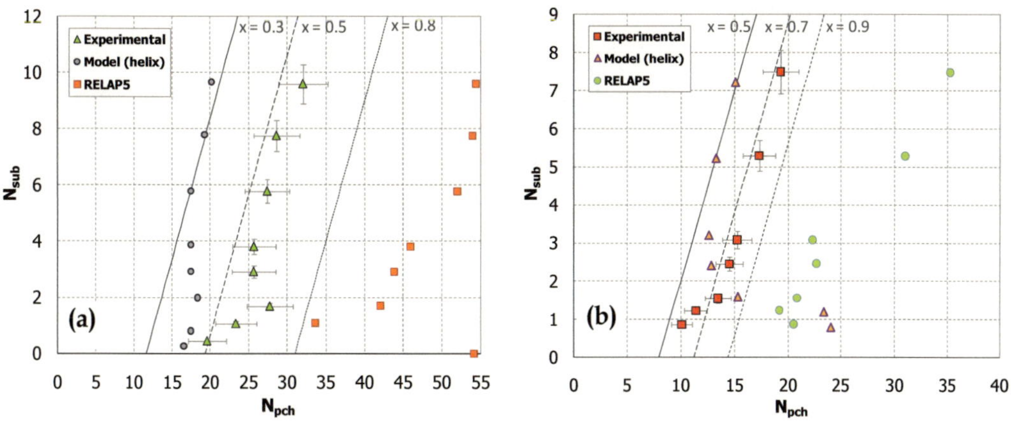

Fig. 18. Comparison between experimental, theoretical and RELAP5 results.
(a) P = 40 bar; G = 200 kg/m^{2}s - (b) P = 80 bar; G = 400 kg/m^{2}s

9. Conclusions

Density wave instability phenomena have been presented in this work, featured as topic of interest in the nuclear area, both to the design of BWR fuel channels and the development of the steam generators with peculiar reference to new generation SMRs.

Parametric discussions about the effects of thermal power, flow rate, inlet subcooling, system pressure, and inlet/exit throttling on the stability of a boiling channel have been stated. Theoretical studies based on analytical and numerical modelling have been presented, aimed at gaining insight into the distinctive features of DWOs as well as predicting instability onset conditions.

An analytical lumped parameter model has been developed. Non-linear features of the modelling equations have permitted to represent the complex interactions between the variables triggering the instability. Proper simulation of two-phase frictional pressure drops - prior to proper representation of the pressure drop distribution within the channel - has been depicted as the most critical concern for accurate prediction of the instability threshold. Dealing with the simple and known-from-literature case of vertical tube geometry, theoretical predictions from analytical model have been validated with numerical results obtained via the RELAP5 and COMSOL codes, which have proved to successfully predict the DWO onset.

The study of the instability phenomena with respect to the helical coil geometry, envisaged for the steam generators of several SMRs, led to a thorough experimental activity by testing two helically coiled parallel tubes. The experimental campaign has shown the peculiar influence of the helical geometry on instability thresholds, evident mostly in a pretty different parametric effect of the inlet subcooling.

The analytical model has been satisfactorily applied to the simulation of the experimental results. Correct representation of the stationary pressure drop distribution (partially accomplished thanks to the experimental tuning of a sound friction correlation) has been identified as fundamental before providing any accurate instability calculations. In this respect, the RELAP5 code cannot be regarded for the time being as a proven tool to study DWO phenomena in helically coiled tubes.

10. Acknowledgments

The Authors wish to thank Gustavo Cattadori, Andrea Achilli as well as all the staff of SIET labs for the high professionalism in the experimental campaign preparation and execution. Dario Colorado (UAEM - Autonomous University of Morelos State) is gratefully acknowledged for the pleasant and fruitful collaboration working on the modelling of helical-coiled steam generator systems.

11. Nomenclature

A	tube cross-sectional area [m^2]
c	specific heat [J/kg°C]
G	mass flux [kg/m^{2}s]
H	tube length (heated zone) [m]
h	specific enthalpy [J/kg]
	heat transfer coefficient, Eqs.(8),(9) [W/m^2°C]
j	volumetric flux $((x/\rho_g + (1-x)/\rho_f) \cdot G_{2\phi})$ [m/s]
k	concentrated loss coefficient [-]
M	tube mass [kg]
N_{pch}	phase change number $(Q/(\Gamma h_{fg}) \cdot v_{fg}/v_f)$ [-]
N_{sub}	subcooling number $(\Delta h_{in}/h_{fg} \cdot v_{fg}/v_f)$ [-]
P	pressure [bar]
Q	thermal power [W]
Q'''	thermal power per unit of volume [W/m^3]
S	heat transfer surface [m^2]
T	temperature [°C]
	period of oscillations, Eq.(2) [s]
t	time [s]
v	specific volume [m^3/kg]
w	liquid velocity [m/s]
X_{tt}	Lockhart-Martinelli parameter $(((1-x)/x)^{0.9} \cdot (\rho_g/\rho_f)^{0.5} \cdot (\mu_f/\mu_g)^{0.1})$ [-]
x	thermodynamic quality [-]
z	tube abscissa [m]
α	void fraction [-]
ΔP	pressure drops [Pa]
Γ	mass flow rate [kg/s]
η	state variable
λ	system eigenvalue
μ	dynamic viscosity [Pa s]
ρ	density [kg/m^3]
τ	heated section transit time [s]
$\Phi^2_{l/lo}$	two-phase friction multiplier $(\Delta P_{tp}/\Delta P_{l/lo})$ [-]
Ω	reaction frequency $(Q/(AH) \cdot v_{fg}/h_{fg})$ [1/s]

Subscripts

acc	accelerative
av	average
BB	boiling boundary
ex	exit
f	saturated liquid
fl	fluid bulk
frict	frictional
g	saturated vapour
grav	gravitational
H	homogeneous model
h	heated wall
in	inlet
l	only-liquid
lo	liquid-only
tot	total
tp	two-phase
1ϕ	single-phase region
2ϕ	two-phase region

12. References

Ambrosini, W., Di Marco, P. & Ferreri, J.C. (2000). Linear and Nonlinear Analysis of Density Wave Instability Phenomena, *International Journal of Heat and Technology*, Vol.18, No.1, pp. 27-36

Ambrosini, W. & Ferreri, J.C. (2006). Analysis of Basic Phenomena in Boiling Channel Instabilities with Different Flow Models and Numerical Schemes, *Proceedings of*

14th International Conference on Nuclear Engineering (ICONE 14), Miami, Florida, USA, July 17-20, 2006

Bouré, J.A., Bergles, A.E. & Tong, L.S. (1973). Review of two-phase flow instability, *Nuclear Engineering and Design*, Vol.25, pp. 165-192

Collins, D.B. & Gacesa, M. (1969). Hydrodynamic Instability in a Full Scale Simulated Reactor Channel, *Proceedings of the Symposium on Two Phase Flow Systems*, Leeds, Institute of Mechanical Engineers, London, UK, 1969, pp. 117-128

Colorado, D., Papini, D., Hernández, J.A., Santini, L. & Ricotti, M.E. (2011). Development and experimental validation of a computational model for a helically coiled steam generator, *International Journal of Thermal Sciences*, Vol.50, pp. 569-580

COMSOL, Inc. (2008). COMSOL Multiphysics® User's Guide, Version 3.5a

Guo Yun, Qiu, S.Z., Su, G.H. & Jia, D.N. (2008). Theoretical investigations on two-phase flow instability in parallel multichannel system, *Annals of Nuclear Energy*, Vol.35, pp. 665-676

Guo Yun, Huang Jun, Xia Genglei & Zeng Heyi (2010). Experiment investigation on two-phase flow instability in a parallel twin-channel system, *Annals of Nuclear Energy*, Vol.37, pp. 1281-1289

Ishii, M. & Zuber, N. (1970). Thermally Induced Flow Instabilities in Two Phase Mixture, *Proceedings of 4th International Heat Transfer Conference*, Paris, France, August 31 - September 5, 1970, Vol.5, paper B5.11

Kakaç, S. & Bon, B. (2008). A Review of two-phase flow dynamic instabilities in tube boiling systems, *International Journal of Heat and Mass Transfer*, Vol.51, pp. 399-433

Lahey Jr., R.T. & Moody, F.J. (1977). *The thermal-hydraulics of a boiling water nuclear reactor*, American Nuclear Society, USA

Masini, G., Possa, G. & Tacconi, F.A. (1968). Flow instability thresholds in parallel heated channels, *Energia Nucleare*, Vol.15, No.12, pp. 777-786

Muñoz-Cobo, J.L., Podowski, M.Z. & Chiva, S. (2002). Parallel channel instabilities in boiling water reactor systems: boundary conditions for out of phase oscillations, *Annals of Nuclear Energy*, Vol.29, pp. 1891-1917

Papini, D. (January 2011). Modelling and experimental investigation of helical coil steam generator for IRIS Small-medium Modular Reactor, *PhD Thesis*, Politecnico di Milano, Department of Energy, cycle XXIII, Milan, Italy

Papini, D., Colombo, M., Cammi, A., Ricotti, M.E., Colorado, D., Greco, M. & Tortora, G. (2011). Experimental Characterization of Two-Phase Flow Instability Thresholds in Helically Coiled Parallel Channels, *Proceedings of ICAPP 2011 - International Congress on Advances in Nuclear Power Plants*, Nice, France, May 2-5, 2011, paper 11183

Rizwan-Uddin (1994). On density-wave oscillations in two-phase flows, *International Journal of Multiphase Flow*, Vol.20, No.4, pp. 721-737

Saha, P., Ishii, M. & Zuber, N. (1976). An Experimental Investigation of the Thermally Induced Flow Oscillations in Two-Phase Systems, *Journal of Heat Transfer – Transactions of the ASME*, Vol.98, pp. 616-622

Schlichting, W.R., Lahey Jr., R.T., Podowski, M.Z. & Ortega Gòmez, T.A. (2007). Stability analysis of a boiling loop in space, *Proceedings of the COMSOL Conference 2007*, Boston, Massachusetts, USA, October 4-6, 2007

Schlichting, W.R., Lahey Jr., R.T. & Podowski, M.Z. (2010). An analysis of interacting instability modes, in a phase change system, *Nuclear Engineering and Design*, Vol.240, pp. 3178-3201

The Math Works, Inc. (2005). SIMULINK® software

Todreas, N.E. & Kazimi, M.S. (1993). *Nuclear Systems I: Thermal Hydraulic Fundamentals*, Taylor and Francis, Washington, DC, USA

US NRC Nuclear Safety Analysis Division (December 2001). RELAP5/MOD3.3 Code Manual, NUREG/CR-5535/Rev 1

Yadigaroglu, G. (1981). Two-Phase Flow Instabilities and Propagation Phenomena, In: Delhaye, J.M., Giot, M. & Riethmuller, M.L., (Eds.), *Thermohydraulics of two-phase systems for industrial design and nuclear engineering*, Hemisphere Publishing Corporation, Washington, DC, USA, 1981, pp. 353-396

Yadigaroglu, G. & Bergles, A.E. (1972). Fundamental and Higher-Mode Density Wave Oscillations in Two-Phase Flow, *Journal of Heat Transfer – Transactions of the ASME*, Vol.94, pp. 189-195

Zhang, Y.J., Su, G.H., Yang, X.B. & Qiu, S.Z. (2009). Theoretical research on two-phase flow instability in parallel channels, *Nuclear Engineering and Design*, Vol.239, pp. 1294-1303

13

Spray Cooling

Zhibin Yan[1], Rui Zhao[1], Fei Duan[1], Teck Neng Wong[1], Kok Chuan Toh[2], Kok Fah Choo[2], Poh Keong Chan[3] and Yong Sheng Chua[3]
[1]*School of Mechanical and Aerospace Engineering, Nanyang Technological University,*
[2]*Temasek Laboratories @ NTU,*
[3]*DSO National Laboratories*
Singapore

1. Introduction

1.1 Categorisation of cooling techniques

The need for higher heat flux cooling techniques is driven very much by the microelectronics and semiconductor industry. In accordance with Moore's Law, continuing advances in the semiconductor industry allow the device feature size to shrink and the transistor density and switching speed to double every one and a half to two years. Correspondingly, the heat dissipation from the chip increases in proportion, if there is no change in the semiconductor technology. In their study on the limits of device scaling and switching speeds, Zhirnov et al. (2003) concluded that "even if entirely different electron transport models are invented for digital logic, their scaling for density and performance may not go much beyond the ultimate limits obtainable with CMOS technology, due primarily to limits on heat removal capacity". For example, maximum heat flux at the localized submillimeter scale hotspots of high performance chips approaches 1 kW/cm^2 (Bar-Cohen et al., 2006). The operating efficiencies and stability of these devices depend on how effectively the heat generated can be removed from the system. Hence, developments in the cooling system have to keep apace with the heat removal requirements, starting with forced air convection being enhanced by compact finned heat sinks, to liquid-cooled microchannel arrays, and ultimately using phase change heat transfer through the boiling phenomena or from atomized sprays and jets. The choice of an appropriate cooling technique is however dependent on the specific application and the critical system factors which must be satisfied, such as the maximum permissible heat flux, total heat load, tight temperature tolerances, reliability considerations or overall power consumption. The operating environment also play a significant part which may necessitate an emphasis on the use of space, complexity of the system's components, relative maturity of the technology or cost.

Table 1 shows comparative cooling technologies and the respective heat fluxes and heat transfer coefficients (Glassman, 2005). There may be other work that list values outside of this table, but the nominal capacities of these cooling technologies in the table can still be viewed as a good reference. In general, cooling methods using sub-cooled flow boiling (SCFB), micro-channel cooling, two-phase jet impingement and spray cooling have achieved very high heat fluxes (over 100 W/cm^2) and heat transfer coefficients compared to the other traditional cooling techniques. However, under the right combination of factors, spray cooling has been found to be preferred over the other high heat flux cooling techniques.

Mechanism	Cooling Method	Heat Transfer Coefficient (W/cm²·K)	Highest Heat Flux (W/cm²)	Reference
Single Phase	Free Air Convection	0.0005-0.0025	15	(Mudawar, 2001; Azar, 2002)
Single Phase	Forced Air Convection, (Heat Sink with a fan)	0.001-0.025	35	(Mudawar, 2001)
Single Phase	Natural Convection with FC	0.1	0.1-3	(Anderson et al., 1989)
Single Phase	Natural Convection with water	0.08-0.2	5-90	(Mudawar, 2001)
Two Phase	Heat Pipes (water)	-NA-	250	(Zuo et al., 2001)
Single Phase	Micro-channel	-NA-	790	(Tukerman et al., 1981)
Electrical	Peltier Cooler	-NA-	125	(Riffat et al., 2004)
Two phase	Pool boiling with porous media	3.7	140	(Rainey et al., 2003a)
Two Phase	Sub-cooled Flow Boiling	2	129	(Sturgis and Mudawar, 1999)
Two Phase	Micro-channel Boiling	10-20	275	(Faulkner et al., 2003)
Two Phase	Spray Cooling	20-40	1200	(Pais et al., 1992)
Two Phase	Jet Impingement	28	1820	(Overholt et al., 2005)

Table 1. Cooling Techniques and Respective Heat Fluxes and Heat Transfer Coefficients (Glassman, 2005)

1.2 Major application areas of spray cooling

Spray cooling utilises a spray of small droplets impinging on a heated surface to increase the effectiveness of heat transfer as a cooling mechanism with phase change (Incropera and Dewitt, 2002). Spray cooling is widely used in various fields: fire protection, cooling of hot gases, dermatological operation and cooling of hot surfaces including hot strip mill and high performance electronic devices.

A fire sprinkler system is a common application of spray cooling for fire protection. A discharge of water through the nozzles into the ambient is atomized into tiny droplets in order to control or suppress the fire. The large surface area of the small droplets in contact with unsaturated ambient air promotes evaporation. As a result of the high latent heat absorbed by the water drops during evaporation, the heat release rate of the fire can be controlled to prevent fire spread.

In the metal production and processing industry, spray cooling also plays an important role for the high temperature (up to 1800 K) steel strip casting and the final microstructure optimization after hot rolling. Typically, a jet of gas carrying water drops is sprayed towards the hot surface to be cooled. Figure 1 shows a boiling curve corresponding to a certain water impact density (Nukiyama curve) in this process.

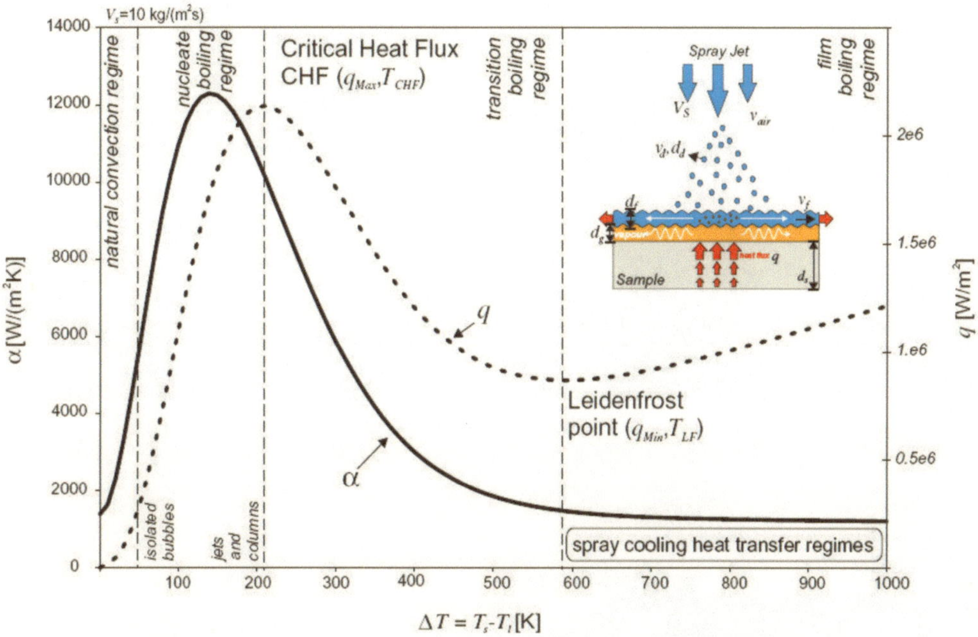

Fig. 1. Typical boiling curve in metal production (Wendelstorf et al., 2008)

In the biomedical industry, cryogenic spray cooling is implemented for selectively precooling of human skin during laser treatment with port wine stain birthmarks and hair removal. To avoid the permanent thermal damage to the skin surface arising from large temperature differences between the epidermis and deeper targeted vessels, a cryogenic spray can be spurted to the skin surface for a short period of time before the laser pulse is applied. Figure 2 shows a cryogenic spray using R134a as a working fluid for contact cooling of human skin.

However, this chapter will be devoted primarily to the study of cooling hot surfaces in high performance electronic devices. In the electronic packaging industry, spray cooling has drawn great attention due to its high heat flux removal ability (1200 W/cm²) while maintaining device temperature below 100 °C with spatial and temporal variations below 10 °C (Pais et al., 1992; Bar-Cohen et al., 2006). Currently, spray cooling have been used in a high performance computer (CRAY X-1) and is a promising solution for the thermal management of a high power insulated gate bipolar transistor (Mertens et al., 2007), laser diode laser arrays (Huddel et al., 2000) and microwave source components (Lin et al., 2004). Two examples of such applications are given in Figure 3 developed by Bar-Cohen et al. (1995) and Tilton et al. (1994).

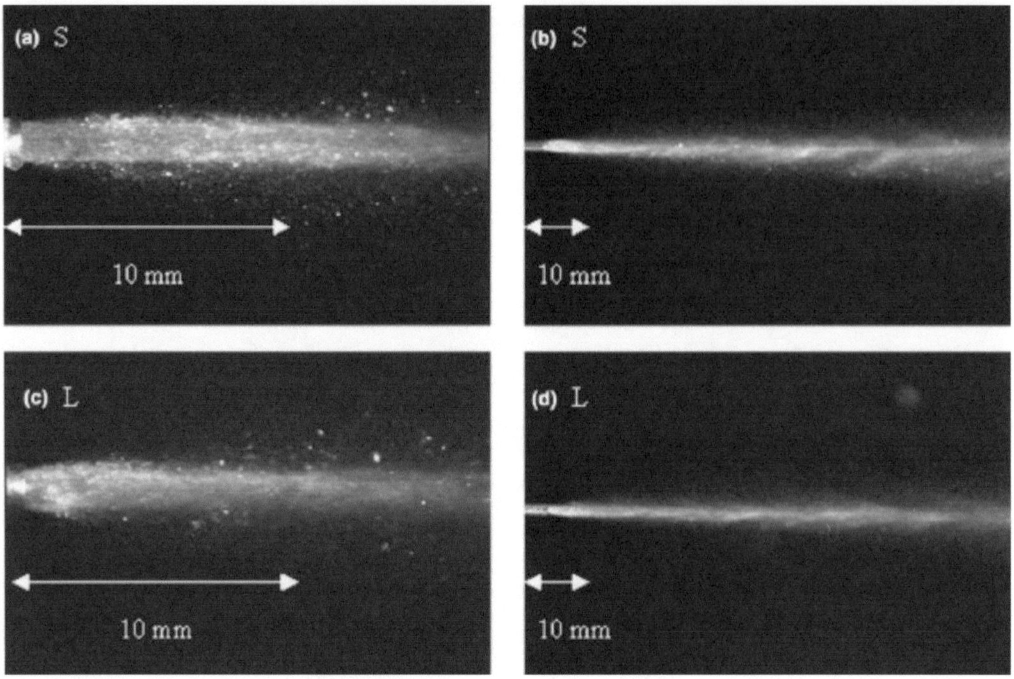

Fig. 2. Images of cryogen sprays for human skins (Aguilar et al., 2001)

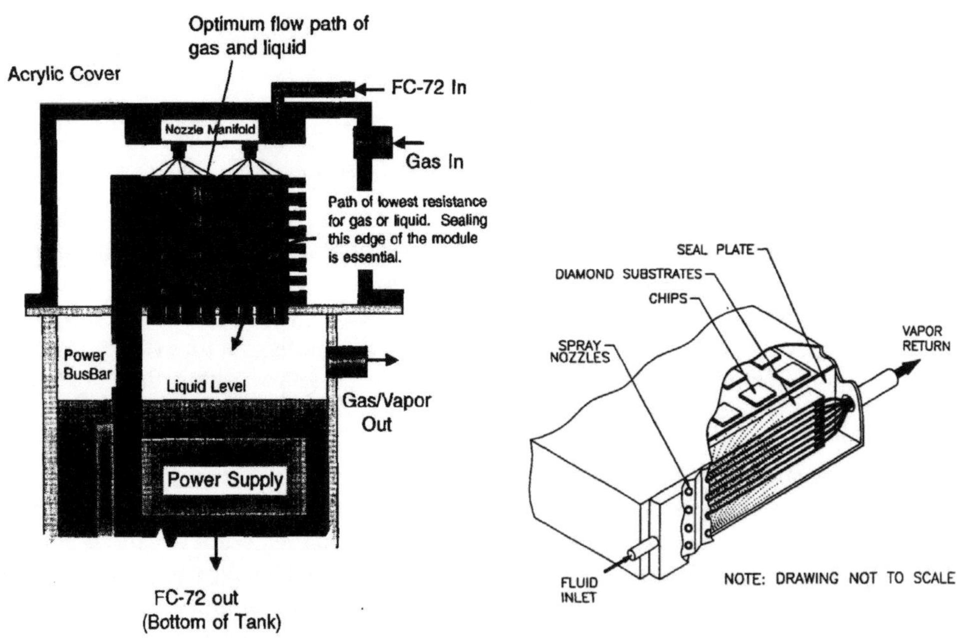

(a) (b)

Fig. 3. Spray cooling system for electronic devices by (a) Bar-Cohen et al. (1995); (b) Tilton et al. (1994)

2. Heat transfer mechanisms and critical heat flux in spray cooling

The heat transfer mechanisms occurring in a spray cooling process have yet to be clearly established, although it is known that spray cooling may comprise several heat transfer mechanisms that contribute to its high heat removal rate (Rini, 2000; Sellers, 2000; Tan, 2001; Selvam, 2006). The combination and interference of these mechanisms makes spray cooling unique compared to other conventional cooling methods such as forced convection which makes use of only a single phase fluid to achieve its cooling purposes.

Four major heat transfer mechanisms were proposed by Pais et al., 1992; Mesler and Mailen, 1993; Yang et al., 1996 and Rini et al., 2002. They are (1) evaporation off surface of the liquid film, (2) forced convection arising from droplet impingement on heated surface, (3) enhancement of nucleation sites on heated surface, and lastly (4) presence of secondary nucleation sites on the surface of spray droplets. Figure 4 illustrates the basic heat transfer mechanisms which will be explained in further detail later in this section. Other researchers suggested alternative mechanisms are at work. Selvam et al. (2005, 2006, 2009) proposed that transient conduction accompanying liquid backfilling the superheated heated surface after bubble departure dominated the high heat transfer in spray cooling according to their 2-D numerical simulation. By correlating the heat transfer data with the contact line lengths, Horacek et al. (2004, 2005) suggested that the contact line heat transfer was crucial for spray cooling.

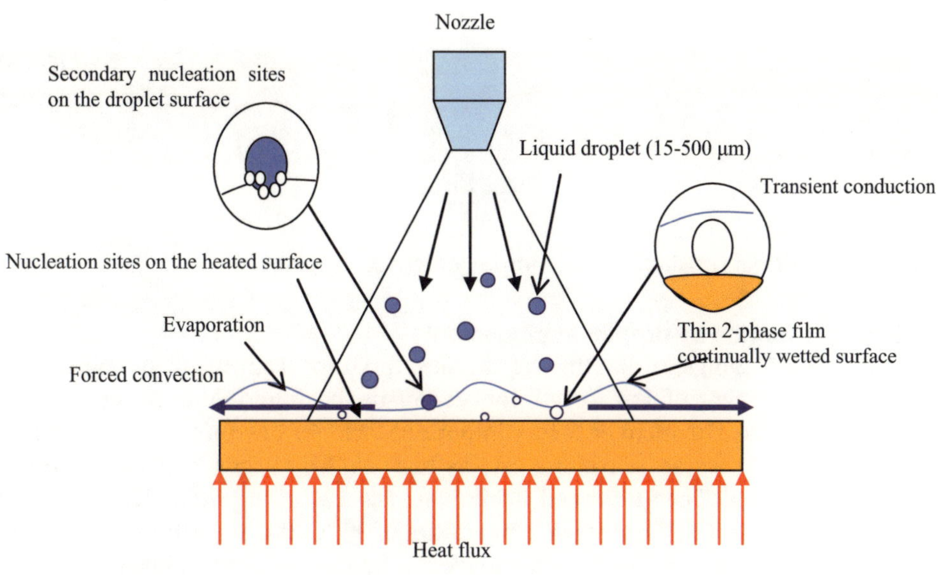

Fig. 4. The heat transfer mechanisms of spray cooling

2.1 Major mechanisms in spray cooling

2.1.1 Evaporation off surface of liquid film

Evaporation of liquid molecules from the surface of liquid film is one of the key factors in the heat transfer mechanism of spray cooling. As shown in Figure 5, a film of liquid is formed over the heated surface when spray cooling is initiated. This film is usually very thin at only a few hundred microns (300-500 μm). The impingement of spray droplets can generate an additional mixing, which decreases the already small effective thermal resistance resulting from the thin film of liquid, and improves the overall heat transfer efficiency considerably. Pais et al. (1992) suggested that evaporation from thin film is the dominant heat transfer mechanism in spray cooling according to their experimental studies on ultrasmooth surfaces. Although the phase change portion of evaporation process was also proposed as a possible enhancement for heat transfer, it is not considered to be the dominant effect (Silk et al., 2008). Silk et al. concluded that spray cooling with moderate evaporation efficiency can reach a higher heat flux compared with spray cooling process with full evaporation of the liquid on the heated surface, based on most experimental investigations they have reviewed.

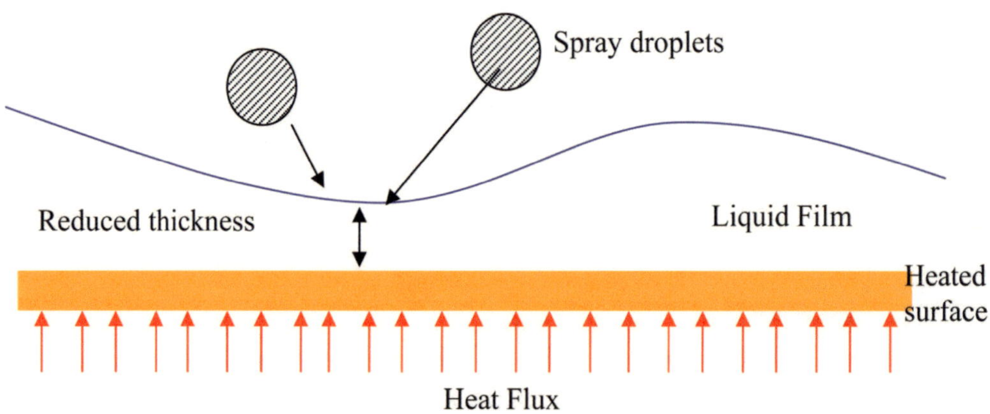

Fig. 5. Reduced thermal resistance due to impingement of droplet

2.1.2 Forced convection by droplet impingement

When the droplets impinge on the thin liquid film, the force from the incoming droplets produce an enhancement of the forced convection in the liquid film as illustrated in Figure 6. This has been proven to be a very important factor in previous works (Tan, 2001) on spray cooling with water. A cooling rate as high as 200 W/cm^2 and with a surface temperature of 99°C has been observed using water as a working fluid (Nevedo, 2000). Since nucleation is absent at the surface temperature of 99 °C, the majority of the heat flux removed has been credited to the forced convection by the droplet impingement for the single phase spray cooling. In the two phase region, the forced convection by droplet impingement is proposed to have the dominant effect at the period of low heat flux and surface superheat. Pautsch and Shedd (2005) and Shedd and Pautsch (2005) conducted a series of spray cooling experiments with single and multiple nozzles and developed an empirical model based on their experimental results. With the aid of visualisation studies, their model indicated that single-phase energy transfer by bulk fluid momentum played the major role in the high heat flux spray cooling, where a thin liquid film had formed on the heated surface.

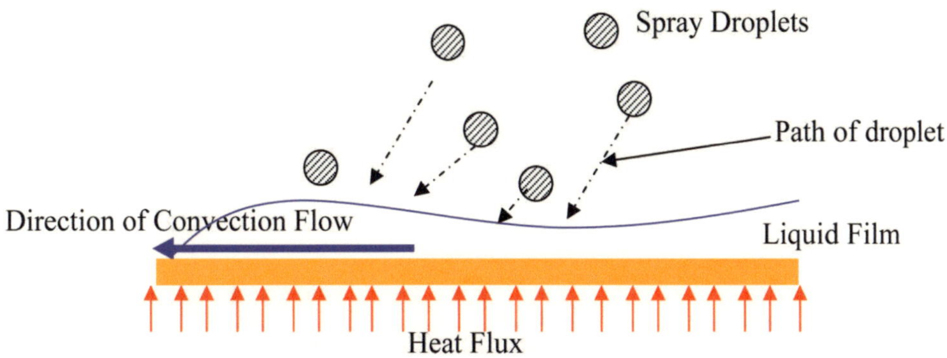

Fig. 6. Schematic of forced convection under droplet impingement

2.1.3 Fixed nucleation sites on heated surface

From previous experiments done on spray cooling, bubbles appear to be growing from fixed nucleation sites on the heated surface. This is possibly due to cavitations on the heated surface that promotes the growth of bubbles (Rini, 2000). The initiation of bubble growth is due to the absorbed heat flux and the temperature of the local nucleus site reaching T_{sat} which results in phase change of the liquid. When this happens, the bubble starts to grow from the nucleus by absorbing the heat from the heated surface and the surface temperature drops. It is also noted that bubbles would not start to grow around an existing nucleation site, probably a result of the existing bubble taking the required heat away from the surrounding surface necessary for another bubble initiation (Carey, 1992; Rohsenow et al., 1998).

In pool boiling, the bubble requires a period of time to gain enough buoyancy force at a certain diameter to overcome the surface tension of liquid and gravity for departure, and the nucleation sites also need time to recover the heat loss and increase in temperature to T_{sat} before a second bubble can be initiated from the same site. However in spray cooling, the momentum available in a droplet enables it to impinge through the liquid film and hit on the heated surface frequently, resulting in the break up of bubbles on the nucleation sites. This causes rapid removal of bubbles at the nucleation sites and a shorter interval time for bubble growth from the same site. Another possible scenario is when the forced convection by the droplet impingement discussed previously clears the bubbles from the surface, resulting in increase of new bubbles nucleating from the sites and reduction of the duration of bubbles anchoring on the heated surface.

These characteristics of spray cooling allow more bubbles to grow on the surface as the 'reduced bubble' sizes allow for more bubbles to grow around the sites and at a more rapid rate as shown in Figure 7. Previous studies (Pais et al., 1992; Sehmbey et al., 1990; Yang et al., 1993; Mudawar et al., 1996; Chen et al., 2002; Hsieh et al., 2004) have shown that the heat transfer in spray cooling is almost an order of magnitude higher than pool boiling (Nishikawa et al., 1967; Mesler et al., 1977; Marto et al., 1977; Hsieh et al., 1999). Though, both cooling methods involve phase change processes, the additional mechanisms and factors present in spray cooling make it favourable for evaporation to take place and make full use of latent heat to cool the heat source.

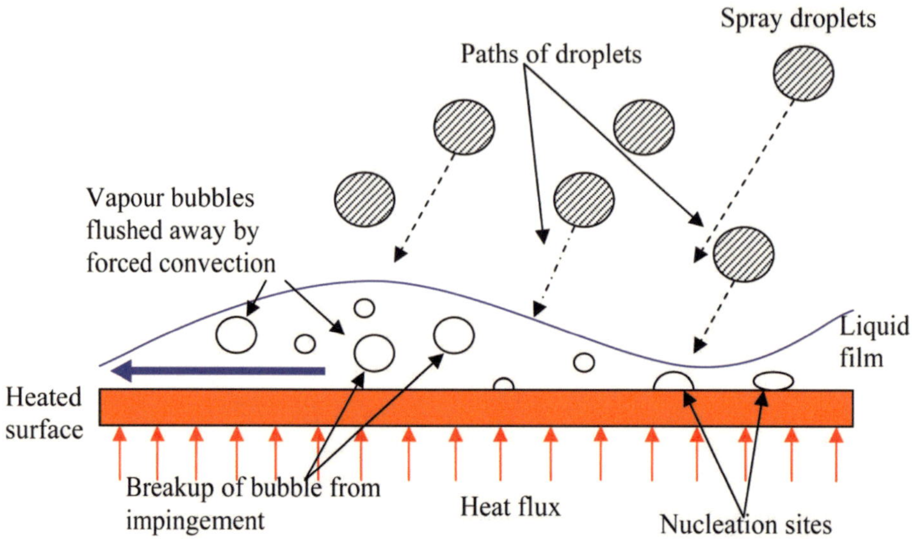

Fig. 7. Schematic of nucleation sites on heated surface under effect of droplets impingement

2.1.4 Secondary nucleation by spray droplets

It was proposed that the large number of secondary nucleation sites entrained by spray droplets is a major reason for spray cooling to remove a higher heat flux from the heated surface than by pool boiling (Rini et al., 2002). Esmailizadeh et al. (1986) and Sigler et al. (1990) both found that the upper surface of a bubble broke into small droplets and fell back to the liquid film when the bubbles impacted the liquid film in pool boiling studies. Thereafter, these small droplets could entrap vapour around them and bring it into the liquid film. Finally, the small vapour bubbles possibly acted as nuclei when they moved close to the heated surface and promoted boiling heat transfer as a result. In spray cooling, a similar phenomenon that the bubbles burst over the liquid film was observed as well. Nevertheless, spray droplets mixed with the vapour around and entrapped vapour bubbles within them. And when the droplets hit the liquid film, the entrapped vapour bubbles act as secondary nuclei sites to grow new bubbles. Hence, spray cooling can produce a lot more bubbles than pool boiling, over 3 to 4 times more (Rini et al., 2002). These additional nuclei sites are very important in the heat transfer mechanism of spray cooling as it provides a lot more nucleation sites for bubbles to grow and to absorb heat from the heated surface.

2.1.5 Transient conduction with liquid backfilling

Transient conduction accompanying liquid backfilling the superheated surface after bubble departure was numerically simulated by Selvam et al. (2006, 2009) using the direct numerical simulation method. Their model suggested that the cold-droplet impingement during impact, rebound of cold liquid after impact and transient conduction attributed to spreading of cold liquid over the dry hot surface played the dominant role in high heat flux spray cooling mechanism. It differs from the widely accepted dominant mechanism which is micro-layer evaporation in saturated pool boiling.

Although there has been no experimental result to support the view that transient conduction is the dominant mechanism in the spray cooling, previous experimental investigations in pool boiling (Demiray et al., 2004) has provided the evidence that transient conduction enhanced the heat transfer of pool boiling. According to the definition of the transient heat flux through conduction in a semi-infinite region with constant surface temperature as Eq. (1) (Incropera et al., 2002), the transient heat flux in the liquid film of spray cooling is determined by the frequency of vapour bubble departure and liquid around bubble flow over the locations occupied by vapour bubble antecedently.

$$\dot{q}'' = \frac{k\left(T_{surface} - T_i\right)}{\sqrt{\pi \alpha t}} \tag{1}$$

2.1.6 Contact line heat transfer

It was proposed by Horacek et al. (2004, 2005) that contact line heat transfer was responsible for the two-phase heat transfer of spray cooling based on their measurements for contact line lengths using total internal reflectance technique (TIR). Their measurement results indicated that the heat flux removal did not depends on the wetted surface area fraction of liquid, but well correlated with the contact line length. It was suggested that the heat flux removal could be improved by controlling the contact line length or the position of the contact line through constructing the surface geometry.

2.2 Critical heat flux of spray cooling

Any two phase cooling technology, including spray cooling, is limited by a condition called critical heat flux (CHF), which is defined as the maximal heat flux in the boiling heat transfer, as shown in Figure 8. The most serious problem is that the boiling limitation can be directly related to the physical burnout of the materials of a heated surface due to the suddenly inefficient heat transfer through a vapour film formed across the surface resulting from the replacement of liquid by vapour adjacent to the heated surface.

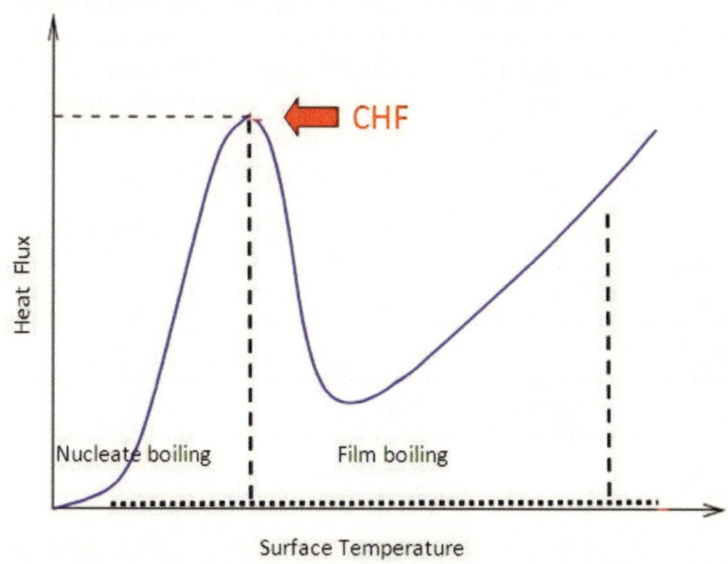

Fig. 8. A typical boiling curve

2.2.1 Theoretical model

Correct CHF estimation requires a clear understanding of the physical phenomenon that triggers the CHF, which remains poorly studied, however. By definition, CHF is the watershed of the nucleate boiling and the film boiling. From the perspective of physical phenomena, the most essential and iconic feature of CHF is the formation of the vapour film in the bulk of the liquid. Following this feature, two possible mechanisms are assumed to be responsible to trigger CHF, the coalescence of bubbles in the film, and the liftoff of the thin liquid layer by the vaporization in the film.

The coalescence of bubble is triggered by the merging of a large amount of homogeneous nucleation bubbles. To activate the growth of homogeneous bubbles, the temperature of the heated surface is required to a certain level, so that homogeneous bubbles absorb enough heat to overcome the critical free energy. A classical theory which gained acceptance is the self-consistent theory (SCT) of nucleation (Girshick et al. 1990). Assuming that the homogeneous bubble is spherical, the critical free energy of the homogeneous bubble is presented as:

$$\Delta G = (4\pi r^2 - A)\sigma - (n-1)k_B T \ln S \tag{2}$$

where ΔG is the critical free energy, k_B the Boltzmann constant, S the supersaturation, and A the surface area of a homogeneous nucleus. Under this theory, the nucleation rate becomes

$$I_{sct} = \frac{\exp(\sigma / k_B T)}{S} I \tag{3}$$

where I is the rate calculated from the classical nucleation theory. The exponential coefficient in the equation takes into account the surface energy of the homogeneous nucleus.

The liftoff mechanism were proposed based on the observation that at conditions just prior to CHF, as shown in Figure 9. Below CHF, vapour bubbles on the surface are separated by the liquid sub-layer. When CHF occurs, the liquid sub-layer among vapour bubbles lifts off from the heated surface, so that the heat conduction between the surface and the liquid sub-layer is cut off, resulting in the sudden drop of the heat transfer rate. This phenomenon was then idealized as a wavy liquid-vapour interface depicted in Figure 10, by assuming the vapour to be periodic, wave-like distributed along the heated surface.

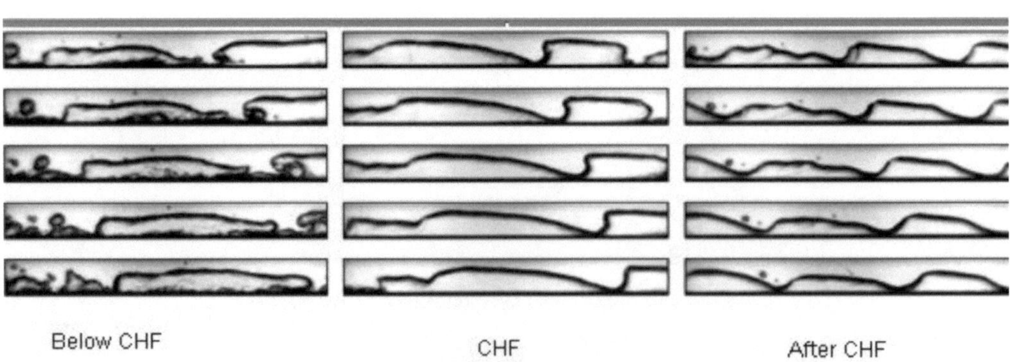

Fig. 9. Images of the liftoff process (Zhang et al., 2005)

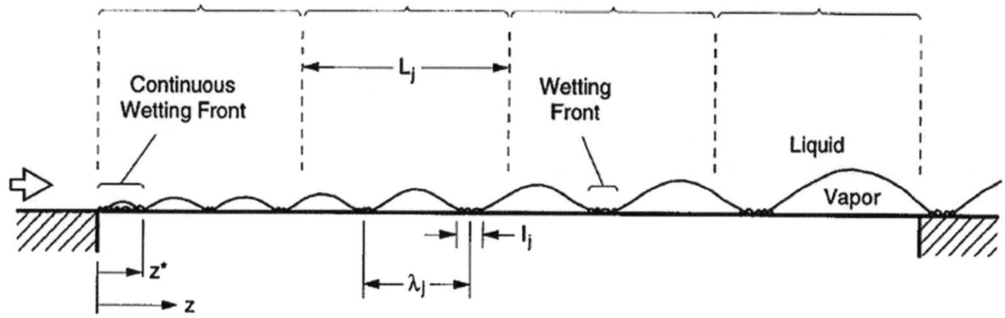

Fig. 10. Idealized periodical, wavelike distribution of vapour on the surface (Sturgis and Mudawar, 1999)

The model for predicting CHF based on this idealization was usually evolved from separated flow model, with the use of the instability analysis, and energy balance analysis, which was well introduced by Sturgis and Mudawar (1999). In the separated flow model, the phase velocity difference caused by the density disparity is responsible for the instability in the boiling. The instability analysis is used to calculate the critical wavelength (the wavelength at which CHF occurs), with the facilitation of energy balance analysis for obtaining the number of wetting fronts.

$$q''_{CHF} = \frac{l_j}{\lambda_j}\rho_v(C_{p,l}\Delta T + h_{fg})(\frac{\overline{p_l - p_v}}{\rho_v})^{1/2} l_j(z^*) \tag{4}$$

where l_j is the wetting front length, λ_j the vapour wave length, p_l-p_v the average pressure jump across the interface.

2.2.2 Empirical model

In spray cooling, empirical models have been developed with the continuous expansion of experimental data bases and applicable systems of interests.

Mudawar and Estes (1996) first attempted an empirical model to predict CHF in spray cooling by correlating CHF with the volumetric flux of liquid and the Sauter Mean Diameter of droplets, as following:

$$\frac{q''_{CHF}}{\rho_v h_{fg} \overline{V''}} = 1.467[(1+\cos(\theta/2))\cos(\theta/2)]^{0.3} \cdot \left(\frac{\rho_l}{\rho_v}\right)^{0.3} \left(\frac{\rho_l \overline{V''^2} d_{32}}{\sigma}\right)^{-0.35} \left[1 + 0.0019\frac{C_{p,l}\Delta T}{\rho_v h_{fg}}\right] \tag{5}$$

where θ is the spray cone angle, d_{32} the Sauter Mean Diameter, σ the surface tension, ΔT the superheat temperature, h_{fg} the evaporative latent heat. To predict CHF using Eq. (5), the nozzle parameters and droplet parameters (pressure drop across the nozzle, volumetric flow rate, inclined angle, and the Sauter Mean Diameter of droplets) have to be tested. In addition, the distance between the nozzle orifice and the surface needs to be chosen carefully, so that the spray cone exactly covers the heated surface. This model was validated by a set of experiments of the spray cooling on a rectangular 1.27×1.27 cm^2 flat surface using refrigerants (FC-72, and FC-87). The volumetric flow rate was regulated inside the range of 16.6 - 216 $m^3.s^{-1}.m^{-2}$. The Sauter Mean Diameter of droplets was inside the range of 110 - 195 μm. The superheat temperature was below 33 °C. The accuracy of this model was claimed to be within ±30%.

Visaria and Mudawar (2008) improved their previous empirical model by adding the effect of inclined spray. They concluded that CHF will decrease by increasing the inclination angle due to the elliptical cone produced by inclined spray decreased both the volumetric flux and spray impact area. An modified correlation was presented as:

$$\frac{q''_{CHF}}{\rho_v h_{fg} \overline{V''}} = 1.467[(1+\cos(\theta/2))\cos(\theta/2)]^{0.3} \cdot \left(\frac{\rho_l}{\rho_v}\right)^{0.3} \left(\frac{\rho_l \overline{V''}^2 d_{32}}{\sigma}\right)^{-0.35} \left[1+0.0019\frac{C_{p,l}\Delta T}{\rho_v h_{fg}}\right] \left(\frac{f_1^{0.3}}{f_2}\right) \tag{6}$$

$$f_1 = \frac{Q''}{\overline{Q''}} \tag{7}$$

$$f_2 = \frac{1}{\left[\frac{\pi}{4}\cos\alpha\sqrt{1-\tan^2\alpha\tan^2\left(\frac{\theta}{2}\right)}\right]} \tag{8}$$

Compared with Eq. (5), additional items f_1 and f_2 correspond to the effect of the reduced volumetric flux and the reduced impact area, respectively. The limitation of this model is the same with Eq. (5). This model was validated by experimental data provided by the authors themselves, with spray inclination angle varying from 0 to 55^0. The accuracy of the model was improved to ±25%.

Another empirical model was developed based on the liftoff model, by Lin and Ponnappan (2002). In this model, there is a slight difference from the traditional liftoff model: the vapour layer not only isolates the liquid layer from the heated surface, but also makes the surface droplet-proof. The empirical correlation was evolved from Eq. (4), presented as:

$$q''_{CHF} = cWe^{-1/3}\rho_v(C_{p,l}\Delta T + h_{fg})\left(\frac{\rho_l}{\rho_v}\right)^n \tag{9}$$

where c and n were unknown beforehand, and then obtained using the experimental CHF data that c=0.386 and n=0.549, with the standard errors of 0.039 for c, 0.0154 for n, and 0.937 for the estimate. Eq. (9) was compared with experimental data of both Lin and Ponnappan (2002), and Mudawar and Estes (1996). The accuracy of of Eq. (9) was ±33%.

Up to now, the applicabilities of all empirical models are limited to their validated conditions. In the future work, the validation of models needs to be conducted with other refrigerants and surface conditions. On the other hand, more factors should be included to the model. For instance, the velocity of droplets was verified to have an essential effect on CHF in spray cooling (Chen et al. 2002), but has not been included in any model.

3. Small area spray cooling with a single nozzle

In the past few decades, there had been great interests on spray cooling with a single nozzle over a small area of the order of 1 cm² as a potential cooling solution for high power electronic chips. In order to further understand the heat transfer mechanism of spray cooling as well as enhance the cooling capacity, researchers have made many efforts to conduct parametric studies on spray cooling, such as mass flow rate (Pais et al., 1992; Estes and Mudawar, 1995; Yang et al., 1996), pressure drop across the nozzle (Lin et al., 2003), gravity (Kato et al., 1995; Yoshida et al., 2001; Baysinger et al., 2004; Yerkes et al., 2006), subcooling of coolant (Hsieh et al., 2004; Viasaria and Mudawar, 2008), surface roughness and configuration (Sehmbey et al., 1990; Pais et al., 1992; Silk et al., 2004, Weickgenannt et al. 2011), and spray nozzle orientation and inclination angle (Rybicki and Mudawar, 2006; Lin and Ponnappan, 2005; Li et al., 2006; Visaria and Mudawar, 2008; Wang et al., 2010). Moreover, it was suggested that spray characteristics, such as spray droplet diameter, droplet velocity and droplet flux, played a paramount role in spray cooling.

Generally, there are two kinds of sprays implemented for spray cooling: pressurised spray and gas-assisted spray. Pressurised sprays are widely utilised in spray cooling researches and applications, which are generated by high pressure drop across the nozzle or with the aid of a swirl structure inside in some cases. Gas-assisted spray is rarely used in spray cooling due to its complex system structure for introducing the secondary gas into the nozzle to provide fine liquid droplets. However, it is found that gas-assisted spray can provide faster liquid droplet speed, smaller droplet size and more even droplet distribution on the heated surface compared with pressurised spray at similar working conditions (Pais et al., 1992; Yang et al., 1996). Eventually, it could provide better heat transfer and higher CHF.

By using the single pressurised spray nozzle on a small heated surface of 3 cm^2, Tilton (1989) obtained heat fluxes of up to 1000 W/cm^2 at surface superheat within 40 °C while the average droplet diameter and the mean velocities of droplets in that study were approximately 80 μm and 10 m/s, respectively. Tilton concluded that a reduction of spray droplet diameter (d_{32}) increased the heat transfer coefficient; the mass flow rate may not be a paramount factor for CHF. Another experimental study also showed that smaller droplets at smaller flow rates can produce the same values of CHF as larger droplets at larger flow rates (Sehmbey et al., 1995).

Estes and Mudawar (1995) performed experiments with a single pressurized nozzle on a copper surface of 1.2 cm^2, and developed correlations for the droplets' Sauter Mean Diameter (SMD, d_{32}) and CHF, which fitted their experimental data within a mean absolute error of 12.6% using water, FC-87 and FC-72 as working fluids. The spray characteristics were captured by a non-intrusive technique: Phase Doppler Anemometry (PDA). It was found that CHF correlated with SMD successfully and reached a higher value for the nozzle which produced smaller droplets.

A different view proposed by Rini et al. (2002) was that the dominant spray characteristic is the droplet number flux (N). Chen et al. (2002) proposed that the mean droplet velocity (V) had the most dominant effect on CHF followed by the mean droplet number flux (N). They also conclude that the SMD (d_{32}) did not appear to have an effect on CHF and the mass flow rate was not a dominant parameter of CHF. The increasing droplet velocity and droplet number flux resulted in increases of CHF and heat transfer coefficient. Experimental results indicated that a dilute spray with large droplet velocities excelled in increasing CHF compared with a denser spray with lower velocities for a certain droplet flux. Recently, Zhao et al. (2010) tested the heat transfer sensitivity of both droplet parameters and the flow rate by a numerical method. They concluded that both finer droplets and higher flow rate are favorable in increasing the heat transfer ability of spray cooling. In addition, the contribution of bubble boiling varies with the superheat temperature of the heated surface.

In the case of low superheat condition, the majority of heat transfer in spray cooling is due to the droplet impingement. The effect of bubble boiling increases with the increment of the surface superheat. At the surface superheat over 30 °C, the bubble boiling is responsible for more than 50% of the total heat transfer in spray cooling.

4. Large area spray cooling with multiple nozzles

4.1 Experimental studies

As mentioned above, the predominant interest of spray cooling in the published literature focused on cooling a small heated surface of the order of 1 cm^2 using a single nozzle or a small array of nozzles. Fewer researchers investigated large area spray cooling, of the order of 10 cm^2 or more using multiple nozzles. Lin et al. (2004) carried out experiments using FC-72 on the heated surfaces (2.54 x 7.6 cm^2) for two orientations using an array of multiple-nozzle plate (4 x 12) as shown in Figure 11. The maximum heat flux measured over the large area surface was 59.5 W/cm^2 with the heater in a horizontal downward-facing position.

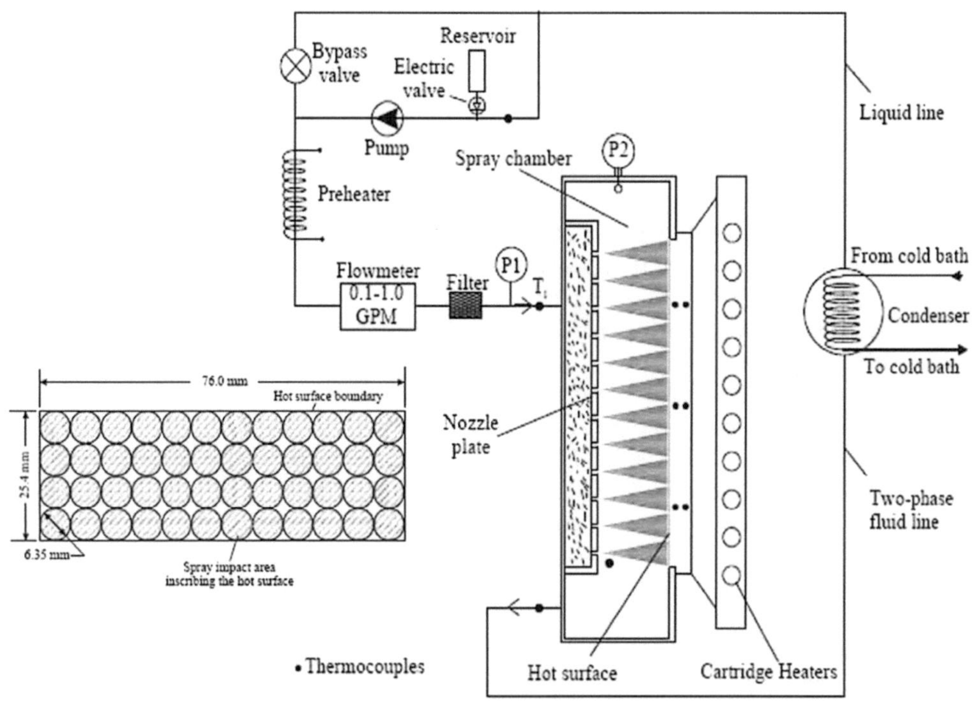

Fig. 11. Schematic of test rig of Lin et al. (2004)

Glassman et al. (2004) conducted an experimental study with a fluid management system for a 4 x 4 nozzle array spray cooler to cool a heated copper plate (4.5 x 4.5 cm^2). With the help of fluid management system or suction system on this 16 spray nozzle array, the heat transfer was improved on the average by 30 W/cm^2 for similar values of superheat above 5 °C. It was concluded that increasing the amount of suction increased the heat flux and thus the heat transfer coefficient. Suction effectiveness was improved greatly by adding extra siphons outside the spray area. Additionally, suction effectiveness was also increased by adding small slits to the sides of the siphons.

Yan et al. (2010a, 2010b) conducted an experimental study on large area spray cooling of the order of 100 cm^2 with multiple nozzles. As illustrated in Figure 12, the experimental facility, using R-134a as the working fluid and a heated plate of up to 1 kW power with built-in thermocouples, enabled a wide range of variables to be explored. A particular investigation is to reduce the spray chamber volume by using an inclined spray. The design of the spray chamber for the inclined spray nozzle kept the heated surface and spray coverage closely similar to that for the normal spray nozzle, as shown in Figure 13, but with a lower spray height (H_N) of 20 mm, which reduced the volume of the spray chamber from 1509.8 cm^3 to 762.3 cm^3. This was achieved by using four gas-assisted nozzles with a spray angle of 70° positioned with an inclination angle of 39° relative to the heated surface in the normal position. Vapour flow through the nozzle was utilized to thin the liquid film on the heated surface through shear forces, sweep away the coolant undergoing heat transfer with the heated surface as well as reduce the vapour partial pressure above the liquid film to enhance evaporative heat transfer.

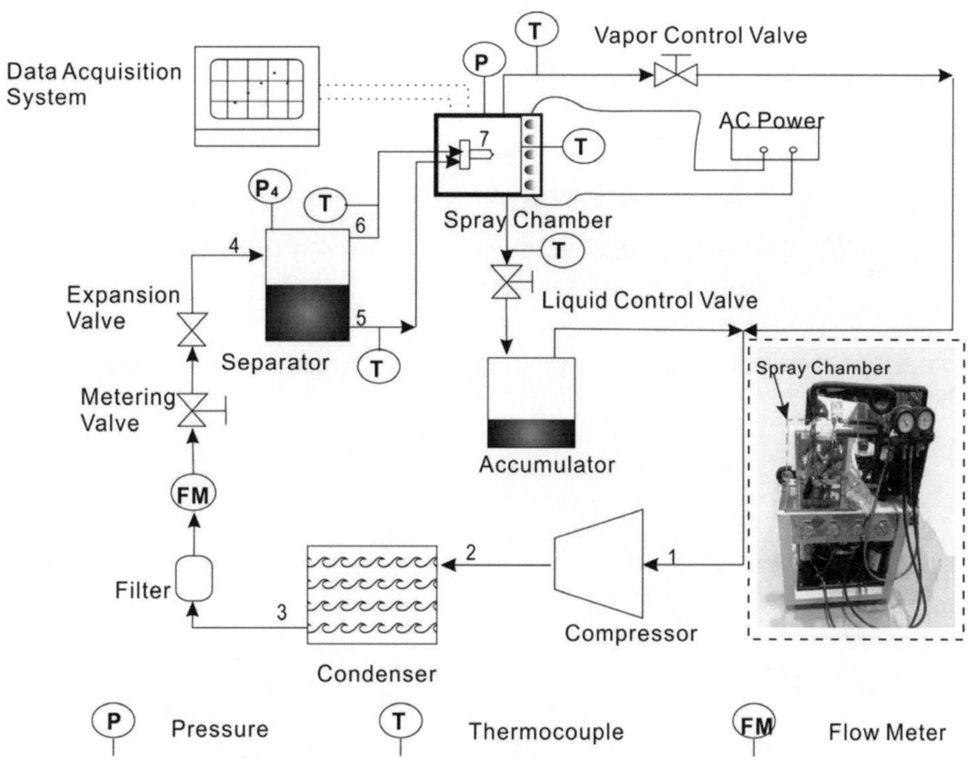

Fig. 12. Experimental set-up of impingement spray cooling (Yan et al., 2010a)

The experimental results suggest that increasing the coolant mass flow rate, nozzle inlet pressure and chamber pressure will have positive effects on the heat transfer effectiveness of impingement spray cooling as shown in Figures 14a, 15a and 16a, . Uniformity of the heated surface temperature can be reached with higher mass flow rate and nozzle inlet pressure; however it is not affected by varying chamber pressure as seen in Figures 14b, 15b and 16b.

Partial liquid accumulation might have occurred on the heated surface, due to interactions between sprays as well as the less effective drainage of un-evaporated coolant on such a large heated surface.

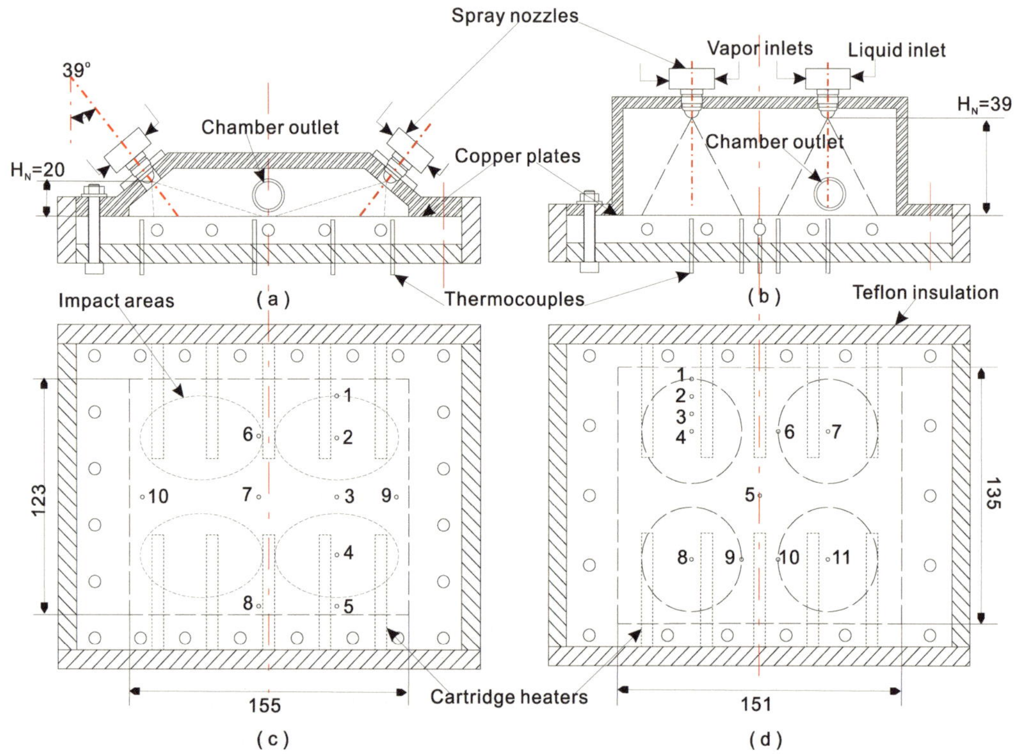

Fig. 13. Schematics of multiple normal spray chamber and inclined spray chamber (Yan et al., 2010c)

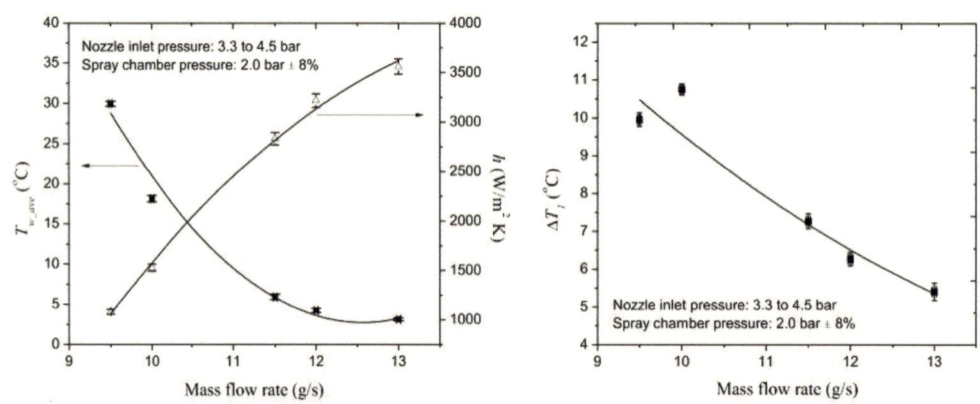

(a) (b)

Fig. 14. Effect of mass flow rate (Yan et al., 2010a)

A comparison of the thermal performances between the normal spray and inclined spray shows that although the heat transfer coefficient of the inclined spray configuration is higher compared with the normal spray configuration, the normal spray produces better surface temperature uniformity. The higher heat transfer coefficient by the inclined spray is attributed to the intensified forced convection in the liquid film caused by the large droplet velocity in the horizontal direction and consequent improvements in nucleate boiling and transient conduction occurring on the heated surface due to the quick refresh of the liquid film. It would intensify turbulent mixing in the liquid film and improve the drainage of the refrigerant in the spray chamber. Better surface temperature uniformity by the normal spray results from its more even volumetric flux distribution over the heated surface compared with that of the inclined spray (Yan et al. 2010c).

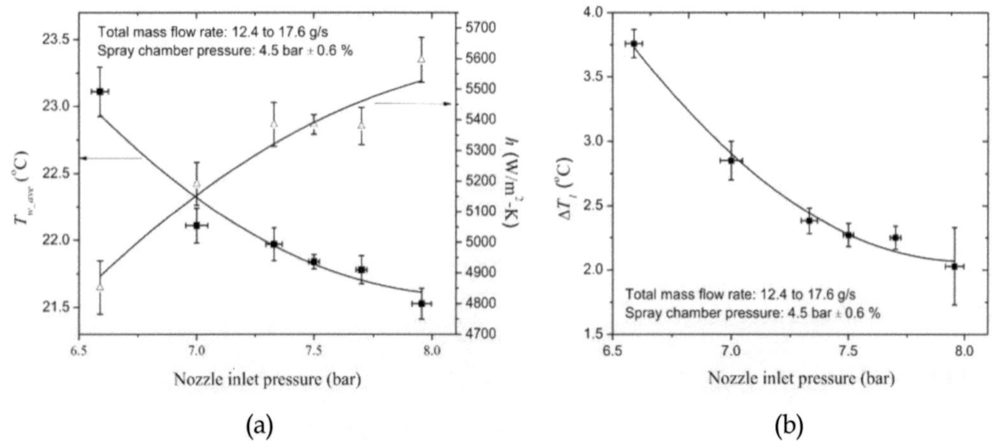

Fig. 15. Effect of nozzle inlet pressure (Yan et al., 2010a)

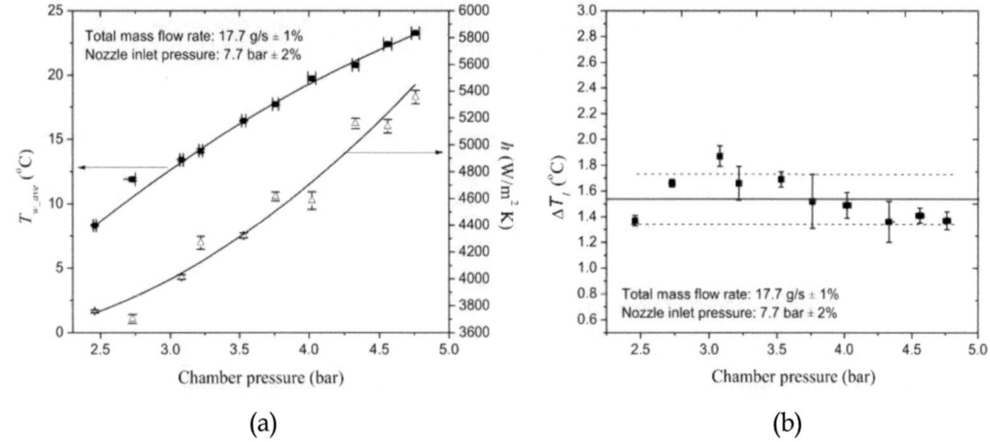

Fig. 16. Effect of spray chamber pressure (Yan et al., 2010a)

The mechanisms of spray cooling heat transfer have been widely debated. Zhao et al. (2010) suggested that two mechanisms responsible for the majority of the heat transfer in spray cooling are the heat transfer due to the droplet impingement and the heat transfer due to the bubble boiling. They built a numerical model based on droplet dynamics, film hydraulics, and bubble boiling, to capture the heat transfer in spray cooling by superposing the heat transfer due to the droplet impingement and the bubble boiling (both fixed sited nuclei and secondary nuclei). The heat transfer due to the droplet impingement was modeled based on an empirical correlation for a single droplet and then extended to the full spray cone. The heat transfer due to the bubble boiling was modeled by numerically simulating the process of the bubble growth in the film and its corresponding heat transfer. The film thickness was obtained by solving the continuum equation and the momentum equation of the film. The microscopic parameters of the droplets SMD (d_{32}), droplet velocity, and droplet number flux) and their distribution were obtained by experimental tests using a Laser Doppler Anemometry (PDA). The laser beam generated by the laser source (see Figure 17) is split by color separation and form two different channels of green light and blue light. These two channels of light will form orthogonal fringes which can measure the two orthogonal velocity components (vertical direction: z, horizontal direction: x) simultaneously. The droplet size can be measured with the use of the image analysis technique as well. The signals received by the detector will be first processed by the signal processor which combines the functions of counter; buffer interface and coincidence filter, and finally recorded by the computer with data processing software.

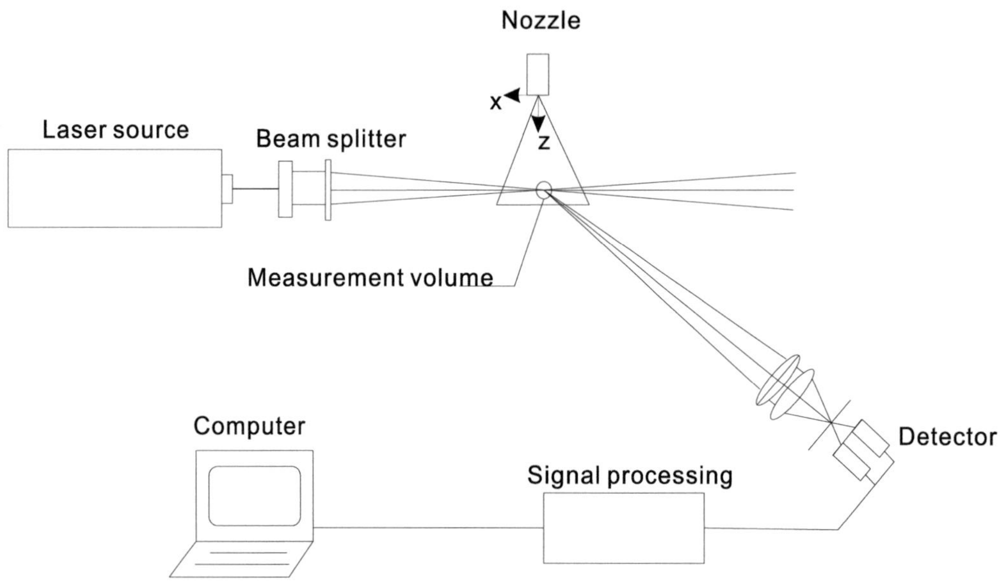

Fig. 17. Schematic of a typical PDA system

Simulations performed for the four-nozzle spray cooling configuration of Figure 15 gave a temperature distribution on the heated surface as shown in Figure 18. It shows that the temperature in the region covered by the spray was lower than outside the spray cones, and the temperature gradient in the center of the heated surface was higher than the edge, which indicates that the heat transfer rate in the center was lower than on the edge due to the liquid congestion between nozzles (Zhao et al., 2011). In addition, the non-uniformity of surface temperature distribution inside the spray cone was also caused by the non-uniform droplet distribution and the resulting non-uniform distribution of film thickness (Zhao et al. 2010).

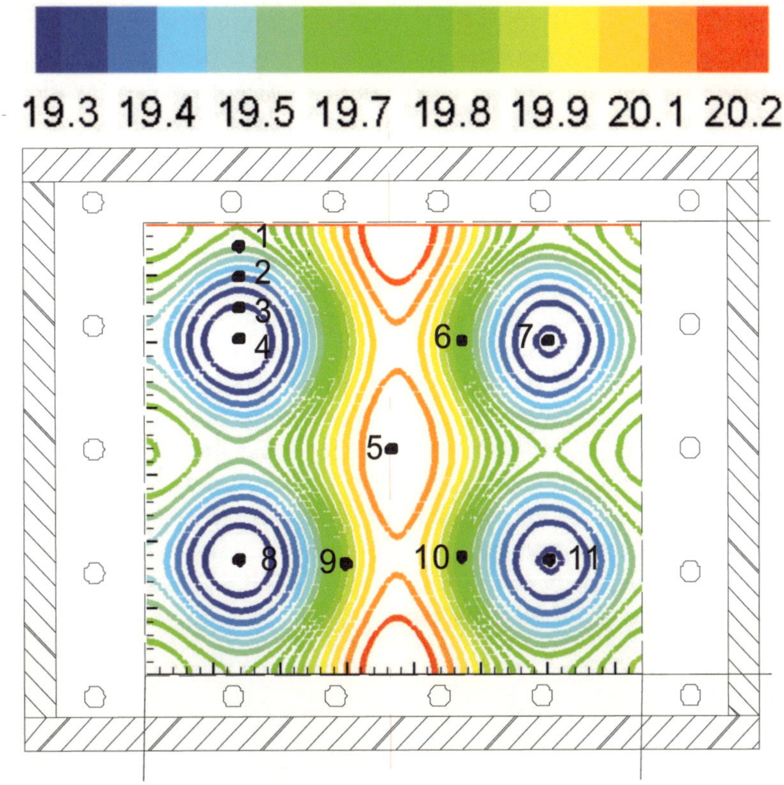

Fig. 18. Simulated surface temperature distribution

No.	***1***	***2***	***3***	***4***	***5***	***6***	***7***	***8***	***9***	***10***	***11***	***Ave.***
Exp.(°C)	19.9	19.8	20.3	19.1	20.1	20.0	19.7	20.0	19.5	20.0	19.9	19.8
Num.(°C)	19.6	19.4	19.3	19.2	20.2	19.9	19.3	19.2	20.0	19.9	19.3	19.6
Dev. (°C)	-0.3	-0.4	-1.0	0.1	0.1	-0.1	-0.4	-0.8	0.5	-0.1	-0.6	±0.2

Table 2. Comparison of simulated temperature distribution with experimental data

Comparisons of the surface temperature with the experimental data are listed in Table 2, and show the validity of the numerical model. The deviation between simulation and experimental temperature is less than ±0.8°C.

4.2 Comparison between large area and small area spray cooling

The maximum heat transfer coefficient and CHF of a large area spray cooling performed by Lin et al. (2004) compared with their previous data for a heated cooling surface area of 2.0 cm^2 are lower by about 30% and 34%, respectively. The heated surface area (203 cm^2) investigated by Yan et al. (2010a) is considerably larger than that by Lin et al. (2 cm^2) (2003), and shows a maximum heat transfer coefficient of 5596 W/cm^2 much lower than that obtained by the latter at a similar level of heat flux, probably a result of un-evaporated liquid accumulating in the chamber. Considering the central region of the heated surface, the interaction of the spray droplets with the counter-current flowing vapor is stronger for the large heated surfaces than the small heated surface as shown in Figure 19. This would result in a thicker liquid film and a smaller heat transfer coefficient, particularly in the central region of the heated surface (Lin et al., 2004). Liquid accumulation at the central region of multiple nozzles was also confirmed by Shedd and Pautsch (2005), and Pautsch and Shedd (2006) through their visualization studies. The liquid film impacted by the four sprays from a multiple nozzle plate experiences a stagnation point in the central region of the heated surface, where virtually all of its initial momentum must be redirected toward the drainage outlet at the edge. Furthermore, it was found that that the fluid motion in the central region was very chaotic and that flow velocities were lower than in the thin film surrounding the sprays using a three-color strobe technique for bubble behaviors (Shedd, 2002). Such flow condition with the slow moving liquid could cause the thicker liquid films and lower heat transfer occurring at the central region of the heated surface, compared with the spray impact region. Recently, the liquid congestion among spray cones was also observed by authors' group in a 54-nozzle spray cooling process, as shown in Figure 20. These results show that, for a larger heated surface with multiple spray nozzles, it is much more difficult to control the evaporation, as well as the fluid flow and effective discharge to the outlets. Proper management of the fluid run-off in impingement spray cooling system may improve the cooling performance further.

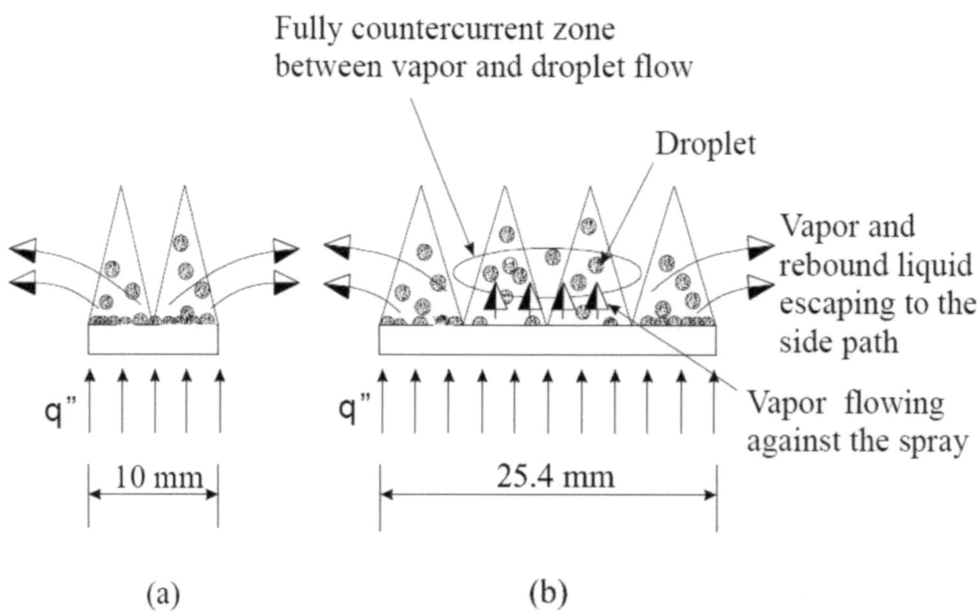

Fig. 19. Interactions between the spray droplets and vapor flow (Lin et al., 2004)

Fig. 20. A transparent surface impinged by a 54-nozzle spray

5. Conclusion

Spray cooling is an appropriate technique for high power and high heat flux applications, especially for temperature sensitive devices. By taking advantage of the liquid's relatively high latent heat, liquid impingement spray cooling has demonstrated to be an effective way of removing high heat power from surfaces, requiring only a small surface superheat as well as low mass flow rate, which are essential requirements for a compact cooling system design for a high powered electronic devices. Major heat transfer mechanisms and the critical heat flux (CHF) in spray cooling have been described based on many experimental and numerical investigations. However, more work is required to fully understand the mechanism of spray cooling. There is abundant work in the literature on parametric studies about CHF on small heated surfaces with high heat flux input. However, studies based on spray cooling with multiple nozzles on larger heated surfaces, which are crucial for the thermal management of high power devices mounted on electronic cards and in data centres, are still relatively scarce.

6. Nomenclature

A	Surface area, m^2
C_p	Heat capacity at constant pressure, $J \cdot kg^{-1} \cdot K^{-1}$
d_{32}	Sauter Mean Diameter, m
ΔG	Critical free energy of the homogeneous bubble, J

h_{fg}	Evaporative latent heat, $J \cdot kg^{-1}$
h_n	Spray height, m
k_B	Boltzmann constant, -
k	Thermal conductivity, W/m·K
l_j	Wetting front length, m
$\dot{q}''$	Heat flux per unit area, W/m^2
p	Pressure, pa
S	Supersaturation, pa
T	Temperature, K
t	Time, s
We	Weber number, -

Greek letters

a	Thermal diffusivity, m^2/s; Spray inclined angle, ^{0}
θ	Spray cone angle, ^{0}
ρ	Density, $kg \cdot m^{-3}$
λ_j	Vapor wave length, m
σ	Surface tension, $N \cdot m^{-1}$

Subscripts

bub	Bubble
I	Initial condition
v	Vapor phase
l	Liquid phase
CHF	Critical heat flux
sat	Saturation

7. References

Aguilar, G., Majaron, B., Verkruysse, W., Zhou, Y., Nelson, J. S. and Lavernia, E. J. Theoretical and experimental analysis of droplet diameter, temperature, and avaporation rate evolution in cryogenic sprays, International Journal of Heat and Mass Transfer 44(17): 3201-3211 (2001).

Anderson T. M., Mudawar I., Microelectronic cooling by enhanced pool boiling of a dielectric fluorocarbon liquid, Journal of Heat Transfer, Vol. 111, pp. 752–759, (1989).

Azar K., Advanced cooling concepts and their challenges, Ed. www.qats.com. Advanced Thermal Solutions, Inc. (2002).

Bar-Cohen, A., Sherwood, G., Hodes, M. and Solbreken, G., Gas-assisted evaporative cooling of high density electronic modules. IEEE transactions on components, packaging, and manufacturing technology. Part A Vol. 18 (3), pp: 502-509 (1995).

Bar-Cohen, A., Arik M., Ohadi, M., Direct Liquid Cooling of High Flux Micro and Nano Electronic Components. Proceeding of IEEE, Vol. 94, pp. 1549-1570 (2006).

Carey V.P., Liquid-vapour phase-change phenomena, Hemisphere Publishing Corporation, (1992).

Chen R.H., Chow L.C., Navedo J.E., Effects of spray characteristics on critical heat flux in sub-cooled water spray cooling, International Journal of Heat and Mass Transfer, Vol. 45, pp. 4033-4043 (2002).

Demiray F., Kim J., Micro-scale heat transfer measurements during pool boiling of FC-72: effect of subcooling. International Journal of Heat and Mass Transfer, Vol. 47, pp. 3257-3268 (2004).

Esmailizadeh L., Mesler R., Bubble entrainment with drops, Journal of Colloid and Interface Science, Vol. 110 (2), pp. 561-574 (1986).

Faulkner, D., Khotan, M., and Shekarriz, R., Practical Design of a 1000 W/cm2 Cooling System, In: 19th IEEE SEMI-THERM Symposium, pp. 223–230, San Jose, USA, (2003).

Girshick, S.L., Chiu, C.-P., Kinetic nucleation theory: A new expression for the rate of homogeneous nucleation from an ideal supersaturated vapor, The Journal of Chemical Physics 93 (2), pp. 1273-1277 (1990)

Glassman B.S., Kuravi S., Du J., Lin Y.-R., Zhao G.C., Chow L.C., A Fluid Management System for a Multiple Nozzle Array Spray Cooler, In: 37th AIAA Thermo-physics Conference, Portland, Oregon, (2004).

Glassman B.S., Spay cooling for land, sea, air and space based applications, a fluid management system for multiple nozzle spray cooing and a guide to high heat flux heater design, Master of Science Thesis, Department of Mechanical, Materials and Aerospace Engineering, University of Central Florida, (2005).

Huddle J.J., Chow L.C., Lei S., Marcos A., Rini D.P., Lindauer S.J., Bass M., Delfyett P. J., Thermal management of Diode laser arrays, In: 16th IEEE SEMI-THERM™ Symposium (2000).

Horacek, B., Kim, J., Kiger, K., Spray cooling using multiple nozzles: visualization and wall heat transfer measurements. IEEE Transactions on Device and Materials Reliability, Vol. 4 (4), pp. 614–625 (2004).

Horacek, B., Kiger, K., Kim, J., Single nozzle spray cooling heat transfer mechanisms. International Journal of Heat and Mass Transfer, Vol. 48 (8), pp. 1425–1438 (2005).

Hsieh, S. S., Weng, C. J. and Chiou, J. J., Nucleate pool boiling on ribbed surfaces with micro-roughness at low and moderate heat flux. Transactions of the ASME. Journal of Heat Transfer Vol. 121 (2), pp: 376-385 (1999).

Hsieh S., Fan T., Tsai H., Spray cooling characteristics of water and R-134a. Part 1: nucleate boiling. International Journal of Heat and Mass Transfer, Vol. 47. pp. 5703-5712 (2004).

Incropera F.P., Dewitt D.P., Fundamentals of Heat and Mass Transfer. 5th ed. New York: John Wiley & Sons (2002).

Li, B. Q., Cader, T., Schwarzkopf, J., Okamoto, K. and Ramaprian, B., Spray angle effect during spray cooling of microelectronics: Experimental measurements and comparison with inverse calculations. Applied Thermal Engineering Vol. 26 (16), pp: 1788-1795 (2006).

Lin, L., Ponnappan, R., Critical heat flux of multi-nozzle spray cooling in a closed loop. Proceedings of the Intersociety Energy Conversion Engineering Conference (2002).

Lin L., Ponnappan R., Yerkes K., Hager B., Large area spray cooling. In: 42nd AIAA Aerospace Sciences Meeting and Exhibit, Reno, Nevada, pp. 10838–10843 (2004).

Lin, L., Ponnappan, R., Two-phase high capacity spray cooling loop - Nozzle orientation effects and performance results. Collection of Technical Papers - 3rd International Energy Conversion Engineering Conference, San Francisco, California (2005).

Marto, P.J., Mackenzie D.K., Rivers A. D., Nucleate boiling in thin liquid films, AIChE Symposium Series, Vol. 73 (164), pp. 228-235 (1977).

Melser R., Mailen G., Nucleate boiling in thin liquid films, AIChE Journal, Vol. 23, pp. 954-957 (1977).

Mertens, R. G., Chow, L., Sundaram, K. B., Cregger, R. B., Rini, D. P., Turek, L. and Saarioos, B. A., Spray cooling of IGBT devices. Journal of Electronic Packaging, Transactions of the ASME 129(3): 316-323 (2007).

Estes, K. A. and Mudawar, I., Correlation of sauter mean diameter and critical heat flux for spray cooling of small surfaces. International Journal of Heat and Mass Transfer Vol. 38 (16), pp: 2985-2996 (1995).

Mudawar I., Estes K.A., Optimizing and predicting CHF in spray cooling of a square surface. Journal of Heat Transfer, Vol. 118, pp. 672–679 (1996).

Mudawar I., Assessment of high-heat flux thermal management schemes, IEEE transactions on Components and Packaging Technologies, Vol. 24 (2), pp. 122-141 (2001).

Nevedo J., Parametric effects of spray characteristics on spray cooling heat transfer, Ph.D. Dissertation, Department of Mechanical Material and Aerospace Engineering, University of Central Florida (2000).

Nishikawa K., Kusuda H., Yamasaki K., and Tanaka K., Nucleate boiling at low levels, Bulletin of JSME, Vol. 10 (38), pp. 328-338 (1967).

Overholt, M.R., McCandless, A., Kelly, K.W., Becnel, C.J., and Motakef, S., Micro-Jet Arrays for Cooling of Electronic Equipment, In: 3rd International Conference on Microchannels and Minichannels, PART B, pp. 249–252 (2005).

Pautsch A.G., Shedd T.A., Spray impingement cooling with single- and multi-nozzle arrays. Part 1: Heat transfer data using FC-72. International Journal of Heat and Mass Transfer, Vol. 48, pp. 3167-3175 (2005).

Pais M.R., Chow L.C., Mahefkey E.T., Surface roughness and its effect on the heat transfer mechanism in spray cooling, Journal of Heat Transfer, Vol. 114, pp. 211–219 (1992).

Rainey K.N., You S.M., Lee S., Effect of pressure, subcooling, and dissolved gas on pool boiling heat transfer from microporous, square pin-finned surfaces in FC-72. International Journal of Heat Transfer, Vol. 46, pp. 23-35 (2003a).

Riffat S.B., Ma X., Improving the coefficient of performance of thermoelectric cooling systems: a review, International Journal of Energy Research, Vol. 28, pp. 753–768 (2004).

Rini D.P., Pool boiling and spray cooling with FC-72, Ph.D. dissertation, Department of Mechanical, Materials and Aerospace Engineering, University of Central Florida, 2000

Rini D.P., Chen R.-H., Chow L.C., Bubble behavior and nucleate boiling heat transfer in saturated FC-72 spray cooling, Journal of Heat Transfer, Vol. 124, pp. 63–72 (2002).

Rohsenow M.W., Hartnett J.P., Ganic E.N., Handbook of Heat Transfer Fundamentals, 2nd edition, McGraw Hill Inc., NY (1985).

Rybicki, J. R. and Mudawar, I., Single-phase and two-phase cooling characteristics of upward-facing and downward-facing sprays. International Journal of Heat and Mass Transfer Vol. 49 (1-2), pp: 5-16 (2006).

Sehmbey M.S., Pais M.R., Chow L.C., Effect of surface material properties and surface characteristics in evaporative spray cooling. In: AIAA/ASME 5th Joint Thermophysics and Heat Transfer Conference, AIAA 90-1728, Seattle, WA (1990).

Sellers S.M., Heat transfer resulting from the evaporation of liquid droplets on a horizontal heated surface, Ph.D. dissertation, School of Mechanical Engineering, Georgia Institute of Technology (2000).

Selvam R.P., Baskara S., Balda J.C., Barlow F., and Elshabini A., Computer Modeling of Liquid Droplet Impact on Heat Transfer During Spray Cooling, American Society of Mechanical Engineers Paper HT2005-72569 (2005).

Selvam R.P., Lin L., Ponnappan R., Direct Simulation of Spray Cooling: Effect of Vapour Bubble Growth and Liquid Droplet Impact on Heat Transfer, International Journal of Heat and Mass Transfer, Vol. 49, Nos. 23–24, pp. 4265–4278 (2006).

Selvam R.P., Sarkar M., Sarkar S., Ponnappan R., and Yerkes K.L., Modeling thermal-boundary-layer effect on liquid-vapour interface dynamics in spray cooling. Journal of Thermophysics and Heat Transfer, Vol. 23(2) pp. 356-370 (2009).

Shedd, T.A., Single- and three-color strobe techniques for bubble/droplet sizing and velocimetry, in: C.-F. Lee (Ed.), ILASS 2002, ILASS Americas, Madison, WI, pp. 376–380 (2002).

Shedd T.A., Pautsch A.G., Spray impingement cooling with single- and multiple-nozzle arrays. Part II: Visualisation and empirical models. International Journal of Heat Mass Transfer, Vol. 48, pp. 3176-3184 (2005).

Sigler J., Mesler R., The behavior of the gas film formed upon drop impact with a liquid surface, International Journal of Colloid and Interface Science, Vol. 134 n2, pp. 459-474 (1990).

Silk E.A., Golliher E.L., Selvam R.P., Spray cooling heat transfer: Technology overview and assessment of future challenges for micro-gravity application. Energy Conversion and Management, Vol. 49(3), pp. 453-468 (2008).

Sturgis J.C., Mudawar I., Critical heat flux in a long, rectangular channel subjected to one-sided heating - II. Analysis of critical heat flux data, International Journal of Heat Mass and Transfer, Vol. 42, pp. 1849-1862 (1999).

Tan S.-W., Computer simulation of a spray cooling system with FC-72, Ph.D. dissertation, Department of Mechanical, Materials and Aerospace Engineering, University of Central Florida, (2001).

Tilton, D. E., Tilton, C. L., Moore, C. J. and Ackerman, R. E., Spray cooling for the 3-D cube computer. In: Intersociety Conference on Thermal Phenomena in Electronic Systems, Washington, DC, USA (1994).

Tuckerman, D.B., and Pease, R.F.W., High-Performance Heat Sink for VLSI, IEEE Electron Device Letters, Vol. 2, pp. 126–129 (1981).

Wang Y., Liu M., Liu D., Xu K., and Chen Y., Experimental study on the effects of spray inclination on water spray cooling performance in non-boiling regime. Experimental Thermal and Fluid Science, Vol. 34, pp. 933-942 (2010).

Weickgenannt, C. M., Zhang, Y., Lembach, A. N., Roisman, I. V., Gambaryan-Roisman, T., Yarin, A. L. and Tropea, C., Nonisothermal drop impact and evaporation on polymer nanofiber mats. Physical Review E - Statistical, Nonlinear, and Soft Matter Physics Vol. 83 (3), (2011).

Wendelstorf, J., Spitzer, K.-H., Wendelstorf, R., Spray cooling heat transfer at high temperature and liquid mass fluxes, International Journal of Heat and Mass Transfer, Vol. 51, pp. 4902-4910 (2008).

Visaria M., Mudawar I., Theoretical and experimental study of the effects of spray inclination on two-phase spray cooling and critical heat flux, International Journal of Heat and Mass Transfer, Vol. 51, pp. 2398-2410 (2008).

Yan, Z. B., Toh, K. C., Duan, F., Wong, T. N., Choo, K. F., Chan, P. K. and Chua, Y. S., Experimental study of impingement spray cooling for high power devices. Applied Thermal Engineering Vol. 30 (10), pp: 1225-1230 (2010a).

Yan, Z. B., Duan, F., Wong, T. N., Toh, K. C., Choo, K. F., Chan, P. K., Chua, Y. S. and Lee, L. W., Large area spray cooling by inclined nozzles for electronic board. 12th Electronics Packaging Technology Conference, EPTC 2010, Singapore (2010b).

Yan, Z. B., Duan, F., Wong, T. N., Toh, K. C., Choo, K. F., Chan, P. K., Chua, Y. S. and Lee, L. W., Large area impingement spray cooling from multiple normal and inclined spray nozzles, submitted (2010c).

Yang J., Spray cooling with an air atomizing nozzle, Ph.D. dissertation, School of Mechanical Engineering, University of Kentucky (1993).

Yang J., Chow L.C., Pais M.R., Nucleate boiling heat transfer in spray cooling, Journal of Heat Transfer, Vol. 188, pp. 668-671 (1996).

Zhang, H., Mudawar, I., Hasan, M. M., Flow boiling CHF in microgravity. International Journal of Heat Mass Transfer, Vol. 48, pp. 3107-3118 (2005).

Zhao, R., Cheng, W. L., Liu, Q. N. and Fan, H. L., Study on heat transfer performance of spray cooling: Model and analysis. Heat and Mass Transfer/Waerme- und Stoffuebertragung Vol. 46 (8-9), pp: 821-829 (2010).

Zhao, R., Duan, F., Wong, T. N., Toh, K. C., Choo, K. F., Chan, P. K., and Chua, Y. S., Numerical simulation of spray cooling heat transfer with multi-nozzle arrays, submitted (2011).

Zhirnov, V.V., Cavin, R.K., Hutchby, J.A., Bourianoff, G.I., 2003. Limits to binary logic switch scaling – a Gedanken model. Proceedings of the IEEE 91 (11), 1934–1939.

Zuo Z.J., North M.T., and Wert K.L., High Heat Flux Heat Pipe Mechanism for Cooling of Electronics, IEEE transactions on Components and Packaging Technologies, Vol. 24 (2), pp. 220-225 (2001).

14

Wettability Effects on Heat Transfer

Chiwoong Choi[1] and Moohwan Kim[2]
[1]University of Wyoming,
[2]Pohang University of Science and Technology
[1]United States
[2]Republic of Korea

1. Introduction

Wettability is an ability of a liquid to maintain contact with a solid surface. Most of heat transfer systems are considered that of an intermediate fluid on a solid surface. Thus, the wettability has a potential of being effective parameter in the heat transfer, especially a two-phase heat transfer. In the two-phase states, there are triple contact lines (TCL), which are the inter-connected lines for all three phases; liquid, gas, and solid. All TCL can be expanded, shrunken, and moved during phase change heat transfer with or without an external forced convection. This dynamic motion of the TCL should be balanced with a dynamic contact, which is governed by the wettability. Recently, interesting phenomena related with superhydrophilic/ hydrophobic have been reported. For example, an enhancement of both the heat transfer and the critical heat flux using the hydrophobic and hydrophilic mixed surface was reported by Betz et al. (2010). Various heat transfer applications related with these special surfaces are accelerated by new micro/nano structured surface fabrication techniques, because the surface wettability can be changed by only different material deposition (Phan et al., 2009b). In addition, many heat transfer systems become smaller, governing forces change from a body force to a surface force. This means that an interfacial force is predominant. Thus, the wettability becomes also one of influential parameters in the heat transfer.

This chapter will be covered by following sub parts. At first, a definition of the wettability will be explained to help an understanding of the wettability effects on various heat transfer mechanisms. Then, previous researches for single phase and two-phase heat transfer will be reviewed. In the single phase, there is no TCL. However, there is an apparent slip flow on a hydrophobic surface. Most studies related to a slip flow focused on the reduction of a frictional pressure loss. However, several studies for wettability effects in a convective heat transfer on a hydrophobic surface were carried out. So, this part will be covered by the slip flow phenomenon and the convective heat transfer related to the slip flow on the hydrophobic surface. In the two-phase flow, various two-phase heat transfers including evaporation, condensation, pool boiling, and flow boiling will be discussed. In evaporation and condensation parts, previous studies related with the wettability effects on the evaporation and the condensation of droplets will be focused on. Most studies for the wettability effects are included in the pool boiling heat transfer field. In the pool boiling heat transfer, bubbles are incepted and departed with removing heat from the heated surface. After meeting a maximum heat flux, which is limited by higher resistance of vapor phase columns on the heating surface, boiling heat transfer is deteriorated before meeting a melting temperature of material of the heating surface. Therefore, how many bubbles are generated on the surface and how frequently bubbles are departed from the surface are important parameters in the nucleate boiling heat transfer. Obviously, there are two-phase interfaces on the heated solid surface like as situations of incepted bubble, moving bubble, and vapor columns. Therefore, these all sequential mechanisms are affected by the wettability. In this part, the wettability effects on bubble inception, nucleate boiling heat transfer, and CHF will be reviewed. Lastly, previous works related with wettability effects on flow boiling in a microchannel will be reviewed.

2. What is wettability?

2.1 Fundamentals of wetting phenomena

The wettability represents an ability of liquid wetting on a solid surface. Surface force (adhesive and cohesive forces) controls the wettability on the surface. The adhesive forces between a liquid and a solid cause a liquid drop to spread across the surface. The cohesive forces within the liquid cause the drop to avoid contact with the surface. A sessile drop on a solid surface is typical phenomena to explain the wettability (Fig. 1).

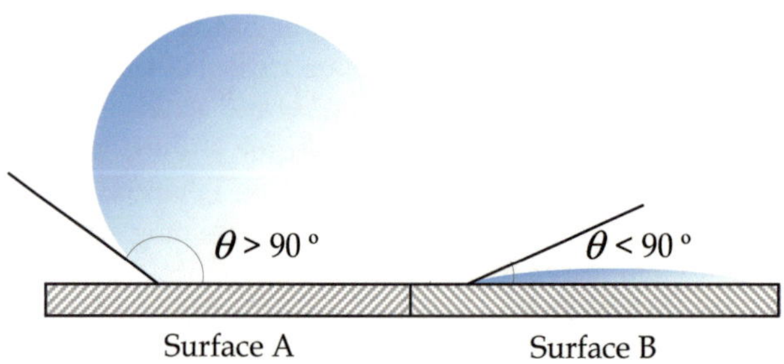

Fig. 1. Water droplets on different wetting surfaces

The surface A shows a fluid with less wetting, while the surface B shows a fluid with more wetting. The surface A has a large contact angle, and the surface B has a small contact angle. The contact angle (θ), as seen in Fig. 1, is the angle at which the liquid-vapor interface meets the solid-liquid interface. The contact angle is determined by the resultant between adhesive and cohesive forces. As the tendency of a drop to spread out over a flat, solid surface increases, the contact angle decreases. Thus, a good wetting surface shows lower a contact angle and a bad wetting surface shows a higher contact angle (Sharfrin et al., 1960). A contact angle less than 90° (low contact angle) usually indicates that wetting of the surface is very favorable, and the fluid will spread over a large area of the surface. Contact angles greater than 90° (high contact angle) usually indicates that wetting of the surface is unfavorable, so the fluid will minimize contact with the surface. For water, a non-wettable surface hydrophobic (Surface A in Fig.1) and a wettable surface may also be termed hydrophilic (Surface B in Fig.1). Super-hydrophobic surfaces have contact angles greater than 150°, showing almost no contact between the liquid drop and the surface. This is sometimes referred to as the Lotus effect. The table 1 describes varying contact angles and their corresponding solid/liquid and liquid/liquid interactions (Eustathopoulos et al., 1999). For non-water liquids, the term lyophilic and lyophobic are used for lower and higher contact angle conditions, respectively. Similarly, the terms omniphobic and omniphilic are used for polar and apolar liquids, respectively.

There are two main types of solid surfaces with which liquids can interact: high and low energy type solids. The relative energy of a solid has to do with the bulk nature of the solid itself. Solids such as metals, glasses, and ceramics are known as 'hard solids' because the chemical bonds that hold them together (e.g. covalent, ionic, or metallic) are very strong. Thus, it takes a large input of energy to break these solids so they are termed high energy. Most molecular liquids achieve complete wetting with high-energy surfaces. The other type of solids is weak molecular crystals (e.g. fluorocarbons, hydrocarbons, etc.) where the molecules are held together essentially by physical forces (e.g. van der waals and hydrogen bonds). Since these solids are held together by weak forces it would take a very low input of energy to break them, and thus, they are termed low energy. Depending on the type of a liquid chosen, low-energy surfaces can permit either complete or partial wetting. (Schrader & Loeb, 1992; Gennes et al., 1985).

Contact angle	Degree of wetting	Strength	
		Solid/Liquid	Liquid/Liquid
$\theta = 0°$	Perfect wetting	strong	weak
$0 < \theta < 90°$	high wettability	strong	strong
$90° \leq \theta < 180°$	low wettability	weak	weak
$\theta = 180°$	Perfectly non-wetting	weak	strong

Table 1. Contact angle and wettability

2.2 Wetting models

There are several models for interface force equilibrium. An ideal solid surface is one that is flat, rigid, perfectly smooth, and chemically homogeneous. In addition, it has zero contact angle hysteresis. Zero hysteresis implies that the advancing and receding contact angles are equal. In other words, there is only one thermodynamically stable contact angle. When a drop of liquid is placed on such a surface, the characteristic contact angle is formed as depicted in Fig. 1. Furthermore, on an ideal surface, the drop will return to its original shape if it is disturbed (John, 1993).

Laplace's theorem is the most general relation for the wetting phenomena. It indicates a relation of pressure difference between inside and outside of an interface as like Eq. (1) (Adamson, 1990),

$$\Delta p = \gamma\left(\frac{1}{R_1 + R_2}\right) = \gamma\kappa \tag{1}$$

where, γ is a surface tension coefficient, R_1 and R_2 are radius of the interface, κ is a curvature of the interface. In equilibrium, the net force per unit length acting along the boundary line among the three phases must be zero. The components of net force in the direction along each of the interfaces are given by Young's equation (Young, 1805),

$$\gamma_{SG} = \gamma_{SL} + \gamma_{LG}\cos\theta \tag{2}$$

which relates the surface tensions among the three phases: solid, liquid and gas. Subsequently this predicts the contact angle of a liquid droplet on a solid surface from knowledge of the three surface energies involved. This equation also applies if the gas phase is another liquid, immiscible with the droplet of the first liquid phase.

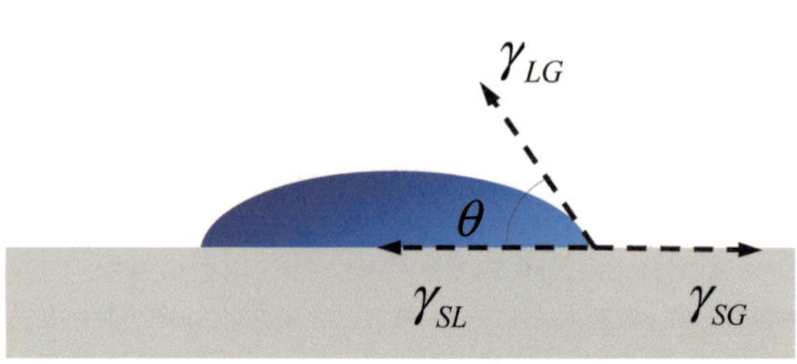

Fig. 2. Contact angle of a liquid droplet wetted to a solid surface

Unlike ideal surfaces, real surfaces do not have perfect smoothness, rigidity, or chemical homogeneity. Such deviations from ideality result in phenomena called contact-angle hysteresis. The contact-angle hysteresis is defined as the difference between the advancing (θ_a) and receding (θ_b) contact angles (Good, 1992):

$$H = \theta_a - \theta_r \tag{3}$$

In simpler terms, contact angle hysteresis is essentially the displacement of a triple contact line (TCL), by either expansion or retraction of the droplet.

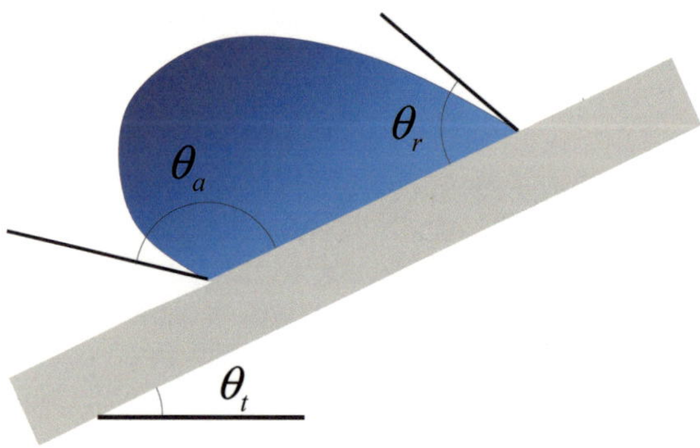

Fig. 3. Schematics of advancing and receding contact angles

Fig. 3 depicts the advancing and receding contact angles. Here, θ_t is an inclined angle. The advancing contact angle is the maximum stable angle, whereas the receding contact angle is the minimum stable angle. The contact-angle hysteresis occurs because there are many different thermodynamically stable contact angles on a non-ideal solid. These varying thermodynamically stable contact angles are known as metastable states (John, 1993). Such motions of a phase boundary, involving advancing and receding contact angles, are known as dynamic wetting. When a contact line advances, covering more of the surface with liquid, the contact angle is increased, it is generally related to the velocity of the TCL (Gennes, 1997). If the velocity of a TCL is increased without bound, the contact angle increases, and as it approaches 180° the gas phase it will become entrained in a thin layer between the liquid and solid. This is a kinetic non-equilibrium effect, which results from the TCL moving at such a high speed, that complete wetting cannot occur.

A well-known departure from an ideality is when the surface of interest has a rough texture. The rough texture of a surface can fall into one of two categories: homogeneous or heterogeneous. A homogeneous wetting regime is where the liquid fills in the roughness grooves of a surface. On the other hand, a heterogeneous wetting regime is where the surface is a composite of two types of patches. An important example of such a composite surface is one composed of patches of both air and solid. Such surfaces have varied effects on the contact angles of wetting liquids. Wenzel and Cassie-Baxter are the two main models that attempt to describe the wetting of textured surfaces. However, these equations only apply when the drop size is sufficiently large compared with the surface roughness scale (Marmur, 2003).

The Wenzel model describes the homogeneous wetting regime, as seen in Fig. 4(a), and is defined by the following equation for the contact angle on a rough surface (Wenzel, 1936):

$$\cos\theta^* = \beta\cos\theta \tag{4}$$

where, θ^* is the apparent contact angle which corresponds to the stable equilibrium state (i.e. minimum free energy state for the system). The roughness ratio, β, is a measure of how surface roughness affects a homogeneous surface. The roughness ratio is defined as the ratio of a true area of the solid surface to the apparent area. Also, θ is the Young contact angle as defined for an ideal surface in Eq. (2). Although Wenzel's equation demonstrates that the contact angle of a rough surface is different from the intrinsic contact angle, it does not describe contact angle hysteresis (Schrader and Loeb, 1992).

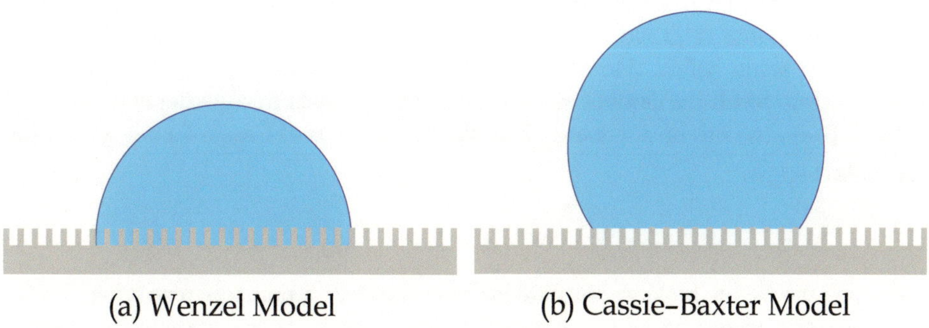

Fig. 4. Models for rough surface: (a) Wenzel model and (b) Cassie-Baxter model

When dealing with a heterogeneous surface, the Wenzel model is not sufficient. This heterogeneous surface, like that seen in Fig. 4(b), is explained by using the Cassie-Baxter equation (Cassie's law): (Cassie & Baxter, 1944; Marmur, 2003)

$$\cos\theta^* = \beta_f f\cos\theta_Y + f - 1 \tag{5}$$

Here the β_f is the roughness ratio of the wet surface area and f is the fraction of solid surface area wet by the liquid. Cassie-Baxter equation with f = 1 and $\beta_f = \beta$ is identical to Wenzel equation. On the other hand, when there are many different fractions of surface roughness, each fraction of the total surface area is denoted by f_i. A summation of all f_i equals 1 or the total surface. Cassie–Baxter can also be recast in the following equation (Whyman et al., 2008):

$$r\cos\theta^* = \sum_{n=1}^{N} f_i\left(\gamma_{i,SG} - \gamma_{i,SL}\right) \tag{6}$$

here, γ is the Cassie-Baxter surface tension between liquid and gas, the $\gamma_{i,SG}$ is the solid gas surface tension of every component and $\gamma_{i,SL}$ is the solid liquid surface tension of every component. A case that is worth mentioning is when the liquid drop is placed on the substrate, and it creates small air pockets underneath it. This case for a two component system is denoted by: (Whyman et al., 2008)

$$\gamma\cos\theta^* = f_1\left(\gamma_{1,SG} - \gamma_{1,SL}\right) + \left(1 - f_1\right)\gamma \tag{7}$$

Here, the key difference in notice is that the there is no surface tension between the solid and the vapor for the second surface tension component. This is because we assume that the surface of air that is exposed is under the droplet and is the only other substrate in the system. Subsequently, the equation is then expressed as (1 - f). Therefore, the Cassie equation can be easily derived from the Cassie–Baxter equation. Experimental results regarding the surface properties of Wenzel versus Cassie–Baxter systems showed the effect of pinning for a Young angle of 180° to 90°, a region classified under the Cassie–Baxter model. This liquid air composite system is largely hydrophobic. After that point a sharp transition to the Wenzel regime was found where the drop wets the surface but no further than edges of the drop. A third state is the penetration state where the drop is in the Wenzel state but also fills a region of the substrate around the drop. A drop placed on a rough surface can be either in Cassie-Baxter, Wenzel or penetration states. Furthermore, can easily change its state if the required barrier energy is gained by the drop, e.g. if the drop is deposited from some height (He et al., 2003) or by applying pressure (Lafuma & Quere, 2003) on the drop to fill the cavities with liquid. The equilibrium state depends on whether, for given θ, β, ϕ_s, the minimum energy is of Wenzel type or of Cassie-Baxter type. With the critical contact angle,

$$\theta_c = \cos^{-1}\left[\left(\phi_s - 1\right) / \left(r - \phi_s\right)\right] \tag{8}$$

such as when $\theta > \theta_c$, the most stable state is Cassie-Baxter' s one, whereas when $\theta < \theta_c$, it is Wenzel' s one. A transition from a metastable (e.g., Cassie-Baxter) state to the most stable (e.g., Wenzel) state is possible only if the required energy barrier is overcome by the drop (e.g., by lightly pressing the drop). These characteristics of models will be shown in literatures related with drop-wise evaporation and condensation in hydrophobic surfaces.

3. Wettability effects on heat transfer

3.1 Convective heat transfer

Wettability is highly related with a two-phase interface on a solid surface. So, there is less investigation for a single phase heat transfer. However, the reduction of drag in a hydrophobic tube is one topic related with wettability effects on a single phase flow (Watanabe, 1999). In a hydrophobic surface generally, a no slip condition is not applicable due to the slip flow. Studies of the slip flow on a hydrophobic surface have been conducted both by using an experimental approach (Zhu & Granick, 2002; Barrat & Bocquet, 1999; Tretheway & Meinhart, 2005) and by using a molecular dynamics (MD) approach (Thomson & Troian, 1997; Nagayama & Cheng, 2004). Fluid molecules tumble along the wall much like two solid surfaces sliding over one another occurs when the forces between the fluid and wall molecules are not strong enough to overcome the shear forces at the wall. This decoupling of the fluid from the wall results in a lower frictional pressure drop. Fig. 5 shows velocity profiles for no slip and slip walls, where u_{slip} is a slip velocity and L_{slip} is a slip length. The velocity for flow between parallel plates with the no slip is given by

$$\frac{u}{u_c} = \left(1 - \left(\frac{y}{w}\right)^2\right) \quad (9)$$

Where u is the fluid velocity, u_c is the maximum velocity, y is the vertical height with centerline of its origin and w is a half of the channel height. In a slip condition, Eq.(9) can be changed to

$$u = u_c\left(1 - \left(\frac{y}{w}\right)^2\right) + u_{slip} \quad (10)$$

Most studies have shown that there is a critical wall shear rate for the onset of the slip. Thomson & Troian (1997) firstly showed the critical shear rate using a MD simulation. Wu & Cheng (2003) reported that the critical shear rate is an order of 50,000 s^{-1} and Zhu & Granick (2002), and Choi et al. (2003) reported that is the order of 10,000 s^{-1}. Usually, slip phenomena have been seen in a microchannel due to a higher shear rate in a smaller dimension. Navier's hypothesis effectively describes the slip velocity at a surface is proportional to the shear rate at the surface (Lamb, 1932).

$$u_{slip} = L_{slip} \left.\frac{du}{dy}\right|_{wall} \quad (11)$$

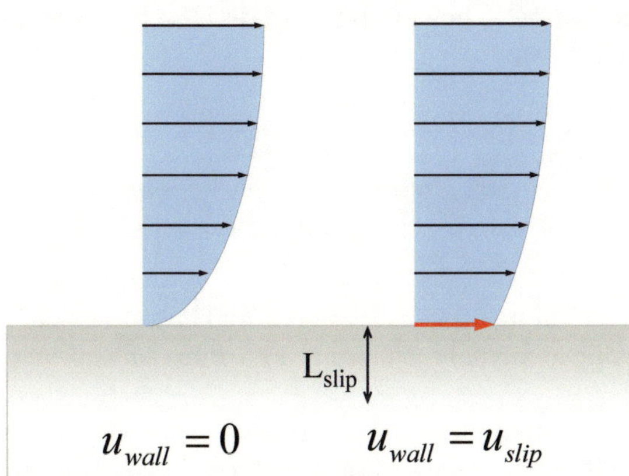

Fig. 5. Schematics of no slip and slip velocity profiles

Various researchers also proposed models for the slip length. Tretheway & Meinhart (2005) suggested possible mechanisms of the slip flow on a hydrophobic surface, which is existence of nanobubbles or a layer of lower density fluid at the surface. Also, they proposed the slip length as a function of an air gap and a plate height with rarefied gas conditions.

Now, we will discuss about wettability effects on a convective heat transfer according to slip flow on a hydrophobic surface. Here we will review three reports for this topic. First, Wu & Cheng (2003) studied surface condition effects on laminar convective heat transfer in microchannels for water. They fabricated 13 different trapezoidal silicon microchannels. Also, three of them were coated with silicon oxide to increase their hydrophilic abilities (Asif et al., 2002). The Nusselt number of microchannels with the hydrophilic silicon oxide surface is higher than that with the hydrophobic silicon surface, which means the hydrophilic capability of the surface enhance the convective heat transfer (Fig. 6). However, they did not explain the physical reason.

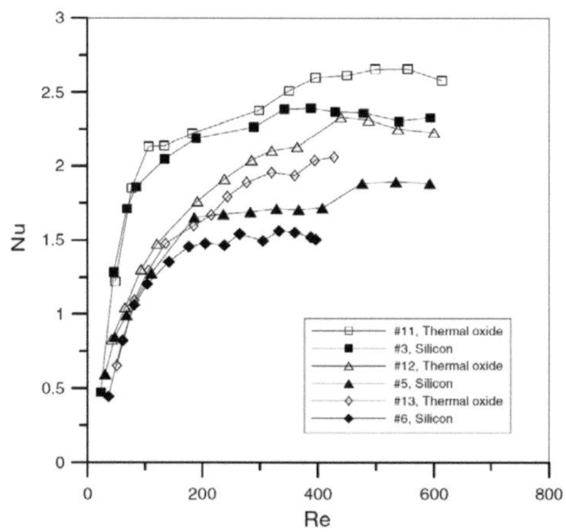

Fig. 6. Effect of surface wettability on Nusselt number: #11(L/D_h~307), #3(L/D_h~310), #12(L/D_h~368), #5(L/D_h~370), #13(L/D_h~451), #6(L/D_h~451) (Wu & Cheng, 2003)

Second, Rogengarten et al. (2006) investigated the effect of contact angle on the convective heat transfer in a microchannel. They analytically derived the Nusselt number using a slip velocity condition, as it follows:

$$Nu_{slip} = \frac{4\left(\frac{4}{3}+2A\right)}{\left[1.32-A\left(3.7+\frac{8}{3}A\right)\right]} \tag{12}$$

where, $A = u_{slip}/u_c$, a ratio of a slip velocity and a maximum velocity. Fig. 7 shows Nusselt number increased by approximately 2% for a 10% ratio of slip velocity as its maximum velocity.

Fig. 8 indicates that higher contact angle surfaces tend to decrease that heat transfer coefficient comparing with lower contact angle surfaces. Also, this deviation can occurred in over the specific Peclet number (Pe~100), which the slip flow occurred.

Lastly, Hsieh & Lin (2009) performed experiments to study the convective heat transfer in rectangular microchannels using deionized (DI) water, methanol, 50 wt% DI water/50 wt% methanol mixture and ethanol solutions. The hydrophilic and hydrophobic surfaces were obtained using Ultra Violet (UV) treatment. They measured flow and temperature fields using a micro particle image velocimetry (μPIV) and a micro laser-induced fluorescence (μLIF), respectively. In their experiments, maximum slip ratio is 10% for water in the hydrophobic microchannel. Also, their results indicate that the hydrophilic microchannel has higher local heat transfer coefficient than the hydrophobic microchannel (Fig. 9).

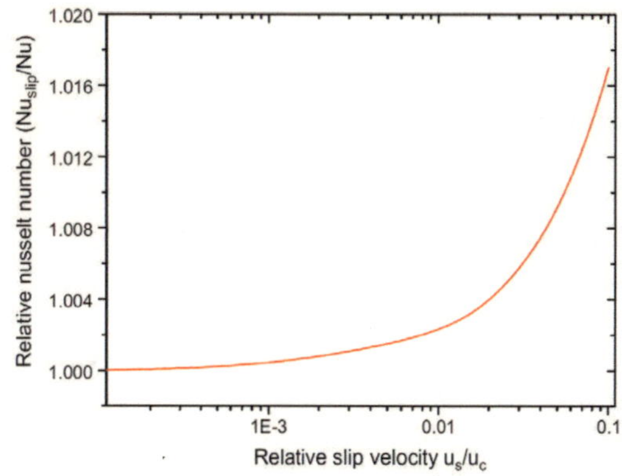

Fig. 7. Relative change in the Nusselt number due to slip induced flow-rate variations (Rogengarten et al., 2006)

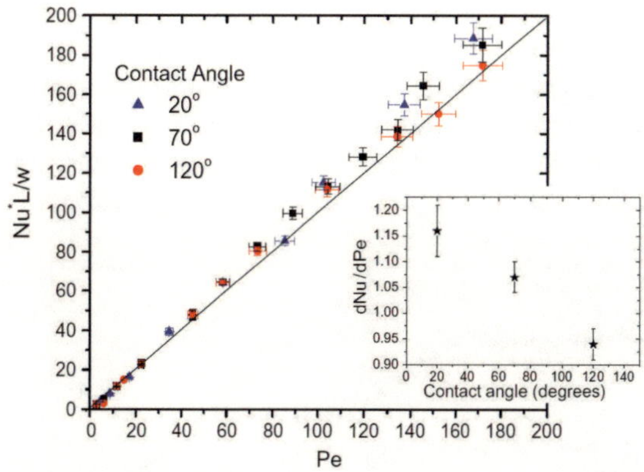

Fig. 8. Ratio of nondimensional heat flux as a function of Pe for a different contact angle. Insert shows the gradient of Nu v.s. Pe graph as a function of contact angel for Pe > 100 (Rogengarten et al., 2006)

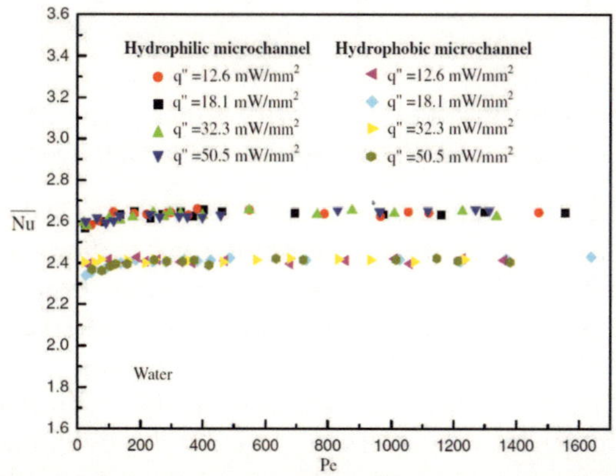

Fig. 9. Nu vs Pe for hydrophilic and hydrophobic microchannels (Hsieh & Lin, 2009)

3.2 Two-phase heat transfer

3.2.1 Evaporation

Evaporation is one of major two-phase heat transfer mechanisms. In an evaporation process, a mass transfer occurs, which means liquid meniscus including a triple contact line (TCL) has a motion. Therefore, we need to consider a dynamic contact angle (advancing and receding contact angles) as shown in Fig. 3. Generally, the advancing contact angle will tend to toward a lower value during evaporation (Picknett & Bexon, 1977). Most of studies for wettability effects on the evaporation fundamentally are focused on an evaporation of a sessile drop. The evaporation process of the droplet can be classified to few steps as shown in Fig.10: Step 1 (saturation of atmosphere), Step 2 (constant contact radius with a decreasing drop height and contact angle), Step 3 (a constant contact angle with a decreasing a contact radius) and Step 4 (final drop disappearance). In most previous studies focused on step 2, 3, and 4.

Chandra et al. (1996) studied on the contact angle effect on the droplet evaporation. Three kinds of droplets of pure water, surfactant 100 ppm and 1000 ppm on a stainless steel surface were visualized. Their results indicate that a reduced contact angle makes a droplet thickness thinner and a contact area larger. Thus, an increased heat transfer area and a decreased conductive resistance enhance the droplet evaporation (Fig. 11). Takata et al. (2004, 2005) measured an evaporation time, a wetting limit and Leidenfrost temperatures on stainless steel, copper and aluminum surfaces. They used a plasma-irradiation to increase a wetting property of those surfaces. Their results indicate that the evaporation time decreases and the wetting limit and the Leidenfrost temperatures increase in hydrophilic surfaces. Therefore, the hydrophilic surface has potentials for the enhancement of evaporation.

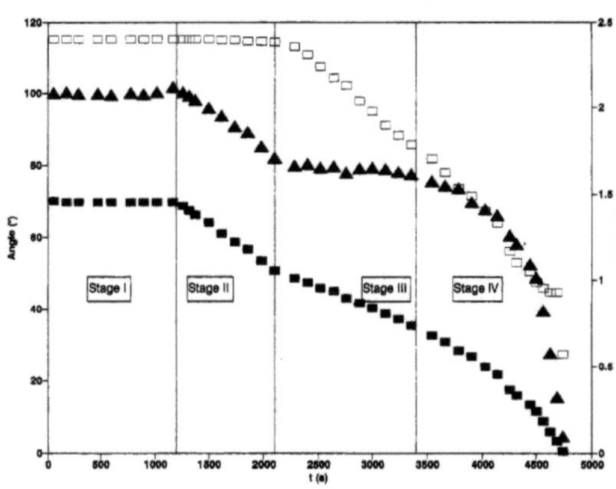

Fig. 10. Evaporation process for water on ETFE with initial drop volume of 5 μL: □ Diameter, ■ Height, and ▲ Angle (Bourges-Monnire & Shanahan, 1995)

Yu et al. (2004) reported an evaporation of water droplets on self-assembled monolayers (SAMs) follows an exclusive trend from a constant contact diameter model to a constant contact angle mode. Shin et al. (2009) investigated droplet evaporations on pure glass, octadecyl-tricholoro-silane (OTS), and alkyl-ketene dimmer (AKD) surfaces. They show that a hydrophilic surface enhances the evaporation heat transfer and a super-hydrophobic surface does not have distinct stages and pinning sections. Kulinich & Farzaneh (2009) investigated a contact angle hysteresis effect on a droplet evaporation using two super-hydrophobic surfaces of the same contact angle but contrasting wetting hysteresis. In their results, the surface of a low contact angle hysteresis was observed to follow the evaporation model normally ascribed to hydrophobic surface (a quasi-static constant angle while constantly decreasing contact diameter). Meanwhile, the surface with a high contact angle hysteresis was found to be behaved in accordance with the evaporation model normally associated with hydrophilic surfaces (constantly the decreasing contact angle and the quasi-static contact diameter).

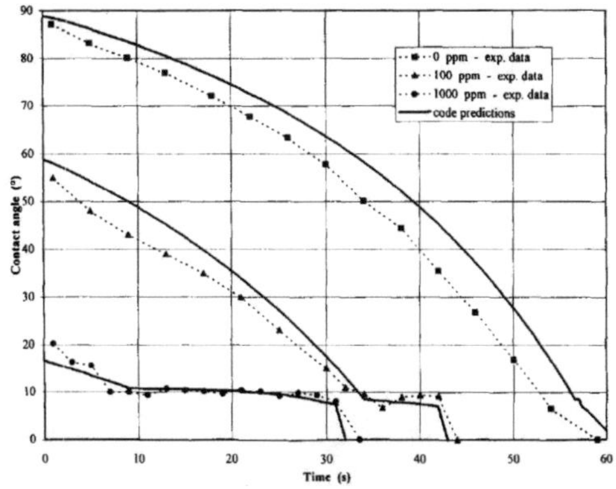

Fig. 11. Evolution of contact angle during evaporation of droplets of pure water, 100 ppm and 1000 ppm surfactant solutions on a stainless steel surface at 80 °C, (Chandra et al., 1996)

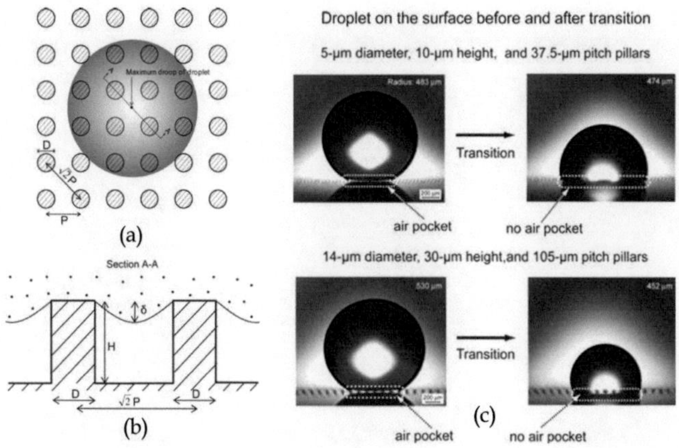

Fig. 12. A small water droplet suspended on a super-hydrophobic surface consisting of a regular array of circular pillars. (a) Plan view. (b) Side view in section A–A, (c) Visualization results for transition (Jung & Bhushan, 2007)

Jung & Bhushan (2007) studied effects of a droplet size on the contact angle by evaporation using droplets with radii ranging from about 300 to 700 µm. In addition, they proposed a criterion where the transition from the Cassie and Baxter regime to the Wenzel regime occurs when the droop of the droplet sinking between two asperities is larger than the depth of the cavity. A small water droplet is suspended on a super-hydrophobic surface consisting of a regular array of circular pillars with diameter D, height H and pitch P as shown in Fig. 12(a). The curvature of a droplet is governed by the Laplace equation, which relates the pressure inside the droplet to its curvature (Adamson, 1990). Therefore, the maximum droop of the droplet (δ) in the recessed region can be found in the middle of two pillars that are diagonally across as shown in Fig. 12(b) which is if the droop is much greater than the depth of the cavity,

$$\left(\sqrt{2}P-D\right)^2 / R \geq H \tag{13}$$

Then, the droplet will just contact the bottom of the cavities between pillars, resulting in the transition from the Cassie and Baxter regime to the Wenzel regime as shown in Fig. 12(c). Before the transition, an air pocket is clearly visible at the bottom area of the droplet, but after the transition air pocket is not found at the bottom area of the droplet.

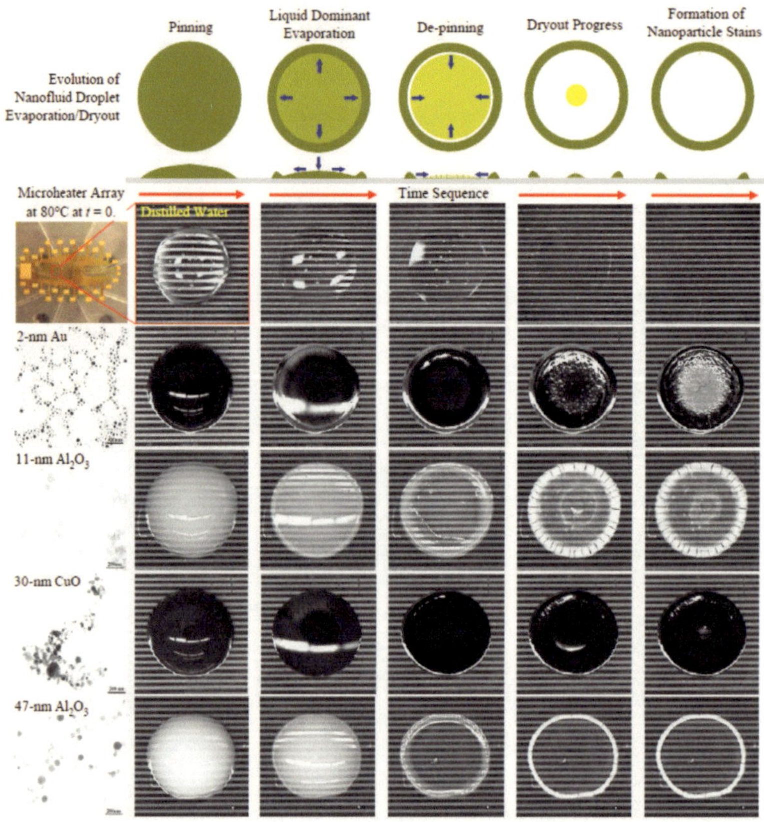

Fig. 13. Evaporation and dryout of various nanofluids on a microheater array, (Chon et al. http://minsfet.utk.edu/Research/2007-update/Evaporation_Dryout.pdf)

Nanofluids have various engineering merits including higher conductivity, enhancement of boiling heat transfer and CHF. Especially, the nano-particle deposited surface shows super-hydrophilic characteristics. Based on this good wetting property, several studies for the evaporation of a nanofluid have been conducted (Leeladhar et al., 2009; Sefiane & Bennacer, 2009; Chen et al., 2010). The initial equilibrium contact angle of the nanofluids was significantly affected by the nanoparticle sizes and concentrations. During evaporation, the evaporation behavior for the nanofluids exhibited a complete different mode from that of the base fluid. In terms of a contact angle, nanofluids shows a slower decrease rate than base fluid. A nanofluid contact diameter remained almost a constant throughout evaporation with a slight change only at the very end of an evaporation stage. The nanofluids also show a clear distinction in the evaporation rates, resulting in a slower rate than base fluid. No abrupt change in a contact angle and a diameter was observed during the evaporation, the deposited nanoparticles after the complete evaporation of a solvent showed unique dry-out patterns depending on nanoparticle sizes and concentrations, e.g., a thick ring-like pattern (as shown in Fig. 13) with larger particle sizes while a uniformly distributed pattern with smaller particles at higher concentrations.

3.2.2 Condensation

Here, we will show short reviews for wettability effects on a condensation including fundamentals and systematic views. Most studies for wettability effects on condensation are also focused on a droplet condensation mechanism like as evaporation. Fritter et al. (1991) has identified different stages of a droplet growth during condensations of a vapor on partially wetting surfaces. An initial stage where a surface coverage by the condensate is very low and there is negligible coalescence, a second stage where in the droplets grow and coalesce with no new droplets appearing in the empty spaces between the already existing drops. The droplet growth then attains a self similar pattern with time. The surface coverage attains a constant value of 0.5 with appearing no new drops. The growth of drops before coalescence is less when compared to the growth after the drops coalescence. They proposed a growth rate of an individual drop and after drop coalescence is exponent of 1/3 and 1 of time, respectively (Fig. 14).

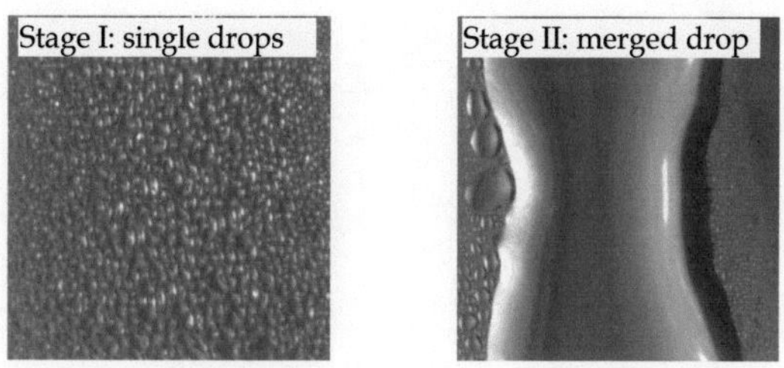

Fig. 14. A condensed drop in the hydrophilic surface: different stages in a condensation (Pulipak, 2003)

It is a well-known experimental fact that, in a drop-wise condensation, most of the heat transfer occurs during the early stages of the formation and the growth of a droplet (Griffith, 1972). Therefore, it must therefore be the aim of any pretreatment of the condenser surface to cause the condensate droplet to depart as early and as quickly from the condenser surface as possible. The departure of the drop, on the other hand, is resisted by the adhesion of the droplet to the condenser surface; this resistance has been attributed to the contact angle hysteresis (Schwartz et al., 1964). A contact angle is formed between a liquid meniscus and solid surface with which it intersects. As a rule, this angle is different in a situation where the liquid advances from the one where it recedes. The actual difference between advancing and receding contact angle is referred to as a contact angle hysteresis. While a contact angle hysteresis stems from dynamic effects, it is to be noted that it also exists under static conditions: advancing a liquid meniscus and stopping it will lead to the static advancing contact angle; receding the meniscus prior to a static measurement will yield the static receding contact angle. The difference between the two contact angles, which is as a rule finite, may be termed as the static contact angle hysteresis. Gokhale et al. (2003) conducted measurements of the apparent contact angle and the curvature of a drop and meniscus during condensation and evaporation processes in a constrained vapor bubble (CVB) cell. A working fluid and a surface material are n-butanol and quartz, respectively. They monitored a growth of a single drop until that drop merges with another drop. They found an apparent contact angle is a constant during condensation. As the rate of condensation increases, the contact angle increases. This means that a dynamic contact angel (shown in Fig. 3) should be considered in drop-wise condensation. Two main causes of static contact angle hysteresis are surface heterogeneity and roughness (Neumann, 1974).

Pulipaka (2003) studied the wettability effects on a heterogeneous condensation as his master thesis. Main objectives of this study are wettability effects on a drop-wise condensation and a drop growth rate. He observed the initial growth rate for the hydrophilic surface is higher than that for the hydrophobic surface. However, at the final stage, there is no difference between the hydrophilic and the hydrophobic surfaces as shown in Fig. 15. An initial growth rate for the hydrophilic and the hydrophobic surfaces are exponent of 0.671 and 0.333, respectively. The condensate growth rate is a strong function of a temperature gradient on the hydrophilic surface than the hydrophobic surface (Fig. 16). The time for initiation of a nucleation is decreased as contact angle decreases.

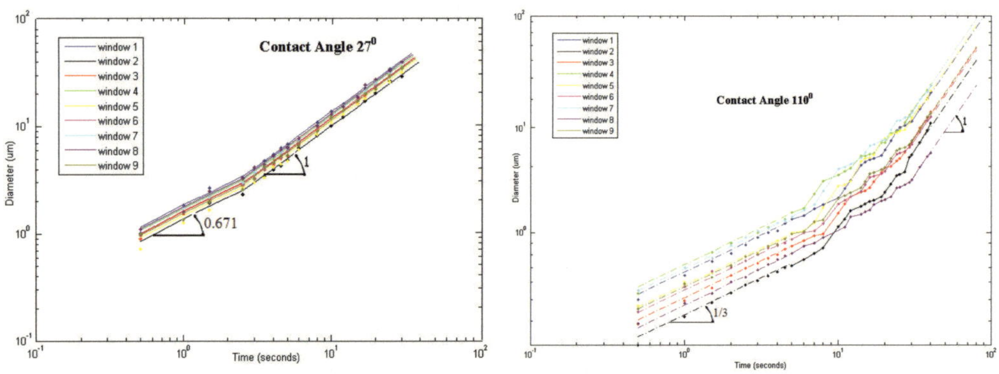

Fig. 15. A diameter of condensed drop for different wettability: left (θ=27 °) and right (θ=110°) (Pulipaka, 2003)

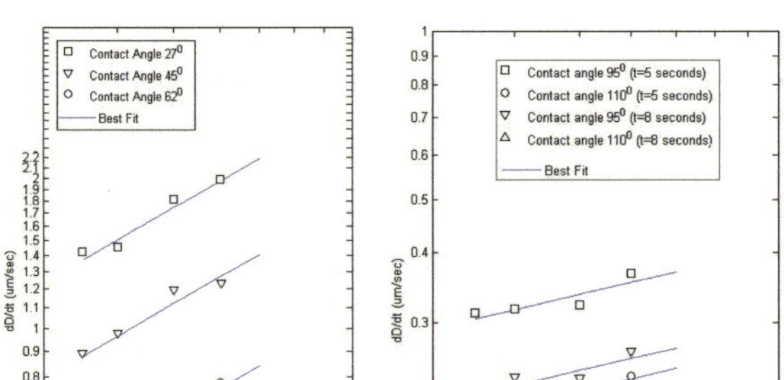

Fig. 16. Drop growth rate with a temperature gradient for different wettabilities (Pulipaka, 2003)

Neumann et al. (1978) studied the effects of varying contact angle hysteresis on the efficiency of a drop-wise condensation heat transfer on a cylinder type condenser. They prepared two kinds of the surface wettability with a coating of Palmitic and Stearic acids. Their results indicate that the heat flux and the heat transfer coefficient increase with the decrease in contact angle hysteresis (increasing the advancing contact angle) (Fig. 17). The limiting size drop to slide on an inclined surface is given in

$$mg\sin\theta_t = \gamma_{LG}\left(\cos\theta_r - \cos\theta_a\right) \quad (14)$$

Therefore, the limiting mass, m for a drop removal will a decrease with decreasing contact angle hysteresis. It enhances the drop-wise condensation heat transfer.

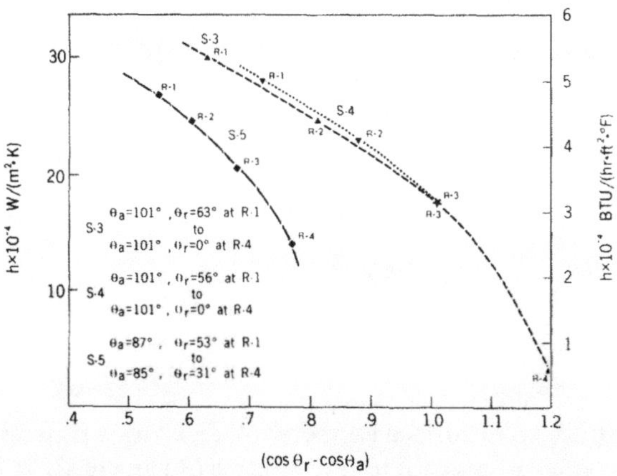

Fig. 17. Heat transfer coefficient, h and contact angle hysteresis (Neumann et al., 1978)

Recently, studies of condensation on the super-hydrophobic surface, which has a micro structured surface have been conducted. Furuta et al. (2010) studied a drop-wise condensation with different hydrophobic surfaces, which are treated with two fluoroalkylsilanes (FAS3 and FAS17). Static contact angles of FAS3 and FAS17 are 146 ° and 160 ° for rough surface and 78 ° and 104 °, respectively. From this study, the contact angles of the FAS3 or FAS17 coatings decreased concomitantly with a decreasing surface temperature. At the dew point, clear inflection points were observed in the temperature dependence of contact angles as shown in Fig. 18, suggesting the change of the interfacial free energy of the solid-gas interface by water adsorption. The contact angle decrease implies a mode transition from Cassie to Wenzel. The decrease was attributed to the surface wettability change and the increase of the condensation amount of water. The contact angle change attributable to heating revealed that the Wenzel mode is more stable than the Cassie mode.
Narhe & Beysens (2006) studied condensation induced a water drop growth on a super-hydrophobic spike surface. They described three main stages according to the size of the drop (Fig. 19). Initial stage is characterized by the nucleation of the drops at the bottom of the spikes. During intermediate stage, large drops are merged with neighboring small drops. The last stage is characterized by Wenzel-type drops, which growing is similar to that on a planar surface. Also, the contact angle in last stage is smaller than that in the initial stage. When the radius of a drop on the top surface reaches the size of the cavities, two phenomena enter in a competition. The drop can either (i) coalesce with the drops in the

cavity and get sucked in, resulting in a spectacular self-drying of the top surface (Narhe & Beysens, 2004), and/or (ii) coalesce with another drop on the top surface, resulting in a Cassie-Baxter drop (Narhe & Beysens, 2007). If the phenomenon (i) occurs first, condensation results in large Wenzel drops connected to the channels in a penetration regime. If the phenomenon (ii) occurs first, condensation proceeds by Cassie-Baxter drops, thus preserving super-hydrophobicity till stage (i) proceeds and penetration drops are formed. Depending on the pattern morphology, this stage may never occur. Nevertheless, even in the penetration case, some features of super-hydrophobicity are still preserved as the top surface of the micro-structures remained almost dry while the cavities were filled with condensed water. Their results show that Wenzel or Cassie–Baxter states of droplet on the super-hydrophobic structured surface are governed by a length scale of the surface pattern and the structure shape.

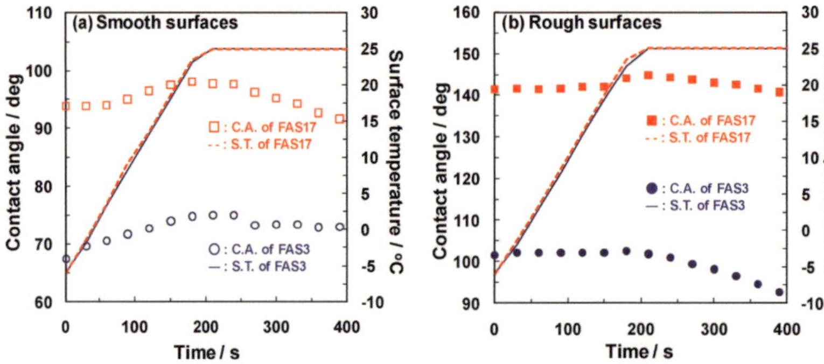

Fig. 18. Contact angle (C.A.) and surface temperature (S.T.) for a different surface wettability and roughness: (a) smooth surfaces, (b) rough surfaces (Furuta et al., 2010)

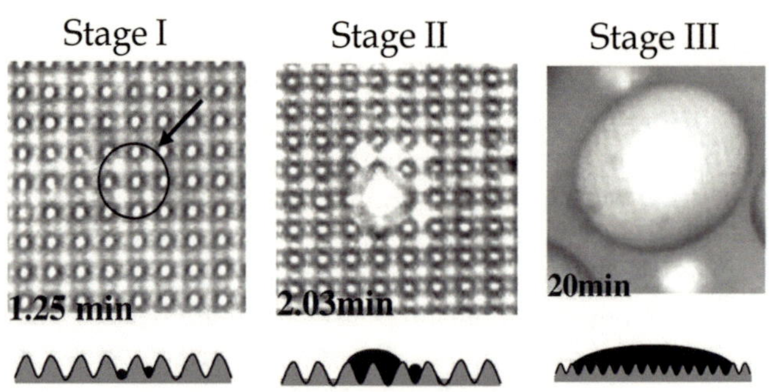

Fig. 19. Three growth stages of condensation (Narhe & Beysens, 2006)

3.2.3 Pool boiling

Many studies of the wettability effects on heat transfer were focused on a pool boiling heat transfer area. A major reason is not related with only the basic two-phase heat transfer mechanism but also the boiling enhancement with nanofluids. In this chapter, we will review previous works for the wettability effects on the pool boiling phenomena including heterogeneous nucleation, nucleate boiling heat transfer and critical heat flux (CHF). Eddington & Kenning (1979) studied the nucleation of gas bubbles from supersaturated solutions of Nitrogen in water and ethanol-water mixtures on two metal surfaces. A decrease in the contact angle decreases the population of active bubble nucleation sites by reducing the effective radii of individual sites. Wang & Dhir (1993) also reported the same results that the good surface wettability causes a decrease of the density of active nucleation sites. Most of two-phase heat transfer mechanisms are highly related with a contact angle hysteresis due to the dynamics motion of the interface. The contact angle hysteresis is affected by a degree of heterogeneity and roughness of the solid surface (Johnson& Dettre, 1969). Fig. 20 represents the general nucleation and growth processes. Lorenz (1972) developed a theoretical heterogeneous model, which shows the ratio of the bubble radius to the cavity radius, R_1/R_0 is a function of a static contact angle (β_s), a dynamic contact angle (β_d), and a conical cavity half angle (φ). When the static contact angle is fixed and the dynamic contact angle increases, R_1/R_0 increases. Especially, for a highly wetting surface (Fig. 21(a)), the ratio is less than a unity and the effect of dynamic contact angle on R_1/R_0 is significant only when a dynamic contact angle is small. Tong, et al. (1990) proposed a modified Lorenz model, which involved both the static and dynamic contact angles.

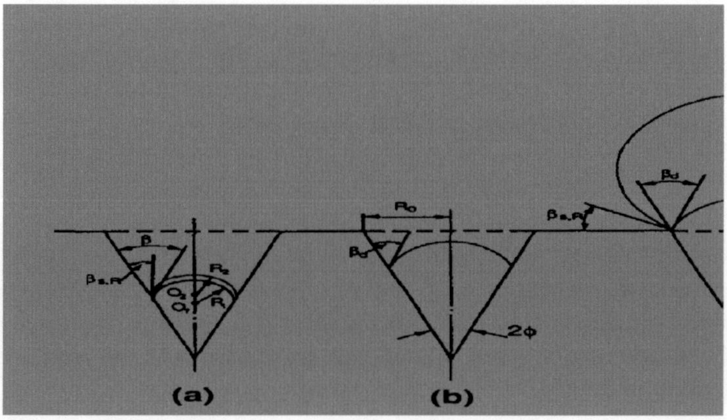

Fig. 20. Bubble growth steps: (a) contact angle readjustment; (b) in-cavity growth; (c) growth on the cavity mouth and the contact angle readjustment; (d) growth on an outer surface (Tong et al, 1990)

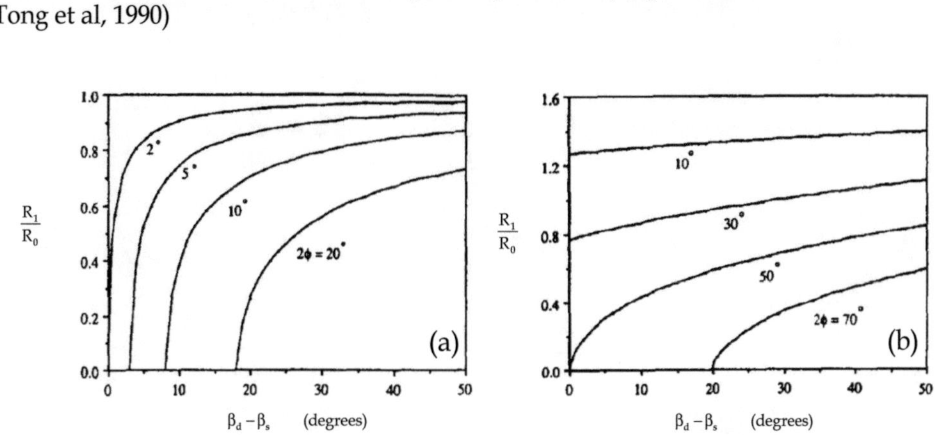

Fig. 21. The effect of the dynamic contact angle on the ratio of embryo radius to the cavity radius for highly wetting liquids: (a) static contact angle = 2°, (b) static contact angle = 50° (Tong et al, 1990)

Yu et al. (1990) conducted experiments of pool boiling using cylindrical heater surfaces of platinum, silicon oxide, and aluminum oxide with dielectric fluids of FC-72 and R-113. They reported the difference in incipience wall superheat value between FC-72 and R-113 was significant, but the surface material effect on a boiling incipience was small.

Harrison & Levine (1958) investigated the wetting effects on the pool boiling heat transfer using different crystal planes of single crystals of copper. In their results, the wetting surface and the non-wetting surface show higher the heat transfer rate in the lower and higher heat flux regions, respectively. The lower heat flux region is governed by a non-boiling natural convection, in which the non-wetting surface represents higher thermal resistance. However, the higher heat flux region is governed by a nucleate boiling, in which the non-wetting surface represents a larger bubble generation due to a higher nucleation cite density (Eddington & Kenning, 1979).

Phan et al. (2009a, 2009b) investigated the wettability effects on a nucleate boiling using various materials deposited on surfaces. In the hydrophobic surface, no bubble departure was noticed and the heat transfer was unstable when the bubbles stayed on the heating surface. In the hydrophilic surface, they measured a departure diameter and a bubble emission frequency. As increased the contact angle, the bubble departure diameter is decreased (Fig. 22a). They compared a following Fritz's correlation (Fritz, 1935), which has linear relation with the contact angle (Eq. 15).

$$D_d = 0.0208\theta\left(\frac{\gamma}{g(\rho_L - \rho_G)}\right)^{0.5} \tag{15}$$

They proposed a new correlation (Eq. 16) for the departure diameter considering the wettability effects using an energy factor, as the ratio of the energy needed to form a bubble with a contact angle to need to form a homogeneous bubble with the same diameter, which is proposed by Bankoff (1967),

$$D_d = 0.626977\left(\frac{2+3\cos\theta-\cos^3\theta}{4}\right)\left(\frac{\gamma}{g(\rho_L - \rho_G)}\right)^{0.5} \tag{16}$$

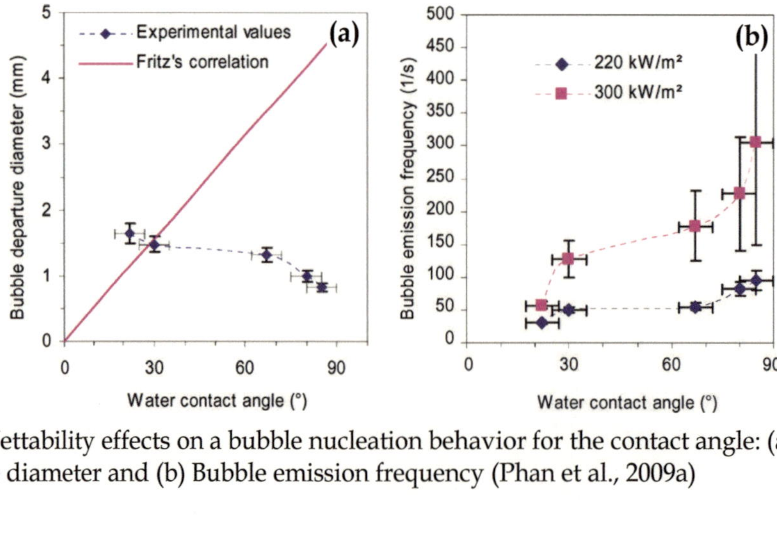

Fig. 22. Wettability effects on a bubble nucleation behavior for the contact angle: (a) Bubble departure diameter and (b) Bubble emission frequency (Phan et al., 2009a)

The decreased contact angle is resulted in the increases of both a bubble growth time (t_g) and a waiting period of the next bubble (t_w) (Fig. 22b). Also, they observed the same trend for density of an active nucleation site with Eddington & Kenning (1979). In their results, a heat transfer coefficient (h) deteriorates with the decrease of the contact angle of between 30 ° and 90 °. When the contact angle is lower than 30 °, its decrease induces an increase of h. Therefore, the highest heat transfer coefficient would be obtained with a surface of which the contact angle of is either 0 ° or 90 °. In contrast, Harada et al. (2010) reported that the bubbles were lifted-off the vertical heated surface of a small contact angle within a shorter period of time after the nucleation than that of a larger contact angle.

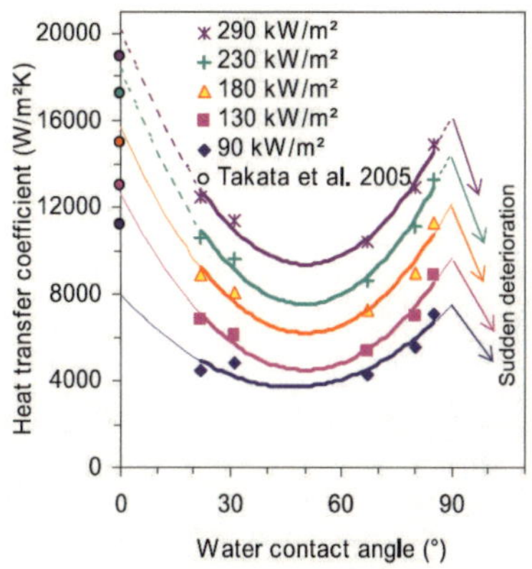

Fig. 23. Heat transfer coefficient versus the contact angles (Phan et al., 2009a)

Except coating methods, a typical way to change the contact angle is the use of surfactant solutions. However, this method changes the surface wettability, the liquid surface tension, and the viscosity simultaneously. It is generally believed that a small amount of surfactant can increase boiling heat transfer. Wasekar & Manglik (1999) reviewed an enhancement of pool boiling using this method. Some studies of wettability effects on the pool boiling with addition of surfactants will be reviewed. Wen & Wang (2010) used water and acetone with different surfactants, 95% sodium dodecyl surfate (SDS), Triton X-100 and octadecylamine. Their result shows that both SDS and Triton X-100 solution can increase the water boiling heat transfer coefficient and the enhancement of heat transfer for SDS solution is obvious. They subtracted only wettability effects on the heat transfer by comparing between SDS and X-100 experiments for the same surface tension and viscosity conditions. The contact angle only for X-100 decreases from 76 to 17 °. It means that the good wettability deteriorates boiling heat transfer.

The most intensively focused topic in the wettability effects in a pool boiling heat transfer is a critical heat flux (CHF), due to its higher dependency of surface characteristics. In the CHF situation, if the surface has ability to supply liquid to evaporate, the CHF can be increased. However, the surface has no ability for that, so the CHF can be decreased, then vapor can cover the entire surface. After reporting the major reason of the CHF enhancement of a nanofluid is wettability (Kim & Kim, 2009). Many researchers have concentrated on the wettability effects on the CHF. Especially, the super-hydrophilic surface that generated during the nanofluid boiling process indicates extremely high CHF value. Gaertner (1965) already reported that a low contact angle results in the higher value of CHF, while a high contact angle results in the lower value of CHF. Kandlikar (2001) proposed a new CHF model considering the contact angle and the orientation of a heating surface. For a horizontal surface, the correlation becomes Eq. (17),

$$q''_{CHF} = h_{fg}\rho_G^{0.5}\left(\frac{1+\cos\theta}{16}\right)\left[\frac{2}{\pi}+\frac{\pi}{4}(1+\cos\theta)\right]^{0.5}\left[\gamma g(\rho_L-\rho_G)\right]^{0.25} \tag{17}$$

Various studies for a nanofluid CHF enhancement reported that the major reason of the CHF enhancement is the nanoparticle coated surface, which is changed to a good wetting

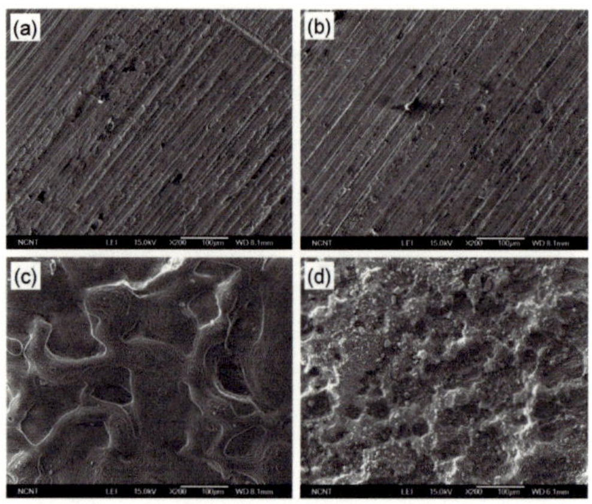

Fig. 24. SEMS images for various copper heater surfaces: (a) fresh, (b) water boiled, (c) alumina-nanofluid boiled, and (d) titania-nanofluid boiled (Kim et al., 2010)

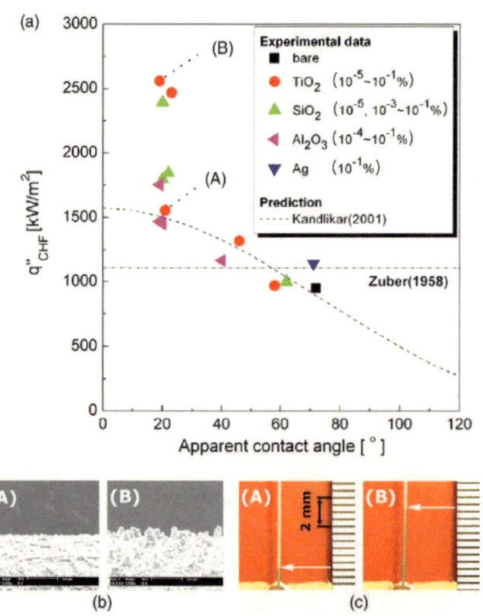

Fig. 25. A relation between CHF and surface characteristics: (a) CHF of pure water vs the contact angle on nanoparticle-deposited surfaces. (b) Scanning electron micrographs and (c) a maximum capillary wicking height of pure water on (A) 10^{-3}% and (B) 10^{-1}% TiO_2 nano-particle deposited surfaces with different CHF values at similar contact angles of approximately 20° (Kim & Kim, 2007)

surface. In the other words, the highly wetting surface, which is a lower contact angle, enhances the CHF of the pool boiling (Kim, S. J. et al., 2007; Coursey & Kim, 2008; Kim & Kim; 2009, & Kim, S. et al, 2010). Fig. 24 shows SEM images of the nanoparticle deposited heater surfaces after achieving the CHF. The nanoparticle deposited surface indicates as a highly wetting surface. Kim & Kim (2007) conducted wicking experiments using nano-particle coated wires, which is coated during a nanofluid boiling process. Fig. 25 shows their CHF value corresponding to the contact angle. Their results well agree with the Kandlikar's correlation (Eq. 17), except some cases of the lowest contact angle. These cases of extraordinarily highest CHF show a micro/nano structured surface and a higher wicking height. Chen et al. (2009) observed the same results for a super-hydrophilic surface coated by a nanowire. Kim et al. (2010) conducted a pool boiling CHF experiment using bare silicon, micro-structured (M), nano-structured (N) and both (NM) surfaces. They reported that a NM surface shows the contact angle of 0 ° (super-hydrophilic) and the highest value of the CHF. Recently, based on the CHF enhancement of the micro/nano structured super-hydrophilic surface, many researchers have been trying to obtain the CHF enhanced surface (Ahn et al., 2010; Truong et al., 2010; Forrest et al., 2010).

3.2.4 Flow boiling

In a conventional system, studies of the wettability effects on a flow boiling are less, because an external flow is dominant comparing with surface force. However, in micro scale, the surface force is predominant because of a higher surface to volume ratio. Choi & Kim (2008) developed a new fabrication technique to study the wettability effects on water flow boiling in a microchannel. They fabricated a single glass rectangular microchannel using a photosensitive glass and six microheaters to measure a local wall temperature and to apply heat to fluid as shown in Fig. 26. A glass was used as a hydrophilic surface and Octadecyl-trichloro-silane (OTS) was coated on a glass surface to obtain a hydrophobic surface. They focused on visualization of the two-phase flow patterns in the microchannel with different wetting surfaces. They observed a new flow pattern in the hydrophobic microchannel, which is named drop-wise slug (Fig. 27). A major flow pattern during a flow boiling in a microchannel is an elongated bubble, which is a very long bubble surrounded with thin liquid film. The evaporation of this thin film is a main heat transfer mechanism in a microchannel (Thome, 2006). Generally, the heat transfer coefficient is initially increased on the lower quality region, gradually decreased at a certain critical quality. A possible reason of this decreasing the heat transfer coefficient is a local dryout (Thome et al., 2004; Dupont et al., 2004). When the local dryout occurred, the liquid film is easily re-wetted on a hydrophilic surface. However, the liquid film is very unstable on a hydrophobic wall (Choi et al, 2010). This unstable pattern is represented to a new flow pattern. His extended work reported the wettability effects on flow boiling in a 500 μm rectangular microchannel for water (Choi et al. (2010). They obtained visualized flow patterns and a local heat transfer coefficient. They observed different flow patterns for different wettability conditions and analyzed heat transfer characteristics based on flow patterns. In the hydrophilic microchannel, flow patterns are similar to previous results for flow boiling in a microchannel. However, in the hydrophobic microchannel, the number of nucleation is increased due to low surface energy as shown in Fig. 28. These results are already reported by the pool boiling studies (Eddington & Kenning, 1979; Wang & Dhir, 1993; Phan et al., 2010a, 2010b). For relatively higher mass flux condition, nucleation is suppressed. They observed a heat transfer trend for different wettabilities and mass fluxes as shown in Fig. 29.

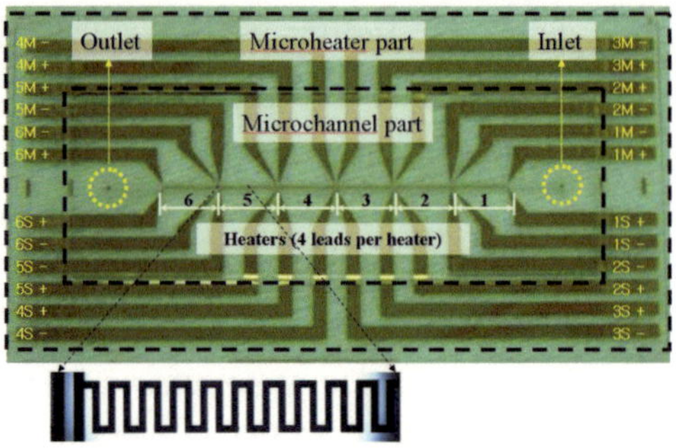

Fig. 26. A single glass microchannel and six gold micro heaters (Choi & Kim, 2008)

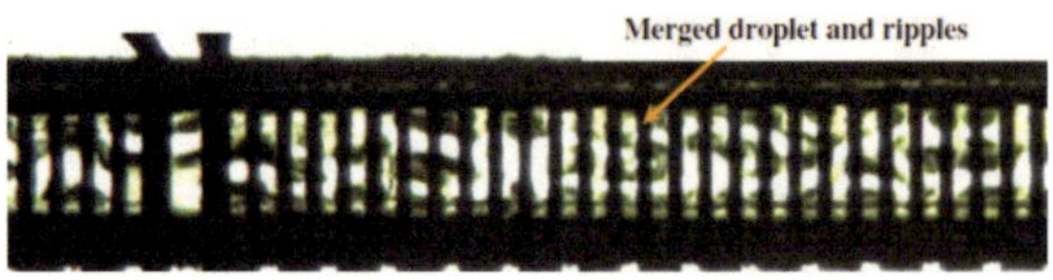

Fig. 27. A drop-wise slug flow pattern in a hydrophobic microchannel (Choi & Kim, 2008)

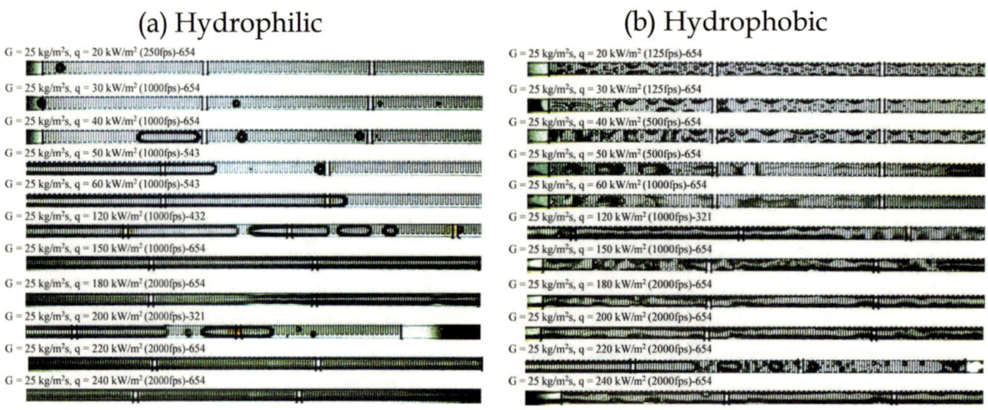

Fig. 28. Two-phase flow patterns in rectangular microchannels for different wettabilities: (a) hydrophilic microchannel, (b) hydrophobic microchannel (Choi et al., 2010)

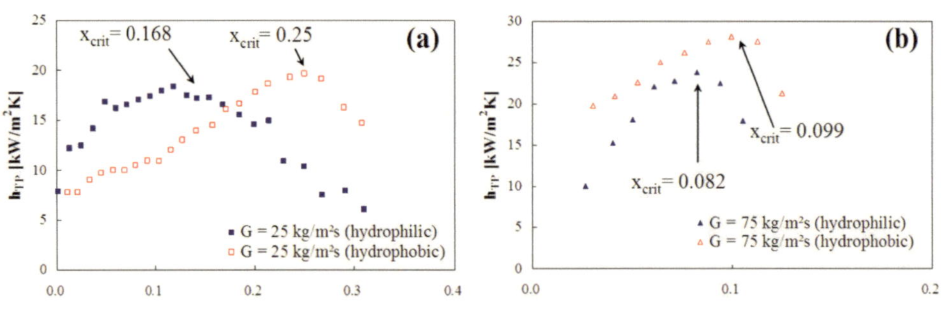

Fig. 29. A local heat transfer coefficient in rectangular microchannels for different wettabilities and mass fluxes: (a) 25 kg/m²s, (b) 75 kg/m²s (Choi et al, 2010)

Zhang et al. (2009) conducted flow boiling experiments with a hydrophobic microchannel with hydrophilic cover glass. They observed wettability effects on two-phase flow patterns as shown in Fig. 30. The tip of the liquid thread (rivulet) penetrates the junction interface of the inlet fluid plenum and the central microchannel at t = 1.0 ms in Fig. 30. Then a churn (chaotic) mushroom cloud, containing a mixture of vapor and liquid, was ejected into the central microchannel. A planar fluid triangle (shrinkage of liquid films), consisting of two contracted liquid films and the mixture of vapor and liquid inside, appears in the central microchannel upstream (see the images for t > 5.0 ms in Fig. 30). In front of the fluid triangle there is a long liquid rivulet populated near the microchannel centerline with the zigzag pattern. The rivulet reached the end of the central microchannel at t = 10.0 ms as shown in Fig. 30(a). For the time t > 12.0 ms, the rivulet was broken in the central microchannel downstream to form isolated droplets (see the circled image at t = 14.0 ms in Fig. 19(a)). The tip of the rivulet is being receded to the central microchannel upstream due to evaporation for t > 12.0 ms in Fig. 30(a), until the whole central microchannel is almost dry out, leaving a short rivulet in the central microchannel upstream (see the images at t=33.0 and 34.0ms in Fig. 30(a)). Then a new rivulet ejection and receding cycle starts. Fig. 30(b) shows the enlarged image for the isolated droplets formed by the breakup of the rivulet. Those new flow patterns are resulted from different wettability and temperature gradient.

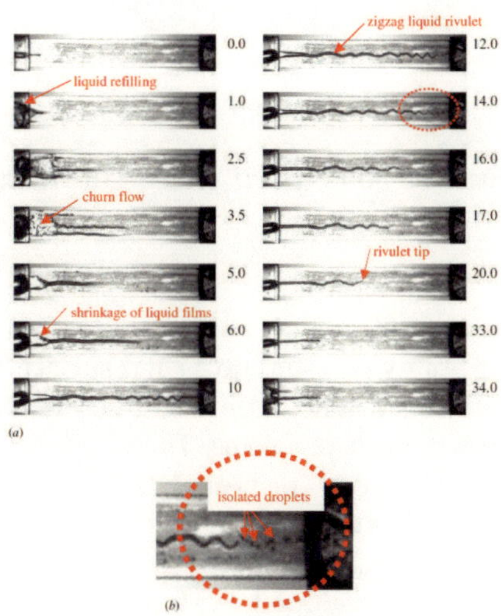

Fig. 30. Periodic liquid rivulet ejection and receding process (Zhang et al., 2009)

There are studies related with the CHF enhancement in the flow boiling in a microchannel. Ahn et al. (2010) conducted experiments with Alumina (Al_2O_3) nanofluid flow boiling on a local small heater to investigate external flow effect. As we discuss previously, nanofluid can enhance CHF in a pool boiling, because a nanofluid makes a super-hydrophilic heating surface during a boiling process. They obtained 40% enhancement of CHF for the highest flow velocity. Also, they measured apparent contact angles for the used heating surfaces. Their results are well agreed with a pool boiling CHF correlation (Eq. 17), except super-hydrophilic surface ($\theta \sim 0^o$) as shown in Fig. 31.

Vafaei & Wen (2010) studied CHF of the subcooled flow boiling of Alumina nanofluids in a 510 μm single microchannel. Their results show 51% enhancement of CHF under nanoparticle concentration of 0.1 vol. %. From their results, a main contribution of CHF enhancement is also a surface modification of nano particles during the boiling process. Sarwar et al. (2007) conducted a flow boiling CHF experiment with a nanoparticle coated porous surface. They reported 25% and 20% enhancement of CHF for Al_2O_3 and TiO_2, respectively. They explained that the enhancement is highly related with a wettability index. In the same group, Jeong et al. (2008) studied the flow boiling CHF with surfactant (TSP) solutions. Their results also show that the surfactant decreases a contact angle of the heating surface, and a CHF enhancement was achieved due to the higher wettability.

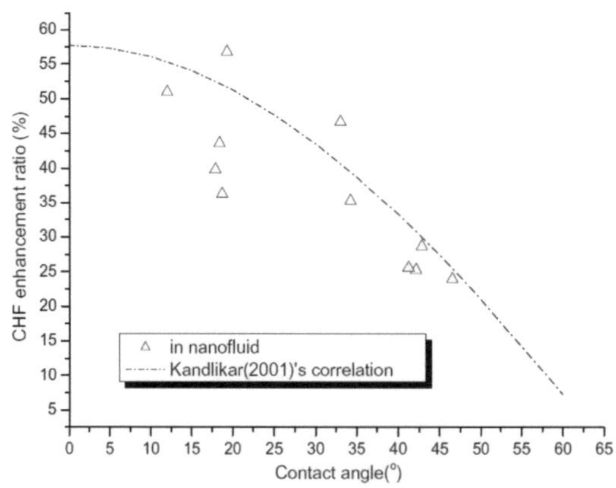

Fig. 31. A relation between the flow boiling CHF enhancement and the contact angle of the heated surface (Ahn et al., 2010)

4. Conclusion

The wettability is an adhesive ability of liquid on a solid surface, which can be characterized with the contact angle. In addition, a solid is used as intermediate to transfer heat thru the working fluid in the most heat transfer problems. Therefore, the wettability has a chance to be one of the important parameters in heat transfer phenomena. Recently, super-hydrophobic/hydrophilic surfaces have shown interesting phenomena, and a major reason of heat transfer enhancement of nanofluids is proven to be a hydrophilic surface coated by oxide nanoparticles. In addition, developed fabrication techniques for the micro/nano structured surface enforce intensive studies for the wettability effects on the heat transfer. In this chapter, we reviewed open literatures related with the wettability effects on the heat transfer. We categorized a single phase and two-phase heat transfers. Moreover, evaporation, condensation, pool boiling, and flow boiling are specifically discussed for the two-phase heat transfer. From these reviews, following consistent conclusions are derived.
The single phase has no TCL, which means that the solid is used as an intermediate to transfer heat thru the working fluid in most heat transfer problems. There is no interface of the two-phase on a solid surface. Therefore, there is less studies related with the wettability effect on the heat transfer. However, there is a slip flow in the hydrophobic surface only when the critical shear rate condition meets. According to previous studies related with the wettability effect on a convective heat transfer shows that the good wetting surface has a higher Nusselt number.

Basically, the wettability is a critical parameter in the two-phase behavior, because the motion of triple contact line (TCL) is highly influenced by a wetting characteristic on the surface. During a phase change heat transfer, mass transfer makes motion of TCL due to a volume expansion or a contraction. Thus, a dynamic wetting including a contact angle hysteresis becomes an influential parameter in the two-phase heat transfer. In evaporation and condensation, we considered the drop-wise heat transfer. In a drop-wise evaporation, the good wetting surface shows a high evaporation rate due to a large heat transfer area and a thin droplet thickness (low heat resistance). In condensation, the wettability effects is dominant on an initial stage of condensation and a good wetting surface shows a higher condensation rate due to the same reason to evaporation. For a super-hydrophilic/hydrophobic surface that was prepared with micro/nano structures, the contact angle hysteresis is the most critical parameter. As well as, morphology is important to understand the heat transfer mechanism in these special surfaces. There are two kinds of modes: Wenzel and Cassie-Baxter, which are governed by the dynamic wetting and the length scale of the surface pattern and the structure shape.

In the pool boiling heat transfer, the wettability is affected on the entire boiling process including a nucleation, a nucleate boiling, and a CHF. The good wettability decreased the density of active nucleation sites and the decreased departure frequency. Therefore, a typical trend for nucleate boiling heat transfer according to wettability effects is that a non-wettable surface indicates higher the heat transfer rate due to a higher nucleation site density. However, there is still unclear understanding for the wettability effects on the nucleate boiling heat transfer, because the nucleate boiling is complicate phenomena mixed surface parameters of a wettability, a roughness, a morphology. In CHF, a good wettability shows the higher value of the CHF due to a liquid supplying ability. For super-hydrophilic surface, there is an additional effect like the morphology for an extraordinary enhancement of the CHF.

In the open literature, there are only few studies related with the wettability effect flow boiling heat transfer owing to fabricational complexities and feasibility in a microscale. Most of studies indicate that the wettability is a critical parameter on the two-phase flow pattern in a microchannel. As same as the CHF in pool boiling, the wettable surface shows a higher value of the CHF in the flow boiling than the non-wettable surface. However, the wettability effects on the heat transfer of the flow boiling are still far from well understanding.

5. References

Adamson, A.V. (1990). *Physical Chemistry of Surfaces.*Wiley, New York, U.S.

Ahn, H. S., Kim, H., Jo, H., Kang, S., Chang, W., & Kim, M. H. (2010). Experimental study of critical heat flux enhancement during forced convective flow boiling of nanofluid on a short heated surface. *Int. J. Multiphase Flow*, Vol. 36, pp. 375-384.

Ahn, H. S., Lee, C., Kim, H., Jo, H., Kang, S., Kim, W., Shin, J., & Kim, M. H. (2010). Pool boiling CHF enhancement by micro/nanoscale modification of Zircaloy-4 surface. *Nuclear Engineering and Design*, Vol. 240, pp. 3350-3360.

Asif, S. A. S., Wahl, K. J. & Colton, R. J. (2002). The influence of oxide and adsorbates on the nanomechanical response of silicon surface. *J. Mater. Res.*, Vol. 15, No. 2, pp. 546-553.

Bankoff, S. G. (1967). Ebullition from solid surfaces in the absence of a pre-existing gaseous phase. *Trans. Am. Mech. Eng.*, Vol. 79, pp. 735-740.

Barrat, J. & Bocquet, L. (1999). Large slip effect at a nonwetting fluid-solid interface. *Phys. Rev. Lett.*, Vol. 82, No. 3, pp. 4671-4674.

Betz, A. R., Xu, J., Qiu, H., & Attinger, D. (2010). Do surface with mixed hydrophilic and hydrophobic area enhance pool boiling? *Appl. Phys. Lett.*, Vol. 97, pp. 141909-1-141909-3.

Bourges-Monnier, C. & Shanahan, M. E. R. (1995). Influence of Evaporation on Contact Angle. *Langmuir*, Vol. 11, pp. 2820-2829.

Cassie, A. B. D.; Baxter, S. (1944). Wettability of porous surfaces. *Trans. Faraday Soc.*, Vol. 40, pp. 546-551.

Chandra, S., di-Marzo, M., Qiao, Y. M. & Tartarini, P. (1996). Effect of Liquid-Solid Contact Angle on Droplet Evaporation. *Fire Safety Journal*, Vol. 27, pp. 141-158.

Chen, R., Lu, M., Srinivasan, V., Wang, Z., Cho, H. & Majumdar, A. (2009). Nanowires for Enhanced Boiling Heat Transfer. *Nano Letters*, Vol. 9, No. 2, pp. 548-553.

Chen, R., Phuoc, T. X., Martello, D. (2010). Effects of nanoparticles on nanofluid droplet evaporation. *Int. J. of Heat Mass Transfer*, Vol. 53, pp. 3677–3682.

Choi, C., Westin, K. J. A. & Breuer, K. S. (2003). Apparent slip flows in hydrophilic and hydrophobic microchannels. *Physics of Fluids*, Vol. 15, No. 10, pp. 2897-2902.

Choi, C. & Kim, M. H. (2008). The fabrication of a single glass microchannel to study the hydrophobicity effect on two-phase flow boiling of water. *J. Micromech. Microeng.* Vol. 18, pp. 105016 (9pp).

Choi, C., Shin, J. S., Yu, D. I. & Kim, M. H. (2010). Flow boiling behaviors in hydrophilic and hydrophobic microchannels. *Exp. Therm. and Fl. Sci.*, Vol. 35, pp. 816-824.

Chon, C. H., Paik, S. W., Tipton Jr., J. B. & Kihm, K. D. Evaporation and Dryout of Nanofluid Droplets on a Microheater Array, In: May,1th, 2011, Available from: <http://minsfet.utk.edu/Research/2007-update/Evaporation_Dryout.pdf>

Colin, S., Lalonde, P. & Caen, R. (2004). Validatin of a second-order slip flow model in rectangular microchannels. *Heat Transfer Eng.*, Vol. 25, No. 3, pp. 23-30.

Coursey, J. S., & Kim, J. (2008). Nanofluid boiling: The effect of surface wettability. *Int. J. Heat Fluid Flow*, Vol. 29, pp. 1577-1586.

Dupont, V., Thome, J. R. & Jacobi, A. M. (2004). Heat transfer model for evaporation in microchannels. Part II: Comparison with the database. *Int. J. Heat Mass Transfer*, Vol. 47, pp. 3387–3401.

Eddington, R. I. & Kenning, D. B. R. (1979). The Effect of Contact Angle on Bubble Nucleation. *Int. J. Heat Mass Transfer*, Vol. 22, pp. 1231-1236.

Eustathopoulos, N., Nicholas, M.G. & Drevet, B. (1999). *Wettability at high temperatures*, Oxford, 0080421466, Pergamon, U.K.

Forrest, E., Williamson, E., Buongiorno, J., Hu, L., Rubner, M. & Cohen, R. (2010). Augmentation of nucleate boiling heat transfer and critical heat flux using nanoparticle thin-film coatings. *Int. J. Heat Mass Transfer*, Vol. 53, pp. 58-67.

Fritter, D., Knobler, C. M. & Beysens, D. (1991). Experiments and Simulation of Growth of Drops on a Surface. *Physical Review A*, Vol. 43, No. 6, pp. 2858-2869.

Fritz, W. (1935). Maximum volume of vapour bubble. *Phys. Z.*, Vol. 36, pp. 379-384.

Furuta, T., Sakai, M., Isobe, T. & Nakajima, A. (2010). Effect of Dew Condensation on the Wettability of Rough Hydrophobic Surfaces Coated with Two Different Silanes. *Langmuir*, Vol. 26, No. 16, pp. 13305-13309.

Gaertner, R. F. (1965). Photographic Study of Nucleate Pool Boiling on Horizontal Surface. *ASME J. Heat Transfer*, Vol. 87, pp. 17-29.

Gennes, P. D. (1997). *Soft Interfaces*. Cambridge University Press, 9780521564175, U.K.

Gennes, P. D. (1985). Wetting: statics and dynamics. *Reviews of Modern Physics*, Vol. 57, No. 3, pp. 827–863.

Gokhale, S. J., Plawsky, J. L. & Wayner Jr., P. C. (2003). Experimental investigation of contact angle, curvature, and contact line motion in dropwise condensation and evaporation. *J. Colloid and Interface Science*, Vol. 259, pp. 354-366.

Good, R. J. (1992). Contact angle, wetting, and adhesion: a critical review. *J. Adhesion Sci. Technol.*, Vol. 6, No. 12, pp. 1269–1302.

Griffith, P. (1972). *Handbook of Heat Transfer*, McGraw-Hill, New York, U. S.

Harada, T., Nagakura, H., & Okawa, T. (2010). Dependence of bubble behavior in subcooled boiling on surface wettability. *Nuclear Engineering and Design*, Vol. 240, pp. 3949-3955.

Harrison, W. B. & Levine, Z. (1958). Wetting effects on boiling heat transfer: the Copper-Stearic Acid System. *AIChE J.*, Vol. 4, No. 4, pp. 409-412.

He, B., Patankar, N. & Lee, J. (2003). Multiple Equilibrium Droplet Shapes and Design Criterion for Rough Hydrophobic Surfaces. *Langmuir*, Vol. 19, pp. 4999-5003.

Hsieh, S. & Lin, C. (2009). Convective heat transfer in liquid microchannels with hydrophobic and hydrophilic surfaces. *Int. J. Heat Mass Transfer*, Vol. 52, pp. 260-270.

Jeong, Y. H., Sarwar, M. S. & Chang, S. H. (2008). Flow boiling CHF enhancement with surfactant solutions under atmospheric pressure. *Int. J. Heat Mass Transfer*, Vol. 51, pp. 1913-1919.

John, C. B. (1993). *Wettability*, Marcel Dekker, 0824790464, New York, U.S.

Johnson Jr., R. E. and Dettre, R. H. (1969). Wettability and contact angle. *Surface and Colloid Science*, Vol. 2, pp. 85-153.

Jung, Y. C. & Bhushan, B. (2008). Wetting behaviour during evaporation and condensation of water microdroplets on superhydrophobic patterned surfaces. *Journal of Microscopy*, Vol. 229, pp. 127–140.

Kandlikar, S. G. (2001). A theoretical model to predict pool boiling CHF incorporating effects of contact angle and orientation. *AMSE J. Heat Transfer*, Vol. 123, pp. 1071-1080.

Kim, S. J., Bang, I. C., Buongiorno, J., & Hu, L. W. (2007). Surface Wettability change during pool boiling of nanofluids and its effect on critical heat flux. *Int. J. Heat Mass Transfer*, Vol. 50, pp. 4105-4116.

Kim, H. D. & Kim, M. H. (2007). Effect of nanoparticle deposition on capillary wicking that influences the critical heat flux in nanofluids. *Applied Physics Letters*, Vol. 91, pp. 014104-1-014104-3.

Kim, H., & Kim, M. (2009) Experimental Study of the characteristics and mechanism of pool boiling CHF enhancement using nanofluids. *Heat Mass Transfer*, Vol. 45, pp. 991-998.

Kim, H., Ahn, H. S., & Kim, M. H. (2010). On the Mechanism of Pool Boiling Critical Heat Flux Enhancement in Nanofluids. ASME J. Heat Transfer, Vol. 132, pp. 061501-1-061501-11.

Kim, S. Kim, H. D., Kim, H., Ahn, H. S., Jo, H., Kim, W., & Kim, M. H. (2010). Effects of nano-fluid and surfaces with nano structure on the increase of CHF, *Exp. Therm. Fl. Sci.*, Vol. 4, pp. 487-495.

Kulinich, S. A. & Farzaneh, M. (2009). Effect of contact angle hysteresis on water droplet evaporation from super-hydrophobic surfaces. *Applied Surface Science*, Vol. 255, pp. 4056-4060.

Lafuma, A. & Quere, D. (2003). Superhydrophobic states. *Nature Mater.*, Vol. 2, pp. 457-460.

Lamb, H. (1932). *Hydrodynamics*, Dover, New York, U.S.

Leeladhar, R., Xu, W., & Choi, C. (2009). Effects of Nanofluids on Droplet Evaporation and Wetting on Nanoporous Superhydrophobic Surfaces, *ASME Second International Conference on Micro/Nanoscale Heat and Mass Transfer*, Vol. 2, No. MNHMT2009-18551 pp. 725-733, Shanghai, China, December, 2009.

Lorenz, J. J. (1972). *The effects of surface conditions of boiling characteristics*, Ph. D Thesis, Massachusetts Institute of Technology, Cambridge, Massachusetts.

Marmur, A. (2003). Wetting of Hydrophobic Rough Surfaces: To be heterogeneous or not to be. *Langmuir*, Vol. 19, pp. 8343–8348.

Nagayama, G. & Cheng, P. (2004). Effects of interface wettability on microscale flow by molecular dynamics simulation. *Int. J. Heat Mass Transfer*, Vol. 47, pp. 501-513.

Narhe, R. D. & Beysens, D. A. (2004). Nucleation and Growth on a Super-hydrophobic Grooved Surface. *Phys. Rev. Lett.*, Vol. 93, 76103-76107.

Narhe, R. D. & Beysens, D. A. (2006). Water condensation on a super-hydrophobic spike surface. *Europhys. Lett.*, Vol. 75, No. 1, pp. 98–104.

Narhe, R. D. & Beysens, D. A., (2007). Growth Dynamics of Water Drops on a Square-Pattern Rough Hydrophobic Surface. *Langmuir*, Vol. 23, pp. 6486-6489.

Neumann, A. W. (1974). Contact angles and their temperature dependence: thermodynamic status: measurement, interpretation and application. *Adv. Colloid Interface Sci.*, Vol. 4, pp. 105-191.

Neumann, A. W., Abdelmessih, A. H. & Hameed, A. (1978). The role of contact angle and contact angle hysteresis in dropwise condensation heat transfer. *Int. J. Heat Mass Transfer*, Vol. 21, pp. 947-953.

Phan, H. T., Caney, N., Marty, P., Colasson, S., & Gavillet, J. (2009a). How does surface wettability influence nucleate boiling? *C.R. Mecanique*, Vol. 337, pp. 251-259.

Phan, H. T, Cabeny, N., Marty, P., Colasson, S., & Gavillet, J. (2009b). Surface wettability control by nanocoating: The effects on pool boiling heat transfer and nucleation mechanism. *Int. J. Heat Mass Transfer*, Vol. 52, pp. 5459-5471.

Picknett, R. G. & Bexon, R. (1977). The Evaporation of Sessile or Pendant Drops in Still Air. *J. Colloid Interface Sci.*, Vol. 61, No. 2, pp. 336-350.

Pulipaka, S. (2008), *The Effect of Surface Wettability on Heterogeneous Condensation*, Master Thesis, University of Cincinnati, Dept. Mechanical Eng.

Sarwar, M. S., Jeong, Y. H. & Chang, S. H. (2007). Subcooled flow boiling CHF enhancement with porous sruface coatings. *Int. J. Heat Mass Transfer*, Vol. 50, pp. 3649-3657.

Sefiane, K., & Bennacer, R. (2009). Nanofluids droplets evaporation kinetics and wetting dynamics on rough heated substrates. *Advances in Colloid and Interface Science*, Vol. 147–148, pp. 263–271.

Schrader, M. E. & Loeb, G.I. (1992). *Modern Approaches to Wettability: Theory and Applications*, Plenum Press, 0306439859, New York, U.S.

Sharfrin, E., Zisman & William, A. (1960). Constitutive relations in the wetting of low energy surfaces and the theory of the retraction method of preparing monolayers. *The Journal of Physical Chemistry*, Vol. 64, No.5, pp. 519–524.

Schwartz, A. M., Rader, C. A. & Huey, E. (1964). Contact angle wettability and adhesion: resistance to flow in capillary systems of positive contact angles. *Adv. Chem. Ser.*, Vol. 43, pp. 250-267.

Shin, D. H., Lee, S. H., Jung, J. & Yoo, J. Y., (2009). Evaporating characteristics of sessile droplet on hydrophobic and hydrophilic surfaces. *Microelectronic Engineering*, Vol. 86, pp. 1350-1353.

Takata, Y., Hidaka, S., Yamashita, A., & Yamamoto, H. (2004). Evaporation of water drop on a plasma-irradiated hydrophilic surface. *Int. J. Heat Fluid Flow*, Vol. 25, pp. 320–328.

Takata, Y., Hidaka, S., Cao, J. M., Nakamura, T., Yamamoto, H., Masuda, M., & Ito, T. (2005). Effect of surface wettability on boiling and evaporation. *Energy*, Vol. 30, pp. 209–220.

Thome, J. R. (2006). State-of-the-Art Overview of Boiling and Two-Phase Flows in Microchannels. *Heat Transfer Engineering*, Vol. 27, No. 9, pp. 4-19.

Thome, J. R., Dupont, V. & Jacobi, A. M. (2004). Heat transfer model for evaporation in microchannels. Part I: Presentation of the model. *Int. J. Heat Mass Transfer*, Vol. 47, pp. 3375–3385.

Thomson, P. & Troian, S. (1997). A general boundary condition for liquid flow at solid surfaces. *Nature*, Vol. 389, pp. 360-362.

Tong, W., Bar-Cohen, A., Simon T. W. & You, S. M. (1990). Contact angle effect on boiling incipience of highly-wetting liquids. *Int. J. Heat Mass Transfer*, Vol. 33, No. 1, pp. 91-103.

Tretheway, D. C. & Meinhart, C. D. (2005). A generating mechanism for apparent fluid slip in hydrophobic microchannel. *Physics of Fluids*, Vol. 17. pp. 103606-103616.

Truong, B., Hu, L., Buongiorno, J., & Mckrell, T. (2010). Modification of sandblasted plate heaters using nanofluids to enhance pool boiling critical heat flux. *Int. J. Heat Mass Transfer*, Vol. 53, pp. 85-94.

Vafaei, S. & Wen, D. (2010). Critical Heat Flux (CHF) of Subcooled Flow Boiling of Alumina Nanofluids in a Horizontal Microchannel. *J. Heat Transfer*, Vol. 132, pp. 102404-1-102404-7.

Wang, C. H. & Dhir, V. K. (1993). Effect of surface wettability on active nucleate site density during pool boiling of water on a vertical surface. *Trans. ASME J. Heat Transfer*, Vol. 115, pp. 670-679.

Wasekar, V. M., & Manglik, R. M. (1999). A review of enhanced heat transfer in nucleate pool boiling of aqueous surfactant and polymeric solutions. J. *Enhanced Heat Transfer*, Vol. 6, pp. 135-150.

Watanabe, K., Yanuar and Udagawa, H. (1999). Drag reduction of Newtonian fluid in a circular pipe with a highly water-repellent wall. *J. Fluid Mech.*, Vol. 381, pp. 225-238.

Wen, D. S., & Wang, B. X. (2002). Effects of surface wettability on nucleate pool boiling heat transfer for surfactant solutions. *Int. J. Heat Mass Transfer*, Vol. 45. pp. 1739-1747.

Wenzel, R. N. (1936). Resistance of solid surface to wetting by water. *Ind. Eng. Chem.*, Vol. 28, pp. 988-994.

Whyman, G., Bormashenko, E. & Stein, T. (2008). The rigirious derivation of Young, Cassie–Baxter and Wenzel equations and the analysis of the contact angle hysteresis phenomenon. *Chemical Physics Letters*, Vol. 450, pp. 355–359.

Wu, H.Y. & Cheng, P. (2003). An experiment study of convective heat transfer in silicon microchannels with different surface conditions. *Int. J. Heat Mass Transfer*, Vol. 46, pp. 2547-2556.

You, S. M., Bar-Cohen, A. & Simon, T. W. (1990). Boiling Incipience and Nucleate Boiling Heat Transfer of Highly Wetting Dielectric Fluids from Electronic Materials. *IEEE Transactions on Components, Hybrids, and Manufacturing Technology*, Vol. 13, No. 4, pp. 1032-1039.

Young, T. (1805). An Essay on the Cohesion of Fluids. *Phil. Trans. R. Soc. Lond.*, Vol. 95, pp. 65–87.

Yu, H., Soolaman, D. M., Rowe, A. W. & Banks, J. T. (2004). Evaporation of Water Microdroplets on Self-Assembled Monolayers: From Pinning to Shrinking. *Chem Phys Chem*, Vol. 5, pp. 1035-1038.

Zhang, W., Liu, G., Xu, J. & Yang, Y. (2009). Effect of channel surface wettability and temperature gradients on the boiling flow pattern in a single microchannel. *J. Micromech. Microeng.*, Vol. 19, pp. 055012 (13pp).

Zhao, H. & Beysens, D. (1995) From Droplet Growth to Film Growth on a Heterogeneous Surface: Condensation Associated with a Wettability Gradient. *Langmuir*, Vol. 11, pp. 627-634.

15

Liquid Film Thickness in Micro-Scale Two-Phase Flow

Naoki Shikazono and Youngbae Han
The University of Tokyo
Japan

1. Introduction

Liquid film formed between confined vapor bubble and tube wall in micro-scale two phase flow plays an important role in heat exchangers and chemical reactors, since local heat and mass transfer is effectively enhanced at the thin liquid film region (Taha and Cui, 2006). However, characteristics of the liquid film in micro-scale two phase flows are not fully understood, and thus designing two-phase flow systems still remains as a difficult task. It is reported that the thickness of the liquid film is one of the most important parameters for predicting two phase flow heat transfer in micro tubes, see Thome et al., 2004; Kenning et al., 2006; Qu and Mudawar, 2004; Saitoh et al., 2007. For example, in the three zone evaporation model proposed by Thome et al. (2004), initial liquid film thickness is one of the three unknown parameters which must be given from experimental studies.
Many researches have been conducted to investigate the characteristics of liquid film both experimentally and theoretically. Taylor (1961) experimentally obtained mean liquid film thickness in a slug flow by measuring the difference between bubble velocity and mean velocity. Highly viscous fluids, i.e. glycerol, syrup-water mixture and lubricating oil, were used so that wide capillary number range could be covered. It was found that the ratio of bubble velocity to mean velocity approaches an asymptotic value of 0.55. This asymptotic value was re-evaluated by Cox (1964), which was reported to be 0.60. Schwartz et al. (1986) investigated the effect of bubble length on the liquid film thickness using the same method as Taylor (1961). It was reported that longer bubbles move faster than shorter ones. Bretherton (1961) proposed an analytical theory for the bubble profile and axial pressure drop across the bubble using lubrication equations. Assuming small capillary number, it is shown that the dimensionless liquid film thickness can be scaled by an exponential function of capillary number, $Ca^{2/3}$. Liquid film thickness can also be measured from the temperature change of the channel wall under the assumption that the whole liquid film on the wall evaporates and the heat is wholly consumed by the evaporation of the liquid film. Cooper (1969) measured liquid film thickness with this method and investigated the bubble growth in nucleate pool boiling. Moriyama and Inoue (1996) measured liquid film thickness during a bubble expansion in a narrow gap. It was reported that liquid film thickness is affected by the viscous boundary layer in the liquid slug when acceleration becomes large. Their experimental data was correlated in terms of capillary number, Bond number and dimensionless boundary layer thickness. Heil (2001) numerically investigated the inertial

force effect on the liquid film thickness. It is shown that the liquid film thickness and the pressure gradient depend on Reynolds number. Aussillous & Quere (2000) measured liquid film thickness of fluids with relatively low surface tension. It was found that the liquid film thickness deviates from the Taylor's data at relatively high capillary numbers. Visco-inertia regime, where the effect of inertial force on the liquid film thickness becomes significant, was demonstrated. Kreutzer et al. (2005) studied liquid film thickness and pressure drop in a micro tube both numerically and experimentally. Predicted liquid film thickness showed almost the same trend as reported by Heil (2001).

Several optical methods have been applied for liquid film thickness measurement, e.g. optical interface detection, laser extinction, total light reflection and laser confocal displacement etc. Ursenbacher et al. (2004) developed a new optical method to detect instantaneous vapor-liquid interface. Interface of stratified two-phase flow in a 13.6 mm inner diameter tube was detected in their experiment. Utaka et al. (2007) measured liquid film thickness formed in narrow gap channels with laser extinction method. Liquid film thickness from 2 to 30 μm was measured in 0.5, 0.3 and 0.15 mm gap channels. It was concluded that the boiling process were dominated by two characteristic periods, i.e., micro-layer dominant and liquid saturated periods. Hurlburt & Newell (1996) developed a device which can measure liquid film thickness from total light reflection. Using the same method, Shedd & Newell (2004) measured liquid film thickness of air/water two-phase flow in round, square and triangular tubes. Other measurement techniques, e.g. acoustical, electrical and nucleonic methods are summarized comprehensively in the review paper of Tibirica et al. (2010).

Although many experiments have been carried out to measure liquid film thickness, quantitative data of local and instantaneous liquid film thicknesses are still limited. To develop precise heat transfer models for micro-scale two phase flows, it is crucial to predict liquid film thickness accurately around the confined bubble. In the present study, local and instantaneous liquid film thicknesses are measured directly with laser confocal displacement meter. Series of experiments is conducted to investigate the effects of parameters such as viscosity, surface tension and inertial forces, cross sectional shapes on the formation of liquid film in micro-scale two phase flow. In addition, under flow boiling conditions, the bubble velocity is not constant but accelerated. Acceleration may affect the balance between viscous, surface tension and inertia forces in the momentum equation. It is thus very important to consider this acceleration effect on the liquid film thickness (Kenning et al., 2006). In the present study, liquid film thickness is measured systematically using laser confocal method, and simple scaling analyses are conducted to obtain predictive correlations for the initial liquid film thickness.

2. Experimental setup and procedures

In this section, experimental setup and procedures are described. Refer to the original papers by the authors for details (Han & Shikazono, 2009a, 2009b, 2010 and Han et al. 2011).

2.1 Test section configuration

Figure 1 shows the schematic diagram of the experimental setup. Circular tubes made of Pyrex glass with inner diameters of $D_h \approx 0.3$, 0.5, 0.7, 1.0 and 1.3 mm, square quartz tubes with $D_h \approx 0.3$, 0.5 and 1.0 mm, and high aspect ratio rectangular quartz tubes with $D_h \approx 0.2$, 0.6 and 1.0 mm were used as test tubes. Table 1 and Fig. 2 show the dimensions and the photographs of the test tubes. Tube diameter was measured with a microscope, and the differences of inlet and outlet inner diameters were less than 1% for all tubes. One side of the tube was connected to the syringe. Actuator motor (EZHC6A-101, Oriental motor) was used to move the liquid in the tube. The velocity of the actuator motor ranged from 0 to 0.6 m/s. Syringes with several cross sectional areas were used to control the liquid velocity in the test section, and the range of liquid velocity in the present experiment was varied from 0 to 6 m/s. The velocity of the gas-liquid interface was measured from the images captured by the high speed camera (Phantom 7.1, Photron SA1.1). The images were taken at several frame rates depending on the bubble velocity. For the highest bubble velocity case, maximum frame rate was 10,000 frames per second with a shutter time of 10 μs. Laser confocal displacement meter (LT9010M, Keyence) was used to measure the liquid film thickness. Laser confocal displacement meter has been used by several researchers for liquid film measurement (Takamasa and Kobayashi, 2000; Hazuku et al., 2005). It is reported that laser confocal displacement meter can measure liquid film thickness very accurately within 1% error (Hazuku et al., 2005). Figure 3 shows the principle of the laser confocal displacement meter. The position of the target surface can be determined by the displacement of objective lens moved by the tuning fork. The intensity of the reflected light becomes highest in the light-receiving element when the focus is obtained on the target surface. The resolution for the present laser confocal displacement meter is 0.01 μm, the laser spot diameter is 2 μm and the response time is 640 μs. Thus, it is possible to measure instantaneous and local liquid film thickness. Measured liquid film thickness is transformed to DC voltage signal in the range of ±10V. Output signal was sent to PC through GPIB interface and recorded with LabVIEW.

	Hydraulic diameter D_h [mm]	H [mm]	W [mm]	Aspect ratio	L_{corner} [mm]
Circular tube	0.305				
	0.487				
	0.715				
	0.995				
	1.305				
Square tube	0.282	0.279	0.284	1.02	0.020
	0.570	0.582	0.558	0.959	0.035
	0.955	0.956	0.953	0.997	0.067
High aspect ratio rectangular tube	0.225	0.116	4.00	34.5	
	0.592	0.309	7.00	22.7	
	0.957	0.504	10.0	19.8	

Table 1. Dimensions of the tested tubes

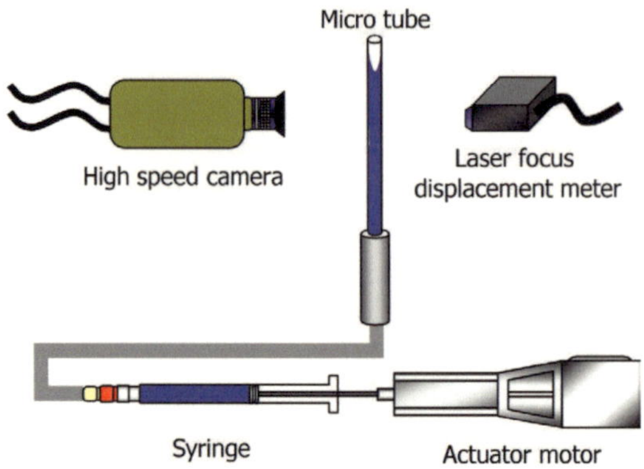

Fig. 1. Schematic diagram of the experimental setup

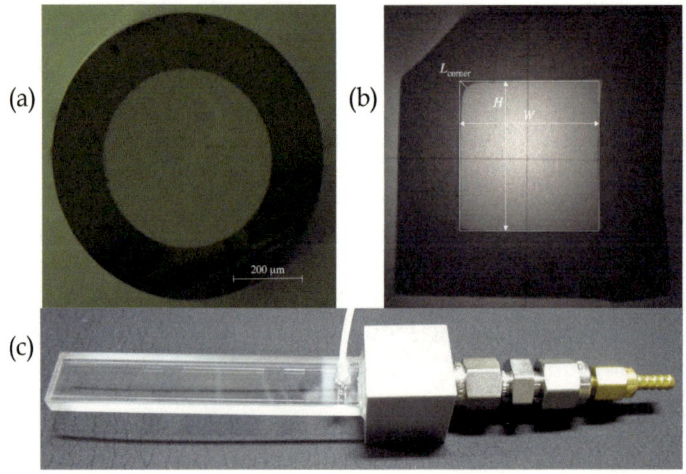

Fig. 2. Tubes tested in the present study. (a) Circular, (b) square and (c) rectangular tubes

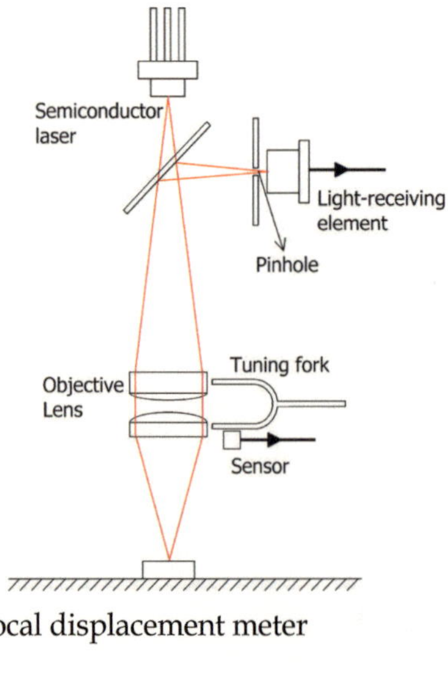

Fig. 3. Principle of laser confocal displacement meter

2.2 Correction for the wall curvature for circular tubes

In the case of circular tubes, focus is scattered within a certain range due to the difference of curvatures between axial and circumferential directions when the laser beam passes through the curved tube surface. Cover glass and glycerol were used to eliminate the curvature effect caused by the outer wall as shown in Fig. 4. Refractive index of glycerol (n = 1.47) is almost the same with that of the Pyrex glass (n = 1.474), so the refraction of laser between glycerol and Pyrex glass can be neglected. Refractive indices of ethanol, water and FC-40 are 1.36, 1.33 and 1.29 under the condition of 1 atm and 25°C. It is difficult to detect inner wall/liquid and liquid/gas interfaces at the same time, because the difference of the refractive indices of the wall and the liquid is small. Therefore, the distance from the cover glass to the inner wall is measured beforehand in a dry condition. Then, total thickness with liquid film is measured. Liquid film thickness is obtained from the difference of these two values. The effect of the inner wall curvature is corrected by the equation suggested by Takamasa & Kobayashi (2000). Figure 5 shows the laser path and refraction through the liquid film. Focus is scattered from δ_1 to δ_2 due to the difference of wall curvatures in X and Z directions. Liquid film thickness is assumed to be the average of δ_1 and δ_2, because the intensity of reflection may become highest at the center of δ_1 and δ_2:

$$\delta = \frac{\delta_1 + \delta_2}{2} . \tag{1}$$

In Eq. (1), δ_1 and δ_2 are the liquid film thicknesses measured in Y-Z and X-Y planes, respectively. Liquid film thickness δ_1 in Y-Z plane can be calculated from Eqs. (2) and (3) as:

$$\delta_1 = y_{\mathrm{m}} \frac{\tan\theta_{\mathrm{w}}}{\tan\theta_{\mathrm{f}}} , \tag{2}$$

$$\frac{\sin\theta_{\mathrm{w}}}{\sin\theta_{\mathrm{f}}} = \frac{n_{\mathrm{f}}}{n_{\mathrm{w}}} , \tag{3}$$

where n_{f} and n_{w} are the refractive indices of the working fluid and the tube wall, respectively. In Eq. (2), y_{m} is the distance of objective lens movement, and it can be obtained from the recorded data during the experiment. The angle of incidence θ_{w} is 14.91° in the present laser confocal displacement meter. The refraction angle θ_{f} is determined from the Snellius's law, Eq. (3). Liquid film thickness δ_2 can be calculated from following equations as:

$$\delta_2 = y_0 + \frac{x_0}{\tan\left(\theta_{\mathrm{w}} - \theta'_{\mathrm{w}} + \theta'_{\mathrm{f}}\right)} , \tag{4}$$

$$x_0^2 + y_0^2 = D y_0 , \tag{5}$$

$$y_0 = y_{\mathrm{m}} - \frac{x_0}{\tan\theta_{\mathrm{w}}} , \tag{6}$$

$$x_0 = \frac{D}{2} \sin\left(\theta_{\mathrm{w}} - \theta'_{\mathrm{w}}\right) , \tag{7}$$

$$\frac{\sin\theta'_{\mathrm{w}}}{\sin\theta'_{\mathrm{f}}} = \frac{n_{\mathrm{f}}}{n_{\mathrm{w}}}, \tag{8}$$

where θ'_{w} and θ'_{f} are the angles of incidence and refraction, and x_0 and y_0 are the intersection points between laser and inner wall in X-Y plane. From Eqs. (4) to (8), δ_2 is calculated as:

$$\delta_2 = y_{\mathrm{m}} + \frac{1}{2} D \sin\left(\theta_{\mathrm{w}} - \theta'_{\mathrm{w}}\right)\left(\frac{1}{\tan\left(\theta_{\mathrm{w}} - \theta'_{\mathrm{w}} + \theta'_{\mathrm{f}}\right)} - \frac{1}{\tan\theta_{\mathrm{w}}}\right). \tag{9}$$

Finally, liquid film thickness δ in circular tubes can be obtained from Eqs. (2) and (9) as follows:

$$\delta = \frac{y_{\mathrm{m}}}{2}\left(\frac{\tan\theta_{\mathrm{w}}}{\tan\theta_{\mathrm{f}}} + 1\right) + \frac{1}{4} D \sin\left(\theta_{\mathrm{w}} - \theta'_{\mathrm{w}}\right)\left(\frac{1}{\tan\left(\theta_{\mathrm{w}} - \theta'_{\mathrm{w}} + \theta'_{\mathrm{f}}\right)} - \frac{1}{\tan\theta_{\mathrm{w}}}\right). \tag{10}$$

The curvature effect on liquid film thickness is not so severe when the liquid film is thin. The difference of δ_1 and δ_2 is less than 2% in the present experiments.

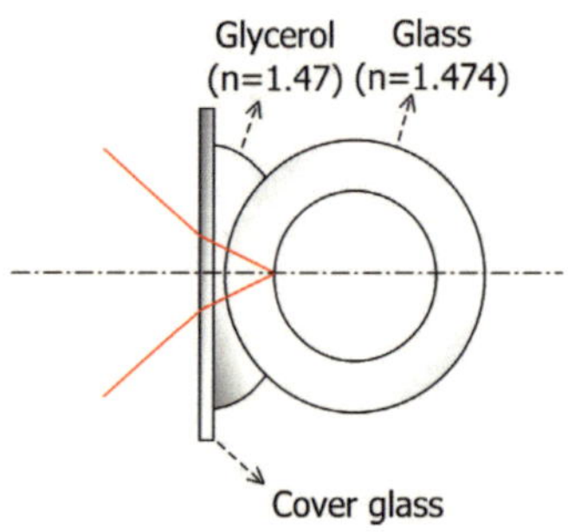

Fig. 4. Correction for the outer wall curvature

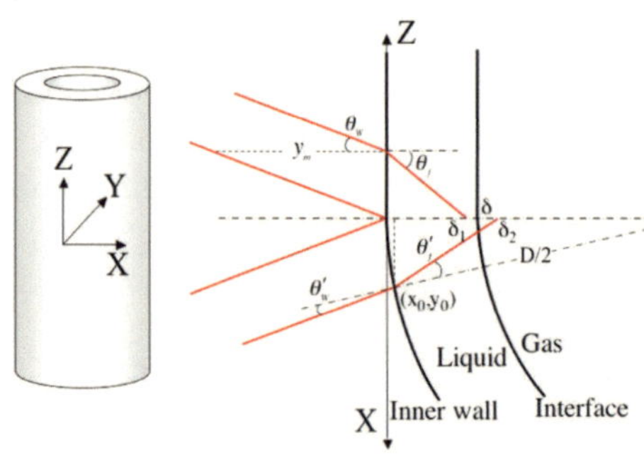

Fig. 5. Correction for the inner wall curvature

2.3 Physical properties of working fluids

It is known that the liquid film thickness in a micro tube is mainly dominated by the force balance between viscous and surface tension forces, i.e. capillary number. However, it is reported that the effects of inertial force should be also considered even in micro tubes at moderate Reynolds numbers (Heil, 2001). To clarify the effects of inertial force on liquid film thickness, three working fluids, water, ethanol and FC-40 were used. For the gas phase, air was always used throughout the experiments. All experiments were conducted under room temperature and 1 atm. Table 2 shows the properties of three liquids at 20 and 25◦C. Figure 6 shows Reynolds and capillary numbers for the present experimental condition. In Fig. 6, viscosity and density of the liquid phase are used for calculating Reynolds and capillary numbers. It can be seen that present experiments can cover wide ranges of Reynolds and capillary numbers by using different diameter tubes and working fluids.

	Temperature T [◦C]	Density ρ [kg/m³]	Viscosity μ [μPa s]	Surface tension σ [mN/m]	Refractive indices n [-]
Water	20	998	1001	72.7	1.33
	25	997	888	72.0	
Ethanol	20	789	1196	22.8	1.36
	25	785	1088	22.3	
FC-40	20	1860	3674	16.3	1.29
	25	1849	3207	15.9	

Table 2. Physical properties of the working fluids at 20 and 25 ◦C

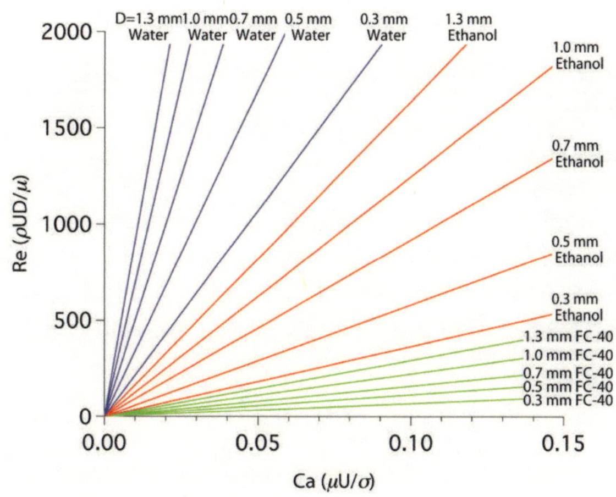

Fig. 6. Reynolds and capillary numbers for the present experiments

2.4 Experimental procedure

Figure 7 shows measured liquid film thickness data for water in a D_h = 1.3 mm circular tube. To investigate the gravitational effect, liquid film thicknesses were measured from four different directions. Three of them are measured in a horizontal flow (top, side and bottom), and one in a vertical downward flow. If the angle of laser and interface becomes larger than 11◦, the reflected light intensity becomes weak and the interface position cannot be detected. Therefore, it is only possible to measure liquid film thickness after the transition region from bubble nose to flat film region. In Fig. 7, liquid film thickness initially decreases and then becomes nearly constant or changes gradually in time. Initial decreasing period corresponds to the transition region between bubble nose and flat film region. Liquid film thickness measured from the top in a horizontal flow decreases linearly, while liquid film thickness increases linearly at the bottom. The lineal change after the initial drop is thus attributed to the gravitational effect. Liquid film flows down slowly due to gravity after liquid film is formed on the tube wall. On the other hand, liquid film thicknesses measured from the side and in a vertical flow remain nearly constant. Regardless of the measuring positions, initial liquid film thicknesses δ_0 are almost identical for all cases.

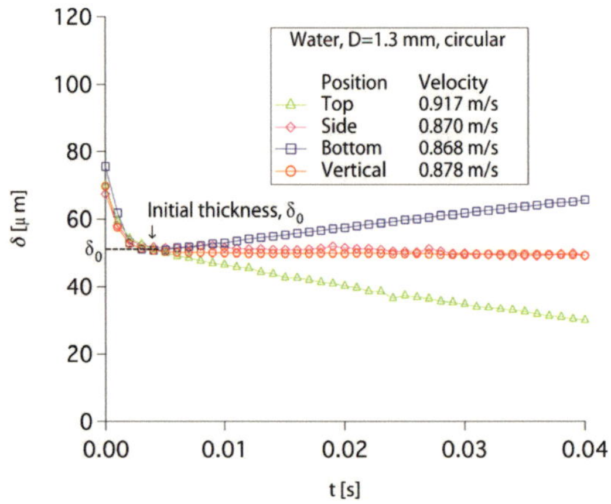

Fig. 7. Liquid film thickness measured from different directions

3. Experimental results

3.1 Steady circular tube flow

3.1.1 Liquid film thickness

Figure 8 (a) shows initial liquid film thicknesses normalized by tube diameter against capillary number, $Ca = \mu U/\sigma$, in steady circular tubes with FC-40. Liquid film thickness is measured from tube side in a horizontal flow. The solid line in Fig. 8 is an empirical fitting curve of Taylor's experimental data proposed by Aussillous and Quere (2000).

$$\frac{\delta_0}{D_h} = \frac{0.67Ca^{\frac{2}{3}}}{1+3.35Ca^{\frac{2}{3}}}, \tag{11}$$

Equation (11) is called Taylor's law. The working fluids in Taylor's experiments were highly viscous such as glycerol and sugar-water syrup. Therefore, Reynolds number in Taylor's experiment was small and the inertial force is negligible. At $Ca < 0.025$, dimensionless initial liquid film thicknesses of five tubes become nearly identical with Taylor's law, which means that inertial force can be ignored, and the dimensionless initial liquid film thickness is determined only by capillary number. As capillary number increases, all data become smaller than the Taylor's law. At $0.025 < Ca < 0.10$, initial liquid film thickness decreases as tube diameter increases. For example, initial liquid film thickness of 1.3 mm inner diameter tube is lower than that of 0.3 mm tube at $Ca \approx 0.05$. Reynolds numbers of 1.3 mm and 0.3 mm tubes are Re = 151 and 34 at Ca = 0.05. However, this trend is inverted as capillary number is increased. At $Ca > 0.15$, initial liquid film thickness starts to increase with Reynolds number.

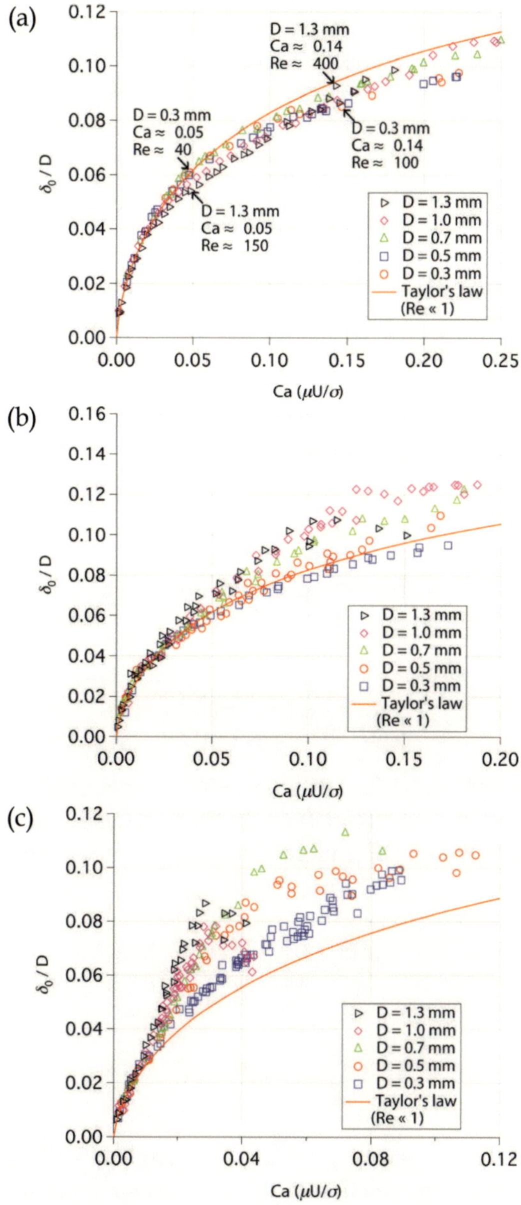

Fig. 8. Initial liquid film thickness in steady circular tubes. (a) FC-40, (b) ethanol and (c) water

Figure 8 (b) shows initial liquid film thickness for ethanol. Again, initial liquid film thickness measured from the tube side is shown. Reynolds number of ethanol is about 6 times larger than that of FC-40, as already shown in Fig. 6. Therefore, the effect of inertial force becomes stronger for ethanol than for FC-40. At Ca < 0.02, dimensionless initial liquid film thicknesses in five different tubes become nearly identical with the Taylor's law as in the case of FC-40. However, the deviation from Taylor's law starts from lower capillary number

for the ethanol case. At large capillary numbers, all data are larger than the Taylor's law. Inertial force is often neglected in micro two phase flows, but it is clear that the inertial force should be considered from this Reynolds number range. In Fig. 8 (b), dimensionless initial liquid film thickness in 1.3 mm inner diameter tube shows different trend at $Ca > 0.12$, showing some scattering. Reynolds number of ethanol in 1.3 mm inner diameter tube becomes $Re \approx 2000$ at $Ca \approx 0.12$. Thus, this different trend is considered to be the effect of flow transition from laminar to turbulent.
Figure 8 (c) shows initial liquid film thickness for water. At $Re > 2000$, initial liquid film thickness does not increase but remains nearly constant with some scattering. This tendency is found again when Reynolds number exceeds approximately $Re \approx 2000$. The deviation from Taylor's law starts from the lower capillary number than FC-40 and ethanol. Dimensionless initial liquid film thickness of water shows much larger values than that of ethanol and Taylor's law. In the case of 1.3 mm inner diameter tube, dimensionless initial liquid film thickness is nearly 2 times larger than the Taylor's law at $Ca \approx 0.03$. It is clearly seen that inertial force has a strong effect on liquid film thickness even in the Reynolds number range of $Re < 2000$.

3.1.2 Scaling analysis for circular tubes

Bretherton (1961) proposed a theoretical correlation for the liquid film thickness with lubrication equations as follows:

$$\frac{\delta_0}{D_h/2} = 0.643\left(\frac{3\mu U}{\sigma}\right)^{\frac{2}{3}}. \tag{12}$$

Aussillous and Quere (2000) modified Bretherton's analysis, and replaced the bubble nose curvature $\kappa = 1/(D_h/2)$ with $\kappa = 1/\{(D_h/2)\text{-}\delta_0\}$. In their analysis, the momentum balance and the curvature matching between the bubble nose and the transition region are expressed as follows:

$$\frac{\rho U^2}{\lambda} \sim \frac{1}{\lambda}\left\{\frac{\sigma}{(D_h/2)-\delta_0}\right\}, \tag{13}$$

$$\frac{\delta_0}{\lambda^2} \sim \frac{\sigma}{(D_h/2)-\delta_0}. \tag{14}$$

where λ is the length of the transition region as shown in Fig. 9. Eliminating λ from Eqs. (13) and (14), they obtained following relation for dimensionless liquid film thickness:

$$\frac{\delta_0}{D_h/2} \sim \frac{Ca^{\frac{2}{3}}}{1+Ca^{\frac{2}{3}}}. \tag{15}$$

In Eq. (15), dimensionless liquid film thickness asymptotes to a finite value due to the term $Ca^{2/3}$ in the denominator. Based on Eq. (15), Taylor's experimental data was fitted as Eq. (11).
If inertial force effect is taken into account, the momentum balance (13) should be expressed as follows:

$$\frac{\mu U}{\delta_0^2} \sim \frac{1}{\lambda}\left\{\frac{\sigma}{(D_h/2)-\delta_0}\right\} - \frac{\rho U^2}{\lambda}, \tag{16}$$

Using Eqs. (14) and (16), we can obtain the relation for initial liquid film thickness δ_0/D_h as:

$$\frac{\delta_0}{D_h} \sim \frac{Ca^{\frac{2}{3}}}{Ca^{\frac{2}{3}} + (1-We')^{\frac{2}{3}}}, \tag{17}$$

where Weber number is defined as $We' = \rho U^2((D_h/2)-\delta_0)/\sigma$. Equation (17) is always larger than Eq. (15) because the sign in front of Weber number is negative. Therefore, Eq. (17) can express the increase of the liquid film thickness with Weber number. In addition, Heil (2001) reported that inertial force makes the bubble nose slender and increases the bubble nose curvature at finite Reynolds numbers. It is also reported in Edvinsson & Irandoust (1996) and Kreutzer et al. (2005) that the curvature of bubble nose increases with Reynolds and capillary numbers. This implies that curvature term $\kappa = 1/\{(D_h/2)-\delta_0\}$ in momentum equation (16) should be larger for larger Reynolds and capillary numbers. We assume that this curvature change can be expressed by adding a modification function of Reynolds and capillary numbers to the original curvature term $\kappa = 1/\{(D_h/2)-\delta_0\}$ as:

$$\kappa = \frac{1+f(\mathrm{Re},Ca)}{(D_h/2)-\delta_0}, \tag{18}$$

Substituting Eq. (18) into Eqs. (14) and (16), we obtain:

$$\frac{\delta_0}{D_h/2} \sim \frac{Ca^{2/3}}{Ca^{\frac{2}{3}} + (1+f(\mathrm{Re},Ca))\left(1-\frac{We'}{1+f(\mathrm{Re},Ca)}\right)^{2/3}}. \tag{19}$$

If all the terms with *Re*, *Ca* and *We* can be assumed to be small, we may simplify Eq. (19) as:

$$\frac{\delta_0}{D_h/2} \sim \frac{Ca^{2/3}}{Ca^{\frac{2}{3}} + 1 + f(\mathrm{Re},Ca) - g(We')}. \tag{20}$$

In the denominator of Eq. (20), $f(Re, Ca)$ term corresponds to the curvature change of bubble nose and contributes to reduce liquid film thickness. On the other hand, when the inertial effect increases, $g(We')$ term contributes to increase the liquid film thickness due to the momentum balance. Weber number in Eq. (17) includes initial liquid film thickness δ_0 in its definition. Therefore, in order to simplify the correlation, Weber number is redefined as $We = \rho U^2 D_h/\sigma$. The experimental data is finally correlated by least linear square fitting in the form as:

$$\left(\frac{\delta_0}{D_h}\right)_{\text{steady}} = \frac{0.670Ca^{\frac{2}{3}}}{1+3.13Ca^{\frac{2}{3}}+0.504Ca^{0.672}\mathrm{Re}^{0.589}-0.352We^{0.629}} \quad (Ca < 0.3,\ Re < 2000), \tag{21}$$

where $Ca = \mu U/\sigma$ and $Re = \rho U D_h/\mu$ and $We = \rho U^2 D_h/\sigma$. As capillary number approaches zero, Eq. (21) should follow Talors's law (11), so the coefficient in the numerator is taken as 0.670. If Reynolds number becomes larger than 2000, initial liquid film thickness is fixed at a constant value at Re = 2000. Figures 10 and 11 show the comparison between the experimental data and the prediction of Eq. (20). As shown in Fig. 11, the present correlation can predict δ_0 within the range of ±15% accuracy.

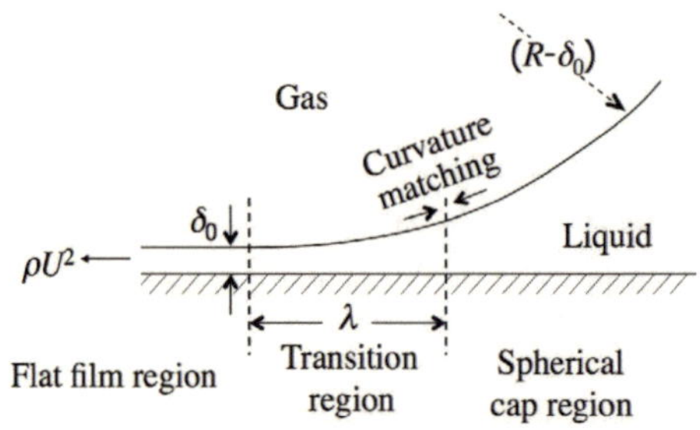

Fig. 9. Schematic diagram of the force balance in bubble nose, transition and flat film regions in circular tube slug flow

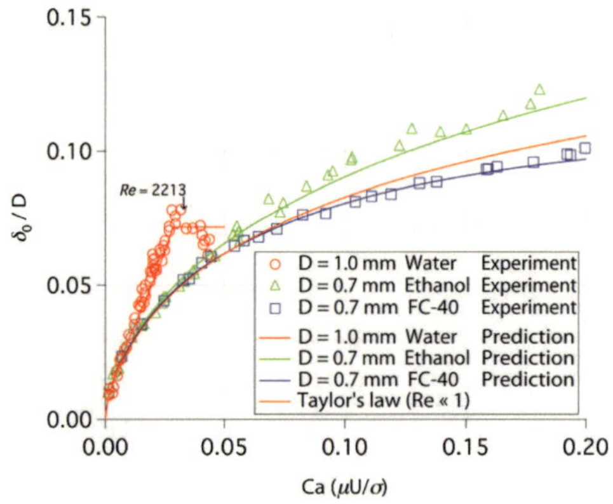

Fig. 10. Predicted initial liquid film thickness δ_0 by Eq. (21)

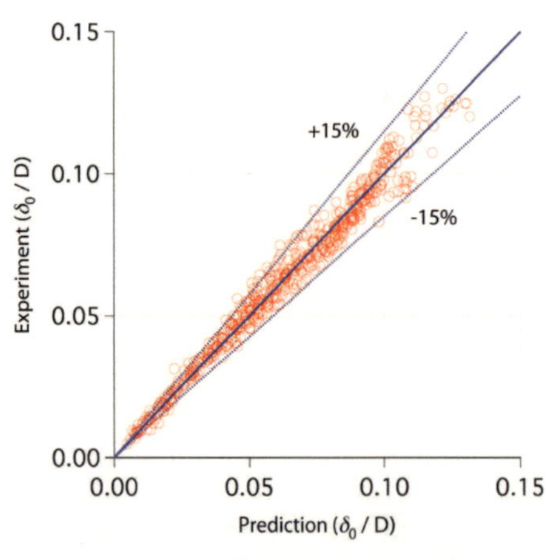

Fig. 11. Comparison between predicted and measured initial liquid film thicknesses δ_0

3.2 Steady square tube flow

3.2.1 Dimensionless bubble radii

Dimensionless bubble radii R_{center} and R_{corner} are the common parameters used in square channels:

$$R_{center} = 1 - \frac{2\delta_{0\_center}}{D_h}, \tag{22}$$

$$R_{corner} = \sqrt{2} - \frac{2\delta_{0\_corner}}{D_h}. \tag{23}$$

It should be noted that initial liquid film thickness at the corner δ_{0_corner} in Eq. (23) is defined as a distance between air-liquid interface and the corner of circumscribed square which is shown as a white line in Fig. 2(b). When initial liquid film thickness at the channel center δ_{0_center} is zero, R_{center} becomes unity. If the interface shape is axisymmetric, R_{center} becomes identical to R_{corner}.

Figure 12(a) shows R_{center} and R_{corner} against capillary number for FC-40. The solid lines in Fig. 12 are the numerical simulation results reported by Hazel & Heil (2002). In their simulation, inertial force term was neglected, and thus it can be considered as the low Reynolds number limit. Center radius R_{center} is almost unity at capillary number less than 0.03. Thus, interface shape is non-axisymmetric for $Ca < 0.03$. For $Ca > 0.03$, R_{center} becomes nearly identical to R_{corner}, and the interface shape becomes axisymmetric. In Fig. 12, measured bubble radii in D_h = 0.3 and 0.5 mm channels are almost identical, and they are larger than the numerical simulation result. On the other hand, the bubble radii in D_h = 1.0 mm channel are smaller than those for the smaller channels. As capillary number approaches zero, liquid film thickness in a micro circular tube becomes zero. In micro square tubes, liquid film δ_{0_corner} still remains at the channel corner even at zero capillary number limit. Corner radius R_{corner} reaches an asymptotic value smaller than $\sqrt{2}$ as investigated in Wong et al.'s numerical study (1995a, b). This asymptotic value will be discussed in the next section.

Figure 12(b) shows R_{center} and R_{corner} for ethanol. Similar to the trend found in FC-40 experiment, R_{center} is almost unity at low capillary number. Most of the experimental data are smaller than the numerical result. Transition capillary number, which is defined as the capillary number when bubble shape changes from non-axisymmetric to axisymmetric, becomes smaller as D_h increases. For D_h = 1.0 mm square tube, R_{center} is almost identical to R_{corner} beyond this transition capillary number. However, for D_h = 0.3 and 0.5 mm tubes, R_{center} is smaller than R_{corner} even at large capillary numbers. At the same capillary number, both R_{center} and R_{corner} decrease as Reynolds number increases. For $Ca > 0.17$, R_{center} and R_{corner} in D_h = 1.0 mm square tube becomes nearly constant. It is considered that this trend is attributed to laminar-turbulent transition. At $Ca \approx 0.17$, Reynolds number of ethanol in D_h = 1.0 mm channel becomes nearly $Re \approx 2000$ as indicated in Fig. 12(b).

Center and coner radii, R_{center} and R_{corner}, for water are shown in Fig. 12(c). Center radius R_{center} is again almost unity at low capillary number. Transition capillary numbers for D_h = 0.3, 0.5 and 1.0 mm square channels are Ca = 0.025, 0.2 and 0.014, respectively. These values are much smaller than those for ethanol and FC-40. Due to the strong inertial effect, bubble diameter of the water experiment is much smaller than those of other fluids and the numerical results. It is confirmed that inertial effect must be considered also in micro square tubes. Bubble diameter becomes nearly constant again for $Re > 2000$. Data points at $Re \approx 2000$ are indicated in Fig. 12(c).

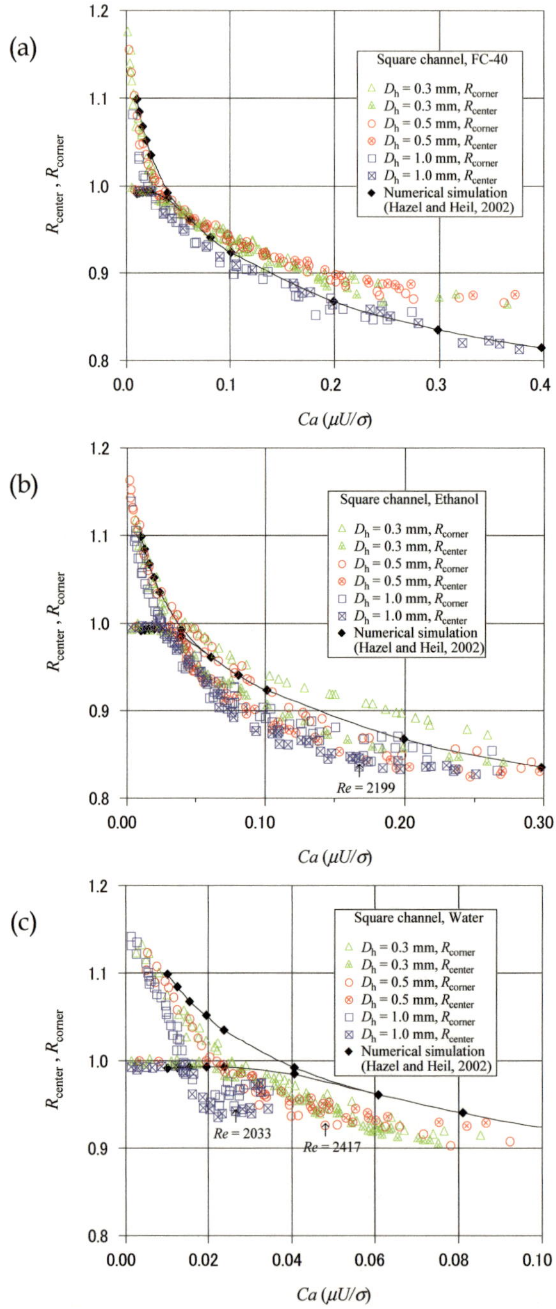

Fig. 12. Dimensionless center and coner radii, R_{center} and R_{corner}, in steady square tubes. (a) FC-40, (b) ethanol and (c) water

3.2.2 Scaling analysis for square tubes

Figure 13 shows the schematic diagram of the force balance in the transition region in square tubes. Momentum equation and curvature matching in the transition region are expressed as follows:

$$\frac{\mu U}{\delta_0^2} \sim \frac{1}{\lambda}\sigma(\kappa_1 - \kappa_2) - \frac{\rho U^2}{\lambda}, \tag{24}$$

$$\frac{\delta_0}{\lambda^2} \sim \kappa_1 - \kappa_2, \tag{25}$$

where, κ_1 and κ_2 are the curvatures of bubble nose and flat film region, respectively. In the present experiment, δ_{0_corner} does not become zero but takes a certain value as $Ca \to 0$. Figure 14 shows the schematic diagram of the interface shape at $Ca \to 0$. In Fig. 14, air-liquid interface is assumed as an arc with radius r. Then, κ_2 can be expressed as follows:

$$\kappa_2 = \frac{1}{r} = \frac{\sqrt{2}-1}{\delta_{0\_corner}}. \tag{26}$$

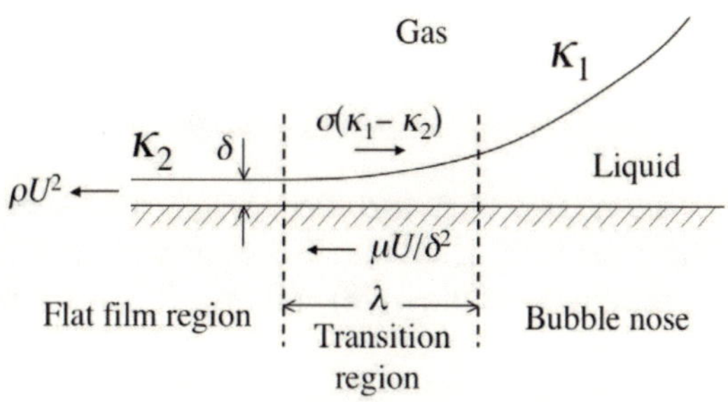

Fig. 13. Schematic diagram of the force balance in bubble nose, transition and flat film regions in square

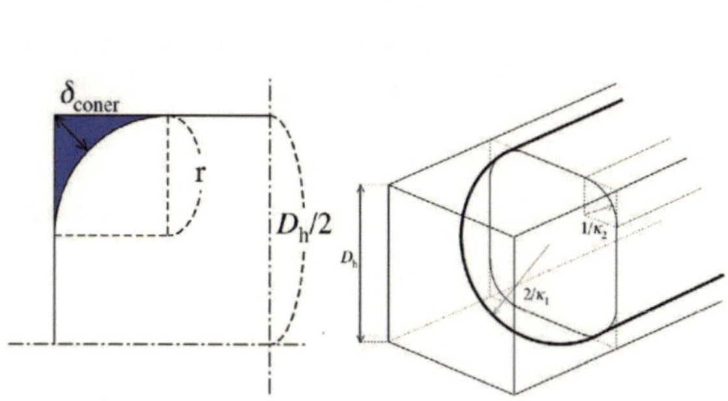

Fig. 14. Schematic diagram of the gas liquid interface profile at $Ca \to 0$

If bubble nose is assumed to be a hemisphere of radius $D_h/2$, the curvature at bubble nose becomes $\kappa_1 = 2/(D_h/2)$. This curvature κ_1 should be larger than the curvature of the flat film region κ_2 according to the momentum balance, i.e. $\kappa_1 \geq \kappa_2$. From this restraint, the relation of D_h and δ_{0_corner} is expressed as follows:

$$\frac{2}{D_h/2} \geq \frac{\sqrt{2}-1}{\delta_{0\_corner}}. \tag{27}$$

From Eqs. (23) and (27), the maximum value of R_{corner} can be determined as follows:

$$R_{corner} \leq 1.171. \tag{28}$$

From Fig. 12, the interface shape becomes nearly axisymmetric as capillary number increases. Here, bubble is simply assumed to be hemispherical at bubble nose and cylindrical at the flat film region, i.e. $R_{corner} = R_{center}$. Under such assumption, the curvatures κ_1 and κ_2 in Eqs. (24) and (25) can be rewritten as follows:

$$\kappa_1 = \frac{2}{D_h/\sqrt{2}-\delta_{0\_corner}}, \tag{29}$$

$$\kappa_2 = \frac{1}{D_h/\sqrt{2}-\delta_{0\_corner}}. \tag{30}$$

We can obtain the relation for δ_{0_corner} from Eqs. (24), (25), (29) and (30) as:

$$\frac{\delta_{0\_corner}}{D_h} \approx \frac{\sqrt{2}Ca^{\frac{2}{3}}}{Ca^{\frac{2}{3}}+(1-We')^{\frac{2}{3}}}, \tag{31}$$

where We' is the Weber number which includes δ_{0_corner} in its definition. Thus, We' is replaced by $We = \rho U^2 D_h/\sigma$ for simplicity. The denominator of R.H.S in Eq. (31) is also simplified with Taylor expansion. From Eqs. (28) and (31), R_{corner} is written as follows:

$$R_{corner} \sim 1.171 - \frac{2\sqrt{2}Ca^{\frac{2}{3}}}{1+Ca^{\frac{2}{3}}-We}. \tag{32}$$

The experimental correlation for R_{corner} is obtained by optimizing the coefficients and exponents in Eq. (32) with the least linear square method as follows:

$$R_{corner} = 1.171 - \frac{2.43Ca^{\frac{2}{3}}}{1+7.28Ca^{\frac{2}{3}}-0.255We^{0.215}} \quad (Re < 2000), \tag{33}$$

$$R_{center} \cong \begin{cases} 1 & (R_{corner} > 1) \\ R_{corner} & (R_{corner} \leq 1) \end{cases} \quad (Re < 2000). \tag{34}$$

From Eq. (34), R_{center} becomes unity at small capillary number. However, δ_{0_center} still has a finite value even at low Ca, which means that R_{center} should not physically reach unity. Further investigation is required for the accurate scaling of δ_{0_center} and R_{center} at low Ca. As capillary number increases, interface shape becomes nearly axisymmetric and R_{center} becomes identical to R_{corner}. As capillary number approaches zero, R_{corner} takes an asymptotic value of 1.171. If Reynolds number becomes larger than 2000, R_{corner} becomes constant due to flow transition from laminar to turbulent. Then, capillary and Weber numbers at Re = 2000 should be substituted in Eq. (33). Figure 15 shows the comparison between the experimental data and the predicted results with Eqs. (33) and (34). As shown in Fig. 16, the present correlation can predict dimensionless bubble diameters within the range of ±5 % accuracy.

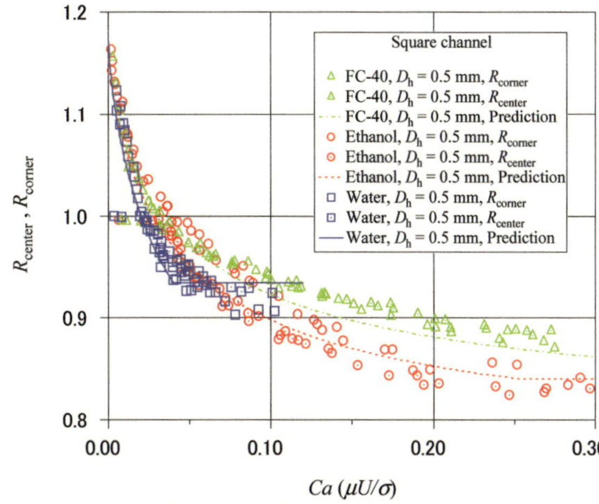

Fig. 15. Predicted bubble diameter in D_h = 0.5 mm square tube

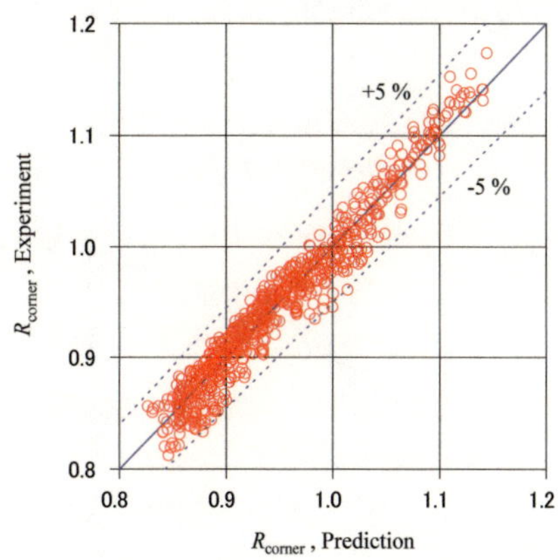

Fig. 16. Comparison between predicted and measured bubble radii

3.3 Steady flow in high aspect ratio rectangular tubes

For high aspect ratio rectangular tubes, interferometer as well as laser confocal displacement meter are used to measure liquid film thickness (Han et al. 2011). Figure 17 shows the initial liquid film thicknesses obtained by interferometer and laser confocal displacement meter. In the case of interferometer, initial liquid film thickness is calculated by counting the number of fringes from the neighbouring images along the flow direction. In Fig. 17, error bars on the interferometer data indicate uncertainty of 95 % confidence. Both results show good agreement, which proves that both methods are effective to measure liquid film thickness very accurately.

From the analogy between flows in circular tubes and parallel plates, it is demonstrated that dimensionless expression of liquid film thickness in parallel plates takes the same form as Eq. (19) if tube diameter D_h is replaced by channel height H (Han, et al. 2011). Figure 18 shows the comparison between experimental data and predicted values with Eq. (21) using hydraulic diameter as the characteristic length for Reynolds and Weber numbers. As can be seen from the figure, Eq (21) can predict initial liquid film thickness in high aspect ratio rectangular tube remarkably well.

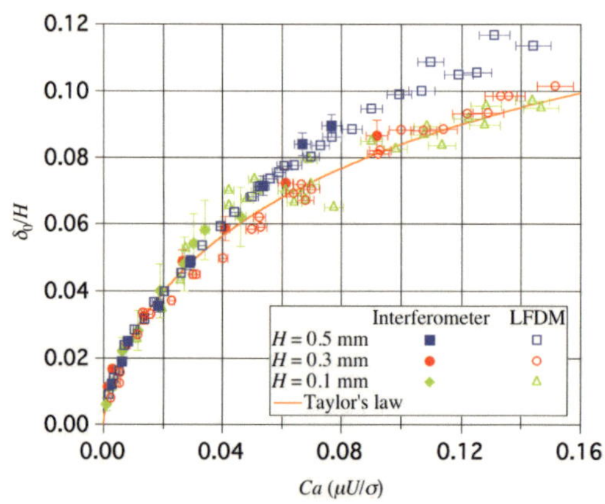

Fig. 17. Measured initial liquid film thickness in high aspect ration rectangular tubes using interferometer and laser confocal displacement meter

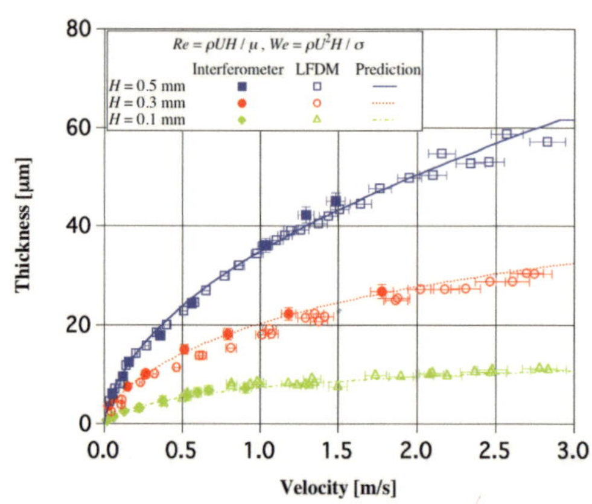

Fig. 18. Comparison between measured and predicted initial liquid film thicknesses by Eq. (21) in high aspect ratio rectangular tubes

3.4 Accelerated circular tube flow

3.4.1 Acceleration experiment

In order to investigate the effect of flow acceleration on the liquid film thickness, measurement points are positioned at Z = 5, 10 and 20 mm away from the initial air-liquid interface position, Z = 0 mm, as shown in Fig. 19. For the convenience in conducting experiments, circular tubes are used. The position of laser confocal displacement meter is fixed by *XYZ* stage accurately with high-speed camera and illumination light. Air/liquid interface is moved to the initial position (Z = 0 mm) with the actuator motor to correctly set the distance between the initial position and the measurement position. The distance is measured from the image captured by the high-speed camera. The bubble acceleration is simply expressed assuming that the acceleration is uniform when the flow is accelerated to a certain velocity as follows:

$$a = \frac{U^2}{2Z}, \tag{35}$$

where U is the bubble velocity at the measurement position. Since measurement position is fixed in the present experiment, acceleration becomes larger for larger capillary numbers. At given capillary number, in other words at given velocity, bubble acceleration decreases as the distance Z increases, which is apparent from Eq. (35). Surface tension of water is much larger than those of ethanol and FC-40, which means that bubble velocity of water is much higher at same capillary number. For example, bubble velocities of water, ethanol and FC-40 at Ca = 0.1 are 7.77, 1.99 and 0.27 m/s, respectively. Therefore, bubble acceleration of water becomes much larger than those of ethanol or FC-40 at fixed capillary number.

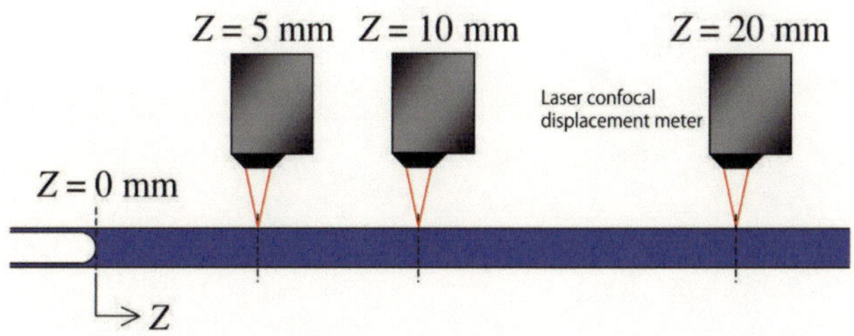

Fig. 19. Initial gas-liquid interface position and the measuring points

3.4.2 Liquid film thicknesses in accelerated flows

Figure 20 shows the dimensionless initial liquid film thickness in D_h = 1.0 mm circular tube for FC-40, ethanol and water. As shown in the figure, initial liquid film thickness under accelerated condition can be divided into two regions. At small capillary numbers, initial liquid film thickness is identical to the steady case. As capillary number increases, initial liquid film thickness deviates from the steady case and becomes much thinner.

3.4.3 Scaling analysis for accelerated flows

Under accelerated condition, velocity profile in the preceding liquid slug is different from that in the steady flow, and bubble nose curvature is affected by this velocity profile change. This is considered to be the reason for the decrease of the liquid film thickness. Under the bubble acceleration condition, bubble nose curvature is modified as:

$$\kappa \sim \frac{1}{\left(\frac{D_h}{2} - \delta_0\right)} \times h, \tag{36}$$

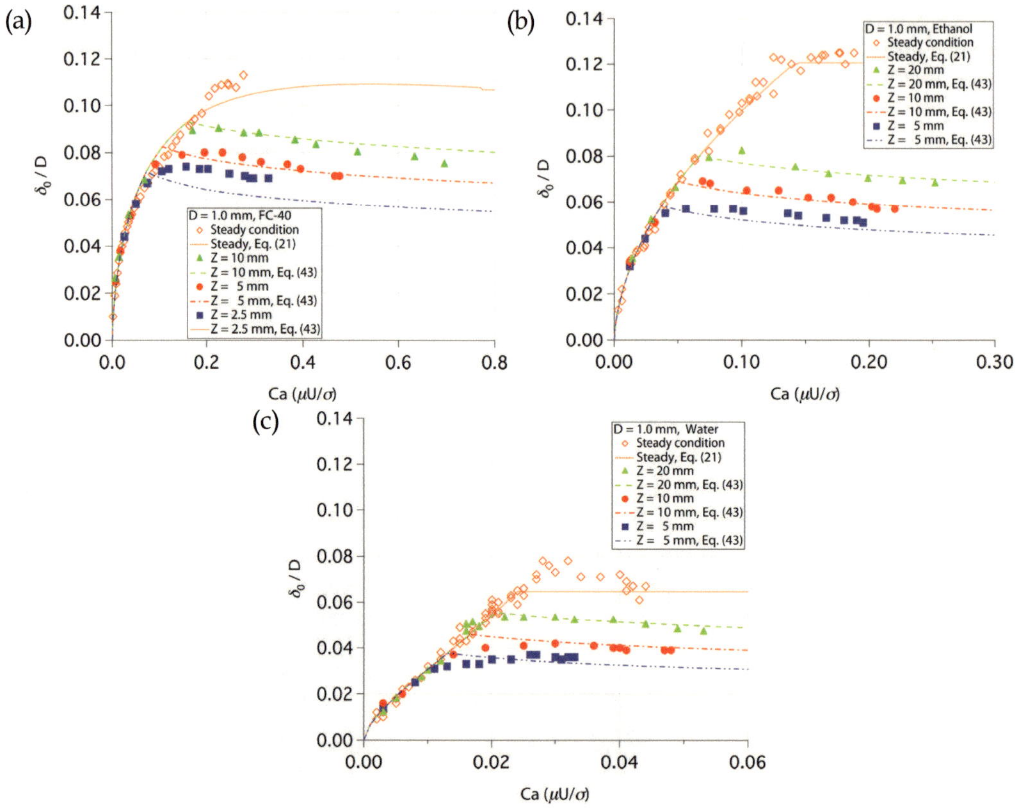

Fig. 20. Initial liquid film thicknesses in accelerated circular tubes. (a) FC-40, (b) ethanol and (c) water

where h is the modification coefficient which accounts for the acceleration effect. If the curvature of bubble nose in the R.H.S. of Eqs. (13) and (14) is replaced by Eq. (36), dimensionless initial liquid film thickness in accelerated flow can be written as follows:

$$\left(\frac{\delta_0}{D_\mathrm{h}}\right)_{\mathrm{acceleration}} \sim \frac{0.67Ca^{2/3}\cdot h^{-1}}{1+3.35Ca^{2/3}\cdot h^{-1}}\,, \tag{37}$$

Modification coefficient h can be expressed from Eq. (37) as:

$$h \sim \frac{0.67Ca^{\frac{2}{3}}}{\left(\delta_0/D_\mathrm{h}\right)_{\mathrm{acceleration}}} - 3.35Ca^{\frac{2}{3}}\,. \tag{38}$$

Moriyama & Inoue (1996) and Aussillous & Quere (2000) reported that liquid film generation is restricted by the viscous boundary layer developed in the liquid slug when viscous boundary layer is thin. Viscous boundary layer thickness δ^* can be scaled as follows:

$$\delta^* \sim \left(\frac{\nu Z}{U}\right)^{1/2}, \tag{39}$$

where ν is the kinematic viscosity. Although viscous boundary layer thickness is independent of tube diameter, absolute liquid film thickness is nearly proportional to the tube diameter as shown in Fig. 20. This indicates that viscous boundary layer is not the proper parameter to scale the acceleration effect. It is considered that surface tension should also play an important role in accelerated flows as in the steady case. Under the accelerated condition, Bond number based on bubble acceleration a is introduced as follows:

$$Bo = \frac{\rho a D^2}{\sigma}. \tag{40}$$

Figure 21 show how modification coefficient h varies with boundary layer thickness δ^* and Bond number Bo. In order to focus on the acceleration effect, the experimental data points that deviate from the steady case in Fig. 20 are used. As shown in Fig. 21, the modification coefficient h can be scaled very well with Bond number. The data points are correlated with a single fitting line:

$$h = 0.692 Bo^{0.414}. \tag{41}$$

Substituting Eq. (41) into Eq. (37), a correlation for the initial liquid film thickness under flow acceleration can be obtained as follows:

$$\left(\frac{\delta_0}{D_{\mathrm{h}}}\right)_{\mathrm{acceleration}} = \frac{0.968 Ca^{\frac{2}{3}} \cdot Bo^{-0.414}}{1 + 4.838 Ca^{\frac{2}{3}} \cdot Bo^{-0.414}}. \tag{42}$$

As shown in Fig. 20, initial liquid film thickness in steady and accelerated flows are identical when capillary number is small. Thus, in the present study, initial liquid film thickness in the whole capillary number range is simply expressed by combining steady and accelerated correlations as follows:

$$\frac{\delta_0}{D_h} = \min\left[\left(\frac{\delta_0}{D_{\mathrm{h}}}\right)_{\mathrm{steady}}, \left(\frac{\delta_0}{D_{\mathrm{h}}}\right)_{\mathrm{acceleration}}\right], \tag{43}$$

where, Eq. (21) is used for $(\delta_0/D_{\mathrm{h}})_{\mathrm{steady}}$ and Eq. (42) is used for $(\delta_0/D_{\mathrm{h}})_{\mathrm{acceleration}}$. The predicted thicknesses by Eq. (43) are plotted together with the experimental data in Fig. 20. As can be seen from the figure, Eq. (43) can predict initial liquid film thickness very accurately for three different working fluids. Figure 22 shows comparison between present correlation and the experimental data. Equation (43) can predict initial liquid film thickness very accurately within the range of ±15 % accuracy.

4. Conclusions

The liquid film thickness in a micro tube is measured by laser confocal displacement meter. The effect of inertial force can not be neglected even in the laminar liquid flow. As capillary number increases, initial liquid film thickness becomes much thicker than the Taylor's law which assumes very low Reynolds number. When Reynolds number becomes larger than roughly 2000, initial liquid film thickness becomes nearly constant and shows some scattering. From the scaling analysis, empirical correlation for the dimensionless initial liquid film thickness based on capillary number, Reynolds number and Weber number is proposed. The proposed correlation can predict the initial liquid film thickness within ±15% accuracy.

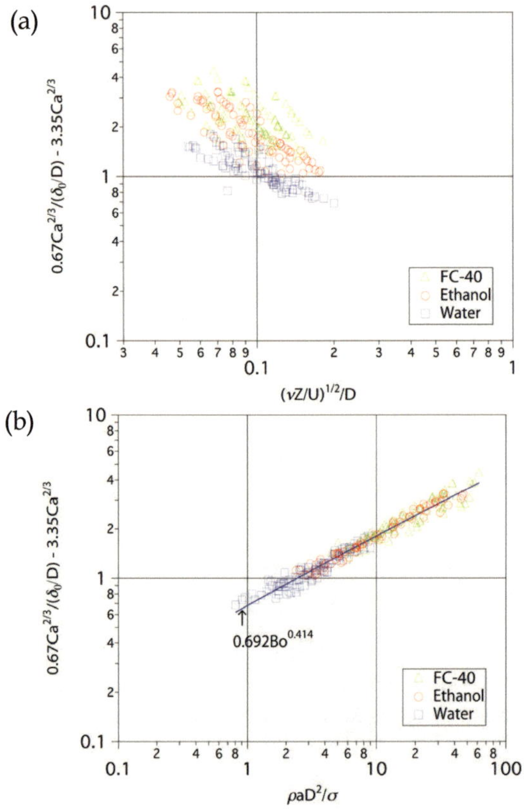

Fig. 21. RHS of Eq. (38) plotted against (a) boundary layer thickness and (b) Bond number

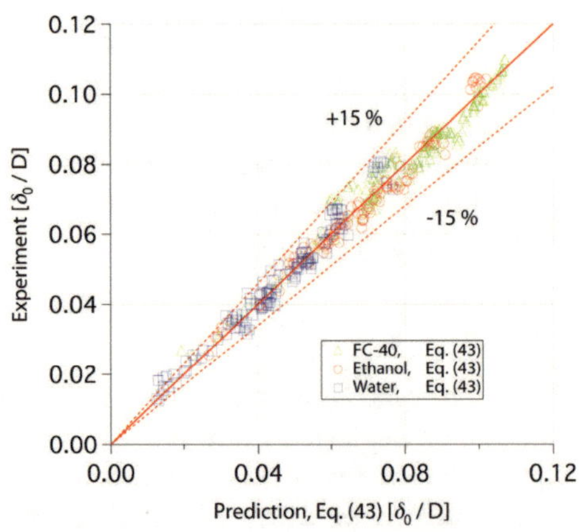

Fig. 22. Comparison between predicted and measured initial liquid film thicknesses δ_0 in accelerated flows

In square tubes, liquid film formed at the center of the side wall becomes very thin at small capillary numbers. However, as capillary number increases, the bubble shape becomes nearly axisymmetric. As Reynolds number increases, flow transits from non-axisymmetric to axisymmetric at smaller capillary numbers.
Initial liquid film thickness in high aspect ratio rectangular tubes can be predicted well using the circular tube correlation provided that hydraulic diameter is used for Reynolds and Weber numbers. It is also shown that results from interferometer and laser confocal displacement meter give nearly identical results, which proves the reliability of both methods.
When the flow is accelerated, velocity profile in the preceding liquid slug strongly affects the liquid film formation. Liquid film becomes much thinner as flow is further accelerated. Experimental correlation for the initial liquid film thickness under accelerated condition is proposed by introducing Bond number. In order to develop precise micro-scale two-phase heat transfer models, it is necessary to consider the effect of flow acceleration on the liquid film formation.

5. Acknowledgment

We would like to thank Prof. Kasagi, Prof. Suzuki and Dr. Hasegawa for the fruitful discussions and suggestions. This work is supported through Grant in Aid for Scientific Research (No. 20560179) and Global COE program, Mechanical Systems Innovation, by MEXT, Japan.

6. References

Aussillous, P. & Quere, D. (2000). Quick deposition of a fluid on the wall of a tube, *Physics of Fluids*, 12(10), 2367-2371.

Bretherton, F. P. (1961). The motion of long bubbles in tubes, *Journal of Fluid Mechanics*, 10(2), 166-188.

Cooper, M. G. (1969). The microlayer and bubble growth in nucleate pool boiling, *International Journal of Heat and Mass Transfer*, 12, 915-933.

Cox, B. G. (1964). An experimental investigation of the streamlines in viscous fluid expelled from a tube, *Journal of Fluid Mechanics*, 20, 193-200.

Edvinsson, R. K. & Irandoust, S. (1996). Finite-element analysis of taylor flow, *AIChE Journal*, 42(7), 1815-1823.

Han, Y. & Shikazono, N. (2009a). Measurement of the liquid film thickness in micro tube slug flow, *International Journal of Heat and Fluid Flow*, 30(5), 842-853.

Han, Y. & Shikazono, N. (2009b). Measurement of liquid film thickness in micro square channel, *International Journal of Multiphase Flow*, 35(10), 896-903.

Han, Y. & Shikazono, N. (2010). The effect of bubble acceleration on the liquid film thickness in micro tubes, *International Journal of Heat and Fluid Flow*, 31(4), 630-639.

Han, Y.; Shikazono, N. & Kasagi, N. (2009b). Measurement of liquid film thickness in a micro parallel channel with interferometer and laser focus displacement meter, *International Journal of Multiphase Flow*, 37(1), 36-45.

Hazel, A. L. & Heil, M. (2002). The steady propagation of a semi-infinite bubble into a tube of elliptical or rectangular cross-section, *Journal of Fluid Mechanics*, 470, 91-114.

Hazuku, T.; Fukamachi, N.; Takamasa, T.; Hibiki, T. & Ishii, M. (2005). Measurement of liquid film in microchannels using a laser focus displacement meter, *Experiments in Fluids*, 38(6), 780-788.

Heil, M. (2001). Finite Reynolds number effects in the Bretherton problem, *Phys. of Fluids*, 13(9), 2517-2521.

Hurlburt, E. T. & Newell, T. A. (1996). Optical measurement of liquid film thickness and wave velocity in liquid film flows, *Experiments in Fluids*, 21, 357-362.

Kenning, D. B. R.; Wen, D. S.; Das, K. S. & Wilson, S. K. (2006). Confined growth of a vapour bubble in a capillary tube at initially uniform superheat: Experiments and modeling, *International Journal of Heat and Mass Transfer*, 49(23-24), 4653-4671.

Kreutzer, M. T.; Kapteijn, F.; Moulijn, J. A.; Kleijn, C. R. & Heiszwolf, J. J. (2005). Inertial and interfacial effects on pressure drop of Taylor flow in capillaries, *AIChE Journal*, 51(9), 2428-2440.

Moriyama, K. & Inoue, A. (1996). Thickness of the liquid film formed by a growing bubble in a narrow gap between two horizontal plates, *Transactions of the ASME*, 118, 132-139.

Qu, W. & Mudawar, I. (2004). Flow boiling heat transfer in two-phase micro-channel heat sink-II. Annular two-phase flow model, *International Journal of Heat Mass Transfer*, 46, 3387-3401.

Saitoh, S.; Daiguji, H. & Hihara, H. (2007). Correlation for boiling heat transfer of R-134a in horizontal tubes including effect of tube diameter, *International Journal of Heat Mass Transfer*, 50, 5215-5225.

Schwartz, L.W.; Princen, H.M. & Kiss, A.D. (1986). On the motion of bubbles in capillary tubes, *Journal of Fluid Mechanics*, 172, 259–275.

Shedd, T. A. & Newell, T. A. (2004). Characteristics of the liquid film and pressure drop in horizontal, annular, two-phase flow through round, square and triangular tubes, *Journal of Fluid Engineering*, 126, 807-817.

Taha, T. & Cui, Z. F. (2006). CFD modelling of slug flow inside square capillaries, *Chemical Engineering Science*, 61, 665-675

Takamasa, T. & Kobayashi, K. (2000). Measuring interfacial waves on film flowing down tube inner wall using laser focus displacement meter, *International Journal of Multiphase Flow*, 26(9), 1493-1507.

Taylor, G. I. (1961). Deposition of a viscous fluid on the wall of a tube, *Journal of Fluid Mechanics*, 10(2), 161-165.

Thome, J. R.; Dupont, V. & Jacobi, A. M. (2004). Heat transfer model for evaporation in microchannels. Part I: presentation of the model, *International Journal of Heat Mass Transfer*, 47(14-16), 3375-3385.

Tibirica, C. B.; Nascimento, F. J. & Ribatski, G. (2010). Film thickness measurement techniques applied to micro-scale two-phase flow systems, *Experimental Thermal and Fluid Science*, 34 (4), 463-473.

Ursenbacher, T.; Wojtan, L. & Thome, J. R. (2004). Interfacial measurements in stratified types of flow. Part I: New optical measurement technique and dry angle measurements, *International Journal of Multiphase Flow*, 30, 107-124.

Utaka, Y.; Okuda, S. & Tasaki, Y. (2007). Structure of micro-layer and characteristics of boiling heat transfer in narrow gap mini-channel system, *Transactions of the JSME*, Series B, 73(733), 1929-1935.

Wong, H., Radke, C. J. & Morris, S. (1995a). The motion of long bubbles in polygonal capillaries. Part 1. Thin films, *Journal of Fluid Mechanics*, 292, 71-94.

Wong, H., Radke, C. J. & Morris, S. (1995b). The motion of long bubbles in polygonal capillaries. Part 2. Drag, fluid pressure and fluid flow, *Journal of Fluid Mechanics*, 292, 95-110.

16

New Variants to Theoretical Investigations of Thermosyphon Loop

Henryk Bieliński
The Szewalski Institute of Fluid-Flow Machinery, Polish Academy of Sciences, Gdańsk Poland

1. Introduction

The purpose of this chapter is to present three variants of the generalized model of thermosyphon loop, using a detailed analysis of heat transfer and fluid flow (Bieliński & Mikielewicz, 2011). This theoretical investigation of thermosyphon loop is based on analytical and numerical calculations. The first variant of thermosyphon loop (HHVCHV) is composed of two heated sides: the lower horizontal and vertical sides and two cooled sides: the upper horizontal and vertical opposite sides. This variant is made for conventional tubes and has a one-phase fluid as the working substance. The second variant of thermosyphon loop (2H2C) is consisted of two lower evaporators: horizontal and vertical and two upper condensers: horizontal and vertical and is made for minichannels. The third variant of thermosyphon loop has an evaporator on the lower horizontal section and a condenser on the upper vertical section. This variant contains minichannels and a supporting minipump (HHCV+P). A two-phase fluid is used as the working substance in the second and third variants.

The new variants reported in the present study is a continuation and an extension of earlier work *"Natural Circulation in Single and Two Phase Thermosyphon Loop with Conventional Tubes and Minichannels."* published by InTech (ISBN 978-953-307-550-1) in book "Heat Transfer. Mathematical Modelling, Numerical Methods and Information Technology", Edited by A. Belmiloudi, pp. 475-496, (2011). This previous work starts a discussion of the generalized model for the thermosyphon loop and describes three variants. In the first variant (HHCH) the lower horizontal side of the thermosyphon loop was heated and its upper horizontal side was cooled. In the second variant (HVCV) the lower part of vertical side of the thermosyphon loop was heated and its upper part at opposite vertical side was cooled. In the third variant (HHCV) a section of the lower horizontal side of the thermosyphon loop was heated and its upper section of vertical side was cooled. A one- and two-phase fluid were used as a working substance in the first and in both second and third variants of the thermosyphon loop, respectively. Additionally, the first variant was made for conventional tubes and the second and third variants were made for minichannels. It was necessary in case of the thermosyphon loop with minichannels to apply some new correlations for the void fraction and the local two-phase friction coefficient in both two-phase regions: adiabatic and diabatic, and the local heat transfer coefficient in flow boiling and condensation. Some other variants to theoretical investigations of the generalized model for thermosyphon loop are demonstrated in (Bieliński & Mikielewicz, 2004, 2005, 2010).

Fluid flow of thermosyphon loop is created by the buoyancy forces that evolve from the density gradients induced by temperature differences in the heating and cooling sections of the loop. An advanced thermosyphon loop is composed of an evaporator and a condenser; a riser and a downcomer connect these parts. A liquid boils into its vapour phase in the evaporator and the vapour condenses back to a liquid in the condenser. The thermosyphon loop is a simple passive heat transfer device, which relies on gravity for returning the liquid to the evaporator. The thermosyphon loops are a far better solution than other cooling systems because they are pumpless. In such cases, when mass flow rate is not high enough to circulate the necessary fluid to transport heat from evaporator to condenser, the use of a pump is necessary. The presented study considers the case where the buoyancy term and the pump term in the momentum equation are of the same order.

The following applications for thermosyphon loops are well-known, such as solar water heaters, thermosyphon reboilers, geothermal systems, emergency cooling systems in nuclear reactor cores, thermal diodes and electronic device cooling. The thermal diode is based on natural circulation of the fluid around the closed-loop thermosyphon (Bieliński & Mikielewicz, 1995, 2001), (Chen, 1998). The closed-loop thermosyphon is also known as a "liquid fin" (Madejski & Mikielewicz, 1971).

Numerous investigations, both theoretical and experimental have been conducted to study of the fluid behaviour in thermosyphon loops. Zvirin (Zvirin, 1981) presented results of theoretical and experimental studies concerned with natural circulation loops, and modelling methods describing steady state flows, transient and stability characteristics. Ramos (Ramos et al., 1985) performed the theoretical study of the steady state flow in the two-phase thermosyphon loop with conventional tube. Greif (Greif, 1988) reviewed basic experimental and theoretical work on natural circulation loops. Vijayan (Vijayan et al., 2005) compared the dynamic behaviour of the single- and two-phase thermosyphon loop with conventional tube and the different displacement of heater and cooler. Misale (Misale et al., 2007) reports an experimental investigations related to rectangular single-phase natural circulation mini-loop.

The present study provides in-depth analysis of heat transfer and fluid flow using three new variants of the generalized model of thermosyphon loop. Each individual variant can be analyzed in terms of single- and two-phase flow in the thermosyphon loop with conventional tubes and minichannels. In order to analyse the numerical results of simulation for the two-phase flow and heat transfer in the thermosyphon loop, the empirical correlations for the heat transfer coefficient in flow boiling and condensation, and two-phase friction factor in diabatic and adiabatic sectors in minichannels, are used. The analysis of the thermosyphon loop is based on the one-dimensional model, which includes mass, momentum and energy balances. The separate two-phase flow model is used in calculations. A numerical investigation for the analysis of the mass flux and heat transfer coefficient in the steady state has been done. The effect of thermal and geometrical parameters of the loop on the mass flux in the steady state is examined numerically.

The El-Hajal correlation for void fraction (El-Hajal et al., 2003), the Zhang-Webb correlation for the friction pressure drop of two-phase flow in adiabatic region (Zhang & Webb, 2001), the Tran correlation for the friction pressure drop of two-phase flow in diabatic region (Tran et al. 2000), the Mikielewicz (Mikielewicz et al., 2007) and the Saitoh (Saitoh et al., 2007) correlations for the flow boiling heat transfer coefficient in minichannels, the Mikielewicz (Mikielewicz et al., 2007) and the Tang (Tang et al., 2000) correlations for condensation heat transfer coefficient in minichannels has been used to evaluate the thermosyphon loop with minichannels.

Finally, theoretical investigations of the variants associated with the generalized model of thermosyphon loop can offer practical advice for technical and research purposes.

2. Single phase thermosyphon loop heated from lower horizontal and vertical side and cooled from upper horizontal and vertical side

This single-phase variant of thermosyphon loop is heated from below horizontal section $(s_0 \le s \le s_1)$ and vertical section $(s_1 \le s \le s_2)$ by a constant heat flux: $\dot{q}_H$. Constant heat flux $\dot{q}_H$ spaced in cross-section area per heated length: L_H. In the upper horizontal section $(s_3 \le s \le s_4)$ and opposite vertical section $(s_4 \le s \le s_5)$ the thermosyphon loop gives heat to the environment. The heat transfer coefficient between the wall and environment, α_C, and the temperature of the environment, T_0, are assumed constant. The heated and cooled parts of the thermosyphon loop are connected by perfectly isolated channels $(s_2 \le s \le s_3 \;;\; s_5 \le s \le s_6)$.

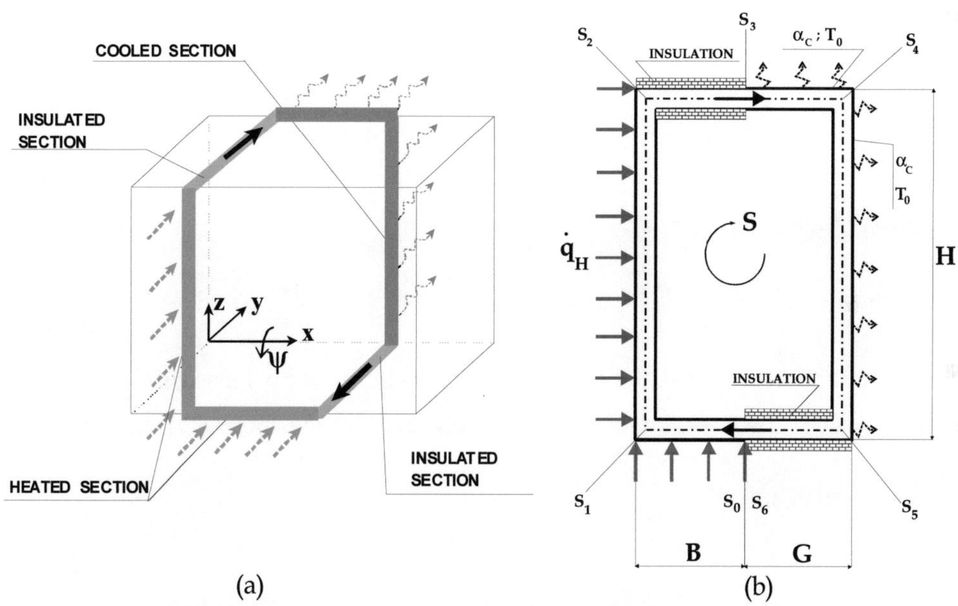

Fig. 1. The variant of single phase thermosyphon loop heated from lower horizontal and vertical side and cooled from upper horizontal and opposite vertical side (HHVCHV). (a) 3Dimensional, (b) 2D

The space co-ordinate s circulates around the closed loop as shown in Fig. 1(b). The total length of the loop is denoted by L, cross-section area of the channel is A, wetted perimeter is U . Thermal properties of fluid: ρ - density, c_p - heat capacity of constant pressure, λ - thermal conductivity.

The following assumptions are used in the theoretical model of natural circulation in the closed loop thermosyphon:

1. thermal equilibrium exists at any point of the loop,
2. incompressibility, because the flow velocity in the natural circulation loop is relatively low compared with the acoustic speed of the fluid under current model conditions,

3. viscous dissipation in fluid is neglected in the energy equations,
4. heat losses in the thermosyphon loop are negligible,
5. $(D/L) << 1$; one-dimensional models are used and the flow is fully mixed. The velocity and temperature variation at any cross section is therefore neglected. The flow is fully developed and the temperature is uniform at the steady state,
6. single-phase fluid can be selected as the working fluid,
7. curvature effects and associated form losses are negligible,
8. fluid properties are constants, except density in the gravity term. The Boussinsq approximation is valid for a single-phase system, then density is assumed to vary as $\rho = \rho_0 \cdot \left[1 - \beta \cdot (T - T_0)\right]$ in the gravity term where $\beta = \frac{1}{\upsilon_0} \cdot \left(\frac{\partial \upsilon}{\partial T}\right)_p$ (υ - specific volume, "0" is the reference of steady state),
9. the effect of superheating and subcooling are neglected.

Under the above assumptions, the governing equations for natural circulation systems can be written as follows:

- conservation of mass:

$$\frac{\partial \rho}{\partial \tau} + \frac{\partial}{\partial s}(\rho \cdot w) = 0 \quad ; \tag{1}$$

where τ - time, w - velocity.

- conservation of momentum:

$$\rho \cdot \left(\frac{\partial w}{\partial \tau} + w \cdot \frac{\partial w}{\partial s}\right) = -\frac{\partial p}{\partial s} + \varepsilon \cdot \rho \cdot \tilde{g} - \tau_w \cdot \frac{U}{A} \quad ; \tag{2}$$

where $\varepsilon = 0$ for $\vec{e} \perp \vec{g}$; $\varepsilon = (+1)$ for $\vec{e} \uparrow \wedge \vec{g} \downarrow$; $\varepsilon = (-1)$ for $\vec{e} \downarrow \wedge \vec{g} \downarrow$; $\tilde{g} = \vec{e} \circ \vec{g} = 1 \cdot g \cdot \cos(\vec{e}, \vec{g})$; $|\vec{g}| = g$; $|\vec{e}| = 1$; $\vec{e}$ is a versor of the coordinate around the loop, and τ_w - wall shear stress.

- conservation of energy:

$$\frac{\partial T}{\partial \tau} + w \cdot \frac{\partial T}{\partial s} = a_0 \cdot \frac{\partial^2 T}{\partial s^2} \begin{cases} +0 & \text{for adiabatic section} \\ -\dfrac{q_C \cdot U_C}{c_{p0} \cdot \rho_0 \cdot A} & \text{for cooled section} \\ +\dfrac{\dot{q}_H \cdot U_H}{c_{p0} \cdot \rho_0 \cdot A} & \text{for heated section} \end{cases} \tag{3}$$

where $a_0 = \frac{\lambda_0}{\rho_0 \cdot c_{p0}}$ - thermal diffusivity,

In order to eliminate the pressure gradient and the acceleration term, the momentum equation in Eq. (2) is integrated around the loop $\oint \left(\frac{\partial p}{\partial s}\right) ds = 0$.

The flow in natural circulation systems which is driven by density distribution is also known as a gravity driven flow or thermosyphonic flow. The momentum and the energy equations in such flows are coupled and for this reason they must be solved simultaneously (Mikielewicz, 1995).
The above governing equations can be transformed to their dimensionless forms by the following scaling:

$$\tau^+ = (a_0 \cdot \tau)/L^2 \ ; \quad s^+ = s/L \ ; \quad \dot{m}^+ = (\dot{m} \cdot L)/(a_0 \cdot \rho_0 \cdot A) \ ; \quad T^+ = \frac{\lambda_0 \cdot (A/U_H) \cdot (T - T_0)}{(\dot{q}_H \cdot L^2)} \ ; \tag{4}$$

The dimensionless momentum equation and the energy equation at the steady state for the thermosyphon loop heated from below can be written as follows:

- momentum equation (with: $K_j = s_j/L$;) and $\theta = \begin{cases} 1 & \text{for laminar flow} \\ 7/4 & \text{for turbulent flow} \end{cases}$;

$$\left(\dot{m}^+\right)^{\theta} = (Ra)^{**}(-1) \cdot \left[\int_0^1 T^+ \cdot \cos(\vec{e}, \vec{g}) \ ds^+ \right] \ ; \tag{5}$$

- energy equation

$$\dot{m}^+ \frac{dT^+}{ds^+} = \frac{d^2T^+}{ds^{+2}} \begin{cases} +0 & & \text{insulated sections} \\ -(Bi)^{**} \cdot T^+ & \text{for} & \text{cooling section} \\ +1 & & \text{heater section} \end{cases} \tag{6}$$

with boundary conditions

$$\begin{gathered} T^+_{A1}(K_2) = T^+_H(K_2) \ ; \quad T^+_{A1}(K_3) = T^+_C(K_3) \ ; \quad T^+_C(K_5) = T^+_{A2}(K_5) \ ; \quad T^+_{A2}(1) = T^+_H(0) \ ; \\ \left.\frac{dT^+_{A1}}{ds^+}\right|_{s^+=K_2} = \left.\frac{dT^+_H}{ds^+}\right|_{s^+=K_2} ; \quad \left.\frac{dT^+_{A1}}{ds^+}\right|_{s^+=K_3} = \left.\frac{dT^+_C}{ds^+}\right|_{s^+=K_3} ; \\ \left.\frac{dT^+_C}{ds^+}\right|_{s^+=K_5} = \left.\frac{dT^+_{A2}}{ds^+}\right|_{s^+=K_5} ; \quad \left.\frac{dT^+_{A2}}{ds^+}\right|_{s^+=1} = \left.\frac{dT^+_H}{ds^+}\right|_{s^+=0} ; \end{gathered} \tag{7}$$

The parameters appearing in the momentum and the energy equations are the modified Biot, Rayleigh and Prandtl numbers.

$$(Bi)^{**} = \frac{\alpha_C \cdot U_C}{\lambda_0} \cdot \frac{L^2}{A} \ ; \tag{8}$$

for laminar flow: $(\theta = 1)$

$$(Ra)^{**}_l = \frac{g \cdot \beta_0 \cdot L^3 \cdot (\dot{q}_H / \lambda_0)}{\nu_0 \cdot a_0} \cdot \frac{A \cdot U_H}{2 \cdot U^2} \ ; \quad (Pr)^{**}_l = 2 \cdot L^2 \cdot \left(\frac{U}{A}\right)^2 \cdot \left(\frac{\nu_0}{a_0}\right) \ ; \tag{9}$$

for turbulent flow: $(\theta = 7/4)$

$$(Ra)_t^{**} = \frac{\sqrt{128}}{0.3164} \cdot \frac{g \cdot \beta_0 \cdot (L)^{15/4} \cdot (\dot{q}_H / \lambda_0)}{(\nu_0)^{1/4} \cdot (a_0)^{7/4}} \cdot \frac{(A)^{1/4} \cdot U_H}{(U)^{5/4}}; \quad (Pr)_t^{**} = \frac{0.3164}{\sqrt{128}} \cdot \left(\frac{L \cdot U}{A}\right)^{5/4} \cdot \left(\frac{\nu_0}{a_0}\right)^{1/4}; \quad (10)$$

In the case of the laminar and turbulent steady-state flow, the dimensionless distributions of temperature around the loop can be obtained analytically from Eq. (6). The distilled water was used as the working fluid.
It has been found that the Biot number has an influence on temperature in the laminar and turbulent flow. The results are shown in Figs. 2 and 3.

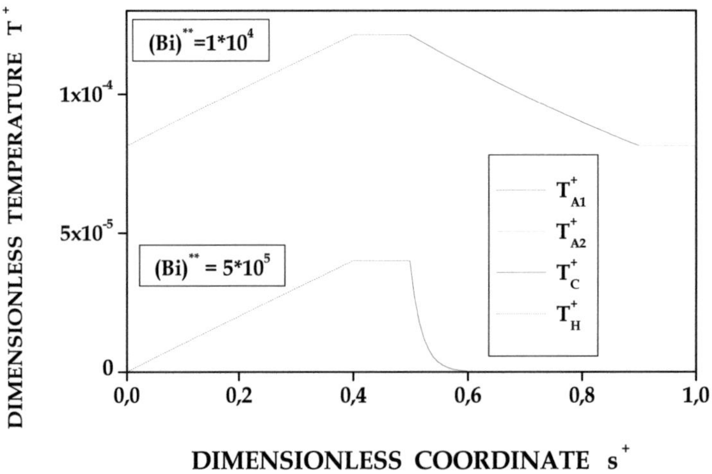

Fig. 2. The effect of Biot number on temperatures in the laminar steady-state flow (HHVCHV)

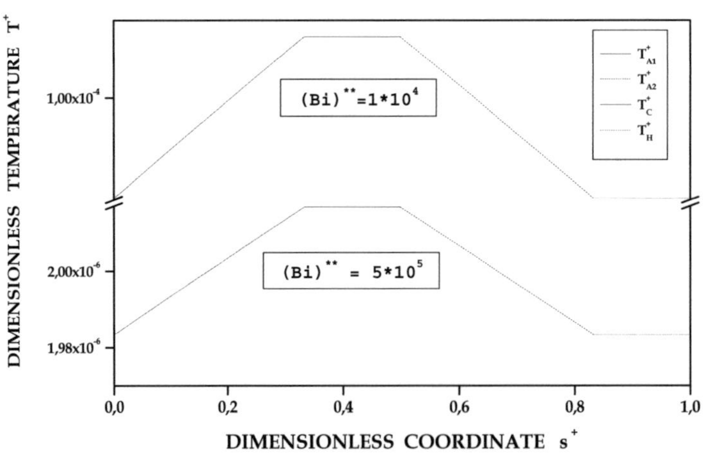

Fig. 3. The effect of Biot number on temperatures in the turbulent steady-state flow (HHVCHV)

The effect of the loop's aspect ratio (breadth B to height H) on the mass flow rate found numerically in the case of laminar flow at the steady state is presented in Fig. 4 .

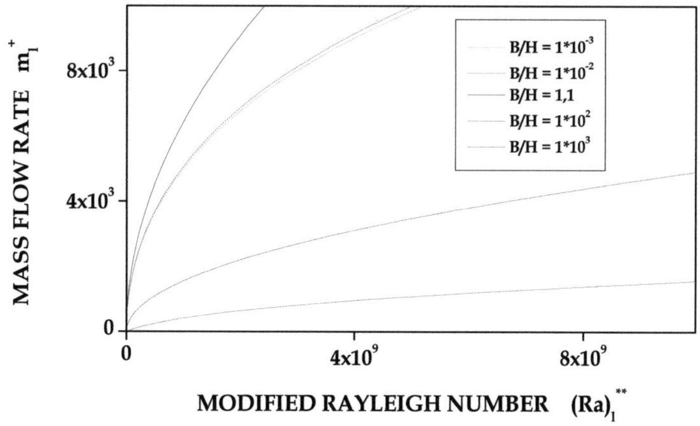

Fig. 4. Mass flow rate for laminar flow at the steady state versus modified Rayleigh number at different B/H ratios (HHVCHV)

For this variant of the thermosyphon loop it has been found that the maximum of the mass flow rate appears for B/H=1,1 .

The effect of geometrical parameter of the loop (length of insulation section G to height H) on the mass flow rate found numerically in the case of laminar flow at the steady state is presented in Fig. 5. The mass flow rate increases with decreasing *G/H* aspect ratio, due to the decreasing frictional pressure term.

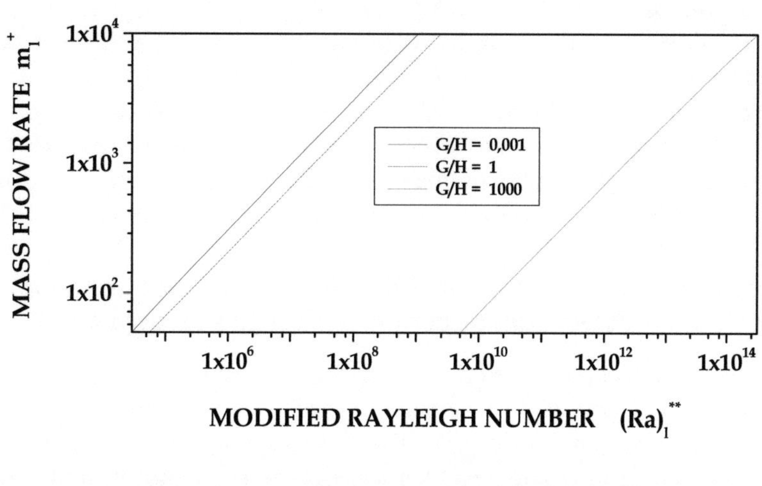

Fig. 5. Mass flow rate for laminar flow at the steady state versus modified Rayleigh number at different G/H ratios (HHVCHV)

This paper presents the case of the onset of motion of the single-phase fluid from a rest state if the loop rotates 90 degrees around the x-axis. The heated sections can be presented in the horizontal plane below the cooled sections. The presented numerical calculations are based on a new method for solution of the problem for the onset of motion in the fluid from the rest (Bieliński & Mikielewicz, 2005). Conditions for the onset of motion in the thermosyphon can be determined by considering the steady solutions with circulation for the limiting case of $\dot{m}_1^+ \to 0$.

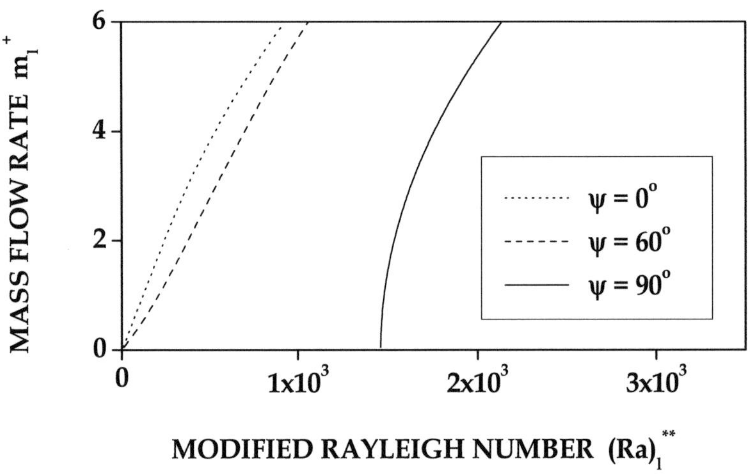

Fig. 6. The case of the onset of motion of the single-phase fluid from a rest state if the loop rotates 90 degrees around the x-axis (HHVCHV+ ψ90°)

The analysis was based on the equations of motion and energy for the steady-state conditions. The heat conduction term has to be taken into account in this approach because the heat transfer due to conduction is becoming an increasingly important factor for decreasing mass flow rates. The fluid starts circulation around the loop, when the Rayleigh number exceeds a critical value, which can be found using the method $\dot{m}_1^+ \to 0$ for the $\psi = 90^o$ angle. The critical Rayleigh number for angles $\psi < 90^o$ is zero. This means that the circulation of the fluid around the loop begins after the start up of the heating (Fig. 6).

3. Two-phase thermosyphon loop with heated from lower horizontal and vertical parts and cooled from upper horizontal and vertical parts

The variant of the two-phase closed thermosyphon loop consists of two heaters and two coolers connected by channels. A schematic diagram of a one-dimensional model of the thermosyphon loop is shown in Fig. 7. The thermosyphon loop is heated from lower horizontal section $(s_0 \le s \le s_1)$ and lower vertical section $(s_3 \le s \le s_4)$ by a constant heat flux: $\dot{q}_{H1}$ and $\dot{q}_{H2}$, respectively and cooled in the upper horizontal section $(s_6 \le s \le s_7)$ and upper vertical section $(s_9 \le s \le s_{10})$ by a constant heat flux: $\dot{q}_{C1}$ and $\dot{q}_{C2}$, respectively.

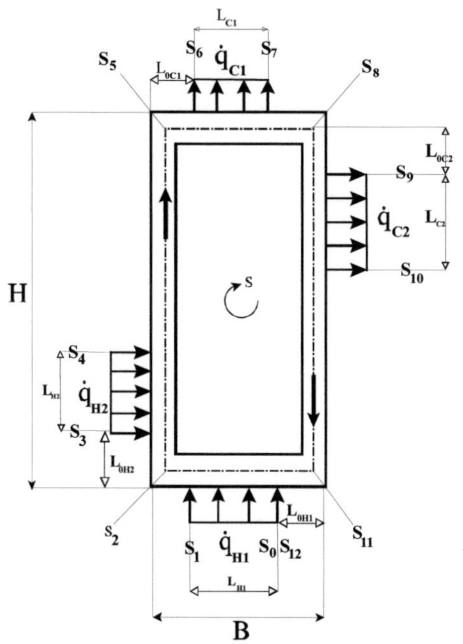

Fig. 7. A schematic diagram of a one-dimensional model of the thermosyphon loop (2H2C)

The constant heat fluxes $\dot{q}_{H1}, \dot{q}_{H2}$ and $\dot{q}_{C1}, \dot{q}_{C2}$ are applied in the cross-section area per heated and cooled length: L_{H1}, L_{H2} and L_{C1}, L_{C2} ,respectively. The heated and cooled parts of the thermosyphon loop are connected by perfectly insulated channels $(s_1 \leq s \leq s_3), (s_4 \leq s \leq s_6), (s_7 \leq s \leq s_9), (s_{10} \leq s \leq s_{12})$.

The coordinate s along the loop and the characteristic geometrical points on the loop are marked with s_j , as shown in Fig. 7. The total length of the loop is denoted by *L*, the cross-section area of the channel by *A* and the wetted perimeter by U. Thermal properties of fluid: ρ - density, c_p - heat capacity of constant pressure, λ - thermal conductivity.

The following additional assumptions are made in this study:

1. heat exchangers in the thermosyphon loop can be equipped by minichannels,
2. two-phase fluid can be selected as the working fluid,
3. friction coefficient is constant in each region of the loop, separate two-phase flow model can be used in calculations for the frictional pressure loss in the heated, cooled and adiabatic two-phase sections; the two-phase friction factor multiplier $R = \phi_{L0}^2$ is used; the density in the gravity term can be approximated as follows: $\rho = \alpha \cdot \rho_V + (1-\alpha) \cdot \rho_L$, where α is a void fraction,
4. quality of vapour in the two-phase regions is assumed to be a linear function of the coordinate around the loop,
5. effect of superheating and subcooling are neglected.

In order to eliminate the pressure gradient and the acceleration term, the momentum equation in Eq. (2) is integrated around the loop $\oint \left(\frac{\partial p}{\partial s} \right) ds = 0$.

After integrating the gravitational term in the momentum equation (2) around the loop, we obtain

$$\oint\{\varepsilon\cdot g\cdot\rho\}ds = g\cdot(\rho_V-\rho_L)\cdot\Big\{(s_3-s_2)\cdot\bar{\alpha}_{\langle s_1;s_3\rangle}+(s_4-s_3)\cdot\bar{\alpha}_{\langle s_3;s_4\rangle}+(s_5-s_4)\cdot\bar{\alpha}_{\langle s_4;s_6\rangle}+ \\ -(s_9-s_8)\cdot\bar{\alpha}_{\langle s_7;s_9\rangle}-(s_{10}-s_9)\cdot\bar{\alpha}_{\langle s_9;s_{10}\rangle}\Big\}=0\;; \tag{11}$$

where $\bar{\alpha}_{\langle s_P;s_K\rangle}=\dfrac{1}{(s_K-s_P)}\cdot\displaystyle\int_{s_P}^{s_K}\alpha_{\langle s_P;s_K\rangle}(s)ds$.

Due to the friction of fluid, the pressure losses in two-phase regions can be calculated as

$$\frac{U}{A}\cdot\tau_w=\left(\frac{-dp}{ds}\right)_{2p}=R\cdot\left(\frac{-dp}{ds}\right)_{L0} \tag{12}$$

where: $\left(\dfrac{dp}{ds}\right)_{L0}=\dfrac{2\cdot f_{L0}^{Chur}\cdot(\dot{G})^2}{D\cdot\rho_L}$ is the liquid only frictional pressure gradient calculated for the total liquid mass velocity, $\dot{G}=\rho\cdot w$, f_{L0}^{Chur} is friction factor of the fluid (Churchill, 1977). After integrating the friction term in Eq. (2) around the loop, the solution is obtained as follows

$$\oint\left(\frac{U}{A}\cdot\tau_w\right)ds=\left(\frac{dp}{ds}\right)_{L0}\cdot\Big\{(s_1-s_0)\cdot\bar{R}_{\langle s_0;s_1\rangle}+(s_3-s_1)\cdot\bar{R}_{\langle s_1;s_3\rangle}+(s_4-s_3)\cdot\bar{R}_{\langle s_3;s_4\rangle}+ \\ +(s_6-s_4)\cdot\bar{R}_{\langle s_4;s_6\rangle}+(s_7-s_6)\cdot\bar{R}_{\langle s_6;s_7\rangle}+(s_9-s_7)\cdot\bar{R}_{\langle s_7;s_9\rangle}+(s_{10}-s_9)\cdot\bar{R}_{\langle s_9;s_{10}\rangle}+(s_{12}-s_{10})\Big\}\;; \tag{13}$$

3.1 Minichannels. Distribution of the mass flux

The following correlations have been used in calculation of the thermosyphon loop with minichannels (Table 1): the El-Hajal correlation for void fraction (El-Hajal et al., 2003), the Zhang-Webb correlation for the friction pressure drop of two-phase flow in adiabatic region (Zhang & Webb, 2001), the Tran correlation for the friction pressure drop of two-phase flow in diabatic region (Tran et al. 2000).

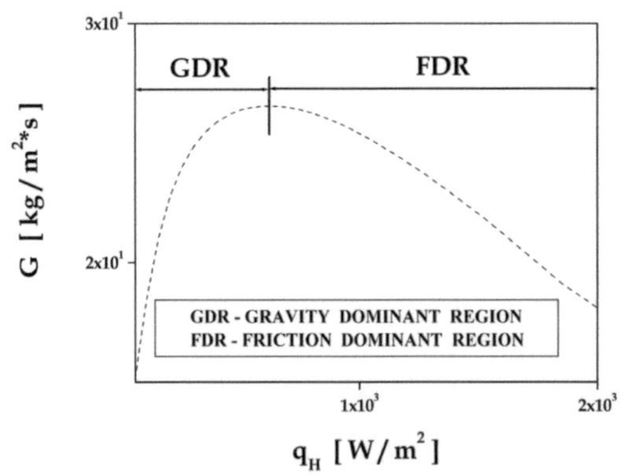

Fig. 8. Minichannels. Mass flux $\dot{G}$ as a function of $\dot{q}_H$ for the steady state (2H2C), (L=0.2 [m], D=0.002 [m], H=0.07 [m], B=0.03 [m], $L_{H1}=L_{H2}=L_{C1}=L_{C2}=0.02$ [m], $L_{H1P}=L_{H2P}=L_{C1P}=L_{C2P}=0.005$ [m])

Researcher	Correlation	
El-Hajal et al., (2003)	$\alpha_{HAJAL} = \frac{\alpha_{HOM} - \alpha_{STEINER}}{\ln\left(\frac{\alpha_{HOM}}{\alpha_{STEINER}}\right)}$; $\alpha_{HOM} = \frac{1}{1 + \frac{1-x}{x} \cdot \left(\frac{\rho_V}{\rho_L}\right)}$; $\alpha_{STEINER} = \left(\frac{x}{\rho_V}\right) \times \left\{ \left[1 + 0.12 \cdot (1-x)\right] \cdot \left[\frac{x}{\rho_V} + \frac{1-x}{\rho_L}\right] + \right.$ $\left. + \frac{1.18 \cdot (1-x) \cdot \left[g \cdot \sigma \cdot (\rho_L - \rho_V)\right]^{0.25}}{\dot{G} \cdot (\rho_L)^{0.5}} \right\}^{(-1)}$;	(14)
Zhang & Webb, (2001)	$\left(\frac{dp}{dl}\right)_{2p}^{Z-W} = \Phi_{L0}^2 \cdot \left(\frac{dp}{dz}\right)_{L0}$; $\Phi_{L0}^2 = (1-x)^2 + 2.87 \cdot (x)^2 \cdot \left(\frac{P}{P_{CRIT}}\right)^{(-1)} +$ $+1.68 \cdot (1-x)^{0.25} \cdot \left(\frac{P}{P_{CRIT}}\right)^{(-1.64)}$;	(15)
Tran et al., (2000)	$\left(\frac{dp}{dl}\right)_{2p}^{TRAN} = \Phi_{L0}^2 \cdot \left(\frac{dp}{dz}\right)_{L0}$; $\Phi_{L0}^2 = 1 + \left(4.3 \cdot Y^2 - 1\right) \cdot \left[N_{CONF} \cdot (x)^{0.875} \cdot (1-x)^{0.875} + (x)^{1.75}\right]$; $N_{CONF} = \frac{\left[\frac{\sigma}{g \cdot (\rho_L - \rho_V)}\right]^{0.5}}{D}$; $Y = \sqrt{\left(\frac{dp}{dz}\right)_{V0} \Big/ \left(\frac{dp}{dz}\right)_{L0}}$;	(16)

Table 1. Minichannels. Correlation for the void fraction and the friction pressure drop of two-phase flow

The mass flux distributions $\dot{G}$ versus heat flux $\dot{q}_H$ for the steady-state conditions and for the minichannels case, is shown in Fig. 8. Two flow regimes can be clearly identified in Fig. 8, namely GDR - gravity dominant regime and FDR – friction dominant regime (Vijayan et al., 2005). Calculations were carried out using the separate model of two-phase flow. The working fluid was distilled water.

3.2 Minichannels. The distributions of heat transfer coefficient in flow boiling

The heat transfer coefficient in flow boiling was calculated for minichannels using the Mikielewicz formula (Mikielewicz et al., 2007) and also calculated using the modified Saitoh formula (Saitoh et al., 2007). The heat transfer coefficient in flow boiling for minichannels h_{TPB} versus heat flux $\dot{q}_{H1}$ in the first evaporator is presented in Fig. 9.

Researcher	Correlation
Mikielewicz et al., (2007)	$\frac{h_{TPB}^{JM}}{h_{REF}}=\sqrt{\left(R_{M-S}\right)^{n}+\frac{1}{1+P}\cdot\left(\frac{h_{PB}}{h_{REF}}\right)^{2}}$; $R_{M-S}=\left[1+2\cdot\left(\frac{1}{f_1}-1\right)\cdot x\cdot\left(N_{CONF}\right)^{(-1)}\right]\cdot(1-x)^{\frac{1}{3}}+x^{3}\cdot\frac{1}{f_{1z}}$; $LAM\Rightarrow n=2$; $\alpha_{REF}^{LAM}=4.36\cdot\left(\frac{\lambda_L}{D}\right);f_1^{LAM}=\left(\frac{\mu_L}{\mu_V}\right)\cdot\left(\frac{\rho_V}{\rho_L}\right);f_{1z}^{LAM}=\left(\frac{\lambda_L}{\lambda_V}\right)$; $TUR\Rightarrow n=0.76$; $h_{REF}=0.023\cdot\frac{\lambda_L}{D}\cdot\left(Re_{L0}\right)^{0.8}\cdot\left(Pr_L\right)^{\frac{1}{3}}$; $f_1^{TUR}=\left(\frac{\mu_L}{\mu_V}\right)^{0.25}\cdot\left(\frac{\rho_V}{\rho_L}\right)$; $f_{1z}^{TUR}=\left(\frac{\mu_V}{\mu_L}\right)^{\frac{7}{15}}\cdot\left(\frac{c_{pL}}{c_{pV}}\right)^{\frac{1}{3}}\cdot\left(\frac{\lambda_L}{\lambda_V}\right)^{\frac{3}{2}}$; $P=2.53\times10^{(-3)}\cdot\left(Re_{L0}\right)^{1.17}\cdot(Bo)^{0.6}\cdot\left(R_{M-S}-1\right)^{(-0.65)}$; $(Bo)=\frac{\dot{q}}{\dot{G}\cdot r}$; $\left(Re_{L0}\right)=\frac{\dot{G}\cdot d}{\mu_L}$; $h_{PB}=55\cdot\dot{q}^{0.67}\cdot M^{(-0.5)}\cdot\left(\frac{P_n}{P_{CRIT}}\right)^{0.12}\cdot\left[-\log_{10}\left(\frac{P_n}{P_{CRIT}}\right)\right]^{(-0.55)}$; (17)
Saitoh et al., (2007)	$h_{TPB}^{SAITOH}=E\cdot h_{REF}+S\cdot h_{POOL}$; $h_{POOL}=207\cdot\left(\frac{\lambda_L}{d_b}\right)\cdot\left(\frac{q\cdot d_b}{\lambda_L\cdot T_{SAT}}\right)^{0.745}\cdot\left(\frac{\rho_G}{\rho_L}\right)^{0.581}\cdot\left(Pr_L\right)^{0.533}$; $h_{REF}=\begin{cases}(Nu)_{LAM}\cdot\left(\frac{\lambda_L}{D}\right); & LAM\\ 0.023\cdot\left(Re_L\right)^{\frac{4}{5}}\cdot\left(Pr_L\right)^{0.4}\cdot\left(\frac{\lambda_L}{D}\right); & TUR\end{cases}$ $E=1+\frac{\left(\frac{1}{X}\right)^{1.05}}{1+\left(We_G\right)^{(-0.4)}}$; $\left(Re_G\right)=\frac{\dot{G}_G\cdot D}{\mu_G}$; $\left(Re_L\right)=\frac{\dot{G}_L\cdot D}{\mu_L}$; $S=\frac{1}{1+0.4\cdot\left[\left(10^{(-4)}\right)\cdot\left(Re_{TP}\right)\right]^{1.4}};d_b=0.51\cdot\left(\frac{2\cdot\sigma}{g\cdot\left(\rho_L-\rho_G\right)}\right)0.5$; $\left(We_G\right)=\frac{\dot{G}_G\cdot D}{\sigma\cdot\rho_G}$; $\left(Re_{TP}\right)=\left(Re_L\right)\cdot(F)^{1.25}$; $\dot{G}_G=\dot{G}\cdot x$; $\dot{G}_L=\dot{G}\cdot(1-x)$; $X=\left(\frac{1-x}{x}\right)^{0.9}\cdot\left(\frac{\rho_G}{\rho_L}\right)^{0.5}\cdot\left(\frac{\mu_L}{\mu_G}\right)^{0.1}$ for $\begin{cases}\left(Re_L\right)>1000\\ \left(Re_G\right)>1000\end{cases}$; $C_G=0.046$; $C_L=16$; $X=\left(\frac{C_L}{C_G}\right)^{0.5}\times\left(Re_G\right)^{(-0.4)}\times\left(\frac{G_L}{G_G}\right)^{0.5}\cdot\left(\frac{\rho_G}{\rho_L}\right)^{0.5}\cdot\left(\frac{\mu_L}{\mu_G}\right)^{0.5}$ for $\begin{cases}\left(Re_L\right)<1000\\ \left(Re_G\right)>1000\end{cases}$; (18)

Table 2. Minichannels. Correlation for the heat transfer coefficient in flow boiling

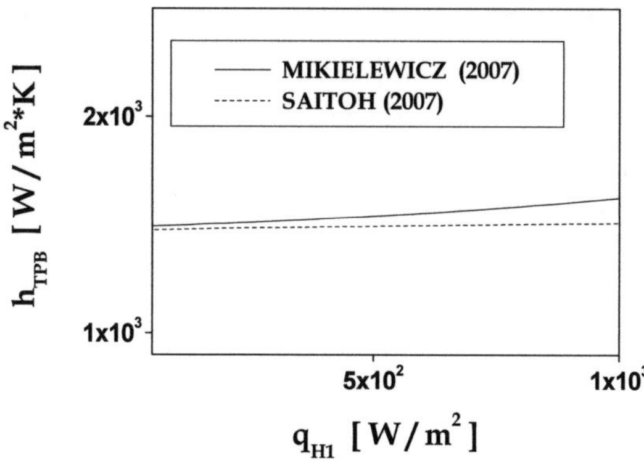

Fig. 9. Minichannels. Heat transfer coefficient in flow boiling h_{TPB} as a function of $\dot{q}_{H1}$ in the first evaporator. (L=0.2 [m], D=0.002 [m], H=0.07 [m], B=0.03 [m], L_{H1}= L_{H2}=L_{C1}= L_{C2}=0.02 [m], L_{H1P}= L_{H2P} =L_{C1P}= L_{C2P} =0.005 [m])

3.3 Minichannels. The heat transfer coefficient in condensation

The condensation heat transfer coefficient for minichannels was calculated using the Mikielewicz formula Eq. (17). The term which describes nucleation process in this formula was neglected. The heat transfer coefficient for condensation in minichannels was also calculated using the modified Tang formula (Tang et al., 2000).

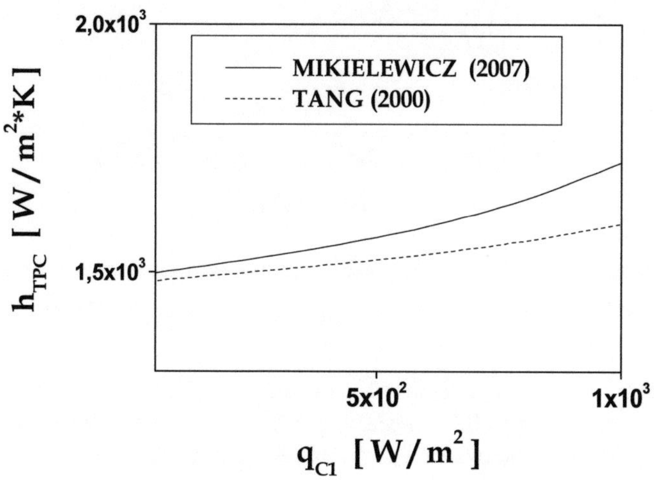

Fig. 10. Minichannels. Heat transfer coefficient h_{TPC} as a function of $\dot{q}_{C1}$ in the first condenser. (L=0.2 [m], D=0.002 [m], H=0.07 [m], B=0.03 [m], L_{H1}= L_{H2}=L_{C1}= L_{C2}=0.02 [m], L_{H1P}= L_{H2P} =L_{C1P}= L_{C2P} =0.005 [m])

The condensation heat transfer coefficient for minichannels h_{TPC} versus heat flux $\dot{q}_{C1}$ in the first condenser is presented in Fig. 10.

Researcher	Correlation	
Mikielewicz et al., (2007)	$\frac{h_{TPB}^{JM}}{h_{REF}} = \sqrt{\left(R_{M-S}\right)^{n}}$;	(19)
Tang et al., (2000)	$h_{TPC}^{TANG} = (Nu) \cdot \left(\frac{\lambda_L}{D}\right) \cdot \left[1 + 4.863 \cdot \left(\frac{(-x) \cdot \left[\ln\left(\frac{p_{SAT}}{p_{CRIT}}\right)\right]}{(1-x)}\right)^{0.836}\right]$;	(20)

Table 3. Minichannels. Correlation for the condensation heat transfer coefficient

3.4 The effect of geometrical and thermal parameters on the mass flux distributions

The effect of the internal diameter tube *D* on the mass flux for the steady-state conditions is presented in Fig. 11. The mass flux rapidly increases with increasing internal diameter tube *D*. The GDR (Gravity Dominant Region) decreases with decreasing internal diameter tube D.

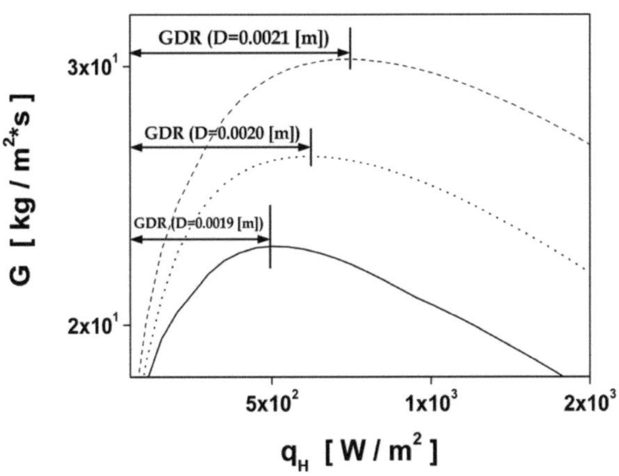

Fig. 11. Mass flux $\dot{G}$ as a function of $\dot{q}_H$ with internal diameter tube D as the parameter (2H2C). (L=0.2 [m], H=0.07 [m], B=0.03 [m], $L_{H1}= L_{H2}=L_{C1}= L_{C2}=0.02$ [m], $L_{H1P}= L_{H2P} =L_{C1P}= L_{C2P} =0.005$ [m])

The effect of length of the heated section L_{H2} on the mass flux is demonstrated in Fig. 13. If the length of horizontal section B is constant, the mass flux increases with increasing length of vertical section H due to the increasing gravitational pressure drop. The increase in length of the vertical section H induces an increase in both the gravitational and frictional pressure drop. However, the gravitational pressure drop grows more in comparison to frictional pressure drop.

The effect of length of the heated section L_{H2} on the mass flux is demonstrated in Fig. 12. The mass flux increases with increasing length of the heated section L_{H2} in gravity dominant region (GDR) but in friction dominant region (FDR) the mass flux decreases with increasing length of the heated section L_{H2} .

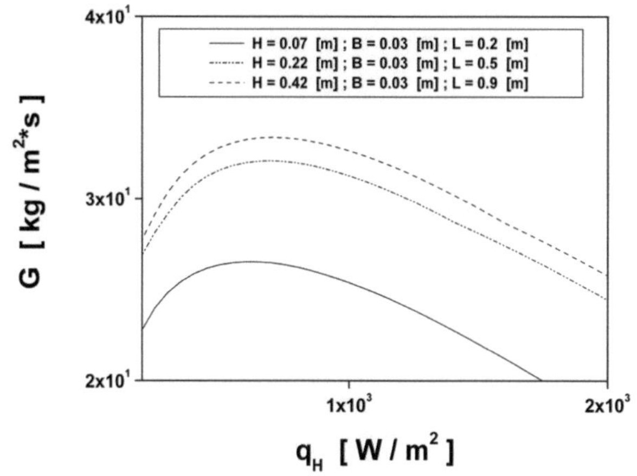

Fig. 12. Mass flux $\dot{G}$ as a function of $\dot{q}_H$ with parameter H (2H2C).
(D=0.002 [m], B=0.03 [m], L_{H1}= L_{H2}=L_{C1}= L_{C2}=0.02 [m], L_{H1P}= L_{H2P} =L_{C1P}= L_{C2P} =0.005 [m])

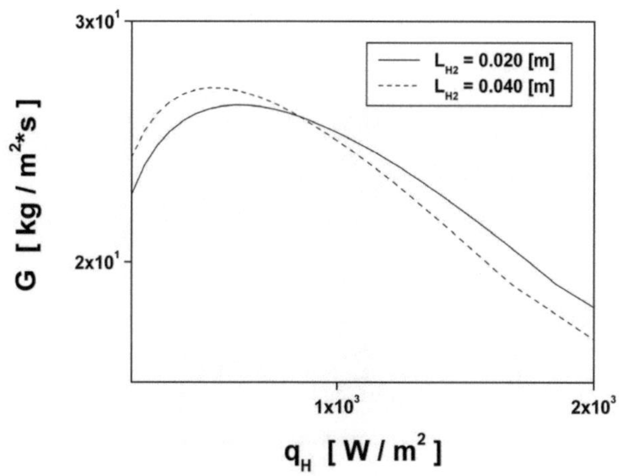

Fig. 13. Mass flux $\dot{G}$ as a function of $\dot{q}_H$ with parameter L_{H2} (2H2C).
(L=0.2 [m], D=0.002 [m], H=0.07 [m], B=0.03 [m], L_{H1}= L_{C1}= L_{C2}=0.02 [m],
L_{H1P}= L_{H2P} =L_{C1P}= L_{C2P} =0.005 [m])

The effect of length of the preheated section L_{H2P} on the mass flux is shown in Fig. 14. The mass flux increases with decreasing length of the preheated section L_{H2P}, in gravity dominant region (GDR) due to the increasing of the gravitational driving force.
The effect of length of the cooled section L_{C2} on the mass flux is given in Fig. 15. The mass flux decreases with increasing length of cooled section L_{C2} due to the increasing length of two-phase friction section $\langle s_9 ; s_{10} \rangle$ and the increasing frictional pressure drop.
The effect of length of the precooled section L_{C2P} on the mass flux is presented in Fig. 16. The mass flux increases with decreasing length of the precooled section L_{C2P} due to the increasing gravitational driving force.

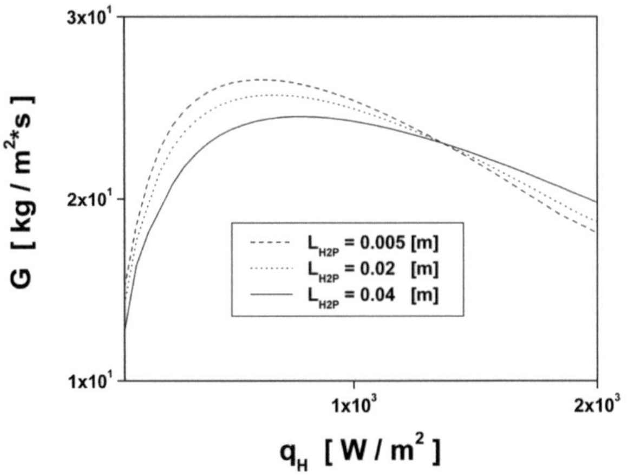

Fig. 14. Mass flux $\dot{G}$ as a function of $\dot{q}_H$ with parameter L_{H2P} (2H2C).
(L=0.2 [m], D=0.002 [m], H=0.07 [m], B=0.03 [m], L_{H1}= L_{H2}=L_{C1}= L_{C2}=0.02 [m], L_{H1P}= L_{C1P}= L_{C2P} =0.005 [m])

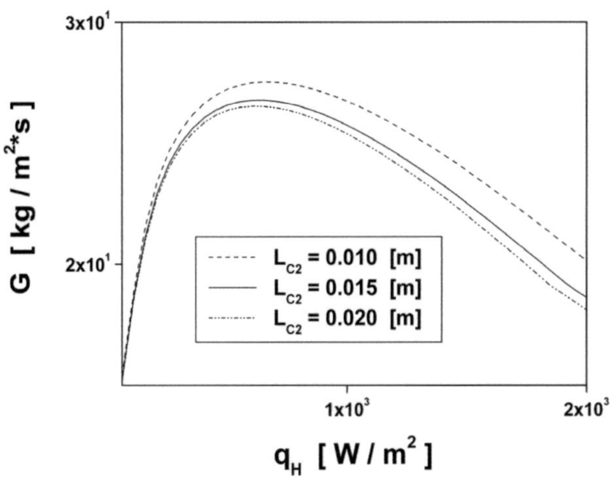

Fig. 15. Mass flux $\dot{G}$ as a function of $\dot{q}_H$ with L_{C2} as a parameter (2H2C).
(L=0.2 [m], D=0.002 [m], H=0.07 [m], B=0.03 [m], L_{H1}= L_{H2}=L_{C1}= 0.02 [m], L_{H1P}= L_{H2P} =L_{C1P}= L_{C2P} =0.005 [m])

The effect of width B of the loop on the mass flux is given in Fig. 17. If the height H of the loop is constant the mass flux decreases with the increasing width B of the loop, due to the increasing frictional pressure drop. No change of the gravitational pressure drop is observed because the height H of the loop is constant.
The effect of heat flux ratio $\dot{q}_{H1}/\dot{q}_{H2}$ on the mass flux $\dot{G}$ versus $\dot{q}_H$ for the steady-state conditions is presented in Fig. 18. The mass flux increases with increasing of heat flux ratio $\dot{q}_{H1}/\dot{q}_{H2}$.

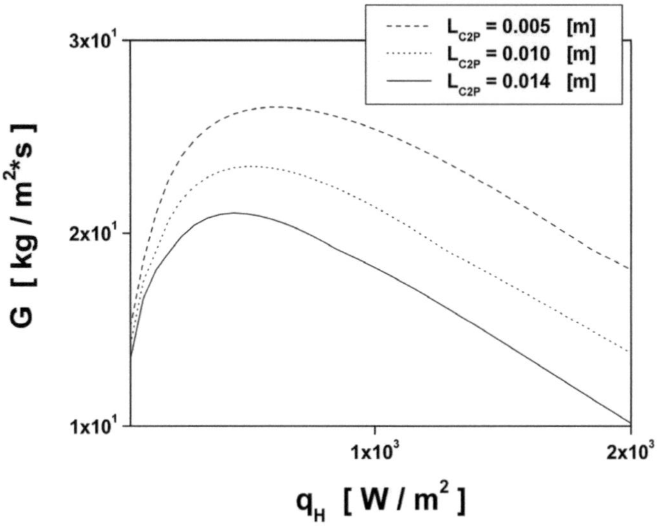

Fig. 16. Mass flux $\dot{G}$ as a function of $\dot{q}_H$ with L_{C2P} as a parameter (2H2C).
(L=0.2 [m], D=0.002 [m], H=0.07 [m], B=0.03 [m], L_{H1}= L_{H2}=L_{C1}= L_{C2}=0.02 [m], L_{H1P}= L_{H2P} =L_{C1P}= 0.005 [m])

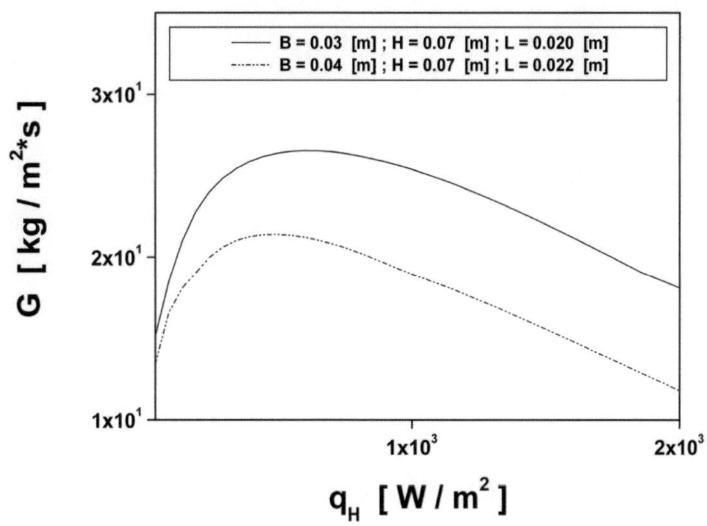

Fig. 17. Mass flux $\dot{G}$ as a function of $\dot{q}_H$ with parameter *B* (width of the loop) (2H2C).
(D=0.002 [m], H=0.07 [m], L_{H1}= L_{H2}=L_{C1}= L_{C2}=0.02 [m], L_{H1P}= L_{H2P} =L_{C1P}= L_{C2P} =0.005 [m])

The effect of heat flux ratio $\dot{q}_{C1}/\dot{q}_{C2}$ on the mass flux $\dot{G}$ versus $\dot{q}_H$ for the steady-state conditions is presented in Fig. 19. The mass flux increases with increasing of heat flux ratio $\dot{q}_{C1}/\dot{q}_{C2}$.

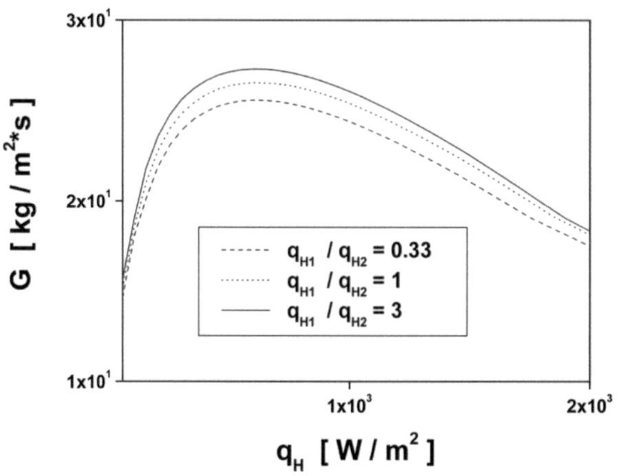

Fig. 18. Mass flux $\dot{G}$ as a function of $\dot{q}_H$ with parameter $\dot{q}_{H1}/\dot{q}_{H2}$ (2H2C). ($L=0.2$ [m], $D=0.002$ [m], $H=0.07$ [m], $B=0.03$ [m], $L_{H1}= L_{H2}=L_{C1}= L_{C2}=0.02$ [m], $L_{H1P}= L_{H2P} =L_{C1P}= L_{C2P} =0.005$ [m])

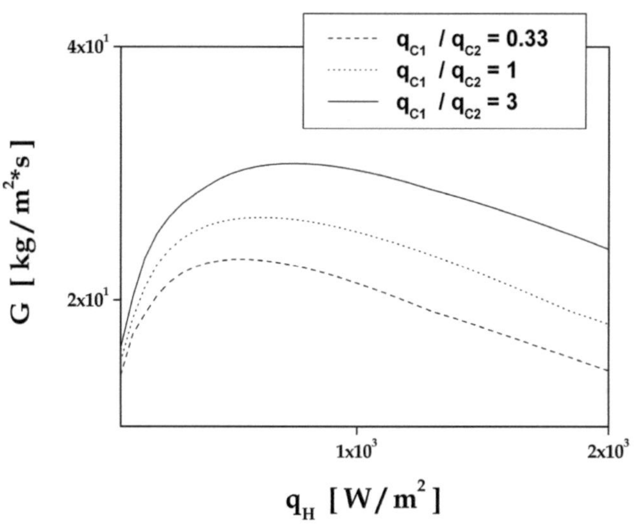

Fig. 19. Mass flux $\dot{G}$ as a function of $\dot{q}_H$ with parameter $\dot{q}_{C1}/\dot{q}_{C2}$ (2H2C). ($L=0.2$ [m], $D=0.002$ [m], $H=0.07$ [m], $B=0.03$ [m], $L_{H1}= L_{H2}=L_{C1}= L_{C2}=0.02$ [m], $L_{H1P}= L_{H2P} =L_{C1P}= L_{C2P} =0.005$ [m])

4. Two-phase thermosyphon loop with minichannels and minipump heated from lower horizontal section and cooled from upper vertical section

A schematic diagram of thermosyphon loop heated from horizontal side and cooled from vertical side with minipump is shown in Fig. 20 . The minipump can be used if the mass flux is not high enough to transport heat from evaporator to condenser. Therefore, the minipump promotes natural circulation. In the equation of motion of the thermosyphon loop with natural circulation, the pressure term of integration around the loop is zero $\oint\left(\frac{dp}{ds}\right)ds = 0$. For the thermosyphon loop with minipump the pressure term is

$\oint\left(\frac{dp}{ds}\right)ds = \Delta p_{PUMP} = \rho_L \cdot g \cdot H_{PUMP}$; $H_{PUMP} = H_{MAX} \cdot \left[1 - \left(\frac{\dot{V}}{\dot{V}_{MAX}}\right)^2\right]$, with $H_{MAX}, \dot{V}_{MAX}$ from minipump curve ($\dot{V}$ - volumetric flow rate).

A schematic diagram of a one-dimensional model of the thermosyphon loop with minipump is shown in Fig. 20.

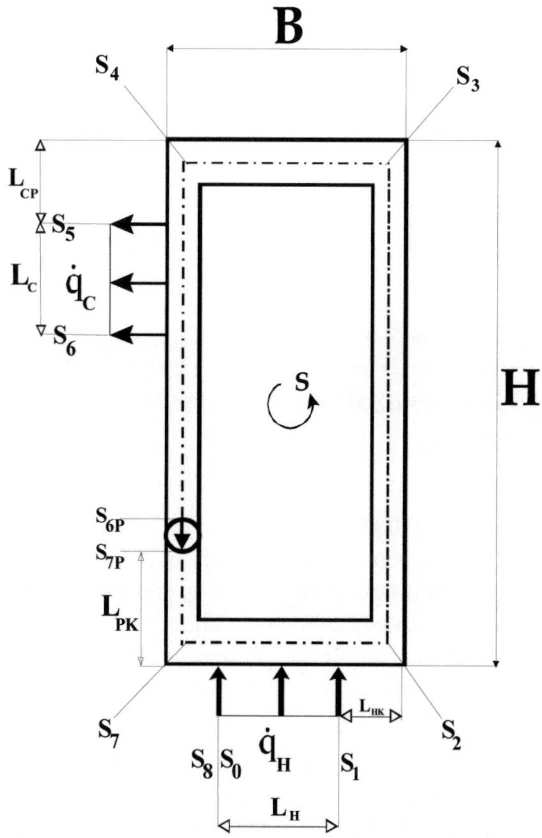

Fig. 20. A schematic diagram of a one-dimensional model of the thermosyphon loop with minipump (HHCV+P)

The mass flux distributions $\dot{G}$ versus heat flux $\dot{q}_H$ for the steady-state conditions and for minichannels, is shown in Fig. 21. Calculations were carried out using the separate model of two-phase flow. The following correlations have been used in the calculation: the El-Hajal correlation (Eq. 21) for void fraction (El-Hajal et al., 2003), the Zhang-Webb correlation (Eq. 22) for the friction pressure drop of two-phase flow in adiabatic region (Zhang & Webb, 2001), the Tran correlation (Eq. 23) for the friction pressure drop of two-phase flow in diabatic region (Tran et al. 2000). The working fluid was distilled water. A miniature pump curve from (Blanchard et. al., 2004) was included in the calculation. The Fig. 21 shows the mass flux $\dot{G}$ decreases with increasing heat flux $\dot{q}_H$ for minichannels with minipump (HHCV+P) for the steady-state condition.

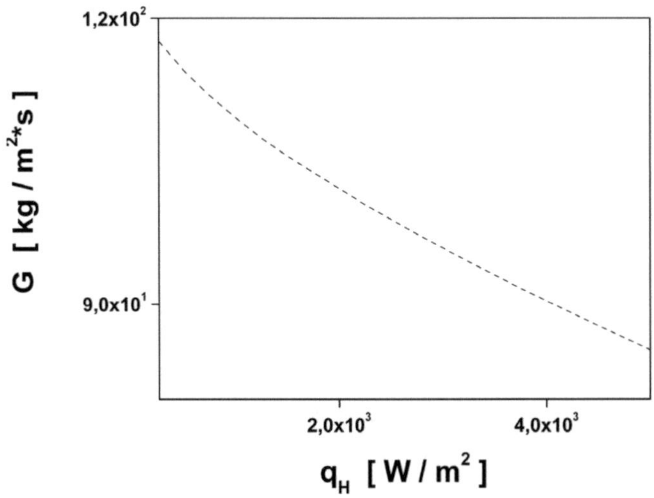

Fig. 21. Distributions of the mass flux $\dot{G}$ versus heat flux $\dot{q}_H$, for the steady-state conditions for minichannels with minipump (HHCV+P). (L=0.2 [m], D=0.002 [m], H=0.09 [m], B=0.01 [m], L_H=L_C=0.008 [m], L_{HP}= L_{CP} =0.0001 [m], L_{PK}=0.0001 [m])

5. Conclusions

The presented new variants (HHVCHV, 2H2C, HHCV+P) and the previous variants (HHCH, HVCV, HHCV) described in the chapter (Bieliński & Mikielewicz, 2011) can be analyzed using the conservation equations of mass, momentum and energy based on the generalized model of the thermosyphon loop. This study shows that the new effective numerical method proposed for solving the problem of the onset of motion in a fluid from the rest can be applied for the following variants: (HHVCHV+ $\psi 90^\circ$) and (HHCH).

The results of this study indicate that the properties of the variants associated with the generalized model of thermosyphon loop depend strongly on their specific technical conditions. For this reasons, the theoretical analysis of the presented variants can be applied, for example, to support the development of an alternative cooling technology for electronic systems. The progress in electronic equipment is due to the increased power levels and miniaturization of devices. The traditional cooling techniques are not able to cool effectively at high heat fluxes. The application of mini-loops can be successful by employing complex geometries, in order to maximize the heat transferred by the systems under condition of single- and two phase flows.

The obtained results show that the one-dimensional two-phase separate flow model can be used to describe heat transfer and fluid flow in the thermosyphon loop for minichannels. The evaluation of the thermosyphon loop with minichannels can be done in calculations using correlations such as the El-Hajal correlation (El-Hajal et al., 2003) for void fraction, the

Zhang-Webb correlation (Zhang & Webb, 2001) for the friction pressure drop of two-phase flow in adiabatic region, the Tran correlation (Tran et al., 2000) for the friction pressure drop of two-phase flow in diabatic region and the Mikielewicz correlation (Mikielewicz et al., 2007) for the heat transfer coefficient in evaporator and condenser.

Two flow regimes such as GDR- gravity dominant regime and FDR - friction dominant regime can be clearly identified (Fig. 8). The distribution of the mass flux against the heat flux approaches a maximum and then slowly decreases for minichannels. The effect of geometrical and thermal parameters on the mass flux distributions was obtained numerically for the steady-state conditions as presented in Figs. 11-19. The mass flux strongly increases with the following parameters: (a) increasing of the internal tube diameter, (b) increasing length of the vertical section H, (c) decreasing length of the precooled section L_{C2P} . The mass flux decreases with the parameters, such as (d) increasing length of the cooled section L_{C2} , (e) increasing length of the horizontal section B, (f) decreasing of the heat flux ratio: $\dot{q}_{H1}/\dot{q}_{H2}$ and $\dot{q}_{C1}/\dot{q}_{C2}$. If the mass flow rate is not high enough to circulate the necessary fluid to transport heat from evaporator to condenser, the minipump can be used to promotes natural circulation. For the steady-state condition as is demonstrated in Fig. 21, the mass flux $\dot{G}$ decreases with increasing heat flux $\dot{q}_H$ for minichannels with minipump (HHCV+P).

Each variant of thermosyphon loop requires an individual analysis of the effect of geometrical and thermal parameters on the mass flux. Two of the reasons are that the variants include the heated and cooled sections in different places on the loop and may have different quantity of heaters and coolers.

In future the transient analysis should be developed in order to characterize the dynamic behaviour of single- and two phase flow for different combination of boundary conditions. Attempts should be made to verify the presented variants based on numerical calculations for the theoretical model of thermosyphon loops with experimental data.

6. References

Bieliński, H.; Mikielewicz, J. (1995). Natural Convection of Thermal Diode., *Archives of Thermodynamics*, Vol. 16, No. 3-4.

Bieliński, H.; Mikielewicz, J. (2001). New solutions of thermal diode with natural laminar circulation., *Archives of Thermodynamics*, Vol. 22, pp. 89-106.

Bieliński, H.; Mikielewicz J. (2004). The effect of geometrical parameters on the mass flux in a two phase thermosyphon loop heated from one side., *Archives of Thermodynamics*, Vol. 29, No. 1, pp. 59-68.

Bieliński, H.; Mikielewicz J. (2004). Natural circulation in two-phase thermosyphon loop heated from below., *Archives of Thermodynamics*, Vol. 25, No. 3, pp. 15-26.

Bieliński, H.; Mikielewicz, J. (2005). A two-phase thermosyphon loop with side heating, *Inżynieria Chemiczna i Procesowa.*, Vol. 26, pp. 339-351 (in Polish).

Bieliński, H.; Mikielewicz, J. (2010). Energetic analysis of natural circulation in the closed loop thermosyphon with minichannels,. *Archiwum Energetyki*, Tom. XL, No 3, pp.3-10,

Bieliński, H.; Mikielewicz, J. (2010). Computer cooling using a two phase minichannel thermosyphon loop heated from horizontal and vertical sides and cooled from vertical side., *Archives of Thermodynamics*, Vol. 31(2010), No. 4, pp. 51-59.

Bieliński, H.; Mikielewicz, J. (2010). A Two Phase Thermosyphon Loop With Minichannels Heated From Vertical Side And Cooled From Horizontal Side, *Inżynieria Chemiczna i Procesowa.*, Vol. 31, pp. 535-551 .

Bieliński, H.; Mikielewicz, J. (2011). Natural Circulation in Single and Two Phase Thermosyphon Loop with Conventional Tubes and Minichannels,. published by InTech (ISBN 978-953-307-550-1) in book *Heat Transfer. Mathematical Modeling, Numerical Methods and Information Technology*, Edited by A. Belmiloudi, pp. 475-496,

Blanchard, D.B., Ligrani, P.M., Gale, B.K. (2004). Performance and Development of a Miniature Rotary Shaft Pump (RSP)., *2004 ASME International Mechanical Engineering Congress and RD&D Expo*, November 13-20, 2004, Anaheim, California USA.

Chen, K. (1988). Design of Plane-Type Bi-directional Thermal Diode., *ASME J. of Solar Energy Engineering*, Vol. 110.

Churchill, S.W. (1977). Friction-Factor Equation Spans all Fluid Flow Regimes., *Chem. Eng.*, pp. 91-92.

El-Hajal, J.; Thome, J.R. & Cavalini A. (2003). Condensation in horizontal tubes, part 1; two-phase flow pattern map., *Int. J. Heat Mass Transfer*, Vol. 46, No. 18, pp. 3349-3363.

Greif, R. (1988). Natural Circulation Loops., *Journal of Heat Transfer*, Vol. 110, pp. 1243-1257.

Madejski, J.; Mikielewicz, J. (1971). Liquid Fin - a New Device for Heat Transfer Equipment, *Int. J. Heat Mass Transfer*, Vol. 14, pp. 357-363.

Mikielewicz, D.; Mikielewicz, J. & Tesmar J. (2007). Improved semi-empirical method for determination of heat transfer coefficient in flow boiling in conventional and small diameter tubes., *Inter. J. Heat Mass Transfe* , Vol. 50, pp. 3949-3956.

Mikielewicz J. (1995). Modelling of the heat-flow processes., *Polska Akademia Nauk Instytut Maszyn Przepływowych, Seria Cieplne Maszyny Przepływowe*, Vol. 17, Ossolineum.

Misale, M.; Garibaldi, P.; Passos, J.C.; Ghisi de Bitencourt, G. (2007). Experiments in a Single-Phase Natural Circulation Mini-Loop., *Experimental Thermal and Fluid Science*, Vol. 31, pp. 1111-1120.

Ramos, E.; Sen, M. & Trevino, C. (1985). A steady-state analysis for variable area one- and two-phase thermosyphon loops, *Int. J. Heat Mass Transfer*, Vol. 28, No. 9, pp. 1711-1719.

Saitoh, S.; Daiguji, H. & Hihara, E. (2007). Correlation for Boiling Heat Transfer of R-134a in Horizontal Tubes Including Effect of Tube Diameter., *Int. J. Heat Mass Tr.*, Vol. 50, pp. 5215-5225.

Tang, L.; Ohadi, M.M. & Johnson, A.T. (2000). Flow condensation in smooth and microfin tubes with HCFC-22, HFC-134a, and HFC-410 refrigerants, Part II: Design equations. *Journal of Enhanced Heat Transfer*, Vol. 7, pp. 311-325.

Tran, T.N.; Chyu, M.C.; Wambsganss, M.W.; & France D.M. (2000). Two –phase pressure drop of refrigerants during flow boiling in small channels: an experimental investigations and correlation development., *Int. J. Multiphase Flow*, Vol. 26, No. 11, pp. 1739-1754.

Vijayan, P.K.; Gartia, M.R.; Pilkhwal, D.S.; Rao, G.S.S.P. & Saha D. (2005). Steady State Behaviour Of Single-Phase And Two-Phase Natural Circulation Loops. 2nd RCM on the IAEA CRP ,Corvallis, Oregon State University, USA.

Zhang, M.; Webb, R.L. (2001). Correlation of two-phase friction for refrigerants in small-diameter tubes. *Experimental Thermal and Fluid Science*, Vol. 25, pp. 131-139.

Zvirin, Y. (1981). A Review of Natural Circulation Loops in PWR and Other Systems., *Nuclear Engineering Design*, Vol. 67, pp. 203-225.

Part 3

Nanofluids

17

Nanofluids for Heat Transfer

Rodolphe Heyd
CRMD UMR6619 CNRS/Orléans University
France

1. Introduction

1.1 A need for energy saving

The global warming and nuclear or ecological disasters are some current events that show us that it is urgent to better consider renewable energy sources. Unfortunately, as shown by figures of the International Energy Agency (IEA), clean energies like solar, geothermal or wind power represent today only a negligible fraction of the energy balance of the planet. During 2008, the share of renewable energies accounted for 86 Mtoe, only 0.7% of the 12,267 Mtoe of global consumption. Unfortunately, the vital transition from fossil fuels to renewable energies is very costly in time and energy, as evidenced by such high costs of design and fabication of photovoltaic panels. Thus it is accepted today that a more systematic use of renewable energy is not sufficient to meet the energy challenge for the future, we must develop other ways such as for example improving the energy efficiency, an area where heat transfers play an important role.
In many industrial and technical applications, ranging from the cooling of the engines and high power transformers to heat exchangers used in solar hot water panels or in refrigeration systems, the low thermal conductivity k of most heat transfer fluids like water, oils or ethylene-glycol is a significant obstacle for an efficient transfer of thermal energy (Table 1).

liquids:	Ethylen Glycol (EG)	Glycerol (Gl)	Water (Wa)	Thermal Compound (TC)	
k (W/mK)	0.26	0.28	0.61	≈ 0.9	
metals:	Iron	Aluminium	Copper	Silver	CNT
k (W/mK)	80	237	400	429	≈ 2500

Table 1. Thermal conductivities k of some common materials at RT.

The improvement of heat transfer efficiency is an important step to achieve energy savings and, in so doing, address future global energy needs. According to Fourier's law $\mathbf{j}_Q = -k\nabla T$, an increase of the thermal conductivity k will result in an increase of the conductive heat flux. Thus one way to address the challenge of energy saving is to combine the transport properties of some common liquids with the high thermal conductivity of some common metals (Table 1) such as copper or novel forms of carbon such as nanotubes (CNT). These composite materials involve the stable suspension of highly conducting materials in nanoparticulate form to the fluid of interest and are named **nanofluids**, a term introduced by Choi in 1995 (Choi, 1995). A nanoparticle (NP) is commonly defined as an assembly of bounded atoms with at least one of its characteristic dimensions smaller than 100 nm. Due to their very high surface to volume ratio, nanoparticles exhibit some remarkable and sometimes new physical and chemical properties, in some way intermediate between those of isolated atoms and those of bulk material.

1.2 Some applications and interests of nanocomposites

Since the first report on the synthesis of nanotubes by Iijima in 1991 (Iijima, 1991), there has been a sharp increase of scientific interest about the properties of the nanomaterials and their possible uses in many technical and scientific areas, ranging from heat exchange, cooling and lubrication to the vectorization of therapeutic molecules against cancer and biochemical sensing or imaging. The metal or metal oxides nanoparticles are certainly the most widely used in these application areas.

It has been experimentally proved that the suspension in a liquid of some kinds of nanoparticles, even in very small proportions (<1% by volume), is capable of increasing the thermal conductivity of the latter by nearly 200% in the case of carbon nanotubes (Casquillas, 2008; Choi et al., 2001), and approximately 40% in the case of copper oxide nanoparticles (Eastman et al., 2001). Since 2001, many studies have been conducted on this new class of fluids to provide a better understanding of the mechanisms involved, and thus enable the development of more efficient heat transfer fluids. The high thermal conductivity of the nanofluids designates them as potential candidates for replacement of the heat carrier fluids used in heat exchangers in order to improve their performances. It should be noted that certain limitations may reduce the positive impact of nanofluids. Thus the study of the performance of cooling in the dynamic regime showed that the addition of nanoparticles in a liquid increases its viscosity and thereby induces harmful losses (Yang et al., 2005). On the other hand, the loss of stability in time of some nanofluids may result in the agglomeration of the nanoparticles and lead to a modification in their thermal conduction properties and to risks of deposits as well as to the various disadvantages of heterogeneous fluid-flow, like abrasion and obstruction. Nevertheless, in the current state of the researches, these two effects are less important with the use of the nanofluids than with the use of the conventional suspensions of microparticles (Daungthongsuk & Wongwises, 2007). We must not forget to take into account the high ecological cost of the synthesis of the NPs, which often involves a large number of chemical contaminants. Green route to the synthesis of the NPs using natural substances should be further developed (Darroudi et al., 2010).

2. Preparation of thermal nanofluids

2.1 Metal nanoparticles synthesis

2.1.1 Presentation

Various physical and chemical techniques are available for producing metal nanoparticles. These different methods make it possible to obtain free nanoparticles, coated by a polymer or encapsulated into a host matrix like mesoporous silica for example. In this last case, they are protected from the outside atmosphere and so from the oxidation. As a result of their very high surface to volume ratio, NPs are extremely reactive and oxidize much faster than in the bulk state. The encapsulation also avoids an eventual agglomeration of the nanoparticles as aggregates (clusters) whose physico-chemical properties are similar to that of the bulk material and are therefore much less interesting. The choice of a synthesis method is dictated by the ultimate use of nanoparticles as: nanofluids, sensors, magnetic tapes, therapeutic molecules vectors,etc. Key factors for this choice are generally: the size, shape, yield and final state like powder, colloidal suspension or polymer film.

2.1.2 Physical route

The simplest physical method consists to subdivide a bulk material up to the nanometric scale. However, this method has significant limitations because it does not allow precise control of size distributions. To better control the size and morphology, we can use other more sophisticated physical methods such as:

- the sputtering of a target material, for example with the aid of a plasma (cathode sputtering), or with an intense laser beam (laser ablation). K. Sakuma and K. Ishii have synthesized magnetic nanoparticles of Co-Pt and Fe with sizes ranging from 4 to 6 nm (Sakuma & Ishii, 2009).
- the heating at very high temperatures (thermal evaporation) of a material in order that the atoms constituting the material evaporate. Then adequate cooling of the vapors allows agglomeration of the vapor atoms into nanoparticles (Singh et al., 2002).

The physical methods often require expensive equipments for a yield of nanoparticles often very limited. The synthesized nanoparticles are mostly deposited or bonded on a substrate.

2.1.3 Chemical route

Many syntheses by the chemical route are available today and have the advantage of being generally simple to implement, quantitative and often inexpensive. Metallic NPs are often obtained via the reduction of metallic ions contained in compounds like silver nitrate, copper chloride, chloroauric acid, bismuth chloride, etc.
We only mention here a few chemical methods chosen among the most widely used for the synthesis of metal and metal oxides NPs:

Reduction with polymers: schematically, the synthesis of metal nanoparticles (M) from a solution of M^+ ions results from the gradual reduction of these ions by a weak reducing polymer (suitable to control the final particle size) such as PVA (polyvinyl alcohol) or PEO (polyethylene oxide). The metal clusters thus obtained are eventually extracted from the host polymer matrix by simple heating. The size of the synthesized metal nanoparticles mainly depends on the molecular weight of the polymer and of the type of metal ions. For example with PVA ($M_w = 10000$) we obtained (Hadaoui et al., 2009) silver nanoparticles with a diameter ranging from 10 to 30 nm and copper nanoparticles with a diameter of about 80 nm.

Gamma radiolysis: the principle of radiolytic synthesis of nanoparticles consists in reducing the metal ions contained in a solution through intermediate species (usually electrons) produced by radiolysis. The synthesis can be described in three parts (i) radiolysis of the solvent, (ii) reduction reaction of metal ions by species produced by radiolysis followed by (iii) coalescence of the produced atoms (Benoit et al., 2009; Ramnani et al., 2007; Temgire et al., 2011).

Thermal decomposition: the synthesis by the thermal decomposition of an organometallic precursor allows to elaborate various systems of nanoparticles (Chen et al., 2007; Liu et al., 2007; Roca et al., 2006; Sun et al., 2004) or carbon nanotubes (Govindaraj & Rao, 2002). This method is widely used because of its ease and of the reproducibility of the synthesis, as well as the uniformity in shape and size of the synthesized particles. Metal particles such as Au, Ag, Cu, Co, Fe, FePt, and oxides such as copper oxides, magnetite and other ferrites have been synthesized by this method. It mainly consists of the decomposition of an organometallic precursor dissolved in an organic solvent (like trioctylamine, oleylamine, etc.) with high boiling points and containing some surfactants (so called capping ligands) like oleic acid, lauric acid, etc. By binding to the surface of the NPs, these surfactants give rise to a steric barrier against aggregation, limiting the growing phase of the nanoparticles. Basing on the choice of the ligand properties (molecular length, decomposition temperature) and on the ligand/precursor ratio, it is possible to control the size and size distribution of the synthesized NPs (Yin et al., 2004).

Using the thermal decomposition of the acetylacetonate copper precursor dissolved in oleylamine in the presence of oleic acid, we have synthesized copper oxide nanoparticles of mean diameter 7 nm with a quasi-spherical shape and low size dispersion (Fig. 1).

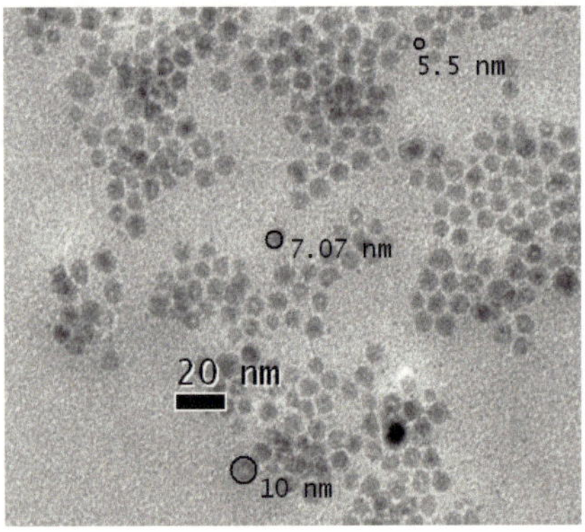

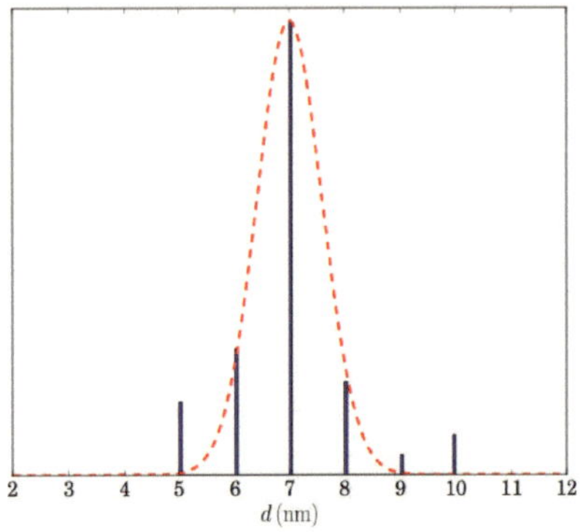

Fig. 1. TEM picture of copper oxides nanoparticles synthesized by the thermal decomposition of acetylacetonate copper precursor dissolved in oleylamine (Hadaoui, 2010).

2.1.4 Characterization of the nanoparticles

Depending on the final state of the nanoparticles, there are several techniques to visualize and characterize them: the X-ray diffraction, electron microscopy (TEM, cryo-TEM, etc.), the atomic force microscopy, photoelectron spectroscopy like XPS. More macroscopic methods like IR spectroscopy and UV-visible spectroscopy are interesting too in the case where there is a plasmonic resonance depending on the size of the NPs like for example in the case of silver and gold.

The Dynamic Light Scattering (DLS) is a well established technique to measure hydrodynamic sizes, polydispersities and aggregation effects of nanoparticles dispersed in a colloidal suspension. This method is based on the measurement of the laser light scattering fluctuations due to the Brownian motion of the suspended NPs. In the case of opaque nanofluids, only the backscattering mode of DLS is able to provide informations on NPs characteristics.

2.2 Stability of colloidal suspensions

2.2.1 Presentation

The nanofluids belong to the class of Solid/Liquid colloidal systems where a solid phase is very finely dispersed in a continous liquid phase. Most of nanofluids are prepared by direct injection of nanoparticles in the host liquid, depending on the nature of this liquid (water, ethylene glycol (EG), oils, glycerol, etc.) it may be necessary to add chemicals to the solution to avoid coagulation and ensure its stability by balancing internal forces exerted on particles and slowing down agglomeration rates. This addition can dramatically change the physical properties of the base liquid and give disappointing results.

2.2.2 Isolated spherical particle immersed in a fluid

We consider a spherical particle of radius a_p, density ρ_p, immersed in a fluid of density ρ_f and dynamical viscosity η, placed at rest in the gravitational field $\mathbf{g}$ assumed to be uniform (Fig. 2(a)). Under the effect of its weight $\mathbf{P} = \rho_p V_p \mathbf{g}$ and of the buoyancy $\mathbf{F}_A = -\rho_f V_p \mathbf{g}$ due to the fluid, the particle moves with velocity $\mathbf{v}$ that obeys to the equation of motion $m_p \frac{\mathrm{d}\mathbf{v}}{\mathrm{d}t} = \Delta\mathbf{F} + \mathbf{F}_v$, where $\Delta\mathbf{F} = \mathbf{P} + \mathbf{F}_A = V_p(\rho_p - \rho_f)\mathbf{g}$ and $\mathbf{F}_v$ is the viscous drag exerted by the fluid on the particle. In the limit of laminar flow at very low Reynolds numbers $\mathrm{Re} = \rho_f v 2a_p/\eta \ll 1$, we can write the Stokes law for a sphere as $\mathbf{F}_v = -6\pi a_p \eta \mathbf{v}$. We deduce from these hypotheses the following equation satisfied by the velocity of the sphere:

$$\frac{\mathrm{d}\mathbf{v}}{\mathrm{d}t} + \frac{6\pi\eta a_p}{\rho_p V_p}\mathbf{v} = \left(1 - \frac{\rho_p}{\rho_f}\right)\mathbf{g} \tag{1}$$

As we can see from (1), if $\rho_p > \rho_f$, agglomeration leads to sedimentation and on the other hand if $\rho_p < \rho_f$ agglomeration leads to skimming. After a characteristic time $\tau = 2\rho_p a_p^2/9\eta$ generally very short, the velocity of the sphere reaches a constant limiting value v_ℓ (Fig. 2(a)) whose magnitude is given by:

$$v_\ell = \frac{2g|\rho_p - \rho_f|a_p^2}{9\eta} \tag{2}$$

Based on previous results, we can preserve the stability of water-based nanofluids by limiting a_p, that is by *limiting the agglomeration* of nanoparticles. In the case of viscous host media (like glycerol or gels), stability is generally guaranteed, even for large agglomerates.

2.2.3 Coagulation of nanoparticles

2.2.3.1 Presentation

The coagulation between two particles may occur if:

1. the particles are brought close enough from each other in order to coagulate. When a colloid is not stable, the coagulation rate depends of the frequency at which the particles collide. This *dynamic process* is mainly a function of the thermal motion of the particles, of the fluid velocity (coagulation due to shear), of its viscosity and of the inter-particles forces (colloidal forces).
2. during the collision the energy of the system is lowered by this process. This decrease in energy originates from the forces, called colloidal forces, acting between the particles in suspension. The colloidal forces are mainly composed of electrostatic repulsive forces

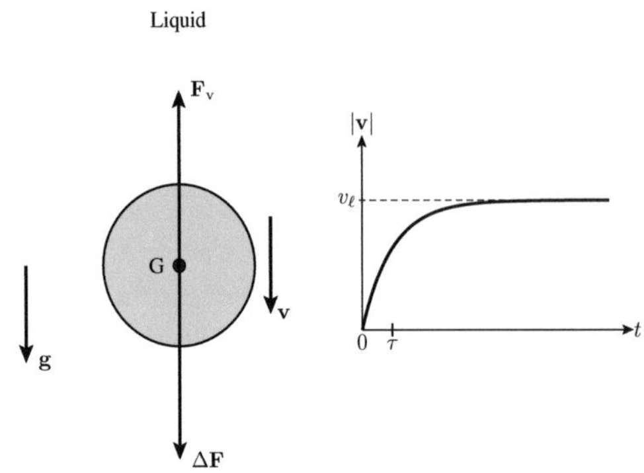

(a) Dynamics of a spherical particle immersed in a liquid at rest.

radius a_p	Water	Glycerol
5 nm	400 d	420531 d
50 nm	4 d	4205 d
100 nm	1 d	1051 d

(b) Values (in days) of the time taken by cupric oxide NPs to travel a distance $h = 1\,\text{cm}$ in different liquids and for various radii.

Fig. 2. A simple mechanical model to discuss the stability of the nanofluids in the terrestrial gravitational field.

and Van der Waals type forces. The electrostatic forces, always present in the case of water-based nanofluids, are due to the presence of ionised species on the surface of the particles, inducing an *electric double layer*. More this double-layer is important, the more the particles repel each other and more stable is the solution. The Van der Waals type forces are due to the interactions between the atoms constituing the NPs.

2.2.3.2 DLVO theory

For a system where the electrostatic forces and the Van der Waals forces are dominant, as in the case of water-based nanofluids, the DLVO theory establishes that a simple combination of the two corresponding interaction energies, respectively $U_e(s)$ and $U_{VW}(s)$, is sufficient to explain any tendency to the aggregation of the suspension. This concept was developed by Derjaguin and Landau and also by Vervey and Overbeck.

In the case of two identical interacting spherical particles with radius a_p, separated by a distance s (Fig. 3), it is possible (Masliyah & Bhattarjee, 2006) to write the DLVO interaction energy $U(s)$ as:

$$
\begin{aligned}
U(s) &= U_e(s) + U_{VW}(s) \\
&= 2\pi a_p \epsilon_r \epsilon_0 \psi_S^2 \ln\left(1 + e^{-s/\kappa^{-1}}\right) - \frac{A_H a_p}{12s}
\end{aligned}
\tag{3}
$$

where A_H is the Hamaker's constant ($A_H \approx 30 \times 10^{-20}$ J for copper NPs in water), ϵ_0 is the permittivity of vacuum, ϵ_r is the dielectric constant of the host fluid ($\epsilon_r = 78.5$ for water at RT), ψ_S is the surface electrical potential of NPs and κ^{-1} is the Debye length defined by:

$$
\kappa^{-1} = \left(\frac{10^3 N_A e^2}{\epsilon_0 \epsilon_r k_B T} \sum_{i=1}^{N} z_i^2 M_i \right)^{-1/2} \tag{4}
$$

where z_i is the valence of ith ionic species and M_i is its moalrity, N_A is the Avogadro number, k_B is the Boltzmann constant, e is the elementary charge and T is the absolute temperature

of the colloid. The Debye length gives an indication of the double layer thickness, thus more κ^{-1} is important, better is the stability of the suspension. Introducing the ionic strength $I = \sum_{i=1}^{N} z_i^2 M_i/2$, we see from (4) that using high values of I makes the suspension unstable. It is therefore recommended to use highly deionized water to prepare water-based nanofluids.
As can be seen on Fig. 3(a), the colloidal suspension is all the more stable that there is a significant energy barrier E_b, preventing the coagulation of nanoparticles.

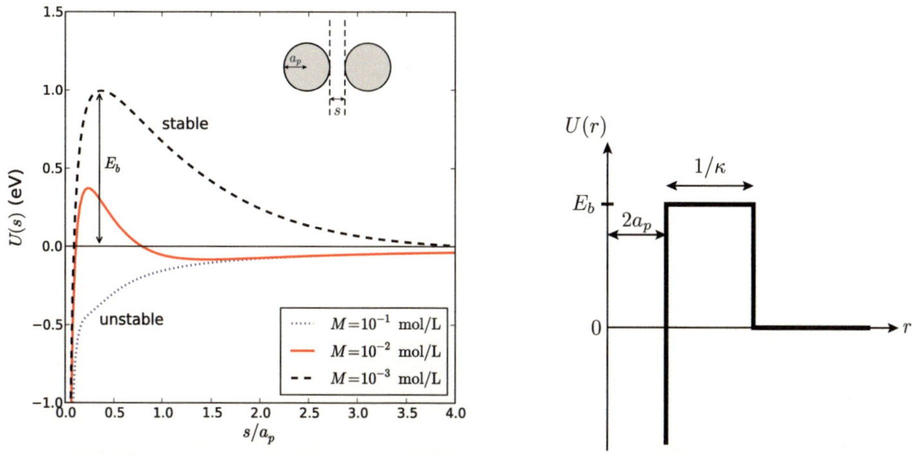

(a) DLVO interaction energy and stability tendencies of copper oxide spherical NPs suspended in water at RT and using symetric electrolytes with different molarities M and $\psi_S = 0.1$ V.

(b) Approximate DLVO interaction potentiel used to calculate the frequency collision function K'.

Fig. 3. DLVO interaction energy in the case of two identical spheres. We recall that $1\,\text{eV} \approx 39\, k_B T$ at RT and $r = s + 2a_p$ is the distance between the centers of two particles.

2.2.3.3 Dynamics of agglomeration

If on the one hand the colloidal forces are a key factor to discuss the stability of a suspension, on the other hand the dynamics of the collisions is another key factor.
We note $J_k^+ > 0$ the rate of formation per unit volume of particles of volume v_k and $J_k^- < 0$ the rate of disappearance per unit volume. With these notations the net balance equation for the kth species is written as:

$$\frac{\mathrm{d}n_k}{\mathrm{d}t} = J_k^+ + J_k^- \tag{5}$$

where n_k is the number of particles of the kth species per unit volume. Von Smoluchowski proposed the following expressions of J_k^+ and J_k^- to describe the formation of any aggregate of volume v_k:

$$J_k^+ = \frac{1}{2} \sum_{i=1;v_i+v_j=v_k}^{i=k-1} \beta_{ij} n_i n_j \tag{6}$$

$$J_k^- = -\sum_{i=1}^{N_p} \beta_{ki} n_i n_k \tag{7}$$

where β_{ij} is the collision frequency function and N_p is the total number of particles species or equivalently of different volumes. The $1/2$ factor in (6) takes care of the fact that $v_i + v_j = v_j + v_i$. The collision frequency function β_{ij} is the key insight of the kinetics of coagulation and is tightly dependent of several factors such as: the Brownian motion (thermal motion) or the deterministic motion (fluid-flow) of the fluid, the nature of the inter-particles forces and of the aggregation ("touch-and-paste" or "touch-and-go", the last case requiring then many collisions before permanent adhesion). If we consider the simplest case of an initially monodisperse colloidal particles modeled as hard spheres and only submitted to Brownian motion, the collision frequency function is given (Masliyah & Bhattarjee, 2006) by:

$$K = \beta_{kk} = \frac{8k_B T}{3\eta} \tag{8}$$

This simple result shows once again that the use of viscous fluids host significantly slows the onset of aggregation of nanofluids.
We now need an estimate of the time $t_{1/2}$ needed for the coagulation for example of one half of the initial population of nanoparticles. For simplicity we suppose that there is only binary collisions of identical particles of kind (1) and volume v_1. We assume that every collision leads by coagulation to the formation of a particle of kind (2) and volume $v_2 = 2v_1$ and that this particle deposits as a sediment without undergoing another collisions. Using relations (5), (6) and (7) we write:

$$\frac{\mathrm{d}n_1}{\mathrm{d}t} = -\beta_{11}n_1^2 \Rightarrow n_1(t) = \frac{n_1(0)}{1+\beta_{11}n_1(0)t} \tag{9}$$

$$\frac{\mathrm{d}n_2}{\mathrm{d}t} = \frac{1}{2}\beta_{11}n_1^2 \Rightarrow n_2(t) = \frac{1/2\beta_{11}n_1^2(0)t}{1+\beta_{11}n_1(0)t} \tag{10}$$

where $n_1(0)$ is the initial number of particles per unit volume. Introducing $t_{1/2} = 1/\beta_{11}n_1(0)$, recalling that the volume fraction of NPs is written as $\phi = 4/3\pi a_p^3 n_1(0)$ and using (8), the time $t_{1/2}$ can be expressed as:

$$t_{1/2} = \frac{\eta\pi a_p^3}{2\phi k_B T} \tag{11}$$

In the case of a water-based nanofluid containing a volume fraction $\phi = 0.1\%$ of identical spherical particles with radius $a_p = 10$ nm, we found with our model that $t_{1/2} = 0.38$ ms at RT, which is a quite small value! The relation (11) qualitatively shows that it is preferable to use low NPs volume fractions suspended in viscous fluids. For the same volume fractions, small NPs aggregate faster than the bigger.
A more sophisticated approach includes the colloidal forces between particles. Using an approximated DLVO potential of the form represented Fig. 3(b) can lead to the following approximated expression of the frequency collision function K' taking into account interactions:

$$K' = 2a_p\kappa \exp\left(-\frac{E_b}{k_B T}\right) K \tag{12}$$

We will retain from this expression that more the colloidal forces are repulsive ($E_b/k_B T \gg 1$), more the coagulation of particles is slow and the solution is stable over time.

2.2.3.4 How to control aggregation in nanofluids?

The preceeding studies have shown that, to control the agglomeration of NPs in the suspension and avoid settling, it is recommended to use:

- viscous host fluids with high value of the dielectric constant, low particles volume fraction ϕ and not too small particles ;
- pure highly desionized water with low values of the ionic strength I (in the case of water-based nanofluids);
- pH outside the region of the *isoelectric point* for the case of amphoteric NPs (like silica and metal oxides) suspended in water. The *isoelectric point* (IEP) may be defined as the pH at which the surface of the NP exhibits a neutral net electrical charge or equivalently a zero *zeta potential* $\zeta = 0$ V. For this particular value of ζ there are only attractive forces of Van der Waals and the solution is not stable. For example in the case of copper oxide NPs suspended in water, IEP(CuO) ≈ 9.5 at RT and a neutral or acid pH $\leqslant 7$ promotes the stability of the suspension.
- surface coating with surfactants or with low molecular weight ($M_w < 10000$) neutral polymers highly soluble in the liquid suspension. They allow to saturate the surface of NPs without affecting the long range repulsive electrostatic force. In contrast this polymeric shell induces steric effects that may dominate the short distances attractive Van der Waals interaction. Thus forces are always repulsive and the solution is stable. In a sense the presence of the polymer shell enhances the value of the energy barrier E_b.
- high power sonication to break agglomerates and disperse particles.

It is important to mention here that the surface treatments we presented above allow to enhance the stability of the suspension and to control the aggregation, but unfortunately they certainly also have a deep impact on the heat transfer properties of the nanofluid and should be considered carefully. The control of the NPs surface using polymer coating, surfactants or ions grafting, introduces unknown thermal interfacial resistances which can dramatically alter the benefit of using highly conductive nanoparticles.

3. Thermal transfer coefficients of nanofluids

3.1 Presentation

The use of suspended nanoparticles in various base fluids (thermal carriers and biomedical liquids for example) can alter heat transfer and fluid flow characteristics of these base fluids. Before any wide industrial application can be found for nanofluids, thorough and systematic studies need to be carried out. Apart of the potential industrial applications, the study of the nanofluids is of great interest to the understanding of the mechanisms involved in the processes of heat transfer to the molecular level. Experimental measurements show that the thermal properties of the nanofluids do not follow the predictions given by the classical theories used to describe the homogeneous suspensions of solid micro-particles in a liquid. Despite the large number of published studies on the subject in recent years, today there is no unique theory that is able to properly describe the whole experimental results obtained on the nanofluids.

Fluids	Particles, size (nm)	ϕ (%)	Improvement (%)
EG	CuO, 18.6	4	20
water	CuO, 18.6	4.3	10
GL	Cu_2O, 7.0	0.6	120
GL	Cu_2O, 150	0.6	60
EG	Cu, 10	0.2	40
PO	Cu, 35	0.06	45
water	Cu, 100	7.5	75
water	TiO_2, 15	4	33
water	TiO_2, 27	4.3	10.6
water	Al_2O_3, 60	5	20
EG	Al_2O_3, 60	5	30
PO	Al_2O_3, 60	5	40
water	Al_2O_3, 10	0.5	100
water	Al_2O_3, 20	1	16
oil	MWCNTs, 25	1.0	$\geqslant 250$
water	MWCNTs, 130	0.6	34

Table 2. Some significant results relating to the improvement of the thermal conductivity of nanofluids at RT. PO: pump oil; EG: ethylene glycol; GL: glycerol

3.2 Experimental results

Since the pioneering works of Choi, many experimental studies have been conducted on thermal nanofluids and have shown very large dispersion in the results. There is a profusion of very varied experimental results, sometimes contradictory, so it is very difficult for the novice and sometimes even for the specialist to identify a trend in the contribution of thermal nanofluids for heat transfer. We have gathered in Tab. 2 some of the the most significant results published to date on the improvement of the thermal conductivity of nanofluids containing metallic particles, oxides particles or CNTs. We can identify several trends and indications

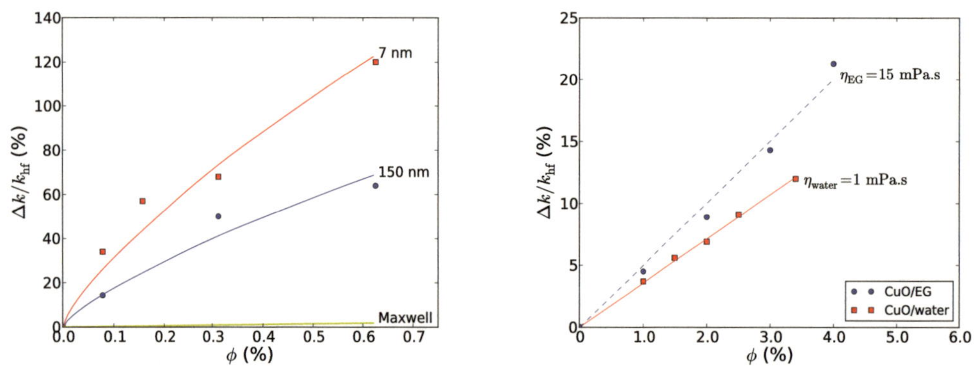

(a) Enhancement as a function of NPs size and volume fraction in the case of Cu_2O/glycerol nanofluid.

(b) Enhancement as a function of host fluid viscosity and volume fraction.

Fig. 4. Thermal conductivity enhancement of nanofluids at RT. k_{hf} is the thermal conductivity of the host fluid at RT.

from the preceding experimental results:

- For the same volume concentrations, the improvement of thermal conductivity $\Delta k/k_{hf}$ obtained with NPs suspensions is much higher than that obtained with equivalent suspensions of micro-particles. The classical laws such as Maxwell-Garnett or Hamilton-Crosser (Tab. 3) are no longer valid in the case of nanofluids (Fig. 4(a)).
- The size d of the nanoparticles has a moderate influence on the improvement of the thermal conductivity. The more the NPs are smaller, the more the increase is significant (Fig. 4(a), Tab. 2). This behavior is not predictable using the classical laws of table 3.
- The viscosity of the host fluid also appears to play a significant role that has not been sufficiently explored so far. As shown by the measurements taken at room temperature with Al_2O_3 in various liquids (water, EG and oil) and the measurements of figure 4(b) about CuO, the improvement of the thermal conductivity increases with the viscosity of the host fluid.
- The nature of the particles and host fluid also plays an important role. However it is very difficult to identify clear trends due to the various NPs surface treatments (surfactants, polymer coating, pH) used to stabilize the suspensions according to the different kinds of interactions NP/fluid and their chemical affinity. Thus we can assume that the surfactants and polymer coatings can significantly modify the heat transfer between the nanoparticles and the fluid.

3.3 Theoretical approaches

3.3.1 Classical macroscopic approach

As mentioned previously, the conventional models (Tab. 3) do not allow to describe the significant increase of the thermal conductivity observed with nanofluids, even at low volume fractions. These models are essentially based on solving the stationary heat equation $\nabla(k\nabla T) = 0$ in a macroscopic way. By using metallic particles or oxides, one may assume that $\alpha = k_p/k_{hf} \gg 1$ (large thermal contrast). Under these conditions, one can write from the (MG) mixing rule: $\phi_{MG} \approx 1/(1 + 3k_{hf}/\Delta k)$. In the case of copper nanoparticles suspended in pump oil at RT (Table 2), it was found that $\Delta k/k_{hf} = 0.45$ for $\phi_{exp} = 0.06\%$ while the corresponding value provided by (MG) is $\phi_{MG} \approx 13\%$, ie 200 times bigger. These results clearly show that the macroscopic approach is generally not suitable to explain the improvement of thermal conductivity of the thermal nanofluids.

3.3.2 Heat transfer mechanisms at nanoscale/new models

We now present the most interesting potential mechanisms allowing to explain the thermal behavior of nanofluids, which are: Brownian motion, ordered liquid layer at the interface between the fluid and the NP, agglomeration across the host fluid.

3.3.2.1 Influence of Brownian motion

The Brownian motion (BM) of the NPs, due to the collisions with host fluid molecules, is frequently mentioned as a possible mechanism for improving the thermal conductivity of nanofluids. There are at least two levels of interpretation:

1. BM induces collisions between particles, in favor of a thermal transfer of solid/solid type, better than that of the liquid/solid type (Keblinski et al., 2002). To discuss the validity of this assumption, we consider the time τ_D needed by a NP to travel a distance L into

Model	Law	Comments
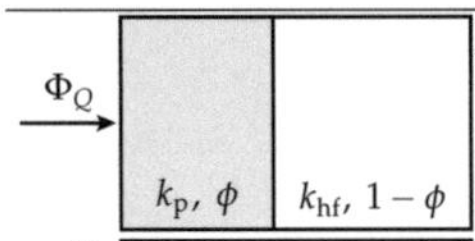	$\frac{1}{k} = \frac{\phi}{k_p} + \frac{1-\phi}{k_{hf}}$	*Series* model. No assumption on particles size and shape. The assembly of particles is considered as a continuous whole.
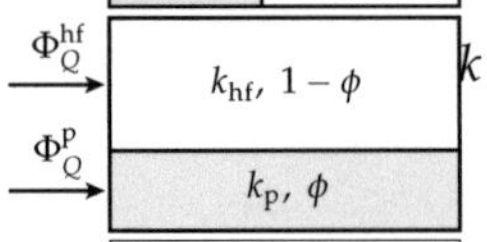	$k = \phi k_p + (1-\phi)k_{hf}$	*Parralel* model. Same comments as before.
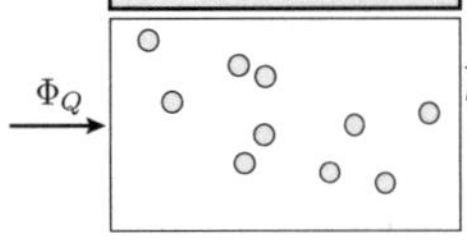	$\frac{k}{k_{hf}} = 1 + \frac{3(\alpha-1)\phi}{\alpha+2-(\alpha-1)\phi}$	*Maxwell-Garnett* mixing rule (MG) with $\alpha = k_p/k_{hf}$. Spherical, micron size noninteracting particles randomly dispersed in a continuous host matrix. Low volume fractions.
	$\phi\left(\frac{k_p-k}{k_p+2k}\right) + (1-\phi)\left(\frac{k_{hf}-k}{k_{hf}+2k}\right) = 0$	*Bruggeman* implicit model for a binary mixture of homogeneous spherical particles. No limitations on the concentration of inclusions. Randomly distributed particles
	$\frac{k}{k_{hf}} = \frac{\alpha+(n-1)+(n-1)(\alpha-1)\phi}{\alpha+(n-1)-(\alpha-1)\phi}$	*Hamilton-Crosser* model. Same hypotheses as Maxwell-Garnett, n is a form factor introduced to take into account non-spherical particles ($n = 6$ for cylindrical particles).

Table 3. Classical models used to describe the thermal conductivity k of micro-suspensions. k_p and k_{hf} are respectively the thermal conductivities of the particles and of the host fluid, ϕ is the volume fraction of particles and Φ_Q is the heat flux.

the fluid due to the Brownian motion. According to the equation of diffusion $\partial n/\partial t - \nabla(D\nabla n) = 0$, this time is of order of $\tau_D = L^2/D$, where $D = k_B T/6\pi\eta a_p$ is the diffusion coefficient for a spherical particle of radius a_p. Considering now the heat transfer time τ_L associated to heat diffusion in the liquid, we obtain from the heat transfer equation $\rho_f c_m \partial T/\partial t - \nabla(k_{hf}\nabla T) = 0$ in a liquid at rest: $\tau_L = L^2/\alpha = \rho_f c_m L^2/k_{hf}$. The ratio of τ_D/τ_L is given by:

$$\frac{\tau_D}{\tau_L} = \frac{3\pi k_{hf}\eta a_p}{\rho_f c_m k_B T} \tag{13}$$

For water at room temperature ($\eta = 10^{-3}$ Pa.s, $\rho_f = 10^3$ kg/m^3, $k_{hf} = 0.58$ W/m.K, $c_m = 4.18$ kJ/kg, $k_B = 1.38\ 10^{-23}$ J/K) and with $a_p = 5$ nm, Eq. (13) gives $\tau_D/\tau_L \approx 3000$. This result shows that the transport of heat by thermal diffusion in the liquid is much faster than Brownian diffusion, even within the limit of very small particles. Thus the collisions induced by BM cannot be considered as the main responsible for the significant increase in thermal conductivity of the nanofluids.

2. BM induces a flow of fluid around the nanoparticles, in favor of an additional heat transfer by Brownian forced micro-convection (Wang et al., 2002). To compare the efficiency of the forced convective heat transfer to the heat transfer by conduction, we express the Nusselt number Nu for a sphere as (White, 1991):

$$\text{Nu} = 2 + 0.3\text{Re}^{0.6}\text{Pr}^{1/3} = 2 + \Delta\text{Nu} \tag{14}$$

where $\mathrm{Re} = 2\rho_f v_{\mathrm{BM}} a_p/\eta$ is the Reynolds number of the flow around a spherical nanoparticle of radius a_p and $\mathrm{Pr} = \eta c_m/k_{\mathrm{hf}}$ is the Prandtl number of the host fluid. In the limiting case where there is no flow, $\Delta\mathrm{Nu} = 0$. Following Chon (Chon et al., 2005), the average Brownian speed of flow is expressed as $v_{\mathrm{BM}} = D/\overline{\ell}_{\mathrm{hf}}$ where $\overline{\ell}_{\mathrm{hf}}$ is the mean free path of the host fluid molecules and again $D = k_B T/6\pi\eta a_p$. If we suppose that the mean free path of water molecules in the liquid phase is of the order of $\overline{\ell}_{\mathrm{hf}} \approx 0.1$ nm at RT, we find $\Delta\mathrm{Nu} \approx 0.09$, which is negligible. Once again, the forced micro-convection induced by BM cannot be considered as the main responsible mechanism.

The preceding results show that the Brownian motion of nanoparticles can not be considered as the main responsible for the significant increase in thermal conductivity of the nanofluids.

3.3.2.2 Ordered liquid layer at the NP surface

In solids heat is mainly carried by phonons, which can be seen as sound waves quanta. The acoustic impedances of solids and liquids are generally very different, which means that the phonons mostly reflect at the solid/liquid interface and do not leave the NP. If some phonons initiated in a NP could be emitted in the liquid and remain long enough to reach another particle, this phonon mediated heat transport could allow to explain the increase of thermal conductivity observed for nanofluids. But unfortunately liquids are disordered and the phonon mean free path is much shorter in the liquid that in the solid. The only solution for a phonon to persist out of the NP is to consider an ordered interfacial layer in the liquid in which the atomic structure is significantly more ordered than in the bulk liquid (Henderson & van Swol, 1984; Yu et al., 2000).
We write the effective radius $a_p^{\mathrm{eff}} = a_p + e_{\mathrm{L}}$ of the NP (e_{L} is the width of the layer) as $a_p^{\mathrm{eff}} = \beta^{1/3} a_p$. The effective volume fraction of the NPs is then given by $\phi^{\mathrm{eff}} = \beta\phi$. Using the approximated MG expression introduced in Par. 3.3.1, we can write the new volume fraction ϕ'_{MG} needed to obtain an enhancement $\Delta k/k_{\mathrm{hf}}$ taking into account the ordered liquid layer as:

$$\phi'_{\mathrm{MG}} = \frac{1}{\beta}\frac{1}{1+3k_{\mathrm{hf}}/\Delta k} = \frac{\phi_{\mathrm{MG}}}{\beta} \tag{15}$$

If we suppose that $a_p^{\mathrm{eff}} = 2a_p$, which is a very optimistic value, we obtain $\beta = 8$. Thus, taking into account the liquid layer at the solid/liquid interface could permit in the best case to obtain an improvement of one order of magnitude, which is not sufficient to explain the whole increase of the thermal conductivity.

3.3.2.3 Influence of clusters

It has been reported in a benchmark study on the thermal conductivity of nanofluids (Buongiorno et al., 2009) that, the thermal conductivity enhancement afforded by the nanofluids increases with increasing particle loading, with particle aspect ratio and with decreasing basefluid thermal conductivity. This observations seem to be an indirect proof of the role of the aggregation and thus of ordered layer assisted thermal percolation in the mechanisms that could explain the thermal conductivity of nanofluids. As we have seen with glycerol based nanofluids, a large thermal conductivity enhancement (Fig. 4(a)) is accompanied by a sharp viscosity increases (Fig. 11(b)) even at low ($\phi < 1\%$) nanoparticle volume fractions, which may be indicative of aggregation effects. In addition, some authors (Putnam et al., 2006; Zhang et al., 2006) have demonstrated that nanofluids exhibiting good dispersion generally do not show any unusual enhancement of thermal conductivity.

By creating paths of low thermal resistance, clustering of particles into local percolating patterns may have a major effect on the effective thermal conductivity (Emami-Meibodi et al., 2010; Evans et al., 2008; Keblinski et al., 2002). Moreover if one takes into account the possibility of an ordered liquid layer in the immediate vicinity of the particle, it can allow a rapid and efficient transfer of thermal energy from one particle to another without any direct contact, avoiding thus large clusters and the settling. Thus the association of local clustering and ordered liquid layer can be the key factor to explain the dramatic enhancement of the thermal conductivity of the nanofluids.

3.4 Measurement methods

Over the years many techniques have been developed to measure the thermal conductivity of liquids. A number of these techniques are also used for the nanofluids. In Fig. 5 we have gathered a basic classification, adapted from Paul (Paul et al., 2010), of the main measurement techniques available today. There are mainly the transient methods and the steady-state methods. Compared to solids, measurement of the thermal properties of nanofluids poses

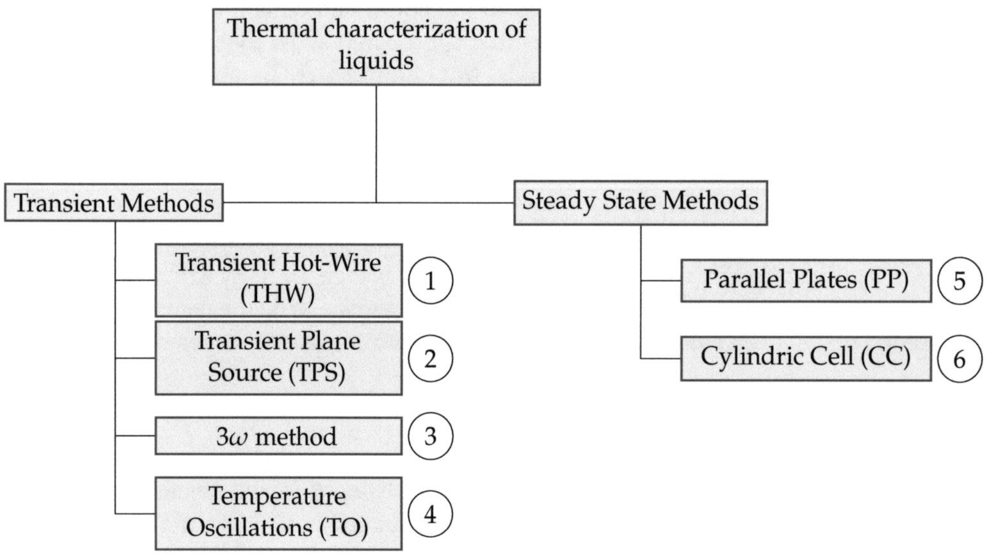

Fig. 5. Different thermal characterization techniques used for nanofluids. The numbers indicate the frequency of occurrence in publications.

many additional issues such as the occurrence of convection, occurrence of aggregates and sedimentation, etc. In the case of the THW method and 3ω method, which are commonly used and relatively easy to implement, conductive end effects are supplementary problems to take into account. To avoid the influence of convection, sedimentation and conductive end-effects on the measurements it is important that the time t_m taken to measure k is both small compared to the time t_{cv} of occurence of convection, compared to the time t_{se} of occurence of sedimentation and compared to the time t_{ce} of occurence of conductive end-effects influence. There are several solutions to ensure that $t_m \ll t_{cv}, t_{se}, t_{ce}$:

Convection will occur if the buoyant force resulting from the density gradient exceeds the viscous drag of the fluid, consequently the low viscosity fluids such as water are more prone to free convection than more viscous fluids such as oils or ethylen-glycol. To ensure that $t_m \ll t_{cv}$ it is preferable to:

- limit the rise $\delta T = T(M,t) - T_i$ in fluid temperature $T(M,t)$ due to thermal excitation at a low value $\delta T \ll T_i$ on the whole domain, with T_i the measurement temperature of the fluid. It should be noted that small increases in fluid temperature also limit the energy transfer by radiation.
- use the low viscosity fluids with either a thickener (such as sodium alginate or agar-agar for water) or a flow inhibitor such as glass fiber. These additions should be set to a minimum so as not to significantly change the thermal properties of the examined nanofluids. If the addition of thickeners, even at minimum values, considerably alters the thermal properties of a nanofluid, it could be very interesting to measure these properties in zero-gravity conditions.
- use the most suitable geometry to limit the influence of convection. In the case of plane geometry, it is preferable to heat the liquid by above rather than by below. In the case of heating by hot wire, vertical positioning is a better choice than horizontal.

Conductive end-effects due to electrical contacts are unavoidable but can be limited, when possible, by using a very long heating wire.

Sedimentation will occur if the suspension is not stable over the time. Settling causes a decrease in particle concentration and thermal conductivity. Under these conditions the measurement of the thermal conductivity of nanofluids is not feasible. It is recommended in this case to implement the remarks of paragraph 2.2.3.4.

3.5 THW and 3ω methods

3.5.1 Presentation

THW and 3ω methods are transient techniques that use the generation of heat in the fluid by means of the Joule heating produced in a thin metallic line put in thermal contact with the sample. One then measures the temporal variation $\delta T_w(t)$ of the temperature of the metallic line that results from the thermal excitation, via the variation of its electrical resistance $\delta R(t)$. The more the thermal conductivity of the surrounding liquid is high, the less the increase in temperature of the immersed heating wire is important. This principle is used to measure the thermal conductivity of the liquid to be characterized. Transient techniques have the following advantages:

- They are generally much faster (few minutes) than the quasi-static methods, thus allowing limiting the influence of convection on the measurements.
- They can allow to determine both the thermal conductivity k and specific heat c_m of the medium to be characterized.
- The heater is used both as the source of thermal excitation and as the thermometer, thereby eliminating the difficult problem of precise relative positioning of the sensor and the heat source.
- The informative signals are electric which greatly facilitates the design of the instrumentation, of its interface and allows easy extraction and automatic treatment of data.
- The ranges of thermal conductivity measurements can be significant: 0.01 W/mK to 100 W/mK.

Obviously these methods also have some inconveniences, however few in number:

- The ratio of the length L of the wire to its diameter d should preferably satisfy the relation $L/d \gg 1$ in order to minimize the errors due to the boundary effects of the electrical contacts and convection. This constraint is not easy to achieve when one must characterize very small samples.
- The sample to be characterized has to be an electrical insulator to ensure that electrical current $i(t)$ does not penetrate the fluid. In the case of electrical conducting liquids, it is possible to use metallic wires coated with a thin sheath made of teflon or kapton.

The theoretical basis of these two methods relies on the same theory of an infinite line heat source developed by Carslaw and Jaeger (Carslaw & Jaeger, 1959). We now present the assumptions of the ideal model of line heater. An infinitely long and infinitely thin line heat source, conductive of electric current, is immersed in an infinite medium at rest whose thermal conductivity has to be measured. The wire and the medium are assumed to be in perfect thermal contact and their physical properties are assumed to be constant. We suppose that the heat is applied in a continuous way between times $t = 0$ and t. With these assumptions, the temperature rise of the medium satisfies the following expression:

$$\delta T(r,t) = \frac{1}{4\pi k} \int_0^t \dot{q}(t') e^{-\frac{r^2}{4\alpha(t-t')}} \frac{\mathrm{d}t'}{t-t'} \tag{16}$$

where $\dot{q}$ is the heat rate per unit length (W/m), $\alpha = k/\rho c_m$ is the thermal diffusivity (m^2/s) of the medium and r is the distance from the line at which temperature is measured. A platinum wire is frequently used as the heat line because of its very low reactivity and high electrical conductivity.

3.5.2 Transient hot wire technique

3.5.2.1 Ideal model

At initial time $t = 0$, the wire is submitted to an abrupt electrical pulse that heats the medium by Joule effect. If we note $\hat{I}$ the constant amplitude of the current intensity flowing across the wire, the rate of heat per unit length can be written as $\dot{q} = R\hat{I}^2/L$ where L is the length of the wire in contact with the medium. Of course, the electrical resistance of a metallic wire is a function of temperature and can be writen as $R = R_{\text{ref}}\left[1 + \alpha_w(T - T_{\text{ref}})\right] = R(T_i) + \alpha_w R_{\text{ref}} \delta T$, where α_w is the temperature coefficient of the wire which is constant in a small range of variation around T_{ref} and T_i is the measurement temperature of the fluid far from the wire. If the amplitude of the electrical pulse is small enough to ensure that $\delta T \ll T_i$ then we can make the linear approximation that consists to write the heat rate per unit length as $\dot{q} = R(T_i)\hat{I}^2/L = \text{cst}$. According to (16) and by virtue of the temperature continuity across the surface $r = a$ between the wire and the medium, the temperature rise of the infinitely long heat line can be written as:

$$\delta T(t) = \frac{\dot{q}}{4\pi k} \int_0^t e^{-\frac{a^2}{4\alpha(t-t')}} \frac{\mathrm{d}t'}{t-t'} = -\frac{\dot{q}}{4\pi k} \mathrm{Ei}\left(-\frac{a^2}{4\alpha t}\right) \tag{17}$$

where Ei is the exponential integral, defined (Abramowitz & Stegun, 1970) for negative argument by:

$$-\mathrm{Ei}(-x) = \int_{x>0}^{\infty} \frac{e^{-t}}{t} \mathrm{d}t \tag{18}$$

where $x = a^2/4\alpha t$. In real situations, if the condition $L \gg a$ is satisfied, then the expression (17) gives the temperature of the whole wire with a very good approximation as long as convection and boundaries heat conductive losses can be neglected. For times verifying $t \gg t_\ell = a^2/4\alpha$, Eq. (17) can be approximated as:

$$\delta T(t) \approx \frac{\dot{q}}{4\pi k}\left(\ln\frac{t}{t_\ell} - \gamma\right) \tag{19}$$

in which $\gamma = 0.57722\ldots$ is Euler's constant. As we can see on Fig. 6(a), a semi-log graph of δT versus $\ln t$ or $\log t$ becomes a straight line (dashed line) for $t \gg t_\ell$, with a slope proportional to $\dot{q}/4\pi k$. The thermal conductivity can be computed from points 1 and 2 belonging to this straight line as:

$$k = \frac{\dot{q}}{4\pi}\frac{\ln t_2/t_1}{\delta T_2 - \delta T_1} \tag{20}$$

On the other hand, for any time $t \gg t_\ell$, points that deviate from the straight line in semi-log scale attest to the onset of the intrinsic limitations of the method such as convection and thermal conduction boundary effects due to the electrical contacts. View the brevity (few

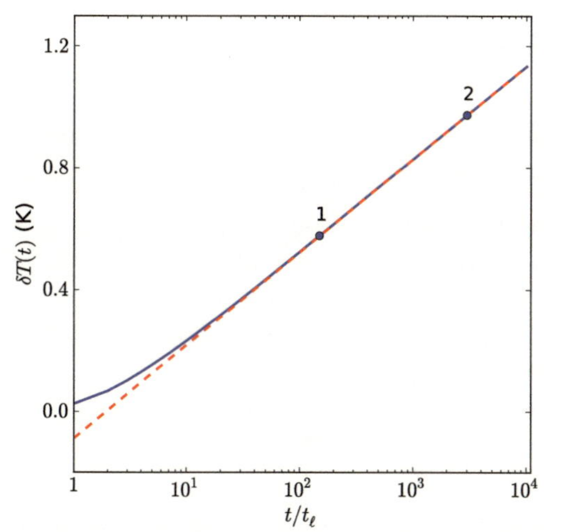

(a) Lin-log plot of δT versus t in the case of the ideal model.

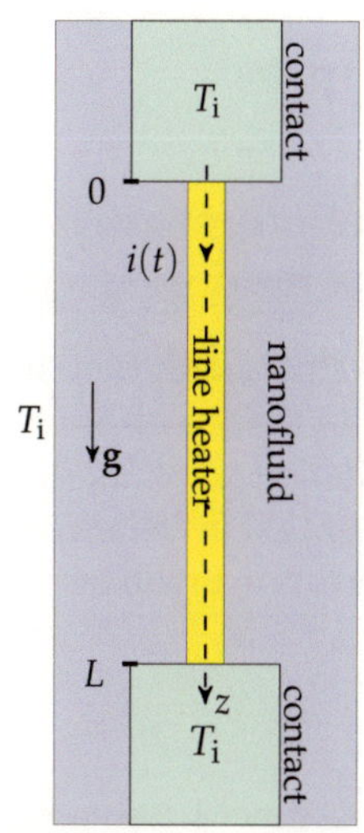

(b) Physical model used for the characterization of nanofluids.

Fig. 6. Exact variation (continuous line) of the temperature rise $\delta T(t)$ of the wire in the case of pure water with $\dot{q} = 1\mathrm{W/m}$, $a = 25\,\mu\mathrm{m}$ and using the THW technique. The amplitude of δT satisfies to the linear approximation.

seconds) of the measurements within the transient technique framework, it is important to quantify the effect of the condition $t \gg t_\ell$ on the accuracy of the method. We have gathered in Table 4 the values of t_ℓ for some common materials and a heater with a radius $a = 25\,\mu$m. In the case of water and glycerol, two liquids commonly used as a host fluids for nanoparticles, the relative error using the approximate expression (19) is less than 1% for measurement times greater than $100t_\ell \approx 0.2$ s.

Materials	Air	Water	Glycerol	Silicon	Platinum
$\alpha \times 10^5$ ($m^2.s^{-1}$)	1.99	1.41×10^{-2}	9.24×10^{-3}	8.94	2.51
t_ℓ (s)	7.8×10^{-6}	1.1×10^{-3}	1.7×10^{-3}	1.7×10^{-6}	6.2×10^{-6}

Table 4. Values of t_ℓ for some common materials at RT.

3.5.2.2 Measuring circuit

The measurement of the temperature rise δT of the wire is achieved through the accurate measurement of its small resistance variation δR. There are mainly two kinds of circuits, the one that uses the classic Wheatstone bridge (Fig. 7) and another that uses a voltage divider.

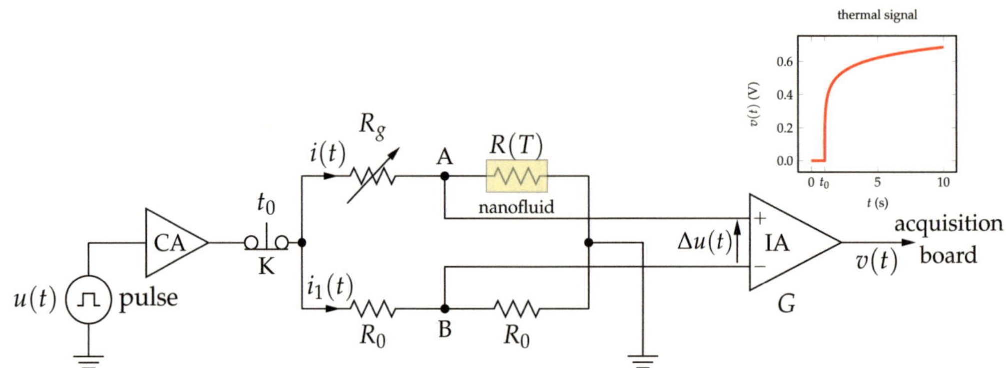

Fig. 7. THW circuit using a Wheatstone bridge.

The R_0 resistors are chosen such that $i_1 \ll i$. R_g and R_0 have a very low temperature coefficient compared to the one of $R(T)$. CA is a low distorsion current buffer (like LT1010) and IA is an instrumentation amplifier (like AD620 or INA126). For each measurement temperature T_i, the bridge must first be balanced by ensuring that $R_g = R(T_i)$. The voltage $v(t)$ delivered by IA is then a function of the temperature rise:

$$v(t) = \alpha_w \frac{G}{4} \frac{R_{\text{ref}}}{R(T_i)} u(t) \delta T(t) \tag{21}$$

At the initial time t_0, the switch K is closed, the current buffer CA imposes through the heating line an electric current of constant intensity $i(t) = \hat{I}$ and thus a constant heat rate per unit length $\dot{q} = R(T_i)\hat{I}^2/L$.

3.5.2.3 Influence of convection and electrical contacts

In practice, the main deviations from the law (19) are caused by natural convection and heat conduction at electrical contacts.

Influence of convection: the difference between the temperature of the wire and that of the fluid far from the wire generates a density gradient in the fluid. This density gradient is then the "engine" of a phenomenon of natural convection that takes place within the system. The convection redistributes the thermal energy in the vicinity of the wire in a quite complex manner. The overall impact of this redistribution is a cooling of the wire that results in an overestimated measure of the thermal conductivity of the fluid.

Influence of electrical contacts: the electrical contacts between the wire and the pulse generator act as heat sinks that cause further cooling of the wire, which also results in an overestimation of the thermal conductivity of the fluid.

As we can see, the convection and electrical contacts lead to an overestimation of the thermal conductivity that can be significant. These two phenomena are not independent and we have to calculate their influence as realistically as possible. To evaluate the effects of the convection and electrical contacts on the measures within the framework of the transient techniques, we have numerically solved the heat and Navier-Stokes equations of the system, mutually coupled by a term of natural convection.

We note $\mathbf{u}$ the eulerian velocity field of the fluid, η is the dynamic viscosity and the pressure P is written as $P = p + \rho_0 g z$. Using the Boussinesq approximation and considering that the fluid is newtonian, the Navier-Stokes equation (NS) is written as:

$$(\text{NS}) \; : \; \rho_0 \frac{\partial \mathbf{u}}{\partial t} + \rho_0 \mathbf{u} \cdot \nabla \mathbf{u} = -\nabla p + \eta \nabla^2 \mathbf{u} - \beta \rho_0 \mathbf{g}\, \delta T \tag{22}$$

where β is the coefficient of thermal expansion of the fluid, related to its density variation $\delta\rho$ by the relation $\delta\rho = -\beta\rho_0\delta T$ and $\rho_0 = \rho(T_i)$ is the density of the fluid in absence of themal excitation. The heat equation (HE) for a flowing fluid without a source term is written as:

$$(\text{HE}) \; : \; \rho_0 c_m \frac{\partial T}{\partial t} - k\nabla^2 T = -\rho_0 c_m \, \mathbf{u} \cdot \nabla T \tag{23}$$

Finally it remains to express the material balance (MB) for an incompressible fluid:

$$(\text{MB}) \; : \; \nabla \cdot \mathbf{u} = 0 \tag{24}$$

Denoting $\partial\Omega$ the frontier delimiting the fluid, the set of boundary conditions that accompanies the system of differential equations (NS, HE, MB) satisfied by the fluid is as follows:

$$T = T_i \text{ and } \mathbf{u} = \mathbf{0} \tag{25}$$

exept at the wire interface where the temperature and heat flux are continuous.

There is no exact solution of this system of coupled equations with the set of boundary conditions (25). To our knowledge, the numerical resolution of this system has not yet been explored in order to clarify the influence of the convection and thermal contacts on the accuracy of the measurements in the case of the transient methods. Knibbe is the only one to have explored a similar set of equations for the same purpose but assuming an infinite wire and a decoupling between the thermal conduction and convection (Knibbe, 1986). We note δT_{id}, δT_{ec} and δT_{tot} the variations of the wire temperature respectively in the ideal case of an infinite wire without convection given by (19), due to the electrical contacts only and due both to the convection and to the electrical contacts. As shown on Figure 8, the influence of electrical contacts is independent of temperature while the influence of convection increases with temperature. One can eventually limit these influences using long wires, however long wires require high volume samples which is not always possible.

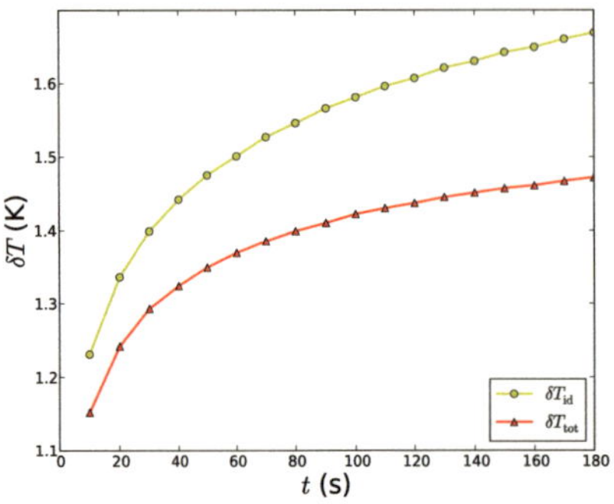

(a) Measurement temperature $T_i = 293$ K. The Influence of convection is totally negligible, $\delta T_{\text{id}} > \delta T_{\text{tot}} = \delta T_{\text{ec}}$.

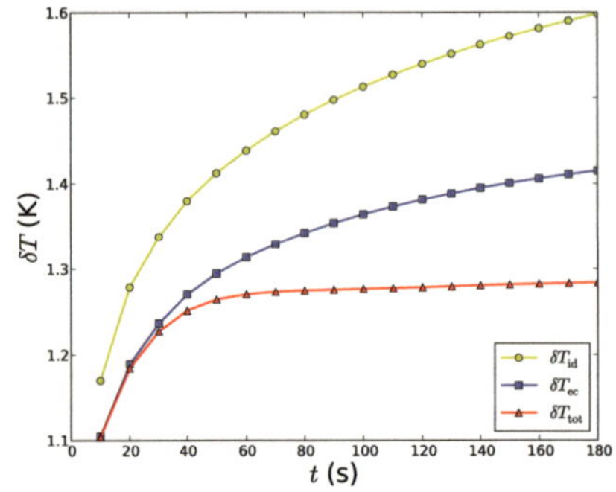

(b) Measurement temperature $T_i = 373$ K. The Influence of convection is not negligible, $\delta T_{\text{id}} > \delta T_{\text{tot}}$.

Fig. 8. Influence of the convection and electrical contacts on the temperature variation of a thin platinum wire immersed in glycerol within the framework of transient hot wire method.

3.5.3 3ω technique

3.5.3.1 Presentation

The 3ω technique, introduced for the first time by Cahill, has been widely used for the characterization of dielectric thin films (Cahill, 1990; Franck et al., 1993; Moon et al., 1996). The adaptation of the method for liquids is relatively recent (Chen et al., 2004; Heyd et al., 2008; Oh et al., 2008; S. R. Choi & Kim, 2008) but its use is increasingly common (Paul et al., 2010) in a variety of applications ranging from anemometry (Heyd et al., 2010) to thermal microscopy (Chirtoc & Henry, 2008).

This method uses the same basic principle as the THW technique but replaces the constant current i through the heater by a sinusoidally varying current $i(t) = \hat{I}\cos\omega t$ where $\omega = 2\pi\nu$. The heat rate per unit length dissipated by Joule effect in the line is written this time as $\dot{q}(t) = \dot{q}_{\max}(1+\cos 2\omega t)/2$. This heat rate generates in the wire a temperature oscillation $\delta T(t)$ that contains a 2ω component $\delta T_{2\omega}(t) = \delta\hat{T}^0_{2\omega}(\nu)\cos 2\omega t + \delta\hat{T}^q_{2\omega}(\nu)\sin 2\omega t$. Since the resistance of the wire is a known function of temperature, the voltage drop $u(t) = R(t)i(t)$ across the wire contains a 3ω component that can be written as $u_{3\omega}(t) = \hat{U}^0_{3\omega}(\nu)\cos 3\omega t + \hat{U}^q_{3\omega}(\nu)\sin 3\omega t$. With the same experimental design as in the case of the transient method, one can use an appropriate synchronous detection to detect the quadrature components of $u_{3\omega}(t)$ and derive then the thermal conductivity k and specific heat c_m of the fluid.

To go further into the analysis, we must express the temperature variation $\delta T(t)$ of the line heater by using the fundamental expression (16), but this time with $\dot{q}(t) = \dot{q}_{\max}(1+\cos 2\omega t)/2$, where $\dot{q}_{\max} = R(T_i)\hat{I}^2/L$:

$$\begin{aligned}\delta T(t) &= \frac{\dot{q}_{\max}}{8\pi k}\int_0^t \left(1+\cos 2\omega t'\right) e^{-\frac{a^2}{4\alpha(t-t')}}\frac{dt'}{t-t'} \\ &= \delta T_{\text{DC}}(t) + \delta T_{2\omega}(t)\end{aligned} \quad (26)$$

The $\delta T_{\text{DC}}(t)$ term corresponds to the transient method, (Par. 3.5.2.1) and will not be discussed here. Furthermore the synchronous detection allows to detect the electrical signals induced

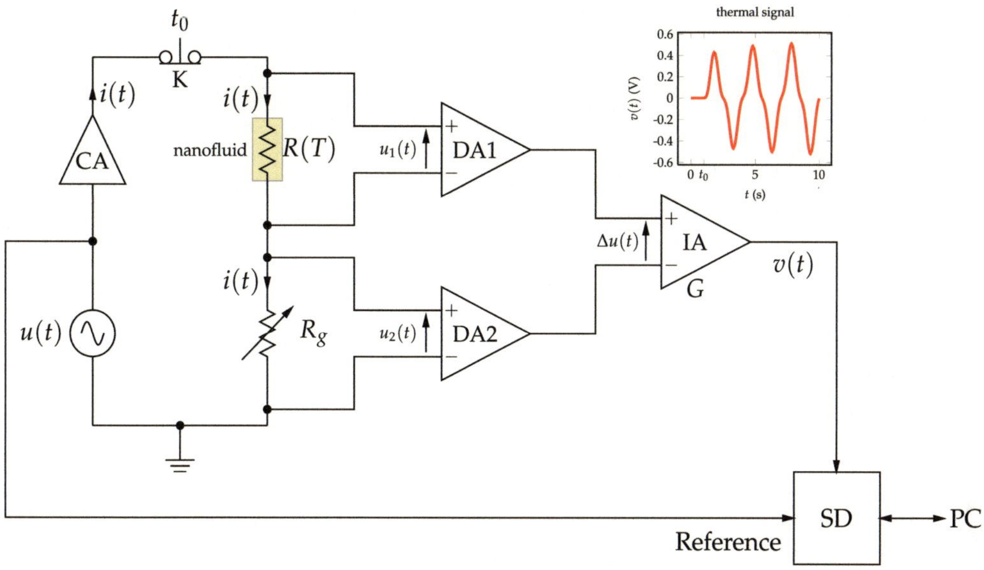

Fig. 9. 3ω circuit using a voltage divider and a dual phase DSP lock-in amplifier (SD) like model 7265 from Signal Recovery.

by $\delta T_{2\omega}(t)$ insensitive to the influence of $\delta T_{\mathrm{DC}}(t)$. Using the $t \gg t_\ell$ usual approximation and introducing $\Lambda = \sqrt{\alpha/2\omega}$ the thermal length of the fluid, it can be shown (Hadaoui, 2010) that:

$$\begin{aligned} \delta T_{2\omega}(t) &= \frac{\dot{q}_{\max}}{4\pi k} \Re\left[\mathrm{K}_0\left(\frac{a}{\Lambda}\mathrm{i}^{\frac{1}{2}}\right)\right]\cos 2\omega t - \frac{\dot{q}_{\max}}{4\pi k} \Im\left[\mathrm{K}_0\left(\frac{a}{\Lambda}\mathrm{i}^{\frac{1}{2}}\right)\right]\sin 2\omega t \\ &= \delta\hat{T}^{0}_{2\omega}\cos 2\omega t + \delta\hat{T}^{\mathrm{q}}_{2\omega}\sin 2\omega t \end{aligned} \tag{27}$$

where $\Re$ and $\Im$ denote respectively the real and the imaginary part and K_0 is the modified Bessel function. The formatting (27) is not easy to use to analyze experimental datas. Using the following approximation:

$$\lim_{x\to 0} \mathrm{K}_0\left(x\,\mathrm{i}^{\frac{1}{2}}\right) = \ln 2 - \gamma - \mathrm{i}\frac{\pi}{4} - \ln x \tag{28}$$

it is possible to propose more suitable expressions of $\delta\hat{T}^{0}_{2\omega}$ and $\delta\hat{T}^{\mathrm{q}}_{2\omega}$ as long as $\Lambda \gg a$:

$$\delta\hat{T}^{0}_{2\omega} = \frac{\dot{q}_{\max}}{4\pi k}\left(\frac{1}{2}\ln\frac{2\alpha}{a^2} - \gamma - \frac{1}{2}\ln\omega\right) \tag{29}$$

$$\delta\hat{T}^{\mathrm{q}}_{2\omega} = \frac{\dot{q}_{\max}}{16k} \tag{30}$$

To check the accuracy of the approximate expressions (29) and (30), we have gathered in Table 5 the values of Λ at room temperature for some common materials and excitation frequencies. As we can see in this Table, in the case of most of the liquids (here water and glycerol) it is not possible to use (29) and (30) for excitation frequencies greater than 1 Hz. This is the main limitation of this technique for the thermal characterization of nanofluids because on the one hand low excitation frequencies require very stable external conditions and on the other hand the measurements take a long time, allowing to the convection and to losses due to electrical contacts to occur.

materials	water	air	glycerol	silicon	platinum
$\nu_0 = 10^{-1}$ Hz, $\Lambda =$	335	3981	271	8433	4469
$\nu_0 = 10^{0}$ Hz, $\Lambda =$	106	1259	86	2667	1413
$\nu_0 = 10^{1}$ Hz, $\Lambda =$	33	398	27	843	447
$\nu_0 = 10^{2}$ Hz, $\Lambda =$	10,6	126	8,6	267	141

Table 5. Values of the thermal length Λ (in μm) at RT for some common materials and usual excitation frequencies.

3.5.3.2 Measurements

As in the case of the Wheatstone bridge configuration, the voltage divider (Fig. 9) must be first balanced for each measurement temperature T_i by ensuring that $R_g = R(T_i)$. The use of two differential amplifiers DA1 and DA2 (AMP03 like) allows to extract the informative signal. This signal $\Delta u(t)$ is a function of the temperature change $\delta T(t)$ of the line that is induced by Joule self-heating and heat exchanges with the fluid. As in the case of the transient technique, the amplitude of $\Delta u(t)$ is very small and needs to be amplified by a factor $G \approx 1000$ using an instrumentation amplifier (IA). The signal delivered by the amplifier includes a 3ω component that can be written as $v_{3\omega}(t) = Gu_{3\omega}(t)$. Using relations (29) and (30), the amplitudes X (in phase) and Y (in quadrature) of the tension $v_{3\omega}(t)$ can be written as:

$$X(\omega) = \frac{\alpha_w R_{\text{ref}} R(T_i) G \hat{I}^3}{8\pi k L} \left(\frac{1}{2} \ln \frac{2\alpha}{a^2} - \gamma - \frac{1}{2} \ln \omega \right) \tag{31}$$

$$Y(\omega) = \frac{\alpha_w R_{\text{ref}} R(T_i) G \hat{I}^3}{32 k L} = \text{cst} \tag{32}$$

As we can see from the relation (31), the amplitude $X(\omega)$ varies linearly with $\ln \omega$ and its theoretical graph is a straight line in a semi-log scale, with a slope $p_X = -\alpha_w R_{\text{ref}} R(T_i) G \hat{I}^3 / 16\pi k L$. Once the physical properties of the experimental setup are precisely known, this expression allows for a very precise determination of the thermal conductivity k by a frequency sweep of the exciting current $i(t)$ and measurements with a lock-in amplifier. As an example we have represented Fig. 10 the measurements obtained for pure glycerol at $T_i = 298$ K. The value of the slope is $p_X = -0.0698$ which leads to a value of the thermal conductivity of the glycerol at RT: $k = 0.289$ W/mK.

3.5.4 Comparison of the two techniques

Both techniques are very similar because they are both derived from the hot wire method and have the same temporal and spatial limitations. The THW method has the advantage of being very fast but requires an important excitation $\delta T(t)$ which can cause significant errors primarily due to non-linearities and to influence of convection and electrical contacts.
In the case of liquids, the 3ω method requires measurement times significantly longer than those of the THW method. This can promote the influence of convection and electrical contacts. However the use of a very sensitive dual-phase synchronous detection allows for low-amplitude excitations within the 3ω framework, thus reducing the influence of non-linearities and spatial limitations.

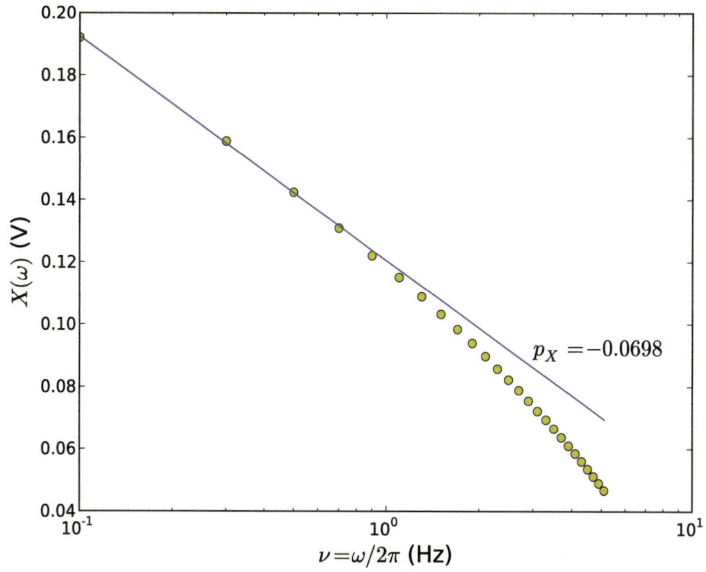

Fig. 10. Measurement of the thermal conductivity of pure glycerol at RT by the 3ω method. Experimental values: $R(T_i) = 1.430\,\Omega$, $R_{\text{ref}} = 1.403\,\Omega$, $G = 993$, $L = 2.5$ cm, $\alpha_w = 3.92 \times 10^{-3}\,\text{K}^{-1}$ and $\hat{I} = 148$ mA.

4. Some basic rheological properties of nanofluids

4.1 Presentation

The viscosity is probably as critical as thermal conductivity in engineering systems that use fluid flow (pumps, engines, turbines, etc.). A viscous flow dissipates mechanic power which volumic density is directly proportionnal to the dynamic viscosity η of the fluid in the case of the laminar flow of a newtonian liquid.

As we have seen, the increase in thermal conductivity of nanofluids reaches values still incompletely explained, it is the same for the viscosity of these suspensions. The rheology of the nanofluids has given rise to much less research than the thermal behavior, and until now, the analysis of rheological properties of the nanofluids remains superficial. The predominance of the surface effects and the influence of aggregation are certainly the two major elements that distinguish a conventional suspension from a nanofluid, both from a thermal point of view than rheological.

4.2 Experimental results

Viscosity measurements concerning nanofluids generally do not obey directly to the classical models (Tab. 6) used to describe the behavior of the micro suspensions viscosity. Although the measures differ much from one study to another, as shwon on figure 11 common facts emerge and should guide future research:

- The size of NPs, that does not appear in the classical models, has an unpredicted influence on the viscosity of nanofluids. The shape of nanoparticles is another factor that may influence the rheology of the host liquid. Thus in most situations, spherical nanoparticles do not change the nature of a Newtonian fluid such as water or glycerol. In contrast the CNTs can dramatically change the nature of the liquid.

- The nature of the host liquid has a great influence on the law of variation of the relative viscosity $\eta_r = \eta/\eta_0$, where η is the dynamic viscosity of the nanofluid and η_0 is the dynamic viscosity of the host fluid taken at the same temperature. For a given host liquide, the nature of nanoparticles with the same shape and with same size has very low influence on the dynamic viscosity of the suspension.

Model	Expression	Comments
Einstein	$\eta_r = 1 + [\eta]\phi + O[\phi^2]$	Effective medium theory for spherical particles and dilute non-interacting suspensions ($\phi < 10\%$). The intrincic viscosity $[\eta]$ has a typical value of 2.5
Brinkman	$\eta_r = \frac{1}{(1-\phi^{2.5})}$	Modified Einstein's equation to a more generalised form. (Brinkman, 1952)
Mooney	$\eta_r = \exp\left(\frac{\xi\phi}{1-k\phi}\right)$	Higher concentrations interacting spherical suspensions. k is a constant called the self-crowding factor ($1.35 < k < 1.91$), and ξ is a fitting parameter chosen to agree with Einstein's value of 2.5. (Mooney, 1951)
Krieger-Dougherty	$\eta_r = \left(1 - \frac{\phi}{\phi_m}\right)^{-[\eta]\phi_m}$	Interactions between neighboring spherical particles are taken into account. ϕ_m is the maximum particle packing fraction and $[\eta] = 2.5$ for spherical particles. (Krieger & Dougherty, 1959)
Batchelor	$\eta_r = 1 + 2.5\phi + 6.2\phi^2$	Spherical particles and semi-dilute suspensions, interaction of pair-particles are considered. (Batchelor & Green, 1972)

Table 6. Some classical models commonly used for viscosity of micro dispersions as a function of the volume fraction ϕ of solid particles. The relative viscosity is defined by $\eta_r = \eta/\eta_0$, where η_0 and η are the dynamic viscosities respectively of the base liquid and of the suspension.

Dynamic Light Scattering (DLS) and cryo-TEM measurements in general show that nanoparticles agglomerate (He et al., 2007; Kwak & Kim, 2005) in the liquid, forming micro-structures that can alter the effective volume fraction of the solid phase. This can be the main reason for the big difference between the viscosity behaviour of micro-suspensions and that of nano-suspensions. These observations suggest that, due to formation of micro-aggregates of nanoparticles, the effective volume fraction ϕ_{eff} of nanofluids can be much higher than the actual solid volume fraction ϕ, which leads to a higher viscosity increase of nanofluids. Using an effective volume fraction that is higher than the initial solid fraction is a way to reconciliate observed results with those predicted by classical models. To justify that the aggregation of nanoparticles leads to an effective volume fraction higher than the initial fraction, some authors Chen et al. (2009) have introduced the fractal geometry to predict this increase in volume fraction. According to the fractal theory, the effective particle volume fraction is given by:

$$\phi_{\text{eff}} = \phi \left(\frac{d_{\text{eff}}}{d}\right)^{3-D} \tag{33}$$

d and d_{eff} are respectively the diameters of primary nanoparticles and aggregates, D is the fractal index having typical values ranging from 1.6 to 2.5 for aggregates of spherical nanoparticles.

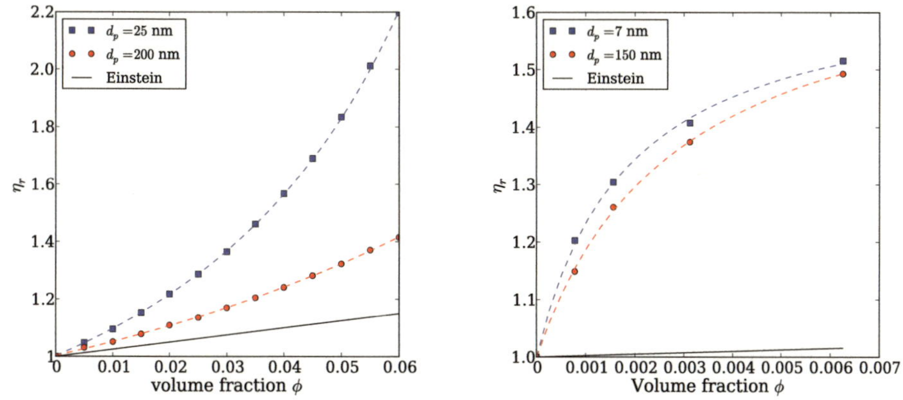

(a) Water-based nanofluids, adapted from (Corcione, 2011).

(b) Glycerol-based nanofluid, adapted from (Hadaoui, 2010).

Fig. 11. Evolution of viscosity as a function of ϕ and NPs diameter d_p.

Using a modified Krieger-Dougherty model where ϕ is replaced by ϕ_{eff} given by (33), it is possible to correctly describe measurements corresponding to a lot of different water-based nanofluids, as shown by dashed lines on Fig. 11(a). The same remark holds for glycerol-based nanofluids but using this time a modified Mooney model where ϕ has been replaced by ϕ_{eff} (dashed lines on Fig. 11(b)).
It is also very interesting to study the evolution of viscosity as a function of temperature. In the case of glycerol-based nanofluids containing spherical copper oxides NPs, we have found (Fig. 12) that the variation of the viscosity vs temperature always obeys a generalized Arrhenius law, regardless of the size and volume fraction of the NPs:

$$\eta = A \exp \frac{B}{T - T_0} \tag{34}$$

As shown on Fig. 12(a) and Tab. 12(b), the dependence of the viscosity with temperature is mainly due to the host fluid. This is reasonable because, as one might expect the loss of viscous fluid by friction on the NPs depends few on temperature, even if the fractal geometry of the micro-aggregates is certainly a function of temperature.

4.3 Perspectives

As we can see, the inclusion of nanoparticles in the host liquid can greatly increase the viscosity even at low volume fractions (<1%). This increase may be a serious obstacle for many applications. In the field of lubrication, for example, an increased viscosity is an advantage for transmission of normal stresses but it is a disadvantage with regard to the friction forces that dissipate more energy within the liquid thereby increasing its temperature.

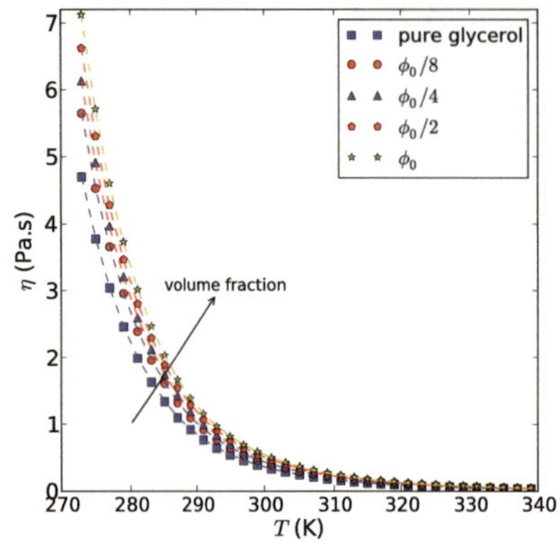

(a) Evolution of Glycerol-based nanofluids dynamic viscosity with temperature and volume fraction. $\phi_0 = 0.625\%$.

ϕ	A (10^{-7} Pa.s)	B (K)	T_0 (K)
0	4.4	4.10	130
$\phi_0/8$	5.5	4.06	131
$\phi_0/4$	5.7	4.08	131
$\phi_0/2$	6.1	4.09	131
ϕ_0	6.5	4.10	130

(b) Evolution of Arrhenius law coefficients as a function of NPs volume fraction.

Fig. 12. The variation ot the viscosity as a function of temperature T follows an Arrhenius law regardless of the NPs volume fraction.

In the biomedical field, functionalized nanoparticles are used or intended for use as contrast agents for medical imaging or (and) grafted with therapeutic molecules used to kill cancer cells in a targeted manner (therapeutic nanocarriers). The hydrodynamic radius of these functionalized NP is often on average equal to almost 100 nm, a value very close to those of aggregates encountered with nanofluids. It is therefore very probable that the results we have outlined above are relevant to predict the rheological behavior of blood products containing nanoparticles functionalized. To our knowledge there are no or very few studies that address the biophysical impact of functionalized NPs on the transport properties of human blood. This study is certainly critical to patient safety and should be considered both as a theoretical point of view using for example molecular dynamics simulations and as an experimental point of view through for example the use of the microfluidic devices available today.

5. Conclusion

The applications of nanofluids are numerous and very promising especially in the area of the transport of thermal energy. The wide dispersion of experimental results and numerical models available show that much remains to be done to identify clear trends and reliable models to describe the heat transfer at the scale of the nanoparticle. Even if the the role of the aggregation and secondarily the role of the ordered interfacial molecular layer seem preponderant in many situations, there is currently no comprehensive model allowing to predict the thermal behavior of all nanofluids. The lack of knowledge about the influence of surface treatment (the use of a polymer coating, the use of surfactants, the grafting of ions) on the heat transfer at the nanoparticle scale is certainly a major reason (by introducing unknown thermal interfacial resistances) of the dispersion of results and numerical models proposed until now. Systematic comparative studies and use of molecular dynamic simulations for transport coefficients modeling and Monte-Carlo simulations for aggregation modeling and control should allow progress on this subject.

If the thermal conductivity is an important quantity for predicting heat transfer and as such has been widely studied, other physical properties and phenomena deserve further investigations like: the viscosity η, the heat transfer coefficient h, the specific heat c_m, nanocomposites changes of state, etc.
On the other hand the concerns of preservation of the nature should be considered more systematically, both at the level of green synthesis of nanoparticles than in terms of their composition. The multifunctional core-shell nanoparticles like SiO_2@M (where M is a metal) partially meet the previous requirements. They have already been studied for medical imaging and should also be considered for the transport of heat.

6. References

Abramowitz, M. & Stegun, I. A. (eds) (1970). *Handbook of Mathematical Functions, with Formulas, Graphs, And Mathematical Tables*, ninth edn, Dover.

Batchelor, G. K. & Green, J. T. (1972). The determination of the bulk stress in a suspension of spherical particles to order c^2, *Journal Fluid Mechanics* 56: 401–427.

Benoit, R., Warmont, F., Meynen, V., Witte, K. D., Cool, P., Delapierre, M. P. & Saboungi, M.-L. (2009). Optimisation of the surface properties of sba-15 mesoporous silica for in-situ nanoparticle synthesis, *Microporous and Mesoporous Materials* 120: 2–6.

Brinkman, H. (1952). The viscosity of concentrated suspensions and solutions, *Journal of Chemical Physics* 20: 571–581.

Buongiorno, J., Venerus, D. C., Prabhat, N., McKrell, T. & Townsend, J. (2009). A benchmark study on the thermal conductivity of nanofluids, *Journal of Applied Physics* 106: 14.

Cahill, D. (1990). Thermal conductivity measurement from 30 to 750 K: the 3ω method, *Rev. Sci. Instrum.* 61: 802.

Carslaw, H. & Jaeger, J. (1959). *Conduction of Heat in Solids*, second edition.

Casquillas, G. V. (2008). *Contrôle de température et étude des transferts thermiques dans des dispositifs microfluidiques*, PhD thesis, Orsay Sciences Faculty, Paris.

Chen, F., Shulman, J., Xue, Y., Chu, C. W. & Nolas, G. S. (2004). Thermal conductivity measurement under hydrostatic pressure using the 3ω method, *Rev. Sci. Instrum.* 75: 4578.

Chen, H., Witharana, S., Jin, Y., Kim, C. & Ding, Y. (2009). Predicting thermal conductivity of liquid suspensions of nanoparticles (nanofluids) based on rheology, *Particuology* 7: 151–157.

Chen, Y., Peng, D., Lin, D. & Luo, X. (2007). Preparation and magnetic properties of nickel nanoparticles via the thermal decomposition of nickel organometallic precursor in alkylamines, *Nanotechnology* 18.

Chirtoc, M. & Henry, J. (2008). 3ω hot wire method for micro-heat transfer measurements: From anemometry to scanning thermal microscopy (sthm), *Eur. Phys. J. Special Topics* 153: 343.

Choi, S., Zhang, Z., Yu, W., Lockwood, F. & Grulke, E. (2001). Anomalous thermal conductivity enhancement in nanotube suspensions, *Applied Physics Letters* 79: 2252–2254.

Choi, U. (1995). Enhancing thermal conductivity of fluids with nanoparticles, *Technical Report FED, vol 231*, ASME, New-York.

Chon, C. H., Kihm, K. D., Lee, S. P. & Choi, S. U. S. (2005). Empirical correlation finding the role of temperature and particle size for nanofluid (Al_2O_3) thermal conductivity enhancement, *Applied Physics Letters* p. 153107.

Corcione, M. (2011). Empirical correlating equations for predicting the effective thermal conductivity and dynamic viscosity of nanofluids, *Energy Conversion and Management* 52: 789–793.

Darroudi, M., Ahmad, M., Abdullah, A., Ibrahim, N. & Shameli, K. (2010). Effect of accelerator in green synthesis of silver nanoparticles, *Int. J. Mol. Sci.* 11: 3898–3905.

Daungthongsuk, W. & Wongwises, S. (2007). A critical review of convective heat transfer of nanofluids, *Renewable and Sustainable Energy Reviews* pp. 797–817.

Eastman, J. A., Choi, S. U. S., Li, S., Yu, W. & Thompson, L. J. (2001). Anomalously increased effective thermal conductivities of ethylene glycol-based nanofluids containing copper nanoparticles, *Applied Physics Letters* 78: 718–720.

Emami-Meibodi, M., Vafaie-Sefti, M., Rashidi, A. M., Amrollahi, A., Tabasi, M. & Sid-Kalal, H. (2010). A model for thermal conductivity of nanofluids, *Materials Chemistry and Physics* 123: 639–643.

Evans, W., Prasher, R., Fish, J., Meakin, P., Phelan, P. & Keblinski, P. (2008). Effect of aggregation and interfacial thermal resistance on thermal conductivity of nanocomposites and colloidal nanofluids, *International Journal of Heat and Mass Transfer* 51: 1431–1438.

Franck, R., Drach, D. & Fricke, J. (1993). Determination of thermal conductivity and specific heat by a combined 3ω/decay technique, *Rev. Sci. Instrum.* 64: 760.

Govindaraj, A. & Rao, C. N. R. (2002). Organometallic precursor route to carbon nanotubes, *Pure Appl. Chem.* 74: 1571–1580.

Hadaoui, A. (2010). *Effects of size and concentration on the thermal and rheological properties of nanofluids*, PhD thesis, Orléans University - France.

Hadaoui, A., Heyd, R., Saboungi, M., Meducin, F., Warmont, F., Aeziane, E., Flyiou, M. & Koumina, A. (2009). Des polymères organiques pour la synthèse de nanoparticules métalliques, *Les VI ièmes Journées sur les Polymères Organiques et leurs Applications (JPOA VI)*, Université Ibn Tofail.

He, Y. R., Jin, Y., Chen, H., Ding, Y., Cang, D. & Lu, H. L. (2007). Heat rransfer and flow behaviour of aqueous suspensions of TiO_2 nanoparticles (nanofluids) flowing upward through a vertical pipe, *International Journal of Heat and Mass Transfer* 50: 2272–2281.

Henderson, J. & van Swol, F. (1984). On the interface between a fluid and a planar wall: theory and simulations of a hard sphere fluid at a hard wall, *Mol. Phys.* 51: 991–1010.

Heyd, R., Hadaoui, A., Ameziane, E., Saboungi, M., Guillot, S. & Milosevic, I. (2008). Thermal properties of biocompatible ferrofluids by the 3ω method, *MSNOW 2008 International Workshop*, Nancy.

Heyd, R., Hadaoui, A., Fliyou, M., Koumina, A., Ameziane, L. E., Outzourhit, A. & Saboungi, M. (2010). Development of absolute hot-wire anemometry by the 3ω method, *Rev. Sci. Instrum.* 81: 044901.

Iijima, S. (1991). Helical microtubules of graphitic carbon, *Nature* p. 354:56.

Keblinski, P., Phillpot, S., Choi, S. & Eastman, J. (2002). Mechanisms of heat flow in suspensions of nano-sized particles(nanofluids), *International Journal of Heat and Mass Transfer* 45: 855–863.

Knibbe, P. (1986). The end-effect error in the determination of thermal conductivity using a hot-wire apparatus, *Int. J. Heat Mass Transfer* 29: 463–473.

Krieger, I. M. & Dougherty, T. J. (1959). A mechanism for non-newtonian flow in suspensions of rigid spheres, *Transactions of The Society of Rheology* 3: 137–152.

Kwak, K. & Kim, C. (2005). Viscosity and thermal conductivity of copper oxide nanofluid dispersed in ethylene glycol, *Korea-Australia Rheology Journal* 17: 35–40.

Liu, X., Geng, B., Du, Q., Ma, J. & Liu, X. (2007). Temperature-controlled self-assembled synthesis of CuO, Cu_2O and Cu nanoparticles through a single-precursor route, *Materials Science and Engineering A* 448: 7–14.

Masliyah, J. & Bhattarjee, S. (2006). *Electrokinetic and colloid transport phenomena*, John Wiley and Sons.

Moon, I., Jeong, Y. & Kwun, S. (1996). The 3ω technique for measuring dynamic specific heat and thermal conductivity of a liquid or solid, *Rev. Sci. Instrum.* 67: 29.

Mooney, M. (1951). The viscosity of a concentrated suspension of spherical particles, *Journal of Colloid Science* 6: 162–170.

Oh, D., Jain, A., Eaton, J. K., Goodson, K. E. & Lee, J. S. (2008). Thermal conductivity measurement and sedimentation detection of aluminum oxide nanofluids by using the 3ω method, *International Journal of Heat and Fluid Flow* 29: 1456.

Paul, G., Chopkar, M., Manna, I. & Das, P. (2010). Techniques for measuring the thermal conductivity of nanofluids: A review, *Renewable and Sustainable Energy Reviews* 14: 1913–1924.

Putnam, S. A., Cahill, D. G. & Braun, P. V. (2006). Thermal conductivity of nanoparticle suspensions, *Journal of Applied Physics* 99: 084308–1–084308–6.

Ramnani, S., Biswal, J. & Sabharwal, S. (2007). Synthesis of silver nanoparticles supported on silica aerogel using gamma radiolysis, *Radiation Physics and Chemistry* 76: 1290–1294.

Roca, A. G., Morales, M. P. & Serna, C. J. (2006). Synthesis of monodispersed magnetite particles from different organometallic precursors, *IEEE TRANSACTIONS ON MAGNETICS* 42: 3025–3029.

Choi, S. R. & Kim, D. (2008). Real-time thermal characterization of 12 nl fluid samples in a microchannel, *Rev. Sci. Instrum.* 79: 064901.

Sakuma, H. & Ishii, K. (2009). Gas flow sputtering: Versatile process for the growth of nanopillars, nanoparticles, and epitaxial thin films, *Journal of Magnetism and Magnetic Materials* 321: 872–875.

Singh, Y., Javier, J., Ehrman, S. H., Magnusson, M. H. & Deppert, K. (2002). Approaches to increasing yield in evaporation/condensation nanoparticle generation, *Journal of Aerosol Science* 33: 1309–1325.

Sun, S., Zeng, H., Robinson, D. B., Raoux, S., Rice, M., Wang, S. X. & Li, G. J. (2004). Monodisperse MFe_2O_4(M = Fe, Co, Mn) nanoparticles, *J. Amer. Chem. Soc.* 126: 273–279.

Temgire, M. K., Bellare, J. & Joshi, S. S. (2011). Gamma radiolytic formation of alloyed ag-pt nanocolloids, *Advances in Physical Chemistry* 2011.

Wang, B., Li, H. & Peng, X. (2002). Research on the heat-conduction enhancement for liquid with nano-particle suspensions, *J. of Thermal Science* 11: 214–219.

White, F. (1991). *Viscous fluid flow*, 2nd edn, McGraw-Hill.

Yang, Y., Zhang, Z., Grulke, A., Anderson, W. & G.Wu (2005). Heat transfer properties of nanoparticle-in-fluid dispersions (nanofluids) in laminar flow, *International Journal of Heat and Mass Transfer* 48: 1107–1116.

Yin, M., Willis, A., Redl, F., Turro, N. & O'Brien, S. P. (2004). Influence of capping groups on the synthesis of $\gamma-Fe_2O_3$ nanocrystals, *J. Mater. Res* 19: 1208–1215.

Yu, C.-J., Richter, A., Datta, A., Durbin, M. & Dutta, P. (2000). Molecular layering in a liquid on a solid substrate: an x-ray reflectivity study, *Physica B* 283: 27–31.

Zhang, X., Gu, H. & Fujii, M. (2006). Experimental study on the effective thermal conductivity and thermal diffusivity of nanofluids, *International Journal of Thermophysics* 27: 569–580.

18

Forced Convective Heat Transfer of Nanofluids in Minichannels

S. M. Sohel Murshed and C. A. Nieto de Castro
Centre for Molecular Sciences and Materials
Faculty of Sciences of the University of Lisbon
Portugal

1. Introduction

Nanofluids are a new class of heat transfer fluids which are engineered by dispersing nanometer-sized metallic or non-metallic solid particles or tubes in conventional heat transfer fluids such as water, ethylene glycol, and engine oil. This is a rapidly emerging interdisciplinary field where nanoscience, nanotechnology, and thermal engineering meet. Since this novel concept of nanofluids was innovated in the mid-last decade (Choi, 1995), this research topic has attracted tremendous interest from researchers worldwide due to their fascinating thermal characteristics and potential applications in numerous important fields such as microelectronics, transportation, and biomedical.

With an ever-increasing thermal load due to smaller features of microelectronic devices and more power output, cooling for maintaining desirable performance and durability of such devices is one of the most important technical issues in many high-tech industries. Although increased heat transfer can be achieved creating turbulence, increasing heat transfer surface area and other way, the heat transfer performance will ultimately be limited due to the low thermal properties of these conventional fluids. If extended heating surface is used to obtain high heat transfer, it also undesirably increases the size of the thermal management system. Thus, these conventional cooling techniques are not suitable to meet the cooling demand of these high-tech industries. There was therefore a need for new and efficient heat transfer liquids that can meet the cooling challenges for advanced devices as well as energy conversion-based applications and the innovation of nanofluids has opened the door to meet those cooling challenges.

In the field of heat transfer, all liquid coolants currently used at low and moderate temperatures exhibit very poor thermal conductivity and heat storage capacity resulting in their poor convective heat transfer performance. Although thermal conductivity of a fluid plays a vital role in the development of energy-efficient heat transfer equipments and other cooling technologies, the traditional heat transfer fluids possess orders-of-magnitude smaller thermal conductivity than metallic or nonmetallic particles. For example, thermal conductivities of water and engine oil are about 5000 times and 21000 times, respectively smaller than that of multi-walled carbon nanotubes (MWCNT) as shown in Table 1 which provides values of thermal conductivities of various commonly used liquids and nanoparticle materials at room temperature. Therefore, the thermal conductivities of fluids that contain suspended metallic or nonmetallic particles or tubes are expected to be significantly higher than those of traditional heat transfer fluids. With this classical idea and applying nanotechnology to thermal fluids, Steve Choi from Argonne National Laboratory of USA coined the term "*nanofluids*" to designate a new class of heat transfer fluids (Choi, 1995). From the investigations performed thereafter, nanofluids were found to show considerably higher conductive, boiling, and convective heat transfer performances compared to their base fluids (Murshed et al., 2005, 2006, 2008a, 2008b & 2011; Das et al., 2006, Murshed, 2007; Yu et al., 2008). These nanoparticle suspensions are stable and Newtonian and they are considered as next generation heat transfer fluids which can respond more efficiently to the challenges of great heat loads, higher power engines, brighter optical devices, and micro-electromechanical systems (Das et al., 2006; Murshed et al., 2008a). Although significant progress has been made on nanofluids, variability and controversies in the heat transfer characteristics still exist (Keblinski et al., 2008; Murshed et al., 2009).

Conventional Fluids and Materials	Thermal Conductivity (W/m·K)	Reference
Deionized water (DIW)	0.607	Kaviany, 2002
Ethylene glycol	0.254	Kaviany, 2002
Engine oil	0.145	Kaviany, 2002
Fe_3O_4	7.2	Slack,1962
TiO_2	8.4	Masuda et al., 1993
CuO	13.5	Lide, 2007
Al_2O_3	40	Slack,1962
Al	237	Lide, 2007
Cu	401	Lide, 2007
Ag	429	Lide, 2007
MWCNT	3000	Kim et al., 2001

Table 1. Thermal conductivities of commonly used liquids and materials at room temperature

As the heat transfer performance of heat exchangers or cooling devices is vital in numerous industries, the impact of nanofluids technology is expected to be great. For example, the transport industry has a need to reduce the size and weight of vehicle thermal management systems and nanofluids can increase thermal transport of coolants and lubricants. When the nanoparticles are properly dispersed, nanofluids can offer numerous benefits besides their anomalously high thermal conductivity. These benefits include improved heat transfer and stability, microchannel cooling without clogging, miniaturized systems and reduction in pumping power. The better stability of nanofluids will prevent rapid settling and reduce clogging in the walls of heat transfer devices. The high thermal conductivity of nanofluids translates into higher energy efficiency, better performance, and lower operating costs. They can reduce energy consumption for pumping heat transfer fluids. Miniaturized systems require smaller inventories of fluids where nanofluids can be used. In vehicles, smaller components result in better gasoline mileage, fuel savings, lower emissions, and a cleaner environment (Murshed et al., 2008a). In addition, because heat transfer takes place at the surface of the particles, it is desirable to use particles with larger surface area. The much larger relative surface areas of nanoparticles compared to micro-particles, provide significantly improved heat transfer capabilities. Particles finer than 20 nm carry 20% of their atoms on their surface, making them instantaneously available for thermal interaction (Choi et al., 2004). Fig. 1 demonstrates that nanoparticles are much better than microparticles in applications (Murshed, 2007). With dispersed nanoparticles, nanofluids can flow smoothly through mini- or micro-channels. Because the nanoparticles are small, they weigh less and chances of sedimentation are also less making nanofluids more stable. With the aforementioned highly desirable thermal properties and potential benefits, nanofluids are considered to have a wide range of industrial and medical applications such as transportation, micromechanics and instrumentation, heating-ventilating and air-conditioning systems, and drug delivery systems. Details of the enhanced thermophysical properties, potential benefits and applications of nanofluids can be found elsewhere (Choi et al., 2004; Das et al., 2006; Yu et al., 2008; Murshed, 2007; Murshed et al., 2008a). As of today, researchers have mostly focused on anomalous thermal conductivity of nanofluids. However, comparatively few research efforts have been devoted to investigate the flow and convective heat transfer features of nanofluids which are very important in order to exploit their potential benefits and applications.

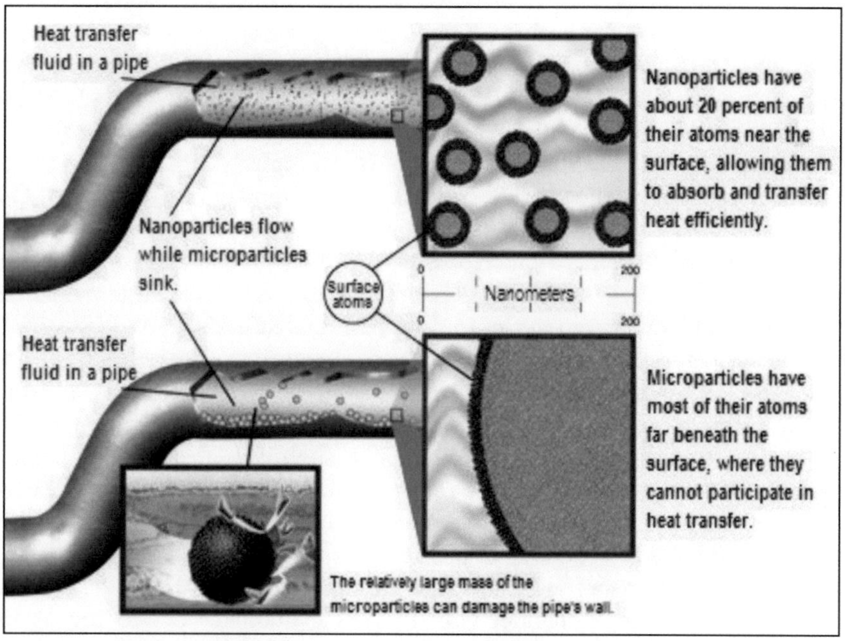

Fig. 1. Comparison between nanoparticles and microparticles flowing in channel

The aim of this chapter is to analyze experimental findings on forced convective heat transfer with nanofluids from literature together with representative results from our experimental investigation on heat transfer characteristics of aqueous TiO_2-nanofluids flowing through a cylindrical minichannel. Effects of Reynolds number and concentration of nanoparticles on the heat transfer performance are also reported and discussed.

2. Literature survey on convective heat transfer with nanofluids

As mentioned before compared to the studies on thermal conductivity, efforts to investigate convective heat transfer of nanofluids are still scarce. For example, according to ISI Web of Knowledge searched results, only 222 convective heat transfer-related publications out of 1363 recorded publications on nanofluids appeared (publications including journal and conference papers, patent, news and editorial and searched by topic "nanofluids" and refined by topic "convective heat transfer" on 12 April 2011). However, the practical applications of nanofluids as advanced heat transfer fluids or cooltants are mainly in flowing systems such as mini- or micro-channels heat sinks and miniaturized heat exchangers. A brief review of forced convective studies (experimental and theoretical) with nanofluids is presented in this section.

The first experiment on convective heat transfer of nanofluids (γ-Al_2O_3/water and TiO_2/water) under turbulent flow conditions was performed by (Pak & Cho, 1998). In their study, even though the Nusselt number (*Nu*) was found to increase with increasing nanoparticle volume fraction (ϕ) and Reynolds number (*Re*), the heat transfer coefficient (*h*) of nanofluids with 3 volume % loading of nanoparticles was 12% smaller than that of pure water at constant average fluid velocity condition. Whereas, (Eastman et al., 1999) later showed that with less than 1 volume % of CuO nanoparticles, the convective heat transfer coefficient of water increased more than 15%. The results of (Xuan & Li, 2003) illustrated that the Nusselt number of Cu/water-based nanofluids increased significantly with the volumetric loading of particles and for 2 volume % of nanoparticles, the Nusselt number increased by about 60%. Wen and Ding investigated the heat transfer behavior of nanofluids at the tube entrance region under laminar flow conditions and showed that the local heat transfer coefficient varied with particle volume fraction and Reynolds number (Wen & Ding, 2004). They also observed that the enhancement is particularly significant at the entrance region. Later (Heris et al., 2006) studied convective heat transfer of CuO and Al_2O_3/water-based nanofluids under laminar flow conditions through an annular tube. Their results showed that heat transfer coefficient increases with particle volume fraction as well as Peclet number. In their study, Al_2O_3/water-based nanofluids found to have larger enhancement of heat transfer coefficient compared to CuO/water-based nanofluids.

An experimental investigation on the forced convective heat transfer and flow characteristics of TiO_2-water nanofluids under turbulent flow conditions is reported by (Daungthongsuk & Wongwises, 2009). A horizontal double-tube counter flow heat exchanger is used in their study. They observed a slightly higher (6–11%) heat transfer coefficient for nanofluid compared to pure water. The heat transfer coefficient increases with increasing mass flow rate of the hot water as well as nanofluid. They also claimed that the use of the nanofluid has a little penalty in pressure drop.

In microchannel flow of nanofluids, the first convective heat transfer experiments with aqueous CNT-nanofluid in a channel with hydraulic diameter of 355 μm at Reynolds numbers between 2 to 17 was conducted by (Faulkner et al., 2004). They found considerable enhancement in heat transfer coefficient of this nanofluid at CNT concentration of 4.4%. Later, a study was performed on heat transfer performance of Al_2O_3/water-based nanofluid in a rectangular microchannel under laminar flow condition by (Jung et al., 2006). Results showed that the heat transfer coefficient increased by more than 32% for 1.8 volume% of nanoparticles and the *Nu* increases with increasing *Re* in the flow regime of 5 $>Re<300$.

An up-to-date overview of the published experimental results on the forced convective heat transfer characteristics of nanofluids is given in Table 2. A comparison of results of Nusselt number versus Reynolds number for both laminar and turbulent flow conditions from various groups is also shown in Fig. 2. Both Table 2 and Fig. 2 demonstrate that the results from various groups are not consistent.

Nanofluids	**Geometry/Flow Nature**	**Findings**	**Reference**
Al_2O_3/water and TiO_2/water	tube/turbulent	At 3 vol. %, *h* was 12% smaller than pure water for a given fluid velocity.	Pak & Cho, 1998
Cu /water	tube/turbulent	A larger increase in *h* with ϕ and *Re* was observed.	Xuan & Li, 2003
Al_2O_3/water	tube/laminar	*h* increases with ϕ and Reynolds number.	Wen & Ding, 2004
CNT/water	tube/laminar	At 0.5 wt. %, *h* increased by 350% at $Re = 800$.	Ding et al., 2006
Al_2O_3/water and CuO /water	tube/laminar	*h* increases with ϕ and *Pe*. Al_2O_3 shows higher increment than CuO.	Heris et al., 2006
Al_2O_3/DIW	tube/laminar	*Nu* increased 8 % for $\phi = 0.01$ and $Re = 270$.	Lai et al., 2006
Al_2O_3 /water	rectangular microchannel/ laminar	*h* increased 15 % for $\phi = 0.018$.	Jung et al., 2006
Al_2O_3 and ZrO_2/water	tube/turbulent	*h* increased significantly.	Williams et al., 2008
Al_2O_3 /water	tube/laminar	*h* increased only up to 8% at $Re = 730$ for $\phi = 0.003$.	Hwang et al., 2009
Al_2O_3,ZnO, TiO_2 and MgO/water	tube/laminar	*h* increased up to 252% at $Re = 1000$ for MgO/water.	Xie et al., 2010
MWCNT/water	tube/laminar and turbulent	*h* increased up to 40% at concentration of 0.25 wt.%.	Amrollahi et al., 2010

Table 2. Summary of forced convection heat transfer experimental studies of nanofluids

Although a growing number researchers have recently shown interest in flow features of nanofluids (Murshed et al., 2011), there is not much progress made on the development of rigorous theoretical models for the convective heat transfer of nanofluids. Researchers investigating convective heat transfer of nanofluids mainly employed existing conventional single-phase fluid correlations such as those attributed to Dittus-Boelter and Shah (Bejan, 2004) to predict the heat transfer coefficient. Some researchers also proposed new correlations obtained by fitting their limited experimental data (Pak & Cho, 1998; Xuan & Li, 2003; Jung et al., 2006). However, none of these correlations were validated with wide range of experimental data under various conditions and thus are not widely accepted. In an attempt to establish a clear explanation of the reported anomalously enhanced convective heat transfer coefficient of nanofluids, (Buongiorno, 2006) considered seven-slip mechanisms and concluded that among those seven only Brownian diffusion and thermophoresis are the two most important particle/fluid slip mechanisms in nanofluids. Besides proposing a new correlation, he also claimed that the enhanced laminar flow convective heat transfer can be attributed to a reduction of viscosity within and consequent thinning of the laminar sublayer.

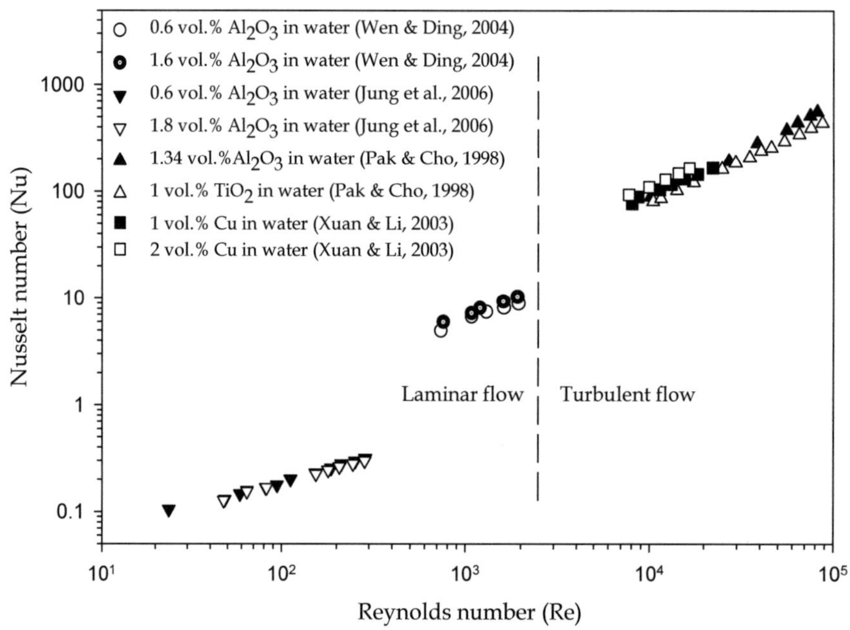

Fig. 2. Convective heat transfer data of nanofluids from various research groups

3. Present laminar flow heat transfer study with nanofluids

The forced convective heat transfer of TiO_2/DIW-based nanofluids flowing through a minichannel under laminar flow and constant heat flux conditions was experimentally studied (Murshed et al., 2008c) and some representative results on nanoparticles concentration and Reynolds number dependence of the convective heat transfer features of this nanofluid are presented together with the exposition on experimental and theoretical bases.

3.1 Experimental

Sample nanofluids were prepared by dispersing different volume percentages (from 0.2% to 0.8%) of TiO_2 nanoparticles of 15 nm diameter in deionized water. To ensure proper dispersion of nanoparticles, sample nanofluids were homogenized by using an ultrasonic dismembrator and a magnetic stirrer. Cetyl Trimethyl Ammonium Bromide (CTAB) surfactant of 0.1mM concentration was added to nanofluid as a dispersant agent to ensure better dispersion of nanoparticles.

An experimental setup was established to conduct experiments on convective heat transfer of nanofluids at laminar flow regime in a cylindrical minichannel. The schematic of experimental facilities used is shown in Fig. 3. The experimental facility consisted of a flow loop, a heating unit, a cooling system, and a measuring and control unit. The flow loop consisted of a pump, a test section, a flow meter, dampener, and a reservoir. The measuring and control unit includes a HP data logger with bench link data acquisition software and a computer. A straight copper tube of 360 mm length, 4 mm inner diameter (D_i) and 6 mm outer diameter (D_o) was used as flowing channel. A peristaltic pump (Cole-Parmer International, USA) with variable speed and flow rate was employed to maintain different flow rates for the desired Reynolds number. In order to minimize the vibration and to ensure steady flow, a flow dampener was also installed between the pump and flow meter. An electric micro-coil heater was used to obtain a constant wall heat-flux boundary condition. Voltmeter and ammeter were connected to the loop to measure the voltage and current, respectively. The heater was connected with the adjustable AC power supply. In order to minimize the heat loss, the entire test section was thermally insulated. Five K-type thermocouples were mounted on the test section at various axial positions from the inlet of the test section to measure the wall temperature distribution. Two thermocouples were further mounted at the inlet and exit of the channel to measure the bulk fluid temperature. A tank with running cold water was used as the cooling system and test fluid was run through the copper coils inside the tank before exiting. During the experiment, the pump flow rate, voltage, and current of the power supply were recorded and the temperature readings from the thermocouples were registered by the data acquisition system. By making use of these temperature readings and supplied heat flux into appropriate expressions, the heat transfer coefficients (h and Nu) were then calculated. Details of the experimental facilities and procedures are reported elsewhere (Murshed et al., 2008c) and will not be elaborated further. Instead formulations for obtaining the heat transfer coefficient of the sample fluids are provided in the subsequent section.

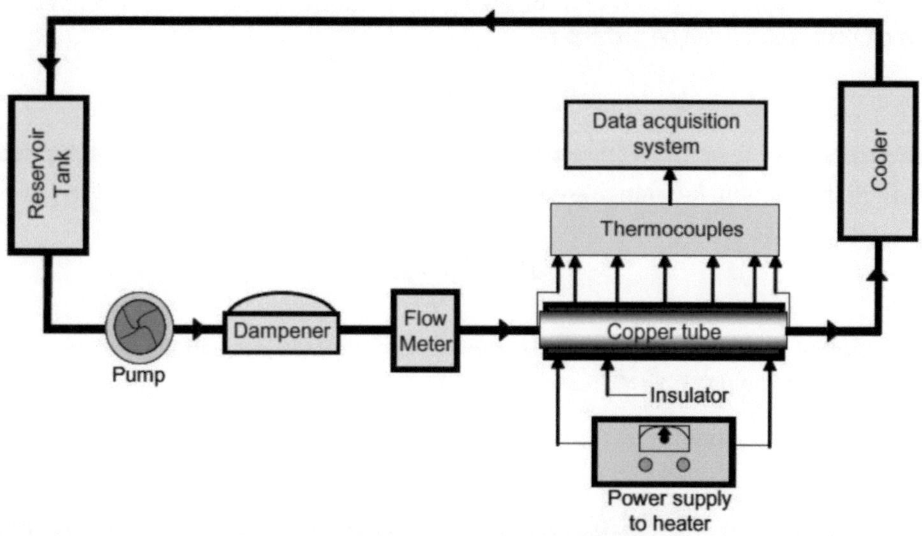

Fig. 3. Schematic of convective heat transfer experimental setup

3.2 Theoretical

The heat transfer feature of sample fluids was determined in terms of the following local convective heat transfer coefficient:

$$h_x = \frac{q''}{T_{i,w}(x) - T_m(x)} \quad (1)$$

where h_x is the local heat transfer coefficient (W/m²K) of sample fluids, $q'' = \dot{m}c_p(T_{out} - T_{in}) / (\pi D_i L)$ is the heat flux (W/m²) of the heat transfer test section, D_i is the inner diameter of the tube (also hydrodynamic diameter), L is the length of the test section, $\dot{m}$ $(= \rho u A_c)$ is the mass flow rate (kg/s), c_p is the specific heat of the fluid, T_{in} and T_{out} are the inlet and outlet fluid temperature, respectively and $T_{i,w}$ (x) and T_m(x) are the inner wall temperature of the tube and the mean bulk fluid temperature at axial position x, respectively.

Since the inner wall temperature of the tube, $T_{i,w}$ (x) could not be measured directly for an electrically heated tube, it can be determined from the heat conduction equation in the cylindrical coordinates as given (Pak et al., 1991)

$$T_{i,w}(x) = T_{o,w}(x) - \frac{q[2D_o^2 \ln(D_o / D_i) - (D_o^2 - D_i^2)]}{4\pi(D_o^2 - D_i^2)k_s x} \quad (2)$$

where $T_{o,w}$ (x) is the outer wall temperature of the tube (measured by thermocouples), q is the heat supplied to the test section (W), k_s is the thermal conductivity of the tube i.e. copper tube, D_o is the outer diameter of the tube, x represents the longitudinal location of the section of interest from the entrance.

The mean bulk fluid temperature, $T_m(x)$ at the section of interest can be determined from an equation based on energy balance in any section of the tube for constant surface heat flux condition. From the first law (energy balance) for the control volume of length, dx of the tube with incompressible liquid and for negligible pressure, the differential heat equation for the control volume can be written as

$$dq_{conv} = q'' p dx = \dot{m}c_p dT_m \quad (3)$$

where perimeter of the cross section, $p = \pi D_i$ and dT_m is the differential mean temperature of the fluid in that section. Rearranging equation (3)

$$dT_m = \frac{q'' \pi D_i}{\dot{m}c_p} dx \quad (4)$$

The variation of T_m with respect to x is determined by integrating equation (4) from $x = 0$ to x and after simplifying using q'' term and $T_m(x = 0) = T_{in}$, we have

$$T_m(x) = T_{in} + \frac{(T_{out} - T_{in})}{L} x \quad (5)$$

Applying equation (2) and equation (5) into equation (1), the following expression for the local heat transfer coefficient of flowing fluid is obtained

$$h_x = \frac{q''}{\{T_{o,w}(x) - \frac{q[2D_o^2 \ln(D_o / D_i) - (D_o^2 - D_i^2)]}{4\pi(D_o^2 - D_i^2)k_s x}\} - \{T_{in} + \frac{(T_{out} - T_{in})}{L} x\}} \tag{6}$$

Once the local heat transfer coefficient is determined from equation (6) and the thermal conductivity of the medium is known, the local Nusselt number is calculated from

$$Nu_x = \frac{h_x D_i}{k_f} \tag{7}$$

where k_f is the thermal conductivity of fluids. The classical Hamilton-Crosser model is used for the determination of effective thermal conductivity of nanofluids (k_{nf}) which is given by (Hamilton & Crosser, 1962)

$$k_{nf} = k_f \left[\frac{k_p + (n-1)k_f - (n-1)\phi(k_f - k_p)}{k_p + (n-1)k_f + \phi(k_f - k_p)} \right] \tag{8}$$

where k_f and k_p are the thermal conductivities of the base liquid and the nanoparticles, respectively, ϕ is the volume fraction of nanoparticles and n is the empirical shape factor, which has a value of 3 for spherical particle.

The Nusselt number can also be determined from the existing correlations. The well-known Shah's correlation for laminar flows under the constant heat flux boundary conditions is used and reproduced as (Bejan, 2004)

$$Nu = 1.953 \left(\mathrm{Re}\,\mathrm{Pr} \frac{D_i}{x} \right)^{1/3} \text{ for } \left(\mathrm{Re}\,\mathrm{Pr} \frac{D_i}{x} \right) \geq 33.3 \tag{9}$$

This correlation is popular and commonly used for thermal entrance region.

For steady and incompressible flow of nanofluids in a tube of uniform cross-sectional area, the Reynolds number (*Re*) and Prandtl number (*Pr*) are defined as follows

$$\mathrm{Re} = \frac{4\dot{m}}{\pi D_i \mu_{nf}} \text{ and } \mathrm{Pr} = \frac{c_{p-nf}\mu_{nf}}{k_{nf}} \tag{10}$$

where μ_{nf} and c_{p-nf} are the viscosity and specific heat of nanofluids, respectively.

The specific heat of nanofluids is calculated using the following volume fractioned-based mixture rule (Pak & Cho, 1998; Jung et al., 2006)

$$c_{p-nf} = \phi c_{p-p} + (1-\phi)c_{p-f} \tag{11}$$

The viscosity of nanofluids is determined from Batchelor's model given by (Batchelor, 1977)

$$\mu_{nf} = \mu_f (1 + 2.5\phi + 6.2\phi^2) \tag{12}$$

where μ_f is the base fluid viscosity. It is noted that other classical models for calculating the viscosity of mixture also yield similar results (Murshed, 2007; Murshed et al., 2008b).

3.3 Results and discussion

Fig. 4 demonstrates the local heat transfer coefficient of DIW for various concentrations of TiO_2 nanoparticles against the axial distance from the entrance of the test section at Reynolds numbers of 1100 and 1700 (Murshed et al., 2008c). The results show that nanofluids exhibits considerably enhanced convective heat transfer coefficient which also increases with volumetric loadings of TiO_2 nanoparticles. For example, at 0.8 volume % of nanoparticles and at position $x/D_i = 25$ (where tube diameter $D_i = 4$ mm), the local heat transfer coefficient of this nanofluid was found to be about 12% and 14% higher compared to deionized water at *Re* of 1100 and 1700, respectively. The enhancement in heat transfer coefficients of nanofluids with particle loading is believed to be because of the enhanced effective thermal conductivity and the acceleration of the energy exchange process in the fluid resulting from the random movements of the nanoparticles. Another reason for such enhancement can be the migration of nanoparticles in base fluids due to shear action, viscosity gradient and Brownian motion in the cross section of the tube. For higher Reynolds number ($Re = 1700$), the heat transfer coefficients (h) of nanofluids of all concentrations showed almost linear decrease along the axial distance from the channel entrance (Fig.4b) while at lower Reynolds number (e.g., $Re = 1100$) clear non-linear trends of decreasing the heat transfer coefficients with axial distance are observed (Fig.4a). The reasons for such paradoxical trends of heat transfer coefficients are not clear at this stage.

Fig. 5 compares experimentally determined Nusselt numbers with the predictions by classical Shah's correlation i.e., equation (9) along the axial distance for DIW at Reynolds numbers of 1100 and 1700 (Murshed et al., 2008c). It is noted that in order to calculate Nusselt numbers at various axial positions by Shah's correlation the values of viscosity and thermal conductivity of DIW at mean temperature between the inlet and outlet (i.e., $T_m=(T_{out} + T_{in})/2$) were used. Although Shah's correlation slightly over-predicts the present results, both the experimental and the prediction data of Nusselt number as a function of axial distance show quite similar trends (Fig. 5). The difference in tube size may be one of the reasons for such over prediction. A relatively small tube was used in our experiment, whereas the Shah's equation was developed on the basis of laminar flow in large channel (Bejan, 2004). Nevertheless, for pure water and at about the same Reynolds numbers (Re = 1050 and 1600), similar over prediction of Nusselt number by Shah's equation was also reported by (Wen and Ding, 2004).

The effect of Reynolds number on Nusselt number at a specific axial location ($x/D_i = 25$) is shown in Fig. 6 (Murshed et al., 2008c). It can be seen that the measured Nusselt numbers for nanofluids are higher than those of DIW and they increase remarkably and non-linearly with Reynolds number. Again, this trend of increasing Nusselt number with increasing Reynolds number is similar to that observed by (Wen and Ding, 2004) from a similar experimental study with Al_2O_3/water nanofluids. It was also found that the enhancement in heat transfer coefficient was particularly significant at the entrance region. The observed enhancement of the Nusselt number could be due to the suppression of the boundary layer, viscosity of nanofluids as well as dispersion of the nanoparticles. As expected, the Nusselt number of this nanofluid also increases with the particle concentration (Fig. 6).

Fig. 7 shows that at $x/D_i = 25$ and $Re = 1100$ the Nusselt number of this nanofluid increases almost linearly with the particle volume fraction (Murshed et al., 2008c). This is not surprising as the higher the particle concentration in base fluids, the larger the number density of nanoparticles and this can intensify the particle migration as well as Brownian force related mechanisms in the base fluids contributing to increase heat transfer rate.

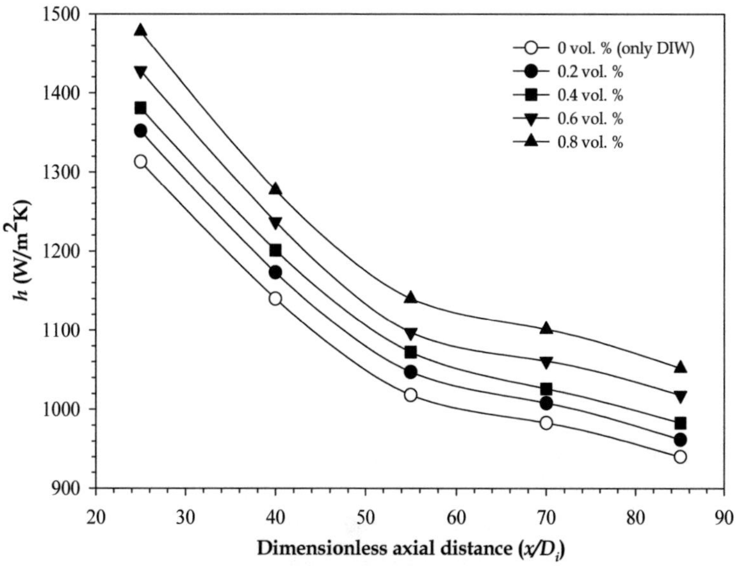

(a)

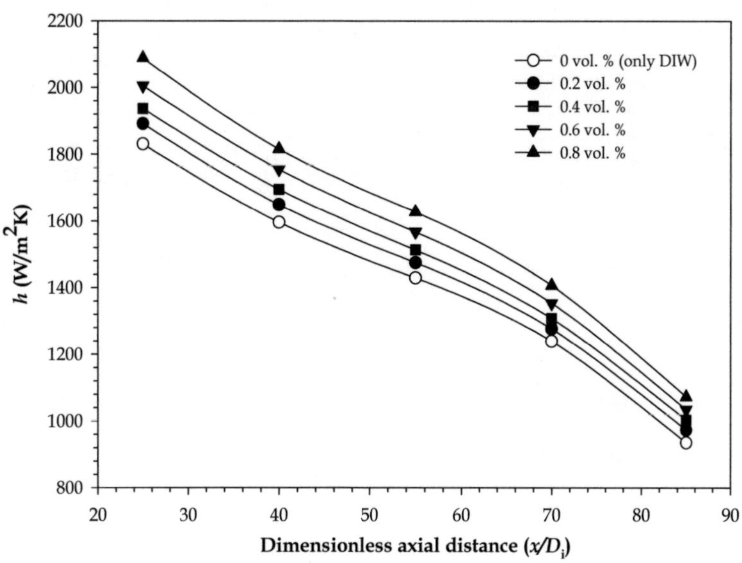

(b)

Fig. 4. Axial profiles of local heat transfer coefficient of DIW for various volumetric loadings of TiO_2 nanoparticles at (a) *Re* = 1700 and (b) *Re* = 1700

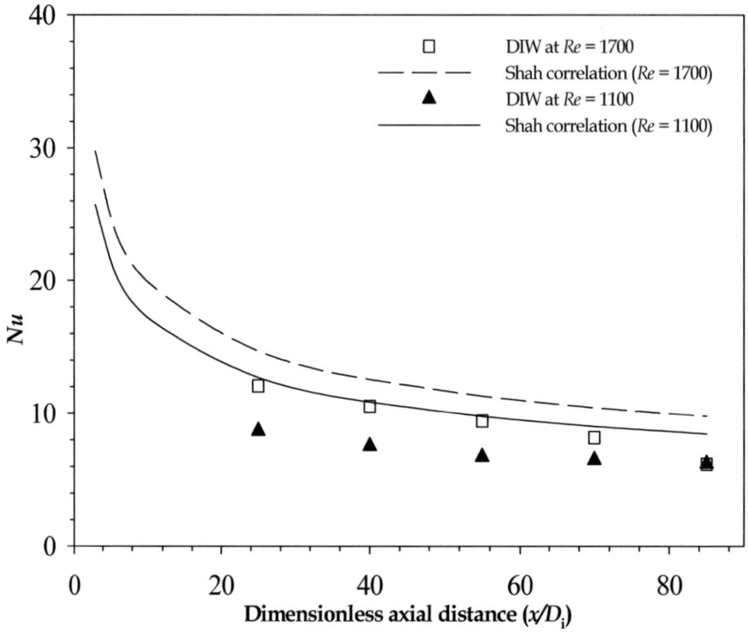

Fig. 5. Comparison with Shah's correlation along axial distance at *Re* = 1100 and 1700

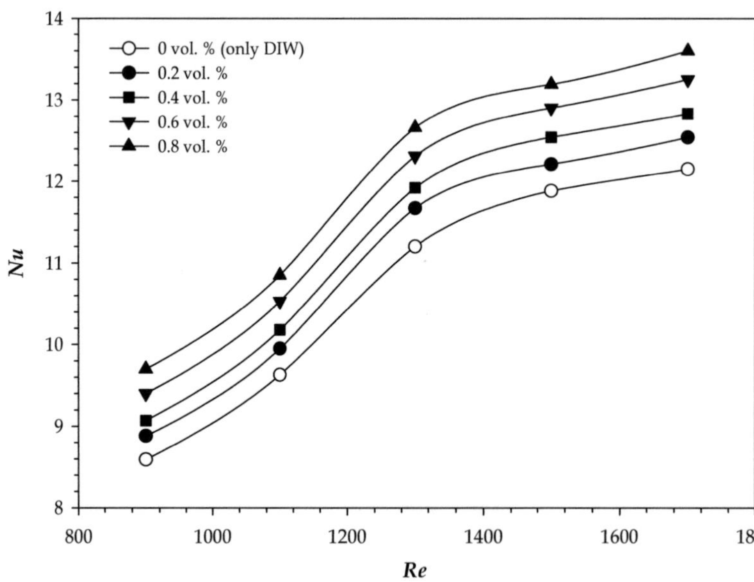

Fig. 6. Effect of Reynolds number and TiO_2 nanoparticle concentrations on Nusselt number

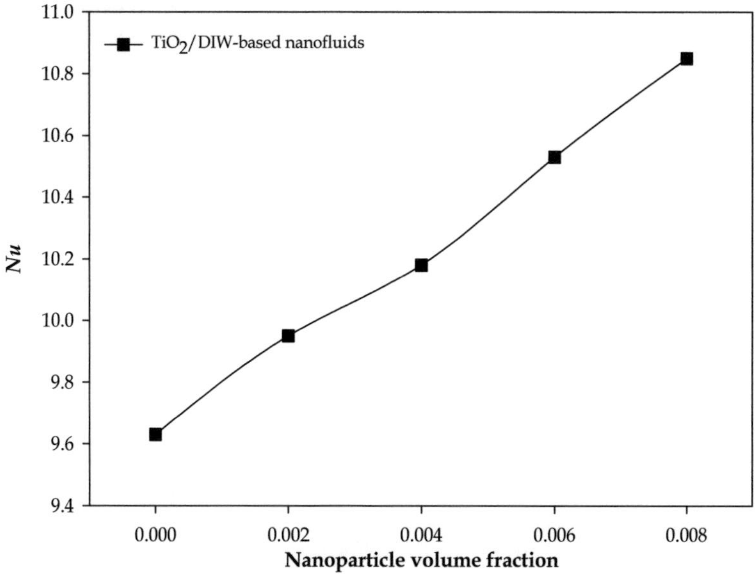

Fig. 7. Nanoparticle concentration-dependent Nusselt number of nanofluids at *Re* = 1100

4. Conclusions

The review of the experimental studies on forced convective heat transfer with nanofluids together with the representative results obtained from our investigation on laminar flow heat transfer features of a nanofluid are presented in this chapter.

Results demonstrate that like most of the literature data, aqueous-TiO_2 nanofluids exhibit enhanced heat transfer coefficient compared to its base fluid. The heat transfer coefficient found to increase significantly with increasing Reynolds number i.e., flow rate. It also shows a strong and linear dependent on the concentration of nanoparticles.

The review showed a considerable chaos and randomness in the reported data on convective heat transfer coefficient from various research groups. Despite of such chaotic and inconsistent data, the applications of nanofluids as advanced heat transfer fluids appear to be promising due to their overall enhanced heat transfer performance in flowing as well as static conditions. However, the advancement toward concrete understanding the mechanisms for the observed heat transfer features of nanofluids remain challenging. There is also not much progress made on the development of rigorous theoretical models for convective heat transfer of nanofluids. Therefore, more careful and systematic investigations on nanofluids preparation and measurements of their heat transfer features as well as rigorous theoretical analysis are needed.

5. Acknowledgments

The authors would like to thank FCT- Fundação para a Ciência e Tecnologia, Portugal for pluriannual funding to CCMM.

6. References

Amrollahi, A., Rashidi, A. M., Lotfi, R., Meibodi, M. E. & Kashefi, K. (2010). Convection heat transfer of functionalized MWNT in aqueous fluids in laminar and turbulent flow at the entrance region. *International Communications in Heat and Mass Transfer*, Vol.37, No.6, pp.717-723.

Batchelor, G. K. (1977). The effect of Brownian motion on the bulk stress in a suspension of spherical particles. *Journal of Fluid Mechanics*, Vol. 83, No.1, pp.97-117.

Bejan, A. (2004). *Convection Heat Transfer*. John Wily & Sons, Inc.: New Jersey.

Buongiorno, J. (2006). Convective transport in nanofluids. *Journal of Heat Transfer*, Vol. 128, No.3, pp.240-250.

Choi, S. U. S. (1995). Enhancing thermal conductivity of fluids with nanoparticles. *ASME FED*, Vol. 231, pp. 99–105.

Choi, S. U. S., Zhang, Z. G. & Keblinski, P. (2004). Nanofluids, *Encyclopedia of Nanoscience and Nanotechnology*, Vol.6, pp.757-773.

Das, S.,Choi, S. U. S. & Patel, H. (2006). Heat transfer in nanofluids - A review. *Heat Transfer Engineering*, Vol. 27, pp.3-19.

Daungthongsuk, W. & Wongwises, S. (2009). Heat transfer enhancement and pressure drop characteristics of TiO2–water nanofluid in a double-tube counter flow heat exchanger. *International Journal of Heat and Mass Transfer*, Vol. 52, Nos.7-8, pp.2059-2067.

Ding, Y., Alias, H., Wen, D. & Williams, A. R. (2006). Heat transfer of aqueous suspensions of carbon nanotubes. *International Journal of Heat and Mass Transfer*, Vol. 49, Nos.1-2, pp.240-250.

Eastman, J. A., Choi, S. U. S., Li, S., Soyez, G., Thompson, L. J. & Dimelfi, R. J. (1999). Novel thermal properties of nanostructured materials. *Materials Science Forum*, Vols. 312-314, pp.629-634.

Faulkner, D., Rector, D. R., Davison, J. J. & Shekarriz, R. (2004). Enhanced heat transfer through the use of nanofluids in forced convection. *Proceedings of ASME International Mechanical Engineering Congress and Exposition*, pp. 219–224, California

Hamilton, R. & Crosser, O. (1962). Thermal Conductivity of Heterogeneous 2-Component Systems. *Industrial & Engineering Chemistry Fundamentals*, Vol. 1, No. 3, 187-191.

Heris, S. Z., Etemad, S. G. & Esfahany, M. S. (2006). Experimental investigation of oxide nanofluids under laminar flow convective heat transfer. *International Communications of Heat and Mass Transfer*, Vol.33, No.4, pp.529-535.

Hwang, K. S., Jang, S. P. & Choi, S. U. S. (2009). Flow and convective heat transfer characteristics of water-based Al_2O_3 nanofluids in fully developed laminar flow regime. *International Journal of Heat and Mass Transfer*, Vol.52, Nos. 1-2, pp.193–199.

Jung, J. Y., Oh, H. S. & Kwak, H. Y. (2006). Forced convective heat transfer of nanofluids in microchannels. *Proceedings of the ASME International Mechanical Engineering Congress and Exposition*, Chicago

Kaviany, M. (2002). *Principles of Heat Transfer*. John Wiley & Sons, Inc.: New Jersey.

Keblinski, P., Prasher, R. & Eapen, J. (2008). Thermal conductance of nanofluids: is the controversy over? *Journal of Nanoparticle Research*, Vol. 10, No. 7, pp. 1089-1097.

Kim, P., Shi, L., Majumdar, A. & McEuen, P. L. (2001). Thermal transport measurements of individual multiwalled nanotubes. *Physical Review Letters*, Vol.87, No.21, pp. 215502-1–215502-4.

Lai, W. Y., Duculescu, B., Phelan, P. E. & Prasher, R. S. (2006). Convective heat transfer with nanofluids in a single 1.02-mm tube. *Proceedings of the ASME International Mechanical Engineering Congress and Exposition*, Chicago

Lide, D. R. (2007). *CRC Handbook of chemistry and physics*. Taylor and Francis: Boca Raton, USA.

Masuda, H., Ebata, A., Teramae, K. & Hishinuma, N. (1993). Alteration of thermal conductivity and viscosity of liquid by dispersing ultra-fine particles (dispersion of γ-Al_2O_3, SiO_2, and TiO_2 ultra-fine particles). *Netsu Bussei*, Vol. 4, No.4, pp.227-233.

Murshed, S. M. S. "Heat transfer characteristics of nanofluids", PhD Thesis, NTU, 2007.

Murshed, S. M. S. (2009). Comment and correction on " thermal conductance of nanofluids: is the controversy over?. *Journal of Nanoparticle Research*, Vol. 11, pp.511-512.

Murshed, S. M. S., Leong, K. C. & Yang, C. (2005). Enhanced thermal conductivity of TiO_2-water based nanofluids. *International Journal of Thermal Sciences*, Vol. 44, pp. 367-373.

Murshed, S. M. S., Leong, K. C. & Yang, C. (2006). Determination of the effective thermal diffusivity of nanofluids by the double hot-wire technique. *Journal of Physics D: Applied Physics*, Vol. 39, pp.5316–5322.

Murshed, S. M. S., Leong, K. C. & Yang, C. (2008a). Thermophysical and electrokinetic properties of nanofluids - A critical review. *Applied Thermal Engineering*, Vol. 28, No.17-18, pp. 2109-2125.

Murshed, S. M. S., Leong, K. C. & Yang, C. (2008b). Investigations of thermal conductivity and viscosity of nanofluids. *International Journal of Thermal Sciences*, Vol. 47, No.5, pp.560-568.

Murshed, S. M. S., Leong, K. C., Yang, C. & Nguyen N. T. (2008c). Convective heat transfer characteristics of aqueous TiO_2 nanofluids under laminar flow conditions. *International Journal of Nanoscience*, Vol. 7, No.6, pp.325-331.

Murshed, S. M. S., Nieto de Castro, C. A., Lourenço, M. J. V., Matos Lopes, M. L. & Santos, F. J. V. (2011). A review of boiling and convective heat transfer with nanofluids. *Renewable and Sustainable Energy Reviews*, Vol. 15, No.5, pp. 2342-2354.

Pak, B. C. & Cho, Y. I. (1998). Hydrodynamic and heat transfer study of dispersed fluids with submicron metallic oxide particles. *Experimental Heat Transfer*, Vol.11, No.2, pp.151-170.

Pak, B. C., Cho, Y. I. & Choi, S. U. S. (1991). A study of turbulent heat transfer in a sudden-expansion pipe with drag-reducing viscoelastic fluid. *International Journal of Heat and Mass Transfer*, Vol. 34, Nos.4-5, pp.1195-1208.

Slack, G. A. (1962). Thermal conductivity of MgO, Al_2O_3, $MgAl_2O_4$, and Fe_3O_4 Crystals from 3° to 300°K. *Physical Review*, Vol.126, No.2, pp. 427–441.

Wen, D., & Ding, Y. (2004). Experimental investigation into convective heat transfer of nanofluids at the entrance region under laminar flow conditions. *International Journal of Heat and Mass Transfer*, Vol. 47, No.24, pp.5181-5188.

Williams, W., Buongiorno, J. & Hu, L. W. (2008). Experimental investigation of turbulent convective heat transfer and pressure loss of alumina/water and zirconia/water

nanoparticle colloids (nanofluids) in horizontal tubes. *Journal of Heat Transfer*, Vol. 130, No.4, pp.1–7.
Xie, H., Li, Y. &Yu W. (2010). Intriguingly high convective heat transfer enhancement of nanofluid coolants in laminar flows. *Physics Letters A*, Vol.374, No.25, pp.2566-2568.
Xuan, Y. & Li, Q. (2003). Investigation on convective heat transfer and flow features of nanofluids. *Journal of Heat Transfer*, Vol.125, No.1, pp.151-155.
Yu, W., France, D. M., Routbort, J. L. & Choi, S. U. S. (2008). Review and comparison of nanofluid thermal conductivity and heat transfer enhancements. *Heat Transfer Engineering*, Vol.29, No.5, pp.432-460.

19

Nanofluids for Heat Transfer – Potential and Engineering Strategies

Elena V. Timofeeva
Energy Systems Division, Argonne National Laboratory, Argonne, IL USA

1. Introduction

In an age of increasing heat fluxes and power loads in applications as diverse as power electronics, renewable energy, transportation, and medical equipment, liquid cooling systems are necessary to enhance heat dissipation, improve energy efficiency, and lengthen device lifetime. To satisfy these increasing thermal management needs, the heat transfer efficiency of conventional fluids must be improved.

Nanofluids are nanotechnology-based heat transfer fluids that are engineered by stably dispersing nanometer-sized solid particles (such as ceramics, metals, alloys, semiconductors, nanotubes, and composite particles) in conventional heat transfer fluids (such as water, ethylene glycol, oil, and mixtures) at relatively low particle volume concentrations. Nanofluids have been considered for applications as advanced heat transfer fluids for almost two decades, since they have better suspension stability compared to micron-sized solid particles, can flow smoothly without clogging the system, and provide enhanced thermal and physical properties.

Nanofluids are in essence nanocomposite materials, with adjustable parameters including, but not limited to nanoparticle material, size, and shape, base fluid, surfactants and other additives. The thermal conductivity of heat transfer fluid is widely recognized as a main factor influencing the heat transfer efficiency. Low thermal conductivity of conventional fluids (i.e. 0.1-0.6 W/mK at 25°C) improves when solid particles with significantly higher thermal conductivity values (i.e. 10-430 W/mK for pure elements) are added. Therefore addition of small solid particles to liquids improves thermal conductivity of suspension, while still allowing for convection heat transfer mechanism of the fluid. The magnitudes of the effects reported in the literature are scattered from few percent (as predicted by effective medium theory (EMT) [1-3]) to hundred percents per nanoparticle volume concentration (i.e. abnormal enhancements [4-6]).

2. Diversity of nanofluids

Theoretical efforts and modeling of the thermal conductivity enhancement mechanisms in nanofluids [7, 8] have not come up with a universal theoretical model that carefully predicts the thermal conductivity for a variety of nanofluid compositions. The macroscopic effective medium theory (EMT) introduced by Maxwell [1] and further developed for non-spherical particle shapes by Hamilton and Crosser [2] predicts that thermal conductivity of two component heterogeneous mixtures is a function of the conductivity of pure materials, the composition of the mixture and the manner in which pure materials distributed throughout the mixture. Hamilton-Crosser model allows calculation of the effective thermal conductivity (k_{eff}) of two component heterogeneous mixtures and includes empirical shape factor, n given by $n = 3/\psi$ (ψ is the sphericity defined as ratio between the surface area of the sphere and the surface area of the real particle with equal volumes):

$$\frac{k_{eff}}{k_0} = \frac{k_p + (n-1)k_0 + (n-1)(k_p - k_0)\phi}{k_p + (n-1)k_0 - (k_p - k_0)\phi}, \qquad (1),$$

where k_p and k_0 are the conductivities of the particle material and the base fluid and ϕ is volume fraction of nanoparticles. Thus, according to this model [2], suspensions of particles with high shape factor (elongated and thin) should have higher thermal conductivities.

Despite the large database supporting EMT, there are many experimental results showing significantly higher or lower thermal conductivity enhancements [4-6] indicating that basic EMT doesn't account for all contributing factors. A number of mechanisms for enhanced thermal conductivity were suggested to explain the experimental data, and include the interaction between nanoparticles and liquids in form of interfacial thermal resistance [9-11], formation of condensed nano-layers around the particles [12-14], the particle size effects [15], agglomeration of nanoparticles [16-18], the microconvection mechanism due to Brownian motion of nanoparticles in the liquid [19-21], surface plasmon resonance [22-24], and near field radiation [25, 26]. None of these mechanisms alone seems to have the capacity of explaining the variety of experimental thermal conductivity enhancements in nanofluids, but it appears that different combinations of suggested mechanisms could explain the majority of experimental results. This is possible when different nanofluid parameters engage additional to EMT thermal conductivity enhancing mechanisms.

Large volume of studies has been devoted to characterization of individual thermo-physical properties of nanofluids, such as thermal conductivity, viscosity, and agglomeration of nanoparticles [5, 8, 27-33]. However no agreement has been achieved on the magnitude of potential benefits of using nanofluids for heat transfer applications because of diversity and complexity of the nanofluid systems.

By the type of nanoparticle material the nanofluid systems can be roughly classified into (1) ceramic (oxides, carbides, nitrides) nanofluids; (2) metallic nanofluids; (3) carbonaceous (graphite, graphene, carbon nanotubes, etc.) nanofluids; and (4) nanodroplet/nanoemulsions. Each class of nanofluids draws a unique set of thermal conductivity enhancement mechanisms that contribute to the heat transfer efficiency of these nanofluids.

Ceramic nanofluids are the most investigated class of nanofluids, because of the low cost, wide availability and chemical stability of ceramic nanomaterials. Most reports on ceramic nanofluids agree that the increases in thermal conductivity fall on or slightly above the prediction of EMT corrected for contribution of interfacial thermal resistance and/or elongated nanoparticle shape [3, 9, 18, 34, 35], with the thermal conductivity of solid-liquid suspensions linearly increasing with the volume fraction of the solid particles (black dashed line, Fig. 1).

Metallic nanofluids are less investigated than ceramic nanofluids because of the limited oxidative stability of many affordable metals and high cost of chemically stable precious metal nanoparticles. However many experimental results for metallic nanofluids report thermal conductivity increases well above the effective medium theory prediction [36-44] as summarized in Figure 1. Data from different research groups are quite scattered, possibly because of the difference in the preparation techniques, particle size, material, base fluids, surfactants, and also uncertainties in measurements of particle concentration and thermal conductivity [3]. It was suggested [23] that metallic nanoparticles possess geometry-dependent localized plasmon resonances (collective oscillations of the metals free electrons upon optical or other excitation), which could be responsible for abnormal thermal conductivity increases in metallic nanofluids. The significant enhancement in thermal conductivity, shown by the majority of metal containing nanofluids, indicates a great potential for revolutionizing industries that are dependent on the performance of heat transfer fluids. Production of metal containing nanofluids faces some major challenges, such as stability towards agglomeration and surface oxidation, availability, cost of materials and manufacturing issues. Use of dry metal nanopowders fabricated in gas phase is limited to precious metals (Au, Pt) resistant to surface oxidation. Generation of nanoparticles directly in the base fluid is recognized to produce more homogeneous nanofluids with fewer agglomerates and also provides better control over the surface state [38].

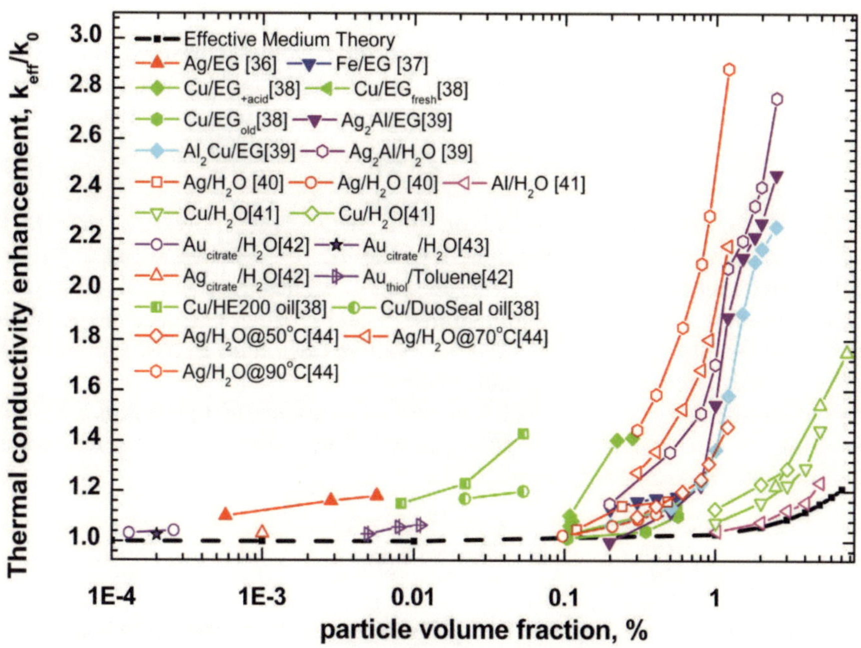

Fig. 1. Summary of published data on the thermal conductivities of metal containing nanofluids in ethylene glycol -EG (solid markers), water (empty markers) and other solvents (semi-empty). Nanoparticle material indicated by color: Ag - red, Fe - blue, Cu - green, Al - magenta, Au - violet

Carbonaceous nanofluids show a wide range of thermal conductivity increases, from very insignificant increase in amorphous carbon black to a 2-3 fold increase in thermal conductivity in some suspensions with carbon nanotubes [45-48] and graphene oxides [49, 50]. A unique nature of anisotropic carbonaceous nanomaterials is most likely responsible

for such a dramatic thermal conductivity increase by engaging additional heat transfer mechanism in suspensions.
Nanoemulsions (liquid/liquid dispersions) [51, 52] are attractive due to their long-term stability, although the potential of nanodroplets in enhancing thermal conductivity is limited, the development of nanoemulsions may open a new direction for thermal fluid studies [53].

3. Factors affecting the fluids cooling efficiency

Attention to nanofluids as advanced heat transfer fluids was initially based on the increased thermal conductivity of nanoparticle suspensions. It is not always realized that the thermal conductivity is not the only property that determines the efficiency of heat transfer fluid in practical applications [54]. In the forced flow systems the coolant is pumped through the pipes of a heat exchanger, introducing convective heat transfer mechanisms and pumping power penalties. Therefore the convective heat transfer coefficient becomes more important than the thermal conductivity value. Evaluation of cooling efficiency, i.e. ability of the heat transfer fluid to remove heat from the heat source depends on the flow regime and includes assessment of contributions from thermal conductivity, viscosity, specific heat, and density of the fluid and can be estimated from the fluid dynamics equations [55] in assumption of a single phase flow.
In the case of hydrodynamically and thermally fully developed laminar flow, the heat transfer coefficient (*h*) is proportional to the thermal conductivity (*k*), and within the acceptable range of inlet/outlet temperature difference is independent of the flow velocity [56]:

$$h \propto k \qquad (2).$$

High viscosity of nanofluids compared to base fluid increases the power required to pump the fluid through the system. When the benefit of the increased heat transfer is larger than the penalty of the increased pumping power, the nanofluid has the potential for commercial viability. Experimental studies have demonstrated good agreement between experimentally measured pressure drops in nanofluid flow and values calculated in assumption of single phase fluid flow with viscosity of the nanofluid [58-60].
An alternative merit criterion for laminar flow [57] was suggested to account for pumping power penalties, for situation, when the tube diameter can be increased for the nanofluid to result in the same heat transfer coefficient:

$$\frac{\mu_{eff}}{\mu_0} \approx 1 + C_\mu \phi; \quad \frac{k_{eff}}{k_0} \approx 1 + C_k \phi; \quad C_\mu / C_k < 4; \qquad (3),$$

where ϕ is the particle volume concentration, μ is the dynamic viscosity of the nanofluid (*eff*) and the base fluid (*0*), and C_μ and C_k are viscosity and thermal conductivity enhancement coefficients, determined from experimental viscosity and thermal conductivity ratios. However this merit criterion is not very practical when efficiencies of two fluids are compared in the same system geometry (i.e. tube diameter).
In turbulent flow regime the heat transfer rate (based on the Dittus-Boelter equation for heating applications) is dependent not only upon the thermal conductivity (*k*), but also on the density (ρ), specific heat (c_p), viscosity (μ) and flow velocity (V) [55]:

$$h \propto \rho^{4/5} c_p^{2/5} \mu^{-2/5} k^{3/5} V^{4/5} \qquad (4).$$

Introduction of nanoparticles to the fluid affects all of thermo-physical properties and should be accounted for in the nanofluid evaluations [61]. Density and specific heat are proportional to the volume ratio of solid and liquid in the system, generally with density increasing and specific heat decreasing with addition of solid nanoparticles to the fluid. According to equation (4) the increase in density, specific heat and thermal conductivity of nanofluids favors the heat transfer coefficient; however the well described increase in the viscosity of nanoparticle suspensions is not beneficial for heat transfer. The velocity term in the equation (4) also represents the pumping power penalties resulting from the increased viscosity of nanofluids [55, 58].

The comparison of two liquid coolants flowing in fully developed turbulent flow regime over or through a given geometry at a fixed velocity reduces to the ratio of changes in the thermo-physical properties:

$$\frac{h_{eff}}{h_0} \approx \left(\frac{\rho_{eff}}{\rho_0}\right)^{4/5} \left(\frac{c_{peff}}{c_{p0}}\right)^{2/5} \left(\frac{\mu_{eff}}{\mu_0}\right)^{-2/5} \left(\frac{k_{eff}}{k_0}\right)^{3/5} \quad (5).$$

The nanofluid is beneficial when h_{eff}/h_0 ratio is above one and not beneficial when it is below one. Similar figure of merit the ratio of Mouromtseff values (Mo) was also suggested for cooling applications [62, 63]. The fluid with the highest Mo value will provide the highest heat transfer rateove the same cooling system geometry.

It is obvious that nanofluids are multivariable systems, with each thermo-physical property dependent on several parameters including nanoparticle material, concentration, size, and shape, properties of the base fluid, and presence of additives, surfactants, electrolyte strength, and pH. Thus, the challenge in the development of nanofluids for heat transfer applications is in understanding of how micro- and macro-scale interactions between the nanoparticles and the fluid affect the properties of the suspensions. Below we discuss how each of the above parameters affects individual nanofluids properties.

4. General trends in nanofluid properties

The controversy of nanofluids is possibly related to the underestimated system complexity and the presence of solid/liquid interface. Because of huge surface area of nanoparticles the boundary layers between nanoparticles and the liquid contribute significantly to the fluid properties, resulting in a three-phase system. The approach to nanofluids as three-phase systems (solid, liquid and interface) (instead of traditional consideration of nanofluids as two-phase systems of solid and liquid) allows for deeper understanding of correlations between the nanofluid parameters, properties, and cooling performance. In this section general experimentally observed trends in nanofluid properties are correlated to nanoparticle and base fluid characteristics with the perspective of interface contributions (Fig. 2).

a. Nanoparticles

Great varieties of nanoparticles are commercially available and can be used for preparation of nanofluids. Nanoparticle material, concentration, size and shape are engineering parameters that can be adjusted to manipulate the nanofluid properties.

Nanoparticle material defines density, specific heat and thermal conductivity of the solid phase contributing to nanofluids properties (subscripts *p*, *0*, and *eff* refer to nanoparticle, base fluid and nanofluid respectively) in proportion to the volume concentration of particles (ϕ):

$$\rho_{eff} = (1-\phi)\rho_0 + \phi\rho_0 \quad (6);$$

$$\left(c_p\right)_{eff} = \frac{(1-\phi)\left(\rho c_p\right)_0 + \phi\left(\rho c_p\right)_p}{(1-\phi)\rho_0 + \phi\rho_p} \quad (7);$$

$$k_{eff} = k_0\left(\frac{k_p + 2k_0 + 2\left(k_p - k_0\right)\phi}{k_p + 2k_0 - \left(k_p - k_0\right)\phi}\right), \text{(for spherical particles by EMT)} \quad (8).$$

As it was mentioned previously materials with higher thermal conductivity, specific heat, and density are beneficial for heat transfer. Besides the bulk material properties some specific to nanomaterials phenomena such as surface plasmon resonance effect [23], increased specific heat [64], and heat absorption [65, 66] of nanoparticles can be translated to the advanced nanofluid properties in well-dispersed systems.

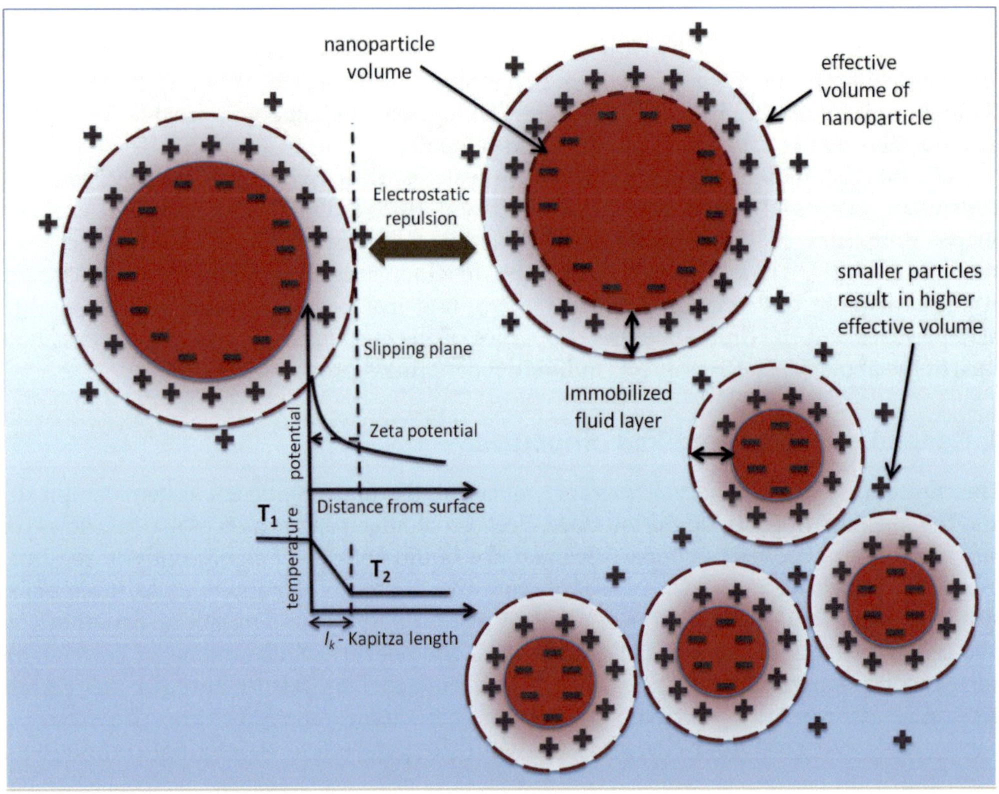

Fig. 2. Interfacial effects in nanoparticle suspensions

The size of nanoparticles defines the surface-to-volume ratio and for the same volume concentrations suspension of smaller particles have a higher area of the solid/liquid interface (Fig. 2). Therefore the contribution of interfacial effects is stronger in such a suspension [15, 34, 35, 67]. Interactions between the nanoparticles and the fluid are manifested through the interfacial thermal resistance, also known as Kapitza resistance (R_k), that rises because interfaces act as an obstacle to heat flow and diminish the overall thermal conductivity of the system [11]. A more transparent definition can be obtained by defining the Kapitza length:

$$l_k = R_k k_0 \quad (9),$$

where k_0 is the thermal conductivity of the matrix, l_k is simply the thickness of base fluid equivalent to the interface from a thermal point of view (i.e. excluded from thermal transport, Fig. 2) [11]. The values of Kapitza resistance are constant for the particular solid/liquid interface and defined by the strength of solid-liquid interaction and can be correlated to the wetting properties of the interface [11]. When the interactions between the nanoparticle surfaces and the fluid are weak (non-wetting case) the rates of energy transfer are small resulting in relatively large values of R_k. The overall contribution of the solid/liquid interface to the macroscopic thermal conductivity of nanofluids is typically negative and was found proportional to the total area of the interface, increasing with decreasing particle sizes [34, 67].

The size of nanoparticles also affects the viscosity of nanofluids. Generally the viscosity increases as the volume concentration of particles increases. Studies of suspensions with the same volume concentration and material of nanoparticles but different sizes [67, 68] showed that the viscosity of suspension increases as the particle size decreases. This behavior is related to formation of immobilized layers of the fluid along the nanoparticle interfaces that move with the particles in the flow (Fig. 2) [69]. The thicknesses of those fluid layers depend on the strength of particle-fluid interactions while the volume of immobilized fluid increases in proportion to the total area of the solid/liquid interface (Fig. 2). At the same volume concentration of nanoparticles the "effective volume concentration" (immobilized fluid and nanoparticles) is higher in suspensions of smaller nanoparticles resulting in higher viscosity. Therefore contributions of interfacial effects, to both, thermal conductivity and viscosity may be negligible at micron particle sizes, but become very important for nanoparticle suspensions. Increased viscosity is highly undesirable for a coolant, since any gain in heat transfer and hence reduction in radiator size and weight could be compensated by increased pumping power penalties. To achieve benefit for heat transfer, the suspensions of larger nanoparticles with higher thermal conductivity and lower viscosity should be used.

A drawback of using larger nanoparticles is the potential instability of nanofluids. Rough estimation of the settling velocity of nanoparticles (V_s) can be calculated from Stokes law (only accounts for gravitational and buoyant forces):

$$V_S = \frac{2}{9}\left(\frac{\rho_p - \rho_0}{\mu}\right) r^2 g \quad (10),$$

where g is the gravitational acceleration. As one can see from the equation (10), the stability of a suspension (defined by lower settling rates) improves if: (a) the density of the solid material (ρ_p) is close to that of the fluid (ρ_0); (b) the viscosity of the suspension (μ) is high, and (c) the particle radius (r) is small.

Effects of the nanoparticles shapes on the thermal conductivity and viscosity of alumina-EG/H_2O suspensions [34] are also strongly related to the total area of the solid/liquid interface. In nanofluids with non-spherical particles the thermal conductivity enhancements predicted by the Hamilton-Crosser equation [2, 70] (randomly arranged elongated particles provide higher thermal conductivities than spheres [71]) are diminished by the negative contribution of the interfacial thermal resistance as the sphericity of nanoparticles decreases [34].

In systems like carbon nanotube [45-48], graphite [72, 73] and graphene oxide [49, 50, 74] nanofluids the nanoparticle percolation networks can be formed, which along with high anisotropic thermal conductivity of those materials result in abnormally increased thermal conductivities. However aggregation and clustering of nanoparticles does not always result in increased thermal conductivity: there are many studies that report thermal conductivity just within EMT prediction in highly agglomerated suspension [71, 75-77].

Elongated particles and agglomerates also result in higher viscosity than spheres at the same volume concentration, which is due to structural limitation of rotational and transitional motion in the flow [77, 78]. Therefore spherical particles or low aspect ratio spheroids are more practical for achieving low viscosities in nanofluids – the property that is highly desirable for minimizing the pumping power penalties in cooling system applications.

b. Base fluid

The influence of base fluids on the thermo-physical properties of suspensions is not very well studied and understood. However there are few publications indicating some general trends in the base fluid effects.

Suspensions of the same Al_2O_3 nanoparticles in water, ethylene glycol (EG), glycerol, and pump oil showed increase in relative thermal conductivity (k_{eff}/k_0) with decrease in thermal conductivity of the base fluid [15, 79, 80]. On the other hand the alteration of the base fluid viscosity [81] (from 4.2 cP to 5500 cP, by mixing two fluids with approximately the same thermal conductivity) resulted in decrease in the thermal conductivity of the Fe_2O_3 suspension as the viscosity of the base fluid increased. Comparative studies of 4 vol% SiC suspensions in water and 50/50 ethylene glycol/water mixture with controlled particle sizes, concentration, and pH showed that relative change in thermal conductivity due to the introduction of nanoparticles is ~5% higher in EG/H_2O than in H_2O at all other parameters being the same [68]. This effect cannot be explained simply by the lower thermal conductivity of the EG/H_2O base fluid since the difference in enhancement values expected from EMT is less than 0.1% [7]. Therefore the "base fluid effect" observed in different nanofluid systems is most likely related to the lower value of the interfacial thermal resistance (better wettability) in the EG/H_2O than in the H_2O-based nanofluids.

Both, thermal conductivity and viscosity are strongly related to the nanofluid microstructure. The nanoparticles suspended in a base fluid are in random motion under the influence of several acting forces such as Brownian motion (Langevin force, that is random function of time and reflects the atomic structure of medium), viscous resistance (Stokes drag force), intermolecular Van-der-Waals interaction (repulsion, polarization and dispersion forces) and electrostatic (Coulomb) interactions between ions and dipoles. Nanoparticles in suspension can be well-dispersed (particles move independently) or agglomerated (ensembles of particles move together). Depending on the particle concentration and the magnitude of particle-particle interaction that are affected by pH, surfactant additives and particle size and shape [82] a dispersion/agglomeration equilibrium establishes in nanoparticle suspension. It should be noted here, that two types of agglomerates are possible in nanofluids. First type of agglomerates occurs when nanoparticles are agglomerated through solid/solid interface and can potentially provide increased thermal conductivity as described by Prasher [17]. When loose single crystalline nanoparticles are suspended each particle acquires diffuse layer of fluid intermediating particle-particle interactions in nanofluid. Due to weak repulsion such nanoparticles can form aggregate-like ensembles moving together, but in this case the interfacial resistance at solid/liquid/solid interface is likely to prevent proposed agglomeration induced enhancement in thermal conductivity.

Relative viscosity was shown to decrease with the increase of the average particle size in both EG/H_2O and H_2O-based suspensions. However at the same volume concentration of nanoparticles relative viscosity increase is smaller in the EG/H_2O than in H_2O-based nanofluids, especially in suspensions of smaller nanoparticles [68]. According to the classic Einstein-Bachelor equation for hard non-interacting spheres [83], the percentage viscosity increase should be independent of the viscosity of the base fluid and only proportional to the particle volume concentration. Therefore the experimentally observed variations in viscosity increase upon addition of nanoparticles to different base fluids increase with base fluids can be related to the difference in structure and thickness of immobilized fluid layers around the nanoparticles, affecting the effective volume concentration and ultimately the viscosity of the suspensions [34, 67, 68].

Viscosity increase in nanofluids was shown to depend not only on the type of the base fluid, but also on the pH value (in protonic fluids) that establishes zeta potential (charge at the particle's slipping plane, Fig. 2). Particles of the same charge repel each other minimizing the particle-particle interactions that strongly affect the viscosity [34, 67, 84]. It was demonstrated that the viscosity of the alumina-based nanofluids can be decreased by 31% by only adjusting the pH of the suspension without significantly affecting the thermal conductivity [34]. Depending on the particle concentration and the magnitude of particle-particle interactions (affected by pH, surfactant additives and particle size and shape) dispersion/agglomeration equilibrium establishes in nanoparticle suspension. Extended agglomerates can provide increased thermal conductivity as described in the literature [17, 85], but agglomeration and clustering of nanoparticles result in undesirable viscosity increase and/or settling of suspensions [75].

Introduction of other additives (salts and surfactants) may also affect the zeta potential at the particle surfaces. Non-ionic surfactants provide steric insulation of nanoparticles preventing Van-der-Waals interactions, while ionic surfactants may serve as both electrostatic and steric stabilization. The thermal conductivity of surfactants is significantly lower than water and ethylene glycol. Therefore addition of such additives, while improving viscosity, typically reduces the thermal conductivity of suspension.

It should be mentioned here that all thermo-physical properties have some temperature dependence. The thermal conductivity of fluids may increase or decrease with temperature, however it was shown that the relative enhancement in the thermal conductivity due to addition of nanoparticles remains constant [71, 86]. The viscosity of most fluids strongly depends on the temperature, typically decreasing with increasing temperature. It was noted in couple of nanofluid systems that the relative increase in viscosity is also reduced as temperature rises [67, 68]. The constant thermal conductivity increase and viscosity decrease with temperature makes nanofluids technology very promising for high-temperature application. The density and specific heat of nanomaterials change insignificantly within the practical range of liquid cooling applications. Stability of nanofluids could be improved with temperature increase due to increase in kinetic energy of particles, but heating also may disable the suspension stability provided by electrostatic or/and steric methods, causing the temperature-induced agglomeration [76]. Further studies are needed in this area.

5. Efficient nanofluid by design

In light of all the mentioned nanofluid property trends, development of a heat transfer nanofluid requires a complex approach that accounts for changes in all important thermo-physical properties caused by introduction of nanomaterials to the fluid. Understanding the correlations between nanofluid composition and thermo-physical properties is the key for engineering nanofluids with desired properties. The complexity of correlations between nanofluid parameters and properties described in the previous section and schematically presented on Figure 3, indicates that manipulation of the system performance requires prioritizing and identification of critical parameters and properties of nanofluids.

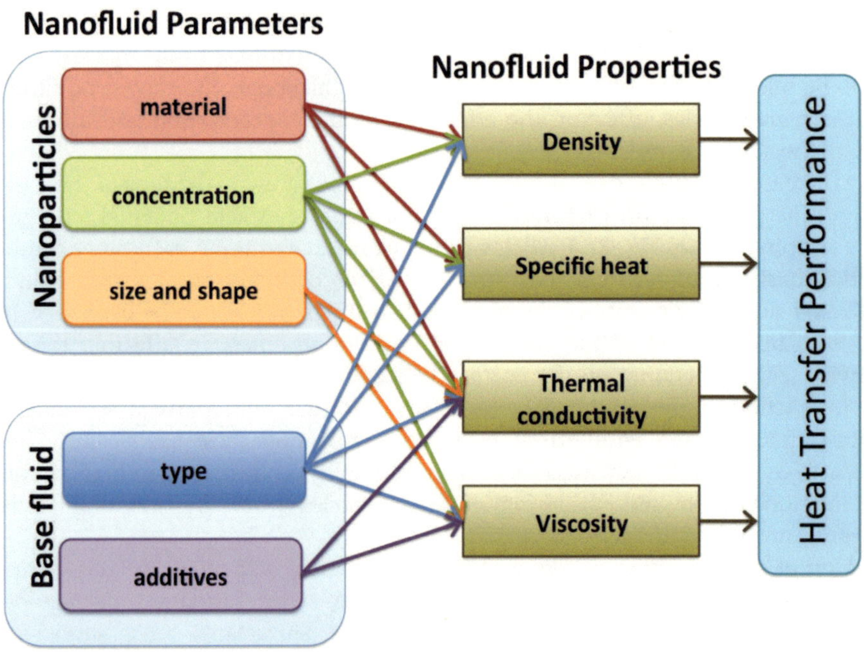

Fig. 3. Complexity and multi-variability of nanoparticle suspensions

Systems engineering is an interdisciplinary field widely used for designing and managing complex engineering projects, where the properties of a system as a whole, may greatly differ from the sum of the parts' properties [87]. Therefore systems engineering can be used to prioritize nanofluid parameters and their contributions to the cooling performance.

The decision matrix is one of the systems engineering approaches, used here as a semi-quantitative technique that allows ranking multi-dimensional nanofluid engineering options [88]. It also offers an alternative way to look at the inner workings of a nanofluid system and allows for design choices addressing the heat transfer demands of a given industrial application. The general trends in nanoparticle suspensions reported in the literature and summarized in previous sections are arranged in a basic decision matrix (Table 1) with each engineering parameter in a separate column and the nanofluid properties listed in rows. Each cell in the table represents the trend and the strength of the contribution of a particular parameter to the nanofluid property.

	NANOFLUID PARAMETERS	Nanoparticle material	Nanoparticle concentration	Nanoparticle shape	Nanoparticle size	Base fluid	Zeta potential/fluid pH	Kapitza resistance	Additives	Temperature
NANOFLUID PROPERTIES										
Stability	⇑	▲	▲	▲	◘↓	○	◘	x	◘	?
Density	⇑	◘	◘↑	x	x	◘	x	x	x	x
Specific Heat	⇑	◘	◘↓	x	x	◘	x	x	x	▲
Thermal Conductivity	⇑	○	◘↑	○	◘↑	▲	○	◘↓	▲	○
Viscosity	⇓	▲	◘↓	◘	◘↓	◘↑	◘	x	○	◘
Heat Transfer Coefficient	⇑	◘	◘↑*	◘	◘↑	◘	◘	◘↓	○	◘
Pumping Power Penalty	⇓	x	◘	◘	◘↑	◘	◘	x	○	◘
Relative Importance		4.0	6.25	3.75	5.0	5.25	4.0	2.0	2.75	3.75

Table 1. Systems engineering approach to nanofluid design. Symbols: ◘- strong dependence; ○- medium dependence; ▲- weak dependence; x - no dependence; ? – unknown or varies from system to system; ⇑ - larger the better;⇓ - smaller the better; ↑- increase with increase in parameter; ↓- decrease with increase in parameter; *-within the linear property increase

Symbols "x", "▲", "○", and "◘"indicating no, weak, medium, and strong dependence on nanofluid parameter respectively are also scored as 0.0, 0.25, 0.5 and 1.0 for importance [88]. The relative importance of each nanofluid parameter for heat transfer can be estimated as a sum of the gained scores (Table 1). Based on that the nanofluid engineering parameters can be arranged by the decreasing importance for the heat transfer performance: particle concentration > base fluid > nanoparticle size > nanoparticle material ≈ surface charge > temperature ≈ particle shape > additives > Kapitza resistance. This is an approximate ranking of nanofluid parameters that assumes equal and independent weight of each of the nanofluid property contributing to thermal transport. The advantage of this approach to decision making in nanofluid engineering is that subjective opinions about the importance of one nanofluid parameter versus another can be made more objective.

Applications of the decision matrix (Table 1) are not limited to the design of new nanofluids, it also can be used as guidance for improving the performance of existing nanoparticle suspensions. While the particle material, size, shape, concentration, and the base fluid parameters are fixed in a given nanofluid, the cooling performance still can be improved by remaining adjustable nanofluid parameters in order of their relative importance, i.e. by adjusting the zeta potential and/or by increasing the test/operation temperatures in the above case. Further studies are needed to define the weighted importance of each nanofluid property contributing to the heat transfer. The decision matrix can also be customized and extended for specifics of nanofluids and the mechanisms that are engaged in heat transfer.

6. Summary

In general nanofluids show many excellent properties promising for heat transfer applications. Despite many interesting phenomena described and understood there are still several important issues that need to be solved for practical application of nanofluids. The winning composition of nanofluids that meets all engineering requirements (high heat transfer coefficients, long-term stability, and low viscosity) has not been formulated yet because of complexity and multivariability of nanofluid systems. The approach to engineering the nanofluids for heat transfer described here includes several steps. First the thermo-physical properties of nanofluids that are important for heat transfer are identified using the fluid dynamics cooling efficiency criteria for single-phase fluids. Then the nanofluid engineering parameters are reviewed in regards to their influence on the thermo-physical properties of nanoparticle suspensions. The individual nanofluid parameter-property correlations are summarized and analyzed using the system engineering approach that allows identifying the most influential nanofluid parameters. The relative importance of engineering parameters resulted from such analysis suggests the potential nanofluid design options. The nanoparticle concentration, base fluid, and particle size appear to be the most influential parameters for improving the heat transfer efficiency of nanofluid. Besides the generally observed trends in nanofluids, discussed here, nanomaterials with unique properties should be considered to create a dramatically beneficial nanofluid for heat transfer or other application.

7. References

[1] Maxwell, J.C., A Treatise on Electricity and Magnetism. 1873, Oxford, UK: Clarendon.

[2] Hamilton, R.L. and O.K. Crosser, Thermal conductivity of heterogeneous two-component systems. *Industrial & Engineering Chemistry Fundamentals*, 1962. 1(3): p. 187-191.

[3] Buongiorno, J., et al., A benchmark study on the thermal conductivity of nanofluids. *Journal of Applied Physics*, 2009. 106(9): p. 094312.

[4] Kabelac, S. and J.F. Kuhnke, Heat transfet mechanisms in nanofluids --experiments and theory--. *Annals of the Assembly for International Heat Transfer Conference*, 2006. 13: p. KN-11.

[5] Yu, W., et al., Review and comparison of nanofluid thermal conductivity and heat transfer enhancements. *Heat Transfer Engineering*, 2008. 29(5): p. 432-460.

[6] Trisaksri, V. and S. Wongwises, Critical review of heat transfer characteristics of nanofluids. *Renewable & Sustainable Energy Reviews*, 2007. 11(3): p. 512-523.

[7] Yu, W., et al., Mechanisms and Models of Effective Thermal Conductivities of Nanofluids. *Journal of Nanoscience and Nanotechnology*, 2010. 10: p. 1-26.

[8] Chandrasekar, M. and S. Suresh, A Review on the Mechanisms of Heat Transport in Nanofluids. *Heat Transfer Engineering*, 2009. 30(14): p. 1136-1150.

[9] Nan, C.W., et al., Effective thermal conductivity of particulate composites with interfacial thermal resistance. *Journal of Applied Physics*, 1997. 81(10): p. 6692-6699.

[10] Wilson, O.M., et al., Colloidal metal particles as probes of nanoscale thermal transport in fluids. *Physical Review* B, 2002. 66(22).

[11] Barrat, J.L. and F. Chiaruttini, Kapitza resistance at the liquid-solid interface. *Molecular Physics*, 2003. 101: p. 1605-1610.

[12] Yu, W. and S.U.S. Choi, The role of interfacial layers in the enhanced thermal conductivity of nanofluids: A renovated Maxwell model. *Journal of Nanoparticle Research*, 2003. 5(1-2): p. 167-171.

[13] Xie, H.Q., M. Fujii, and X. Zhang, Effect of interfacial nanolayer on the effective thermal conductivity of nanoparticle-fluid mixture. *International Journal of Heat and Mass Transfer*, 2005. 48(14): p. 2926-2932.

[14] Leong, K.C., C. Yang, and S.M.S. Murshed, A model for the thermal conductivity of nanofluids - the effect of interfacial layer. *Journal of Nanoparticle Research*, 2006. 8(2): p. 245-254.

[15] Xie, H.Q., et al., Thermal conductivity enhancement of suspensions containing nanosized alumina particles. *Journal of Applied Physics*, 2002. 91(7): p. 4568-4572.

[16] Wang, B.X., L.P. Zhou, and X.F. Peng, A fractal model for predicting the effective thermal conductivity of liquid with suspension of nanoparticles. International *Journal of Heat and Mass Transfer*, 2003. 46(14): p. 2665-2672.

[17] Prasher, R., et al., Effect of aggregation on thermal conduction in colloidal nanofluids. *Applied Physics Letters*, 2006. 89(14).

[18] Evans, W., et al., Effect of aggregation and interfacial thermal resistance on thermal conductivity of nanocomposites and colloidal nanofluids. *International Journal of Heat and Mass Transfer*, 2008. 51(5-6): p. 1431-1438.

[19] Prasher, R., P. Bhattacharya, and P.E. Phelan, Brownian-motion-based convective-conductive model for the effective thermal conductivity of nanofluids. *Journal of Heat Transfer-Transactions of the Asme*, 2006. 128(6): p. 588-595.

[20] Jang, S.P. and S.U.S. Choi, Role of Brownian motion in the enhanced thermal conductivity of nanofluids. *Applied Physics Letters*, 2004. 84(21): p. 4316-4318.

[21] Prasher, R., P. Bhattacharya, and P.E. Phelan, Thermal conductivity of nanoscale colloidal solutions (nanofluids). *Physical Review Letters*, 2005. 94(2): p. 025901-4.

[22] Hartland, G.V., Measurements of the material properties of metal nanoparticles by time-resolved spectroscopy. *Physical Chemistry Chemical Physics*, 2004. 6(23): p. 5263-5274.

[23] Lee, K.H., et al., Surface Plasmon Enhanced Thermal Properties of Noble Metallic Nanofluids. *Advanced Science Letters*, 2010. 3(2): p. 149-153.

[24] Kim, I. and K.D. Kihm, Measuring near-field nanoparticle concentration profiles by correlating surface plasmon resonance reflectance with effective refractive index of nanofluids. *Optics Letters*, 2010. 35(3): p. 393-395.

[25] Rad, P.M. and C. Aghanajafi, The Effect of Thermal Radiation on Nanofluid Cooled Microchannels. *Journal of Fusion Energy*, 2009. 28(1): p. 91-100.

[26] Mu, L.J., Q.Z. Zhu, and L.L. Si, Radiative properties of nanofluids and performance of a direct solar absorber using nanofluids. *Mnhmt*2009, Vol 1, 2010: p. 549-553.

[27] Ozerinc, S., S. Kakac, and A.G. Yazicioglu, Enhanced thermal conductivity of nanofluids: a state-of-the-art review. *Microfluidics and Nanofluidics*, 2010. 8(2): p. 145-170.

[28] Li, Y.J., et al., A review on development of nanofluid preparation and characterization. *Powder Technology*, 2009. 196(2): p. 89-101.
[29] Cheng, L.X., E.P. Bandarra, and J.R. Thome, Nanofluid Two-Phase Flow and Thermal Physics: A New Research Frontier of Nanotechnology and Its Challenges. *Journal of Nanoscience and Nanotechnology*, 2008. 8(7): p. 3315-3332.
[30] Murshed, S.M.S., K.C. Leong, and C. Yang, Thermophysical and electrokinetic properties of nanofluids - A critical review. *Applied Thermal Engineering*, 2008. 28(17-18): p. 2109-2125.
[31] Choi, S.U.S., Nanofluids: From Vision to Reality Through Research. *Journal of Heat Transfer-Transactions of the Asme*, 2009. 131(3).
[32] Wen, D.S., et al., Review of nanofluids for heat transfer applications. *Particuology*, 2009. 7(2): p. 141-150.
[33] Wang, X.Q. and A.S. Mujumdar, Heat transfer characteristics of nanofluids: a review. *International Journal of Thermal Sciences*, 2007. 46(1): p. 1-19.
[34] Timofeeva, E.V., J.L. Routbort, and D. Singh, Particle shape effects on thermophysical properties of alumina nanofluids. *Journal of Applied Physics*, 2009. 106: p. 014304.
[35] Timofeeva, E.V., et al., Base Fluid and Temperature Effects on the Heat Transfer Characteristics of SiC in EG/H_2O and H_2O Nanofluids. *Journal of Applied Physics*, 2011. 109: p. 014914 (5pp).
[36] Cho, T., et al., Preparation of nanofluids containing suspended silver particles for enhancing fluid thermal conductivity of fluids. *Journal of Industrial and Engineering Chemistry*, 2005. 11(3): p. 400-406.
[37] Hong, T.K., H.S. Yang, and C.J. Choi, Study of the enhanced thermal conductivity of Fe nanofluids. *Journal of Applied Physics*, 2005. 97(6).
[38] Eastman, J.A., et al., Anomalously increased effective thermal conductivities of ethylene glycol-based nanofluids containing copper nanoparticles. Applied Physics Letters, 2001. 78(6): p. 718-720.
[39] Chopkar, M., et al., Development and characterization of Al2Cu and Ag2Al nanoparticle dispersed water and ethylene glycol based nanofluid. *Materials Science and Engineering B-Solid State Materials for Advanced Technology*, 2007. 139(2-3): p. 141-148.
[40] Kang, H.U., S.H. Kim, and J.M. Oh, Estimation of thermal conductivity of nanofluid using experimental effective particle volume. *Experimental Heat Transfer*, 2006. 19(3): p. 181-191.
[41] Li, Q. and Y.M. Xuan, Experimental investigation on transport properties of nanofluids. *Heat Transfer Science and Technology* 2000, 2000: p. 757-762.
[42] Patel, H.E., et al., Thermal conductivities of naked and monolayer protected metal nanoparticle based nanofluids: Manifestation of anomalous enhancement and chemical effects. *Applied Physics Letters*, 2003. 83(14): p. 2931-2933.
[43] Venerus, D.C., et al., Study of thermal transport in nanoparticle suspensions using forced Rayleigh scattering. *Journal of Applied Physics*, 2006. 100(9).
[44] Godson, L., D.M. Lal, and S. Wongwises, Measurement of Thermo Physical Properties of Metallic Nanofluids for High Temperature Applications. *Nanoscale and Microscale Thermophysical Engineering*, 2010. 14(3): p. 152-173.
[45] Sastry, N.N.V., et al., Predicting the effective thermal conductivity of carbon nanotube based nanofluids. *Nanotechnology*, 2008. 19.
[46] Choi, S.U.S., et al., Anomalous thermal conductivity enhancement in nanotube suspensions. *Applied Physics Letters*, 2001. 79(14): p. 2252-2254.

[47] Zhang, X., H. Gu, and M. Fujii, Effective thermal conductivity and thermal diffusivity of nanofluids containing spherical and cylindrical nanoparticles. *Journal of Applied Physics*, 2006. 100(4).

[48] Hwang, Y., et al., Stability and thermal conductivity characteristics of nanofluids. *Thermochimica Acta*, 2007. 455(1-2): p. 70-74.

[49] Yu, W., H.Q. Xie, and D. Bao, Enhanced thermal conductivities of nanofluids containing graphene oxide nanosheets. *Nanotechnology*, 2010. 21(5).

[50] Yu, W., et al., Significant thermal conductivity enhancement for nanofluids containing graphene nanosheets. *Physics Letters* A, 2011. 375(10): p. 1323-1328.

[51] Yang, B. and Z.H. Han, Thermal conductivity enhancement in water-in-FC72 nanoemulsion fluids. *Applied Physics Letters*, 2006. 88(26).

[52] Han, Z.H. and B. Yang, Thermophysical characteristics of water-in-FC72 nanoemulsion fluids. *Applied Physics Letters*, 2008. 92(1).

[53] Han, Z.H., F.Y. Cao, and B. Yang, Synthesis and thermal characterization of phase-changeable indium/polyalphaolefin nanofluids. *Applied Physics Letters*, 2008. 92(24).

[54] Mohapatra, S.C. (2006) An Overview of Liquid Coolants for Electronics Cooling. *ElectronicsCooling* 12, ttp://electronics-cooling.com/articles/2006/2006_may_a2.php.

[55] Yu, W., et al., Thermophysical property-related comparison criteria for nanofluid heat transfer enhancement in turbulent flow. *Applied Physics Letters*, 2010. 96: p. 213109-3.

[56] Etherington, H., ed. *Nuclear Engineering Handbook*. 1958, McGraw-Hill Book Company, Inc.: New York, USA.

[57] Prasher, R., et al., Measurements of nanofluid viscosity and its implications for thermal applications. *Applied Physics Letters*, 2006. 89(13): p. 133108-133110.

[58] Routbort, J.L., et al., Pumping power of nanofluids in a flowing system. *Journal of Nanoparticle Research*, 2011. 12.

[59] Williams, W., J. Buongiorno, and L.W. Hu, Experimental investigation of turbulent convective heat transfer and pressure loss of alumina/water and zirconia/water nanoparticle colloids (nanofluids) in horizontal tubes. *Journal of Heat Transfer-Transactions of the Asme*, 2008. 130(4): p. 042412-7.

[60] Xuan, Y.M. and Q. Li, Investigation on convective heat transfer and flow features of nanofluids. *Journal of Heat Transfer-Transactions of the Asme*, 2003. 125(1): p. 151-155.

[61] Murshed, S.M.S., K.C. Leong, and C. Yang, Investigations of thermal conductivity and viscosity of nanofluids. *International Journal of Thermal Sciences*, 2008. 47(5): p. 560-568.

[62] Mouromtseff, I.E., Water and forced-air cooling of vacuum tubes. *Proceedings of the Institute of Radio Engineers*, 1942: p. 190-205.

[63] Simons, R.E. (2006) Comparing Heat Transfer Rates of Liquid Coolants Using the Mouromtseff Number. *Electronics Cooling* 12, ttp://electronics-cooling.com/articles/2006/2006_may_cc.php.

[64] Likhachev, V.N., et al., Anomalous heat capacity of nanoparticles. *Russian Journal of Physical Chemistry* B, 2007. 1(1): p. 74-78.

[65] Tyagi, H., P. Phelan, and R. Prasher, Predicted Efficiency of a Low-Temperature Nanofluid-Based Direct Absorption Solar Collector. *Journal of Solar Energy Engineering-Transactions of the Asme*, 2009. 131(4).

[66] Otanicar, T.P., et al., Nanofluid-based direct absorption solar collector. *Journal of Renewable and Sustainable Energy*, 2010: p. 033102 (13 pp.).

[67] Timofeeva, E.V., et al., The Particle Size and Interfacial Effects on Thermo-physical and Heat Transfer Characteristics of Water Based a-SiC Nanofluids. *Nanotechnology*, 2010. 21(21): p. 215703-13.

[68] Timofeeva, E.V., et al., Base Fluid and Temperature Effects on the Heat Transfer Characteristics of SiC in EG/H_2O and H_2O Nanofluids. *Journal of Applied Physics*, 2010.

[69] Li, L., et al., An investigation of molecular layering at the liquid-solid interface in nanofluids by molecular dynamics simulation. *Physics Letters* A, 2008. 372(25): p. 4541-4544.

[70] Zhu, H.T., et al., Novel synthesis and thermal conductivity of CuO nanofluid. *Journal of Physical Chemistry* C, 2007. 111(4): p. 1646-1650.

[71] Timofeeva, E.V., et al., Thermal conductivity and particle agglomeration in alumina nanofluids: Experiment and theory. Physical Review E, 2007. 76: p. 061203-16.

[72] Zhu, H.T., et al., Preparation and thermal conductivity of suspensions of graphite nanoparticles. *Carbon*, 2007. 45(1): p. 226-228.

[73] Shaikh, S., K. Lafdi, and R. Ponnappan, Thermal conductivity improvement in carbon nanoparticle doped PAO oil: An experimental study. *Journal of Applied Physics*, 2007. 101(6): p. 064302.

[74] Baby, T.T. and S. Ramaprabhu, Investigation of thermal and electrical conductivity of graphene based nanofluids. *Journal of Applied Physics*, 2010: p. 124308 (6 pp.).

[75] Gharagozloo, P.E. and K.E. Goodson, Aggregate fractal dimensions and thermal conduction in nanofluids. *Journal of Applied Physics*, 2010. 108(7).

[76] Gharagozloo, P.E. and K.E. Goodson, Temperature-dependent aggregation and diffusion in nanofluids. *International Journal of Heat and Mass Transfer*, 2011. 54(4): p. 797-806.

[77] Anoop, K.B., et al., Rheological and flow characteristics of nanofluids: influence of electroviscous effects and particle agglomeration. *Journal of Applied Physics*, 2009: p. 034909 (7 pp.).

[78] Yang, Y., et al., Rheological behavior of carbon nanotube and graphite nanoparticle dispersions. *Journal of Nanoscience and Nanotechnology*, 2005. 5: p. 571-579.

[79] Xie, H.Q., et al., Dependence of the thermal conductivity of nanoparticle-fluid mixture on the base fluid. *Journal of Materials Science Letters*, 2002. 21(19): p. 1469-1471.

[80] Lee, J.K., et al., Thermal conductivity and lubrication characteristics of nanofluids. Current Applied Physics | *Current Applied Physics*, 2006. 6: p. e67-71.

[81] Tsai, T.H., et al., Effect of viscosity of base fluid on thermal conductivity of nanofluids. *Applied Physics Letters*, 2008. 93(23).

[82] Sposito, G., ed. The Environmental Chemistry of Aluminum. 2nd ed. 1996, CRC, Lewis Publishers: Boca Raton, FL.

[83] Vold, R.D. and M.J. Vold, Colloid and interface chemistry. 1983, *Reading*, Massachusetts: Addison-Wesley Publishing Company, Inc.

[84] Zhao, J.-F., et al., Dependence of nanofluid viscosity on particle size and pH value. *Chinese Physics Letters*, 2009: p. 066202 (4 pp.).

[85] Eapen, J., et al., The Classical Nature of Thermal Conduction in Nanofluids. *Journal of Heat Transfer-Transactions of the Asme*, 2010. 132(10).

[86] Singh, D., et al., An investigation of silicon carbide-water nanofluid for heat transfer applications. *Journal of Applied Physics*, 2009. 105(6): p. 064306-6.

[87] Kossiakoff, A. and W.N. Sweet, Systems Engineering: Principles and Practice. *Systems Engineering and Management*, ed. A. Sage. 2003: Wiley-IEEE. 463.

[88] Pugh, S., D. Clausing, and R. Andrade, *Creating innovative products using total design: the living legacy of Stuart Pugh*. 1996: Addison-Wesley Pub. Co.

20

Heat Transfer in Nanostructures Using the Fractal Approximation of Motion

Maricel Agop[1,2], Irinel Casian Botez[3],
Luciu Razvan Silviu[4] and Manuela Girtu[5]
[1]*Laboratoire de Physique des Lasers, Atomes et Molécules (UMR 8523), Université des Sciences et Technologies de Lille,*
[2]*Physics Department, "Ghe. Asachi" Technical University, Iasi,*
[3]*Department of Electronics, Telecommunication and Information Technology, "Gh. Asachi" Technical University, Iasi,*
[4]*Faculty of Civil Engineering, "Ghe. Asachi" Technical University, Iasi,*
[5]*"Vasile Alecsandri" University of Bacau, Department of Mathematics, Bacau*
[1]*France*
[2,3,4,5]*Romania*

1. Introduction

If at a macroscopic scale the heat transfer mechanism implies either diffusion type conduction or phononic type conduction (Zhang, 2007; Rohsenow et al., 1998), at a microscopic scale the situation is completely different. This happens because the macroscopic familiar concepts cannot be applied at a microscopic scale, e.g. the concept of a distribution function of both coordinates and momentum used in the Boltzmann equation (Wang et al., 2008). Moreover, fundamental concepts such a temperature cannot be defined in the conventional sense, *i.e.* as a measure of thermodynamic equilibrium (Chen, 2000). Thus anomalies might occur: the thermal anomaly of the nanofluids (Wang&Xu, 1999; Keblinski et al., 2002; Patel et al., 2003), etc.

According to our opinion, anomalies become normalities if their specific measures depend on scales: heat conduction in nanostructures differs significantly from that in macrostructures because the characteristic length scales associated with heat carriers, *i.e.* the mean free path and the wavelength, are comparable to the characteristic length of nanostructures (Chen, 2000). Therefore, we expect to replace the usual mechanisms (ballistic thermal transport, etc.) by something more fundamental: a unique mechanism in which the physical measures should depend not only on spatial coordinates and time, but also on scales. This new way will be possible through the Scale Relativity (SR) theory (Notalle, 1992, 2008a, 2008b, 2007). Some applications of the SR theory at the nanoscale was given in (Casian Botez et al., 2010; Agop et al. 2008). In the present paper, a new model of the heat transfer on nanostructures, considering that the heat flow paths take place on continuous but non-differentiable curves, i.e. an fractals, is established.

2. Consequences of non-differentiability in the heat transfer processes

Let us suppose that the heat flow take place on continuous but non-differentiable curves (fractal curves). The non-differentiability implies the followings (Notalle, 1992, 2008a, 2008b, 2007):

i. A continuous and a non-differentiable curve (or almost nowhere differentiable) is explicitly scale dependent, and its length tends to infinity, when the scale interval tends to zero. In other words, a continuous and non-differentiable space is fractal, in the general meaning given by Mandelbrot to this concept (Mandelbrot, 1982);
ii. There is an infinity of fractals curves (geodesics) relating any couple of its points (or starting from any point), and this is valid for all scales;
iii. The breaking of local differential time reflection invariance. The time-derivative of the temperature field T can be written two-fold:

$$\frac{dT}{dt} = \lim_{dt \to 0} \frac{T(t+dt) - T(t)}{dt}$$
$$\frac{dT}{dt} = \lim_{dt \to 0} \frac{T(t) - T(t-dt)}{dt} \quad (1a,b)$$

Both definitions are equivalent in the differentiable case. In the non-differentiable situation these definitions fail, since the limits are no longer defined. In the framework of fractal theory, the physics is related to the behavior of the function during the "zoom" operation on the time resolution δt, here identified with the differential element dt ("substitution principle"), which is considered as an independent variable. The standard temperature field $T(t)$ is therefore replaced by a fractal temperature field $T(t,dt)$, explicitly dependent on the time resolution interval, whose derivative is undefined only at the unobservable limit $dt \to 0$. As a consequence, this lead us to define the two derivatives of the fractal temperature field as explicit functions of the two variables t and dt,

$$\frac{d_+T}{dt} = \lim_{dt \to 0_+} \frac{T(t+dt,dt) - T(t,dt)}{dt}$$
$$\frac{d_-T}{dt} = \lim_{dt \to 0_-} \frac{T(t,dt) - T(t-dt,dt)}{dt} \quad (2a,b)$$

The sign, +, corresponds to the forward process and, -, to the backward process;

iv. the differential of the fractal coordinates, $d_\pm X(t,dt)$, can be decomposed as follows:

$$d_\pm X(t,dt) = d_\pm x(t) + d_\pm \xi(t,dt) \quad (3a,b)$$

where $d_\pm x(t)$ is the "classical part" and $d_\pm \xi(t,dt)$ is the "fractal part".

v. the differential of the "fractal part" of $d_\pm X$ satisfies the relation (the fractal equation)

$$d_\pm \xi^i = \lambda_\pm^i (dt)^{1/D_F} \quad (4a,b)$$

where $\lambda_\pm^i$ are some constant coefficients, and D_F is a constant fractal dimension. We note that for the fractal dimension we can use any definition (Kolmogorov, Hausdorff

(Notalle, 1992, 2008a, 2008b, 2007; Casian Botez et al., 2010; Agop et al. 2008; Mandelbrot, 1982), etc.);

vi. the local differential time reflection invariance is recovered by combining the two derivatives, d_+/dt and d_-/dt, in the complex operator:

$$\frac{\hat{d}}{dt}=\frac{1}{2}\left(\frac{d_+ + d_-}{dt}\right)-\frac{i}{2}\left(\frac{d_+ - d_-}{dt}\right) \tag{5}$$

Applying this operator to the "position vector" yields a complex speed

$$\hat{V}=\frac{\hat{d}\mathbf{X}}{dt}=\frac{1}{2}\left(\frac{d_+\mathbf{X}+d_-\mathbf{X}}{dt}\right)-\frac{i}{2}\left(\frac{d_+\mathbf{X}-d_-\mathbf{X}}{dt}\right)=\frac{\mathbf{V}_+ + \mathbf{V}_-}{2}-i\frac{\mathbf{V}_+ - \mathbf{V}_-}{2}=\mathbf{V}-i\mathbf{U} \tag{6}$$

with

$$\mathbf{V}=\frac{\mathbf{V}_+ + \mathbf{V}_-}{2}$$
$$\mathbf{U}=\frac{\mathbf{V}_+ - \mathbf{V}_-}{2} \tag{7a,b}$$

The real part, $\mathbf{V}$, of the complex speed, $\hat{\mathbf{V}}$, represents the standard classical speed, which is differentiable and independent of resolution, while the imaginary part, $\mathbf{U}$, is a new quantity arising from fractality, which is non-differentiable and resolution-dependent;

vii. the average values of the quantities must be considered in the sense of a generalized statistical fluid like description. Particularly, the average of $d_\pm\mathbf{X}$ is

$$\langle d_\pm\mathbf{X}\rangle = d_\pm\mathbf{x} \tag{8a,b}$$

with

$$\langle d_\pm\xi\rangle = 0 \tag{9a,b}$$

viii. in such an interpretation, the "particles" are indentified with the geodesics themselves. As a consequence, any measurement is interpreted as a sorting out (or selection) of the geodesics by the measuring devices.

3. Covariant total derivative in the heat transfer processes

Let us now assume that the curves describing the heat flow (continuous but non-differentiable) is immersed in a 3-dimensional space, and that $\mathbf{X}$ of components $X^i\,(i=\overline{1,3})$ is the position vector of a point on the curve. Let us also consider the fractal temperature fluid $T(\mathbf{X},t)$, and expand its total differential up to the third order:

$$d_\pm T=\frac{\partial T}{\partial t}dt+\nabla T\cdot d_\pm\mathbf{X}+\frac{1}{2}\frac{\partial^2 T}{\partial X^i\partial X^j}d_\pm X^i d_\pm X^j+\frac{1}{6}\frac{\partial^3 T}{\partial X^i\partial X^j\partial X^k}d_\pm X^i d_\pm X^j d_\pm X^k \tag{10a,b}$$

where only the first three terms were used in the Nottale's theory (*i.e.* second order terms in the equation of motion). The relations (10a,b) are valid in any point of the space manifold and also for the points $\mathbf{X}$ on the fractal curve which we have selected in relations (10a,b). From here, the forward and backward average values of this relation take the form:

$$\begin{aligned}\langle d_\pm T\rangle = \left\langle \frac{\partial T}{\partial t}dt\right\rangle + \langle \nabla T\cdot d_\pm \mathbf{X}\rangle + \frac{1}{2}\left\langle \frac{\partial^2 T}{\partial X^i \partial X^j} d_\pm X^i d_\pm X^j\right\rangle + \\ + \frac{1}{6}\left\langle \frac{\partial^3 T}{\partial X^i \partial X^j \partial X^k} d_\pm X^i d_\pm X^j d_\pm X^k\right\rangle\end{aligned} \tag{11a,b}$$

We make the following stipulation: the mean value of the function f and its derivatives coincide with themselves, and the differentials $d_\pm X^i$ and dt are independent, therefore the average of their products coincide with the product of averages. Thus, the equations (11a,b) become:

$$d_\pm T = \frac{\partial T}{\partial t}dt + \nabla T\cdot\langle d_\pm \mathbf{X}\rangle + \frac{1}{2}\frac{\partial^2 T}{\partial X^i \partial X^j}\langle d_\pm X^i d_\pm X^j\rangle + \frac{1}{6}\frac{\partial^3 T}{\partial X^i \partial X^j \partial X^k}\langle d_\pm X^i d_\pm X^j d_\pm X^k\rangle \tag{12a,b}$$

or more, using equations (3a,b) with the property (9a,b),

$$\begin{aligned}d_\pm T = \frac{\partial T}{\partial t}dt + \nabla T\cdot d_\pm \boldsymbol{x} + \frac{1}{2}\frac{\partial^2 T}{\partial X^i \partial X^j}\left(d_\pm x^i d_\pm x^j \langle d_\pm \xi^i d_\pm \xi^j\rangle\right) + \\ + \frac{1}{6}\frac{\partial^3 T}{\partial X^i \partial X^j \partial X^k}\left(d_\pm x^i d_\pm x^j d_\pm x^k \langle d_\pm \xi^i d_\pm \xi^j d_\pm \xi^k\rangle\right)\end{aligned} \tag{13a,b}$$

Even the average value of the fractal coordinate, $d_\pm \xi^i$ is null (see (9a,b)), for the higher order of the fractal coordinate average the situation can be different. First, let us focus on the mean $\langle d_\pm \xi^i d_\pm \xi^j\rangle$. If $i \neq j$, this average is zero due the independence of $d_\pm \xi^i$ and $d_\pm \xi^j$. So, using (4a,b), we can write:

$$\langle d_\pm \xi^i d_\pm \xi^j\rangle = \lambda_\pm^i \lambda_\pm^j (dt)^{(2/D_F)-1}dt \tag{14a,b}$$

Then, let us consider the mean $\langle d_\pm \xi^i d_\pm \xi^j d_\pm \xi^k\rangle$. If $i \neq j \neq k$, this average is zero due the independence of $d_\pm \xi^i$ on $d_\pm \xi^j$ and $d_\pm \xi^k$. Now, using equations (4a,b), we can write:

$$\langle d_\pm \xi^i d_\pm \xi^j d_\pm \xi^k\rangle = \lambda_\pm^i \lambda_\pm^j \lambda_\pm^k (dt)^{(3/D_F)-1}dt \tag{15a,b}$$

Then, equations (13a,b) may be written under the form:

$$\begin{aligned}d_\pm T = \frac{\partial T}{\partial t}dt + d_\pm \boldsymbol{x}\cdot\nabla T + \frac{1}{2}\frac{\partial^2 T}{\partial X^i \partial X^j}d_\pm x^i d_\pm x^j + \\ + \frac{1}{2}\frac{\partial^2 T}{\partial X^i \partial X^j}\lambda_\pm{}^i \lambda_\pm{}^j (dt)^{(2/D_F)-1}dt + \\ + \frac{1}{6}\frac{\partial^3 T}{\partial X^i \partial X^j \partial X^k}d_\pm x^i d_\pm x^j d_\pm x^k + \\ + \frac{1}{6}\frac{\partial^3 T}{\partial X^i \partial X^j \partial X^k}\lambda_\pm{}^i \lambda_\pm{}^j \lambda_\pm{}^k (dt)^{(3/D_F)-1}dt\end{aligned} \tag{16a,b}$$

If we divide by dt and neglect the terms which contain differential factors (for details on the method see (Casian Botez et al., 2010; Agop et al. 2008)), the equations (16a,b) are reduced to:

$$\frac{d_\pm T}{dt}=\frac{\partial T}{\partial t}+\mathbf{V}_\pm\cdot\nabla T+\frac{1}{2}\frac{\partial^2 T}{\partial X^i\partial X^j}\lambda_\pm^i\lambda_\pm^j(dt)^{(2/D_F)-1}+ \\ +\frac{1}{6}\frac{\partial^3 T}{\partial X^i\partial X^j\partial X^k}\lambda_\pm^i\lambda_\pm^j\lambda_\pm^k(dt)^{(3/D_F)-1} \tag{17a,b}$$

These relations also allows us to define the operator:

$$\frac{d_\pm}{dt}=\frac{\partial}{\partial t}+\mathbf{V}_\pm\cdot\nabla+\frac{1}{2}\frac{\partial^2}{\partial X^i\partial X^j}\lambda_\pm^i\lambda_\pm^j(dt)^{(2/D_F)-1}+ \\ +\frac{1}{6}\frac{\partial^3}{\partial X^i\partial X^j\partial X^k}\lambda_\pm^i\lambda_\pm^j\lambda_\pm^k(dt)^{(3/D_F)-1} \tag{18a,b}$$

Under these circumstances, let us calculate $\left(\hat{\partial}T/\partial t\right)$. Taking into account equations (18a,b), (5) and (6) we obtain:

$$\begin{aligned}
\frac{\hat{\partial}T}{\partial t}&=\frac{1}{2}\left[\frac{d_+T}{dt}+\frac{d_-T}{dt}-i\left(\frac{d_+T}{dt}-\frac{d_-T}{dt}\right)\right]=\frac{1}{2}\frac{\partial T}{\partial t}+\frac{1}{2}\mathbf{V}_+\cdot\nabla T+\\
&+\lambda_+^i\lambda_+^j\frac{1}{4}(dt)^{(2/D_F)-1}\frac{\partial^2 T}{\partial X^i\partial X^j}+\lambda_+^i\lambda_+^j\lambda_+^k\frac{1}{12}(dt)^{(3/D_F)-1}\frac{\partial^3 T}{\partial X^i\partial X^j\partial X^k}+\\
&+\frac{1}{2}\frac{\partial T}{\partial t}+\frac{1}{2}\mathbf{V}_-\cdot\nabla T+\lambda_-^i\lambda_-^j\frac{1}{4}(dt)^{(2/D_F)-1}\frac{\partial^2 T}{\partial X^i\partial X^j}+\\
&+\lambda_-^i\lambda_-^j\lambda_-^k\frac{1}{12}(dt)^{(3/D_F)-1}\frac{\partial^3 T}{\partial X^i\partial X^j\partial X^k}-\frac{i}{2}\frac{\partial T}{\partial t}-\frac{i}{2}\mathbf{V}_+\cdot\nabla T-\\
&-\lambda_+^i\lambda_+^j\frac{i}{2}(dt)^{(2/D_F)-1}\frac{\partial^2 T}{\partial X^i\partial X^j}-\lambda_+^i\lambda_+^j\lambda_+^k\frac{i}{12}(dt)^{(3/D_F)-1}\frac{\partial^3 T}{\partial X^i\partial X^j\partial X^k}+\\
&+\frac{i}{2}\frac{\partial T}{\partial t}+\frac{i}{2}\mathbf{V}_-\cdot\nabla T+\lambda_-^i\lambda_-^j\frac{i}{2}(dt)^{(2/D_F)-1}\frac{\partial^2 T}{\partial X^i\partial X^j}+\\
&+\lambda_-^i\lambda_-^j\lambda_-^k\frac{i}{12}(dt)^{(3/D_F)-1}\frac{\partial^3 T}{\partial X^i\partial X^j\partial X^k}=\\
&=\frac{\partial T}{\partial t}+\left(\frac{\mathbf{V}_++\mathbf{V}_-}{2}-i\frac{\mathbf{V}_++\mathbf{V}_-}{2}\right)\cdot\nabla T+\\
&+\frac{(dt)^{(2/D_F)-1}}{4}\left[\left(\lambda_+^i\lambda_+^j+\lambda_-^i\lambda_-^j\right)-i\left(\lambda_+^i\lambda_+^j-\lambda_-^i\lambda_-^j\right)\right]\frac{\partial^2 T}{\partial X^i\partial X^j}+\\
&+\frac{(dt)^{(3/D_F)-1}}{12}\left[\left(\lambda_+^i\lambda_+^j\lambda_+^k+\lambda_-^i\lambda_-^j\lambda_-^k\right)-i\left(\lambda_+^i\lambda_+^j\lambda_+^k-\lambda_-^i\lambda_-^j\lambda_-^k\right)\right]\frac{\partial^3 T}{\partial X^i\partial X^j\partial X^k}=\\
&=\frac{\partial T}{\partial t}+\hat{\mathbf{V}}\cdot\nabla T+\frac{(dt)^{(2/D_F)-1}}{4}\left[\left(\lambda_+^i\lambda_+^j+\lambda_-^i\lambda_-^j\right)-i\left(\lambda_+^i\lambda_+^j-\lambda_-^i\lambda_-^j\right)\right]\frac{\partial^2 T}{\partial X^i\partial X^j}+\\
&+\frac{(dt)^{(3/D_F)-1}}{12}\left[\left(\lambda_+^i\lambda_+^j\lambda_+^k+\lambda_-^i\lambda_-^j\lambda_-^k\right)-i\left(\lambda_+^i\lambda_+^j\lambda_+^k-\lambda_-^i\lambda_-^j\lambda_-^k\right)\right]\frac{\partial^3 T}{\partial X^i\partial X^j\partial X^k}
\end{aligned} \tag{19a,b}$$

This relation also allows us to define the fractal operator:

$$\frac{\hat{\partial}}{\partial t}=\frac{\partial}{\partial t}+\hat{\mathbf{V}}\cdot\nabla+\frac{(dt)^{(2/D_F)-1}}{4}\left[\left(\lambda_+^i\lambda_+^j+\lambda_-^i\lambda_-^j\right)-i\left(\lambda_+^i\lambda_+^j-\lambda_-^i\lambda_-^j\right)\right]\frac{\partial^2}{\partial X^i\partial X^j}+$$
$$+\frac{(dt)^{(3/D_F)-1}}{12}\left[\left(\lambda_+^i\lambda_+^j\lambda_+^k+\lambda_-^i\lambda_-^j\lambda_-^k\right)-i\left(\lambda_+^i\lambda_+^j\lambda_+^k-\lambda_-^i\lambda_-^j\lambda_-^k\right)\right]\frac{\partial^3}{\partial X^i\partial X^j\partial X^k} \tag{20}$$

Particularly, by choosing:

$$\lambda_+^i\lambda_+^j=-\lambda_-^i\lambda_-^j=2\mathrm{D}\delta^{ij}$$
$$\lambda_+^i\lambda_+^j\lambda_+^k=\lambda_-^i\lambda_-^j\lambda_-^k=2\sqrt{2}\mathrm{D}^{3/2}\delta^{ijk} \tag{21a,b}$$

the fractal operator (20) takes the usual form:

$$\frac{\hat{\partial}}{\partial t}=\frac{\partial}{\partial t}+\hat{V}\cdot\nabla-i\mathrm{D}(dt)^{(2/D_F)-1}\Delta+\frac{\sqrt{2}}{3}\mathrm{D}^{3/2}(dt)^{(3/D_F)-1}\nabla^3 \tag{22}$$

We now apply the principle of scale covariance, and postulate that the passage from classical (differentiable) mechanics to the "fractal" mechanics can be implemented by replacing the standard time derivative operator, d/dt, by the complex operator $\hat{\partial}/\partial t$ (this results in a generalization of the principle of scale covariance given by Nottale in (Nottale, 1992)). As a consequence, we are now able to write the equation of the heat flow in its covariant form:

$$\frac{\hat{\partial}T}{\partial t}=\frac{\partial T}{\partial t}+\left(\hat{V}\cdot\nabla\right)T-i\mathrm{D}(dt)^{(2/D_F)-1}\Delta T+\frac{\sqrt{2}}{3}\mathrm{D}^{3/2}(dt)^{(3/D_F)-1}\nabla^3 T=0 \tag{23}$$

This means that at any point of a fractal heat flow path, the local temporal term, $\partial_t T$, the non-linearly (convective) term, $\left(\hat{V}\cdot\nabla\right)T$, the dissipative term, ΔT and the dispersive one, $\nabla^3 T$, make their balance. Moreover, the behavior of a fractal fluid is of viscoelastic or of hysteretic type, *i.e.* the fractal fluid has memory. Such a result is in agreement with the opinion given in (Ferry& Goodnick, 1997; Chiroiu et al., 2005): the fractal fluid can be described by Kelvin-Voight or Maxwell rheological model with the aid of complex quantities e.g. the complex speed field, the complex structure coefficients.

4. The dissipative approximation in the heat transfer processes

4.1 Standard thermal transport

In the dissipative approximation of the fractal heat transfer, the relation (23) becomes a Navier-Stokes type equation for the temperature field:

$$\frac{\hat{\partial}T}{\partial t}=\frac{\partial T}{\partial t}+\left(\hat{V}\cdot\nabla\right)T-i\mathrm{D}(dt)^{(2/D_F)-1}\Delta T=0 \tag{24}$$

with an imaginary viscosity coefficient:

$$\eta=i\mathrm{D}(dt)^{2/D_F-1} \tag{25}$$

Separating the real and imaginary parts in (24), *i.e.*

$$\frac{\partial T}{\partial t}+\boldsymbol{V}\cdot\nabla T=0$$
$$-\boldsymbol{U}\cdot\nabla T=\mathsf{D}(dt)^{(2/D_F)-1}\Delta T \qquad (26a,b)$$

We can add these two equations and obtain the thermal transfer equation in the form:

$$\frac{\partial T}{\partial t}+(\boldsymbol{V}-\boldsymbol{U})\cdot\nabla T=\mathsf{D}(dt)^{(2/D_F)-1}\Delta T \qquad (27)$$

The standard equation for the thermal transport, *i.e.*:

$$\frac{\partial T}{\partial t}=\alpha\Delta T,\quad \alpha=\mathsf{D}(dt)^{(2/D_F)-1} \qquad (28a,b)$$

results from (27) on the following assertions

i. the fractal heat flow are of Peano's type (Nottale, 1992), i.e. for $D_F=2$;
ii. the movements at differentiable and non-differentiable scales are synchronous, i.e. $\boldsymbol{V}=\boldsymbol{U}$;
iii. the structure coefficient D, proper to the fractal-nonfractal transition, is identified with the diffusivity coefficient α, i.e. $\alpha\equiv\mathsf{D}$.

In the form

$$\frac{\partial\bar{T}}{\partial\bar{t}}=\left(\frac{\partial^2}{\partial\bar{x}^2}+\frac{\partial^2}{\partial\bar{y}^2}\right)\bar{T} \qquad (29)$$

where we used the normalized quantities

$$\bar{t}=\omega t,\quad \bar{x}=kx,\quad \bar{y}=ky,\quad \bar{T}=\frac{T}{T_0} \qquad (30a\text{-}d)$$

and the restriction

$$\frac{\mathsf{D}k^2}{\omega}=1 \qquad (31)$$

the equation (29) can by solved with the following initial and boundaries conditions:

$$\bar{T}(0,\bar{x},\bar{y})=\frac{1}{4},\text{for } 0\le\bar{x}\le1 \text{ and } 0\le\bar{y}\le1 \qquad (32a,b)$$

$$\bar{T}(\bar{t},0,\bar{y})=1/4,\bar{T}(\bar{t},1,\bar{y})=1/4$$
$$\bar{T}(\bar{t},\bar{x},0)=\exp\left[-\left(\frac{\bar{t}-1/2}{1/2}\right)^2\right]\exp\left[-\left(\frac{\bar{x}-1/2}{1/2}\right)^2\right],\bar{T}(\bar{t},\bar{x},1)=1/4 \qquad (33a\text{-}d)$$

In the Figures (1a-j) we present the solutions obtained with the finite differences method (Zienkievicz &Taylor, 1991). Furthermore, using tha same method from (Zienkievicz

&Taylor, 1991), if the thermal transport occurs in the presence of a "wall", condition which involves substituting (33d) with

$$\frac{\partial \bar{T}}{\partial \bar{y}}\left(\bar{t},\bar{x},1\right)=0 \tag{34}$$

then obtain the numerical solutions from the figures (2a-j). It results that the perturbation of the thermal field, either disappear because of the rheological properties of the fractal environment (Figures 1a-j), or it regenerates (Figures 2a-j).

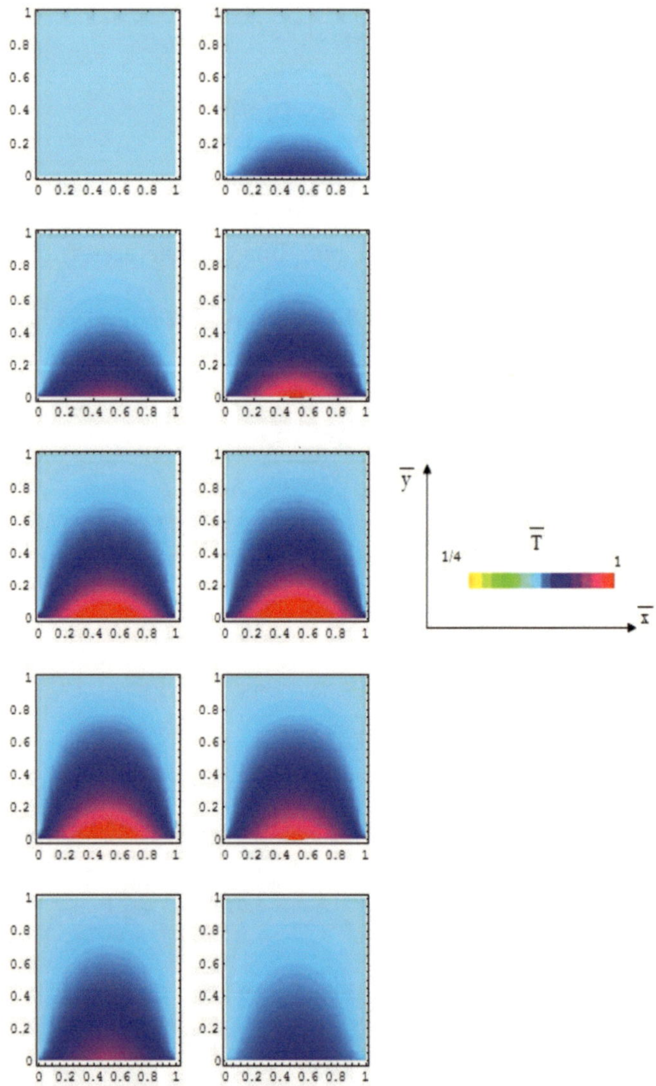

Fig. 1. a-j. Numerical 2D contour curves of the normalized temperature field in the absence of a "wall". Thermal field perturbation disappears due to the rheological properties of the fractal environment

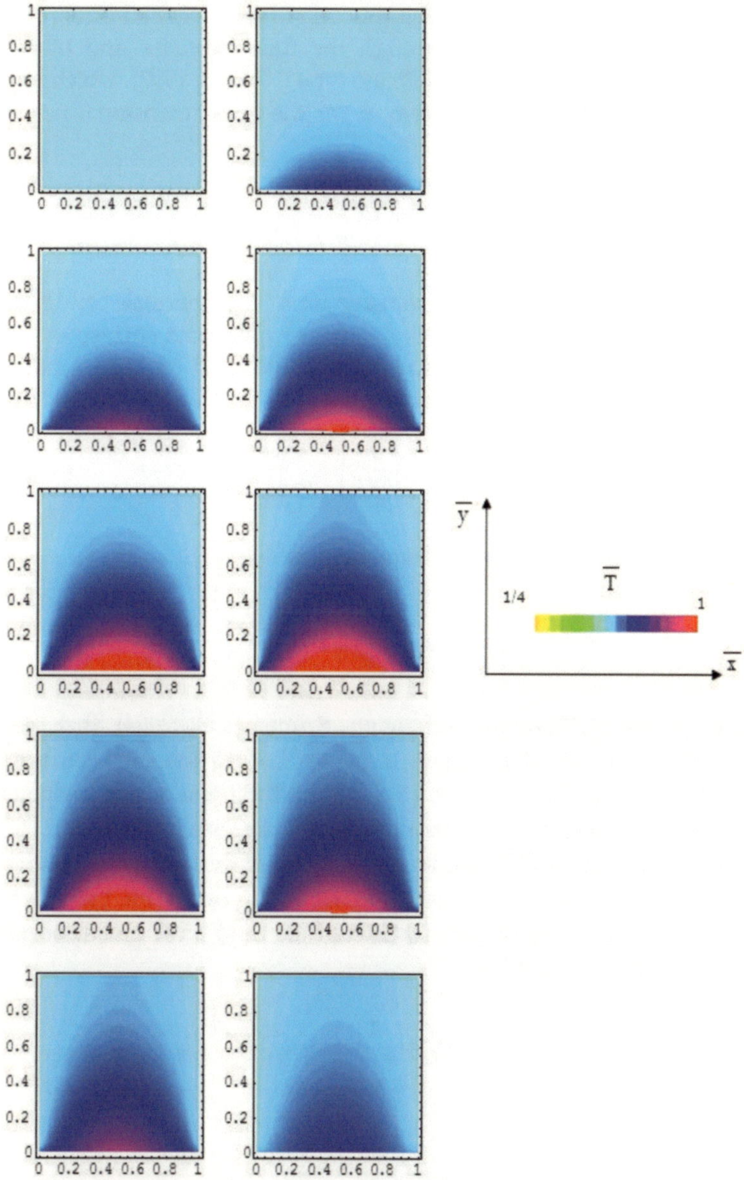

Fig. 2. a-j. Numerical 2D contour curves of the normalized temperature field in the presence of a "wall". Thermal field perturbation regenerates in the presence of a "wall"

4.2 Thermal anomaly of the nanofluids

The equation (28a) is implied by the Fourier type law

$$j(T) = -k\nabla T \tag{35}$$

with $j(T)$ the thermal current density and k the thermal conductivity.

Let us apply the previous formalism for the heat transfer in nanofluids, assuming the following: (i) there are two different paths (fractal curves of fractal dimension D_F) of heat flow through the "suspension", one through the fluid particles and other through the nanoparticles; (ii) the fractal curves are of Peano type (Nottale, 1992), which implies $D_F=2$. The overall heat transfer rate of the system, q, for the one-dimensional heat flow, may be expressed as:

$$q=q_f+q_p=-k_fA_f\left(\frac{dT}{dX}\right)_f-k_pA_p\left(\frac{dT}{dX}\right)_p \tag{36}$$

where A, k, (dT/dX) denote the heat transfer area, the thermal conductivity and the temperature gradient, while the subscripts f, p denote quantities corresponding to the fluid and the particle phase, respectively. Assuming that the fluid and the nanoparticles are in local thermal equilibrium at each location, we can set:

$$\left(\frac{dT}{dX}\right)_f=\left(\frac{dT}{dX}\right)_p=\left(\frac{dT}{dX}\right) \tag{37}$$

Now the overall heat transfer rate can be expressed as

$$q_t=-k_fA_f\left(\frac{dT}{dX}\right)\left[1+\frac{k_pA_p}{k_fA_f}\right] \tag{38}$$

We propose, using the method from (Hemanth Kumar et al., 2004), that the ratio of heat transfer areas, (A_p/A_f), could be taken in proportion to the total surface areas of the nanoparticles (S_p) and the fluid species (S_f) per unit volume of the "suspension". Taking both the fluid and the suspended nanoparticles to be spheres of radii r_f and r_p respectively, the total surface area can be calculated as the product of the number of particles n and the surface area of the particle for each constituent. Denoting by ε the volume fraction of the nanoparticle and by $(1-\varepsilon)$ the volume fraction of the fluid, the number of particles for the two constituents can be calculated as :

$$\begin{aligned} n_f&=\frac{1}{\frac{4}{3}\pi r_f^3}(1-\varepsilon)\\ n_p&=\frac{1}{\frac{4}{3}\pi r_p^3}\varepsilon \end{aligned} \tag{39a,b}$$

The corresponding surface areas of the fluid and the nanoparticle phase are given by:

$$\begin{aligned} S_f&=n_f4\pi\left(r_f\right)^2=\frac{3}{r_f}(1-\varepsilon)\\ S_p&=n_p4\pi\left(r_p\right)^2=\frac{3}{r_p}\varepsilon \end{aligned} \tag{40a,b}$$

Taking

$$\frac{S_f}{S_p}=\frac{A_f}{A_p} \tag{41}$$

and using the previous relations, the expression for the heat transfer rate becomes:

$$q=-k_f A_f\left(\frac{dT}{dX}\right)\left[1+\frac{k_p\varepsilon r_f}{k_f(1-\varepsilon)r_p}\right]=-k_{ef}A_f\left(\frac{dT}{dX}\right) \tag{42}$$

where the effective thermal conductivity, k_{eff} is expressed as:

$$\frac{k_{eff}}{k_f}=1+\frac{k_p\varepsilon r_f}{k_f(1-\varepsilon)r_p} \tag{43}$$

We present in Figures 3a-c the dependencies: $k_{eff}/k_f\left(k_p/k_f=\text{const.},\varepsilon,r_p/r_f\right)$ (a), $k_{eff}/k_f\left(k_p/k_f,\varepsilon,r_p/r_f=\text{const.}\right)$ (b) and $k_{eff}/k_f\left(k_p/k_f,\varepsilon=\text{const.},r_p/r_f\right)$ (c).
In the above expression, it is seen that the enhancement is directly proportional to the ratio of the conductivities, volume fraction of the nanoparticle (for $\varepsilon\ll 1$) and is inversely proportional to the nanoparticle radius.
Next we determine the temperature dependence of k_{eff}. The thermal conduction of nanoparticle based on Debye's model is:

$$k_p=\frac{n\hat{c}_v l}{3}\left\langle u_p\right\rangle \tag{44}$$

where l is the mean free path, $\hat{c}_v$ is the specific heat per particle, n is the particle concentration and $\left\langle u_p\right\rangle$ the average particle speed. Because the particle's movement in fluid is a Brownian one, so it can be approximate by a fractal with fractal dimension $D_F=2$, we can use a Stokes-Einstein's type formula for the definition of D from Eqs. (21a, b)

$$\mathsf{D}\sim\frac{k_B T}{\pi\eta r_p} \tag{45}$$

with k_B the Boltzmann's constant, T the temperature and η the dynamic viscosity of the fluid. For a choice of the form:

$$\mathsf{D}\sim\left\langle u_p(T)\right\rangle r_p \tag{46}$$

which implies

$$\left\langle u_p(T)\right\rangle\sim\frac{k_B T}{\pi\eta r_p^2} \tag{47}$$

the equation (44) becomes:

$$k_p\sim k_p(T_0)t_r,\ t_r=\frac{T}{T_0},\ k_p(T_0)=\frac{n\hat{C}_v l}{3}\left\langle u_p(T_0)\right\rangle,\ \left\langle u_p(T_0)\right\rangle\sim\frac{k_B T_0}{\pi\eta r_p^2} \tag{48a-d}$$

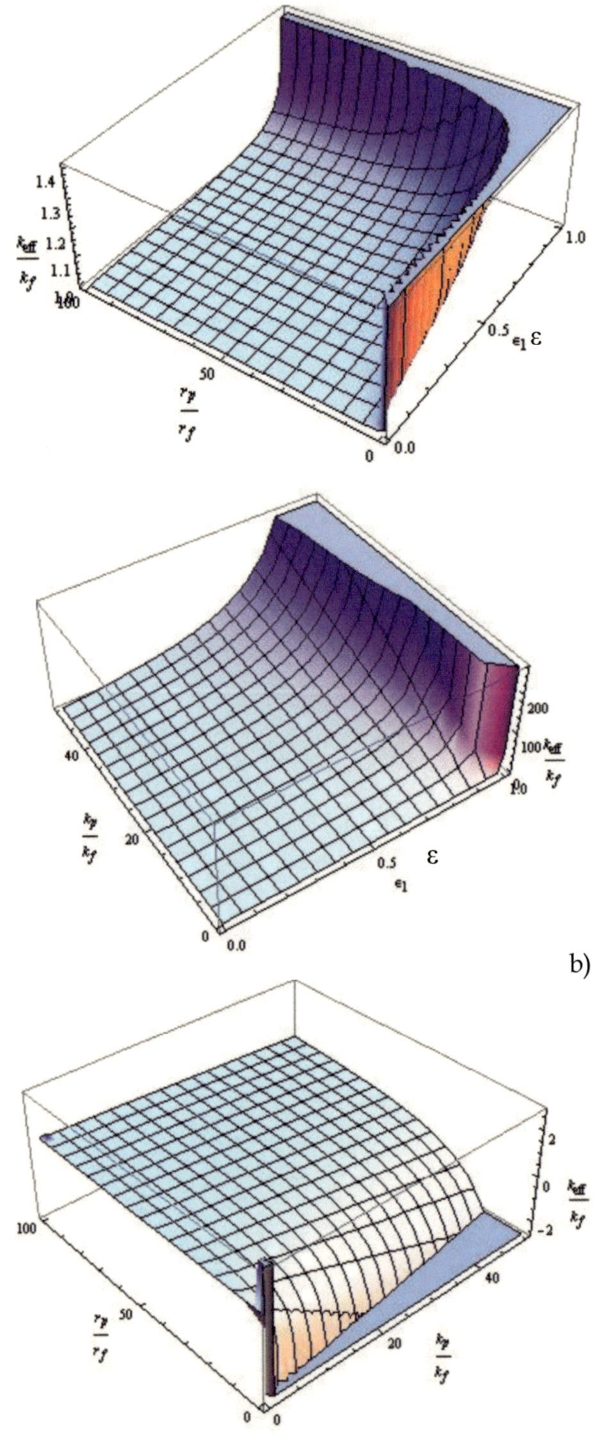

a)

b)

c)

Fig. 3. Dependence of the effective thermal conductivity k_{eff} on: (a) $r_p/r_f, \varepsilon$; (b) $k_p/k_f, \varepsilon$; (c) $r_p/r_f, k_p/k_f$

So, the dependence of k_{eff} on the reduced temperature t_r takes the form (see also Fig.4):

$$\frac{k_{eff}}{k_f}=1+\nu t_r,\nu=\frac{k_p(T_0)\varepsilon r_f}{k_f(1-\varepsilon)r_p} \quad (49a,b)$$

Obviously, Eq.(49a) it more complicated if we accept the dependence $\eta=\eta(t_r)$.

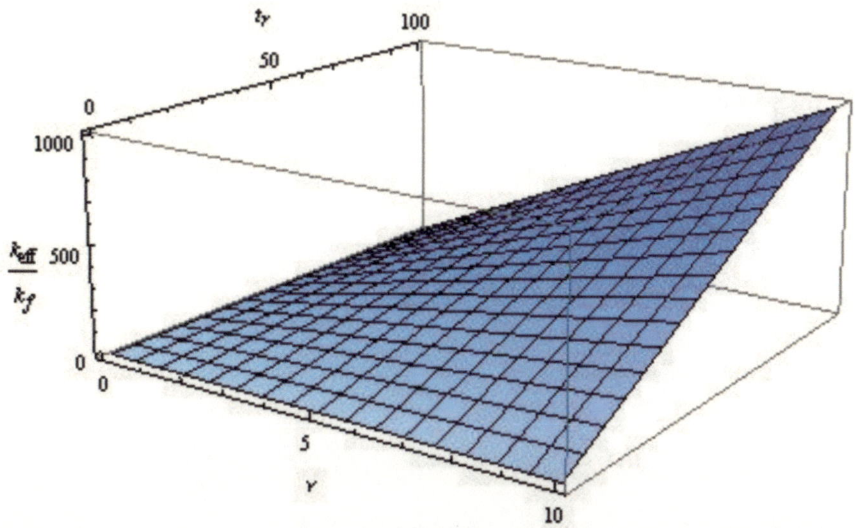

Fig. 4. Dependence of the effective thermal conductivity k_{eff} on the reduced temperature t_r and ν

We remark that the theoretical model describes not only qualitative but also quantitative the thermal behavior of the nanofluids experimentally observed (the increasing of the heat transfer in nanofluids-thermal anomaly of the nanofluids) (Wang&Xu, 1999; Keblinski, 2002; Hemanth Kumar et al., 2004).

4.3 Negative differential thermal conductance effect

Applying the fractal operator (22) in the dispersive approximation of motions to the complex speed field (fractal function), $\hat{V}$ we obtain the inertial principle in the form of a Navier-Stokes type equation:

$$\frac{\hat{\partial} T}{\partial t}=\frac{\partial T}{\partial t}+\hat{V}\cdot\nabla T+\frac{\sqrt{2}}{3}\mathrm{D}^{3/2}(dt)^{(3/D_F)-1}\nabla^3 T=0 \quad (50)$$

with a imaginary viscosity coefficient (25).

This means that the local complex acceleration field, $\partial\hat{V}/\partial t$, the convective term, $\hat{V}\cdot\nabla\hat{V}$, and the dissipative one, $\nabla\hat{V}$, reciprocally compensate in any point of the fractal curve.

In the case of the irrotational motions:

$$\nabla\times\hat{V}=0 \quad (51)$$

so that the complex speed field (6) can be expressed through the gradient of a complex scalar function Φ,

$$\hat{V} = \nabla \Phi \tag{52}$$

named the scalar potential of the complex speed field.
Substituting equation (52) in equation (50) it results

$$\nabla\left[\frac{\partial \Phi}{\partial t} + \frac{1}{2}(\nabla \Phi)^2 - i\mathrm{D}(dt)^{(2/D_F)-1}\Delta \Phi\right] = 0 \tag{53}$$

and by an integration, a Bernoulli type equation

$$\frac{\partial \Phi}{\partial t} + \frac{1}{2}(\nabla \Phi)^2 - i\mathrm{D}(dt)^{(2/D_F)-1}\Delta \Phi = F(t) \tag{54}$$

with $F(t)$ function which depends only on time. Particularly, for Φ of the form:

$$\Phi = -2i\mathrm{D}(dt)^{(2/D_F)-1}\ln \psi \tag{55}$$

where ψ is a new complex scalar function, the equation (54) takes the form:

$$\mathrm{D}^2(dt)^{(4/D_F)-1}\Delta \psi + i\mathrm{D}(dt)^{(2/D_F)-1}\frac{\partial \psi}{\partial t} + \frac{F(t)}{2}\psi = 0 \tag{56}$$

From here, a Schrödinger type equation result for $F(t) \equiv 0$ *i.e.*

$$\mathrm{D}^2(dt)^{(4/D_F)-1}\Delta \psi + i\mathrm{D}(dt)^{(2/D_F)-1}\frac{\partial \psi}{\partial t} = 0 \tag{57}$$

Moreover, for the movement on fractal curves of Peano's type, *i.e.* in the fractal dimension $D_F = 2$, and Compton's length, λ, and temporal, τ, scales,

$$\lambda = \frac{\hbar}{m_0 c}$$

$$\tau = \frac{\hbar}{m_0 c^2} \tag{58a,b}$$

equation (57) takes the Schrödinger standard form:

$$\frac{\hbar^2}{2m_0}\Delta \psi + i\hbar\frac{\partial \psi}{\partial t} = 0 \tag{59}$$

In the relations (58 a,b) and (59) $\hbar$ is the reduced Plank's constant, c the speed of light on the vacuum and m_0 the rest mass of the particle test.
Let us apply the previous mathematical model in the description of two fractal fluids interface dynamics in the fractal dimension D_F. Consider two fractal fluids, 1 and 2, separated by an interface as shown in Figure 5. If the interface is thick enough so that the

fractal fluids are "isolated" from each other, the time-dependent Schrödinger type equation for each side is:

$$im_0 2D\frac{d\psi_1}{dt} = H_1\psi_1 \tag{60}$$

$$im_0 2D\frac{d\psi_2}{dt} = H_2\psi_2 \tag{61}$$

with

$$D = \mathsf{D}(dt)^{(2/D_F)-1} \tag{62}$$

where ψ_i and H_i, i = 1, 2 are the scalar potentials of the complex speed fields and respectively the "Hamiltonians" on either side of the interface. We assume that a temperature field, $2T$, is applied between the two fractal fluids. If the zero point of the temperature field is assumed to occur in the middle of the interface, the fractal fluid 1 will be at the temperature field $-T$, while the fractal fluid 2 will be at the temperature field $+T$.

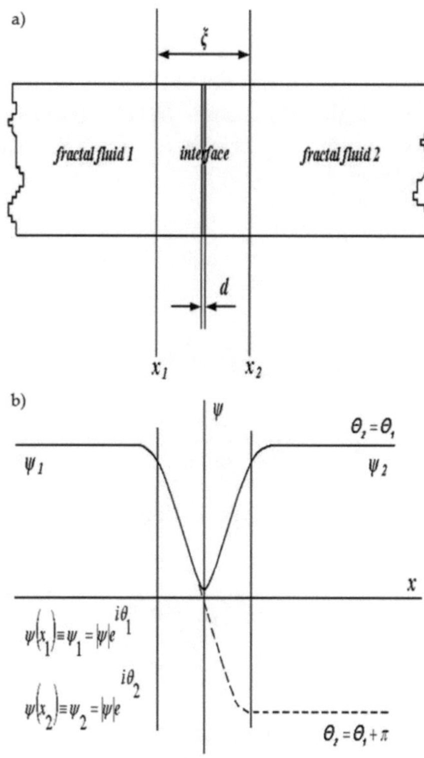

Fig. 5. Interface generated through the interaction of two fractal fluids (d is the geometrical thickness, before the self-structuring of the interface and ξ is the physical thickness, after the self-structuring of the interface) (a) and the variation of the speed field with the fractal coordinates (b)

The presence of the interface couples together the two previous Equations (60) and (61) in the form:

$$im_0 2D\frac{d\psi_1}{dt} = \alpha T\psi_1 + \Gamma\psi_2 \tag{63}$$

$$im_0 2D\frac{d\psi_2}{dt} = -\alpha T\psi_2 + \Gamma\psi_1 \tag{64}$$

where a is a constant which specifies the thermal transfer type in the fractal fluid (Vizureanu&Agop, 2007) and Γ is the coupling constant for the scalar potentials of the complex speed fields across the interface. Since the square of each scalar potential of the complex speed fields is also a probability density (Notalle, 1992, 2008a, 2008b, 2007), the two scalar potentials of the complex speed fields can be written in the form:

$$\psi_1 = \sqrt{\rho_1}e^{i\theta_1} \tag{65}$$

$$\psi_2 = \sqrt{\rho_2}e^{i\theta_2} \tag{66}$$

$$\Theta = \theta_2 - \theta_1 \tag{67}$$

where ρ_1 and ρ_2 are the densities of particles in the two fractal fluids and Θ is the phase difference across the interface. If the two scalar potentials of the complex speed fields (65) and (66) are substituted in the coupled Equations (63) and (64) and the results separated into real and imaginary parts, we obtain equations for the time dependence of the particle densities and the phase difference:

$$\frac{d\rho_1}{dt} = -\frac{\Gamma}{m_0 D}\sqrt{\rho_1\rho_2}\sin\Theta \tag{68}$$

$$\frac{d\rho_2}{dt} = -\frac{\Gamma}{m_0 D}\sqrt{\rho_1\rho_2}\sin\Theta \tag{69}$$

$$\frac{d\Theta}{dt} = \frac{\alpha T}{m_0 D} = \overline{\Omega} \tag{70}$$

We can specify the heat flux in terms of the difference between Equations (69) and (70) which multiplies with ε:

$$j = \varepsilon\frac{d}{dt}(\rho_1 - \rho_2) \tag{71}$$

It results

$$j = j_c \sin\Theta \tag{72}$$

where

$$j_c = \frac{2\varepsilon\Gamma\sqrt{\rho_1\rho_2}}{m_0 D} \tag{73}$$

and ε is the elementary amount of energy transferred trough the interface (Vizureanu&Agop, 2007).
Equations (70) and (72) define the thermal transport inside the interface. If the temperature field from Equation (70) is zero, a constant heat flux of any value between $-j_c$ and j_c may flow through the junction according to the Equation (72).
We return to Equations (69), (70) and (72) and apply a constant temperature field T_0 to the junction that is:

$$\Theta(t)=\frac{\alpha}{m_0 D}T_0 t+\Theta_0\,,\ \Theta_0=\text{const.} \tag{74a,b}$$

A variable heat flux:

$$j(t)=j_c\sin\left(\Omega_0 t+\Theta_0\right)$$

$$\Omega_0=\frac{\alpha}{m_0 D}T_0 \tag{75 a,b}$$

results, although a constant temperature field is applied.
If one overlay an "alternative" temperature field over the constant temperature field:

$$T(t)=T_0+\overline{T}_0\cos\left(\Omega t\right) \tag{76}$$

one obtains a "frequency" modulation of the "heat flux":

$$\begin{aligned} j&=j_c\sin\left(\Omega_0 t+\frac{\alpha\overline{T}_0}{m_0\Omega D}\sin\left(\Omega t\right)+\overline{\Theta}_0\right)= \\ &=j_c\sum_{n=-\infty}^{+\infty}(-1)^n J_n\left(\frac{\alpha\overline{T}_0}{m_0\Omega D}\right)\sin\left[\left(\Omega_0-n\Omega\right)t+\overline{\Theta}_0\right] \end{aligned}$$

$$\overline{\Theta}_0=\text{const.} \tag{77a,b}$$

J_n is the Bessel function of integer index (Nikitov&Ouvanov, 1974). We note that, in the first approximation, for any "arbitrary" thermal signal we can always perform a Fourier's decomposition (Jackson, 1991).
Since j versus T characteristic is drawn for the average thermal flux $j\approx\left\langle j(t)\right\rangle$, and since the sine term averages to zero unless $\Omega_0=n\Omega$, there are spikes appearing on this characteristic for temperature field equal to:

$$T_n=n\frac{m_0 D}{\alpha}\Omega \tag{78}$$

with the maximum amplitude

$$j_{\max}=j_c J_n\left(\frac{\alpha\overline{T}_0}{m_0\Omega D}\right) \tag{79}$$

occurring for the phase $\bar{\Theta} = \pi/2$. Figure 6 shows these spikes at intervals proportional to the thermal source "frequency" and indicates their maximum amplitude range. The value of the heat flux can be anywhere along a particular heat flux spike, depending on the initial phase.

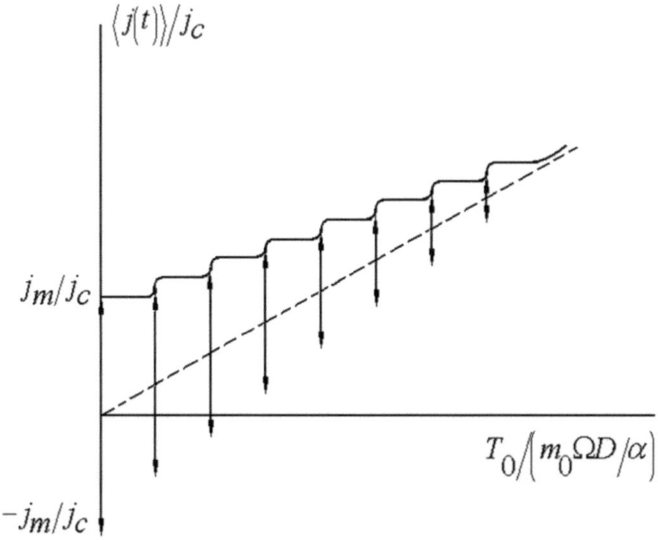

Fig. 6. Theoretical heat flux-temperature characteristic

It results the following:

i. The presence of the spikes in the average heat flux specifies a negative differential thermal "conductance" which corresponds to the interface self-structuring. This is a Josephson thermal type effect;
ii. Condition (78) corresponds to the "modulation" of the interface "oscillations" under the influence of an external thermal signal.

4.4 Numerical simulations of the heat transfer in nanofluids

Replacing the complex speed field (6) in equation (50) and separating the real and imaginary parts, we obtain:

$$\begin{gathered} m_0 \frac{\partial \boldsymbol{V}}{\partial t} + m_0 \boldsymbol{V} \cdot \nabla \boldsymbol{V} = -\nabla(Q) \\ \frac{\partial \boldsymbol{U}}{\partial t} + \nabla(\boldsymbol{V} \cdot \boldsymbol{U}) + D(dt)^{(2/D_F)-1} \Delta \boldsymbol{V} = 0 \end{gathered} \tag{80a,b}$$

where Q is the fractal potential,

$$Q = -\frac{m_0 \boldsymbol{U}^2}{2} - m_0 D(dt)^{(2/D_F)-1} \nabla \cdot \boldsymbol{U} \tag{81}$$

The explicit form of the complex speed field is given by means the expression:

$$\psi = \sqrt{\rho}\, e^{iS} \tag{82}$$

with ρ the amplitude and S the phase. Then equation (55) with

$$\Phi = -2iD(dt)^{(2/D_F)-1} \ln\left(\sqrt{\rho}\, e^{iS}\right) \tag{83}$$

involves the real and imaginary speed field components

$$\boldsymbol{V} = 2D(dt)^{(2/D_F)-1} \nabla S$$
$$\boldsymbol{U} = D(dt)^{(2/D_F)-1} \nabla \ln \rho \tag{84a,b}$$

while the fractal potential (81) is given by the simple expression

$$Q = -m_0 D^2 (dt)^{(4/D_F)-2} \frac{\Delta\sqrt{\rho}}{\sqrt{\rho}} \tag{85}$$

With equations (84 a, b), the relation (80 b) takes the form:

$$\nabla\left(\frac{\partial \ln \rho}{\partial t} + \boldsymbol{V}\cdot\nabla \ln \rho + \nabla\cdot\boldsymbol{V}\right) = 0 \tag{86}$$

or, by integration with $\rho \neq 0$:

$$\frac{\partial \rho}{\partial t} + \nabla\cdot(\rho \boldsymbol{V}) = T(t) \tag{87}$$

with $T(t)$ a function which depends only on time.
Equation (80 a) corresponds to the momentum conservation law, while equation (87), with $T(t) \equiv 0$ to the probability density conservation law. So, equations:

$$m_0\left(\frac{\partial \boldsymbol{V}}{\partial t} + \boldsymbol{V}\cdot\nabla\boldsymbol{V}\right) = -\nabla(Q)$$
$$\frac{\partial \rho}{\partial t} + \nabla\cdot(\rho\boldsymbol{V}) = 0 \tag{88a,b}$$

with Q given by (81) or (85), from the fractal hydrodynamic equations in the fractal dimension D_F. The fractal potential (81) is induced by the non-differentiability of the space coordinates.
Now, by multiplying equation (88 b) with ε, *i.e.*

$$\frac{\partial(\rho\varepsilon)}{\partial t} + \nabla\cdot(\rho\varepsilon\boldsymbol{V}) = \rho\left(\frac{\partial\varepsilon}{\partial t} + \boldsymbol{V}\cdot\nabla\varepsilon\right) \tag{89}$$

and considering the null value of the right term of Eq. (89), the conservation law for ε is found in the form:

$$\frac{\partial(\rho\varepsilon)}{\partial t} + \nabla\cdot(\rho\varepsilon\boldsymbol{V}) = 0 \tag{90}$$

Particularly, if ε is the energy density of a fluid (Landau&Lifshitz, 1987), $\varepsilon = e + (p/\rho) + v^2/2$, the "classical" form of the energy conservation law results (the physical significances of e and p are given in (Landau&Lifshitz, 1987)).
Several numerical investigations of the nanofluid heat transfer have been accomplished in (Maiga et al., 2005, 2004; Patankar, 1980). Akbarnia and Behzadmehr (Akbarnia & Behzadmehr, 2007) reported a Computational Fluid Dynamics (CFD) model based on single phase model for investigation of laminar convection of water-Al_2O_3 nanofluid in a horizontal curved tube. In their study, effects of buoyancy force, centrifugal force and nanoparticle concentration have been discussed.
In that follows we shall perform numerical studies on the nanofluid heat transfer (water-based nanofluids, Al_2O_3 with 10 nm particle-sizes) in a coaxial heat exchanger.
The detailed turbulent flow field for the single-phase flow in a circular tube with constant wall temperature can be determined by solving the volume-averaged fluid equations, as follows:

i. continuity equations (88 b)

$$\frac{\partial \rho}{\partial t} + \nabla(\rho \mathbf{V}) = 0 \tag{91}$$

ii. momentum equation (88 a) in the form:

$$\frac{\partial}{\partial t}(\rho \mathbf{V}) + \nabla(\rho \mathbf{V}\,\mathbf{V}) = -\nabla P + \nabla \tau + B \tag{92}$$

where we supposed that (Harvey, 1966; Albeverio&Hoegh-Krohn, 1974):

$$-\nabla Q = -\nabla P + \nabla \tau + B \tag{93}$$

P, τ and B having the significances from (Fard et al., 2009);

iii. energy equation (90) in the form:

$$\frac{\partial \rho}{\partial t}(\rho H) + \nabla(\rho \mathbf{V} C_p T) = \nabla(k \nabla T - C_p \rho \mathbf{V} T) \tag{94}$$

where H is the enthalpy, C_p is the specific heat capacity and T is the temperature field.
In order to solve above-mentioned equations the thermo physical parameters of nanofluids such as density, heat capacity, viscosity, and thermal conductivity must be evaluated. These parameters are defined as follows:

i. density and heat capacity. The relations determinate by Pak si Cho (Pak&Cho, 1998), have the form:

$$\rho_{nf} = (1-\varepsilon)\rho_f + \varepsilon \rho_p \tag{95}$$

$$C_{nf} = (1-\varepsilon)C_f + \varepsilon C_p \tag{96}$$

ii. thermal conductivity. The effective thermal conductivity of a mixture can be calculated by using relation (43):

$$\frac{k_{eff}}{k_f} = 1 + 0.043 \frac{k_p \varepsilon}{k_f (1-\varepsilon)} \tag{97}$$

where we consider that $r_f/r_p \approx 0{,}043$ as in (Kumar et al., 2004; Jang&Choi, 2004; Prasher, 2005) and $k_{eff}= k_{nf}$,

iii. viscosity. We choose the polynomial approximation based on experimental data Nguyen (Nguyen et al., 2005), for water - Al_2O_3 nanofluid:

$$\mu_{nf} = \left(306\varepsilon^2 - 0.19\varepsilon + 1\right)\mu_f \tag{98}$$

These equations were used to perform the calculation of temperature distribution and transmission fields in the geometry studied.

Figure 7 shows the geometric configuration of the studied model which consists of a coaxial heat exchanger with length *L=64 cm*; inner tube diameter *d=10 mm* and outer tube diameter *D=20 mm*. By inner tube will circulate a nanofluid as primary agent, and by the outer tube will circulate pure water as secondary agent. The nanofluid used is composed of aluminum oxide Al_2O_3 particles dispersed in pure water in different concentrations (1%, 3% and 5%).

Fig. 7. Geometry of coaxial heat exchanger

The continuity, momentum, and energy equations are non-linear partial differential equations, subjected to the following boundary conditions: at the tubes inlet, "velocity inlet" boundary condition was used. The magnitude of the inlet velocity varies for the inner tube between 0,12 m/s and 0,64 m/s, remaining constant at the value of 0,21 m/s for the outer tube. Temperatures used are 60, 70, 90 degrees C for the primary agent and for the secondary agent is 30 degrees C. Heat loss to the outside were considered null, imposing the heat flux = 0 at the outer wall of heat exchanger. The interior wall temperature is considered equal to the average temperature value of interior fluid. Using this values for velocity, the flow is turbulent and we choose a corresponding model *(k-ε)* for solve the equations (Mayga&Nguyen, 2006; Bianco et al., 2009).

For mixing between the base fluid and the three types of nanofluids were performed numerical simulations to determinate correlations between flows regime, characterized by Reynold's number, and convective coefficient values.

The convective coefficient value *h* is calculated using Nusselt number for nanofluids ($Al_2O_3+H_2O$), relation established following experimental determinations by Vasu and all (Vasu et al., in press):

$$Nu_{nf} = 0.0023 \cdot \mathrm{Re}_{nf}^{0.8} \cdot \mathrm{Pr}_{nf}^{0.4} \tag{99}$$

where the Reynolds number is defined by:

$$\mathrm{Re}_{nf} = \frac{\rho_{nf} v_m d}{\mu_{nf}} \tag{100}$$

and Prandtl number is :

$$\mathrm{Pr}_{nf} = \frac{v_{nf}}{\alpha_{nf}} \tag{101}$$

and then, results :

$$h = \frac{Nuk_{nf}}{d} \tag{102}$$

The temperature and velocity profiles can be viewed post processing. In figure 8 is illustrated one example of visualization the temperature profile in a case study, depending by the boundary conditions imposed.

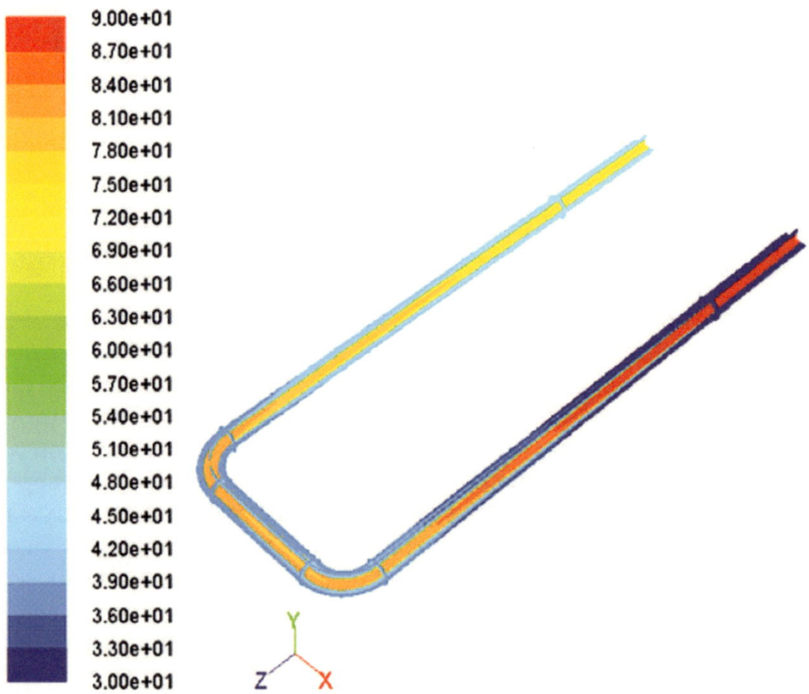

Fig. 8. Temperature profile

Following we analyze the variation of convective heat transfer coefficient in comparison with flow regime, temperature and nanofluids concentrations.

Figures 9-11 highlights the results of values of water and three types of nanofluids used depending on the Reynolds number and the primary agent temperature.

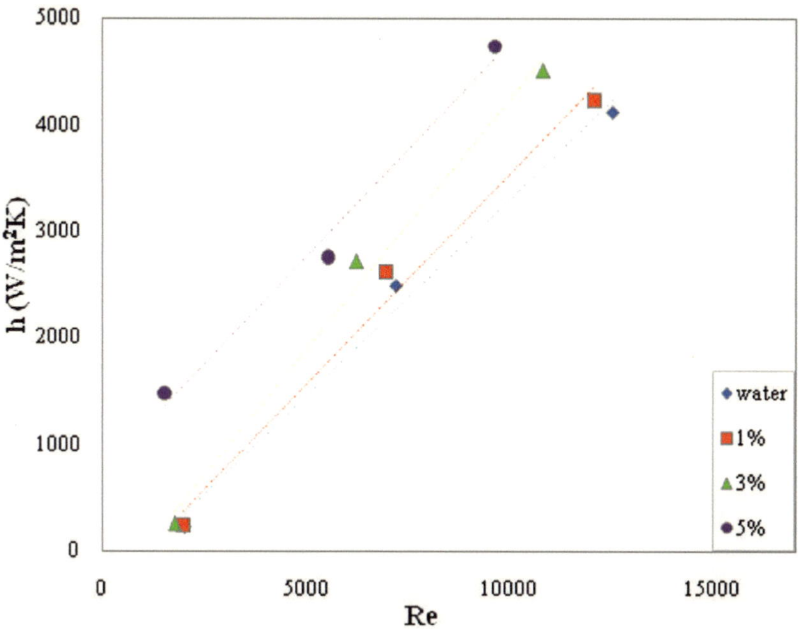

Fig. 9. Variation of convective heat transfer coefficient based on the Reynolds number at the T=60°C

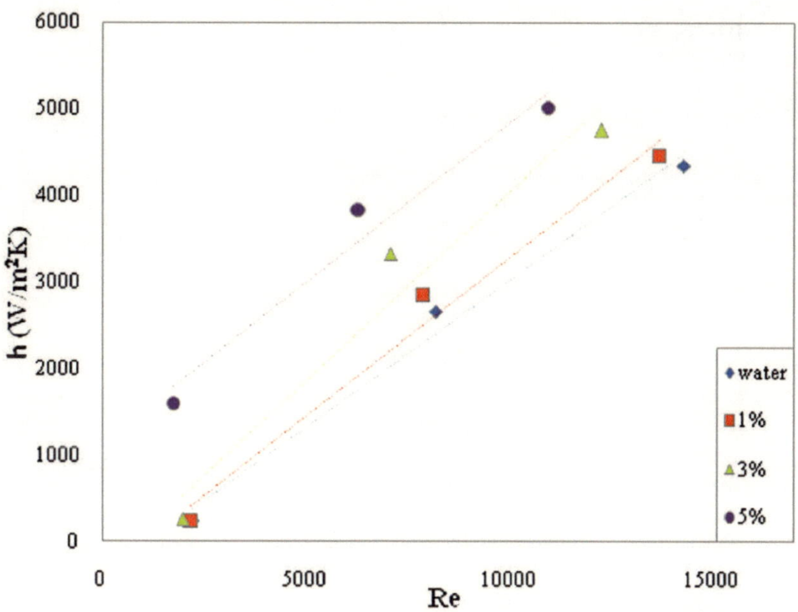

Fig. 10. Variation of convective heat transfer coefficient based on the Reynolds number at the T=70°C

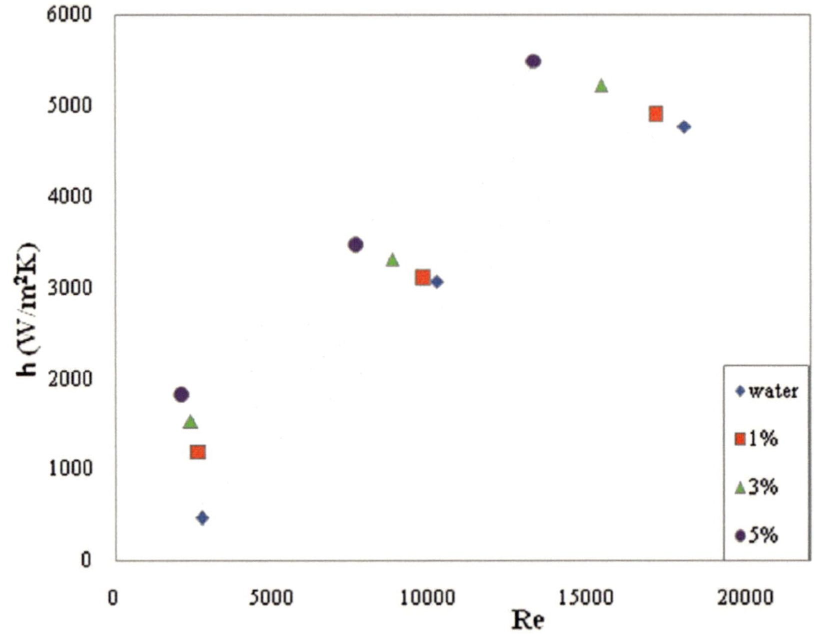

Fig. 11. Variation of convective heat transfer coefficient based on the Reynolds number at the T=90°C

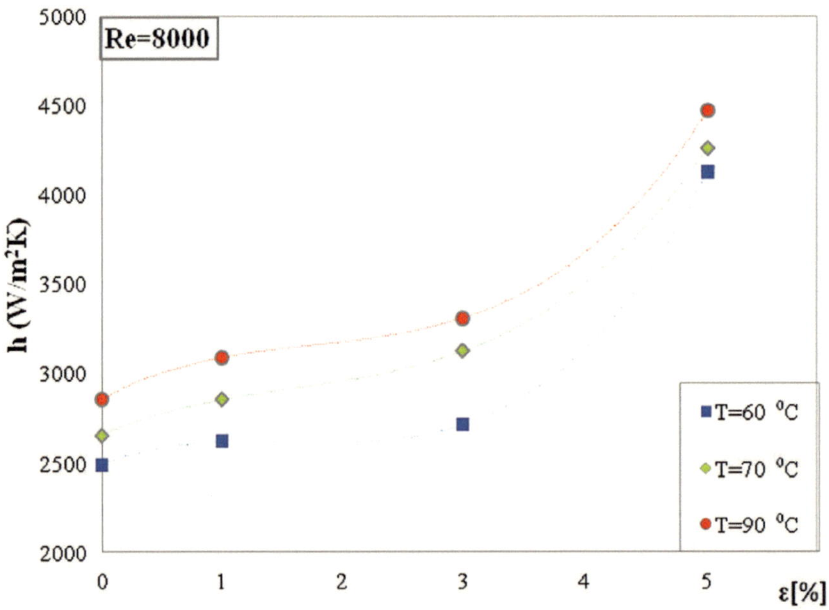

Fig. 12. Variation of convective heat transfer coefficient based on temperature at Reynolds number equal to 8000

It can be seen that the value of convective heat transfer coefficient h for water is about 13% lower than the nanofluids, also parietal heat transfer increases with increasing the primary agent temperature and implicitly with increasing of volume concentration.
In Figure 12 is represented the variation of convective heat transfer coefficient h depending on the volume concentration of particles at imposed temperatures (60, 70 and 90 degree C) for Reynold's number equal to 8000.
We can notice a significant increase of approximately 50% for convective heat transfer coefficient for nanofluid at 5% concentration, compared with water at 90 degree C.

5. The dispersive approximation in the heat transfer processes

In the dispersive approximation of the fractal heat transfer the relation becomes a Korteweg de Vries type equation for the temperature field

$$\frac{\hat{\partial} T}{\partial t}=\frac{\partial T}{\partial t}+\hat{\boldsymbol{V}}\cdot\nabla T+\frac{\sqrt{2}}{3}\mathsf{D}^{3/2}(dt)^{(3/D_F)-1}\nabla^3 T=0 \tag{103}$$

Separating the real and imaginary parts in Eq.(103), *i.e.*

$$\begin{aligned}&\frac{\partial T}{\partial t}+\boldsymbol{V}\cdot\nabla T+\frac{\sqrt{2}}{3}\mathsf{D}^{3/2}(dt)^{(3/D_F)-1}\nabla^3 T=0\\&-\boldsymbol{U}\cdot\nabla T=0\end{aligned} \tag{104a,b}$$

and adding them the heat transfer equation is obtained as:

$$\frac{\partial T}{\partial t}+(\boldsymbol{V}-\boldsymbol{U})\cdot\nabla T+\frac{\sqrt{2}}{3}\mathsf{D}^{3/2}(dt)^{(3/D_F)-1}\nabla^3 T=0 \tag{105}$$

From Eq.(104b) we see that at the fractal scale there isn't any thermal convection.
Assuming that $|\boldsymbol{V}-\boldsymbol{U}|=\sigma T$, with $\sigma=\text{constant}$ (for this assumption see (Agop et al., 2008)), in the one-dimensional case, the equation (52), with the dimensionless parameters

$$\tau=\omega t,\ \xi=kx,\ \phi=\frac{T}{T_0} \tag{106a-c}$$

and the normalizing conditions

$$\frac{\sigma T_0 k}{6\omega}=\frac{\sqrt{2}}{3}\frac{\mathsf{D}^{3/2}(dt)^{(3/D_F)-1}k^3}{\omega}=1 \tag{107}$$

takes the form:

$$\partial_\tau\phi+6\phi\,\partial_\xi\phi+\partial_{\xi\xi\xi}\phi=0 \tag{108}$$

Through the substitutions

$$w(\theta)=\phi(\tau,\xi),\ \theta=\xi-u\tau \tag{109a,b}$$

the Eq.(108), by double integration, becomes

$$\frac{1}{2}w'^2 = F(w) = -\left(w^3 - \frac{u}{2}w^2 - gw - h\right) \tag{110}$$

with g, h two integration constants and u the normalized phase velocity. If $F(w)$ has real roots, the equation (108) has the stationary solution

$$\phi(\xi,\tau,s) = 2a\left(\frac{E(s)}{K(s)} - 1\right) + 2a\cdot \mathrm{cn}^2\left[\frac{\sqrt{a}}{s}\left(\xi - \frac{u}{2}\tau + \xi_0\right);s\right] \tag{111}$$

where cn is the Jacobi's elliptic function of s modulus (Bowman, 1953), a is an amplitude, ξ_0 is a constant of integration and

$$K(s) = \int_0^{\pi/2}\left(1 - s^2\sin^2\varphi\right)^{-1/2} d\varphi,\ E(s) = \int_0^{\pi/2}\left(1 - s^2\sin^2\varphi\right)^{1/2} d\varphi \tag{112a,b}$$

are the complete elliptic integrals (Bowman, 1953). As a result, the heat transfer is achieved by one-dimensional cnoidal oscillation modes of the temperature field (see Fig.13a). This process is characterized through the normalized wave length (see Fig.13b):

$$\lambda = \frac{2sK(s)}{\sqrt{a}} \tag{113}$$

and normalized phase velocity (see Fig.13c):

$$u = 4a\left[3\frac{E(s)}{K(s)} - 1 - \frac{1}{s^2}\right] \tag{114}$$

In such conjecture, the followings result:

i. the parameter s becomes a measure of the heat transfer. The one-dimensional cnoidal oscillation modes contain as subsequences for $s=0$ the one-dimensional harmonic waves while for $s \to 0$ the one-dimensional waves packet. These two subsequences describe the heat transfer through the non-quasi-autonomous regime. For $s=1$, the solution (111) becomes a one-dimensional soliton, while for $s \to 1$ the one-dimensional solitons packet results. These last two subsequences describe the heat transfer through the quasi-autonomous regime;

ii. by eliminating the parameter a from relations (113) and (114), one obtains the relation:

$$\begin{aligned} &u\lambda^2 = A(s) \\ &A(s) = 16\left[3s^2E(s)K(s) - \left(1 - s^2K^2(s)\right)\right] \end{aligned} \tag{115a,b}$$

We observe from Fig.13d that only for $s = 0 \div 0.7$, $A(s) \approx \text{const.}$, and $u\lambda^2 \approx \text{const.}$. According with previous transport regimes, this dispersion relation is valid only for the non-quasi-autonomous regime. For the quasi-autonomous regime it has no signification. Moreover, these two regimes (non-quasi-autonomous and quasi-autonomous) are separated by the 0.7 experimental structure (Chiatti et al., 1970). We note that the cnoidal oscillation modes can be assimilated to a non-linear Toda lattice (Toda, 1989). In such conjecture, the ballistic thermal phononic transport can be emphasized.

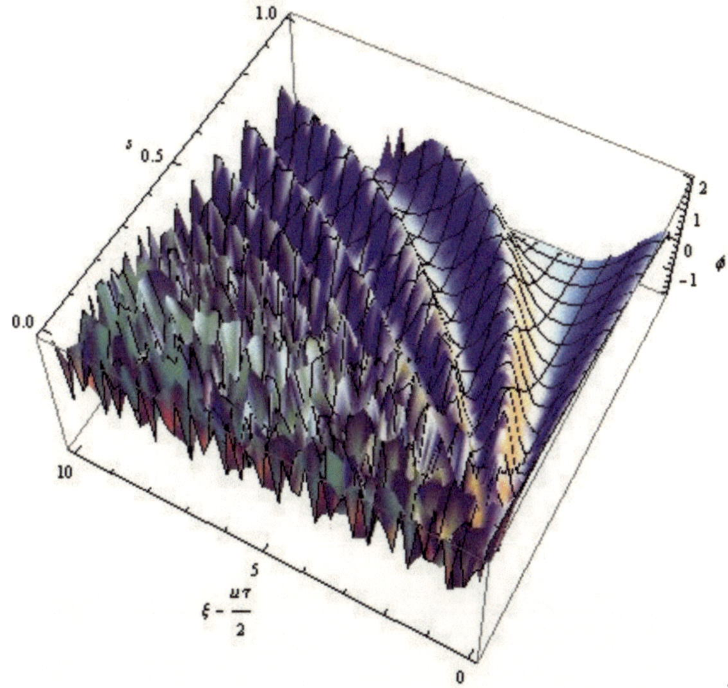

a)

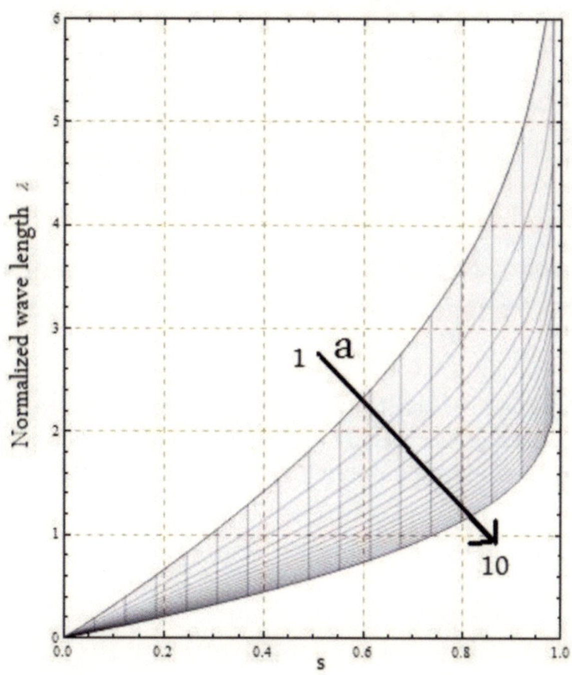

b)

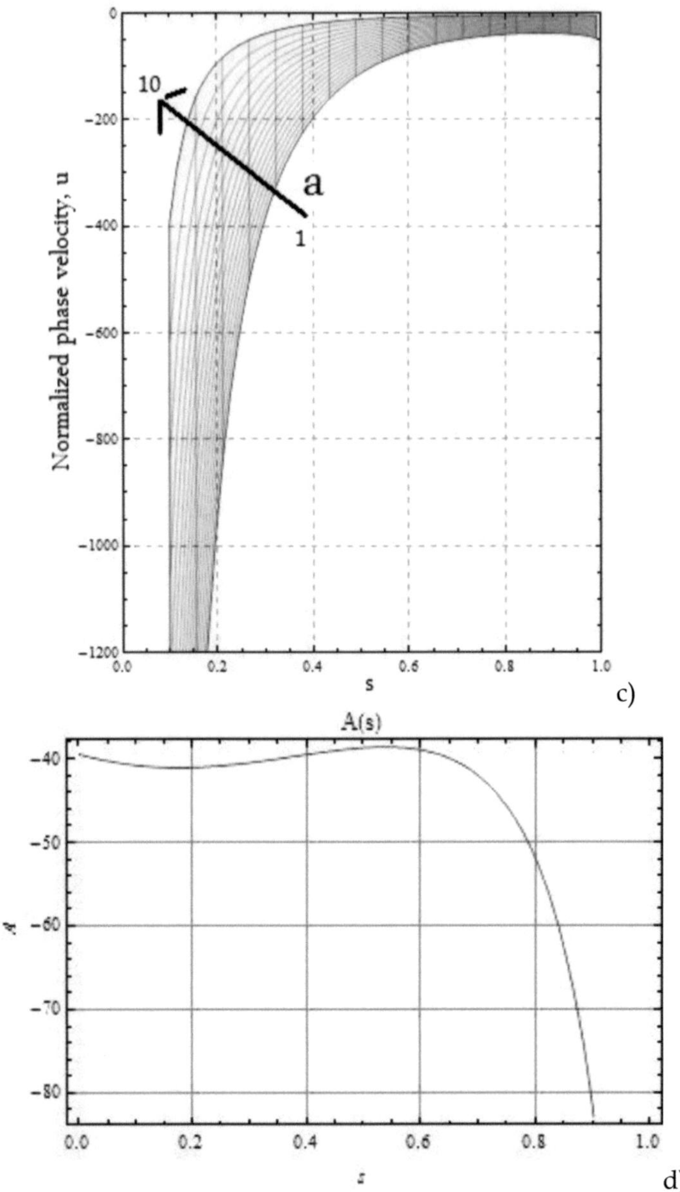

Fig. 13. One-dimensional cnoidal oscillation modes of the temperature field (a) ; normalized wave length (b); normalized phase velocity (c); separation of the thermal flowing regimes (non-quasi-autonomous and quasi-autonomous) by means of the 0.7 experimental structure (Jackson, 1991)

Let us study the influence of fractality on the heat transfer. This can be achieved by the substitutions:

$$w = \frac{u}{4} f^2, \frac{2\theta}{\sqrt{u}} = i\beta \tag{116a,b}$$

and the restriction $h=0$ in Eq.(110). We obtained a Ginzburg-Landau (GL) type equation (Jackson, 1991; Poole et al., 1995):

$$\partial_{\beta\beta} f = f^3 - f \tag{117}$$

The following result:

i. The β coordinate has dynamic significations and the variable f has probabilistic significance;
ii. The general solution of GL equation (Jackson, 1991):

$$f = \sqrt{\frac{2s^2}{1+s^2}} \operatorname{sn}\left(\frac{\beta-\beta_0}{\sqrt{1+s^2}};s\right), \beta_0 = \text{const.} \tag{118a,b}$$

where sn is the Jacobi elliptic function of s modulus (Bowman, 1953) (see Fig14), i.e. the fractalisation of the thermal flowing regime, implies the dependence on s of the following parameters:

i. The relative pair breaking time

$$\tau_r = (1+s^2)K^2(s) \tag{119}$$

ii. The relative concentration

$$n_r = \frac{2}{1+s^2}\left(1-\frac{E(s)}{K(s)}\right) \tag{120}$$

iii. The relative thermal conductivity

$$k_r = 2K(s)(K(s)-E(s)) \tag{121}$$

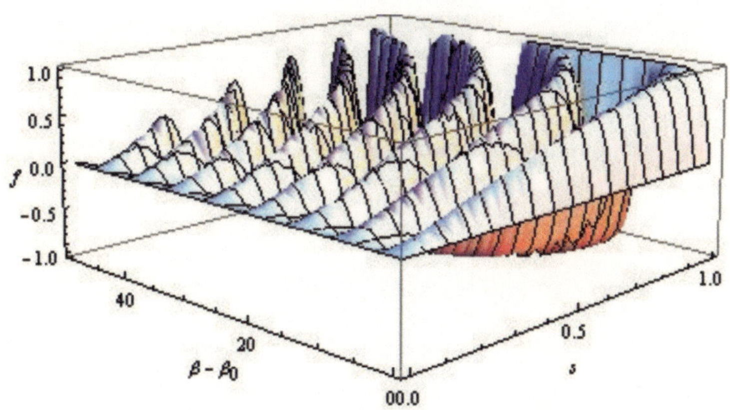

Fig. 14. The fractalisation of the thermal flowing regime is introduced by means of GL equation

These parameters are discontinuous at $s=1$ (see Figs 15a-c), which allows us to say that this singularity can be associated with a phase transition, e.g. from self-structuring to normal state.

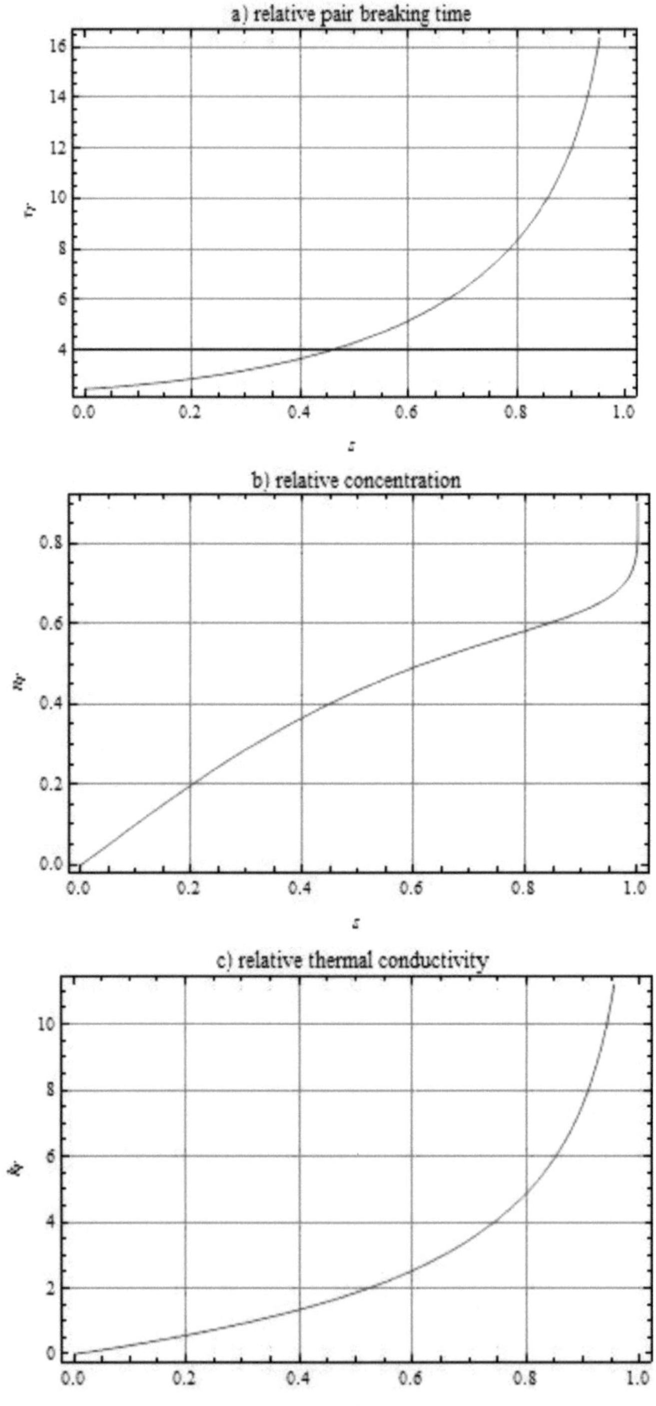

Fig. 15. The dependences on s for: relative pair breaking time τ_r (a); relative concentration n_r (b); relative thermal conductivity k_r (c)

Since the general solution of GL equation is (118a), the self-structuring process is controlled by means of the normalized fractal potential,

$$Q(\beta,s)=-\frac{1}{f}\frac{d^2 f}{d\beta^2}=\left(1-f^2\right)=\frac{1-s^2}{1+s^2}+\frac{2s^2}{1+s^2}\mathrm{cn}^2\left(\frac{\beta-\beta_0}{\sqrt{1+s^2}};s\right) \tag{122}$$

also through cnoidal modes. Thus, for $s\to 0$ it results the non-quasi-autonomous regime (of wave packet type),

$$Q(\beta,s\to 0)=\frac{1-s^2}{1+s^2}+\frac{2s^2}{1+s^2}\cos^2\left(\frac{\beta-\beta_0}{\sqrt{1+s^2}};s\right) \tag{123}$$

and for $s\to 1$ the quasi-autonomous regime (of soliton packet type),

$$Q(\beta,s\to 1)=\frac{1-s^2}{1+s^2}+\frac{2s^2}{1+s^2}\mathrm{sech}^2\left(\frac{\beta-\beta_0}{\sqrt{1+s^2}};s\right) \tag{124}$$

For $s=1$ the soliton (118a) is reduced to the fractal kink,

$$f_k(\beta)=\tanh\left(\frac{\beta-\beta_0}{\sqrt{2}}\right) \tag{125}$$

and we can build a field theory with spontaneous symmetry breaking. The fractal kink spontaneously breaks the vacuum symmetry by tunneling and generates pairs of Copper's type (Chaichian&Nelipa, 1984).

iv. The normalized fractal potential (122) take a very simple expression which is proportional with the density of states of the Cooper pairs type. When the density of states of the Cooper pairs type, f^2, becomes zero, the fractal potential takes a finite value, $Q=1$. The fractal fluid is normal (it works in a non-quasi-autonomous regime) and there are no coherent structures (Cooper pairs type) in it. When f^2 becomes 1, the fractal potential is zero, *i.e.* the entire quantity of energy of the fractal fluid is transferred to its coherent structures, *i.e.* to the Cooper pairs type. Then the fractal fluid becomes coherent (it works in a quasi-autonomous regime). Therefore, one can assume that the energy from the fractal fluid can be stocked by transforming all the environment's entities into coherent structures (Cooper pairs type) and then "freezing" them. The coherent fluid acts as an energy accumulator through the fractal potential (122).

6. Conclusions

A new model on the heat transfer processes in nanostructures considering that the heat flow paths take place on fractal curves is obtained. It results:

i. In the dissipative approximation of the heat transfer process, for Peano type heat flow paths and synchronous movements at differentiable and non-differentiable scales, the thermal transfer mechanism is of diffusive type. In such conjecture, numerical solutions in the absence and in the presence of "walls" are obtained.

For a nanofluid, the increasing of the thermal conductivity depends on the ratio of conductivitie (nano-particle/fluid), volume fraction of the nanoparticle and the nanoparticle radius. Moreover, a temperature dependence of the thermal conductivity is olso given.

ii. In the dispersive approximation of the heat transfer process, both at differentiable and non-differentiable scales, the thermal transfer mechanism is given through the cnoidal oscillation modes of the temperature field. Two thermal flow regimes result: one by means of waves and wave packets and the other by means of solitons and soliton packets. These two regimes are separated by the 0.7 experimental "structure".
Since the cnoidal oscillation modes can be assimilated with a non-linear Toda lattice, a ballistic thermal phononic transport can be emphasized.

iii. It result an unique mechanism of thermal transfer in nanostructures in which the usual ones (diffusive type, ballistic phononic type, etc.) can be seen as approximations of the present approach.

iv. For convective type behavior of a complex fluid, numerical studies of a coaxial heat exchanger using nanofluids are presented.

Then single-phase model have been used for prediction of flow field and calculation of heat transfer coefficient. The study present here indicate the thermal performances of a particular nanofluid composed of aluminum oxide (Al_2O_3) particles dispersed in water for various concentrations ranging from 0 to 5 %. Results have shown that heat transfer coefficient clearly increases with an increase in particle concentration.

The results clearly show that the addition of particles in a base fluid produces a great increase in the heat transfer (≈50%). Intensification of heat transfer increases proportionally with increasing of volume concentration of these nanoparticles.

In the present model the values of convective heat transfer coefficient are dependent of flow regime and temperature values. When temperature is higher, the value of this coefficient increases.

7. References

Agop M., Forna N., Casian Botez I., Bejenariu C., J. (2008), New Theoretical Approach of the Physical Processes in Nanostructures, *Comput. Theor. Nanos*, Vol. 5, No. 4, pp.483-489

Akbarinia A., Behzadmehr A. (2007), Numerical study of laminar mixed convection of ananofluid in horizontal curved tube, *Applied Thermal Science*, Vol. 27, No. 8-9, pp. 1327-1337

Albeverio S., Hoegh-Krohn R. (1974), A remark on the connection between stochastic mechanics and the heat equation, *Journal of Mathematical Physics*, Vol 15., No 10, pp. 1745-1747

Agop M., Paun V., Harabagiu A. (2008), El Naschie's $\varepsilon(\infty)$ theory and effects of nanoparticle clustering on the heat transport in nanofluids, *Chaos Solitons & Fractals*, Vol. 37, No. 5, pp. 1269-1278

Bianco V., Chiacchio F., Manca O., Nardini (2009), Numerical investigation of nanofluids forced convection in circular tube, *Applied Thermal Engineering*, Vol. 29, No. 17-18, pp. 3632-3642

Bowman F. (1953), *Introduction to Elliptic Functions with Applications*, English Universities Press, London

Chen G. (2000), Particularities of Heat Conduction in Nanostructures, *J.Nanopart. Res.*, Vol. 2, No. 2, pp. 199-204

Casian Botez I., Agop M., Nica P., Paun V., Munceleanu G.V. (2010), Conductive and Convective Types Behaviors at Nano-Time Scales, *J. Comput. Theor. Nanos.*, Vol. 7, No. 11, pp. 2271-1180

Chiroiu V., Stiuca P., Munteanu L., Danescu S. (2005), *Introduction in nanomechanics*, Roumanian Academy Publishing House, Bucuresti,

Chiatti O., Nicholls J.T., Proskuryakov Y.Y., Lumpkin N., Farrer I., Ritchie D.A. (2006), Quantum thermal conductance of electrons in a one-dimensional wire, *Phys. Rev. Lett.*, Vol. 97, No. 5

Chaichian M., Nelipa N.F (1984), *Introduction to Gauge Field Theories. Texts and Monographs in Physics*, Springer-Verlag Berlin-Heidelberg-New York-Tokyo

Ferry D.K., Goodnick S.M. (1997), *Transport in Naostructures*, Cambridge University Press, Cambridge, U.K.

Fard M. H., Esfahany M. N. , Talaie M.R. (2009 in press), Numerical study of convective heat transfer of nanofluids in a circular tube two-phase model versus single-phase model, *International Communications in Heat and Mass Transfer*

Hemanth Kumar D., Patel H.E., Rajeev Kumar V.R., Sundararajan Pradeep T., Das S.K. (2004), Model for Heat Conduction in Nanofluids, *Phys. Rev. Lett.*, Vol. 93, No. 14, p. 144301

Harvey R.J. (1966), Navier-Stokes Analog of Quantum Mechanics, *Physical Review*, Vol 152, No 4, p 1115

Jang S.P., Choi S.U. (2004), Role of Brownian motion in the enhaced thermal conductivity of nanofluids, *Applied Physics Letters*, Vol. 84, No. 21, p. 4316

Jackson E. A. (1991), *Perspectives in Nonlinear Dynamics*, Vol. 1, 2, Cambridge University Press, Cambridge, U. K.

Keblinski P., Phillpot S.R., Choi S.U.S., Eastman J.A. (2002), Mechanisms of heat flow in suspensions of nano-sized particles (nanofluids), *Int. J. Heat and Mass. Transfer*, Vol. 45, No. 4, pp. 855-863

Kumar D. H., Patel H. E., Rajeev Kumar V.R., Sundararajan T., Pradeep T., Das S.K. (2004), Model for Heat Conduction in Nanofluids, *Physical Review Letters*, Vol. 93, No. 14, p. 144301

Landau L., Lifshitz E. (1987), *Fluid Mechanics*, Butterworth-Heinemann, Oxford

Mandelbrot B. (1982), *The Fractal Geometry of Nature*, Freeman, San Francisco, U.S.A.

Maiga S.E.B., Palm S.J., et al. (2005), Heat transfer enhancement by using nanofluids in forced convection flows, *International Journal of Heat and Fluid Flow*, Vol. 26, No.4, pp. 530–546

Maiga S.E.B., Nguyen C.T., Galanis N., Roy G. (2004), Heat transfer behavior of nanofluids in a uniformly heated tube, *Superlattices and Microstructures*, Vol. 35, No. 3-6,pp. 543–557

Maiga S.E.B, Nguyen C.T. (2006), Heat transfer enchancement in turbulent tube flow using Al2O3 nanoparticles suspension, *International Journal of Numerical Methods for Heat and Fluid Flow*, Vol 16, No 3, pp. 275 - 292

Nottale L. (1992), *Fractal Space-Time and Microphysics: Towards a Theory of Scale Relativity*, Word Scientific, Singapore

Nottale L., Ch. Auffray (2008), Scale relativity theory and integrative systems biology: 2 Macroscopic quantum-type mechanics, *Prog. Biophys. Mol. Bio.*, Vol. 97, No. 1, pp. 115-157

Nottale L. (2008), *Scale relativity and fractal space-time: theory and applications*, First International Conference on the Evolution and Development of the Universe, Paris

Notalle L. (2007), Scale Relativity: A Fractal Matrix for Organization in Nature, *Electronic Journal of Theoretical Physics*, Vol. 4, No.16 (III), pp. 15-102

Nikitov A. and Ouvanov V. (1974), *Élémentes de la Théorie des Functions Spéciales*, Mir, Moscow

Nguyen C. T., Roy G., Lajoie P.R. (2005), *Refroidissement des microprocesseurs à haute performance en utilisant des nano fluides*, Congrès Français de Thermique, SFT Reims

HE Patel, SK Das, T. Sundararajan, AS Nair, B. George, T. Pradeep (2003), Thermal conductivities of naked and monolayer protected metal nanoparticle based nanofluids: Manifestation of anomalous enhancement and chemical effects, *Appl.Phys.Lett.*,Vol. 83, No.14, p. 2931

Patankar S.V. (1980), *Numerical heat transfer and fluid flow*, Hemisphere Publishing Corporation, Taylor and Francis Group, New York

Pak, B. C. et Cho, Y. I. (1998), Hydrodynamic and Heat Transfer Study of Dispersed Fluids with Submicron Metallic Oxide Particles, *Experimental Heat Transfer*, Vol. 11, No. 2, pp. 151-170

Poole Ch.P. Jr., Farach H.A., Creswick R.J. (1995), *Textbook of Superconductivity*, Academic Press, San Diego

Prasher R. (2005), Thermal Conductivity of Nanoscale Colloidal Solutions (nanofluids), *Physical Review Letters*, Vol. 94, No.2, p. 025901

Rohsenow HW.M., Hartnett J.P., Cho Y.I. (1998), *Handbook of Heat Transfer*, McGraw Hill, U.S.A.

Toda M. (1981), *Theory of Nonlinear Lattices*, Springer Series in Solid-State Sciences 20, Springer-Verlag

Vizureanu P., Agop M. (2007), A Theoretical Approach of the Heat Transfer in Nanofluids, *Materials Transactions*, Vol. 48, No. 11, pp. 3021-3023

Vasu V., Rama K.K., Kumar A.C.S. (Article in press), Empirical correlations to predict thermophysical and heat transfer characteristics of nanofluids, *Thermal Science Journal*, Vol. 12, No. 3

Wang J.-S., Wang J. and Lii J.T. (2008), Quantum thermal transport in nanostructures, *Eur. Phys. Jour. B*, Vol 62, No. 4, pp. 381-404

Wang X., Xu X., J. (1999), Thermal Conductivity of Nanoparticle-Fluid Mixture, *Jour. Thermophys. And Heat Transfer*, Vol. 13, No. 4, pp. 474-480

Zhang Z. (2007), *Nano-Microscale Heat Transfer*, McGraw Hill, U.S.A.

Zienkievicz O.C., Taylor R.L. (1991), *The Finite Element Method*, McGraw-Hill, New York, U.S.A.

21

Heat Transfer in Micro Direct Methanol Fuel Cell

Ghayour Reza
The Noshirvani Babol university of technology in Mazandaran
Iran

1. Introduction

1.1 The micro-fuel cell power supply

This invention is a simple high energy per unit mass fuel cell electrical power system for cellular phones, portable computers and portable electrical devices. We believe this is the best initial consumer niche market for fuel cell technology, rather than larger power systems. The micro-fuel cell utilizes vacuum thin film deposition techniques to coat pattern etched-nuclear-particle-track plastic membranes. The process forms catalytically active surface hydrogen/oxygen electrodes on either side of a single structured proton-exchange-membrane electrolyte. A series stack of cells is built onto a single structured membrane by geometrically engineering the cells on the membrane to allow through-membrane contacts, through-cell water control, thin film electrodes, and electrode breaks. These production techniques are well suited to roll-to-roll production processes and minimize the use of expensive catalysts. To improve reliability, an integrated system of fault correction is used to ensure the operation of the cell stack if there is cell damage. The fuel cells will be directly fueled with liquid hydrocarbon fuels such as methanol and ethanol, by incorporating new direct conversion catalysts. The Micro-Fuel Cell bridges the final gap in portable electronics with an energy source that is smaller, lighter, simpler, cleaner, and less expensive.
Comment on this chapter is that first a brief explanation about the methods of prediction methods for computing fluid dynamics analysis (CFD) is one of them is be provided.
Among the applications considered finite volume and finite element software for the calculation of the FLUENT CFD May be used with more ability and are more and more wide spread, so familiar with this part of the software are presented. Simulation for the micro fuel cell design to optimal dimensions for the design of channels was brought to get. Also, a heat transfer analysis was performed for the cell. At the end of the simulation the result can be validity.

2. Prediction methods

Predicting heat transfer and fluid flow processes into two main methods are performed:
1. Laboratory
2. Theoretical calculations

Accurate information about a physical process often determine by Experimental measurement. Laboratory researches on a system that exactly the same size as that real dimensions use to predict that how similar work version of the system under these same conditions, but in most cases do such experiments due to large size of the device being very

expensive and is often impossible, so tests on models with a smaller scale can be done, though here the issue of expansion of information obtained from ever smaller samples of all aspects of the device the original simulation does not often important aspects such as the combustion of model experiments to be excluded. These limits are further decreased useful results. Finally, should be remembering that in many cases, exist serious problems measurement and measurement instruments also not are out of error.
A theoretical prediction, use maximum application of mathematical model to comparison with the experimental results will be less used to. We are looking for physical processes; mathematical model essentially follows a series of differential equations. If the classical mathematical methods used in solving these equations, not exist predicting the possibility for many Utility phenomena. With little attention to a classic text on fluid mechanics or heat transfer can be determined that there are a few numbers of scientific problems that can count indefinite parameters with the equations needed to find. Moreover, these results often are include unlimited series, special functions, algebraic equations, specific values etc. So that may be, their numerical solution is not easy. Fortunately, numerical methods development and availability of large processors to ensure there has, for almost every issue of the practical implications of a mathematical model can be used.

3. Advantage of the theoretical calculation

3.1 Low cost

The most important point of a predictive computational cost is low. In most applications, the cost of applying a computer program costs far less than the same research laboratory, the physical status of the agent when the study is large and more complex, gaining more importance and that while the price of items currently being much more. The computational cost will be less likely in the future.

3.2 Speed

One study calculated that a can significantly speed is performed, the designer can concepts combining hundreds of different conditions in less than a day to study, to select the optimum design. On the other hand, simply can well imagine maturity or laboratory research will require much time.

3.3 Complete information

Computer Solution a problem give me the necessary information and complete details and will give value all the dependent variables (such as velocity, pressure, temperature, chemical concentration samples, turbulence intensity) across the field to your favorite loses. Unlike adverse conditions that are happen also during test, inaccessible places in a low computational job are decrease and don't exist flow turbulence due to measurement devices.

3.4 Ability to real simulate conditions

In a theoretical calculation, since the actual conditions can easily be simulated, there is no need to model the small scale and we resort to cold flow. For a computer program, having geometric dimensions too small or too big, apply very low or very high temperatures, to act with flammable or toxic materials, processes follow very fast or very slow to does not create a major problem.

3.5 Ability to simulate the ideal conditions

Sometimes a prediction method is used for studying the base phenomenon instead a complex engineering application. To study the phenomenon, the person concerned on a few main parameters focused and will be removed other aspect. Thus, under ideal conditions as much may be considered optimal conditions, for example, it can be two dimensional, constant densities, despite an adiabatic surface, or having an unlimited rate interplay named in a computational work, these conditions are easily and precisely can be established. Moreover, even in a practical test can be accurate to the near ideal conditions hardly.

4. Inadequacy of the theoretical calculation

According above, prominences are effective enough that the person encourage computer analysis. However, creation blind interest to any cause is not desirable. So that would be helpful to be aware of the obstacles and limitations. As previously mentioned, the computer analyzes used to concepts of a mathematical model. So a mathematical model importance, is limited the usefulness of the computational work. It should be noted, the final results of the person who used computer analysis, depend on the mathematical model and the numerical method. So that applying a mathematical model is inappropriate up can cause a numerical technique ideal to produce uncertainly results.

5. Choice prediction method

Discussion about relative suitability of the computer analysis and laboratory researches is not recommendations for laboratory work. Recognize the strong and weaknesses of these are essential to select the proper technique. Indubitable, test is the method of research about a new fundamental phenomenon. In this case, test leads and calculating will follow. In combination of some phenomenon known and effective to apply the calculation is useful. Even in these conditions also required to give validity to the results of calculations are compared with experimental calculations. On the other hand, to design a device through the experiment, the initial calculations were most helpful and if you practical research, is added the calculation, can often be decrease significant number of experiments. Therefore, the appropriate volume of activity should be combined a prediction to perform of rational calculations and test. Value of each of these compounds depends on the nature of problem and predictive purposes, economic issues and other specific conditions.

6. What is CFD?

In theory methods, in first, with the observation of physical phenomenon beginning the expression of the relevant differential equations and then extend to the algebraic equations governing the issue outlines. There is a problem that unlike phenomena which mathematical models suitable for them are offered (such as laminar flow), there are some phenomena mathematical model that still has not found suitable for them (such as two-phase flows). Hence use of the numerical methods as a third way to solve their problems. So on the other division into fluid dynamics can be divided into three parts:

- Experiment Fluid dynamics
- Theory Fluid dynamics

- Computational Fluid Dynamics

Computational fluid dynamics or CFD analysis of expression systems include fluid flow, heat transfer and associated phenomena such as chemical reactions, based on computer simulation that is CFD method can be very able, so that include a wide range of industrial applications in the industrial. Some examples include:

- Aircraft aerodynamic and vehicles
- Ship Hydrodynamic
- Power: combustion motor and gas turbines

And...

Therefore, a CFD has been as a major component in industrial production and design process increasingly. In addition, CFD fluid system designs of multi a unique advantage compared to the experimental methods have:

- Major reduction time and cost in new design
- Ability to study a system that tests on them are difficult or impossible (such as very large systems)
- Ability study systems under randomized more than usual about them
- Very high level of detail results.

6.1 CFD program

Structure of the CFD program is numerical method. There are general three methods for separate numerical methods that include:

1. Finite difference
2. Finite element
3. Spectral methods

6.2 Capability of program

FLUENT software can be able to simulation and modeling the following:

- Flow in complex geometry of two dimensional and three dimensional with the possible resolution of network optimization,
- Current density, compressibility and non-reversible,
- Persistent or transient analysis,
- Flows slimy, slow and turbulent,
- Newtonian and non-Newtonian fluids,
- Heat transfer, free convection or forced,
- Combined heat transfer / guidance,
- Radiation heat transfer,
- Rotating frames or static models,
- Slider and the network of networks by moving,
- Chemical reactions, including combustion and reaction models,
- Add optional volume terms of heat, mass, momentum, turbulence and chemical composition,
- Flow in porous media,
- Heat exchangers, blower, the radiators and their efficiency,
- Two-phase and multiphase flows
- Free surface flows with complex surface shapes.

This capabilities allows that the FLUENT to be used in the wide range in many industries

- Application Process Equipment in chemistry, energy (power), oil, gas,
- Applications of environmental (change climate conditions), air space,
- Turbo machine, car,
- Heat exchangers, electronics (semiconductors and electronic components cooling)
- Air conditioning and refrigeration, process materials and fire investigation and design architects.

In other words, FLUENT a suitable choice for modeling compressibility and non compressibility fluid flow can be complex.

7. Numerical analysis of a micro direct methanol fuel cell

7.1 Assumptions for flow and pressure distribution analysis

As was expressed in the anode, reaction begins when produce the CO_2 bubbles, so our actual flow will be two-phase. According to the process for production parts the surface quality of spark is not perfectly polished level. The pump flow is completely uniform because not using a pressure circuit breakers, was not to provide the desired flow.

But in this analysis were the following assumptions:

1. Fluid phase is Single and the gas in the fluid was regardless.
2. Fluid resistance with surface channels was regardless.
3. Inlet flow rate was considered uniform completely.

Full analysis was performed as symmetrical. Therefore, analysis was performed on half the model. The line of symmetry is aligned with 135 degrees angle line. For network selected triangular elements and are used 378,640 elements totally in the model. Mesh models is given in figure (1).

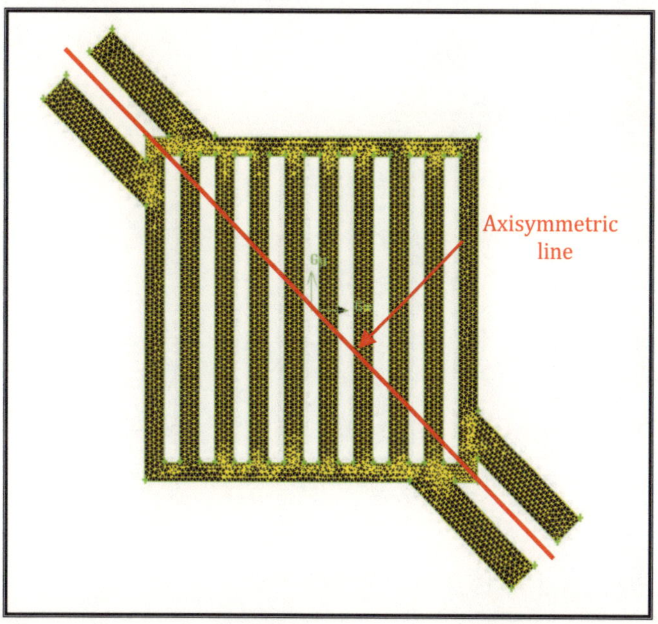

Fig. 1. Meshing model and axisymmetric line

For this simulation model is used the second order momentum equation that is given in formula (4-1) and the momentum coefficient have been used 0.7.

7.2 Momentum equation

The equation is shown in equation (1):

$$\frac{\partial}{\partial t}(\rho_m v_m) + \nabla.(\rho_m v_m v_m) = \\ -\nabla p + \nabla.\left[\mu_m(\nabla v_m + \nabla v_m{}^T\right] + \rho_m g + F + \nabla.\left(\sum_{k=1}^{n} \alpha_k \rho_k \upsilon_{dr,k} \upsilon_{dr,k}\right) \tag{1}$$

To evaluate the distribution flow in flow field, parallel and cross strip field of this analysis is given. Figure (2) contour flow distribution in parallel flow channel depth of Z=0.3 and flow rate $\dot{m} = 0.3cc/\min$ is shown. Figure (3) contour of the current distribution in the cross strip flow field is shown. The figure denote uniformity and dispersal distribution cross strip flow field in comparison with the parallel flow field is much higher and this may seem at first glance appears one of the important factors in the high efficiency cell that is reactive. If the path of liquid methanol in the parallel flow field is traced, we observe that the area around the flow field path and center of flow field have a little velocity. However, if parallel compared to cross strip flow field, which is observed uniformity in all area of flow field except in the corner and it shows that in terms of flow field analysis. It can give higher efficiency compared with parallel the flow field. After simulation, cross strip flow field is superior to parallel. Figure (4) show flow vector in inlet and Figure (5) show flow vector in outlet channels cross strip flow field.

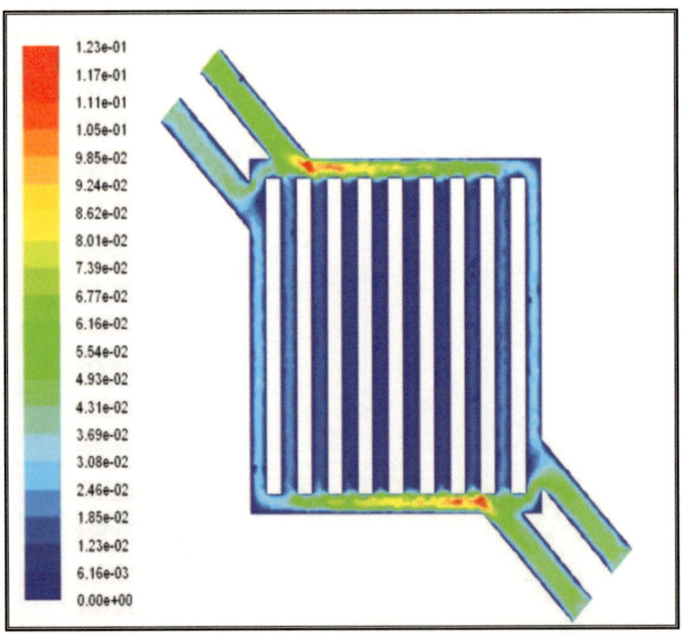

Fig. 2. Flow contour in parallel

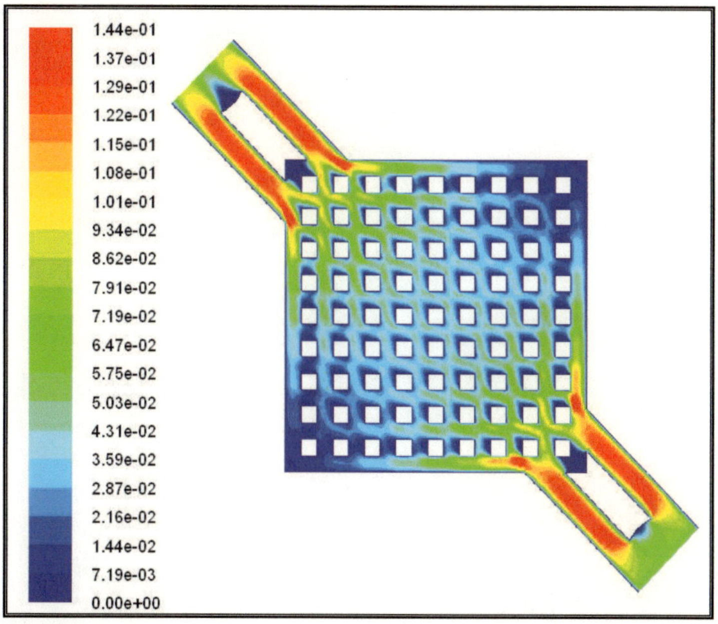

Fig. 3. Flow contour in cross strip

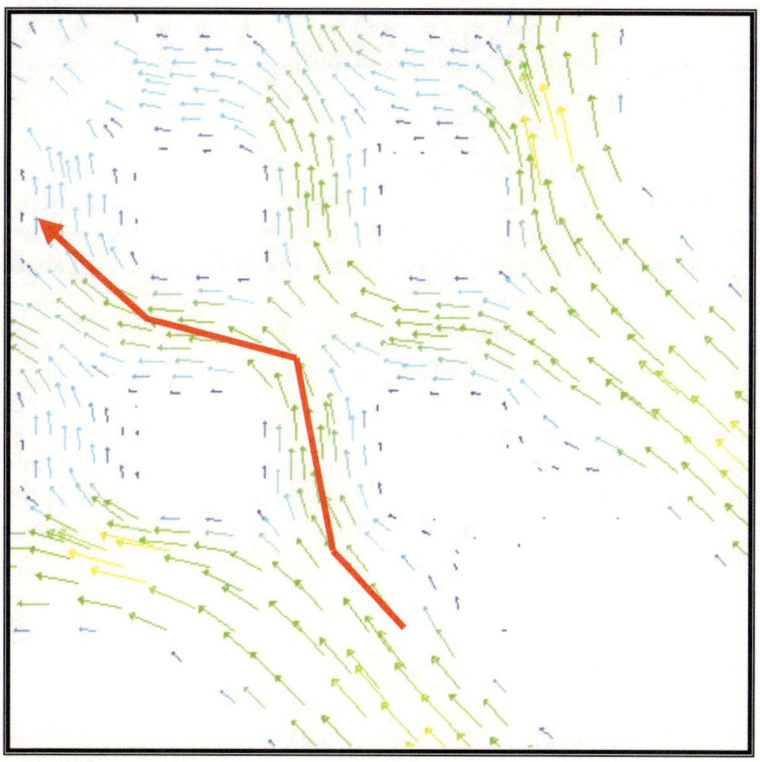

Fig. 4. Flow of parallel in inlet

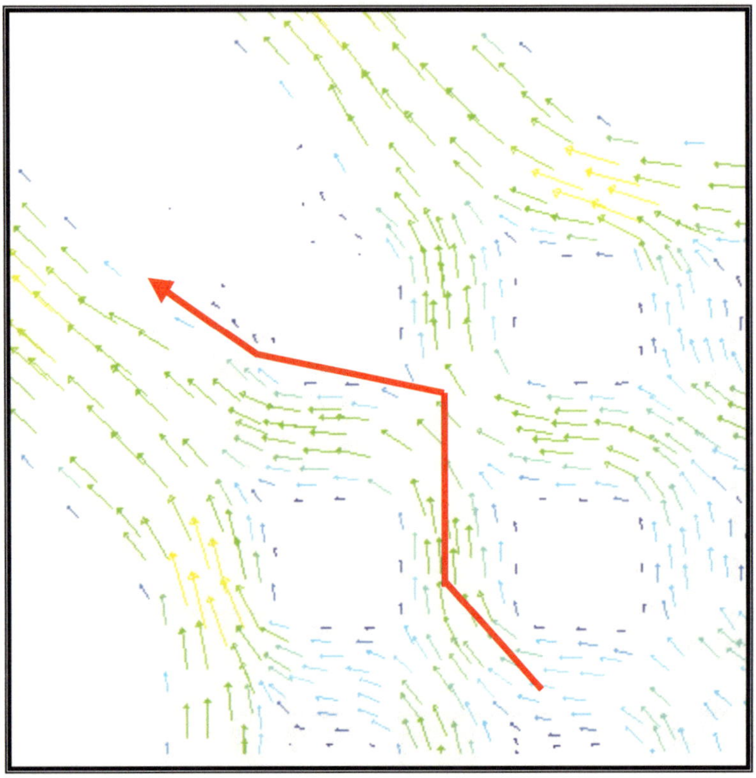

Fig. 5. Flow of cross strip in outlet

7.3 Assumptions of heat transfer analysis

In real estate, total area of MEA surface does not participate in chemical reaction uniformly for this reason that MEA has not a good efficiency and safety of the membrane. In analysis of thermal conductivity in the steel body of the cell that tried simplifying about reaction in the cell membrane that is given below:

- The total membrane surface response to in reaction.
- The total membrane area reacts in uniformly.
- There are similar rates of heat generation.
- The existence of gas bubbles in channels is apart.

Thus, flow is considered as single-phase and slow regimen for fluid motion. Heat generation is simulated by the MEA with a generation temperature area that total area generates heat with a constant rate. There for analysis done with these assumptions and use the energy equation in the calculations.

7.4 Energy equation

The energy equation is defined by below form:

$$\frac{\partial}{\partial t}(\rho v)+\nabla.(v(\rho E+p))=\nabla.\left(k_{eff}\nabla T-\sum_{j}h_{j}J_{j}+(\tau_{eff}.v)\right)+S_{h} \quad (2)$$

So that k_{eff} is effective conductivity equal to $k+k_t$ that k_t is thermal conductivity turbulence and that is defined accord to the turbulence model. J_j is the gush of components influence. Three term of Right side of the above equation shows energy transfer due to conduction, different influence and viscous waste regularity.

S_h is including heat of the chemical reaction or other heat source that is defined. With simplify the above equations have:

$$E = h - \frac{p}{\rho} + \frac{v^2}{2} \tag{3}$$

So that h is defined as the sensible enthalpy for ideal gas and that is in the following form:

$$h = \sum_j Y_j h_j \tag{4}$$

For incompressible fluid we have:

$$h = \sum_j Y_j h_j + \frac{p}{\rho} \tag{5}$$

Y_j is mass fraction of the samples j and

$$h_j = \int_{T_{ref}}^{T} c_{p,j} dT \tag{6}$$

So that is $T_{ref} = 298.15^\circ K$. Thermal analysis is applied by using of energy formula for cross strip flow field for the incompressible fluid that is presented in equation (3). Results are reported in continue. For analysis, thermal characteristics are given in Table (1).

MATERIAL	METHANOL SOLUTION	STEEL-316
Density (Kg/m^3)	785	8030
Specific heat capacity (j/Kg.k)	2534	502.48
Heat transfer coefficient (W/m.k)	0.2022	16.27

Table 1. Thermal characteristics

After analyzing with the different mass flows ($\dot{m}$), highest temperature with consideration by conduction heat transfer from the wall with displacement transfer coefficient $10 W/m^2K$ for air are listed in Table (2). Cell temperature is $300^\circ K$ in normal state. The number of iterations to converge to solutions in Figure (6) is given. Heat transfer contour in tangent membrane on the page in Figure (7) is shown.

In this analysis, show the effects of the temperature distribution around heat generation membrane with contours that is specified more clearly with red lines that high light in figure. The contour dispersals are to output side. This term of view performance is also acceptable. That is Because of temperature generation and high transfer rate of mass flow in micro channel that because the temperature contours aggregation in outlet gate and temperature dispersal in outlet is more that seems quite reasonable.

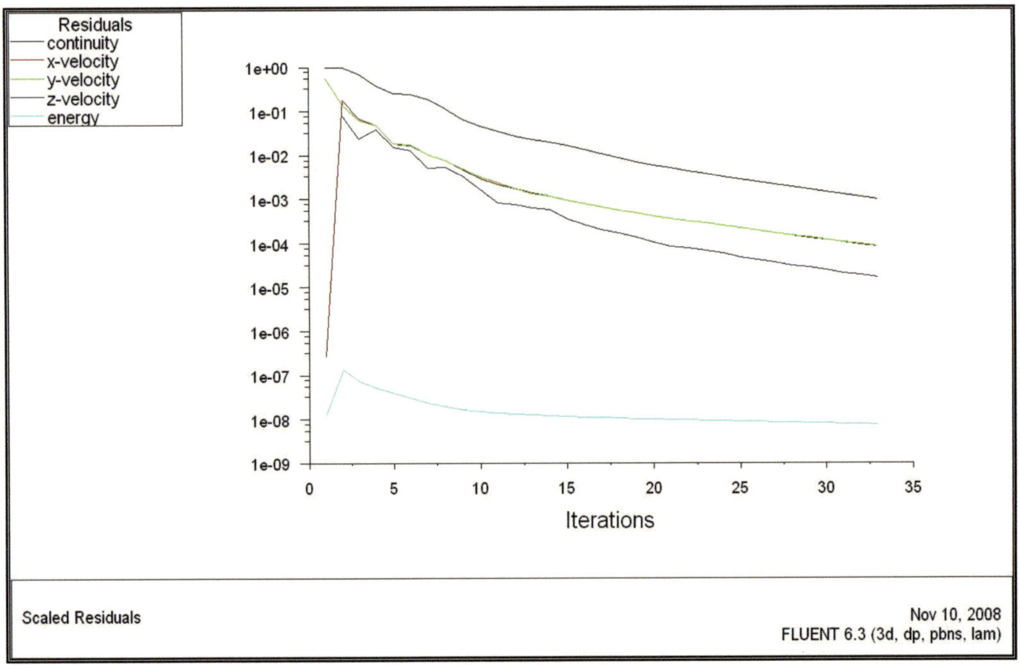

Fig. 6. Converge to solutions

$T_{max}(K^\circ)$	$\dot{m}(mLit/s)$
312.5	*0.3*
310.7	*0.6*
307.8	*0.9*

Table 2. Highest temperature generate with heat transfer

Figure (8) is shown heat transfer in cross section of steel plate of channel. Following this study, heat transfer existence in cross is the micro reactor. In this cross section is observed the temperature gradient contour is put away with a sharp slope relatively. But in comparison with heat transfer plate mode convention is small relatively. Because temperature displacement because of mass transfer of micro-channels compared to the dimensions of micro channels is more effective than heat-conduction in touch with the hot membrane. High speed of mass transfer in micro channels prevents conduction heat transfer.

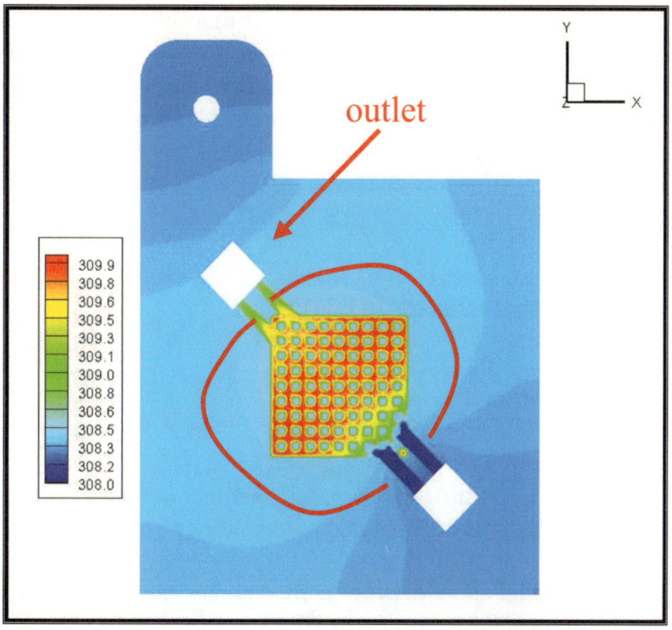

Fig. 7. Heat transfer for Steel plate

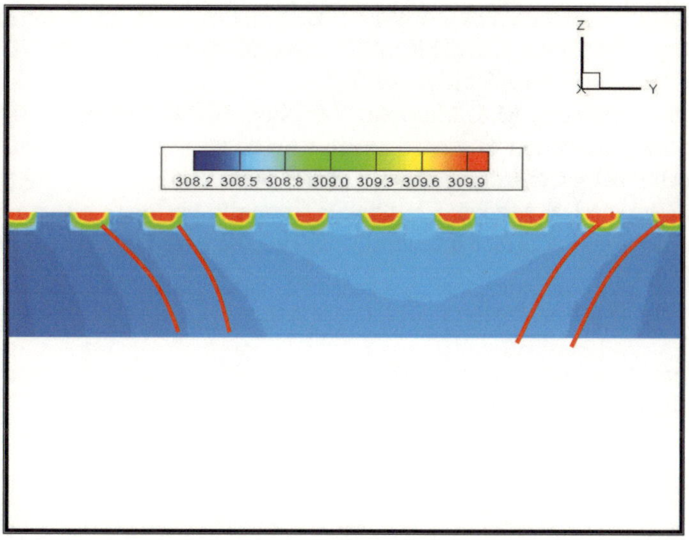

Fig. 8. Heat transfer of steel cross section plate

8. Conclusion

Performing the numerical simulation can be determined very uniform distribution cross strip flow field rather than parallel flow field. So with simulation can be determined distribution of methanol in the membranes. Because if we have good distribution, we have more uniform fuel distribution in the anode side and result in good performance in reaction.

With simulation of heat transfer, is found heat distribution in the cell and can be show the small scale of the chemical reaction in steel surface areas that are more affected by temperature, even at very low temperatures different from doing the chemical reaction.
Finally, the comparison between two kind of flow field and give the best distribution in cross strip flow field and good reaction other than parallel flow field.

9. Acknowledgment

Special thanks for Dr. Shakeri Mohsen and fuel cell research center in Babol university of mazandaran and all people that assist me in this project.

10. References

Arico, A.S.& Srinivasan S.& Antonucci, V. (2001), 1, No.2. DMFCs, From Fundamental Aspects to Technology Development, FUEL CELLS.

Cao, J. & Zou, Zh. (2008). Planar air-breathing micro-direct methanol fuel cell stacks based on micro-electronic-mechanical-system technology. *Journal of Power Sources* 185 (2008) 433-438.

Kulikovsky, A. (2005). Model of the flow with bubbles in the anode channel and ... *Electrochemistry Communications*, 7, pp.237,

Lu, G. Q & Lim, P. C. & Liu, F. Q. & Wang, C. Y. (2005). On mass transport in an air-breathing DMFC stack. *J. Energy Res.;* 29:1041-1050.

Lu, G. Q. & Lim, P. C. & Liu, F. Q. & Wang, C. Y. (2005). On mass transport in an air-breathing DMFC stack. INTERNATIONAL JOURNAL OF ENERGY RESEARCH Int. J. Energy Res. 2005; 29:1041-1050.

Motokawa, Sh.& Mohamedi, M.& Momma, T.& Shoji, Sh. T. Osaka, (2004). MEMS-based design and fabrication of a new concept micro direct methanol fuel cell (μDMFC), Electrochemistry Communications 6 (2004) 562-565.

Valeri, A. D. & Jongkoo L.& Moona, Ch. (2006). Three-dimensional, two-phase, CFD model for the design of a direct methanol fuel cell, Received 11 April 2006; accepted 26 July 2006.

Van wailer, Thermo dynamic book.

www.fctec.com.

www.fleunt.com.

www.microbialfuelcell.com.

22

Heat Transfer in Complex Fluids

Mehrdad Massoudi
U.S. Department of Energy, National Energy Technology Laboratory (NETL), Pittsburgh USA

1. Introduction

Amongst the most important constitutive relations in Mechanics, when characterizing the behaviour of complex materials, one can identify the (Cauchy) stress tensor **T**, the heat flux vector **q** (related to heat conduction) and the radiant heating (related to the radiation term in the energy equation). Of course, the expression 'complex materials' is not new. In fact, at least since the publication of the paper by Rivlin & Ericksen (1955), who discussed fluids of complexity n (Truesdell & Noll, 1992)], to the recently published books (Deshpande et al., 2010), the term complex fluids refers in general to fluid-like materials whose response, namely the stress tensor, is 'non-linear' in some fashion. This non-linearity can manifest itself in variety of forms such as memory effects, yield stress, creep or relaxation, normal-stress differences, etc. The emphasis in this chapter, while focusing on the constitutive modeling of complex fluids, is on granular materials (such as coal) and non-linear fluids (such as coal-slurries).

One of the main areas of interest in energy related processes, such as power plants, atomization, alternative fuels, etc., is the use of slurries, specifically coal-water or coal-oil slurries, as the primary fuel (Papachristodoulou & Trass, 1987; Roh et al., 1995; Tsai & Knell, 1986). Some studies indicate that the viscosity of coal-water mixtures depends not only on the volume fraction of solids, and the mean size and the size distribution of the coal, but also on the shear rate, since the slurry behaves as shear-rate dependent fluid (Gupta & Massoudi, 1993). There are also studies which indicate that preheating the fuel results in better performance (Tsai, et al., 1988; Saeki & Usui, 1995), and as a result of such heating, the viscosity changes. Constitutive modeling of these non-linear fluids, commonly referred to as non-Newtonian fluids, has received much attention (Schowalter, 1978; Larson 1999). Most of the naturally occurring and synthetic fluids are non-linear fluids, for example, polymer melts, suspensions, blood, coal-water slurries, drilling fluids, mud, etc… It should be noted that sometimes these fluids show Newtonian (linear) behavior for a given range of parameters or geometries; there are many empirical or semi-empirical constitutive equations suggested for these fluids (Massoudi & Vaidya, 2008). There have also been many non-linear constitutive relations which have been derived based on the techniques of continuum mechanics (Batra, 2006; Haupt, 2002). The non-linearities oftentimes appear due to higher gradient terms or time derivatives. When thermal and or chemical effects are also important, the (coupled) momentum and energy equations can give rise to a variety of interesting problems, such as instability, for example the phenomenon of double-diffusive convection in a fluid layer (Straughan, 1998, 2008).

When a coal stockpile is stored in the presence of air, slow oxidation of the carbonaceous materials occurs and heat is released. The self-heating of coal stockpiles has a long history of posing significant problems to coal producers because it lowers the quality of coal and may result in hazardous thermal runaway. The prediction of the self-heating process is, therefore, necessary in order to identify and evaluate control measures and strategies for safe coal mining, storage and transportation; this requires an accurate estimate of the various processes associated with the self-heating which are impossible unless the appropriate phenomenological coefficients are known. In such storage-type problems, the critical ignition temperature θ_{cr} also known as the critical storage temperature, is an important design and control parameter, since at higher temperatures than this θ_{cr}, thermal ignition occurs, possibly giving rise to a variety of instabilities and problems.

Most complex fluids are multi-component mixtures. In many applications, these fluids are treated as a single continuum suspension with non-linear material properties and the techniques and models used in rheology or mechanics of non-linear fluids can generally be used to study such problems (Larson, 1999). In this case, global or macroscopic information about the variables such as the velocity or temperature fields for the whole suspension can be obtained. In many other applications, however, there is a need to know the details of the field variables such as velocity, concentration, temperature, etc., of each component and in such cases one needs to resort to the multi-component modeling approaches (Rajagopal & Tao, 1995; Massoudi, 2008, 2010). Examples of complex fluids whereby both approaches can be used are coal-slurries, many of the biological fluids such as blood and the synovial fluid, and many chemically- reacting fluids.

Granular materials exhibit non-linear phenomena like yield stress and normal stress differences, the latter usually being referred to as *dilatancy* (Reynolds, 1885, 1886). The normal-stress phenomenon is a characteristic of non-linear fluids and non-linear elastic solids. The central role played by this phenomenon in determining the character of granular materials was recognized early in the development of the theories for modeling granular materials. Interestingly, a constitutive model that was proposed for wet sand (Reiner, 1945), enjoyed a good bit of popularity as a model for non-Newtonian fluids before losing its appeal. One approach in the modeling of granular materials is to treat it as a *continuum,* which assumes that the material properties of the ensemble may be represented by continuous functions so that the medium may be divided infinitely without losing any of its defining properties. Since granular materials conform to the shape of the vessel containing them, they can be considered fluid-like. However, unlike fluids, they can be heaped. Characterizing bulk solids is difficult mainly because small variations in some of the primary properties such as size, shape, hardness, particle density, and surface roughness can result in very different behavior. Furthermore, secondary factors (such as the presence or absence of moisture, and ambient temperature) that are not directly associated with the particles, but are associated with the environment can have a significant effect on the behavior of the bulk solids (Massoudi, 2004).

Recently, Mehrabadi et al., (2005) have derived a set of conservation laws and constitutive relations of a density-gradient-dependent viscous fluid as a multipolar continuum where the connection between their model and the materials of Korteweg type (Truesdell & Noll, 1992) is also discussed. To replace the classical theory of capillarity, which specifies a jump condition at the surface separating homogeneous fluids possessing different densities, Korteweg proposed smooth constitutive equations for the stresses that depend on density gradient[1]. Massoudi & Phuoc (2008) studied the flow of a compressible (density-gradient-dependent) non-linear fluid down an inclined plane, subject to radiation boundary condition. They assumed that the heat of reaction appears as a source term in the energy equation; in a sense they did not allow for a chemical reaction to occur and thus the conservation equation for the chemical species was ignored. A more general approach is, for example, that of Straughan & Tracey (1999) where the density is assumed to be not only a function of temperature, but also of (salt) concentration and there is an additional balance equation (the diffusion equation). In recent years, chemically reacting flows have been studied in a variety of applications. A class of problems where for example heat and salinity concentration compete with each other, and as a result the density distribution can be affected, has received much attention (Straughan, 2002, 2007). The phenomenon of double-diffusive convection in a fluid layer presents a challenging problem not only to engineers, but also to mathematicians since the stability of the flow is also of concern and interests.

In this Chapter, we provide a brief discussion of the important constitutive aspects of heat transfer in flows of complex fluids. We study the flow of a compressible (density gradient type) non-linear fluid down an inclined plane, subject to radiation boundary condition (For a full treatment of this problem, we refer the reader to Massoudi & Phuoc, 2008). The convective heat transfer is also considered where a source term, similar to the Arrhenius type reaction, is included. The non-dimensional forms of the equations are solved numerically and the competing effects of conduction, dissipation, heat generation and radiation are discussed.

2. Nomenclature

Symbol	**Explanation**
$\mathbf{b}$	body force vector
$\mathbf{D}$	Symmetric part of the velocity gradient
g	acceleration due to gravity
H	characteristic length
$\mathbf{1}$	identity tensor
k	thermal conductivity
K_0	reaction rate
$\mathbf{L}$	gradient of the velocity vector
N	dimensionless average volume fraction
$\mathbf{q}$	heat flux vector
t	time
$\mathbf{T}$	Cauchy stress tensor
u_0	reference velocity
$\mathbf{x}$	spatial position occupied at time t

[1] Korteweg's equation in modern notation is (Truesdell & Noll, 1992, p. 514):

$$T_{ij} = (-p + \alpha \rho_{,k} \rho_{,k} + \beta \rho_{,kk})\delta_{ij} + \gamma \rho_{,i} \rho_{,j} + \nu \rho_{,ij} + \lambda D_{kk} \delta_{ij} + 2\mu D_{ij},$$

where p, α, β, γ, ν , λ, and μ, are functions of ρ and θ alone. It is interesting to note that if we replace the density ρ by the temperature θ, we obtain equations very similar to those proposed by Maxwell (1876), who proposed constitutive equations for stresses in rarified gases that arise from inequalities of temperature.

y	direction normal to the inclined plane
(Y) or $\overline{y}$	dimensionless y
β_i	granular material constitutive coefficients, i = 0 to 5
ν	volume fraction
ρ	bulk density
ρ_0	reference density
θ	temperature
div	divergence operator
∇	gradient symbol
$\otimes$	outer product

3. Governing equations

The balance laws, in the absence of chemical and electromagnetic effects, are the conservation of mass, linear momentum, angular momentum and energy (Truesdell & Noll, 1992). The conservation of mass in the Eulerian form is given by:

$$\frac{\partial \rho}{\partial t} + \mathrm{div}(\rho \mathbf{u}) = 0 \tag{1}$$

where $\mathbf{u}$ is the velocity, ρ is the density, and $\partial/\partial t$ is the partial derivative with respect to time. The balance of linear momentum is

$$\rho \frac{d\mathbf{u}}{dt} = \mathrm{div}\mathbf{T} + \rho \mathbf{b} \tag{2}$$

where d/dt is the total time derivative, given by

$$\frac{d(.)}{dt} = \frac{\partial(.)}{\partial t} + [\mathrm{grad}(.)]\mathbf{u}\,, \tag{3}$$

where $\mathbf{b}$ is the body force, and $\mathbf{T}$ is the Cauchy stress tensor. The balance of angular momentum (in the absence of couple stresses) yields the result that the Cauchy stress is symmetric. The energy equation in general can have the form:

$$\rho \frac{d\varepsilon}{dt} = \mathbf{T.L} - \mathrm{div}\mathbf{q} + \rho r + QC_0K_0 \tag{4}$$

where ε denotes the specific internal energy, $\mathbf{q}$ is the heat flux vector, r is the radiant heating, Q is the heat of reaction, C_0 is the initial concentration of the reactant species, K_0 is the reaction rate expression which is a function of temperature, and $\mathbf{L}$ is the velocity gradient. For most common applications where there are no chemical reactions or heat generation, the last term on the right hand side is ignored. It should also be noted that the form of the energy equation for a complex fluid is in general not the same as the standard energy equation given in many books and articles, where the substantial (or total) time derivative of the temperature appears on the left hand side of Eqn (4) instead of the internal energy. For the detailed derivation of Eqn (4) and the assumptions implicit in obtaining this form using the First Law of Thermodynamics, see Appendix A.

Thermodynamical considerations require the application of the second law of thermodynamics or the entropy inequality. The local form of the entropy inequality is given by (Liu, 2002, p. 130):

$$\rho\dot{\eta} + \operatorname{div}\boldsymbol{\varphi} - \rho s \geq 0 \tag{5}$$

where $\eta(\mathbf{x},t)$ is the specific entropy density, $\phi(\mathbf{x},t)$ is the entropy flux, and s is the entropy supply density due to external sources, and the dot denotes the material time derivative. If it is assumed that $\boldsymbol{\varphi} = \frac{1}{\theta}\mathbf{q}$, and $s = \frac{1}{\theta}r$, where θ is the absolute temperature, then Equation (5) reduces to the Clausius-Duhem inequality

$$\rho\dot{\eta} + \operatorname{div}\frac{\mathbf{q}}{\theta} - \rho\frac{r}{\theta} \geq 0 \tag{6}$$

Even though we do not consider the effects of the Clausius-Duhem inequality in this Chapter, for a complete thermo-mechanical study of a problem, the Second Law of Thermodynamics has to be considered (Müller, 1967; Ziegler, 1983; Truesdell & Noll, 1992; Liu, 2002).
Constitutive relations for complex materials can be obtained in different ways, for example, by using: (a) continuum mechanics, (b) physical and experimental models, (c) numerical simulations, (d) statistical mechanics approaches, and (e) ad-hoc approaches. In the next section, we provide brief description of the constitutive relations that will be used in this Chapter. In particular, we mention the constitutive relation for the stress tensor **T** and the heat flux vector **q**. A look at the governing equation (1-4) reveals that constitutive relations are required for **T**, **q**, Q, ε, and r. Less obvious[2] is the fact that in many practical problems involving competing effects such as temperature and concentration, the body force **b**, which in problems dealing with natural convection oftentimes depends on the temperature and is modeled using the Boussinesq assumption (Rajagopal et al., 2009), now might have to be modeled in such a way that it is also a function of concentration [see for example, Equation (2.2) of Straughan and Walker (1997)].

4. Stress tensor and viscous dissipation

One of the most widely used and successful constitutive relations in fluid mechanics is the Navier-Stokes model, where the stress **T** is explicitly and linearly related to the symmetric

[2] In certain applications, such as the flow of chemically reactive fluids, the conservation of concentration $\frac{\partial c}{\partial t} + \operatorname{div}(c\mathbf{u}) = f$ where c is the concentration and f is a constitutive function also needs to be considered. This equation is also known as the convection-reaction-diffusion equation. For example, for the concentration flux, Bridges & Rajagopal (2006) suggested $f = -\operatorname{div}\mathbf{w}$ where $\mathbf{w}$ is a flux vector, related to the chemical reactions occurring in the fluid and is assumed to be given by a constitutive relation similar to the Fick's assumption, namely $\mathbf{w} = -K_1\nabla c$, where K_1 is a material parameter which is assumed to be a scalar-valued function of (the first Rivlin-Ericksen tensor) $\mathbf{A}_1$, $K_1 = K_1(\mathbf{A}_1) = \kappa\|\mathbf{A}_1^2\|$, where κ is constant, and $\|.\|$ denotes the trace-norm. Clearly K_1 can also depend on the concentration and temperature as well as other constitutive variables.

part of the velocity gradient **D**. From a computational point of view, it is much easier and less cumbersome to solve the equations for the explicit models[3]. For many fluids such as polymers, slurries and suspensions, some generalizations have been made to model shear dependent viscosities. These fluids are known as the power-law models or the generalized Newtonian fluid (GNF) models, where

$$\mathbf{T} = -p\mathbf{1} + \mu_0\left(\mathrm{tr}\mathbf{A}_1^2\right)^m \mathbf{A}_1 \tag{7}$$

where p is the indeterminate part of the stress due to the constraint of incompressibility, and **1** is the identity tensor, μ_0 is the coefficient of viscosity, m is a power-law exponent, a measure of non-linearity of the fluid related to the shear-thinning or shear-thickening effects, *tr* is the trace operator and $\mathbf{A}_1$ is related to the velocity gradient. A sub-class of the GNF models is the chemically reacting fluids which offer many technological applications ranging from the formation of thin films for electronics, combustion reactions, catalysis, biological systems, etc. (Uguz & Massoudi, 2010). Recently, Bridges & Rajagopal (2006) have proposed constitutive relations for chemically reacting fluids where

$$\mathbf{T} = -\pi\mathbf{1} + \mu(c, \mathbf{A}_1)\mathbf{A}_1 \tag{8}$$

where π is the constraint due to incompressibility and

$$\mathbf{A}_1 = \mathbf{L} + \mathbf{L}^T ; \mathbf{L} = \mathrm{grad}\mathbf{u} ; c = \frac{\rho_r}{\rho_r + \rho} \tag{9}$$

where ρ is the density of the fluid and ρ_r denotes the density of the (coexisting) reacting fluid. Furthermore they assumed

$$\mu(c, \mathbf{A}_1) = \mu^*(c)[1 + \alpha \mathrm{tr}(\mathbf{A}^2{}_1)]^n \tag{10}$$

where n determines whether the fluid is shear-thinning (n<0), or shear-thickening (n>0). A model of this type where μ^* is constant, i.e., when μ does not depend on c, has been suggested by Carreau et al., (1997) to model the flows of polymeric liquids. The viscosity is assumed to depend on the concentration c; depending on the form of $\mu^*(c)$ the fluid can be either a chemically-thinning or chemically-thickening fluid, implying a decrease or an increase in the viscosity, respectively, as c increases. The second law of thermodynamics requires the constant $\alpha \geq 0$ [Bridges & Rajagopal, 2006). Clearly, in general, it is possible to define other sub-classes of the GNF models where the viscosity can also be function of temperature, pressure, electric or magnetic fields, etc.

Another class of non-linear materials which in many ways and under certain circumstances behave as non-linear fluids is granular materials which exhibit two unusual and peculiar characteristics: (i) normal stress differences, and (ii) yield criterion. The *first* was observed by

[3] There are, however, cases [such as Oldroyd (1984) type fluids and other rate-dependent models] whereby it is not possible to express **T** explicitly in terms of **D** and other kinematical variables. For such cases, one must resort to implicit theories, for example, of the type (Rajagopal, 2006) $\mathbf{f}(\mathbf{T}, \mathbf{D}, \theta) = \mathbf{0}$, where θ is the temperature.

Reynolds (1885, 1886) who called it 'dilatancy.' Dilatancy is described as the phenomenon of expansion of the voidage that occurs in a tightly packed granular arrangement when it is subjected to a deformation. Reiner (1945, 1948) proposed and derived a constitutive relation for wet sand whereby the concept of dilatancy is given a mathematical structure. This model does not take into account how the voidage (volume fraction) affects the stress. Using this model, Reiner showed that application of a non-zero shear stress produces a change in volume. The constitutive relation of the type $S_{lm} = F_0\delta_{lm} + 2\eta D_{lm} + 4\eta_c D_{lj} D_{jm}$ describing the rheological behavior of a non-linear fluid was named by Truesdell (Truesdell & Noll, 1992) as the Reiner–Rivlin (Rivlin, 1948) fluid, where in modern notation the stress tensor **T** is related to **D** (Batra, 2006, p. 221):

$$\mathbf{T} = -p(\rho)\mathbf{I} + f_1\mathbf{D} + f_2\mathbf{D}^2 \tag{11}$$

where f's are function of $\rho, \mathrm{tr}\mathbf{D}, \text{and } \mathrm{tr}\mathbf{D}^2$. Perhaps the simplest model which can predict the normal stress effects (which could lead to phenomena such as 'die-swell' and 'rod-climbing', which are manifestations of the stresses that develop orthogonal to planes of shear) is the second grade fluid, or the Rivlin-Ericksen fluid of grade two (Rivlin & Ericksen, 1955; Truesdell & Noll, 1992). This model has been used and studied extensively and is a special case of fluids of differential type. For a second grade fluid the Cauchy stress tensor is given by:

$$\mathbf{T} = -p\mathbf{1} + \mu\mathbf{A}_1 + \alpha_1\mathbf{A}_2 + \alpha_2\mathbf{A}_1^2 \tag{12}$$

where p is the indeterminate part of the stress due to the constraint of incompressibility, μ is the coefficient of viscosity, α_1 and α_2 are material moduli which are commonly referred to as the normal stress coefficients. The kinematical tensor $\mathbf{A}_2$ is defined through

$$\mathbf{A}_2 = \frac{d\mathbf{A}_1}{dt} + \mathbf{A}_1\mathbf{L} + (\mathbf{L})^T\mathbf{A}_1 \tag{13}$$

where $\mathbf{A}_1$ and $\mathbf{L}$ are given by Eqn (9). The thermodynamics and stability of fluids of second grade have been studied in detail by Dunn & Fosdick (1974). They show that if the fluid is to be thermodynamically consistent in the sense that all motions of the fluid meet the Clausius-Duhem inequality and that the specific Helmholtz free energy of the fluid be a minimum in equilibrium, then

$$\begin{aligned} &\mu \geq 0, \\ &\alpha_1 \geqq 0, \\ &\alpha_1 + \alpha_2 = 0 \end{aligned} \tag{14}$$

It is known that for many non-Newtonian fluids which are assumed to obey Equation (12), the experimental values reported for α_1 and α_2 do not satisfy the restriction $(14)_{2,3}$. In an important paper, Fosdick & Rajagopal (1979) show that irrespective of whether $\alpha_1 + \alpha_2$ is positive, the fluid is unsuitable if α_1 is negative. It also needs to be mentioned that second grade fluids (or higher order models) raise the order of differential equations by introducing higher order derivates into the equations. As a result, in general, one needs additional

boundary conditions; for a discussion of this issue, see Rajagopal (1995), and Rajagopal & Kaloni (1989).
The *second* peculiarity is that for many granular materials there is often a yield stress. This yield condition is often related to the angle of repose, friction, and cohesion among other things. Perhaps the most popular yield criterion for granular materials is the Mohr-Coulomb one, although by no means the only one (Massoudi & Mehrabadi, 2001). Overall, it appears that many of the bulk solids behave as visco-plastic fluids. Bingham (1922, p. 215) proposed a constitutive relation for a visco-plastic material in a simple shear flow where the relationship between the shear stress (or stress **T** in general), and the rate of shear (or the symmetric part of the velocity gradient **D**) is given by (Prager, 1989, p. 137)

$$2\mu D_{ij} = \begin{Bmatrix} 0 & \text{for} \quad F < 0 \\ FT'_{ij} & \text{for } F \geq 0 \end{Bmatrix} \tag{15}$$

where T'_{ij} denotes the stress deviator and F, called the yield function, is given by

$$F = 1 - \frac{K}{II_2'^{1/2}} \tag{16}$$

where II'_2 is the second invariant of the stress deviator, and in simple shear flows it is equal to the square of the shear stress and K is called yield stress (a constant). For one dimensional flow, these relationships reduce to the ones proposed by Bingham (1922), i.e.

$$F = 1 - \frac{K}{|T_{12}|} \tag{17}$$

And

$$2\mu D_{12} = \begin{Bmatrix} 0 & \text{forF} < 0 \\ FT_{12} & \text{forF} \geq 0 \end{Bmatrix} \tag{18}$$

The constitutive relation given by Eqn (15) is known as Bingham model (Zhu et al., 2005).
We now provide a brief description of a model due to Rajagopal & Massoudi (1990) which will be used in this Chapter; this model is capable of predicting both of the above mentioned non-linear effects, namely possessing a yield stress and being capable of demonstrating the normal-stress differences. The Cauchy stress tensor **T** in a flowing granular material may depend on the manner in which the material is distributed, *i.e.*, the volume fraction ν and possibly also its gradient, and the symmetric part of the velocity gradient tensor **D**. Based on this observation, Rajagopal & Massoudi (1990) derived a constitutive model that predicts the possibility of both normal stress-differences and is properly frame invariant (Cowin, 1974; Savage, 1979):

$$\begin{aligned} \mathbf{T} = [\beta_o(\rho) + \beta_1(\rho)\, \nabla\rho \cdot \nabla\rho + \beta_2(\rho)\, \mathrm{tr}\, \mathbf{D}]\, \mathbf{1} \\ + \beta_3(\rho)\mathbf{D} + \beta_4(\rho, \nabla\rho)\, \nabla\rho \otimes \nabla\rho + \beta_5(\rho)\, \mathbf{D}^2 \end{aligned} \tag{19}$$

where β's are material properties, and $\mathbf{D}=\frac{1}{2}\left[\nabla\mathbf{u}+(\nabla\mathbf{u})^{T}\right]$. In what follows we will use the concept of volume fraction[4] ν, and use this instead of the density ρ, as a variable, where ν is represented as a continuous function of position and time $0\le\nu(\mathbf{x},t)<1$ and is related to the classical mass density or bulk density ρ, through $\rho=\rho_{10}\nu$ where ρ_{10} is the reference density (a constant value). That is, in some sense we have normalized the density through the introduction of volume fraction. Now if the material is flowing, the following representations are proposed for the β's :

$$\beta_o = f\nu; \quad f<0 \quad \left\{\begin{array}{l} \beta_1=\beta_1^*\left(1+\nu+\nu^2\right) \\ \beta_2=\beta_2^*\left(\nu+\nu^2\right) \\ \beta_3=\beta_3^*\left(\nu+\nu^2\right) \\ \beta_4=\beta_4^*\left(1+\nu+\nu^2\right) \\ \beta_5=\beta_5^*\left(\nu+\nu^2\right) \end{array}\right\} \tag{20}$$

The above representation can be viewed as Taylor series approximation for the material parameters [Rajagopal, et al (1994)]. Such a quadratic dependence, at least for the viscosity $\beta_{3,}$ is on the basis of dynamic simulations of particle interactions (Walton & Braun, 1986a,1986b). Furthermore, it is assumed (Rajagopal & Massoudi, 1990) that

$$\beta_{30}=\beta_{20}=\beta_{50} \tag{21}$$

In their studies, Rajagopal et al. (1992) proved existence of solutions, for a selected range of parameters, when, $\beta_1+\beta_4>0$, and f <0. Rajagopal & Massoudi (1990) gave the following rheological interpretation to the material parameters: β_0 is similar to pressure in a compressible fluid or the yield stress and is to be given by an equation of state, β_2 is like the second coefficient of viscosity in a compressible fluid, β_1 and β_4 are the material parameters connected with the distribution of the granular materials, β_3 is the viscosity of the granular materials, and β_5 is similar to what is referred to as the 'cross-viscosity' in a Reiner-Rivlin fluid. The distinct feature of this model is its ability to predict the normal stress differences which are often related to the dilatancy effects. The significance of this model is discussed by Massoudi (2001), and Massoudi & Mehrabadi (2001). If the material is just about to yield, then

---

[4] The volume fraction field $\nu(\mathbf{x},t)$ plays a major role in many of the proposed continuum theories of granular materials. In other words, it is assumed that the material properties of the ensemble are continuous functions of position. That is, the material may be divided indefinitely without losing any of its defining properties. A distributed volume, $V_t=\int \nu dV$ and a distributed mass, $M=\int \rho_s \nu dV$ can be defined, where the function ν is an independent kinematical variable called the volume distribution function and has the property $0\le\nu(\mathbf{x},t)\le\nu_m<1$. The function ν is represented as a continuous function of position and time; in reality, ν in such a system is either one or zero at any position and time, depending upon whether one is pointing to a granule or to the void space at that position. That is, the real volume distribution content has been averaged, in some sense, over the neighborhood of any given position. The classical mass density or bulk density, ρ is related to ρ_s and ν through $\rho=\rho_s\nu$.

Massoudi & Mehrabadi (2001) indicate that if the model is to comply with the Mohr-coulomb criterion, the following representations are to be given to the material parameters in Eqn (19):

$$\beta_o = c \cot \phi$$
$$\beta_1 = \frac{\beta_4}{2}\left(\frac{1}{\sin \phi} - 1\right) \tag{22}$$

where ϕ is the internal angle of friction and c is a coefficient measuring cohesion. Rajagopal et al., (2000) and Baek et al., (2001) discuss the details of experimental techniques using orthogonal and torsional rheometers to measure the material properties β_1 and β_4. Rajagopal et al., (1994) showed that by using an orthogonal rheometer, and measuring the forces and moments exerted on the disks, one can characterize the material moduli β's.
Finally, we can see from Eqn (4) that the term usually referred to as the viscous dissipation is given by the first term on the right hands side of Eqn (4), that is

$$\zeta = \mathbf{T.L} \tag{23}$$

Thus, there is no need to model the viscous dissipation term independently, since once the stress tensor for the complex fluid is derived or proposed, ζ can be obtained from the definition given in Eqn (23).

5. Heat flux vector (Conduction)

For densely packed granular materials, as particles move and slide over each other, heat is generated due to friction and therefore in such cases the viscous dissipation should be included. Furthermore, the constitutive relation for the heat flux vector is generally assumed to be the Fourier's law of conduction where

$$\mathbf{q} = -k\nabla\theta \tag{24}$$

where k is an effective or modified form of the thermal conductivity. In general, k can also depend on concentration, temperature, etc., and in fact, for anisotropic material, k becomes a second order tensor. There have been many experimental and theoretical studies related to this issue and in general the flux **q** could also include additional terms such as the Dufour and Soret effects. Assuming that **q** can be explicitly described as a function of temperature, concentration, velocity gradient, etc., will make the problem highly non-linear. Kaviany (1995, p.129) presents a thorough review of the appropriate correlations for the thermal conductivity of packed beds and the effective thermal conductivity concept in multiphase flows. Massoudi (2006a, 2006b) has recently given a brief review of this subject and has proposed and derived a general constitutive relation for the heat flux vector for a flowing granular media. It is important to recognize that in the majority of engineering applications, the thermal conductivity of the material is assumed (i) *a priori* to be based on the Fourier's heat conduction law, and (ii) is a measurable quantity (Narasimhan, 1999). Jeffrey (1973) derived an expression for the effective thermal conductivity which includes the second order effects in the volume fraction (Batchelor & O'Brien, 1977):

$$k = \kappa_M[1 + 3\xi\nu + \hat{\xi}\nu^2] + O(\nu^3) \tag{25}$$

where

$$\hat{\xi} = 3\xi^2 + \frac{3\xi^3}{4} + \frac{9\xi^3}{16}\left(\frac{\omega+2}{2\omega+3}\right) + \frac{3\xi^4}{26} + \dots \quad (26)$$

where

$$\xi = \frac{\omega-1}{\omega+2} \quad (27)$$

$$\omega = \frac{k_2}{k_1} \quad (28)$$

where ω is the ratio of conductivity of the particle to that of the matrix, κ the effective conductivity of the suspension, κ_M the conductivity of the matrix, and ν is the solid volume fraction (Bashir & Goddard, 1990). Massoudi (2006a, 2006b) has conjectured, based on arguments in mechanics, that the heat flux vector for a 'reasonably' dense assembly of granular materials where the media is assumed to behave as a continuum in such a way that as the material moves and is deformed, through the distribution of the voids, the heat flux is affected not only by the motion but also by the density (or volume fraction) gradients. To keep things simple, it was assumed that the interstitial fluid does not play a major role (some refer to this as 'dry' granular medium), and as a result a frame-indifferent model for the heat flux vector of such a continuum was derived to be:

$$\mathbf{q} = a_1\mathbf{n} + a_2\mathbf{m} + a_3\mathbf{Dn} + a_4\mathbf{Dm} + a_5\mathbf{D}^2\mathbf{n} + a_6\mathbf{D}^2\mathbf{m} \quad (29)$$

where

$$\mathbf{m} = \text{grad}\rho \quad (30)$$

$$\mathbf{n} = \text{grad}\theta \quad (31)$$

where the a's in general have to be measured experimentally; within the context of the proposed theory they depend on the invariants and appropriate material properties. It was shown that (i) when $a_2 = a_3 = a_4 = a_5 = a_6 = 0$, and a_1 =constant=-k, then we recover the standard Fourier's Law:

$$\mathbf{q} = -k\nabla\theta \quad (32)$$

And (ii) when a_1 =constant=-k, and a_2 =constant, we have

$$\mathbf{q} = -k\nabla\theta + a_2\nabla\nu \quad (33)$$

Soto et al., (1999) showed that based on molecular dynamics (MD) simulations of inelastic hard spheres (IHS), the basic Fourier's law has to be modified for the case of fluidized granular media. It is noted that Wang (2001) also derived a general expression for the heat flux vector for a fluid where heat convection is also important; he assumed that

$\mathbf{q} = \mathbf{f}(\theta, \nabla\theta, \mathbf{v}, \mathbf{L}, X)$ where $\mathbf{f}$ is a vector-valued function, θ temperature, $\nabla\theta$ is the gradient of temperature, $\mathbf{v}$ the velocity vector, $\mathbf{L}$ its gradient, and X designates other scalar-valued thermophysical parameters.

6. A brief discussion of other constitutive parameters

Looking at Eqn (4), it can be seen that constitutive relations are also needed for K_0, r, and ε. As shown by Dunn & Fosdick (1974), the specific internal energy ε, in general, is related to the specific Helmholtz free energy ψ through:

$$\varepsilon = \psi + \theta\eta = \varepsilon(\theta, \mathbf{A}_1, \mathbf{A}_2) = \hat{\varepsilon}(y) \tag{34}$$

where η is the specific entropy and θ is the temperature. In the problem considered in this chapter, due to the nature of the kinematical assumption about $\mathbf{u}$ and θ, it can be seen that $\frac{d\varepsilon}{dt} = 0$. We now discuss briefly the constitutive modeling of K_0 and r.

We assume that the heat of reaction appears as a source term in the energy equation; in a sense we do not allow for a chemical reaction to occur and thus the conservation equation for the chemical species is ignored. This is only to be considered as a first approximation; a more general approach is, for example, that of Straughan & Tracey (1999) where the density is assumed to be not only a function of temperature, but also of (salt) concentration and there is an additional balance equation (the diffusion equation). We assume that K_0 is given by (Boddington et al., 1983)

$$K_0(\theta) = A_0 \left(\frac{\bar{k}\theta}{\bar{v}h}\right)^m \exp\left(\frac{-E}{R\theta}\right) \tag{35}$$

where A_0 is the rate constant, E is the activation energy, R is the universal gas constant, h is the Planck's number, $\bar{k}$ is the Boltzmann's constant, $\bar{v}$ is the vibration frequency and m is an exponent related to the type of reaction; for example, $m \in \{0.5, 0, -2\}$ correspond to Bimolecular temperature dependence, Arrhenius or zero order reaction and sensitized temperature dependence. As indicated by Boddington et al., (1977), "Even when reactions are kinetically simple and obey the Arrhenius equation, the differential equations for heat balance and reactant consumption cannot be solved explicitly to express temperatures and concentrations as functions of time unless strong simplifications are made." One such simplification is to assume that there is no reactant consumption, which as mentioned earlier, is the approach that we have taken in the present study. Furthermore, although in this paper we assume A_0 to be constant and K_0 to be a function of temperature only, in reality, we expect K_0 (and/or A_0) to be function of volume fraction (density).

Combined heat transfer processes, such as convection-radiation, play a significant role in many chemical processes (Siegel & Howell, 1981) involving combustion, drying, fluidization, MHD flows, etc (Zel'dovich & Raizer, 1967; Pomraning, 1973). In general, the radiative process either occurs at the boundaries or as a term in the energy equation. The latter case is usually accomplished by a suggestion due to Rosseland (Clouet, 1997) where the radiative term is approximated as a flux in such a way that the term corresponding to radiation in the heat transfer (energy) equation now appears as a gradient term similar to the Fourier's conduction term. This method has found much favor among many researchers especially those working with viscoelastic fluids and MHD flows. Alternatively, radiation effects can be incorporated at the boundaries through appropriate (constitutive) assumption, such as the Stefan-Boltzmann condition. Free surface flows present a challenging problem to engineers as the combined convection-radiation at the boundaries has major applications in many industries (Miller & Weaver, 2003). At the free surface, the no-traction boundary condition is imposed on the stress tensor, and as a result we obtain two expressions for the velocity gradient, and for the temperature we apply the Stefan-Boltzmann condition (Saldanha da Gama, 2004)

$$q = \gamma\sigma(\theta_h^4 - \theta_\infty^4) \tag{36}$$

where γ is surface emissivity, σ is the Stefan-Boltzmann constant, the surrounding temperature is designated as θ_∞ and the temperature at the free surface is θ_h. Finally, in order to study the phenomenon of self-ignition or spontaneous combustion in a coal stockpile, a multiphase flow approach [see for example, Salinger et al., (1994) or Akgun & Essenhigh, 2001) should be used where the effects of moisture content, oxidation, etc., are also considered.

7. Flow down an inclined plane

Flow down an inclined plane occurs naturally as in the cases of avalanches and mudslides; it is also used for transporting and drying of bulk solids (such as agricultural and pharmaceutical products). It is a viscometric flow (Truesdell, 1974) and one which amends itself to fundamental theoretical and experimental studies. Studies have shown that if the effects of viscous dissipation are included, strong non-linearities in the temperature profiles are observed (Massoudi & Anand, 2004). It is assumed that the flow is fully developed [see Figure 1]. The free surface is exposed to high ambient temperature and as a result a modified Stefan-Boltzmann correlation is used at that surface (Fuchs 1996, p.331).

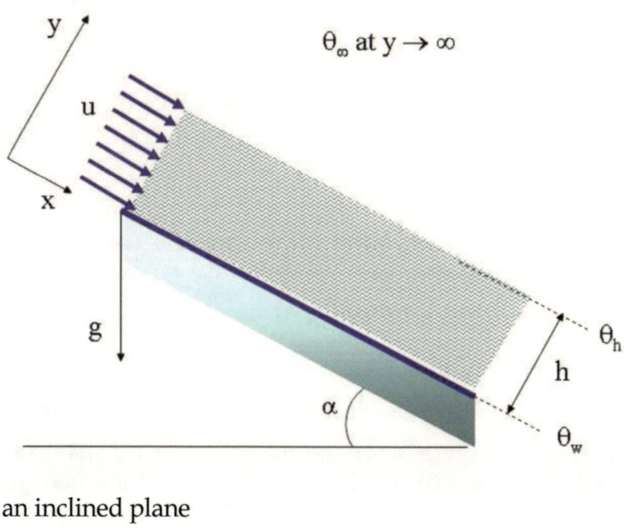

Fig. 1. Flow down an inclined plane

For the problem under consideration, we make the following assumptions:

i. the motion is steady,
ii. the effects of radiant heating 'r' are imposed at the free surface,
iii. the constitutive equation for the stress tensor is given by Equation (19) and the constitutive equation for the heat flux vector is that of Fourier's law, given by Equations (24)-(25);
iv. the heat of reaction is given by equation (35)
v. the density (or volume fraction), velocity and temperature fields are of the form

$$\begin{Bmatrix} \nu = \nu(y) \\ \mathbf{u} = u(y)\mathbf{i} \\ \theta = \theta(y) \end{Bmatrix} \tag{38}$$

With the above assumptions, the conservation of mass is automatically satisfied and by defining the dimensionless distance $\bar{y}$, the velocity $\bar{u}$ and the temperature $\bar{\theta}$ by the following equations (Na, 1979):

$$\bar{y} = \frac{y}{H}; \quad \bar{u} = \frac{u}{u_0}; \quad \bar{\theta} = \frac{\theta}{\theta_w} \tag{39}$$

where u_0 is a reference velocity, θ_w is the wall temperature[5], and H is the constant height to the free surface, the dimensionless form of the equations are:

$$R_1 \frac{d\nu}{d\bar{y}} + R_2\left(1+\nu+\nu^2\right)\frac{d\nu}{d\bar{y}}\frac{d^2\nu}{d\bar{y}^2} + R_2(1+2\nu)\left(\frac{d\nu}{d\bar{y}}\right)^3 + R_5(1+2\nu)\frac{d\nu}{d\bar{y}}\left(\frac{d\bar{u}}{d\bar{y}}\right)^2 + 2R_5\nu(1+\nu)\left(\frac{d\bar{u}}{d\bar{y}}\right)\left(\frac{d^2\bar{u}}{d\bar{y}^2}\right) = \nu\cos\alpha \tag{40}$$

$$R_3\nu(1+\nu)\frac{d^2\bar{u}}{d\bar{y}^2} + R_3(1+2\nu)\frac{d\nu}{d\bar{y}}\frac{d\bar{u}}{d\bar{y}} = -\nu\sin\alpha \tag{41}$$

$$\left(1+a\nu+b\nu^2\right)\frac{d^2\bar{\theta}}{d\bar{y}^2} + (a+2b\nu)\frac{d\nu}{d\bar{y}}\frac{d\bar{\theta}}{d\bar{y}} + R_7\bar{\theta}^m e^{\frac{-1}{\zeta\bar{\theta}}} = -R_4\nu(1+\nu)\left(\frac{d\bar{u}}{d\bar{y}}\right)^2 \tag{42}$$

[5] It needs to be mentioned that it is possible to use another reference temperature for this problem, namely a proper dimensionless quantity as it appears in the exponent of the heat of reaction. For example, as Boddington et al. (1983, p. 249) show, if $\theta = \frac{T-T_a}{(RT_a^2/E)}$ and $\varepsilon = \frac{RT_a}{E}$ are used, then "the concepts of explosion and criticality are appropriate so long as the activation energy E is not too low or the ambient temperature T_a is not too high, i.e., so that $\varepsilon = \frac{RT_a}{E} < \varepsilon_{tr}$". If one uses this, then one obtains a relationship which expresses the balance between the heat generated and the heat conducted, as for example in the Frank-Kamenetskii (1969) approach. However, since in our problem we also have radiation at the free surface, we have decided to use the wall temperature as the reference temperature.

where

$$R_1=\frac{f}{\rho_{10}gH};\quad R_2=\frac{2(\beta_1^*+\beta_4^*)}{\rho_{10}gH^3};\quad R_3=\frac{\beta_3^* u_0^2}{2H^2\rho_{10}g};\quad R_4=\frac{\beta_3^* u_w^2}{K_M\theta_w};$$
$$R_5=\frac{\beta_5^* u^2_w}{\rho_{10}gH^3};\quad R_6=\frac{\gamma\sigma\theta_w^3 H}{K_M};R_7=\frac{H^2QC_0A_0\bar{k}^m\theta_w^{m-1}}{K_M h^m\bar{v}^m};\zeta=\frac{R\theta_w}{E} \tag{43}$$

and the boundary conditions become [At the wall surface of the inclined we assume the no-slip condition for the velocity and a constant temperate θ_w.]:

$$\text{at } \bar{y}=0:\quad \begin{cases}\bar{u}=0\\ \bar{\theta}=1\end{cases} \tag{44}$$

At the free surface, the no-traction boundary condition is imposed on the stress tensor, and as a result we obtain two expressions for the velocity gradient and the volume fraction [see below], and for the temperature we apply the Stefan-Boltzmann[6] condition (Saldanha da Gama, 2004; Wright, 2007;Wright et al., 2002; Agudelo & Cortes, 2010) when the surrounding temperature is designated as θ_∞ and the temperature at the free surface is θ_H.

$$\text{at } \bar{y}=1:\quad \begin{cases}\dfrac{d\bar{u}}{d\bar{y}}=0\\ R_1\nu+\dfrac{R_2}{2}(1+\nu+\nu^2)\left(\dfrac{d\nu}{d\bar{y}}\right)^2+\dfrac{R_5}{4}(1+\nu+\nu^2)\left(\dfrac{d\bar{u}}{d\bar{y}}\right)^2=0\\ \dfrac{d\bar{\theta}}{d\bar{y}}=\dfrac{-R_6}{1+a\nu+b\nu^2}\left(\bar{\theta}^4_{\bar{y}=1}-\bar{\theta}^4_\infty\right)\end{cases} \tag{45}$$

We can see that we still need an additional boundary condition for ν. Two options are available to us: (i) we can impose a distribution function, which could be a constant number for ν at the wall, based on experimental results (practically this may mean gluing particles), or (ii) we can give an average value for ν integrated over the cross section (a measure of the amount of particles in the system).
Case a

$$\begin{Bmatrix}\nu=\nu_o & \text{at } \bar{y}=0\\ \nu=\nu_H & \text{at } \bar{y}=1\end{Bmatrix} \tag{46}$$

or
Case b:

$$\begin{Bmatrix}\nu=\nu_o & \text{at } \bar{y}=0\\ N=\int_0^1 \nu d\bar{y} & \end{Bmatrix} \tag{47}$$

[6] Equation (36) is really our first approximation (Wu & Chu, 1999; Miller & Weaver, 2003) and a more appropriate one for the case of granular materials might be to introduce into the equation a function for the dependence of the volume fraction, for example, $q=f(\nu)\varepsilon\sigma\left(\theta_H^4-\theta_s^4\right)$

And

$$\bar{\theta}_{\infty} = \frac{\theta_{\infty}}{\theta_w} \tag{48}$$

These dimensionless parameters can be given the following physical interpretations: R_1 could be thought of as the ratio of the pressure force to the gravity force, R_2 is the ratio of forces developed in the material due to the distribution of the voids to the force of gravity, R_4 is a measure of viscous dissipation, which is the product of the Prandtl number and the Eckert number, R_5 is related to the normal stress coefficient, R_6 is a measure of the emissivity of the particles to the thermal conductivity, and R_7 is a measure of the heat generation due to chemical reaction. It follows from Rajagopal & Massoudi (1990) that R_1, must always be less than zero for the solution to exist and all the other non-dimensional parameters, i.e., R_3 and R_4 must be greater than zero, since the viscosity is positive. In addition to these dimensionless numbers, the value of the volume fraction at the lower plate, N a, b, and α are also parameters which need to be specified.

8. Numerical solution and concluding remarks

The volume fraction equation, Eqn. (40) and the velocity equation, Eqn. (41) are coupled and must be solved simultaneously. Once these solutions are obtained the temperature distribution can be found by integrating equation (42). For equation (40) the boundary conditions $\nu = \nu_o$ at $\bar{y} = 0$ and $N_o = \int_0^1 \nu d\bar{y}$ are assumed *a priori*, but $d\nu/d\bar{y}$ at $\bar{y} = 0$ is unknown. For equation (41) the boundary conditions are $\bar{u} = 0$ at $\bar{y} = 0$ and $(d\bar{u}/d\bar{y})_{\bar{y}=1} = 0$ but $(d\bar{u}/d\bar{y})_{\bar{y}=0}$ is unknown. The unknown boundary conditions must be assumed so that the integration can be performed. That is, it is necessary to correct the initial guesses to be such that the derivative of the velocity at the edge of the solution domain and the distribution of volume fraction satisfy the corresponding known conditions given by equations (33) and (34). Procedures for such corrections are given by Massoudi & Phuoc (2005, 2007) and they will be used here.

The effect of R_7 on the distribution of the dimensionless temperature is shown in Fig. 2. The results indicate that the temperature is always higher inside the domain than the inclined surface temperature and the free surface temperature. Since R_7 is the measure of the heat generation due to chemical reaction, when the reaction is frozen ($R_7 = 0.0$) the temperature distribution would depend only on R_1, and R_2, representing the effects of the pressure force developed in the material due to the distribution, R_3 and R_4 viscous dissipation, R_5 the normal stress coefficient, R_6 the measure of the emissivity of the particles to the thermal conductivity, etc. When the flow is not frozen ($R_7 > 0$) the temperature inside the flow domain is much higher than those at the inclined and free surfaces. As a result, heat is transferred away from the flow toward both the inclined surface and the free surface with a rate that increases as R_7 increases.

The effect of the reaction can also be investigated in terms of the activation energy parameter ζ. To see this, we integrate the energy equation with ζ varying from 0.5 to 20 while keeping all other parameters constant. The temperature distributions are shown in Fig. 3. For a given temperature, an increase in ζ implies that the activation energy is smaller and thus, the reaction rate is increased leading to an increase in the heat of the reaction. As a result the flow is chemically heated and its temperature increase. The results shown here indicate that for all values of ζ used the chemical effects are significant and the temperature is always higher than both the surface temperature and the free surface temperature. The heat transfer is always from the flow toward both the inclined surface and the free stream.

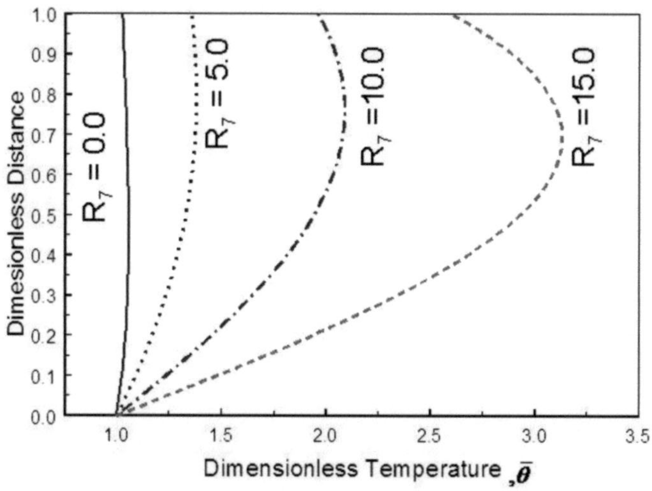

Fig. 2. Effect of R_7 on the dimensionless temperature profiles (a = 0.75, b = 1.0, R_1 = -3.0; R_2 = 10.0; R_3 = 0.05, R_4 = 0.1, R_5 = 0.01, R_6 = 0.1,ν_w = 0.4; N = 0.3; α = 30°, m = 0.5, ζ = 0.5, and $\bar{\theta}_\infty = 0.5$)

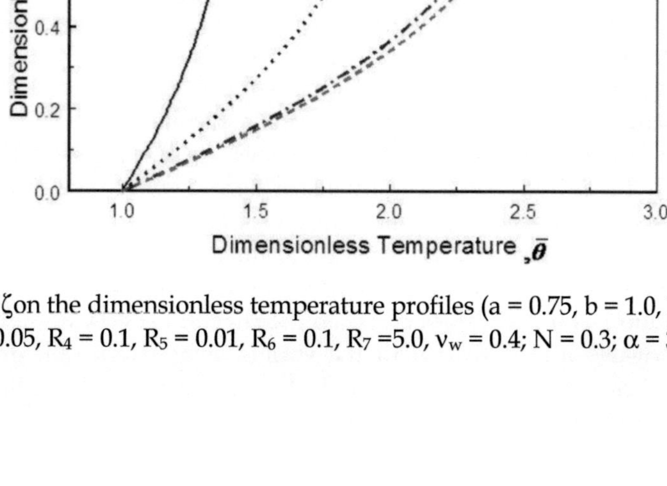

Fig. 3. Effect of ζon the dimensionless temperature profiles (a = 0.75, b = 1.0, R_1 = -3.0; R_2 = 10.0; R_3 = 0.05, R_4 = 0.1, R_5 = 0.01, R_6 = 0.1, R_7 =5.0, ν_w = 0.4; N = 0.3; α = 30°, m = 0.5, and $\bar{\theta}_\infty = 0.5$)

The effects of the reaction order m on the distribution of the dimensionless temperature and the heat transfer rate at the inclined and free surfaces are shown in Fig 4. For all values of m chosen here, the temperature is higher than the surface and the free stream temperature. The heat transfer at the inclined surface and at the free stream increase slowly for negative values of m to about m=0.5, but it begins to significantly increase for m greater than 0.5

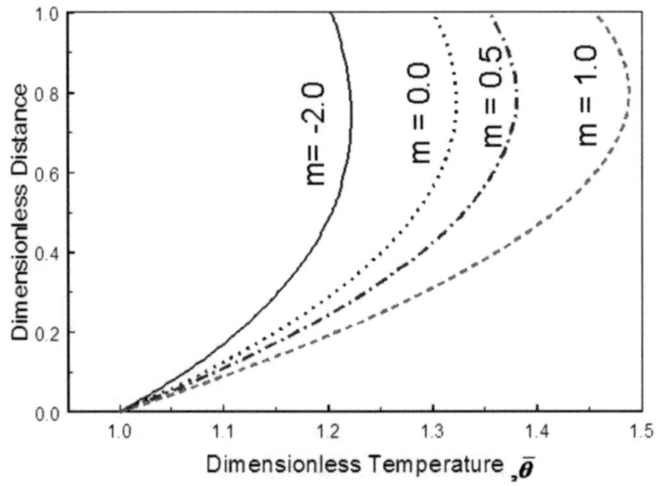

Fig. 4. Effect of the reaction order m on the dimensionless temperature profiles (a = 0.75, b = 1.0, R_1 = -3.0; R_2 = 10.0; R_3 = 0.05, R_4 = 0.1, R_5 = 0.01, R_6 = 0.1, R_7 =5.0, ζ = 0.5, ν_w = 0.4; N = 0.3; α = 30°, and $\overline{\theta}_\infty = 0.5$)

In Conclusion, we have studied the flow of a compressible (density gradient type) non-linear fluid down an inclined plane, subject to radiation boundary condition. The heat transfer is also considered where a source term, similar to the Arrhenius type reaction, is included. The non-dimensional forms of the equations are solved numerically and the competing effects of conduction, dissipation, heat generation and radiation are discussed. It is observed that the velocity increases rapidly in the region near the inclined surface and is slower in the region near the free surface. Since R_7 is a measure of the heat generation due to chemical reaction, when the reaction is frozen (R_7=0.0) the temperature distributions would depend only on R_1, and R_2, representing the effects of the pressure force developed in the material due to the distribution, R_3 and R_4 viscous dissipation, R_5 the normal stress coefficient, R_6 the measure of the emissivity of the particles to the thermal conductivity, etc. When the flow is not frozen ($R_7 > 0$) the temperature inside the flow domain is much higher than those at the inclined and free surfaces. As a result, heat is transferred away from the flow toward both the inclined surface and the free surface with a rate that increases as R_7 increases. For a given temperature, an increase in ζ implies that the activation energy is smaller and thus, the reaction rate is increased leading to an increase in the heat of the reaction. As a result the flow is chemically heated and its temperature increase. The results shown here indicate that for all values of ζ used the chemical effects are significant and the temperature is always higher than both the surface temperature and the free surface temperature. The heat transfer is always from the flow toward both the inclined surface and the free stream. It is also noticed that for all values of m chosen in this study, the temperature is higher than the surface and the free stream temperature. The heat transfer at the inclined surface and at the free stream increase slowly for negative values of m to about m=0.5, but it begins to significantly increase for m greater than 0.5.

9. Appendix A

In order to show that the primary focus of the formulation for heat conduction in complex materials should be on the derivation of the heat flux vector and not on the thermal conductivity, we start with the general statement of the balance of energy, also known as the first law of thermodynamics. The second law of thermodynamics, also known as the entropy law, entropy inequality, or in its various forms as Clausius-Duhem inequality, the dissipation inequality, etc., is very much a subject matter of controversy[7] as there does not seem to be a consensus whether this law should be applied locally, i.e., to certain parts of the system, or to the whole system; there is, however, no disagreement on the generality, acceptance, and applicability of the first law of thermodynamics (Truesdell, 1984, p.67) which states:

$$\dot{E} = W + Q \tag{A-1}$$

where E is the internal energy of a body, W is the net working on it, and Q is the heating associated with it. By definition the net working W at time t on the body is given by

$$W \equiv P - \dot{K} \tag{A-2}$$

where P is the mechanical power and K is the kinetic energy. Furthermore, according to a theorem proved by Stokes (Truesdell, 1984, p.109)

$$W = \int_B w dV \tag{A-3}$$

where w is called the stress power and is given by

$$w = \mathbf{T} \cdot \text{grad}\mathbf{u} = \mathbf{T.L} \tag{A-4}$$

where $\mathbf{T}$ is the Cauchy stress tensor and $\mathbf{u}$ is the velocity vector. It is also assumed that Q is composed of two types of heating: one associated with the body and its interactions with the outside environment, Q_b , and the other , Q_c , is concerned with the contacts between different parts of the body:

$$\begin{aligned} Q &= Q_b + Q_c \\ &= \int_{\partial B} h dA + \int_B r dM \end{aligned} \tag{A-5}$$

where Q_b and Q_c are often described as radiation and conduction, h is called the influx of heating (related to the heat flux vector $\mathbf{q}$), and r is the heating supply (related to the

---

[7] This is in fact exacerbated further for the granular materials as the concept of entropy has been given different meanings by different people (Mehta, (1994).

radiation effect). If one assumes that E is given by a continuous additive set function ε (called the specific internal energy):

$$E = \int_B \varepsilon dM \tag{A-6}$$

then it can be shown, by using the divergence theorem, that for sufficiently smooth fields, using Equations (A-4) -(A-6), Equation (A-1) can be written as:

$$\rho\dot{\varepsilon} = w\text{-div}\mathbf{q} + \rho r \tag{A-7}$$

where

$$h = -\mathbf{q}.\mathbf{n} \tag{A-8}$$

where $\mathbf{q}$ is the heat flux vector and $\mathbf{n}$ is the outward unit normal vector to the surface. Note that in the notation used in this Chapter $w = \xi$. Equation (A-7) is often regarded as the local or the differential form of the first law of thermodynamics, whereas, we can see that it is derived based on a series of definitions along with using Cauchy's laws of motion: $\rho\frac{d\mathbf{u}}{dt} = \text{div}\mathbf{T} + \rho\mathbf{b}$ and $\mathbf{T} = \mathbf{T}^T$, where **b** is the body force vector.

10. References

Agudelo, A., & C. Cortes. (2010). Thermal radiation and the second law. *Energy,* Vol. 35, pp. 670-691.

Akgun, F.& R. H. Essenhigh (2001). Self-ignition characteristics of coal stockpiles: theoretical prediction from a two-dimensional unsteady-state model. *Fuel,* Vol. 80, pp. 409-415.

Baek, S.; K. R. Rajagopal, & A. R. Srinivasa (2001). Measurements related to the flow of granular materials in a torsional rheometer. *Particulate Sci. Tech.,* Vol. 19, pp. 175-186.

Bashir, Y. H., & J. D. Goddard (1990). Experiments on the conductivity of suspensions of ionically-conductive spheres. *AIChE J.,* Vol. 36, pp. 387-396.

Batra, Romesh C. (2006) *Elements of Continuum Mechanics.* American Institute of Aeronautics and Astronautics (AIAA) Inc., Reston, VA.

Batchelor, G. K., & R. W. O'Brien (1977). Thermal or electrical conduction through a granular material. *Proc. R. Soc. Lond.* A. Vol. 355, pp. 313-333.

Bingham, E. C. (1922). *Fluidity and Plasticity.* McGraw Hill. New York.

Boddington, T.; Gray, P. & Wake, G. C. (1977) Criteria for thermal explosions with and without reactant consumption, *Proc. Royal Society London* A, Vol. 357, pp. 403-422.

Boddington, T.; Feng, C. G., & Gray, P. (1983). Thermal explosions, criticality and the disappearance of criticality in systems with distributed temperatures .1. Arbitrary Biot-number and general reaction-rate laws, *Proc. Royal Society London* A, Vol. 390, pp. 247-264.

Bridges, C., & Rajagopal, K. R. (2006). Pulsatile flow of a chemically-reacting nonlinear fluid. *Computers and Mathematics with Applications,* Vol. 52, pp. 1131-1144.

Carreau, P. J.; D. De Kee, & R. J. Chhabra. (1997). *Rheology of Polymeric Systems.* Hanser/Gardner Publications. Cincinnati, OH.

Clouet, J. -F. (1997). The Rosseland approximation for radiative transfer problems in heterogeneous media. *Journal of Quantitative Spectroscopy and Radiative Transfer,* Vol. 58, pp. 33-43.

Cowin, S.C. (1974). A theory for the flow of granular material. *Powder Tech.*, Vol. 9, pp. 61-69.

Deshpande, A. P.; Krishnan, J. M., & P. B. Sunil (Eds.). (2010) *Rheology of Complex Fluids.* 1st Edition. Springer, ISBN: 978-1-4419-6493-9.

Dunn, J. E., & R. L. Fosdick. (1974). Thermodynamics, stability, and boundedness of fluids of complexity 2 and fluids of second grade, *Arch. Rational Mech. Anal.*, Vol. 56 , pp. 191-252.

Fosdick, R. L., & K. R. Rajagopal. (1979). Anomalous features in the model of "second order fluids". *Arch. Rational Mech. Anal.*, Vol. 70, pp.145-152.

Frank-Kamenetskii, D. (1969). A. *Diffusion and Heat Transfer in Chemical Kinetics.* 2nd Edition. New York: Plenum Press.

Fuchs, H. U. (1996). *The Dynamics of Heat.* Springer-Verlag, Inc., New York.

Gupta, G. & M. Massoudi. (1993). Flow of a generalized second grade fluid between heated plates. *Acta Mechanica,* Vol. 99, pp. 21-33.

Haupt, P. (2002). *Continuum Mechanics and Theory of Materials.* 2nd edition. Springer. Berlin.

Jeffrey, D. J. (1973). Conduction through a random suspension of spheres. *Proc. R. Soc. Lond.* A. Vol. 335, pp. 355-367.

Kaviany, M. (1995). *Principles of Heat Transfer in Porous Media.* Second edition. Springer-Verlag, New York.

Larson, R. G. (1999). *The Structure and Rheology of Complex Fluids.* Oxford University Press. New York.

Liu, I. S. (2002). *Continuum Mechanics.* Springer-Verlag. Berlin.

Massoudi, M. (2001). On the flow of granular materials with variable material properties. *Int. J. Non-Linear Mech.*, Vol. 36, pp. 25-37.

Massoudi, M. (2004). Constitutive Modelling of Flowing Granular Materials: A Continuum Approach. In *Granular Materials: Fundamentals and Applications.* Edited by S. J. Antony, W. Hoyle, and Y. Ding. The Royal Society of Chemistry. Cambridge, UK, 2004, pp.63-107.

Massoudi, M. (2006a). On the heat flux vector for flowing granular materials, Part I: Effective thermal conductivity and background. *Math. Methods Applied Sci.*, Vol. 29, pp. 1585-1598.

Massoudi, M. (2006b) On the heat flux vector for flowing granular materials, Part II: Derivation and special cases. *Math. Methods Applied Sci.*, Vol. 29, pp. 1599-1613.

Massoudi, M. (2008). A note on the meaning of mixture viscosity using the classical continuum theories of mixtures. *International Journal of Engineering Science,* Vol. 46, pp.677-689

Massoudi, M. (2010). A Mixture Theory formulation for hydraulic or pneumatic transport of solid particles. *International Journal of Engineering Science.* Vol. 48, pp. 1440-1461.

Massoudi, M. & M. M. Mehrabadi. (2001). A continuum model for granular materials: Considering dilatancy, and the Mohr-Coulomb criterion. *Acta Mech.*, Vol. 152, pp. 121-138.

Massoudi, M. & N. K. Anand. (2004). A theoretical study of heat transfer to flowing granular materials. *International Journal of Applied Mechanics and Engineering*, Vol. 9, pp. 383-398.

Massoudi, M. & Phuoc, T. X. (2005). Heat transfer in flowing granular materials: The effects of radiation boundary condition. *Int. J. of Applied Mechanics and Engineering*, Vol. 10, pp. 489-503.

Massoudi, M. & T. X. Phuoc. (2007). Conduction and dissipation in the shearing flow of granular materials modeled as non-Newtonian fluids. *Powder Technology*, Vol. 175, pp.146-162.

Massoudi, M. & A. Vaidya. (2008). On some generalizations of the second grade fluid model, *Nonlinear Analysis, Part II, Real World Applications,* Vol. 9, pp.1169-1183.

Massoudi M. & T. X. Phuoc. (2008). Flow of a non-linear (density-gradient-dependent) viscous fluid with heat generation, viscous dissipation and radiation. *Mathematical Methods in the Applied Sciences*, Vol. 31, pp.1685-1703.

Maxwell, J. C. (1876). On stresses in rarified gases arising from inequalities of temperature. *Phil. Trans. Roy. Soc. Lond.*, Vol. 170, pp. 231-256.

Mehrabadi, M. M.; S. C. Cowin, & M. Massoudi. (2005). Conservation laws and constitutive relations for density-gradient-dependent viscous fluids. *Continuum Mechanics and Thermodynamics*, Vol. 17, pp. 183-200.

Mehta, A. (Editor). (1994). *Granular matter*. Springer-Verlag. New York.

Miller, J. R., & P. M. Weaver. (2003). Temperature profiles in composites plates subject to time-dependent complex boundary conditions. Vol. 59, pp. 267-278.

Müller, I. (1967). On the entropy inequality. *Arch. Rat. Mech. and Anal.*, Vol. 26, pp. 118-14.

Na, T. Y. (1979). *Computational Methods in Engineering Boundary Value Problems.* Academic Press, New York.

Narasimhan, T. N. (1999). Fourier's heat conduction equation: History, influence, and connections. *Rev. Geophys.*, Vol. 37, pp.151-172.

Oldroyd, J. G. (1984). An approach to non-Newtonian fluid mechanics. *J. Non-Newtonian Fluid Mech.*, 14, pp. 9-46.

Papachristodoulou, G. & Trass, O. Coal slurry fuel technology. (1987). *Canadian J. Chem. Engng*, Vol. 65, pp. 177-201.

Pomraning, G. C. (1973). *The Equations of Radiative Hydrodynamics*. Dover Publications, Inc., Mineola, NY.

Prager, W. (2004). *Introduction to Mechanics of Continua.* Dover Publications, Inc., Mineola, NY.

Rajagopal, K. R. (1995). On boundary conditions for fluids of differential type, in: A. Sequeira (Ed.) *Navier-Stokes Equations and Related Nonlinear Problems*. Plenum Press, New York, 1995, pp. 273-278.

Rajagopal, K. R. (2006). On implicit constitutive theories for fluids. *J. Fluid Mech.*, Vol. 550, pp. 243-249.

Rajagopal, K. R. & P. N. Kaloni. (1989). Some remarks on boundary conditions for flows of fluids of the differential type. In: *Continuum Mechanics and its Applications*, Hemisphere Press, 1989, pp. 935-942.

Rajagopal, K. R. & M. Massoudi. (1990). *A Method for Measuring Material Moduli of Granular Materials: Flow in an Orthogonal Rheometer.* Topical Report, DOE/PETC/TR-90/3, 1990.

Rajagopal, K. R., W.C. Troy & M. Massoudi. (1992). Existence of solutions to the equations governing the flow of granular materials. *European J. Mech., B/Fluids*, Vol. 11, pp. 265-276.

Rajagopal, K. R., M. Massoudi, & A. S. Wineman. (1994). Flow of granular materials between rotating disks. *Mech. Research Comm.*, Vol. 21, pp. 629-634.

Rajagopal, K. R., & L. Tao. (1995). *Mechanics of Mixtures.* New Jersey: World Scientific Publishing.

Rajagopal, K. R., G. Gupta, & R. C. Yalamanchili. (2000). A rheometer for measuring the properties of granular materials. *Particulate Sci. Tech.*, Vol. 18, pp.39-55.

Rajagopal, K. R.., G. Saccomandi, & L. Vergori. (2009). On the Oberbeck-Boussinesq approximation for fluids with pressure dependent viscosities. *Nonlinear Anal. Real World Applcs.*, Vol. 10, pp. 1139-1150.

Reiner, M. (1945). A mathematical theory of dilatancy. *American J. Math.*, Vol. 67, pp. 350-362.

Reiner, M. (1948). Elasticity beyond the elastic limit. *Amer. J. Math.*, Vol. 70, pp. 433-466.

Reynolds, O. (1885). On the dilatancy of media composed of rigid particles in contact with experimental illustrations. *Phil. Mag., Series 5*, Vol. 20, pp. 469-481.

Reynolds, O. (1886). Experiments showing dilatancy, a property of granular material, possibly connected with gravitation. *Proc. Roy. Inst. of Gr. Britain*, Vol. 11, pp.354-363.

Rivlin, R. S. (1948). The hydrodynamics of non-Newtonian fluids, I. *Proc. Royal Soc. Lond.*, Vol. 193, pp. 260-281.

Rivlin, R. S. & Ericksen, J. L. (1955). Stress deformation relations for isotropic materials, *J. Rat. Mech. Anal.* Vol. 4, pp.323-425.

Roh, N.S., Shin, D. Y., Kim, D. C., & Kim, J. D. (1995). Rheological behavior of coal-water mixtures: 1. Effects of coal type, loading and particle size. *Fuel*, Vol. 74, pp. 1220-1225.

Saeki, T, & Usui, H. (1995). Heat transfer characteristics of coal-water mixtures. *Canadian J. Chem. Engng.*, Vol. 73, pp. 400-404.

Saldanha da Gama, R. M. (2004). On the conduction/radiation heat transfer problem in a body with wavelength-dependent properties. *Appl. Math. Modelling*, Vol. 28, pp. 795-816.

Salinger, A. G., Aris, R., & Derby, J. J. (1994). Modeling the spontaneous ignition of coal stockpiles , *AICHE Journal*, Vol. 40, pp. 991-1004.

Savage, S.B. (1979). Gravity Flow of Cohesionless Granular Materials in Chutes and Channels. *J. Fluid Mech.*, Vol. 92, pp. 53-96.

Schowalter, E. R. (1978). *Mechanics of Non-Newtonian Fluids*. Pergamon Press, New York.

Siegel, R., & J. R. Howell. (1981). *Thermal Radiation Heat Transfer.* 2nd edition. Hemisphere Publishing Company. New York.

Soto, R., M. Mareschal, & D. Risso. (1999). Departures from Fourier's law for fluidized granular media. *Phys. Rev. Lett.*, Vol. 83, pp. 5003-5006.

Straughan, B. (1998). *Explosive Instabilities in Mechanics*. Springer Verlag. New York.

Straughan, B. (2002). Global stability for convection induced absorption of radiation. *Dyn. Atmos. Oceans*, Vol. 35, pp.351-361.

Straughan, B. (2007). A note on convection with nonlinear heat flux. *Ricerche mat.*, Vol. 56, pp. 229-239.

Straughan. B. (2008). *Stability and wave motion in porous media.* Springer-Verlag, New York.
Straughan, B., & D. W. Walker. (1997). Multi-component diffusion and penetrative convection. *Fluid Dyn. Research,* Vol. 19, pp. 77-89.
Straughan, B., & J. Tracey. (1999). Multi-component convection-diffusion with internal heating or cooling. *Acta Mech.*, Vol. 111, pp.219-238.
Truesdell, C. (1976). The meaning of viscometry in fluid mechanics. *Annual Rev. Fluid Mech.*, Vol. 6, pp. 111-146.
Truesdell, C. & W. Noll. (1992). *The Non-Linear Field Theories of Mechanics.* Springer-Verlag, New York.
Tsai, C. Y., Navack, M., & Roffe, G. (1988). *Rheological and heat transfer characteristics of flowing coal-water mixtures.* DOE Report, DOE/MC/23255-2763, December 1988.
Tsai, S. C., & Knell, E. W. (1986). Viscosity and rheology of coal water slurry. *Fuel,* Vol. 65, pp. 566-571.
Uguz, A. K., & M. Massoudi. (2010). Heat transfer and Couette flow of a chemically-reacting non-linear fluid. *Mathematical Methods in the Applied Sciences,* Vol. 33, pp.1331-1341.
Walton, O.R. & R.L. Braun. (1986a). Stress calculations for assemblies of inelastic spheres in uniform shear. *Acta Mechanica,* Vol. 63, pp. 73-86.
Walton, O.R. & R.L. Braun. (1986b). Viscosity, granular-temperature, and stress calculations for shearing assemblies of inelastic, frictional disks. *J. Rheology,* Vol. 30, pp.949-980.
Wang, L. (2001). Vector-field theory of heat flux in convective heat transfer. *Nonlinear Anal.*, Vol. 47, pp. 5009-5020.
Wright, S. E. (2007). The Clausius inequality corrected for heat transfer involving radiation. *Int. J. Eng. Sci.*, Vol. 45, pp. 1007-1016.
Wright, S. E., M. A. Rosen, D. S. Scott, & J. B. Haddow. (2002). The exergy flux of radiative heat transfer with an arbitrary spectrum. *Exergy,* Vol. 2, pp. 69-77.
Wu, J. W., & H. S. Chu. (1999). Combined conduction and radiation heat transfer in plane-parallel packed beds with variable porosity. *J. Quant. Spectrosc. Radiat. Transfer,* Vol. 61, pp. 443-452.
Zhu, H., Y. D. Kim, & D. De Kee. (2005). Non-Newtonian fluids with a yield stress. *J. Non-Newtonian Fluid Mech.*, Vol. 129, pp.177-181.
Zel'dovich, Ya. B., & Yu. P. Raizer. (1967). *Physics of Shock Waves and High Temperature Hydrodynamic Phenomena.* Dover Publications, Inc., Mineola, NY.
Ziegler, H. (1983). *An Introduction to Thermomechanics.* Second Revised Edition. North-Holland Publishing Company. Amsterdam.

Part 4

Phase Change

23

A Numerical Study on Time-Dependent Melting and Deformation Processes of Phase Change Material (PCM) Induced by Localized Thermal Input

Yangkyun Kim[1], Akter Hossain[1], Sungcho Kim[2] and Yuji Nakamura[1]
[1]*Hokkaido University,*
[2]*Sunchon National University*
[1]*Japan*
[2]*Korea*

1. Introduction

Deep understanding of fire damage triggered by combustion of electric wires is one of important issue in terms of the fire safety of automated facilities, such as factories, power plant etc. Combustion process of electric wire is, nevertheless, quite complicated since it consists of multi-phase, multi-dimensional time-dependent heat and mass transfer with chemical reactions in each phase and several fundamental processes are equally important so that it is relatively hard to simplify the system. Unlikely the conventional solid combustion, the metal rod in the wire could play an important role to determine the combustion process of the wire (Bakhman et al., 1981a, 1981b). In this way, the thermal interaction between the metal rod and surrounded insulated matter (mainly polymeric materials) is a leading key process in understanding the fire character of the wire (Umemura et al., 2002). However, this is not only the matter of concern; we have much serious problem to face with. As pointed, the combustible of electric wire is mainly the polymeric material surrounded by the (conductive) metal rod and the polymer does "melt" during the fire event. The shape of liquefied polymer freely modifies and sometimes tremendously deforms, thus, the precise tracking of the liquid-gas interface is one of important task since the major chemical reaction at the interface should govern the overall gasification rate (Blasi, 1991; Ross, 1994), i.e., gas-phase combustion behavior. As summarized, in order to predict the precise process of electric wire, the following three processes need to be modeled properly: 1) three-phase induced by chemical reactions (e.g., degraded pyrolysis), 2) deformation of interface of liquid phase, 3) heat transfer between metal rod and surrounded polymer (either melted and solid). Our ultimate goal is to understand each contribution properly and develop simplified model of wire combustion.

To this date, the precise experimental observation of combustion behavior of electric wire has been performed by authors' group (Nakamura et al., 2008a, 2008b, 2009), as shown schematically in Fig. 1. It shows the magnified still image of spreading flame over the specially-designed "model" wire (polyethylene-coated on the several kind of metal wires.

For details, see above references). During the combustion event, the coated polymer first liquefies to form large molten ball, and then decomposes to produce fuel gas released into the atmosphere. As notified clearly, it includes complex phenomena associated with the formation of molten layer; e.g., deformation of outer shape, bubble formation and its internal motion in the molten polymer etc. In our previous studies, it has been found that the size of molten polymer gradually increased during the flame spread over the wire. As a result of the size growth, "falls-off" of molten layer is frequently observed. Our precise observation data would be useful to validate the simulation and modelling, which is our goal as stated.

To achieve our ultimate goal; such as establishment of complete model of wire combustion, since the target is quite complex to handle as shown, it is preferable to take step-by-step. In this paper, let us consider the most fundamental case that there is no species transport and reaction, then main part to be modelled is the following two folds; one is how to consider the size change of the molten phase, and the other is how to handle the complex melting process. To simulate this, the governing equation requires the treatments of the discontinuity at the melting front caused by a higher energy than the latent heat of fusion at their interface, which is well known as Stefan problem. This results in transport properties varying considerably between phases, and hugely different rates of energy, mass and momentum transport from one phase to another.

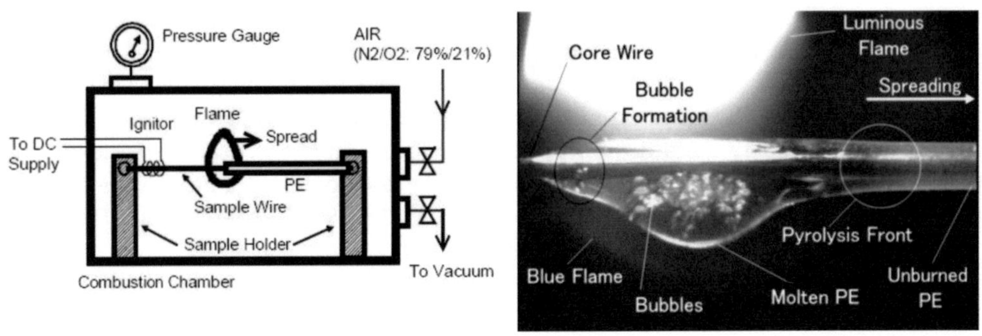

Fig. 1. Experimental set-up (left) and a typical observation of flame spreading (right) over polyethylene (PE) coated electric wire (Nakamura et al., 2009)

In the past, a few analytical methods offered an exact solution (Neumann, 1863). Even though they were mathematically robust, applicable ranges of solution are limited to one-dimensional cases of an infinite or semi-infinite region with simple initial and boundary conditions and constant thermal properties. Therefore treatments were extended to numerical analyses with finite difference and finite element methods. Particularly, because of their simplicity in formulation, finite difference methods are still used for a wide range of industrial processes. The essential feature of finite difference methods is that the latent heat absorption or release is accounted for in the governing energy equation by defining either a total enthalpy (Voller, 1986, 1987a; Gong, Z. X et al., 1997, 1999) or a specific heat capacity (Yang & He, 2010). Consequently, the numerical solution can be carried out on a space grid that remains fixed throughout the calculation, the so-called fixed grid method (Voller,

1987b). In contrast to the variable grid method, domain or coordinate transformation is not required, implying a low computational cost. One of approaches in the fixed grid method, enthalpy method taking account of latent heat evolution, is applied in our calculation. A major advantage of the enthalpy method is that it can calculate the melting with convection by the simple concept of porosity (Brent, 1988). In other words, the combined Enthalpy-Porosity method can accommodate the zero velocity condition which is required as a liquid region turns to solid. Mathematical treatment of this Enthalpy-Porosity method is very simple, and has a wide range of application such as energy storage systems and to casting processes (Yvan et al., 2011; Lamberg et al., 2004; Dawei et al., 2005). For this reason, it was chosen in the current study, and this allows the estimation of the latent heat of melting and the position of the melting front.

A particularly difficult part of the modelling is to compute as a function of time the interface motion and deformation at a flexible free-surface boundary which co-exist with the melting surface. In the case of melting, modelling focuses on the latent heat change with convection flow inside the liquid and melting position of the interface between the liquid and the solid phases, but the key to understanding the free surface motion and the deformation of the melting surface is the surface tension force as well as the tracking free surface. In such problems involving change of phase, diverse approaches exist according to combination of the governing equation and the tracking method, and are divided into roughly two main sectors. These are the Lagrangian or Eulerian approaches for tracking the position of interface based on one or two sets of conservation equations for the phase change. Although two sets of conservation equations with the Lagrangian tracking approaches such as Maker and cell (MAC) methods and the front tracking method (Deen et al., 2009) are quite accurate, nowadays one set conservation equations with the Eulerian approach is more generally used because numerical problems arise when a re-meshing process in Lagrangian tracking approaches is required to model high distortions of interfaces or interface break up. A famous set of conservation equations with Eulerian approach is the VOF (volume of fluid) method, which was pioneered by Hirt and Nichols (Hirt & Nichols, 1981). In this method, the interface is given implicitly by the volume fraction of one of the phases within each cell. A reconstruction of the interface is made, and is propagated implicitly by updating the volume fraction using the transport equation.

Much of the earlier work was performed using the Enthalpy-Porosity method and the VOF method, and have been gradually improved. In order to extend these methods to three phases as in the present study, a combination of melting and free surface tracking is required (Assis et al., 2007; Ganaoui et al., 2002; Jeong et al., 2010; Kamnis & Gu, 2005). For this reason, in the present study numerical model including scalar transport and a source term in the governing equation is considered, and these combined methods are applied to investigate the phenomena during a melting and falls-off process of suspended liquified matter beneath the wire. By exploiting a combination of these two methods melting combined with a three-phase problem is properly considered. Furthermore, for an accurate calculation of the melting and dropping process, temperature dependent surface tension and piecewise polynomial approximation for material properties between solid-liquid phases are additionally applied. In the following, in order to observe the basic process of flame spreading over polymer-coated wire combustion, we are going to model a melting and falls-off process of polymer (i.e., phase change material: PCM) subjected to the local heating without considering any species transport and generation/consumption due to the chemical reactions. This study is done with commercial software (FLUENT 12.0) based on the finite volume method.

2. Numerical model

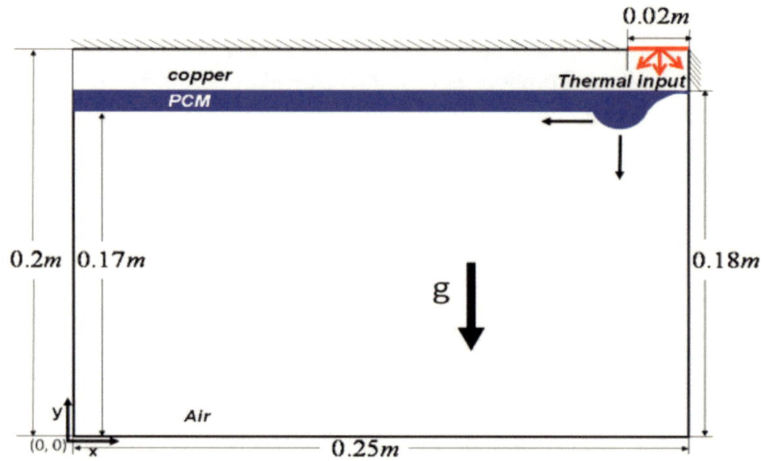

Fig. 2. Schematic description of the numerical model

Fig. 2 is a schematic illustration of the physical configuration. The 2D domain width and height are 0.25 m and 0.2 m respectively, and initially the numerical domain consists of solid (only in the top portion) and gas phases. Solid phase includes copper plate with polymer (phase change material; PCM) whose thickess is 1 mm as shown in Fig.1. Normal gravity, 9.81 m/s^2, is applied in the downward direction. Three materials are used in the calculation, and their properties are described in Table 1. Two phases, liquid & solid, of PCM are included. A localized thermal input is used on the top part of the copper surface. Heat from the localized thermal input is conducted through the copper, and then PCM changes phase from solid to liquid with absorbance of the equivalent latent heat. The free surface of the PCM is then deformed, and liquid PCM moves to the left following the growth of a molten PCM which eventually falls-off via gravity drag.

2.1 Governing equations

Melting of the PCM is governed by the two-dimensional unsteady Navier-Stokes equations in the form of equations for continuity, momentum, and energy.

$$\nabla \cdot (\beta \vec{v}) = 0, \tag{1}$$

$$\beta \frac{\partial \vec{v}}{\partial t} + \nabla \cdot (\beta \vec{v}\vec{v}) = -\frac{\beta}{\rho} \nabla p + \frac{\beta}{\rho} \nabla \cdot [\mu(\nabla \vec{v}) + (\nabla \vec{v})^T] + \beta F_{ST} + \vec{g} + \vec{S}, \tag{2}$$

$$\rho \frac{\partial h}{\partial t} + \nabla \cdot (\rho \vec{v} h) = \nabla \cdot (k\ \nabla T) - S_h. \tag{3}$$

Parameter	Symbol	Value	Units
Air (gas phase)			
Density	ρ_g	1.225	kg/m³
Thermal conductivity	k_g	0.0242	W/(m K)
Specific heat	$c_{p,g}$	1006.43	J/(kg K)
Viscosity	μ_g	1.789×10^{-5}	kg/(m s)
Copper (solid phase)			
Density	ρ_c	8978	kg/m³
Thermal conductivity	k_c	387.6	W/(m K)
Specific heat	$c_{p,c}$	381	J/(kg K)
PCM (solid phase)			
Density	ρ_s	980	kg/m³
Thermal conductivity	k_s	0.24	W/(m K)
Specific heat	$c_{p,s}$	4800	J/(kg K)
Latent heat of melting	L	1.8×10^{5}	J/kg
Melting temperature	T_m	400	K
PCM (liquid phase)			
Density	ρ_l	900	kg/m³
Thermal conductivity	k_l	0.15	W/(m K)
Specific heat	$c_{p,l}$	4200	J/(kg K)
Viscosity	μ_l	0.005	kg/(m s)
Solidification temperature	T_s	350	K

Table 1. Physical properties of the phase change material

Here, β is the liquid fraction, $\vec{v}$ is velocity, ρ is density, μ is viscosity, p is pressure, g is gravity, F_{ST} is surface tension force, $\vec{S}$ is the momentum source term, T is temperature, k is conductivity and h is enthalpy. Surface tension is modeled as a smooth variation of capillary pressure across the interface. Following Brackbill et al (Brackbill, 1992), it is represented as a continuum surface force (CSF), and is specified as a volumetric source term in the momentum equation as

$$F_{ST} = \sigma \frac{\rho \kappa_{c,g} \nabla F_g}{0.5(\rho_l + \rho_g)}. \tag{4}$$

Here subscripts g, l and s represent the gas, liquid and solid phase respectively. σ, the surface tension coefficient, is modeled as linear function of temperature, as shown in Fig. 3 . κ_c is the curvature of free surface and is defined in terms of the divergence of the unit normal $\hat{n}$ as

$$\kappa_c = \nabla \bullet \hat{n} \quad \text{with} \quad \hat{n} = \frac{\nabla F}{|\nabla F|}. \tag{5}$$

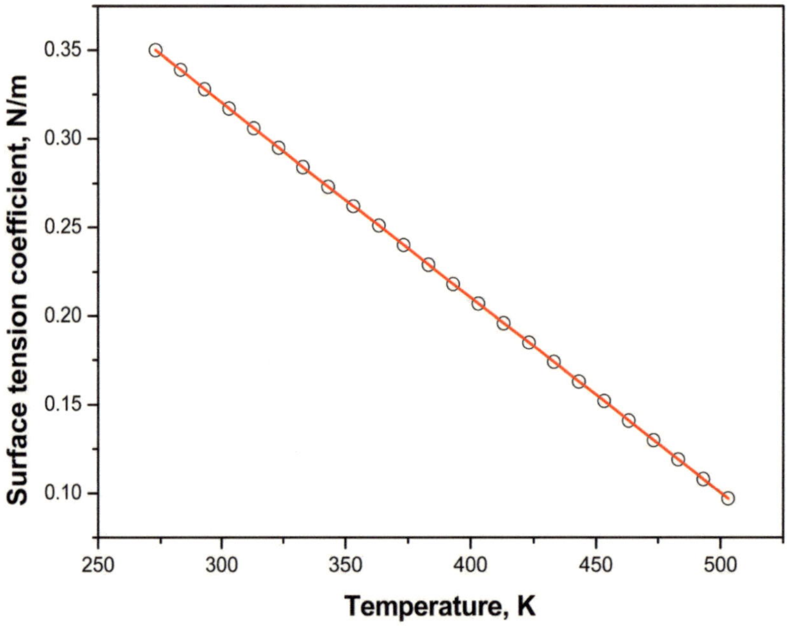

Fig. 3. Surface tension coefficient as a function of temperature

Because surface tension plays an important role in the process of interface reconstruction, a piecewise-linear interpolation scheme developed by Youngs (Youngs, 1982) is used for the interface reconstruction. It assumes that the interface between two fluids has a linear slope within each cell, and uses this linear shape for calculating the advection of fluid through the faces of the computational cell.

In order to model the solid phase, it is necessary to impose a zero velocity on a liquid with the appropriate solid physical parameter. Several methods can be used to achieve this, including velocity switch-off, variable viscosity, and Darcy law approaches (Sanchez-Palencia, 1987). In this work all computational fluid cells were modelled as porous media by adjusting the parameter β . And the Carman-Kozeny equations (Voller, 1987b; Brent, 1988), based on the Darcy law, were used for the source term to describe the flow in the porous medium with the following the momentum equation:

$$\nabla p = -\left[A_{mush} \frac{(1-\beta)^2}{\beta^3} \right] \vec{v}, \tag{6}$$

where A_{mush} is a constant (1.0×10^6) accounting for the mushy region morphology. In order to achieve this behavior, we implemented a source term in the momentum equation for the mushy zone (a region in which the liquid fraction lies between 0 and 1):

$$\vec{S} = -A_{mush} \frac{(1-\beta)^2}{(\beta^3 + \varepsilon)} \vec{v}, \tag{7}$$

where ε is a computational constant (0.001) introduced to prevent division by zero.
In the energy equation, h is the sensible enthalpy, which is

$$h = h_{ref} + \int_{T_{ref}}^{T} c_p dT, \tag{9}$$

where, h_{ref} is the reference enthalpy, T_{ref} is the reference temperature and c_p is specific heat. In the continuity and momentum equation, β determines whether a computational cell is solid or not. β is a function of temperature, and can be described as

$$\beta = \begin{cases} 0 \ if \ T < T_{solidus}, \\ 1 \ if \ T > T_{liquidus}, \\ (T - T_{solidus}) / (T_{liquidus} - T_{solidus}) \ if \ T_{solidus} < T < T_{liquidus}. \end{cases} \tag{10}$$

Furthermore, the energy equation takes into account latent heat as the volume source for the heat transfer condition at the melting front, S_h :

$$S_h = \frac{\partial(\rho \Delta H)}{\partial t} + \nabla \cdot (\rho \vec{v} \Delta H), \tag{11}$$

where ΔH is latent heat, and is defined as $\Delta H = \beta L$, where L is latent heat of PCM material. To represent the free surface of the melting region adjacent to the gas phase, the VOF method is used. In this method, function F is a scalar field, which defines the state of a particular cell in the computational domain:

$$F = \begin{cases} 1 = liquid \ or \ solid, \\ 0 < F < 1 = partial \ gas, \\ 0 = gas, \end{cases} \tag{12}$$

and F also satisfies the conservation equation

$$\frac{DF}{Dt} = \frac{\partial(\beta F)}{\partial t} + \nabla \cdot (\beta \vec{v} F) = 0, \tag{13}$$

and the material properties involved in equations (1) to (3) are written as follows:

$$\rho = \rho_s + \beta(\rho_g - \rho_s) + \beta F(\rho_l - \rho_g), \;\; \mu = \beta\mu_g + \beta F(\mu_l - \mu_g)$$
$$k = k_s + \beta(k_g - k_s) + \beta F(k_l - k_g), \;\; c_p = c_{p,s} + \beta(c_{p,g} - c_{p,s}) + \beta F(c_{p,l} - c_{p,g}). \tag{14}$$

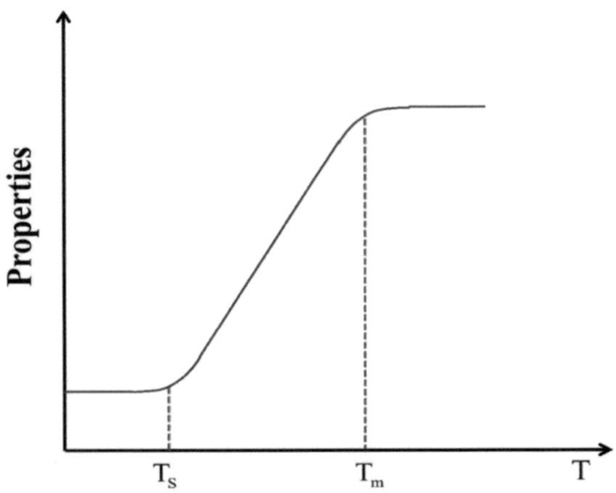

Fig. 4. Temperature dependent smoothed function for modeling properties intermediate between the solid and liquid phases

A smoothed piecewise-polynomial profile, which is a function of temperature, is used due to discontinuities in properties between solid and liquid PCM. This is shown in Fig. 4.

2.2 Initial and boundary conditions

The initial temperature of domain is 300 K, and the localized thermal input temperature is 500 K. The conjugated thermal boundary condition is applied between the copper and the solid PCM, and the heat balance equation between the PCM and air. The boundary conditions are expressed as follows:
at x = 0

$$T = 300\ K;$$

at interface between the PCM and air

$$k_l \frac{\partial T_l}{\partial n} - k_g \frac{\partial T_g}{\partial n} = 0\ ; \tag{15}$$

at interface between the solid and liquid PCM

$$k_s \frac{\partial T_s}{\partial n} - k_l \frac{\partial T_l}{\partial n} = \frac{k}{l}(T_s - T_l)\ ;$$

at other boundaries

$$\frac{\partial T}{\partial x} = 0 \text{ or } \frac{\partial T}{\partial y} = 0.$$

3. Results and discussion

3.1 Model validation

To validate the model, a simple melting problem of gallium in a cavity by the use of Enthalpy-Porosity method was solved and compared with experimental results. Fig. 5 shows the schematic illustration of the physical configuration of gallium melting. Solid gallium occupies the whole domain, T_H = 311 K is heated wall temperature, and T_C = 301.3 K is cold wall temperature. The boundaries of the top and bottom surfaces are isothermal walls. The width W = 8.89 cm and the height H = 6.35 cm. Normal gravity is applied in the downward. Details of the applied material properties and information on the experimental setup are described in Brent's work (Brent, 1988). Once the calculation is started, the solid gallium melts. Fig. 6 shows the shape and location of the solid-liquid interface at several times during the melting process. The black and red lines indicate the experimental (Brent, 1988) and calculated data respectively. Before a time of 2 minutes, the shape of the interface is nearly flat because convection is still weak and melting is driven by conduction. After 2 minutes, the interface becomes wavy due to the circular flow inside the molten region. The position of the melt front near the top surface in the calculation before a time of 12.5 minutes is over-estimated compared to experiment, and after 19 minutes, it is underestimated. However, the overall trend shows good agreement with experiment and we can safely said that our model and code are fairly validated to track the melting boundary satisfactorily. It is well known that a key point in the calculation of melting is the exact interface position between the solid and liquid phases. But in case of a convection-driven melting problem, such exact prediction is difficult due to the complex convection flow inside the liquid. For this reason, numerical studies for convection flow inside molten liquids require more attention (Noureddine, 2003).

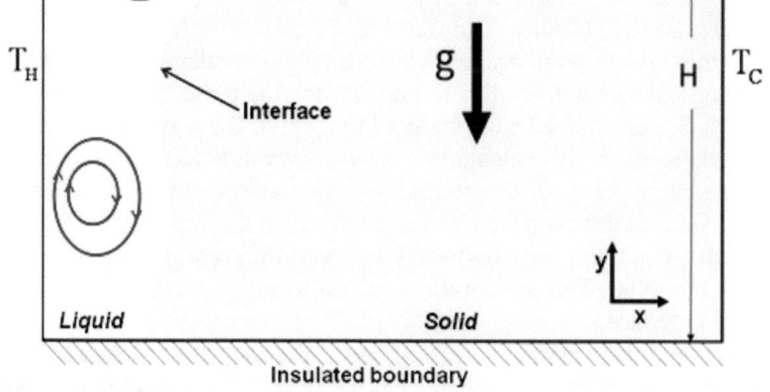

Fig. 5. Schematic of gallium melting

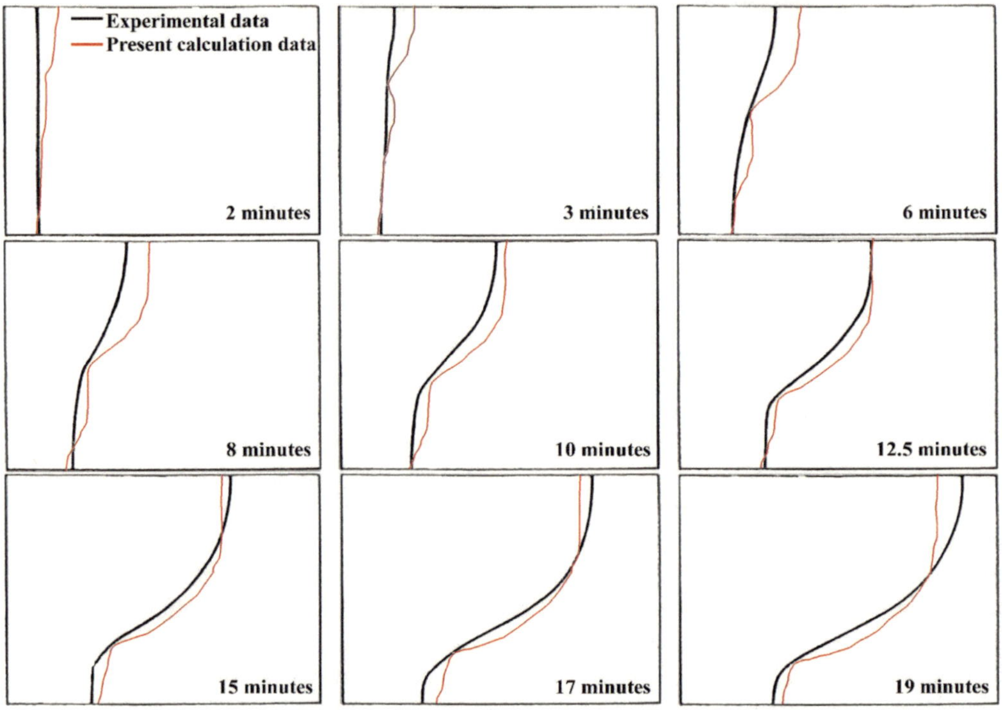

Fig. 6. Comparison of experiment (Brent, 1988) and current numerical model: position of melt front with time

3.2 Expansion to three phase problem

The two dimensional continuity and Navier-Stokes equations are solved with the Enthalpy-Porosity and the VOF methods in order to simulate a melting and falls-off PCM and we can safely said that our model and code are fairly validated to track the melting boundary satisfactorily hereafter. For precise calculation the free interface between liquid PCM and air and linear surface tension, which is function of temperature, are considered. And to reduce the numerical oscillation at the interface discontinuity, a piecewise polynomial profile between the solid and liquid state PCM materials is used.

Energy determines critical point of melting and most physical and transport properties vary with it in melting phenomena. For this reason, at first, the temperature profiles as a function of time at 0, 1, 2, 3.5, 3.9 and 4.2 s are shown in Fig. 7. At 3.9 s, melted PCM separates from the ceiling and falls-off. In this calculation, convection mode heat transfer can be negligible due to no force flow. Heat is transferred by conduction through the copper from the localized thermal input imposed from the right corner at the top surface, and then passed to the PCM and air. At the interface boundary between different materials, a discontinuity in temperature is observed. The temperature profile in all regions shows a decrease over a wide range of y in the air.

Because convection flow inside molten PCM affects the shape of the melt front directly, flow inside molten PCM is shown in Fig. 8 as velocity vectors. During molten PCM growth, the velocity vector is generated inside the molten PCM and then moves to the left. At 3.5 s, a relatively high surface velocity near the molten ball is observed. When falls-off of molten ball is experienced at 3.9 s, a high velocity driven by gravity is observed.

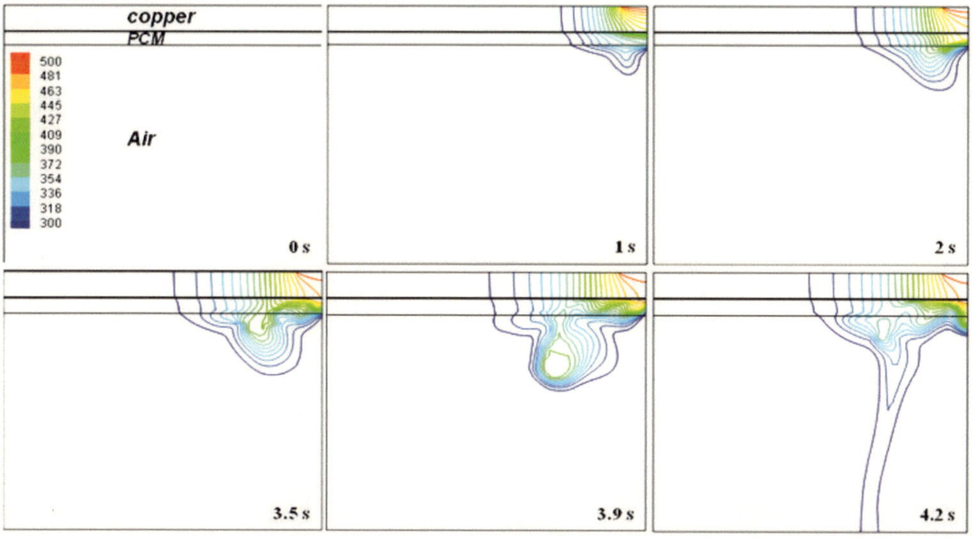

Fig. 7. Temperature distribution in copper, PCM and air as a function of time (localized thermal input is imposed from right side on the top surface of copper)

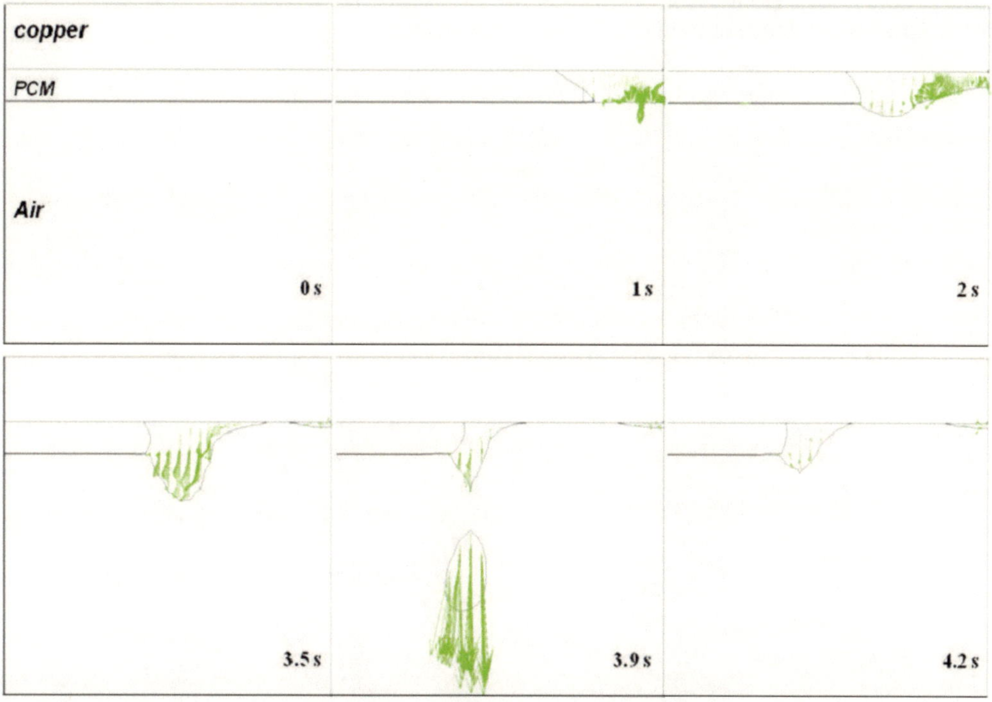

Fig. 8. Velocity vector field and solid-liquid interface at t = 0, 1, 2, 3.5, 3.9 and 4.2 s

Fig. 9 shows the volume fraction, F. In this figure, change of free surface interface between gas and PCM are observed. Free surface interface becomes to strech from 2 s, and then free surface interface moves to left direction. It is important to note that the melted region cannot be distinguished solely by F.

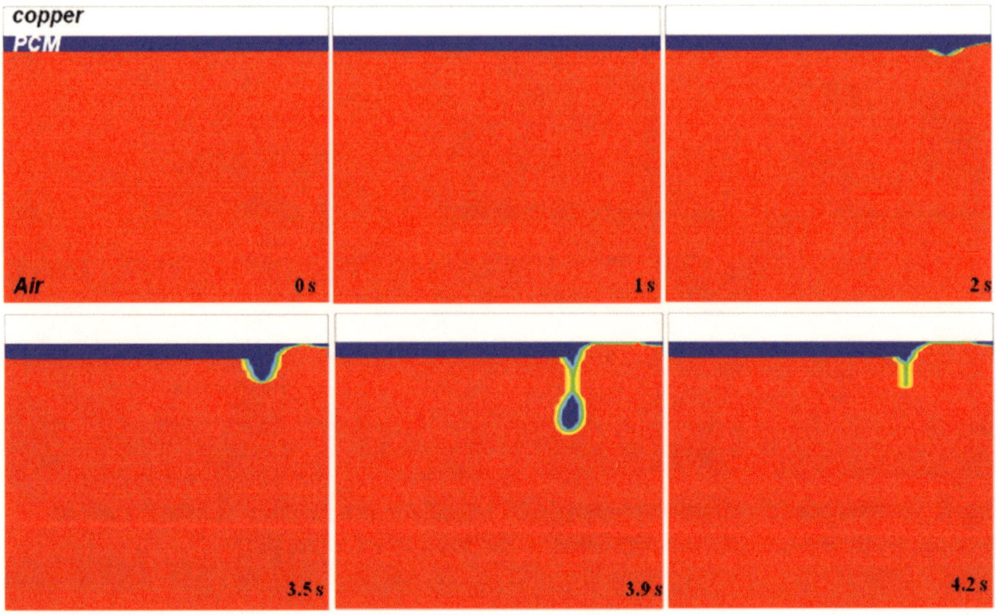

Fig. 9. Time dependence of the volume fraction distribution

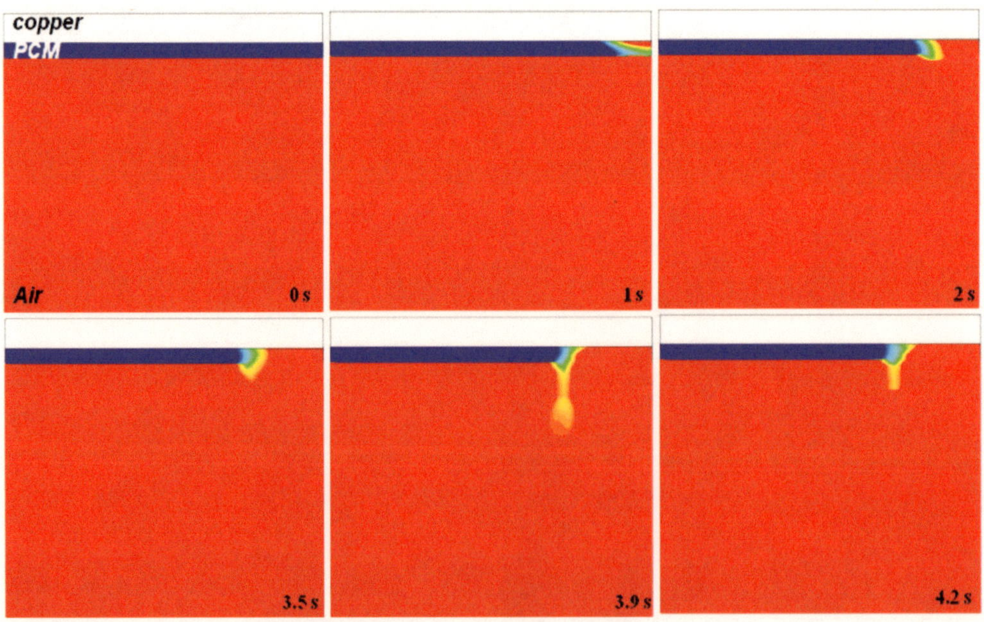

Fig. 10. Time dependence of the liquid fraction distribution

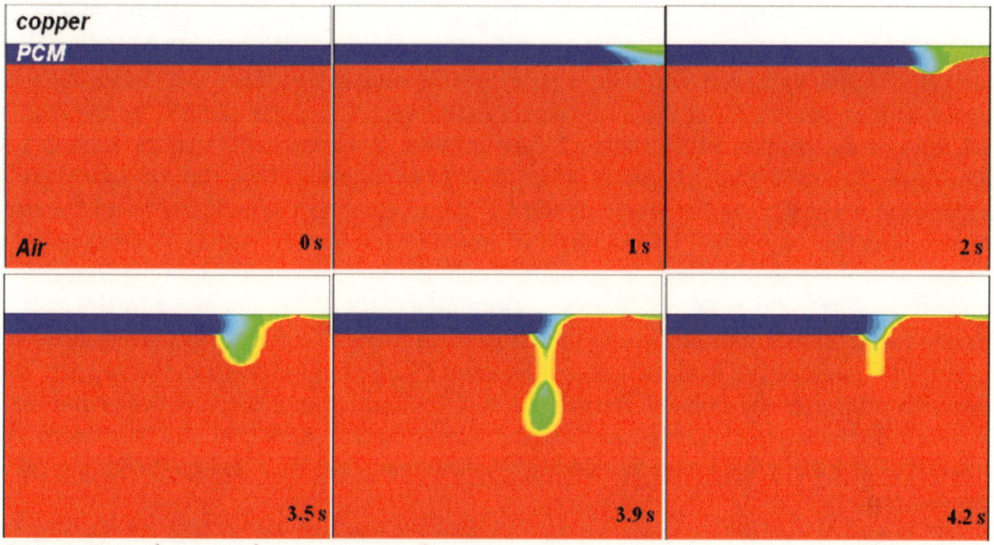

Fig. 11. Distribution of $(\beta + F)/2$ with respect to time

Fig. 10 illustrates the melting processes by use of liquid fraction β. β determines the melt front by both solidus and liquidus temperature. When cell temperature is lower than solidus temperature, $\beta = 0$, mass and momentum equations are turned off, and energy equation is only solved. When cell temperature is higher than liquidus temperature, $\beta = 1$, all equations are solved. If temperature is between solidus and liquidus temperature, $0 < \beta < 1$, cell is treated as partial liquid region, which is represents a mushy region. Here blue is solid region, and red means gas or liquid region. Figure at 1 s shows that melting of PCM begins to happen at the right conner of top surface. After that, melting front advances to left, and then molten ball falls-off at 3.9 s, as stated. But it is hard to distinguish where is liquid and gas region when melt front touch the gas phase. To the end, in order to visualize the three phases together, the simple combined relation, $(\beta + F)/2$, is shown in Fig. 11. When $(\beta + F)/2 = 1$, all computational cells are shown in red, and this represents the gas phase. When $(\beta + F) = 0$, all computational cells are shown in blue, and this represents the solid phase. When $0<(\beta + F)/2<1$, intermediate colors are used to represent the liquid region. Melting in the solid state PCM initially takes place due to absorption of heat from the adjacent copper by localized thermal input. When heat reaches to the free surface between the liquid PCM and air, free surface starts to deform. After that, molten PCM moves to the left and starts to form a molten ball, as shown at 3.5 s. Molten PCM is sustained till 3.9 s, and then the molten ball falls-off eventually. By introducing $(\beta + F)/2$ for identification of edge of each phase, we can see a melting as well as falls-off process clearly.

Fig. 12 represents the melt fraction as a function of time. It is estimated that 24% of the PCM is melted during 4.2 s. Melting of PCM is started at 0.25 s. The melt fraction variation with time exhibits a different gradient after 1.8 s. This behaviour can be categorized by two regimes: regime 1 from the starting point of melting to the point at which the molten ball begins to grow; regime 2 from the point of the initiation of molten ball growth and the point at which molten ball starts to drop. These two regimes can be explained by different conduction modes. In regime 1, the conduction from copper governs the heat transfer to the solid PCM, and this directly affects the melt fraction. However, liquefied PCM on the right hand side moves to the left, and then it generates the molten ball. Therefore, when the melt front becomes isolated from the localized thermal input, it is more affected by the molten ball than by the copper. So in regime 2, heat transfer by conduction from the molten ball dominates the melt fraction rather than that from copper. This can be more easily understood by observing the shape of solid PCM adjacent to the melt front and the melt fraction after the molten ball falls-off (as it is shown by the inset in Fig.12). Within regime 1, the top part of the solid PCM is more melted than the bottom part because the conduction mode of heat transfer from the copper mainly affects the PCM. However in the case of regime 2, the bottom part of the solid PCM is more melted than the top part because the molten ball governs the heat transfer to the solid PCM rather than from the copper. It is also seen that after the falls-off the molten ball, the melt speed is dramatically reduced. This fact could support above-mentioned thermal status, such that the heat from the molten ball is mainly governed by melting phenomena in the PCM before the falling-off is experienced.

$(\beta+F)/2$ are shown with various surface tension coefficients, [σ] in Figs. 13, 14 and 15. Falling-off of molten phase is only happen in Fig. 13 (surface tension coefficient; [σ] = 0.15), and is repeated. But when relatively high surface tension is forced, free surface of molten PCM is sustained along the copper, and melted region is broadening out, which is shown in Figs. 14 and 15. Especially, in case of surface tension [σ] = 0.35, surface becomes wavy, and molten ball is not generated till 4.2 s. The surface tension force is a tensile force tangential to the interface separating pair of fluids, and it tries to keep the fluid molecules at the free surface. Therefore, molten PCM can be sustained with growth of forced surface tension.

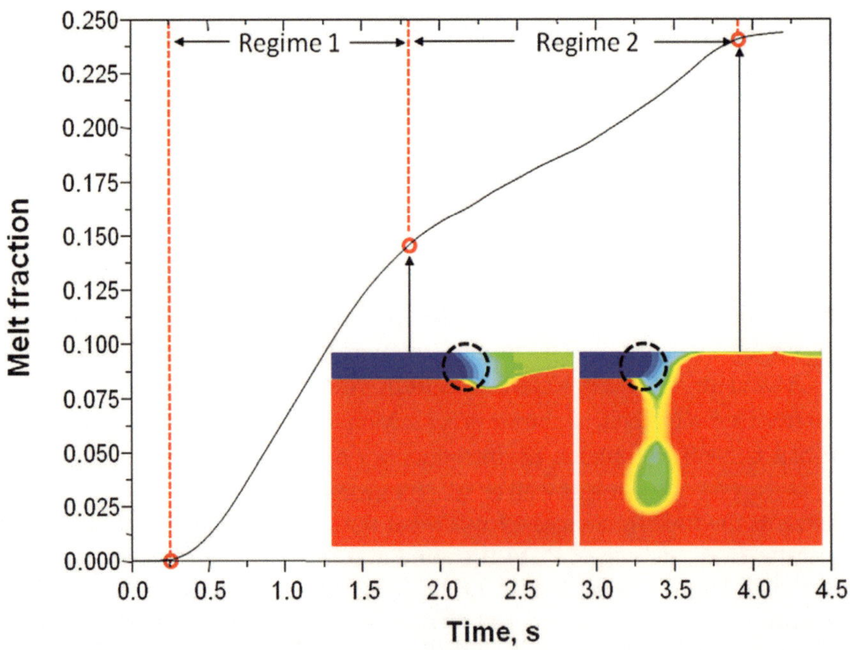

Fig. 12. Melt fraction with time, showing two regimes

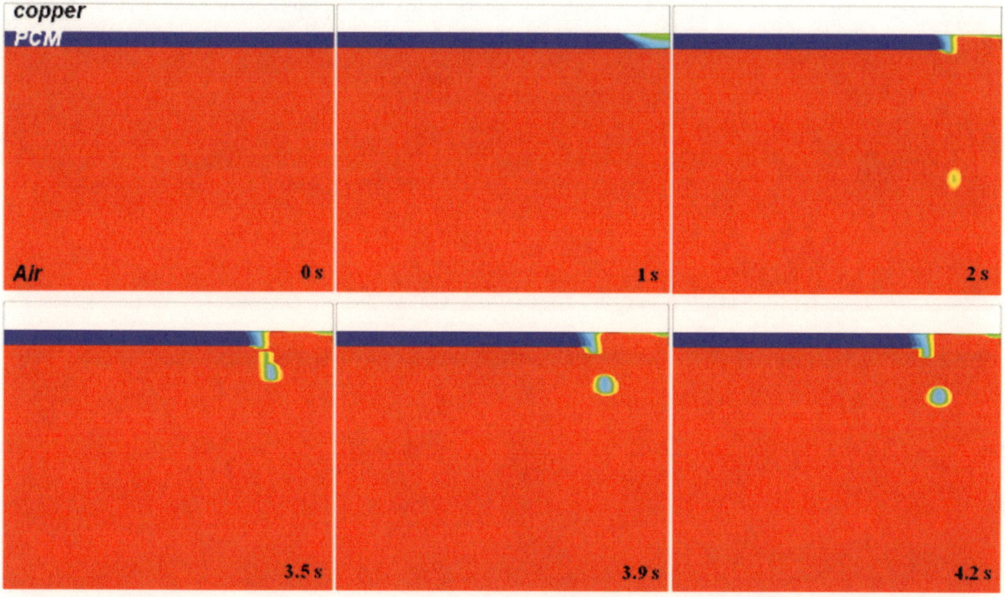

Fig. 13. Distribution of $(\beta + F)/2$ with respect to time (surface tension coefficient, [σ] = 0.15)

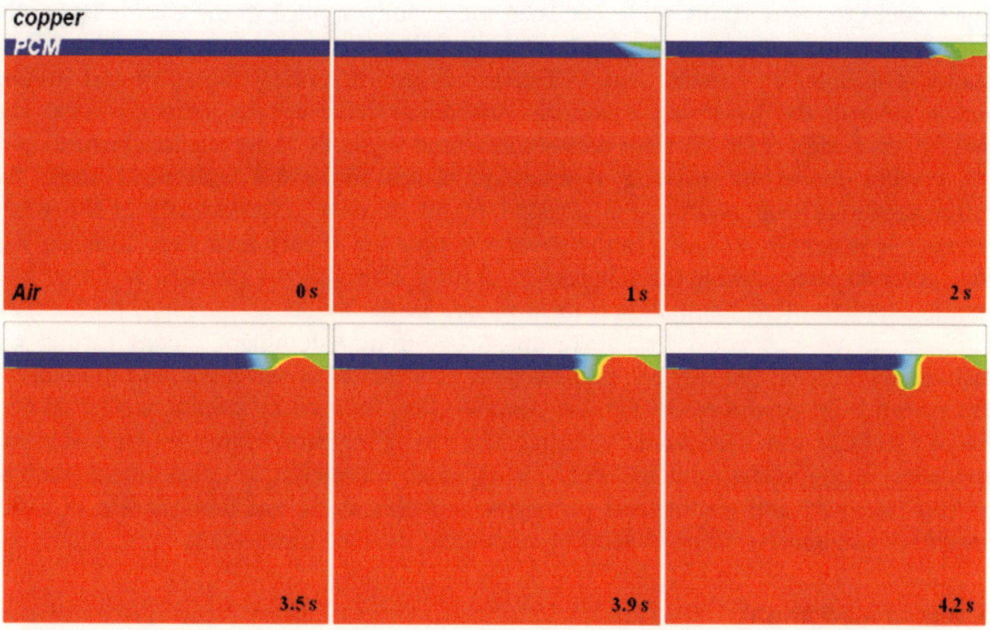

Fig. 14. Distribution of $(\beta + F)/2$ with respect to time ([σ] = 0.25)

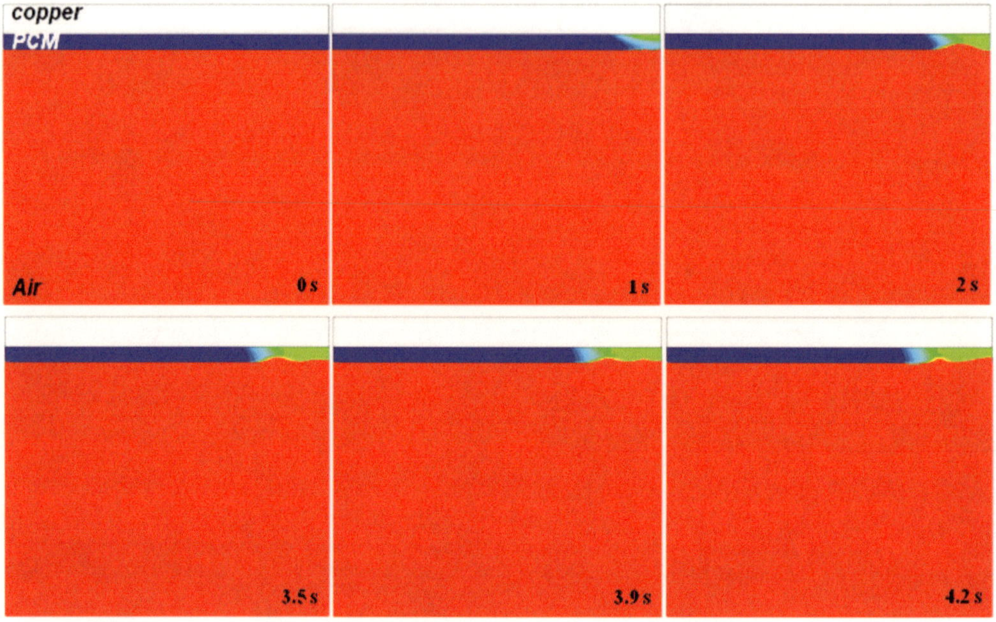

Fig. 15. Distribution of $(\beta + F)/2$ with respect to time ([σ] = 0.35)

4. Conclusion

The model proposed in this study has been successfully applied in the elucidation of the melting process involving three phases and the falling-off phenomena of sustained solid matter. The Enthalpy-Porosity and VOF methods generate scalar transport and involve source term in the governing equations. Additional treatment for surface tension and material properties at the interface between solid and liquid PCM are applied. Validation of the current model by existing experiment shows reasonable agreement from the mathematical as well as from the physical points of view. Discontinuity at the phase interface is inherently included in the governing equation at each time step. However this may generate errors during the progression of time. Therefore we precisely included heat transfer, motion of molten ball and melting rate in the model to minimize such errors. Furthermore we suggested that there are two different dominant modes during the melting and falls-off process: one is the copper conduction driven mode and the other is the molten PCM driven mode. Finally, possible effect induced by surface tension on heat transfer in PCM was elucidated. Although the model requires further development and validation of the model with the inclusion of much more complex phenomena such as species transport and combustion processes, and this study has brought one of major insights of teat transfer which possibly occurs during the wire combustion.

5. Acknowledgment

The authors gratefully acknowledge the financial support for this research provided by JSPS (Grants-in-aid for Young Scientists: #21681022; PI: YN) and the Japan Nuclear Energy Safety

Organization (JNES). The first author (YK) also would like to express his sincere appreciation to the Ministry of Education, Culture, Sports, Science and Technology, Japan for providing him the MEXT Scholarship for conducting this research.

6. References

Assis, E.; Katsman, L.; Ziskind, G. & Letan, R. (2007). Numerical and Experimental Study of Melting in a Spherical Shell, *International Journal of Heat and Mass Transfer*, Vol. 50, pp. 1790-1804.

Bakhman, N. N.; Aldabaev, L. I.; Kondrikov, B. N. & Filippov, V. A. (1981a). Burning of Polymeric Coatings on Copper Wires and Glass Threads : I. Flame Propagation Velocity, *Combust. Flame*, Vol. 41, pp. 17-34.

Bakhman, N. N.; Aldabaev, L. I.; Kondrikov, B. N. & Filippov, V. A. (1981b). Burning of Polymeric Coatings on Copper Wires and Glass Threads : II. Critical Conditions of Burning, *Combust. Flame*, Vol. 41, pp. 35-43.

Brackbill, J. U.; Kothe, D. B. & Zemach, C. (1992). A Continuum Method for Modeling Surface Tension, *Journal of Computational Physics*, Vol. 100, No. 2, pp. 335-354.

Brent, A. D.; Voller, V. R. & Reid, K. J. (1988). The Enthalpy-Porosity Technique for Modeling Convection-Diffusion Phase Change : Application to the Melting of a Pure Metal, *Numerical Heat Transfer*, Vol. 13, pp. 297-318.

Dawei, S.; Suresh, V. G.; Sanjeev, S. & Neelam, N. (2005). Numerical and Experimental Investigation of the Melt Casting of Explosives, *Propellants, Explosives, Pyrotechnics*, Vol. 30, No. 5, pp. 369-380.

Deen, N. G.; Annaland, M. V. S. & Kuipers, J. A. M. (2009). Direct Numerical Simulation of Complex Multi-fluid Flows Using a Combined Front Tracking and Immersed Boundary Method, *Chemical Engineering Science*, Vol. 64, pp. 2186-2201.

Di Blasi, C.; Crescitelli, S. & Russo, G. (1991). Model of Oscillatory Phenomena of Flame Spread along the Surface of Liquid Fuels, *Comp. Meth. App. Mech. Eng*, Vol. 90, pp. 643-657.

FLUENT 12. 0 User's Guide, Available from http://www.ansys.com

Ganaoui, M. E.; Lamazouade, A. ; Bontoux, P. & Morvan, D. (2002). Computational Solution for Fluid Flow under Solid/liquid Phase Change Conditions, *Computers & Fluids*, Vol. 31, pp. 539-556.

Gong, Z. X. & Mujumdar, A. S. (1997). Flow and Heat Transfer in Convection-dominated Melting in a Rectangular Cavity Heated from Below, *International Journal of Heat and Mass Transfer*, Vol. 41, No. 17, pp. 2573-2580.

Gong, Z. X. ; Devahastin, S. & Mujumdar, A. S. (1999). Enhanced Heat Trasnfer in Free Convection-dominated Melting in a Rectangular Cavity with an Isothermal Vertical Wall, *Applied Thermal Engineering*, Vol. 19, No. 12, pp. 1237-1251.

Hirt, C. W. & Nichols, B. D. (1981). Volume of Fluid (VOF) Method for the Dynamics of Free Boundaries, *Journal of computational Physics*, Vol. 39, pp. 201-225.

Jeong, H.; Lee, Y.; Ji, M. ; Lee, G. & Chung, H. (2010). The Optimum Solidification and Crucible Rotation in Silicon Czochralski Crystal Growth, *Journal of Mechanical Science and Technology*, Vol. 24, pp. 407-414.

Kamnis, S. & Gu, S. (2005). Numerical Modelling of Droplet Impingement, *Journal of Physics D: Applied Physics*, Vol. 38, pp. 3664-3673.

Lamberg, P.; Lehtiniemi, R. & Henell, A. (2004). Numerical and Experimental Investigation of Melting and Freezing Processes in Phase Change Material Storage, *International Journal of Thermal Sciences*, Vol. 43, No. 3, pp. 277-287.

McCabe, W. L.; Smith, J. C. & Harriot, P. (2005). *Unit Operations of Chemical Engineering* (7th ed.), McGraw-Hill, New York, pp. 163-165.

Nakamura, Y.; Yoshimura, N.; Ito, H.; Azumaya, K. & Fujita, O. (2008a). Flame Spread over Electric Wire in Sub-atmospheric Pressure, *Proceedings of the Combustion Institute*, Vol. 32, No. 2, pp. 2559-2562.

Nakamura, Y.; Yoshimura, N.; Matsumura, T.; Ito, H. & Fujita, O. (2008b). Opposed-wind Effect on Flame Spread of Electric Wire in Sub-atmospheric Pressure, *Thermal Sci. Tech*, Vol. 3, No. 3, pp. 430-441.

Nakamura, Y.; Azumaya, K.; Ito, H. & Fujita, O. (2009). Time-dependent Flame Spread Behavior of Electric Wire in Sub-atmospheric Pressure, *9th Proc. Asia-Pacific Conference on Combustion*, pp. 101, Taipei, Taiwan May, 2009.

Neumann, F. (1863). Experiments on the Thermal Conductivity of Solids, *Phill. Mag.* 25, 63.

Noureddine H. (2003). Resolving the Controversy over Tin and Gallium Melting in a Rectangular Cavity Heated from the Side, *Numerical Heat Transfer, Part B*, Vol. 44, pp. 253-276.

Ross, H. D. (1994). Ignition of and Flame Spread over Laboratory-scale Pools of Pure Liquid Fuels, *Prog. Energy Combust. Sci*, Vol. 20, pp. 17-63.

Sanchez-Palencia, E. (1987). Homogenization Techniques for Composite Media, *Lecture Notes in Physics*, Springer-Verlag, New York.

Umemura, A.; Uchida, M.; Hirata, T. & Sato, J. (2002). Physical Model Analysis of Flame Spreading along an Electric Wire in Microgravity, *Combust. Inst*, Vol. 29, pp. 2535-2543.

Voller, V. R. (1986). An Implicit Enthalpy Solution for Phase Change Problems : With Application to a Binary Alloy Solidifiaction, *Applied Mathematical Modelling*, Vol.11, No.2 pp. 110-116.

Voller, V. R. (1987a). An Enthalpy Method for Convection/diffusion Phase Change, *International Journal for Numeirical Methods in Engineering*, Vol. 24, pp. 271-284.

Voller, V. R. (1987b). A Fixed Grid Numerical Modelling Methodology for Convection-diffusion Mushy Region Phase-change Problems, *International Journal of Heat and Mass Transfer*, Vol. 30, No. 8, pp. 1709-1719.

Yang, H. & He, Y. (2010). Solving Heat Transfer Problems with Phase Change via Smoothed Effective Heat Capacity and Element-free Galerkin Methods, *International Communications in Heat and Mass Transfer*, Vol. 37, No. 4, pp. 385-392.

Youngs, D. L. (1982). Time Dependent Multimatierial Flow with Large Fluid Distortion, *Numerical Methods for Fluid Dynamics*, pp. 273-285.

Yvan, D.; Daniel, R. R.; Nizar, B. S.; Stéphane L. & Laurent, Z. (2011). A Review on Phase-change Materials : Mathematical Modeling and Simulations, *Renewable and Sustainable Energy Reviews*, Vol. 15, pp. 112-330.

24

Thermal Energy Storage Tanks Using Phase Change Material (PCM) in HVAC Systems

Motoi Yamaha[1] and Nobuo Nakahara[2]
[1]*Chubu University,*
[2]*Nakahara Laboratory, Environmental Syst.-Tech.*
Japan

1. Introduction

Thermal energy storage (TES) systems, which store energy as heat, can compensate for energy imbalances between heat generation and consumption (Tamblyn, 1977). Thermal energy storage systems designed for use with solar energy can accumulate unstable solar insolation. These systems can also shave the peak heat demand to off-peak hours. As such, the required capacity of refrigeration machines can be reduced by extending the time during which these machines are operated. These system also offer other advantages, such as load leveling for the energy supply side. Electric utility companies in Japan offer discount rates during nighttime to promote peak shaving.

Methods of storing heat can be classified as sensible, latent, or chemical storage methods. Sensible heat storage uses heat capacity obtained through a temperature difference. Latent heat storage utilizes the heat to produce a phase change. Considering the associated volume expansion, the phase change between a liquid and a solid is generally used. Reversible chemical thermal reactions can also be used to store heat.

For latent heat storage, various phase change materials (PCM) for different temperature ranges have been investigated. Since these materials should be inexpensive, abundant, and safe, water or ice are the most attractive storage materials for use in the heating, ventilation, and air conditioning (HVAC) field. Water has a relatively high heat of fusion and a melting temperature that is suitable for cooling. The freezing point is suitable for comfort cooling, even though the low evaporation temperature of the refrigeration cycle decreases the efficiency of the machine. Since the tank volume is smaller than the water tank, heat losses from the tank are also smaller. Buildings that do not have sufficient space for water storage still can take advantage of TES through the use of ice storage tanks.

Although ice storage tanks have been used successfully in commercial applications, their use is limited to cooling applications and lowers the efficiency of refrigeration machines due to the lower evaporative temperature associated with these tanks. Phase change materials other than ice have been studied for various purposes. Paraffin waxes, salt hydrates, and eutectic mixtures are materials for use in building applications. Compared to ice storage, these PCMs are used in a passive manner such as the stabilization of room temperature by means of the thermal inertia of phase change.

In this chapter, performance indices are discussed for ice storage and an estimation method is demonstrated experimentally. Furthermore, PCM storage using paraffin waxes in a passive method is evaluated.

2. Analysis of performance of ice thermal storage in HAVC systems

Ice thermal storage is the most common type of latent heat storage. Although a large number of applications exist in countries with warm climates, the performance of ice thermal storage in HVAC systems has not been analyzed. Since the heat of fusion of water is relatively large, the performance of ice thermal storage is usually evaluated from the viewpoint of the amount of heat. However, the temperature response at the outlet of the ice storage tank should be considered if the transient status of the entire HVAC system is discussed.

Ice storage systems can be classified as static systems, in which ice is fixed around a heat exchanger, or slurry ice systems, in which ice floats inside the storage tank. In the following sections, definitions of efficiency are presented, and the effect on the efficiency of the conditions at the inlet for both types is analyzed experimentally.

2.1 Definitions of efficiency for evaluating tanks

Efficiencies should be defined when evaluating the performance of storage tanks. Therefore, the present author has proposed several definitions of efficiencies:

2.2 Response-based efficiency η

A tank is modeled as shown in Figure 1. The heat removed from the tank (Ht) until time T can be calculated according to the following equation, when a step input of temperature θ_{in} and flow rate Q is assumed.

$$Ht = \rho c Q \int_0^T (\theta_{in} - \theta_{out}) dt \tag{1}$$

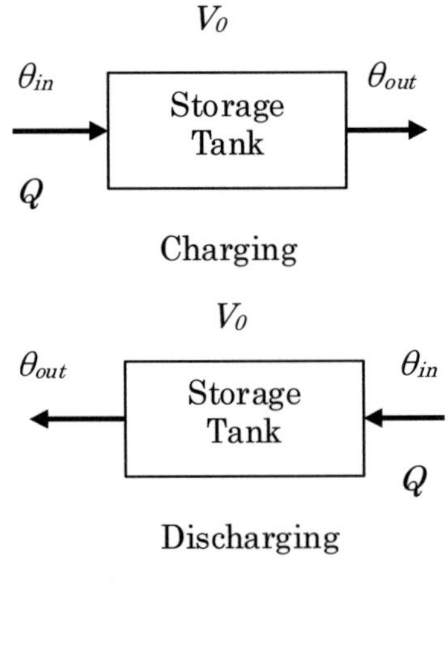

Fig. 1. Model of a tank

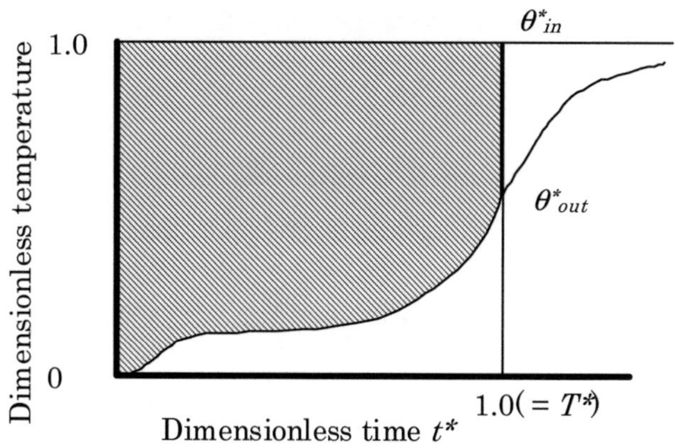

Fig. 2. Response-based efficiency η

Since θ_{in} is constant, the heat discharged until the water in the tank is completely changed ($T = Vo/Q$) is calculated as follows:

$$Ht = \rho c Q\left[\theta_{in}T - \int_0^T \theta_{out}\,dt\right] \quad (2)$$

The above equation is normalized by the following dimensionless variables:

$$\theta^*_{out} = \frac{\theta_{out} - \theta_0}{\theta_{in} - \theta_0} \quad (3)$$

$$t^* = \frac{Q}{V_0}t \quad (4)$$

Substituting these variables and considering that $T^* = 1$, the following equation is obtained:

$$\frac{Ht}{\rho c(\theta_{in} - \theta_0)V_0} = 1 - \int_0^1 \theta^*_{out}\,dt^* \quad (5)$$

The left-hand side of Equation (5) represents the ratio of discharged heat to possible heat to be stored. The efficiency, which can be obtained from the dimensionless response, is indicated by the hatched area in Figure 2.

2.2.1 System efficiency η_0

In actual applications, the outlet water from a storage tank is supplied to secondary systems, i.e., air handling units. The temperature of the water is raised by a certain temperature difference by exchanging heat at the coils of the air handling units, and the water is then returned to the tank. Although the heat from the tank can be calculated using Equation (5), in this case, the inlet temperature varies. The heat is supplied until the outlet temperature of the storage reaches a specific temperature, which is higher than the temperature required for cooling and dehumidification. This temperature is defined as the limit temperature (θ_c) of the coils of the air handling units. Assuming that the time is T_c when the outlet temperature reaches the limit temperature, if the temperature difference for discharge is constant as $\Delta\theta = \theta_{in} - \theta_{out}$, then Equation (6) can be rewritten as follows:

$$Ht_c = \rho c Q \Delta\theta T_c \tag{7}$$

which is normalized according to Equations (3) and (4) to obtain

$$\frac{H_{Tc}}{\rho c(\theta_{in} - \theta_0)V_0} = \frac{Q}{V_0} T_c = T_c^* \tag{8}$$

In Figure 3, the efficiency is represented by the hatched area between the inlet and outlet curves until the limit temperature is reached.

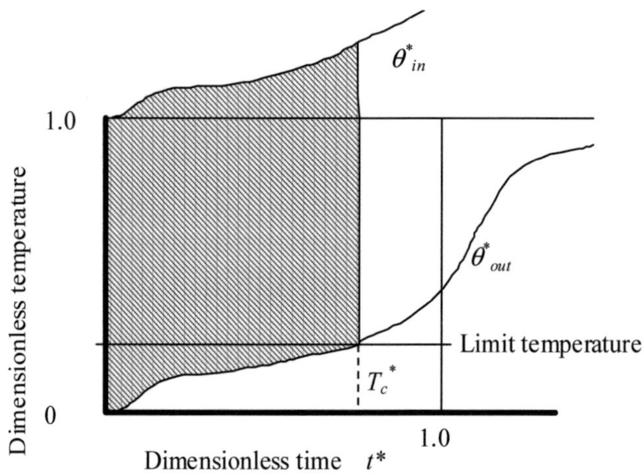

Fig. 3. System-based efficiency η_0

$$Ht_c = \rho c Q \int_0^{T_c} (\theta_{in} - \theta_{out})dt \tag{6}$$

2.2.2 Volumetric efficiency η_v

Efficiency can also be defined based on the temperature profile. The heat obtained from the tank can therefore be indicated by the hatched area between the two curves on the left-hand side of Figure 4. The volumetric efficiency is defined as the ratio of the hatched area to the rectangular area. For an ice storage tank, an equivalent temperature difference ($\Delta\theta_i$), which is the quotient of the stored latent heat and specific heat of water, was introduced in order to represent the latent heat in terms of temperature. The volumetric efficiency is defined as follows:

$$\eta_v = \frac{H_t}{c\rho\Delta\theta_0 V_0} \tag{9}$$

Since $\Delta\theta_0$ in Equation (9) is the temperature difference at the coil of an air handling unit, the definition of efficiency can be adapted to both ice and water storage tanks. Since the value of $\eta_{v\_}$ can be greater than unity by definition, the excess can be considered to represent the reduction in tank volume due to ice storage by latent heat.

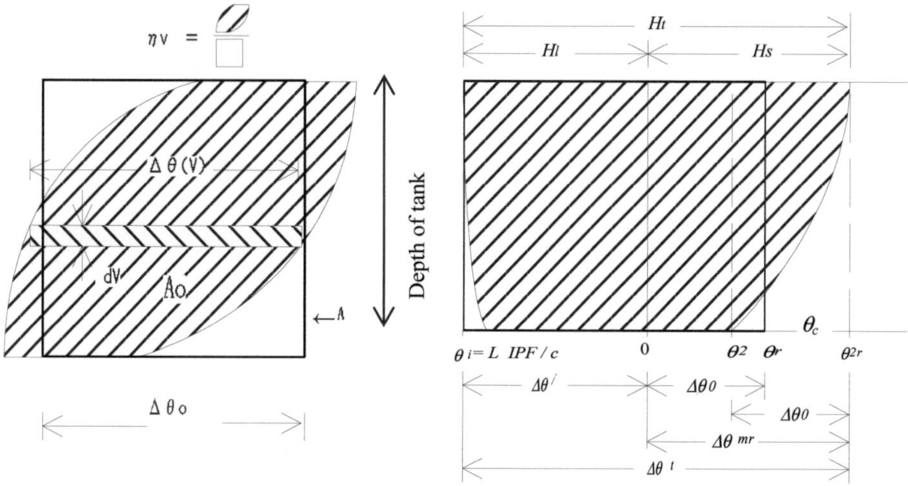

(a) water storage tank (b) ice storage tank

Fig. 4. Definition of tank volume efficiency

2.3 Thermal response of the ice-on-coil ice storage tank

2.3.1 Experimental setup and conditions

Figure 5 shows the experimental setup of an ice-on-coil ice storage tank. The input temperature could be maintained constant by conditioned water supplied from a hot water tank and a chilled water tank. The flow rate to the experimental tank was controlled by the difference in water level between a high tank and the experimental tank. The experimental tank consisted of transparent acrylic plates. The coil was constructed from polyethylene pipes, as shown in Figure 6. Temperature was measured by thermocouples and the quantity of ice was calculated by measuring the water level of the tank. The ice packing factor (IPF), which is the volumetric ratio of ice to water (V_{ice}/V_0), was calculated from the measured quantity of ice.

Factors for thermal response are chosen considering fluid dynamics and heat transfer. Reynolds number and Archimedes number are the dominant dimensionless numbers used in analyzing non-isothermal fluid flow, although experiments for water thermal storage tanks indicate that the Reynolds number is less influential. Therefore, the Archimedes number at the inlet of the tank, as defined by the following equation, is the dominant dimensionless number:

$$\mathrm{Ar}_{in} = \frac{d_{in} g(\Delta\rho / \rho_0)}{u_{in}^{\ 2}} \tag{10}$$

Furthermore, the enthalpy flow at the inlet is also an important factor with respect to the thermal response of an ice storage tank. The dimensionless enthalpy flow rate is defined as follows:

$$Q^{*} = \frac{\rho c Q \theta_{in}}{\rho c V_0 \theta_{in} + \rho_{ice} V_0 IPF \cdot L} \tag{11}$$

The experimental conditions are listed in Tables 1 through 4.

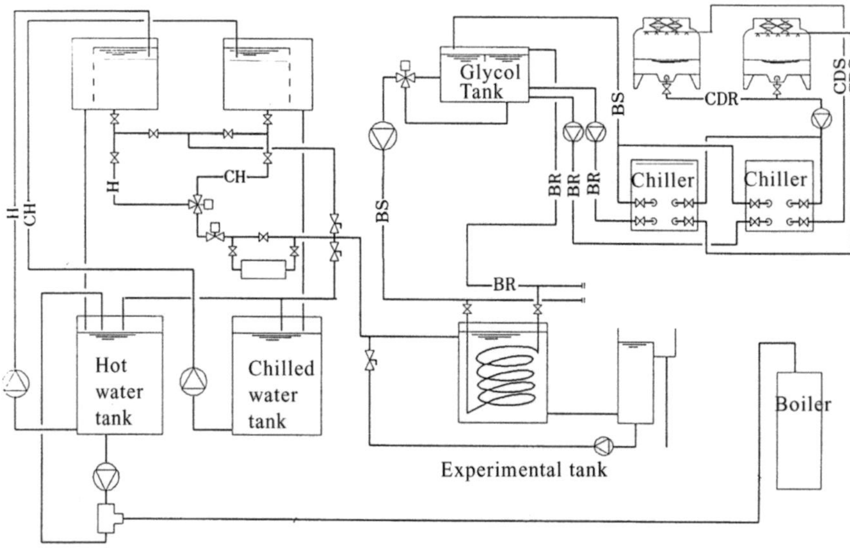

Fig. 5. Schematic diagram of the experimental setup

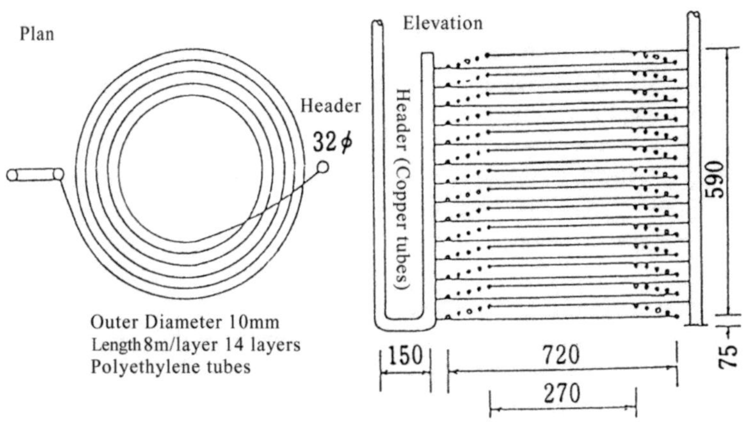

Fig. 6. Structure of the ice making coil

2.4 Results

Figure 7 shows the temperature response of the upper and lower parts of the tank during the freezing process. With the exception of the upper part of the coil, the temperature in the tank decreased uniformly. Soon after the temperature at the bottom of the tank reached 4°C, at which the density of water is maximum, the temperature of the upper part of the tank decreased quickly. When the temperature reached 0°C, ice first formed on the header of the coils and then formed on the entire coils. The patterns for the ice making process were approximately the same throughout the experiments.

The dimensionless response of the outlet temperature during the melting process is shown in Figures 8 through 10 for various Archimedes numbers and enthalpy flow rates. For the results shown in Figure 8, the outlet temperature increased immediately after the discharge process began and remained lower than 4°C until all of the ice in the tank had melted. The upper part of the tank was warmed by the inlet water and stratification developed. As the inlet enthalpy flow rate was large enough to maintain stratification, melting occurred primarily beneath the stratification. Since the inlet water was cooled by the remaining ice as the water passed through the tank, the outlet water remained at a lower temperature. The results of experiments conducted using a smaller enthalpy flow rate are shown in Figure 9. The outlet temperature gradually increased to 4°C and remained constant. Once the inlet water entered the tank, the water was cooled by melting ice and was mixed due to buoyancy effects. Melting occurred uniformly in the tank, and the temperature was maintained at 4°C during melting. For both conditions, the thermal characteristics were the same as for a stratified water tank, after complete melting. In Figure 10, the outlet temperature exceeded 4°C immediately after the start of the experiment. Since the Archimedes number was small for this condition, the momentum of the entering water from the inlet exceeded the buoyancy force, and hence the inside of the tank was completely mixed. Comparison of dimensionless responses for the same conditions, with the exception of the IPF, showed no significant differences. The IPF, which represents the quantity of ice, determined the duration of ice melting. However, the IPF had little effect on the dimensionless response.

Based on the above results, the dominant factors affecting mixing inside the tank and the outlet response are the Archimedes number and the inlet enthalpy flow rate. The response pattern is determined by the Archimedes number, and the melting pattern is determined by the enthalpy flow rate.

Exp. no	Initial temp. [°C]	Charging time [hr:min]	IPF [%]
SA01-11-1	14.9	3:45	10
SA01-21-1	9.3	2:55	10
SA01-31-1	15.3	3:30	10
SA01-12-1	10.1	2:55	10
SA01-22-1	13.1	3:15	10
SA01-32-1	18.7	3:00	10
SA01-42-1	18.8	3:26	10
SA01-13-1	10.0	2:55	10
SA01-23-1	12.7	3:25	10
SA01-33-1	14.7	3:25	10
SA01-43-1	18.9	3:40	10

Table 1. Experimental conditions of the freezing process for the ice-on-coil ice storage tank with IPF 10%

Exp. no	Initial temp. [°C]	Charging time [hr:min]	IPF [%]
SA01-11-2	7.6	5:00	20
SA01-21-2	7.8	5:30	20
SA01-31-2	15.3	4:30	20
SA01-12-2	12.9	4:20	20
SA01-22-2	14.1	4:50	20
SA01-32-2	15.5	4:30	20
SA01-42-2	12.4	4:27	20
SA01-13-2	12.5	4:30	20
SA01-23-2	17.2	4:45	20
SA01-33-2	--	--	20
SA01-43-2	15.2	4:15	20

Table 2. Experimental conditions of the freezing process for the ice-on-coil ice storage tank with IPF 20%

Exp. no	Input temp. [°C]	Flow rate [L/min]	Ar_{in} [-]	Inlet heat [kW]
SA01-11-1	10.7	5.9	2.62E-02	4.4
SA01-21-1	12.7	5.1	7.18E-02	4.5
SA01-31-1	15.4	4.1	2.03E-01	4.4
SA01-12-1	14.7	11.4	2.24E-01	11.6
SA01-22-1	18.3	8.9	6.72E-02	11.4
SA01-32-1	25.3	8.1	1.77E-01	14.3
SA01-42-1	10.9	16.0	4.10E-03	12.2
SA01-13-1	14.7	35.7	2.10E-02	36.6
SA01-23-1	18.4	27.8	6.39E-02	35.6
SA01-33-1	24.3	20.7	2.23E-01	35.1
SA01-43-1	15.3	32.3	3.11E-03	34.4

Table 3. Experimental conditions of the melting process for the ice-on-coil ice storage tank with IPF 10%

Exp. no	Input temp. [°C]	Flow rate [L/min]	Ar_{in} [-]	Inlet heat [kW]
SA01-11-2	10.8	6.0	2.76E-02	4.5
SA01-21-2	13.0	5.0	7.83E-02	4.5
SA01-31-2	15.4	4.0	2.03E-01	4.3
SA01-12-2	14.5	11.3	2.16E-01	11.4
SA01-22-2	18.3	8.9	6.78E-02	11.4
SA01-32-2	25.2	7.9	1.85E-01	13.9
SA01-42-2	10.5	15.5	3.61E-03	11.4
SA01-13-2	14.7	35.8	2.08E-02	36.7
SA01-23-2	18.3	27.7	6.30E-02	35.2
SA01-33-2	24.5	20.8	2.27E-01	35.6
SA01-43-2	15.3	33.8	2.87E-03	36.0

Table 4. Experimental conditions of the melting process for the ice-on-coil ice storage tank with IPF 10%

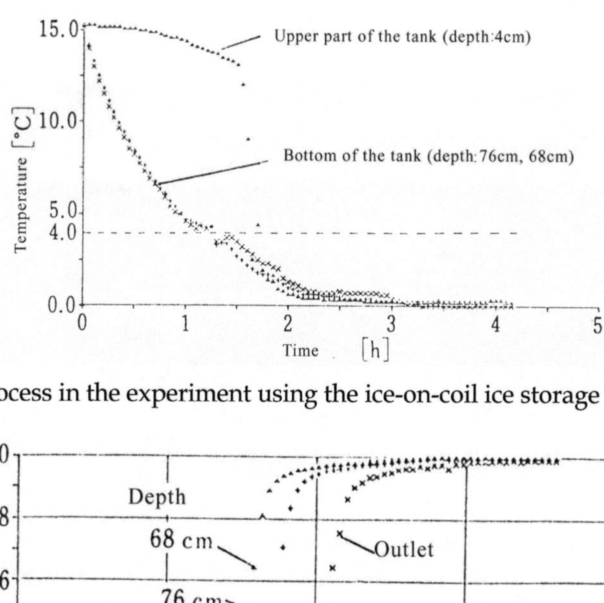

Fig. 7. Freezing process in the experiment using the ice-on-coil ice storage tank

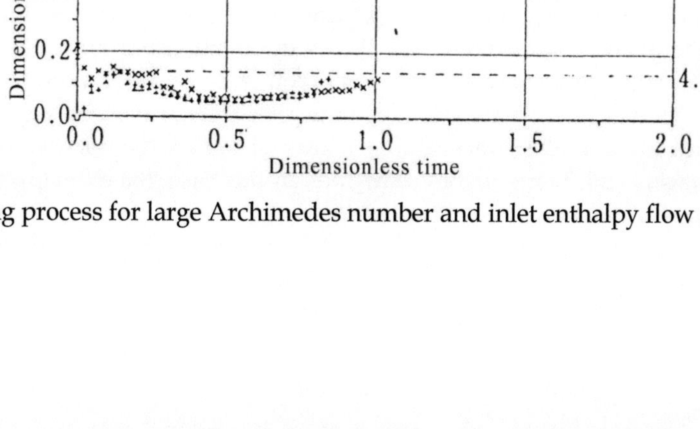

Fig. 8. Melting process for large Archimedes number and inlet enthalpy flow rate

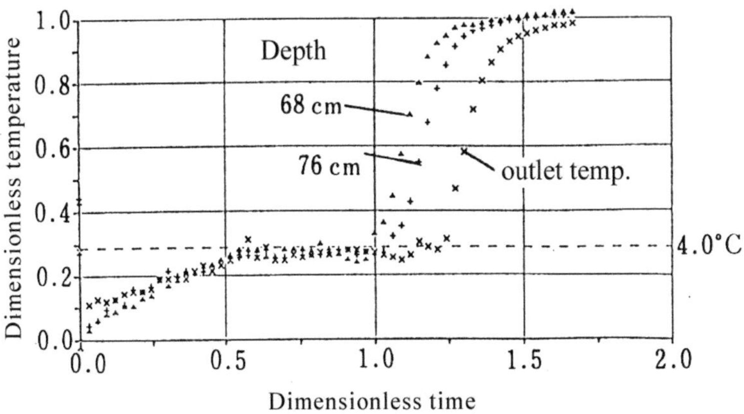

Fig. 9. Melting process for large Archimedes number and moderate inlet enthalpy flow rate

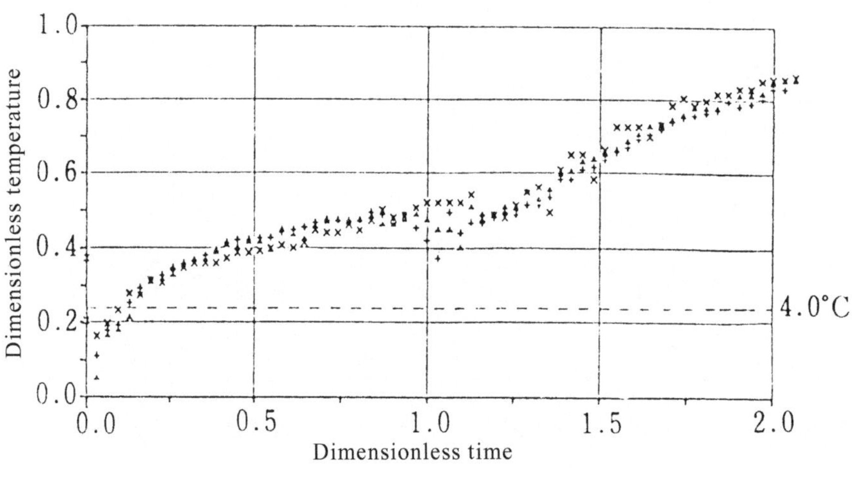

Fig. 10. Melting process for small Archimedes number

2.5 Effect of main parameters on efficiencies

The relationship among efficiency, Archimedes number, and inlet enthalpy flow rate is analyzed in this section. The efficiency depends on the limit temperature to the coils of the air handling units. Even though the value of the limit temperature depends on the design conditions of the air handling units, in the present study, the limit temperature was set to 4°C based on the above results. Figure 11 shows the relationship among η, Archimedes number, and inlet enthalpy flow rate. The effect on outlet response is more pronounced for the Archimedes number than for the enthalpy flow rate. This means that larger Archimedes numbers produce lower outlet temperatures. Figure 12 shows the relationship among η_0, Archimedes number, and inlet enthalpy flow rate. In this case, the enthalpy flow rate has more influence on the response than in the case of η.

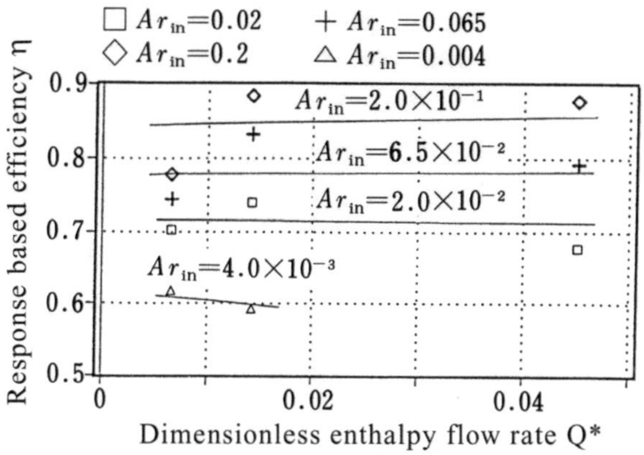

Fig. 11. Relationship between response-based efficiency η and inlet conditions

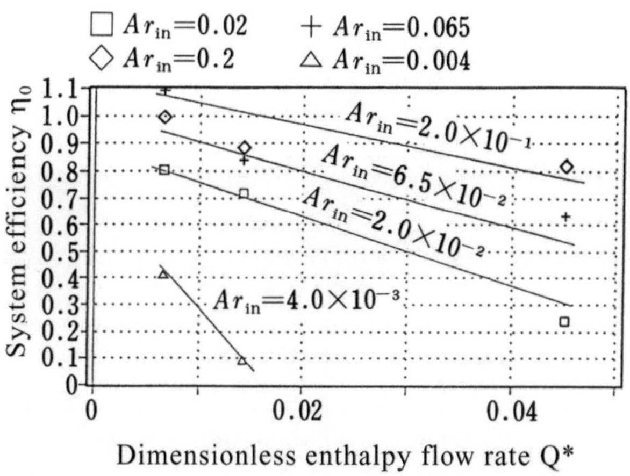

Fig. 12. Relationship between system efficiency η_0 and inlet conditions

2.6 Thermal response of the slurry ice storage tank

The dynamic ice making method, which makes ice using an additional device, is an alternative to the ice-on-coil ice storage tank. Since ice is intermittently or continuously removed from the surface of an ice making heat exchanger, no thermal resistance occurs, as in the case of the ice-on-coil ice storage tank. There are several types of dynamic ice making processes, which use a diluted glycol solution or the sub-cooling phenomenon of water. In the present paper, experiments were conducted on a dynamic ice storage tank using sub-cooled water.

2.6.1 Experimental setup and conditions

The experimental setup is shown in Figure 13 and includes a sub-cooling heat exchanger, which cools water to 2°C below the freezing point. The sub-cooled water was injected into the tank and collided with a plate at which the sub-cooled state was released.

The flow rates of the glycol solution and the input water for melting were measured by electromagnetic flow meters. Temperature profiles from 10 vertical points at two locations, as well as the inlet and outlet temperatures, were measured. Melting was performed by spray nozzles at the upper part of the tank.

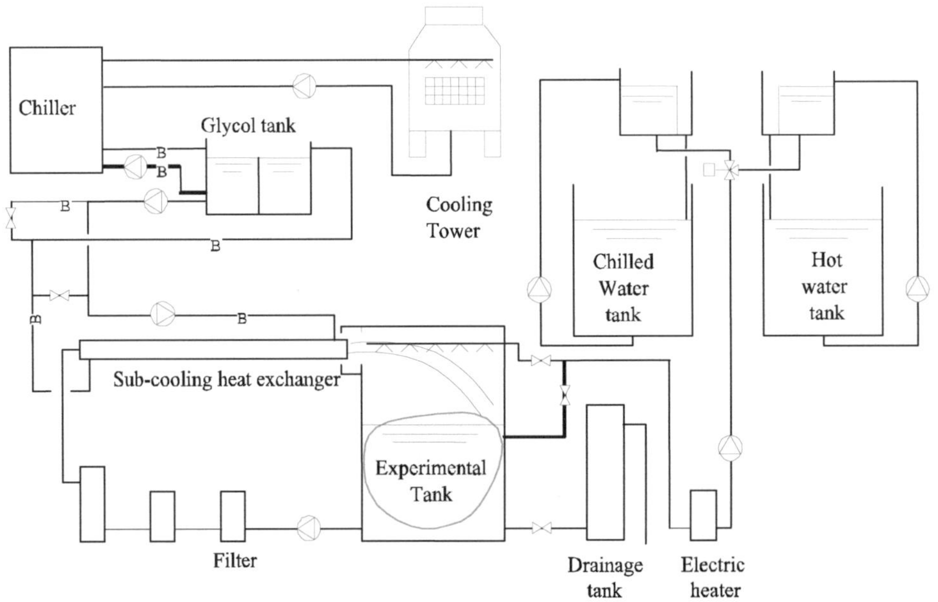

Fig. 13. Schematic diagram of the experimental setup for slurry ice storage

Exp. no.	Initial temp. [°C]	Charging time [hr:min]	IPF [%]
SD101C	15.8	4:30	43.9
SD102C	19.6	4:35	17.4
SD103C	16.4	4:20	58
SD104C	14.4	------	27.2
SD105C	11.7	4:30	44.6
SD106C	15.6	4:55	44.3
SD107C	13.0	4:40	34.4
SD108C	5.3	3:50	33.9
SD109C	16.1	4:40	45.8
SD110C	13.5	4:10	30.5
SD111C	16.8	4:05	31.9
SD112C	14.5	4:10	31.8

Table 5. Experimental conditions for the freezing process for the slurry ice storage tank

Exp. no.	Inlet temp. [°C]	Flow rate [l/min]	Inlet heat [kW]
SD101H	38.5	12.6	33.8
SD102H	29.7	16.1	33.4
SD103H	24.8	19.4	33.6
SD104H	17.5	27.3	33.3
SD105H	29.7	11.1	23.0
SD106H	24.6	12.9	22.1
SD107H	17.1	19.8	23.6
SD108H	13	24.9	22.6
SD109H	18	8.7	10.9
SD110H	12.3	10.6	9.1
SD111H	12.6	12.2	10.2
SD112H	9.9	15.7	10.8

Table 6. Experimental conditions for the freezing process for the slurry ice storage tank

2.7 Results

Figure 14 shows the temperature variation of the tank and the glycol solution during a freezing process. Since sub-cooled water was injected from the heat exchanger into the tank, the inside of the tank was completely mixed so that the temperature profile was uniform. The temperature of the tank decreased from the beginning of the experiment and reached 0°C after two hours. Once the inside of the tank reached the freezing temperature, heat extraction from the heat exchanger was used to form ice. Therefore, the temperature of the glycol solution was maintained at approximately 4°C below the freezing point.

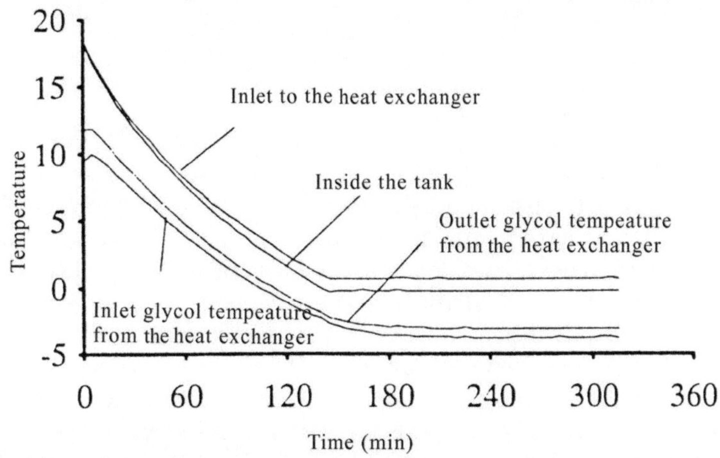

Fig. 14. Freezing process of the slurry ice storage tank

The injected water was released from its sub-cooled state by the collision, and 2% of the water was frozen. Ice in the shape of tiny flakes was observed to float inside the tank. There was no constraint on ice formation, which was different from that in the ice-on-coil ice storage tank. After a certain amount of ice flakes was produced, a lump of ice formed by agglomeration of the ice flakes. Experiments to examine the freezing process were continued until the lump of ice extended to the bottom of the tank. The value of the IPF was calculated from the heat balance between the extracted heat by the glycol solution and the sensible and latent heat of water inside the tank. The IPF reached a higher value than that for the ice-on-coil ice storage tank, in which the thickness of the ice was limited by the space between the ice making coils.

Dimensionless output responses of melting processes are shown in Figures 15 and 16. Since the temperature at the maximum density of water, i.e., 4°C, is also important for the slurry ice type, the points at which the outlet temperature exceeded 4°C are indicated by filled circles in the figures. The outlet temperature was maintained at temperature lower than 4°C from the beginning of the experiments and increased to dimensionless temperatures of 0.7 to 1.0. The response shape indicated complete mixing and a lack of significant difference between experimental conditions. The dimensionless time, when the response increased, appeared earlier for larger inlet enthalpy flow rates.

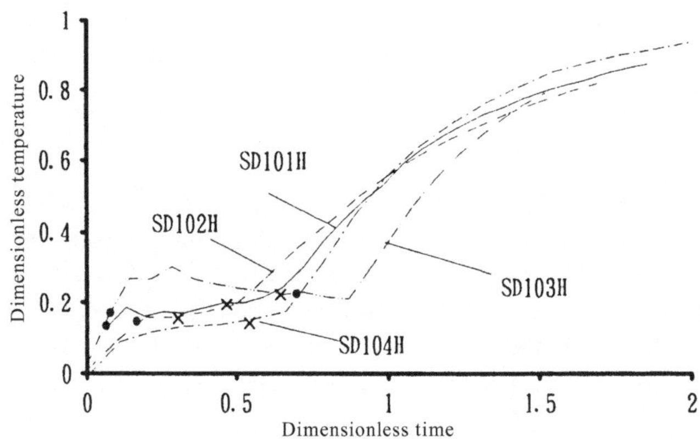

Fig. 15. Dimensionless response of the melting process for slurry ice storage for large inlet enthalpy flow rate

Considering the time at which the outlet temperature exceeded 4°C, the real temperature before response increase differed for different inlet conditions. The temperature exceeded 4°C at a dimensionless time of approximately 0.1 for certain conditions. However, the temperature remained above 4°C until a dimensionless time of approximately 0.8 for other conditions. The dimensionless times at which the inlet enthalpy became equal to the latent heat of the ice are indicated in the figures by cross symbols. As observed from the figures, the temperature had already increased when ice remained present in the tank.

The time at which the outlet temperature exceeded 4°C is considered to depend on the relationship between the enthalpy flow rate and the heat transfer to the ice. The ice in the slurry ice tank was in the form of particles and was distributed over the entire tank. Therefore, heat transfer occurred over a larger area than for the ice-on-coil ice storage tank, and depended strongly on the state of mixing inside the tank. As the Archimedes number became small, which indicates a higher velocity at the inlet, mixing inside the tank was accelerated and so the heat transfer between ice and water was enhanced. Consequently, the outlet temperature remained lower for small Archimedes numbers.

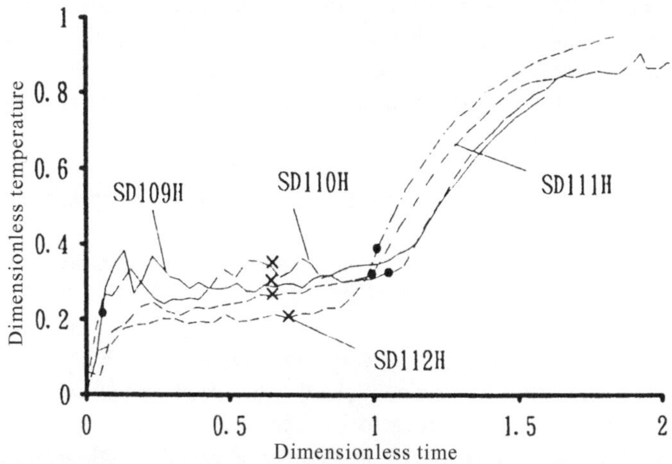

Fig. 16. Dimensionless response of the melting process of slurry ice storage for small inlet enthalpy flow rate

The temperature of the outlet flow and its duration below 4°C are important for system utilization. The efficiency defined by the dimensionless response was difficult to apply to slurry ice storage, because the outlet temperature sometimes exceeded 4°C. Therefore, the relationship between efficiencies and experimental conditions is not discussed for the case of slurry ice storage.

3. Evaluation of a PCM storage system using paraffin waxes

Phase change materials other than ice and water have been extensively investigated as a TES medium. In recent years, various commercially available materials have been developed. Research on the use of PCMs in buildings have been conducted. The thermal characteristics of building materials with PCMs, which could stabilize the temperature of a room, were measured (Mehling, 2002). Organic compounds, such as fatty acids and paraffin waxes, have also attracted attention as TES media. The melting temperature of a binary mixture of these materials is adjustable to climate requirements (Kauranen et al. 1991). The heats of fusion of these materials were from 120 to 160 kJ/kg (Feldman et al. 1989). Both heating and cooling applications are attractive for use with binary mixtures of tetradecane and hexadecane (He et al. 1999).

Several studies on building materials containing PCM have been conducted. Gypsum boards combined with a mixture of fatty acids could reduce the fluctuation of room temperature in the wintertime (Shilei et al. 2006). Floor panels mixed with PCM in an under-floor electrical heating system were evaluated because of the availability of inexpensive electricity during the nighttime (Lin et al. 2003). Applications of PCMs to ceilings and wallboards, which were cooled during the nighttime and released stored energy for cooling during the day, were examined (Barnard and Setterwall 2003, Lin et al. 2003 and Feldman et

al. 1995). These studies focused on the use of natural heat resources in conjunction with TES technologies.
On the other hand, TES is commonly used in warm countries, because the electric peak demand may be problematic. In such countries, electric consumption of heating, ventilating, and air conditioning (HVAC) systems is concentrated during warm summer afternoons. Therefore, the demand for electricity has a steep peak. This peak should be shaved to off-peak hours in order to avoid electricity shortages. Water and ice storage can be used for this purpose. Ice storage has become common, because the volume of the storage tank is smaller than water storage tank due to the latent heat of water. However, chilling machines are less efficient than ordinary machines used for comfort cooling. The use of a PCM having a higher melting temperature than ice is promising because the operating temperature need not be changed from ordinary operation.
Phase change material storage devices can be installed in the water circuit or the air circuit of HVAC systems. Since the temperature difference between the PCM and the heat transfer medium is needed in order to solidify or liquefy, an air circuit with a wide temperature range was considered to be suitable. We proposed a system with PCM containers in the air ducts. The materials selected in the present study were mixtures of various paraffin waxes, which allowed the melting temperature to be adjusted by adjusting the concentration of each material. Simple methods by which to determine the thermal properties of the PCM were proposed by comparing the temperature response of the PCM samples with water (Zheng et al. 1999 and Martin et al. 2003). In the present study, the thermal characteristics of the mixtures were measured using a simple apparatus and simulations of an HVAC system were conducted in order to evaluate various properties, such as the melting temperature or the quantity of the mixture. The performance of the proposed system was evaluated using a system simulation program.

3.1 Research methods

The melting temperature can be changed by adjusting the concentrations of paraffin waxes (He et al. 1999). We used industrial grade paraffin waxes. Table 7 lists the concentrations of the mixtures. The use of flammable liquids at 20°C in buildings is prohibited by Japanese building codes. A fatty acid, namely, stearic acid with a high melting temperature, was added to solidify the mixture of paraffin waxes. The apparatus shown in Figure 17 was used to measure the thermal properties of the mixtures. The apparatus consisted of foam polystyrene covered with acrylic plates. A cavity was located in the center of the apparatus, which was filled with the mixture. The surface areas of the cavity were covered with heat flux transducers. Thermocouples were placed inside the cavity.

	Estimated melting temp.	Concentration of paraffin wax (t_m: 18°C)	Concentration of paraffin wax (t_m: 28°C)	Concentration of stearic acid	Mass of PCM (g)
MT 17	17°C (62.6°F)	40%	40%	20%	39.1
MT 19	19°C (66.2°F)	28%	52%	20%	40.4
MT 21	21°C (69.8°F)	24%	56%	20%	40.0
MT 23	23°C (73.4°F)	16%	64%	20%	38.5

Table 7. Concentrations of paraffin waxes and fatty acid used in the present study
t_m: melting temperature

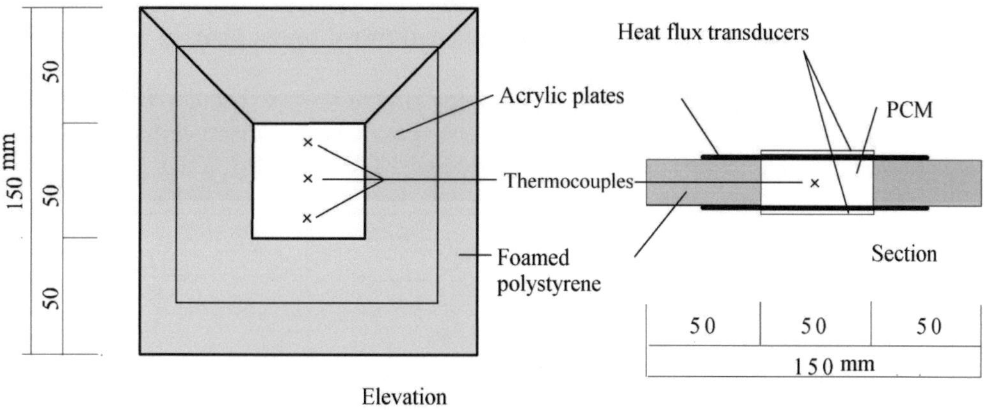

Fig. 17. Experimental apparatus used to measure the thermal properties of the mixtures

The apparatus was placed in a small thermal chamber in which both temperature and humidity could be controlled. The temperature inside the chamber was raised from -5°C to 30°C over seven hours. The temperature inside the chamber was maintained at 30°C for three hours and decreased to -5°C over seven hours, before being maintained constant for seven hours. One cycle of the experiment was continued over 24 hours, and seven cycles were repeated for each measurement. The first and last cycles were not used for analysis because of the instability of the experimental conditions.

3.2 Results

The results for the MT17 mixture are shown in Figure 18. The left-hand figure shows the sum of the heat through the heat flux transducers versus the average temperature of the thermocouples for five cycles. The specific heat could be obtained by differentiating the curve as is shown on the right-hand side of the figure. The measured enthalpy was integrated as latent heat in the temperature range for the phase change observed in Figure 2(b), where the temperature ranged from 11.5°C to 20.5°C for freezing and from 10.0°C to 21.5°C for melting. The results for all of the mixtures are listed in Table 2. The latent heat of

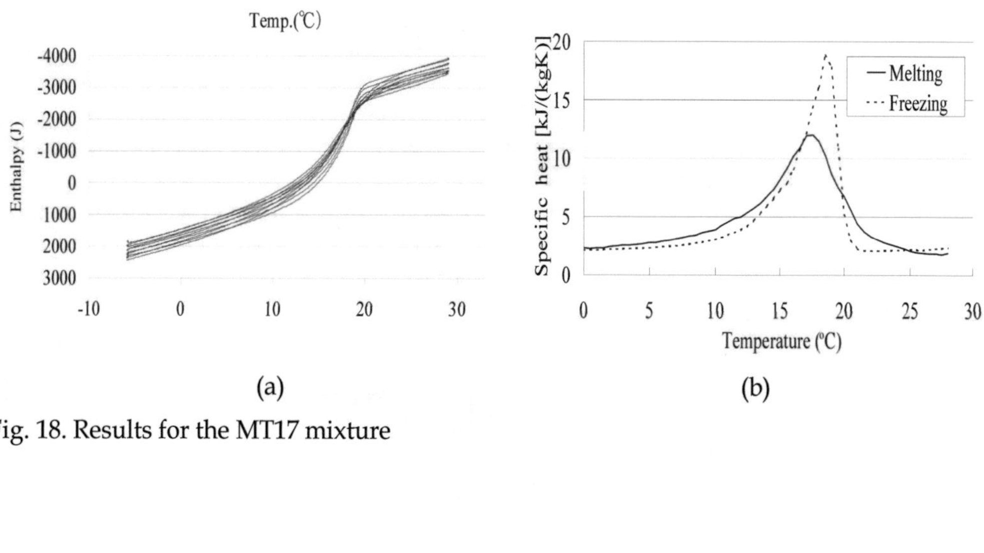

Fig. 18. Results for the MT17 mixture

pure paraffin wax is approximately 200 kJ/kg. The mixtures had smaller latent heats than the pure material. The measured latent heat was equivalent to the heat for a temperature difference of 20°C for water.

The curves shown in Figure 18(b) were used for simulations, which used the enthalpy method of the PCM. In the simulation program, the specific heat of the materials varied with temperature according to the curves shown in the figure (Yamaha et al. 2001).

Materials	Operations	Peak temperature [°C]	Amount of latent heat [kJ/kg]
MT 17	Freezing	18.5	86
	Melting	17.5	77
MT 19	Freezing	21.5	87
	Melting	20.5	86
MT 21	Freezing	21.5	85
	Melting	20.5	87
MT 23	Freezing	21.5	76
	Melting	22.0	83

Table 8. Thermal properties of materials

3.3 System simulations

The use of the mixtures was evaluated through computer simulations. The section and plan of the building used in the simulations are shown in Figure 19, and a schematic diagram of the system is shown in Figure 20. An air conditioning system for an office building was assumed. The calculated area was part of one floor of an office building with a floor area of 73.8 m^2 that was assumed to be located in Nagoya City, Japan. The room had windows of 6.5 m^2 facing south, and the weather data used to calculate the peak load was the data for a summer day. The wall was constructed using lightweight concrete and was insulated with 25-mm-thick foam urethane.

For charging operation, the air runs through the closed circuit of the PCM storage tank and the air conditioner (Figure 20, (1)). After the end of the charging cycle, the ordinary air conditioning operation was started. The conditioned air is projected into the room and returned to the air conditioner after mixing with a volume of outdoor air. In this operation, the air is assumed to bypass the PCM storage tank (Figure 20, (2)). For the discharging operation, the air passes into the room through the PCM storage tank. In the charging and discharging operations, the airflow rate is reduced to half that of the ordinary air conditioning in order to store and recover heat effectively (Figure 20, (3)). The discharging period started at 13:00 and ended at 16:00. In Japan, utility companies offer special discount rates for peak shaving during this period.

Calculation was conducted using the enthalpy method, which assumed the heat of fusion of PCM to be a specific heat $c_p(\theta)$ that varied with temperature. The temperature of the PCM was calculated by combining the experimental results shown in Figure 2 with the one-dimensional heat conduction equation:

$$\frac{\partial}{\partial t}\left[\rho c_p(\theta)\theta_p\right] = \frac{\partial}{\partial x}\left(\lambda_p \frac{\partial \theta_p}{\partial x}\right) + \frac{S}{dz_p} \tag{12}$$

where S is heat flux through the PCM capsule wall, which is calculated as follows:

$$S = \frac{1}{1/h + 1/\lambda_c}\left(\theta_a - \theta_p\right) \tag{13}$$

The heat from the PCM to the circulating air was calculated by heat convection on the surface of the PCM containers. The convection coefficient was calculated using the following empirical equation for a flat surface (Incorpera et al. 1996):

$$Nu = 0.037\,\mathrm{Re}^{0.8}\,\mathrm{Pr}^{1/3} \tag{14}$$

The heat transfer between a container of PCM and air in the duct was enhanced by fins extended toward the air. The fins increased the surface 18.2 times as compared to a flat surface. The heat balance among the air entering the room, the heat transfer from outdoor air, and the internal heat gain determined the temperature of room is as follows:

$$c_r \frac{d\theta_r}{dt} = UA\left(\theta_o - \theta_r\right) + V\left(\theta_i - \theta_r\right) \tag{15}$$

Charging was conducted for three hours, from 5:00 to 8:00, followed by ordinary air conditioning from 9:00. Discharging started at 13:00 and ended at 16:00. The charging hours were set to be equal to the discharging hours. The inlet temperature to the PCM storage tank for the charging operation was 12°C, and the inlet temperature to the room (θ_i) during ordinary air conditioning was 16°C. No temperature control was performed during the discharging operation. During the ordinary air conditioning, the air flow rate to the room was controlled in order to maintain the temperature of the room at 26°C. The mixture quantities were 50, 100, 150, 200, 250, 300, 350, and 400 kg.
The room temperature was set to 25°C, as calculated by solving the heat balance for the heat transfer through walls and windows, internal heat, and release of stored cooling from the PCM. The calculation was conducted for two days for each condition. The results shown herein are the results for the second day.

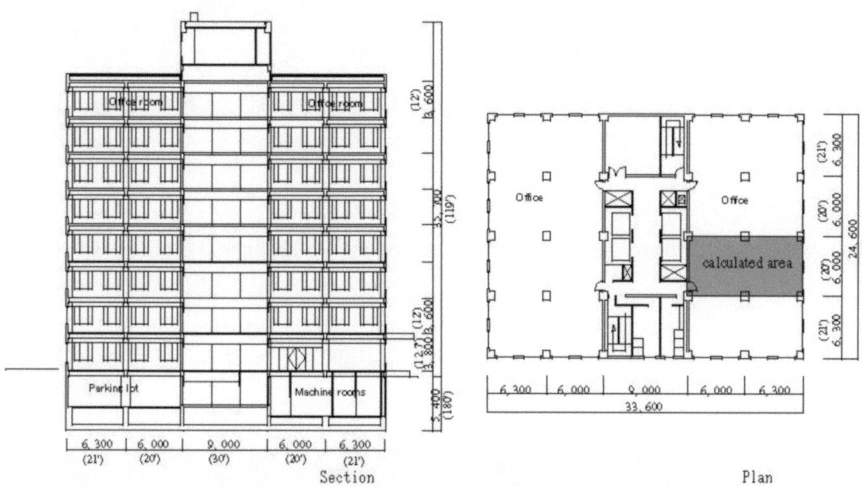

Fig. 19. Section and plan of the building used for simulation

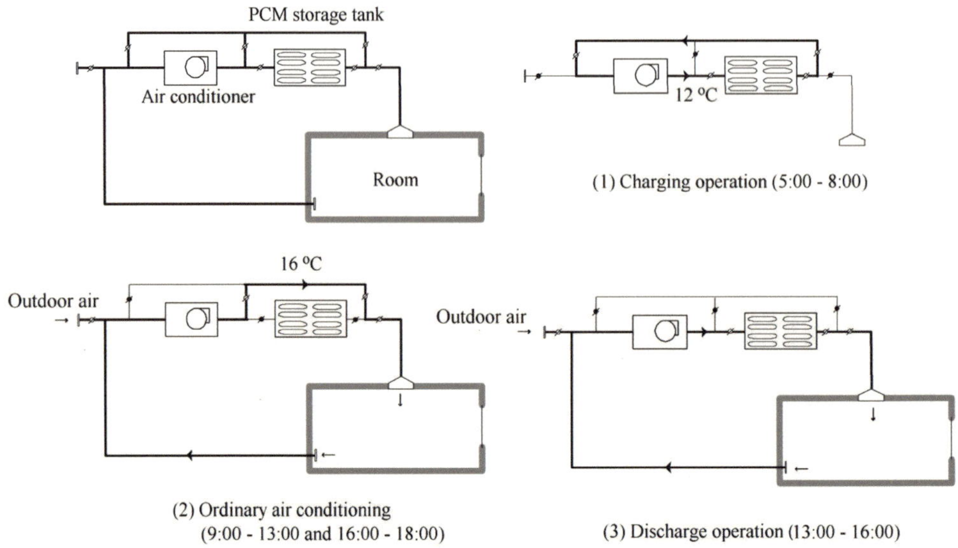

Fig. 20. Schematic diagrams of the HVAC systems used in the simulations

The results are shown in Figure 21 for 100 and 400 kg of PCM. In the left-hand figure, the PCM mixture was cooled to air temperature (12°C) as soon as the charging operation started. During the discharging operation, the stored heat was not large enough to maintain the room temperature. Consequently, the room temperature was raised to 35°C. The right-hand figure shows the results for 400 kg. The temperature during charging and discharging operations decreased gradually due to latent heat. The stored heat had sufficient capacity to maintain the room temperature near the set point.

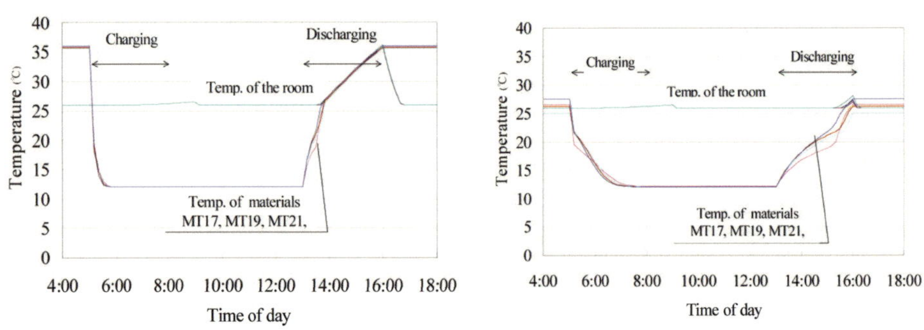

Fig. 21. Comparison of temperature fluctuation using 100 kg or 400 kg of PCM

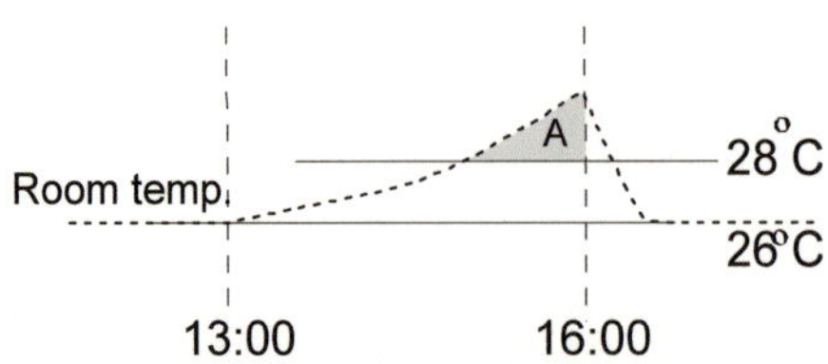

Fig. 22. Index used to evaluate the investigated effect

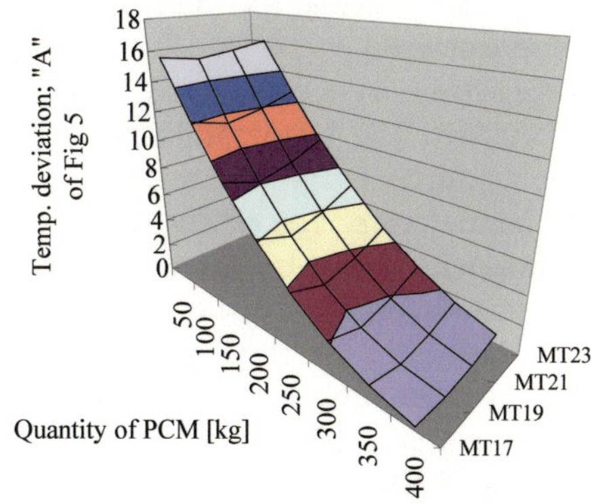

Fig. 23. Relationship among the index, the materials, and the quantities

3.4 Discussion

The purpose of this system was to control the temperature increase while the refrigeration machines were stopped. The evaluation of the system focused on the degree to which the temperature fluctuated. Assuming that 28°C is the allowed indoor temperature, the area A shown in Figure 22, which is the difference between the room temperature and 28°C, was used as an index of temperature deviation. This index increases as the temperature in the room increases.

Figure 23 shows the relationship between the index, the quantity of PCM, and the PCM mixture. The temperature deviation decreased as the quantity of PCM mixture increased. The index or the temperature deviation was very small for 400 kg of PCM, which was equivalent to 5.4 kg/m^2 of PCM. The differences among the various materials were not significant. The index was larger for materials with higher melting temperatures (MT23, MT21). Because of its lower melting temperature, the most effective material was MT19. Moreover, MT 17 melted too quickly.

In the system discussed in the present paper, the PCM would be maintained in containers and installed in air ducts. The heat transfer between the surface of the container and the air in the duct would be a significant problem. Since thermal conductivities of paraffin waxes are small, the material would not be sufficiently melted or frozen, unless some enhancements, such as fins, were adopted. Although, in the present study, fins were adopted, for real applications, the structure of the container should be simple in order to decrease the cost of construction.

In the present study, there was no consideration of the humidity because the program only treated the heat transfer problem. The humidity has a large influence on thermal comfort. The dew point of 26°C and RH 50% air is lower than 17°C, so the humidity of the room would increase during the discharging operation. The humidity should be calculated because the sensible heat load is relatively small in an office building.

4. Conclusions

Thermal energy storage systems are used to shift peak heat load to off-peak hours. The performance depends on the design and installation of such systems. The performances of two types of TES, which use ice and paraffin waxes, were analyzed. Ice storage systems were analyzed as HVAC system components, and a storage system using paraffin waxes was evaluated for use by a passive method.

Ice-on-coil and slurry ice storage system were considered. Several definitions of efficiency as indices of evaluation were discussed. The temperature response of an ice-on-coil storage system depends on the mixing condition. Large Archimedes numbers at the inlet result in a longer duration of low outlet temperature. The effects of the operating conditions on the energy and response-based efficiencies were also examined. The response-based efficiency was more sensible to the normalized inlet enthalpy flow rate. For the slurry ice storage tank, the time at which the outlet temperature reached 4°C varied according to experimental conditions. Since the ice in the slurry ice tank consisted of tiny floating particles, the higher velocity could enhance heat transfer and result in lower outlet temperatures

For storage system using paraffin waxes, an air distribution system with the PCM tank in the air ducts was proposed. The system was used for cooling and could take advantage of discounted electricity rates at night. The materials that could be used in the system, were obtained by mixing paraffin waxes and fatty acids. The thermal properties of the materials were measured. The melting temperature could be controlled by adjusting the concentration of each material, although the latent heat of the measured mixtures was less than that of the pure paraffin wax.

The system performance was examined through a computer simulation, and the necessary quantity of material was evaluated. The PCM was cooled from 5:00 to 8:00 am using discounted electricity. The stored heat was discharged from 13:00 to 16:00, when the peak load of cooling occurred. As the refrigeration machines were stopped during this period, the temperature of the room fluctuated. The temperature deviation was taken as an index, and the system was evaluated. For an ordinary office building in Nagoya City, which is located in the same climate as major cities with more than two million inhabitants in Japan, 400 kg of PCM for 73.8 m^2 of room surface (or 5.4 kg/m^2 of PCM) could maintain the room temperature to be constant without any cold source operation. The melting temperature suitable for the system was approximately 19°C, which could be achieved using MT19.

5. Nomenclature

A : wall surface area
Ar_{in} : Archimedes number at the inlet
c : specific heat
d_{in} : diameter of the inlet of the tank
dz : thickness of PCM
g : gravitational acceleration
h: convective coefficient
H_t : heat removed from a storage tank
H_{tc} : heat removed until the outlet temperature reaches the limit temperature
IPF : (Ice Packing Factor) ratio of ice volume to tank volume (= V_{ice}/V_0)
L : heat of fusion of water
Nu : Nusselt number
Pr : Prandtl number
q : heat flow from coil
Q^*: dimensionless enthalpy flow rate
Q : flow rate of inlet water

Re : Reynolds number
T, t : time
Tc : limit temperature to the coils of the air handling units
u_{in}: velocity of inlet water
u: velocity of water inside the tank
U : average overall heat transfer coefficient
V : airflow rate to the room
V_0 : volume of tank
V_{ice} : volume of ice
x : length in the flow direction,
η : response-based efficiency
η_0 : system efficiency
η_v : volumetric efficiency
θ_0 : initial temperature
θ_{in} : temperature of the inlet water
θ_{out} : temperature of the outlet water
θ_c : limit temperature to the coils of the air handling units
$\Delta\theta_i$: equivalent temperature difference for ice storage (= L • IPF/c)
$\Delta\theta_0$: temperature difference of the coils of the air handling units
ρ: density of inlet water
ρ_0 : density of water at the initial temperature
ρ_{ice} : density of ice
$\Delta\rho$: density difference between the inlet water to the tank and the initial temperature of water in the tank
λ : thermal conductivity
θ_a: temperature of air
θ_p: temperature of PCM
θ_r: temperature of the room
* indicates a dimensionless value

6. References

Barnard, N and Setterwall, F, (2003), Thermal Mass and Night Ventilation - Utilising "hidden" Thermal Mass, *Proceedings of Workshop IEA Annex 17*, Indore. Mar. 2003.

Feldman, D, Shapirom, M M, Banu, D and Fuks, C J, (1989), Fatty Acids and Their Mixtures as Phase-Change Materials for Thermal Energy Storage. *Solar Energy Material,* Vol. 18, Issue 3-4, pp. 201-216. ISSN 0927-0248

Feldman, D, Banu, D, and Hawes, D W, (1995), Development and Application of Organic Phase Change Mixtures in Thermal Storage Gypsum Wallboard, *Solar Energy Materials and Solar Cells,* Vol. 36, Issue 2, pp. 147-157. ISSN 0927-0248

He, B, Gustafsson, M, and Setterwall, F, (1999), Tetradecane and Hexadecane Binary Mixtures as Phase Change Materials (Pcms) for Cool Storage in District Cooling Systems. *Journal of Energy,* Vol. 24, Issue 12, 1015-1028. ISSN: 0360-5442

Incropera, F and DeWitt, D, (1996), *Fundamentals of Heat and Mass Transfer,* John Wiley & Sons., ISBN 0-471-30460-3, New York

Kauranen, P, Peippo, K, and Lund, P D, (1991), An Organic PCM Storage System with Adjustable Melting Temperature. *Solar Energy,* Vol. 46, Issue 5, pp. 275-278. ISSN: 0038-092X

Lin, K, Zhang, Y, and Jiang, Y, (2003), Simulation and Evaluation of the Thermal Performance of PCM Wallboard Rooms Located in Different Climate Regions of China in Summer, *Proceedings of the ASME/JSME Thermal Engineering Joint Conference:* 71, Hawaii, Mar. 2003

Mehling, H, (2002), News on the Application of PCMs for Heating and Cooling of Buildings. *Proceedings of Workshop IEA Annex 17,* Tokyo, Sept. 2002.

Shilei, L, Neng, Z, and Gouhui, F, (2006), Impact of Phase Change Wall Room on Indoor Thermal Environment in Winter. *Energy and Buildings*, Vol. 38: 18-24.

Tamblyn, R T, (1977), Thermal storage: it saves and saves and saves. *ASHRAE Transaction* Vol. 83, Part 1, pp.677-684, ISSN: 0001-2505

Yamaha, M, Shuku, K, and Misaki, S, (2001), A Study on Thermal Characteristics of Thermal Storage Tank Using Phase Change Material Installed in an Air Distribution System, *Transaction of AIJ.* No. 549, pp. 51-57. ISSN 1348-0685.

Heat Transfer and Phase Change in Deep CO_2 Injector for CO_2 Geological Storage

Kyuro Sasaki and Yuichi Sugai
Department of Earth Resource Engineering, Kyushu University
Japan

1. Introduction

CO_2 capture and storage (CCS) is expected to reduce CO_2 emissions into the atmosphere. Various underground reservoirs and layers exist where CO_2 may be stored such as aquifers, depleted oil and gas reservoirs as well as unmined coal seams.

Coal seams are feasible for CCS because coal can adsorb CO_2 gas with roughly twice volume compared with CH_4 gas originaly stored (Yee et al., 1993). However, the coal matrix is swelling with adsorption CO_2 and its permeability is reduced. Supercritical CO_2 has a higher injection rate of CO_2 into coal seams than liquid CO_2 because its viscosity is 40% lower than the liquid CO_2 (see Harpalani and Chen, 1993).

The Japanese consortium carried out the test project on Enhanced Coal Bed Methane Recovery by CO_2 injection (CO_2-ECBMR) at Yubari City, Hokkaido, Japan during 2004 to 2007 [Yamaguchi et al. (2007), Fujioka et al.(2010)]. The target coal seam at Yubari was located about 890 to 900 m below the surface (Yasunami et al., 2010). However, liquid CO_2 was injected from the bottom holes because of heat loss along the deep injection tubing. The absolute pressure and temperature at the bottom hole was approximately 15.5MPa and 28°C. The regular tubing was replaced with thermally insulated tubing that included an argon gas layer but the temperature at the bottom was still lower than the critical temperature of CO_2.

This chapter provides a numerical model of heat transfer and calculation procedure for the prediction of CO_2 temperature and pressure that includes a phase change (supercritical or liquid) by considering the heat loss from the injector to surrounding casing pipes and rock formation. Furthermore, this study provides numerical simulation results of the temperature distribution of the coal seam after the injection of CO_2.

2. Prediction model for CO_2 injection temperature

2.1 CO_2 flow rate injected into a reservoir

As shown in Fig. 1, a schematic radial flow model in a reservoir, such as coal seam or aquifer, is targeted for CO_2 injection with a vertical injection well (injector). The reservoir with radius R and thickness h_R, is saturated with water and open with constant pressure at its outer boundary. Assume omitting well pressure loss, the initial CO_2 mass flow rate , $M(0)$, at time t = 0, that is injected into the reservoir from its bottom hole, is equal to radial water flow rate in the reservoir [Michael et al. (2008) and Sasaki & Akibayashi (1999)],

$$M(0)=\rho_{BH}\frac{P_{BH}(0)-P_R}{\frac{\mu_w}{2\pi K_w h_R}\cdot\ln\left(\frac{R}{r_w}\right)} \quad ; \quad P_{BH}(0)=P_{WH}(0)+g\int_0^H \rho(x,0)\,dx \tag{1}$$

where $\rho(x,t)$ and $\rho_{BH}=\rho(H,t)$ are CO_2 density in the injector and bottom hole respectively, g is acceleration of gravity, r_w is outer radius of the bottom hole, K_w is reservoir permeability, P_{WH}, P_{BH} and P_R are pressures at well head, bottom hole and outer boundary, μ_w is water viscosity in the reservoir, and H is length of vertical injector. The reservoir's initial pressure is also equal to P_R.

After starting CO_2 injection, the CO_2 mass flow rate $M(t)$ and bottom hole pressure $P_{BH}(t)$ are changing with elapsed time t, since bottom hole pressure depends on CO_2 density distribution through the injector and water is replaced with CO_2. Therefore, flow rate after becoming steady-state Q is given with P_{BH} and CO_2 viscosity μ_f at $t=\infty$.

$$M(\infty)=\rho_{BH}(\infty)\frac{P_{BH}(\infty)-P_R}{\frac{\mu_f}{2\pi K_w h_R}\cdot\ln\left(\frac{R}{r_w}\right)} \quad ; \quad P_{BH}(\infty)=P_{WH}(\infty)+g\int_0^H \rho(x,\infty)\,dx \tag{2}$$

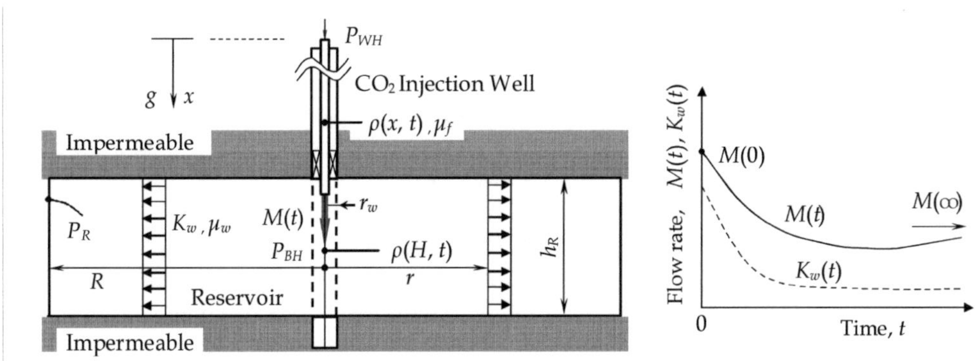

Fig. 1. Schematic radial flow model for injected CO_2 into a reservoir filled with water

Generally, CO_2 viscosity (30°C, 15MPa) is much smaller than water (roughly 1/30), thus the flow rate increases with t. Furthermore, viscosity of supercritical CO_2 is smaller than liquid CO_2. On the other hand, the flow rate Q strongly depends on reservoir permeability times height ($=K_w h_R$). Especially coal seams have relatively low permeability of order 10^{-15} m^2. It has been reported by some projects that permeability of coal seams decreased with rough ratio of 1/10 to 1/100 after CO_2 injection due to swelling of coal matrix by CO_2 adsorption [Clarkson et al. (2008) and Sasaki et al. (2009)].

2.2 Unsteady heat conduction equation

Figure 2 shows schematic diagram of radial heat loss from a vertical injection well (injector) that is consisting tubing pipe, casing pipes and well annulus. CO_2 is flowed down through the tubing pipe, and injected from bottom of the well with perforated holes. The annulus between two coaxial pipes is not used for CO_2 injection, and possibly needed to prevent heat loss from the tubing.

In present analytical approaches, inside area of the casing pipe is assumed as quasi-steady and outer region of the casing pipe ($r \geq r_{cao}$) is analyzed by unsteady equation of heat conduction. For the outer cement and rock region at a level, Fourier's second law in cylindrical coordinates (r, x) is expressed as;

$$\frac{\partial \theta}{\partial t} = a_r \left(\frac{\partial^2 \theta}{\partial r^2} + \frac{1}{r}\frac{\partial \theta}{\partial r} + \frac{\partial^2 \theta}{\partial x^2} \right) \cong a_r \left(\frac{\partial^2 \theta}{\partial r^2} + \frac{1}{r}\frac{\partial \theta}{\partial r} \right) \quad (3)$$

where θ (°C) is rock temperature, t(s) is elapsed time, r(m) is radius, a_r(m²/s) is the heat diffusivity of rock. Heat conduction in vertical direction, x, can be omitted by comparing with that of radial direction. Analytical solution has been presented by Starfield & Bleloch (1983) for unsteady-state rock temperature distribution around underground airways. Especially, they presented a method to simulate internal surface temperature using with Biot number and elapsed time factor function of Fourier number (see section 2.7).

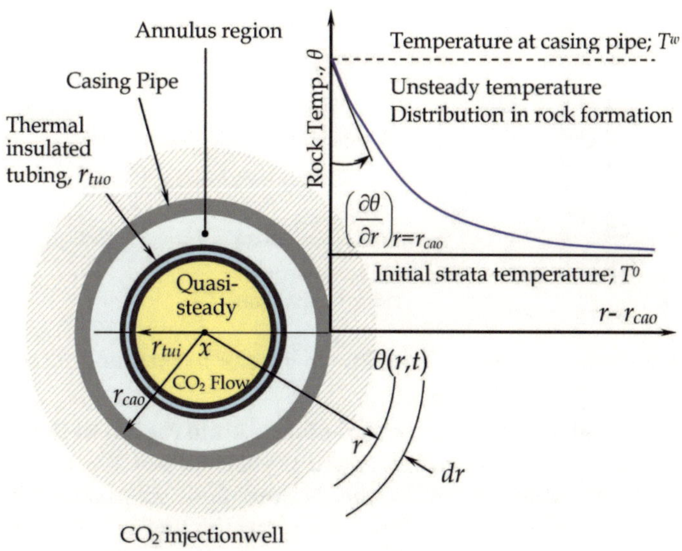

Fig. 2. Schematic diagram of radial heat flow from a vertical injection well (cross section)

2.3 Four thermal phenomena considered along CO2 injection well

Figure 3 shows a schematic of heat transfer phenomena at an injection well. Four thermal phenomena were considered for the construction of the numerical model that is used for predicting CO_2 temperature and pressure at the bottom hole.

1. Natural convection in the annulus, filled with N_2 or water, increases heat transfer from tubing to casing, cement and rock formation. The heat transfer coefficient or Nusselt number at a specific depth is determined by using a formula reported by. Choukairy et al. (2004).
2. The thermal performance of insulated tubing containing an argon shield layer was evaluated by considering the vertical convection flow of argon, thermal radiation between inner surfaces of the argon layer and thermal conduction at the tubing joints. Thermal characteristics of the insulated tubing are able to be corrected against the

original heat conductivity of argon gas using a number n determined by a field test and also by well logging data (see section 2.5).
3. The CO_2 phase was determined by its specific enthalpy which can be calculated from the pressure, temperature and heat loss along the well.
4. An unsteady analytical solution of the outer-surface temperature of casing pipe, expressed with Eq.(1), can be applied against the elapsed time from the start of CO_2 injection.

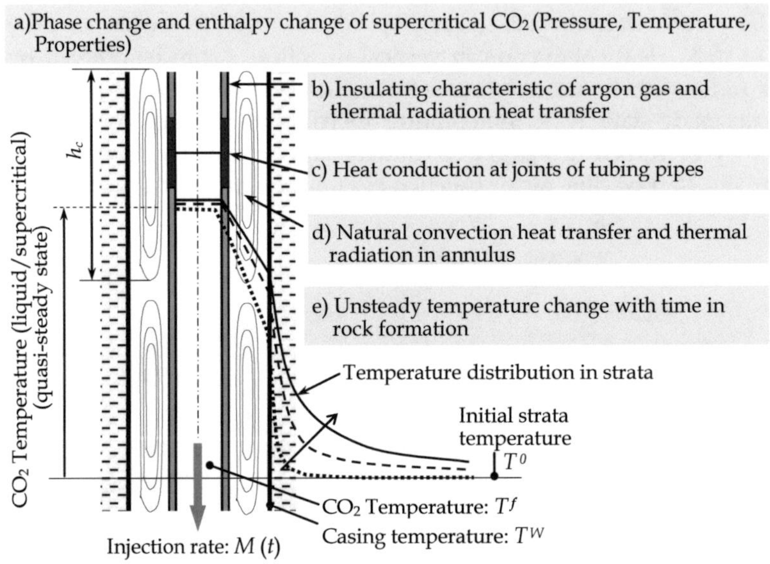

Fig. 3. Heat transfer phenomena from fluid flow in injector to surrounding rock formation

2.4 Overall thermal conductivity of the quasi-steady state region of the injection well

Figure 4 shows an example of the well structure (Yubari CO_2-ECBMR pilot-test site). CO_2 heat loss occurs during flow down to the bottom and propagates through various cylindrical combinations of steels and fluids with various thermal properties in the well configuration. To evaluate heat loss the overall heat conductivity that consists of conductivities of well materials and convective heat transfer rates of fluid flows that are contained in the well are important. Equations (4) and (5) represent single tubing and thermally insulated tubing, respectively (Nag, 2006).

$$\lambda = \frac{1}{\dfrac{\ln\frac{r_{cao}}{r_{cai}}}{\lambda_{Steal}} + \dfrac{\ln\frac{r_{cai}}{r_{tuo}}}{Nu\cdot\lambda_f} + \dfrac{\ln\frac{r_{tuo}}{r_{tui}}}{\lambda_{Steal}} + \dfrac{1}{r_{tui}\alpha_i}} \tag{4}$$

$$\lambda = \frac{1}{\dfrac{\ln\frac{r_{cao}}{r_{cai}}}{\lambda_{Steal}} + \dfrac{\ln\frac{r_{cai}}{r_{thco}}}{N_u\cdot\lambda_f} + \dfrac{\ln\frac{r_{thco}}{r_{thci}}}{\lambda_{Steal}} + \dfrac{\ln\frac{r_{thci}}{r_{tho}}}{n\cdot\lambda_{Ar}} + \dfrac{\ln\frac{r_{tho}}{r_{thi}}}{\lambda_{Steal}} + \dfrac{1}{r_{thi}\alpha_{thi}}} \tag{5}$$

where a_{thi} is the heat transfer coefficient at the inner wall of the tubing pipe, λ_f is the heat conductivity of the fluid (water) in the annulus, λ_{Steal} is the heat conductivity of the casing and tubing pipes, N_u is the Nusselt number for the annulus and n is a correction number to adjust the heat conductivity of the argon gas layer in the insulated tubing.

2.5 Evaluation of performance of thermal insulated tubing

Thermal insulated tubing pipe is sometime used for geo-thermal wells through cold formation in order to prevent heat loss from produced hot spring water/steam. In case of the Yubari injected CO_2-ECBMR test, connected thermal insulated tubing pipes 20 m in length were used partially in 2005-2006 and totally in 2007. The insulated tubing includes argon gas shield layer is enclosed between inner and outer pipes to prevent heat loss from inside ideally with low thermal conductivity of argon gas; 0.116 W/m°C. However, joints between pipes are not shielded, and natural gas convection flow in the shield is expected to make increase the heat loss trasfered from the flow to outer tubing.

Fig. 4. Test to evaluate of equivalent thermal conductivity in the thermal insulated tubing using by pulsed heating carried at Yubari CO_2-ECBMR test field (Oct. 10, 2006) (see Yasunami et al., 2010)

To evaluate the thermal performance of the insulated tubing, tests using a insulated tubing pipe were carried out by pulsed heating from inside and measurements of outer and inner surface temperatures of the pipe placed horizontally as shown Fig. 4. Furthermore, the equivalent thermal conductivity was analyzed with Choukairy et al.'s equation (see section 2.5) and the history matching study for the well logging data. The thermal conductivity correction factor for conductivity of argon gas, n, is evaluated as shown in Fig. 5.

The equivalent heat conductivity including inside convective heat transfer was evaluated as three times larger as that of original argon gas without longitudinal heat loss through to connected tubing pipes. The correction factor, n, was introduced to adjust the equivalent heat conductivity of the tubing based on the original heat conductivity of argon gas. It was determined to be n = 3 but heat loss through the joints that are between the insulated tubing was not included in the test. The thermal equivalent conductivity of the insulated tubing was determined to be n = 4 or λ = 0.21W/m°C based on the well logging temperature at the Yubari CO_2-ECBMR test site and the measurement data were obtained from the heater response test carried out in the test field.

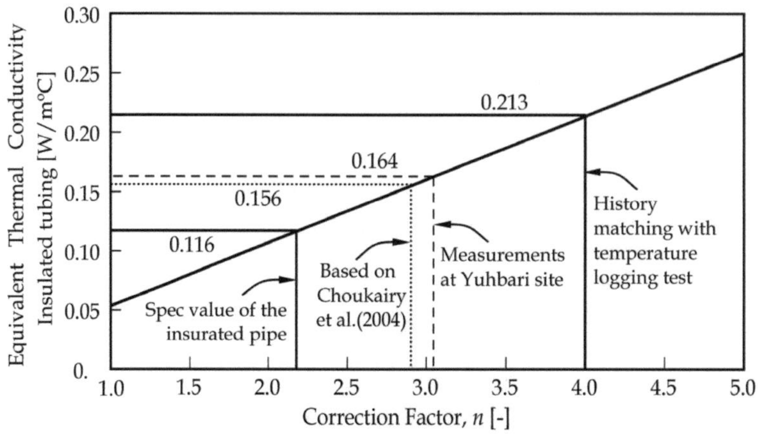

Fig. 5. Thermal conductivity correction factor for shielding with argon gas (*; spec value provided by a steel pipe maker)

2.6 Convective heat transfer in the annulus

Natural convection of annulus fluids makes influences on the heat transfer rate from the tubing pipe to the surrounding casing pipe and the formation. Choukairy et al. (2004) presented the following formula for the Nusselt number, N_u, for natural convection flow in an annulus with various radius ratios:

$$N_u = \frac{\alpha_f L}{\lambda_f} = \frac{\kappa}{mA}(P_r R_a)^{1/4} \cdot T_m^{5/4} \tag{6}$$

where α_f denotes the natural convection heat transfer coefficient on the inner surface of the casing, L ($=r_{cai}$ - r_{tuo}) is the width of the annulus, κ is the radius ratio, m is a constant defined by Choukairy et al., A is the aspect ratio, P_r is the Prandtl number, R_a is the Rayleigh number and T_m is a dimensionless temperature defined by following equations:

$$A = \frac{h}{L} \tag{7}$$

$$\kappa = \frac{r_{cai}}{r_{tuo}} \tag{8}$$

$$R_a = \frac{g\beta_T (T^f - T^w) \cdot h_c^3}{\alpha_f \cdot \upsilon_f} \tag{9}$$

$$T_m = \frac{1}{1 - \kappa^{4/5}} \tag{10}$$

where h_c is the circulation height of natural convection flow, g is the acceleration of gravity, β_T is the coefficient of thermal expansion of the fluid, υ_f is the dynamic viscosity and α_f is heat diffusivity of fluid in the annulus. The Nusselt number, N_u, calculated by Eq.(4) was used for each elevation.

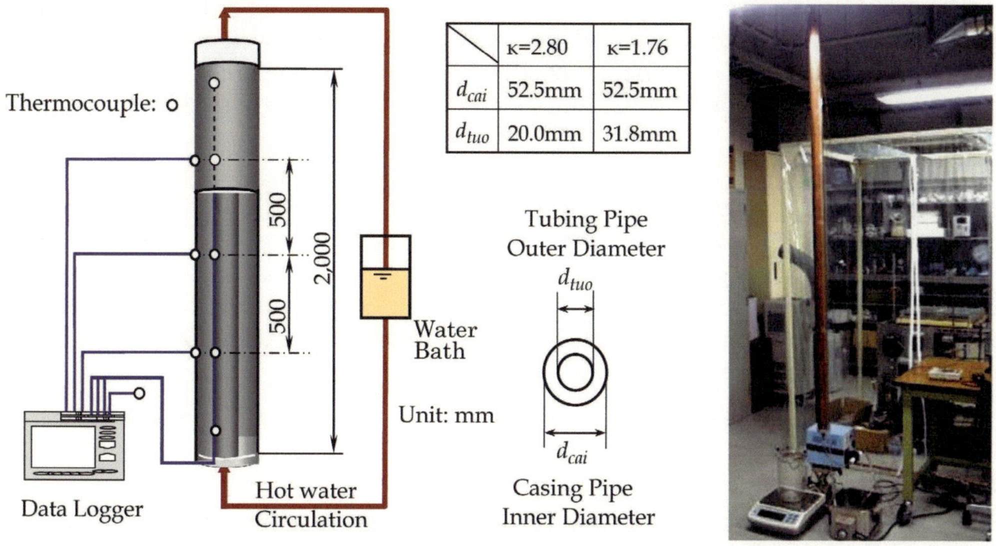

Fig. 6. Experimental setup to verify natural convection heat transfer coefficient in the annulus (Yasunami et al., 2010)

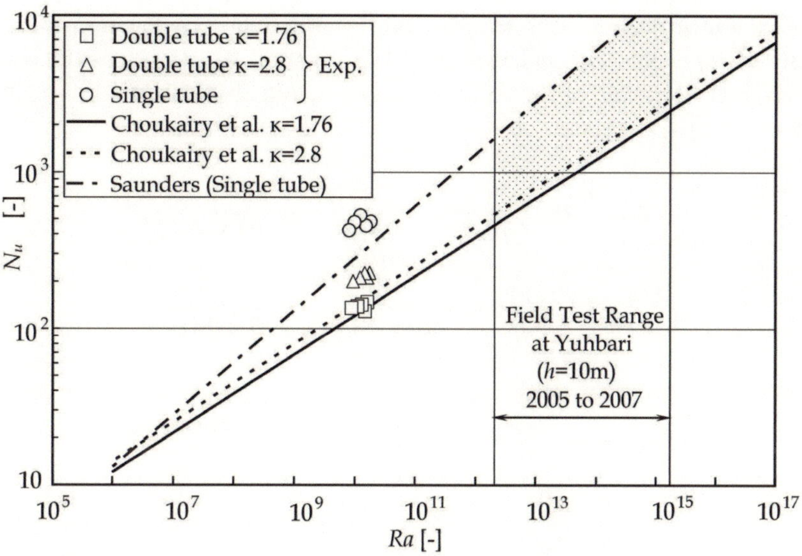

Fig. 7. Experimental results of Nusselt number for convective heat transfer in annulus (Yasunami et al., 2010)

Laboratory experiments were carried out to verify the reliability of Choukairy's equation and to investigate the heat transfer rate using the well models consisting of two copper pipes with different diameters as shown in Fig. 6. Hot water at 40 to 60 °C was circulated through the inner pipe instead of CO_2. Pipe temperatures were measured by T-thermocouples that were placed on the pipe surfaces. Figure 7 shows experimental results obtained for N_u and compared with those from Choukairy's equation. In addition, measured values of N_u on the outer surface of the single tubing determined using the equation proposed by Saunders [after Rohsenow et al. (1998)] were also compared in Fig. 7. Based on these results, we have found that Choukairy's equation is able to evaluate the heat transfer rate in the annulus.

2.7 Unsteady casing temperature

On the other hand, the temperature of the formation outside the casing pipe (outer surface) increases gradually after the injection. Assume T^0 is the initial strata formation temperature and T^{an} is the temperature in the annulus, the temperature at outer surface of the casing T^w, can be given by the solution for the unsteady heat conduction equation; Eq. (3). It has been presented by Starfield and Bleloch (1983):

$$T^w = T^{an} + \frac{\eta_t}{\eta_t + B_i}(T^0 - T^{an}) \tag{11}$$

where η_t is defined as the elapsed time factor and B_i is the non-dimensional Biot number, and B_i is defined by following equation:

$$B_i = \frac{\alpha_{ca} \cdot r_{cao}}{\lambda_r} \tag{12}$$

where α_{ca} is the apparent heat transfer rate at the inner casing and λ_r is the heat conductivity of rock. Starfield and Bleloch (1983) reported equations for the elapsed time factor η_t, which is a function of the Fourier number, τ, and Sasaki & Dindiwe (2002) revised it for $\tau \leq 1.5$ as:

$$\tau \leq 1.5 \quad \eta_t = \frac{1}{[0.9879 + 0.3281(\ln\tau) + 0.03064(\ln\tau)^2} \tag{13}$$

$$1.5 \leq \tau \leq 10 \quad \eta_t = \frac{1}{[0.979813 + 0.383760(\ln\tau)} \tag{14}$$

$$10 \leq \tau \leq 100 \quad \eta_t = \frac{1}{[0.839337 + 0.444718(\ln\tau)} \tag{15}$$

$$1000 \leq \tau \quad \eta_t = \frac{2\Lambda(1 - \Lambda - \Lambda^2 - \Lambda^3)}{0.57722} \tag{16}$$

$$\Lambda = \frac{0.57722}{[\ln(4\tau) - 1.15444)} \tag{17}$$

$$\tau = \frac{\alpha_r t}{r_{cao}^2} \tag{18}$$

The elapsed time factor η_t vs. Fourier number τ calculated by equations (13) to (18), is presented in Fig. 8.

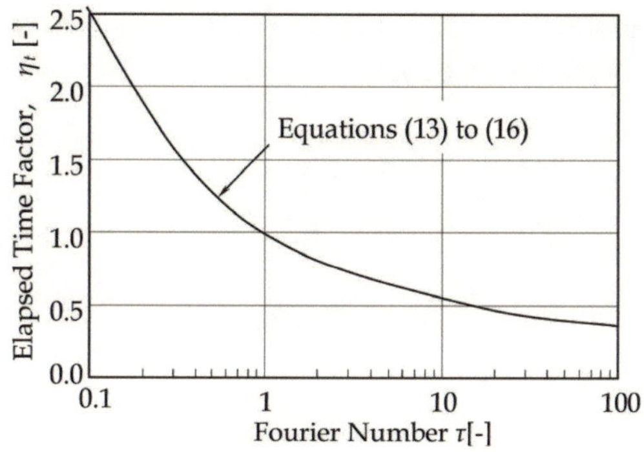

Fig. 8. Elapsed time factor vs. Fourier number

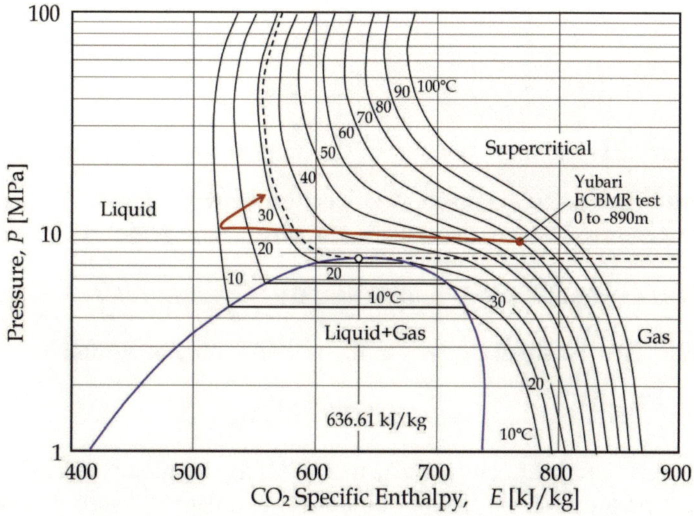

Fig. 9. CO_2 pressure-specific enthalpy and phase diagram calculated with PROPATH(2008) for 10 to 100 °C and 1 to 100 MPa (○; Critical point; 31.1°C and 7.38MPa)

2.8 Numerical equations for the determination of the CO_2 specific enthalpy

Changes in CO_2 temperature and phase (gas, liquid and supercritical) are accompanied by a specific enthalpy change. CO_2 specific enthalpy, $E(P,T)$ may be expressed by:

$$E(P,T) = \int_{T_0}^{T} C_p dT^f + \int_{P_0}^{P} V(1 - T_i\beta)dP \tag{19}$$

where V is the specific volume, β is the coefficient of thermal expansion, T_0 and P_0 are triple point temperature (=-56.57°C) and pressure (=0.5185MPa). The diagram CO_2 pressure-specific enthalpy for temperature range 10 to 100 °C and pressure range 1 to 100 MPa, that is calculated by PROPATH(2008), is shown in Fig. 9.

The specific enthalpy of CO_2 decreases with depth x by heat loss from CO_2 flow to the formation around the injection well.

$$\Delta q = 2\pi\lambda(T^w - T^f)\Delta x \tag{20}$$

where T_f is the CO_2 temperature in the tubing, Δx is the length of the element and T_w is the temperature at the outer surface of the casing.

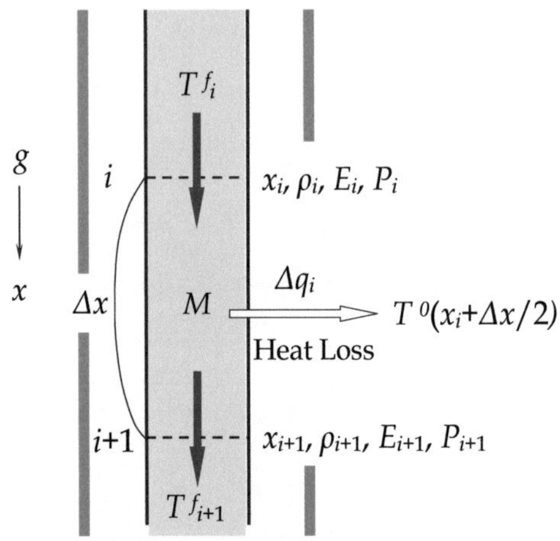

Fig. 10. The numerical calculation model for CO_2 temperature and pressure in the injector

CO_2 temperature Tf_i was calculated using the function shown in Fig. 10. The function used to calculate the temperature Tf_i from the specific enthalpy E_i and pressure P_i is defined as:

$$T_i^f = \theta(E_i, P_i) \tag{21}$$

The heat flow rate, Δq_i, of a small element in the well, Δx_i, may be written as:

$$\Delta q_i = 2\pi\lambda_i (T_i^f - T_i^w)\Delta x_i \tag{22}$$

where λ_i is the equivalent heat conductivity at x_i, T_i^f is the temperature of CO_2 in the tubing and T_i^w is the temperature of the casing outer surface at each element denoted i . The heat generation by flow friction with internal surface of the tubing can be omitted due to very small pipe friction factor and low fluid viscosity for CO_2 flow.
The specific enthalpy of CO_2, E_{i+1} at $x_{i+1}=x_i+\Delta x_i$ is obtained from:

$$E_{i+1} = E_i + \frac{\Delta W - \Delta q_i}{M} \tag{23}$$

where M is the mass flow rate of CO_2 and ΔW is heat generated by a heater during x_i to x_{i+1}. Using the function $\rho(P_i, T_i)$, calculation of the CO_2 density from P_i and T_i and the CO_2 pressure at x_{i+1}, P_{i+1} is given by;

$$P_{i+1} = P_i + \rho(P_i, T_i)\left(g - f\frac{v^2}{4r_{tui}}\right)\Delta x_i \tag{24}$$

where f and v are friction factor and average velocity of tubing pipe. Then the temperature of CO_2 at x_{i+1} can be obtained from:

$$T_{i+1}^f = \theta(E_{i+1}, P_{i+1}) \tag{25}$$

In these numerical simulations, $E(P,T)$, $\theta(P,T)$ and $\rho(P,T)$ and other fluids properties are calculated using a corresponding software subroutines, such as PROPATH(Propath Group, 2008) and NIST (2007). Calculation step Δx_i = 1.0m can be used to get enough accuracy (Yasunami et al., 2010).

2.9 Required values in the numerical calculations

For these numerical calculations, three values for each depth are required.

1. Heat diffusivity of formation.
   In Yubari ECBMR test project introduced in this book, no rock core drilling was carried out from o m to -800 m, thus we had to estimate rock properties (Fujioka et al., 2010). The heat conductivity λ_r and the heat diffusivity a_f of the rock formation outer casing have not been measured previously, so values of a_r=1.30×10^{-6} m^2/s and λ_r=1.30 W/mK were assumed and this was based on standard heat properties of sedimentary rocks (Yasunami et al., 2010).
2. Circulation height of natural convection flow in the annulus.
   It was difficult to measure the circulation height h of natural convection in the annulus at the Yubari site. However, the bottom hole temperature was not sensitive to h, even when h changed from 5 to 20 m. Thus h =10m was assumed as an appropriate value since natural convection was not observed at lower than 2m in the experiments described in the previous section.
3. Heat capacity of the tubing or casing.
   We assumed that temperature changes of tubing and casing pipes were quasi-steady and thus the heat capacity of these pipes was not included in the equations.

3. Results of Yubari ECBMR test project

3.1 Injection well formation

Figure 11 shows a well structure and formation used at the Yubari CO_2-ECBMR test project in 2005. CO_2 heat loss occurs during flow down to the bottom and propagates through various cylindrical combinations of steels and fluids with various thermal properties in the well configuration. Table 1 shows conditions used for the models from 2005 to 2007 carried out in the project denoted as;

a. Model 2005:
   The well was drilled in 2005 (hereafter denoted as Model 2005) and consisted of thermally insulated tubing 180 m in length from the well head.
b. Model 2006:
   In 2006, thermally insulated tubing of 180m in length was used at the head (0 to 180m) and the bottom (650 to 890m) while the annulus was filled with liquid CO_2.
c. Model 2007:
   In 2007 all the injection pipe tubing was replaced with thermally insulated tubing of 890 m in length and H_2O was used to fill the annulus. This was done to minimize heat loss from the tubing and thus keep CO_2 in its supercritical condition.
d. Heater Model 2007:
   To overcome the difficulty of low temperature and low injection rate, numerical predictions were done considering the use of an electric line heater to heat up CO_2 flow at the position of 180m from the surface. The heater capacity of W = 1.43kW was chosen because of the cable strength and restrictions of materials against corrosion of supercritical CO_2.

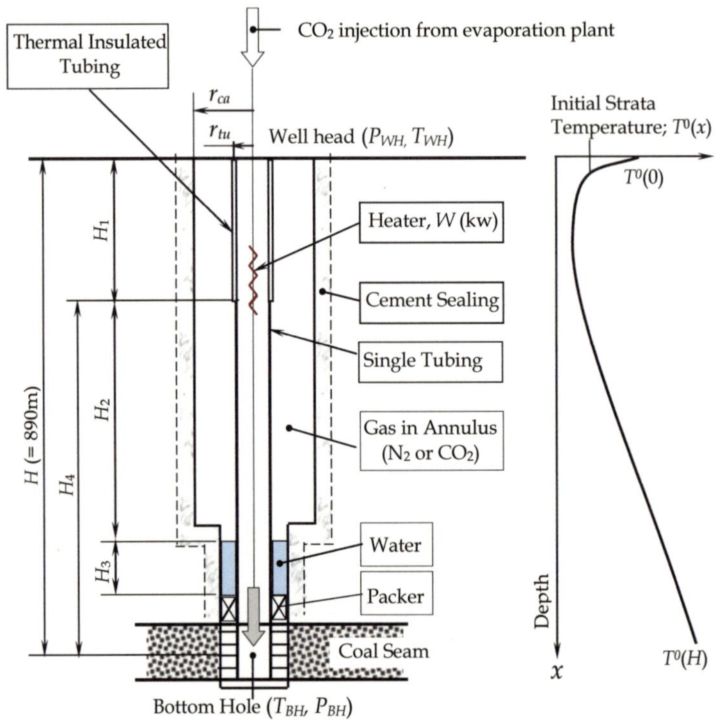

Fig. 11. An example of CO_2 injection well formation, initial strata temperature and schematic annulus formation (Yubari CO_2-ECBMR test project, Model 2005)

Term/Model		Model 2005	Model 2006	Model 2007	Model 2007+ Heater
Temp. and Press. At well head (T_{WH}, P_{WH})		70 °C 9.0 MPa	70 °C 9.0 MPa	70 °C 8.6 MPa	70 °C 8.6 MPa
S. Enthalpy at well head; E_{WH}(kJ/kg)		766.34	766.34	771.27	771.27
Injection rate M(kg/day)		3000	3000	3000	11000
Tubing	H_1; x=0~180m	Insulated tube	Insulated tube	Insulated tube	Insulated Tube
	H_2; x=180~667m	Single tube	Single tube	Insulated tube	Insulated Tube
	H_3; x=690~890m	Single tube	Insulated tube	Insulated tube	Insulated Tube
Fluid in annulus	for H_1	N_2 Gas	Liquid CO_2	Water	Water
	for H_2	N_2 Gas	Liquid CO_2	Water	Water
	for H_3	Water	Water	Water	Water
Heater output; W(kW) (x=0~255m)		0	0	0	1,430

Table 1. Parameters of injection well formation for CO_2 injection

3.2 Effect of natural convection in the annulus

The results of temperature prediction against depth after one day by the heat conduction model (N_u=1 and n=1) and the heat convection model for an injection temperature of 70°C, an injection pressure of 9MPa and an injection rate of 3.0ton/day is shown in Fig. 12.

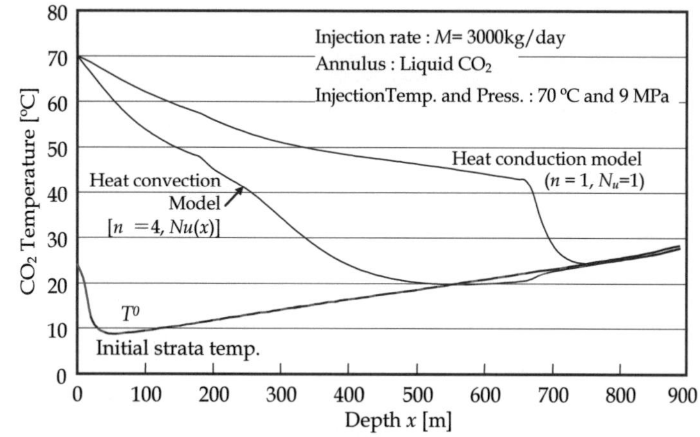

Fig. 12. A comparison of CO_2 temperatures after 1 day between heat conduction and heat convection models (Model 2005, 180m insulated tubing was partly used from well head)

Figure 13 shows comparisons of CO_2 temperature and pressure at the bottom hole. Numerical simulation results for the data, obtained in 2005 at the Yubari field, show that the heat convection model is better than the conduction model. This is because the temperature of the CO_2 decreased by heat loss caused by natural convection in the annulus. The bottom pressure increased because of the increase in CO_2 density that resulted from the CO_2 supercritical to liquid phase change.

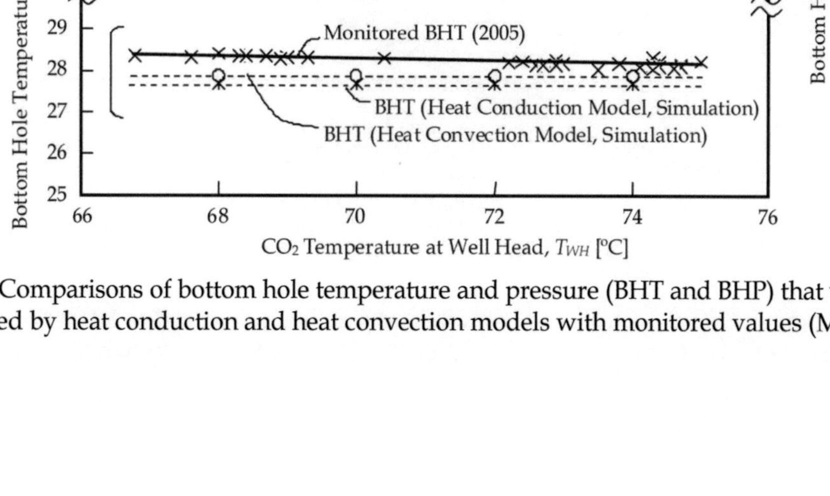

Fig. 13. Comparisons of bottom hole temperature and pressure (BHT and BHP) that were simulated by heat conduction and heat convection models with monitored values (Model 2005)

Figures 14 and 15 show comparisons of CO_2 temperature and pressure between simulations and the well logging data for injection conditions of 68.54°C, 9MPa and 4.5ton/day at the well head. Since logging from the surface to a level of -890m took 2.4hours (Prensky,1992), simulated CO_2 temperatures against depth were plotted for each time segment. The reason for the rise in the measured pressure near the well head of about of 0.3 MPa is unknown at present.

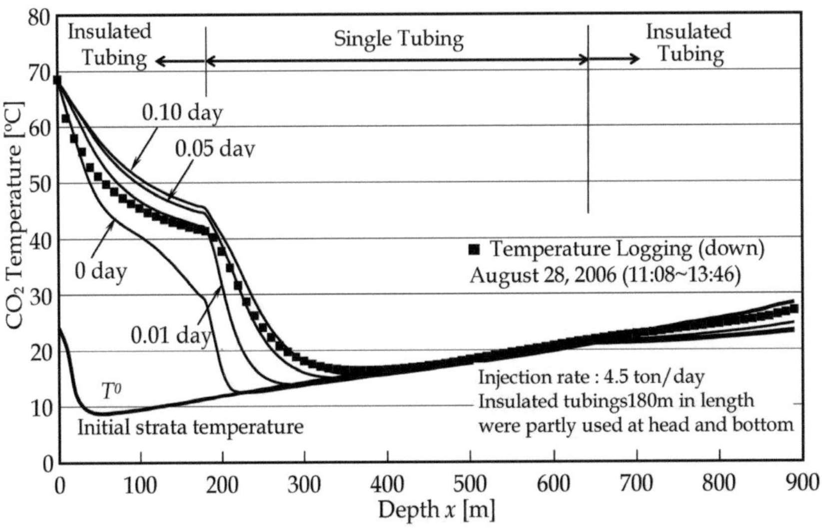

Fig. 14. Comparison between logged temperature and simulation results for Model 2006 (Logging data was obtained on August 28, 2006 (11:08 to 13:46) at the Yubari ECBMR test site)

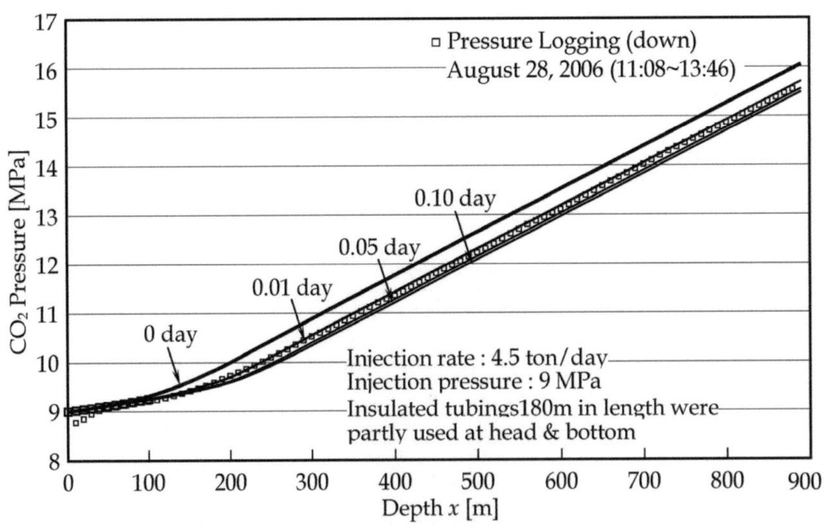

Fig. 15. Comparison between logged pressure and simulation results (Model 2006) (Logging data was obtained on August 28,2006 (11:08 to 13:46) at the Yubari test site)

3.3 Thermal insulated tubing partly used at the well head and bottom (Model 2006)

For the case of Model 2006 of Yubari ECBMR test, numerical simulations at 0, 22 and 68 days are shown in Figure 16. Figures 17 and 18 show the Nusselt number, the heat conductivity, the density and the specific enthalpy versus depth after 1 day.

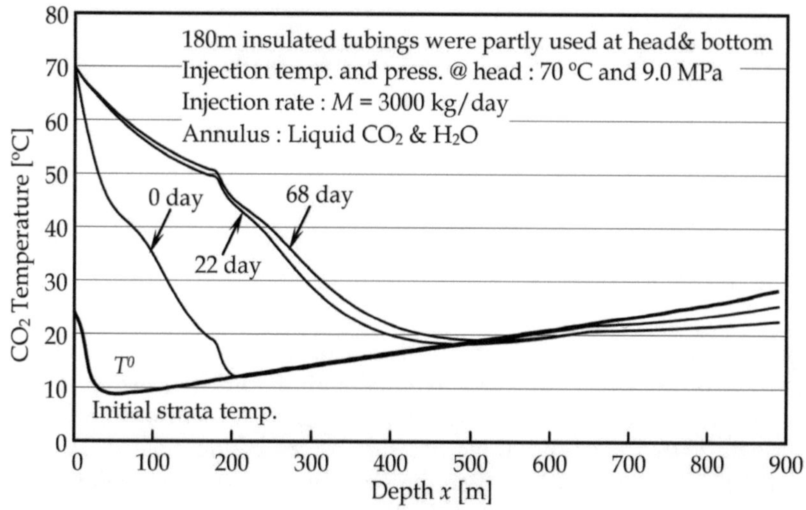

Fig. 16. CO_2 temperature distribution vs. depth (Model 2006)

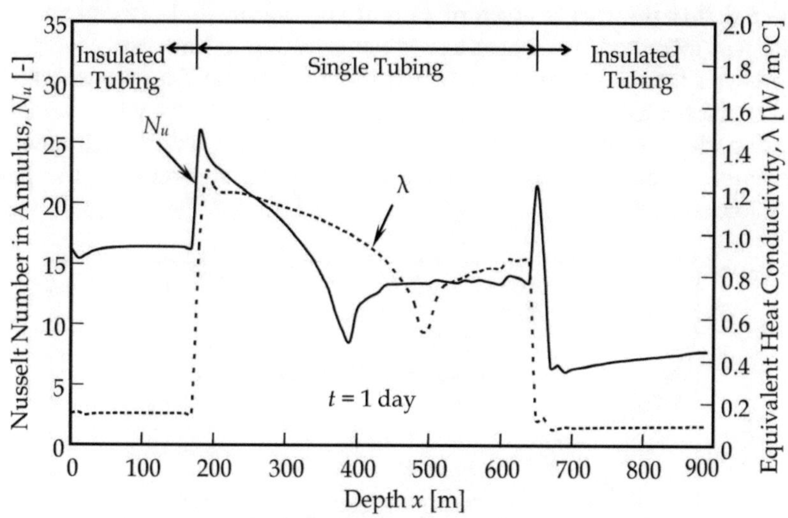

Fig. 17. Nusselt number of convective heat transfer in the annulus vs. depth (Model 2006)

The temperature was still lower than the supercritical temperature (=31.4°C) at the bottom hole because liquid CO_2 filled the annulus and cold CO_2 flow was maintained from 650 to 890m for the insulated tubing despite the formation temperature increasing with depth. The line in Fig. 9 shows s typical phase changes in the injection tubing on the CO_2 pressure-specific enthalpy diagram.

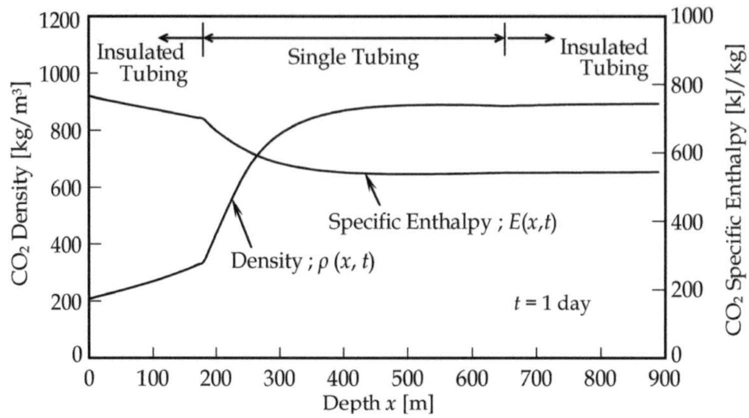

Fig. 18. CO_2 density and specific enthalpy vs. depth (Model 2006)

3.4 All usage of thermal insulated tubing (Model 2007)

In 2007, the all injection tubing pipe was replaced with thermally insulated tubing of 890 m in length and the annulus was filled with water. Figure 13 shows numerical calculation results for Model 2007. The predicted temperature for the bottom hole at an injection rate of 3.0ton/day is 26.0°C, which is lower than the observed temperature at the outer surface of the annulus of 27.5°C. This was influenced by the formation temperature in the annulus.

3.5 The effect of injection rate on the bottom hole temperature

It was expected that the temperature of CO_2 at the bottom hole would increase as the injection rate was increased, since heat loss is not sensitive to flow rate. Figure 19 shows a sensitivity analysis for temperature versus the injection rate at the bottom hole for Model 2007. The CO_2 phase was supercritical at the bottom hole after 1 day when the injection rate was over 12ton/day as shown in this figure. An operation like a hydraulic fracture is required to improve permeability, since the injection rate depends on the permeability around the injection well.

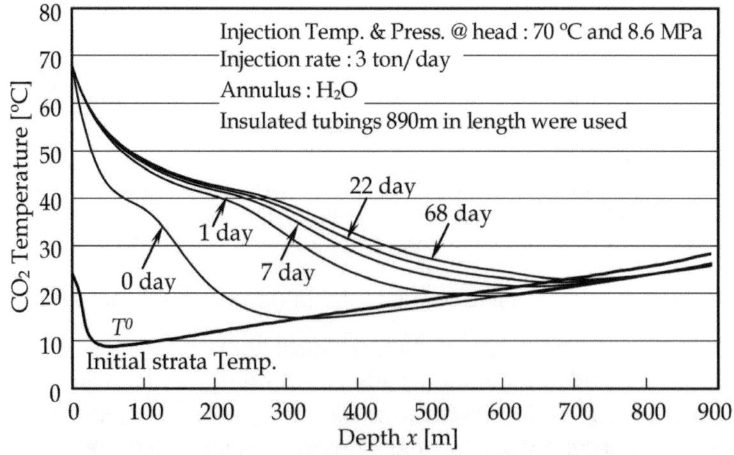

Fig. 19. CO_2 temperature distribution vs. depth for H=H_1 (Model 2007)

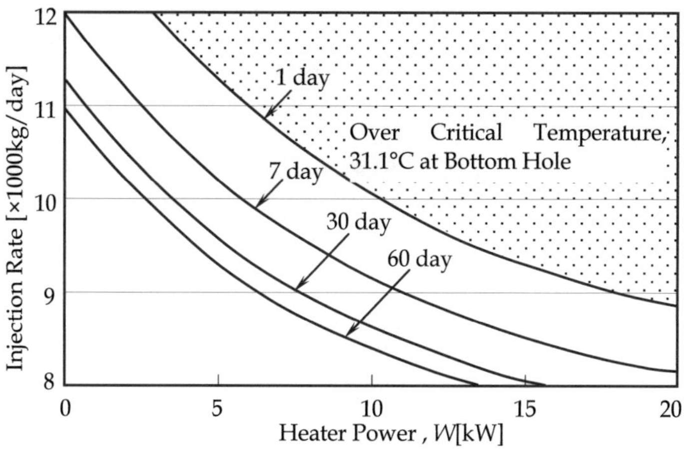

Fig. 20. Control map for maintaining the supercritical condition at the bottom hole (Model 2007+Heater, Injection temperature and pressure at well head; 70 °C and 8.6 MPa, Annulus; H_2O, Insulated tubing 890m in length was used)

3.6 Prediction of CO_2 temperature using a line heater

All tubing was replaced with thermally insulated tubing but the bottom hole temperature was still not adequate to maintain CO_2 in its critical condition. To overcome the difficulty of injection, numerical predictions were done considering the use of an electric line heater with 1.43kW of heating from the surface to 180m (denoted as Heater Model 2007). The heater capacity of 1.43kW was chosen because of the cable strength and because of restrictions of materials for supercritical CO_2. Table 1 shows conditions used in the calculation. The temperature at the bottom hole from Heater Model 2007 is 5°C higher than that from Model 2007. Even if the energy efficiency of CO_2 injection becomes lower by heating in the injector, it is better that CO_2 temperature is in a supercritical condition at the bottom hole to keep larger CO_2 injection rate into the coal seam. Figure 15 shows a control map for the CO_2 injection rate to maintain the supercritical condition at the bottom. This model shows that the critical temperature increases with the heater power and the elapsed time from the start of CO_2 injection.

4. Summary

In this chapter, a numerical model of heat transfer and calculation procedure for flow and heat transfer phenomena, related to CO_2 flow in a vertical deep injector, has been focused in order to predict CO_2 temperature, pressure and phase change (supercritical or liquid CO_2) in the well. Especially, it was considered that the heat loss from the injector to surrounding casing pipes and rock formation including natural convection heat transfer in annulus and insulated tubing pipes. Furthermore, numerical simulations have been presented for the Yubari CO_2-ECBMR test project carried out from 2005 to 2007.

The results are summarized as follows:

1. The bottom hole pressure and temperature in the injector at Yubari CO_2-ECBMR test field were successfully simulated by considering heat loss accelerated by natural convection flow in the annulus.

2. The thermal equivalent conductivity of the insulated tubing was determined to be 0.21W/m°C based on the well logging temperature carried out at the Yubari test site.
3. A control map showing targeted injection rates against the heater power for elapsed time as a parameter was compiled to maintain the supercritical condition at the bottom hole of the injectior.
4. CO_2 at the bottom hole is expected to be supercritical at a CO_2 injection rate over 12 ton/day without any heating or 11 ton/day using the 1.43kW line heater in the injector.

5. Acknowledgment

Authors would like to express their gratitude to Mr. Tetsu Yasunami, who was a graduate student, Kyushu University for his efforts on numerical simulations. We also thank his kind discussion to Mr. Ferian Angara, who is a PhD student, Kyushu University.

6. Nomenclature

a_f = heat diffusivity of fluid [m²/s]
a_r = heat diffusivity of rock [m²/s]
A = aspect ratio [-]
B_i = Biot number [-]
C_p = isobaric specific heat [kJ/(kg°C)]
E = specific enthalpy [kJ/kg]
E_{WH} = specific enthalpy at well head (x=0) [kJ/kg]
f = friction factor of tubing pipe [-]
g = acceleration of gravity [m/s²]
h_c = circulation height of natural convection flow [m]
h_R = reservoir height [m]
K_w = permeability of reservoir [m²]
L = width of annulus [m]
m = constant number defined by Choukairy et al. (2004) [-]
M = CO_2 mass flow rate [kg/s]
n = correction to adjust heat conductivity in thermally insulated tubing [-]
N_u = Nusselt number [-]
P_{BH} = pressure at bottom hole [MPa]
P_r = Prandtl number ($=\upsilon_f/\alpha_f$) [-]
P_R = pressure at reservoir outer boundary [MPa]
P_{WH} = pressure at well head (x=0) [MPa]
Q = CO_2 flow rate [m³/s]
r_{cao} = outer radius of casing [m]
r_{cai} = internal radius of casing [m]
r_{tuo} = outer radius of single tubing [m]
r_{tui} = internal radius of single tubing [m]
r_{thco} = outer radius of outer thermal insulated tubing [m]
r_{thci} = internal radius of outer thermal insulated tubing [m]
r_{tho} = outer radius of inner thermal insulated tubing [m]
r_{thi} = internal radius of inner thermal insulated tubing [m]
R_a = Rayleigh number [-]

T^0 = initial strata temperature [°C]
T^{an} = temperature of fluid in the annulus [°C]
T_{BH} = temperature at bottom hole [°C]
T^f = CO_2 temperature in tubing [°C]
T_m = dimensionless temperature [-]
T^w = temperature at outer surface of casing [°C]
T_{WH} = temperature at well head (x=0) [°C]
v = average velocity of CO_2 flow in tubing pipe [m/s]
V = specific volume [m³/kg]
x = length from surface (depth) [m]
α_f = heat transfer rate at inner surface of casing [W/(m²°C)]
$\alpha_{thi\ i}$ = heat transfer rate at inner surface of tubing [W/(m²°C)]
α_{ca} = equivalent heat transfer rate at inner casing [W/(m²°C)]
β = coefficient of thermal expansion of CO_2 [1/K]
β_T = coefficient of thermal expansion of the fluid [1/K]
η_t = elapsed time factor [-]
κ = radius ratio [-]
λ = overall heat conductivity [W/(m°C)]
λ_{Ar} = heat conductivity of fluid (Ar) in thermal insulated tubing [W/(m°C)]
λ_f = heat conductivity of fluid (N_2, CO_2 or water) in annulus [W/(m°C)]
λ_r = heat conductivity of rock [W/(m°C)]
λ_{Steal} = heat conductivity of casing and tubing [W/(m°C)]
μ_f = CO_2 viscosity [Pas]
μ_w = water viscosity [Pas]
v_f = dynamic viscosity [m²/s]
τ = Fourier number [-]
Δq = heat flow rate at tubing element [W]
ΔW = heat generated by a heater during x_i to x_{i+1} [W]
Δx = length of tubing element [m]

7. References

Clarkson, C.R., Pan, Z., Palmer, I. & Harpalani, S. (2008). Predicting Sorption-Induced Strain and Permeability Increase With Depletion for CBM Reservoirs, *Proceedings of SPE Annual Technical Conference and Exhibition* (August, 2008), SPE114778-MS, DOI 10.2118/114778-MS, Society of Petroleum Engineers

Choukairy, K., Eennacer, R. & Vasseur, P. (2004) , Natural Convection in a Vertical Annulus Boarded By An Inner Wall of Finite Thickness, *International Communications in Heat and Mass Transfer*, Vol. 31, pp.501-512, ISSN 0735-1933

Fujioka, M., Yamaguchi, S. & Nako, M. (2010). CO_2-ECBM field tests in the Ishikari Coal Basin of Japan, *International Journal of Coal Geology*, Volume 82, Issues 3-4, 1 June 2010, pp. 287-298, ISSN 0166-5162

Rohsenow, W., Hartnett, J. & Cho, Y. (1998). *An Introduction to Heat Transfer* (May 1998), McGraw-Hill Professional, ISBN-10 0070535558

Michael, A. M., Khepar, S. D. & Sondhi, S. K. (2008). *Water Wells and Pumps*, Tata McGraw-Hill, ISBN(13) 978-0-07-065706-9, New Delhi

Nag, P.K. (2006). *Heat And Mass Transfer.* Tata McGraw-Hill, ISBN 9780070606531, New Delhi

National Institute Standard Technology (NIST) (2010). *Thermophysical Properties of Fluid Systems*, http://webbook.nist.gov/chemistry/fluid/

Sasaki, K. & Akibayashi, S. (1999), A Calculation Model for Liquid CO2 Injection into Shallow Sub-seabed Aquifer, *Annals of New York Academy of Sciences*, Vol. 912, 1999, pp.211-225, ISSN1749-6632

Sasaki, K. & Dindiwe, C. (2002). Integrated mine ventilation simulator "MIVENA Ver.6" and its applications, *Proceedings of North American/Ninth U.S. Mine Ventilation Symposium*, pp. 243-251, ISBN 9789058093875, CRC Press, Kingston, Canada, June 8-12, 2002

Sasaki, K., Yasunami, T. & Sugai, Y. (2009). Prediction model of Bottom Hole Temperature and Pressure at Deep Injector for CO_2 Sequestration to Recover Injection Rate, *Energy Procedia*, Volume 1, Issue 1 (February 2009), pp. 2999-3006, ISSN 1876-6102

Starfield, A.M. & Bleloch, A.L. (1983). A new Method for The Computation of Heat and Moisture Transfer in a partly Wet Airway, *Journal of South African Institute of Mining and Metallurgy*, Vol. 83, pp.263-269 (November/December, 1983), ISSN 0038-223X

Propath Group (2008). *Manual of PROPATH Version 13.1* (April, 2008), ISSN 0911-1743

Prensky, S. (1992). Temperature Measurements in Boreholes-An Overview of Engineering and Scientific Applications, *The log analyst: a journal of formation evaluation and reservoir description*, Vol. 33-3, pp.313-333, ISSN 0024-581X

Yamaguchi, S., Oga, K., Fujioka, M. & Nako, M. (2007). History Matching on Micro-Pilot Test of CO_2 Sequestration and ECBMR in the Ishikari Coal Field (Coalbed methane(CBM), *Journal of the Japan Institute of Energy*, Vol. 86-2, 2007, pp.80-86, ISSN 0916-8753

Yasunami, T., Sasaki, K. & Sugai, Y. (2010). CO_2 Temperature Prediction System in Injection Tubing Considering Supercritical Condition at Yubari ECBM Pilot-Test, *Journal of Canadian Petroleum Technology (Society of Petroleum Engineers)*, Vol. 49-4 (April, 2010), pp. 44-50, ISSN 00219487

Yee, D., Seidle, J.P. & Hanson, W.B. (1993). Gas Sorption on Coal and Measurement of Gases content, *AAPG Studies in Geology*, Vol. 38 (May, 1983), pp. 203-218, ISSN 0 89181-049-8